THE CD-ROM

After reading about psychological disorders in this text, you can *see* and *hear* real patients who have been diagnosed with these disorders being interviewed by skilled clinicians. Look for the green video icons in the margin, and then go to the CD-ROM to see these videos:

VIDEO 3.1
Administration of Projective Tests
Dr. Ruth Munroe

VIDEO 4.1
Client-Centered Therapy
Dr. Carl Rogers

VIDEO 6.1
Panic Disorder
The Case of Jerry

VIDEO 6.2
Obsessive-Compulsive Disorder
The Case of Ed

VIDEO 7.1
Dissociative Identity Disorder
The Three Faces of Eve

VIDEO 7.2
Dissociative Identity Disorder
Dr. Holliday Milby

VIDEO 8.1
Depression
The Case of Helen

VIDEO 8.2
Bipolar Disorder
The Case of Craig

VIDEO 9.1
Antisocial Personality Disorder
The Case of Paul

VIDEO 10.1
Substance Abuse
Therapist Jean Obert

VIDEO 10.2
Substance Abuse
Therapist Louise Roberts

VIDEO 11.1
Eating Disorders
Nutritionist Alise Thresh

VIDEO 11.2
Anorexia
The Case of Tamora

VIDEO 11.3
Bulimia
The Case of Ann

VIDEO 12.1
Gender Identity Disorder
The Case of Denise

VIDEO 13.1
Schizophrenia
The Case of Georgiana

VIDEO 14.1
Autism
Dr. Kathy Pratt

VIDEO 14.2
ADHD
Dr. Raun Melmed

VIDEO 15.1
Alzheimer's Disease
The Case of Wilburn "John" Johnson

VIDEO 16.1
Child Sexual Abuse
The Case of Karen

FIFTH EDITION

ABNORMAL PSYCHOLOGY IN A CHANGING WORLD

Media and Research Update

JEFFREY S. NEVID
St. John's University

SPENCER A. RATHUS
New York University

BEVERLY GREENE
St. John's University

PEARSON
Prentice
Hall

Upper Saddle River, New Jersey 07458

Editor-in-Chief: Leah Jewell
Executive Editor: Stephanie Johnson
Editorial Assistant: Catherine Fox
Executive Marketing Manager: Sheryl Adams
Marketing Assistant: Ron Fox
AVP/Director of Production and Manufacturing: Barbara Kittle
Senior Production Editor: Shelly Kupperman
Manufacturing Manager: Nick Sklitsis
Prepress and Manufacturing Buyer: Tricia Kenny

Line Art Coordinator: Guy Ruggiero
Artist: Maria Piper
Creative Design Director: Leslie Osher
Interior and Cover Designer: Anne DeMarinis
Director, Image Resource Center: Melinda Reo
Image Specialist: Beth Boyd
Photo Researcher: Melinda Alexander
Cover Art: Naoki Okamoto, Untitled, Living—Asian. B. 1990

This book was set in 10/12 Minion by TSI Graphics
Group and was printed and bound by Von Hoffmann.
The cover was printed by Coral Graphics.

Acknowledgments begin on page 603, which
constitutes a continuation of this copyright page.

© 2005, 2000, 1997, 1994, 1991 by Pearson Education, Inc.
Upper Saddle River, New Jersey 07458

Printed in the United States of America
10 9 8 7 6 5 4 3 2 1

ISBN 0-13-118962-X

Pearson Education LTD., London
Pearson Education Australia PTY, Limited, Sydney
Pearson Education Singapore, Pte. Ltd
Pearson Education North Asia Ltd, Hong Kong
Pearson Education Canada, Ltd., Toronto
Pearson Educación de Mexico, S.A. de C.V.
Pearson Education – Japan, Tokyo
Pearson Education Malaysia, Pte. Ltd
          ...tion, Upper Saddle River, New Jersey

MEDIA AND RESEARCH UPDATE CONTENTS

Chapter 1 Introduction and Methods of Research

In Chapter 1 we discuss research methods designed to disentangle the influences on behavior of nature (genetics) and nurture (environment). Here, Danielle M. Dick and Richard J. Rose review recent developments in behavior genetics, the scientific field that explores the influences on behavior of genetic factors and the interaction of genes and environments.

Behavior Genetics: What's New? What's Next?

Danielle M. Dick and Richard J. Rose[1]
Department of Psychology, Indiana University, Bloomington, Indiana

Through most of its brief history, behavior genetics had a single and simple goal: to demonstrate that some of the variation in behavior is attributable to genetic variance. Now, a diverse array of behaviors has been investigated with twin and adoption designs, yielding evidence that genetic variation contributes to individual differences in virtually all behavioral domains (McGuffin, Riley, & Plomin, 2001). Is behavior genetics, then, a thing of the past, a field whose success makes it obsolete? Not at all: Never has behavior genetic research held more promise. Investigators now possess analytic tools to move from estimating latent, unmeasured sources of variance to specifying the genes and environments involved in behavioral development, and the ways in which they interact. Our modest aim in this essay is to describe the questions now asked by behavior geneticists and to sketch the role that the field will assume in the emerging era of behavioral genomics.

A Developmental Perspective

Traditional behavior genetic analyses divide observed behavioral variance into three unobserved (latent) sources: variance attributable to genetic effects, that due to environmental influences shared by siblings (e.g., family structure and status), and that arising in unshared environmental experience that makes siblings differ from one another. Estimates of the magnitude of these genetic and environmental effects are usually obtained from statistical path models that compare identical twins, who share all their genes, with fraternal twins, who like ordinary siblings, on average, share one half their genes. Behavior genetic research now identifies developmental changes in the importance of genetic dispositions and environmental contexts in accounting for individual differences in behavior. Such changes can be dramatic and rapid. For example, we assessed substance use in a sample of adolescent Finnish twins on three occasions from ages 16 to 18 1/2; we found that genetic contributions to individual differences in drinking frequency increased over time, accounting for only a third of the variation at age 16, but half of it just 30 months later (Rose, Dick, Viken, & Kaprio,

2001). Concurrently, the effects of sharing a common environment decreased in importance. Interestingly, parallel analyses of smoking found little change in the importance of genetic and environmental effects, illustrating the trait-specificity of gene-environment dynamics: Some effects are stable across a developmental period; others change.

Different Behaviors, Same Genes?

It is well known that certain behaviors tend to co-occur, as do certain disorders, but the causes of such covariance are much less understood. Behavior genetic models assess the degree to which covariation of different disorders or behaviors is due to common genetic influences, common environmental influences, or both. An example can be found in the significant, albeit modest, correlations observed between perceptual speed (the minimum time required to make a perceptual discrimination, as assessed with computer display methods) and standard IQ test scores (Posthuma, de Geus, & Boomsma, in press); those correlations were found to be due entirely to a common genetic factor, hypothesized to reflect genetic influences on neural transmission. Another example is found in our study of behavioral covariance between smoking and drinking during adolescence. Genes contributing to the age when teens started smoking and drinking correlated nearly 1.0 (suggesting that the same genes influence an adolescent's decision to begin smoking and to begin drinking), but once smoking or drinking was initiated, genes influencing the frequency with which an adolescent smoked or drank were quite substance-specific, correlating only about .25.

Gene-Environment Interaction and Correlation

The interaction of genes and environments has been difficult to demonstrate in human behavioral data, despite consensus that interaction must be ubiquitous. New behavior genetic methods are demonstrating what was long assumed. These methods use information from twins who vary in specified environmental exposure to test directly for the differential expression of genes across different environments. For example, genetic effects played a larger role in the use of alcohol among twin women who had been reared in nonreligious households than among those who had been reared in religious households (Koopmans, Slutske, van Baal, & Boomsma, 1999). Similarly, we found greater genetic effects on adolescent alcohol use among Finnish twins living in urban environments than among those living in rural environments (Rose, Dick, et al., 2001).

These demonstrations of gene-environment interaction used simple dichotomies of environmental measures. But subsequently, we explored underlying processes in the interaction effect of urban versus rural environments by employing new statistical techniques to accommodate more continuous measures of the characteristics of the municipalities in which the Finnish twins resided. We hypothesized that communities spending relatively

more money on alcohol allow for greater access to it, and communities with proportionately more young adults offer more role models for adolescent twins, and that either kind of community enhances expression of individual differences in genetic predispositions. And that is what we found: up to a 5-fold difference in the importance of genetic effects among twins residing in communities at these environmental extremes (Dick, Rose, Viken, Kaprio, & Koskenvuo, 2001), suggesting that the influence of genetic dispositions can be altered dramatically by environmental variation across communities.

Analysis of gene-environment interaction is complemented by tests of gene-environment correlation. Individuals' genomes interact with the environmental contexts in which the individuals live their lives, but this process is not a passive one, for genetic dispositions lead a person to select, and indeed create, his or her environments. Perhaps the most salient environment for an adolescent is found in the adolescent's peer relationships. In a study of 1,150 sixth-grade Finnish twins, we (Rose, in press) obtained evidence that they actively selected their friends from among their classmates. This result is consistent with the inference that people's genetic dispositions play some role in their selection of friends. People like other people who are like themselves, and genetically identical co-twins make highly similar friendship selections among their classmates.

Measuring Effects of the Environment in Genetically Informative Designs

In traditional behavior genetic designs, environmental influences were modeled, but not measured. Environmental effects were inferred from latent models fit to data. Such designs understandably received much criticism. Now, behavior geneticists can incorporate specific environmental measures into genetically informative designs and, by doing so, are demonstrating environmental effects that latent models failed to detect. Thus, we have studied effects of parental monitoring and home atmosphere on behavior problems in 11- to 12-year-old Finnish twins; both parental monitoring and home atmosphere contributed significantly to the development of the children's behavior problems, accounting for 2 to 5% of the total variation, and as much as 15% of the total common environmental effect. Recent research in the United Kingdom found neighborhood deprivation influenced behavior problems, too, accounting for about 5% of the effect of shared environment. Incorporation of specific, measured environments into genetically informative designs offers a powerful technique to study and specify environmental effects.

In other work, new research designs have been used to directly assess environmental effects in studies of unrelated children reared in a common neighborhood or within the same home. We have investigated neighborhood environmental effects on behavior in a large sample of 11- to 12-year-old same-sex Finnish twins. For each twin, we included a control classmate of the same gender and similar age, thus enabling us to compare three kinds of dyads: co-twins, each twin and his or her control classmate, and the two control classmates for each pair of co-twins. These twin-classmate dyads were sampled from more than 500 classrooms throughout Finland. The members of each dyad shared the same neighborhood, school, and classroom, but only the co-twin dyads shared genes and common household experience. For some behaviors, including early onset of smoking and drinking, we found significant correlations for both control-twin and control-control dyads; fitting models to the double-dyads formed by twins and their controls documented significant contributions to behavioral variation from nonfamilial environments—schools, neighborhoods, and communities (Rose, Viken, Dick, Pulkkinen, & Kaprio, 2001).

A complementary study examined genetically unrelated siblings who were no more than 9 months apart in age and who had been reared together from infancy in the same household. An IQ correlation of .29 was reported for 50 such dyads, and in another analysis, 40 of these dyads were only slightly less alike than fraternal co-twins on a variety of parent-rated behaviors (Segal, 1999). Clearly, appropriate research designs can demonstrate effects of familial and extrafamilial environmental variation for some behavioral outcomes at specific ages of development.

Integrating Behavior and Molecular Genetics[2]

Where do the statistical path models of behavior geneticists fit into the emerging era of behavioral genomics (the application of molecular genetics to behavior)? In the same way that specific, measured environments can be incorporated into behavior genetic models, specific information about genotypes can be included, as well, to test the importance of individual genes on behavior. Additionally, the kinds of behavior genetic analyses we have described can be informative in designing studies that maximize the power to detect susceptibility genes. Many efforts to replicate studies identifying genes that influence clinically defined diagnoses have failed. Those failures have stimulated the study of alternatives to diagnoses. When several traits are influenced by the same gene (or genes), that information can be used to redefine (or refine) alternatives to study, to enhance gene detection. For example, because heavy smoking and drinking frequently co-occurred in the Collaborative Study of the Genetics of Alcoholism sample, combined smoking and alcohol dependence was studied (Beirut et al., 2000). The combined dependency yielded greater evidence of linkage with a chromosomal region than did either tobacco dependence or alcohol dependence alone.

This approach is not limited to co-occurring behavioral disorders. It applies to normative behavioral differences, as well: A multidisciplinary international collaboration (Wright et al., 2001) has initiated a study of covariation among traditional and experimental measures of cognitive ability and will employ the correlated measures, once found, in subsequent molecular genetic analyses. And in a complementary way, behavior genetic methods can be useful to identify behavioral outcomes that are highly heritable, because these outcomes are most

likely informative for genetic studies: When the definition of major depression was broadened, genetic factors assumed a larger role in women's susceptibility to this disorder (Kendler, Gardner, Neale, & Prescott, 2001), and, interestingly, this broader definition of depression suggested that somewhat different genes may influence depression in men and women.

A second strategy to enhance the power of molecular genetic analyses is to more accurately characterize trait-relevant environmental factors and also incorporate them more accurately in the analyses. In searching for genes, traditional genetic research effectively ignored the interplay of genetic and environmental influences in behavioral and psychiatric traits. Now, new analytic methods are being developed to incorporate environmental information better (Mosley, Conti, Elston, & Witte, 2000). But which specific environmental information is pertinent to a particular disorder? And how does a specific risk-relevant environment interact with genetic dispositions? Behavioral scientists trained in the methods of behavior genetics will play a key role in answering these questions.

Beyond Finding Genes

The traditional endpoint for geneticists is finding the gene (or genes) involved in a behavior or disorder. At that point, psychologists should become instrumental in using this genetic information. Applying genetic research on complex disorders to clinical practice will be complicated, because gene-behavior correlations will be modest and nonspecific, altering risk, but rarely determining outcome. Genes confer dispositions, not destinies. Research examining how risk and protective factors interact with genetic predispositions is critical for understanding the development of disorders and for providing information to vulnerable individuals and their family members. Far from ousting traditional psychological intervention, advances in genetics offer opportunities to develop interventions tailored to individual risks in the context of individual lifestyles. Enhanced understanding of the interactions between genetic vulnerabilities and environmental variables may dispel public misconceptions about the nature of genetics and correct erroneous beliefs about genetic determinism. Informed psychologists can play a vital role in disseminating the benefits of genetic research to families whose members experience behavioral and psychiatric disorders, and to the public in general.

Conclusions

Research questions now addressed by behavior geneticists have grown dramatically in scope: The questions have expanded into developmental psychology and sociology, as researchers have employed measures of the home and community, and utilized longitudinal designs. And behavior geneticists now study the effect of measured genotypes, a study traditionally left to geneticists. These developments create new and compelling research questions and raise new challenges. One such challenge is in addressing the complexity of behavioral development despite current reliance on methods that largely assume additive, linear effects. People who appreciate the complex, interactive, and unsystematic effects underlying behavioral development may be skeptical that the genomic era will profoundly

advance understanding of behavior. But there is a preliminary illustration that advance will occur, even within the constraints of additive models: the identification of a gene (ApoE) that increases risk for Alzheimer's disease, and the interaction of that gene with head trauma (Mayeux et al., 1995). Further, new analytic techniques are being developed to analyze simultaneously hundreds of genes and environments in attempts to understand how gene-gene and gene-environment interactions contribute to outcome (Moore & Hahn, 2000). These techniques are beginning to capture the systems-theory approach long advocated by many researchers as an alternative to linear additive models.

This is not to deny that unresolved problems remain. For example, we are enthusiastic about including measured environmental information in genetic research designs, but we note, with disappointment, that the magnitude of shared environmental effects detected to date has been modest. Equally disappointing are the results of recent research efforts to specify nonshared environmental effects (Turkheimer & Waldron, 2000). Such findings underscore a problem acutely evident in contemporary behavior genetics: an imperative need for better measures of trait-relevant environments. Now that researchers have tools to search for measured environmental effects, what aspects of the environment should they measure—and with what yardsticks? These are questions that psychologists are uniquely positioned to address.

Another set of challenging questions will arise from the ethical, legal, and social issues to be confronted once genes conferring susceptibility to disorders are identified. How should information about the nature and meaning of susceptibility genes be conveyed to the media, the public, and the courts? How can erroneous beliefs about genetic determinism be dispelled effectively? Such issues will be even more salient once dispositional genes for normal behavioral variation are identified: Ethical issues surrounding prevention of behavioral disorders are undeniably complex, but surely they are less so than the ethical issues surrounding enhancement of selected behavioral traits.

Results from the first phase of behavior genetics research convincingly demonstrated that genes influence behavioral development. In the next phase, that of behavioral genomics, psychologists will begin to identify specific genes that exert such influence, seek understanding of how they do so, and accept the challenge to interpret that understanding to the public.

Acknowledgments—We gratefully acknowledge the contributions of Lea Pulkkinen, Jaakko Kaprio, Markku Koskenvuo, and Rick Viken to FinnTwin research, and support from the National Institute on Alcohol Abuse and Alcoholism (AA00145, AA09203, and AA08315) awarded to R.J.R. Manuscript preparation was supported by the Indiana Alcohol Research Center (AA07611) and by a National Science Foundation Pre-Doctoral Fellowship awarded to D.M.D.

Notes

1. Address correspondence to Richard Rose, Indiana University, Department of Psychology, 1101 East 10th St., Bloomington, IN 47405.

2. We use the term molecular genetics broadly to include statistical genetic techniques that test for gene-behavior associations.

References

Beirut, L., Rice, J., Goate, A., Foroud, T., Edenberg, H., Crowe, R., Hesselbrock, V., Li, T.K., Nurnberger, J., Porjesz, B., Schuckit, M., Begleiter, H., & Reich, T. (2000). Common and specific factors in the familial transmission of substance dependence. *American Journal of Medical Genetics, 96,* 459.

Dick, D.M., Rose, R.J., Viken, R.J., Kaprio, J., & Koskenvuo, M. (2001). Exploring gene-environment interactions: Socio-regional moderation of alcohol use. *Journal of Abnormal Psychology, 110,* 625–632.

Kendler, K.S., Gardner, C.O., Neale, M.C., & Prescott, C.A. (2001). Genetic risk factors for major depression in men and women: Similar or different heritabilities and same or partly distinct genes? *Psychological Medicine, 31,* 605–616.

Koopmans, J.R., Slutske, W.S., van Baal, G.C.M., & Boomsma, D.I. (1999). The influence of religion on alcohol use initiation: Evidence for genotype × environment interaction. *Behavior Genetics, 29,* 445–453.

Mayeux, R., Ottman, R., Maestre, G., Ngai, C., Tang, M.X., Ginsberg, H., Chun, M., Tycko, B., & Shelanski, M. (1995). Synergistic effects of traumatic head injury and apolipoprotein-E4 in patients with Alzheimer's disease. *Neurology, 45,* 555–557.

McGuffin, P., Riley, B., & Plomin, R. (2001). Toward behavioral genomics. *Science, 291,* 1232–1249.

Moore, J.H., & Hahn, L.W. (2000). A cellular automata approach to identifying gene-gene and gene-environment interactions. *American Journal of Medical Genetics, 96,* 486–487.

Mosley, J., Conti, D.V., Elston, R.C., & Witte, J.S. (2000). Impact of preadjusting a quantitative phenotype prior to sib-pair linkage analysis when gene-environment interaction exists. *Genetic Epidemiology, 21*(Suppl. 1), S837–S842.

Posthuma, D., de Geus, E.J.C., & Boomsma, D.I. (in press). Perceptual speed and IQ are associated through common genetic factors. *Behavior Genetics.*

Rose, R.J. (in press). How do adolescents select their friends? A behavior-genetic perspective. In L. Pulkkinen & A. Caspi (Eds.), *Paths to successful development.* Cambridge, England: Cambridge University Press.

Rose, R.J., Dick, D.M., Viken, R.J., & Kaprio, J. (2001). Gene-environment interaction in patterns of adolescent drinking: Regional residency moderates longitudinal influences on alcohol use. *Alcoholism: Clinical and Experimental Research, 25,* 637–643.

Rose, R.J., Viken, R.J., Dick, D.M., Pulkkinen, L., & Kaprio, J. (2001, July). *Shared environmental effects on behavior: Distinguishing familial from non-familial sources with data from twins and their classmate controls.* Paper presented at the annual meeting of the Behavior Genetics Association, Cambridge, England.

Segal, N.L. (1999). *Entwined lives.* New York: Penguin Putnam.

Turkheimer, E., & Waldron, M. (2000). Nonshared environment: A theoretical methodological, and quantitative review. *Psychological Bulletin, 126,* 78–108.

Wright, M., de Geus, E., Ando, J., Luciano, M., Posthuma, D., Ono, Y., Hansell, N., Van Baal, C., Hiraishi, K., Hasegawa, T., Smith, G., Geffen, G., Geffen, L., Kanba, S., Miyake, A., Martin, N., & Boomsma, D. (2001). Genetics of cognition: Outline of a collaborative twin study. *Twin Research, 4,* 48–56.

Chapter 4 Methods of Therapy and Treatment

In Chapter 4, we note that you can do most anything on the Internet these days, from ordering concert tickets to downloading music or whole books. But what about counseling or therapy services? Would you be willing to seek help from an online therapy? In this review, C. Barr Taylor and Kristine Luce bring us up-to-date on the developing uses of the computer and the Internet in providing psychotherapy interventions.

Computer- and Internet-Based Psychotherapy Interventions

C. Barr Taylor[1] and Kristine H. Luce
Department of Psychiatry, Stanford University Medical Center, Stanford, California

In recent years, the increasing number of users of computer and Internet technology has greatly expanded the potential of computer- and Internet-based therapy programs. Computer- and Internet-assisted assessment methods and therapy programs have the potential to increase the cost-effectiveness of standardized psychotherapeutic treatments by reducing contact time with the therapist, increasing clients' participation in therapeutic activities outside the standard clinical hour, and streamlining input and processing of clients' data related to their participation in therapeutic activities. Unfortunately, the scientific study of these programs has seriously lagged behind their purported potential, and these interventions pose important ethical and professional questions.

Computer-Based Programs

Information A number of studies have demonstrated that computers can provide information effectively and economically. An analysis of a large number of studies of computer-assisted instruction (CAI) found that CAI is consistently effective in improving knowledge (Fletcher-Flinn & Gravatt, 1995). Surprisingly, few studies evaluating the use of CAI for providing information related to mental health or psychotherapy have been conducted.

Assessment Traditional paper-based self-report instruments are easily adapted to the computer format and offer a number of advantages that include ensuring data completeness and standardization. Research has found that computer-administered assessment instruments work as well as other kinds of self-report instruments and as well as therapist-administered ones. Clients may feel less embarrassed about reporting sensitive or potentially stigmatizing information (e.g., about sexual behavior or illegal drug use) during a computer-assisted assessment than during a face-to-face assessment, allowing for more accurate estimates of mental health behaviors. Studies show that more symptoms, including suicidal thoughts, are reported during computer-assisted interviews than face-to-face interviews. Overall, the evidence suggests that computers can make assessments more efficient, more accurate, and less expensive. Yet computer-based assessment interviews do not allow for clinical intuition and nuance, assessment of behavior, and nonverbal emotional expression, nor do they foster a therapeutic alliance between client and therapist as information is collected.

Recently, handheld computers or personal digital assistants (PDAs) have been used to collect real-time, naturalistic data on a variety of variables. For example, clients can record their thoughts, behaviors, mood, and other variables at the same time and when directed to do so by an alarm or through instructions from the program. The assessment of events as they occur avoids retrospective recall biases. PDAs can be programmed to beep to cue a response and also to check data to determine, for instance, if responses are in the right range. The data are easily downloaded into computer databases for further analysis. PDAs with interactive transmission capabilities further expand the potential for real-time data collection. Although PDAs have been demonstrated to be useful for research, they have not been incorporated into clinical practice.

Computer-Assisted Psychotherapy Much research on computer-based programs has focused on anxiety disorders (Newman, Consoli, & Taylor, 1997). Researchers have developed computer programs that direct participants through exercises in relaxation and restfulness; changes in breathing frequency, regularity, and pattern; gradual and progressive exposure to aspects of the situation, sensation, or objects they are afraid of; and changes in thinking patterns. Although the majority of studies report symptom reduction, most are uncontrolled trials or case studies and have additional methodological weaknesses (e.g., small sample sizes, no follow-up to assess whether treatment gains are maintained, focus on individuals who do not have clinical diagnoses).

Computer programs have been developed to reduce symptoms of simple phobias, panic disorder, obsessive-compulsive disorder (OCD), generalized anxiety disorder, and social phobia. In a multicenter, international treatment trial (Kenardy et al., 2002), study participants who received a primary diagnosis of panic disorder were randomly assigned to one of four groups: (a) a group that received 12 sessions of therapist-delivered cognitive behavior therapy (CBT), (b) a group that received 6 sessions of therapist-delivered CBT augmented by use of a handheld computer, (c) a group that received 6 sessions of therapist-delivered CBT augmented with a manual, or (d) a control group that was assigned to a wait list. Assessments at the end of treatment and 6 months later showed that the 12-session CBT and the 6-session CBT with the computer were equally effective. The results suggested that use of a handheld computer can reduce therapist contact time without compromising outcomes and may speed the rate of improvement.

An interactive computer program was developed to help clients with OCD, which is considered one type of anxiety disorder. The computer provided three weekly 45-min sessions of therapy involving vicarious exposure to their obsessive thoughts and response prevention (a technique by which clients with OCD are taught and encouraged not to engage in their customary rituals when they have an urge to do so). Compared with a control group, the clients who received the intervention had significantly greater improvement in symptoms. In a follow-up study with clients diagnosed with OCD, computer-guided telephone behavior therapy was effective; however, clinician-guided behavior therapy was even more effective. Thus, computer-guided behavior therapy can be a helpful first step in treating patients with OCD, particularly when clinician-guided behavior therapy is unavailable. Computers have also been used to help treat individuals with other anxiety disorders, including social phobia and generalized anxiety disorder, a condition characterized by excessive worry and constant anxiety without specific fears or avoidances.

CBT also has been adapted for the computer-delivered treatment of depressive disorders. Selmi,

Klein, Greist, Sorrell, and Erdman (1990) conducted the only randomized, controlled treatment trial comparing computer- and therapist-administered CBT for depression. Participants who met the study's criteria for major, minor, or intermittent depressive disorder were randomly assigned to computer-administered CBT, therapist-administered CBT, or a wait-list control. Compared with the control group, both treatment groups reported significant improvements on depression indices. The treatment groups did not differ from each other, and treatment gains were maintained at a 2-month follow-up.

Little information exists on the use of computer-assisted therapy for treating patients with complicated anxiety disorders or other mental health problems. Thus, further study is needed.

The Internet

Internet-based programs have several advantages over stand-alone computer-delivered programs. The Internet makes health care information and programs accessible to individuals who may have economic, transportation, or other restrictions that limit access to face-to-face services. The Internet is constantly available and accessible from a variety of locations. Because text and other information on the Internet can be presented in a variety of formats, languages, and styles, and at various educational levels, it is possible to tailor messages to the learning preferences and strengths of the user. The Internet can facilitate the collection, coordination, dissemination, and interpretation of data. These features allow for interactivity among the various individuals (e.g., physicians, clients, family members, caregivers) who may participate in a comprehensive treatment plan. As guidelines, information, and other aspects of programs change, it is possible to rapidly update information on Web pages. The medium also allows for personalization of information. Users may select features and information most relevant to them, and, conversely, programs can automatically determine a user's needs and strengths and display content accordingly.

Information Patients widely search the Internet for mental health information. For example, the National Institute of Mental Health (NIMH) public information Web site receives more than 7 million "hits" each month. However, the mental health information on commercial Web sites is often inaccurate, misleading, or related to commercial interests. Sites sponsored by nonprofit organizations provide better and more balanced information, but search engines often list for-profit sites before they generate nonprofit sites. Furthermore, education Web sites rarely follow solid pedagogical principles.

Screening and Assessment Many mental health Web sites have implemented screening programs that assess individuals for signs or symptoms of various psychiatric disorders. These programs generally recommend that participants who score above a predetermined cutoff contact a mental health provider for further assessment. The NIMH and many other professional organizations provide high-quality, easily accessible information combined with screening instruments. Houston and colleagues (2001) evaluated the use of a Web site that offered a computerized version of the Center for Epidemiological Studies' depression scale (CES-D;

Ogles, France, Lunnen, Bell, & Goldfarb, 1998). The scale was completed 24,479 times during the 8-month study period. Fifty-eight percent of participants screened positive for depression, and fewer than half of those had previously been treated for depression. The Internet can incorporate interactive screening, which already has been extensively developed for desktop computers. Screening can then be linked to strategies that are designed to increase the likelihood that a participant will accept a referral and initiate further assessment or treatment.

On-Line Support Groups Because Internet-delivered group interventions can be accessed constantly from any location that has Internet access, they offer distinct advantages over their face-to-face counterparts. Face-to-face support groups often are difficult to schedule, meet at limited times and locations, and must accommodate inconsistent attendance patterns because of variations in participants' health status and schedules. On-line groups have the potential to help rural residents and individuals who are chronically ill or physically or psychiatrically disabled increase their access to psychological interventions.

A wide array of social support groups is available to consumers in synchronous (i.e., participants on-line at the same time) or asynchronous formats. The Pew Internet and American Life Project (www.pewinternet .org) estimated that 28% of Internet users have attended an on-line support group for a medical condition or personal problem on at least one occasion. After a morning television show featured Edward M. Kennedy, Jr., promoting free on-line support groups sponsored by the Wellness Community (www.wellness-community .org), the organization received more than 440,000 inquiries during the following week! The majority of published studies on Internet-based support groups suggest that the groups are beneficial; however, scientific understanding of how and when is limited. Studies that examine the patterns of discourse that occur in these groups indicate that members' communication is similar to that found in face-to-face support groups (e.g., high levels of mutual support, acceptance, positive feelings).

Only a few controlled studies have examined the effects of Internet-based support programs. One such study investigated the effects of a program named Bosom Buddies on reducing psychosocial distress in women with breast cancer (Winzelberg et al., in press). Compared with a wait-list control group, the intervention group reported significantly reduced depression, cancer-related trauma, and perceived stress.

On-Line Consultation On-line consultation with "experts" is readily available on the Internet. There are organizations for on-line therapists (e.g., the International Society for Mental Health Online, www.ismpo .org) and sites that verify the credentials of on-line providers. However, little is known about the efficacy, reach, utility, or other aspects of on-line consultation.

Advocacy The Internet has become an important medium for advocacy and political issues. Many organizations use the Internet to facilitate communication among members and to encourage members to support public policy (e.g., the National Alliance for the Mentally Ill, www.nami.org).

Internet-Based Psychotherapy The Internet facilitates the creation of treatment programs that combine a variety of interactive components. The basic components that can be combined include psychoeducation; social support; chat groups; monitoring of symptoms, progress, and use of the program; feedback; and interactions with providers. Although many psychotherapy programs developed for desktop computers and manuals are readily translatable to the Internet format, surprisingly few have been adapted in this way, and almost none have been evaluated. Studies show that Internet-based treatments are effective for reducing symptoms of panic disorder. Compared with patients in a wait-list control group, those who participated in an Internet-based posttraumatic stress group reported significantly greater improvements on trauma-related symptoms. During the initial 6-month period of operation, an Australian CBT program for depression, MoodGYM, had more than 800,000 hits (Christensen, Griffiths, & Korten, 2002). In an uncontrolled study of a small subsample of participants who registered on this site, program use was associated with significant decreases in anxiety and depression. Internet-based programs also have been shown to reduce symptoms of eating disorders and associated behaviors. Users consistently report high satisfaction with these programs.

Treatment programs for depression, mood swings, and other mental health disorders are being designed to blend computer-assisted psychotherapy and psychoeducation with case management (in which a therapist helps to manage a client's problems by following treatment and therapy guidelines) and telephone-based care. These programs might also include limited face-to-face interventions, medication, and support groups. The effectiveness of these programs remains to be demonstrated.

Eventually, the most important use of the Internet might be to deliver integrated, home-based, case-managed, psychoeducational programs that are combined with some face-to-face contact and support groups. Unfortunately, although a number of such programs are "under development," none have been evaluated in controlled trials.

Ethical and Professional Issues

Web-based interventions present a number of ethical and professional issues (Hsiung, 2001). Privacy is perhaps the most significant concern. The Internet creates an environment where information about patients can be easily accessed and disseminated. Patients may purposely or inadvertently disclose private information about themselves and, in on-line support groups, about their peers. Although programs can be password-protected, and electronic records must follow federal privacy guidelines, participants must be clearly informed that confidentiality of records cannot be guaranteed.

Internet interventions create the potential that services will be provided to patients who have not been seen by a professional or who live in other states or countries where the professionals providing the services are not licensed to provide therapy. Professional organizations are struggling to develop guidelines to address these concerns (e.g., Hsiung, 2001; Kane & Sands, 1998).

Because of its accessibility and relative anonymity, patients may use the Internet during crises and report suicidal and homicidal thoughts. Although providers who use Internet support groups develop statements to clearly inform patients that the medium is not to be used for psychiatric emergencies, patients may ignore these instructions. Thus, providers need to identify ancillary procedures to reduce and manage potential crises.

Given the continuing advances in technology and the demonstrated effectiveness and advantages of computer- and Internet-based interventions, one might expect that providers would readily integrate these programs into their standard care practice. Yet few do, in part because programs that are easy to install and use are not available, there is no professional or market demand for the use of computer-assisted therapy, and practitioners may have ethical and professional concerns about applying this technology in their clinical practice. Thus, in the near future this technology may primarily be used for situations in which the cost-effectiveness advantages are particularly great.

Conclusion

Computers have the potential to make psychological assessments more efficient, more accurate, and less expensive. Computer-assisted therapy appears to be as effective as face-to-face therapy for treating anxiety disorders and depression and can be delivered at lower cost. However, applications of this technology are in the early stages.

A high priority is to clearly demonstrate the efficacy of this approach, particularly compared with standard face-to-face, "manualized" treatments that have been shown to be effective for common mental health disorders. Studies that compare two potentially efficacious treatments require large samples for us to safely conclude that the therapies are comparable if no statistically significant differences are found. Kenardy et al. (2002) demonstrated that multisite, international studies sampling large populations could be conducted relatively inexpensively, in part because the intervention they examined was standardized. If a treatment's efficacy is demonstrated, the next step would be to determine if the therapy, provided by a range of mental health professionals, is useful in large, diverse populations. Examination of combinations of therapies (e.g., CBT plus medication) and treatment modalities (Taylor, Cameron, Newman, & Junge, 2002) should follow. As the empirical study of this technology advances, research might examine the utility and cost-effectiveness of adapting these approaches to treating everyone in a community who wants therapy.

Continued use of the Internet to provide psychosocial support and group therapy is another promising avenue. As in the case of individual therapy, research is needed to compare the advantages and disadvantages between Internet and face-to-face groups, determine which patients benefit from which modality, compare the effectiveness of professionally moderated groups and self- or peer-directed groups, and compare the effectiveness of synchronous and asynchronous groups.

As research progresses, new and exciting applications can be explored. Because on-line text is stored, word content can be examined. This information may teach us more about the therapeutic process or may automatically alert providers to patients who are depressed, dangerous, or deteriorating.

Although research in many aspects of computer-assisted therapy is needed, and the professional and ethical concerns are substantial, computers and the Internet are likely to play a progressively important role in providing mental health assessment and interventions to clients. Thus, mental health professionals will need to decide how they will incorporate such programs into their practices.

Note

1. Address correspondence to C. Barr Taylor, Department of Psychiatry, Stanford University Medical Center, Stanford, CA 94305-5722; e-mail: btaylor@stanford.edu.

References

Christensen, H., Griffiths, K.M., & Korten, A. (2002). Web-based cognitive behavior therapy: Analysis of site usage and changes in depression and anxiety scores. *Journal of Medical Internet Research, 4*(1), Article e3. Retrieved July 16, 2002, from http://www.jmir.org/2002/1/e3

Fletcher-Flinn, C.M., & Gravatt, B. (1995). The efficacy of computer assisted instruction (CAI): A meta-analysis. *Journal of Educational Computing Research, 3,* 219–241.

Houston, T.K., Cooper, L.A., Vu, H.T., Kahn, J., Toser, J., & Ford, D.E. (2001). Screening the public for depression through the Internet. *Psychiatric Services, 52,* 362–367.

Hsiung, R.C. (2001). Suggested principles of professional ethics for the online provision of mental health services. *Medinfo, 10,* 296–300.

Kane, B., & Sands, D.Z. (1998). Guidelines for the clinical use of electronic mail with patients: The AMIA Internet Working Group, Task Force on Guidelines for the Use of Clinic-Patient Electronic Mail. *Journal of the American Medical Informatics Association, 5,* 104–111.

Kenardy, J.A., Dow, M.G.T., Johnston, D.W., Newman, M.G., Thompson, A., & Taylor, C.B. (2002). *A comparison of delivery methods of cognitive behavioural therapy for panic disorder: An international multicentre trial.* Manuscript submitted for publication.

Newman, M.G., Consoli, A., & Taylor, C.B. (1997). Computers in assessment and cognitive behavioral treatment of clinical disorders: Anxiety as a case in point. *Behavior Therapy, 28,* 211–235.

Ogles, B.M., France, C.R., Lunnen, K.M., Bell, M.T., & Goldfarb, M. (1998). Computerized depression screening and awareness. *Community Mental Health Journal, 34*(1), 27–38.

Selmi, P.M., Klein, M.H., Greist, J.H., Sorrell, S.P., & Erdman, H.P. (1990). Computer-administered cognitive-behavioral therapy for depression. *American Journal of Psychiatry, 147,* 51–56.

Taylor, C.B., Cameron, R., Newman, M., & Junge, J. (2002). Issues related to combining risk factor reduction and clinical treatment for eating disorders in defined populations. *The Journal of Behavioral Health Services and Research, 29,* 81–90.

Winzelberg, A.J., Classen, C., Alpers, G., Roberts, H., Koopman, C., Adams, N., Ernst, H., Dev, P., & Taylor, C.B. (in press). An evaluation of an Internet support group for women with primary breast cancer. *Cancer.*

Chapter 5   Stress, Psychological Factors, and Health

As you'll discover in Chapter 5, stress is implicated in a wide range of physical and psychological problems. Here, Margaret Kemeny examines the latest developments in our understanding of the psychobiology of stress.

The Psychobiology of Stress

Margaret E. Kemeny[1]
Department of Psychiatry, University of California, San Francisco, San Francisco, California

The term stress is used in the scientific literature in a vague and inconsistent way and is rarely defined. The term may refer to a stimulus, a response to a stimulus, or the physiological consequences of that response. Given this inconsistency, in this review I avoid using the term stress (except when discussing the field of stress research) and instead differentiate the various components of stress. *Stressors,* or stressful life experiences, are defined as circumstances that threaten a major goal, including the maintenance of one's physical integrity (physical stressors) or one's psychological well-being (psychological stressors; Lazarus & Folkman, 1984). *Distress* is a negative psychological response to such threats and can include a variety of affective and cognitive states, such as anxiety, sadness, frustration, the sense of being overwhelmed, or helplessness. Researchers have proposed a number of stressor taxonomies, most of which differentiate threats to basic physiological needs or physical integrity, social connectedness, sense of self, and resources. A number of properties of stressful circumstances can influence the severity of the psychological and physiological response. These properties include the stressor's controllability (whether responses can affect outcomes of the stressor), ambiguity, level of demand placed on the individual, novelty, and duration.

Physiological Effects of Exposure to Stressful Life Experience

Extensive research in humans and other animals has demonstrated powerful effects of exposure to stressors on a variety of physiological systems. These specific changes are believed to have evolved to support the behaviors that allow the organism to deal with the threat (e.g., to fight or flee). In order for the organism to respond efficiently, physiological systems that are needed to deal with threats are mobilized and physiological systems that are not needed are suppressed. For example, when responding to a threat, the body increases available concentrations of glucose (an energy source) to ready the organism for physical activity; at the same time, the body inhibits processes that promote growth and reproduction. Although the body is adapted to respond with little ill effect to this acute mobilization, chronic or repeated activation of systems that deal with threat can have adverse long-term physiological and health effects (McEwen, 1998; Sapolsky, 1992). A wide array of physiological systems have been shown to change in response to stressors; in this section, I summarize the effects on the three most carefully studied systems (Fig. 1).

Impact on the Autonomic Nervous System Since Walter Cannon's work on the fight-or-flight response in the 1930s, researchers have been interested in the effects of stressful experience on the sympathetic adrenomedullary system (the system is so named because the sympathetic nervous system and adrenal medulla are its key components; see Fig. 1). Cannon correctly proposed that exposure to emergency situations results in the release of the hormone epinephrine from the adrenal medulla (the core of the adrenal gland, located above the kidney). This effect was shown to be accomplished

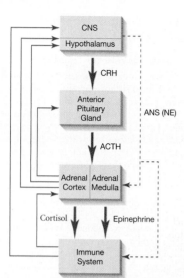

Fig. 1.
Schematic representation of interrelationships among the central nervous system (CNS), the hypothalamic-pituitary-adrenal axis, the autonomic nervous system (ANS), and the immune system. Dashed lines indicate ANS neural pathways, and solid lines indicate hormonal pathways. ACTH = adrenocorticotropic hormone; CRH = corticotropin-releasing hormone; NE = norepinephrine.

by the activity of the autonomic nervous system (ANS). The ANS has two components: the *parasympathetic nervous system,* which controls involuntary resting functions (activation of this system promotes digestion and slows heart rate, e.g.), and the *sympathetic nervous system,* which comes into play in threatening situations and results in increases in involuntary processes (e.g., heart rate and respiration) that are required to respond to physical threats. Fibers of the sympathetic nervous system release the neurotransmitter norepinephrine at various organ sites, including the adrenal medulla, causing the release of epinephrine (also known as adrenaline) into the bloodstream. Research has demonstrated that exposure to a variety of stressors can activate this system, as manifested by increased output of norepinephrine and epinephrine, as well as increases in autonomic indicators of sympathetic arousal (e.g., increased heart rate). This extremely rapid response system can be activated within seconds and results in the "adrenaline rush" that occurs after an encounter with an unexpected threat.

Impact on the Hypothalamic-Pituitary-Adrenal Axis A large body of literature suggests that exposure to a variety of acute psychological stressors (e.g., giving a speech, doing difficult cognitive tasks), for relatively short durations, can cause an increase in the levels of the hormone cortisol in the blood, saliva, and urine. This increase is due to activation of the hypothalamic-pituitary-adrenal (HPA) axis (see Fig. 1). Neural pathways link perception of a stressful stimulus to an integrated response in the hypothalamus, which results in the release of corticotropin-releasing hormone. This hormone stimulates the anterior part of the pituitary gland to release adrenocorticotropic hormone, which then travels through the blood stream to the adrenal glands and causes the adrenal cortex (the outer layer of the adrenal gland) to release

cortisol (in rodents this hormone is called corticosterone). The activation of this entire system occurs over minutes rather than seconds (as in the case of the ANS). The peak cortisol response occurs 20 to 40 min from the onset of acute stressors. Recovery, or the return to baseline levels, occurs 40 to 60 min following the end of the stressor on average (Dickerson & Kemeny, 2002).

Impact on the Immune System Exposure to stressful experiences can diminish a variety of immune functions. For example, stressful life experiences, such as bereavement, job loss, and even taking exams, can reduce circulating levels of classes of immunological cells called lymphocytes; inhibit various lymphocyte functions, such as the ability to proliferate when exposed to a foreign substance; and slow integrated immune responses, such as wound healing (Ader, Felten, & Cohen, 2001). Individuals' autonomic reactivity to stressors correlates with the degree to which their immune system is affected by acute laboratory stressors. Extensive evidence that autonomic nerve fibers innervate (enter into) immune organs and alter the function of immune cells residing there supports the link between the ANS and the immune system. In addition, some of the immunological effects of stressors are due to the potent suppressive effects of cortisol on immunological cells. Cortisol can inhibit the production of certain cytokines (chemical mediators released by immune cells to regulate the activities of other immune cells) and suppress a variety of immune functions.

Exposure to stressors can also enhance certain immune processes, for example, those closely related to inflammation. Inflammation is an orchestrated response to exposure to a pathogen that creates local and systemic changes conducive to destroying it (e.g., increases in core body temperature). However, chronic, inappropriate inflammation is at the root of a host of diseases, including certain autoimmune diseases such as rheumatoid arthritis, and may play a role in others, such as cardiovascular disease. There is a great deal of current interest in factors that promote inappropriate inflammation outside the normal context of infection. Exposure to some psychological stressors can increase circulating levels of cytokines that promote inflammation, perhaps because stressful experience can reduce the sensitivity of immune cells to the inhibitory effects of cortisol (Miller, Cohen, & Ritchey, 2002).

Not only can the brain and peripheral neural systems (systems that extend from the brain to the body—e.g., the ANS and HPA axis) affect the immune system, but the immune system can affect the brain and one's psychological state. In rodents, certain cytokines can act on the central nervous system, resulting in behavioral changes that resemble sickness (e.g., increases in body temperature, reduction in exploratory behavior) but also appear to mimic depression (e.g., alterations in learning and memory, anorexia, inability to experience pleasure, reductions in social behavior, alterations in sleep, behavioral slowing). Emerging data indicate that these cytokines can induce negative mood and alter cognition in humans as well. These effects may explain affective and cognitive changes that have been observed to be associated with inflammatory conditions. They may also explain some depressive symptoms associated with stressful conditions (Maier & Watkins, 1998).

Health Implications Activation of these physiological systems during exposure to a stressor is adaptive in the short run under certain circumstances but can become maladaptive if the systems are repeatedly or chronically activated or if they fail to shut down when the threat no longer exists. McEwen (1998) has coined the term *allostatic load* to refer to the cumulative toll of chronic overactivation of the physiological systems that are designed to respond to environmental perturbations. For example, evidence suggests that chronic exposure to stressors or distress (as in posttraumatic stress disorder and chronic depression) can cause atrophy in a part of the brain called the hippocampus, resulting in memory loss. Chronic exposure to stressful circumstances has also been shown to increase vulnerability to upper respiratory infections in individuals exposed to a virus. Researchers have observed effects on other health outcomes as well, but complete models of stress and health that document all the mediating mechanisms from the central nervous system to the pathophysiological processes that control disease are not yet available (Kemeny, 2003).

Generality Versus Specificity in the Physiological Response to Stressors

The central dogma of most stress research today is that stressors have a uniform effect on the physiological processes I have just described. Hans Selye shaped the thinking of generations of researchers when he argued that the physiological response to stressful circumstances is nonspecific, meaning that all stressors, physical and psychological, are capable of eliciting the triad of physiological changes he observed in his rodent research: shrinking of the thymus (a central immune organ), enlargement of the adrenal gland (which produces corticosterone), and ulceration of the gastrointestinal tract. Very little research has directly tested this *generality model* by determining whether or not differences in stressful conditions are associated with distinctive physiological effects in humans. Modern versions of the generality model propose that if stressors lead to the experience of distress (or perceived stress), then a stereotyped set of physiological changes will be elicited in the systems I have described. These models also emphasize the important role of a variety of psychological and environmental factors that can moderate the relationships among stressor exposure, distress, and physiological activation (see Fig. 2). However, these newer versions are essentially generality models because all of the factors are

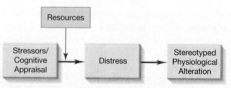

Fig. 2.
The generality model of stress. This model proposes that exposure to stressors and the cognitive appraisals of those events can lead to distress. The nature of this relationship depends on the resources available to deal with the stressors (e.g., coping skills, social support, personality factors, genetics, environmental resources). Elevations in distress cause a stereotyped physiological alteration in stress-responsive systems. Bidirectional relationships between many components of the model are assumed but are not indicated here.

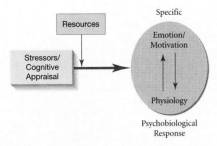

Specific

Psychobiological
Response

Fig. 3.
The integrated specificity model of stress. This model proposes
that exposure to specific stressful conditions and cognitive
appraisals of those conditions shape the specific nature of
an integrated psychobiological response (including emotion-
motivation and physiology) to promote adaptive responses
to the threat. For example, threats that are appraised as
uncontrollable may lead to an integrated psychobiological
response that includes disengagement from the goal that is
threatened by the stressor (manifested in withdrawal,
inactivity, and reduced effort), related affective states
(e.g., depression), and physiological changes that support
disengagement. Threats appraised as controllable may lead
to an integrated response involving engagement with the
threat and physiological responses supporting active coping
processes. As in the generality model, resources available
to deal with the stressors can moderate this relationship.

considered relevant to the extent that they buffer
against or exacerbate the experience of distress,
without considering that different kinds of distress
(e.g., different emotional responses) might have
distinctive physiological correlates. According to
these models, distress has a uniform relationship to
physiology.

There is, however, increasing evidence for specificity in the relationship between stressors and
physiology. Weiner (1992) advocated an integrated
specificity model of stressor physiology, arguing
that "organisms meet . . . challenges and dangers by
integrated behavioral, physiological patterns of
response that are appropriate to the task" (p. 33).
According to this model, both behavior and physiology are parts of an integrated response to address
a specific environmental condition (see Fig. 3), and
specific conditions or environmental signals elicit a
patterned array of hormonal and neural changes
that are designed to ready the organism to deal with
the specific nature of the threat. In animals, specific
neural and peripheral changes occur in concert
with behaviors such as fighting, fleeing, defending,
submitting, exerting dominance, and hunting prey,
among others. Distinctive behaviors (fight, flight,
and defeat) have also been elicited by activating
specific regions of the brain with excitatory amino
acids.

Cognitive Appraisals Shape Physiological Responses

Cognitive appraisal processes can profoundly shape
the specific nature of the physiological response to
stressful circumstances and play a central role in the
integrated specificity model. Cognitive appraisal is
the process of categorizing a situation in terms of its
significance for well-being (Lazarus & Folkman,
1984). Primary appraisal relates to perceptions of
goal threat, whereas secondary appraisal relates to
perceptions of resources available to meet the
demands of the circumstance (e.g., intellectual,
social, or financial resources). Three categories of

cognitive appraisals have been shown to elicit
distinctive affective and physiological responses.

Threat Versus Challenge According to Blascovich
and Tomaka (1996), the experience of threat results
when the demands in a given situation are perceived to outweigh the resources. When resources
are perceived to approximate or exceed demands,
however, the individual experiences a challenge
response. These two motivational states are associated with distinctive ANS alterations. In situations
that require active responses to obtain a goal, challenge is associated with increases in sympathetic
arousal (increased cardiac performance) coupled
with reduced or unchanged peripheral resistance
(resistance to blood flow). These changes parallel
those observed with metabolically demanding
aerobic exercise. Threat, in contrast, although also
associated with sympathetic arousal involving
increased cardiac performance, is associated with
increased peripheral resistance, leading to increased
blood pressure. Thus, different cognitive appraisals
can result in distinctive patterns of ANS reactivity
with potentially distinguishable implications for
health. The issue here is not degree of activation of
the sympathetic nervous system, but rather distinctive qualities of activation depending on the
specific nature of the cognitive appraisal process.

Perceived Control Animal and human research
demonstrates that uncontrollable circumstances, or
those perceived as uncontrollable, are more likely to
activate key stressor-relevant systems than are
circumstances that the organism perceives to be
controllable. For example, when rodents with and
without control over exposure to identical stressors
are compared, those with control show a reduced
cortisol response. A meta-analysis (a statistical
analysis that summarizes findings across studies)
has demonstrated that humans who are exposed to
stressors in an acute laboratory context are significantly more likely to experience HPA activation if
the stressors are uncontrollable than if they are controllable (Dickerson & Kemeny, 2002). Threats that
are appraised as controllable but in fact are uncontrollable have been shown to elicit less severe physiological alterations (e.g., in the immune system)
than those appraised as uncontrollable.

Social Cognition The social world has a powerful
effect on stress-relevant physiological systems
(Cacioppo, 1994). For example, social isolation has
a very significant effect on health, which is likely
mediated by the physiological systems described
here. Other social processes can regulate physiological systems as well. For example, place in a dominance hierarchy has a significant effect on physiological systems. Subordinate animals, who have low
social status, demonstrate a more activated HPA
axis, higher levels of cytokines that promote
inflammation, and other physiological changes
compared with their dominant counterparts. A
meta-analytic review has demonstrated that
demanding performance tasks elicit HPA activation
when one's social status or social self-esteem is
threatened by performance failures, but these
effects are greatly diminished when this social-sta-
tus threat is not present (Dickerson & Kemeny,
2002). Cognitive appraisals of social status and
social self-esteem appear to play an important role
in these effects (Dickerson, Gruenewald, & Kemeny,
in press).

Conclusions

The research findings on cognitive appraisal and
physiological systems lead to two important conclusions. First, depending on the nature of the eliciting conditions, different patterns of physiological
response can occur. Second, when cognitive
appraisals of conditions are manipulated, distinctive physiological effects can be observed within the
same context. Therefore, the way the individual
thinks about the situation may override the impact
of the specific nature of the conditions themselves.

In the integrated specificity model of stressful
experience, stressful conditions and appraisals of
them elicit integrated psychobiological responses
(including emotion and physiology) that are tied to
the nature of the threat experienced. A number of
researchers have found that different neural and
autonomic pathways are activated during different
emotional experiences. Thus, specific emotions, in
all likelihood, play a central role in the nature of the
physiological response to stressful conditions. A
more intensive evaluation of the role of distinct
emotions would be an important contribution to
future stress research. It is most likely that distinctions will be observed when researchers evaluate
patterns of physiological change across systems,
rather than relying on single response systems (e.g.,
cortisol level), and when emotional behavior is
assessed in conjunction with self-report data.

Acknowledgments—This article is dedicated to
the memory of Herbert Weiner, a pioneer in the
field of stress research, who profoundly shaped the
thinking of the generations of stress researchers
he trained.

Note

1. Address correspondence to Margaret E. Kemeny,
Health Psychology Program, Department of Psychiatry, Laurel Heights Campus, University of California,
3333 California St., Suite 465, San Francisco, CA
94143.

References

Ader, R., Felten, D.L., & Cohen, N. (2001). *Psychoneuroimmunology* (3rd ed.). New York: Academic Press.

Blascovich, J., & Tomaka, J. (1996). The biopsychosocial
model of arousal regulation. *Advances in Experimental
Social Psychology, 28,* 1–51.

Cacioppo, J.T. (1994). Social neuroscience: Autonomic,
neuroendocrine, and immune responses to stress.
Psychophysiology, 31, 113–128.

Dickerson, S.S., Gruenewald, T.L., & Kemeny, M.E. (in
press). When the social self is threatened: Shame,
physiology and health. *Journal of Personality.*

Dickerson, S.S., & Kemeny, M.E. (2002). *Acute stressors and
cortisol responses: A theoretical integration and synthesis
of laboratory research.* Manuscript submitted for
publication.

Kemeny, M.E. (2003). An interdisciplinary research model
to investigate psychosocial cofactors in disease: Application to HIV-1 pathogenesis. *Brain, Behavior &
Immunity, 17,* 562–572.

Lazarus, R.S., & Folkman, S. (1984). *Stress, appraisal, and
coping.* New York: Springer.

Maier, S.F., & Watkins, L.R. (1998). Cytokines for psychologists: Implications of bidirectional immune-to-brain
communication for understanding behavior, mood,
and cognition. *Psychological Review, 105,* 83–107.

McEwen, B.S. (1998). Protective and damaging effects of
stress mediators. *New England Journal of Medicine, 338,*
171–179.

Miller, G.E., Cohen, S., & Ritchey, A.K. (2002). Chronic psychological stress and the regulation of pro-inflammatory cytokines: A glucocorticoid resistance model. *Health Psychology, 21,* 531–541.

Sapolsky, R.M. (1992). Neuroendocrinology of the stress-response. In J.B. Becker, S.M. Breedlove, & D. Crews (Eds.), *Behavioral endocrinology* (pp. 287–324). Cambridge, MA: MIT Press.

Weiner, H. (1992). *Perturbing the organism: The biology of stressful experience.* Chicago: University of Chicago Press.

Chapter 7   Dissociative and Somatoform Disorders

In Chapter 7, you'll read about the controversy about recovered memories of childhood abuse. At the heart of the controversy is the question of whether such memories are believable. Here, Richard McNally examines what laboratory studies may teach us about recovering memories of past trauma.

Recovering Memories of Trauma: A View From the Laboratory

Richard J. McNally[1]
Department of Psychology, Harvard University, Cambridge, Massachusetts

How victims remember trauma is among the most explosive issues facing psychology today. Most experts agree that combat, rape, and other horrific experiences are unforgettably engraved on the mind (Pope, Oliva, & Hudson, 1999). But some also believe that the mind can defend itself by banishing traumatic memories from awareness, making it difficult for victims to remember them until many years later (Brown, Scheflin, & Hammond, 1998).

This controversy has spilled out of the clinics and cognitive psychology laboratories, fracturing families, triggering legislative change, and determining outcomes in civil suits and criminal trials. Most contentious has been the claim that victims of childhood sexual abuse (CSA) often repress and then recover memories of their trauma in adulthood.[2] Some psychologists believe that at least some of these memories may be false—inadvertently created by risky therapeutic methods (e.g., hypnosis, guided imagery; Ceci & Loftus, 1994).

One striking aspect of this controversy has been the paucity of data on cognitive functioning in people reporting repressed and recovered memories of CSA. Accordingly, my colleagues and I have been conducting studies designed to test hypotheses about mechanisms that might enable people either to repress and recover memories of trauma or to develop false memories of trauma.

For several of our studies, we recruited four groups of women from the community. Subjects in the *repressed-memory group* suspected they had been sexually abused as children, but they had no explicit memories of abuse. Rather, they inferred their hidden abuse history from diverse indicators, such as depressed mood, interpersonal problems with men, dreams, and brief, recurrent visual images (e.g., of a penis), which they interpreted as "flashbacks" of early trauma. Subjects in the *recovered-memory group* reported having remembered their abuse after long periods of not having thought about it.[3] Unable to corroborate their reports, we cannot say whether the memories were true or false. Lack of corroboration, of course, does not mean that a memory is false. Subjects in the *continuous-memory group* said that they had never forgotten their abuse, and subjects in the *control group* reported never having been sexually abused.

Personality Traits and Psychiatric Symptoms

To characterize our subjects in terms of personality traits and psychiatric symptoms, we asked them to complete a battery of questionnaires measuring normal personality variation (e.g., differences in absorption, which includes the tendency to fantasize and to become emotionally engaged in movies and literature), depressive symptoms, posttraumatic stress disorder (PTSD) symptoms, and dissociative symptoms (alterations in consciousness, such as memory lapses, feeling disconnected with one's body, or episodes of "spacing out"; McNally, Clancy, Schacter, & Pitman, 2000b).

There were striking similarities and differences among the groups in terms of personality profiles and psychiatric symptoms. Subjects who had always remembered their abuse were indistinguishable from those who said they had never been abused on all personality measures. Moreover, the continuous-memory and control groups did not differ in their symptoms of depression, posttraumatic stress, or dissociation. However, on the measure of negative affectivity—proneness to experience sadness, anxiety, anger, and guilt—the repressed-memory group scored higher than did either the continuous-memory or the control group, whereas the recovered-memory group scored midway between the repressed-memory group on the one hand and the continuous-memory and control groups on the other.

The repressed-memory subjects reported more depressive, dissociative, and PTSD symptoms than did continuous-memory and control subjects. Repressed-memory subjects also reported more depressive and PTSD symptoms than did recovered-memory subjects, who, in turn, reported more dissociative and PTSD symptoms than did control subjects. Finally, the repressed- and recovered-memory groups scored higher than the control group on the measure of fantasy proneness, and the repressed-memory group scored higher than the continuous-memory group on this measure.

This psychometric study shows that people who believe they harbor repressed memories of sexual abuse are more psychologically distressed than those who say they have never forgotten their abuse.

Forgetting Trauma-Related Material

Some clinical theorists believe that sexually molested children learn to disengage their attention during episodes of abuse and allocate it elsewhere (e.g., Terr, 1991). If CSA survivors possess a heightened ability to disengage attention from threatening cues, impairing their subsequent memory for them, then this ability ought to be evident in the laboratory. In our first experiment, we used directed-forgetting methods to test this hypothesis (McNally, Metzger, Lasko, Clancy, & Pitman, 1998). Our subjects were three groups of adult females: CSA survivors with PTSD, psychiatrically healthy CSA survivors, and nonabused control subjects. Each subject was shown, on a computer screen, a series of words that were either trauma related (e.g., *molested*), positive (e.g., *charming*), or neutral (e.g., *mailbox*). Immediately after each word was presented, the subject received instructions telling her either to remember the word or to forget it. After this encoding phase, she was asked to write down all the words she could remember, irrespective of the original instructions that followed each word.

If CSA survivors, especially those with PTSD, are characterized by heightened ability to disengage attention from threat cues, thereby attenuating memory for them, then the CSA survivors with PTSD in this experiment should have recalled few trauma words, especially those they had been told to forget. Contrary to this hypothesis, this group exhibited memory deficits for positive and neutral words they had been told to remember, while demonstrating excellent memory for trauma words, including those they had been told to forget. Healthy CSA survivors and control subjects recalled remember-words more often than forget-words regardless of the type of word. Rather than possessing a superior ability to forget trauma-related material, the most distressed survivors exhibited difficulty banishing this material from awareness.

In our next experiment, we used this directed-forgetting approach to test whether repressed- and recovered-memory subjects, relative to nonabused control subjects, would exhibit the hypothesized superior ability to forget material related to trauma (McNally, Clancy, & Schacter, 2001). If anyone possesses this ability, it ought to be such individuals. However, the memory performance of the repressed- and recovered-memory groups was entirely normal: They recalled remember-words better than forget-words, regardless of whether the words were positive, neutral, or trauma related.

Intrusion of Traumatic Material

The hallmark of PTSD is involuntary, intrusive recollection of traumatic experiences. Clinicians have typically relied on introspective self-reports as confirming the presence of this symptom. The emotional Stroop color-naming task provides a quantitative, nonintrospective measure of intrusive cognition. In this paradigm, subjects are shown words varying in emotional significance, and are asked to name the colors the words are printed in while ignoring the meanings of the words. When the meaning of a word intrusively captures the subject's attention despite the subject's efforts to attend to its color, Stroop interference—delay in color naming—occurs. Trauma survivors with PTSD take longer to name the colors of words related to trauma than do survivors without the disorder, and also take longer to name the colors of trauma words than to name the colors of positive and neutral words or negative words unrelated to their trauma (for a review, see McNally, 1998).

Using the emotional Stroop task, we tested whether subjects reporting either continuous, repressed, or recovered memories of CSA would exhibit interference for trauma words, relative to nonabused control subjects (McNally, Clancy, Schacter, & Pitman, 2000a). If severity of trauma motivates repression of traumatic memories, then subjects who cannot recall their presumably repressed memories may nevertheless exhibit interference for trauma words. We presented a series of trauma-related, positive, and neutral words on a computer screen, and subjects named the colors of the words as quickly as possible. Unlike patients with PTSD, including children with documented abuse histories (Dubner & Motta, 1999), none of the groups exhibited delayed color naming of trauma words relative to neutral or positive ones.

Memory Distortion and False Memories in the Laboratory

Some psychotherapists who believe their patients suffer from repressed memories of abuse will ask them to visualize hypothetical abuse scenarios, hoping that this guided-imagery technique will unblock the presumably repressed memories. Unfortunately, this procedure may foster false memories.

Using Garry, Manning, Loftus, and Sherman's (1996) methods, we tested whether subjects who have recovered memories of abuse are more susceptible than control subjects to this kind of memory distortion (Clancy, McNally, & Schacter, 1999). During an early visit to the laboratory, subjects rated their confidence regarding whether they had experienced a series of unusual, but nontraumatic, childhood events (e.g., getting stuck in a tree). During a later visit, they performed a guided-imagery task requiring them to visualize certain of these events, but not others. They later rerated their confidence that they had experienced each of the childhood events. Nonsignificant trends revealed an inflation in confidence for imagined versus non-imagined events. But the magnitude of this memory distortion was more than twice as large in the control group as in the recovered-memory group, contrary to the hypothesis that people who have recovered memories of CSA would be especially vulnerable to the memory-distorting effects of guided imagery.

To use a less-transparent paradigm for assessing proneness to develop false memories, we adapted the procedure of Roediger and McDermott (1995). During the encoding phase in this paradigm, subjects hear word lists, each consisting of semantically related items (e.g., *sour, bitter, candy, sugar*) that converge on a nonpresented word—the *false target*—that captures the gist of the list (e.g., *sweet*). On a subsequent recognition test, subjects are given a list of words and asked to indicate which ones they heard during the previous phase. The false memory effect occurs when subjects "remember" having heard the false target. We found that recovered-memory subjects exhibited greater proneness to this false memory effect than did subjects reporting either repressed memories of CSA, continuous memories of CSA, or no abuse (Clancy, Schacter, McNally, & Pitman, 2000). None of the lists was trauma related, and so we cannot say whether the effect would have been more or less pronounced for words directly related to sexual abuse.

In our next experiment, we tested people whose memories were probably false: individuals reporting having been abducted by space aliens (Clancy, McNally, Schacter, Lenzenweger, & Pitman, 2002). In addition to testing these individuals (and control subjects who denied having been abducted by aliens), we tested individuals who believed they had been abducted, but who had no memories of encountering aliens. Like the repressed-memory subjects in our previous studies, they inferred their histories of trauma from various "indicators" (e.g., a passion for reading science fiction, unexplained marks on their bodies). Like subjects with recovered memories of CSA, those reporting recovered memories of alien abduction exhibited pronounced false memory effects in the laboratory. Subjects who only believed they had been abducted likewise exhibited robust false memory effects.

Conclusions

The aforementioned experiments illustrate one way of approaching the recovered-memory controversy. Cognitive psychology methods cannot ascertain whether the memories reported by our subjects were true or false, but these methods can enable testing of hypotheses about mechanisms that ought to be operative if people can repress and recover memories of trauma or if they can develop false memories of trauma.

Pressing issues remain unresolved. For example, experimentalists assume that directed forgetting and other laboratory methods engage the same cognitive mechanisms that generate the signs and symptoms of emotional disorder in the real world. Some therapists question the validity of this assumption. Surely, they claim, remembering or forgetting the word *incest* in a laboratory task fails to capture the sensory and narrative complexity of autobiographical memories of abuse. On the one hand, the differences between remembering the word *incest* in a directed-forgetting experiment, for example, and recollecting an episode of molestation do, indeed, seem to outweigh the similarities. On the other hand, laboratory studies may underestimate clinical relevance. For example, if someone cannot expel the word *incest* from awareness during a directed-forgetting experiment, then it seems unlikely that this person would be able to banish autobiographical memories of trauma from consciousness. This intuition notwithstanding, an important empirical issue concerns whether these tasks do, indeed, engage the same mechanisms that figure in the cognitive processing of traumatic memories outside the laboratory.

A second issue concerns attempts to distinguish subjects with genuine memories of abuse from those with false memories of abuse. Our group is currently exploring whether this might be done by classifying trauma narratives in terms of how subjects describe their memory-recovery experience. For example, some of the subjects in our current research describe their recovered memories of abuse by saying, "I had forgotten about that. I hadn't thought about the abuse in years until I was reminded of it recently." The narratives of other recovered-memory subjects differ in their experiential quality. These subjects, as they describe it, suddenly realize that they are abuse survivors, sometimes attributing current life difficulties to these long-repressed memories. That is, they do not say that they have remembered forgotten events they once knew, but rather indicate that they have learned (e.g., through hypnosis) the abuse occurred. It will be important to determine whether these two groups of recovered-memory subjects differ cognitively. For example, are subjects exemplifying the second type of recovered-memory experience more prone to develop false memories in the laboratory than are subjects exemplifying the first type of experience?

Acknowledgments—Preparation of this article was supported in part by National Institute of Mental Health Grant MH61268.

Notes

1. Address correspondence to Richard J. McNally, Department of Psychology, Harvard University, 1230 William James Hall, 33 Kirkland St., Cambridge, MA 02138; e-mail: rjm@wjh.harvard.edu.

2. Some authors prefer the term *dissociation* (or *dissociative amnesia*) to *repression*. Although these terms signify different proposed mechanisms, for practical purposes these variations make little difference in the recovered-memory debate. Each term implies a defensive process that blocks access to disturbing memories.

3. However, not thinking about a disturbing experience for a long period of time must not be equated with an inability to remember it. Amnesia denotes an inability to recall information that has been encoded.

References

Brown, D., Scheflin, A.W., & Hammond, D.C. (1998). *Memory, trauma treatment, and the law.* New York: Norton.

Ceci, S.J., & Loftus, E.F. (1994). 'Memory work': A royal road to false memories? *Applied Cognitive Psychology, 8,* 351–364.

Clancy, S.A., McNally, R.J., & Schacter, D.L. (1999). Effects of guided imagery on memory distortion in women reporting recovered memories of childhood sexual abuse. *Journal of Traumatic Stress, 12,* 559–569.

Clancy, S.A., McNally, R.J., Schacter, D.L., Lenzenweger, M.F., & Pitman, R.K. (2002). Memory distortion in people reporting abduction by aliens. *Journal of Abnormal Psychology, 111,* 455–461.

Clancy, S.A., Schacter, D.L., McNally, R.J., & Pitman, R.K. (2000). False recognition in women reporting recovered memories of sexual abuse. *Psychological Science, 11,* 26–31.

Dubner, A.E., & Motta, R.W. (1999). Sexually and physically abused foster care children and posttraumatic stress disorder. *Journal of Consulting and Clinical Psychology, 67,* 367–373.

Garry, M., Manning, C.G., Loftus, E.F., & Sherman, S.J. (1996). Imagination inflation: Imagining a childhood event inflates confidence that it occurred. *Psychonomic Bulletin & Review, 3,* 208–214.

McNally, R.J. (1998). Experimental approaches to cognitive abnormality in posttraumatic stress disorder. *Clinical Psychology Review, 18,* 971–982.

McNally, R.J., Clancy, S.A., & Schacter, D.L. (2001). Directed forgetting of trauma cues in adults reporting repressed or recovered memories of childhood sexual abuse. *Journal of Abnormal Psychology, 110,* 151–156.

McNally, R.J., Clancy, S.A., Schacter, D.L., & Pitman, R.K. (2000a). Cognitive processing of trauma cues in adults reporting repressed, recovered, or continuous memories of childhood sexual abuse. *Journal of Abnormal Psychology, 109,* 355–359.

McNally, R.J., Clancy, S.A., Schacter, D.L., & Pitman, R.K. (2000b). Personality profiles, dissociation, and absorption in women reporting repressed, recovered, or continuous memories of childhood sexual abuse. *Journal of Consulting and Clinical Psychology, 68,* 1033–1037.

McNally, R.J., Metzger, L.J., Lasko, N.B., Clancy, S.A., & Pitman, R.K. (1998). Directed forgetting of trauma cues in adult survivors of childhood sexual abuse with and without posttraumatic stress disorder. *Journal of Abnormal Psychology, 107,* 596–601.

Pope, H.G., Jr., Oliva, P.S., & Hudson, J.I. (1999). Repressed memories: The scientific status. In D.L. Faigman, D.H. Kaye, M.J. Saks, & J. Sanders (Eds.), *Modern scientific evidence: The law and science of expert testimony* (Vol. 1, pocket part, pp. 115–155). St. Paul, MN: West Publishing.

Roediger, H.L., III, & McDermott, K.B, (1995). Creating false memories: Remembering words not presented in lists. *Journal of Experimental Psychology: Learning, Memory, and Cognition, 21*, 803–814.

Terr, L.C. (1991). Childhood traumas: An outline and overview. *American Journal of Psychiatry, 148*, 10–20.

Chapter 12 Gender Identity Disorder, Paraphilias, and Sexual Dysfunctions

Gender differences are an important aspect of our study of abnormal behavior. In Chapter 12 we examine gender differences in sexual response, sexual dysfunctions, and paraphilias. In Chapter 16 we consider gender differences in sexual aggression. Here, Letitia Anne Peplau examines ways in which men and women differ with respect to sexuality and sexual aggression.

Human Sexuality: How Do Men and Women Differ?

Letitia Anne Peplau[1]

Psychology Department, University of California, Los Angeles, Los Angeles, California

A century ago, sex experts confidently asserted that men and women have strikingly different sexual natures. The rise of scientific psychology brought skepticism about this popular but unproven view, and the pendulum swung toward an emphasis on similarities between men's and women's sexuality. For example, Masters and Johnson (1966) captured attention by proposing a human sexual response cycle applicable to both sexes. Feminist scholars cautioned against exaggerating male-female differences and argued for women's sexual equality with men. Recently, psychologists have taken stock of the available scientific evidence. Reviews of empirical research on diverse aspects of human sexuality have identified four important male-female differences. These gender differences are pervasive, affecting thoughts and feelings as well as behavior, and they characterize not only heterosexuals but lesbians and gay men as well.

Sexual Desire

Sexual desire is the subjective experience of being interested in sexual objects or activities or wishing to engage in sexual activities (Regan & Berscheid, 1999). Many lines of research demonstrate that men show more interest in sex than women (see review by Baumeister, Catanese, & Vohs, 2001). Compared with women, men think about sex more often. They report more frequent sex fantasies and more frequent feelings of sexual desire. Across the life span, men rate the strength of their own sex drive higher than do their female age-mates. Men are more interested in visual sexual stimuli and more likely to spend money on such sexual products and activities as X-rated videos and visits to prostitutes.

Men and women also differ in their preferred frequency of sex. When heterosexual dating and marriage partners disagree about sexual frequency, it is usually the man who wants to have sex more often than the woman does. In heterosexual couples, actual sexual frequency may reflect a compromise between the desires of the male and female partners. In gay and lesbian relationships, sexual frequency is decided by partners of the same gender,

and lesbians report having sex less often than gay men or heterosexuals. Further, women appear to be more willing than men to forgo sex or adhere to religious vows of celibacy.

Masturbation provides a good index of sexual desire because it is not constrained by the availability of a partner. Men are more likely than women to masturbate, start masturbating at an earlier age, and do so more often. In a review of 177 studies, Oliver and Hyde (1993) found large male-female differences in the incidence of masturbation. In technical terms, the meta-analytic effect size[2] (d) for masturbation was 0.96, which is smaller than the physical sex difference in height (2.00) but larger than most psychological sex differences, such as the performance difference on standardized math tests (0.20). These and many other empirical findings provide evidence for men's greater sexual interest.

Sexuality and Relationships

A second consistent difference is that women tend to emphasize committed relationships as a context for sexuality more than men do. When Regan and Berscheid (1999) asked young adults to define sexual desire, men were more likely than women to emphasize physical pleasure and sexual intercourse. In contrast, women were more likely to "romanticize" the experience of sexual desire, as seen in one young woman's definition of sexual desire as "longing to be emotionally intimate and to express love for another person" (p. 75). Compared with women, men have more permissive attitudes toward casual premarital sex and toward extramarital sex. The size of these gender differences is relatively large, particularly for casual premarital sex ($d = 0.81$; Oliver & Hyde, 1993). Similarly, women's sexual fantasies are more likely than men's to involve a familiar partner and to include affection and commitment. In contrast, men's fantasies are more likely to involve strangers, anonymous partners, or multiple partners and to focus on specific sex acts or sexual organs.

A gender difference in emphasizing relational aspects of sexuality is also found among lesbians and gay men (see review by Peplau, Fingerhut, & Beals, in press). Like heterosexual women, lesbians tend to have less permissive attitudes toward casual sex and sex outside a primary relationship than do gay or heterosexual men. Also like heterosexual women, lesbians have sex fantasies that are more likely to be personal and romantic than the fantasies of gay or heterosexual men. Lesbians are more likely than gay men to become sexually involved with partners who were first their friends, then lovers. Gay men in committed relationships are more likely than lesbians or heterosexuals to have sex with partners outside their primary relationship.

In summary, women's sexuality tends to be strongly linked to a close relationship. For women, an important goal of sex is intimacy; the best context for pleasurable sex is a committed relationship. This is less true for men.

Sexuality and Aggression

A third gendered pattern concerns the association between sexuality and aggression. This link has been demonstrated in many domains, including individuals' sexual self-concepts, the initiation of sex in heterosexual relationships, and coercive sex.

Andersen, Cyranowski, and Espindle (1999) investigated the dimensions that individuals use to characterize their own sexuality. Both sexes evaluated themselves along a dimension of being romantic, with some individuals seeing themselves as very passionate and others seeing themselves as not very passionate. However, men's sexual self-concepts were also characterized by a dimension of aggression, which concerned the extent to which they saw themselves as being aggressive, powerful, experienced, domineering, and individualistic. There was no equivalent aggression dimension for women's sexual self-concepts.

In heterosexual relationships, men are commonly more assertive than women and take the lead in sexual interactions (see review by Impett & Peplau, 2003). During the early stages of a dating relationship, men typically initiate touching and sexual intimacy. In ongoing relationships, men report initiating sex about twice as often as their female partners or age-mates. To be sure, many women do initiate sex, but they do so less frequently than their male partners. The same pattern is found in people's sexual fantasies. Men are more likely than women to imagine themselves doing something sexual to a partner or taking the active role in a sexual encounter.

Rape stands at the extreme end of the link between sex and aggression. Although women use many strategies to persuade men to have sex, physical force and violence are seldom part of their repertoire. Physically coercive sex is primarily a male activity (see review by Felson, 2002). There is growing recognition that stranger and acquaintance rape are not the whole story; some men use physical force in intimate heterosexual relationships. Many women who are battered by a boyfriend or husband also report sexual assaults as part of the abuse.

In summary, aggression is more closely linked to sexuality for men than for women. Currently, we know little about aggression and sexuality among lesbians and gay men; research on this topic would provide a valuable contribution to our understanding of gender and human sexuality.

Sexual Plasticity

Scholars from many disciplines have noted that, in comparison with men's sexuality, women's sexuality tends to have greater plasticity. That is, women's sexual beliefs and behaviors can be more easily shaped and altered by cultural, social, and situational factors. Baumeister (2000) systematically reviewed the scientific evidence on this point. In this section, I mention a few of the many supportive empirical findings.

One sign of plasticity concerns changes in aspects of a person's sexuality over time. Such changes are more common among women than among men. For example, the frequency of women's sexual activity is more variable than men's. If a woman is in an intimate relationship, she might have frequent sex with her partner. But following a breakup, she might have no sex at all, including masturbation, for several months. Men show less temporal variability: Following a romantic breakup, men may substitute masturbation for interpersonal sex and so maintain a more constant frequency of sex. There is also growing evidence that women are more likely than men to change their sexual orientation over time. In an illustrative longitudinal study (Diamond, 2003), more than 25% of 18- to 25-year-old women who initially identified as lesbian or bisexual changed their sexual identity during the next 5 years. Changes such as these are less common for men.

A further indication of malleability is that a person's sexual attitudes and behaviors are responsive to social and situational influences. Such factors as education, religion, and acculturation are more strongly linked to women's sexuality than to men's. For example, moving to a new culture may have more impact on women's sexuality than on men's. The experience of higher education provides another illustration. A college education is associated with more liberal sexual attitudes and behavior, but this effect is greater for women than for men. Even more striking is the association between college education and sexual orientation shown in a recent national survey (Laumann, Gagnon, Michael, & Michaels, 1994). Completing college doubled the likelihood that a man identified as gay or bisexual (1.7% among high school graduates vs. 3.3% among college graduates). However, college was associated with a 900% increase in the percentage of women identifying as lesbian or bisexual (0.4% vs. 3.6%).

Conclusion and Implications

Diverse lines of scientific research have identified consistent male-female differences in sexual interest, attitudes toward sex and relationships, the association between sex and aggression, and sexual plasticity. The size of these gender differences tends to be large, particularly in comparison to other male-female differences studied by psychologists. These differences are pervasive, encompassing thoughts, feelings, fantasies, and behavior. Finally, these male-female differences apply not only to heterosexuals but also to lesbians and gay men.

Several limitations of the current research are noteworthy. First, much research is based on White, middle-class American samples. Studies of other populations and cultural groups would be valuable in assessing the generalizability of findings. Second, although research findings on lesbians and gay men are consistent with patterns of male-female difference among heterosexuals, the available empirical database on homosexuals is relatively small. Third, differences between women and men are not absolute but rather a matter of degree. There are many exceptions to the general patterns described. For instance, some women show high levels of sexual interest, and some men seek sex only in committed relationships. Research documenting male-female differences has advanced further than research systematically tracing the origins of these differences. We are only beginning to understand the complex ways in which biology, experience, and culture interact to shape men's and women's sexuality.

These four general differences between women's and men's sexuality can illuminate specific patterns of sexual interaction. For example, in heterosexual couples, it is fairly common for a partner to engage in sex when he or she is not really interested or "in the mood." Although both men and women sometimes consent to such unwanted sexual activity, women are more often the compliant sexual partner (see review by Impett & Peplau, 2003). Each of the gender differences I have described may contribute to this pattern. First, the stage is set by a situation in which partners have differing desires for sex, and the man is more often the partner desiring sex. Second, for compliant sex to occur, the more interested partner must communicate his or her desire. Men typically take the lead in expressing sexual interest. Third, the disinterested partner's reaction is pivotal: Does this partner comply or, instead, ignore or reject the request? If women view sex as a way to show love and caring for a partner, they may be more likely than men to resolve a dilemma about unwanted sex by taking their partner's welfare into account. In abusive relationships, women may fear physical or psychological harm from a male partner if they refuse. Finally, sexual compliance illustrates the potential plasticity of female sexuality. In this case, women are influenced by relationship concerns to engage in a sexual activity that goes against their personal preference at the time.

The existence of basic differences between men's and women's sexuality has implications for the scientific study of sexuality. Specifically, an adequate understanding of human sexuality may require separate analyses of sexuality in women and in men, based on the unique biology and life experiences of each sex. Currently, efforts to reconceptualize sexual issues have focused on women's sexuality. Three examples are illustrative.

Rethinking Women's Sexual Desire How should we interpret the finding that women appear less interested in sex than men? One possibility is that researchers have inadvertently used male standards (e.g., penile penetration and orgasm) to evaluate women's sexual experiences and consequently ignored activities, such as intimate kissing, cuddling, and touching, that may be uniquely important to women's erotic lives. Researchers such as Wallen (1995) argue that it is necessary to distinguish between sexual desire (an intrinsic motivation to pursue sex) and arousability (the capacity to become sexually aroused in response to situational cues). Because women's sexual desire may vary across the menstrual cycle, it may be more appropriate to describe women's desire as periodic rather than weak or limited. In contrast, women's receptivity to sexual overtures and their capacity for sexual response may depend on situational rather than hormonal cues. Other researchers (e.g., Tolman & Diamond, 2001) argue that more attention must be paid to the impact of hormones that may have special relevance for women, such as the neuropeptide oxytocin, which is linked to both sexuality and affectional bonding.

Rethinking Women's Sexual Orientation Some researchers have proposed new paradigms for understanding women's sexual orientation (e.g., Peplau & Garnets, 2000). Old models either assumed commonalities among homosexuals, regardless of gender, or hypothesized similarities between lesbians and heterosexual men, both of whom are attracted to women. In contrast, empirical research has documented many similarities in women's sexuality, regardless of their sexual orientation. A new model based on women's experiences might highlight the centrality of relationships to women's sexual orientation, the potential for at least some women to change their sexual orientation over time, and the importance of sociocultural factors in shaping women's sexual orientation.

Rethinking Women's Sexual Problems Finally, research on women's sexuality has led some scientists to question current systems for classifying sexual dysfunction among women. The widely used *Diagnostic and Statistical Manual of Mental Disorders* (*DSM*) of the American Psychiatric Association categorizes sexual dysfunction on the basis of Masters and Johnson's (1966) model of presumed normal and universal sexual functioning. Critics (e.g., Kaschak & Tiefer, 2001) have challenged the validity of this model, its applicability to women, and its use as a basis for clinical assessment. They have also faulted the *DSM* for ignoring the relationship context of sexuality for women. Kaschak and Tiefer have proposed instead a new "woman-centered" view of women's sexual problems that gives prominence to partner and relationship factors that affect women's sexual experiences, and also to social, cultural, and economic factors that influence the quality of women's sexual lives.

Notes

1. Address correspondence to Letitia Anne Peplau, Psychology Department, Franz 1285, University of California, Los Angeles, CA 90095-1563; e-mail: lapeplau@ucla.edu.

2. In a meta-analysis, the findings of multiple studies are analyzed quantitatively to arrive at an overall estimate of the size of a difference between two groups, in this case, between men and women. This effect size (known technically as *d*) is reported using a common unit of measurement. By convention in psychological research, 0.2 is considered a small effect size, 0.5 is a moderate effect size, and 0.8 is a large effect size.

References

Andersen, B.L., Cyranowski, J.M., & Espindle, D. (1999). Men's sexual self-schema. *Journal of Personality and Social Psychology, 76,* 645–661.

Baumeister, R.F. (2000). Gender differences in erotic plasticity. *Psychological Bulletin, 126,* 347–374.

Baumeister, R.F., Catanese, K.R., & Vohs, K.D. (2001). Is there a gender difference in strength of sex drive? *Personality and Social Psychology Review, 5,* 242–273.

Diamond, L.M. (2003). Was it a phase? Young women's relinquishment of lesbian/bisexual identities over a 5-year period. *Journal of Personality and Social Psychology, 84,* 352–364.

Felson, R.B. (2002). *Violence and gender reexamined.* Washington, DC: American Psychological Association.

Impett, E., & Peplau, L.A. (2003). Sexual compliance: Gender, motivational, and relationship perspectives. *Journal of Sex Research, 40,* 87–100.

Kaschak, E., & Tiefer, L. (Eds.). (2001). *A new view of women's sexual problems.* New York: Haworth Press.

Laumann, E., Gagnon, J., Michael, R., & Michaels, S. (1994). *The social organization of sexuality.* Chicago: University of Chicago Press.

Masters, W.H., & Johnson, V.E. (1966). *Human sexual response.* Boston: Little, Brown, & Co.

Oliver, M.B., & Hyde, J.S. (1993). Gender differences in sexuality: A meta-analysis. *Psychological Bulletin, 114,* 29–51.

Peplau, L.A., Fingerhut, A., & Beals, K. (in press). Sexuality in the relationships of lesbians and gay men. In J. Harvey, A. Wenzel, & S. Sprecher (Eds.), *Handbook of sexuality in close relationships.* Mahwah, NJ: Erlbaum.

Peplau, L.A., & Garnets, L.D. (Eds.). (2000). Women's sexualities: New perspectives on sexual orientation and gender [Special issue]. *Journal of Social Issues, 56*(2).

Regan, P.C., & Berscheid, E. (1999). *Lust: What we know about human sexual desire.* Thousand Oaks, CA: Sage.

Tolman, D.L., & Diamond, L.M. (2001). Desegregating sexuality research: Cultural and biological perspectives on gender and desire. *Annual Review of Sex Research, 12,* 33–74.

Wallen, K. (1995). The evolution of female sexual desire. In P. Abramson & S.D. Pinkerton (Eds.), *Sexual nature/sexual culture* (pp. 57–79). Chicago: University of Chicago Press.

Chapter 13 Schizophrenia and Other Psychotic Disorders

As we note in Chapter 13, mounting evidence connects schizophrenia to brain abnormalities that may arise in early development. In this article, Heather Conklin and William Iacono adopt a neurodevelopmental perspective that may lead to a better understanding of the etiology of this puzzling psychological disorder.

Schizophrenia: A Neurodevelopmental Perspective

Heather M. Conklin and William G. Iacono[1]
Department of Psychology, University of Minnesota, Minneapolis, Minnesota

The past decade has seen a proliferation of research findings in the field of schizophrenia, with provocative developments in molecular genetics, neurobiology, neuroimaging, neuropsychology, and studies of high-risk individuals. Although the etiology of schizophrenia remains enigmatic, scientists are gaining ground in developing plausible models of vulnerability to this disorder. In the past, most research findings have provided insights into selected aspects of the disorder without yielding a comprehensive theory that has received broad-based approval. Recently emerging neurodevelopmental models of schizophrenia, however, are capable of accommodating diverse findings and are receiving widespread support among schizophrenia investigators.

Neurodevelopmental models propose that vulnerability to schizophrenia results from a disruption in forebrain development during the perinatal period. A brain lesion that occurs early in development is hypothesized to lie dormant until normal brain maturational events trigger the appearance of traditional diagnostic signs, typically in adolescence or early adulthood (Weinberg, 1987). Such models are supported by reports of increased intrauterine and perinatal complications among individuals with schizophrenia, as well as by demonstrations that neurological, neuropsychological, and physical abnormalities predate the onset of psychosis. Although this evidence is far from conclusive, neurodevelopmental models hold immense promise as a heuristic for bridging research in multiple domains and posing questions central to discovering the etiology of this disorder.

Genetic and Environmental Vulnerability

Well-replicated findings from family, twin, and adoption studies indicate that there is a substantial genetic component to the predisposition for schizophrenia. The likelihood that this genetic predisposition involves multiple genes and the possibility that different genetic variants underlie the risk for schizophrenia have made the search for genes via standard molecular techniques daunting. Although research findings have identified several chromosomal sites where there may be genes that confer susceptibility to schizophrenia (i.e., genetic linkage), a failure to replicate these findings has become the norm rather than the exception. A recent study, which examined the entire genome of individuals in families with high rates of schizophrenia, provided evidence for schizophrenia susceptibility on chromosome 1 (Brzustowicz, Hodgkinson, Chow, Honer, & Bassett, 2000). This finding is promising in that the evidence for genetic linkage was unusually strong, a factor that should facilitate the search for a specific gene on this chromosome in these families.

It is reasonable to propose that alteration of gene expression (i.e., production of proteins coded for by genes), during critical phases of early development, contributes to neurodevelopmental abnormalities seen in schizophrenia. Brain development is a delicate process that requires a precise cascade of events orchestrated by the timing and specificity of gene expression. However, until one or more schizophrenia-susceptibility genes have been identified, the link between genetic variations and neurodevelopmental abnormalities remains largely theoretical. For example, neurodevelopmental disturbances in schizophrenia may result from the improper function of proteins that regulate the movement of neurons to their final destination in the brain (neuronal migration) and the formation of neural connections (synaptogenesis).

If schizophrenia were entirely due to heredity, all identical twins with schizophrenia would have co-twins who also have the disorder because identical twins share all of their genes. In fact, the co-twins of affected identical twins develop schizophrenia only about half the time. Thus, environmental factors must also influence schizophrenia's development. From a neurodevelopmental perspective, events occurring early in life are of greatest interest as potential environmental risk factors. A higher rate of obstetric complications has been found for schizophrenia patients relative to normal comparison subjects, psychiatric comparison subjects, and well siblings. A recent report suggests that the risk for schizophrenia is correlated with the number of hypoxia-associated obstetric complications (i.e., complications that can result in oxygen deprivation) an individual may have experienced (Cannon, Rosso, Bearden, Sanchez, & Hadley, 1999). The risk for schizophrenia appears to be conferred from an interaction between genetic predisposition and obstetric complications, rather than obstetric complications alone. In addition, *in utero* viral exposure has been studied as an environmental risk factor for schizophrenia because of the higher number of winter births than births in other seasons among schizophrenia patients and the increased frequency of viral epidemics in the fall. For example, an increased rate of schizophrenia was demonstrated among individuals who were exposed during their second trimester to an influenza epidemic in Helsinki in 1957 (Mednick, Machon, Huttunen, & Bonett, 1988).

Neurological Abnormalities

The longest-held finding in support of the neurodevelopmental model is the increased size of fluid-filled spaces (lateral ventricles) in the brain that is present in first-episode schizophrenia patients and appears to remain static over time. It appears, then, that brain abnormalities are not just an index of the disorder's progression, but more likely constitute a preexisting vulnerability to the disorder. Post mortem histological studies have produced convergent evidence for neurological anomalies at the cellular level. Cellular abnormalities in the brain, such as increased neuronal spacing and altered arrangement of neuronal layers in temporal and frontal lobes areas,[2] have suggested that the predisposition for schizophrenia may involve disruption in neuronal migration. Furthermore, histological studies have failed to find signs of gliosis (a neuronal indicator of injury to a mature brain or of a neuropathological process), again suggesting the cellular deviations occurred early in life.

Neuroimaging studies have demonstrated structural and metabolic abnormalities in the medial-temporal lobe and frontal lobe of schizophrenia patients. For example, reduced frontal cerebral blood flow (hypofrontality) during tasks that require frontal activation has been observed, with the degree of frontal blood flow correlating with task performance. Although a review of recent neuroimaging findings in schizophrenia is beyond the scope of this article, there have been increasing efforts to parse out specific areas within the medial-temporal and frontal lobes that may be compromised in schizophrenia. Temporal lobe dysfunction likely contributes to positive symptoms, consisting of delusions and hallucinations, and frontal lobe dysfunction likely contributes to negative symptoms, such as impoverished thought, lack of goal-directed activities, and social withdrawal.

The performance of schizophrenia patients on neuropsychological tasks has been used to elucidate cognitive deficits that may be secondary to brain abnormalities in these patients, as well as to develop hypotheses about the location of their neuropathology. Schizophrenia patients have been found to be impaired on a range of tasks, including ones purported to measure abstraction, sustained attention, language, and memory. Recently, Bilder et al. (2000) evaluated the performance of first-episode schizophrenia patients using a comprehensive neuropsychological test battery. They reported a large generalized deficit in schizophrenia patients with additional specific deficits in memory and executive functions. These results are not open to previous criticisms that cognitive deficits in schizophrenia merely reflect factors associated with chronic mental illness (e.g., long-term treatment) or depict global impairment. The findings are consistent with histological and neuroimaging findings that implicate temporal and frontal lobe involvement in schizophrenia.

Although it is now recognized that multiple neurotransmitters likely contribute to the etiology of schizophrenia, dopamine continues to be the primary neurotransmitter of interest.[3] The dopamine hypothesis, which originally asserted that schizophrenia results from a diffuse excess of dopamine in the brain, has been revised to suggest a dysregulation of dopamine resulting in an excess of dopamine in temporal areas and a depletion of dopamine in frontal areas. Further, it has now been proposed that the alteration in dopamine neurotransmission may not result from a primary deficit in dopamine neurons or receptors, but rather may result from abnormalities in the regulation of dopamine by limbic (medial-temporal lobe structures responsible for motivated and emotional behaviors) and frontal regions (More, West, & Grace, 1999). These are the same brain areas implicated by histological, neuroimaging, and neuropsychological studies. The dysregulation of dopamine neurotransmission that appears to occur in schizophrenia corresponds with behavioral and cognitive processes that are altered in this disorder. For example, within the frontal lobe, dopamine appears to specifically mediate aspects of working memory and motor planning that are impaired in schizophrenia (Goldman-Rakic, 1996). Dopamine and its interaction with other neurotransmitters, such as glutamate and gamma amino butyric acid (GABA), continue to be central to etiological models of schizophrenia.

Animal models[4] of schizophrenia hold promise for testing etiological theories, including neurodevelopmental models. Administration of neurotoxins in developing animals has been used to create disruptions in prenatal neuronal migration, perinatal oxygen deprivation has been used to imitate hypoxia associated with obstetric complications, and neonatal lesions to the hippocampus have been used to re-create structural brain abnormalities. To date, animal models have been able to reproduce a surprisingly broad range of neurobiological, behavioral, and cognitive aspects of schizophrenia. For example, some models have reproduced schizophrenia-like post mortem histological changes, impairment on working memory tasks, and withdrawn social behavior. In addition, animal models have demonstrated that some deficits are specific to neonatal rather than adult lesions, some symptoms show delayed emergence in adulthood, and some functions are returned to normal with the administration of drugs used to treat schizophrenia (neuroleptics). Behavioral outcomes can also vary with the genetic strain of an animal, suggesting an interaction between genes and environment. Although animal models integrate findings across research areas well, they have obvious limitations, including the fact that animal behaviors may be insufficient proxies for certain complex human behaviors.

Prospective and High-Risk Studies

Neurodevelopmental models implicitly predict that signs of disorder predate the onset of florid psychosis. Indeed, research has demonstrated that individuals who later develop schizophrenia exhibit motor, cognitive, and behavioral abnormalities during childhood. In an innovative archival study, Walker and Lewine (1990) showed that preschizophrenic children could be reliably differentiated from their well siblings in home videos taken during early childhood, primarily on the basis of abnormal movements and reduced facial expression. Jones, Rodgers, Murray, and Marmot (1994) studied a British cohort of 4,746 children born in 1946, of which 30 later developed schizophrenia. The preschizophrenic individuals were more likely than control subjects to have exhibited delayed early motor development; obtained low educational test scores at ages 8, 11, and 15; preferred solitary play at ages 4 and 6; and been rated by teachers as anxious in social situations at age 15.

Researchers have also investigated abnormalities in the unaffected first-degree relatives of schizophrenia patients. These individuals are at genetic risk because they share on average half of their genes with schizophrenia patients. Healthy relatives have been observed to demonstrate both behavioral and neurobiological impairments that are similar to those seen in affected patients. For nearly a century, higher rates of schizophrenia-related disorders, such as schizotypal personality disorder,[5] have been seen in these relatives compared with the general population. The most consistent finding in relatives has been eye movement dysfunction, a finding consistent with frontal involvement in the genetic diathesis for schizophrenia. The impaired performance of relatives on certain neuropsychological measures, such as working memory tasks, provides further convergent evidence for frontal lobe dysfunction. Relatives who are deviant on more than one of these measures may be at the greatest risk for schizophrenia and may be most informative when included in genetic studies of this disorder. Associations among schizophrenia-related disorders, cognitive task performance, and the quality of eye movements in relatives of schizophrenia patients are being investigated (for discussion, see Iacono & Grove, 1993).

Velocardiofacial Syndrome (VCFS) As An Integrative Example

VCFS is a congenital syndrome that affects multiple body systems and is associated with a small deletion of genetic material in a specific area of chromosome 22. The symptom profile of individuals with VCFS is variable but commonly includes facial malformations, oral palatal anomalies, nasal voice, and cardiac abnormalities. Various studies have demonstrated that the rate of schizophrenia among individuals with VCFS is approximately 25 times the rate found in the population overall (i.e., 1%), leading investigators to suggest that VCFS is a genetic subtype of schizophrenia (Bassett et al., 1998). The inverse relationship also holds, with multiple studies demonstrating that the rate of this deletion on chromosome 22 in schizophrenia patients is approximately 80 times the general-population rate of 1 in 4,000. VCFS and preschizophrenic individuals show strikingly similar developmental characteristics. Specifically, children with VCFS exhibit delayed motor development, below-average IQ, a tendency toward concrete thinking, bland affect, and lowered levels of social interaction.

Research has begun to suggest potentially shared pathophysiology for VCFS and schizophrenia that may stem from the deletion on chromosome 22. One theory proposes that both VCFS and schizophrenia are neurodevelopmental disorders that affect midline body structures, an idea consistent with the physical abnormalities seen in VCFS. It may be that the pathology also includes migration of cells destined to be midline brain structures, including medial-temporal lobe structures. VCFS and schizophrenia have been associated with similar neuropathology (e.g., enlarged ventricles and an underdeveloped cerebellum), as revealed by magnetic resonance imaging; these structural changes may play a role in predisposing individuals to psychosis (Vataja & Elomaa, 1998). Another potential mechanism stems from the observation that the chromosomal area deleted in VCFS is close to the catechol-O-methyl transferase (COMT) gene (Dunham, Collins, Wadey, & Scambler, 1992). COMT is an enzyme that metabolizes certain neurotransmitters, including dopamine. It has been proposed that a predisposition to psychosis could arise through either a decrease in the metabolism of these neurotransmitters in the brain or an increase in exposure to them during neurodevelopment. Although there are limitations to the notion that VCFS is a schizophrenia subtype, the case of VCFS illustrates how research can be integrated to handle multiple aspects of schizophrenia, including genetic predisposition to illness, presence of signs of disorder that predate psychosis, neurochemical deviations, and developmental brain abnormalities.

Future Directions

As much as schizophrenia research is yielding provocative findings, there continue to be important unanswered questions regarding etiology. To date, investigators have not been able to reliably identify susceptibility genes for schizophrenia, precluding mapping the pathway from genetic vulnerability to brain abnormalities. A better understanding of the dormancy period between early brain lesions and adult onset of the disorder is needed. Animal models have failed to support the idea that hormonal changes in puberty may trigger the appearance of symptoms, and theories suggesting that the onset of diagnostic symptoms coincides with ongoing frontal lobe development need to be more adequately investigated. The identification of environmental stressors that contribute substantially to risk for schizophrenia is required. Perinatal complications, such as obstetric complications and viral exposure *in utero*, are some of the leading risk contenders; however, they are likely insufficient to account for the 50% of identical twins who have schizophrenia but whose co-twins do not. In addition, these environmental events make different theoretical predictions based on their timing, the stage of brain development implicated, and the mechanism of action.

Although the neurodevelopmental model is making great strides in integrating diverse research findings, it may be but one of several useful models that ultimately characterize schizophrenia's multiple etiologies. The lack of cohesion of some of the research evidence may be due to schizophrenia resulting from different etiologies in different individuals. Such etiological heterogeneity confounds research into the cause (or causes) of schizophrenia, as study samples likely include individuals for whom the underlying cause of the disorder is not the same. One way to obtain samples with greater etiological homogeneity would be to supplement traditional diagnostic systems with measurement of traits that are likely more direct manifestations of the biological predisposition. For example, an investigator could select study samples of individuals who not only meet current diagnostic criteria for schizophrenia, but also demonstrate signs of neurodevelopmental origin for this disorder, such as those reviewed in this article. Research using a selection procedure such as this, one that is theoretically driven and also supported by recent research findings, likely holds the greatest promise for yielding etiological insight.

Notes

1. Address correspondence to William G. Iacono, Department of Psychology, University of Minnesota, N218 Elliott Hall, 75 East River Rd., Minneapolis, MN 55455; e-mail: wiacono@tfs.psych.umn.edu.

2. The temporal lobe is located laterally in the brain, near the temples. A primary ability supported by medial-temporal lobe structures (e.g., the hippocampus) is memory. In addition, individuals with damage to the temporal lobe may experience hallucinations. The frontal lobe is located in the most anterior part of the brain. Primary abilities supported by the frontal lobe include attention, as well as higher-level planning and organizing skills sometimes referred to as executive functions. Individuals with damage to the frontal lobe may demonstrate working memory impairment (i.e., an inability to temporarily store and manipulate information needed to execute a task) and eye movement dysfunction (i.e., an inability to produce certain kinds of eye movements in experimental paradigms).

3. Dopamine is one of many identified neurotransmitters, chemicals that allow for communication between nerve cells (neurons). Neurotransmitters are typically released into the space between neurons (a synapse), where they may exert their effect by binding to specific neuroanatomical sites (receptors) of adjacent neurons. In this manner, neurotransmitters may serve to propagate electrochemical signals throughout the nervous system.

4. Animal models attempt to imitate or re-create some aspect of human functioning in animals in order to study specific processes under greater experimental control. For example, animal models of schizophrenia may create any combination of signs and symptoms of the disorder in order to gain better understanding of its etiology or treatments.

5. Schizotypal personality disorder is characterized by disturbances in interpersonal relationships, distorted thoughts or perceptions, and odd speech or behavior. These symptoms are generally believed to be similar, but sub-threshold, to schizophrenia symptoms.

References

Bassett, A.S., Hodgkinson, K., Chow, E.W.C., Correia, S., Scutt, L.E., & Weksberg, R. (1998). 22q11 deletion syndrome in adults with schizophrenia. *American Journal of Medical Genetics, 81,* 328–337.

Bilder, R.M., Goldman, R.S., Robinson, D., Reiter, G., Bell, L., Bates, J.A., Pappadopulos, E., Wilson, D.F., Alvir, J.M.J., Woerner, M.G., Geisler, S., Kane, J.M., & Lieberman, J.A. (2000). Neuropsychology of first-episode schizophrenia: Initial characterization and clinical correlates. *American Journal of Psychiatry, 157,* 549–559.

Brzustowicz, L.M., Hodgkinson, K.A., Chow, E.W.C., Honer, W.G., & Bassett, A.S. (2000). Location of a major susceptibility locus for familial schizophrenia on chromosome 1q21-q22. *Science, 288,* 678–682.

Cannon, T.D., Rosso, I.M., Bearden, C.E., Sanchez, L.E., & Hadley, T. (1999). A prospective cohort study of neurodevelopmental processes in the genesis and epigenesis of schizophrenia. *Development and Psychopathology, 11,* 467–485.

Dunham, I., Collins, J., Wadey, R., & Scambler, P. (1992). Possible role for COMT in psychosis associated with velo-cardio-facial syndrome. *The Lancet, 340,* 1361–1362.

Goldman-Rakic, P.S. (1996). Regional and cellular fractionation of working memory. *Proceedings of the National Academy of Sciences, USA, 93,* 13473–13480.

Iacono, W.G., & Grove, W.M. (1993). Schizophrenia research: Toward an integrative genetic model. *Psychological Science, 4,* 273–276.

Jones, P., Rodgers, B., Murray, R., & Marmot, M. (1994). Child developmental risk factors for adult schizophrenia in the British 1946 birth cohort. *The Lancet, 344,* 1398–1402.

Mednick, S.A., Machon, R.A., Huttunen, M.O., & Bonett, D. (1988). Adult schizophrenia following prenatal exposure to an influenza epidemic. *Archives of General Psychiatry, 45,* 189–192.

Moore, H., West, A.R., & Grace, A.A. (1999). The regulation of forebrain dopamine transmission: Relevance to the pathophysiology and psychopathology of schizophrenia. *Biological Psychiatry, 46,* 40–55.

Vataja, R., & Elomaa, E. (1998). Midline brain anomalies and schizophrenia in people with CATCH 22 syndrome. *British Journal of Psychiatry, 172,* 518–520.

Walker, E., & Lewine, R.J. (1990). Prediction of adult-onset schizophrenia from childhood home movies of the patients. *American Journal of Psychiatry, 147,* 1052–1056.

Weinberger, D.R. (1987). Implications of normal brain development for the pathogenesis of schizophrenia. *Archives of General Psychiatry, 44,* 660–669.

Chapter 14   Abnormal Behavior in Childhood and Adolescence

In Chapter 14 we discuss psychological disorders of childhood and adolescence. As Elaine Walker notes in this article, adolescence is a pivotal time for the development of some forms of psychopathology. She adopts a neurodevelopmental framework that focuses on the role of maturational processes in the development of abnormal behavior.

Adolescent Neurodevelopment and Psychopathology

Elaine F. Walker[1]
Department of Psychology, Emory University, Atlanta, Georgia

The notion that adolescence is a period of storm and stress has been highly controversial among psychological theorists (Cote, 1994). The debate was sparked by Margaret Mead's contention that Western culture generated a stereotype of tumultuous adolescence—one that did not apply to non-Western societies. But the controversy has gradually subsided, and the weight of the empirical literature does suggest that adolescence is a period of heightened anxiety and stress across many cultural contexts. The data also indicate that a substantial number of teenagers experience adjustment problems and dysphoria (Arnett, 1999). Although in most cases these difficulties do not persist into adulthood, for a subgroup the problems escalate, reflecting the prodromal (precursor) stage of serious mental illness. There is now a growing body of evidence that the onset of puberty marks the entry into a sensitive developmental period with respect to the neural circuits involved in mental health and illness (Benes, 1999). The developmental changes associated with adolescence are reflected in behavior, endocrinology, and brain structure.

Adolescence and Behavioral Adjustment

Adolescence is also associated with a rise in a variety of adjustment problems. There is a precipitous increase in self-reported negative emotional experiences, and in rates of risk taking, substance abuse, and clinical depression (Arnett, 1999; Spear, 2000). Although social and cultural factors undoubtedly contribute to these problems, the fact that similar developmental trends are observed in diverse cultures suggests that biological factors also play a role.

The onset of depression during adolescence is especially pernicious because it is linked with a poorer long-term prognosis. That is, adolescents who manifest clinical depression are much more likely to have a chronic course with repeated episodes than are individuals who first experience depression in adulthood. Although the postpubertal rise in depression is observed in both sexes, it is most pronounced among girls (Hankin et al., 1998; Silberg et al., 1999). Further, girls who show an early onset of puberty manifest the highest rates of mood disorders. It is noteworthy that there is some evidence that the rate of adolescent depression has increased in recent cohorts of youth. The onset of puberty is also occurring earlier in recent cohorts, and this could be related to the escalation in adolescent mood disorders.

Although psychotic disorders, such as schizophrenia, usually have their onset in the early 20s, the subclinical signs are typically apparent during the teenage years (Walker, Baum, & Diforio, 1998). In fact, the majority of individuals who are eventually diagnosed with schizophrenia and other psychotic illnesses show a steep increase in adjustment problems through adolescence. Social withdrawal, anxiety, academic difficulties, and thought problems become more common with each year between the ages of 12 and 18 in this group.

As with teenage depression, there are sex differences in the prodromal course of psychotic disorders. Boys who are subsequently diagnosed with schizophrenia show more severe adjustment problems than do girls. The prodromal phase for boys is also characterized by more disruptive behavior. Sex differences persist through the early course of schizophrenia; females tend to be diagnosed with the illness 2 to 3 years later than males, and they have a more favorable long-term prognosis. It has been suggested that these differences are due to hormones, with estrogen serving to delay the onset and ameliorate the course of the illness. Specifically, the activity of the neurotransmitter dopamine, which has been implicated in the neuropathology of schizophrenia, is dampened by estrogen.

Some childhood-onset mental disorders undergo a change in clinical expression during adolescence. For example, children with Tourette's syndrome often experience an amelioration of symptoms after the onset of puberty. In contrast, many forms of epilepsy have their onset following puberty. Again, these developmental trends suggest that brain maturation has implications for vulnerability to various neuropsychiatric syndromes.

One of the most fascinating findings from behavioral genetic studies is that the heritability of some behavioral propensities and mental disorders increases with age. In other words, the proportion of the variance accounted for by genetic factors rises, particularly during adolescence. This holds for cognitive and personality traits, as well as clinical depression (Silberg et al., 1999). The reason for the increase in heritability is not known; however, as I discuss later, hormones may exert a major influence.

Adolescent Neurodevelopment

Brain Changes During Adolescence New technologies for studying the brain in vivo have quickened the pace of research on brain development in humans. As a result, significant postpubertal brain development has now been documented. In general, these changes entail a maturation and refinement of neural circuitry. There are normative maturational changes in the volume of several brain regions, including the frontal and temporal cortex, amygdala, and hippocampus (Giedd et al., 1996, 1999; Sowell & Jernigan, 1998). Specifically, limbic structures, including the hippocampus and amygdala, tend to show an increase in volume. The limbic system is a group of interconnected brain structures that play an important role in human emotion. Also, gray matter volume in some areas of the cortex decreases through adolescence. The gray matter is the outer layer of the cortex where the cell bodies of neurons are concentrated. In addition, there is protracted maturation of fiber pathways in the white matter throughout childhood and adolescence. The white matter of the brain contains neural fibers that are covered with myelin, and the maturation of these pathways includes increased myelination of the hippocampus and associated limbic regions, and increased white matter density in fiber tracts that connect regions of the cortex with each other and with the spinal cord. The age-related changes in white matter density may reflect increases in axon diameter or myelination.

Frontal brain activity, as measured with functional MRI (magnetic resonance imaging) and electrophysiology, is enhanced during adolescence (Casey, Giedd, & Thomas, 2000; Rubia et al., 2000). This increased activation is assumed to contribute to advances in higher-level cognitive processes. For example, abstract reasoning and attentional capacities improve following puberty and into young adulthood. Interest in social activities and interpersonal awareness also increases (Spear, 2000). It is likely that these normative changes in cognitive capacities and behavior, as well as risk for certain forms of psychopathology, are a consequence of changes in the brain that are linked with sexual maturation.

Hormonal and Neurotransmitter Changes There are well-established developmental changes in activity of what is called the hypothalamic-pituitary-gonadal (HPG) axis as the child advances through puberty. The HPG axis is the neural system that controls the rise in sex hormones (e.g., estrogen and testosterone). These maturational processes result from the genetic program that prepares the organism for reproduction.

More recently, researchers have documented adolescent changes in the secretion of thyroid and adrenal hormones. Most relevant to the issue of adolescent "stress and storm" is the increased activation of another neural system, the hypothalamic-pituitary-adrenal (HPA) axis, during the teenage years. The HPA axis, which comprises the hypothalamus, pituitary, and adrenal gland, plays a central role in the biological stress response. The HPA axis subserves a cascade of biochemical events: The hypothalamus releases corticotropin-releasing hormone, which activates pituitary secretion of adreno-corticotropin, hormone, which, in turn, stimulates the adrenal gland to release glucocorticoids, most notably cortisol in primates. Studies of humans have revealed a gradual rise in cortisol levels beginning in early adolescence (see the Recommended Reading). These and other findings have led some researchers to conclude that adolescence is a period of heightened stress sensitivity (Kiess et al., 1995; Spear, 2000).

Levels of neurotransmitters also change with the onset of puberty. There appears to be a generalized decrease in serotonin, whereas dopamine activity increases in some cortical regions. Certain enzymes that play a role in the synthesis and degradation of neurotransmitters also increase during the teenage years. It has been hypothesized that the increased risk for the onset of psychosis during adolescence and early adulthood may be due to the elevation in dopamine activity.

Hormones and the Brain: Potential Neural Mechanisms in Adolescent-Onset Psychopathology When researchers examine the relation between gonadal hormone levels and behavior in youth, they typically find only a modest linear association. This is consistent with the assumption that hormonal effects on behavior are mediated by changes in brain structure and function. Thus, hormones trigger changes in brain structure and function that, in turn, influence behavior. There is also evidence of threshold effects of hormones, so, rising hormones may have no effect on behavior until they exceed a certain level. As a result, the relations between baseline circulating levels of hormones and behavior are likely to be nonlinear.

Hormones play a pivotal role in neuromaturation. They have organizational as well as activational effects on the brain. In other words, they affect the brain's structural development as well as its immediate functional properties. The organizational effects of gonadal hormones are pronounced during the prenatal period, when sexually dimorphic aspects of the central nervous system arise. Then later, during puberty, gonadal hormones play a role in brain maturation, and, in turn, influence cognition, mood, and behavior.

It has been shown that the behavioral influences exerted by gonadal and adrenal hormones are partially mediated by their effects on gene expression (i.e., the activation of the gene's program; McEwen, 1994; Watson & Gametchu, 1999). There are hormone receptors on the surface of neurons as well as inside the cell body. In general, it appears that the surface receptors mediate short-term effects on behavior. These are referred to as *nongenomic* effects. The hormone receptors that reside in a cell's nucleus are responsible for hormones' *genomic* effects. These effects can be long term because they can permanently alter the brain. When hormones bind to receptors inside the nucleus, they can increase gene expression by changing the expression of messenger RNA that codes for specific proteins. These proteins, in turn, influence neuronal structure and function, including neuronal growth, neurotransmitter synthesis, and receptor density and sensitivity. For example, in rodents, stress hormones change the expression of genes that code for the production of brain growth factors, which are substances that can induce neuronal development in the hippocampus. Hormones are also capable of augmenting the expression of genes that affect the survival of neurons. Thus, cell death (apoptosis) may result from abnormal levels of hormones.

Research with rodents has shown that hormones can trigger the expression of genes that control postpubertal maturational processes. Thus, some of the normative brain changes observed in human adolescents are assumed to result from the effects of hormones on the expression of genes that govern maturational processes such as the proliferation and elimination of neuronal processes. This raises the possibility that the hormonal changes occurring during adolescence may also be capable of triggering genes that contribute to vulnerability for mental disorders. The postpubescent increase in heritability for behavioral traits and disorders suggests that hormonal maturation results in the expression of genes that were previously silent. If the individual possesses genes that code for aberrant brain function, and gonadal or adrenal hormones trigger the expression of these "vulnerability" genes, then signs of behavioral disorder may first become apparent in adolescence. For example, the rise in hormones during puberty may result in the expression of a gene that codes for abnormal dopamine neurotransmission. This, in turn, may give rise to the brain abnormality that confers susceptibility to schizophrenia. Similarly, vulnerability to depression might result if hormone surges trigger the expression of a gene that leads to a defect in one of the neurotransmitter systems involved in this illness, such as the serotonin system.

Hormonal deficiency may also be involved in neurodevelopmental abnormality. It is plausible that insufficient levels of gonadal or adrenal hormones lead to the failure of expression of genes that are critical for adolescent brain maturation, resulting in psychopathology. In this connection, it has been suggested that schizophrenia involves a deficit in the pruning of neural connections that is normally triggered by puberty. In other words, deficient elimination of neural processes may result in faulty neuronal interconnections.

Finally, adjustment problems may arise during adolescence when there is a preexisting abnormality in a brain region that comes "on line" during this period. Thus, genetically programmed brain maturation could lead to maladaptive behavior if one or more components of a newly emerging circuit is defective. In this way, a previously "silent" brain lesion could begin to negatively influence behavior after the onset of puberty.

Future Research Directions

Our understanding of adolescent development has increased dramatically. The convergence of advances in neuroimaging, molecular genetics, and endocrinology has elucidated the nature of adolescent neurodevelopment. At the same time, developmental research on various forms of psychopathology has demonstrated that adolescence is a pivotal period for the onset of certain symptoms and syndromes.

But there is still much to be learned about both normal and abnormal neuromaturation. It is generally agreed that normal developmental changes in hormones arise from genetic programs that govern the maturation of the HPA and HPG axes. But we have little information on the temporal ordering of the changes in hormones, brain structure, and behavior in humans. To what extent are adolescent changes in brain structure and activity driven by hormonal changes? Further, what direct and indirect effects do hormones and brain structure have on behavior? Answering questions such as these will require comprehensive, longitudinal studies of normal adolescent development. The optimal approach will be one that combines measures of behavior with biological indices, such as hormonal activity and brain structure. Data from repeated assessments beginning before pubescence and extending to the postpubescent years will allow investigators to chart the temporal course for each measure and determine the temporal ordering of maturational events. Taking this line of investigation to the molecular level will involve studies of gene expression. Such work is now well underway with animals, and advances in technology may soon make it possible to pursue this kind of research with humans.

In addition to charting the course of normal neurodevelopmental processes, investigators should give high priority to longitudinal research on the development of at-risk adolescents, such as those at genetic risk for psychopathology, or those who are manifesting excessive adjustment problems following the onset of puberty. One salient set of questions concerns the role of hormonal and brain changes in the emergence of mental disorder. Does the emergence of psychopathology parallel maturational changes in hormones or brain characteristics? Taking this question to the molecular level raises questions about the effect of hormones on the expression of vulnerability genes that result in aberrant neurodevelopment. Do hormones trigger the expression of genes that lead to depression or schizophrenia? If the answer is "yes," a host of intriguing questions about prevention will ensue. Of course, before we can explore the factors that trigger the expression of vulnerability genes, we must be able to identify such genes. To date, genetic research has not identified a specific gene or set of genes that leads to any particular form of psychopathology, but there are some extremely promising leads.

Acknowledgments—This work was supported by Research Scientist Development Award No. K01 MH00876 from the National Institute of Mental Health.

Note

1. Address correspondence to Elaine F. Walker, Department of Psychology, Emory University, Atlanta, GA 30322; e-mail: psyefw@emory.edu.

References

Arnett, J. (1999). Adolescent storm and stress, reconsidered. *American Psychologist, 54,* 317–326.

Benes, F. (1999). Neurodevelopmental approach to the study of mental illness. *Developmental Neuropsychology, 16,* 359–360.

Casey, B., Giedd, J., & Thomas, K. (2000). Structural and functional brain development and its relation to cognitive development. *Biological Psychology, 54,* 241–257.

Cote, J. (1994). *Adolescent storm and stress.* Hills-dale, NJ: Erlbaum.

Giedd, J., Jeffries, N., Blumenthal, J., Castellanos, F., Vaituzis, A., Fernandez, T., Hamburger, S., Liu, H., Nelson, J., Bedwell, J., Tran, L., Lenane, M., Nicolson, R., & Rapoport, J. (1999). Childhood-onset schizophrenia: Progressive brain changes during adolescence. *Biological Psychiatry, 46,* 892–898.

Giedd, J., Vaituzis, A., Hamburger, S., Lange, N., Rajapakse, J., Kaysen, D., Vauss, Y.C., & Rapoport, J. (1996). Quantitative MRI of the temporal lobe, amygdala, and hippocampus in normal human development: Ages 4–18 years. *Journal of Comparative Neurology, 366,* 223–230.

Hankin, B., Abramson, L., Moffitt, T., Silva, P., McGee, R., & Angell, K. (1998). Development of depression from preadolescence to young adulthood: Emerging gender differences in a 10-year longitudinal study. *Journal of Abnormal Psychology, 107,* 128–140.

Kiess, W., Meidert, A., Dressendorfer, R, Scheiver, K., Kessler, U., & Konig, A. (1995). Salivary cortisol levels throughout childhood and adolescence. *Pediatric Research, 37,* 502–506.

McEwen, B. (1994). Steroid hormone actions on the brain: When is the genome involved? *Hormones & Behavior, 28,* 396–405.

Rubia, K., Overmeyer, S., Taylor, E., Brammer, M., Williams, S., Simmons, A., Andrew, C., & Bullmore, E. (2000). Functional frontalisation with age: Mapping neurodevelopmental trajectories with fMRI. *Neuroscience & Biobehavioral Reviews, 24,* 13–19.

Silberg, J., Pickles, A., Rutter, M., Hewitt, J., Simonoff, E., Maes, H., Carbonneau, R., Murrelle, L., Foley, D., & Eaves, L. (1999). The influence of genetic factors and life stress on depression among adolescent girls. *Archives of General Psychiatry, 56,* 225–232.

Sowell, E., & Jernigan, T. (1998). Further MRI evidence of late brain maturation: Limbic volume increases and changing asymmetries during childhood and adolescence. *Developmental Neuropsychology, 14,* 599–617.

Spear, L.P. (2000). The adolescent brain and age-related behavioral manifestations. *Neuroscience & Biobehavioral Reviews, 24,* 417–463.

Walker, E., Baum, K., & Diforio, D. (1998). Developmental changes in the behavioral expression of the vulnerability for schizophrenia. In M. Lenzenweger & R. Dworkin (Eds.), *Origins and development of schizophrenia* (pp. 469–492). Washington, DC: American Psychological Association Press.

Watson, C., & Gametchu, B. (1999). Membrane-initiated steroid actions and the proteins that mediate them. *Proceedings of the Society for Experimental Biology & Medicine, 220,* 9–19.

BRIEF CONTENTS

CONTENTS

CHAPTER NINE

Personality Disorders 266

CHAPTER TEN

Substance Abuse and Dependence 298

CHAPTER ELEVEN

Eating Disorders, Obesity, and Sleep Disorders 340

CHAPTER TWELVE

Gender Identity Disorder, Paraphilias, and Sexual Dysfunctions 370

CHAPTER SIXTEEN

Violence and Abuse 500

CHAPTER SEVENTEEN

Abnormal Psychology and Society 536

PREFACE

Integrated Approach

With the fifth edition of *Abnormal Psychology in a Changing World*, we launch the first fully integrated textbook in abnormal psychology. We bring to our writing a focus on integrating issues of diversity, theoretical perspectives, and multimedia content.

Integration of Diversity

We are gratified by the many comments we have received over the years about our incorporation of material on diversity and multicultural issues in the field of abnormal psychology. We believe that issues of diversity are inseparable from the discussion of disorders and their treatments, and as a result, we now integrate material relating to diversity directly within the body of the text rather than setting it off in boxed features.

Integration of Theoretical Perspectives

Students often feel as though one theoretical perspective must ultimately be right and all the others wrong. The "Tying It Together" features helps students integrate the theoretical discussions and examine possible causal pathways involving interactions of psychological, sociocultural, and biological factors in explaining many forms of abnormal behavior, including anxiety disorders, dissociative disorders, mood disorders, substance abuse and dependence, and schizophrenia. We hope to impress upon students the importance of taking a broader view of complex problems by considering the influences of multiple factors and their interactions.

Integration of Multimedia

With this edition, we have enhanced the quality of our multimedia supplements *and* made them easier to use. We've reorganized and strengthened the material on our Companion Website™ to make it a more useful study tool for students. In addition, every copy of the fifth edition comes with a free CD-ROM that includes video interviews with patients, clinicians, and researchers.

QUIZ   RESEARCH UPDATE   VIDEO   WEB LINK

Web sites and CD-ROMs won't help, though, if it isn't clear how and when you should use them. That's why we've integrated the content on the Companion Website and CD-ROM with the textbook through the use of marginal icons. Throughout the text, you'll notice four different types of green icons and a brief title in the margins; the icons signal Quizzes, Web Links, Research Updates, and Videos. So when you see a green icon, you can go to the Companion Website or CD-ROM to find material that relates to that section of the text. Each icon is numbered to make it easier to find the corresponding material on the site. For example, as you're reading through Chapter 7 and come to an icon for "Quiz 7.1," go to the Nevid fifth edition Companion Website, click on Chapter 7, and then click on the "Quiz" button. This will bring up all of the quizzes for Chapter 7, including the first one— "Quiz 7.1, Dissociative Disorders."

CD-ROM with Video Case Examples

New to this edition is a free CD-ROM featuring 20 video case vignettes. The video case examples are indicated in the margins of the text with a Video/CD-ROM icon, so students can easily see how the case examples relate to the text material. (See the front endpapers of this text for a full list of video cases found on the CD-ROM.) These video case examples provide students with an opportunity to see and hear individuals who are diagnosed with a range of psychological disorders, from depression to schizophrenia. Students can now read about the clinical features of specific disorders and with a few clicks of a computer mouse see a case example illustrating the concepts discussed in the text. The video case examples supplement the many case examples we include in the text itself. Putting a human face on the subject matter helps make complex material more accessible.

Companion Website™

Icons in the margins of the text also highlight related Web content that helps students reinforce and expand their learning. By visiting the Companion Website, students can take quizzes that help them review what they've learned and find related resources on the Web that expand their learning. We also provide a new Web-based feature, "Research Update," which provides abstracts of the latest research developments in the field that have appeared since the book was published. Students may use these updates to write term papers, and instructors may find them helpful in keeping abreast of the latest research findings.

Also New to the Fifth Edition

As with previous editions of this book, we believe that a textbook should do more than offer a portrait of a field of knowledge. It should primarily be a teaching device—a means of presenting information that arouses student interest and encourages understanding and critical thinking. This new edition of *Abnormal Psychology in a Changing World* helps make the material more accessible to a new generation of students in a rapidly changing world. We sought to make this edition an even better learning experience for students and teaching experience for their instructors by incorporating the following new chapter organization and additional pedagogical features.

New Chapter Organization

We have reorganized the early chapters to provide students with a firm foundation in current theoretical perspectives on abnormal behavior and methods of assessment and treatment before they begin examining specific clinical disorders. The first 15 chapters cover the essential bases of abnormal psychology and all of the major diagnostic groupings. Chapter 16 ("Violence and Abuse") expands the focus to consider the roots of aggressive behavior and how violent and abusive behavior represent forms of abnormal behavior. In Chapter 17 ("Abnormal Psychology and Society") we review the legal and ethical issues that relate to the interface of society and abnormal behavior, as in, for example, the insanity defense and psychiatric commitment.

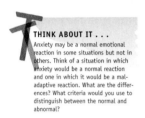

THINK ABOUT IT . . .
Anxiety may be a normal emotional reaction in some situations but not in others. Think of a situation in which anxiety would be a normal reaction and one in which it would be a maladaptive reaction. What are the differences? What criteria would you use to distinguish between the normal and abnormal?

NEW Feature: "Think About It"

With this edition we do a good deal more to promote critical thinking skills. In Chapter 1 we outline the skills of critical thinking and invite students to apply these skills in answering the new "Think About It" features that are interspersed throughout the text. Students are encouraged to think critically about the topics they encounter and to examine how these topics relate to their own personal experiences.

This new feature poses questions that encourage critical thinking, asks students to review key concepts, and helps them see the connections between the text material and their own experiences. Here are some examples of these "Think About It" features:

Critical Thinking Questions

- How would you recognize abnormal behavior? What criteria would you use to distinguish abnormal behavior from normal behavior? (Chapter 1)
- How do judgments about abnormal behavior reflect the cultural context in which they are made? In your answer, give at least one specific example. (Chapter 1)
- Anxiety may be a normal emotional reaction in some situations but not in others. Think of a situation in which anxiety would be a normal reaction and one in which it would be a maladaptive reaction. What are the differences? What criteria would you use to distinguish between the normal and abnormal? (Chapter 6)
- Why is the diagnosis of dissociative identity disorder controversial? Do you believe that people with dissociative identity disorder are merely playing a role they have learned? Why or why not? (Chapter 7)
- Are some personality disorders more likely to be diagnosed in men or in women because of societal expectations rather than because of real underlying pathology? Have you ever assumed that women are "just dependent or hysterical" or that men are "just narcissists or antisocial"? What kinds of problems do these underlying assumptions pose for clinicians and researchers? (Chapter 9)

- Where should we draw the line between normal and abnormal sexual behavior? What criteria should we use? (Chapter 12)

Review Questions

- What cultural issues do therapists need to consider when working with members of diverse cultural and racial groups? (Chapter 4)
- What role does childhood physical and sexual abuse play in dissociative disorders? (Chapter 7)
- What is Alzheimer's disease? What have we learned about the biological underpinnings of the disease? What don't we know? (Chapter 15)
- What is the difference between the concept of competency to stand trial and the legal defense of insanity? (Chapter 17)

Personal Reflection Questions

- Whom would you consider to be a self-actualizer? What about yourself? Are you a self-actualizer? Why or why not? (Chapter 2)
- What type of therapy would you prefer if you were seeking treatment for a psychological disorder? Why? (Chapter 4)
- Can you think of examples in your own life in which you have been hampered by performance anxiety of one kind or another? What did you do about it? (Chapter 12)
- Have you ever been subjected to sexual harassment? What was the outcome? Would you do anything differently if it were to happen again? (Chapter 16)

NEW Feature: Marginal Glossary

New to this edition is a running glossary in the text margins so students will not need to thumb to the back of the book for definitions of key terms. Key terms are in boldface type in the text and are defined in both the glossary in the back of the book and in the margins of the text on the two-page spread where the terms appear. The origins of key terms are often discussed. By learning to attend to commonly found Greek and Latin word origins, students can acquire skills that will help them decipher the meanings of new words. These decoding skills are a valuable objective for general education as well as a specific asset for the study of abnormal psychology.

NEW Feature: "Overview" Feature

Overview of Mood Disorders

TYPES OF MOOD DISORDERS	Description	Features
Major Depressive Disorder	Episodes of severe depression	• A range of features may be present, from downcast mood to appetite and sleep disturbance, to lack of interest and motivation • Seasonal affective disorder and postpartum depression are subtypes of major depression
Dysthymic Disorder	Long-standing mild depression	• Feeling "down in the dumps" most of the time, but not as severely depressed as people with major depressive disorder • Double depression is characterized by major depressive episodes occurring during the course of dysthymia
Bipolar Disorder	Mood swings between extreme elation and severe depression	• The two general subtypes are bipolar I disorder and bipolar II disorder • In rapid cycling, mania and major depression alternate without intervening periods of normal mood
Cyclothymia	Milder mood swings than bipolar disorder	• Chronic, cyclical pattern of shifting mood states from hypomania to states of mild depression • Frequent periods of depressed mood or loss of interest or pleasure in activities, but not at the level of severity of a

One of the most challenging aspects of this course is mastering and organizing the vast amounts of information about all of the disorders. To help students accomplish this more successfully, we have included a new "Overview" feature that helps students organize information by providing a visual summary of the major types of disorders, their causal factors, and the treatment approaches available. The "Overviews" are presented in a consistent format, so students can see "at a glance" how the information presented in the chapter fits together.

NEW Feature: Summing Up

In this new edition we developed a question-and-answer format for the chapter summary, in place of the traditional narrative summary. We believe that students will learn better when material is framed in terms of questions to answer rather than just narrative rewording of the text.

Maintaining Our Focus

Abnormal Psychology in a Changing World, 5th edition, is a complete learning and teaching package that represents our focus on four major objectives: (1) engaging student interest by incorporating student-oriented features; (2) integrating an interactionist or biopsychosocial model of abnormal behavior; (3) underscoring the importance of issues of diversity to the understanding and treatment of psychological disorders; and (4) maintaining currency with recent developments in the field.

Focus on Student-Oriented Features

We continue to provide students with opportunities to gain insight into their attitudes and behavior patterns. In addition to the new "Think About It" features described above, there are other student-focused features, as illustrated below.

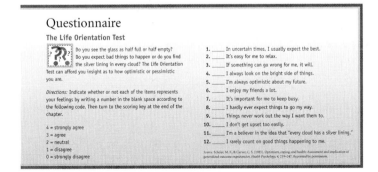

Self-Scoring Questionnaires

Questionnaires involve students in the discussion at hand and permit them to evaluate their own attitudes and behavior patterns. In some cases, students may become more aware of troubling concerns, such as states of depression or problems with drug or alcohol use, which they may wish to bring to the attention of a professional. We have screened the questionnaires to ensure that

they will provide students with useful information upon which to reflect as well as to serve as a springboard for class discussion. This allows students to have immediate scoring and feedback. Questionnaires include:

- The Life Orientation Test (Optimism Scale) (Chapter 5)
- Are You Type A? (Chapter 5)
- The Dissociative Experiences Scale (Chapter 7)
- Are You Depressed? (Chapter 8)
- The Fear of Fat Scale (Chapter 11)
- Examining Your Attitudes Toward Aging (Chapter 15)

This book also contains a number of features that are intended to keep it "on the beam" as a vehicle for instruction and learning, as with the following features.

"Truth or Fiction?" Chapter Openers

Each chapter begins with "Truth or Fiction?" statements that whet students' appetites for the subject matter within the chapter. Some items challenge preconceived ideas and common folklore and debunk myths and misconceptions, while others highlight new research in the field. Throughout the chapter, we give students feedback about the accuracy of their preconceptions by revisiting the "Truth or Fiction?" statements, at the points where the topics are discussed. Instructors and students have repeatedly reported that these items stimulate and challenge students. Examples include:

- Researchers find that people report more personal problems when interviewed by human interviewers than by computers.
- In some ways, many "mentally healthy" people see things less realistically than people who are depressed.
- People who threaten suicide are only seeking attention.
- Being able to "hold your liquor" better than most people helps prevent the development of problem drinking.
- The male sex hormone testosterone is produced by the body in women as in men.
- Dementia is a normal part of the aging process.
- Women are more likely to be raped by men they know than by strangers.

"A Closer Look" Feature

These features highlight new developments and controversies in the field and offer applications or resources that students can apply in their own lives. Examples include:

- Thinking Critically About Abnormal Psychology (Chapter 1)
- How Do I Find a Psychologist? (Chapter 4)
- Internet Counseling: Psychological Help May Be Only a Few Mouse Clicks Away (Chapter 4)
- Psychological Methods for Lowering Arousal (Chapter 5)
- EMDR: A Fad or a Find? (Chapter 6)
- Coping with a Panic Attack (Chapter 6)
- The Recovered Memory Controversy (Chapter 7)

- St. John's wort—A Natural "Prozac"? (Chapter 8)
- Suicide Prevention (Chapter 8)
- Did Samson Have Antisocial Personality Disorder? (Chapter 9)
- Gender Identity Disorder: A Disorder or Culture-Specific Creation? (Chapter 12)
- Anger Management (Chapter 16)
- Rape Prevention (Chapter 16)
- The Duty to Warn (Chapter 17)

Focus on Interactionist Approaches

We approach our writing with the belief that a better understanding of abnormal psychology is gained by adopting a biopsychosocial orientation that takes into account the roles of biological, psychological, and sociocultural factors and their interactions in the development of abnormal behavior patterns. We emphasize the value of taking an interactionist approach as a running theme throughout the text.

Focus on Issues of Diversity

We examine relationships between abnormal behavior patterns and issues of diversity relating to ethnicity, cultural factors, gender, sexual orientation, and socioeconomic status. We believe that students need to understand how issues of diversity affect both the conceptualization of abnormal behavior as well as the diagnosis and treatment of psychological disorders. Among the many issues relating to diversity that we explore in the text are the following:

- Cultural bases of abnormal behavior (Chapter 1)
- Cultural issues in diagnostic evaluation (Chapter 3)
- Surgeon General's 2001 report on culture, race, ethnicity, and mental health (Chapter 4)
- Multicultural issues in psychotherapy (Chapter 4)
- Relationship between acculturation and mental health (Chapter 5)
- Culture-bound syndromes (Chapters 3 and 7)
- Gender differences in prevalence of depression (Chapter 8)
- Sociocultural factors in substance use and abuse (Chapter 10)
- Sociocultural factors in eating disorders (Chapter 11)
- Cultural differences in expressed emotion (Chapter 13)
- Cultural differences in beliefs about abnormal behavior in childhood (Chapter 14)
- Sociocultural perspectives on aggression (Chapter 16)

Focus on Recent Developments in the Field

We help the reader keep abreast of the ever-changing subject matter, in the field. This new edition has also been thoroughly updated to incorporate information from the 2000 edition of the *DSM-IV-TR*.

Here is a small sample of the extensive coverage of new research included in this edition:

- The 1999 U.S. Surgeon General's report on the state of the nation's mental health
- Computerized clinical interviews and computer-assisted therapy
- Controversies over online counseling services
- New findings on validity of projective tests and comparisons of validities of psychological and medical tests
- Use of fMRI brain imaging in studying brain function
- Effectiveness of psychotherapy in ordinary clinical practice
- New evidence on specific versus nonspecific factors in psychotherapy
- Update on effects of stress on the immune system functioning
- New evidence on effects of expressive writing on psychological and physical well-being
- Genetic links between OCD and tic disorders
- Update on vulnerability factors in PTSD
- Classical conditioning model of panic disorder
- New information on role of GABA in anxiety disorders
- Update on treatment approaches for anxiety disorders and mood disorders
- Update on EMDR
- Update on St. John's wort
- Update on childhood abuse and development of dissociative disorders
- Update on phototherapy for SAD
- Relationships between dysfunctional attitudes and proneness to depression and between stress and depression
- Update on genetic factors in mood disorders
- Update on effectiveness of psychological and pharmacological treatment for depression
- The 2001 U.S. Surgeon General's report on suicide
- Recent developments in the treatment of personality disorders
- Updated prevalence rates of drug use and abuse
- Abuse of prescription opioids, especially OxyContin
- Psychological and physical effects of the drug known as ecstasy
- Update on biochemical bases of drug use and abuse
- Update on genetic factors in alcoholism and substance abuse
- Update on sociocultural factors in drug use in adolescents
- Update on treating substance abuse and dependence
- Update on factors underlying eating disorders
- Biochemical causes of narcolepsy
- Need evidence of brain abnormalities in schizophrenia
- Latest estimates of the prevalence of autism
- MRI and PET scan studies of autistic children and adults

- New evidence on brain abnormalities in children with ADHD
- New evidence on combining drug treatment and behavior modification in treating ADHD
- Latest research on causal factors and treatment of Alzheimer's disease
- Research evidence on psychological and drug treatment of geriatric depression
- New evidence on the psychological profile of batterers
- Update on effects of child abuse and child sexual abuse on psychological functioning
- Update on the accuracy of clinician predictions of dangerousness

Ancillaries

No matter how comprehensive a textbook is, today's instructors and students require a complete teaching package to advance teaching and comprehension. *Abnormal Psychology in a Changing World, Fifth Edition,* is accompanied by the following ancillaries:

For Students

Videos in Abnormal Psychology CD-ROM

With every new copy of *Abnormal Psychology, Fifth Edition,* students will receive a free CD-ROM with video clips showing skilled clinicians interviewing real patients who have been diagnosed with various disorders. Disorders represented include panic disorder, schizophrenia, anorexia, bulimia, and others. Icons in the text margins indicate when students should go to the CD-ROM to find video case interviews.

Companion Website™ (www.prenhall.com/nevid)

Fred Whitford of Montana State University, along with the text authors, has carefully created and selected all of the resources on the text-matched Companion Website to reinforce students' understanding of the concepts in the fifth edition. The Web resources are tightly integrated with the text through icons found in the text margins. These icons indicate when material on the Web site corresponds to material in the text. Students can take online quizzes and get immediate scoring and feedback; link to related Web sites; and find research updates to keep up with recent developments in the field. Students can also link from the Companion Website to the video segments found on the *Abnormal Psychology* CD-ROM.

ContentSelect Research Database

Prentice Hall and EBSCO, the world leader in online journal subscription management, have developed a customized research database for students of psychology. The database provides unlimited access to the text of dozens of peer-reviewed psychology publications. Student access codes can be packaged *free* with *Abnormal Psychology, Fifth Edition.* To see for yourself how this site works, ask your local Prentice Hall representative for a free Instructor Access Code.

Study Guide (0-13-049508-5)

Gwen Parsons of Hillsborough Community College has created a study guide that includes numerous review and study questions, crossword puzzles, and other learning aids to help reinforce students' understanding of the concepts covered in the text.

Print Supplements for Instructors

Instructor's Resource Manual (0-13-049509-3)

Nancy Simpson of Trident Technical College has prepared an instructor's resource manual with many useful features, including "Lecture and Discussion" suggestions, "Student Activities," "Classroom Demonstration" ideas, and interesting suggestions on how to integrate the new *Abnormal Psychology* CD-ROM into your course.

Test Item File (0-13-049505-0)

Developed by Joanne Karpinen of Hope College, this comprehensive test bank has been updated to include new questions on revised text material. It contains over 4,000 multiple-choice, true/false, short answer, and essay questions.

Color Transparencies for Abnormal Psychology, Series II (0-13-080451-7)

This set of full-color transparencies includes illustrations, figures, and graphs from the text as well as images from a variety of other sources. It has been designed with lecture hall visibility and convenience in mind.

Media and Online Resources for Instructors

Test Manager (0-13-049507-7)

One of the best-selling test-generating software programs on the market, Test Manager is available in Windows and Macintosh formats (both of which are included on one CD-ROM). The Test Manager includes a Gradebook, On-Line Network Testing, and many tools to help you edit and create tests quickly and easily.

PsychologyCentral Web Site (www.prenhall.com/psychology)

This site is password-protected for instructors' use only and allows you online access to all Prentice Hall psychology supplements at any time. You'll find a multitude of resources (both text-specific and non-text-specific) for teaching abnormal psychology—and many other psychology courses too. From this site, you can download any of the key supplements for Nevid et al., fifth edition: Instructor's Resource Manual, Test Item File, and PowerPoint presentations. Contact your local sales representative for the User ID and Password to access this site.

PowerPoint Presentations (on the Companion Website and the *PsychologyCentral* Web site)

Fred Whitford of Montana State University has created two sets of PowerPoint presentations—one with graphics and one without—

to give you even greater flexibility in using PowerPoint in your lectures. Both presentations highlight all of the key points in the fifth edition of *Abnormal Psychology*.

Online Course Management

For instructors interested in using online course management, Prentice Hall offers fully customizable courses in BlackBoard and Course Compass to accompany this textbook. These online courses are preloaded with material for *Abnormal Psychology, Fifth Edition,* including the Test Item File. Contact your local Prentice Hall representative or visit www.prenhall.com/demo for more information.

Video Resources for Instructors
ABC News Videos for Abnormal Psychology, Series III

Qualified adopters can obtain this series consisting of segments from the *ABC Nightly News* with Peter Jennings, *Nightline, 20/20, Prime Time Live,* and *The Health Show*. The programs cover issues such as drugs and alcoholism, psychotherapy, autism, crime motivation, depression, and others. Contact your Prentice Hall representative for more details.

Patients as Educators: Video Cases in Abnormal Psychology

This video was created by James H. Scully, Jr., M.D., and Alan M. Dahms, Ph.D., Colorado State University, and is available to qualified adopters. It includes a series of ten patient interviews that illustrate a range of disorders. Each interview is preceded by a brief history of the patient and a synopsis of some major symptoms of the disorder and ends with a summary and brief analysis. Contact your local sales representative for more details.

Acknowledgments

The field of abnormal psychology is a moving target, as the literature base that informs our understanding is continually expanding. We are deeply indebted to a number of talented individuals who helped us hold our camera steady in taking a portrait of the field, focus in on the salient features of our subject matter, and develop our snapshots through prose.

First, our professional colleagues, who reviewed our manuscript through the first several versions and continue to help us refine and strengthen the material:

Reviewers of the Fifth Edition
Heinz Fischer, *Long Beach City College*
John H. Forthman, *Vermilion Community College*
Pam Gibson, *James Madison University*
John K. Hall, *University of Pittsburgh*
Shay McCordick, *San Diego State University*
Linda L. Morrison, *University of New England*
Ari Solomon, *Williams College*
Theresa Wadkins, *University of Nebraska at Kearney*

Reviewers of Previous Editions
Sally Bing, *University of Maryland Eastern Shore*
Christiane Brems, *University of Alaska Anchorage*
Bernard Gorman, *Nassau Community College*
Gary Greenberg, *Connecticut College*
Bob Hill, *Appalachian State University*
Robert Kapche, *California State University, Long Beach*
Stuart Keeley, *Bowling Green State University*
Joseph J. Palladino, *University of Southern Indiana*
Carol Pandey, *Los Angeles Pierce College*
J. Langhinrichsen-Rohling, *University of Nebraska-Lincoln*
Esther D. Rosenblum, *University of Vermont*
Harold Siegel, *Nassau Community College*
Larry Stout, *Nicholls State University*
Max Zwanziger, *Central Washington University*

Second, but by no means second-rate, are the publishing professionals at Prentice Hall who helped guide the development of this edition, especially Stephanie Johnson, Executive Editor; Rochelle Diogenes, Associate Editor-in-Chief for Development; Elaine Silverstein, Developmental Editor; Shelly Kupperman, Senior Production Editor; Sheryl Adams, Executive Marketing Manager; Karen Branson, Media Editor; Mindy DePalma, Media Editor; Katie Fox, Editorial Assistant; and Ronald Fox, Marketing Assistant. A special thanks to Leslie Osher, Creative Design Director, and Anne DeMarinis, freelance designer, for the beautiful new design of the fifth edition. We would also like to thank the entire Prentice Hall sales force for their enthusiastic and diligent efforts on behalf of our text.

Finally, we especially wish to thank two people without whose inspiration and support this effort would never have materialized or been completed, Judith Wolf-Nevid and Lois Fichner-Rathus.

J.S.N.

S.A.R.

B.A.G.

ABOUT THE AUTHORS

Jeffrey S. Nevid is a professor of psychology at St. John's University in New York, where he directs the Doctoral Program in Clinical Psychology; teaches graduate courses in research methods, psychological assessment, and behavior therapy; and supervises doctoral students in clinical practicum work. He received his doctorate in clinical psychology from the State University of New York at Albany and was awarded a National Institute of Mental Health (NIMH) Postdoctoral Fellowship in Mental Health Evaluation Research. He has published numerous articles in the areas of clinical and community psychology, health psychology, training models in clinical psychology, and methodological issues in clinical research. He holds a diplomate in clinical psychology from the American Board of Professional Psychology, is a fellow of the Academy of Clinical Psychology (FAClinP), has served on the editorial boards of several journals, and is presently an associate editor of *The Journal of Consulting and Clinical Psychology*. He is also an author of several leading textbooks in psychology and related fields and was keynote speaker in 2002 at the 16th Annual Conference on Undergraduate Teaching of Psychology.

Spencer A. Rathus received his doctorate from the State University of New York at Albany. He is on the faculty at the New York University School of Continuing and Professional Studies. His areas of interest include psychological assessment, cognitive behavior therapy, and deviant behavior. He is the originator of the Rathus Assertiveness Schedule, which has become a Citation Classic. He has authored several books, including *Psychology in the New Millennium*, *Essentials of Psychology*, and *The World of Children*. He has coauthored *Making the Most of College* with Lois Fichner-Rathus; *AIDS: What Every Student Needs to Know* with Susan Boughn;

Behavior Therapy, Psychology and the Challenges of Life and *Health in the New Millennium* with Jeffrey S. Nevid; and *Human Sexuality in a World of Diversity* with Jeffrey S. Nevid and Lois Fichner-Rathus. His professional activities include service on the American Psychological Association Task Force on Diversity Issues at the Precollege and Undergraduate Levels of Education in Psychology and on the Advisory Panel, American Psychological Association, Board of Educational Affairs (BEA) Task Force on Undergraduate Psychology Major Competencies.

Beverly Greene is a professor of psychology at St. John's University and is a fellow of the American Psychological Association, the American Orthopsychiatric Association, and the Academy of Clinical Psychology. She holds a diplomate in clinical psychology from the American Board of Professional Psychology and serves on the editorial boards of numerous scholarly journals. She received her doctorate in clinical psychology from Adelphi University and is founding coeditor of *Psychological Perspectives on Lesbian, Gay and Bisexual Issues* and coeditor of *Education, Research and Practice in Lesbian, Gay, Bisexual and Transgendered Psychology: A Resource Manual* (Vol. 5, 2000). The author of nearly 70 professional publications, Dr. Greene was the recipient of the 1996 Outstanding Achievement Award from the American Psychological Association's Committee on Lesbian, Gay and Bisexual Concerns, the 2000 Heritage Award from the APA Division of the Psychology of Women, and the 1995, 1996, and 2000 (co-recipient) of the Psychotherapy with Women Research Award from The Society for the Psychology of Women. One of her papers was honored with the 2000 Women of Color Psychologies Publication Award, an award she previously received in 1991 and 1995. Her coedited book, *Psychotherapy with African American Women: Innovations in Psychodynamic Perspectives and Practice*, was also the recipient of the Association for Women in Psychology's 2001 Distinguished Publication Award.

ABNORMAL PSYCHOLOGY IN A CHANGING WORLD

CHAPTER ONE

Introduction and Methods of Research

Wassily Kandinsky
Sweet Pink

Truth OR Fiction?

- Psychological disorders actually affect only relatively few of us. (p. 4)

- Behavior deemed abnormal in one society may be perceived as perfectly normal in another. (p. 6)

- The modern medical model of abnormal behavior can be traced to the work of a Greek physician some 2,500 years ago. (p. 10)

- Innocent people were drowned in medieval times as a way of certifying they were not possessed by the devil. (p. 11)

- A night's entertainment in London a few hundred years ago might have included peering at the inmates at the local asylum. (p. 12)

- Finding that two variables are closely linked together means that one is a cause of the other. (p. 21)

- A survey of 1,500 Americans may provide a more accurate reflection of voting attitudes and preferences of the American public than one based on millions of participants. (p. 25)

- Case studies have been conducted on people who have been dead for hundreds of years. (p. 27)

Abnormal behavior might seem the concern of only a few. After all, only a minority of the population will ever be admitted to a psychiatric hospital. Most people never seek the help of a **psychologist** or **psychiatrist.** Only a few people plead not guilty to crimes on grounds of insanity. Many of us have what we call an "eccentric" relative, but few of us have relatives we would consider truly bizarre.

The truth of the matter is that abnormal behavior affects virtually everyone in one way or another. Abnormal behavior patterns that involve a disturbance of psychological functioning or behavior are classified by mental health professionals as **psychological disorders,** or *mental disorders*. The term *mental illness* refers collectively to all of the diagnosable mental disorders, including anxiety disorders, mood disorders, schizophrenia, sexual dysfunctions, and substance use disorders (USDHHS, 1999a). If we confine our definition of abnormal behavior to diagnosable mental disorders, about one in two of us have been directly affected (R. C. Kessler, 1994). About one in five people in the United States are affected by mental disorders in a given year (USDDHS, 1999a). Figure 1.1 shows the lifetime and past-year rates of several major classes of psychological (or mental) disorders based on a representative sample of the adult U.S. population (R. C. Kessler et al., 1993, 1994).[1] Psychological disorders were most common among people in the 25- to 32-year-old age range and declined with increasing age. Problems involving anxiety and depression were more common among women. Alcohol and substance abuse problems more commonly affected men. If we also include the mental health problems of our family members, friends, and coworkers, and take into account those who foot the bill for treatment in the form of taxes and health insurance premiums and lost productivity due to sick days, disability leaves, and impaired job performance inflating product costs, then perhaps none of us remains unaffected ("Mental Health Problems," 2000).

In December 1999, the U.S. Surgeon General issued a major report on the state of the nation's mental health. Here let us highlight some key conclusions in the report (USDHHS, 1999b; Satcher, 2000):

- Mental health and illness reflects a complex interaction of brain functioning and environmental influences.

- A range of effective treatments exists for most mental disorders, including psychological interventions such as psychotherapy and counseling, and psychopharmacologic or drug therapies. Treatment is often more effective when psychological and pharmacological treatments are combined.

- Progress in developing effective prevention programs in the mental health field has been slow, as we continue to lack clear knowledge about the underlying causes of mental disorders or ways of altering known casual influences, such as genetic predispositions. Nonetheless, some effective prevention programs have been developed.

- Though about 15% of adult Americans receive some form of mental health assistance in a given year, a critical gap continues to exist between the numbers of people needing help and those receiving it.

- Mental health problems are best understood when we take a broader view and consider the social and cultural contexts in which they occur.

- Mental health services need to be designed and delivered in a culturally sensitive manner that takes into account the viewpoints and needs of racial and ethnic minorities.

The Surgeon General's findings form a backdrop for our study of abnormal psychology. As we shall see throughout the text, the understanding of abnormal behavior is best viewed through a lens that takes into account complex interactions involving biological and environmental factors. We shall also see the importance of social and cultural (or *sociocultural*) factors in attempting to understand mental disorders and in developing men-

---

[1]To be precise, the survey was not quite national, as the sample was limited to people residing in the 48 contiguous U.S. states.

WWW Web Link **1.1**
Mental Disorders in America

psychologist A person with advanced graduate training in psychology.

psychiatrist A physician who specializes in the diagnosis and treatment of emotional disorders.

psychological disorders Abnormal behavior patterns that involve a disturbance of psychological functioning or behavior.

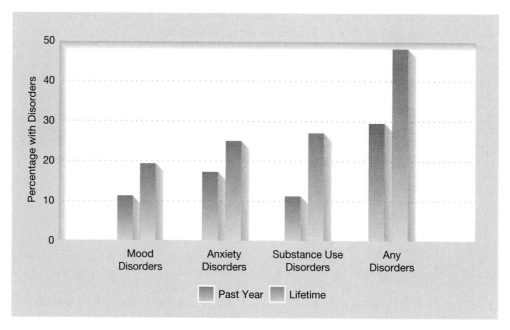

FIGURE 1.1 Lifetime and past-year prevalences of psychological disorders.
This graph shows the percentages of adults in the United States in the 15- to 49-year-old age range who show evidence of having diagnosable psychological disorders in either the past year or lifetime. The data are shown for several major diagnostic categories. The mood disorders category includes major depressive episode, manic episode, and dysthymia (discussed in Chapter 8). Anxiety disorders includes panic disorder, agoraphobia without panic disorder, social phobia, specific phobia, and generalized anxiety disorder (discussed in Chapter 6). Substance use disorders include abuse or dependence disorders involving alcohol or other drugs (discussed in Chapter 10).
Source. National Comorbidity Survey, (Kessler et al., 1994).

Web Link **1.2**
Mental Health: A Report of the
Surgeon General

abnormal psychology The branch of psychology that deals with the description, causes, and treatment of abnormal behavior patterns.

medical model A biological perspective in which abnormal behavior is viewed as symptomatic of underlying illness.

tal health services for people from diverse cultural backgrounds. We shall also survey the range of effective treatment approaches that are now available to help people who are affected by mental disorders.

Abnormal psychology is the branch of psychology that seeks to understand abnormal behavior patterns and ways of helping people who are affected by them. Abnormal psychology encompasses a broader view of abnormal behavior than the study of mental (or psychological) disorders. For example, rape is certainly a form of abnormal behavior, even though it is not classified as a psychological disorder. However, our attention throughout the text is focused on understanding the nature and treatment of mental disorders.

Let us pause for a moment to consider our use of terms. Though the terms *mental disorder* and *psychological disorder* are often used interchangeably, we generally prefer using the term *psychological disorder*. There are several reasons we have adopted this approach. First, the term *psychological disorder* puts the study of abnormal behavior squarely within the purview of the field of psychology. Another reason is that the term *mental disorder* is generally associated with the **medical model** perspective that considers abnormal behavior patterns to be symptoms of underlying illnesses or disorders. Although the medical model remains a prominent perspective for understanding abnormal behavior patterns, we will show that other perspectives, including psychological and sociocultural perspectives, also inform our understanding of abnormal behavior. In addition, the term *mental disorder* reinforces the traditional distinction between mental and physical phenomena. As we'll see, there is increasing awareness of the interrelationships between the body and the mind that calls into question this distinction.

In this chapter we first address the task of defining abnormal behavior. We see that throughout history, and even in prehistory, abnormal behavior has been viewed from different perspectives, or models. We chronicle the development of concepts of abnormal behavior and its treatment. We see that, historically speaking, treatment usually referred to what was done *to*, rather than *for*, people with abnormal behavior. Finally, we describe the ways in which psychologists and other scholars study abnormal behavior today.

How Do We Define Abnormal Behavior?

Most of us become anxious or depressed from time to time, but our behavior is not deemed abnormal. It is normal to become anxious in anticipation of an important job interview or a final examination. It is appropriate to feel depressed when you have lost someone close to you or when you have failed at a test or on the job. But when do we cross the line between normal and abnormal behavior?

One answer is that emotional states such as anxiety and depression may be considered abnormal when they are not appropriate to the situation. It is normal to feel down because of failure on a test, but not when one's grades are good or excellent. It is normal to feel anxious during a college admissions interview, but not whenever entering a department store or boarding a crowded elevator.

Abnormal behavior may also be suggested by the magnitude of the problem. Although some anxiety is normal enough before a job interview, feeling that your heart is hammering away so relentlessly that it might leap from your chest—and consequently canceling the interview—are not. Nor is it normal to feel so anxious in this situation that your clothing becomes soaked with perspiration.

Criteria for Determining Abnormality

Mental health professionals apply various criteria in making judgments about whether behavior is abnormal. The most commonly used criteria include the following:

1. *Behavior is unusual.* Behavior that is unusual is often considered abnormal. Only a few of us report seeing or hearing things that are not really there; "seeing things" and "hearing things" are almost always considered abnormal in our culture, except, perhaps, in cases of certain religious experiences in which "hearing voices" or "seeing visions" of religious figures are not unusual (USDHHS, 1999a). Moreover, "hearing voices" and others forms of hallucinations under some circumstances are not considered unusual in some preliterate societies.

Becoming overcome with feelings of panic when entering a department store or when standing in a crowded elevator is uncommon and considered abnormal in our culture. But uncommon behavior is not in itself abnormal. Only one person can hold the record for swimming or running the fastest 100 meters. The record-holding athlete differs from the

Cultural sensitivity in a diverse society. The recent Surgeon General's report on mental health emphasizes the importance of providing mental health services in a culturally sensitive manner.

When is anxiety abnormal? Negative emotions such as anxiety are considered abnormal when they are judged to be excessive or inappropriate to the situation. Anxiety is generally regarded as normal when it is experienced during a job interview (left), so long as it is not so severe that it prevents the interviewee from performing adequately. Anxiety is deemed to be abnormal if it is experienced whenever one boards an elevator (right).

paranoid Referring to irrational suspicions.

rest of us but, again, is not considered abnormal. Thus rarity or statistical deviance is not a sufficient basis for labeling behavior abnormal; nevertheless, it is one yardstick often used to judge abnormality.

2. *Behavior is socially unacceptable or violates social norms.* All societies have norms (standards) that define the kinds of behaviors acceptable in given contexts. Behavior deemed normal in one culture may be viewed as abnormal in another. In our society, standing on a soapbox in a park and repeatedly shouting "Kill!" to passersby would be labeled abnormal; shouting "Kill!" in the grandstands at an important football game is usually within normal bounds, however tasteless it may seem. Although the use of norms remains one of the important standards for defining abnormal behavior, we should be aware of some limitations of this definition.

One implication of basing the definition of abnormal behavior on social norms is that norms reflect relative standards, not universal truths. What is normal in one culture may be abnormal in another. For example, Americans who assume strangers are devious and try to take advantage are usually regarded as distrustful, perhaps even **paranoid.** But such suspicions were justified among the Mundugumor, a tribe of cannibals studied by anthropologist Margaret Mead (1935). Within that culture, male strangers, even the male members of one's own family, *were* typically malevolent toward others.

Clinicians need to weigh cultural differences in determining what is normal and abnormal. In the case of the Mundugumor, this need is more or less obvious. Sometimes, however, differences are more subtle. For example, what is seen as normal, outspoken behavior by most American women might be interpreted as brazen behavior when viewed in the context of another, more traditional culture. Moreover, what strikes one generation as abnormal may be considered by others to fall within the normal spectrum. For example, until the mid-1970s homosexuality was classified as a mental disorder by the psychiatric profession (see Chapter 11). Today, however, the psychiatric profession no longer considers homosexuality a mental disorder, and many people argue that contemporary societal norms should include homosexuality as a normal variation in behavior.

Another implication of basing normality on compliance with social norms is the tendency to brand nonconformists as mentally disturbed. We may come to brand behavior we do not like or understand as "sick" rather than accept that that behavior may be normal, even if it offends or puzzles us.

3. *Perception or interpretation of reality is faulty.* Normally speaking, our sensory systems and cognitive processes permit us to form accurate mental representations of the

Is this abnormal? One of the criteria used to determine whether or not behavior is abnormal is whether it deviates from acceptable standards of conduct or social norms. The behavior and attire of these men might be considered abnormal in a classroom or workplace, but not perhaps at a football game.

environment. But seeing things and hearing voices that are not present are considered **hallucinations,** which in our culture are often taken as signs of an underlying disorder. Similarly, holding unfounded ideas or **delusions,** such as **ideas of persecution** that the CIA or the Mafia are out to get you, may be regarded as signs of mental disturbance—unless, of course, they *are.* (A former secretary of state is credited with having remarked that he might, indeed, be paranoid; his paranoia, however, did not mean he was without enemies.)

It is normal in the United States to say that one "talks" to God through prayer. If, however, a person claims to have literally seen God or heard the voice of God—as opposed to, say, being divinely inspired—we may come to regard her or him as mentally disturbed.

4. *The person is in significant personal distress.* States of personal distress caused by troublesome emotions, such as anxiety, fear, or depression, may be considered abnormal. As we noted earlier, however, anxiety and depression are sometimes appropriate responses to the situation. Real threats and losses occur from time to time, and *lack* of an emotional response to them would be regarded as abnormal. Appropriate feelings of distress are not considered abnormal unless they become prolonged or persist long after the source of anguish has been removed (after most people would have adjusted) or if they are so intense that they impair the individual's ability to function.

5. *Behavior is maladaptive or self-defeating.* Behavior that leads to unhappiness rather than self-fulfillment can be regarded as abnormal. Behavior that limits our ability to function in expected roles, or to adapt to our environments, may also be considered abnormal. According to these criteria, heavy alcohol consumption that impairs health or social and occupational functioning may be viewed as abnormal. **Agoraphobic** behavior, characterized by intense fear of venturing into public places, may be considered abnormal in that it is both uncommon and also maladaptive because it impairs the individual's ability to fulfill work and family responsibilities.

6. *Behavior is dangerous.* Behavior that is dangerous to oneself or other people may be considered abnormal. Here, too, the social context is crucial. In wartime, people who sacrifice themselves or charge the enemy with little apparent concern for their own safety may be characterized as courageous, heroic, and patriotic. But people who threaten or attempt suicide because of the pressures of civilian life are usually considered abnormal.

Football and hockey players, even adolescent boys who occasionally get into altercations, may be normal enough. Given the cultural demands of the sports, unaggressive football and hockey players would not last long in college or professional ranks. But individuals involved in frequent unsanctioned fights may be regarded as abnormal. Physically aggressive behavior is most often maladaptive in modern life. Moreover, outside the contexts of sports and warfare, physical aggression is discouraged as a way of resolving interpersonal conflicts—although it is by no means uncommon.

Abnormal behavior thus has multiple definitions. Depending on the case, some criteria may be weighted more heavily than others. But in most cases, a combination of these criteria is used to define abnormality.

It is one thing to recognize and label behavior as abnormal; it is another to understand and explain it. Philosophers, physicians, natural scientists, and psychologists have used various approaches, or *models,* in the effort to explain abnormal behavior. Some approaches have been based on superstition; others have invoked religious explanations. Some current views are predominantly biological; others, psychological. We consider various historical and contemporary approaches to understanding abnormal behavior. First, let us look further at the importance of cultural beliefs and expectations in determining which behavior patterns are deemed abnormal.

Cultural Bases of Abnormal Behavior

Behavior that is considered normal in one culture may be deemed abnormal in another. Hallucinations (hearing voices or seeing things that are not in fact present) are a common experience among Australian aborigines but are generally taken as a sign of abnormality in our culture. Aborigines also believe they can communicate with the spirits of their ancestors

hallucination A perception that occurs in the absence of an external stimulus and that is confused with reality.

delusion A firmly held but inaccurate belief that persists despite evidence that it has no basis in reality.

ideas of persecution A form of delusional thinking characterized by false beliefs that one is being persecuted or victimized by others.

agoraphobic Relating to excessive, irrational fear of open places.

THINK ABOUT IT
How would you recognize abnormal behavior? What criteria would you use to distinguish abnormal behavior from normal behavior?

wWw **Web Link 1.3**
Online Guide to Mental Health

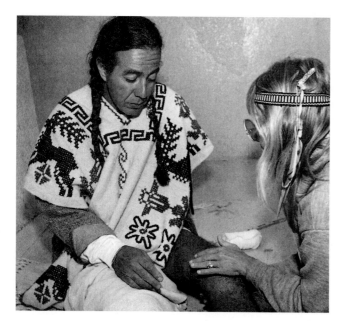

A traditional Native American healer. Many traditional Native Americans distinguish between illnesses that are believed to arise from influences external to their own culture (thus "White man's sicknesses") and those that emanate from a lack of harmony with traditional tribal life and thought ("Indian sicknesses"). Tribal healers (such as the one shown here) may be called on to treat "Indian sickness," whereas "White man's medicine" may be sought for people with problems that have causes seen as lying outside the traditional community, such as alcoholism and drug addiction.

Web Link **1.4**
Mental Health: Culture, Race, and Ethnicity WWW

THINK ABOUT IT

How do judgments about abnormal behavior reflect the cultural context in which they are made? Give at least one specific example.

demonology The idea that abnormal behavior is caused by supernatural forces.

worldview The prevailing view of the times (English translation of German term *Weltanschaung).*

and that dreams are shared among people, especially close relatives. Such beliefs may be regarded in Western culture as delusions (fixed false beliefs). Hallucinations and delusions are taken to be common features of schizophrenia in Western culture. Should we thus conclude that aborigines are seriously disturbed or have schizophrenia? What standards should be applied in judging abnormal behavior in other cultures? Even aborigines perceive "madness" in some members of their community, although the criteria they use to label someone as mentally disturbed may differ from those used by health professionals in Western society.

Kleinman (1987) offers an example of "hearing voices" among Native Americans to underscore the ways in which judgments about abnormal behavior are embedded within a cultural context:

> Ten psychiatrists trained in the same assessment technique and diagnostic criteria who are asked to examine 100 American Indians shortly after the latter have experienced the death of a spouse, a parent or a child may determine with close to 100% consistency that those individuals report hearing, in the first month of grieving, the voice of the dead person calling to them as the spirit ascends to the afterworld. [While such judgments may be consistent across observers] the determination of whether such reports are a sign of an abnormal mental state is an interpretation based on knowledge of this group's behavioural norms and range of normal experiences of bereavement. (p. 453)

To many Native Americans, bereaved people who report hearing the spirits of the deceased calling to them as they ascend to the afterlife are regarded as normal. Kleinman's example leads us to recognize that behavior should not be considered abnormal when it is normative within the cultural setting in which it occurs. Concepts of health and illness may also have different meanings in different cultures. Many traditional Native American cultures distinguish between illnesses that are believed to arise from influences outside the culture, called "White man's sicknesses," such as alcoholism and drug addiction, from those that emanate from a lack of harmony with traditional tribal life and thought, which are called "Indian sicknesses" (Trimble, 1991). Traditional healers, shamans, and medicine men and women are called on to treat and cure "Indian sickness." When the problem is thought to have its cause outside the community, help may be sought from "White man's medicine."

The very words that Western cultures use to describe psychological disorders—words such as depression or even mental health—may have very different meanings in other cultures or no equivalent meaning at all. In many non-Western societies, depression may be closer in meaning to the concept of "soul loss" than to Western concepts involving a sense of loss of purpose and meaning in life (Shweder, 1985).

Abnormal behavior patterns may also take different forms in different cultures (USDHHS, 1999a). Westerners may experience anxiety, for example, in the form of excessive worrying about paying the mortgage, losing a job, and so on. Yet "[I]n a number of African cultures, anxiety is expressed as fears of failure in procreation, in dreams and complaints about witchcraft" (Kleinman, 1987). Some Australian aborigines develop intense fears of sorcery, which may be accompanied by the belief that one is in mortal danger from evil spirits (D. J. Spencer, 1983). Trancelike states in which young aboriginal women are mute, immobile, and unresponsive are also quite common. If women do not recover from the trance within hours or, at most, a few days, they may be brought to a sacred site for healing.

Depression may also be expressed differently in different cultures (Bebbington, 1993; Thakker & Ward, 1998). This doesn't mean that depression doesn't exist in other cultures. Rather, it suggests we need to consider how people in different cultures experience states of emotional distress, including depression and anxiety, rather than imposing our perspectives on their experiences. Among some Far Eastern peoples, such as the Chinese, depression is often expressed through physical symptoms, such as headaches, fatigue, or weakness, rather than by feelings of guilt or sadness that are common in Western cultures (American Psychiatric Association, 2000; Parker, Gladstone, & Chee, 2001).

Cultural differences in how abnormal behavior patterns are expressed lead us to realize that we must determine that our concepts of abnormal behavior are recognizable and valid before they are applied to other cultures (Bebbington, 1993). The reverse is equally true. The concept of "soul loss" characterizes psychological distress in some non-Western societies, but it has little or no relevance to middle-class North Americans. Evidence from multinational studies conducted by the World Health Organization (WHO) in the 1960s and 1970s shows that the behavior pattern we characterize as schizophrenia exists in countries as far flung as Colombia, India, China, Denmark, Nigeria, and the former Soviet Union, among others (Jablensky et al., 1992). Rates of schizophrenia and its general features were actually quite similar among the countries studied. However, some differences have been observed in the specific features of schizophrenia across cultures (Thakker & Ward, 1998).

Societal views of abnormal behavior vary across cultures. In our culture, models based on medical disease and psychological factors have achieved prominence in explaining abnormal behavior. But in traditional cultures, concepts of abnormal behavior often invoke supernatural causes, such as possession by demons or the devil (Lefley, 1990). In Filipino folk society, for example, psychological problems are often attributed to the influence of "spirits" or the possession of a "weak soul" (Edman & Johnson, 1999). The notion of supernatural causation, or **demonology,** also held prominence in Western society until the Age of Enlightenment.

possession A superstitious belief in which abnormal behavior is taken as a sign that the person is possessed by demons or the devil.

trephination A harsh, prehistoric practice of cutting a hole in a person's skull, possibly in an attempt to release demons.

demonological model The model that explains abnormal behavior in terms of supernatural forces.

THINK ABOUT IT

What behaviors have you observed in members of other cultural groups that might be considered abnormal in your own? What behaviors in your own cultural group might members of other groups consider abnormal?

 Quiz **1.1**
How Do We Define Abnormal Behavior?

Historical Perspectives on Abnormal Behavior

Throughout the history of Western culture, concepts of abnormal behavior have been shaped, to some degree, by the prevailing **worldview** of the time. Throughout much of history, beliefs in supernatural forces, demons, and evil spirits held sway. Abnormal behavior was often taken as a sign of **possession.** In more modern times, the predominant—but by no means universal—worldview has shifted toward beliefs in science and reason. Abnormal behavior has come to be viewed in our culture as the product of physical and psychosocial factors, not demonic possession.

The Demonological Model

Let us begin our journey with an example from prehistory. Archaeologists have unearthed human skeletons from the Stone Age with egg-sized cavities in the skull. One interpretation of these holes is that our prehistoric ancestors believed abnormal behavior reflected the invasion of evil spirits. Perhaps they used the harsh method—called **trephination**—of creating a pathway through the skull to provide an outlet for those irascible spirits. Fresh bone growth indicates that some people managed to survive the ordeal.

Threat of *trephining* may have persuaded people to comply with group or tribal norms to the best of their abilities. Because no written records or accounts of the purposes of trephination exist, other explanations are possible. Perhaps trephination was used as a primitive form of surgery to remove shattered pieces of bone or blood clots that resulted from head injuries (Maher & Maher, 1985).

Explanation of abnormal behavior in terms of supernatural or divine causes is termed the **demonological model.** The ancients explained natural forces in terms of divine will and spirits. The

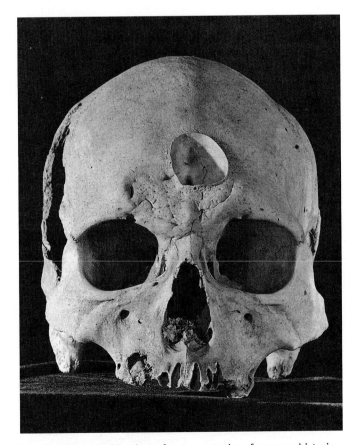

Trephination. Trephination refers to a practice of some prehistoric cultures by which a hole was chipped into a person's skull. Some investigators speculate that the practice represented an ancient form of surgery. Perhaps trephination was intended to release demons that were believed responsible for abnormal behavior.

humors According to the ancient Hippocratic belief system, the vital bodily fluids (phlegm, black bile, blood, yellow bile).

phlegmatic Slow and solid.

melancholia A state of severe depression.

sanguine Having a cheerful disposition.

choleric Having or showing bad temper.

exorcism A ritual intended to expel demons from a person believed to be possessed.

Truth OR Fiction? REVISITED

The modern medical model of abnormal behavior can be traced to the work of a Greek physician some 2,500 years ago.

TRUE. The foundations of what is known as the modern medical model can be traced to the Greek physician Hippocrates, who lived some 2,500 years ago.

Exorcism. This medieval woodcut illustrates the practice of exorcism, which was used to expel evil spirits who were believed to have possessed people.

ancient Babylonians believed the movements of the stars and the planets were fashioned by the adventures and conflicts of the gods. The ancient Greeks believed their gods toyed with humans; when aroused to wrath, they could unleash forces of nature to wreak havoc on disrespectful or arrogant humans, even cloud their minds with madness.

In ancient Greece, people who behaved abnormally were often sent to temples dedicated to Aesculapius, the god of healing. Priests believed that Aesculapius would visit the afflicted persons while they slept in the temple and offer them restorative advice through dreams. Rest, a nutritious diet, and exercise were also believed to contribute to treatment. Incurables might be driven from the temple by stoning.

Origins of the Medical Model: In "Ill Humor"

Not all ancient Greeks believed in the demonological model. The seeds of naturalistic explanations of abnormal behavior were sown by Hippocrates and developed by other physicians in the ancient world, especially Galen.

Hippocrates (ca. 460–377 B.C.E.), the celebrated physician of the Golden Age of Greece, challenged the prevailing beliefs of his time by arguing that illnesses of the body and mind were the result of natural causes, not possession by supernatural spirits. He believed the health of the body and mind depended on the balance of **humors,** or vital fluids, in the body: phlegm, black bile, blood, and yellow bile. An imbalance of humors, he thought, accounted for abnormal behavior. A lethargic or sluggish person was believed to have an excess of phlegm, from which we derive the word **phlegmatic.** An overabundance of black bile was believed to cause depression, or **melancholia.** An excess of blood created a **sanguine** disposition: cheerful, confident, and optimistic. An excess of yellow bile made people "bilious" and **choleric**—quick-tempered, that is.

Though we no longer subscribe to Hippocrates's theory of bodily humors, his theory is of historical importance because of its break from demonology. It also foreshadowed the development of the modern medical model, the view that abnormal behavior results from underlying biological processes. Hippocrates made many contributions to modern thought and, indeed, to modern medical practice. Hippocrates had even begun to classify abnormal behavior patterns, using three main categories that find some equivalents today: *melancholia* to characterize excessive depression, *mania* to refer to exceptional excitement, and *phrenitis* (from the Greek "inflammation of the brain") to characterize the bizarre kinds of behavior that might today typify schizophrenia. Medical schools continue to pay homage to Hippocrates by having new physicians swear the Hippocratic oath in his honor.

Galen (ca. 130–200 C.E.), a Greek physician who attended Roman emperor-philosopher Marcus Aurelius, adopted and expanded on the teachings of Hippocrates. Among Galen's contributions was the discovery that arteries carry blood, not air, as had been formerly believed.

Medieval Times

The Middle Ages, or medieval times, cover the millennium of European history from about 476 C.E. through 1450 C.E. After the passing of Galen, belief in supernatural causes, especially the doctrine of possession, increased in influence and eventually dominated medieval thought. The doctrine of possession held that abnormal behaviors were a sign of possession by evil spirits or the devil. This belief was embodied within the teachings of the Roman Catholic Church, which became the unifying force in western Europe following the decline of the Roman Empire. Although belief in possession antedated the Church and is found in ancient Egyptian and Greek writings, the Church revitalized it. The treatment of choice for abnormal behavior was **exorcism.** Exorcists were employed to persuade evil spirits that the bodies of their intended victims were basically uninhabitable. Methods included prayer, waving a cross at the victim, beating and flogging, even starving the victim. If the victim still displayed unseemly behavior, there were yet more powerful remedies, such as the rack, a device of torture. It seems clear that recipients of these "remedies" would be motivated to conform their behavior to social expectations as best they could.

The Renaissance—the great European revival in learning, art, and literature—began in Italy in the 1400s and spread gradually throughout Europe. The Renaissance is considered the transition from the medieval world to the modern. Therefore, it is ironic that fear of witches also reached its height during the Renaissance.

Witchcraft

The late 15th through the late 17th centuries were especially dangerous times to be unpopular with your neighbors. These were times of massive persecutions of people, particularly women, who were accused of witchcraft. Officials of the Roman Catholic Church believed witches made pacts with the devil, practiced satanic rituals, and committed heinous acts, such as eating babies and poisoning crops. In 1484, Pope Innocent VIII decreed that witches be executed. Two Dominican priests compiled a manual for witch-hunting, called the *Malleus Maleficarum* (The Witches' Hammer), to help inquisitors identify suspected witches. Over 100,000 accused witches were killed in the next two centuries.

There were also creative "diagnostic" tests for detecting possession and witchcraft. In the case of the water-float test, innocent people were drowned in medieval times as a way of certifying they were not possessed by the devil. The water-float test was based on the principle that pure metals settle to the bottom during smelting, whereas impurities bob up to the surface. Suspects who sank and were drowned were ruled pure. Suspects who were able to keep their heads above water were regarded as being in league with the devil. Then they were in real trouble. This trial is the source of the phrase, "Damned if you do and damned if you don't."

Modern scholars once believed the so-called witches of the Middle Ages and the Renaissance were actually people who were mentally disturbed. They were believed to be persecuted because their abnormal behavior was taken as evidence they were in league with the devil. It is true that many suspected witches confessed to impossible behaviors, such as flying or engaging in sexual intercourse with the devil. At face value such confessions might suggest disturbances in thinking and perception that are consistent with a modern diagnosis of a psychological disorder, such as schizophrenia. Most of these confessions can be discounted, however, because they were extracted under torture by inquisitors who were bent on finding evidence to support accusations of witchcraft (Spanos, 1978). In other cases, the threat of torture and other forms of intimidation were sufficient to extract false confessions. Although some of those who were persecuted as witches probably did show abnormal behavior patterns, most did not (Schoenman, 1984). Rather, accusations of witchcraft appeared to be a convenient means of disposing of social nuisances and political rivals, of seizing property, and of suppressing heresy (Spanos, 1978). In English villages, many of the accused were poor, unmarried elderly women who were forced to beg their neighbors for food. If misfortune befell people who declined to help, the beggar might be accused of causing the misery by having cast a curse on the uncharitable family. If the woman was generally unpopular, accusations of witchcraft were more likely to be followed up.

Although demons were believed to play roles both in abnormal behavior and witchcraft, there was a difference between the two. Victims of possession may have been perceived to be afflicted as retribution for wrongdoing, but some people who showed abnormal behavior were considered to be innocent victims of demonic possession. Witches, however, were believed to have voluntarily entered into a pact with the devil and renounced God. Witches were generally seen as more deserving of torture and execution (Spanos, 1978).

Historical trends do not follow straight lines. Although the demonological model held sway during the Middle Ages and much of the Renaissance, it did not universally

The water-float test. This so-called test was one way in which medieval authorities sought to detect possession and witchcraft. Managing to float above the water line was deemed a sign of impurity. In the lower right-hand corner, you can see the bound hands and feet of one poor unfortunate who failed to remain afloat, but whose drowning would have cleared away any suspicions of possession.

Truth OR Fiction? REVISITED

Innocent people were drowned in medieval times as a way of certifying they were not possessed by the devil.

TRUE. Drowning was thought to be evidence that a person was not possessed by the devil.

"Bedlam." The bizarre antics of the patients at St. Mary's of Bethlehem Hospital in London in the 18th century were a source of entertainment for the well-heeled gentry of the town, such as the two well-dressed women in the middle of the painting.

supplant belief in naturalistic causes (Schoenman, 1984). In medieval England, for example, demonic possession was only rarely invoked as the cause of abnormal behavior in cases in which a person was held to be insane by legal authorities (Neugebauer, 1979). Most explanations for unusual behavior involved natural causes, such as physical illness or trauma to the brain. In England, in fact, some disturbed people were kept in hospitals until they were restored to sanity (Alldridge, 1979). The Renaissance Belgian physician Johann Weyer (1515–1588) also took up the cause of Hippocrates and Galen by arguing that abnormal behavior and thought patterns were caused by physical problems.

Asylums

By the late 15th and early 16th centuries, asylums, or madhouses, began to crop up throughout Europe. Many were former leprosariums, which were no longer needed because of a decline in leprosy that occurred during the late Middle Ages. Asylums often gave refuge to beggars as well as the disturbed, and conditions were generally appalling. Residents were often chained to their beds and left to lie in their own waste or wander about unassisted. Some asylums became public spectacles. In one asylum in London, St. Mary's of Bethlehem Hospital—from which the word *bedlam* is derived—the public could buy tickets to observe the bizarre antics of the inmates, much as we would view a sideshow in a circus or animals at a zoo.

The Reform Movement and Moral Therapy

The modern era of treatment can be traced to the efforts of individuals such as the Frenchmen Jean-Baptiste Pussin and Philippe Pinel in the late 18th and early 19th centuries. They argued that people who behave abnormally suffer from diseases and should be treated humanely. This view was not at all popular at the time. Deranged people were generally regarded as threats to society, not as sick people in need of treatment.

From 1784 to 1802, Pussin, a layman, was placed in charge of a ward for people considered "incurably insane" at La Bicêtre, a large mental hospital in Paris. Although Pinel is often credited with freeing the inmates of La Bicêtre from their chains, Pussin was actually the first official to unchain a group of the "incurably insane." These unfortunates had been considered too dangerous and unpredictable to be left unchained. But Pussin believed that if they were treated with kindness, there would be no need for chains. As he predicted, most of the shut-ins became manageable and calm when their chains were removed. They could walk the hospital grounds and take in fresh air. Pussin also forbade the staff from treating the residents harshly, and he discharged any employees who disregarded his directives.

Pinel (1745–1826) became medical director for the incurables' ward at La Bicêtre in 1793 and continued the humane treatment Pussin had begun. He stopped harsh practices, such as bleeding and purging, and moved patients from darkened dungeons to well-ventilated, sunny rooms. Pinel also spent hours talking to inmates, in the belief that showing understanding and concern would help restore them to normal functioning.

The philosophy of treatment that emerged from these efforts was labeled **moral therapy.** It was based on the belief that providing humane treatment in a relaxed and decent environment could restore functioning. Similar reforms were instituted at about this time in England by William Tuke and later in the United States by Dorothea Dix. Another influential figure was the American physician Benjamin Rush (1745–1813)— also a signatory to the Declaration of Independence and an early leader of the antislavery movement (Farr, 1994). Rush, considered the father of American psychiatry, penned the first American textbook on psychiatry in 1812: *Medical Inquiries and Observations Upon the Diseases of the Mind.* He believed that madness is caused by engorgement of the blood vessels of the brain. To relieve pressure, he recommended bloodletting and other

moral therapy A 19th-century treatment approach that emphasized treating hospitalized patients with care and understanding.

harsh treatments such as purging and ice-cold baths. But he did advance humane treatment by encouraging the staff of his Philadelphia Hospital to treat patients with kindness, respect, and understanding. He also favored the therapeutic use of occupational therapy, music, and travel (Farr, 1994). His hospital became the first in the United States to admit patients for psychological disorders.

Dorothea Dix (1802–1887), a Boston schoolteacher, traveled about the country decrying the deplorable conditions in the jails and almshouses where deranged people were often placed. As a direct result of her efforts, 32 mental hospitals were established throughout the United States.

A Step Backward

In the latter half of the 19th century, however, the belief that abnormal behaviors could be successfully treated or cured by moral therapy fell into disfavor (USDHHS, 1999a). A period of apathy ensued in which patterns of abnormal behavior were deemed incurable (Grob, 1994). Mental institutions in the United States grew in size and came to provide little more than custodial care. Conditions deteriorated. Mental hospitals became frightening places. It was not uncommon to find residents "wallowing in their own excrements," in the words of a New York State official of the time (Grob, 1983). Straitjackets, handcuffs, cribs, straps, and other devices were used to restrain excitable or violent patients.

Deplorable hospital conditions remained commonplace through the middle of the 20th century. By the mid-1950s, the population in mental hospitals had risen to half a million patients. Although some good state hospitals provided decent and humane care, many were described as little more than human *snakepits*. Residents were crowded into wards that lacked even rudimentary sanitation. Mental patients in back wards were essentially *warehoused*. That is, they were left to live out their lives with little hope or expectation of recovery or return to the community. Many received little professional care and were abused by poorly trained and supervised staffs. By the mid-20th century, the appalling conditions that many mental patients were forced to endure led to increasing calls for reforms of the mental health system.

The unchaining of inmates at La Bicêtre by 18th-century French reformer Philippe Pinel.
Continuing the work of Jean-Baptiste Pussin, Pinel stopped harsh practices, such as bleeding and purging, and moved inmates from darkened dungeons to sunny, airy rooms. Pinel also took the time to converse with inmates, in the belief that understanding and concern would help restore them to normal functioning.

deinstitutionalization The policy of discharging hospitalized mental patients into the community and of reducing the need for new admissions through alternative treatment approaches.

phenothiazines A group of antipsychotic drugs ("major tranquilizers") used to treat schizophrenia.

The Community Mental Health Movement: The Exodus from State Hospitals

In response to the growing call for reform of the mental health system, Congress in 1963 established a nationwide system of community mental health centers (CMHCs) that was intended to offer an alternative to long-term custodial care in bleak institutions. CMHCs were charged with providing continuing support and care to former hospital residents who were released from state mental hospitals under a policy of **deinstitutionalization.** Another factor that spurred the exodus from mental hospitals was the advent of a new class of drugs—the *phenothiazines.* The **phenothiazines,** a group of antipsychotic drugs that helped quell the most flagrant behavior patterns associated with schizophrenia, were introduced in the 1950s. They reduced the need for indefinite hospital stays and permitted many people with schizophrenia to be discharged to less restrictive living arrangements in the community, such as halfway houses, group homes, and independent living. The mental hospital population across the United States plummeted from more than 550,000 in 1955 to fewer than 130,000 by the late 1980s (D. Braddock, 1992; Kiesler & Sibulkin, 1987). Some mental hospitals were closed entirely (Salokangas & Saarinen, 1998).

The community mental health movement was predicated on the belief—the hope perhaps—that mental patients could return to their communities and assume more independent and fulfilling lives. Critics contend that the exodus from state hospitals abandoned tens of thousands of marginally functioning people to communities that lacked adequate housing and other forms of support. Many homeless people we see wandering city streets and sleeping in bus terminals and train stations are discharged mental patients. In Chapter 4, we take a closer look at the policy of deinstitutionalization and the problems faced by the psychiatric homeless population.

THINK ABOUT IT
How have beliefs about abnormal behavior changed over time? What changes have occurred in how society treats people considered mentally disturbed?

Contemporary Perspectives on Abnormal Behavior: From Demonology to Science

Beliefs in possession or demonology persisted until the rise of the natural sciences in the late 17th and 18th centuries. Society at large began to turn toward reason and science as ways of explaining natural phenomena and human behavior. The nascent sciences of biology, chemistry, physics, and astronomy offered promise that knowledge could be derived from scientific methods of observation and experimentation. The 18th and 19th centuries witnessed rapid developments in medical science. Scientific discoveries uncovered the microbial causes of some kinds of diseases and gave rise to preventive measures. Models of abnormal behavior also began to emerge, including models representing biological, psychological, sociocultural, and biopsychosocial perspectives. We will briefly discuss each of these models here, particularly in terms of their historical background, which will lead to a fuller discussion in Chapter 2.

The Biological Perspective Against the backdrop of advances in medical science, the German physician Wilhelm Griesinger (1817–1868) argued that abnormal behavior was rooted in diseases of the brain. Griesinger's views influenced another German physician, Emil Kraepelin (1856–1926), who wrote an influential textbook on psychiatry in 1883 in which he likened mental disorders to physical diseases. Griesinger and Kraepelin paved the way for the development of the modern medical model, which attempts to explain abnormal behavior on the basis of underlying biological defects or abnormalities, not evil spirits. According to the medical model, people behaving abnormally suffer from mental illnesses or disorders that can be classified, like physical illnesses, according to their distinctive causes and symptoms. Not all adopters of the medical model believe every pattern of abnormal behavior is a product of defective biology, but they maintain that patterns of abnormal behavior can be likened to physical illnesses in that their features can be conceptualized as symptoms of underlying disorders, whatever their cause.

Kraepelin specified two main groups of mental disorders or diseases: **dementia praecox** (from roots meaning "precocious [premature] insanity"), which we now call schizophrenia, and manic-depressive psychosis, which is now labeled *bipolar disorder*. Kraepelin believed that dementia praecox was caused by a biochemical imbalance and manic-depressive psychosis by an abnormality in body metabolism. But his major contribution was the development of a classification system that forms the cornerstone for current diagnostic systems.

Much of the terminology in current use reflects the influence of the medical model. Because of the medical model, many professionals and laypeople speak of people whose behavior is deemed abnormal as being mentally *ill*. It is because of the medical model that so many speak of the *symptoms* of abnormal behavior, rather than the features or characteristics of abnormal behavior. Other terms spawned by the medical model include *mental health, syndrome, diagnosis, patient, mental patient, mental hospital, prognosis, treatment, therapy, cure, relapse,* and *remission.*[2]

The medical model is a major advance over demonology. It inspired the idea that abnormal behavior should be treated by learned professionals rather than punished. Compassion supplanted hatred, fear, and persecution.

The Psychological Perspective Although the medical model was gaining influence in the 19th century, there were those who believed organic factors alone could not explain the many forms of abnormal behavior. In Paris, a highly respected neurologist, Jean-Martin Charcot (1825–1893), experimented with the use of **hypnosis** in treating *hysteria,* a condition in which people present with physical symptoms like paralysis or numbness that could not be explained by any underlying physical cause. The thinking at the time was that they must have an affliction of the nervous system, which caused their symptoms. Yet Charcot and his associates demonstrated that these symptoms could be removed in hysterical patients or actually induced in normal patients by means of hypnotic suggestions.

Among those who attended Charcot's demonstrations was a young Austrian physician named Sigmund Freud (1856–1939). Freud reasoned that if hysterical symptoms could be made to disappear or appear through hypnosis—the mere "suggestion of ideas"—they must be psychological in origin (E. Jones, 1953). He concluded that whatever psychological factors give rise to hysteria, they must lie outside the range of conscious awareness. This was the kernel of the idea that underlies the first psychological perspective on abnormal behavior—the **psychodynamic model.** Freud believed that the causes of abnormal behavior lie in the interplay of forces within the unconscious mind. "I received the proudest impression," Freud wrote of his experience with Charcot, "of the possibility that there could be powerful mental processes which nevertheless remained hidden from the consciousness of men" (as cited in Sulloway, 1983, p. 32).

Freud was also influenced by the Viennese physician, Joseph Breuer (1842–1925), 14 years his senior. Breuer too had used hypnosis to treat a 21-year-old woman, Anna O., with hysterical complaints for which there was no apparent medical basis, such as paralysis in her limbs, numbness, and disturbances of vision and hearing (E. Jones, 1953). A

dementia praecox The term given by Kraepelin to the disorder now called schizophrenia.

hypnosis A trancelike state, induced by suggestion, in which the individual responds to the commands of the hypnotist.

psychodynamic model The theoretical model of Freud and his followers, in which abnormal behavior is viewed as the product of clashing forces within the personality.

Charcot's teaching clinic. Parisian neurologist Jean-Martin Charcot presents a woman patient who exhibits the highly dramatic behavior associated with hysteria, such as falling faint at a moment's notice. Charcot was an important influence on the young Sigmund Freud.

[2]Because the medical model is not the only way of viewing abnormal behavior patterns, we adopt a more neutral language in this text in describing abnormal behavior patterns. For example, we often refer to "features" or "characteristics" of abnormal behavior patterns or psychological disorders rather than to "symptoms." But our adoption of non-medical jargon is not an absolute rule. In some cases, there may be no handy substitutes for terms that derive from the medical model, such as the term *remission* or the reference to patients in mental hospitals as "mental patients." In other cases we may use terms such as *disorder, therapy,* and *treatment* because they are commonly used by psychologists who "treat" "mental disorders" with psychological "therapies."

catharsis The purging or free expression of feelings.

"paralyzed" muscle in her neck prevented her from turning her head. Immobilization of the fingers of her left hand made it all but impossible for her to feed herself. Breuer believed there was a strong psychological component to the symptoms. He treated her by encouraging her to talk about them, sometimes under hypnosis. Recalling and talking about events connected with the appearance of the symptoms—especially events that evoked feelings of fear, anxiety, or guilt—appeared to provide symptom relief, at least for a time. Anna referred to the treatment as the "talking cure" or, when joking, as "chimney sweeping."

The hysterical symptoms were taken to represent the transformation of these blocked-up emotions, forgotten but not lost, into physical complaints. In Anna's case, the symptoms seemed to disappear once the emotions were brought to the surface and "discharged." Breuer labeled the therapeutic effect **catharsis,** a Greek term meaning purgation or purification of feelings. Cases of hysteria, such as that of Anna O., seemed to have been a common occurrence in the later Victorian period, but are relatively rare today (Spitzer et al., 1989).

Freud's theoretical model was the first major psychological model of abnormal behavior. As we'll see in Chapter 2, other psychological perspectives on abnormal behavior soon followed based on behavioral, humanistic, and cognitive models. We'll also see that each of these perspectives, well as the contemporary medical model, spawned particular forms of therapy to treat psychological disorders.

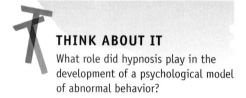

THINK ABOUT IT

What role did hypnosis play in the development of a psychological model of abnormal behavior?

The Sociocultural Perspective Sociocultural theorists believe that we must consider the broader social contexts in which behavior occurs to understand the roots of abnormal behavior. They believe the causes of abnormal behavior may be found in the failures of society rather than in the person. Psychological problems may be rooted in the social ills of society, such as poverty, social decay, racial and gender discrimination, and lack of economic opportunity.

According to the more radical sociocultural theorists, such as the psychiatrist Thomas Szasz, mental illness is a myth—a label used to stigmatize and subjugate people whose behavior is socially deviant (T. S. Szasz, 1961, 2000). Szasz states that so-called mental illnesses are really "problems in living," not actual diseases like influenza, AIDS, and cancer. Szasz argues that people who offend others or engage in socially deviant behavior are perceived as threats by the establishment. Labeling them as sick allows others to deny the validity of their problems and to put them away in institutions.

Sigmund Freud and Bertha Pappenheim. Freud is shown here at around age 30, a few years after he treated Bertha Pappenheim. Pappenheim (1859–1936) is known more widely in the psychological literature as "Anna O." Freud believed that her hysterical symptoms represented the transformation of blocked-up emotions into physical complaints.

Sociocultural theorists maintain that once the label of "mental illness" is applied to a person, it is difficult to remove. The label also affects other people's responses to the "patient." Mental patients are stigmatized and socially degraded. Job opportunities may be denied, friendships may dissolve, and the "patient" may become increasingly alienated from society. Szasz argues that treating people as mentally ill strips them of their dignity because it denies them responsibility for their own behavior and choices. He claims that troubled people should be encouraged to take more responsibility for managing their lives and solving their problems.

Although not all sociocultural theorists subscribe to Szasz's radical views, all do emphasize the importance of taking sociocultural factors into account in understanding people whose behavior leads them to be perceived as mentally ill or abnormal. Sociocultural factors may include those related to gender, race, ethnicity, lifestyle, or social ills such as poverty and discrimination.

The Biopsychosocial Perspective Many leading scholars today believe that patterns of abnormal behavior are too complex to be understood from any one model or perspective. They endorse the view that abnormal behavior is best understood by taking into account the interaction of multiple causes representing the biological, psychological, and sociocultural domains. The biopsychosocial perspective, or *interactionist model*, informs the approach we take in this text toward understanding the origins of abnormal behavior. We believe we need to consider the interplay of biological, psychological, and sociocultural factors in the development of psychological disorders. Though we recognize that our understanding of these causal factors may be incomplete, we encourage the reader to consider possible causal pathways that take into account the influences of multiple factors and their interactions.

Perspectives on psychological disorders provide a framework not only for explanation but also for treatment (see Chapter 4). They also lead to formulations of predictions, or *hypotheses*, that guide research. The medical model, for example, fosters inquiry into genetic and biochemical treatment methods. In the next section, we consider the ways in which psychologists and other mental health professionals study abnormal behavior.

Quiz **1.2**
Historical Perspectives on Abnormal Behavior

Research Methods in Abnormal Psychology

Abnormal psychology is a branch of the scientific discipline of psychology, which means research in the field is based on the application of the **scientific method.** Here we examine how researchers apply the scientific method in investigating abnormal behavior.

Let us begin by asking you to imagine you are a brand-new graduate student in psychology and are sitting in your research methods course on the first day of the term. The professor, a distinguished woman of about 50, enters the class. She is carrying a small wire-mesh cage that holds a white rat. She smiles and sets the cage on her desk.

The professor removes the rat from the cage and places it on the desk. She asks the class to observe its behavior. As a serious student, you attend closely. The animal moves to the edge of the desk, pauses, peers over the edge, and seems to jiggle its whiskers at the floor below. It maneuvers along the edge of the desk, tracking the perimeter. Now and then the rat pauses and vibrates its whiskers downward in the direction of the floor.

The professor picks up the rat and returns it to the cage. She asks the class to describe the animal's *behavior.*

A student responds, "The rat seems to be looking for a way to escape."

Another student says, "It is reconnoitering its environment, examining it." "Reconnoitering?" you think. That student has seen too many war movies.

The professor writes each response on the blackboard. Another student raises her hand. "The rat is making a visual search of the environment," she says. "Maybe it's looking for food."

The professor prompts other students for their descriptions.

"It's looking around," says one.

scientific method A method of conducting scientific research in which theories or assumptions are examined in the light of evidence.

"Trying to escape," says another.

Your turn arrives. Trying to be scientific, you say, "We can't say what its motivation might be. All we know is that it's scanning its environment."

"How so?" the professor asks.

"Visually," you reply, confidently.

The professor writes the response and then turns to the class, shaking her head. "Each of you observed the rat," she said, "but none of you described its *behavior*. Each of you made certain *inferences*, that the rat was 'looking for a way down' or 'scanning its environment' or 'looking for food,' and the like. These are not unreasonable inferences, but they are inferences, not descriptions. They also happen to be wrong. You see, the rat is blind. It's been blind since birth. It couldn't possibly be looking around, at least not in a visual sense."

Description, Explanation, Prediction, and Control: The Objectives of Science

Description is one of the primary objectives of science. To understand abnormal behavior, we must first learn to describe it. Description allows us to recognize abnormal behavior and provides the basis for explaining it.

Descriptions should be clear, unbiased, and based on careful observation. Our anecdote about the blind rat illustrates the point that our observations and our attempts to describe them can be influenced by our expectations, or biased. Our expectations reflect our models of behavior, and they may incline us to perceive events—such as the rat's movements and other people's behavior—in certain ways. Describing the rat in the classroom as "scanning" and "looking" for something is an **inference,** or conclusion, we draw from our observations based on our model of how animals explore their environments. In contrast, description would involve a precise accounting of the animal's movements around the desk, measuring how far in each direction it moves, how long it pauses, how it bobs its head from side to side, and so on.

Inference is also important in science, however. Inference allows us to jump from the particular to the general—to suggest laws and principles of behavior that can be woven into a model or **theory** of behavior. In Chapter 2 we consider the major theoretical perspectives or models of abnormal behavior. Here let us note that without a way of organizing our descriptions of phenomena in terms of models and theories, we would be left with a buzzing confusion of unconnected observations.

Theories help scientists explain puzzling behavior and predict future behavior. Prediction entails the discovery of factors that anticipate the occurrence of events. Geology, for example, seeks clues in the forces affecting the earth that can forecast natural events such as earthquakes and volcanic eruptions. Scientists who study abnormal behavior seek clues in overt behavior, biological processes, family interactions, and so forth, to predict the development of abnormal behaviors as well as factors that might predict response to various treatments. It is not sufficient for theoretical models to help us explain or make sense of events or behaviors that have already occurred. Useful theories must allow us to predict the occurrence of particular behaviors.

The idea of controlling human behavior—especially the behavior of people with serious problems—is controversial. The history of societal response to abnormal behaviors, including abuses such as exorcism and cruel forms of physical restraint, render the idea particularly distressing. Within science, however, the word *control* does not imply that people are coerced into doing the bidding of others, like puppets dangling on strings. Psychologists, for example, are committed to the dignity of the individual, and the concept of human dignity requires that people be free to make decisions and exercise choices. Within this context, *controlling behavior* means using scientific knowledge to help people shape their own goals and more efficiently use their resources to accomplish them. Today, in the United States, even when helping professionals restrain people who are violently disturbed, their goal is to assist them to overcome their agitation and regain the ability to exercise

description The representation of observations without making interpretations or drawing inferences.

inference A conclusion that is drawn from data.

theory A formulation of the relationships underlying observed events.

meaningful choices in their lives.[3] Ethical standards prohibit the use of injurious techniques in research or practice.

Psychologists and other scientists use the *scientific method* to advance the description, explanation, prediction, and control of abnormal behavior.

The Scientific Method

The scientific method involves systematic attempts to test our assumptions and theories about the world through gathering objective evidence. Various means are used in applying the scientific method, including observational and experimental methods. Here let us focus on the basic steps involved in using the scientific method in experimentation:

1. *Formulating a research question.* Scientists derive research questions from their observations and theories of events and behavior. For instance, based on their clinical observations and understandings of the underlying mechanisms in depression, they may formulate questions about whether certain experimental drugs or particular types of psychotherapy can help people overcome depression.

2. *Framing the research question in the form of a hypothesis.* A **hypothesis** is a precise prediction about behavior that is examined through research. For example, scientists might hypothesize that people who are clinically depressed will show greater improvement on measures of depression if they are given an experimental drug than if they receive an inert placebo ("sugar pill").

3. *Testing the hypothesis.* Scientists test hypotheses through carefully controlled observation and experimentation. They might test the hypothesis about the experimental drug by setting up an experiment in which one group of people with depression is given the experimental drug and another group is given the placebo. They would then administer tests to see if the people who received the active drug showed greater improvement over a period of time than those who received the placebo.

4. *Drawing conclusions about the hypothesis.* In the final step, scientists draw conclusions from their findings about the correctness of their hypotheses. Psychologists use statistical methods to determine the likelihood that differences between groups are **significant** as opposed to chance fluctuations. Psychologists are reasonably confident that group differences are significant—that is, not due to chance—when the probability that chance alone can explain the difference is less than 5%. When well-designed research findings fail to bear out hypotheses, scientists can modify the theories from which the hypotheses are derived. Research findings often lead to modifications in theory, new hypotheses, and, in turn, subsequent research.

Let us consider the major research methods used by psychologists and others in studying abnormal behavior: the naturalistic-observation, correlational, experimental, epidemiological, kinship, and case-study methods. Before we do so, however, let us consider some of the principles that guide ethical conduct in research.

Ethics in Research

Ethical principles are designed to promote the dignity of the individual, protect human welfare, and preserve scientific integrity (McGovern, 1991). Psychologists are prohibited by the ethical standards of their profession from using methods that cause psychological or physical harm to subjects or clients (APA, 1992). Psychologists also must follow ethical guidelines that protect animal subjects in research.

Institutions such as universities and hospitals have review committees, called *institutional review boards* (IRBs), that review proposed research studies in the light of ethical guidelines. Investigators must receive IRB approval before they are permitted to begin

hypothesis An assumption that is tested through experimentation.

significant In statistics, a magnitude of difference that is taken as indicating meaningful differences between groups.

---

[3]Here we are talking about violently confused and disordered behavior, not criminal behavior. Criminals and disturbed people may both be dangerous to others, but with criminals the intention of restraint is usually limited to protecting society.

their studies. Two of the major principles on which ethical guidelines are based are (1) *informed consent* and (2) *confidentiality*.

The principle of **informed consent** requires that people be free to choose whether they wish to participate in research studies. They must be given sufficient information in advance about the study's purposes and methods, and its risks and benefits, to allow them to make an informed decision about their participation. Subjects must also be free to withdraw from a study at any time without penalty. In some cases, researchers may withhold certain information until all the data are collected. For instance, subjects in placebo-control studies of experimental drugs are told that they may receive an inert placebo rather than the active drug. After the study is concluded, participants who received the placebo would be given the option of receiving the active treatment. In studies in which information was withheld or deception was used, subjects must be **debriefed** afterward. That is, they must receive an explanation of the true methods and purposes of the study and why it was necessary to keep them in the dark.

Subjects also have a right to expect that their identities will not be revealed. Investigators are required to protect their **confidentiality** by keeping the records of their participation secure and by not disclosing their identities to others.

We turn now to discussion of the research methods used to investigate abnormal behavior.

The Naturalistic-Observation Method

The **naturalistic-observation method** is used to observe behavior in the field, where it happens. Anthropologists have lived in preliterate societies in order to study human diversity. Sociologists have followed the activities of adolescent gangs in inner cities. Psychologists have spent weeks observing the behavior of homeless people in train stations and bus terminals. They have even observed the eating habits of slender and overweight people in fast-food restaurants, searching for clues to obesity.

Scientists take every precaution to ensure their naturalistic observations are **unobtrusive,** so as to prevent any interference with the behavior they observe. Otherwise, the presence of the observer may distort the behavior that is observed.

Naturalistic observation provides a good deal of information on how subjects behave, but it does not necessarily reveal why they do so. Men who frequent bars and drink, for example, are more likely to get into fights than men who do not. But such observations do not show that alcohol *causes* aggression. As we see in the following pages, questions of cause and effect are best approached by means of controlled experiments.

The Correlational Method

A **correlation** is a statistical measure of the relationships between two factors, or **variables.** In the naturalistic-observation study that occurred in the fast-food restaurant, eating behaviors were related—or correlated—to patrons' weights. They were not directly manipulated. In other words, the investigators did not manipulate the weights or eating rates of their subjects, but merely measured the two variables in some fashion and examined whether they were statistically related to each other. When one variable (weight level) increases as the second variable (rate of eating) increases, there is a **positive correlation** between them. If one variable decreases as the other increases, there is a **negative correlation** between the variables.

The correlational method tests the statistical relationship between variables. However, it does not prove that correlated variables are causally related to each other. Sometimes there is no causal connection between variables that are merely correlated. For example, children's foot size is correlated with their vocabulary development, but changes in foot size certainly do not determine growth of vocabulary. Depression and negative thoughts are also correlated, as we shall see in Chapter 8. Though depression may be caused by negative thinking, it is possible that the direction of causality works

Web Link **1.5**

Ethical Issues in Research Involving wWw Human Participants

informed consent The principle that subjects should receive enough information about an experiment beforehand to decide freely whether to participate.

debriefed To be fully informed about an experiment after it takes place.

confidentiality Protection of the identity of participants by keeping records secure and not disclosing their identities.

naturalistic-observation method A research method in which subjects' behavior is observed and measured in their natural environments.

unobtrusive Not interfering or conspicuous.

correlation A relationship or association between variables.

variables Conditions that are measured (dependent variables) or manipulated (independent variables) in experiments.

positive correlation A statistical relationship between two variables such that increases in one are associated with increases in the other.

negative correlation A statistical relationship between two variables such that increases in one are associated with decreases in the other.

the other way—that depression gives rise to negative thinking. Or perhaps the direction of causality works both ways, with negative thinking contributing to depression and depression in turn influencing negative thinking. Then again, depression and negative thinking may both reflect a common causative factor, such as stress, and not be causally related to each other at all.

Although correlational research does not reveal cause and effect, it can be used to serve the scientific objective of prediction. When two variables are correlated, we can use one to predict the other. Knowledge of correlations among alcoholism, family history, and attitudes toward drinking helps us predict which adolescents are at great risk of developing problems with alcohol, although causal connections are complex and somewhat nebulous. But knowing which factors predict future problems may help us direct preventive efforts toward these high-risk groups to help prevent these problems from developing.

The Longitudinal Study One type of correlational study is the **longitudinal study,** in which subjects are studied at periodic intervals over lengthy periods, perhaps for decades. By studying people over time, researchers can investigate the events associated with the onset of abnormal behavior and, perhaps, learn to identify factors that predict the development of such behavior. However, this type of research is time consuming and costly. It requires a commitment that may literally outlive the original investigators. Therefore, long-term longitudinal studies are relatively uncommon. In Chapter 13 we examine one of the best known longitudinal studies, the Danish high-risk study that has tracked, since 1962, a group of children whose mothers had schizophrenia and who were therefore themselves at increased risk of developing the disorder (Mednick, Parnas, & Schulsinger, 1987; Parnas et al., 1993).

Naturalistic observation. Anthropologists learn about other cultures by observing how members of these other societies live from day to day, in some cases actually living for a time in the societies they study. Here an American anthropologist is shown sitting among members of an African pygmy tribe.

The Experimental Method

Prediction is based on the *correlation* between events or factors that are separated in time. As in other forms of correlational research, we must be careful not to infer *causation* from *correlation*. A *causal relationship* between two events involves a time-ordered relationship in which the second event is the direct result of the first. We need to meet two strict conditions to posit a causal relationship between two factors:

1. The effect must follow the cause in a time-ordered sequence of events.
2. Other plausible causes of the observed effects (rival hypotheses) must be eliminated.

The **experimental method** allows scientists to demonstrate causal relationships by first manipulating the causal factor and then measuring its effects under controlled conditions that minimize the risk of other factors explaining these effects.

The term *experiment* can cause some confusion. Broadly speaking, an experiment is a trial or test of a hypothesis. From this vantage point, any method that actually seeks to test a hypothesis could be considered experimental—including naturalistic observation and correlational studies. But investigators usually limit the use of the term *experimental method* to refer to studies in which researchers seek to uncover cause-and-effect relationships by manipulating possible causal factors directly.

The factors or variables hypothesized to play a causal role are manipulated or controlled by the investigator in experimental research. These are called the **independent variables.** The observed effects are labeled **dependent variables,** because changes in them are believed to depend on the independent or manipulated variable. Dependent variables are observed and measured, not manipulated, by the experimenter. Examples of independent and dependent variables of interest to investigators of abnormal behavior are shown in Table 1.1.

Truth OR Fiction? **REVISITED**

Finding that two variables are closely linked together means that one is a cause of the other.

FALSE. Two variables may be linked or correlated without being causally related to one another.

longitudinal study A research study in which subjects are followed over time.

experimental method A scientific method that aims to discover cause-and-effect relationships by manipulating independent variables and observing the effects on the dependent variables.

independent variables Factors that are manipulated in experiments.

dependent variables Outcomes of an experiment believed to be dependent on the effects of an independent variable.

TABLE 1.1   Examples of Independent and Dependent Variables in Experimental Research

Independent Variables	Dependent Variables
Type of treatment: for example, different types of drug treatments or psychological treatments	Behavioral variables: for example, measures of adjustment, activity levels, eating behavior, smoking behavior
Treatment factors: for example, brief vs. long-term treatment, inpatient vs. outpatient treatment	Physiological variables: for example, measures of physiological responses such as heart rate, blood pressure, and brain wave activity
Experimental manipulations: for example, types of beverage consumed (alcoholic vs. nonalcoholic)	Self-report variables: for example, measures of anxiety, mood, or marital or life satisfaction

---

THINK ABOUT IT

Why should we not assume that because two variables are correlated they are causally linked?

experimental subjects In an experiment, subjects who receive the experimental treatment.

control subjects In an experiment, subjects who do not receive the experimental treatment.

selection factor A type of bias in which differences between experimental and control groups result from differences in the subjects placed in the groups, not from the independent variable.

blind A state of being unaware of whether one has received an experimental treatment.

In an experiment, subjects are exposed to an *independent variable*, for example, the type of beverage (alcoholic vs. nonalcoholic) they consume in a laboratory setting. They are then observed or examined to determine whether the independent variable makes a difference in their behavior, or, more precisely, whether the independent variable affects the dependent variable—for example, whether they behave more aggressively if they consume alcohol.

Experimental and Control Subjects Well-controlled experiments assign subjects to experimental and control groups at random. **Experimental subjects** are given the experimental treatment; **control subjects,** are not. Care is taken to hold other conditions constant for each group. By using random assignment and holding other conditions constant, experimenters can be reasonably confident that the experimental treatment, and not uncontrolled factors, such as room temperature or differences between the types of subjects in the experimental and control groups, brought about the differences in outcome between the experimental and control groups (Ioannidis & Karassa, 2001).

Why should experimenters assign subjects to experimental and control groups at random? Consider a study intended to investigate the effects of alcohol on behavior. Let's suppose we allowed subjects themselves to decide whether or not they wanted to be in an experimental group that drank alcohol or a control group that drank a nonalcoholic beverage. If this were the case, then differences between the groups might be to due to an underlying selection factor rather than the experimental manipulation. For example, subjects who *chose* the alcoholic beverage might differ in their personalities from those who chose the control beverage. They might be more willing to explore or to take risks, for example. Therefore, we would not know whether the independent variable (type of beverage) or a **selection factor** (difference in the kinds of subjects making up the groups) was ultimately responsible for observed differences in behavior. Random assignment controls for selection factors by ensuring that subject characteristics are randomly distributed across groups. Thus it is reasonable to assume that differences between groups result from the treatments they receive rather than from differences between the subjects making up the groups. Still, it is possible that apparent treatment effects stem from subjects' expectancies about the treatments they receive rather than from the active components in the treatments themselves. In other words, knowing you are being given an alcoholic beverage to drink might affect your behavior, quite apart from the alcoholic content of the beverage itself.

Controlling for Subject Expectancies To control for subject expectancies, experimenters rely on procedures that render subjects **blind,** or uninformed about, as to what treatments they are receiving. For example, the taste of an alcoholic beverage such as vodka may be masked by mixing it with tonic water in certain amounts, so as to keep subjects unaware of whether the drinks they receive contain alcohol or tonic water only. In this way, subjects who truly receive alcohol should have no different expectations than those receiving the nonalcoholic control beverage. Similarly, drug treatment studies are often designed to control for subjects' expectations by keeping subjects in the dark as to whether they are receiving the experimental drug or an *inert* placebo control.

The term **placebo** derives from the Latin meaning "I shall please," referring to the fact that belief in the effectiveness of a treatment (its pleasing qualities) may inspire hopeful expectations that help people mobilize themselves to overcome their problems—regardless of whether the substance they receive is chemically active or inert. In medical research on chemotherapy, a placebo—also referred to as a "sugar pill"—is an inert substance that physically resembles an active drug. By comparing the effects of the active drug with those of the placebo, the experimenter can determine whether the drug has specific effects beyond those accounted for by expectations.

In a *single-blind placebo-control study*, subjects are randomly assigned to treatment conditions in which they receive an active drug (experimental condition) or a placebo (placebo-control condition), but they are kept blind, or uninformed, about which drug they are receiving. It is also helpful to keep the dispensing researchers blind as to which substances the subjects are receiving, lest the researchers' expectations come to affect the results. So in the case of a *double-blind placebo design*, neither the researcher nor the subject is told whether an active drug or a placebo is being administered. Of course, this approach assumes the subjects and the experimenters cannot "see through" the blind. In some cases, however, telltale side effects or obvious drug effects may break the blind (Basoglu et al., 1997). Still, the double-blind placebo control is among the strongest and most popular experimental designs, especially in drug treatment research.

Though placebos are routinely used in clinical research, evidence suggests that the effects of placebos are generally weak (Hrobjartsson & Gotzsche, 2001; Bailar, 2001). Evidence of placebo effects is strongest in pain studies, presumably because pain is a subjective experience that may be influenced more by the power of suggestion than other medical conditions that rely on objective measures, such as blood pressure ("Doubt Cast," 2001).

Placebo-control groups have also been used in psychotherapy research to control for subject expectancies. Assume you were to study the effects of therapy method A on mood. It would be inadequate to assign the experimental group to therapy A randomly and the control group to a no-treatment waiting list. The experimental group might show improvement because of group participation, not because of therapy method A. Participation might raise expectations of success, and these expectations might be sufficient to engender improvement. Changes in control subjects placed on the "waiting list" would help to account for effects due to the passage of time, but they would not account for placebo effects, such as the benefits of therapy that result from instilling a sense of hope.

An *attention-placebo* control group design can be used to separate the effects of a particular form of psychotherapy from placebo effects. In an attention-placebo group, subjects are exposed to a believable or credible treatment that contains the nonspecific factors that all therapies share—such as the attention and emotional support of a therapist—but not the specific ingredients of therapy represented in the active treatment. Attention-placebo treatments commonly substitute general discussions of participants' problems for the specific ingredients of therapy contained in the experimental treatment. Unfortunately, although attention-placebo subjects may be kept blind as to whether or not they are receiving the experimental treatment, the therapists themselves are generally aware of which treatment is being administered. Therefore, the attention-placebo method may not control for therapists' expectations.

Experimental Validity Experimental studies are judged on whether they are valid, or sound. The concept of experimental validity has multiple meanings, and we consider three of them: *internal validity, external validity,* and *construct validity.* We will see in Chapter 3 that the term *validity* is also applied in the context of tests and measures to refer to the degree to which these instruments measure what they purport to measure.

placebo An inert medication or bogus treatment that is intended to control for expectancy effects.

THINK ABOUT IT
Why is a double-blind experimental design preferable to a single-blind design? How can a therapist's knowledge or expectations affect the results of an attention-placebo study? How are these two problems related?

internal validity The degree to which manipulation of the independent variables can be causally related to changes in the dependent variables.

external validity The degree to which experimental results can be generalized to other settings and conditions.

construct validity The degree to which treatment effects can be accounted for by the theoretical mechanisms (constructs) represented in the independent variables.

Experiments are said to have **internal validity** when the observed changes in the dependent variable(s) can be causally related to the independent or treatment variable. Assume a group of depressed subjects is treated with a new antidepressant medication (the independent variable), and changes in their mood and behavior (the dependent variables) are tracked over time. After several weeks of treatment, the researcher finds most subjects have improved and claims the new drug is an effective treatment for depression. "Not so fast," you think to yourself. "How does the experimenter know that the independent variable and not some other factor was causally responsible for the improvement? Perhaps the subjects improved naturally as time passed, or perhaps they were exposed to other events responsible for their improvement." Experiments lack internal validity to the extent they fail to control for other factors (called *confounds*, or threats to validity) that might pose rival hypotheses for the results.

Experimenters randomly assign subjects to treatment and control groups to help control for such rival hypotheses. Random assignment helps ensure that subjects' attributes—intelligence, motivation, age, race, and so on—and presumably the life events they experience are randomly distributed across the groups and are not likely to favor one group over the other. Through the random assignment to groups, researchers can be reasonably confident that significant differences between the treatment and control groups reflect the effects of independent (treatment) variables and not confounding selection factors.

External validity refers to the generalizability or applicability of the results of an experimental study to other subjects and settings and at other times. In most cases, researchers are interested in generalizing the results of a specific study (for example, effects of a new antidepressant medication on a sample of people who are depressed) to a larger population (people in general who are depressed). The external validity of a study is strengthened to the degree the *sample* is representative of the target population. In studying the problems of the urban homeless, it is essential to make the effort to recruit a representative sample of the homeless population, for example, rather than focusing on a few homeless people who happen to be available. One way of obtaining a representative sample is by means of random sampling. In a *random sample*, every member of the target population has an equal chance of being selected.

Researchers may seek to extend the results of a particular study by replication, which refers to the process of repeating the experiment in other settings, with samples drawn from other populations, or at other times. A treatment for hyperactivity may be helpful with economically deprived children in an inner city classroom but not with children in affluent suburbs or rural areas. The external validity of the treatment may be limited if its effects do not generalize to other samples or settings. That does not mean the treatment is less effective, but rather that its range of effectiveness may be limited to certain populations or situations.

Construct validity represents a conceptually higher level of validity—the degree to which treatment effects can be accounted for by the theoretical mechanisms or constructs represented in the independent variables. A drug, for example, may have predictable effects but not for the theoretical reasons claimed by the researchers.

Consider a hypothetical experimental study of a new antidepressant medication. The research may have internal validity in the form of solid controls and external validity in the form of generalizability across samples of seriously depressed people. However, it may lack construct validity if the drug does not work for the reasons proposed by the researchers. Perhaps the researchers assumed that the drug would work by raising the levels of certain chemicals in the nervous system, whereas the drug actually works by increasing the sensitivity of receptors for those chemicals. "So what?" you may think. After all, the drug still works. True enough—in terms of immediate clinical applications. However, a better understanding of why the drug works can advance theoretical knowledge of depression and give rise to the development of yet more effective treatments.

We can never be certain about the construct validity of research. Scientists recognize that their current theories about why their results occurred may eventually be toppled by other theories that better account for the findings.

The Epidemiological Method

The **epidemiological method** studies the rates of occurrence of abnormal behavior in various settings or population groups. One type of epidemiological study is the **survey method,** which relies on interviews or questionnaires. Surveys are used to ascertain the rates of occurrence of various disorders in the population as a whole and in various subgroups classified according to such factors as race, ethnicity, gender, or social class. Rates of occurrence of a given disorder are expressed in terms of **incidence,** the number of new cases occurring during a specific period of time, and **prevalence,** the overall number of cases of a disorder existing in the population during a given period of time. Prevalence rates, then, include both new and continuing cases.

Epidemiological studies may point to potential causal factors in illnesses and disorders, even though they lack the power of experiments. By finding that illnesses or disorders "cluster" in certain groups or locations, researchers may be able to identify distinguishing characteristics that place these groups or regions at higher risk. Yet such epidemiological studies cannot control for selection factors—that is, they cannot rule out the possibility that other unrecognized factors might play a causal role in putting a certain group at greater risk. Therefore they must be considered suggestive of possible causal influences that must be tested further in experimental studies.

Samples and Populations In the best of possible worlds, we would conduct surveys in which every member of the **population** of interest would participate. In that way, we could be sure the survey results accurately represent the population we wish to study. In reality, unless the population of interest is rather narrowly defined (say, for example, designating the population of interest as the students living on your dormitory floor), chances are it is extremely difficult, if not impossible, to survey every member of a given population. Even census takers can't count every head in the general population. Consequently, most surveys are based on a **sample,** or subset, of the population. Researchers take steps when constructing a sample to ensure that it *represents* the target population. A researcher who sets out to study smoking rates in a local community by interviewing people drinking coffee in late-night cafés will probably overestimate its true prevalence.

One method of obtaining a representative sample is random sampling. A **random sample** is drawn in such a way that each member of the population of interest has an equal probability of selection. Epidemiologists sometimes construct random samples by surveying at random a given number of households within a target community. By repeating this process in a random sample of U.S. communities, the overall sample can approximate the general U.S. population, based on even a tiny percentage of the overall population.

Random sampling is often confused with random assignment. Random sampling refers to the process of randomly choosing individuals within a target population to participate in a survey or research study. By contrast, random assignment refers to a process by which members of a research sample are assigned at random to different experimental conditions or treatments.

Kinship Studies

Kinship studies attempt to disentangle the roles of heredity and environment in determining behavior. Heredity plays a critical role in determining a wide range of traits. The structures we inherit make our behavior possible (humans can walk and run) and at the same time place limits on us (humans cannot fly without artificial equipment). Heredity plays a role in determining not only our physical characteristics (hair color, eye color, height, and the like) but also many of our psychological characteristics. The science of heredity is called **genetics.**

Genes are the basic building blocks of heredity. They regulate the development of traits. **Chromosomes,** rod-shaped structures that house our genes, are found in the nuclei of the body's cells. A normal human cell contains 46 chromosomes, organized into 23 pairs.

epidemiological method A method of research that involves tracking the rates of occurrence of a disorder among different groups.

survey method A research method in which large samples of people are questioned by means of a survey instrument.

incidence The number of new cases of a disorder that occurs within a specific period of time.

prevalence The overall number of cases of a disorder in a population within a specific period of time.

population A total group of people, other organisms, or events.

sample Part of a population.

random sample A sample that is drawn in such a way that every member of a population has an equal chance of being included.

genetics The science of heredity.

genes The units, found on chromosomes, that carry heredity.

chromosomes The structures found in the nuclei of cells that carry the units of heredity, or genes.

genotype The set of traits specified by an individual's genetic code.

phenotype An individual's actual or expressed traits.

proband The case first diagnosed of a given disorder.

monozygotic (MZ) twins Twins that develop from the same fertilized egg and therefore share identical genes.

dizygotic (DZ) twins Twins that develop from separate fertilized eggs.

concordance Agreement.

Chromosomes consist of large complex molecules of deoxyribonucleic acid (DNA). Genes occupy various segments along the length of chromosomes. There are an estimated 30,000 to 40,000 genes in the nucleus of a human body cell (N. Wade, 2001a, 2001b).

The set of traits specified by our genetic code is referred to as our **genotype.** Our appearance and behavior are not determined by our genotype alone. We are also influenced by environmental factors such as nutrition, learning, exercise, accident and illness, learning, and culture. The constellation of our actual or expressed traits is called our **phenotype.** Our phenotype represents the interaction of genetic and environmental influences. People who possess genotypes for particular psychological disorders are said to have a *genetic predisposition* that makes them more likely to develop the disorder in response to stress or other factors, such as physical or psychological trauma.

The more closely people are related, the more genes they have in common. Children receive half their genes from each parent. There is thus a 50% overlap in genetic heritage between each parent and his or her offspring. Siblings (brothers and sisters) similarly share half their genetic heritage. Aunts and uncles related by blood to their nephews and nieces have a 25% overlap; first cousins, a 12.5% overlap (see Figure 1.2).

To determine whether abnormal behavior runs in a family, as we would expect if genetics plays a role, researchers would locate a person with the disorder and then study how the disorder is distributed among the person's family members (Nestadt et al., 2000; Tillfors et al., 2001). The case first diagnosed is referred to as the index case, or **proband.** If the distribution of the disorder among family members of the proband approximates their degree of kinship, there may be a genetic involvement in the disorder. However, the closer their kinship, the more likely people also are to share environmental backgrounds. For this reason, twin and adoptee studies are of particular value.

Twin Studies Sometimes a fertilized egg cell (or *zygote*) divides into two cells that separate, so each develops into a separate person. In such cases, there is a 100% overlap in genetic makeup, and the offspring are known as identical twins, or **monozygotic (MZ) twins.** Sometimes a woman releases two egg cells, or ova, in the same month, and they are both fertilized. In such cases, the *zygotes* (fertilized egg cells) develop into fraternal twins, or **dizygotic (DZ) twins.** DZ twins overlap 50% in their genetic heritage, just as other siblings do.

Identical, or MZ, twins are important in the study of the relative influences of heredity and environment because differences between MZ twins are the result of environmental rather than genetic influences. MZ twins look more alike and are closer in height than DZ twins. In twin studies, researchers identify probands for a given disorder who are members of MZ or DZ twin pairs and then study the other twins in the pairs. A role for genetic factors is suggested when MZ twins are more likely than DZ twins to share a disorder. Differences in the rates of **concordance** (agreement for the given trait or disorder) for MZ versus DZ twins are found for some forms of abnormal behavior, such as schizophrenia and bipolar disorder. Even among MZ twins, though, environmental influences cannot be ruled out. Parents and teachers, for example, often encourage MZ twins to behave in similar ways. Put in another way: If one twin does X, everyone expects the other to do X also. Expectations have a way of influencing behavior and making for self-fulfilling prophecies. We should also note that twins might not be typical of the general population, so we need to be cautious when generalizing the results of twin studies to the larger population. Twins tend to have had shorter gestational periods, lower birth weights, and a greater frequency of congenital malformations than nontwins (Kendler, 1994). Perhaps differences in prenatal experiences influence their later development in ways that set them apart from nontwins.

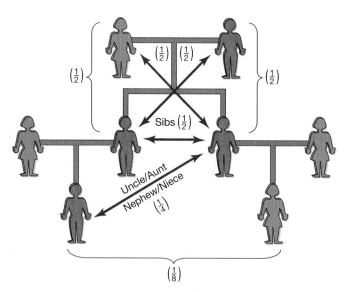

FIGURE 1.2 A family tree showing the proportion of shared inheritance among relatives.
The more closely people are related, the more genes they have in common. Kinship studies, including twin studies and adoptee studies, afford researchers insight into the heritability of various patterns of abnormal behavior.

Adoptee Studies **Adoptee studies** can provide powerful arguments for or against a role for genetic factors in the appearance of psychological traits and disorders. Assume that children are reared by adoptive parents from a very early age—perhaps from birth. The children share environmental backgrounds with their adoptive parents but not their genetic heritages. Then assume we compare the traits and behavior patterns of these children to those of their biological parents and their adoptive parents. If the children show a greater similarity to their biological parents than their adoptive parents on certain traits or disorders, we have strong evidence indeed for genetic factors in these traits and disorders.

The study of monozygotic twins reared apart might provide even more dramatic testimony to the relative roles of genetics and environment in shaping abnormal behavior. However, this situation is so uncommon that few examples exist in the literature. Although adoptee studies may represent the strongest source of evidence for genetic factors in explaining abnormal behavior patterns, we should recognize that adoptees, like twins, may not be typical of the general population. In later chapters we explore the role that adoptee and other kinship studies play in ferreting out genetic and environmental influences in many psychological disorders.

The Case-Study Method

Case studies have been important influences in the development of theories and treatment of abnormal behavior. Freud developed his theoretical model primarily on the basis of case studies, such as that of Anna O. Therapists representing other theoretical viewpoints have also reported cases studies.

Types of Case Studies **Case studies** involve intensive studies of individuals. Some case studies are based on historical material, involving subjects who have been dead for hundreds of years. Freud, for example, conducted a case study of the Renaissance artist and inventor Leonardo da Vinci. More commonly, case studies reflect an in-depth analysis of an individual's course of treatment. They typically include detailed histories of the subject's background and response to treatment. The therapist attempts to glean information from a particular client's experience in therapy that may be of help to other therapists treating similar clients.

Despite the richness of clinical material that case studies can provide, they are much less rigorous as research designs than experiments. Distortions or gaps in memory are bound to occur when people discuss historical events, especially those of their childhoods. Some people may intentionally color events to make a favorable impression on the interviewer; others aim to shock the interviewer with exaggerated or fabricated recollections. Interviewers themselves may unintentionally guide subjects into slanting the histories they report in ways that are compatible with their own theoretical perspectives.

Single-Case Experimental Designs The lack of control available in the traditional case-study method led researchers to develop more sophisticated methods, called **single-case experimental designs** (sometimes called *single-participant research designs*) in which subjects are used as their own controls (Morgan & Morgan, 2001). One of the most common forms of the single-case experimental design is the A-B-A-B, or **reversal design** (see Figure 1.3). The reversal design consists of the repeated measurement of clients' behavior across four successive phases:

1. A baseline phase (A). The baseline phase, which occurs prior to the inception of treatment and is characterized by repeated measurement of the target problem

adoptee studies Studies that compare the traits and behavior patterns of adopted children to those of their biological parents and their adoptive parents.

case study A carefully drawn biography based on clinical interviews, observations, and psychological tests.

single-case experimental design A type of case study in which the subject is used as his or her own control.

reversal design An experimental design that consists of repeated measurement of a subject's behavior through a sequence of alternating baseline and treatment phases.

THINK ABOUT IT
How do investigators attempt to separate out the effects of heredity and environment?

Truth OR Fiction?   REVISITED

Case studies have been conducted on people who have been dead for hundreds of years.

TRUE. Case studies have been conducted on people who have been dead for hundreds of years, such as Freud's study of Leonardo. Such studies rely on historical records rather than interviews.

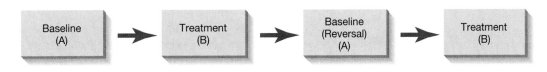

FIGURE 1.3 Diagram of an A-B-A-B reversal design.

baseline The rate at which a behavior occurs before treatment.

critical thinking Adoption of a questioning attitude and careful scrutiny of claims and arguments in the light of evidence.

behaviors at periodic intervals. This measurement allows the experimenter to establish a **baseline** rate for the behavior before treatment begins.

2. A treatment phase (B). Now the target behaviors are measured as the client undergoes treatment.

3. A second baseline phase (A, again). Treatment is now temporarily withdrawn or suspended. This is the reversal in the reversal design, and it is expected that the positive effects of treatment should now be reversed because the treatment has been withdrawn.

4. A second treatment phase (B, again). Treatment is reinstated and the target behaviors are assessed yet again.

Clients' target behaviors or response patterns are compared from one phase to the next to determine the effects of treatment. The experimenter looks for evidence of a correspondence between a subject's behavior and the particular phase of the design to determine whether the independent variable (that is, the treatment) has produced the intended effects. If the behavior improves whenever treatment is introduced (during the first and second treatment phases) but returns (or is reversed) to baseline levels during the reversal phase, the experimenter can be reasonably confident the treatment had the intended effect.

The method is illustrated by a case in which Azrin and Peterson (1989) used a controlled blinking treatment to eliminate a severe eye tic—a form of squinting in which her eyes shut tightly for a fraction of a second—in a 9-year-old girl. The tic occurred about 20 times a minute when the girl was at home. In the clinic, the rate of eye tics or squinting was measured for 5 minutes during a baseline period (A). Then the girl was prompted to blink her eyes softly every 5 seconds (B). The experimenters reasoned that voluntary "soft" blinking would activate motor (muscle) responses incompatible with those producing the tic, thereby suppressing the tic. As you can see in Figure 1.4, the tic was virtually eliminated in but a few minutes of practicing the incompatible, or competing, response ("soft" blinking) but returned to near baseline levels during the reversal phase (A) when the competing response was withdrawn. The positive effects were quickly reinstated during the second

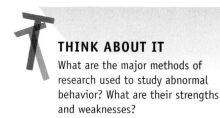

THINK ABOUT IT
What are the major methods of research used to study abnormal behavior? What are their strengths and weaknesses?

FIGURE 1.4 Treatment results from the Azrin and Peterson study (an A-B-A-B design).
Notice how the target response, eye tics per minute, decreased when the competing response was introduced in the first "B" phase. The rate then increased to near baseline levels when the competing response was withdrawn during the second "A" phase. It decreased again when the competing response was reinstated in the second "B" phase.

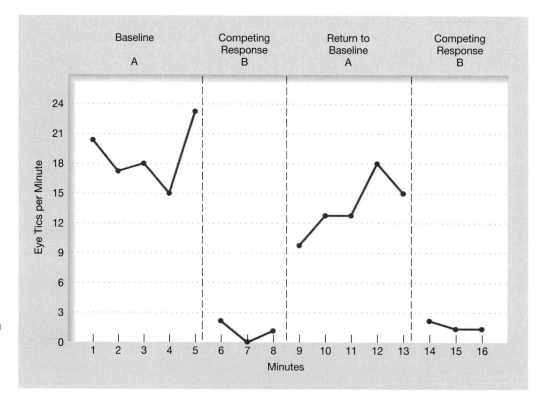

treatment period (B). The child was also taught to practice the blinking response at home during scheduled 3-minute practice periods and whenever the tic occurred or she felt an urge to squint. The tic was completely eliminated during the first 6 weeks of the treatment program and remained absent at a follow-up evaluation 2 years later.

Although reversal designs offer better controls than traditional treatment case studies, it is not always possible or ethical to reverse certain behaviors or treatment effects. Participants in a stop-smoking program who reduce or quit smoking during treatment may not revert to their baseline smoking rates when treatment is temporarily withdrawn during a reversal phase.

The *multiple-baseline design* is a type of single-case experimental design that does not require a reversal phase. In a multiple-baseline design *across behaviors*, treatment is applied, in turn, to two or more behaviors following a baseline period. A treatment effect is inferred if changes in each of these behaviors corresponded to the time at which each was subjected to treatment. Because no reversal phase is required, many of the ethical and practical problems associated with reversal designs are avoided.

A multiple-baseline design was used to evaluate the effects of a social skills training program in the treatment of a shy, unassertive 7-year-old girl named Jane (Bornstein, Bellack, & Hersen, 1977). The program taught Jane to maintain eye contact, speak more loudly, and make requests of other people through modeling (therapist demonstration of the target behavior), rehearsal (practice), and therapist feedback regarding the effectiveness of practice. However, the behaviors were taught sequentially, not simultaneously. Measurement of each behavior and an overall rating of assertiveness were obtained during a baseline period from observations of Jane's role-playing of social situations with other children, such as playing social games at school and conversing in class. As shown in Figure 1.5, Jane's performance of each behavior that were improved following treatment. The rating of overall assertiveness showed more gradual improvement as the number of behaviors that were included in the program increased. Treatment gains were generally maintained at a follow-up evaluation.

To show a clear-cut treatment effect, changes in target behaviors should occur only when they are subjected to treatment. In some cases, however, changes in the treated behaviors may lead to changes in the yet untreated behaviors, apparently because of generalization of the effect. Fortunately though, generalization effects have tended to be the exception rather than the rule in experimental research (Kazdin, 1992).

No matter how tightly controlled the design, or how impressive the results, single-case designs suffer from weak external validity because they do not show whether a treatment effective for one person is effective for others. Replication with other individuals is essential to help strengthen external validity. If these results prove encouraging, they may lead to controlled experiments to provide even more convincing evidence of treatment effectiveness.

Scientists may use different methods to study phenomena of interest to them. But they share in common a skeptical, hard-nosed way of thinking called critical thinking. **Critical thinking** involves a willingness to challenge conventional wisdom and common knowledge that many of us take for granted. It also means finding *reasons* to support beliefs rather than relying on feelings or gut impressions. When people think critically, they maintain open minds. They suspend their beliefs until they have obtained and evaluated evidence that either supports or refutes them. In the "A Closer Look" feature on page 30, we examine the features of critical thinking and how they can be applied in our study of abnormal psychology.

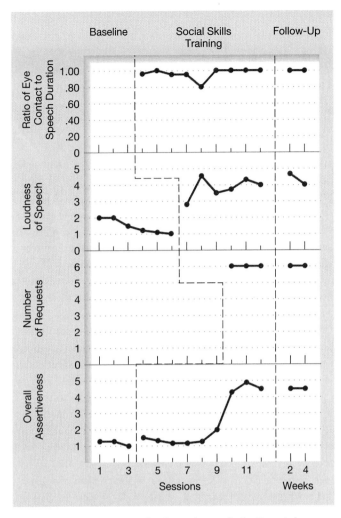

FIGURE 1.5 Treatment results from the study by Bornstein, Bellack, and Hersen.
The dotted line shows the point at which social skills training was applied to each of the targeted behaviors. Here we see that the targeted behaviors (eye contact, loudness of speech, and number of requests) improved only when they were subject to the treatment approach (social skills training). We thus have evidence that the treatment—and not another, unidentified factor—accounted for the results. The section on the bottom shows ratings of Jane's overall level of assertiveness during the baseline assessment period, the social skills training program, and the follow-up period.

Source. Bornstein, M. R., Bellack, A. S., & Hersen, M. (1977). Social-skills training for unassertive children: A multiple-baseline analysis. *Journal of Applied Behavior Analysis, 10*, pp. 183–195. Reprinted with permission.

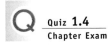

Quiz **1.3**
Research Methods in Abnormal Psychology

Quiz **1.4**
Chapter Exam

A Closer Look

Thinking Critically About Abnormal Psychology

 We are exposed to a flood of information about mental health streaming down to us through the popular media—television, radio, and print media, including books, magazines, and newspapers, and increasingly, the Internet. We may hear a news report touting a new drug as a "breakthrough" in the treatment of anxiety, depression, or obesity, only to learn some time later that the so-called breakthrough doesn't live up to expectations or carries serious side effects. Some reports in the media are accurate and reliable, while others are misleading, biased, or contain half-truths, exaggerated claims, or unsupported conclusions.

To sort through the welter of sometimes confusing information, we need to arm ourselves with the skills of critical thinking, which involves adopting a questioning attitude toward information you hear and read. Critical thinkers carefully weigh the available evidence to see if claims people make can stand up to scrutiny. Becoming a critical thinker means never taking claims at face value. It means looking carefully at both sides of the argument. Sad to say, most of us take certain "truths" for granted. Critical thinkers, however, never say, "This is true because so-and-so says it is true." They seek to evaluate assertions and claims for themselves.

We encourage you to apply critical thinking skills to the questions posed in the "Think About It" features in each chapter. Critical thinkers adopt a skeptical attitude toward information they receive. They carefully examine the definitions of terms, evaluate the logical bases of arguments, and evaluate claims in the light of available evidence. Here are some key features of critical thinking:

1. *Maintain a skeptical attitude.* Don't take anything at face value, not even claims made by respected scientists or textbook authors. Consider the evidence yourself and seek additional information to help you evaluate claims made by others.

2. *Consider the definitions of terms.* Statements may be true or false depending on how the terms that are used are defined. Consider the statement, "Stress is bad for you." If we define the concept *stress* in terms of hassles and work or family pressures that stretch to the max our ability to cope, then there is perhaps substance to the statement. However, if we define stress (see Chapter 5) to include any factors that impose a demand on us to adjust, including events such as a new marriage or the birth of a child, then perhaps certain types of stress can be positive, even if they are stressful. Perhaps, as we'll see, we all need some amount of stress to be energized and alert.

3. *Weigh the assumptions or premises on which arguments are based.* Consider a case in which we are comparing differences in the rates of psychological disorders across racial or ethnic groups in our society. Assuming we find differences, should we conclude that ethnicity or racial identity accounts for these differences? This conclusion might be valid if we can assume that all other factors that distinguish one racial or ethnic group from another are held constant. However, ethnic or racial minorities in the United States and Canada are disproportionately represented among the poor, and the poor are more apt to develop more severe psychological disorders. Differences among racial or ethnic groups may thus be a function of poverty, not race or ethnicity per se. These differences may also be due to negative stereotyping of racial minorities by clinicians in making diagnostic judgments rather than to differences in underlying rates of the disorder.

4. *Bear in mind that correlation is not causation.* Critical thinkers recognize that correlation is not causation. Consider the relationship between depression and stress. Evidence shows a positive correlation between these variables, which means depressed people tend to have higher levels of stress in their lives (Hammen & de Mayo, 1982; Pianta & Egeland, 1994). But does stress cause depression? Perhaps it does. Or perhaps depression leads to greater stress. After all, depressive symptoms may be stressful in themselves and may lead to additional stress as the person finds it increasingly difficult to meet life responsibilities, such as keeping up with work at school or on the job. It is also possible that the two variables are not causally linked at all but are linked through a third variable, perhaps an underlying genetic factor. It is conceivable that people inherit clusters of genes that make them more prone to encounter both depression and stress.

5. *Consider the kinds of evidence on which conclusions are based.* Some conclusions, even seemingly "scientific" conclusions, are based on anecdotes and personal endorsements. They are not founded on sound research. There is much controversy today about so-called recovered memories that may suddenly arise in adulthood, usually during psychotherapy or hypnosis, and usually involving incidents of sexual abuse committed during childhood by the person's parents or family members. But are such memories accurate? (See Chapter 7.)

6. *Do not oversimplify.* Consider the statement, "Alcoholism is inherited." In Chapter 10, we review evidence suggesting that genetic factors may create a predisposition to alcoholism, at least in males. But the origins of alcoholism, as well as of schizophrenia, depression, and physical health problems such as cancer and heart disease, are more complex, reflecting a complicated interplay of biological and environmental factors. In only a few cases are diseases the direct result of a single defective gene or genes. People may even inherit a predisposition to develop a particular psychological or physical disorder but can avoid developing it if they are raised in a supportive family environment and learn to manage stress effectively.

7. *Do not overgeneralize.* In Chapter 7, we consider evidence showing that a history of severe abuse in childhood figures prominently in the great majority of cases of people who later develop multiple personalities. Does this mean that all (or even most) abused children go on to develop multiple personalities? Actually, very few do.

Summing Up

How Do We Define Abnormal Behavior?

What criteria do mental health professionals use to determine that behavior is abnormal? Psychologists generally consider behavior abnormal when it meets some combination of the following criteria: (1) unusual or statistically infrequent; (2) socially unacceptable or in violation of social norms; (3) fraught with misperceptions or misinterpretations of reality; (4) associated with states of severe personal distress; (5) maladaptive or self-defeating; or (6) dangerous.

What are psychological disorders? Psychological disorders (also called *mental disorders)* involve abnormal behavior patterns associated with disturbances in mental health or psychological functioning.

How do views about abnormal behavior vary across cultures? Behaviors deemed normal in one culture may be considered abnormal in another. Concepts of health and illness may also have different meanings in different cultures. Abnormal behavior patterns may also take different forms in different cultures, and societal views or models explaining abnormal behavior also vary across cultures.

Historical Perspectives on Abnormal Behavior

How have views about abnormal behavior changed over time? Ancient societies attributed abnormal behavior to divine or supernatural forces. In medieval times, belief in possession held sway, and exorcists were used to rid people who behaved abnormally of the evil spirits that were believed to possess them. The 19th-century German physician Wilhelm Griesinger argued that abnormal behavior was caused by diseases of the brain. He, along with another German physician who followed him, Emil Kraepelin, were influential in the development of the modern medical model, which likens abnormal behavior patterns to physical illnesses.

How has the treatment of people with mental disorders changed over time? Asylums, or madhouses, began to crop up throughout Europe in the late 15th and early 16th centuries. Conditions in these asylums were dreadful. With the rise of moral therapy in the 19th century, conditions in mental hospitals improved. Proponents of moral therapy believed that mental patients could be restored to functioning if they were treated with dignity and understanding. The decline of moral therapy in the latter part of the 19th century led to a period of apathy and to the belief the "insane" could not be successfully treated. Conditions in mental hospitals deteriorated, and they offered little more than custodial care. Not until the middle of the 20th century did public outrage and concern about the plight of mental patients mobilize legislative efforts toward the development of community mental health centers as alternatives to long-term hospitalization.

What are the major contemporary models of abnormal behavior? The medical model conceptualizes abnormal behavior patterns, like physical diseases, in terms of clusters of symptoms, called syndromes, which have distinctive causes that are presumed to be biological in nature. Psychological models focus on the psychological roots of abnormal behavior and derive from psychoanalytic, behavioral, humanistic, and cognitive perspectives. The sociocultural model emphasizes a broader perspective that takes into account the social contexts in which abnormal behavior occurs. Today, many theorists subscribe to a biopsychosocial model that posits that multiple causes representing biological, psychological, and sociocultural domains interact in complex ways in the development of abnormal behavior patterns.

Research Methods in Abnormal Psychology

What are the basic objectives of the scientific method, and what steps are involved in applying it? The scientific approach focuses on four general objectives: description, explanation, prediction, and control. There are four steps to the scientific method: formulating a research question, framing the research question in the form of a hypothesis, testing the hypothesis, and drawing conclusions about the correctness of the hypothesis. Psychologists follow the ethical principles of the profession that govern research.

What are the methods psychologists use to study abnormal behavior? The naturalistic-observation method allows scientists to measure behavior under naturally occurring conditions. The correlational method explores the relationship between variables, which may help predict future behavior and suggest possible underlying causes of behavior. But correlational research does not directly test cause-and-effect relationships. Longitudinal research is a correlational method in which a sample of subjects is repeatedly studied at periodic intervals over long periods of time, sometimes spanning decades.

In the experimental method, the investigator directly controls (manipulates) the independent variable under controlled conditions to demonstrate cause-and-effect relationships. Experiments use random assignment as the basis for determining which subjects (called experimental subjects) receive an experimental treatment and which others (called control subjects) do not. Experiments are evaluated in terms of internal, external, and construct validity.

The epidemiological method examines the rates of occurrence of abnormal behavior in various population groups or settings. Kinship studies, such as twin studies and adoptee studies, attempt to disentangle the contributions of environment and heredity.

Case-study methods can provide a richness of clinical material, but they are limited by difficulties of obtaining accurate and unbiased client histories, by possible therapist biases, and by the lack of control groups. Single-case experimental designs are intended to help researchers overcome some of the limitations of the case-study method.

CHAPTER TWO

Contemporary Perspectives on Abnormal Behavior

Alejandro Xul Solar
Patria B, 1925

Truth OR Fiction?

• Messages are transmitted through the nervous system by chemical messengers. (p. 34)

• Depressant drugs are drugs that cause depression. (p. 37)

• Freud likened the mind to a giant iceberg, with only the tip rising into conscious awareness. (p. 38)

• Freud believed that an ancient Greek legend about a king who slew his father and married his mother contained key insights into the nature of the development of the human psyche. (p. 43)

• Punishment does not eliminate undesirable behavior. (p. 51)

• Children may acquire a distorted self-concept that mirrors what others expect them to be but which does not reflect who they truly are. (p. 53)

• According to a leading cognitive theorist, states of emotional distress are caused by the beliefs people hold about their life experiences, not by the experiences themselves. (p. 55)

• Rates of mental disorders are generally higher among African Americans than Euro-Americans, even when we account for income differences between these groups. (p. 58)

Since earliest times humans have sought explanations for strange or deviant behavior. As we saw in Chapter 1, in ancient times and through the Middle Ages, beliefs about abnormal behavior centered on the role of demons and other supernatural forces. But even in ancient times, there were some scholars, such as Hippocrates and Galen, who sought natural explanations of abnormal behavior. In contemporary times, superstition and demonology have given way to theoretical models engendered by the natural and social sciences. These approaches pave the way not only for a scientifically based understanding of abnormal behavior but also for ways of treating people with psychological disorders.

In this chapter we examine major contemporary perspectives on abnormal behavior, including the biological, psychological, and sociocultural perspectives. Each of these major perspectives provides a window for examining abnormal behavior. Each contributes to our understanding of abnormal behavior, but none captures a complete view of our subject matter. Many scholars today believe that abnormal behavior patterns are complex phenomena that are best understood by adopting an interactionist or biopsychosocial perspective that takes into account the interaction of factors representing biological, psychological, and sociocultural domains.

The Biological Perspective

The medical model, inspired by physicians from Hippocrates through Kraepelin, remains a powerful force in contemporary understanding of abnormal behavior. The medical model represents a biological perspective on abnormal behavior. We prefer to use the term *biological perspective* rather than *medical model* to refer to approaches that emphasize the role of biological factors in explaining abnormal behavior and the use of biologically based treatments in treating psychological disorders. We can speak of biological perspectives without adopting the tenets of the medical model, which treats abnormal behavior patterns as *disorders* and their features as *symptoms*. For example, certain behavior patterns (shyness or a lack of musical ability) may have a strong genetic component but not be considered "symptoms" of underlying "disorders."

Knowledge of the biological underpinnings of abnormal behavior has grown with great speed in recent years. In Chapter 1 we focused on the methods of studying the role of heredity or genetics. Genetics plays a large role in many forms of abnormal behavior, as we shall see throughout the text.

We also know that other biological factors, especially the functioning of the nervous system, are involved in the development of abnormal behavior (Cravchik & Goldman, 2000). To better understand the role of the nervous system in abnormal behavior patterns, we first need to learn how the nervous system is organized and how nerve cells communicate with each other.

The Nervous System

Perhaps you could not be nervous if you did not have a nervous system—neither could you see, hear, perceive touch or pain, or move—but even calm people have nervous systems. The nervous system is made up of nerve cells called **neurons.** Neurons communicate with one another, or transmit "messages." These messages account for events as diverse as sensing an itch from a bug bite, coordinating a figure skater's vision and muscles, composing a symphony, solving an architectural equation, and, in the case of hallucinations, hearing or seeing things that are not really there.

Every neuron has a cell body, or **soma,** dendrites, and an axon (see Figure 2.1). The cell body contains the nucleus of the cell and metabolizes oxygen to carry out the work of the cell. Short fibers called **dendrites** project from the cell body to receive messages from adjoining neurons. Each neuron has a single **axon** projecting trunklike from the cell body. Axons can extend as long as several feet if they are conveying messages between the toes and the spinal cord. They may branch and project in various directions. Axons terminate

neurons Nerve cells.

soma A cell body.

dendrites The rootlike structures at the ends of neurons that receive nerve impulses from other neurons.

axon The long, thin part of a neuron along which nerve impulses travel.

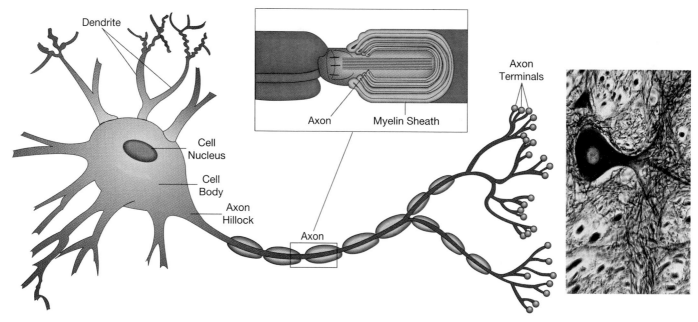

FIGURE 2.1 Anatomy of a neuron.
Neurons typically consist of cells bodies (or somas), dendrites, and one or more axons. The axon of this neuron is wrapped in a myelin sheath, which insulates it from the bodily fluids surrounding the neuron and facilitates transmission of neural impulses (messages that travel within the neuron).

Truth OR Fiction?   REVISITED

Messages are transmitted through the nervous system by chemical messengers.

TRUE. Chemicals called neurotransmitters carry messages from one neuron to another.

terminals The small branching structures at the tips of axons.

knobs The swollen endings of axon terminals.

neurotransmitters Chemical substances that transmit messages from one neuron to another.

synapse The junction between the terminal knob of one neuron and the dendrite or soma of another through which nerve impulses pass.

receptor site A part of a dendrite on a receiving neuron that is structured to receive a neurotransmitter.

Alzheimer's disease A progressive brain disease characterized by gradual loss of memory and intellectual functioning, personality changes, and eventual loss of ability to care for oneself.

in small branching structures that are aptly termed **terminals.** Swellings called **knobs** are found at the tips of axon terminals. Neurons convey messages in one direction, from the dendrites or cell body along the axon to the axon terminals. The messages are then conveyed from terminal knobs to other neurons, muscles, or glands.

Neurons transmit messages to other neurons by means of chemical substances called **neurotransmitters.** Neurotransmitters induce chemical changes in receiving neurons. These changes cause axons to conduct the messages in electrical form.

The junction between a transmitting neuron and a receiving neuron is termed a **synapse.** A transmitting neuron is termed *presynaptic.* A receiving neuron is said to be *postsynaptic.* A synapse consists of an axon terminal from a transmitting neuron, a dendrite of a receiving neuron, and a small fluid-filled gap between the two called the *synaptic cleft.* The message does not jump the synaptic cleft like a spark. Instead, axon terminals release neurotransmitters into the cleft like myriad ships casting off into the seas (Figure 2.2).

Each kind of neurotransmitter has a distinctive chemical structure. It will fit only into one kind of harbor, or **receptor site,** on the receiving neuron. Consider the analogy of a lock and key. Only the right key (neurotransmitter) operates the lock, causing the postsynaptic neuron to forward the message.

Once released, some molecules of a neurotransmitter reach port at receptor sites of other neurons. "Loose" neurotransmitters may be broken down in the synaptic clefts by enzymes or be reabsorbed by the axon terminal (a process termed *reuptake*), so as to prevent the receiving cell from continuing to fire.

Irregularities in the workings of neurotransmitter systems in the brain are closely related to abnormal behavior patterns (see Table 2.1). For example, depression is linked to dysfunctions involving the neurotransmitters *norepinephrine* and *serotonin* (see Chapter 8). Irregularities of serotonin functioning are also implicated in eating disorders (see Chapter 11). **Alzheimer's disease,** a brain disease in which there is a progressive loss of memory and cognitive functioning, is associated with reductions in the levels of the neurotransmitter *acetylcholine* in the brain. Irregularities involving the neurotransmitter *dopamine* appear to be involved in schizophrenia (see Chapter 13). People with schizophrenia may use more of

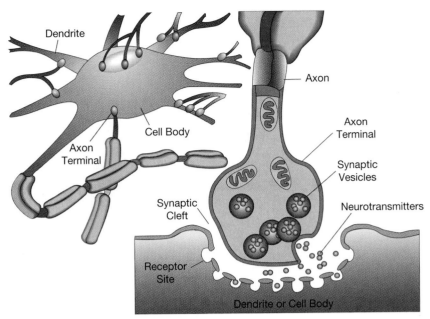

FIGURE 2.2 Transmission of neural impulses across the synapse.
The diagram here shows the structure of the neuron and the mode of transmission of neural impulses between neurons. Neurons transmit messages, or neural impulses, across synapses, which consist of the axon terminal of the transmitting neuron, the gap or synaptic cleft between the neurons, and the dendrite of the receiving neuron. The "message" consists of neurotransmitters that are released into the synaptic cleft and taken up by receptor sites on the receiving neuron. Somehow the patterns of firing of many thousands of neurons give rise to psychological events such as thoughts and mental images. Many patterns of abnormal behavior have been associated with irregularities in the transmission or reception of neural messages.

the dopamine that is available in their brains than do people without schizophrenia. The result may be hallucinations, incoherent speech, and delusional thinking. Antipsychotic drugs used to treat schizophrenia apparently work by blocking dopamine receptors in the brain. Serotonin is linked not only to depression but also to anxiety disorders, sleep disorders, and eating disorders (Lesch et al., 1996; Mann et al., 1996; McBride, Anderson, & Shapiro, 1996). Although neurotransmitter systems are implicated in many psychological disorders, the precise causal mechanisms remain to be determined.

Parts of the Nervous System The nervous system consists of two major parts, the **central nervous system** and the **peripheral nervous system.** The two parts are also divided. The central nervous system consists of the brain and spinal cord. The peripheral nervous system is made up of nerves that (1) receive and transmit sensory messages (messages from sense organs such as the eyes and ears) to the brain and spinal cord, and (2) transmit messages from the brain or spinal cord to the muscles, causing them to contract, and to glands, causing them to secrete hormones.

Central Nervous System We begin our overview of the parts of the central nervous system with the back of the head, where the spinal cord meets the brain, and work forward (see Figure 2.3). The lower part of the brain, or *hindbrain*, consists of the medulla, pons, and

central nervous system The brain and spinal cord.

peripheral nervous system The somatic and autonomic nervous systems.

TABLE 2.1 Neurotransmitter Functions and Relationships with Abnormal Behavior Patterns

Neurotransmitter	Functions	Associations with Abnormal Behavior
Acetylcholine (ACh)	Control of muscle contractions and formation of memories	Reduced levels found in patients with Alzheimer's disease
Dopamine	Regulation of muscle contractions and mental processes involving learning, memory, and emotions	Overutilization of dopamine in the brain may be involved in the development of schizophrenia
Norepinephrine	Mental processes involved in learning and memory	Imbalances linked with mood disorders such as depression
Serotonin	Regulation of mood states, satiety, and sleep	Irregularities may be involved in depression and eating disorders

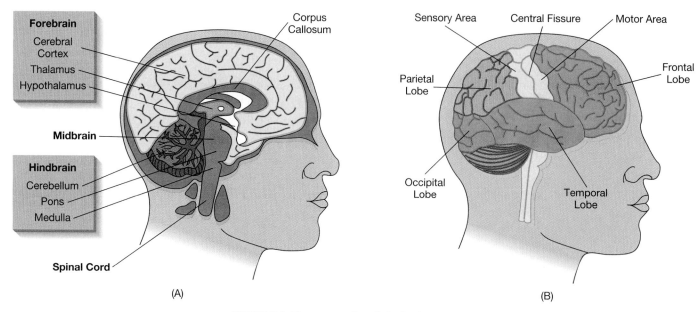

FIGURE 2.3 The geography of the brain.
Part A shows parts of the hindbrain, midbrain, and forebrain. Part B shows the four lobes of the cerebral cortex: frontal, parietal, temporal, and occipital. In B, the sensory (tactile) and motor areas lie across the central fissure from one another. Researchers are investigating the potential relationships between various patterns of abnormal behavior and irregularities in the formation or functioning of the structures of the brain.

Web Link **2.1** wWw
Neuroscience of Mental Health

medulla An area of the hindbrain involved in regulation of heartbeat and respiration.

pons A structure in the hindbrain involved in respiration.

cerebellum A structure in the hindbrain involved in coordination and balance.

reticular activating system Brain structure involved in processes of attention, sleep, and arousal.

comatose In a coma, a state of deep, prolonged unconsciousness.

thalamus A structure in the forebrain involved in relaying sensory information to the cortex and in processes related to sleep and attention.

hypothalamus A structure in the forebrain involved in regulating body temperature, emotion, and motivation.

limbic system A group of forebrain structures involved in learning, memory, and basic drives.

basal ganglia An assemblage of neurons located between the thalamus and cerebrum, involved in coordinating motor (movement) processes.

cerebellum. Many nerves that link the spinal cord to higher brain levels pass through the **medulla.** The medulla plays roles in such vital functions as heart rate, respiration, and blood pressure, and also in sleep, sneezing, and coughing. The **pons** transmits information about body movement and is involved in functions related to attention, sleep, and respiration.

Behind the pons is the **cerebellum** (Latin for "little brain"). The cerebellum is involved in balance and motor (muscle) behavior. Injury to the cerebellum may impair motor coordination and cause stumbling and loss of muscle tone.

The midbrain lies above the hindbrain and contains nerve pathways that link the hindbrain with the forebrain. The **reticular activating system** (RAS) starts in the hindbrain and rises through the midbrain into the lower forebrain. The RAS, which consists of a weblike network of neurons, plays vital roles in sleep, attention, and arousal. RAS injury may leave an animal **comatose.** RAS stimulation triggers messages that heighten alertness. *Depressant drugs*, such as alcohol, which dampen central nervous system activity, lower RAS activity.

Important areas in the frontal part of the brain, or *forebrain*, are the thalamus, hypothalamus, limbic system, basal ganglia, and cerebrum. The **thalamus** relays sensory information (such as touch and vision) to higher brain regions. The thalamus is also involved in sleep and attention, in coordination with other structures, such as the RAS.

The **hypothalamus** is a tiny structure located between the thalamus and the pituitary gland. The hypothalamus is vital in regulating body temperature, concentration of fluids, storage of nutrients, and motivation and emotion. By implanting electrodes in parts of the hypothalamus of animals and observing the effects when a current is switched on, researchers have found that the hypothalamus is involved in a range of motivational drives and behaviors, including hunger, thirst, sex, parenting behaviors, and aggression.

The hypothalamus, together with parts of the thalamus and other structures, make up the **limbic system.** The limbic system plays a role in memory and in regulating the more basic drives involving hunger, thirst, and aggression. The **basal ganglia** lie in front of the thalamus and help to regulate postural movements and coordination.

The **cerebrum** is your "crowning glory" and is responsible for the round shape of the human head. The surface of the cerebrum is convoluted with ridges and valleys. This surface is the **cerebral cortex,** the thinking, planning, and executive center of the brain. The two hemispheres, of the cerebral cortex are connected by the **corpus callosum,** a thick fiber bundle.

Peripheral Nervous System The peripheral nervous system connects the brain to the outer world. Without the peripheral nervous system, people could not perceive the world or act on it. The two main divisions of the peripheral nervous system are the *somatic nervous system* and the *autonomic nervous system.*

The **somatic nervous system** transmits messages about sights, sounds, smells, temperature, body position, and so on, to the brain. Messages from the brain and spinal cord to the somatic nervous system regulate intentional body movements, such as raising an arm, winking, or walking; breathing; and subtle movements that maintain posture and balance.

Psychologists are particularly interested in the **autonomic nervous system** (ANS) because its activities are linked to emotional response. *Autonomic* means "automatic." The ANS regulates the glands and **involuntary** activities such as heart rate, breathing, digestion, and dilation of the pupils of the eyes, even when we are sleep.

The ANS has two branches or subdivisions, the **sympathetic** and the **parasympathetic.** These branches have mostly opposing effects. Many organs and glands are served by both branches of the ANS. The sympathetic division is most involved in processes that mobilize the body's resources in times of stress, such as drawing energy from stored reserves to prepare the person to deal with imposing threats or dangers (see Chapter 5). When we face a threat or dangerous situation, the sympathetic branch of the ANS accelerates the heart rate and breathing rate, which helps prepare our bodies to either fight or flee. Sympathetic activation in the face of a threatening stimulus is associated with emotional responses such as fear or anxiety. When we relax, the parasympathetic branch decelerates the heart rate. The parasympathetic division is most active during processes that replenish energy reserves, such as digestion. Because the sympathetic branch dominates when we are fearful or anxious, fear or anxiety can lead to indigestion because activation of the sympathetic nervous system curbs digestive activity.

The Cerebral Cortex The human activities of thought and language involve the two hemispheres of the cerebrum. Each hemisphere is divided into four parts, or lobes, as shown in Figure 2.3. The *occipital lobe* is primarily involved in vision; the *temporal lobe* is involved in processing sounds or auditory stimuli. The *parietal lobe* is involved in determining sensations of touch, temperature, and pain. The *sensory area* of the parietal lobe receives messages from skin sensors all over the body. Neurons in the motor area (or *motor cortex*) of the *frontal lobe* are involved in controlling muscular responses, which enables us to move our limbs. The *prefrontal cortex* (the part of the frontal lobe that lies in front of the motor cortex) is involved in higher mental functions such as thinking, problem solving, and use of language.

Evaluating Biological Perspectives on Abnormal Behavior

There is no question that biological structures and processes are involved in many patterns of abnormal behavior, as we will see in later chapters. Factors such as disturbances in neurotransmitter functioning and underlying brain abnormalities or defects are implicated in many psychological disorders. For some disorders, such as Alzheimer's disease, biological processes play the direct causative role. Even then, however, the precise causes remain unknown. In other cases, such as schizophrenia, biological factors, especially genetics, appear to interact with stressful environmental factors in the development of the disorder.

Genetic influences are implicated in a wide range of psychological disorders, including schizophrenia, bipolar (manic-depressive) disorder, major depression, alcoholism, autism, dementia due to Alzheimer's disease, anxiety disorders, dyslexia, and antisocial personality disorder (DiLalla et al., 1996; Plomin et al., 1997). Where genetic

cerebrum The large mass of the forebrain, consisting of the two cerebral hemispheres.

cerebral cortex The wrinkled surface area of the cerebrum, it is responsible for processing sensory stimuli and controlling higher mental functions, such as thinking and use of language.

corpus callosum A thick bundle of fibers that connects the two cerebral hemispheres.

somatic nervous system The division of the peripheral nervous system that relays information from the sense organs to the brain and transmits messages from the brain to the skeletal muscles.

autonomic nervous system The division of the peripheral nervous system that regulates the activities of the glands and involuntary functions.

involuntary Automatic or without conscious direction.

sympathetic Pertaining to the division of the autonomic nervous system whose activity leads to heightened states of arousal.

parasympathetic Pertaining to the division of the autonomic nervous system whose activity reduces states of arousal and regulates bodily processes that replenish energy reserves.

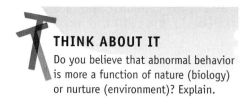

THINK ABOUT IT
Do you believe that abnormal behavior is more a function of nature (biology) or nurture (environment)? Explain.

Quiz **2.1** Q
The Biological Perspective

Truth OR Fiction? REVISITED

Freud likened the mind to a giant iceberg, with only the tip rising into conscious awareness.

TRUE. Freud believed that the larger part of the mind remains below the surface of consciousness.

Web Link **2.2**
The American Psychoanalytic wWw
Association

psychoanalytic theory The theoretical model of personality developed by Sigmund Freud; also called psychoanalysis.

conscious To Freud, the part of the mind that corresponds to our present awareness.

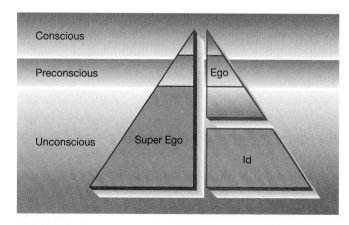

FIGURE 2.4 The parts of the mind, according to Freud.
In psychodynamic theory, the mind is akin to an iceberg in that only a small part of it rises to conscious awareness at any moment in time. Although material in the preconscious mind may be brought into consciousness by focusing our attention on it, the impulses and ideas in the unconscious tend to remain veiled in mystery.

factors play a role, they involve a complex interaction of multiple genes. We have yet to find any specific mental health disorder that can be explained by defects or variations on a single gene (USDHHS, 1999a). Nor do genetic factors alone account for any particular mental health disorder (Carey & DiLalla, 1994). Environmental factors also play important roles.

While we continue to learn more about the biological foundations of abnormal behavior patterns, the interface between biology and behavior can be construed as a two-way street. Researchers have uncovered links between psychological factors and many physical disorders and conditions (see Chapter 5). Researchers are also investigating whether the combination of psychological and drug treatments for such problems as depression, anxiety disorders, and substance abuse disorders, among others, may increase the therapeutic benefits of either of the two approaches alone. Although American psychiatry has become increasingly medicalized in recent years, some within the psychiatric community have warned their colleagues not to overlook the role of psychological factors in explaining and treating mental health problems (e.g., van Praag, 1988).

The Psychological Perspective

At about the time that biological models of abnormal behavior were beginning to achieve prominence with the contributions of Kraepelin, Griesinger, and others, another approach to understanding the bases of abnormal behavior began to emerge. This approach emphasized the psychological roots of abnormal behavior and was most closely identified with the work of the Austrian physician Sigmund Freud. Over time other psychological models would emerge from the behaviorist, humanistic, and cognitivist traditions. Let us begin our study of psychological perspectives with Freud's contribution and the development of psychodynamic models.

Psychodynamic Models

Psychodynamic theory is based on the contributions of Sigmund Freud and his followers. The psychodynamic model espoused by Freud, called **psychoanalytic theory,** is based on the belief that psychological problems such as hysteria are derived from unconscious psychological conflicts that can be traced to childhood. Freud held that much of our behavior is driven by unconscious motives and conflicts of which we are unaware. These underlying conflicts revolve around primitive sexual and aggressive instincts or drives and the need to keep these primitive impulses out of direct awareness. Why? Because awareness of these primitive impulses, including murderous urges and incestuous im-pulses, would flood the conscious self with crippling anxiety. Within the Freudian view, abnormal behavior patterns such as hysteria represent "symptoms" of the dynamic struggles taking place within the mind. In the case of hysteria, the "symptom" represents the *conversion* of an unconscious psychological conflict into a physical problem.

The Structure of the Mind Freud's clinical experiences led him to conclude that the mind is like an iceberg (Figure 2.4). Only the tip of an iceberg is visible above the surface of the water. The great mass of the iceberg lies below the surface. Freud came to believe that people, similarly, perceive but a few of the ideas, wishes, and impulses that dwell within them and determine their behavior. Freud held that the larger part of the mind, which includes our deepest wishes, fears, and instinctual urges, remains below the surface of consciousness. Freud labeled the region that corresponds to our present awareness the **conscious** part of the mind. The regions that lie beneath the surface of awareness were labeled the *preconscious* and the *unconscious*.

Ego and Id. Psychodynamic theorists believe the ego curbs the instinctual demands of id. The ego seeks socially acceptable ways of channeling these demands. When you share a meal with other people, you do not grab their food or snatch away the serving dish.

In the **preconscious** is the part of the mind are found memories of experiences that are not in awareness, but that can be brought into awareness by focusing on them. Your telephone number, for example, remains in the preconscious until you focus on it. The **unconscious** is the part of the mind, the largest part of the mind, remains shrouded in mystery. Its contents can only be brought to awareness with great difficulty, if at all. Freud believed the unconscious is the repository of biological drives, or instincts, such as sex and aggression.

preconscious To Freud, the part of the mind whose contents lie outside of present awareness but can be brought into awareness by focusing attention.

unconscious To Freud, the part of the mind that lies outside the range of ordinary awareness and that contains instinctual urges.

The Structure of Personality

According to Freud's **structural hypothesis,** the personality is divided into three mental entities, or **psychic** structures: the *id, ego,* and *superego*. Psychic structures cannot be seen or measured directly, but their presence is suggested by observable behavior and expressed in thoughts and emotions.

The **id** is the only psychic structure present at birth. It is the repository of our baser drives and instinctual impulses, including hunger, thirst, sex, and aggression. The id, which operates completely in the unconscious, was described by Freud as "a chaos, a cauldron of seething excitations" (1933/1964, p. 73). The id follows the **pleasure principle.** It demands instant gratification of instincts without consideration of social rules or customs or the needs of others. It operates by **primary process thinking,** which is a mode of relating to the world through imagination and fantasy. This enables the id to achieve gratification by conjuring up the mental image of the object of desire.

During the first year of life, the child discovers that every demand is not instantly gratified. He or she must learn to cope with the delay of gratification. The **ego** develops during this first year to organize reasonable ways of coping with frustration. Standing for "reason and good sense" (Freud, 1933/1964, p. 76), the ego seeks to curb the demands of the id and to direct behavior in keeping with social customs and expectations. Gratification can thus be achieved, but not at the expense of social disapproval. The id floods your consciousness with hunger pangs. Were it to have its way, the id might also prompt you to wolf down any food at hand or even to swipe someone else's plate. But the ego creates the ideas of walking to the refrigerator, making yourself a sandwich, and pouring a glass of milk.

The ego is governed by the **reality principle.** It considers what is practical and possible, as well as the urgings of the id. The ego engages in **secondary process thinking**—the remembering, planning, and weighing of circumstances that permit a compromise between the fantasies of the id and the realities of the world outside. The ego lays the groundwork for the development of the conscious sense of oneself as a distinct individual.

structural hypothesis The belief that the clashing forces within the personality can be divided into three structures: id, ego, and superego.

psychic Relating to mental phenomena.

id The unconscious psychic structure, present at birth, that contains primitive instincts and is regulated by the pleasure principle.

pleasure principle The governing principle of the id, involving demands for immediate gratification of needs.

primary process thinking In infancy, the mental process by which the id seeks gratification by imagining that it possesses what it desires; thinking that is illogical or magical.

ego The psychic structure that corresponds to the concept of the self, governed by the reality principle and characterized by the ability to tolerate frustration.

reality principle The governing principle of the ego, which involves considerations of social acceptability and practicality.

secondary process thinking The reality-based thinking processes and problem-solving activities of the ego.

superego The psychic structure that incorporates the values of the parents and important others and that is governed by the moral principle; consists of two parts, the conscience and the ego ideal.

identification The process of incorporating the personality or behavior of others.

moral principle The principle that governs the superego to set and enforce moral standards.

ego ideal The set of higher social values and moral ideals embodied in the superego.

defense mechanisms The reality-distorting strategies used by the ego to shield the self from awareness of anxiety-provoking materials.

repression A defense mechanism involving the unconscious ejection of anxiety-provoking ideas, images, or impulses.

During middle childhood, the **superego** develops. The moral standards and values of parents and other key people become internalized through a process of **identification.** The superego operates according to the **moral principle;** it demands strict adherence to moral standards. The superego represents the moral values of an ideal self, called the **ego ideal.** It also serves as a conscience, or internal moral guardian, that monitors the ego and passes judgment on right and wrong. It metes out punishment in the form of guilt and shame when it finds that ego has failed to adhere to the superego's moral standards. Ego stands between the id and the superego. It endeavors to satisfy the cravings of the id without offending the moral standards of the superego.

Defense Mechanisms Although part of the ego rises to consciousness, some of its activity is carried out unconsciously. In the unconscious, the ego serves as a kind of watchdog, or censor, that screens impulses from the id. It uses **defense mechanisms** (psychological defenses) to prevent socially unacceptable impulses from rising into consciousness. If it were not for these defenses, or defense mechanisms, the darkest sins of our childhoods, the primitive demands of our ids, and the censures of our superegos might disable us psychologically. **Repression,** or motivated forgetting (the banishment of unacceptable ideas or motives to the unconscious), is considered the most basic of the defense mechanisms. A number of these defense mechanisms are described in Table 2.2.

A dynamic unconscious struggle thus takes place between the id and the ego. It pits biological drives that strive for expression (the id) against the ego, which seeks to restrain

TABLE 2.2 Some Defense Mechanisms of the Ego, According to Psychodynamic Theory

Defense Mechanism	Definition	Examples
Repression	The ejection of anxiety-evoking ideas from awareness.	A student forgets a difficult term paper is due.
		A patient in therapy forgets an appointment when anxiety-evoking material is to be discussed.
Regression	The return, under stress, to a form of behavior characteristic of an earlier stage of development.	An adolescent cries when forbidden to use the family car.
		An adult becomes highly dependent on his parents following the breakup of his marriage.
Rationalization	The use of self-deceiving justifications for unacceptable behavior.	A student blames her cheating on her teacher's leaving the room during a test.
		A man explains his cheating on his income tax by saying, "Everyone does it."
Displacement	The transfer of ideas and impulses from threatening or unsuitable objects onto less threatening objects.	A worker picks a fight with her spouse after being criticized sharply by her supervisor.
Projection	The thrusting of one's own unacceptable impulses onto others so that others are assumed to harbor them.	A hostile person perceives the world as being a dangerous place.
		A sexually frustrated person interprets innocent gestures of others as sexual advances.
Reaction formation	Assumption of behavior in opposition to one's genuine impulses in order to keep impulses repressed.	A person who is angry with a relative behaves in a "sickly sweet" manner toward that relative.
		A sadistic individual becomes a physician.
Denial	Refusal to accept the true nature of a threat.	Belief that one will not contract cancer or heart disease although one smokes heavily ("It can't happen to me").
Sublimation	The channeling of primitive impulses into positive, constructive efforts.	A person paints nudes for the sake of "beauty" and "art."
		A hostile person directs aggressive energies into competitive sports.

Source. From *Essentials of Psychology, 6th edition,* by S. A. Rathus, © 2001. Reprinted with permission of Brooks/Cole, an imprint of the Wadsworth Group, a division of Thomson Learning. FAX 800-730-2215.

them or channel them into socially acceptable outlets. When these conflicts are not resolved smoothly, they can lead to the development of symptoms or features associated with psychological disorders, such as hysterical symptoms, phobias, and behavioral problems. Because we cannot view the unconscious mind directly, Freud developed a method of mental detective work called *psychoanalysis*, which is described in Chapter 4.

The use of defense mechanisms to cope with feelings such as anxiety, guilt, and shame is considered normal. These mechanisms enable us to constrain impulses from the id as we go about our daily business. In his work *The Psychopathology of Everyday Life*, Freud noted that slips of the tongue and ordinary forgetfulness could represent hidden motives that are kept out of consciousness by repression. If a friend means to say, "I hear what you're saying," but it comes out, "I hate what you're saying," perhaps the friend is expressing a repressed emotion. If a lover storms out in anger but forgets his umbrella, perhaps he is unconsciously creating an excuse for returning. Defense mechanisms may also give rise to abnormal behavior, however. The person who regresses to an infantile state under pressures of enormous stress is clearly not acting adaptively to the situation.

Stages of Psychosexual Development Freud aroused heated controversy by arguing that sexual drives are the dominant factors in the development of personality, even in childhood. Freud believed that the child's basic relationship to the world in its first several years of life is organized around the pursuit of sensual or sexual pleasure. In Freud's view, all activities that are physically pleasurable, such as eating or moving one's bowels, are in essence "sexual." The word *sensuality* is probably closer in present-day meaning to what Freud meant by *sexuality*.

The drive for sexual pleasure represents, in Freud's view, the expression of a major life instinct, which he called **Eros**—the basic drive to preserve and perpetuate life. The |energy contained in Eros that allows it to fulfill its function was termed **libido,** or sexual energy. Freud believed libidinal energy is expressed through sexual pleasure in different body parts, called **erogenous zones** as the child matures. In Freud's view, the stages of human development are **psychosexual** in nature, because they correspond to the transfer of libidinal energy from one erogenous zone to another. Freud proposed the existence of five psychosexual stages of development: oral, anal, phallic, latency, and genital.

The Oral Stage In the first year of life, the **oral stage,** infants achieve sexual pleasure by sucking their mothers' breasts and by mouthing anything that happens to be nearby. Oral stimulation, in the form of sucking and biting, is a source of both sexual gratification and nourishment.

Denial? Denial is a defense mechanism in which the ego fends off anxiety by preventing recognition of the true nature of a threat. Failing to take seriously warnings of health risks from cigarette smoking can be considered a form of denial.

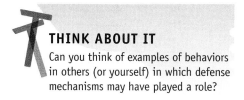

THINK ABOUT IT
Can you think of examples of behaviors in others (or yourself) in which defense mechanisms may have played a role?

Eros Freud's concept of the basic life instinct that seeks to preserve and perpetuate life.

libido The energy of Eros; sexual drive or energy.

erogenous zone A part of the body that is sensitive to sexual stimulation.

psychosexual Pertaining to Freud's stages of development, in which libido becomes expressed through different erogenous zones during different stages.

oral stage The psychosexual stage during infancy in which pleasure is sought primarily through oral activities.

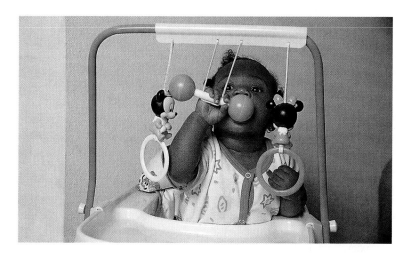

The oral stage of psychosexual development? According to Freud, the child's early encounters with the world are largely experienced through the mouth.

weaning The process of accustoming a child to eat solid food.

fixation Arrested development in the form of attachment to objects of an earlier developmental stage.

anal stage The psychosexual stage during toddlerhood in which pleasure is sought primarily through anal activities.

anal fixation Attachment to objects and behaviors characteristic of the anal stage.

anal retentive Excessive need for self-control and orderliness.

anal expulsive A loosening of restraint, as seen in extreme sloppiness of messiness.

phallic stage A psychosexual stage in early childhood during which pleasure is sought primarily through the phallic region and the child develops incestuous desires for the parent of the opposite sex.

Oedipus complex The conflict that occurs during the phallic stage of development, in which the young boy desires his mother and perceives his father as a rival.

Are young children interested in sex? According to Freud, even young children have sexual impulses. Freud's view of childhood sexuality shocked the scientific establishment of his day, and many of Freud's own followers believe that Freud placed too much emphasis on sexual motivation.

One of Freud's central beliefs is that the child may encounter conflict during each of the psychosexual stages of development. Conflict during the oral stage centers around the issue of whether or not the infant receives adequate oral gratification. Too much gratification could lead the infant to expect that everything in life is given with little or no effort on his or her part. In contrast, early **weaning** might lead to frustration. Too little or too much gratification at any stage could lead to **fixation** in that stage, which leads to the development of personality traits characteristic of that stage. Oral fixations could include an exaggerated desire for "oral activities," which could become expressed in later life in smoking, alcohol abuse, overeating, and nail biting. Like the infant who depends on the mother's breast for survival and gratification of oral pleasure, orally fixated adults may also become clinging and dependent in their interpersonal relationships.

The Anal Stage During the **anal stage** of psychosexual development, the child experiences sexual gratification through contraction and relaxation of the sphincter muscles that control elimination of bodily waste. Although elimination had been controlled reflexively during much of the first year of life, the child now learns that she or he is able, although perhaps not reliably at first, to exercise voluntary muscular control over elimination.

Now the child begins to learn that she or he can delay gratification of the need to eliminate when the urge is felt. During toilet training, the issue of self-control may become a source of conflict between the parent and the child. **Anal fixations** that derive from this conflict are associated with two sets of traits. Harsh toilet training may lead to the development of **anal-retentive** traits, which involve excessive needs for self-control. These include perfectionism and extreme needs for orderliness, cleanliness, and neatness. By contrast, excessive gratification during the anal period might lead to **anal-expulsive** traits, which include carelessness and messiness.

The Phallic Stage The next stage of psychosexual development, the **phallic stage,** generally begins during the third year of life. The major erogenous zone during the stage is the phallic region (the penis in boys, the clitoris in girls). Conflict between parent and child may occur over masturbation—the rubbing of the phallic areas for sexual pleasure—to which parents may react with threats and punishments. Perhaps the most controversial of Freud's beliefs was his suggestion that phallic-stage children develop unconscious incestuous wishes for the parent of the opposite gender and begin to view the parent of the same sex as a rival. Freud dubbed this conflict the **Oedipus complex,** after the legendary Greek king Oedipus who unwittingly slew his father and married his mother. The female version of the Oedipus complex has been named by some followers (although not by Freud himself) the **Electra complex,** after the character of Electra, who, according to Greek legend, avenged the death of her father, King Agamemnon, by slaying her father's murderers—her own mother and her mother's lover.

Freud believed the Oedipus conflict represents a central psychological conflict of early childhood, the resolution of which has far-reaching consequences in later development and in determining the acquisition of **gender roles.** He also believed that **castration anxiety** plays an important role in resolving the complex for boys. Adults sometimes threaten boys with castration to try to get them to stop touching themselves. Freud documented such castration threats from parents or nurses in several case studies. At some point boys discover that girls are different—they do not have penises. Freud conjectured that boys might imagine that girls had lost their penises as a form of punishment. Going further, Freud hypothesized that boys develop castration anxiety, based on the fantasy that their rivals for their mother's affections, namely their fathers, would seek to punish them for their incestuous wishes by removing the organ that has become connected with sexual pleasure. To prevent castration, Freud argued, boys repress their incestuous wishes for their mothers and identify with their fathers. Keep in mind that Freudian theory posits that these developments (incestuous wishes and castration anxiety) are largely unconscious and are part and parcel of normal development. Successful resolution of the Oedipus complex involves the boy repressing his incestuous wishes for his mother and identifying with his father. This identification leads to development of the aggressive, independent characteristics associated with the traditional masculine gender role.

The Oedipus complex in girls is somewhat of a mirror image of the one in boys. Freud believed little girls naturally become envious of boys' penises. This jealousy leads them to become resentful toward their mothers, whom they blame for bringing them into the world so "ill-equipped." Girls develop the desire to possess their fathers, in a way substituting their fathers' penises for their own missing ones. But the rivalry with their mothers for their fathers' affection places them in peril of losing their mothers' love and protection.

Successful resolution of the complex for the girl involves repression of the incestuous wishes for her father and identification with her mother, leading to the acquisition of the more passive, dependent characteristics traditionally associated with the feminine sex role. Eventually, the wish for a penis is transformed into the desire to marry a man and bear children, which represents the ultimate adjustment of surrendering the wish "to be a man" by accepting a baby as a form of penis substitute. Freud hypothesized that, in adulthood, women who retain the unconscious wish for a penis of their own ("to be a man") can become maladjusted and develop masculine-typed characteristics such as competitiveness and dominance and even a lesbian sexual orientation.

The Oedipus complex comes to a point of resolution, whether fully resolved or not, by about the age of 5 or 6. From the identification with the parent of the same gender comes the internalization of parental values in the form of the superego. Children then enter the **latency stage** of psychosexual development, a period of late childhood during which sexual impulses remain in a latent state. Interests become directed toward school and play activities.

The Genital Stage Sexual drives are once again aroused with the **genital stage,** beginning with puberty, which reaches fruition in mature sexuality, marriage, and the bearing of children. The sexual feelings toward the parent of the opposite gender that had remained repressed during the latency period emerge during adolescence but are displaced, or transferred, onto socially appropriate members of the opposite gender. Boys might still look for girls "just like the girl that married dear old dad," and, in parallel girls might still be attracted to boys who resemble their "dear old dads."

In Freud's view, successful adjustment during the genital stage involves attaining sexual gratification through sexual intercourse with someone of the opposite gender, presumably within the context of marriage. Other forms of sexual expression, such as oral or anal stimulation, masturbation, and homosexual activity, are considered **pregenital** fixations, or immature forms of sexual conduct.

Other Psychodynamic Theorists

Freud left us a rich intellectual legacy that has stimulated the thinking of many theorists. Psychodynamic theory has been shaped over the years by the contributions of other psychodynamic theorists who shared certain central tenets in common with Freud, such as the belief that behavior reflects unconscious motivation, inner conflict, and the operation of defensive responses to anxiety. They tended to place lesser emphasis than Freud on the roles of basic instincts such as sex and aggression, and to place greater emphasis on roles for conscious choice, self-direction, and creativity. These theorists also differed from each other in various ways.

One of the most prominent of the early psychodynamic theorists was Carl Jung (1875–1961), a Swiss psychiatrist who was formerly a member of Freud's inner circle. His break with Freud came when he developed his own psychodynamic theory, which he called **analytical psychology.** Like Freud, Jung believed that unconscious processes are important in explaining behavior. Jung believed that an understanding of human behavior must incorporate the facts of self-awareness and self-direction as well as the impulses of the id and the mechanisms of defense. He believed that not only do we have a *personal* unconscious, a repository of repressed memories and impulses, but we also inherit a **collective unconscious.** To Jung, the collective unconscious represents the accumulated experience of humankind, which he believed is passed down genetically through the generations. The

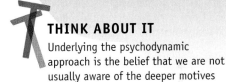

THINK ABOUT IT
Underlying the psychodynamic approach is the belief that we are not usually aware of the deeper motives and impulses that drive our behavior. Do you agree? Why or why not?

Electra complex The conflict that occurs during the phallic stage of development, in which the young girl desires her father and perceives her mother as a rival.

gender roles The characteristic ways in which males and females are expected to behave in a given culture.

castration anxiety The young boy's unconscious fear that he will be castrated as punishment for his incestuous desire for his mother.

latency stage The psychosexual stage in middle childhood characterized by repression of sexual impulses.

genital stage The final stage of psychosexual development, characterized by expression of libido through sexual intercourse with an adult of the opposite sex.

pregenital Referring to characteristics typical of psychosexual stages that precede the genital stage.

analytical psychology Jung's theory, emphasizing the collective unconscious, archetypes, and the self as the unifying force of personality.

collective unconscious The storehouse of archetypes and racial memories.

archetypes Primitive images or concepts that reside in the collective unconscious.

inferiority complex The feelings of inferiority that Adler believed to be a central source of motivation.

powerful drive for superiority Complex of feelings that motivates us to achieve prominence and social dominance.

creative self To Adler, the self-aware part of the personality that strives to achieve its potential.

individual psychology Adler's psychodynamic theory.

neo-Freudians Theorists, such as Jung, Adler, Horney, and Sullivan, who, in comparison with Freud, placed greater emphasis on the importance of cultural and social influences and lesser emphasis on sexual impulses.

ego psychology Modern psychodynamic approach that focuses more on the conscious strivings of the ego than on the hypothesized unconscious functions of the id.

ego analysts Psychodynamically oriented therapists who are influenced by ego psychology.

Web Link **2.3** wWw
Jungian Resources

collective unconscious is believed to contain primitive images, or **archetypes,** which reflect upon the history of our species, including vague, mysterious mythical images like the all-powerful God, the fertile and nurturing mother, the young hero, the wise old man, and themes of rebirth or resurrection. Although archetypes remain unconscious, in Jung's view, they influence our thoughts, dreams, and emotions and render us responsive to cultural themes in stories and films.

Alfred Adler (1870–1937), like Jung, had held a place in Freud's inner circle, but broke away as he developed his own beliefs that people are basically driven by an **inferiority complex,** not by the sexual instinct as Freud had maintained. For some people, feelings of inferiority are based on physical deficits and the resulting need to compensate for them. But all of us, because of our small size during childhood, encounter feelings of inferiority to some degree. These feelings lead to a **powerful drive for superiority**, which motivates us to achieve prominence and social dominance. In the healthy personality, however, strivings for dominance are tempered by devotion to helping other people.

Adler, like Jung, believed self-awareness plays a major role in the formation of personality. Adler spoke of a **creative self,** a self-aware aspect of personality that strives to overcome obstacles and develop the individual's potential. With the hypothesis of the creative self, Adler shifted the emphasis of psychodynamic theory from the id to the ego. Because our potentials are uniquely individual, Adler's views have been termed **individual psychology.**

Many other psychodynamic models have arisen with the work of Freud's followers, who are sometimes referred to collectively as **neo-Freudians.** Some psychodynamic theorists, such as Karen Horney (1885–1952) and Harry Stack Sullivan (1892–1949), focused on the social context of psychological problems and stressed the importance of child-parent relationships in determining the nature of later interpersonal relationships. Sullivan, for example, maintained that children of rejecting parents tend to become self-doubting and anxious. These personality features persist and impede the development of close relationships in adult life.

More recent psychodynamic models also place a greater emphasis on the self or the ego and less emphasis on the sexual instinct than Freud. Today, most psychoanalysts see

The power of archetypes. One of the reasons we may find the *Star Wars* saga so compelling is that it features archetypes such as the struggle between good and evil characters.

Karen Horney.

Erik Erikson.

Margaret Mahler.

people as motivated on two tiers: by the growth-oriented, conscious pursuits of the ego as well as by the more primitive, conflict-ridden drives of the id. Heinz Hartmann (1894–1970) was one of the originators of **ego psychology,** which posits that the ego has energy and motives of its own. Freud, remember, believed ego functions are fueled by the id, are largely defensive, and are perpetually threatened by the irrational. Hartmann and other **ego analysts** find Freud's views of the ego—and of people in general—too pessimistic and ignoble. Hartmann argued that the cognitive functions of the ego could be free of conflict. The choices to seek an education, dedicate oneself to art and poetry, and further humanity are not merely defensive forms of sublimation, as Freud had seen them.

Another ego analyst, Erik Erikson (1902–1994), attributed more importance to children's social relationships than to unconscious processes. Whereas Freud's developmental theory ends with the genital stage, beginning in early adolescence, Erikson focused on developmental processes that he believed continue throughout adulthood. The goal of adolescence, in Erikson's view, is not genital sexuality, but rather the attainment of **ego identity.** Adolescents who achieve ego identity develop a clearly defined and firm sense of who they are and what they believe in. Adolescents who drift without purpose or clarity of self remain in a state of **role diffusion** and are especially subject to negative peer influences.

One popular contemporary psychodynamic approach is termed **object-relations theory,** which focuses on how children come to develop symbolic representations of important others in their lives, especially their parents. One of the major contributors to object-relations theory was Margaret Mahler (1897–1985), who saw the process of separating from the mother during the first 3 years of life as crucial to personality development (discussed further in Chapter 9).

According to psychodynamic theory, we **introject,** or incorporate, into our own personalities, parts of parental figures in our lives. For example, you might introject your father's strong sense of responsibility or your mother's eagerness to please others. Introjection is more powerful when we fear losing others because of death or rejection. Thus we might be particularly apt to incorporate elements of people who *disapprove* of us or who see things differently.

In Mahler's view, these symbolic representations, which are formed from images and memories of others, come to influence our perceptions and behavior. We experience internal conflict as the attitudes of introjected people battle with our own. Some of our perceptions may be distorted or seem unreal to us. Some of our impulses and behavior may seem unlike us, as if they come out of the blue. With such conflict, we may not be able to tell where the influences of other people end and our "real selves" begin. The aim of Mahler's

ego identity The achievement of a firm sense of personal identity.

role diffusion A state of confusion, aimlessness, and heightened susceptibility to the suggestions of others, associated with failure to acquire a firm sense of identity during adolescence.

object-relations theory The psychodynamic viewpoint that focuses on the influences of internalized representations of the personalities of parents and other strong attachment figures (called "objects").

introject To unconsciously incorporate features of another person's personality into one's own ego structure.

neurosis A nonpsychotic form of disturbed behavior characterized by problems involving anxiety.

psychosis A severe form of disturbed behavior characterized by impaired ability to interpret reality and difficulty meeting the demands of daily life.

therapeutic approach was to help clients separate their own ideas and feelings from those of the introjected objects so they could develop as individuals—as their own persons.

Psychodynamic Views on Normality and Abnormality Freud believed that there is a thin line between the normal and the abnormal. Both normal and abnormal behavior are motivated or driven by irrational drives of the id. The difference may be largely a matter of degree. Mental health is a function of the dynamic balance among the psychic structures of id, ego, and superego (USDHHS, 1999a). In mentally healthy people, the ego is strong enough to control the instincts of the id and to withstand the condemnation of the superego. The presence of acceptable outlets for the expression of some primitive impulses, such as the expression of mature sexuality in marriage, decreases the pressures within the id and, at the same time, lessens the burdens of the ego in repressing the remaining impulses. Being reared by reasonably tolerant parents might prevent the superego from becoming overly harsh and condemnatory.

In people with psychological disorders, the balance among the psychic structures is lopsided. Some unconscious impulses may "leak," producing anxiety or leading to the development of **neuroses,** such as hysteria and phobias. The symptom expresses the conflict among the parts of the personality while it protects the self from recognizing the inner turmoil. A fear of knives, for example, shields the self from awareness of threatening unconscious impulses to use a knife to murder someone or attack the self. So long as the symptom is maintained (and the person avoids knives), the murderous or suicidal impulses are kept at bay. If the superego becomes overly powerful, it may create excessive feelings of guilt and lead to depression. An underdeveloped superego is believed to play a role in explaining the antisocial tendencies of people who intentionally hurt others without feelings of guilt.

Freud believed that the underlying conflicts in neuroses have childhood origins that are buried in the depths of the unconscious. Through psychoanalysis, he sought to help people uncover and learn to deal with these underlying conflicts to free themselves of the need to maintain the overt symptom.

Perpetual vigilance and defense take their toll. The ego can weaken and, in extreme cases, lose the ability to keep a lid on the id. **Psychosis** results when the urges of the id spill forth, untempered by an ego that is either weakened or underdeveloped. The fortress of the ego is overrun, and the person loses the ability to distinguish between fantasy and reality. Behavior becomes detached from reality. Primary process thinking and bizarre behavior rule the day. Psychoses are characterized, in general, by more severe disturbances of functioning than neuroses, by the appearance of bizarre behavior and thoughts, and by faulty perceptions of reality, such as hallucinations ("hearing voices" or seeing things that are not present). Speech may become incoherent and there may be bizarre posturing and gestures. The most prominent form of psychosis is schizophrenia, discussed in Chapter 13.

Freud equated psychological health with the *abilities to love and to work*. The normal person can care deeply for other people, find sexual gratification in an intimate relationship, and engage in productive work. To accomplish these ends, there must be an opportunity for sexual impulses to be expressed in a relationship with a partner of the opposite gender. Other impulses must be channeled (sublimated) into socially productive pursuits, such as work, enjoyment of art or music, or creative expression. When some impulses are expressed directly and others are sublimated, the ego has a relatively easy time repressing those that remain in the boiling cauldron.

Other psychodynamic theorists, such as Jung and Adler, emphasized the need to develop a differentiated self—the unifying force that provides direction to behavior and helps develop a person's potential. Adler also believed that psychological health involves efforts to compensate for feelings of inferiority by striving to excel in one or more of the arenas of human endeavor. For Mahler, similarly, abnormal behavior derives from failure to separate ourselves from those we have psychologically brought within us. The notion of a guiding self provides bridges between psychodynamic theories and other theories, such as humanistic theories (which also speak of a self and the fulfillment of inner potential) and social-cognitive theory (which speaks in terms of self-regulatory processes).

Evaluating Psychodynamic Models Psychodynamic theory has had a pervasive influence, not only on concepts of abnormal behavior but more broadly on art, literature, philosophy, and the general culture. It has focused attention on our inner lives—our dreams, fantasies, and hidden motives. People unschooled in Freud's writings nevertheless look for the symbolic meanings of each other's slips of the tongue and assume that abnormalities can be traced to early childhood. Terms like *ego* and *repression* have become commonplace, although their everyday meanings do not fully overlap with those intended by Freud.

One of the major contributions of the psychodynamic model was the increased awareness that people may be motivated by hidden drives and impulses of a sexual or aggressive nature. Freud's beliefs about childhood sexuality were both illuminating and controversial. Before Freud, children were perceived as *pure innocents*, free of sexual desire. Freud recognized, however, that young children, even infants, seek pleasure through stimulation of the oral and anal cavities and the phallic region. Yet his beliefs that primitive drives give rise to incestuous desires, intrafamily rivalries and conflicts, and castration anxiety and penis envy remain sources of controversy, even within psychodynamic circles. For one thing, these processes are deemed to occur largely if not entirely at an unconscious level and so are difficult if not impossible to study, let alone validate, by scientific means. For another, there is little evidence to support even the existence of the Oedipus complex, let alone its universality (Kupfersmid, 1995).

Freud's views of female psychosexual development have been roundly attacked by women and by modern-day psychoanalysts. One of the most prominent critics, the psychoanalyst Karen Horney, argued that Freud's views on women reflect underlying cultural prejudices in Western society. To Horney, cultural expectations play a greater role in shaping women's self-images than does penis envy. She argued that if women feel inferior, it is because they are relegated to second-class status in our society, not because they lack a penis. From birth, women are exposed to a male-dominated culture that treats women as an inferior sex. Horney's own views of child development take us in a different direction than Freud's. She emphasized the importance of parent-child relationships. She believed that when parents are harsh or uncaring, children may develop deep-seated feelings of anxiety and hostility that lead them to relate to others in unhealthy and rigid ways later in life.

In fairness to Freud, we should note that his theories should be viewed in the context of his day and time. In Freud's day, motherhood and family life were, by and large, the only socially proper avenues of fulfillment for women. Today, the choices available to women are more varied, and normality is not conceptualized in terms of rigidly defined gender roles.

Many critics, including some of Freud's followers, believe he placed too much emphasis on sexual and aggressive impulses and underemphasized social relationships. Critics have also argued that the psychic structures—the id, ego, and superego—may be little more than useful fictions, poetic ways to represent inner conflict. Many critics argue that Freud's hypothetical mental processes are not scientific concepts because they cannot be directly observed or tested. Therapists can speculate, for example, that a client "forgot" about an appointment because "unconsciously" she or he did not want to attend the session. Such unconscious motivation may not be subject to scientific verification, however. On the other hand, psychodynamically oriented researchers have developed scientific approaches that they believe make it possible to test many of Freud's concepts (Westen, 1998).

Learning Models

The psychodynamic models of Freud and his followers were the first major psychological theories of abnormal behavior, but other relevant psychologies were also taking shape early in the 20th century. Among the most important was the behavioral perspective, which is identified with contributions by the Russian physiologist Ivan Pavlov (1849–1936), the discoverer of the conditioned reflex, and the American psychologist John B. Watson (1878–1958), the father of **behaviorism.** The behavioral perspective focuses on the role of learning in explaining both normal and abnormal behavior. From a learning perspective, abnormal behavior represents the acquisition, or learning, of inappropriate, maladaptive behaviors.

behaviorism The school of psychology that defines psychology as the study of observable behavior.

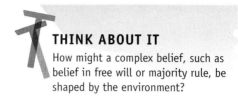

Ivan Pavlov. Russian physiologist Ivan Pavlov (center, with white beard) demonstrates his apparatus for classical conditioning to students. How might the principles of classical conditioning explain the acquisition of excessive irrational fears that we refer to as phobias?

B. F. Skinner.

From the medical and psychodynamic perspectives, abnormal behavior is *symptomatic*, respectively, of underlying biological or psychological problems. From the learning perspective, however, abnormal behavior need not be symptomatic of anything. The abnormal behavior itself is the problem. Abnormal behavior is regarded as learned in much the same way as normal behavior. Why, then, do some people behave abnormally?

One reason is found in situational factors: Their learning histories, that is, might differ from most people's. For example, harsh punishment for early exploratory behavior, such as childhood sexual exploration in the form of masturbation, might give rise to adult anxieties over autonomy or sexuality. Poor child-rearing practices, such as the lack of praise or rewards for good behavior and harsh and capricious punishment for misconduct, might give rise to antisocial behavior. Then, too, children with abusive or neglectful parents might learn to pay more attention to inner fantasies than to the world outside, giving rise, at worst, to difficulty in distinguishing reality from fantasy.

Watson and other behaviorists, such as Harvard University psychologist B. F. Skinner (1904–1990), believed that human behavior is the product of genetic endowment and environmental or situational influences. Like Freud, Watson and Skinner discarded concepts of personal freedom, choice, and self-direction. But whereas Freud saw us as driven by irrational forces, behaviorists see us as products of environmental influences that shape and manipulate our behavior. To Watson and Skinner, even the belief that we have free will is determined by the environment. Behaviorists focus on the roles of two major forms of learning in shaping normal and abnormal behavior, classical conditioning and operant conditioning.

Role of Classical Conditioning The Russian physiologist Ivan Pavlov discovered the conditioned reflex (now called a *conditioned response*) quite by accident. In his laboratory, he harnessed dogs to an apparatus like that in Figure 2.5 to study their salivary response to food. Yet he observed that the animals would start salivating and secreting gastric juices even before they started eating. These responses appeared to be elicited by the sounds made by his laboratory assistants when they wheeled in the food cart. So Pavlov undertook a clever experimental program that showed that animals could learn to salivate in response to other stimuli, such as the sound of a bell, if these stimuli were *associated* with feeding.

FIGURE 2.5 The apparatus used in Ivan Pavlov's experiments on conditioning.
Pavlov used an apparatus such as this to demonstrate the process of conditioning. To the left is a two-way mirror, behind which a researcher rings a bell. After ringing the bell, meat is placed on the dog's tongue. Following several pairings of the bell and the meat, the dog learns to salivate in response to the bell. The animal's saliva passes through the tube to a vial, where its quantity may be taken as a measure of the strength of the conditioned response.

Because dogs don't normally salivate to the sound of bells, Pavlov reasoned that they had acquired this response, called a **conditioned response** (CR), or conditioned reflex, because it had been paired with a stimulus, called an **unconditioned stimulus** (US)—in this case, food—which naturally elicits salivation (see Figure 2.6). The salivation to food, an unlearned response, is called the **unconditioned response** (UR), and the bell, a previously neutral stimulus, is called the **conditioned stimulus** (CS).

Can you recognize classical conditioning in your everyday life? Do you flinch in the waiting room at the sound of the dentist's drill? The drill sounds may be conditioned stimuli for conditioned responses of fear and muscle tension.

Phobias or excessive fears may be acquired by classical conditioning. For instance, a person may develop a phobia for riding on elevators following a traumatic experience on an elevator. In this example, a previously neutral stimulus (elevator) becomes paired or associated with an aversive stimulus (trauma), which leads to the conditioned response (phobia).

conditioned response In classical conditioning, a learned response to a previously neutral stimulus.

unconditioned stimulus A stimulus that elicits an unlearned response.

unconditioned response An unlearned response.

conditioned stimulus A previously neutral stimulus that evokes a conditioned response after repeated pairings with an unconditioned stimulus that had previously evoked that response.

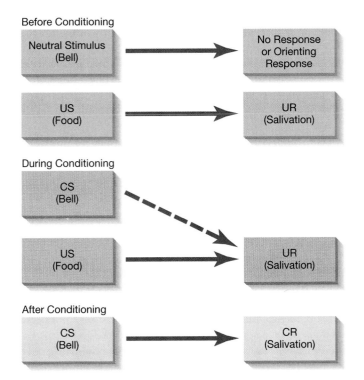

FIGURE 2.6 Schematic diagram of the process of classical conditioning.
Before conditioning, food (an unconditioned stimulus, or US) placed on a dog's tongue will naturally elicit salivation (an unconditioned response, or UR). The bell, however, is a neutral stimulus that may elicit an orienting response but not salivation. During conditioning, the bell (the conditioned stimulus, or CS) is rung while food (the US) is placed on the dog's tongue. After several conditioning trials have occurred, the bell (the CS) will elicit salivation (the conditioned response, or CR) when it is rung, even though it is not accompanied by food (the US). The dog is said to have been *conditioned,* or to have learned, to display the conditioned response (CR) in response to the conditioned stimulus (CS). Learning theorists have suggested that irrational excessive fears of harmless stimuli may be acquired through principles of classical conditioning.

reinforcement A stimulus or event that increases the frequency of the response that it follows.

reward A pleasant stimulus or event that increases the frequency of the response that it follows.

positive reinforcers Reinforcers that, when introduced, increase when the frequency of behavior.

negative reinforcers Reinforcers that on removal increase the frequency of behavior.

primary reinforcers Reinforcers that fulfill basic needs, such as water, food, warmth, and relief from pain.

secondary reinforcers Stimuli that gain reinforcement value through their association with established reinforcers, such as money and social approval.

punishments Unpleasant stimuli that reduce the frequency of the behaviors they follow.

From the learning perspective, normal behavior involves responding adaptively to stimuli, including conditioned stimuli. After all, if we do not learn to be afraid of drawing our hand too close to a hot stove after one or two experiences of being burned or nearly burned, we might suffer unnecessary burns. On the other hand, acquiring inappropriate and maladaptive fears on the basis of conditioning may cripple our efforts to function in the world. Chapter 6 explains how conditioning may help explain anxiety disorders such as phobias and posttraumatic stress disorder.

Role of Operant Conditioning Operant conditioning involves the acquisition of behaviors, called *operant behaviors,* that are emitted by the organism and that operate upon, or manipulate, the environment to produce certain effects. The psychologist B. F. Skinner (1938) showed that food-deprived pigeons would learn to peck buttons when food pellets drop into their cages as a result. It takes a while for the birds to happen on the first peck, but after a few repetitions of the association of button pecking and food, pecking behavior, an operant response, becomes fast and furious until the pigeons have had their fill.

In operant conditioning, organisms acquire responses or skills that lead to **reinforcement.** Reinforcers are changes in the environment (stimuli) that increase the frequency of the preceding behavior. A **reward** is a *pleasant* stimulus that increases the frequency of behavior, and so it is a type of reinforcer. Skinner found the concept of reinforcement to be preferable to that of reward because it is defined in terms of relationships between observed behaviors and environmental effects. In contrast to *reward*, the meaning of reinforcement does not depend on "mentalistic" conjectures about what is pleasant to another person or lower animal. Many psychologists use the words *reinforcement* and *reward* interchangeably, however.

Positive reinforcers boost the frequency of behavior when they are presented. Food, money, social approval, and the opportunity to mate are examples of positive reinforcers. **Negative reinforcers** increase the frequency of behavior when they are *removed.* Fear, pain, discomfort, and social disapproval are examples of negative reinforcers. We learn responses that lead to their removal (like learning to turn on the air conditioner to remove unpleasant heat and humidity from a room).

Adaptive, normal behavior involves learning responses or skills that permit us to obtain positive reinforcers and to avoid or remove negative reinforcers. Thus we learn adaptive behaviors that permit us to obtain such positive reinforcers as money, food, and social approval and to avoid or remove such negative reinforcers as fear, pain, and social condemnation. But if our early learning environments do not provide opportunities for learning new skills, we might be hampered in our efforts to develop the skills needed to obtain reinforcers. A lack of social skills, for example, may reduce opportunities for social reinforcement (approval or praise from others), especially when a person withdraws from social situations. This may lead to depression and social isolation. In Chapter 8, we examine links between changes in reinforcement levels and the development of depression.

We can also differentiate *primary* and *secondary,* or conditioned, reinforcers. **Primary reinforcers** influence behavior because they satisfy basic physical needs. We do not learn to respond to these basic reinforcers; we are born with that capacity. Food, water, sexual stimulation, and escape from pain are examples of primary reinforcers. **Secondary reinforcers** influence behavior through their association with established reinforcers. Thus we learn to respond to secondary reinforcers. People learn to seek money—a secondary reinforcer—because it can be exchanged for such primary reinforcers as food and heat (or air conditioning).

Punishments are aversive stimuli that decrease or suppress the frequency of the preceding behavior when they are applied. Negative reinforcers, by contrast, increase the frequency of the preceding behavior when they are removed. A loud noise, for example, can be either a punishment (if by its introduction the probability of the preceding behavior increases) or a negative reinforcer (if by its removal the probability of the preceding behavior decreases).

Punishment, especially physical punishment, may suppress but not eliminate undesirable behavior. The behavior may return when the punishment is withdrawn. One lim-

Web Link 2.4 www
B. F. Skinner Foundation

itation of punishment is that it does not lead to the development of more desirable alternative behaviors. Another is that it may also encourage people to withdraw from such learning situations. Punished children may cut classes, drop out of school, or run away. Punishment may generate anger and hostility rather than constructive learning. Finally, because people also learn by observation, punishment may become imitated as a means for solving interpersonal problems.

Rewarding desirable behavior is thus generally preferable to punishing misbehavior. But rewarding good behavior requires paying attention to it, not just to misbehavior. Some children who develop conduct problems can gain the attention of other people only by misbehaving. They learn that when they act out, others will pay attention to them. To them punishment may actually serve as a positive reinforcer, increasing the rate of response of the behavior it follows. Learning theorists point out that it is not sufficient to expect good conduct from children. Instead, adults need to teach children proper behavior and regularly reinforce them for emitting it.

Let us now consider a contemporary model of learning, called *social-cognitive theory* (formerly called *social-learning theory*), which broadens the focus of traditional learning theory by considering the role of cognitive factors in learning and behavior.

Social-Cognitive Theory **Social-cognitive theory** represents the contributions of theorists such as Albert Bandura, Julian B. Rotter, and Walter Mischel. Social-cognitive theorists emphasize the roles of thinking or cognition and of learning by observation, or **modeling**, in human behavior. For example, social-cognitive theorists suggest that phobias may be learned *vicariously*, by observing the fearful reactions of others in real life, on television, or in the movies.

Social-cognitive theorists view people as having an impact on their environments, just as their environment has an impact on them (Bandura, 2001). They see people as self-aware and purposeful learners who seek information about their environments, who do not just respond automatically to the stimuli that impinge on them. Social-cognitive theorists concur with traditional behaviorists that theories of human nature should be tied to observable behavior. They assert, however, that factors *within* the person should also be considered in explaining human behavior. Rotter (1990), for example, argues that behavior cannot be predicted from situational factors alone. Whether or not people behave in certain ways also depends on certain cognitive factors, such as the person's **expectancies** about the outcomes of behavior. For example, we see in Chapter 10 that people who hold more positive expectancies about the outcomes of using drugs are more likely to use them and to use them in larger quantities.

social-cognitive theory A learning-based theory that emphasizes observational learning and incorporates roles for both situational and cognitive variables in determining behavior.

modeling Learning by observing and imitating the behavior of others.

expectancies Beliefs about expected outcomes.

Observational learning. According to social-cognitive theory, much human behavior is acquired through modeling, or observational learning.

Carl Rogers and Abraham Maslow, two of the principal forces in humanistic psychology.

![Think about it icon]

THINK ABOUT IT

How has your present behavior been influenced by your learning history? What learning principles (classical conditioning, operant conditioning, observational learning) can you use to account for your behavior, both normal and abnormal?

Evaluating Learning Models One of the principal values of learning models, in contrast to psychodynamic approaches, is their emphasis on observable behavior and environmental factors, such as rewards and punishments, that can be systematically manipulated to observe their effects on behavior. Learning perspectives have spawned a major model of therapy, called *behavior therapy* (also called *behavior modification*), which involves the systematic application of learning principles to help people make adaptive behavioral changes (see Chapter 4). Behavior therapy techniques have been applied to helping people overcome a wide range of psychological problems, including phobias and other anxiety disorders, sexual dysfunctions, and depression. Moreover, reinforcement-based programs are now widely used in helping parents learn better parenting skills and helping children learn in the classroom.

Web Link **2.5**
Association for Humanistic WWW
Psychology

Critics contend that behaviorism cannot explain the richness of human behavior and that human experience cannot be reduced to observable responses. Many learning theorists, too—especially social-cognitive theorists—have been dissatisfied with the strict behavioristic view that environmental influences—rewards and punishments—mechanically control our behavior. Humans experience thoughts and dreams and formulate goals and aspirations; behaviorism does not seem to address much of what it means to be human. Social-cognitive theorists have broadened the scope of traditional behaviorism, but critics claim that social-cognitive theory places too little emphasis on genetic contributions to behavior and has failed to provide a meaningful account of self-awareness.

Self-Actualization. Humanistic theorists believe that there exists in each of us a drive toward self-actualization—to become all that we are capable of being. In the humanistic view, each of us, like artist Faith Ringgold—is unique. No two people follow quite the same pathway toward self-actualization.

Humanistic Models

A "third force" in modern psychology emerged during the mid-20th century—humanistic psychology. Humanistic theorists such as American psychologists Carl Rogers (1902–1987) and Abraham Maslow (1908–1970) believed that human behavior could not be explained as the product of either unconscious conflicts or simple conditioning. Rejecting the determinism implicit in these theories, these theorists saw people as *actors* in the drama of life, not *reactors* to instinctual or environmental pressures. They focused on the importance of subjective conscious experience and self-direction. Humanistic psychology is closely linked with the school of European philosophy called *existentialism*. The existentialists, notably the philosophers Martin Heidegger (1889–1976) and Jean-Paul Sartre (1905–1980), focused on the search for meaning and the importance of choice in human existence. Existentialists believe our humanness makes us responsible for the directions our lives will take.

The humanists maintain that people have an inborn tendency toward **self-actualization**—to strive to become all they are capable of being. Each of us possesses a singular cluster of traits and talents that gives rise to an individual set of feelings and needs and grants us a unique perspective on life. Despite the finality of death, we can each imbue our lives with meaning and purpose if we recognize and accept our genuine needs and feelings. By being true to ourselves, we live *authentically*. We may not decide to act out every wish and fancy, but self-awareness of authentic feelings and subjective experiences can help us make more meaningful choices.

To understand abnormal behavior, in the humanist's view, we need to understand the roadblocks that people encounter in striving for self-actualization and authenticity. To accomplish this, psychologists must learn to view the world from clients' own perspectives because their subjective views of their world lead them to interpret and evaluate their experiences in either self-enhancing or self-defeating ways. The humanistic viewpoint is sometimes called the *phenomenological* perspective because it involves the attempt to understand the subjective or phenomenological experience of others, the stream of conscious experiences people have of "being in the world."

Humanistic Concepts of Abnormal Behavior

Rogers developed the most influential humanistic account of abnormal behavior (Rogers, 1951). His central belief was that abnormal behavior results from the development of a distorted concept of the self. When parents show children **conditional positive regard**—accept them only when they behave in an approved manner—the children may learn to disown the thoughts, feelings, and behaviors their parents have rejected. With conditional positive regard, children may learn to develop **conditions of worth,** to think of themselves as worthwhile only if they behave in certain approved ways. For example, children who are valued by their parents only when they are compliant may deny to themselves ever having feelings of anger. Children in some families learn it is unacceptable to hold their own ideas, lest they depart from their parents' views. Parental disapproval causes them to see themselves as rebels and their feelings as wrong, selfish, or evil. If they wish to retain self-esteem, they may have to deny their genuine feelings or disown parts of themselves. They may thus develop a distorted *self-concept*, or view of themselves, and become strangers to their true selves.

Rogers believed that anxiety might arise when we begin to sense that our feelings and ideas are inconsistent with the distorted self-concept we have developed that mirrors what others expect us to be. Because anxiety is unpleasant, we may deny to ourselves that these feelings and ideas even exist. And so the actualization of our authentic self is bridled by the denial of important ideas and emotions. Psychological energy is channeled toward continued denial and self-defense, not toward growth. Under such conditions, we cannot hope to perceive our genuine values or personal talents, leading to frustration and setting the stage for abnormal behavior.

So we cannot fulfill all of the wishes of others and remain true to ourselves. This does not mean that self-actualization invariably leads to conflict. Rogers was more optimistic about human nature than Freud. Rogers believed that people hurt one another or become antisocial in their behavior only when they are frustrated in their endeavors to reach their unique potentials. But when parents and others treat children with love and tolerance for their differences, children, too, grow to be loving—even if some of their values and preferences differ from their parents' choices.

In Rogers's view, the pathway to self-actualization involves a process of self-discovery and self-acceptance, of getting in touch with our true feelings, accepting them as our own, and acting in ways that genuinely reflect them. These are the goals of Rogers's method of psychotherapy, called *client-centered therapy* or *person-centered therapy*.

self-actualization In humanistic psychology, the tendency to strive to become all that one is capable of being. The motive that drives one to reach one's full potential and express one's unique capabilities.

conditional positive regard Valuing other people on the basis of whether their behavior meets one's approval.

conditions of worth Standards by which one judges the worth or value of oneself or others.

Truth OR Fiction? REVISITED

Children may acquire a distorted self-concept that mirrors what others expect them to be but which does not reflect who they truly are.

TRUE. According to Rogers, children can develop a distorted self-concept that mirrors what others expect them to be but which is not true to themselves.

The makings of unconditional positive regard. Rogers believed that parents can help their children develop self-esteem and set them on the road toward self-actualization by showing them unconditional positive regard—prizing them on the basis of their inner worth, regardless of their behavior of the moment.

Web Link **2.6** wWw
Online Self-Esteem Test

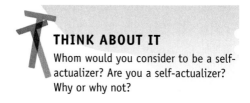

THINK ABOUT IT

Whom would you consider to be a self-actualizer? Are you a self-actualizer? Why or why not?

Evaluating Humanistic Models The strength of humanistic models in understanding abnormal behavior lies largely in their focus on conscious experience and their innovation of therapy methods that assist people along pathways of self-discovery and self-acceptance. The humanistic movement put concepts of free choice, inherent goodness, responsibility, and authenticity back on center stage and brought them into modern psychology. Ironically, the primary strength of the humanistic approach—its focus on conscious experience—may also be its primary weakness. Conscious experience is private and subjective. Therefore, the validity of formulating theories in terms of consciousness has been questioned. How can psychologists be certain they accurately perceive the world through the eyes of their clients?

Nor can the concept of self-actualization—which is so basic to Maslow and Rogers—be proved or disproved. Like a psychic structure, a self-actualizing force is not directly measurable or observable. It is inferred from its supposed effects. Self-actualization also yields circular explanations for behavior. When someone is observed engaging in striving, what do we learn by attributing striving to a self-actualizing tendency? The source of the tendency remains a mystery. Similarly, when someone is observed not to be striving, what do we gain by attributing the lack of endeavor to a blocked or frustrated self-actualizing tendency? We must still determine the source of frustration or blockage.

Cognitive Models

The word *cognitive* derives from the Latin *cognitio*, meaning "knowledge." Cognitive theorists study the cognitions—the thoughts, beliefs, expectations, and attitudes—that accompany and may underlie abnormal behavior. They focus on how reality is colored by our expectations, attitudes, and so forth, and how inaccurate or biased processing of information about the world—and our places within it—can give rise to abnormal behavior. Cognitive theorists believe that our interpretations of the events in our lives, and not the events themselves, determine our emotional states. Several of the more prominent cognitive models of abnormal behavior patterns are information-processing approaches and the models developed by psychologist Albert Ellis and psychiatrist Aaron Beck.

Information-Processing Models Many cognitive psychologists are influenced by concepts of computer science. Computers process information to solve problems. Information is fed into the computer (encoded so it can be accepted by the computer as input). Then it is placed in *memory* while it is manipulated. You can also place the information permanently in *storage*, on a floppy disk, a hard disk, or another device. Information-processing theorists apply these processes to human cognition. They think in terms such as *input* (based on perception), *manipulation* (interpreting or transforming information), *storage* (placing information in memory), *retrieval* (accessing information from memory), and *output* (acting on the information). They view psychological disorders as disturbances in these processes. Disturbances can be caused by the blocking or distortion of input or by faulty storage, retrieval, or manipulation of information. Any of these can lead to lack of output or to distorted output (e.g., bizarre behavior). People with schizophrenia, for example, frequently jump from topic to topic in a disorganized fashion, which may reflect problems in retrieving and manipulating information. They also seem to have difficulty focusing their attention and filtering out extraneous stimuli, such as distracting noises. This may represent problems relating to initial processing of input from their senses.

Manipulation of information may also be distorted by what cognitive therapists call *cognitive distortions*, or errors in thinking. For example, people who are depressed tend to develop an unduly negative view of their personal situation by exaggerating the importance of unfortunate events they experience (Meichenbaum, 1993). Cognitive theorists such as Albert Ellis and Aaron Beck have postulated that distorted or irrational thinking patterns can lead to emotional problems and maladaptive behavior.

Social-cognitive theorists, who share many basic ideas with the cognitive theorists, focus on the ways in which social information is encoded. For example, aggressive boys and adolescents are likely to incorrectly encode other people's behavior as threatening (see

Albert Ellis and Aaron Beck, two of the leading cognitive theorists.

Chapter 14). They assume other people intend them ill when they do not. Aggressive children and adults may behave in ways that elicit coercive or hostile behavior from others, which serves to confirm their aggressive expectations (Meichenbaum, 1993). Rapists, especially date rapists, may misread a woman's expressed wishes. They may wrongly assume, for example, that the woman who says "no" really means yes and is merely playing "hard to get."

Albert Ellis Psychologist Albert Ellis (1977b, 1993), a prominent cognitive theorist, believes that troubling events in themselves do not lead to anxiety, depression, or disturbed behavior. Rather, it is the irrational beliefs we hold about unfortunate experiences that foster negative emotions and maladaptive behavior. Consider someone who loses a job and becomes anxious and despondent about it. It may seem that being fired is the direct cause of the person's misery, but the misery actually stems from the person's beliefs about the loss, not directly from the loss itself.

Ellis uses an "ABC approach" to explain the causes of the misery. Being fired is an *activating event* (A). The ultimate outcome, or *consequence* (C), is emotional distress. But the activating event (A) and the consequences (C) are mediated by various *beliefs* (B). Some of these beliefs might include "That job was the major thing in my life," "What a useless washout I am," "My family will go hungry," "I'll never be able to find another job as good," "I can't do a thing about it." These exaggerated and irrational beliefs compound depression, nurture helplessness, and distract us from evaluating what to do. For instance, the beliefs "I can't do a thing about it" and "What a useless washout I am" promote helplessness.

The situation can be diagrammed like this:

Activating Event ➔ Belief ➔ Consequences

Ellis points out that apprehension about the future and feelings of disappointment are perfectly normal when people face losses. However, the adoption of irrational beliefs leads people to **catastrophize** their disappointments, leading to profound distress and states of depression. By intensifying emotional responses and nurturing feelings of helplessness, such beliefs impair coping ability. Examples of irrational beliefs include "I must have the love and approval of nearly everyone who is important to me or else I'm a worthless and unlovable person," and "I must be competent in virtually everything I do or else I'm an inadequate and incompetent person." In his later writings, Ellis emphasized the demanding nature of irrational or self-defeating beliefs—tendencies to impose "musts" and "shoulds" on ourselves (Ellis, 1993, 1997). Ellis notes that the desire for others' approval is understandable, but it is irrational to assume that one must have it to survive or to feel

wWw Web Link 2.7
     Albert Ellis Institute

catastrophize To exaggerate the negative consequences of events.

THINK ABOUT IT
Can you think of examples from your personal life in which your thinking style reflected one or more of the cognitive distortions identified by Beck—selective abstraction, over-generalization, magnification, or absolutist thinking? What effects did these thought patterns have on your moods? On your level of motivation? Do you think you can change how you think about your experiences? Why or why not?

Web Link **2.8** WWW
Beck Institute

Quiz **2.2** Q
The Psychological Perspective

Roots of abnormal behavior? Sociocultural theorists believe that the roots of abnormal behavior are found not in the individual but in the social ills of society, such as poverty, social decay, discrimination based on race and gender, and lack of economic opportunity.

worthwhile. It would be marvelous to excel in everything we do, but it's absurd to demand it of ourselves or believe that we couldn't stand it if we failed to measure up. Ellis developed a model of therapy, called *rational-emotive behavior therapy* (REBT), to help people dispute these irrational beliefs and substitute more rational ones. Ellis admits that childhood experiences are involved in the origins of irrational beliefs, but cognitive appraisal—the here and now—causes people misery. For most people who are anxious and depressed, the key to greater happiness does not lie in discovering and liberating deep-seated conflicts, but in recognizing and modifying irrational self-demands.

Aaron Beck Another prominent cognitive theorist, psychiatrist Aaron Beck, proposes that depression may result from "cognitive errors," such as judging oneself entirely on the basis of one's flaws or failures and interpreting events in a negative light (as though wearing blue-colored glasses) (A. T. Beck et al., 1979). Beck stresses the pervasive roles of four basic types of cognitive errors that contribute to emotional distress:

1. *Selective abstraction.* People may *selectively abstract* (focus exclusively on) the parts of their experiences that reflect on their flaws and ignore evidence of their competencies. For example, a student may focus entirely on the one mediocre grade he got on a math test and ignore all the higher grades.
2. *Overgeneralization.* People may *overgeneralize* from a few isolated experiences. For example, they may see their futures as hopeless because they were laid off or believe they will never marry because they were rejected by a dating partner.
3. *Magnification.* People may blow out of proportion, or *magnify*, the importance of unfortunate events. For example, a student may catastrophize a bad test grade by jumping to the conclusion that she will flunk out of college and her life will be ruined.
4. *Absolutist thinking.* Absolutist thinking is seeing the world in black and white terms, rather than in shades of gray. Absolutist thinkers may assume any grade less than a perfect "A," or a work evaluation less than a rave, is a total failure.

Like Ellis, Beck has developed a major model of therapy, called *cognitive therapy*, that focuses on helping individuals with psychological disorders identify and correct faulty ways of thinking.

Evaluating Cognitive Models As we'll see in later chapters, cognitive theorists have had an enormous impact on our understanding of abnormal behavior patterns and development of therapeutic approaches. The overlap between the learning-based and cognitive approaches is best represented by the emergence of *cognitive-behavioral therapy* (CBT), a form of therapy that focuses on modifying self-defeating beliefs in addition to overt behaviors.

A major issue concerning cognitive perspectives is their range of applicability. Cognitive therapists have largely focused on emotional disorders relating to anxiety and depression. They have had less impact on the development of treatment approaches, or conceptual models, of more severe forms of disturbed behavior, such as schizophrenia. Moreover, in the case of depression, it remains unclear, as we see in Chapter 8, whether distorted thinking patterns are causes of depression or are themselves effects of depression.

The Sociocultural Perspective

Does abnormal behavior arise from forces within the person, as the psychodynamic theorists propose, or from learning maladaptive behaviors, as the learning theorists suggest? Or, as the sociocultural perspective proposes, must a fuller accounting of abnormal behavior require that we consider the roles of social and cultural factors, including factors relating to ethnicity, gender, and social class? As we noted in Chapter 1, sociocultural theorists seek causes of abnormal behavior that may reside in the failures of society rather than in the person. Some of the more radical psychosocial theorists, like Thomas Szasz, even deny the existence of psychological disorders or mental illness. Szasz (1961, 2000) argues that "abnormal" is merely a label society attaches to people whose behavior deviates from accepted social norms. According to Szasz, this label is used to stigmatize and subjugate social deviants.

Throughout the text we examine relationships between abnormal behavior patterns and sociocultural factors such as gender, ethnicity, and socioeconomic status. Here let us examine recent research on relationships between ethnicity and mental health.

Ethnicity and Mental Health

When Europeans first arrived on America's shores, the land was populated solely by Native Americans. By the time the United States achieved nationhood, an ethnicity[1] profile would show that the numbers of people of European descent were approaching those of Native Americans. During the 19th century, the nation became predominantly populated by White people. Although Euro-Americans (also called European Americans or non-Hispanic White Americans) remain in the majority today, the nation is becoming increasingly ethnically diverse, as a result of both an excess of births over deaths among various U.S. ethnic groups and contemporary trends in immigration.

Figure 2.7 shows the ethnic composition of the U.S. population. African Americans, whose ancestors were forcibly brought to this country and enslaved, remain the largest non-White population group, constituting about 12% of the population. Hispanic Americans (Latinos) account for 11% of the population, while Asian Americans/Pacific Islanders account for 4%, and Native Americans for nearly 1%. During the early part of the 21st century, Hispanic Americans are expected to surpass African Americans as the country's largest ethnic minority group (Sachs, 2001; Rodriguez, 2001). The terms *Hispanic American* or *Latino(a)* refer to persons of Mexican, Puerto Rican, Cuban, or other Central and South American or Spanish origin (USDHHS, 1999a). The population of Asian Americans/Pacific Islanders—whose backgrounds and ancestries include peoples from areas as diverse as China, Japan, Korea, Indochina, Thailand, the Philippines, India, and Pakistan—represents the fastest growing ethnic minority group in the United States. ("America 2000," 2000; Clemetson, 2000). Their numbers in the U.S. population rose by more than 40% during the 1990s.

The term *minority* is quickly becoming something of a misnomer, as traditionally identified minority groups now comprise the majority in many U.S. cities and in the nation's most populous state, California (Purdum, 2001, Schmitt, 2001c). Euro-Americans will constitute but the barest majority of the population by the year 2050 (see Figure 2.8).

Ethnic designations, such as African American, Hispanic American or Latino, Asian American, Euro-American, or Native American, are general categories that encompass many different subgroups. For example, Latinos includes Spanish-speaking people who may trace their heritage to Mexico, Puerto Rico, or Colombia. Asian Americans may perceive themselves as Filipino Americans or Chinese Americans rather than Asian Americans per se. When considering racial or ethnic distinctions, we need to take into account differences among cultural and ethnic subgroups within our own culture. Yet traditional racial or ethnic distinctions are becoming blurry as increasing numbers of Americans and Canadians identify themselves as biracial, multiracial,

[1]The word *ethnicity* is derived from the Greek word *ethnikos*, meaning "people or nation."

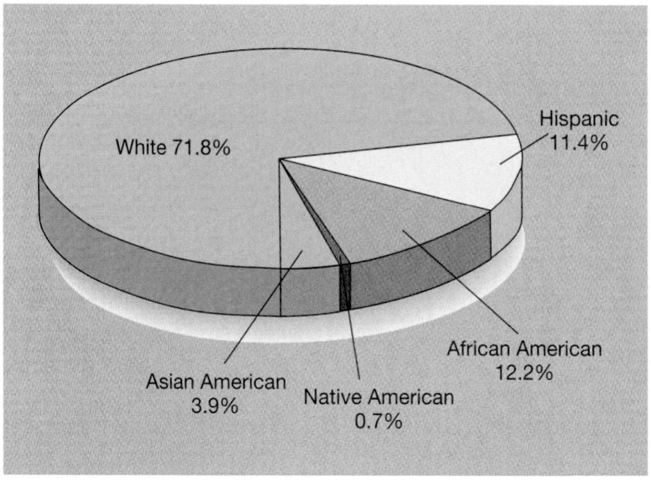

FIGURE 2.7 Ethnic/racial breakdown of the U.S. population in the year 2000.

Source. U.S. Bureau of the Census. (2000). *Resident population of the United States: Middle series projections, 1996–2000, by sex, race, and Hispanic origin, with median age.* Washington, DC: Author.

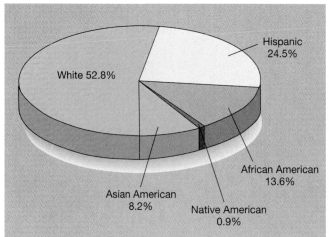

FIGURE 2.8 Projected ethnic/racial breakdown of the U.S. population in the year 2050.

Source. U.S. Bureau of the Census. (1996). *Resident population of the United States: Middle series projections, 2035–2050, by sex, race, and Hispanic origin, with median age.* Washington, DC: Author.

or multiethnic (Meacham, 2000; Miller, 2000). Individuals of multiracial background, such as the golfer Tiger Woods, the baseball player Derek Jeter, and the singer Mariah Carey, cannot easily be classified according to traditional racial groupings (See, 1999). Nearly seven million U.S. residents described themselves as multiracial in the most recent population census (Schmitt, 2001a, 2001b). Young people today are twice as likely to consider themselves multiracial than were their parents (Takahashi, 2001).

Given the increasing ethnic diversity of the U.S. population, researchers have begun to study ethnic group differences in the prevalence of psychological disorders. Knowing that a disorder disproportionately affects one group or another can help planners direct prevention and treatment programs to the groups that are most in need. Researchers recognize that income level or socioeconomic status needs to be considered when comparing rates of a given diagnosis across ethnic groups. We also need to account for differences among ethnic subgroups, such as differences among the various subgroups that comprise the Hispanic American and Asian American populations. We find, for example, higher levels of depression among Hispanic immigrants to the United States from Central America than from Mexico, even when considering differences in educational backgrounds (Salgado de Snyder, Cervantes, & Padilla, 1990).

Some ethnic groups have been underrepresented in previous research. For example, no nationwide surveys of the prevalence of psychological disorders among Asian Americans have been reported (Sue et al., 1995). However, the available evidence indicates that psychological disorders are not significantly lower among Asian Americans than other ethnic groups, which stands in contrast to the popular perception of Asian Americans as a group generally free of mental health problems (Sue et al., 1995; Zane & Sue, 1991).

We should be cautious—and think critically—when interpreting ethnic group differences in rates of diagnoses of psychological disorders. Might these differences reflect ethnic or racial differences, or differences on other factors on which groups may vary, such as socioeconomic level, living conditions, or cultural backgrounds?

Prevalence rates of mental disorders are found to be higher among African Americans than among Euro-Americans (USDHHS, 1999a). However, these differences disappear once one controls for socioeconomic status (SES). In other words, the higher rates of mental disorder among African Americans are a function of their generally lower SES, not their race or ethnicity. Evidence also shows few differences in rates of mental disorders between Hispanic Americans and Euro-Americans (USDHHS, 1999a).

Native Americans, on the whole, are among the most impoverished ethnic groups in the United States and Canada. Like other socially and economically disadvantaged groups, Native Americans also suffer from a much greater prevalence of mental health problems, including alcoholism, depression, suicide, drug abuse, and delinquency (T. J. Young & French, 1996). Native Americans, for example, have alcohol-related disorders at a rate six times that of other Americans (Rabasca, 2000a). The death rate due to suicide among adolescents in the 10- to 14-year age range is about four times higher among Native Americans than among other ethnic groups. Male Native American adolescents and young adults have the highest suicide rates in the nation (USDHHS, 1999a).

When you envision stereotypes such as hula dancing, luaus, and wide tropical beaches, you may assume that Native Hawaiians are a carefree people. Reality paints a different picture, however. One reason for studying the relationship between ethnicity and abnormal behavior is to debunk erroneous stereotypes. Native Hawaiians, like other Native American groups, are economically disadvantaged and suffer a disproportionate share of physical diseases and mental health problems. The death rate for Native Hawaiians is 34% higher than that of the general U.S. population, largely because of an increased rate of serious diseases, including cancer and heart disease (Mokuau, 1990). Native Hawaiians also have a 5- to 10-year lower life expectancy than other groups in Hawaii. Compared to other Hawaiians, Native Hawaiians experience higher rates of mental health problems, including higher suicide rates among males, higher rates of alcoholism and drug abuse, and higher rates of antisocial behavior.

Truth OR Fiction?   REVISITED

Rates of mental disorders are generally higher among African Americans than Euro-Americans, even when we account for income differences between these groups.

FALSE. Rates of mental disorders overall are no higher among African Americans than those of Euro-Americans when differences in socioeconomic levels are taken into account.

In addition to economic disadvantage, the mental health problems of Native Americans, including Native Hawaiians, may at least partly reflect alienation and disenfranchisement from the land and a way of life that resulted from colonization by European cultures (Rabasca, 2000a). Native peoples often attribute mental health problems, especially depression and alcoholism, to the collapse of their traditional culture brought about by colonization (Timpson et al., 1988). Researchers recount how a Native Canadian elder in northwestern Ontario explained depression in his people (Timpson et al., 1988, p. 6):

> Before the White Man came into our world we had our own way of worshipping the Creator. We had our own church and rituals. When hunting was good, people would gather together to give gratitude. This gave us close contact with the Creator. There were many different rituals depending on the tribe. People would dance in the hills and play drums to give recognition to the Great Spirit. It was like talking to the Creator and living daily with its spirit. Now people have lost this. They can't use these methods and have lost conscious contact with this high power. The more distant we are from the Creator the more complex things are because we have no sense of direction. We don't recognize where life is from.

The depression so common among indigenous or native peoples apparently reflects the loss of a relationship with the world that was based on maintaining harmony with nature (Timpson et al., 1988). The description of the loss of this special relationship reminds us of the Western concept of alienation.

Whatever the underlying differences in psychopathology among ethnic groups, members of ethnic minority groups tend to underutilize mental health services compared to European (non-Hispanic White) Americans (USDHHS, 1999a). Those who do seek services are more likely to drop out prematurely from treatment. In Chapter 4 we consider barriers that limit the utilization of mental health services by various ethnic minority groups in our society.

Evaluating the Sociocultural Perspective

Lending support to the linkage between social class and psychological disturbance, classic research in New Haven, CT, showed that people from the lower socioeconomic groups were more likely to be institutionalized for psychiatric problems (Hollingshead & Redlich, 1958). One reason perhaps is that the poor have less access to private outpatient care.

An alternative view is that people from the lower socioeconomic groups may be at greater risk of severe behavior problems because living in poverty subjects them to a greater level of social stress than that faced by the more well-to-do people. Yet another view, the **downward drift hypothesis,** suggests that problem behaviors, such as alcoholism, may lead people to drift downward in social status, thereby explaining the linkage between low socioeconomic status and severe behavior problems.

Certainly it is desirable for social critics such as Szasz to focus our attention on the political implications of our responses to deviance. The views of Szasz and other critics of the mental health establishment have been influential in bringing about much needed changes to better protect the rights of mental patients in psychiatric institutions. Many professionals, however, believe that more radical sociocultural theorists like Szasz go too far in arguing that mental illness is merely a fabrication invented by society to stigmatize social deviants.

Sociocultural theorists have focused much needed attention on the social stressors that may lead to abnormal behavior. Throughout the text we consider how sociocultural factors relating to gender, race, ethnicity, and lifestyle inform our understanding of abnormal behavior and our response to people deemed mentally ill. In Chapter 4, we consider how issues relating to race, culture, and ethnicity impact the therapeutic process.

THINK ABOUT IT
How can researchers distinguish the effects of socioeconomic status from that of ethnicity?

Quiz **2.3**
The Sociocultural Perspective

downward drift hypothesis The theory that explains the linkage between low socioeconomic status and behavior problems by suggesting that problem behaviors lead people to drift downward in social status.

diathesis-stress model A model that posits that abnormal behavior problems involve the interaction of a vulnerability or predisposition and stressful life events or experiences.

diathesis A vulnerability or predisposition to a particular disorder.

The Biopsychosocial Perspective

We have seen that there are several models or perspectives for understanding and treating psychological disorders. The fact that there are different ways of looking at the same phenomenon doesn't mean that one model must be right and the others wrong. No one theoretical perspective can account for the many complex forms of abnormal behavior we encounter in this text. Each perspective contributes something to our understanding, but none offers a complete view. Many theorists today adopt a biopsychosocial perspective that considers how multiple factors representing biological, psychological, and sociocultural domains interact in the development of particular disorders. We are only beginning to ferret out the subtle and often complex interactions of multiple factors that give rise to abnormal behavior patterns.

The biopsychosocial perspective invites us to consider how biological, psychological, and social factors are linked in the development of abnormal behavior patterns (Kiesler, 1999). For some disorders, the causes may be primarily or even exclusively biological in nature. For instance, certain forms of mental retardation have clear-cut biological causes, such as chromosomal abnormalities (see Chapter 14) or maternal alcohol consumption during pregnancy (see Chapter 10). Other disorders may arise directly from learning experiences. For example, phobias may be acquired based on associations or pairings of particular objects or situations with traumatic or painful experiences (see Chapter 6). But in most psychological disorders, multiple causes, representing biological, psychological, and sociocultural domains, are involved. We must consider not only the contributions of multiple causes, but also the interactions among them. We are only beginning to unravel the complex web of factors that underlie many types of disorders. Here, let us consider a leading contemporary model that examines how the interaction of multiple causes may be involved in the development of psychological disorders—the diathesis-stress model.

The Diathesis-Stress Model

The **diathesis-stress model** holds that disorders arise from a combination or interaction of a **diathesis** (vulnerability or predisposition) with stress (see Figure 2.9). In most versions of the model, the diathesis is conceptualized as a biological vulnerability, generally genetic in nature, which increases the risks of developing a particular disorder. Yet whether the disorder actually develops depends on the type and severity of stressors the person experiences. These stressors may include prenatal or childhood trauma, birth complications, physical illness, childhood sexual or physical abuse and family conflict, prolonged unemployment, loss of loved ones, or other negative life circumstances or changes.

In some cases, people with a diathesis for a particular disorder may remain free of the disorder or develop a milder form of the disorder if the level of stress in their lives remains low or if they develop effective coping responses for handling the stress they encounter. However, the stronger the diathesis, the less stress is generally needed to produce the disorder. In some cases the diathesis may be so strong that the disorder develops even under the most benign life circumstances.

The diathesis-stress hypothesis was originally developed as an explanatory framework for understanding schizophrenia (see Chapter 13). It has since been applied to other psycho-

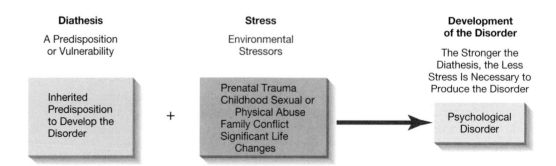

FIGURE 2.9 The diathesis-stress model.

logical disorders, including depression (Lewinsohn, Joiner, & Rohde, 2001; Ormel et al., 2001). The diathesis-stress model is not the only biopsychosocial account of how abnormal behavior patterns develop. We also consider other models that posit roles for biological and psychosocial influences, such as the cognitive model of panic disorder (see Chapter 6).

Not all forms of the diathesis-stress model are based on an interaction of a biological diathesis and life stress. Psychological diatheses may also be involved, such as dysfunctional thinking patterns or personality traits that increase the risk of developing a particular disorder in the face of life stress (Lewinsohn, Joiner, & Rohde, 2001). For example, the tendency to find fault with oneself for negative life events may put individuals at greater risk of developing depression following negative life events or stressors, such as divorce or job loss (see Chapter 8) (Just, Abramson, & Alloy, 2001).

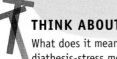

THINK ABOUT IT
What does it mean to state that the diathesis-stress model as formulated here is an interactionist approach to explaining abnormal behavior? Give an example of how your own behavior reflects interactions of biological, psychological, and sociocultural influences.

Evaluating the Biopsychosocial Perspective

The strength of the biopsychosocial model—its very complexity—may also be its greatest weakness. The model endorses the view that with few exceptions, psychological disorders or other patterns of abnormal behavior are complex phenomena that arise from multiple causal factors. We cannot pinpoint any one cause that leads to the development of schizophrenia or panic disorder, for example. Adding to the complexity is the multiple causal pathways that are involved—that is, different people may develop the same disorder based on different sets of causal influences. Yet the complexity of understanding the interplay of underlying causes of abnormal behavior patterns should not deter us from the effort. The accumulation of a body of knowledge is a continuing process. We know a great deal more today than we did a few short years ago. We will surely know more in the years ahead.

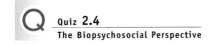
Quiz **2.4**
The Biopsychosocial Perspective

Quiz **2.5**
Chapter Exam

Summing Up

The Biological Perspective

How is the nervous system organized? The nervous system consists of two major parts, the central nervous system and the peripheral nervous system. The central nervous system consists of the brain and spinal cord. The peripheral nervous system consists of two major divisions, the somatic nervous system, which transmits messages between the central nervous system and the sense organs and muscles, and the autonomic nervous system, which controls involuntary bodily processes. The autonomic nervous system or ANS has two branches or subdivisions, the sympathetic and the parasympathetic. The nervous system is composed of nerve cells, or neurons, that communicate with one another through chemical messengers, called neurotransmitters, that transmit nerve impulses across the tiny gaps, or synapses, between neurons.

What are the biological underpinnings of abnormal behavior? Biological factors implicated in the development of abnormal behavior include disturbances in neurotransmitter functioning in the brain, heredity, and underlying brain abnormalities.

The Psychological Perspective

What are the major psychological models of abnormal behavior? Psychodynamic perspectives reflect the views of Freud and his followers, who believed that abnormal behavior stemmed from psychological causes based on underlying psychic forces within the personality. Learning theorists posit that the principles of learning can be used to explain both abnormal and normal behavior. Humanistic theorists believe it is important to understand the obstacles that people encounter as they strive toward self-actualization and authenticity. Cognitive theorists focus on the role of distorted and self-defeating thinking in explaining abnormal behavior.

The Sociocultural Perspective

What is the basic idea underlying the sociocultural perspective on abnormal behavior? Sociocultural theorists believe we need to broaden our outlook on abnormal behavior by taking into account the role of social ills in society, including poverty, racism, and lack of opportunity, in the development of abnormal behavior patterns.

The Biopsychosocial Perspective

What is the distinguishing feature of the biopsychosocial perspective? The biopsychosocial perspective seeks an understanding of abnormal behavior based on the interplay of biological, psychological, and sociocultural factors in abnormal behavior.

What is the diathesis-stress model? The diathesis-stress model holds that a person may have a predisposition, or diathesis, for a particular disorder, but whether the disorder actually develops depends on the interaction of the diathesis with stress-inducing life experiences.

CHAPTER THREE

Classification and Assessment of Abnormal Behavior

Jean Dubuffet
Ontogenese, 1975

Truth OR Fiction?

- Some men in India develop a psychological disorder involving excessive concerns or anxiety over losing semen. (p. 69)

- A psychological test must be valid in order to be reliable. (p. 73)

- Researchers find that people report more personal problems when interviewed by human interviewers than by computers. (p. 76)

- The most widely used personality inventory includes a number of questions that bear no obvious relationship to the traits the instrument purports to measure. (p. 80)

- Some clinicians examine how people interpret inkblots in order to uncover underlying aspects of their personalities. (p. 83)

- Weight-loss program participants who were more conscientious about monitoring what they ate lost more weight than those who were less reliable monitors. (p. 90)

- Despite advances in technology, physicians today still need to perform surgery to study the workings of the brain. (p. 92)

----

ystems of classification of abnormal behavior date to ancient times. Hippocrates classified abnormal behaviors on the basis of his theory of humors. Although his theory proved to be flawed, he arrived at some diagnostic categories that generally correspond to those in modern diagnostic systems. His description of melancholia, for example, is similar to present conceptions of depression. During the Middle Ages some so-called authorities classified abnormal behaviors according to those that represented demonic possession and those that represented natural causes. The 19th-century German psychiatrist Emil Kraepelin is generally considered the first modern theorist to develop a comprehensive model of classification based on the distinctive features, or "symptoms," associated with abnormal behavior patterns. The most commonly used classification system today is largely an outgrowth and extension of Kraepelin's work: the *Diagnostic and Statistical Manual of Mental Disorders (DSM)*, published by the American Psychiatric Association. The *DSM* classifies abnormal behavior patterns as mental disorders on the basis of specified diagnostic criteria.

Why is it important to classify abnormal behavior? For one thing, classification is the core of science. Without labeling and organizing patterns of abnormal behavior, researchers could not communicate their findings to one another, and progress toward understanding these disorders would come to a halt. Moreover, important decisions are made on the basis of classification. Certain psychological disorders respond better to one therapy than another or to one drug than another. Classification also helps clinicians predict behavior. Some patterns of abnormal behavior, such as schizophrenia, follow more or less predictable courses of development. Classification also helps researchers identify populations with similar patterns of abnormal behavior. By classifying groups of people as depressed, for example, researchers might be able to identify common factors that help explain the origins of depression.

This chapter reviews the classification and assessment of abnormal behavior, beginning with the major system clinicians use to classify abnormal behavior patterns: the *Diagnostic and Statistical Manual of Mental Disorders (DSM)*.

Classification of Abnormal Behavior Patterns

The *DSM* was first introduced in 1952. The latest version of the *DSM*, published in 2000 by the American Psychiatric Association, is the *DSM-IV-TR*, the Text Revision (TR) of the Fourth Edition (*DSM-IV*) (APA, 2000). We focus on the *DSM* as a method of classification because of its widespread adoption by mental health professionals. However, many psychologists and other professionals criticize the *DSM* on several grounds, such as relying too strongly on the medical model. Our focus on the *DSM* reflects recognition of its widespread use, not an endorsement.

In the *DSM*, abnormal behavior patterns are classified as "mental disorders." *Mental disorders* involve either emotional distress (typically depression or anxiety) and/or significant impairment in psychological functioning. *Impaired functioning* involves difficulties in meeting responsibilities at work, within the family, or within society at large. It also includes behavior that places people at risk for personal suffering, pain, or death.

Diagnosis of mental disorders within the *DSM* requires that the behavior pattern not represent an expected or culturally appropriate response to a stressful event, such as the loss of a loved one. People who show signs of bereavement or grief following the death of loved ones are not considered disordered, even if their behavior is significantly impaired. If their behavior remains significantly impaired over an extended period of time, however, a diagnosis of a mental disorder might become appropriate.

The *DSM* and Models of Abnormal Behavior

The *DSM* system adheres in some important respects to the medical model. It treats abnormal behaviors as signs or symptoms of underlying pathologies called mental disorders. Unlike the strictest form of the medical model, however, the manual does not assume that abnormal behaviors necessarily reflect biological causes or defects. It recognizes that the causes of most mental disorders remain uncertain: Some disorders may have purely biological causes. Some may have psychological causes. Still others are likely to reflect a multifactorial model, or the interaction of biological, psychological, social (socioeconomic, sociocultural, and ethnic), and physical environmental factors.

Nor does the *DSM* subscribe to a particular theory of abnormal behavior. With the introduction in 1980 of the third edition of the *DSM*, the *DSM-III*, terms linked to specific theories (such as *neurosis*, which was originally a psychodynamic term) were deemphasized in favor of descriptive terms such as *anxiety disorders* and *mood disorders.* Disorders are classified on the basis of their clinical features and behavior patterns, not on the basis of inferences about underlying theoretical mechanisms. Because the *DSM* does not endorse particular theoretical models unless evidence of causal factors is overwhelming, it can be used by practitioners of diverse theoretical persuasions. They can agree on the criteria for diagnosing various disorders, even if they disagree on their causes and proper treatments. Perhaps because of its emphasis on diagnostic criteria, critics contend that the *DSM* is something of a hodgepodge of disorders that are grouped together in various clusters without a consistent conceptual framework (Kutchins & Kirk, 1995).

The authors of the *DSM* recognize that their use of the term *mental disorder* is problematic because it perpetuates a long-standing but dubious distinction between mental and physical disorders (American Psychiatric Association, 1994, 2000). They point out that there is much that is "physical" in "mental" disorders and much that is "mental" in "physical" disorders. The diagnostic manual continues to use the term *mental disorder* because its developers have not been able to agree on an appropriate substitute. In this text we use the term *psychological disorder* in place of *mental disorder* because we feel it is more appropriate to place the study of abnormal behavior more squarely within a psychological context. Moreover, the term *psychological* has the advantage of encompassing behavioral patterns as well as strictly "mental" experiences such as emotions, thoughts, beliefs, and attitudes.

Psychologist Jerome Wakefield (1992a, 1992b, 1997, 2001) proposed that the term *disorder* be conceptualized as "harmful dysfunction." A harmful dysfunction represents a failure of a mental or physical system to perform its natural function, resulting in negative consequences or harm to the individual. By this definition, dysfunction alone is not enough to constitute a disorder. For example, even though the body was naturally designed to have two kidneys, and it would be dysfunctional to have but one, a failure of one kidney to function properly (or even the loss of a kidney) may not be harmful to the individual's well-being. By contrast, a dysfunction involving a breakdown in the brain's ability to store or retrieve information would constitute a disorder if it leads to harmful consequences such as memory deficits that make it difficult for the person to function effectively. We find Wakefield's conceptualization of disorders as harmful dysfunctions to be instructive, although we recognize that not all psychologists share his viewpoint (see Lilienfeld & Marino, 1995). One problem is that we may lack agreement on what constitutes the "natural function" of mental systems (Bergner, 1997).

Finally, we should recognize that the *DSM* is used to classify disorders, not people. This is an important distinction that has a bearing on the terminology we use to describe people who display abnormal behavior patterns. Rather than classify someone as a *schizophrenic* or a *depressive*, we refer to *an individual with schizophrenia* or *a person with major depression.* This difference in terminology is not simply a matter of semantics. To label someone a schizophrenic carries an unfortunate and stigmatizing implication that a person's identity is defined in terms of a disorder he or she may have or exhibit.

Features of the *DSM* The *DSM* is descriptive, not explanatory. It describes the diagnostic features—or, in medical terms, symptoms—of abnormal behaviors rather than attempting to explain their origins. Let us consider a number of features of the *DSM* classification system.

1. *Specific diagnostic criteria are used.* The clinician arrives at a diagnosis by matching a client's behaviors with the criteria that define particular patterns of abnormal behavior ("mental disorders"). Diagnostic categories are described in terms of *essential features*

Web Link **3.1** wWw
Diagnosis of Mental Disorders

TABLE 3.1 Sample Diagnostic Criteria for Generalized Anxiety Disorder

1. Occurrence of excessive anxiety and worry on most days during a period of six months or longer.

2. Anxiety and worry are not limited to one or a few concerns or events.

3. Difficulty controlling feelings of worry.

4. The presence of a number of features associated with anxiety and worry, such as the following:

   a. experiencing restlessness or feelings of edginess

   b. becoming easily fatigued

   c. having difficulty concentrating or finding one's mind going blank

   d. feeling irritable

   e. having states of muscle tension

   f. having difficulty falling asleep or remaining asleep or having restless, unsatisfying sleep

5. Experiencing emotional distress or impairment in social, occupational, or other areas of functioning as the result of anxiety, worry, or related physical symptoms.

6. Worry or anxiety is not accounted for by the features of another disorder.

7. The disturbance does not result from the use of a drug of abuse or medication or a general medical condition and does not occur only in the context of another disorder.

Source. Adapted from *DSM-IV-TR* (APA, 2000).

(criteria that must be present for the diagnosis to be made) and *associated features* (criteria often associated with the disorder but not essential to making a diagnosis). An example of diagnostic criteria for generalized anxiety disorder is shown in Table 3.1

2. *Abnormal behavior patterns that share clinical features are grouped together.* Abnormal behavior patterns are categorized according to their shared clinical features, not theoretical speculation about their causes. For example, abnormal behavior patterns chiefly characterized by anxiety are classified as anxiety disorders. Behaviors chiefly characterized by disruptions in mood are categorized as mood disorders.

3. *The system is multiaxial.* The *DSM* employs a *multiaxial,* or multidimensional, system of assessment that provides a broad range of information about the individual's functioning, not just a diagnosis (see Table 3.2). The system contains the following axes:

   a. *Axis I includes a classification of Clinical* **Syndromes,** which incorporates a wide range of diagnostic classes. These include anxiety disorders, mood disorders, schizophrenia and other psychotic disorders, adjustment disorders, and disorders usually first diagnosed during infancy, childhood, or adolescence (except for mental retardation, which is coded on Axis II). Axis I also includes a classification of *Other Conditions That May Be a Focus of Clinical Attention.* These are conditions or problems that may be the focus of diagnosis and treatment, such as relationship problems, academic or occupational problems, or bereavement, but that do not in themselves constitute definable psychological disorders. These conditions also include a category of psychological factors that affect medical conditions, such as

syndromes Clusters of symptoms that are characteristic of particular disorders.

TABLE 3.2   The Multiaxial Classification System of the *DSM-IV-TR*

Axis	Type of Information	Brief Description
Axis I	Clinical Disorders	The patterns of abnormal behavior ("mental disorders") that impair functioning and are stressful to the individual
	Other Conditions That May Be a Focus of Clinical Attention	Other problems that may be the focus of diagnosis or treatment but do not constitute mental disorders, such as academic, vocational, or social problems, and psychological factors that affect medical conditions (such as delayed recovery from surgery due to depressive symptoms)
Axis II	Personality Disorders Mental Retardation	Personality disorders involve excessively rigid, enduring, and maladaptive ways of relating to others and adjusting to external demands. Mental retardation involves a delay or impairment in the development of intellectual and adaptive abilities.
Axis III	General Medical Conditions	Chronic and acute illnesses and medical conditions that are important to the understanding or treatment of the psychological disorder or that play a direct role in causing the psychological disorder
Axis IV	Psychosocial and Environmental Problems	Problems in the social or physical environment that affect the diagnosis, treatment, and outcome of psychological disorders
Axis V	Global Assessment of Functioning	Overall judgment of current functioning with respect to psychological, social, and occupational functioning; the clinician may also rate the highest level of functioning occurring for at least a few months during the past year

Source. Adapted from the *DSM-IV-TR* (APA, 2000).

TABLE 3.3 Psychosocial and Environmental Problems

Problem Categories	Examples
Problems with Primary Support Group	Death of family members; health problems of family members; marital disruption in the form of separation, divorce, or estrangement; sexual or physical abuse within the family; child neglect; birth of a sibling
Problems Related to the Social Environment	Death or loss of a friend; social isolation or living alone; difficulties adjusting to a new culture (acculturation); discrimination; adjustment to transitions occurring during the life cycle, such as retirement
Educational Problems	Illiteracy; academic difficulties; problems with teachers or classmates; inadequate or impoverished school environment
Occupational Problems	Work-related problems including stressful workloads and problems with bosses or coworkers; changes in employment; job dissatisfaction; threat of loss of job; unemployment
Housing Problems	Inadequate housing or homelessness; living in an unsafe neighborhood; problems with neighbors or landlord
Economic Problems	Financial hardships or extreme poverty; inadequate welfare support
Problems with Access to Health Care Services	Inadequate health care services or availability of health insurance; difficulties with transportation to health care facilities
Problems Related to Interaction with the Legal System/Crime	Arrest or imprisonment; becoming involved in a lawsuit or trial; being a victim of crime
Other Psychosocial Problems	Natural or human-made disasters; war or other hostilities; problems with caregivers outside the family, such as counselors, social workers, and physicians; lack of availability of social service agencies

Source. Adapted from the *DSM-IV-TR* (APA, 2000).

---

hypothyroidism A physical condition, caused by deficiency of the hormone thyroxin, characterized by sluggishness and lowered metabolism.

Assessment of level of functioning. The assessment of functioning takes into account the individual's ability to manage the responsibilities of daily living. Here we see a group home for people with mental retardation. The residents assume responsibility for household functions.

anxiety that exacerbates an asthmatic condition, or depressive symptoms that delay recovery from surgery.

b. *Axis II, Personality Disorders*, includes the more enduring and rigid patterns of maladaptive behavior that generally impair interpersonal relationships and social adaptation, including antisocial, paranoid, narcissistic, and borderline personality disorders (see Chapter 9). Mental retardation is also coded on Axis II.

   Separating the diagnostic categories into two axes provides greater flexibility in reaching diagnostic impressions. People may be given either Axis I or Axis II diagnoses, or a combination of the two when both apply. For example, a person may receive a diagnosis of an anxiety disorder (Axis I) and a second diagnosis of a personality disorder (Axis II) if the diagnostic criteria for both are met.

c. *Axis III, General Medical Conditions*, lists medical conditions and diseases that may be important to the understanding or treatment of the individual's mental disorder. For example, if **hypothyroidism** were a direct cause of an individual's mood disorder (such as major depression), it would be coded under Axis III. Medical conditions that affect the understanding or treatment of a mental disorder but are not direct causes of the disorder are also listed on Axis III. For instance, the presence of a heart condition may determine whether a particular course of drug therapy should be used with a depressed person.

d. *Axis IV, Psychosocial and Environmental Problems*, lists psychosocial and environmental problems believed to affect the diagnosis, treatment, or outcome of a mental disorder. Psychosocial and environmental problems include negative life events (such as a job termination or a marital separation or divorce), homelessness or inadequate housing, lack of social support, the death or loss of a friend, or exposure to war or disasters. Some positive life events may also be listed, such as a job promotion, but only when they create problems for the individual, such as difficulties adapting to a new job. A listing of these types of problems is found in Table 3.3.

e. *Axis V, Global Assessment of Functioning,* refers to the clinician's overall judgment of the client's psychological, social, and occupational functioning. Using a scale similar to that shown in Table 3.4, the clinician rates the client's current level of functioning and may also indicate the highest level of functioning achieved for at least a few months during the preceding year. The level of current functioning is taken to indicate the current need for treatment or intensity of care. The level of highest functioning is suggestive of the level of functioning that might be restored.

An example of a diagnosis in the *DSM* multiaxial system is shown in Table 3.5.

Culture-Bound Syndromes The *DSM* recognizes that some patterns of abnormal behavior, called **culture-bound syndromes,** occur in only one culture, or perhaps in only a few cultures. The fact that some forms of abnormal behavior flourish in some cultures but not in others suggests that culture and social environment have an important influence on the development of abnormal behavior (Osborne, 2001).

Culture-bound syndromes may reflect exaggerated forms of common folk superstitions and belief patterns within a particular culture. For example, the psychiatric disorder **taijin-kyofu-sho** (TKS) is common in Japan but rare elsewhere. The disorder is characterized by excessive fear that one may behave in ways that will embarrass or offend other

culture-bound syndrome A pattern of abnormal behavior that is found within only one or a few cultures.

taijin-kyofu-sho A psychiatric syndrome, found in Japan, involving excessive fear of offending or embarrassing others.

TABLE 3.4 Global Assessment of Functioning (GAF) Scale

Code	Severity of Symptoms	Examples
91–100	Superior functioning across a wide variety of activities of daily life	Lacks symptoms Handles life problems without them "getting out of hand"
81–90	Absent or minimal symptoms, no more than everyday problems or concerns	Mild anxiety before exams Occasional argument with family members
71–80	Transient and predictable reactions to stressful events, OR no more than slight impairment in functioning	Difficulty concentrating after argument with family Temporarily falls behind in schoolwork
61–70	Some mild symptoms, OR some difficulty in social, occupational, or school functioning, but functioning pretty well	Feels down, mild insomnia Occasional truancy or theft within household
51–60	Moderate symptoms, OR moderate difficulties in social, occupational, or school functioning	Occasional panic attacks Few friends, conflicts with coworkers
41–50	Serious symptoms, OR any serious impairment in social, occupational, or school functioning	Suicidal thoughts, frequent shoplifting Unable to hold job, has no friends
31–40	Some impairment in reality testing or communication, OR major impairment in several areas	Speech illogical Depressed man or woman unable to work, neglects family, and avoids friends
21–30	Strong influence on behavior of delusions or hallucinations, OR serious impairment in communication or judgment, OR inability to function in almost all areas	Grossly inappropriate behavior, speech sometimes incoherent Stays in bed all day, no job, home, or friends
11–20	Some danger of hurting self or others, OR occasionally fails to maintain personal hygiene, OR gross impairment in communication	Suicidal gestures, frequently violent Smears feces
1–10	Persistent danger of severely hurting self or others, OR persistent inability to maintain minimal personal hygiene, OR seriously suicidal act	Largely incoherent or mute Serious suicidal attempt, recurrent violence

Source. Adapted from the *DSM-IV-TR* (APA, 2000).

reliable In psychological assessment, the consistency of a measure or diagnostic instrument or system.

validity The degree to which a test or diagnostic system measures the traits or constructs it purports to measure.

predictive validity The degree to which a test score is predictive of some future behavior or outcome.

TABLE **3.5**   **Example of a Diagnosis in the Multiaxial *DSM-* System**

Axis I	Generalized Anxiety Disorder
Axis II	Dependent Personality Disorder
Axis III	Hypertension
Axis IV	Problem with Primary Support Group (marital separation); Occupational Problem (unemployment)
Axis V	GAF = 62

Web Link **3.2**   wWw
DSM-IV: Questions and Answers

Taijin-kyofu-sho. TKS is a culture-bound syndrome that is common in Japan. It is characterized by excessive fear that one may embarrass or offend other people. The syndrome primarily affects young Japanese men and is apparently connected with the Japanese cultural emphasis on being polite and avoiding embarrassing other people.

people (McNally, Cassiday, & Calamari, 1990). People with TKS may dread blushing in front of others for fear of causing them embarrassment, not for fear of embarrassing themselves. In our culture, an excessive fear of social embarrassment is called a *social phobia* (see Chapter 6). Unlike people with TKS, however, people with social phobias have excessive concerns that they will be rejected by, or embarrassed in front of, others, not that they will embarrass other people. People with TKS may also fear mumbling thoughts aloud, lest they inadvertently offend others. The syndrome primarily affects young Japanese men and is believed to be related to an emphasis in Japanese culture on not embarrassing others as well as deep concerns over issues of shame (McNally et al., 1990; Spitzer et al., 1994). Chang (1984) reports that TKS is diagnosed in 7% to 36% of the people treated by psychiatrists in Japan. Table 3.6 lists some other culture-bound syndromes identified in the *DSM-IV-TR*.

We generally think of culture-bound syndromes as abnormal behavior patterns associated with folk cultures in non-Western societies. Yet some abnormal behavior patterns, such as anorexia nervosa (discussed in Chapter 11) and dissociative identity disorder (formerly called *multiple personality disorder*; discussed in Chapter 7), may be considered culture-bound syndromes occurring in some technological societies, including our own, but that are essentially unknown in less developed cultures.

Evaluation of the *DSM* System   Two basic criteria used in evaluating a diagnostic system such as the *DSM* are its reliability and validity. A diagnostic system may be considered **reliable,** or consistent, if various diagnosticians using the system are likely to arrive at the same diagnoses when they evaluate the same cases. The most appropriate test of the **validity** of a diagnostic system for psychological disorders is its correspondence with behavioral observations. Validity is often tested by examining whether people who receive a particular diagnosis display behaviors that correspond to those represented by the diagnostic category. Evidence supports the reliability and validity of most *DSM* anxiety disorder and mood disorder categories (T. A. Brown et al., 2001; Turner et al., 1986). However, the validity of some other diagnostic classes, such as personality disorders, remains a subject of debate in the scientific community, as does the validity of Axis V, Global Assessment of Functioning (Moos, McCoy, & Moos, 2000).

Another yardstick of validity, called **predictive validity,** is based on the ability of the diagnostic system to predict the course the disorder is likely to follow or its response to treatment. Evidence is accumulating that persons classified in certain categories respond better to certain types of medication. Persons with bipolar disorder, for example, respond reasonably well to the drug lithium (see Chapter 8). Specific forms of psychological treatment may also be more effective with certain diagnostic groupings. For example, persons who have specific phobias (such as fear of heights) are generally highly responsive to behavioral techniques for reducing fears (see Chapter 6).

Many observers (e.g., Eisenbruch, 1992; Fabrega, 1992) have argued that the *DSM* should become more sensitive to diversity in culture and ethnicity. The behaviors included as diagnostic criteria in the *DSM* are determined by consensus of mostly U.S.-trained psychiatrists, psychologists, and social workers. Had the American Psychiatric Association asked

Asian-trained or Latin American–trained professionals to develop their diagnostic manual, for example, there might have been some different or some revised diagnostic categories.

In fairness to the *DSM*, however, the latest edition does place greater emphasis than did earlier editions on weighing cultural factors when assessing abnormal behavior (DeAngelis, 1994b; Nathan, 1994). It recognizes that clinicians unfamiliar with an individual's cultural background may incorrectly classify the individual's behavior as abnormal when it in fact falls within the normal spectrum in the individual's culture. In Chapter 1 we noted the same behavior might be deemed normal in one culture but abnormal in another. The *DSM* specifies that for a diagnosis of a mental disorder to be made, the behavior in question must not merely represent a culturally expectable and sanctioned response to a particular event, even though it may seem odd in the light of the examiner's

TABLE **3.6**   **Examples of Culture-Bound Syndromes**

Culture-Bound Syndrome	Description
amok	A disorder principally occurring in men in southeastern Asian and Pacific Island cultures, as well as in traditional Puerto Rican and Navajo cultures in the West, it describes a type of dissociative episode (a sudden change in consciousness or self-identity) in which an otherwise normal person suddenly goes berserk and strikes out at others, sometimes killing them. During these episodes, the person may have a sense of acting automatically or robotically. Violence may be directed at people or objects and is often accompanied by perceptions of persecution. A return to the person's usual state of functioning follows the episode. In the West, we use the expression "running amuck" to refer to an episode of losing oneself and running around in a violent frenzy. The word *amuck* is derived from the Malaysian word *amoq*, meaning "engaging furiously in battle." The word passed into the English language during colonial times when British colonial rulers in Malaysia observed this behavior among the native people.
ataque de nervios ("attack of nerves")	A way of describing states of emotional distress among Latin American and Latin Mediterranean groups, it most commonly involves features such as shouting uncontrollably, fits of crying, trembling, feelings of warmth or heat rising from the chest to the head, and aggressive verbal or physical behavior. These episodes are usually precipitated by a stressful event affecting the family (e.g., receiving news of the death of a family member) and are accompanied by feelings of being out of control. After the attack, the person returns quickly to his or her usual level of functioning, although there may be amnesia for events that occurred during the episode.
dhat syndrome	A disorder (described further in Chapter 7) affecting males found principally in India that involves intense fear or anxiety over the loss of semen through nocturnal emissions, ejaculations, or excretion with urine (despite the folk belief, semen doesn't actually mix with urine). In Indian culture, there is a popular belief that loss of semen depletes the man of his vital natural energy.
falling out or blacking out	Occurring principally among southern U.S. and Caribbean groups, the disorder involves an episode of sudden collapsing or fainting. The attack may occur without warning or be preceded by dizziness or feelings of "swimming" in the head. Although the eyes remain open, the individual reports an inability to see. The person can hear what others are saying and understand what is occurring but feels powerless to move.
ghost sickness	A disorder occurring among American Indian groups, it involves a preoccupation with death and with the "spirits" of the deceased. Symptoms associated with the condition include bad dreams, feelings of weakness, loss of appetite, fear, anxiety, and a sense of foreboding. Hallucinations, loss of consciousness, and states of confusion may also be present, among other symptoms.
koro	Found primarily in China and some other South and East Asian countries, the syndrome (also discussed further in Chapter 7) refers to an episode of acute anxiety involving the fear that one's genitals (the penis in men and the vulva and nipples in women) are shrinking and retracting into the body and that death may result.
zar	A term used in a number of countries in North Africa and the Middle East to describe the experience of spirit possession. Possession by spirits is often used in these cultures to explain dissociative episodes (sudden changes in consciousness or identity) that may be characterized by periods of shouting, banging of the head against the wall, laughing, singing, or crying. Affected people may seem apathetic or withdrawn or refuse to eat or carry out their usual responsibilities.

Source. Adapted from the *DSM-IV-TR* (APA, 2000); Osborne, 2001; and other sources.

own cultural standards. The *DSM-IV* also recognizes that abnormal behaviors may take different forms in different cultures and that some abnormal behavior patterns are culturally specific (see Table 3.6). All told, the *DSM-IV* is widely recognized as an improvement over previous editions, but questions still remain about the reliability and validity of certain diagnostic categories (Langenbucher et al., 2000; Thakker & Ward, 1998; Widiger & Clark, 2000).

Advantages and Disadvantages of the *DSM* System Many consider the major advantage of the *DSM* to be its designation of specific diagnostic criteria. The *DSM* permits the clinician to readily match a client's complaints and associated features with specific standards to see which diagnosis best fits the case. The multiaxial system paints a comprehensive picture of clients by integrating information concerning abnormal behaviors, medical conditions that affect abnormal behaviors, psychosocial and environmental problems that may be stressful to the individual, and level of functioning. The possibility of multiple diagnoses prompts clinicians to consider presenting current problems (Axis I) along with the relatively long-standing personality problems (Axis II) that may contribute to them.

Criticisms have also been leveled against the *DSM* system. As noted, questions remain about the system's reliability and validity. Some critics challenge specific diagnostic criteria, such as the requirement that major depression be present for 2 weeks before diagnosis (Kendler & Gardner, 1998). Others challenge the reliance on the medical model. In the *DSM* system, problem behaviors are viewed as symptoms of underlying mental disorders in much the same way that physical symptoms are signs of underlying physical disorders. The very use of the term *diagnosis* presumes the medical model is an appropriate basis for classifying abnormal behaviors. Some clinicians feel that behavior, abnormal or otherwise, is too complex and meaningful to be treated merely as symptomatic. They assert that the medical model focuses too much on what may happen within the individual and not enough on external influences on behavior, such as social factors (socioeconomic, sociocultural, and ethnic) and physical environmental factors.

Another concern is that the medical model focuses on categorizing psychological (or mental) disorders rather than describing people's behavioral strengths and weaknesses. Nor does the *DSM* attempt to place behavior within a contextual framework that examines the settings, situations, and cultural contexts in which behavior occurs (Follette & Houts, 1996; Wulfert, Greenway, & Dougher, 1996). To behaviorally oriented psychologists, the understanding of behavior, abnormal or otherwise, is best approached by examining the interaction between the person and the environment. The *DSM* aims to determine what "disorders" people "have"—not what they can "do" in particular situations. An alternative model of assessment, the behavioral model, focuses more on behaviors than on underlying processes—more on what people "do" than on what they "are" or "have." Behaviorists and behavior therapists also use the *DSM*, of course, in part because mental health centers and health insurance carriers require the use of a diagnostic code, in part because they want to communicate in a common language with practitioners of other theoretical persuasions. Many behavior therapists view the *DSM* diagnostic code as a convenient means of labeling patterns of abnormal behavior, a shorthand for a more extensive behavioral analysis of the problem.

Another concern about the *DSM* system is the potential for stigmatization of people labeled with psychiatric diagnoses. Our society is strongly biased against people who are labeled as mentally ill. They are often shunned by others, including even family members, and subjected to discrimination in housing and employment. The negative stereotyping of people identified as mentally ill is labeled **sanism** (Perlin, 1994), the counterpart to other forms of prejudice and discrimination that exist in our society, such as racism, sexism, and ageism.

The *DSM* system, despite its critics, has become part and parcel of the everyday practice of most U.S. mental health professionals. It may be the one reference manual found on the bookshelves of nearly all professionals and dog-eared from repeated use. Perhaps the *DSM* is best considered a work in progress, not a final product.

THINK ABOUT IT

What are the advantages and disadvantages of using the *DSM* system to classify abnormal behavior patterns? Can you think of other ways we might classify abnormal behavior patterns?

---

sanism The negative stereotyping of people who are identified as mentally ill.

Now let us consider various ways of assessing abnormal behavior. We begin by considering the basic requirements for methods of assessment—that they be reliable and valid.

Q Quiz **3.1**
Classification of Abnormal Behavior Patterns

Issues of Reliability and Validity in Assessment

Important decisions are made on the basis of classification and assessment. For example, recommendations for specific treatment techniques vary according to our assessment of the problems that clients exhibit. Therefore, methods of assessment, like diagnostic categories, must be *reliable* and *valid.*

Reliability

The reliability of a method of assessment, like that of a diagnostic system, refers to its consistency. A gauge of height would be unreliable if people looked taller or shorter at every measurement. A reliable measure of abnormal behavior must also yield comparable results on different occasions. Also, different people should be able to check the yardstick and agree on the measured height of the subject. A yardstick that shrinks and expands markedly with the slightest change in temperature will be unreliable. So will one that is difficult to read.

There are three main approaches for demonstrating the reliability of assessment techniques.

Internal Consistency Correlational techniques are used to show whether the different parts or items of an assessment instrument, such as a personality scale or test, yield results that are consistent with one another and with the instrument as a whole. **Internal consistency** is crucial for tests intended to measure single traits or construct dimensions. When the individual items or parts of a test are highly correlated with each other, we can assume they are measuring a common trait or construct. For example, if responses to a set of items on a depression scale are not highly correlated with each other, there is no basis for assuming that the items measure a single common dimension or construct—in this case, depression.

Some tests are multidimensional in content. They contain subscales or factors that measure different construct dimensions. One such test is the Minnesota Multiphasic Personality Inventory (MMPI), which assesses various dimensions of abnormal behavior. In such cases, subscales within the test intended to measure individual traits, such as the hypochondriasis and depression subscales, are expected to show internal consistency. Subscales need not correlate with each other, however, unless the traits they are presumed to measure are interrelated.

Temporal Stability Reliable methods of assessment also have **temporal stability** (stability over time). They yield similar results on separate occasions. We would not trust a bathroom scale that yielded different results each time we weighed ourselves—unless we had stuffed or starved ourselves between weighings. The same principle applies to methods of psychological assessment. Temporal stability is measured by **test-retest reliability,** which represents the correlation between two administrations of the test separated by a period of time. The higher the correlation, the greater the temporal stability or test-retest reliability of the test.

Interrater Reliability Interrater reliability—also referred to as *interjudge reliability*—is usually of greatest importance for making diagnostic decisions and for measures requiring ratings of behavior. A diagnostic system is not reliable unless expert raters agree as to their diagnoses made on the basis of the system. For example, two teachers may be asked to use a behavioral rating scale to evaluate a child's aggressiveness, hyperactivity, and sociability. The level of agreement between the raters would be an index of the reliability of the scale.

internal consistency Cohesiveness or interrelationships of items on a test or scales.

temporal stability The consistency of test responses over time, as measured by test-retest reliability.

test-retest reliability A method of measuring the reliability of a test by means of comparing the scores of the same subjects on different occasions.

interrater reliability Consistency of or agreement between raters.

content validity The degree to which the content of a test covers a representative sample of the content it is designed to measure.

face validity The degree to which the content of a test bears an apparent relationship to the constructs it is designed to measure.

criterion validity The degree to which a test correlates with an independent, external criterion or standard.

concurrent validity A type of test validity based on the statistical relationship between the test and a criterion measure taken at the same time.

sensitivity The ability of a diagnostic instrument to correctly identify people who have the disorder the test is intended to detect.

specificity The ability of a diagnostic instrument to avoid classifying people as having a characteristic or disorder when they truly do not have the characteristic or disorder.

false negative An incorrect appraisal that a person is free of a disorder, when in fact he or she has the disorder.

false positive An incorrect appraisal that a person has a particular disorder.

construct validity The degree to which a test measures the hypothetical construct that it purports to measure.

THINK ABOUT IT
Suppose you wanted to develop a new psychological test or measure. How would you go about demonstrating that it was reliable and valid?

Validity

The validity of assessment techniques or measures refers to the degree to which the instruments in question measure what they are intended to measure. There are various kinds of validity, such as *content, criterion,* and *construct validity.*

Content Validity The **content validity** of an assessment technique is the degree to which its content covers a representative sample of the behaviors associated with the construct dimension or trait in question. For example, depression includes features such as sadness and lack of participation in previously enjoyed activities. To have content validity, techniques assessing depression should thus have features or items that address these areas. One type of content validity, called **face validity,** is the degree to which questions or test items bear an apparent relationship to the constructs or traits they purport to measure. A face-valid item on a test of assertiveness could be, "I have little difficulty standing up for my rights." An item that lacks face validity as a measure of assertiveness could read, "I usually subscribe to magazines that contain features about world events."

The limitation of face validity is its reliance on subjective judgment in determining whether or not the test measures what it is supposed to measure. The apparent or face validity of an assessment technique is not sufficient to establish its scientific value. A scientific test may also be valid if its results relate to some standard or criterion, even though the items themselves do not have high face validity. This brings us to criterion validity.

Criterion Validity Criterion validity represents the degree to which the assessment technique correlates with an independent, external criterion (standard) of what the technique is intended to assess. There are two general types of criterion validity: concurrent validity and predictive validity.

Concurrent validity is the degree to which test responses predict scores on criterion measures taken at about the same time. Most psychologists presume intelligence is in part responsible for academic success. The concurrent validity of intelligence test scores is thus frequently studied by correlating test scores with criteria such as school grades and teacher ratings of academic abilities.

A test of depression might be validated in terms of its ability to identify people who meet diagnostic criteria for depression. Two related concepts are important here: **sensitivity** and **specificity.** Sensitivity refers to the degree to which a test correctly identifies people who have the disorder the test is intended to detect. Tests that lack sensitivity produce a high number of **false negatives**—individuals identified as not having the disorder who truly have the disorder. Specificity refers to the degree to which the test avoids classifying people as having a particular disorder who truly do not have the disorder. Tests that lack specificity produce a high number of **false positives**—people identified as having the disorder who truly do not have the disorder. By taking into account sensitivity and specificity of a given test, we can determine the ability of a test to classify individuals correctly.

We noted that predictive validity refers to the ability of a test to predict some future behavior outcome. A test of academic aptitude may be validated in terms of its ability to predict school performance in that particular area.

Construct Validity **Construct validity** is the degree to which a test corresponds to the theoretical model of the underlying construct or trait it purports to measure. Consider a test that purports to measure anxiety. Anxiety is not a concrete object or phenomenon. It can't be measured directly, counted, weighed, or touched. Anxiety is a theoretical construct that helps explain phenomena like a pounding heart or sudden inability to speak when you ask an attractive person out on a date. Anxiety may be indirectly measured by such means as self-report (rating one's own level of anxiety) and physiological techniques (measuring the level of sweat on the palms of one's hands).

The construct validity of a test of anxiety requires the results of the test to predict other behaviors that would be expected given your theoretical model of anxiety. Assume your theoretical model predicts that socially anxious college students would experience greater difficulties than calmer students in speaking coherently when asking someone for a date, but not when they are merely rehearsing the invitation in private. If the speech behavior of high and low scorers on a test purported to measure social anxiety fit these predicted patterns, we can say the evidence supports the construct validity of the test. Construct validity involves a continuing process of testing relationships among variables that are predicted from a theoretical framework. We can never claim to have proven the construct validity of a test because it is always possible to come up with an alternative theoretical account of these relationships.

A test may be reliable (give you consistent responses) but still not measure what it purports to measure (be invalid). A test of musical aptitude might have excellent reliability but be invalid as a measure of general intelligence. Nineteenth-century **phrenologists** believed they could gauge people's personalities by measuring the bumps on their heads. Their calipers provided reliable measures of their subjects' bumps and protrusions; the measurements, however, did not provide valid estimates of subjects' psychological traits. The phrenologists were bumping in the dark, so to speak.

Sociocultural and Ethnic Factors in the Assessment of Abnormal Behavior

Researchers and clinicians also need to be aware of sociocultural and ethnic factors when they assess personality traits and psychological disorders. Assessment techniques may be reliable and valid within one culture but not within another, even when they are translated accurately (Bolton, 2001; Kleinman, 1987). In one study, Chan (1991) administered a Chinese-language version of the Beck Depression Inventory (BDI), a widely used inventory of depression in the United States, to a sample of Chinese students and psychiatric patients in Hong Kong. The Chinese BDI met tests of reliability, as judged by internal consistency, and of validity, as judged by its ability to distinguish people with depression from nondepressives among a small sample of Chinese psychiatric patients. Yet other investigators found that Chinese people in both Hong Kong and the People's Republic of China tended to achieve higher scores on a subscale of the Chinese MMPI, which is suggestive of deviant responses (Cheung, Song, & Butcher, 1991). These higher scores appeared to reflect cultural differences, however, rather than greater psychopathology (Cheung et al., 1991; Cheung & Ho, 1997).

A study in our own culture put the recently revised MMPI, called the MMPI-2, under a cultural microscope. Researchers found the test was as accurate in predicting the psychological adjustment of African Americans as of non-Hispanic White Americans (Timbrook & Graham, 1994). Moreover, researchers found small differences in the average test scores of African Americans and non-Hispanic White Americans when factors such as age, education, and income were taken into account. Another study found no evidence of cultural bias on the MMPI-2 between African American and non-Hispanic White clients at a mental health center (McNulty et al., 1997).

Other investigators found a greater prevalence of depression among Mexican Americans than among non-Hispanic White Americans in Los Angeles (Garcia & Marks, 1989). Here again the meaning of this difference was unclear. The difference may have reflected linguistic or sociocultural factors rather than differences in the prevalence of depression (Fabrega, 1992). Researchers thus need to disentangle psychopathology from sociocultural factors.

Most diagnostic schedules consider culture to some degree, but researchers believe they fail to provide adequate norms for different cultural and ethnic groups. Translations of instruments should not only translate words, but also provide instructions that encourage examiners to address the importance of cultural beliefs, norms, and values, so diagnosticians and interviewers will be prompted to consider the individual's background seriously when making assessments of abnormal behavior patterns.

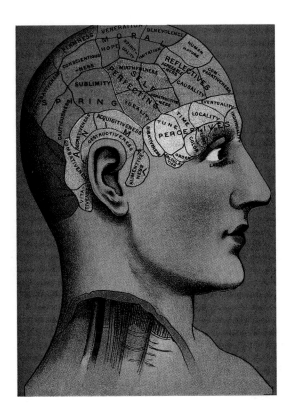

Phrenology. In the 19th century, some people believed that mental faculties and abilities were based in certain parts of the brain and that people's acumen in such faculties could be assessed by gauging the protrusions and indentations of the skull.

Truth OR Fiction? REVISITED

A psychological test must be valid in order to be reliable.

FALSE. A test may be reliable (give you consistent responses) but still not measure what it purports to measure.

wWw **Web Link 3.3**
  Phrenology Page

phrenologist Someone who studies the bumps on a person's head to determine the person's underlying traits.

Interviewers need also be sensitized to problems that can arise when interviews are conducted in a language other than the client's mother tongue. Hispanics, for example, often are judged more disturbed when interviewed in English (Fabrega, 1990). Problems can also arise when interviewers who use a second language fail to appreciate the idioms and subtleties of the language. The first author recalls a case in a U.S. mental hospital in which the interviewer, a foreign-born and -trained psychiatrist, reported that a patient exhibited the delusional belief that he was outside his body. This assessment was based on the patient's response to a question posed by the psychiatrist. The psychiatrist had asked the patient if he was feeling anxious and the patient replied, "Yes, Doc, I feel like I'm jumping out of my skin at times."

Quiz 3.2
Issues of Reliability and Validity in Assessment

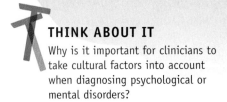

THINK ABOUT IT

Why is it important for clinicians to take cultural factors into account when diagnosing psychological or mental disorders?

Building rapport. By developing rapport and feelings of trust with a client, the skillful interviewer helps put the client at ease and encourages candid communication.

Methods of Assessment

Here we explore methods of assessment that clinicians use to arrive at diagnostic impressions, including interviews, psychological testing, self-report questionnaires, behavioral measures, and physiological measures. The role of assessment, however, goes further than classification. A careful assessment provides a wealth of information about clients' personalities and cognitive functioning. This information helps clinicians acquire a broader understanding of their clients' problems and recommend appropriate forms of treatment.

The Clinical Interview

The clinical interview is the most widely used means of assessment. It is employed by all helping professionals and paraprofessionals. The interview is usually the client's first face-to-face contact with a clinician. Clinicians often begin by asking clients to describe the presenting complaint in their own words. They may say something like, "Can you describe to me the problems you've been having lately?" (Therapists learn not to ask, "What brings you here?" to avoid receiving such answers as, "A car," "A bus," or "My social worker.") The clinician will then usually probe aspects of the presenting complaint, such as behavioral abnormalities and feelings of discomfort, the circumstances regarding the onset of the problem, history of past episodes, and how the problem affects the client's daily functioning. The clinician may explore possible precipitating events, such as changes in life circumstances, social relationships, employment, or schooling. The interviewer encourages the client to describe the problem in her or his own words in order to understand it from the client's viewpoint.

Although the format of the intake process may vary from clinician to clinician, most interviews cover topics such as these:

1. *Identifying data.* Information regarding the client's sociodemographic characteristics: address and telephone number, marital status, age, gender, racial/ethnic characteristics, religion, employment, family composition, and so on.

2. *Description of the presenting problem(s).* How does the client perceive the problem? What troubling behaviors, thoughts, or feelings are reported? How do they affect the client's functioning? When did they begin?

3. *Psychosocial history.* Information describing the client's developmental history: educational, social, and occupational history; early family relationships.

4. *Medical/psychiatric history.* History of medical and psychiatric treatment and hospitalizations: Is the present problem a recurrent episode of a previous problem? How was the problem handled in the past? Was treatment successful? Why or why not?

5. *Medical problems/medication.* Description of present medical problems and present treatment, including medication. The clinician is alert to ways in which medical problems may affect the presenting psychological problem. For example, drugs for certain medical conditions can affect people's moods and general levels of arousal.

Interview Formats There are three general types of clinical interviews: unstructured interviews, semi-structured interviews, and structured interviews. In an **unstructured interview,** the clinician adopts his or her own style of questioning rather than following any standard format. In a **semi-structured interview,** the clinician follows a general outline of questions designed to gather essential information but is free to ask the questions in any particular order and to branch off into other directions in order to follow up clinically important information. In a **structured interview,** the interview follows a preset series of questions in a particular order.

The major advantage of the unstructured interview is its spontaneity and conversational style. There is an active give-and-take between the interviewer and the client, because the interviewer is not bound to follow any specific set of questions. The major disadvantage is the lack of standardization. Different interviewers may ask questions in different ways. For example, one interviewer might ask, "How have your moods been lately?" while another might pose the question, "Have you had any periods of crying or tearfulness during the past week or two?" The clients' responses may depend to a certain extent on how the questions are asked. Another drawback is that the conversational flow of the interview may fail to touch on important clinical information needed to form a diagnostic information. A semi-structured interview provides more structure and uniformity, but at the possible expense of spontaneity. Clinicians may seek to strike a balance by conducting a semi-structured interview in which they follow a general outline of questions but allow themselves the flexibility to depart from the interview protocol to pursue issues that seem important to them.

Structured interviews (also called *standardized interviews*) provide the highest level of reliability and consistency in reaching diagnostic judgments, which is why they are used frequently in research settings. Yet many clinicians prefer using a semi-structured approach because of its greater flexibility. A leading example of a structured interview protocol is the Structured Clinical Interview for the *DSM* (SCID). The SCID includes **closed-ended questions** to determine the presence of behavior patterns that suggest specific diagnostic categories and **open-ended questions** that allow clients to elaborate their problems and feelings. The SCID guides the clinician in testing diagnostic hypotheses as the interview progresses. Recent research supports the reliability of the SCID across various clinical settings (J. B. Williams et al., 1992).

In the course of the interview, the clinician may also conduct a more formal assessment of the client's cognitive functioning by administering a **mental status examination.** This involves a formal assessment of client appearance (appropriateness of attire and grooming), mood, attention, perceptual and thinking processes, memory, orientation (knowing who they are, where they are, and the present date), level of awareness or insight into their problems, and judgment in making life decisions.

The interviewer compiles all the information available from the interview and review of the client's background and presenting problems to arrive at a diagnostic impression.

Psychological Tests

Psychological tests are structured methods of assessment used to evaluate reasonably stable traits such as intelligence and personality. Tests are usually standardized on large numbers of subjects and provide norms that compare clients' scores with the average. By comparing test results from samples of people who are free of psychological disorders with those of people who have diagnosable psychological disorders, we may gain some insights into the types of response patterns that are indicative of abnormal behavior. A recent analysis showed that the validity of many psychological tests are comparable to those of many medical tests when judged by their ability to predict criterion variables, such as underlying conditions or future outcomes (Daw, 2001; Meyer et al., 2001) (see Figure 3.1). Here we examine two major types of psychological tests: intelligence tests and personality tests.

Intelligence Tests The assessment of abnormal behavior often includes an evaluation of intelligence. Formal tests of intelligence are used to help diagnose mental retardation.

unstructured interview Interview in which the clinician adopts his or her own style of questioning rather than following any standard format.

semi-structured interview Interview in which the clinician follows a general outline of questions designed to gather essential information but is free to ask them in any order and to branch off in other directions.

structured interview Interview that follows a preset series of questions in a particular order.

closed-ended questions Questionnaire or test items with a limited range of response options.

open-ended questions Questions that provide an unlimited range of response options.

mental status examination A structured clinical assessment to determine various aspects of the client's mental functioning.

A Closer Look

Would You Tell Your Problems to a Computer?

 Picture yourself seated before a computer screen in the not-too-distant future. The message on the screen asks you to type in your name and press the return key. Not wanting to offend, you comply. This message then comes on the screen: "Hello, my name is Sigmund. I'm programmed to ask you a set of questions to learn more about you. May I begin?" You nod your head yes, momentarily forgetting that the computer can only "perceive" keystrokes. You type "yes" and the interview begins.

The future, as the saying goes, is now. Computerized clinical interviews have been used for more than 25 years. Computers offer some advantages over us traditional human interviewers (Farrell, Camplair, & McCullough, 1987):

1. Computers can be programmed to ask a specific set of questions in a predetermined order, whereas human beings may omit critical items or steer the interview toward less important topics.

2. The client may be less embarrassed about relating personal matters to the computer because computers do not show emotional responses to clients' responses.

3. Computerized interviews can free clinicians to spend more time providing direct clinical services.

Consider a computerized interview system named CASPER. Interview questions and response options, such as the following, are presented on the screen:

"About how many days in the past month did you have difficulty falling asleep, staying asleep, or waking too early (include sleep disturbed by bad dreams)?"

"During the past month, how have you been getting along with your spouse/partner? (1) Very satisfactory; (2) Mostly satisfactory; (3) Sometimes satisfactory, sometimes unsatisfactory; (4) Mostly unsatisfactory; (5) Very unsatisfactory."

Farrell et al., 1987, p. 692

The subject presses a numeric key to respond to each item. CASPER is a branching program that follows up on problems suggested by the clients' responses. For example, if the client indicates difficulty in falling or remaining asleep, CASPER asks whether or not sleep has become a major problem—"something causing you great personal distress or interfering with your daily functioning" (p. 693). If the client indicates yes, the computer will return to the problem after other items have been presented and ask the client to rate the duration and intensity of the problem. Clients may also add or drop complaints—change their minds, that is.

Research with computer interviewing systems shows that people reveal as much if not more personal information to a computer than they do to a human interviewer (Kobak et al., 1997; Kalb, 2001). The computer interview may be especially helpful in identifying problems

Interview by computer. Would you be more likely, or less likely, to tell your problems to a computer than to a person? Computerized clinical interviews have been used for more than 20 years, and some research suggests that the computer may be more sensitive than its human counterpart in teasing out problems.

that clients are embarrassed or unwilling to report to humans. Perhaps people feel less self-conscious if someone isn't looking at them when they are interviewed (Kalb, 2001). Or perhaps the computer seems more willing to take the time to note all complaints.

Truth OR Fiction?   REVISITED

Researchers find that people report more personal problems when interviewed by human interviewers than by computers.

FALSE. Evidence shows that people reveal as much if not more about themselves when interviewed by computers than by humans. Perhaps people are less concerned about being "judged" by computers.

Reviews of research suggest that computer programs are as capable as skilled clinicians at obtaining information from clients and reaching an accurate diagnosis, and are less expensive and more time efficient (Bloom, 1992; Kobak et al., 1996). It seems that most of the resistance to using computer interviews for this purpose comes from clinicians rather than clients.

Computer-assisted treatments for mental health problems have also become available, including systems designed to help people overcome phobias and test anxiety. Almost all of these are aids to therapy, not substitutes for a live therapist (Gilroy et al., 2000; I. Marks et al., 1998a). But with the rapid pace of technological developments today, there may well come a day when computerized programs with interactive voice technology will be used as stand-alone "therapists."

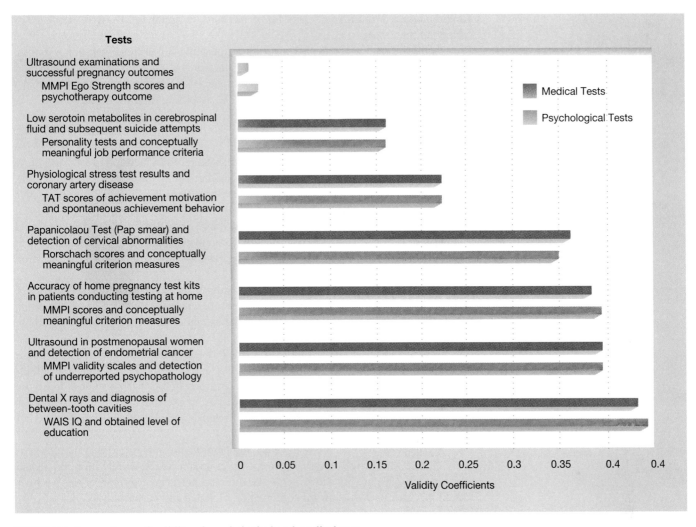

Tests

Ultrasound examinations and successful pregnancy outcomes
   MMPI Ego Strength scores and psychotherapy outcome
Low serotoin metabolites in cerebrospinal fluid and subsequent suicide attempts
   Personality tests and conceptually meaningful job performance criteria
Physiological stress test results and coronary artery disease
   TAT scores of achievement motivation and spontaneous achievement behavior
Papanicolaou Test (Pap smear) and detection of cervical abnormalities
   Rorschach scores and conceptually meaningful criterion measures
Accuracy of home pregnancy test kits in patients conducting testing at home
   MMPI scores and conceptually meaningful criterion measures
Ultrasound in postmenopausal women and detection of endometrial cancer
   MMPI validity scales and detection of underreported psychopathology
Dental X rays and diagnosis of between-tooth cavities
   WAIS IQ and obtained level of education

Medical Tests
Psychological Tests

Validity Coefficients

FIGURE 3.1 Comparisons of validity of psychological and medical tests.
Many psychological tests compare favorably with many medical tests in predicting many criterion variables.

Source. Adapted from Meyer et al., 2001.

They evaluate the intellectual impairment that may be caused by other disorders, such as organic mental disorders caused by damage to the brain. They also provide a profile of the client's intellectual strengths and weaknesses to help develop a treatment plan suited to the client's competencies.

Intelligence is a controversial concept in psychology, however. Even attempts at definition stir debate. David Wechsler (1975), the originator of a widely used series of intelligence tests, defined intelligence as "capacity . . . to understand the world . . . and . . . resourcefulness to cope with its challenges." From his perspective, intelligence has to do with the ways in which we (1) mentally represent the world, and (2) adapt to its demands. There are various intelligence tests, including group tests and those that are administered individually, such as the Stanford-Binet Intelligence Scale (SBIS) and the Wechsler scales. Individual tests allow examiners to observe the behavior of the respondent as well as record answers. Examiners can thus gain insight as to whether factors such as testing conditions, language problems, illness, or level of motivation contribute to a given test performance.

The SBIS was originated by the Frenchmen Alfred Binet and Theodore Simon in 1905 in response to the French public school system's need for a test that could identify children who might profit from special education. The initial Binet-Simon scale yielded a score called a **mental age** (MA) that represented the child's overall level of intellectual functioning. The child who received an MA of 8 was functioning like the typical 8-year-old.

intelligence (1) The capacity to understand the world and respond to its challenges; (2) the trait measured by intelligence tests.

mental age The age equivalent that corresponds to a person's level of intelligence as measured by the Stanford-Binet Intelligence Scale.

Source. Fernald, D. (1997). *Psychology*. Upper Saddle River, NJ: Prentice Hall, p. 242.

TABLE 3.7 Items Similar to Those on the Stanford-Binet

Age	Sample Item
2	"Point to your toes."
6	"Tell me what's next: A minute is short; an hour is _____."
10	"Try to repeat these numbers: 8-9-4-2-6-1."
11	"How are 'beginning' and 'end' alike?"
Adult	"What does this mean? 'The watched pot never boils'?"

Children received "months" of credit for correct answers, and their MAs were calculated by adding up their scores.

Louis Terman of Stanford University adapted the Binet-Simon test for American children in 1916, which is why it is now called the *Stanford-Binet Intelligence Scale* (SBIS). The SBIS yields an **intelligence quotient (IQ),** not an MA, which reflected the relationship between a child's MA and chronological age (CA), according to this formula:

$$IQ = \frac{MA}{CA} \times 100$$

Examination of this formula shows that children who received identical mental age scores might differ markedly in IQ, with the younger child attaining the higher IQ. For example, an 8-year-old with a mental age of 10 would have an IQ of 125, while a 10-year-old with a mental age of 10 would have an IQ of 100.

Binet assumed that intelligence grew as children developed, so older children would obtain more answers that are correct. He thus age-graded his questions and arranged them according to difficulty level, a practice carried over into the Stanford-Binet, as shown in Table 3.7.

Today the SBIS is used with children and adults, and test takers' IQ scores are based on their deviation from the norms of their age group. A score of 100 is defined as the mean. People who answer more items correctly than the average obtain IQ scores above 100; those who answer fewer items correctly obtain scores of less than 100.

This method of deriving an IQ score, called the **deviation IQ,** was used by psychologist David Wechsler in developing various intelligence tests for children and adults, known as the Wechsler scales. The Wechsler scales group questions into subtests like those shown in Table 3.8, each of which measures a different intellectual task. The Wechsler scales are thus designed to offer insight into a person's relative strengths and weaknesses, and not simply yield an overall score.

Wechsler's scales include both *verbal* and *performance* subtests. Verbal subtests generally require knowledge of verbal concepts; performance subtests rely more on spatial relations skills. (Figure 3.2 shows items like those on performance scales of the Wechsler scales.) Wechsler's scales allow for computation of verbal and performance IQs.

intelligence quotient (IQ) A measure of intelligence based on scores on an intelligence test; the ratio between a respondent's mental age and actual age.

deviation IQ An intelligence quotient obtained by determining the deviation between the person's score and the norm (mean).

TABLE 3.8 Examples of Subtests from the Wechsler Adult Intelligence Scale (WAIS)

Verbal Subtests	Performance Subtests
Information Who wrote *The Odyssey?*	**Digit Symbol** Given a key showing a set of symbols that correspond to particular numbers, fill in the correct symbols for a series of numbers.
Comprehension Why are people required to register their cars?	**Picture Completion** Identify the missing parts of a picture.
Arithmetic John wanted to buy a pair of pants that cost $47.25, but only had $19. How much more money would he need to buy the pants?	**Block Design** Use blocks like those in Figure 3.2 to match particular designs.
Similarities How are truth and honor alike?	**Picture Arrangement** Place a set of storybook pictures in the correct order to tell a coherent story.
Digit Span (Forward order) After listening to this series of numbers, repeat them in the same order: 5 2 4 9 (Backward order) After listening to this series of numbers, repeat them backward: 4 9 6 1	**Object Assembly** Arrange the pieces of a jigsaw puzzle so that they form a particular object.
Vocabulary What does the word *augment* mean?	

Source. From "Subtests from the Wechsler Adult Intelligence Scale Revised (WAIS-R)" for S. A. Ratus, *Essentials of Pshychology* (6th ed.), © 2001. Reprinted with permission of Brooks/Cole, on imprint of the Wadsworth Group, a division of Thomson Learning. FAX 800-730-2215.

Picture Arrangement
These pictures tell a story but they are in the wrong order. Put them in the right order so that they tell a story.

Picture Completion
What part is missing from this picture?

Block Design
Put the blocks together to make this picture.

Object Assembly
Put the pieces together as quickly as you can.

FIGURE 3.2 Items similar to those found on the performance subtests of the Wechsler Intelligence Scale (WAIS).
The Wechsler scales yield verbal and performance IQs that are based on the extent to which an individual's test scores deviate from the norm for her or his age group.

Source. Copyright (c) 1981 by the Psychological Corporation. Reproduced by permission. All rights reserved.

Students from various backgrounds yield different profiles. College students, generally speaking, perform better on verbal subtests than on performance subtests. Australian Aboriginal children outperform White Australian children on performance-type tasks that involve visual-spatial skills (Kearins, 1981). Such skills are likely to foster survival in the harsh Australian outback. Intellectual attainments, like psychological adjustment, are connected with the demands of particular sociocultural and physical environmental settings.

Wechsler IQ scores are based on how respondents' answers deviate from those attained by their age-mates. The mean whole test score at any age is defined as 100. Wechsler distributed IQ scores so that 50% of the scores of the population would lie within a "broad average" range of 90 to 110.

Most IQ scores cluster around the mean (see Figure 3.3). Just 5% of them are above 130 or below 70. Wechsler labeled people who attained scores of 130 or above as "very superior" and those with scores below 70 as "intellectually deficient." IQ scores below 70 are one of the criteria used in diagnosing mental retardation.

Next we consider the tests psychologists use to assess personality. We consider two types of personality tests: *self-report personality tests* and *projective tests*.

Web Link 3.4
Test Locator Services from Educational Testing Service (ETS)

self-report personality test A structured personality test in which individuals give information about themselves by responding to items that require a limited type of response, such as "yes-no" or "agree-disagree."

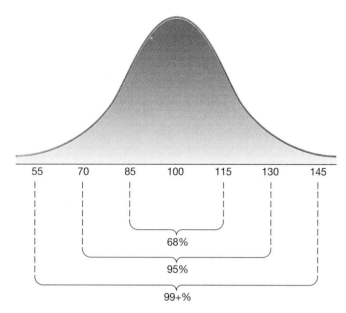

FIGURE 3.3 Normal distribution of IQ scores.
The distribution of IQ scores is based on a bell-shaped curve, which is referred to by psychologists as a *normal curve*. Wechsler defined the deviation IQ in such a way that 50% of the scores fall within the broad average range of 90 to 110.

Truth OR Fiction? REVISITED

The most widely used personality inventory includes a number of questions that bear no obvious relationship to the traits the instrument purports to measure.

TRUE. A leading personality inventory, the MMPI, contains items that bear no apparent relationship to the traits being measured. However, these items did differentiate between the response patterns of clinical diagnostic groups and normal reference groups.

objective tests Tests that allow a limited range of response options and can therefore be scored objectively.

forced-choice formats Test questions that require respondents to select from among a limited number of choices.

contrasted groups approach A method of determining concurrent validity that uses a test's ability to differentiate between members of two or more comparison groups.

Self-Report Personality Tests In **self-report personality tests,** individuals respond to a set of items about their feelings, thoughts, concerns, attitudes, interests, beliefs, and the like. Responses may be given in "yes-no," "true-false," or "agree-disagree" formats. Some self-report personality tests are intended to measure a particular trait or construct, such as anxiety or depression. The Beck Depression Inventory (BDI) (A. T. Beck et al., 1961), for instance, is a widely used measure of depression. In many clinic sites, such as the training clinic where the first author supervises clinical psychology students, the BDI is used routinely to screen new clients for depression. Some personality tests measure multiple dimensions of personality. Here we focus on two of the more widely used multidimensional personality tests in clinical settings, the Minnesota Multiphasic Personality Inventory (MMPI; now the MMPI-2) and the Millon Clinical Multiaxial Inventory (MCMI).

Do you like automobile magazines? Are you easily startled by noises in the night? Are you bothered by periods of anxiety or shakiness? Self-report inventories use structured items, similar to these, to measure personality traits such as anxiety, depression, emotionality, masculinity-femininity, and introversion. Comparison of clients' responses on scales measuring these traits to those of a normative sample reveals their relative standing.

Self-report personality inventories are also called **objective tests.** They are objective in that the range of possible responses to items is limited. Empirical objective standards—rather than psychological theory—are also used to derive test items. Tests might ask respondents to check adjectives that apply to them, to mark statements as true or false, to select preferred activities from lists, or to indicate whether items apply to them "always," "sometimes," or "never." Tests with **forced-choice formats** require respondents to mark which of a group of statements is truest for them, or to select their most preferred activity from a list. They cannot answer "none of the above."

With objective personality tests, items are selected according to some empirical standard. With the development of the original MMPI, the standard was whether items differentiated clinical diagnostic groups from normal comparison groups, not whether they bore an apparent relationship to the disorder itself.

Minnesota Multiphasic Personality Inventory (MMPI-2) The MMPI-2 contains more than 500 true-false statements that assess interest patterns, habits, family relationships, somatic complaints, attitudes, beliefs, and behaviors characteristic of psychological disorders. It is widely used as a test of personality as well as assisting in the diagnosis of abnormal behavior patterns. The MMPI-2 consists of a number of individual scales composed of items that tended to be answered differently by members of carefully selected diagnostic groups, such as patients diagnosed with schizophrenia or depression, than by members of normal comparison groups.

Consider a hypothetical item: "I often read detective novels." If groups of depressed people tended to answer the item in a direction different from normal groups, the item would be placed on the depression scale—regardless of whether or not the item had face validity. Many items that discriminate normal people from clinical groups are transparent in meaning, such as "I feel down much of the time." Some items are more subtle in meaning or bear no obvious relationship to the measured trait.

Derivation of scales on the basis of their ability to distinguish the response patterns of comparison groups such as clinical and normal groups is called the **contrasted groups approach.** The contrasted groups technique establishes concurrent validity; group membership is the criterion by which the validity of the test is measured.

Eight clinical scales were derived through the contrasted groups approach. Two additional clinical scales were developed by using nonclinical comparison groups: a scale measuring masculine–feminine interest patterns and one measuring social introversion. The clinical scales are described in Table 3.9. The MMPI-2 also has **validity scales** that assess tendencies to distort test responses in a favorable ("faking good") or unfavorable ("faking bad") direction. The scale also contains additional validity scales and a set of scales, called *content scales*, which measure an individual's specific complaints and concerns, such as anxiety, anger, family problems, and problems of low self-esteem.

The respondent's raw score for each of the clinical scales on the MMPI scale is simply the number of items scored in a clinical direction. Raw scores are converted into **standard scores** with a mean of 50 and a standard deviation of 10. A standard score of 65 or higher on a particular scale places an individual at approximately the 92nd percentile or higher of the revised normative sample and is considered clinically significant.

The MMPI-2 is interpreted according to individual scale elevations and interrelationships among scales. For example, a "2–7 profile," commonly found among people

validity scales Groups of test items that are used to detect whether the results of a test are valid.

standard scores Scores that indicate the relative standing of raw scores in relation to the distribution of normative scores.

TABLE 3.9 Clinical Scales of the MMPI-2

Scale Number	Scale Label	Items Similar to Those Found on MMPI Scale	Sample Traits of High Scorers
1	Hypochondriasis	My stomach frequently bothers me. At times, my body seems to ache all over.	Many physical complaints, cynical defeatist attitudes, often perceived as whiny, demanding
2	Depression	Nothing seems to interest me anymore. My sleep is often disturbed by worrisome thoughts.	Depressed mood; pessimistic, worrisome, despondent, lethargic
3	Hysteria	I sometimes become flushed for no apparent reason. I tend to take people at their word when they're trying to be nice to me.	Naive, egocentric, little insight into problems, immature; develops physical complaints in response to stress
4	Psychopathic Deviate	My parents often disliked my friends. My behavior sometimes got me into trouble at school.	Difficulties incorporating values of society, rebellious, impulsive, antisocial tendencies; strained family relationships; poor work and school history
5	Masculinity-Femininity	I like reading about electronics. (M) I would like to work in the theater. (F)	Males endorsing feminine attributes: have cultural and artistic interests, effeminate, sensitive, passive Females endorsing male interests: Aggressive, masculine, self-confident, active, assertive, vigorous
6	Paranoia	I would have been more successful in life but people didn't give me a fair break. It's not safe to trust anyone these days.	Suspicious, guarded, blames others, resentful, aloof, may have paranoid delusions
7	Psychasthenia	I'm one of those people who have to have something to worry about. I seem to have more fears than most people I know.	Anxious, fearful, tense, worried, insecure, difficulties concentrating, obsessional, self-doubting
8	Schizophrenia	Things seem unreal to me at times. I sometimes hear things that other people can't hear.	Confused and illogical thinking, feels alienated and misunderstood, socially isolated or withdrawn, may have blatant psychotic symptoms such as hallucinations or delusional beliefs, or may lead detached, schizoid lifestyle
9	Hypomania	I sometimes take on more tasks than I can possibly get done. People have noticed that my speech is sometimes pressured or rushed.	Energetic, possibly manic, impulsive, optimistic, sociable, active, flighty, irritable, may have overly inflated or grandiose self-image or unrealistic plans
10	Social Introversion	I don't like loud parties. I was not very active in school activities.	Shy, inhibited, withdrawn, introverted, lacks self-confidence, reserved, anxious in social situations

seeking therapy, refers to a test pattern in which scores for scales 2 ("Depression") and 7 ("Psychasthenia") are clinically significant. Clinicians may refer to "atlases," or descriptions, of people who usually attain various profiles.

MMPI-2 scales are regarded as reflecting continua of personality traits associated with the diagnostic categories represented by the test. For example, a high score on *psychopathic deviation* suggests that the respondent holds a higher-than-average number of nonconformist beliefs and may be rebellious, which are characteristics often found in people with antisocial personality disorder. However, because it is not tied specifically to *DSM* criteria, this score cannot be used to establish a diagnosis of antisocial personality disorder or any other psychological disorder. Perhaps it is unfair to expect that the MMPI, which was originally developed in the 1930s and 1940s under a largely outmoded diagnostic system, should provide diagnostic judgments consistent with the current version of the *DSM* system. Even so, MMPI profiles may suggest possible diagnoses that can be considered in the light of other evidence. Moreover, many clinicians use the MMPI to gain general information about respondents' personality traits and attributes that may underlie their psychological problems, rather than a diagnosis per se.

The validity of the original MMPI and the MMPI-2 is supported by a large body of research findings (Kubiszyn et al., 2000). The test successfully discriminates between psychiatric patients and controls and between groups of people with different psychological disorders, such as anxiety versus depressive disorders (Ganellen, 1996; Graham, 2000). Moreover, the content scales of the MMPI-2 provide additional information to that provided by the clinical scales, which can help clinicians learn more about the client's specific problems (Graham, 2000; Strassberg, 1997).

The Millon Clinical Multiaxial Inventory (MCMI) The MCMI (Millon, 1982) was developed to help the clinician make diagnostic judgments within the multiaxial *DSM* system, especially in the personality disorders found on Axis II. The MCMI is the only objective personality test that focuses on personality style and disorders. The MMPI-2, in contrast, focuses on personality patterns associated with Axis I diagnoses, such as mood disorders, anxiety disorders, and schizophrenic disorders. Using the MCMI and MMPI-2 in combination may help the clinician make more subtle diagnostic distinctions than are possible with either test alone, because they assess different patterns of psychopathology (Antoni et al., 1986). However, relationships between the MCMI and the underlying personality disorders they are meant to assess remain under study. Though the MCMI may help clinicians discriminate among various Axis I and Axis II disorders (Ganellen, 1996; Kubiszyn et al., 2000), some researchers voice concern that it may overdiagnose personality disorders (Guthrie & Mobley, 1994; Wetzler & Marlowe, 1993).

Web Link 3.5 wWw
Online Links to Personality Tests

Evaluation of Self-Report Inventories Self-report tests have the benefits of relative ease and economy of administration. Once the examiner has read the instructions to clients and ascertained they can read and comprehend the items, clients can complete the tests unattended. Because the tests permit limited response options, such as marking items either true or false, they can be scored with high interrater reliability. Moreover, the accumulation of research findings on respondents provides a quantified basis for interpreting test responses. Such tests often reveal information that might not be revealed during a clinical interview or by observing the person's behavior.

A disadvantage of self-rating tests is that they rely on clients as the source of data. Test responses may therefore reflect underlying response biases, such as tendencies to answer items in a socially desirable direction, rather than accurate self-perceptions. For this reason, self-report inventories, like the MMPI, contain validity scales to help ferret out response biases. Yet even these validity scales may not detect all sources of bias (Bagby, Nicholson, & Buis, 1998; Nicholson et al., 1997). Examiners may also look for corroborating information, such as interviewing others who are familiar with the client's behavior.

Tests are also only as valid as the criteria that were used to validate them. The original MMPI was limited in its role as a diagnostic instrument by virtue of the obsolete diagnostic categories that were used to classify the original clinical groups. Moreover, if a test does nothing more than identify people who are likely to belong to a particular diagnostic category, its utility is usurped by more economical means of arriving at diagnoses, such as the structured clinical interview. We expect more from personality tests than diagnostic classification, and the MMPI has shown its value in showing personality characteristics associated with people with certain response patterns. Psychodynamically oriented critics suggest that self-report instruments tell us little about possible unconscious processes. The use of such tests may also be limited to relatively high functioning individuals who can read well, respond to verbal material, and focus on a potentially tedious task. Clients who are disorganized, unstable, or confused may not be able to complete the tests.

Projective Tests **Projective tests,** unlike objective tests, offer no clear, specified response options. Clients are presented with ambiguous stimuli, such as vague drawings or inkblots, and asked to describe what the stimuli look like or to relate stories about them. The tests are called *projective* because they were derived from the psychodynamic projective hypothesis, the belief that people impose, or "project," their psychological needs, drives, and motives, much of which may lie in the unconscious, onto their interpretations of unstructured or ambiguous stimuli.

The psychodynamic model holds that potentially disturbing impulses and wishes, often of a sexual or aggressive nature, are often hidden from consciousness by defense mechanisms. Defense mechanisms may thwart direct probing of threatening material. Indirect methods of assessment, however, such as projective tests, may offer clues to unconscious processes. More behaviorally oriented critics contend, however, that the results of projective tests are based more on clinicians' subjective interpretations of test responses than on empirical evidence.

Many projective tests have been developed, including tests based on how people fill in missing words to complete sentence fragments or how they draw human figures and other objects. The two most prominent projective techniques are the Rorschach Inkblot Test and the Thematic Apperception Test (TAT).

The Rorschach Test The Rorschach test, in which a person's responses to inkblots are used to reveal aspects of his or her personality, was developed by a Swiss psychiatrist, Hermann Rorschach (1884–1922). As a child, Rorschach was intrigued by the game of dripping ink on paper and folding the paper to make symmetrical figures. He noted that people saw different things in the same blot, and he believed their "percepts" reflected their personalities as well as the stimulus cues provided by the blot. Rorschach's fraternity nickname was *Klex*, which means "inkblot" in German ("Time Capsule," 2000). As a psychiatrist, Rorschach experimented with hundreds of blots to identify those that could help in the diagnosis of psychological problems. He finally found a group of 15 blots that seemed to do the job and could be administered in a single session. Ten blots are used today because Rorschach's publisher did not have the funds to reproduce all 15 blots in the first edition of the text on the subject. Rorschach never had the opportunity to learn how popular and influential his inkblot test would become. The year following its publication, at the age of 38, he died of complications from a ruptured appendix.

Five of the inkblots are black and white and the other five have color (see Figure 3.4). Each inkblot is printed on a separate card, which is handed to subjects in sequence. Subjects are asked to tell the examiner what the blot might be or what it reminds them of. A follow-up inquiry explores what features of the blot (its color, form, or texture) the person used in forming an impression of what it resembled.

Clinicians who use the Rorschach tend to interpret responses in the following ways: Clients who use the entire blot in their responses show ability to perceive part–whole relationships and integrate events in meaningful ways. People whose responses are based solely on minor details of the blots may have obsessive-compulsive tendencies that, in psychodynamic theory,

projective tests Psychological tests that present ambiguous stimuli onto which the examinee is thought to project his or her personality and unconscious motives.

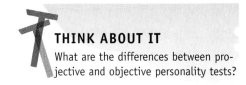

THINK ABOUT IT
What are the differences between projective and objective personality tests?

Truth OR Fiction? REVISITED

Some clinicians examine how people interpret inkblots in order to uncover underlying aspects of their personalities.

TRUE. Some clinicians do use a psychological test—the Rorschach—in which a person's responses to inkblots are used to reveal aspects of his or her personality.

FIGURE 3.4 An inkblot similar to those found on the Rorschach Inkblot Test. What does the blot look like to you? What could it be? Rorschach assumed that people project their personalities into their responses to ambiguous inkblots.

reality testing The ability to perceive the world accurately and to distinguish between reality and fantasy.

protect them from having to cope with the larger issues in their lives. Clients who respond to the negative (white) spaces tend to see things in their own way, suggestive of negativism or stubbornness.

Relationships between form and color are suggestive of clients' capacity to control impulses. When clients use the color of the blot but are primarily guided by the form of the blots, they are believed capable of feeling deeply but also of holding their feelings in check. When color predominates—as in perceiving any reddened area as "blood"—clients may not be able to exercise control over impulses. A response consistent with the form or contours of the blot is suggestive of adequate **reality testing.** People who see movement in the blots may be revealing intelligence and creativity. Content analysis may shed light on underlying conflicts. For example, adult clients who see animals but no people may have problems relating to people. Clients who appear confused about whether or not percepts of people are male or female may, according to psychodynamic theory, be in conflict over their own gender identity.

VIDEO **3.1**

Administration of Projective Tests:
Dr. Ruth Munroe

The Thematic Apperception Test (TAT) The Thematic Apperception Test (TAT) was developed by psychologist Henry Murray (1943) at Harvard University in the 1930s. *Apperception* is a French word that can be translated as "interpreting (new ideas or impressions) on the basis of existing ideas (cognitive structures) and past experience." The TAT consists of a series of cards, like that shown in Figure 3.5, each of which depicts an ambiguous scene. Respondents are asked to construct stories about the cards. It is assumed their tales reflect their experiences and outlooks on life—and, perhaps, also shed light on deep-seated needs and conflicts.

Respondents are asked to describe what is happening in each scene, what led up to it, what the characters are thinking and feeling, and what will happen next. Psychodynamically oriented clinicians assume that respondents identify with the protagonists in their stories and project their psychological needs and conflicts into the events they *apperceive.* On a more superficial level, the stories also suggest how respondents might interpret or behave in similar situations in their own lives. TAT results are also suggestive of clients' attitudes toward others, particularly family members and lovers.

The TAT has been used extensively in research on motivation as well as in clinical practice. For example, psychologist David McClelland (e.g., McClellan, Alexander, & Marks, 1982) pioneered use of the TAT in assessing social motives such as the needs for achievement and power. The rationales for this research are that we are likely to be somewhat preoccupied with our needs, and our needs are projected into our reactions to ambiguous stimuli and situations.

FIGURE 3.5 Thematic Apperception Test (TAT).
Psychologists ask test-takers to provide their impressions of what is happening in the scene depicted in the drawing. They ask test-takers what led up to the scene and how it will turn out. How might your responses reveal aspects of your own personality?

Evaluation of Projective Techniques The reliability and validity of projective techniques has been the subject of extensive research and debate. One problem is the lack of a standard scoring procedure. Interpretation of a person's responses depends to some degree on the subjective judgment of the examiner. For example, two examiners may interpret the same Rorschach or TAT response differently.

Recent attempts to develop a comprehensive scoring approach for the Rorschach, such as the Exner system (Exner, 1991, 1993), have advanced the effort to standardize scoring of responses. But the debate over the reliability of the Rorschach, including the Exner system, continues (see Acklin et al., 2000; G. J. Meyer, 1997; Wood, Nezworski, & Stejskal, 1996, 1997). Even if a Rorschach response can be scored reliably, the interpretation of the response—what it means—remains an open question.

Critics and even some proponents of the Rorschach technique, such as Hertz (1986), recognize that evidence is lacking to support the interpretation of particular responses. However, evidence has accumulated that supports the validity of some specific Rorschach responses (e.g., Blais et al., 2001; Kubiszyn et al., 2000; Leavitt & Labott, 1997; G. J. Meyer, 2001; Viglione, 1999). For example, investigators find that specific Rorschach indicators can distinguish between different types of psychological disorders (Kubiszyn et al., 2000), as well as predict psychotherapy outcomes (G. J. Meyer, 2000) and some types of behaviors, such as dependency behaviors (Bornstein, 1999). Though some reviewers (e.g., Meyer et al., 2001) find the validity of the Rorschach and TAT overall to be generally on par with that of other psychological tests, others claim that these tests have not yet met tests of scientific utility or validity (Hunsley & Bailey, 1999; Goode, 2001a; Lilienfeld, Wood, & Garb, 2000).

One criticism of the TAT is that the stimulus properties of some of the cards, such as cues depicting sadness or anger, may exert too strong a "stimulus pull" on the subject. The pictures themselves may pull for certain types of stories. If so, clients' responses may represent reactions to the stimulus cues rather than projections of their personalities (Murstein & Mathes, 1996). The validity of the TAT in eliciting deep-seated material or tapping underlying psychopathology also remains to be demonstrated. However, evidence does indicate that it can discriminate between different types of Axis I and Axis II disorders (Kubiszyn et al., 2000).

One general problem with projective instruments such as the TAT and Rorschach is that the more healthy test takers talk or see in response to projective instruments, the more likely they will be judged as having psychological problems (Murstein & Mathes, 1996). However, proponents of projective testing argue that in skilled hands, tests like the TAT and the Rorschach can yield meaningful material that might not be revealed in interviews or by self-rating inventories (Stricker & Gold, 1999). Moreover, allowing subjects freedom of expression through projective testing reduces the tendency of individuals to offer socially desirable responses. Despite the lack of direct evidence for the projective hypothesis, the appeal of projective tests among clinicians and internship training directors remains strong (Clemence & Handler, 2001; Lubin et al., 1985).

THINK ABOUT IT
Consider the debate over the use of projective tests. Do you believe that a person's response to inkblots or other unstructured stimuli might reveal aspects of his or her underlying personality? Why or why not?

Neuropsychological Assessment

Neuropsychological assessment is used to evaluate whether psychological problems reflect underlying neurological damage or brain defects. When neurological impairment is suspected, a neurological evaluation may be requested from a *neurologist*—a medical doctor who specializes in disorders of the nervous system. A clinical *neuropsychologist* may also be consulted to administer neuropsychological assessment techniques, such as behavioral observation and psychological testing, to reveal signs of possible brain damage. Neuropsychological testing may be used together with brain-imaging techniques such as the MRI and CT to shed light on relationships between brain function and underlying abnormalities (Fiez, 2001). The results of neuropsychological testing may not only suggest whether patients suffer from brain damage but also point to the parts of the brain that may be affected.

The Bender Visual Motor Gestalt Test One of the first neuropsychological tests to be developed was the Bender Visual Motor Gestalt Test (Bender, 1938). "The Bender" consists of geometric figures that illustrate various Gestalt principles of perception. The client is asked to copy nine geometric designs (see Figure 3.6). Signs of possible brain damage include rotation of the figures, distortions in shape, and incorrect sizing of the figures in relation to one another. The examiner then asks the client to reproduce the designs from memory, because neurological damage can impair memory functioning.

Although the Bender remains a convenient and economical means of uncovering possible organic impairment, it has been criticized for producing too many false negatives—that is, persons with neurological impairment who make satisfactory drawings (Bigler & Ehrhenfurth, 1981). In recent years, more sophisticated tests have been developed. Two of

neuropsychological Pertaining to the relationships between the brain and behavior.

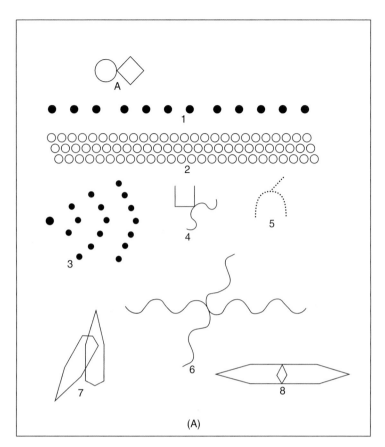
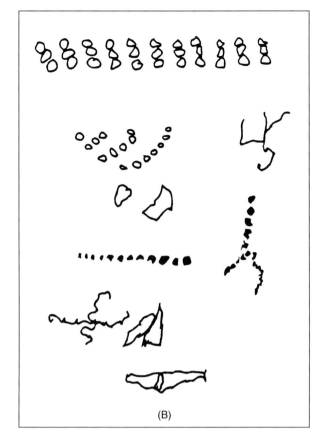

(A)

(B)

FIGURE 3.6 The Bender Visual Motor Gestalt Test.
The "Bender" is intended to assess organic impairment. Part A shows the series of figures
respondents are asked to copy. Part B shows the drawings of a person who is known to be
brain-damaged.

the more widely used neuropsychological inventories today are the Halstead-Reitan Neuropsychological Battery and the Luria Nebraska Test Battery.

The Halstead-Reitan Neuropsychological Battery Psychologist Ralph Reitan developed the battery by adapting tests used by his mentor, Ward Halstead, an experimental psychologist, to study brain-behavior relationships among organically impaired individuals. The battery contains tests that measure perceptual, intellectual, and motor skills and performance. A battery of tests permits the psychologist to observe patterns of results, and various patterns of performance deficits are suggestive of certain kinds of organic defects. The tests in the battery include the following:

1. *The Category Test.* This test measures abstract thinking ability, as indicated by the individual's proficiency at forming principles or categories that relate different stimuli to one another. A series of groups of stimuli that vary in shape, size, location, color, and other characteristics are flashed on a screen. The subject's task is to discern the principle that links them, such as shape or size, and to indicate which stimuli in each grouping represent the correct category by pressing a key. By analyzing the patterns of correct and incorrect choices, the subject normally learns to identify the principles that determine the correct choice. Performance on the test is believed to reflect functioning in the frontal lobe of the cerebral cortex.

2. *The Rhythm Test.* This is a test of concentration and attention. The subject listens to 30 pairs of tape-recorded rhythmic beats and indicates whether the beats in each pair are the same or different. Performance deficits are associated with damage to the right temporal lobe of the cerebral cortex.

3. *The Tactual Performance Test.* This test requires the blindfolded subject to fit wooden blocks of different shapes into corresponding depressions on a form board. Afterward, the subject draws the board from memory as a measure of visual memory.

The Luria Nebraska Test Battery The Luria Nebraska Test Battery is based on the work of the Russian neuropsychologist A. R. Luria and was developed by psychologists at the University of Nebraska (C. J. Golden, Hammeke, & Purisch, 1980). Like the Halstead-Reitan, the Luria Nebraska reveals patterns of skill deficits that are suggestive of particular sites of brain damage. The Luria Nebraska is more efficiently administered than the Halstead-Reitan, requiring about one-third the time to complete.

A wide range of skills is assessed. Tests measure tactile, kinesthetic, and spatial skills; complex motor skills; auditory skills; receptive and expressive speech skills; reading, writing, and arithmetic skills; and general intelligence and memory functioning.

Neuropsychological tests attempt to reveal underlying brain abnormalities without the need to resort to surgical procedures. Researchers find that when clinicians use batteries of neuropsychological tests, they can form reliable and accurate judgments about impaired cognitive functioning resulting from underlying brain damage (Garb, 2000; Kubiszyn et al., 2000). Moreover, these judgments cannot be derived simply on the basis of interviews or casual observations of patients' behaviors. We later consider other contemporary techniques that allow us to probe the workings of the brain without surgery.

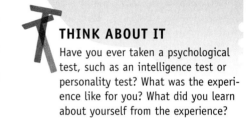

THINK ABOUT IT
Have you ever taken a psychological test, such as an intelligence test or personality test? What was the experience like for you? What did you learn about yourself from the experience?

Behavioral Assessment

The traditional model of assessment, the **psychometric approach,** holds that psychological tests reveal *signs* of reasonably stable traits or dispositions that largely determine people's behavior. The psychometric approach aims to classify people in terms of personality types according to traits such as anxiety, introversion-extraversion, obsessiveness, hostility, impulsivity, and aggressiveness. This model inspired development of trait-based tests such as the Rorschach, TAT, and the MMPI.

The alternative model of **behavioral assessment** treats test results as samples of behavior that occur in specific situations rather than as signs of underlying personality types or traits. According to the behavioral approach, behavior is primarily determined by environmental or situational factors, such as stimulus cues and reinforcements.

The behavioral model has inspired the development of techniques that aim to sample an individual's behavior in settings as similar as possible to the real-life situation, thus maximizing the relationship between the testing situation and the criterion. Behavior may be observed and measured in such settings as the home, school, or work environment. The examiner may also try to simulate situations in the clinic or laboratory that serve as **analogues** of the problems the individual confronts in daily life.

The examiner may conduct a **functional analysis** of the problem behavior—relating it to the *antecedents*, or stimulus cues that trigger it, and the *consequences*, or reinforcements that maintain it. Knowledge of the environmental conditions in which a problem behavior occurs may help the therapist work with the client and the family to change the conditions that trigger and maintain it. The examiner may conduct a **behavioral interview** by posing questions to learn more about the history and situational aspects of problem behavior. If a client seeks help because of panic attacks, the behavioral interviewer might ask how the client experiences these attacks—when, where, how often, under what circumstances. The interviewer looks for precipitating cues, such as thought patterns (e.g., thoughts of dying or losing control) or situational factors (e.g., entering a department store) that may provoke an attack. The interviewer also seeks information about reinforcers that may maintain the panic. Does the client flee the situation when an attack occurs? Is escape reinforced by relief from anxiety? Has the client learned to lessen anticipatory anxiety by avoiding exposure to situations in which attacks have occurred?

The examiner may also use observational methods to connect the problem behavior to the stimuli and reinforcements that help maintain it. Consider the case of Kerry:

psychometric approach An assessment method that relies on psychological tests to identify and measure the traits that compose an individual's personality.

behavioral assessment The approach to clinical assessment that focuses on the objective recording and description of the problem behavior.

analogue Something that resembles something else.

functional analysis Analysis of behavior in terms of antecedent stimuli and reinforcement consequences.

behavioral interview Clinical interview that focuses on relating the problem behavior to antecedent stimuli and reinforcement consequences.

Kerry, the "Royal Terror"

A 7-year-old boy, Kerry, is brought by his parents for evaluation. His mother describes him as a "royal terror." His father complains he won't listen to anyone. Kerry throws temper tantrums in the supermarket, screaming and stomping his feet if his parents refuse to buy him what he wants. At home, he breaks his toys by throwing them against the wall and demands new ones. Sometimes, though, he appears sullen and won't talk to anyone for hours. At school he appears inhibited and has difficulty concentrating. His progress at school is slow and he has difficulty reading. His teachers complain he has a limited attention span and doesn't seem motivated.

—The Authors' Files

■

The psychologist may use direct home observation to assess the interactions between Kerry and his parents. Alternatively, the psychologist may observe Kerry and his parents through a one-way mirror in the clinic. Such observations may suggest interactions that explain the child's noncompliance. For example, Kerry's noncompliance may follow parental requests that are vague (e.g., a parent says, "Play nicely now," and Kerry responds by throwing toys) or inconsistent (e.g., a parent says, "Go play with your toys but don't make a mess," to which Kerry responds by scattering the toys). Observation may suggest ways in which Kerry's parents can improve communication and cue and reinforce desirable behaviors.

Direct observation, or behavioral observation, is the hallmark of behavioral assessment. Through behavioral observation, clinicians can observe and quantify problem behavior. Observations may be videotaped to permit subsequent analysis of behavioral patterns. Observers are trained to identify and record targeted patterns of behavior. Behavior coding systems have been developed that enhance the reliability of recording.

There are advantages and disadvantages to direct observation. One advantage is that direct observation does not rely on the client's self-reports, which may be distorted by efforts to make a favorable or unfavorable impression. In addition to providing accurate measurements of problem behavior, behavioral observation can suggest strategies for intervention. A mother might report that her son is so hyperactive he cannot sit still long enough to complete homework assignments. By using a one-way mirror, the clinician may discover the boy becomes restless only when he encounters a problem he cannot solve right away. The child may thus be helped by being taught ways of coping with frustration and of solving certain kinds of academic problems.

Direct observation also has its drawbacks. One issue is the possible lack of consensus in defining problems in behavioral terms. In coding the child's behavior for hyperactivity, clinicians must agree on which aspects of the child's behavior represent hyperactivity. Another potential problem is a lack of reliability, or inconsistency, of measurement across time or between observers. Reliability is reduced when an observer is inconsistent in the coding of specific behaviors or when two or more observers code behavior inconsistently.

Observers may also show response biases. An observer who has been sensitized to expect that a child is hyperactive may perceive normal variations in behavior as subtle cues of hyperactivity and erroneously record them as instances of hyperactive behavior. Such expectations are less likely to affect behavioral ratings when the target behaviors are defined concretely (S. L. Foster & Cone, 1986).

Reactivity is another potential problem. Reactivity refers to the tendency for the behavior being observed to be influenced by the way in which it is measured. With respect to behavioral observation, people may put their best feet forward when they know they are being observed. Using covert observation techniques, such as hidden cameras or one-way mirrors, may reduce reactivity. Covert observation may not be feasible, however, because of ethical concerns or practical constraints. Another approach is to accustom subjects to observation by watching them a number of times before collecting data. Another potential problem is *observer drift*—the tendency of observers, or groups of raters, to deviate from the coding

reactivity The tendency for the behavior being observed to be influenced by the way in which it is measured.

system in which they were trained as time elapses. One suggestion to help control this problem is to regularly retrain observers to ensure continued compliance with the coding system (Kazdin, 1992). As time elapses, observers may also become fatigued or distracted. It may be helpful to limit the duration of observations and to provide frequent breaks.

Behavioral observation is limited to measuring overt behaviors. Many clinicians also wish to assess subjective or private experiences—for example, feelings of depression and anxiety or distorted thought patterns. Such clinicians may combine direct observation with forms of assessment that permit clients to reveal internal experiences. Staunch behavioral clinicians tend to consider self-reports unreliable and to limit their data to direct observation.

In addition to behavioral interviews and direct observation, behavioral assessment may involve the use of other techniques, such as self-monitoring, contrived or analogue measures, and behavioral rating scales.

Self-Monitoring Training clients to record or monitor the problem behavior in their daily lives is another method of relating problem behavior to the settings in which it occurs. In **self-monitoring,** clients assume the responsibility for assessing the problem behavior in the settings in which it naturally occurs (Cone, 1999; Korotitsch & Nelson-Gray, 1999).

Self-monitoring permits direct measurement of the problem behavior when and where it occurs. Behaviors that can be easily counted, such as food intake, cigarette smoking, nail biting, hair pulling, study periods, or social activities are well suited for self-monitoring. Clients are usually best aware of the frequency of these behaviors and their situational contexts. Self-monitoring can also produce highly accurate measurement, because the behavior is recorded as it occurs, not reconstructed from memory.

There are various devices for keeping track of the targeted behavior. A behavioral diary or log is a handy way to record calories ingested or cigarettes smoked. Such logs are organized in columns and rows to track the frequency of occurrence of the problem behavior and the situations in which it occurs (time, setting, feeling state, etc.). A record of eating may include entries for the type of food eaten, the number of calories, the location in which the eating occurred, the feeling states associated with eating, and the consequences of eating (e.g., how the client felt afterward). In reviewing an eating diary with the clinician, a client can identify problematic eating patterns, such as eating when feeling bored or in response to TV food commercials, and devise better ways of handling these cues.

Behavioral diaries can also help clients increase desirable but low-frequency behaviors, such as assertive behavior and dating behavior. Unassertive clients might track occasions that seem to warrant an assertive response and jot down their actual responses to each occasion. Clients and clinicians then review the log to highlight problematic situations and rehearse assertive responses. A client who is anxious about dating might record social contacts with the opposite gender. To measure the effects of treatment, clinicians may encourage clients to engage in a baseline period of self-monitoring before treatment is begun.

Self-monitoring, though, is not without its disadvantages. Some clients are unreliable and do not keep accurate records. They become forgetful or sloppy, or they underreport undesirable behaviors, such as overeating or smoking, because of embarrassment or fear of criticism. To offset these biases, clinicians may, with clients' consent, corroborate the accuracy of self-monitoring by gathering information from other parties, such as clients' spouses. Private behaviors such as eating or smoking alone cannot be corroborated in this way, however. Sometimes other means of corroboration, such as physiological measures, are available (Jackson, 1999). For example, blood alcohol levels can be used to verify self-reports of alcohol use, or analysis of carbon monoxide levels in clients' breath samples can be used to corroborate reports of abstinence from smoking.

Another issue in self-monitoring is reactivity (Korotitsch & Nelson-Gray, 1999). Some clients may change undesirable behaviors merely as a consequence of focusing on them or recording them. When reactivity leads to more adaptive behavior, it renders the measurement process an effective therapeutic tool, although it can make it difficult to tease out the effects due to measurement from those due to treatment.

self-monitoring The process of observing or recording one's own behaviors, thoughts, or emotions.

Behavioral approach task. One form of behavioral assessment of phobia involves measurement of the degree to which the person can approach or interact with the phobic stimulus. Here we see a woman with a snake phobia tentatively reaching out to touch the phobic object. Other people with snake phobias would not be able to touch the snake or even remain in its presence unless it was securely caged.

Truth OR Fiction? REVISITED

Weight-loss program participants who were more conscientious about monitoring what they ate lost more weight than those who were less reliable monitors.

TRUE. Investigators found that the more consistently weight-loss program participants monitored what they ate, the more weight they lost.

analogue measure A measure taken in a contrived situation meant to simulate a real-life situation.

behavioral rating scale A scale used to record the frequency of occurrence of target behaviors.

Self-monitoring may actually be an important, perhaps even necessary feature of some behavior change programs, such as weight-management programs. In one study, the more consistently participants monitored what they ate, the more weight they lost (Baker & Kirschenbaum, 1993). This is not to imply that self-monitoring alone is sufficient to produce a desired behavior change. Motivation to change and skills needed to make behavior changes are also important.

Analogue Measures **Analogue measures** are intended to simulate the setting in which the behavior naturally takes place but are carried out in laboratory or controlled settings. Role-playing exercises are common analogue measures. Clinicians cannot follow clients who have difficulty expressing dissatisfaction to authority figures throughout the day. Instead, clinicians may rely on role-playing exercises, such as having the clients enact challenging an unfair grade. A scene might be described to the client as follows: "You've worked very hard on a term paper and received a very poor grade, say a D or an F. You approach the professor, who asks, 'Is there some problem?' What do you do now?" The client's enactment of the scene may reveal deficits in self-expression that can be addressed in therapy or assertiveness training.

The Behavioral Approach Task, or BAT (Lang & Lazovik, 1963), is a popular analogue measure of a phobic person's approach to a feared object, such as a snake. Approach behavior is broken down into levels of response, such as looking in the direction of the snake from about 20 feet, touching the box holding the snake, and touching the snake. The BAT provides direct measurement of a response to a stimulus in a controlled situation. The subject's approach behavior can be quantified by assigning a score to each level of approach.

Behavioral Rating Scales A **behavioral rating scale** is a checklist that provides information about the frequency, intensity, and range of problem behaviors. Behavioral rating scales differ from self-report personality inventories, in that items assess specific behaviors rather than personality characteristics, interests, or attitudes.

Behavioral rating scales are often used by parents to assess children's problem behaviors. The Child Behavior Problem Checklist (CBCL) (Achenbach, 1978; Achenbach & Edelbrock, 1979), for example, asks parents to rate their children on more than 100 specific problem behaviors, including the following:

____ refuses to eat
____ is disobedient
____ hits
____ is uncooperative
____ destroys own things

The scale yields an overall problem behavior score and subscale scores on dimensions such as delinquency, aggressiveness, and physical problems. The clinician can compare the child's score on these dimensions with norms based on samples of age-mates.

Cognitive Assessment

Cognitive assessment involves the measurement of *cognitions*—thoughts, beliefs, and attitudes. Cognitive therapists believe that people who hold self-defeating or dysfunctional cognitions are at greater risk of developing emotional problems, such as depression, in the face of stressful or disappointing life experiences. They help clients replace dysfunctional thinking patterns with self-enhancing, rational thought patterns.

Several methods of cognitive assessment have been developed. One of the most straightforward is the thought record or diary. Depressed clients may carry such diaries to record dysfunctional thoughts as they arise. Aaron Beck (A. T. Beck et al.,

1979) designed a thought diary or "Daily Record of Dysfunctional Thoughts" to help clients identify thought patterns connected with troubling emotional states. Each time the client experiences a negative emotion such as anger or sadness, entries are made to identify

1. The situation in which the emotional state occurred,

2. The automatic or disruptive thoughts that passed through the client's mind,

3. The type or category of disordered thinking that the automatic thought(s) represented (e.g., selective abstraction, overgeneralization, magnification, or absolutist thinking—see Chapter 2),

4. A rational response to the troublesome thought,

5. The emotional outcome or final emotional response.

A thought diary can become part of a treatment program in which the client learns to replace dysfunctional thoughts with rational alternative thoughts.

The Automatic Thoughts Questionnaire (ATQ-30; Hollon & Kendall, 1980) has clients rate the weekly frequency and degree of conviction associated with 30 automatic negative thoughts. (Automatic thoughts are thoughts that seem to just pop into our minds.) Sample items include the following:

> I don't think I can go on.
> I hate myself.
> I've let people down.

A total score is obtained by summing the frequencies of occurrence of each item. Higher scores are considered typical of depressive thought patterns. The scale discriminates between depressed and nondepressed subjects, and higher scores are indicative of more severe depressive symptoms (Blankstein & Segal, 2001). The 30-item ATQ has been statistically sorted into four categories or factors of related thoughts (see Table 3.10).

Another cognitive measure, the Dysfunctional Attitudes Scale (DAS; A. N. Weissman & Beck, 1978), consists of an inventory of a relatively stable set of underlying attitudes or assumptions associated with depression (Blankstein & Segal, 2001). Examples include "I

TABLE 3.10 Items Defining Factors on the Automatic Thoughts Questionnaire

Factor 1: Personal Maladjustment and Desire for Change	Something has to change. What's the matter with me? I wish I were a better person. What's wrong with me? I'm so disappointed in myself.
Factor 2: Negative Self-Concept and Negative Expectations	My future is bleak. I'm a failure. I'll never make it. My life's not going the way I wanted it to. I'm a loser. Why can't I ever succeed? I'm no good.
Factor 3: Low Self-Esteem	I'm worthless. I hate myself.
Factor 4: Giving Up/Helplessness	I can't finish anything. It's just not worth it.

Source. Adapted from Hollon & Kendall (1980).

galvanic skin response (GSR) A measure of the change in electrical activity of the skin that accompanies sympathetic nervous system arousal.

electroencephalograph (EEG) An instrument for measuring the electrical activity of the brain.

electromyograph (EMG) An instrument for measuring muscle tension.

computed tomography (CT scan) Computer-enhanced imaging of the internal structures of the brain by passing a narrow X-ray beam through the head.

Truth OR Fiction? REVISITED

Despite advances in technology, physicians today still need to perform surgery to study the workings of the brain.

FALSE. Advances in brain-imaging techniques make it possible to observe the workings of the brain without invasive surgery.

FIGURE 3.7 The Electroencephalograph (EEG). The EEG can be used to study differences in brain waves between groups of normal people and people with problems such as schizophrenia or organic brain damage.

feel like I'm nothing if someone I love doesn't love me back." Subjects use a 7-point scale to rate the degree to which they endorse each belief. The DAS taps underlying assumptions believed to predispose individuals to depression, so it may be sensitive to detecting vulnerability to depression (DeRubeis, Tang, & Beck, 2001; Ingram, Miranda, & Segal, 1998). However, some evidence indicates that the DAS may actually measure depression itself, rather than vulnerability to depression (Calhoon, 1996). Whatever the case, it clearly taps into a style of thinking associated with depression.

Cognitive assessment opens a new domain to the psychologist in understanding how disruptive thoughts are related to abnormal behavior. Only in the past two decades or so have cognitive and cognitive-behavioral therapists begun to explore what B. F. Skinner labeled the "black box"—people's internal states—to learn how thoughts and attitudes influence emotional states and behavior.

The behavioral objection to cognitive techniques is that clinicians have no direct means of verifying clients' subjective experiences, their thoughts and beliefs. These are private experiences that can be reported but not observed and measured directly. Even though thoughts remain private experiences, reports of cognitions in the form of rating scales or checklists can be quantified and validated by reference to external criteria.

Physiological Measurement

We can also learn about abnormal behavior by studying people's physiological responses. Anxiety, for example, is associated with arousal of the sympathetic division of the autonomic nervous system (see Chapter 2). Anxious people therefore show elevated heart rates and blood pressure, which can be measured directly by means of the pulse and a blood pressure cuff. People also sweat more heavily when they are anxious. When we sweat, our skin becomes wet, increasing its ability to conduct electricity. Sweating can be measured by means of the *electrodermal response* or **galvanic skin response** (GSR). (*Galvanic* is named after the Italian physicist and physician, Luigi Galvani, who was a pioneer in research in electricity.) Measures of the GSR assess the amount of electricity that passes through two points on the skin, usually of the hand. We assume the person's anxiety level correlates with the amount of electricity conducted across the skin.

The GSR is just one example of a physiological response measured through probes or sensors connected to the body. Another example is the **electroencephalograph** (EEG), which measures brain waves by attaching electrodes to the scalp (Figure 3.7).

Changes in muscle tension are also often associated with states of anxiety or tension. They can be detected through the **electromyograph** (EMG), which monitors muscle tension through sensors attached to targeted muscle groups. (*Myo-* derives from the Greek *mys*, meaning "mouse" or "muscle." The Greeks observed that muscles moved mouselike beneath the skin.) Placement of EMG probes on the forehead can indicate muscle tension associated with tension headaches.

Brain-Imaging and Recording Techniques Advances in medical technology have made it possible to study the workings of the brain without the need for surgery. One of the most common is the electroencephalograph (EEG), which is a record of the electrical activity of the brain. The EEG detects minute amounts of electrical activity in the brain, or brain waves, that are conducted between electrodes. Certain brain wave patterns are associated with mental states such as relaxation and with the different stages of sleep. The EEG is used to examine brain wave patterns associated with psychological disorders, such as schizophrenia, and with brain damage. It is also used to study various abnormal behavior patterns. The EEG is also used by medical personnel to reveal brain abnormalities such as tumors.

Brain-imaging techniques generate images that reflect the structure and functioning of the brain. In **computed tomography** (CT scan), a narrow X-ray beam is aimed at the head (Figure 3.8). The radiation that passes through is measured from multiple angles. The CT scan (also called CAT scan for *comp-*

uterized axial tomography) reveals abnormalities in shape and structure that may be suggestive of lesions, blood clots, or tumors. The computer enables scientists to integrate the measurements into a three-dimensional picture of the brain. Evidence of brain damage that was once detectable only by surgery may now be displayed on a monitor.

Another imaging method, **positron emission tomography (PET scan),** is used to study the functioning of various parts of the brain (Figure 3.9). In this method, a small amount of a radioactive compound or tracer is mixed with glucose and injected into the bloodstream. When it reaches the brain, patterns of neural activity are revealed by measurement of the positrons—positively charged particles—emitted by the tracer. The glucose metabolized by parts of the brain generates a computer image of neural activity. Areas of greater activity metabolize more glucose. The PET scan has been used to learn which parts of the brain are most active (metabolize more glucose) when we are listening to music, solving a math problem, or using language. It can also be used to reveal differences in brain activity in people with schizophrenia (see Chapter 13).

A third imaging technique is **magnetic resonance imaging (MRI).** In MRI, the person is placed in a donut-shaped tunnel that generates a strong magnetic field. Radio waves of certain frequencies are directed at the head. As a result, parts of the brain emit signals that can be measured from several angles. As with the CT scan, the signals are integrated into a computer-generated image of the brain, which can be used to investigate brain abnormalities associated with schizophrenia (see Chapter 13) and other disorders, such as obsessive-compulsive disorder. A new type of MRI, called **functional magnetic resonance imaging (fMRI),** is used to identify parts of the brain that become active when people engage in particular tasks, such as vision, memory, or use of speech (Carpenter, 2000; Ingram & Siegle, 2001; Stern & Silbersweig, 2001) (see Figure 3.10). A recent fMRI study showed that when cocaine-addicted subjects experienced cocaine cravings, they showed greater activity than healthy subjects did in parts of the brain that were engaged when healthy subjects watched depressing videotapes (Wexler et al., 2001). This suggests there may be a physiological link between depressive feelings and drug cravings.

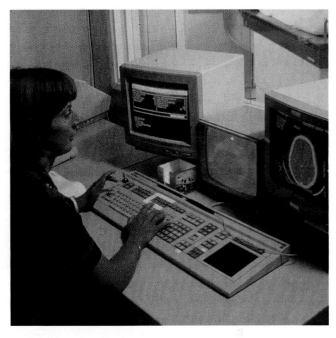

FIGURE 3.8 The Computed Tomography (CT) Scan. The CT scan aims a narrow X-ray beam at the head, and the resultant radiation is measured from multiple angles as it passes through. The computer enables researchers to consolidate the measurements into a three-dimensional image of the brain. The CT scan reveals structural abnormalities in the brain that may be implicated in various patterns of abnormal behavior.

positron emission tomography (PET scan) An imaging technique that forms a computer-generated image by tracing the amount of glucose used in various regions of the brain.

magnetic resonance imaging (MRI) A computer-generated image of the brain formed by measuring the signals emitted when the head is placed in a strong magnetic field.

functional magnetic resonance imaging (fMRI) Type of MRI used to identify parts of the brain that become active when people engage in particular tasks.

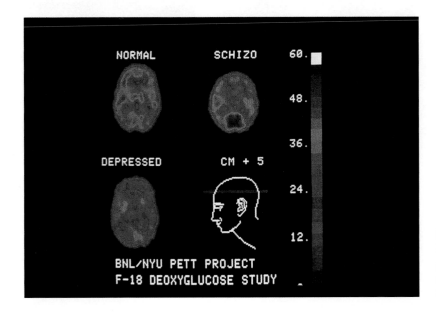

FIGURE 3.9 Positron Emission Tomography (PET) Scan. These PET scan images suggest differences in the metabolic processes of the brains of people with depression, schizophrenia, and controls who are free of psychological disorders.

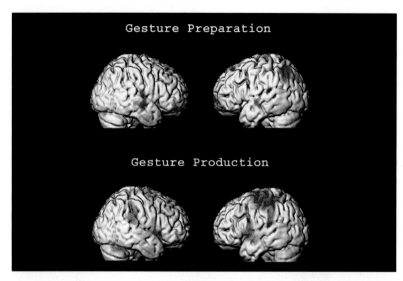

FIGURE 3.10 **Functional Magnetic Resonance Imaging (fMRI).** A fMRI is a specialized type of MRI that allows investigators to determine the parts of the brain that are activated during particular tasks. The areas depicted in red become activated when a person thinks about performing certain gestures (top), such as using a hammer or writing with a pen, and when the person actually performs these gestures (bottom). The right hemisphere is shown on the left side of the photographs and the left hemisphere is shown on the right side.

brain electrical activity mapping (BEAM) Imaging technique involving computer analysis of data from multiple electrodes to reveal areas of the brain with relatively high or low levels of activity.

Brain electrical activity mapping (BEAM), a sophisticated type of EEG, uses the computer to analyze brain wave patterns and reveal areas of relative activity and inactivity from moment to moment (Figure 3.11) (F. H. Duffy, 1994; Silberstein et al., 1998). Twenty or more electrodes are attached to the scalp and simultaneously feed information about brain activity to a computer. The computer analyzes the signals and displays the pattern of brain activity on a color monitor, providing a vivid image of the electrical activity of the brain at work. BEAM and other similar techniques have been helpful in studying the brain activity of people with schizophrenia and children with attention-deficit hyperactivity disorder, among other physical and psychological disorders. In later chapters we see how modern imaging techniques are furthering our understanding of various patterns of abnormal behavior.

In conclusion, people's psychological problems, which are no less complex than people themselves, are thus assessed in many ways. Clients are generally asked to explain their problems as best they can, and sometimes a computer does the asking. Psychologists can also draw on batteries of tests that assess intelligence, personality, and neuropsychological integrity. Many psychologists prefer to observe people's behavior directly. Modern technology has provided several means of studying the structure and function of the brain. The methods of assessment selected by clinicians reflect the problems of their clients, their theoretical orientations, and their mastery of specialized technologies.

THINK ABOUT IT

Jamie complains of feeling depressed since the death of her brother in a car accident last year. What methods of assessment might a psychologist use to evaluate her mental condition?

Web Link **3.6** wWw
The Basics of Brain Imaging

Quiz **3.3**
Methods of Assessment

Quiz **3.4**
Chapter Exam

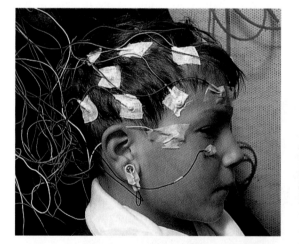

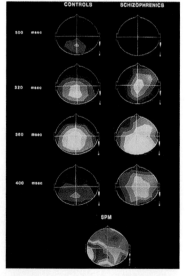

FIGURE 3.11 **Brain Electrical Activity Mapping (BEAM).** BEAM is a type of EEG in which electrodes are attached to the scalp (Part A) to measure electrical activity in various regions of the brain. The left column of Part B shows the average level of electrical activity in the brains of 10 normal people ("controls") at 4 time intervals. The column to the right shows the average level of activity of subjects with schizophrenia during the same intervals. Higher activity levels are represented in increasing order by yellows, reds, and whites. The computer-generated image in the bottom center summarizes differences in activity levels between the brains of normal subjects and those with schizophrenia. Areas of the brain depicted in blue show small differences between the groups. White areas represent larger differences.

Summing Up

Classification of Abnormal Behavior Patterns

What is the DSM and what are its major features? The *Diagnostic and Statistical Manual of Mental Disorders (DSM)* is the most widely accepted system for classifying mental disorders. The *DSM* uses specific diagnostic criteria to group patterns of abnormal behaviors that share common clinical features and a multiaxial system of evaluation.

Why is the DSM considered a multiaxial system? The *DSM* system consists of five axes of classification: Axis I (Clinical Syndromes), Axis II (Personality Disorders and Mental Retardation), Axis III (General Medical Conditions), Axis IV (Psychosocial and Environmental Problems), and Axis V (Global Assessment of Functioning).

What are the major strengths and weaknesses of the DSM? Strengths of the *DSM* include its use of specified diagnostic criteria and a multiaxial system to provide a comprehensive picture of the person's functioning. Weaknesses include questions about reliability and validity of certain diagnostic categories, and to some, the adoption of a medical model framework for classifying abnormal behavior patterns.

Issues of Reliability and Validity in Assessment

What are the standards by which methods of assessment are judged? Methods of assessment must be reliable and valid. Reliability of assessment techniques is shown in various ways, including internal consistency, temporal stability, and interrater reliability. Validity is measured by means of content validity, criterion validity, and construct validity.

Why is it important to take cultural or ethnic factors into account in psychological assessment? We need to ensure that tests that are validated in one culture are reliable and valid when used with members of another culture.

Methods of Assessment

What is a clinical interview? A clinical interview involves the use of a set of questions designed to elicit relevant information from people seeking treatment.

What are the three major types of clinical interviews? The three major types of clinical interviews are unstructured interviews (clinicians use their own style of questioning rather than follow a particular script), semi-structured interviews (clinicians follow a general outline in directing their questioning but are free to branch off in other directions), and structured interviews (clinicians strictly follow a preset order of questions).

What are psychological tests? Psychological tests are structured methods of assessment used to evaluate reasonably stable traits such as intelligence and personality.

What are the major types of psychological tests? Tests of intelligence, such as the Stanford-Binet Intelligence Scale and the Wechsler scales, are used for various purposes in clinical assessment, including determining evidence of mental retardation or cognitive impairment, and assessing strengths and weaknesses. Self-report personality inventories, such as the MMPI, use structured items to measure psychological characteristics or traits, such as anxiety, depression, and masculinity-femininity. These tests are considered objective in the sense that they make use of a limited range of possible responses to items and are based on an empirical, or objective, method of test construction. Projective personality tests, such as the Rorschach and TAT, require subjects to interpret ambiguous stimuli in the belief their answers may shed light on their unconscious processes.

What is neuropsychological assessment? Neuropsychological assessment involves the use of psychological tests to indicate possible neurological impairment or brain defects. The Halstead-Reitan Neuropsychological Battery and Luria Nebraska Test Battery measure perceptual skills, cognitive skills, and motor skills and performance that relate to specific areas of brain function.

What are some of the methods used in behavioral assessment? In behavioral assessment, test responses are taken as samples of behavior rather than as signs of underlying traits or dispositions. The behavioral examiner may conduct a functional assessment, which relates the problem behavior to its antecedents and consequents. Methods of behavioral assessment include behavioral interviewing, self-monitoring, use of analogue or contrived measures, direct observation, and behavioral rating scales.

What is cognitive assessment? Cognitive assessment focuses on the measurement of thoughts, beliefs, and attitudes in order to help identify distorted thinking patterns. Specific methods of assessment include the use of a thought record or diary and the use of rating scales such as the Automatic Thoughts Questionnaire (ATQ) and the Dysfunctional Attitudes Scale (DAS).

How do clinicians and researchers study physiological functioning? Measures of physiological functioning include heart rate, blood pressure, galvanic skin response (GSR), muscle tension, and brain wave activity. Brain-imaging and recording techniques such as EEG, CT scans, PET scans, MRI, and BEAM probe the inner workings and structures of the brain.

CHAPTER FOUR

Methods of Treatment

Paul Klee
Variation II

Truth OR Fiction?

- Some psychologists have been trained to prescribe drugs. (p. 98)

- In classical psychoanalysis, you are asked to express whatever thought happens to come to mind, no matter how seemingly trivial or silly. (p. 101)

- More psychotherapists identify with an eclectic approach than with any specific school of therapy. (p. 110)

- The average client who receives psychotherapy is no better off than control clients who go without it. (p. 113)

- Despite beliefs that it is a wonder drug, the antidepressant Prozac has not been shown to be more effective than the earlier generation of antidepressants. (p. 119)

- Severely depressed people who have failed to respond to other treatments may show rapid improvement from electroconvulsive therapy. (p. 121)

arla, a 19-year-old college sophomore, had been crying more or less continuously for several days. She felt that her life was falling apart, that her college aspirations were in a shambles, and that she was a disappointment to her parents. The thought of suicide had crossed her mind. She could not seem to drag herself out of bed in the morning and had withdrawn from her friends. Her misery had seemed to descend on her from nowhere, although she could pinpoint some pressures in her life: a couple of poor grades, a recent breakup with a boyfriend, some adjustment problems with roommates.

The psychologist who examined her arrived at a diagnosis of major depressive disorder. Had she broken her leg, her treatment from a qualified professional would have followed a fairly standard course. Yet the treatment that Carla or someone else with a psychological disorder receives is likely to vary not only with the type of disorder involved but also with the therapeutic orientation and professional background of the helping professional. A psychiatrist might recommend a course of antidepressant medication, perhaps in combination with some form of psychotherapy. A cognitively oriented psychologist might suggest a program of cognitive therapy to help Carla identify dysfunctional thoughts that may underlie her depression, whereas a psychodynamic therapist might recommend she begin therapy to uncover inner conflicts originating in childhood that may lie at the root of her depression.

In this chapter we focus on ways of treating psychological disorders. About one out of every seven people in the United States receives some form of mental health treatment in a given year (USDHHS, 1999a). In later chapters we examine the kinds of treatment approaches applied to particular disorders, but here we focus on the treatments themselves. We will see that the biological and psychological perspectives have spawned corresponding approaches to treatment. First, however, we consider the major types of mental health professionals who treat psychological or mental disorders and the different roles they play.

Types of Mental Health Professionals

Many people are confused about the differences in qualifications and training of the various types of mental health providers (Farberman, 1997). It is little wonder people are confused, as there exist many different types of mental health professionals who represent a wide range of training backgrounds and areas of practice. The major professional groupings of mental health professionals include psychologists, psychiatrists, social workers, nurses, and counselors (see Table 4.1). Unfortunately, many states do not limit the use of the titles *therapist* or *psychotherapist* to trained professionals. In such states, anyone can set up shop as a psychotherapist and practice "therapy" without a license. Thus, people seeking help are advised to inquire about the training and licensure of helping professionals. If you or someone you know should seek the services of a psychologist, how would you find one? The nearby "A Closer Look" feature, "How Do I Find a Psychologist?" offers some suggestions.

Another reason for confusion is that all different types of mental health providers, such as psychologists, psychiatrists, and clinical social workers, practice psychotherapy, or "talk therapy"—a psychologically based method of treatment involving a series of verbal interchanges between clients and therapists taking place over a period of time, usually on a one-session-per-week basis. The particular approach used by psychotherapists reflects their theoretical orientation, such as psychodynamic, behavioral, humanistic, cognitive, and so on. Some therapists adopt an eclectic orientation, which means they draw on the theories and techniques espoused by two or more theoretical orientations.

We now consider the major types of psychotherapy and their relationships to the theoretical models from which they derive.

Psychotherapy

Psychotherapy is a systematic interaction between a client and a therapist that incorporates psychological principles to help bring about changes in the client's behaviors,

psychotherapy A structured form of treatment derived from a psychological framework which consists of one or more verbal interactions or treatment sessions between a client and a therapist.

TABLE 4.1 Major Types of Mental Health Professionals

Type	Description
Clinical Psychologists	Have earned a doctoral degree in psychology (either a Ph.D., or Doctor of Philosophy, a Psy.D., or Doctor of Psychology, or an Ed.D., Doctor of Education) from an accredited college or university. Training in clinical psychology typically involves 4 years of graduate coursework, followed by a year-long internship and completion of a doctoral dissertation. Clinical psychologists specialize in administering psychological tests, diagnosing psychological disorders, and practicing psychotherapy. Psychologists cannot prescribe psychiatric drugs, except for a handful of specially trained psychologists within a special government program (Sammons & Brown, 1997; Seppa, 1997). The granting of prescription privileges to psychologists remains a hotly contested issue between psychologists and psychiatrists and within the field of psychology itself (for example, see Foxhall, 2000a, 2000b, and Gutierrez & Silk, 1998).
Counseling Psychologists	Also hold doctoral degrees in psychology and have completed graduate training preparing them for careers in college counseling centers and mental health facilities. They typically provide counseling to people with psychological problems falling in a milder range of severity than those treated by clinical psychologists, such as difficulties adjusting to college or uncertainties regarding career choices.
Psychiatrists	Have earned a medical degree (M.D.) and completed a residency program in psychiatry. Psychiatrists are physicians who specialize in the diagnosis and treatment of psychological disorders. As licensed physicians, they can prescribe psychiatric drugs and may employ other medical interventions, such as electroconvulsive therapy (ECT). Many also practice psychotherapy based on training they receive during their residency programs or in specialized training institutes.
Clinical or Psychiatric Social Workers	Have earned a master's degree in social work (M.S.W.) and use their knowledge of community agencies and organizations to help people with severe mental disorders receive the services they need. For example, they may help people with schizophrenia make a more successful adjustment to the community once they leave the hospital. Many clinical social workers practice psychotherapy or specific forms of therapy, such as marital or family therapy.
Psychoanalysts	Typically are either psychiatrists or psychologists who have completed extensive additional training in psychoanalysis. They are required to undergo psychoanalysis themselves as part of their training.
Counselors	Have typically earned a master's degree by completing a graduate program in a counseling field. Counselors work in many settings, including public schools, college testing and counseling centers, and hospitals and health clinics. Many specialize in vocational evaluation, marital or family therapy, rehabilitation counseling, or substance abuse counseling. Counselors may focus on providing psychological assistance to people with milder forms of disturbed behavior or those struggling with a chronic or debilitating illness or recovering from a traumatic experience. Some are clergy members who are trained in pastoral counseling programs to help parishioners cope with personal problems.
Psychiatric Nurses	Typically are R.N.s who have completed a master's program in psychiatric nursing. They may work in a psychiatric facility or in a group medical practice where they treat people suffering from severe psychological disorders.

Source. Adapted from Nevid, J. S. (2003). *Psychology: Concepts & applications.* Boston: Houghton Mifflin.

Truth OR Fiction? REVISITED

Some psychologists have been trained to prescribe drugs.

TRUE. Some psychologists have been trained in an experimental program to prescribe psychotropic medications.

THINK ABOUT IT

What are the major types of mental health professionals? How do they differ in their training and the types of roles they perform?

thoughts, and feelings in order to help the client overcome abnormal behavior, solve problems in living, or develop as an individual. Let us take a closer look at these features of psychotherapy:

1. *Systematic interaction.* The process of psychotherapy involves systematic interactions between clients and therapists. "Systematic" means that therapists structure these interactions with plans and purposes that reflect their theoretical points of view.

2. *Psychological principles.* Psychotherapists draw on psychological principles, research, and theory in their practice.

3. *Behavior, thoughts, and feelings.* Psychotherapy may be directed at behavioral, cognitive, and emotional domains to help clients overcome psychological problems and lead more satisfying lives.

4. *Abnormal behavior, problem solving, and personal growth.* At least three groups of people are assisted by psychotherapy. First are people with abnormal behavior problems such as mood disorders, anxiety disorders, or schizophrenia. Second are people who seek help for personal problems that are not regarded as abnormal, such as social shyness or confusion about career choices. Third are people who seek personal

A Closer Look

How Do I Find a Psychologist?

 To find a psychologist, ask your physician or another health professional. Call your local or state psychological association. Consult a local university or college department of psychology. Ask family and friends. Contact your area community mental health center. Inquire at your church or synagogue.

What to Consider When Making the Choice . . .

Psychologists and clients work together. The right match is important. Most psychologists agree that an important factor in determining whether or not to work with a particular psychologist, once that psychologist's credentials and competence are established, is your level of personal comfort with that psychologist. A good rapport with your psychologist is critical. Choose a psychologist with whom you feel comfortable and at ease.

Questions to Ask . . .

- Are you a licensed psychologist? How many years have you been practicing psychology?
- I have been feeling (anxious, tense, depressed, etc.), and I'm having problems (with my job, my marriage, eating, sleeping, etc.). What experience do you have helping people with these types of problems?
- What are your areas of expertise—for example, working with children and families?
- What kinds of treatments do you use, and have they been proven effective for dealing with my kind of problem or issue?
- What are your fees? (Fees are usually based on a 45- to 50-minute session.) Do you have a sliding-scale fee policy? How much therapy would you recommend?
- What types of insurance do you accept? Will you accept direct billing to/payment from my insurance company? Are you affiliated with any managed care organizations? Do you accept Medicare/Medicaid insurance?

Finances . . .

Many insurance companies provide coverage for mental health services. If you have private health insurance coverage (typically through an em-

ployer), check with your insurance company to see whether mental health services are covered and, if so, how you may obtain these benefits. This also applies to persons enrolled in HMOs and other types of managed care plans. Find out how much the insurance company will reimburse for mental health services and what limitations on the use of benefits may apply.

If you are not covered by a private health insurance plan or employee assistance program, you may decide to pay for psychological services out of pocket. Some psychologists operate on a sliding-scale fee policy, where the amount you pay depends on your income.

Another potential source of mental health services involves government-sponsored health care programs—including Medicare for individuals age 65 or older, as well as health insurance plans for government employees, military personnel, and their dependents. Community mental health centers throughout the country are another possible alternative for receiving mental health services. And some state Medicaid programs for economically disadvantaged individuals provide for limited mental health services from psychologists.

Credentials to Look For . . .

After graduation from college, psychologists spend an average of seven years in graduate education training and research before receiving a doctoral degree. As part of their professional training, they must complete a supervised clinical internship in a hospital or organized health setting and at least one year of postdoctoral supervised experience before they can practice independently in any health-care arena. It's this combination of doctoral-level training and clinical internship that distinguishes psychologists from many other mental health care providers.

Psychologists must be licensed by the state or jurisdiction in which they practice. Licensure laws are intended to protect the public by limiting licensure to those persons qualified to practice psychology as defined by state law. In most states, renewal of this license depends upon the demonstration of continued competence and requires continuing education. In addition, members of the American Psychological Association (APA) adhere to a strict code of professional ethics.

Source. Copyright © 1995 by the American Psychological Association. Reprinted with permission.

growth. For them, psychotherapy is a means of self-discovery that may help them reach their potentials as, for example, parents, creative artists, performers, or athletes.

Psychotherapies share other features as well. For one, psychotherapies involve verbal interactions. Psychotherapies are "talking therapies," forms of interchange between clients and therapists that involve talking or conversation. In some cases, there is much discussion between clients and therapists. In others, such as traditional psychoanalysis, clients do most of the talking. In each case, skillful therapists are attentive listeners. Attentive listening is an

wWw **Web Link 4.1**
Overview of Psychotherapy

The therapeutic relationship. In the course of successful psychotherapy, a therapeutic relationship is forged between the therapist and patient. Therapists use attentive listening to understand as clearly as possible what the client is experiencing and attempting to convey. Skillful therapists are also sensitive to clients' nonverbal cues, such as gestures and posture, that may indicate underlying feelings or conflicts.

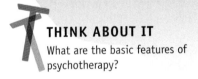

THINK ABOUT IT

What are the basic features of psychotherapy?

psychoanalysis The method of psychotherapy developed by Sigmund Freud.

psychodynamic therapy Therapy that helps individuals gain insight into, and resolve, unconscious conflicts.

active, not a passive, activity. Therapists listen carefully to what clients are saying in order to understand as clearly as possible what they are experiencing and attempting to convey. Skillful therapists are also sensitive to clients' nonverbal cues, such as gestures that may indicate underlying feelings or conflicts. Therapists also seek to convey empathy through words as well as nonverbal gestures, such as establishing eye contact and leaning forward to indicate interest in what the client is saying. Therapist empathy is a consistent predictor of therapy outcome. Clients of therapists who are perceived as warmer and more empathic show greater improvement than clients of other therapists, whether the therapists are psychodynamic (Luborsky et al., 1988) or cognitive-behavioral (Burns & Nolen-Hoeksema, 1992) in their therapeutic approach.

Another common feature of psychotherapies is the instilling in clients of a sense of hope of improvement. Clients generally enter therapy with expectations of receiving help to overcome their problems. Responsible therapists do not promise results or guarantee cures. They do instill hope, however, that they can help clients deal with their problems. Positive expectancies can become a type of self-fulfilling prophecy by leading clients to mobilize their efforts toward overcoming their problems. Responses to positive expectancies are termed *placebo effects* or *expectancy effects.*

The common features of psychotherapy that are not specific to any one form of therapy, such as the encouragement of hope and the display of empathy and attentiveness on the part of the therapist, are often referred to as *nonspecific treatment factors.* Nonspecific factors may have therapeutic benefits in addition to the specific benefits of particular forms of therapy. We will discuss these factors in greater detail in the section on Evaluating Methods of Treatment.

Psychodynamic Therapy

Sigmund Freud was the first theorist to develop a psychological model—the *psychodynamic model*—of abnormal behavior (see Chapter 2). He was also the first to develop a model of psychotherapy, which he called **psychoanalysis,** to help people who suffered from psychological disorders. Psychoanalysis was the first **psychodynamic therapy.** Psychodynamic therapy helps individuals gain insight into, and resolve, the unconscious conflicts believed to lie at the root of abnormal behavior. Working through these conflicts, the ego would be freed of the need to maintain defensive behaviors—such as phobias, obsessive-compulsive behaviors, hysterical complaints, and the like—that shield it from recognition of inner turmoil.

Freud summed up the goal of psychoanalysis by saying, "Where id was, there shall ego be." This meant, in part, that psychoanalysis could help shed the light of awareness, represented by the conscious ego, on the inner workings of the id. But Freud did not expect, or intend, that clients should seek to become conscious of all repressed material—of all their impulses, wishes, fears, and memories. The aim, rather, was to replace defensive behavior with more adaptive behavior. By so doing, clients could find gratification without incurring social or self-condemnation.

Through this process a man with a phobia of knives might become aware he had been repressing impulses to vent a murderous rage against his father. His phobia keeps him from having contact with knives, thereby serving a hidden purpose of keeping his homicidal impulses in check. Another man might come to realize that unresolved anger toward his dominating or rejecting mother has sabotaged his intimate relationships with women during his adulthood. A woman with a loss of sensation in her hand that could not be explained medically might come to see that she harbored guilt over urges to masturbate. The loss of sensation might have prevented her from acting on these urges. Through confronting hidden impulses and the conflicts they produce, clients learn to sort out their feelings and find more constructive and socially acceptable ways of handling their impulses and wishes. The ego is then freed to focus on more constructive interests.

The major methods that Freud used to accomplish these goals were free association, dream analysis, and analysis of the transference relationship.

Freud's consulting room in London. Here we see the consulting room used by Freud after his arrival in London. The patient lay on the couch, and Freud sat on the chair at the left, out of view.

free association The method of verbalizing thoughts as they occur without a conscious attempt to edit or censure them.

compulsion to utter The urge to verbally express repressed material.

resistance The blocking of thoughts or feelings that would evoke anxiety if they were consciously experienced.

insight The attainment of awareness and understanding of one's true motives and feelings.

manifest content The reported content or apparent meaning of dreams.

latent content The underlying or symbolic content of dreams.

Free Association You are asked to lie down on a couch and to say anything that enters your mind. The psychoanalyst (or *analyst* for short) sits in a chair behind you, out of direct view. For the next 45 or 50 minutes, you let your mind wander, saying whatever pops in, or saying nothing at all. The analyst remains silent most of the time, prompting you occasionally to utter whatever crosses your mind, no matter how seemingly trivial, no matter how personal. This process continues, typically for three or four sessions a week, for several years. At certain points in the process, the analyst offers an *interpretation*, drawing your attention to connections between your disclosures and unconscious conflicts.

    Free association is the process of uttering uncensored thoughts as they come to mind. Free association is believed to gradually break down the defenses that block awareness of unconscious processes. Clients are told not to censor or screen out thoughts, but to let their minds wander "freely" from thought to thought. Psychoanalysts do not believe that the process of free association is truly free. Repressed impulses press for expression or release, leading to a **compulsion to utter.** Although free association may begin with small talk, the compulsion to utter eventually leads the client to disclose more meaningful material.

    The ego, however, continues to try to avert the disclosure of threatening impulses and conflicts. Consequently, clients may show **resistance,** an unwillingness or inability to recall or discuss disturbing or threatening material. Clients might report that their minds suddenly go blank when they venture into sensitive areas. They might switch topics abruptly, or accuse the analyst of trying to pry into material that is too personal or embarrassing to talk about. Or they might conveniently "forget" the next appointment after a session in which sensitive material is touched upon. The analyst monitors the dynamic conflict between the "compulsion to utter" and resistance. Signs of resistance are often suggestive of meaningful material. Now and then, the analyst brings interpretations of this material to the attention of the client to help the client gain better **insight** into deep-seated feelings and conflicts.

Dream Analysis To Freud, dreams represented the "royal road to the unconscious." During sleep, the ego's defenses are lowered and unacceptable impulses find expression in dreams. Because the defenses are not completely eliminated, the impulses take a disguised or symbolized form. In psychoanalytic theory, dreams have two levels of content:

1. **Manifest content:** the material of the dream the dreamer experiences and reports, and
2. **Latent content:** the unconscious material the dream symbolizes or represents.

Truth OR Fiction? REVISITED

In classical psychoanalysis, you are asked to express whatever thought happens to come to mind, no matter how seemingly trivial or silly.

TRUE. In classical psychoanalysis, clients are asked to report any thoughts that come to mind. The technique is called free association.

Dream analysis. Freud believed that dreams represent the "royal road to the unconscious." Dream interpretation was one of the principal techniques that Freud used to uncover unconscious material.

displacing Transferring impulses toward threatening or unacceptable objects onto more acceptable or safer objects.

transference relationship The client's transfer onto the analyst of feelings or attitudes the client holds toward important figures in his or her life.

countertransference The transfer of feelings or attitudes that the analyst holds toward other persons onto the client.

A man might dream of flying in an airplane. Flying is the apparent or manifest content of the dream. Freud believed that flying may symbolize erection, so perhaps the latent content of the dream reflects unconscious issues related to fears of impotence. Such symbols may vary from person to person. Analysts therefore ask clients to free-associate to the manifest content of the dream to provide clues to the latent content. Though dreams may have a psychological meaning, as Freud believed, there remains no independent way of determining what dreams mean (Squier & Domhoff, 1998).

Transference Freud found that clients responded to him not only as an individual but also in ways that reflected their feelings and attitudes toward other important people in their lives. A young female client might respond to him as a father figure, **displacing,** or transferring, onto Freud her feelings toward her own father. A man might also view him as a father figure, responding to him as a rival in a manner that Freud believed might reflect the man's unresolved Oedipus complex.

The process of analyzing and working through the **transference relationship** is considered an essential component of psychoanalysis. Freud believed that the transference relationship provides a vehicle for the reenactment of childhood conflicts with parents. Clients may react to the analyst with the same feelings of anger, love, or jealousy they felt toward their own parents. Freud termed the enactment of these childhood conflicts the *transference neurosis*. This "neurosis" had to be successfully analyzed and worked through for clients to succeed in psychoanalysis.

Childhood conflicts usually involve unresolved feelings of anger, rejection, or need for love. For example, a client may interpret any slight criticism by the therapist as a devastating blow, transferring feelings of self-loathing that the client had repressed from childhood experiences of parental rejection. Transferences may also distort or color the client's relationships with others, such as a spouse or employer. Clients might relate to their spouses as they had to their parents, perhaps demanding too much from them or unjustly accusing them of being insensitive or uncaring. Or they might not give new friends or lovers the benefit of a fair chance, if they had been mistreated by others who played similar roles in their past. The analyst helps the client recognize transference relationships, especially the therapy transference, and work through the residues of childhood feelings and conflicts that lead to self-defeating behavior in the present.

According to Freud, transference is a two-way street. Freud felt he transferred his underlying feelings onto his clients, perhaps viewing a young man as a competitor or a woman as a rejecting love interest. Freud referred to the feelings that he projected onto clients as **countertransference.** Psychoanalysts in training are expected to undergo psychoanalysis themselves to help them uncover motives that might lead to countertransferences in their therapeutic relationships. In their training, psychoanalysts learn to monitor their own reactions in therapy, so as to become better aware of when and how countertransferences intrude on the therapy process.

Although the analysis of the therapy transference is a crucial element of psychoanalytic therapy, it generally takes months or years for a transference relationship to develop and be resolved. This is one reason why psychoanalysis is typically a lengthy process.

Modern Psychodynamic Approaches Although some psychoanalysts continue to practice traditional psychoanalysis in much the same manner as Freud, briefer and less intensive forms of psychodynamic treatment have emerged (Strupp, 1992). These newer approaches are often referred to as "psychoanalytic psychotherapy," "psychoanalytically oriented therapy", or "psychodynamic therapy." They are able to reach clients who are seeking briefer and less costly forms of treatment, perhaps once or twice a week.

Like Freudian psychoanalysis, the newer psychodynamic approaches aim to uncover unconscious motives and break down resistances and psychological defenses. Yet they focus more on the client's present relationships and encourage the client to make adaptive behavior changes. Because of the briefer format, therapy may entail a more open dialogue and direct exploration of the client's defenses and transference relationships

Modern psychodynamic psychotherapy.
Modern psychodynamic therapists engage in more direct, face-to-face interactions with clients than do traditional Freudian psychoanalysts. Modern psychodynamic approaches are also generally briefer and focus more on the direct exploration of clients' defenses and transference relationships.

than was traditionally the case (Messer, 2001b). Unlike the traditional approach, the client and therapist generally sit facing each other. Rather than offer an occasional interpretation, the therapist engages in more frequent verbal give-and-take with the client, as in the following vignette. Note how the therapist uses interpretation to help the client, Mr. Arianes, achieve insight into how his relationship with his wife involves a transference of his childhood relationship with his mother:

A Case Vignette of Psychodynamic Therapy

MR. ARIANES: I think you've got it there, Doc. We weren't communicating. I wouldn't tell her [his wife] what was wrong or what I wanted from her. Maybe I expected her to understand me without saying anything.

THERAPIST: Like the expectations a child has of its mother.

MR. ARIANES: Not my mother!

THERAPIST: Oh?

MR. ARIANES: No, I always thought she had too many troubles of her own to pay attention to mine. I remember once I got hurt on my bike and came to her all bloodied up. When she saw me she got mad and yelled at me for making more trouble for her when she already had her hands full with my father.

THERAPIST: Do you remember how you felt then?

MR. ARIANES: I can't remember, but I know that after that I never brought my troubles to her again.

THERAPIST: How old were you?

MR. ARIANES: Nine, I know that because I got that bike for my ninth birthday. It was a little too big for me still, that's why I got hurt on it.

THERAPIST: Perhaps you carried this attitude into your marriage.

MR. ARIANES: What attitude?

THERAPIST: The feeling that your wife, like your mother, would be unsympathetic to your difficulties. That there was no point in telling her about your experiences because she was too preoccupied or too busy to care.

MR. ARIANES: But she's so different from my mother. I come first with her.

THERAPIST: On one level you know that. On another, deeper level there may well be the fear that people—or maybe only women, or maybe only women you're close to—are all the same, and you can't take a chance at being rejected again in your need.

MR. ARIANES: Maybe you're right, Doc, but all that was so long ago, and I should be over that by now.

THERAPIST: That's not the way the mind works. If a shock or a disappointment is strong enough, it can permanently freeze our picture of ourselves and our expectations of the world. The rest of us grows up—that is, we let ourselves learn about life from experience and from what we see, hear, or read of the experiences of others, but that one area where we really got hurt stays unchanged. So what I mean when I say you might be carrying that attitude into your relationship with your wife is that when it comes to your hopes of being understood and catered to when you feel hurt or abused by life, you still feel very much like that nine-year-old boy who was rebuffed in his need and gave up hope that anyone would or could respond to him.

—*From* Doing psychotherapy *by M. F. Basch. Copyright © 1980 by Basic Books, pp. 29–30. Reprinted with permssion of Basic Books, a member of Perseus Books L. L. C.*

object relations The person's relationships to the internalized representations, or "objects," of others' personalities that have been introjected within the person's ego structure.

behavior therapy The therapeutic application of learning-based techniques.

systematic desensitization A behavior therapy technique for overcoming phobias by means of exposure to progressively more fearful stimuli while one remains deeply relaxed.

gradual exposure A behavior therapy technique for overcoming fears through direct exposure to increasingly fearful stimuli.

modeling A behavior therapy technique for helping an individual acquire a new behavior by means of having a therapist or another individual demonstrate a target behavior that is then imitated by the client.

Modeling. Modeling techniques are often used to help people overcome phobic behaviors. Here a woman models approaching and petting a dog to a phobic child. As the phobic child observes the woman harmlessly engage in the desired behavior, he is more likely to imitate the behavior.

Some modern psychodynamic therapies focus more on the role of the ego and less on the role of the id. Therapists adopting this view believe Freud placed too much emphasis on sexual and aggressive impulses and underplayed the importance of the ego. These therapists, such as Heinz Hartmann, are generally described as *ego analysts.* Other modern psychoanalysts, such as Melanie Klein and Margaret Mahler, are identified with object-relations approaches to psychodynamic therapy. **Object-relations** therapists focus on helping people separate their own ideas and feelings from the elements of others they have incorporated or introjected within themselves. They can then develop more as individuals—as their own persons, rather than trying to meet the expectations they believe others have of them.

Behavior Therapy

Behavior therapy is the systematic application of the principles of learning to the treatment of psychological disorders. Because the focus is on changing behavior—not on personality change or deep probing into the past—behavior therapy is relatively brief, lasting typically from a few weeks to a few months. Behavior therapists, like other therapists, seek to develop warm therapeutic relationships with clients, but they believe the special efficacy of behavior therapy derives from the learning-based techniques rather than from the nature of the therapeutic relationship.

Behavior therapy first gained widespread attention as a means of helping people overcome fears and phobias, problems that had proved resistant to insight-oriented therapies. Among these methods are systematic desensitization, gradual exposure, and modeling. **Systematic desensitization** involves a therapeutic program of exposure (in imagination or by means of pictures or slides) to progressively more fearful stimuli while one remains deeply relaxed. First the person uses a relaxation technique, such as progressive relaxation (discussed in Chapter 5), to become deeply relaxed. The client is then instructed to imagine (or perhaps view, as through a series of slides) progressively more anxiety-arousing scenes. If fear is evoked, the client focuses on restoring relaxation. The process is repeated until the scene can be tolerated without anxiety. The client then progresses to the next scene in the *fear-stimulus hierarchy.* The procedure is continued until the person can remain relaxed while imagining the most distressing scene in the hierarchy.

In **gradual exposure** (also called *in vivo,* meaning "in life," exposure), people troubled by phobias purposely expose themselves to the stimuli that evoke their fear. Like systematic desensitization, the person progresses at his or her own pace through a hierarchy of progressively more anxiety-evoking stimuli. The person with a fear of snakes, for example, might first look at a harmless, caged snake from across the room and then gradually approach and interact with the snake in a step-by-step process, progressing to each new step only when feeling completely calm at the prior step. Gradual exposure is often combined with cognitive techniques that focus on replacing anxiety-arousing irrational thoughts with calming rational thoughts.

In **modeling,** individuals learn desired behaviors by observing others perform them (Braswell & Kendall, 2001). For example, the client may observe and then imitate others who interact with fear-evoking situations or objects. After observing the model, the client may be assisted or guided by the therapist or the model in performing the target behavior. The client receives ample reinforcement from the therapist for each attempt. Modeling approaches were pioneered by Albert Bandura and his colleagues, who had remarkable success using modeling techniques with children to treat various phobias, especially fears of animals, such as snakes and dogs (Bandura, Jeffery, & Wright, 1974; Braswell & Kendall, 2001).

Behavior therapists also use techniques based on operant conditioning, or systematic use of rewards and punishments, to shape desired behavior. For example, parents and teachers may be trained to systematically reinforce children for appropriate behavior by showing appreciation and to extinguish inappropriate behavior by ignoring it. In institutional settings, **token economy** systems seek to increase adaptive behavior by allowing patients to earn tokens for performing appropriate behaviors, such as self-grooming and making their beds. The tokens can eventually be exchanged for desired rewards. Token systems have also been used to treat children with conduct disorder problems.

Other techniques of behavior therapy discussed in later chapters include aversive conditioning (used in the treatment of substance abuse problems like smoking and alcoholism), social skills training (used in the treatment of social anxieties and skills deficits associated with schizophrenia), and self-control techniques (used in helping people reduce excess weight and quit smoking).

Humanistic Therapy

Psychodynamic therapists tend to focus on unconscious processes, such as internal conflicts. By contrast, humanistic therapists focus on clients' subjective, conscious experiences. Like behavior therapists, humanistic therapists also focus more on what clients are experiencing in the present—the here and now—than on the past. But there are also similarities between the psychodynamic and humanistic therapies. Both assume the past affects present behavior and feelings and both seek to expand clients' self-insight. The major form of humanistic therapy is **person-centered therapy** (also called **client-centered therapy**), which was developed by the psychologist Carl Rogers.

Person-Centered Therapy
Rogers (1951) believed that people have natural motivational tendencies toward growth, fulfillment, and health. In Rogers's view, psychological disorders develop largely from the roadblocks that others place in the journey toward self-actualization. When others are selective in their approval of our childhood feelings and behavior, we may come to disown the criticized parts of ourselves. To earn social approval, we may don social masks or facades. We learn "to be seen and not heard" and may become deaf even to our own inner voices. Over time, we may develop distorted self-concepts that are consistent with others' views of us but are not of our own making and design. As a result, we may become poorly adjusted, unhappy, and confused as to who and what we are.

Well-adjusted people make choices and take actions consistent with their personal values and needs. *Person-centered therapy* creates conditions of warmth and acceptance in the therapeutic relationship that help clients become more aware and accepting of their true selves. Rogers was a major shaper of contemporary psychotherapy and was rated the single most influential psychotherapist in a survey of therapists (D. Smith, 1982). Rogers did not believe therapists should impose their own goals or values on their clients. His focus of therapy, as the name implies, is the person.

Person-centered therapy is *nondirective*. The client, not the therapist, takes the lead and directs the course of therapy. The therapist uses *reflection*—the restating or paraphrasing of the client's expressed feelings without interpreting them or passing judgment on them. This encourages the client to further explore his or her feelings and get in touch with deeper feelings and parts of the self that had become disowned because of social condemnation.

Rogers stressed the importance of creating a warm therapeutic relationship that would encourage the client to engage in self-exploration and self-expression. The effective therapist should possess four basic qualities or attributes: *unconditional positive regard, empathy, genuineness*, and *congruence*. First, the therapist must be able to express **unconditional positive regard** for clients. In contrast to the conditional approval the client may have received from parents and others in the past, the therapist must be unconditionally accepting of the client as a person, even if the therapist sometimes objects to the client's choices or behaviors. Unconditional positive regard provides clients with a sense of security that encourages them to explore their feelings without fear of disapproval. As clients feel accepted or prized for themselves, they are encouraged to accept themselves in turn. To Rogers, every human being has intrinsic worth and value. Traditional psychodynamic theory holds that people are basically motivated by primitive forces, such as sexual and aggressive impulses. Rogers believed, however, that people are basically good and are motivated to pursue *pro*social goals.

token economy Behavioral treatment program in which a controlled environment is constructed such that people are reinforced for desired behaviors by receiving tokens that may be exchanged for desired rewards.

person-centered therapy The establishment of a warm, accepting therapeutic relationship that frees clients to engage in self-exploration and achieve self-acceptance.

client-centered therapy Another term for *person-centered therapy*.

unconditional positive regard The expression of unconditional acceptance of another person's basic worth as a person.

VIDEO **4.1**
Client-Centered Therapy:
Dr. Carl Rogers

empathy The ability to understand someone's experiences and feelings from that person's point of view.

genuineness The ability to recognize and express one's true feelings.

congruence The fit between one's thoughts, behaviors, and feelings.

Therapists who display **empathy** are able to reflect or mirror accurately their clients' experiences and feelings. Therapists try to see the world through their clients' eyes or frames of reference. They listen carefully to clients and set aside their own judgments and interpretations of events. Showing empathy encourages clients to get in touch with feelings of which they may be only dimly aware.

Genuineness is the ability to be open about one's feelings. Rogers admitted he had negative feelings at times during therapy sessions, typically boredom, but he attempted to express these feelings openly rather than hide them (Bennett, 1985).

Congruence refers to the fit between one's thoughts, feelings, and behavior. The congruent person is one whose behavior, thoughts, and feelings are integrated and consistent. Congruent therapists serve as models of psychological integrity to their clients.

Here Rogers (C.R.) uses reflection to help a client focus more deeply on her inner feelings:

Reflection in Person-Centered Therapy

JILL: I'm having a lot of problems dealing with my daughter. She's 20 years old; she's in college; I'm having a lot of trouble letting her go. And I have a lot of guilt feelings about her; I have a real need to hang on to her.

C.R.: A need to hang on so you can kind of make up for the things you feel guilty about. Is that part of it?

JILL: There's a lot of that. Also, she's been a real friend to me, and filled my life. And it's very hard . . . a lot of empty places now that she's not with me.

C.R.: The old vacuum, sort of, when she's not there.

JILL: Yes. Yes. I also would like to be the kind of mother that could be strong and say, you know, "Go and have a good life," and this is really hard for me, to do that.

C.R.: It's very hard to give up something that's been so precious in your life, but also something that I guess has caused you pain when you mentioned guilt.

JILL: Yeah. And I'm aware that I have some anger toward her that I don't always get what I want. I have needs that are not met. And, uh, I don't feel I have a right to those needs. You know . . . she's a daughter; she's not my mother. Though sometimes I feel as if I'd like her to mother me . . . it's very difficult for me to ask for that and have a right to it.

C.R.: So, it may be unreasonable, but still, when she doesn't meet your needs, it makes you mad.

JILL: Yeah I get very angry, very angry with her.

C.R.: (*Pause*) You're also feeling a little tension at this point, I guess.

JILL: Yeah. Yeah. A lot of conflict . . . (C.R.: M-hm.). A lot of pain.

C.R.: A lot of pain. Can you say anything more about what that's about?

—*From Farber, Brink, & Raskin, 1996*, The psychotherapy of Carl Rogers: Cases and commentary, *pp. 74–75. Reprinted with permission of The Guilford Press.*

■

Cognitive Therapy

. . . there is nothing either good or bad, but thinking makes it so.

—Shakespeare, *Hamlet*

In these words, Shakespeare did not mean to imply that misfortunes or ailments are painless or easy to manage. His point, rather, is that the ways in which we evaluate upsetting events can heighten our discomfort and impair our ability to cope. Several hundred years later, cognitive therapists adopted this simple but elegant expression as a kind of motto for their approach to therapy.

Cognitive therapists focus on helping clients identify and correct maladaptive beliefs, automatic types of thinking, and self-defeating attitudes that create or compound emotional problems. They believe that negative emotions such as anxiety and depression are caused by the interpretations we place on troubling events, not on the events themselves. Here we focus on the contributions of two prominent types of cognitive therapy: Albert Ellis's rational-emotive behavior therapy, and Aaron Beck's cognitive therapy.

Rational-Emotive Behavior Therapy Albert Ellis (1977b, 1993, 2001; Dryden & Ellis, 2001) believes that the adoption of irrational, self-defeating beliefs gives rise to psychological problems and negative feelings. Consider the irrational belief that one must have the approval almost all of the time of the people who are important to you. Ellis finds it understandable to want other people's approval and love, but he argues that it is irrational to believe we cannot survive without it. Another irrational belief is that we must be thoroughly competent and achieving in virtually everything we seek to accomplish or else it would be awful and unbearable. We are doomed to eventually fall short of these irrational expectations. When we do fall short, we may experience negative emotional consequences, such as depression and lowered self-esteem. Emotional difficulties such as anxiety and depression are not directly caused by negative events, but rather by how we distort their meaning by viewing them through the dark-colored glasses of self-defeating beliefs. Imposing "musts" and "shoulds" on ourselves transforms challenging events, such as forthcoming examinations, into looming disasters (e.g., "It would be just so awful if I did poorly that I wouldn't be able to stand it."). In Ellis's **rational-emotive behavior therapy (REBT),** therapists actively *dispute* clients' irrational beliefs and the premises on which they are based and help clients to develop alternative, adaptive beliefs in their place.

Ellis and Dryden (1987) describe the case of a 27-year-old woman, Jane, who was socially inhibited and shy, particularly with attractive men. Through REBT, Jane identified some of her underlying irrational beliefs, such as "I must speak well to people I find attractive" and "When I don't speak well and impress people as I should, I'm a stupid, inadequate person!" (p. 68). REBT helped Jane discriminate between these irrational beliefs and rational alternatives, such as "If people do reject me for showing them how anxious I am, that will be most unfortunate, but I can stand it" (p. 68). REBT encouraged Jane to debate or dispute irrational beliefs by posing challenging questions to herself: (1) "*Why* must I speak well to people I find attractive?" and, (2) "When I don't speak well and impress people, how does that make me a *stupid and inadequate person*?" (p. 69). Jane learned to form rational responses to her self-questioning, for example, (1) "There is no reason I must speak well to people I find attractive, but it would be desirable if I do so, so I shall make an effort—but not kill myself—to do so," and, (2) "When I speak poorly and fail to impress people, that only makes me a *person who spoke unimpressively this time*—not a *totally stupid or inadequate person*" (p. 69).

Jane also rehearsed more rational ideas several times a day. Examples included, "I would like to speak well, but I never *have to*," and, "When people I favor reject me, it often reveals more about them and their tastes than about me" (pp. 69–70). After 9 months of REBT, Jane was able to talk comfortably to men she found attractive and was preparing to take a job as a teacher, a position she had previously avoided due to fear of facing a class.

Ellis recognizes that irrational beliefs may be formed on the basis of early childhood experiences. Changing them requires finding rational alternatives in the here and now, however. Rational-emotive behavior therapists also help clients substitute more effective interpersonal behavior for self-defeating or maladaptive behavior. Ellis often gives clients specific tasks or homework assignments, such as disagreeing with an overbearing relative or asking someone for a date. He assists them in practicing or rehearsing adaptive behaviors.

Beck's Cognitive Therapy As formulated by psychiatrist Aaron Beck and his colleagues (Beck, 1976; Beck et al., 1979; DeRubeis, Tang, & Beck, 2001), cognitive therapy, like REBT,

rational-emotive behavior therapy (REBT) A therapeutic approach that focuses on helping clients replace irrational, maladaptive beliefs with alternative, more adaptive beliefs.

focuses on clients' maladaptive cognitions. Cognitive therapists encourage clients to recognize and change errors in their thinking, called *cognitive distortions*, which affect their moods and impair their behavior, such as tendencies to magnify negative events and minimize personal accomplishments.

Cognitive therapists have clients record the thoughts that are prompted by upsetting events they experience and note the connections between their thoughts and their emotional responses. They then help them to dispute distorted thoughts and replace them with rational alternatives. Therapists also use behavioral homework assignments, such as encouraging depressed clients to fill their free time with structured activities, such as gardening or completing work around the house. Carrying out such tasks serves to counteract the apathy and loss of motivation that tend to characterize depression and may also provide concrete evidence of competence, which helps combat self-perceptions of helplessness and inadequacy.

Another type of homework assignment involves reality testing. Clients are asked to test out their negative beliefs in the light of reality. For example, a depressed client who feels unwanted by everyone might be asked to call two or three friends on the phone to gather data about the friends' reactions to the calls. The therapist might then ask the client to report on the assignment: "Did they immediately hang up the phone? Or did they seem pleased you called? Did they express any interest at all in talking to you again or getting together sometime? Does the evidence support the conclusion that *no one* has any interest in you?" Such exercises help clients replace distorted beliefs with rational alternatives.

Consider this case in which a depressed man was encouraged to test his belief he was about to be fired from his job. The case also illustrates several cognitive distortions or errors in thinking, such as selectively perceiving only one's flaws (in this case, self-perceptions of laziness) and expecting the worst (expectations of being fired):

Kyle Tests His Irrational Beliefs

Kyle, a 35-year-old frozen foods distributor, had suffered from chronic depression since his divorce six years earlier. During the past year the depression had worsened and he found it increasingly difficult to call upon customers or go to the office. Each day that he avoided working made it more difficult for him to go to the office and face his boss. He was convinced that he was in imminent danger of being fired since he had not made any sales calls for more than a month. Since he had not earned any commissions in a while, he felt he was not adequately supporting his two daughters and was concerned that he wouldn't have the money to send them to college. He was convinced that his basic problem was laziness, not depression. His therapist pointed out the illogic in his thinking. First of all, there was no real evidence that his boss was about to fire him. His boss had actually encouraged him to get help and was paying for part of the treatment. His therapist also pointed out that judging himself as lazy was unfair because it overlooked the fact that he had been an industrious, successful salesman before he became depressed. While not fully persuaded, the client agreed to a homework assignment in which he was to call his boss and also make a sales call to one of his former customers. His boss expressed support and reassured him that his job was secure. The customer ribbed him about "being on vacation" during the preceding six weeks but placed a small order. The client discovered that the small unpleasantness he experienced in facing the customer and being teased paled in comparison to the intense depression he felt at home while he was avoiding work. Within the next several weeks he gradually worked himself back to a normal routine, calling upon customers and making future plans. This process of viewing himself and the world from a fresh perspective led to a general improvement in his mood and behavior.

—Adapted from Burns & Beck, 1978, pp. 124–126

■

REBT and Beck's cognitive therapy have much in common, especially the focus on helping clients replace self-defeating thoughts and beliefs with more rational ones. Perhaps the major difference between the two approaches is one of therapeutic style. REBT therapists tend to be more confrontational and forceful in their approach to disputing client's irrational beliefs (A. Ellis, Young, & Lockwood, 1989). Cognitive therapists tend to adopt a more gentle, collaborative approach in helping clients discover and correct the distortions in their thinking.

Cognitive-Behavioral Therapy

Today, most behavior therapists identify with a broader model of behavior therapy called **cognitive-behavioral therapy** (**CBT**) (also called *cognitive behavior therapy*). Cognitive-behavioral therapy attempts to integrate therapeutic techniques that focus on helping individuals make changes not only in their overt behavior but also in their underlying thoughts, beliefs, and attitudes. Cognitive-behavioral therapy draws on the assumption that thinking patterns and beliefs affect behavior and that changes in these cognitions can lead to desirable behavioral changes (Dobson & Dozois, 2001; McGinn & Sanderson, 2001).

Cognitive-behavioral therapists use an assortment of behavioral and cognitive techniques in therapy. The following case illustration shows how behavioral techniques (exposure to fearful situations) and cognitive techniques (changing maladaptive thoughts) were used in the treatment of *agoraphobia*, a type of anxiety disorder characterized by excessive fears of venturing out in public:

> ### The Use of CBT to Treat Agoraphobia
>
> *Mrs. X was a 41-year-old woman with a 12-year history of agoraphobia. She feared venturing into public places alone and required her husband or children to accompany her from place to place. In-vivo (actual) exposure sessions were arranged in a series of progressively more fearful encounters—a fear-stimulus hierarchy. The first step in the hierarchy, for example, involved taking a shopping trip while accompanied by the therapist. After accomplishing this task, she gradually moved upwards in the hierarchy. By the third week of treatment, she was able to complete the last step in her hierarchy—shopping by herself in a crowded supermarket. Cognitive restructuring was conducted along with the exposure training. Mrs. X was asked to imagine herself in various fearful situations and to report the self-statements (self-talk) she experienced. The therapist helped her identify disruptive self-statements, such as "I am going to make a fool of myself." This particular self-statement was challenged by questioning whether it was realistic to believe that she would actually lose control, and, secondly, by disputing the belief that the consequences of losing control, were it to happen, would truly be disastrous. She progressed rapidly with treatment and became capable of functioning more independently. But she still harbored concerns about relapsing in the future. The therapist focused at this point on deeper cognitive structures involving her fears of abandonment by the people she loved if she were to relapse and be unable to attend to their needs. In challenging these beliefs, the therapist helped her realize that she was not as helpless as she perceived herself to be and that she was loved for other reasons than her ability to serve others. She also explored the question, "Who am I improving for?" She realized that she needed to find reasons to overcome her phobia that were related to meeting her own personal needs, not simply the needs of her loved ones. At a follow-up interview nine months after treatment, she was functioning independently, which allowed her to pursue her own interests, such as taking night courses and seeking a job.*
>
> —Adapted from Biran, 1988, pp. 173–176

cognitive-behavioral therapy (CBT)
A learning-based approach to therapy incorporating cognitive and behavioral techniques.

eclectic therapy An approach to psychotherapy that incorporates principles or techniques from various systems or theories.

It could be argued that any behavioral method involving imagination or mental imagery, such as systematic desensitization, bridges behavioral and cognitive domains. Cognitive therapies such as Ellis's rational-emotive behavior therapy and Beck's cognitive therapy might also be regarded as forms of cognitive-behavioral therapy because they incorporate cognitive and behavioral treatment methods. The dividing lines between the psychotherapies may not be as clearly drawn as authors of textbooks—who are given the task of classifying them—might desire. Not only are traditional boundaries between therapies blurring, but many therapists today endorse an *eclectic* orientation in which they incorporate principles and techniques derived from different schools of therapy.

Eclectic Therapy

Each of the major psychological models of abnormal behavior—the psychodynamic, learning theory, humanistic and cognitive approaches—has spawned its own approaches to psychotherapy. Although many therapists identify with one or another of these schools of therapy, an increasing number of therapists practice **eclectic therapy,** in which they draw on techniques and teachings of multiple therapeutic approaches. Eclectic therapists look beyond the theoretical barriers that divide one school of psychotherapy from another in an effort to define what is common among the schools of therapy and what is useful in each of them. They seek to enhance their therapeutic effectiveness by incorporating principles and techniques from different therapeutic orientations. An eclectic therapist might use behavior therapy techniques to help a client change specific maladaptive behaviors, for example, along with psychodynamic techniques to help the client gain insight into the childhood roots of the problem.

A greater percentage of clinical and counseling psychologists identify with an eclectic or integrative orientation than any other therapeutic orientation (Bechtoldt et al., 2001; see Figure 4.1). Therapists who adopt an eclectic approach tend to be older and more experienced (Beitman, Goldfried, & Norcross, 1989). Perhaps they have learned through experience of the value of drawing on diverse contributions to the practice of therapy.

Eclecticism has different meanings for different therapists. Some therapists are *technical eclectics.* They draw on techniques from different schools of therapy without necessarily adopting the theoretical positions that spawned the techniques (Beutler, Harwood, & Caldwell, 2001; Lazarus, 1992). They assume a pragmatic approach in using techniques from different therapeutic approaches that they believe are most likely to work with a given client. The therapist attempts to match the therapeutic approach to the particular characteristics of the client, rather than apply the same therapeutic approach to all clients presenting with a given diagnosis or type of problem. Thus, the eclectic therapy offered to one client will be different than the eclectic therapy offered to another (Beutler, 1995).

Other eclectic therapists are *integrative eclectics.* They attempt to synthesize and integrate diverse theoretical approaches—to bring together different theoretical concepts and therapeutic approaches under the roof of one integrated model of therapy (Beutler, Harwood, & Caldwell, 2001; Stricker & Gold, 2001). Though various approaches to integrative

FIGURE 4.1 Therapeutic orientations of clinical and counseling psychologists. An eclectic/integrative orientation is the most widely endorsed therapeutic orientation among clinical and counseling psychologists today.

Source. Adapted from Bechtoldt, H., Norcross, J. C., Wyckoff, L. A., Pokrywa, M. L., & Campbell, L. F., 2001.

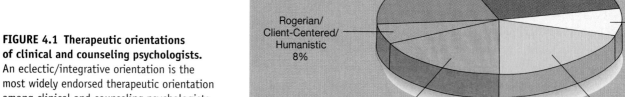

Cognitive 18%

Psychoanalytic/ Psychodynamic 20%

Behavioral 6%

Rogerian/ Client-Centered/ Humanistic 8%

Eclectic/Integrative 28%

Other 20%

A Closer Look

Internet Counseling: Psychological Help May Be Only a Few Mouse Clicks Away

You can do most anything on the Internet these days, from ordering concert tickets to downloading music or whole books. You can also receive counseling or therapy services from an online therapist. By 2001, more than 250 Web sites were offering counseling services online (Kalb, 2001a). But as the numbers of online counseling services mushroom, many professionals voice concerns about the clinical, ethical, and legal issues regarding their use (Reed, McLaughlin, & Milholland, 2000; Rabasca, 2000b; Jacobs et al., 2001; Jerome et al., 2000).

One problem is that while psychologists are licensed in particular states, Internet communications easily cross state and international borders. It remains unclear whether psychologists or other mental health professionals can legally provide online services to residents of states in which they are not licensed. Then too are ethical problems and liability issues psychologists and other helping professionals may face in offering services to clients they never meet in person. Many therapists also express concerns that interacting with a client by computer would prevent them from evaluating nonverbal cues and gestures that might signal deeper levels of distress than are verbally reported or typed on a keyboard.

Yet another problem is that online therapists living at great distances from their clients may not be able to provide the more intensive services that clients need during times of emotional crisis. Professionals also express concern about the potential for unsuspecting clients to be victimized by unqualified practitioners or "quacks." We presently lack a system for ensuring that online therapists are licensed and otherwise qualified practitioners (Lauerman, 2000; Stamm & Perednia, 2000).

Despite these drawbacks, many professionals believe that online consultation and counseling services have potential value. For one thing, the distance of online consultation may encourage people to seek help who have hesitated out of shyness or embarrassment to consult a helping professional (Rabasca, 2000b). Online consultation may also make people feel more comfortable about receiving help and become a first step toward meeting a therapist in person. Online therapy may also provide people living in remote areas where finding a therapist is difficult, or those lacking mobility, with services they might not otherwise receive. Recently, investigators found that participants in an Internet-delivered behavioral program for weight loss achieved better results than a comparison group that was simply given a list of weight-loss education sites on the Web (Tate, Wing, & Winett, 2001).

The bottom line about Internet counseling, says Russ Newman, executive director for professional practice of the American Psychological Association, is the need for monitoring and evaluating this emerging technology (cited in Lauerman, 2000). Psychologists are not writing off so-called e-therapy, but they remain cautious in endorsing its widespread use.

---

psychotherapy have been proposed, there is as yet no clear agreement as to the principles and practices that constitute therapeutic integration (Garfield, 1994). Perhaps multiple approaches are needed (Safran & Messer, 1997).

Not all therapists subscribe to the view that therapeutic integration is a desirable or achievable goal. They believe that combining elements of different therapeutic approaches will lead to a hodgepodge of techniques that lack a cohesive conceptual framework. Still, interest in the professional community in therapeutic integration is growing, and we expect to see new models emerging that aim at tying together the contributions of different approaches.

Group, Family, and Marital Therapy

Some approaches to therapy expand the focus of treatment to include groups of people, families, and couples.

Group Therapy In **group therapy**, a group of clients meet together with a therapist or pair of therapists. Group therapy has several advantages over individual treatment. For one, group therapy is less costly to individual clients, because several clients are treated at the same time. Many clinicians also believe that group therapy is more effective in treating groups of clients who

group therapy Therapy method in which a group of clients meet together with a therapist.

Group therapy. What are some of the advantages of group therapy over individual therapy? What are some of its disadvantages?

family therapy Therapy in which the family, not the individual, is the unit of treatment.

couples therapy Therapy that focuses on resolving conflicts in distressed couples.

have similar problems, such as complaints relating to anxiety, depression, lack of social skills, or adjustment to divorce or other life stresses. The group format provides clients with the opportunity to learn how people with similar problems cope and provides the social support of the group as well as the therapist. Group therapy also provides members with opportunities to work through their problems in relating to others. For example, the therapist or other members may point out to a particular member when he or she acts in a bossy manner or tends to withdraw when criticized, patterns of behavior that may mirror the behavior the client shows in relationships with others outside the group. Group members may also rehearse social skills with one another in a supportive atmosphere.

Despite these advantages, clients may prefer individual therapy for various reasons. For one, clients might not wish to disclose their problems to others in a group. Some clients prefer the individual attention of the therapist. Others are too socially inhibited to feel comfortable in a group setting, even though they might be the ones who could most profit from a group experience. Because of such concerns, group therapists require that group disclosures be kept confidential, that group members relate to each other supportively and nondestructively, and that group members receive the attention they need.

Family Therapy In **family therapy,** the family, not the individual, is the unit of treatment. Family therapy aims to help troubled families resolve their conflicts and problems so the family functions better as a unit and individual family members are subjected to less stress from family conflicts.

Faulty patterns of communications within the family often contribute to problems. In family therapy, family members learn to communicate more effectively and to air their disagreements constructively. Family conflicts often emerge at transitional points in the life cycle, when family patterns are altered by changes in one or more members. Conflicts between parents and children, for example, often emerge when adolescent children seek greater independence or autonomy. Family members with low self-esteem may be unable to tolerate different attitudes or behaviors from other members of the family and may resist their efforts to change or become more independent. Family therapists work with families to resolve these conflicts and help them adjust to life changes.

Family therapists are sensitive to tendencies of families to scapegoat one family member as the source of the problem, or the "identified client." Disturbed families seem to adopt a sort of myth: Change the identified client, the "bad apple," and the "barrel," or family, will once again become functional. Family therapists encourage families to work together to resolve their disputes and conflicts, instead of resorting to scapegoating.

Many family therapists adopt a *systems approach* to understanding the workings of the family and problems that may arise within the family. They see problem behaviors of individual family members as representing a breakdown in the system of communications and role relationships within the family. For example, a child may feel in competition with other siblings for a parent's attention and develop enuresis, or bed-wetting, as a means of securing attention. Operating from a systems perspective, the family therapist may focus efforts on helping family members understand the hidden messages in the child's behavior and then assist the family to make changes in their relationships to meet the child's needs more adequately.

Couples Therapy **Couples therapy** focuses on resolving conflicts in distressed couples, including married and unmarried couples. Like family therapy, couples therapy focuses on improving communication and analyzing role relationships in order to improve the relationship. For example, one partner may play a dominant role and resist any request to share power. The couples therapist helps bring these role relationships into the open, so that partners can explore alternative ways of relating to one another that would lead to a more satisfying relationship.

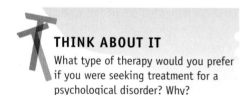

THINK ABOUT IT
What type of therapy would you prefer if you were seeking treatment for a psychological disorder? Why?

Family therapy. In family therapy, the family, not the individual, is the unit of treatment. Family therapists help family members communicate more effectively with one another, for example, to air their disagreements in ways that are not hurtful to individual members. Family therapists also try to prevent one member of the family from becoming the scapegoat for the family's problems.

Evaluating Methods of Treatment

What, then, of the effectiveness of psychotherapy? Does psychotherapy work? Are some forms of therapy more effective than others? Are some forms of therapy more effective for some types of clients or for some types of problems than for others?

The effectiveness of psychotherapy receives strong support from the research literature. Reviews of the scientific literature often utilize a statistical technique called **meta-analysis,** which averages the results of a large number of studies in order to determine an overall level of effectiveness.

In the most frequently cited meta-analysis of psychotherapy research, M. L. Smith and Glass (1977) analyzed the results of some 375 controlled studies comparing various types of therapies (psychodynamic, behavioral, humanistic, etc.) against control groups. The results of their analyses showed that the average psychotherapy client in these studies was better off than 75% of the clients who remained untreated. In 1980, Smith and Glass and their colleague Miller reported the results of a larger analysis based on 475 controlled outcome studies, which showed the average person who received therapy was better off at the end of treatment than 80% of those who did not (M. L. Smith, Glass, & Miller, 1980).

Other meta-analyses also show positive outcomes for psychotherapy, including analyses of behavior therapy (Bowers & Clum, 1988; Lipsey & Wilson, 1993, 1995), brief psychodynamic therapy (E. M. Anderson & Lambert, 1995; Crits-Christoph, 1992), and group psychotherapy (McDermut, Miller, & Brown, 2001). Evidence indicates that psychotherapy is effective not only in the confines of clinical research centers, but also in settings that are more typical of ordinary clinical practice (Shadish et al., 2000). Although not all researchers endorse the use of meta-analysis as a methodological tool, the technique has achieved widespread acceptance within psychology and has provided some of the strongest evidence to date supporting the effectiveness of psychotherapy.

Evidence also shows that the greatest gains in psychotherapy are typically achieved in the first several months of treatment (Barkham et al., 1996; Howard et al., 1986). About 50% of patients show clinically significant change in about 3 or 4 months of treatment; by about 6 months, this figure rises to about 75% (E. M. Anderson & Lambert, 2001; Goode, 1998; Messer, 2001a).

Meta-analyses show only negligible differences, overall, in outcomes among the various therapies when such therapies are compared to control groups (Crits-Christoph, 1992; M. L. Smith, Glass, & Miller, 1980; Wampold et al., 1997a, 1997b). Such minor differences suggest that the effectiveness of psychotherapies may have more to do with the features they have in common than with the specific techniques that set them apart (M. J. Lambert & Bergin, 1994). These common features are called **nonspecific factors.** Nonspecific or common factors include expectations of improvement and features of the therapist–client relationship, including the following: (1) empathy, support, and attention shown by the therapist; (2) *therapeutic alliance*, or the attachment the client develops toward the therapist and the therapy process; and (3) the *working alliance*, or the development of an effective working relationship in which the therapist and client work together to identify and confront the important issues and problems the client faces (J. L. Binder & Strupp, 1997; Connors et al., 1997; M. J. Lambert & Okiishi, 1997; Perlman, 2001).

Should we conclude that different therapies are about equally effective? One possibility is that different therapies are about equal in their effects overall but may not be equal in their effects with every patient (Wampold et al., 1997a). That is, a given therapy may be more effective for a particular patient or for a particular type of problem. All in all, the question of whether differences exist in the relative effectiveness of different forms of therapy remains unresolved (Nathan, Stuart, & Dolan, 2000).

Another approach to the question of determining which therapies are effective for which types of problems was undertaken by a task force commissioned by the Clinical Psychology Division of the American Psychological Association. The task force concluded that enough evidence now exists from controlled trials to support the therapeutic efficacy of various psychological interventions (listed in Table 4.2) for specific psychological problems or disorders (Chambless & Ollendeck, 2001; Weisz et al., 2000).

meta-analysis A statistical technique for combining the results of different studies into an overall average.

nonspecific factors Factors not specific to any one form of psychotherapy, such as therapist attention and support, and the engendering of positive expectancies of change.

Truth OR Fiction?   REVISITED

The average client who receives psychotherapy is no better off than control clients who go without it.

FALSE. The average psychotherapy client is better off than about 75% or 80% of control clients who do not receive psychotherapy.

Nonspecific factors. Are the benefits of psychotherapy due to nonspecific factors that various psychotherapies share in common, such as the mobilization of hope, the attention and support provided by the therapist, and the development of a good working alliance between the client and therapist? It appears that both specific and nonspecific factors are involved in accounting for therapeutic change.

Other treatment interventions may be added to the list of these empirically supported treatments or ESTs as scientific evidence attesting to their effectiveness becomes available. We should caution you not to infer that the inclusion of a particular treatment guarantees that it is effective in every case.

The effort to develop a listing of ESTs comes at a time when health care professionals are facing increasing pressure to demonstrate the effectiveness of the treatments they use. As task force member William Sanderson ("Task Force," 1995) said, "More than ever before, psychologists—and all health care providers—are being called on to show the efficacy of their interventions. Society wants proof that a treatment works—whether it be medication, surgery or psychotherapy—before it is administered" (p. 5).

It is thus insufficient to ask which therapy works best. We must ask, Which therapy works best for which type of problem? Which clients are best suited for which type of therapy? What are the advantages and limitations of particular therapies? Behavior therapy, for example, has shown impressive results in treating various types of anxiety disorders, sleep disorders, and sexual dysfunctions and in improving the adaptive functioning of people with schizophrenia and mental retardation. Psychodynamic and humanistic approaches may be most effective in fostering self-insight and personality growth. Cognitive therapy has demonstrated impressive results in treating depression and anxiety disorders. By and large, however, the process of determining which treatment, practiced by whom, and under what conditions, is most effective for a given client remains a challenge.

All in all, psychotherapy is a complex process that incorporates common features along with specific techniques that foster adaptive change. A strong therapeutic alliance between client and therapist is associated with better therapy outcome (Barber et al., 2000; Martin, Garske, & Davis, 2000). But therapeutic gains are not accounted for entirely by nonspecific factors (Oei & Shuttlewood, 1996; Grissom, 1996). In fact, investigators believe that specific techniques may account for about twice the magnitude of therapeutic change as nonspecific factors that different therapies have in common (Stevens, Hynan, & Allen, 2000). In the final analysis, therapeutic change most likely

---

TABLE 4.2 Examples of Empirically Supported Treatments (ESTs)

Treatment	Conditions for Which Treatment Is Effective (Chapter in text where treatment is discussed is shown in parentheses.)
Cognitive therapy	Headache (Ch. 5) Depression (Ch. 8)
Behavior therapy or Behavior modification	Depression (Ch. 8) Persons with developmental disabilities (Ch. 14) Enuresis (Ch. 14)
Cognitive-behavior therapy	Panic disorder with and without agoraphobia (Ch. 6) Generalized anxiety disorder (Ch. 6) Smoking cessation (Ch. 10) Bulimia (Ch. 11)
Exposure treatment	Agoraphobia and specific phobia (Ch. 6)
Exposure and response prevention	Obsessive-compulsive disorder (Ch. 6)
Interpersonal psychotherapy	Depression (Ch. 8)
Parent training programs	Children with oppositional behavior (Ch. 14)

Source. Adapted from Chambless et al., 1998.

depends on the influence of specific and nonspecific factors, as well as their interactions (Ilardi & Craighead, 1994).

Managed Care or Managed Costs?   This is an appropriate juncture to note that the practice of psychotherapy has been influenced by changes in the general health care environment in recent years, especially the increasing role of **managed care systems,** such as health maintenance organizations (HMOs). Managed care systems typically impose limits on the number of treatment sessions they will approve for payment and the fees they will allow for reimbursement. Consequently, there is greater emphasis today on briefer, more direct forms of treatment, including cognitive-behavioral therapy and shorter-term psychodynamic therapies. Traditional long-term psychodynamic psychotherapy is likely to become a luxury that is available to only a very few (Strupp, 1992). Moreover, managed care has curbed costly inpatient mental health treatment, primarily through limiting the lengths of stay of patients in psychiatric hospitals (Wickizer, Lessler, & Travis, 1996; USDHHS, 1999a). However, many people express concerns about the risks of sacrificing quality of care in the interests of cutting costs.

Though health care providers understand the need to curtail the spiraling costs of care, they are understandably concerned that the cost-cutting emphasis of managed care plans may discourage needful people with identifiable psychological disorders from seeking help or receiving an adequate level of care (Landerman et al., 1994). According to the recent Surgeon General's report, "Excessively restrictive cost-containment strategies and financial incentives to providers and facilities to reduce specialty referrals, hospital admissions, or length or amount of treatment may ultimately contribute to lowered access and quality of care" (cited in USDDHS, 1999a, Chapter 6).

Overzealous cost-cutting policies may also be financially short-sighted because the failure to provide adequate mental health care when problems arise may lead to an increased need for more expensive care at some later point. Evidence shows that for people with severe psychological disorders, such as schizophrenia, bipolar disorder, and borderline personality disorder, psychotherapy actually reduces health care costs by reducing the need for hospitalization and reducing work impairment (Fraser, 1996; Gabbard et al., 1997).

Multicultural Issues in Psychotherapy

We live in a multicultural society in which people bring to therapy not only their personal backgrounds and individual experiences but also their cultural learning and values. Therapists need to be sensitive to cultural differences and how they may affect the therapeutic process. They also need to avoid ethnic stereotyping and to demonstrate sensitivity to the values, languages, and cultural beliefs of members of racial or ethnic groups that are different than their own (Comas-Diaz & Griffith, 1988; Lee & Richardson, 1991). Let us touch on some of the issues involved in treating members of the major ethnic minority groups in our society: African Americans, Asian Americans, Hispanic Americans, and Native Americans.

African Americans   The cultural history of African Americans must be understood in the context of a history of extreme racial discrimination (Boyd-Franklin, 1989; Greene, 1990). African Americans have needed to develop coping mechanisms for managing the pervasive racism they encounter in such areas as employment, housing, education, and access to health care (Greene, 1993a, 1993b). For example, the sensitivity of many African Americans to the potential for maltreatment and exploitation has been a survival tool that may take the form of a heightened level of suspiciousness or reserve (Greene, 1986). Therapists need to be aware of the tendency of African American clients to minimize their vulnerability by being less self-disclosing, especially in early stages of therapy (Ridley, 1984). Therapists should not confuse such suspiciousness with paranoia (Boyd-Franklin, 1989; Greene, 1986).

" IT'S YOUR INSURANCE COMPANY, THEY SAY YOU'RE CURED. "

Managed Care or Managed Care Costs

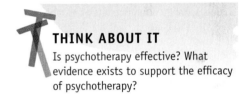

THINK ABOUT IT
Is psychotherapy effective? What evidence exists to support the efficacy of psychotherapy?

WWW   Web Link **4.2**
Financing Mental Health Services

managed care systems Health care delivery systems that impose limits on the number of treatment sessions they will approve for payment and the fees they will allow for reimbursement.

Cultural sensitivity. Therapists need to be sensitive to cultural differences and how they may affect the therapeutic process. They also need to avoid ethnic stereotyping and to demonstrate sensitivity to the values, languages, and cultural beliefs of members of racial or ethnic groups that are different than their own. Clients who are not fluent in English profit from having therapists who can conduct therapy in their own languages.

In addition to whatever psychological problems an African American client may present, the therapist often needs to help the client develop coping mechanisms to deal with societal racial barriers. Therapists also need to be attuned to tendencies of some African Americans to internalize within their self-concepts the negative stereotypes about Blacks that are perpetuated in the dominant culture (Greene, 1985, 1992b, 1992c; Pinder-hughes, 1989; Nickerson, Helms, & Terrell, 1994).

To be culturally competent, therapists not only must develop a better awareness of the cultural traditions and languages of the groups with which they work, but also must come to an understanding of their own racial and ethnic attitudes and how their underlying attitudes affect their clinical practice (Greene, 1985, 1992b, 1992c; Nickerson, Helms, & Terrell, 1994; Pinderhughes, 1989). Therapists are exposed to the same negative stereotypes about African Americans as other people in society and must recognize how the incorporation of these stereotypes, if left unexamined, can become destructive to the therapeutic relationships they form with African American clients. In effect, therapists must be willing to confront their own racism and prejudices and work to replace these attitudes with more realistic appraisals of African Americans (Mays, 1985).

Therapists must also be aware of the cultural characteristics associated with African American families, such as strong kinship bonds between family members, often including people who are not biologically related (for example, a close friend of a parent may have some parenting role and may be addressed as "aunt"), strong religious and spiritual orientation, multigenerational households, adaptability and flexibility of gender roles (African American women have a long history of working outside the home), and distribution of child-care responsibilities among different family members (Boyd-Franklin, 1989; Collins, 1990; Ferguson-Peters, 1985; Greene, 1990; USDHHS, 1999a).

Asian Americans Culturally sensitive therapists not only understand the beliefs and values of other cultures but also integrate this knowledge within the therapy process. Generally speaking, Asian cultures, including Japanese culture, value restraint in talking about oneself and one's feelings. Therapists thus need to be patient and not expect instant self-disclosures from Asian clients (Henkin, 1985). Public expression of emotions is also discouraged in Asian cultures. Suppression of emotions, especially negative emotions, is valued, and failure to keep one's feelings to oneself is believed to reflect poorly on one's upbringing (Huang, 1994). Asian clients who appear emotionally restrained or constricted when judged by Western standards may be responding in ways that are culturally appropriate.

Clinicians also note that Asian clients often express psychological complaints in terms of physical symptoms. However, this tendency to *somaticize* emotional problems may be attributed in part to differences in communication styles (Zane & Sue, 1991). That is, Asians may use somatic terms to convey emotional distress.

In some cases, there may also be inherent role conflicts between the goals of therapy and the values of a particular culture. The individualism of American society, which becomes expressed in therapeutic interventions in Western society that focus on development of the self, contrasts sharply with the group- and family-centered values of Asian cultures (Huang, 1994). Therapeutic approaches that emphasize the importance of individuality and self-determination may be inappropriate when applied to Asian clients who adhere strongly to traditional Asian cultural values, which emphasize the importance of the group over the individual (Ching et al., 1995; Henkin, 1985).

Hispanic Americans Although Hispanic American subcultures differ in various respects, many of them share certain cultural values and beliefs, such as adherence to a strong patriarchal (male-dominated) family structure and strong kinship ties. De la Cancela and Guzman (1991) identify some other values shared by many Hispanic Americans:

> One's identity is in part determined by one's role in the family. The male, or *macho*, is the head of the family, the provider, the protector of the family honor, and the final decision maker. The woman's role (*marianismo*) is to care for the family and the children. Obviously, these roles are changing, with women entering the work force and achieving

greater educational opportunities. Cultural values of *respeto* (respect), *confianza* (trust), *dignidad* (dignity), and *personalismo* (personalism) are highly esteemed and are important factors in working with many [Hispanic Americans]. (p. 60)

Therapists need to recognize that value conflicts may occur between the traditional Hispanic American value of interdependency on the family with the values of independence and self-reliance, which are stressed in the mainstream U.S. culture (De la Cancela & Guzman, 1991). Psychotherapeutic interventions should respect differences in values rather than attempt to impose values of majority cultures on people from ethnic minority groups. Therapists should also be trained to reach beyond the confines of their offices to work within the Hispanic American community itself, in settings that have an impact on the daily lives of Hispanic Americans, such as social clubs, *bodegas* (neighborhood groceries), and neighborhood beauty and barber shops. We can further break down barriers that may impede utilization of mental health services by Hispanic Americans by recruiting bicultural/bilingual staff and creating a welcoming therapeutic atmosphere that is accepting of Hispanic American cultural values (Guarnaccia & Rodriguez, 1996).

Native Americans Among all the ethnic minority groups in the United States, Native Americans may be most in need of effective mental health treatment. Lifetime prevalence of psychological disorders may exceed 50% of the population of some Native American tribes. Despite the need, Native Americans remain severely underserved by mental health professionals, in part because of the cultural gap that exists between providers and recipients of these services.

Kahn (1982) argues that if mental health professionals are to be successful in helping Native Americans, they must do so within a context that is relevant and sensitive to Native Americans' customs, culture, and values. For example, many Native Americans expect the therapist will do most of the talking and they will play a passive role in treatment. These expectations are in keeping with the traditional healer role but may conflict with the client-focused approach of many forms of conventional therapy. There may yet be other differences in gestures, eye contact, facial expression, and other modes of nonverbal expression that can impede effective communication between therapist and client (Renfrey, 1992).

Psychologists recognize the importance of bringing elements of tribal culture into mental health programs for American Indians (Rabasca, 2000a). For example, therapists can use indigenous ceremonies that are part of the client's cultural or religious traditions. To do so, mental health professionals need to become knowledgeable about traditional Native cultures as well as their own and attempt to integrate the two (Timpson et al., 1988). Lefley (1990) notes that purification and cleansing rites are therapeutic for many Native American peoples in the United States and elsewhere, as among the African Cuban *Santeria*, the Brazilian *umbanda*, and the Haitian *vodoun*. Cleansing rites are often sought by people who believe their problems are caused by failure to placate malevolent spirits or to perform mandatory rituals (Lefley, 1990).

Respect for cultural differences is a keynote feature of culturally sensitive therapies. Training in multicultural therapy is becoming more widely integrated into training programs for therapists (e.g., Neville et al., 1996). Culturally sensitive therapies adopt a respectful attitude that encourages people to tell their own personal story as well as the story of their culture (Coronado & Peake, 1992).

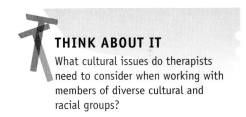

THINK ABOUT IT

What cultural issues do therapists need to consider when working with members of diverse cultural and racial groups?

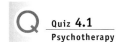

Quiz **4.1**
Psychotherapy

Biomedical Therapies

There is a growing emphasis in American psychiatry on biomedical therapies, especially the use of psychotherapeutic drugs (also called *psychotropic drugs*). Biomedical therapies are generally administered by medical doctors, many of whom have specialized training in psychiatry or **psychopharmacology.** Many family physicians or general practitioners also prescribe psychotherapeutic drugs for their patients, however.

Biomedical approaches have had dramatic success in treating some forms of abnormal behavior, though they also have their limitations. For one, drugs may have unwelcome

psychopharmacology The field of study that examines the effects of therapeutic or psychiatric drugs.

antianxiety drugs Drugs that combat anxiety and reduce states of muscle tension.

tolerance Physical habituation to use of a drug.

rebound anxiety The experiencing of strong anxiety following withdrawal from a tranquilizer.

antipsychotic drugs Drugs used to treat schizophrenia or other psychotic disorders.

Web Link **4.3** wWw
Psychiatric Medications

or dangerous side effects. There is also the potential for abuse. One of the most commonly prescribed minor tranquilizers, Valium, has become a major drug of abuse among people who become psychologically and physiologically dependent on it. Psychosurgery has been all but eliminated as a form of treatment because of serious harmful effects of earlier procedures.

Drug Therapy

Different classes of psychotropic drugs are used in the treatment of various types of mental health problems. These include antianxiety drugs, antipsychotic drugs, antidepressants, and lithium which is used to treat mood swings in people with bipolar disorder. The use of other psychotropic drugs, such as stimulants, will be discussed in later chapters.

Antianxiety Drugs Antianxiety drugs (also called *anxiolytics*, from the Greek *anxietas*, meaning "anxiety," and *lysis*, meaning "bringing to an end") are drugs that combat anxiety and reduce states of muscle tension. They include mild tranquilizers, such as those of the *benzodiazepines* class of drugs, including *diazepam* (Valium) and *alprazolam* (Xanax), as well as hypnotic-sedatives, such as *triazolam* (Halcion) and *flurazepam* (Dalmane).

Antianxiety drugs depress the level of activity in certain parts of the central nervous system (CNS). In turn, the CNS decreases the level of sympathetic nervous system activity, reducing the respiration rate and heart rate and lessening states of anxiety and tension. Mild tranquilizers such as Valium grew in popularity when physicians became concerned about the use of more potent depressants, such as barbiturates, which are highly addictive and extremely dangerous when taken in overdoses or mixed with alcohol. Unfortunately, it has become clear that these tranquilizers also can, and often do, lead to physiological dependence (addiction). People who are dependent on Valium may go into convulsions when they abruptly stop taking it. Deaths have been reported among people who mix mild tranquilizers with alcohol or who are unusually sensitive to them. There are other less severe side effects, such as fatigue, drowsiness, and impaired motor coordination, that might nonetheless impair the ability to function or to operate an automobile. Regular usage of benzodiazepines can also produce **tolerance,** a physiological sign of dependence, which refers to the need over time for increasing dosages of a drug to achieve the same effect. Quite commonly, patients become involved in tugs of war with their physicians as they demand increased dosages despite their physicians' concerns about the potential for abuse and dependence.

When used on a short-term basis, antianxiety drugs can be safe and effective in treating anxiety and insomnia. Yet drugs by themselves do not teach people more adaptive ways of solving their problems and may encourage them to rely on a chemical agent to cope with stress rather than develop active means of coping. Drug therapy is thus often combined with psychotherapy to help people with anxiety complaints deal with the psychological and situational bases of their problems. However, combining drug therapy and psychotherapy may present special problems and challenges. For one, drug-induced relief from anxiety may reduce clients' motivation to try to solve their problems. For another, medicated clients who develop skills for coping with stress in psychotherapy may fail to retain what they have learned once the tranquilizers are discontinued, or find themselves too tense to employ their newly acquired skills.

Rebound anxiety is another problem associated with regular use of tranquilizers. Many people who regularly use antianxiety drugs report that anxiety or insomnia returns in a more severe form once they discontinue them. For some, this may represent a fear of not having the drugs to depend on. For others, rebound anxiety might reflect changes in biochemical processes that are not well understood at present.

Antipsychotic Drugs Antipsychotic drugs, also called *neuroleptics*, are commonly used to treat the more flagrant features of schizophrenia or other psychotic disorders, such as hallucinations, delusions, and states of confusion. Many of these drugs, including *chlorpromazine* (Thorazine), *thioridazine* (Mellaril), and *fluphenazine* (Prolixin), belong to the *phenothiazine* class of chemicals. Phenothiazines appear to control psychotic features by blocking the action of the neurotransmitter dopamine at receptor sites in the brain. Although the underlying causes of schizophrenia remain unknown, researchers suspect an irregularity in the dopamine system in the brain may be involved (see Chapter 13). *Clozapine* (Clozaril), a neuroleptic of a different chemical class than the phenothiazines, has been shown to be effective in treating many people with schizophrenia whose symptoms were unresponsive to other neuroleptics (see Chapter 13). The use of clozapine must be carefully monitored, however, because of potentially dangerous side effects.

The use of neuroleptics has greatly reduced the need for more restrictive forms of treatment for severely disturbed patients, such as physical restraints and confinement in padded cells, and has lessened the need for long-term hospitalization. The introduction of the first generation of antipsychotic drugs in the mid-1950s was one of the major factors that led to a massive exodus of chronic mental patients from state institutions. Many formerly hospitalized patients have been able to resume family life and hold jobs while continuing to take their medications.

Neuroleptics are not without their problems, including potential side effects such as muscular rigidity and tremors. Although these side effects are generally controllable by use of other drugs, long-term use of antipsychotic drugs (possibly excepting clozapine) can produce a potentially irreversible and disabling motor disorder called *tardive dyskinesia* (see Chapter 13), which is characterized by uncontrollable eye blinking, facial grimaces, lip smacking, and other involuntary movements of the mouth, eyes, and limbs. Researchers are experimenting with lowered dosages, intermittent drug regimens, and use of new medications to reduce the risk of such complications.

Antidepressants Three major classes of **antidepressants** are used in treating depression: **tricyclics**, **monoamine oxidase (MAO) inhibitors**, and **selective serotonin-reuptake inhibitors (SSRIs)**. The first two kinds of antidepressants, tricyclics and MAO inhibitors, increase the availability of the neurotransmitters norepinephrine and serotonin in the brain. Some of the more common tricyclics are *imipramine* (Tofranil), *amitriptyline* (Elavil), and *doxepin* (Sinequan). The MAO inhibitors include such drugs as *phenelzine* (Nardil) and *tranylcypromine* (Parnate). Tricyclic antidepressants (TCAs) are more commonly favored over MAO inhibitors because of potentially serious side effects associated with MAO inhibitors.

The third class of antidepressants, selective serotonin-reuptake inhibitors, or SSRIs, have more specific effects on serotonin function in the brain. Drugs in this class include *fluoxetine* (Prozac), now the most widely prescribed antidepressant on the market, and *sertraline* (Zoloft). They increase the availability of serotonin in the brain by interfering with its reuptake by the transmitting neuron.

By the latest estimates, it appears that slightly more than half of the people with clinically significant depression who are treated with antidepressants of the tricyclic class will respond favorably (Depression Guideline Panel, 1993b). A favorable response to treatment does not mean depression is relieved, however. Overall, the effects of tricyclic antidepressants (TCAs) appear to be modest (Greenberg et al., 1992). Nor does any particular antidepressant appear to be clearly more effective than any other (Depression Guideline Panel, 1993b). Even Prozac, which was hailed by some as a "wonder drug," produces about the same level of therapeutic benefit as the older generation of antidepressants, the TCAs (Greenberg et al., 1994). Prozac and other SSRIs may be preferred, however, because they are associated with fewer side effects, such as weight gain, and have a lower risk of lethal overdoses than the older tricyclics (Depression Guideline Panel, 1993b).

Antidepressants also have beneficial effects in treating a wide range of psychological disorders, including panic disorder (see Chapter 6), obsessive-compulsive disorder (also in Chapter 6), and eating disorders (see Chapter 11). As research into the underlying causes of these disorders continues, we may find that irregularities of neurotransmitter functioning in the brain plays a key role in their development.

antidepressants Drugs used to treat depression.

tricyclics A group of antidepressant drugs that increase the activity of norepinephrine and serotonin by interfering with the reuptake of these neurotransmitters.

monoamine oxidase (MAO) inhibitors A group of antidepressant drugs that increase the availability of neurotransmitters in the brain by inhibiting the actions of an enzyme that breaks down neurotransmitters.

selective serotonin-reuptake inhibitors (SSRIs) A group of antidepressant drugs that increase the availability of serotonin in the brain by interfering with its reuptake by the transmitting neuron.

Truth OR Fiction? REVISITED

Despite beliefs that it is a wonder drug, the antidepressant Prozac has not been shown to be any more effective than the earlier generation of antidepressants.

TRUE. Though Prozac may have fewer side effects than the older generation of antidepressants, it has not been shown to provide any greater therapeutic benefit.

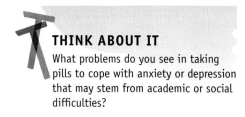

THINK ABOUT IT
What problems do you see in taking pills to cope with anxiety or depression that may stem from academic or social difficulties?

Lithium Lithium carbonate, a salt of the metal lithium in tablet form, helps in many cases to stabilize the dramatic mood swings of patients with bipolar disorder (formerly manic depression) (discussed in Chapter 8). Like people with diabetes who must take insulin through their lifetimes to control their disease, people with bipolar disorder may have to continue using lithium indefinitely to control the disorder. Because of potential toxicity associated with lithium, the blood levels of patients maintained on the drug must be carefully monitored.

Table 4.3 lists psychotropic drugs according to their drug class and category.

TABLE 4.3   Major Psychotropic Drugs

Category	Drug Class	Generic Name	Trade Name
Antianxiety agents (also called anxiolytics)	Benzodiazepines	Diazepam	Valium
		Chlordiazepoxide	Librium
		Clorazepate	Tranxene
		Oxazepam	Serax
		Lorazepam	Ativan
		Alprazolam	Xanax
	Barbiturates	Meprobamate	Miltown
			Equanil
	Hypnotics	Flurazepam	Dalmane
		Triazolam	Halcion
		Zolpidem	Ambien
	Other anxiolytics	Busipirone	BuSpar
Antipsychotic drugs (also called neuroleptics or major tranquilizers)	Phenothiazines	Chlorpromazine	Thorazine
		Thioridazine	Mellaril
		Mesoridazine	Serentil
		Perphenazine	Trilafon
		Trifluoperazine	Stelazine
		Fluphenazine	Prolixin
	Thioxanthenes	Thiothixene	Navane
	Butyrophenones	Haloperidol	Haldol
	Dibenzoxazepines	Loxapine	Loxitane
	Dibenzodiazepines	Clozapine	Clozaril
Antidepressants	Tricyclic antidepressants (TCAs)	Imipramine	Tofranil
		Desipramine	Norpramin
		Amitriptyline	Elavil
		Doxepin	Sinequan
		Clomipramine	Anafranil
	MAO inhibitors (MAOIs)	Phenelzine	Nardil
		Tranylcypromine	Parnate
	Selective serotonin-reuptake inhibitors (SSRIs)	Fluoxetine	Prozac
		Sertraline	Zoloft
		Paroxetine	Paxil
		Fluvoxamine	Luvox
		Citalopram	Celexa
	Other antidepressants	Bupropion	Wellbutrin
		Nefazodone	Serzone
		Venlafaxine	Effexor
Antimanic agents		Lithium carbonate	Eskalith
		Carbamazepine	Tegretol
		Divalproex	Depakote
		Valproate	Depakene
Stimulants		Methylphenidate	Ritalin
		Pemoline	Cylert

Ethnic Differences in Response to Psychotropic Medication

Cultural or ethnic factors may contribute to differences in responsiveness to psychotropic medications (Lefley, 1990; Lesser, 1992). African Americans, for example, tend to show a better response to antidepressants and phenothiazines than other groups. Hispanic Americans tend to show lower effective dosage levels (Lawson, 1986). However, some research suggests that African Americans are at greater risk of experiencing potentially serious side effects from psychiatric drugs, especially phenothiazines (Jeste et al., 1996). Differences in response patterns and risks of side effects among ethnic groups brings into perspective the need to conduct psychopharmacological research on diverse groups. Unfortunately, people of color, including African Americans, have been underrepresented in drug trials (Lawson, 1996).

Electroconvulsive Therapy

In 1939, the Italian psychiatrist Ugo Cerletti introduced the technique of **electroconvulsive therapy (ECT)** in psychiatric treatment. Cerletti had observed the practice in some slaughterhouses of using electric shock to render animals unconscious. He observed that the shocks also produced convulsions. Cerletti incorrectly believed, as did other researchers in Europe at the time, that convulsions of the type found in epilepsy were incompatible with schizophrenia and that a treatment method that induced convulsions might be used to cure schizophrenia.

After the introduction of the phenothiazines in the 1950s, the use of ECT became generally limited to the treatment of severe depression. The introduction of antidepressants has limited the use of ECT even further today. However, evidence indicates that about 50% of people with major depression who fail to respond to antidepressants show significant improvement following ECT (Prudic et al., 1996).

ECT remains a source of controversy for several reasons. First, many people, including many professionals, are uncomfortable about the idea of passing an electric shock through a person's head, even if the level of shock is closely regulated and the convulsions are controlled by drugs. Second are the potential side effects. ECT often produces dramatic relief from severe depression, but concerns remain about its potential for inducing cognitive deficits, such as memory loss. Permanent loss of memory may occur for events that happen during the months that precede ECT and for several weeks afterwards (Glass, 2001). Third are questions of relative efficacy. The relative effectiveness of ECT as compared to antidepressant drugs, to sham (simulated) ECT, and to cognitive-behavioral therapy remains under study. Fourth, no one yet knows why ECT works, although it is suspected that it might help correct neurotransmitter imbalances in the brain. Fifth, evidence shows a high rate of relapse following ECT treatment (Sackeim et al., 2001).

Although controversies concerning the use of ECT persist, increasing evidence supports its effectiveness in helping people overcome severe depression that fails to respond to psychotherapy or antidepressant medication (Sackeim et al., 2001). However, ECT is usually considered a treatment of last resort, after less intrusive methods have been tried and failed.

Psychosurgery

Psychosurgery is yet more controversial than ECT and is rarely practiced today. Although no longer performed, the most widely used form of psychosurgery was the **prefrontal lobotomy,** in which the nerve pathways linking the thalamus to the prefrontal lobes of the brain are surgically severed. The operation was based on the theory that extremely disturbed patients suffer from

electroconvulsive therapy (ECT) A method of treating severe depression by administering electrical shock to the head.

prefrontal lobotomy A form of psychosurgery, no longer in use, in which certain neural pathways in the brain are severed in order to control disturbed behavior.

Truth OR Fiction?   REVISITED

Severely depressed people who have failed to respond to other treatments may show rapid improvement from electroconvulsive therapy.

TRUE. ECT is actually helpful in many cases of severe depression that do not respond to other forms of treatment.

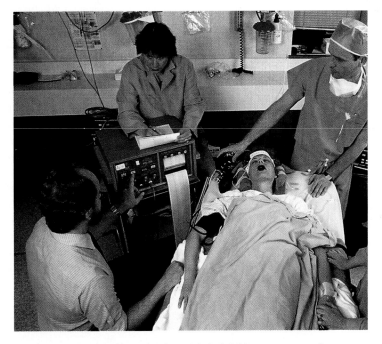

Electroconvulsive therapy (ECT). ECT is helpful in many cases of severe or prolonged depression that do not respond to other forms of treatment. Still, its use remains controversial.

overexcitation of emotional impulses that emanate from the lower brain centers, such as the thalamus and hypothalamus. It was believed that by severing the connections between the thalamus and the higher brain centers in the frontal lobe of the cerebral cortex, the patient's violent or aggressive tendencies could be controlled. The prefrontal lobotomy was developed by the Portuguese neurologist António Egas Moniz and was introduced to the United States in the 1930s. More than 1,000 mental patients received the operation by 1950. Although the operation did reduce violent and agitated behavior in many cases, it was not always successful. In a cruel ironic twist, a patient whom Moniz had treated later shot him, leaving him paralyzed from a bullet that lodged in his spine.

Many distressing side effects are associated with the prefrontal lobotomy, including hyperactivity, impaired learning ability and reduced creativity, distractibility, apathy, overeating, withdrawal, epileptic-type seizures, and even death. The occurrence of these side effects, combined with the introduction of the phenothiazines, led to the elimination of the operation.

More sophisticated psychosurgery techniques have been introduced in recent years. Generally speaking, they are limited to smaller parts of the brain and produce less damage than the prefrontal lobotomy. These operations have been performed to treat such problems as intractable aggression, depression, and psychotic behavior; chronic pain; some forms of epilepsy; and persistent obsessive-compulsive disorder (Baer et al., 1995; Irle et al., 1998; Sachdev & Hay, 1996). Follow-up studies of such procedures have shown marked improvement in about one-quarter to one-half of cases. But concerns about possible complications, including impaired intellectual functioning, have greatly reduced their use (Irle et al., 1998). Before leaving this topic, let us understand that psychosurgery should only be considered as a treatment of last resort.

Evaluation of Biological Approaches

There is little doubt that the use of psychotropic drugs has helped many people with severe psychological problems. Many thousands of people with schizophrenia who were formerly hospitalized are able to function more effectively in the community because of antipsychotic drugs. Antidepressant drugs have helped relieve depression in many cases and have shown therapeutic benefits in treating other disorders, such as panic disorder, obsessive-compulsive disorder, and eating disorders. ECT is helpful in relieving depression in many people who have been unresponsive to other treatments.

On the other hand, it may be that some forms of psychotherapy are as effective as drug therapy in treating anxiety disorders and depression (see Chapters 6 and 8). Moreover, problems persist with respect to the side effects of various psychotropic drugs. In addition, antianxiety agents, such as Valium, have often become drugs of abuse among people who become dependent on them for relieving the effects of stress rather than seeking more adaptive ways of solving their problems. Medical practitioners have often been too quick to use their prescription pads to help people with anxiety complaints, rather than to help them examine their lives or refer them for psychological treatment. Physicians often feel pressured, of course, by patients who seek a chemical solution to their life problems.

While we continue to learn more about the biological foundations of abnormal behavior patterns, the interface between biology and behavior can be construed as a two-way street. Researchers have uncovered links between psychological factors and many physical disorders and conditions (see Chapter 5). Researchers are also investigating whether the combination of psychological and drug treatments for such problems as depression, anxiety disorders, and substance abuse disorders, among others, may increase the therapeutic benefits of either of the two approaches alone.

Quiz 4.2
Biomedical Therapies **Q**

Hospitalization and Community-Based Care

People receive mental health services within various settings, including hospitals, outpatient clinics, community mental health centers, and private practices. In this section we explore the purposes of hospitalization and the movement toward community-based care. Due to deinstitutionalization—the policy of shifting the burden of care from the state hospitals to community-based treatment settings—an exodus has taken place from state mental hospitals. We will see that deinstitutionalization has had a profound impact on the delivery of mental health services as well as on the larger community.

Roles for Hospitalization

Different types of hospitals provide different types of mental health treatment. State mental hospitals provide care to people with severe psychological problems. Municipal and community-based hospitals tend to focus on short-term care for people with serious psychological problems who need a structured hospital environment to help them through an acute crisis. In such cases, psychotropic drugs and other biological treatments, such as ECT for severe cases of depression, are often used in combination with short-term psychotherapy. Hospitalization may be followed by outpatient treatment. Many private care hospitals provide longer-term care or are specialized to help people withdraw safely from alcohol or drugs.

Most state hospitals today are better managed and provide more humane care than those of the 19th and early 20th centuries, but here and there deplorable conditions persist. Today's state hospital is generally more treatment oriented and focuses on preparing residents to return to community living. State hospitals today often function as part of an integrated, comprehensive approach to treatment. They provide the structured environment needed for people who are unable to function in a less restrictive community setting. When hospitalization restores patients to a higher level of functioning, the patients are reintegrated in the community and provided with follow-up care and transitional residences, if needed, to help them adjust to community living. Patients may be rehospitalized as needed in a state hospital if a community-based hospital is not available or if they require more extensive care than a community hospital can provide. For younger and less intensely disturbed people, the state hospital stay is typically briefer than it was in the past, lasting only until their condition allows them to reenter society. Older chronic patients may be unprepared to handle the most rudimentary tasks (shopping, cooking, cleaning, and so on) of independent life, however—in part because the state hospital may be the only home such patients have known as adults.

deinstitutionalization The policy of shifting care for patients with severe or chronic mental health problems from inpatient facilities to community-based facilities.

wWw **Web Link 4.4**
Treatment Facilities

Modern psychiatric hospital. The modern psychiatric hospital is better managed and provides more humane care than those of earlier times, many of which housed patients under the most abysmal conditions. Here we see the bright and spacious dayroom in a modern psychiatric hospital.

halfway houses Supervised community residences that provide a bridge between institutional facilities and independent community living.

primary prevention Efforts designed to prevent problems from arising.

secondary prevention Efforts to ameliorate existing problems at an early stage.

The Community Mental Health Center

Community mental health centers (CMHCs) perform many functions in the effort to reduce the need for hospitalization of new patients and rehospitalization of formerly hospitalized patients. A primary function of the CMHC is to help discharged mental patients adjust to the community by providing continuing care and closely monitoring their progress. Unfortunately, not enough CMHCs have been established to serve the needs of the hundreds of thousands of ex-hospitalized patients and to try to prevent the need for hospitalization of new patients by providing intervention services and alternatives to full hospitalization, such as day hospital programs. Patients in day hospitals attend structured therapy and vocational rehabilitation programs in a hospital setting during the day but are returned to their families or homes at night. Many CMHCs also administer transitional treatment facilities in the community, such as **halfway houses,** which provide a sheltered living environment to help discharged mental patients gradually adjust to the community as well as to provide people in crisis with an alternative to hospitalization. CMHCs also serve in consultative roles to other professionals in the community, such as training police officers to handle disturbed people.

One of the major functions of the community mental health center is prevention. "An ounce of prevention is worth a pound of cure"—so goes the saying. Today we stockpile vital supplies such as grain and oil to lessen the effects of shortages. In medical science, the development of vaccines has helped protect people from contracting such diseases as smallpox and polio. In the mental health system, however, resources are generally directed toward treating mental health problems rather than attempting to prevent them from developing. A recent report by the prestigious Institute of Medicine (IOM) called for increased support for research on prevention and for development of programs to promote psychological well-being and reduce the risks of mental health disorders (Munoz, Mrazek, & Haggerty, 1996).

The Spectrum of Prevention Traditionally, the term *prevention* has been applied to interventions that run the gamut from programs designed to prevent the onset of mental disorders to those that attempt to reduce the impact of disorders once they develop (Kaplan, 2000). The IOM report, initiated by the U.S. Congress, limits the term *prevention* to interventions that occur before the onset of a diagnosable disorder (Munoz, Mrazek, & Haggerty, 1996). Interventions focusing on lessening the impact of already developed disorders are classified as *treatment interventions* rather than prevention.

The IOM report conceptualizes a mental health spectrum of interventions ranging from prevention efforts through treatment and maintenance interventions (see Figure 4.2). Three categories of prevention programs are identified: universal, selective, and indicated.

Universal preventive interventions are targeted toward the whole population or general public, such as programs designed to enhance prenatal health or childhood nutrition. *Selective preventive interventions* are targeted toward individuals or groups known to be at higher than average risk of developing mental disorders, such as children of schizophrenic parents. **Primary prevention** efforts—programs designed to prevent problems from arising in the first place, can be either universal or selective preventive interventions depending on whether they are focused on the general population or "at-risk" groups.

Indicated preventive interventions are directed toward individuals with early signs or symptoms that foreshadow the development of a mental disorder but don't yet meet diagnostic criteria for the particular disorder. This form of prevention, commonly called **secondary prevention,** attempts to nip in the bud developing problems. For example, secondary preventive programs aimed at changing the drinking habits of high-risk drinkers or early

An ounce of prevention. Obtaining good prenatal care can help prevent health problems in both the mother and the fetus. Mental health professionals face the challenge of developing programs to reduce the risks of psychological disorders.

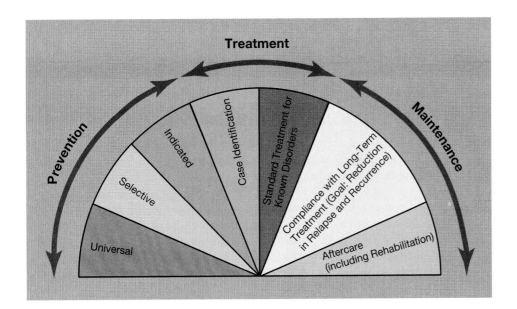

FIGURE 4.2 The mental health intervention spectrum for mental disorders.

Source. Mazrek, P. J., & Haggerty, R. J., *Reducing risks for mental disorders: Frontiers for preventive Intervention Research.* Copyright© 1994 by the National Academy of Sciences. Courtesy of the National Academy Press, Washington, D.C. Reprinted with permission.

problem drinkers may forestall the onset of more severe alcohol-related problems or alcohol dependence (Botelho & Richmond, 1996; Marlatt et al., 1998).

We have had some success in the health arena in developing effective prevention programs for reducing the risks of teenage pregnancies, sexually transmitted diseases, and some forms of drug abuse (e.g., Blackman, 1996; Stover et al., 1996). Psychologist Martin Seligman and his colleagues have shown that teaching cognitive skills involved in disputing catastrophic, negative thoughts reduced the risk of depression in both college students and school-age children (Jaycox et al., 1994; Seligman, 1998). Still, we have much to learn about developing effective prevention programs to prevent psychological disorders. The development of effective preventive programs rests in large part on expanding our knowledge base about the underlying causes of these disorders and mounting controlled investigations that examine ways of preventing them (Munoz, Mrazek, & Haggerty, 1996).

The challenge of preventing psychological disorders is before us. The question is whether the nation can muster the political will and financial resolve to meet the challenge.

Ethnic Group Differences in Use of Mental Health Services

A 2001 report by the U.S. Surgeon General concluded that members of racial and ethnic minority groups typically have less access to mental health care and receive lower quality care than do other Americans (Goode, 2001f; USDHHS, 2001; see Table 4.4). A major reason for this disparity is that a disproportionate number of minority group members remain uninsured or underinsured, leaving many of them unable to afford mental health care. Consequently, minorities shoulder a greater burden of mental health problems that go undiagnosed and untreated (Stenson, 2001a).

Cultural factors are yet another reason for underutilization of mental health services by minority groups. Mental health clinics are not typically the first places where African Americans go for help for emotional problems. They are more likely to turn first to the church and second to the emergency room of the local general hospital (Lewis-Hall, 1992). The National Survey of African Americans found that slightly more than half (54%) of those who reported experiencing feelings of a "nervous breakdown" failed to consult any type of professional for help with their problems (Neighbors, 1992). Another study found that only about 1 in 10 African Americans in a community-based sample who experienced major depression consulted a mental health professional (D. R. Brown, Ahmed, Gary, & Milburn, 1995).

Hispanic Americans who encounter emotional problems are more likely to seek assistance from friends and relatives, or from spiritualists, than to reach out to mental health facilities, which they perceive as cold and impersonal institutions (De La Cancela &

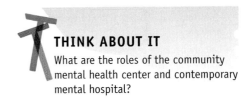

THINK ABOUT IT
What are the roles of the community mental health center and contemporary mental hospital?

TABLE 4.4 *Culture, Race, Ethnicity, and Mental Health:* Major Findings of the Surgeon General's Report

- The percentage of African Americans receiving needed care for mental health problems is only half that of non-Hispanic Whites. African Americans have less access to mental health care than Whites, partly because a greater percentage of African Americans lack health insurance.

- Of all American ethnic groups, Hispanic Americans are the least likely to have health insurance. Moreover, the limited availability of Spanish-speaking mental health professionals means that many Hispanic Americans who speak little or no English lack the opportunity to receive care from linguistically similar treatment providers.

- Largely because of lingering stigma and shame associated with mental illness, Asian Americans/Pacific Islanders often fail to seek care until their problems are more advanced than is the case with other groups. Moreover, accessibility is limited by scarcity of treatment providers with appropriate language skills.

- American Indians/Alaska Natives have a suicide rate that is 50% higher than the national average, but little is known about how many people within these groups receive needed care. In addition, the rural, isolated locations in which many Native Americans live places a severe constraint on the availability of mental health services.

Source. Adapted from Stenson, 2001a; USDHHS, 2001.

Web Link 4.5
Ending Discrimination WWW
in Health Insurance

Guzman, 1991). Hispanic people are also more likely to seek assistance for emotional problems from primary care physicians than from psychologists or psychiatrists. Asian American/Pacific Islanders are also less likely than Euro-Americans to seek help from mental health providers (Breaux, Matsuoka, & Ryujin, 1995).

We may better understand low rates of utilization of outpatient mental health services by ethnic minorities by examining the barriers that exist to receiving treatment, which include the following (adapted from Cheung, 1991; USDHHS, 1999a; Woodward, Dwinell, & Arons, 1992):

1. *Cultural mistrust.* People from minority groups often fail to use mental health services because they are fearful of government-operated services or believe such services will be unresponsive to their needs. Mistrust may stem from a cultural or personal history of oppression and discrimination. In some cases, cultural insensitivity and outright discrimination on the part of mental health workers contribute to underutilization of their services by ethnic minorities (Sanchez & Mohl, 1992). If ethnic minority clients perceive majority therapists and the institutions in which they work to be cold and insensitive, they are less likely to place their trust in them.

2. *Institutional barriers.* Facilities may be inaccessible to minority group members because they are located at a considerable distance from their homes or because of lack of public transportation. Most facilities only operate during daytime work hours, which means they are inaccessible to minority group members who are unable to take time off. Moreover, minority group members feel staff members often make them feel stupid for not being familiar with clinic procedures and their requests for assistance often become tangled in red tape.

3. *Cultural barriers.* Many recent immigrants, especially those from Southeast Asian countries, have had little, if any, previous contact with mental health professionals. They may hold different conceptions of mental health problems or view mental health problems as less severe than physical problems. In some ethnic minority subcultures, the family is expected to take care of members who have psychological problems and may resist seeking outside assistance because of guilt engendered by the belief that seeking outside help would represent rejection of the family member and would embarrass the family. Other cultural barriers include cultural differences between typically lower socioeconomic strata minority group members and mostly White, middle-class staff members and incongruence between the cultural practices of minority group members and techniques used by mental health professionals. For example, Asian immigrants may find little value in talking about their problems or may be uncomfortable expressing their feelings to strangers. In many ethnic minority groups, personal and interpersonal problems are brought to trusted elders in the family or religious leaders, not to outside professionals.

4. *Language barriers.* Differences in language make it difficult for minority group members to describe their problems or obtain needed services. Many mental health services do not have staff members who can communicate in the languages used by ethnic minority residents in their communities.

5. *Economic and accessibility barriers.* As mentioned above, financial barriers are often a major determination of underutilization of mental health services by ethnic minorities, many of whom live in economically distressed areas with limited resources. Moreover, many minority group members live in rural or isolated areas where mental health services may be lacking or inaccessible (USDHHS, 2001).

Cheung (1991) concludes that greater utilization of mental health services will depend to a great extent on the ability of the mental health system to develop programs that consider these cultural factors and build staffs that consist of culturally sensitive providers, including minority mental health professionals and paraprofessionals. Cultural mistrust of the mental health system among minority group members may be grounded in the perception that many mental health professionals are racially biased in how they evaluate and treat members of minority groups. Let's take a closer look at whether the evidence bears out this perception.

Racial Stereotyping and the Mental Health System

If you are African American, you are more likely to be admitted to a mental hospital, and more likely to be involuntarily committed, than if you are White (Lindsey & Paul, 1989). You are also more likely to be diagnosed with schizophrenia (Coleman & Baker, 1994; USDHHS, 1999a). The question is, why?

Relationships between ethnicity and diagnostic and admission practices are complex. They depend in part on differences in rates of mental disorders among different ethnic groups. If the rate of a given disorder is higher in a particular group, then it stands to reason that more members of the group will be diagnosed with the disorder. We know that African Americans as a group are no more likely to develop schizophrenia, a severe psychological disorder that often leads to hospitalization, than are Euro-Americans of the same socioeconomic level (USDHHS, 1999a). However, we also know that African Americans are overrepresented among lower socioeconomic groups in our society, and people in the lower strata on the socioeconomic ladder are more likely to have severe psychological disorders, such as schizophrenia. Thus, differences in socioeconomic backgrounds offer at least a partial explanation of ethnic/racial differences in diagnostic practices and rates of psychiatric hospitalization.

Ethnic stereotyping by mental health professionals may also contribute to an overdiagnosis of severe psychological problems requiring hospitalization. Evidence of clinician bias comes from research showing that whereas African Americans and Hispanic Americans are more likely than Euro-Americans to be diagnosed with schizophrenia, independent evidence fails to justify such differences (Garb, 1997; Lawson, 1994). African Americans are also more likely than Euro-Americans to receive psychiatric medication, including antipsychotic medication (Segal, Bola, & Watson, 1996). Investigators believe that clinician biases rather than clinical criteria may account for differences in prescription patterns (Frackiewicz et al., 1999).

How might clinician biases come to affect their clinical judgments? As the recent Surgeon General's report on mental health points out, diagnostic and treatment decisions in mental health settings are heavily weighted on behavioral signs and patient reporting of symptoms rather than more objective laboratory tests (USDHHS, 1999a). Consequently, clinician judgment plays an important role in determining whether or not someone receives a schizophrenia diagnosis and is deemed to be in need of hospitalization or antipsychotic medication.

Evaluation of Deinstitutionalization

Let us return to the issue of deinstitutionalization. Has this policy achieved its goal of successfully reintegrating mental patients into society, or does it remain a promise that is largely unfulfilled? Deinstitutionalization has often been criticized for failing to live up to its expectations. The criticism seems to be well founded. Among the most frequent criticisms is the charge that many hospital patients were merely dumped into the community and not provided with the community-based services they needed to adjust to demands of community living. A 1998 national study found that fewer than half of patients with schizophrenia were receiving adequate care (Winerip, 1999).

Though the community mental health movement has had some successes, a great many patients with severe and persistent mental health problems fail to receive the range of mental health and social services they need to adjust to life in the community (Jacobs, Newman, & Burns, 2001). One of the major challenges facing the community mental system is the problem of psychiatric homelessness.

Deinstitutionalization and the Psychiatric Homeless Population The federal government estimates that nearly one-third of the homeless people in the United States

Psychiatric homeless population. Many homeless people have severe psychological problems but fall through the cracks of the mental health and social service systems.

THINK ABOUT IT

What do you believe should be done about the problem of psychiatric homelessness?

Quiz **4.3**
Hospitalization and Community-Based Care

Quiz **4.4**
Chapter Exam

suffer from severe psychological disorders (Center for Mental Health Services, 1994). Many ex-hospitalized mental patients were essentially dumped into local communities following discharge and left with little if any support. Lacking adequate support, they often face more dehumanizing conditions on the street, under deinstitutionalization, than they did in the hospital. Many compound their problems by turning to illegal street drugs such as crack. Also, some of the younger psychiatric homeless population might have been hospitalized in earlier times but are now, in the wake of deinstitutionalization, directed toward community support programs, when they are available. The lack of available housing and transitional care facilities and effective case management play important roles in accounting for homelessness among people with psychiatric problems. Some homeless people with severe psychiatric problems are repeatedly hospitalized for brief stays in community-based hospitals during acute episodes. They move back and forth between the hospital and the community as though caught in a revolving door. Frequently, they are released from the hospital with inadequate arrangements for housing and community care. Some are left essentially to fend for themselves. While many state hospitals closed their doors and others slashed the number of beds, the states never funded the support services in the community that were supposed to replace the need for long-term hospitalization (Winerip, 1999).

Problems of homelessness are especially compounded for children in homeless families. Not surprisingly, homeless children tend to have more behavior problems than housed children (Schteingart et al., 1995). The problem of psychiatric homelessness is not limited to urban areas, although it is on our city streets that the problem is most visible. The pattern in rural areas tends to be one of inconsistent housing and unstable living arrangements, rather than outright homelessness (Drake et al., 1991).

The mental health system alone does not have the resources to resolve the multifaceted problems faced by the psychiatric homeless population. Helping the psychiatric homeless escape from homelessness requires an integrated effort involving mental health and alcohol and drug abuse programs; access to decent, affordable housing; and provision of other social services (Dixon et al., 1997). It also requires more effective means of evaluating the mental health needs of homeless people and matching services to their specific needs (Jacobs, Newman, & Burns, 2001; Tolomiczenko, Sota, & Goering, 2000).

Another difficulty in helping meet the challenge of psychiatric homelessness is that homeless people with severe psychological problems typically do not seek out mental health services. More intensive outreach and intervention efforts that focus on helping homeless people connect with the types of services they need are likely to produce the best outcomes (Rosenheck, 2000). All in all, the problems of the psychiatric homeless population remain complex, vexing problems for the mental health system and society at large.

Deinstitutionalization: A Promise as Yet Unfulfilled Although the net results of deinstitutionalization may not have yet lived up to expectations, a number of successful community-oriented programs are available. However, they remain underfunded and unable to reach many people needing ongoing community support. Deinstitutionalization has worked best for those who experience acute episodes of disturbed behavior, who are hospitalized briefly and then returned to their homes, families, and jobs (Shadish et al., 1989). If deinstitutionalization is to eventually succeed, patients must be provided with continuing care and afforded opportunities for decent housing, gainful employment, and training in social and vocational skills.

New, promising services exist to improve community-based care for people with chronic psychological disorders—for example, psychosocial rehabilitation centers, family psychoeducational groups, supported housing and work programs, and social skills training. Unfortunately, too few of these services exist to meet the needs of many patients who might benefit from them. The community mental health movement continues to need expanded community support and adequate financial resources if it is to succeed in fulfilling its original promise.

Summing Up

Types of Mental Health Professionals

How do the three major groups of mental health professionals— clinical psychologists, psychiatrists, and psychiatric social workers—differ in their training backgrounds? Clinical psychologists complete graduate training in clinical psychology, typically at the doctoral level. Psychiatrists are medical doctors who specialize in psychiatry. Psychiatric social workers are trained in graduate schools of social work or social welfare, generally at the master's level.

Psychotherapy

What is psychotherapy? Psychotherapy involves a systematic interaction between a therapist and clients that incorporates psychological principles to help clients overcome abnormal behavior, solve problems in living, or develop as individuals.

What is psychodynamic therapy? Psychodynamic therapy originated with psychoanalysis, the approach to treatment developed by Freud. Psychoanalysts use techniques such as free association and dream analysis to help people gain insight into their unconscious conflicts and work through them in the light of their adult personalities. Contemporary psychodynamic therapy is typically briefer and more direct in its approach to exploring the patient's defenses and transference relationships.

What is behavior therapy? Behavior therapy applies the principles of learning to help people make adaptive behavioral changes. Behavior therapy techniques include systematic desensitization, gradual exposure, modeling, operant conditioning approaches, and social skills training. Cognitive-behavioral therapy integrates behavioral and cognitive approaches in treatment.

What is humanistic therapy? Humanistic therapy focuses on the client's subjective, conscious experience in the here and now. Rogers's person-centered therapy helps people increase their awareness and acceptance of inner feelings that had met with social condemnation and been disowned. The effective person-centered therapist possesses the qualities of unconditional positive regard, empathy, genuineness, and congruence.

What are two major approaches to cognitive therapy? Cognitive therapy focuses on modifying the maladaptive cognitions that are believed to underlie emotional problems and self-defeating behavior. Ellis's rational emotive behavior therapy focuses on disputing the irrational beliefs that occasion emotional distress and substituting adaptive beliefs and behavior. Beck's cognitive therapy focuses on helping clients identify, challenge, and replace distorted cognitions, such as tendencies to magnify negative events and minimize personal accomplishments.

What is cognitive-behavioral therapy? Cognitive-behavioral therapy is a broader form of behavior therapy that integrates cognitive and behavioral techniques in treatment.

What are the two major forms of eclectic therapy? These are technical eclecticism, a pragmatic approach that draws on techniques from different schools of therapy without necessarily subscribing to the theoretical positions represented by these schools, and integrative eclecticism, an approach that attempts to synthesize and integrate diverse theoretical approaches in an integrative model of therapy.

What are the general aims of group therapy, family therapy, and marital therapy? Group therapy provides opportunities for mutual support and shared learning experiences within a group setting to help individuals overcome psychological difficulties and develop more adaptive behaviors. Family therapists work with conflicted families to help them resolve their differences. Family therapists focus on clarifying family communications, resolving role conflicts, guarding against scapegoating individual members, and helping members develop greater autonomy. Marital therapists focus on helping couples improve their communications and resolve their differences.

Does psychotherapy work? Evidence from meta-analyses of psychotherapy outcome studies that compare psychotherapy with control groups supports the value of various approaches to psychotherapy. The question of whether there are differences in the effectiveness of different types of psychotherapy remains under study.

Biomedical Therapies

What are the major biomedical approaches to treating psychological disorders and how effective are they? The major biomedical therapies are drug therapy and electroconvulsive therapy (ECT). Antianxiety drugs, such as Valium, may relieve short-term anxiety but do not directly help people solve their problems or cope with stress. Antipsychotics help control flagrant psychotic symptoms, but regular use of these drugs are associated with the risk of serious side effects. Antidepressants can help relieve depression, and lithium is helpful in many cases in stabilizing mood swings in people with bipolar disorder. ECT often leads to dramatic relief from severe depression. Psychosurgery has all but disappeared as a form of treatment because of adverse consequences.

Hospitalization and Community-Based Care

What roles do mental hospitals and community mental health centers play in the mental health system? Mental hospitals provide structured treatment environments for people in acute crisis and for those who are unable to adapt to community living. Community mental health centers seek to prevent the need for psychiatric hospitalization by providing intervention services and alternatives to full hospitalization.

What factors account for underutilization of mental health services by racial or ethnic minorities in the United States? These include cultural factors regarding preferences for other forms of help, cultural mistrust of the mental health system, cultural barriers, linguistic barriers, and economic and accessibility barriers.

How successful is the policy of deinstitutionalization? Deinstitutionalization has greatly reduced the population of state mental hospitals, but it has not yet fulfilled its promise of providing the quality of care needed to restore discharged patients to a reasonable quality of life in the community. One example of the challenges yet to be met are the many homeless people with severe psychological problems who are not receiving adequate care in the community.

CHAPTER FIVE

Stress, chological Factors, and Health

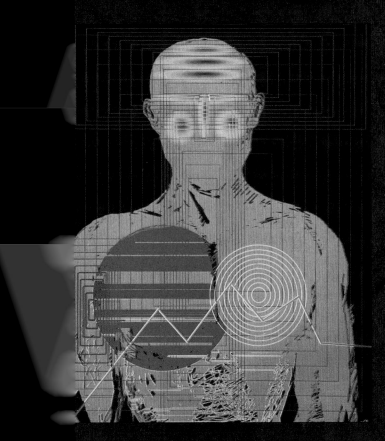

Diana Ong
Medicine Man B, 1940

The relationship between the mind and the body is the subject of an age-old debate. Mental functioning certainly depends on the brain, but there is continuing temptation to regard them separately. The 17th-century French philosopher René Descartes (1596–1650) influenced modern thinking with his belief in *dualism*, or separateness, between the mind and body. Today, scientists and clinicians recognize that mind and body are more closely intertwined than would be suggested by a dualistic model—that psychological factors both influence and are influenced by physical functioning. In other words, mental health and physical health are inseparable (Kendler, 2001; USDHHS, 1999a). Psychologists who study the interrelationships between psychological factors and physical health are called **health psychologists** (Schneiderman et al., 2001).

We begin focusing on relationships between mind and body by examining the role of stress in both mental and physical functioning. The term *stress* refers to pressure or force placed on a body. In the physical world, tons of rocks that crash to the ground in a landslide cause stress on impact, forming indentations or craters when they land. In psychology, we use the term **stress** to refer to a pressure or demand that is placed on an organism to adapt or adjust. A **stressor** is a source of stress. Stressors (or stresses) include psychological factors, such as examinations in school and problems in social relationships, and life changes, such as the death of a loved one, divorce, or a job termination. They also include daily hassles, such as traffic jams, and physical environmental factors, such as exposure to extreme temperatures or noise levels. The term *stress* should be distinguished from **distress,** which refers to a state of physical or mental pain or suffering. Some degree of stress is probably healthy for us; it helps keep us active and alert. But stress that is prolonged or intense can overtax our coping ability and lead to emotional distress, such as states of anxiety or depression, and physical complaints, such as fatigue and headaches.

Stress is implicated in a wide range of physical and psychological problems. We begin our study of the effects of stress by discussing a category of psychological disorders called *adjustment disorders*, which involve maladaptive reactions to stress. We then consider the role of stress and other psychological and sociocultural factors in physical disorders.

Adjustment Disorders

Adjustment disorders are the first psychological disorders we discuss in this book, and they are among the mildest. An **adjustment disorder** is a maladaptive reaction to an identified stressor that develops within a few months of the onset of the stressor. The maladaptive reaction is characterized by significant impairment in social, occupational, or academic functioning, or by states of emotional distress that exceed those normally induced by the stressor. For the diagnosis to apply, the stress-related reaction must not be sufficient to meet the diagnostic criteria for other clinical syndromes, such as anxiety disorders or mood disorders. The maladaptive reaction may be resolved if the stressor is removed or the individual learns to cope with it. If the maladaptive reaction lasts for more than 6 months after the stressor (or its consequences) have been removed, the diagnosis may be changed.

If your relationship with someone comes to an end (an identified stressor) and your grades are falling off because you are unable to keep your mind on schoolwork, you may fit the bill for an adjustment disorder. If Uncle Harry has been feeling down and pessimistic since his divorce from Aunt Jane, he too may be diagnosed with an adjustment disorder. So too might Cousin Billy if he has been cutting classes and spraying obscene words on the school walls or showing other signs of disturbed conduct. There are several subtypes of adjustment disorders that vary in terms of the type of maladaptive reaction (see Table 5.1).

The concept of "adjustment disorder" as a *mental disorder* highlights some of the difficulties in attempting to define what is normal and what is not. When something important goes wrong in life, we should feel bad about it. If there is a crisis in business, if we are victimized by a crime, if there is a flood or a devastating hurricane, it is understandable that we might become anxious or depressed. There might, in fact, be something more seriously wrong with us if we did not react in a "maladaptive" way, at least temporarily. However, if our emotional reaction exceeds an expectable response, or our ability to function is impaired

Truth OR Fiction? REVISITED

If you have trouble concentrating on your schoolwork because of the breakup of a recent romance, you could be experiencing a psychological disorder.

TRUE. If you have trouble concentrating on your schoolwork following the breakup of a romantic relationship, you may have a mild type of psychological disorder called an adjustment disorder.

health psychologist A psychologist who studies the relationships between psychological factors and physical illness.

stress A demand made on an organism to adapt or adjust.

stressor A source of stress.

distress A state of physical or emotional pain or suffering.

adjustment disorder A maladaptive reaction to an identified stressor, which is characterized by impaired functioning or signs of emotional distress that exceed what would normally be expected.

131

TABLE 5.1 Subtypes of Adjustment Disorders	
Disorder	**Chief Features**
Adjustment Disorder with Depressed Mood	Sadness, crying, and feelings of hopelessness.
Adjustment Disorder with Anxiety	Worrying, nervousness, and jitters (or in children, separation fears from primary attachment figures).
Adjustment Disorder with Mixed Anxiety and Depressed Mood	A combination of anxiety and depression.
Adjustment Disorder with Disturbance of Conduct	Violation of the rights of others or violation of social norms appropriate for one's age. Sample behaviors include vandalism, truancy, fighting, reckless driving, and defaulting on legal obligations (e.g., stopping alimony payments).
Adjustment Disorder with Mixed Disturbance of Emotions and Conduct	Both emotional disturbance, such as depression or anxiety, and conduct disturbance (as described above).
Adjustment Disorder Unspecified	A residual category that applies to cases not classifiable in one of the other subtypes.

Source. Adapted from the *DSM-IV-TR* (APA, 2000).

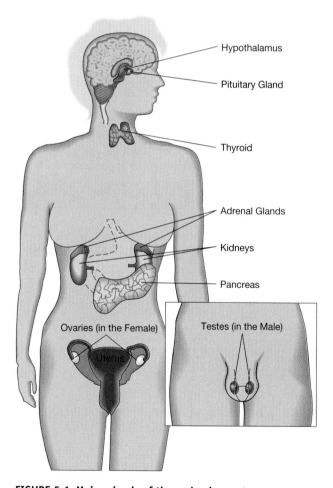

FIGURE 5.1 Major glands of the endocrine system.
The glands of the endocrine pour their secretions—called hormones—directly into the bloodstream. Although hormones may travel throughout the body, they act only on specific receptor sites. Many hormones are implicated in stress reactions and various patterns of abnormal behavior.

(e.g., avoidance of social interactions, difficulty getting out of bed, or falling behind in our schoolwork), then a diagnosis of adjustment disorder may be indicated. Thus, if you are having trouble concentrating on your schoolwork following the breakup of a romantic relationship and your grades are slipping, you may have an adjustment disorder.

Stress and Illness

Psychological sources of stress not only diminish our capacity for adjustment, but also may adversely affect our health. Many visits to physicians, perhaps even most, can be traced to stress-related illness. Stress increases the risk of various types of physical illness, ranging from digestive disorders to heart disease (e.g., Cohen et al., 1993).

The field of **psychoneuroimmunology** studies relationships between psychological factors, especially stress, and the workings of the endocrine system, the immune system, and the nervous system (Kiecolt-Glaser & Glaser, 1992; Maier, Watkins, & Fleshner, 1994). Here we examine what we've learned about these relationships.

Stress and the Endocrine System

Stress has a domino effect on the **endocrine system,** the body's system of glands that release their secretions, called **hormones,** directly into the bloodstream. (Other glands, such as the salivary glands that produce saliva, release their secretions into a system of ducts.) The endocrine system consists of glands distributed throughout the body. Figure 5.1 shows the major endocrine glands in the body.

Several endocrine glands are involved in the body's response to stress. First, the hypothalamus, a small structure in the brain, releases a hormone that stimulates the nearby pituitary gland to secrete *adrenocorticotrophic hormone* (ACTH). ACTH, in turn, stimulates the adrenal glands, which are located above the kidneys. Under the influence of ACTH, the outer layer of the adrenal glands, called the *adrenal cortex*, releases a group of **steroids** (cortisol and cortisone are examples). These cortical steroids (also called *corticosteroids*) are hormones that have a number of different functions in the body. They boost resistance to stress; foster muscle development; and induce the liver to release sugar, which provides needed bursts of energy for responding to a threatening stressor (for example, a lurking predator or assailant) or an emergency situation. They also help the body defend against allergic reactions and inflammation.

The sympathetic branch of the autonomic nervous system, or ANS, stimulates the inner layer of the adrenal glands, called the *adrenal medulla*, to release a mixture of chemicals called **catecholamines**—epinephrine (adrenaline) and norepinephrine (noradrenaline). These chemicals function as hormones when released into the bloodstream. Norepinephrine is also produced in the nervous system and functions as a neurotransmitter. The mixture of epinephrine and norepinephrine mobilizes the body to deal with a threatening stressor by accelerating the heart rate and by also stimulating the liver to release stored glucose (sugar), making more energy available where it can be of use in protecting ourselves in a threatening situation.

The stress hormones produced by the adrenal glands help the body prepare to cope with an impending threat or stressor. Once the stressor has passed, the body returns to a normal state. During states of chronic stress, however, the body may continue to pump out stress hormones, which can have damaging effects throughout the body, including suppressing the ability of the immune system to protect us from various infections and disease ("Can Stress Make You Sick?" 1998).

Difficulty in concentrating or adjustment disorder? An adjustment disorder is a maladaptive reaction to a stressor that may take the form of impaired functioning at school or at work, such as having difficulties keeping one's mind on one's studies.

Quiz **5.1**
Adjustment Disorders

Stress and the Immune System

Given the intricacies of the human body and the rapid advance of scientific knowledge, we might consider ourselves dependent on highly trained medical specialists to contend with illness. Actually our bodies cope with most diseases on their own, through the functioning of the immune system.

The **immune system** is the body's system of defense against disease. It combats disease in a number of ways. Your body is constantly engaged in search-and-destroy missions against invading microbes, even as you're reading this page. Millions of white blood cells, or **leukocytes,** are the immune system's foot soldiers in this microscopic warfare. Leukocytes systematically envelop and kill **pathogens** like bacteria, viruses, and fungi; worn-out body cells; and cells that have become cancerous.

Leukocytes recognize invading pathogens by their surface fragments, called **antigens,** literally *antibody generators*. Some leukocytes produce **antibodies,** specialized proteins that attach to these foreign bodies, inactivate them, and mark them for destruction.

Special "memory lymphocytes" (lymphocytes are a type of leukocyte) are held in reserve rather than marking foreign bodies for destruction or going to war against them. They can remain in the bloodstream for years and form the basis for a quick immune response to an invader the second time around.

Evidence is accumulating that stress can make us more vulnerable to disease by weakening the immune system (Adler, 1999; Dougall & Baum, 2001; Sternberg, 2000). A weakened immune system can make us more vulnerable to common illnesses, such as colds and the flu, and may increase our risks of developing chronic diseases, including cancer.

Exposure to physical sources of stress such as cold or loud noise, especially when intense or prolonged, can dampen immunological functioning. So too can various psychological stressors ranging from sleep deprivation to final examinations (Maier, Watkins, & Fleshner, 1994). Medical students, for example, show poorer immune functioning during

psychoneuroimmunology The study of relationships between psychological factors and immunological functioning.

endocrine system The system of ductless glands that secrete hormones directly into the bloodstream.

hormones Substances secreted by endocrine glands that regulate body functions and promote growth and development.

steroids A group of hormones that includes testosterone, estrogen, progesterone, and corticosteroids.

catecholamines A group of substances that includes neurotransmitters (dopamine and norepinephrine) and hormones (epinephrine and norepinephrine).

immune system The body's system of defense against disease.

leukocytes White blood cells.

pathogens Disease-causing organisms.

antigens Substances that trigger an immune response.

antibodies Substances produced by white blood cells that identify and target antigens for destruction.

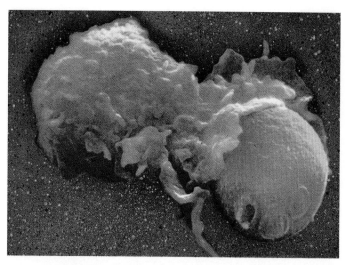

White blood cells attacking and engulfing pathogens. White blood cells, or *leukocytes,* form part of the body's immune system.

exam time than they do a month before exams, when their lives are less stressful (Glaser et al., 1987). Traumatic stress, such as exposure to earthquakes, hurricanes, or other natural or technological disasters, or to violence, can also dampen immunological functioning (Ironson et al., 1997; Solomon et al., 1997). Life stressors such as divorce and chronic unemployment can also take a toll on the immune system (O'Leary, 1990). Chronic stress may also make it take longer for wounds to heal (Kiecolt-Glaser et al., 1995).

Social support appears to moderate the harmful effects of stress on the immune system. For example, investigators find that medical and dental students with large numbers of friends show better immune functioning than students with fewer friends (Jemmott et al., 1983; Kiecolt-Glaser et al., 1984). Consider too that lonely students show a greater suppression of the immune response than do students with greater social support (Glaser et al., 1985). Newly separated and divorced people also show evidence of suppressed immune response, especially those who remain more attached to their ex-partners (Kiecolt-Glaser et al., 1987b, 1988).

Exposure to stress is linked to an increased risk of developing a common cold. In one study, people who reported higher levels of daily stress, such as pressures at work, showed lower levels in their blood streams of antibodies that fend off cold viruses (Stone et al., 1994). In another study, exposure to severe chronic stress lasting a month or longer of the type linked to underemployment, unemployment, or interpersonal problems with family members or friends was associated with a greater risk of developing a common cold after exposure to cold viruses (Cohen et al., 1998). Yet social support may boost resistance to the common cold. Researchers found that people who have more varied types of social relationships—with spouses, children, other relatives, friends, colleagues, members of organizations and religious groups, and so on— were less likely than others to come down with a cold after exposure to cold viruses (Cohen et al., 1997; Gilbert, 1997b). And when they did get sick, they tended to develop milder symptoms.

We should caution that much of the research in the field of psychoneuroimmunology is correlational in nature. Researchers examine immunological functioning in relation to different indices of stress, but do not (nor would they!) directly manipulate stress to observe its effect on subjects' immune systems or general health. Correlational research helps us better understand relationships between variables and may point to possible underlying causal factors, but does not in itself demonstrate causal connections.

Evidence indicates that writing about stressful events may enhance both psychological and physical well-being and perhaps even boost immune system responses (Carpenter, 2001b; Esterling et al., 1999; Smyth & Pennebaker, 2001). Writing about stressful or traumatic events has even reduced symptoms in asthma and arthritis patients (Smyth et al., 1999; Stone et al., 2000). Keeping thoughts and feelings about traumatic events tightly under wraps may place a stressful burden on the autonomic nervous system, which in turn may weaken the immune system, increasing susceptibility to certain stress-related disorders (Petrie, Booth, & Pennebaker, 1998). We should caution, however, that more research is needed before we can reach any definite conclusions about the effects of writing or other psychological interventions on the workings of the immune system (Miller & Cohen, 2001).

In the face of disaster. Exposure to traumatic stress, such as the World Trade Center disaster, can impair immunological functioning, increasing the risk of physical health problems.

The General Adaptation Syndrome

Stress researcher Hans Selye (1976) coined the term **general adaptation syndrome (GAS)** to describe a common biological response pattern to prolonged or excessive stress. Selye pointed out that our bodies respond similarly to many kinds of unpleasant stressors, whether the source of stress is an invasion of microscopic disease organisms, a divorce, or the aftermath of a flood. The GAS model suggests that our bodies, under stress, are like clocks with alarm systems that do not shut off until their energy is perilously depleted.

The GAS consists of three stages: the alarm reaction, the resistance stage, and the exhaustion stage. Perception of an immediate stressor (for example, a car that swerves in front of your own on the highway) triggers the **alarm reaction.** The alarm reaction mobilizes the body for defense. It is initiated by the brain and regulated by the endocrine system and the sympathetic branch of the autonomic nervous system (ANS). In 1929, Harvard University physiologist Walter Cannon termed this response pattern the **fight-or-flight reaction.** We noted earlier how the endocrine system responds to stress. During the alarm reaction, the adrenal glands, under control by the pituitary gland in the brain, pumps out cortical steroids and catecholamines that help mobilize the body's defenses (see Table 5.2).

The fight-or-flight reaction most probably helped our early ancestors cope with the many perils they faced. The reaction may have been provoked by the sight of a predator or by a rustling sound in the undergrowth. But our ancestors usually did not experience prolonged activation of the alarm reaction. Once a threat was eliminated, the body reinstates a lower level of arousal. Our ancestors fought off predators or they fled quickly; if not, they failed to contribute their genes to the genetic pools of their groups. In short, they died. Sensitive alarm reactions bestowed survival. Yet our ancestors did not invest years in the academic grind, struggle to balance the budget each month, or face any of the many daily stresses that repeatedly or persistently tax our body's ability to cope—everything from battling traffic in the morning to balancing school and work, or rushing from job to job. Consequently, much of the time our alarm system is turned on, which may eventually increase the likelihood of developing stress-related disorders.

When a stressor is persistent, we progress to the **resistance stage,** or adaptation stage, of the GAS. Endocrine and sympathetic system responses (release of stress hormones, for example) remain at high levels, but not quite as high as during the alarm reaction. During this stage the body tries to renew spent energy and repair damage. But when stressors continue to persist or new ones enter the picture, we may advance to the final or **exhaustion stage** of the GAS. Although there are individual differences in capacity to resist stress, all of us will eventually exhaust or deplete our bodily resources. The exhaustion stage is characterized by dominance of the parasympathetic branch of the ANS. Consequently, our heart and respiration rates decelerate. Do we benefit from the respite? Not necessarily. If the source of stress persists, we may

THINK ABOUT IT
How does the body's immune system help protect us from disease? What are the relationships between psychological factors, especially stress, and the functioning of the immune system?

Truth OR Fiction? REVISITED

Writing about traumatic experiences may be good for one's health.

TRUE. Talking or writing about your feelings may be good for the immune system and so bolster one's health.

TABLE 5.2 Stress-Related Changes in the Body Associated with the Alarm Reaction

Corticosteroids are released
Epinephrine and norepinephrine are released
Heart rate, respiration rate, and blood pressure increase
Muscles tense
Blood shifts from the internal organs to the skeletal muscles
Digestion is inhibited
Sugar is released by the liver
Blood-clotting ability is increased
Stress triggers the alarm reaction. The reaction is defined by secretion of corticosteroids, catecholamines, and activity of the sympathetic branch of the ANS. The alarm reaction mobilizes the body for combat or flight.

general adaptation syndrome (GAS) The body's three-stage response to states of prolonged or intense stress.

alarm reaction The first stage of the GAS, characterized by heightened sympathetic activity.

fight-or-flight reaction The inborn tendency to respond to a threat by either fighting or fleeing.

resistance stage The second stage of the GAS, involving the body's attempt to withstand prolonged stress and preserve resources.

exhaustion stage The third stage of the GAS, characterized by lowered resistance, increased parasympathetic activity, and possible physical deterioration.

develop what Selye termed "diseases of adaptation." These range from allergic reactions to heart disease—and, at times, even death. The lesson is clear: Chronic stress can damage our health, leaving us more vulnerable to a range of diseases and other physical health problems.

Cortical steroids are perhaps one reason that persistent stress may eventually lead to health problems. Although cortical steroids in some ways help the body cope with stress, persistent secretion of these steroids suppresses the activity of the immune system. Cortical steroids have negligible effects when they are only released periodically. Continuous secretion, however, weakens the immune system by disrupting the production of antibodies. As a result, we may become more vulnerable to various diseases, even the common cold (Cohen, Tyrrell, & Smith, 1991).

Although Selye's model speaks to the general response pattern of the body under stress, different biological processes may be involved in response to particular kinds of stressors. For example, persistent exposure to excessive noise may invoke different bodily processes than other sources of stress, such as overcrowding, or psychological sources of stress, such as divorce or separation.

Stress and Life Changes

Another way in which researchers have investigated the stress-illness connection is by quantifying life stress in terms of *life changes* (also called *life events*). Life changes become sources of stress when they impose demands on us to adjust. They include both positive events, such as getting married, and negative events, such as experiencing the death of a loved one. You can gain insight into the level of stressful life changes you may have experienced during the past year by completing the College Life Stress Inventory.

Investigators report links between exposure to life stressors, including life changes and daily hassles, and the risk of developing physical health problems, and even the risk of suffering sports injuries (Kanner et al., 1981; Smith, Smoll, & Ptacek, 1990; Stewart et al., 1994). Again, we need to be cautious in interpreting these findings. The reported links are correlational and not experimental. In other words, researchers did not (and would not!) assign subjects to conditions in which they were exposed to either a high or low level of life changes to see what effects these conditions might have on their health over time. Rather, existing data are based on observations of relationships, say, between life changes on the one hand and physical health problems on the other. Such relationships are open to other

THINK ABOUT IT

What are the major changes in the body that occur during each of the phases of the general adaptation syndrome?

Web Link **5.1** wWw

Stress: How and When to Get Help

For better or for worse. Life changes such as marriage and the death of loved ones are sources of stress that require adjustment. The death of a spouse may be one of the most stressful life changes that people ever face.

Questionnaire

Going Through Changes

 How stressful has your life been lately? The College Life Stress Inventory contains a listing of stressful events that college students may face. Circle each of the events that you have experienced in the past year. Then compute your total, and look at the guide at the end of the chapter to interpreting your score.

Event	Stress Rating
Being raped	100
Finding out that you are HIV-positive	100
Being accused of rape	98
Death of a close friend	97
Death of a close family member	96
Contracting a sexually transmitted disease(other than AIDS)	94
Concerns about being pregnant	91
Finals week	90
Concerns about your partner being pregnant	90
Oversleeping for an exam	89
Flunking a class	89
Having a boyfriend or girlfriend cheat on you	85
Ending a steady dating relationship	85
Serious illness in a close friend or family member	85
Financial difficulties	84
Writing a major term paper	83
Being caught cheating on a test	83
Drunk driving	82
Sense of overload in school or work	82
Two exams in one day	80
Cheating on your boyfriend or girlfriend	77
Getting married	76
Negative consequences of drinking or drug use	75
Depression or crisis in your best friend	73

Event	Stress Rating
Difficulties with parents	73
Talking in front of a class	72
Lack of sleep	69
Change in housing situation (hassles, moves)	69
Competing or performing in public	69
Getting in a physical fight	66
Difficulties with a roommate	66
Job changes (applying, new job, work hassles)	65
Declaring a major or concerns about future plans	65
A class you hate	62
Drinking or use of drugs	61
Confrontations with professors	60
Starting a new semester	58
Going on a first date	57
Registration	55
Maintaining a steady dating relationship	55
Commuting to campus or work, or both	54
Peer pressures	53
Being away from home for the first time	53
Getting sick	52
Concerns about your appearance	52
Getting straight A's	51
A difficult class that you love	48
Making new friends; getting along with friends	47
Fraternity or sorority rush	47
Falling asleep in class	40
Attending an athletic event (e.g., football game)	20

Source. Renner, M. J., & Mackin, R. S. (1998). A life stress instrument for classroom use. *Teaching of Psychology, 25,* 46–48. Reprinted with permission.

interpretations. It could be that physical symptoms are sources of stress in themselves and lead to more life changes. Physical illness may cause disruptions of sleep or financial burdens, and so forth. Hence, in some cases at least, the causal direction may be reversed: Health problems may lead to life changes. Existing research does not allow us to tease out the possible cause-and-effect relationships (Suls, Wan, & Blanchard, 1994).

Although both positive and negative life changes can be stressful, positive life changes seem to be less disruptive than negative life changes (Thoits, 1983). In other words, marriage tends to be less stressful than divorce or separation. Or to put it another way, a change for the better may be a change, but it is less of a hassle. Let us also note that "eventlessness" (i.e.,

THINK ABOUT IT

Why must evidence linking life changes and stress be correlational rather than experimental?

Adapting to a new culture. The relationship between acculturation and mental health is complex and depends on such factors as financial status, economic opportunities, linguistic differences, and availability of strong family ties.

the absence of life changes) can also be stressful and may be as strongly linked to the risk of physical health problems as negative life events (Theorell, 1992).

Acculturative Stress: Making It in America

Should Hindu women who immigrate to the United States give up the sari in favor of California casuals? Should Soviet immigrants continue to teach their children Russian in the home? Should African American children be acquainted with the music and art of African peoples? Should women from traditional Islamic societies remove the veil and enter the competitive workplace? How do the stresses of acculturation affect the psychological well-being of immigrants and their families?

Sociocultural theorists have alerted us to the importance of accounting for social stressors in explaining abnormal behavior. One of the primary sources of stress imposed on immigrant groups, or on native groups living in the larger mainstream culture, is the need to adapt to a new culture. The term **acculturation** refers to the process of adaptation in which immigrants and native groups identify with the new culture through making behavioral and attitudinal changes (Rogler, Cortes, & Malgady, 1991).

Consider the challenges faced by Hispanic Americans. There are two general theories of the relationships between acculturation and adjustment (Griffith, 1983). One theory, dubbed the *melting pot theory*, holds that acculturation helps people adjust to living in the host culture. From this perspective, Hispanic Americans might adjust better by replacing Spanish with English and adopting the values and customs associated with mainstream American culture. A competing theory, the *bicultural theory*, holds that psychosocial adjustment is fostered by identification with both traditional and host cultures. That is, the ability to adapt to the ways of the new society, combined with a supportive cultural tradition and a sense of ethnic identity, may predict good adjustment. From a bicultural perspective, immigrants maintain their ethnic identity and traditional values while learning to adapt to the language and customs of the host culture.

We first must be able to measure acculturation if we are to investigate its relationship to mental health among immigrant and native groups. Measures of acculturation vary. In assessing acculturation among Hispanic Americans, for example, researchers assess variables such as the degree to which people favor English or Spanish in social situations, when reading, or while watching media such as TV; preferences for types of food and styles of clothing; and self-perceptions of ethnic identity. Using such measures, researchers find that the relationships between acculturation and adjustment are quite complex.

Let us summarize some of the principal findings concerning relationships between acculturation and psychological disorders in Hispanic Americans:

- Highly acculturated Hispanic American women in a large national survey were nine times more likely than relatively unacculturated women to be heavy drinkers (Caetano, 1987). In Latin American cultures, men tend to drink much more alcohol than women, largely because gender-based cultural prohibitions against drinking constrain alcohol use among women. These constraints appear to have loosened among Hispanic American women who adopt "mainstream" U.S. attitudes and values.

- Third-generation Mexican American male adolescents—who are more likely to be acculturated than first- or second-generation Mexican Americans—were at higher risk of delinquency (Buriel, Calzada, & Vasquez, 1982).

acculturation The process of adapting to a new culture.

- Acculturation is associated with an increased risk of smoking among Hispanic adolescents (Ribisl et al., 2000; Unger, Cruz, & Rohrbach, 2000).

- Studies show poorer mental health among U.S.-born Mexican Americans than among Mexican nationals and Mexican immigrants (Burnam et al., 1987; Escobar & Vega, 2000; Escobar, Hoyos Nervi, & Gara, 2000).

- More acculturated Hispanic Americans are more likely to experience a psychological disorder than their less acculturated counterparts (Ortega et al., 2000).

- Highly acculturated Hispanic American high school girls were more likely than their less acculturated counterparts to show test scores associated with anorexia (an eating disorder characterized by excessive weight loss and fears of becoming fat—see Chapter 11) on an eating attitudes questionnaire (Pumariega, 1986). Acculturation apparently made these girls more vulnerable to the demands of striving toward the contemporary American ideal of the (very!) slender woman.

- Despite associations of acculturation with mental health problems, researchers have found that Mexican Americans who are *less* proficient in English show *more* signs of depression and anxiety than those who are more proficient (Salgado de Snyder, 1987; Warheit et al., 1985).

In sum, evidence relating acculturation status to mental health outcomes is mixed. Inconsistencies in research results may partly reflect differences in the indices by which mental health is measured (problem drinking vs. depression, for example) and the complexities of acculturative processes. We need to recognize that relationships between mental health and psychological adjustment are complex. Among unacculturated groups, factors such as social stress resulting from financial hardship, limited opportunities, and linguistic differences may contribute to adjustment problems (e.g., Ryder, Alden, & Paulhus, 2000). On the other hand, the erosion of traditional family networks that may accompany acculturation might operate to increase the risk of psychological disorders in more acculturated groups (Ortega et al., 2000).

Consider a study of Mexican American elders (Zamanian et al., 1992). Those who were minimally acculturated showed higher levels of depression than did those who were either acculturated or bicultural. The bicultural and highly acculturated groups were similar in levels of depression. This evidence shows that low acculturation status was associated with a greater risk of depression. However, people who held a bicultural identity in which they maintained an identification with their original culture while adapting to the new culture experienced no greater vulnerability to depression.

Low acculturation status is often a marker for low socioeconomic status (SES). People who are minimally acculturated often face economic hardship. Financial difficulties add to the stress of adapting to the host culture, which can increase the risk of depression and other psychological problems. Yet SES isn't the only, or necessarily the most important, determinant of mental health in immigrant groups. In a northern California sample, researchers found better mental health profiles among Mexican immigrants than among people of Mexican descent born in the United States, despite the socioeconomic disadvantages faced by the immigrant group (Vega et al., 1998). Acculturation and "Americanization" may have damaging effects on the mental health of Mexican Americans, and the retention of cultural traditions may have a protective or "buffer" effect (Escobar, 1998).

Other studies also point to the benefits of adapting to the host culture while maintaining ties to the

Maintaining ethnic identity. Some studies point to psychological benefits in immigrant groups that adapt to the host culture while maintaining ethnic identity.

emotion-focused coping A coping style that attempts to minimize emotional responsiveness rather than deal with the stressor directly.

problem-focused coping A coping style that attempts to confront the stressor directly.

THINK ABOUT IT

Does the evidence presented in the text seem to argue for or against a melting-pot model of American culture? What evidence presented suggests that maintaining a strong ethnic identity may be beneficial?

traditional culture. Among Asian Americans, establishing contacts with the majority culture while maintaining one's ethnic identity appears to generate less stress than withdrawal and separation from the host culture (Huang, 1994; Phinney, Lochner, & Murphy, 1990). Withdrawal fails to prepare the individual to make the adjustments necessary to function in a multicultural society, which often results in maladjustment. Maintaining one's ethnic identity also seems to hold a psychological benefit. Studies with Asian American adolescents show that those who have achieved an ethnic identity are better adjusted psychologically and have higher self-esteem (Huang, 1994; Phinney, 1989; Phinney & Alipuria, 1990).

Moreover, some outcomes need careful interpretation. For example, does the finding that highly acculturated Hispanic American women are more likely to drink heavily argue in favor of placing greater social constraints on women? The point would seem to be that a loosening of restraints is a double-edged sword, and that all people—male and female, Hispanic and non-Hispanic—may encounter adjustment problems when they gain new freedoms.

Other research appears to bear out this point. There is a strong relationship in Hispanic immigrants between the stress of adapting to a new culture and environment and states of psychological distress. In one study, female immigrants showed higher levels of depression than male immigrants (Salgado de Snyder, Cervantes, & Padilla, 1990). Their depression may be linked to the greater level of stress women encountered in adjusting to changes in family and personal issues, such as the greater freedom of gender roles for men and women in U.S. society. Because they were reared in cultures in which men are expected to be breadwinners and women homemakers, immigrant women may encounter more family and internal conflict when they enter the workforce, regardless of whether their job entry results from economic necessity or personal choice. Given these factors, we shouldn't be surprised by recent findings that greater marital distress was reported by wives in more acculturated Mexican American couples (Negy & Snyder, 1997).

Psychological Factors That Moderate Stress

Stress may be a fact of life, but the ways in which we handle stress help determine our ability to cope with it. Individuals react differently to stress depending on psychological factors such as the meaning they ascribe to stressful events. For example, whether a major life event, such as pregnancy, is a positive or negative stressor depends on a couple's desire for a child and their readiness to care for one. We can say the stress of pregnancy is moderated by the perceived value of children in a couple's eyes and their self-efficacy—their confidence in their ability to raise a child. As we see next, psychological factors such as coping styles, self-efficacy expectancies, psychological hardiness, optimism, social support, and ethnic identity may moderate or buffer the effects of stress.

Styles of Coping What do you do when faced with a serious problem? Do you pretend it does not exist? Like Scarlett O'Hara in *Gone With the Wind*, do you say to yourself "I'll think about it tomorrow" and then banish it from your mind? Or do you take charge and confront it squarely?

Pretending that problems do not exist is a form of denial. Denial is an example of **emotion-focused coping** (Lazarus & Folkman, 1984). In emotion-focused coping, people take measures that immediately reduce the impact of the stressor, such as denying its existence or withdrawing from the situation. Emotion-focused coping, however, does not eliminate the stressor (a serious illness, for example) or help the individual develop better ways of managing the stressor. In **problem-focused coping,** by contrast, people examine the stressors they face and do what they can to change them or modify their own

Problem-focused coping. Unlike emotion-focused coping, in which people attempt to distance themselves from sources of stress through denial or avoidance, problem-focused coping helps people meet their stressors head-on. When it comes to serious medical problems, problem-focused strategies such as seeking information and keeping a hopeful outlook may be adaptive and improve the chances of recovery.

reactions to render stressors less harmful. These basic styles of coping—emotion focused and problem focused—have been applied to ways in which people respond to illness.

Denial of illness can take various forms, including the following:

1. Failure to recognize the seriousness of the illness,

2. Minimization of the emotional distress the illness causes,

3. Misattribution of symptoms to other causes (for example, assuming the appearance of blood in the stool represents nothing more than a local abrasion), and

4. Ignoring threatening information about the illness.

Denial can be dangerous to your health, especially if it leads to avoidance of, or non-compliance with, needed medical treatment. Avoidance is another form of emotion-based coping. In one study, people who had a more avoidant style of coping with cancer (for example, by trying not to think or talk about it) showed greater disease progression when evaluated a year later than did people who more directly confronted the illness (Epping-Jordan, Compas, & Howell, 1994). Like denial, avoidance may deter people from complying with medical treatments, which can lead to a worsening of their medical conditions. It's also possible that avoidance may contribute to heightened emotional distress and arousal, which may impair immunological functioning.

Another form of emotion-focused coping, the use of wish-fulfillment fantasies, is also linked to poorer adjustment in coping with serious illness. Examples of wish-fulfillment fantasies include ruminating about what might have been had the illness not occurred and longing for better times. Wish-fulfillment fantasy offers the patient no means of coping with life's difficulties other than an imaginary escape.

Does this mean that people are invariably better off when they know all the facts concerning their illnesses? Not necessarily. Whether or not you will be better off knowing all the facts may depend on your preferred style of coping. A mismatch between the individual's style of coping and the amount of information provided may hamper recovery. In one study, cardiac patients with a repressive style of coping (relying on denial) who received information about their conditions showed a higher incidence of medical complications than repressors who were largely kept in the dark (Shaw et al., 1985). Sometimes ignorance helps people manage stress—at least temporarily.

Problem-focused coping involves strategies to deal directly with the source of stress, like seeking information about the illness through self-study and medical consultation. Information seeking may help the individual maintain a more optimistic frame of mind by creating an expectancy that the information will prove to be useful.

Self-Efficacy Expectancies Self-efficacy expectancies refer to our expectations regarding our abilities to cope with the challenges we face, to perform certain behaviors skillfully, and to produce positive changes in our lives (Bandura, 1982, 1986). We may be better able to manage stress, including the stress of coping with illness, if we feel confident (have higher self-efficacy expectancies) in our ability to cope effectively. A forthcoming exam may be more or less stressful depending on your confidence in your ability to achieve a good grade. Researchers find that spider-phobic women show high levels of the stress hormones epinephrine and norepinephrine when they interact with the phobic object, such as by allowing a spider to crawl on their laps (Bandura et al., 1985). As their confidence or self-efficacy expectancies for coping with these tasks increased, the levels of these stress hormones declined. Epinephrine and norepinephrine arouse the body by way of the sympathetic branch of the ANS. As a consequence, we are likely to feel shaky, to have "butterflies in the stomach" and general feelings of nervousness. Because high self-efficacy expectancies appear to be associated with lower secretion of catecholamines, people who believe they can cope with their problems may be less likely to feel nervous.

Psychological Hardiness Psychological hardiness refers to a cluster of traits that may help people manage stress. Research on the subject is largely indebted to Suzanne Kobasa (1979) and her colleagues who investigated business executives who resisted illness despite

psychological hardiness A cluster of stress-buffering traits characterized by commitment, challenge, and control.

internal locus of control Perception of one's ability to control reinforcements or affect outcomes.

heavy burdens of stress. Three key traits distinguished the psychologically hardy executives (Kobasa, Maddi, & Kahn, 1982, pp. 169–170):

1. The hardy executives were high in *commitment*. Rather than feeling alienated from their tasks and situations, they involved themselves fully. That is, they believed in what they were doing.

2. The hardy executives were high in *challenge*. They believed change was the normal state of things, not sterile sameness or stability for the sake of stability.

3. The hardy executives were also high in perceived *control* over their lives (Maddi & Kobasa, 1984). They believed and acted as though they were effectual rather than powerless in controlling the rewards and punishments of life. In terms suggested by social-cognitive theorist Julian Rotter (1966), psychologically hardy individuals have an **internal locus of control.**

Psychologically hardy people appear to cope more effectively with stress by using more active, problem-solving approaches (Williams, Wiebe, & Smith, 1992). They are also likely to report fewer physical symptoms and less depression in the face of stress than non-hardy people (Ouellette & DiPlacido, 2001; Pengilly & Thomas, 2000). Kobasa suggests that hardy people are better able to handle stress because they perceive themselves as *choosing* their stress-creating situations. They perceive the stressors they face as making life more interesting and challenging, not as simply burdening them with additional pressures. A sense of control is a key factor in psychological hardiness.

Optimism Research suggests that seeing the glass as half full is healthier than seeing it as half empty (Scheier & Carver, 1992). In one study on the relationships between optimism and health, Scheier and Carver (1985) administered a measure of optimism, the Life Orientation Test (LOT), to college students. The students also tracked their physical symptoms for 1 month. It turned out that those students who received higher optimism scores reported fewer symptoms such as fatigue, dizziness, muscle soreness, and blurry vision. (Subjects' symptoms at the beginning of the study were statistically taken into account, so it could not be argued that the study simply shows that healthier people are more optimistic.)

Other research also reveals links between optimism and better health outcomes. For example, pain patients who expressed more pessimistic thoughts during flare-ups of pain reported more severe pain and distress (Gil et al., 1990). The pessimistic thoughts included, "I can no longer do anything," "No one cares about my pain," and "It isn't fair I have to live this way." In a study of first-year law school students, optimism was associated with better mood and better immune system responses (Segerstrom et al., 1998). Among pregnant women, optimism is linked to a lower likelihood of postpartum depression (depression following childbirth) and higher infant birth weights (Carver & Gaines, 1987; Lobel et al., 2000). More optimistic women also suffered less depression and anxiety in the months following a diagnosis of breast cancer (Epping-Jordan et al., 1999). In separate studies, heart disease patients with more optimistic attitudes showed less depression when evaluated a year later (Shnek et al., 2001) and other patients undergoing coronary artery bypass procedure who had more optimistic attitudes about the procedure showed better outcomes (fewer complications requiring additional hospitalization or surgery) than did more pessimistic patients (Scheier et al., 1999).

Research to date shows only correlational links between optimism and health. Perhaps we shall soon learn whether learning to alter attitudes—to learn to see the glass as half filled—plays a causal role in maintaining or restoring health. You can evaluate your own level of optimism by completing the nearby Life Orientation Test.

Social Support The role of social support as a buffer against stress is well documented (e.g., Wills & Filer Fegan, 2001). In one study, having a broader network of social contacts was associated with greater resistance to developing an infection following exposure to a common cold virus (Cohen et al., 1997). The investigators believe that having a wider range of social contacts may help protect the body's immune system by serving as a buffer against stress. Researchers in Sweden, as well as in the United States, find that people with a

Truth OR Fiction? REVISITED

Optimistic people recover more rapidly than pessimistic people from coronary artery bypass surgery.

TRUE. Investigators find that optimistic patients tend to recover more rapidly than pessimistic patients following coronary artery bypass surgery.

Questionnaire

The Life Orientation Test

 Do you see the glass as half full or half empty? Do you expect bad things to happen or do you find the silver lining in every cloud? The Life Orientation Test can afford you insight as to how optimistic or pessimistic you are.

Directions: Indicate whether or not each of the items represents your feelings by writing a number in the blank space according to the following code. Then turn to the scoring key at the end of the chapter.

4 = strongly agree
3 = agree
2 = neutral
1 = disagree
0 = strongly disagree

1. _____ In uncertain times, I usually expect the best.
2. _____ It's easy for me to relax.
3. _____ If something can go wrong for me, it will.
4. _____ I always look on the bright side of things.
5. _____ I'm always optimistic about my future.
6. _____ I enjoy my friends a lot.
7. _____ It's important for me to keep busy.
8. _____ I hardly ever expect things to go my way.
9. _____ Things never work out the way I want them to.
10. _____ I don't get upset too easily.
11. _____ I'm a believer in the idea that "every cloud has a silver lining."
12. _____ I rarely count on good things happening to me.

Source. Scheier, M. F., & Carver, C. S. (1985). Optimism, coping, and health: Assessment and implication of generalized outcome expectancies. *Health Psychology, 4,* 219–247. Reprinted by permission.

higher level of social support are likely to live longer (Goleman, 1993e). In the Swedish study, researchers followed middle-aged men who experienced a high level of emotional stress due to such factors as financial trouble or serious problems with a family member. Men who were highly stressed but lacked social support were three times more likely to die within a period of 7 years as were those whose lives were low in stress (Goleman, 1993e). Yet men with highly stressed lives who had ample amounts of emotional support in their lives showed no higher death rates. Having other people available may help people find alternative ways of coping with stressors or simply provide them with the emotional support they need during difficult times.

THINK ABOUT IT

Examine your own personality and behavior patterns. How might they be helping to promote your health? In what ways might these patterns damage your health or increase your risk of developing health-related problems? What changes can you make in your lifestyle to adopt healthier behaviors?

Ethnic Identity African Americans, on the average, stand a greater risk than Euro-Americans of developing chronic health problems, such as obesity, hypertension, heart disease, diabetes, and certain types of cancer (Angier, 2000b; Anderson, 1991). The particular stressors that African Americans often face, such as racism, poverty, violence, and overcrowded living conditions, may contribute to their heightened risks of serious health-related problems (Anderson, 1991). Yet African Americans often demonstrate a high degree of resilience in coping with stress (Cutrona et al., 2000). Among the factors that help buffer stress among African Americans are strong social networks of family and friends, beliefs in one's ability to handle stress (self-efficacy), coping skills, and ethnic identity. Ethnic identity appears to be more strongly related to psychological well-being among African Americans than it is among White Americans (Gray-Little & Hafdahl, 2000). Acquiring and maintaining pride

Ethnic pride as a moderator of the effects of stress. Pride in one's racial or ethnic identity may help the individual withstand the stress imposed by racism and intolerance.

Quiz **5.2**
Stress and Illness

in one's racial identity and cultural heritage may help African Americans and other ethnic minorities withstand stresses imposed by racism. Although more research is needed to elucidate the links among racial identity, self-esteem, and tolerance of stress, the available evidence suggests that African Americans who become alienated from their culture develop more negative self-images and stand a greater risk of developing not only physical and psychological disorders, but also academic underachievement and marital conflicts (Anderson, 1991).

Psychological Factors and Physical Disorders

We noted at the start of the chapter that psychological factors can influence physical functioning; physical factors can also influence mental functioning. In these next sections we take a look at the role of psychological factors in various physical disorders. Physical disorders in which psychological factors are believed to play a causal or contributing role have traditionally been termed **psychosomatic** or *psychophysiological*. The term *psychosomatic* is derived from the Greek roots *psyche*, meaning "soul" or "intellect," and *soma*, which means "body." Disorders that involve psychological components range from asthma and headaches to heart disease.

Ulcers are another ailment traditionally identified as psychosomatic disorders. Ulcers affect about 1 in 10 people in the United States. However, their status as a psychosomatic disorder has been reevaluated in the light of recent landmark research that showed that a bacterium, *H. pylori*, not stress or diet, is the cause of the great majority of peptic ulcers (Boren et al., 1993; Mason, 1994). Researchers suspect that ulcers arise when the bacterium damages the protective lining of the stomach or intestines. Treatment with a regimen of antibiotics can help cure ulcers by attacking the bacterium directly (Altman, 1994a). We don't yet know why some people with the bacterium develop ulcers and others don't. The virulence of the particular strain of *H. pylori* may be involved in determining whether infected people develop peptic ulcers (Spechler, Fischbach, & Feldman, 2000). It is also conceivable that psychological stress is involved as well (Levenstein et al., 1999).

The field of psychosomatic medicine was developed to explore the possible health-related connections between the mind and the body. Today, evidence points to the importance of psychological factors in a much wider range of physical disorders than those traditionally identified as psychosomatic. In this section we discuss several of the traditionally identified psychosomatic disorders as well as two other diseases in which psychological factors may play a role in the course or treatment of the disease—cancer and AIDS.

Headaches

Headaches are symptomatic of many medical disorders. When they occur in the absence of other symptoms, however, they may be classified as stress related. By far the most frequent kind of headache is the tension headache (Mark, 1998). Stress can lead to persistent contractions of the muscles of the scalp, face, neck, and shoulders, giving rise to periodic or chronic tension headaches. Such headaches develop gradually and are generally characterized by dull, steady pain on both sides of the head and feelings of pressure or tightness. A survey in the Baltimore area showed that 38% of respondents complained of occasional tension headaches, with women reporting a 16% higher rate of these headaches than men (B. S. Schwartz et al., 1998).

Most other headaches, including the severe migraine headache, are believed to involve changes in the blood flow to the brain. Migraine headaches affect more than 28 million Americans ("Headache Coping," 2000; "New Research Could Open Doors," 2000). Typical migraines last for hours or days. They may occur as often as daily or as seldom as every other month. They are characterized by piercing or throbbing sensations on one side of the head only, or centered behind an eye. They can be so intense that they seem intolerable. Coping with the misery of brutal migraine attacks can take its toll, impairing the quality of life and leading to disturbances of sleep, mood, and thinking processes (Lipton et al., 2000b).

psychosomatic Pertaining to a physical disorder in which psychological factors play a causal or contributing role.

Migraine attacks typically last from 4 to 72 hours. There are two major types of migraines: migraine without aura (formerly called *common migraine*) and migraine with aura (formerly called *classic migraine*) (Olesen, 1994). An *aura* is a cluster of warning sensations that precedes the attack. Auras are typified by perceptual distortions, such as flashing lights, bizarre images, or blind spots. About 1 in 5 migraine sufferers experience auras. Other than the presence or absence of the aura, the two types of migraine are the same.

Theoretical Perspectives   Why, under stress, do some people develop tension headaches? One possible answer is found in the principle of **individual response specificity,** which holds that people may respond to a stressor in idiosyncratic ways. In classic research, Malmo and Shagass (1949) induced pain in patients with muscular complaints (backaches) and in patients with hypertension (high blood pressure). The hypertensive patients responded to the stimulus with larger changes in the heart rate, whereas the backache group showed greater muscle contractions. Tension headache sufferers may thus be more likely to respond to stress by tensing the muscles of the forehead, shoulders, and neck.

The underlying causes of migraine headaches are poorly understood. Investigators suspect that imbalances of the brain chemical serotonin may be involved (Edelson, 1998). Falling levels of serotonin may cause blood vessels in the brain to contract (narrow) and then dilate (expand). This stretching stimulates nerve endings that give rise to the throbbing, piercing sensations associated with migraine.

Given a genetic predisposition to migraines, many factors may trigger an individual's migraine attacks. These include stress; stimuli such as bright lights; changes in barometric pressure; pollen; certain drugs; the chemical monosodium glutamate (MSG), which is often used to enhance the flavor of food; red wine; and even hunger (Martin & Seneviratne, 1997). Hormonal changes of the sort that affect women prior to and during menstruation can also trigger attacks, and the incidence of migraines among women is about twice that among men.

Treatment   Commonly available pain relievers, such as aspirin, ibuprofen, and acetaminophen, may reduce or eliminate pain associated with tension headaches. A recent study reported that a combination of acetaminophen, aspirin, and caffeine (the ingredients in the over-the-counter pain reliever *Excedrin*) produced greater relief from the pain of migraine headaches than a placebo control (Lipton et al., 1998). Drugs that constrict dilated blood vessels in the brain or help regulate serotonin activity are used to treat the pain from migraine headache (Lipton et al., 2000a; Lohman, 2001; Silberstein et al., 2000).

Psychological treatment can also help relieve tension or migraine headache pain in many cases. These treatments include training in biofeedback, relaxation, coping skills training, and some forms of cognitive therapy (Blanchard & Diamond, 1996; Gatchel, 2001; Holroyd et al., 2001). **Biofeedback training (BFT)** helps people gain control over various bodily functions, such as muscle tension and brain waves, by giving them information (feedback) about these functions in the form of auditory signals (e.g., "bleeps") or visual displays. People learn to make the signal change in the desired direction. Training people to use relaxation skills combined with biofeedback has also been shown to be effective. *Electromyographic* (EMG) biofeedback is a form of BFT that involves relaying information about muscle tension in the forehead. EMG biofeedback thus heightens awareness of muscle tension in this region and provides cues that people can use to learn to reduce it.

Some people have relieved the pain of migraine headaches by raising the temperature in a finger. This biofeedback technique, called thermal BFT, modifies patterns of blood flow throughout the body, including blood flow to the brain, which helps to control migraine headaches (Blanchard et al., 1990; Gauthier, Ivers, & Carrier, 1996). One way of providing thermal feedback is by attaching a **thermistor** to a finger. A console "bleeps" more slowly[1] as the temperature rises. The temperature rises because more blood is flowing into the limb—away from the head. The client can imagine the finger growing warmer to bring about changes in the body's distribution of blood.

---

[1]Or more rapidly. The choice of direction is decided by the therapist or therapist and client.

Truth OR Fiction?   REVISITED

People can relieve the pain of migraine headaches by raising the temperature in a finger.

TRUE. Some people have relieved migraine headaches by raising the temperature in a finger. This biofeedback technique modifies patterns of blood flow throughout the body.

individual response specificity   The belief that people respond to the same stressor in different ways.

biofeedback training (BFT)   A method of feeding back to the individual information about bodily functions so that the person can gain some degree of control over these functions.

thermistor   A device for registering body temperature.

A Closer Look

Psychological Methods for Lowering Arousal

 Stress induces bodily responses such as excessive levels of sympathetic nervous system arousal, which if persistent may impair our ability to function optimally and possibly increase the risk of stress-related illnesses. Psychological treatments have been shown to lower states of bodily arousal that may be prompted by stress. In this feature, we consider two widely used psychological methods of lowering arousal: meditation and progressive relaxation.

Meditation

Meditation comprises several ways of narrowing consciousness to moderate the stressors of the outer world. Yogis (adherents to Yoga philosophy) study the design on a vase or a mandala. The ancient Egyptians riveted their attention on an oil-burning lamp, which is the inspiration for the tale of Aladdin's lamp. In Turkey, Islamic mystics called whirling dervishes, fix on their motion and the cadences of their breathing.

There are many meditation methods, but they share the common thread of narrowing one's attention by focusing on repetitive stimuli. Through passive observation, the regular person–environment connection is transformed. Problem solving, worry, planning, and routine concerns are suspended, and consequently, levels of sympathetic arousal are reduced.

Many thousands of Americans regularly practice **transcendental meditation (TM),** a simplified kind of Indian meditation brought to the United States in 1959 by Maharishi Mahesh Yogi. Practitioners of TM repeat **mantras**—relaxing sounds like *ieng* and *om.*

Benson (1975) studied TM practitioners ages 17 to 41—students, businesspeople, artists. His subjects included relative novices and veterans of 9 years of practice. Benson found that TM yields a so-called relaxation response in many people. The relaxation response is typically characterized by a reduced heart rate and metabolic rate, and by reduced blood pressure in people with hypertension (Benson, Manzetta, & Rosner, 1973; Brody, 1996a; Gatchel, 2001). Meditators also produced more alpha waves, brain waves connected with relaxation. Critics of meditation do not hold that meditation is without value; they suggest, instead, that meditation may have no distinct effects when compared to a restful break from a stressful routine.

Meditation can also produce measurable health benefits. Evidence shows that it can lower blood pressure and actually reduce the amount of fatty deposits on artery walls, both of which are major risk factors for heart attacks and strokes (Ready, 2000).

Going with the flow. Meditation is a popular method of managing the stresses of the outside world by reducing states of bodily arousal. This young woman practices yoga, a form of meditation. She "goes with the flow," allowing the distractions of her environment to in a sense "pass through." Contrast her meditative state with the apparently stressful features of the young man sitting behind her.

Although there are differences among meditative techniques, the following suggestions illustrate some general guidelines:

1. Try meditation once or twice a day for 10 to 20 minutes at a time.
2. Keep in mind that when you're meditating, what you *don't* do is more important than what you do. So embrace a passive attitude: Tell yourself, "What happens, happens." In meditation, you take what you get. You don't *strive* for more. Striving of any kind hinders meditation.
3. Place yourself in a hushed, calming environment. For example, don't face a light directly.
4. Avoid eating for an hour before you meditate. Avoid caffeine (found in coffee, tea, many soft drinks, and chocolate) for at least 2 hours.
5. Get into a relaxed position. Modify it as needed. You can scratch or yawn if you feel the urge.
6. For a focusing device, you can concentrate on your breathing or sit in front of a serene object like a plant or incense. Benson suggests "perceiving" (not "mentally saying") the word *one* each time you breathe out. That is, think the word, but "less actively" than you

---

transcendental meditation (TM) A form of meditation that focuses on repeating a mantra to induce a meditative state.

mantra A word or phrase that is repeated to induce a state of relaxation and narrowing of consciousness.

Cardiovascular Disease

Cardiovascular disease (heart and artery disease) is the leading cause of death in the United States, claiming about 1 million lives annually and accounting for more than 4 in 10 deaths, most often as the result of heart attacks or strokes (NCHS, 1996b). *Coronary heart disease* (CHD) is the major form of cardiovascular disease, accounting for about 700,000

normally would. Other researchers suggest thinking the word *in* as you breathe in and *out*, or *ah-h-h*, as you breathe out. They also suggest mantras like *ah-nam, rah-mah*, and *shi-rim*.

7. When preparing for meditation, repeat your mantra aloud many times—if you're using a mantra. Enjoy it. Then say it progressively more softly. Close your eyes. Focus on the mantra. Allow thinking the mantra to become more and more "passive" so you "perceive" rather than think it. Again, embrace your "what happens, happens" attitude. Keep on focusing on the mantra. It may become softer or louder, or fade and then reappear.

8. If unsettling thoughts drift while you're meditating, allow them to "pass through." Don't worry about squelching them, or you may become tense.

9. Remember to take what comes. Meditation and relaxation cannot be forced. You cannot force the relaxing effects of meditation. Like sleep, you can only set the stage for it and then permit it to happen.

10. Let yourself drift. (You won't get lost.) What happens, happens.

Progressive Relaxation

Progressive relaxation was originated by University of Chicago physician Edmund Jacobson in 1938. Jacobson noticed that people tense their muscles under stress, intensifying their uneasiness. They tend to be unaware of these contractions, however. Jacobson reasoned that if muscle contractions contributed to tension, muscle relaxation might reduce tension. But clients who were asked to focus on relaxing muscles often had no idea what to do.

Jacobson's method of progressive relaxation teaches people how to monitor muscle tension and relaxation. With this method, people first tense, then relax, selected muscle groups in the arms; facial area; the chest, stomach, and lower back muscles; the hips, thighs, and calves; and so on. The sequence heightens awareness of muscle tension and helps people differentiate feelings of tension from relaxation. The method is progressive in that people progress from one group of muscles to another in practicing the technique. Since the 1930s, progressive relaxation has been used by a number of behavior therapists, including Joseph Wolpe and Arnold Lazarus (1966).

The following instructions from Wolpe and Lazarus (1966, pp. 177–178) illustrate how the technique is applied to relaxing the arms. Relaxation should be practiced in a favorable setting. Settle back on a recliner, a couch, or a bed with a pillow. Select a place and time when you're unlikely to be disturbed. Make the room warm and comfortable. Dim sources of light. Loosen tight clothing. Tighten muscles about two thirds as hard as you could if you were trying your hardest. If you sense that a muscle could have a spasm, you are tightening too much. After tensing, let go of tensions completely.

Relaxation of Arms (time: 4–5 minutes) *Settle back as comfortably as you can. Let yourself relax to the best of your ability . . . Now, as you relax like that, clench your right fist, just clench your fist tighter and tighter, and study the tension as you do so. Keep it clenched and feel the tension in your right fist, hand, forearm . . . and now relax. Let the fingers of your right hand become loose, and observe the contrast in your feelings . . . Now, let yourself go and try to become more relaxed all over . . . Once more, clench your right fist really tight . . . hold it, and notice the tension again . . . Now let go, relax; your fingers straighten out, and you notice the difference once more . . . Now repeat that with your left fist. Clench your left fist while the rest of your body relaxes; clench that fist tighter and feel the tension . . . and now relax. Again enjoy the contrast . . . Repeat that once more, clench the left fist, tight and tense . . . Now do the opposite of tension—relax and feel the difference. Continue relaxing like that for a while . . . Clench both fists tighter and together, both fists tense, forearms tense, study the sensations . . . and relax; straighten out your fingers and feel that relaxation. Continue relaxing your hands and forearms more and more . . . Now bend your elbows and tense your biceps, tense them harder and study the tension feelings . . . all right, straighten out your arms, let them relax and feel that difference again. Let the relaxation develop . . . Once more, tense your biceps; hold the tension and observe it carefully . . . Straighten the arms and relax; relax to the best of your ability . . . Each time, pay close attention to your feelings when you tense up and when you relax. Now straighten your arms, straighten them so that you feel most tension in the triceps muscles along the back of your arms; stretch your arms and feel that tension . . . And now relax. Get your arms back into a comfortable position. Let the relaxation proceed on its own. The arms should feel comfortably heavy as you allow them to relax . . . Straighten the arms once more so that you feel the tension in the triceps muscles; straighten them. Feel that tension . . . and relax. Now let's concentrate on pure relaxation in the arms without any tension. Get your arms comfortable and let them relax further and further. Continue relaxing your arms even further. Even when your arms seem fully relaxed, try to go that extra bit further; try to achieve deeper and deeper levels of relaxation.*

deaths annually, mostly from heart attacks. It may surprise you to learn that more women die from CHD than from breast cancer (Ansell, 2001).

About 10% of the population, some 22 million Americans, have CHD. In coronary heart disease, the flow of blood to the heart is insufficient to meet its needs. The underlying disease process in CHD is **arteriosclerosis,** or "hardening of the arteries," a condition in which artery walls become thicker, harder, and less elastic, which makes it

cardiovascular disease A disease or disorder of the cardiovascular system, such as coronary heart disease or hypertension.

arteriosclerosis A disease involving thickening and hardening of the arteries.

atherosclerosis The buildup of fatty deposits along artery walls that leads to the formation of artery-clogging plaque.

myocardial infarction A breakdown of heart tissue due to an obstruction in the blood vessels that supply blood to the heart.

stroke Blocking of a blood vessel that supplies the brain due to a blood clot.

Type A behavior pattern (TABP) A behavior pattern characterized by a sense of time urgency, competitiveness, and hostility.

Web Link **5.2** wWw
Test Your Heart Disease IQ

Reducing Type A behavior. Slowing down the pace of your daily life and making time for loved ones are among the ways of reducing Type A behavior. Can you think of other ways that can help you decrease Type A behavior?

more difficult for blood to flow freely. The major underlying cause of arteriosclerosis is **atherosclerosis,** a process involving the build-up of fatty deposits along artery walls that leads to the formation of artery-clogging plaque. If a blood clot should form in an artery narrowed by plaque, it may nearly or completely block the flow of blood to the heart. The result is a heart attack (also called **myocardial infarction**), a life-threatening event in which heart tissue dies due to a lack of oxygen-rich blood. If a blood clot chokes off the supply of blood in an artery serving the brain, a **stroke** may occur, leading to death of brain tissue that can result in loss of function controlled by the part of the brain, coma, or even death.

Risk factors for CHD include some factors you can't control, such as age and family history. But a number of risk factors can be controlled through medical treatment or lifestyle changes—factors such as high cholesterol, hypertension, smoking, overeating, heavy drinking, consuming a high-fat diet, and leading a sedentary lifestyle (Fox, 2001; I-M. Lee et al., 2001; Pinel, Assanand, & Lehman, 2000; Noble, 2000; Stamler et al., 1999). Unfortunately, many of these factors remain uncontrolled. A recent study, for example, found that only about one in four adults with hypertension were taking medications to control their blood pressures (Chobanian, 2001; Hyman & Pavlik, 2001). Rates of uncontrolled hypertension were highest among older adults.

Psychological factors, such as negative emotional states like anger and anxiety, are also risk factors for cardiovascular disorders. Investigators have also identified a personality pattern, called the **Type A behavior pattern (TABP),** that poses yet another psychological risk factor in CHD.

Type A Behavior Pattern The Type A behavior pattern, a style of behavior that characterizes people who are hard-driving, ambitious, impatient, and highly competitive, has been associated with a modestly higher risk of CHD (T. Q. Miller et al., 1991). Evidence indicates that psychological interventions focused on helping people reduce their Type A behavior can significantly reduce the risk of subsequent heart attacks in people who have already suffered one (Brody, 1996c; Friedman et al., 1986). Perhaps there is a lesson in this for us all.

Hostility—quickness to anger—is the element of the Type A behavior pattern most closely linked to cardiovascular risk (Donker, 2000; Matthews et al., 2000) (see "A Closer Look: Emotions and the Heart" feature, p. 150). People with TABP tend to have "short fuses" and are prone to get angry easily.

The questionnaire on page 152 "Are You Type A?" helps you assess whether or not you fit the Type A profile. If you would like to begin modifying Type A behavior, a good place to start is with lessening your sense of time urgency. Here are some suggestions (Friedman & Ulmer, 1984):

1. Increase social activity with family and friends.

2. Each day, spend a few minutes recalling distant events. Peruse photos of family and old friends.

3. Read books—biographies, literature, drama, politics, nature, science, science fiction. (Books on business and on climbing the corporate ladder are not recommended!)

4. Visit art galleries and museums. Consider works for their aesthetic value, not their prices.

5. Go to the movies, theater, concerts, ballet.

6. Write letters to family and old friends.

7. Take an art course; start violin or piano lessons.

8. Keep in mind that life is by nature unfinished. You needn't have all your projects finished by a certain date.

9. Ask family members what they did during the day. *Listen* to the answer.

Here are some additional suggestions for reducing anger and hostility, the elements believed to be the most toxic components of the Type A profile (Brody, 1996b; Friedman & Ulmer, 1984):

1. Don't get involved in discussions that you know lead to pointless arguments.
2. When others do things that disappoint you, consider situational factors that might explain their behavior. Don't jump to the conclusion that others intend to get you upset.
3. Focus on the beauty and pleasure in things.
4. Don't curse.
5. Express appreciation to people for their support and assistance.
6. Play for the fun of it, not to beat your opponent.
7. Check out your face in the mirror from time to time. Look for signs of anger and aggravation; ask yourself if you really need to look like that.
8. Don't sweat the small stuff. Let it go. Avoid grudges, and let bygones be bygones.

Social Environmental Stress Social environmental stress also appears to heighten the risk of CHD (Krantz et al., 1988). Such factors as overtime work, assembly-line labor, and exposure to conflicting demands are linked to increased risk of CHD (C. D. Jenkins, 1988). The stress-CHD connection is not straightforward, however. For example, the effects of demanding occupations may be moderated by factors such as psychological hardiness and whether or not people find their work meaningful (Krantz et al., 1988).

Other forms of stress are also linked to increased cardiovascular risk. Researchers in Sweden, for example, find that among women, marital stress triples the risk of recurrent cardiac events, including heart attacks and cardiac death (Foxhall, 2001b; Orth-Gomér et al., 2000).

Ethnicity and CHD Coronary heart disease is not an equal opportunity destroyer. The disease burden and CHD-related death rates fall disproportionately on African Americans (see Figure 5.2).

Racial differences in deaths due to CHD reflect underlying differences in risk factors (Winkleby et al., 1998). Consider hypertension, a major risk factor for CHD. As shown in Figure 5.3 (p.151), non-Hispanic Black Americans are more likely than non-Hispanic White Americans to have hypertension (USDHHS, 1991b). In addition, African Americans have a higher prevalence of obesity and diabetes, two other major risk factors for CHD. Moreover, a dual standard of care limits access to quality health care of minority group members. Evidence shows that African Americans with CHD and who suffer heart attacks typically receive less aggressive and potentially life-saving treatments than do their White counterparts (Chen et al., 2001; Peterson et al., 1997; Stolberg, 2001). This dual standard of care may reflect discrimination as well as cultural factors limiting utilization of services, such as cultural mistrust of African Americans toward the medical establishment.

We finish this section with encouraging news. Americans have begun to take better care of their health. The incidence of CHD and deaths from heart disease have been declining steadily during the past 50 years, thanks largely to reductions in smoking, to improved treatment of heart patients, and perhaps also

THINK ABOUT IT
Consider the level of stress in your own life. Might the stress you are encountering be affecting your psychological or physical health? In what ways? How might you reduce the level of stress in your life? How might you learn ways of coping more effectively with the stress you do encounter?

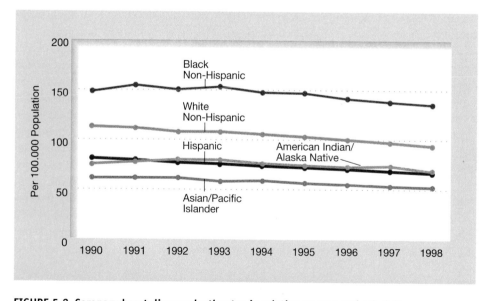

FIGURE 5.2 Coronary heart disease death rates in relation to race and ethnicity.
Black (non-Hispanic) Americans are much more likely to die from CHD than other ethnic or racial groups in the United States. What factors might contribute to these differences?
Source. Centers for Disease Control/National Clearinghouse for Health Statistics, National Vital Statistics System.

A Closer Look

Emotions and the Heart

 Might your emotions be putting you at risk of developing coronary heart disease? It appears so. Evidence shows that both anxiety and anger are hazardous to a person's cardiovascular health (Suinn, 2001).

The Anxious Heart

Investigators have linked phobic anxiety, the type of anxiety characterized by unfounded fears and panicky feelings, to a greater risk of death in men as the result of irregular heart rhythms. A study of some 34,000 men, none of whom were diagnosed at the outset of the study with coronary heart disease, showed those scoring at the high end of an index of phobic anxiety were six times more likely to suffer sudden coronary death over a 2-year period than were less anxious men (Hilchey, 1994; Kawachi et al., 1994). The researchers suspect that persistent, high levels of anxiety may produce "electrical storms" in the heart, resulting in irregular heart rhythms that may lead to sudden coronary death. Fortunately, the number of cardiac-related deaths during the 2-year study period was relatively small (only 16 among 34,000). Other investigators have also linked states of anxiety and tension with an increased risk of coronary symptoms and death in people with established CHD (Denollet et al., 1996; Gullette et al., 1997).

Researchers also find a connection between anxiety in middle-age men and the later risk of developing hypertension, a major risk factor for CHD (Markovitz et al., 1993). Highly anxious men were about twice as likely as their more relaxed counterparts to develop hypertension. We don't yet know whether this relationship also applies to women.

Anger and Hostility

Occasional feelings of anger may not damage the heart in healthy people, but chronic anger—the type of anger you see in people who seem angry all of the time—is linked to an increased risk of CHD and may even be as dangerous a risk factor as smoking, obesity, family history, or a high-fat diet (Brody, 1996c; Clay, 2001a; J. E. Williams et al., 2000). Anger is closely associated with hostility—an attitude characterized by tendencies to blame others and to perceive the world in negative terms (Eckhardt, Barbour, & Stuart, 1997). Hostile people are quick to anger and become angry more often and more intensely when they feel they have been mistreated than do nonhostile people. Young people with high levels of hostility stand an increased risk of developing early signs of coronary heart disease (Clay, 2001a; Matthews et al., 2000).

Although anger may not be a direct cause of heart disease, it is associated with an increased risk of death from cardiovascular disease (Suinn, 2001). Moreover, episodes of acute anger can actually trigger heart attacks and sudden cardiac death in people with established heart disease (Clay, 2001b).

Linking Emotions and the Heart

More research is needed to better understand the underlying mechanism linking negative emotions to heart disease, but investigators suspect that the stress hormones epinephrine and norepinephrine play significant roles (Januzzi & DeSanctis, 1999; Melani, 2001). Anxiety or anger triggers the adrenal glands to release these stress hormones, which then mobilize the body's resources to deal with threatening situations. They increase the heart rate, breathing rate, and blood pressure, which increases the flow of oxygen-rich blood to the muscles to prepare for defensive action—to fight or to flee—in the face of a threatening stressor. When people are persistently or repeatedly anxious or angry, the body may remain overaroused for long periods of time, continuing to pump out these stress hormones, which eventually may have damaging effects on the heart and blood vessels. Stress hormones also appear to increase the stickiness of the clotting factors in blood, which might increase the chances that potentially dangerous blood clots may form (Januzzi & DeSanctis, 1999).

Anxiety and anger may also compromise the cardiovascular system by increasing blood levels of cholesterol, the fatty substance that clogs arteries and increases the risk of heart attacks (Suinn, 2001). People with higher levels of hostility also tend to have higher blood pressures than their less hostile counterparts (Räikkönen et al., 1999). High blood pressure (hypertension) is a major risk factor for heart attacks and strokes.

Cognitive-behavioral therapists are helping chronically angry people learn to control their emotional responses in anxiety-provoking or angering situations (e.g., Deffenbacher et al., 2000). Helping angry people learn to remain calm in provocative situations may have beneficial effects on the heart as well as the mind (Gidron & Davidson, 1996). Along these lines, a recent study reported that men with CHD who received a hostility-reduction program showed less hostility and lower blood pressures after treatment than did controls (Gidron, Davidson, & Bata, 1999).

Investigators are finding additional links between coronary heart disease and other forms of emotional stress, including depression (Carney, Freedland, & Jaffe, 2001; Ferketich et al., 2000; Orth-Gomér et al., 2000). In one recent study, people without cardiac disease who were suffering from major depression were nearly four times more likely than nondepressed people to die from heart-related causes over a 4-year study period (Penninx et al., 2001).

to other changes in lifestyle habits, such as reduced overall intake of dietary fat (McGovern et al., 1996; Traven et al., 1995). Better educated people are also more likely to modify unhealthful behavior patterns and reap the benefits of change. Is there a message in there for you?

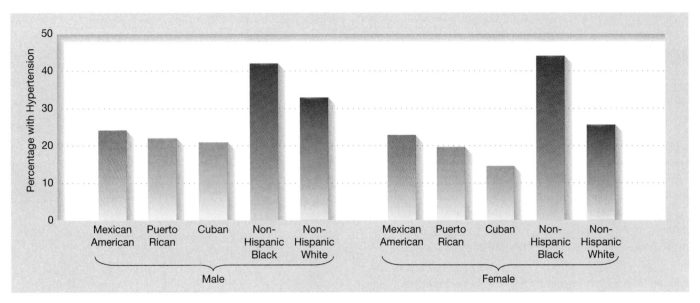

FIGURE 5.3 Hypertension among people ages 20 to 74, according to race/ethnicity.
Non-Hispanic Black Americans are more likely than non-Hispanic White Americans to have high
blood pressure, and non-Hispanic White Americans are more likely to have high blood pressure
than Hispanic Americans. Except in the case of non-Hispanic Black Americans, men ages 20 to 74
are more likely than women in the same age group to have high blood pressure.

Source. USDHHS, Public Health Service (1991), *Health, United States 1990.* DHHS Pub. No. (PHS) 91-1232.

Asthma

Asthma is a respiratory disorder in which the main tubes of the windpipe—the bronchi—
constrict and become inflamed, and large amounts of mucus are secreted. During asthma
attacks, people wheeze, cough, and struggle to breathe in enough air. They may feel as
though they are suffocating.

According to the Centers for Disease Control (CDC), nearly 15 million adults in the
United States are affected by asthma ("Asthma Affects," 2001; CDC, 2001). About 5 million
American children are also affected. Rates of asthma are on the rise, having doubled since
1980. Attacks can last from just a few minutes to several hours and vary notably in intensity. Series of attacks can harm the bronchial system, causing mucus to collect and muscles
to lose their elasticity. Sometimes the bronchial system is weakened to the point where a
subsequent attack is lethal.

Theoretical Perspectives Many causes are implicated in asthma, including allergic
reactions; exposure to environmental pollutants, including cigarette smoke and smog; and
genetic and immunological factors (Cookson & Moffatt, 1997; Giembycz & O'Connor,
2000). Asthmatic reactions in susceptible people can be triggered by exposure to allergens
such as pollen, mold spores, and animal dander; by cold, dry air; and by emotional
responses such as anger or even laughing too hard (Brody, 1988a). Psychological factors,
such as emotional stress, loss of loved ones, and intense disappointment, appear to increase
susceptibility to asthmatic attacks (Moran, 1991). Asthma, moreover, has psychological
consequences. Some sufferers avoid strenuous activity, including exercise, for fear of increasing their demand for oxygen and tripping attacks.

Treatment Although asthma cannot be cured, it can be controlled by reducing exposure
to allergens, by desensitization therapy ("allergy shots") to help the body acquire more resistance to allergens, by use of inhalers, and by drugs that open bronchial passages during
asthma attacks (called *bronchodilators*) and others (called *anti-inflammatories)* that reduce
future attacks by helping to keep bronchial tubes open. Psychological treatment may also

Questionnaire

Are You Type A?

 People with the Type A behavior pattern are impatient, competitive, and aggressive. They feel rushed, under pressure; they keep one eye glued to the clock. They are prompt and often arrive early for appointments. They walk, talk, and eat rapidly. They grow restless when others work slowly.

Type A people don't just stroll out on the tennis court to bat the ball around. They scrutinize their form, polish their strokes, and demand consistent self-improvement.

Are you Type A? The following questionnaire may afford you insight.

Directions: Write a checkmark under the Yes if the behavior pattern described is typical of you. Place a checkmark under the No if it is not. Work rapidly and answer all items. Then check the scoring key at the end of the chapter.

DO YOU: YES   NO

1. Strongly emphasize important words in your ordinary speech? ___ ___
2. Walk briskly from place to place or meeting to meeting? ___ ___
3. Think that life is by nature dog-eat-dog? ___ ___
4. Get fidgety when you see someone complete a job slowly? ___ ___
5. Urge others to complete what they're trying to express? ___ ___
6. Find it exceptionally annoying to get stuck in line? ___ ___
7. Envision all the things you have to do even when someone is talking to you? ___ ___
8. Eat while you're getting dressed, or jot notes down while you're driving? ___ ___
9. Catch up on work during vacations? ___ ___

DO YOU: YES   NO

10. Direct the conversation to things that interest you? ___ ___
11. Feel as if things are going to pot because you're relaxing for a few minutes? ___ ___
12. Get so wrapped up in your work that you fail to notice beautiful scenery passing by? ___ ___
13. Get so wrapped up in money, promotions, and awards that you neglect expressing your creativity? ___ ___
14. Schedule appointments and meetings back to back? ___ ___
15. Arrive early for appointments and meetings? ___ ___
16. Make fists or clench your jaws to drill home your views? ___ ___
17. Think that you have achieved what you have because of your ability to work fast? ___ ___
18. Have the feeling that uncompleted work must be done *now* and fast? ___ ___
19. Try to find more efficient ways to get things done? ___ ___
20. Struggle always to win games instead of having fun? ___ ___
21. Interrupt people who are talking? ___ ___
22. Lose patience with people who are late for appointments and meetings? ___ ___
23. Get back to work right after lunch? ___ ___
24. Find that there's never enough time? ___ ___
25. Believe that you're getting too little done, even when other people tell you that you're doing fine? ___ ___

Source. From Rathus, S. A. (1996). Copyright © 2001. Reprinted with permission of Brooks/Cole, an imprint of Wadsworth Group, a division of Thomson Learning. FAX 800-730-2215.

play a role by helping asthma sufferers apply the skills of muscle relaxation to improve their breathing (Lehrer et al., 1994), and, for asthmatic children, family therapy that helps reduce family conflict (Lehrer et al., 1992).

Cancer

The word *cancer* is arguably the most feared word in the English language and rightly so: One of every four deaths in the United States is caused by cancer (Stolberg, 1998a). Cancer claims about a half a million lives in the United States annually, one every 90 seconds (Andersen, Golden-Kreutz, & DiLillo, 2001). Men have a one in two chance of developing cancer at some point in their lives; for women the odds are one in three. Yet there is good news to report: The number of new cancer cases and deaths from cancer are declining. Cancer cases are on the decline due largely to reductions in smoking, while the declining death rate is attributed largely to increased screening and better treatments ("Cancer Rates," 1999).

Cancer is characterized by development of aberrant, or mutant, cells that form growths (tumors) that spread to healthy tissue. Cancerous cells can take root anywhere—the blood, the bones, lungs, digestive tract, and genital organs. When they are not contained early, cancer may metastasize, or establish colonies throughout the body, leading to death.

There are many causes of cancer, including regular exposure to cancer-causing chemicals in the environment and genetic factors, such as defective or mutant genes. But many behavior patterns also contribute to the development of cancer, including dietary practices (high fat intake), heavy alcohol consumption, smoking, and sunbathing (ultraviolet light causes skin cancer). On the other hand, regular intake of a healthy daily supply of fruits and vegetables may lower the risk of some forms of cancer. Death rates from cancer are lower in Japan than in the United States, where people ingest more fat, especially animal fat. The difference is not genetic or racial, however, because Japanese Americans whose fat intake approximates that of other Americans show similar death rates from cancer.

Stress and Cancer A weakened or compromised immune system may increase susceptibility to cancer. We've seen that psychological factors, such as exposure to stress, may affect the immune system. Research with animals has shown that exposure to stress can hasten the onset of a virus-induced cancer (Riley, 1981). Might exposure to stress in humans increase the risk of cancer? Some studies show an increased incidence of stressful life events, such as the loss of loved ones, preceding the development of some forms of cancer (e.g., Levenson & Bemis, 1991). However, other studies show no linkage between exposure to stress and development of cancer (e.g., McKenna et al., 1999). Clearly, the links between stress and cancer require further study (Delahanty & Baum, 2001; Dougall & Baum, 2001).

Psychological Factors in Treatment and Recovery Cancer is a physical disease treated medically by means of surgery, radiation, and chemotherapy. Yet psychologists and mental health professionals can play key roles in helping cancer patients deal with the emotional consequences of coping with the disease. Feelings of hopelessness and helplessness are common reactions to receiving a cancer diagnosis, but such feelings may hinder recovery (Andersen, 1992), perhaps by depressing the patient's immune system.

Evidence shows that breast cancer patients who maintain a "fighting spirit" experience better outcomes than those who resign themselves to their illness (Pettingale, 1985). This 10-year follow-up of breast cancer patients found that patients who met their diagnosis with anger and a fighting spirit rather than stoic acceptance showed significantly higher survival rates. The will to fight the illness may help to increase survival.

Social support may also help. Women with metastatic breast cancer who participated in a group support program survived a year and half longer on the average than did women assigned to a no-treatment control group (Spiegel et al., 1989). However, how psychological approaches affect the course of cancer is unclear. One possible mode of action is enhancement of the immune system (Andersen, 1992).

Investigators have examined the value of training cancer patients to use coping skills, such as relaxation, stress management, and coping thoughts, to relieve the stress and pain of coping with cancer. These interventions may also help cancer patients cope with the anticipatory side effects of chemotherapy. Cues associated with chemotherapy, such as the hospital environment itself, may become conditioned stimuli that elicit nausea and vomiting even before the drugs are administered (Redd, 1995). By pairing relaxation, pleasant imagery, and attentional distraction with these cues, investigators find that nausea and vomiting can be lessened (Redd, 1995; Redd & Jacobsen, 2001). Playing video games as a form of distraction has also helped lessen the discomfort of chemotherapy in children with cancer (Kolko & Rickard-Figueroa, 1985).

Psychosocial interventions can also have positive effects on emotional and behavioral adjustment, and quality of life, of cancer patients (Andersen, Golden-Kreutz, & DiLillo, 2001; Compas et al., 1998; Meyer & Mark, 1995). It is too early to tell whether psychological interventions can prolong life expectancy of cancer patients, but preliminary evidence indicates that it may (Fawzy & Fawzy, 1994; Kogon et al., 1997).

Truth OR Fiction? REVISITED

Cancer patients who maintain a "fighting spirit" experience no better outcomes than those who resign themselves to their illness.

FALSE. In a sample of breast cancer patients, those who maintained a "fighting spirit" had higher survival rates than those who became resigned to their illness.

wWw Web Link **5.3**
Therapy and Cancer

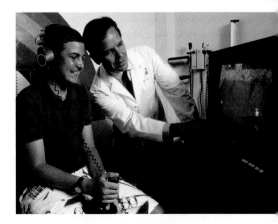

Coping with discomfort. The use of relaxation and distraction techniques may help cancer patients cope with the discomfort of chemotherapy.

acquired immunodeficiency syndrome (AIDS) An immunological disease caused by HIV.

human immunodeficiency virus (HIV) The virus that causes AIDS.

Learning to modify expectations is also important. Cancer patients who are able to maintain or restore their psychological well-being appear to be able to do so by readjusting their expectations of themselves in line with their present capabilities (Heidrich, Forsthoff, & Ward, 1994).

Acquired Immunodeficiency Syndrome (AIDS)

Acquired immunodeficiency syndrome (AIDS) is a disease caused by the **human immunodeficiency virus (HIV).** HIV attacks the person's immune system, leaving it helpless to fend off diseases it normally would hold in check. AIDS is one of history's worst epidemics, claiming nearly 22 million lives worldwide by 2001 and showing no signs of relenting (Altman, 2001; Begley, 2001a; Wren, 2001).

HIV is transmitted by sexual contact (vaginal and anal intercourse; oral-genital contact); direct infusion of contaminated blood, as from transfusions of contaminated blood, accidental pricks from needles used previously on an infected person, or needle sharing among injecting drug users; and from an infected mother to a child during pregnancy or childbirth or through breast-feeding. AIDS is not contracted by donating blood; by airborne germs; by insects; or by casual contact, such as using public toilets, holding or hugging infected people, sharing eating utensils with them, or living or going to school with them. Routine screening of the blood supplies for HIV have reduced the risk of infection from blood transfusions to virtually nil.

HIV infection and AIDS cut across all boundaries of race, ethnicity, income level, gender, sexual orientation, and drug use classification. You needn't be a sexually active gay male or an IV-drug user to become infected.

There is no cure or vaccine for HIV infection, but the introduction of highly active antiretroviral drugs has revolutionized treatment of the disease, raising hopes that it can become a chronic but manageable disease (Cowley, 2001c; Gallant, 2000; Sherbourne et al., 2000). However, hopes are tempered by the fact that many patients fail to derive or maintain any benefit from the newer antiviral drug combinations (Catz & Kelly, 2001).

The lack of a cure or effective vaccine means that prevention programs focusing on reducing or eliminating risky sexual and injection practices represent our best hope for controlling the epidemic (Begley, 2001a). Psychologists have become involved in the fight against AIDS because behavior is the major determinant of the risk of contracting the deadly virus and because AIDS, like cancer, has devastating psychological effects on persons affected by the disease, their families and friends, and society at large.

AIDS support group. AIDS support groups offer emotional support and assistance to people with HIV/AIDS, their families, and their friends.

Adjustment of People with HIV and AIDS Given the nature of the disease and the stigma suffered by people with HIV and AIDS, it is not surprising that many people with HIV, although certainly not all, develop psychological problems, most commonly anxiety and depression (Catz & Kelly, 2001; Ciesla & Roberts, 2001; Sherbourne et al., 2000). Recently, investigators reported that greater levels of depressive symptoms were associated with more rapid disease progression in women with HIV (Ickovics et al., 2001).

Psychological and Psychopharmacological Interventions Behavior change programs focus on reducing risky sexual and injection practices (Ickovics, Thayaparnan, & Ethier, 2001; Kelly et al., 1998). These training programs have been shown to be effective with groups of sexually active gay men (Kelly, Brasfield, & St. Lawrence, 1991) and with adolescents, including substance-dependent adolescents (St. Lawrence et al., 1995a, 1995b).

Psychological treatment, typically in the form of support groups, self-help groups, and organized therapy groups, have also been used to provide psychological assistance to people with HIV/AIDS and their families and friends. Treatment may incorporate training in active coping skills, such as stress management techniques like self-relaxation and positive mental imagery, and cognitive strategies to control intrusive negative thoughts and preoccupations. The importance of stress management skills is highlighted by recent findings that stressful life events and passive coping (use of denial) were associated with faster progression to AIDS in HIV-infected men (Leserman et al., 2000). Coping skills training and cognitive-behavioral therapy have been shown to help improve psychological functioning and ability to handle stress in people living with HIV or AIDS, and to reduce their feelings of depression and anxiety (Lutgendorf et al., 1997). Antidepressant medication has also been found to be helpful in treating depression in people with HIV (Elliott et al., 1998; Markowitz et al., 1998). Whether treatment of depression or coping skills training for handling stress can improve immunological functioning or prolong life in people with HIV and AIDS remains an open question.

The advent of AIDS presents the mental health community with unparalleled challenge to help prevent the spread of AIDS and to treat people who have been infected with HIV and who have developed AIDS. As frightening as AIDS may be, it is preventable, as noted in the next section.

Preventing AIDS For the first time, a generation of young people has come of age at a time when the threat of AIDS hangs over every sexual encounter. People may decrease the risk of being infected by HIV and other sexually transmitted diseases (STDs) by taking the following measures. Only the first two are sure paths to avoiding the sexual transmission of HIV. The others reduce the risk of infection, but cannot be certified as perfectly safe. If we are going to be sexually active without knowing (not guessing) whether we or our partners are infected with HIV or some other STD, we can speak only of safe(r) sex—not of perfectly safe sex.

1. *Maintaining lifelong celibacy.*

2. *Remaining in a lifelong monogamous relationship with an uninfected person who is doing the same thing.* Although these first two sexual career paths guarantee safety, they are not followed by the majority of students or other Americans.

3. *Being discerning in one's choice of sex partners.* Get to know another person before engaging in sexual activity. Still, getting to know a person is no guarantee the person is uninfected with HIV. Avoid contact with multiple partners, or with people who are likely to have multiple partners.

4. *Being assertive with sex partners.* It is important to communicate concerns about AIDS clearly and assertively with sex partners.

5. *Inspecting one's partner's sex organs.* There are no obvious signs of HIV infection, but people who are infected with HIV are often infected by other sexually transmitted diseases as well. It may be feasible to visually inspect your partner's sex organs for rashes, chancres, blisters, discharges, warts, and lice during foreplay. Consider any disagreeable odor a warning sign.

6. *Using latex condoms.* Condoms protect men from infected vaginal fluids and stop infected semen from entering women. All condoms (including so-called natural condoms made of animal intestines or "skins") act as barriers to sperm, but only latex condoms can prevent transmission of HIV.

7. *Using spermicides.* Spermicides containing the ingredient nonoyxnol-9 kill HIV as well as sperm. Spermicides should be used along with latex condoms, not as a substitute for condoms.

8. *Consulting a physician following suspected exposure to a sexually transmitted disease (STD).* Antibiotics following unprotected sex may guard against bacterial STDs, but they are of no use against viral STDs such as genital herpes and HIV/AIDS. Consult with a physician before using any medications, including medications you may have stored away in your medicine cabinet.

THINK ABOUT IT
What are the psychological factors implicated in physical disorders and diseases such as headaches, cardiovascular disorders, asthma, cancer, and AIDS? What role do psychological techniques play in the treatment of physical health disorders and conditions?

9. *Seeking regular medical checkups.* Checkups and appropriate laboratory tests enable you to learn about and treat disorders that might have gone unnoticed.

10. *Avoiding sexual activity if there are doubts about safety.* None of the safer sex practices listed guarantees protection. Why not avoid sexual activity when doubts of safety exist?

We end this section on a sobering note. Information about risk reduction alone is not sufficient to induce widespread changes in sexual behavior (Kelly et al., 1995). Despite awareness of the dangers, many people practice risky sexual and injection behaviors (Kalichman, 2000). People not only need to know about the dangers of unsafe sexual practices, they also need to know how to change their behavior (e.g., learning how to refuse invitations to engage in unsafe sex and how to communicate effectively with one's partner(s) about safer sex), and they must be motivated to change their risk behavior. Unfortunately, motivation has been waning and evidence points to increasingly risky behavior among the young (Begley, 2001a). Other factors not to be overlooked in prevention efforts are drug and alcohol use and peer group norms. The likelihood of people engaging in safer sex practices is linked to the avoidance of alcohol and drugs before sex and to the perception that safer sex practices are the social norm within one's peer group.

In this chapter we focused on relationships between stress and health, and on the psychological factors involved in health. Psychology has much to offer in the understanding and treatment of physical disorders. Psychological approaches may help in the treatment of such physical disorders as headaches and coronary heart disease. Psychologists also help people reduce the risks of contracting health problems such as cardiovascular disorders, cancer, and AIDS. Emerging fields like psychoneuroimmunology promise to further enhance our knowledge of the intricate relationships between mind and body.

Quiz **5.3**
Psychological Factors
and Physical Disorders

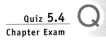

Quiz **5.4**
Chapter Exam

Research Update
Chapter 5

Summing Up

Adjustment Disorders

What are adjustment disorders? Adjustment disorders are maladaptive reactions to identified stressors.

What are their features? Adjustment disorders are characterized by emotional reactions that are greater than normally expected given the circumstances or by evidence of significant impairment in functioning. Impairment usually takes the form of problems at work or school, or in social relationships or activities.

Stress and Illness

How is stress linked to physical illness? Evidence links exposure to stress to weakened immune system functioning, which in turn can increase vulnerability to physical illness. However, since this evidence is correlational, questions of cause and effect remain.

What is the general adaptation syndrome? This is the name given by Hans Selye to the generalized pattern of response of the body to persistent or enduring stress, as characterized by three stages: the alarm reaction, the resistance stage, and the exhaustion stage.

How are life changes related to physical health problems? Again, links are correlational, but evidence shows that people who experience more life stress in the form of life changes and daily hassles are at an increased risk of developing physical health problems.

What psychological factors buffer the effects of stress? These factors include coping styles, self-efficacy expectancies, psychological hardiness, optimism, and social support.

Psychological Factors and Physical Disorders

What roles do psychological factors play in the onset of headaches and their treatment? The most common headache is the muscle-tension headache, which is often stress related. Behavioral methods of relaxation training and biofeedback are of help in treating various types of headaches.

What behavioral or lifestyle factors increase the risk of coronary heart disease? Psychological factors that increase the risk of coronary heart disease include patterns of consumption, leading a sedentary lifestyle, Type A behavior pattern, and persistent negative emotions.

What role do psychological factors play in asthma? Psychological factors such as emotional stress, loss of loved ones, and sudden or intense disappointment may trigger asthma attacks in susceptible individuals.

What role do psychological factors play in the development of cancer and its treatment? Although relationships between stress and risk of cancer remain under study, behavioral risk factors for cancer include dietary practices (especially high fat intake), heavy alcohol use, smoking, and excessive sun exposure. Research shows that a fighting spirit may help people recover from cancer. Psychological interventions help cancer patients cope better with the symptoms of the disease and its treatment.

What roles do psychologists play in the prevention of HIV/AIDS and treatment of people with HIV? Our behavior patterns influence our risk for contracting AIDS. Psychologists have become involved in the prevention and treatment of AIDS because AIDS, like cancer, has devastating psychological effects on victims, their families and friends, and society at large, and because AIDS can be prevented through reducing risky behavior.

Scoring Key for "The College Life Stress Inventory" Though we have no national norms by which to compare your score, the test developers obtained an average (mean) score of 1,247 based on a sample of 257 introductory psychology students. About two of three students obtained scores in the range of 806 to 1,688.

Computing your total score helps you gauge how you compare to the students in the original study sample in terms of your overall stress level. Bear in mind, however, that the same level of stress may affect different people differently. Your ability to cope with stress depends on many factors, including your coping skills and the level of social support you have available. If you are experiencing a high level of stress, you may wish to examine the sources of stress in your life. Perhaps you can reduce the level of stress you experience or learn more effective ways of handling the sources of stress you can't avoid.

Scoring Key for "The Life Orientation Test" To arrive at your total score for the test, first *reverse* your score on items 3, 8, 9, and 12. That is,

4 is changed to 0
3 is changed to 1
2 remains the same
1 is changed to 3
0 is changed to 4

Now add the numbers of items 1, 3, 4, 5, 8, 9, 11, and 12. (Items 2, 6, 7, and 10 are "fillers"; that is, your responses are not scored as part of the test.) Your total score can vary from 0 to 32.

Scheier and Carver (1985) provide the following norms for the test, based on administration to 357 undergraduate men and 267 undergraduate women. The average (mean) score for men was 21.03 (standard deviation = 4.56), and the mean score for women was 21.41 (standard deviation = 5.22). All in all, approximately 2 out of 3 undergraduates obtained scores between 16 and 26. Scores above 26 may be considered quite optimistic, and scores below 16, quite pessimistic. Scores between 16 and 26 are within a broad average range, and higher scores within this range are relatively more optimistic.

Answer Key for "Are You Type A?" Yesses are suggestive of the Type A behavior pattern (TABP). In appraising whether or not you show the TABP, you need not be concerned with the precise number of yes answers. We have no normative data for you. As Friedman and Rosenman (1974, p. 85) note, however, you should have little trouble spotting yourself as "hard core" or "moderately afflicted"—that is, if you are honest with yourself.

CHAPTER SIX

Anxiety Disorders

Miriam Schapiro
Free Fall, 1985

Truth OR Fiction?

- Some people who experience panic attacks believe they are having a heart attack, even though there is nothing wrong with their heart. (p. 162)

- Some people are so fearful of leaving their homes that they are unable to venture outside even to mail a letter. (p. 168)

- It may take an hour or more for people with obsessive-compulsive disorder to leave the house. (p. 169)

- Men are more than twice as likely as women to develop posttraumatic stress disorder (PTSD). (p. 171)

- Some theorists believe we are genetically programmed to more readily acquire fears of some classes of stimuli, including snakes. (p. 175)

- Misinterpretations of bodily sensations may set into motion a spiraling cycle of anxiety that culminates in a full-fledged panic attack. (p. 179)

- The same drugs used to treat schizophrenia are also used to control panic attacks. (p. 183)

- Peering over a virtual ledge 20 stories up has helped some people overcome their fear of actual heights. (p. 188)

Anxiety is a generalized state of apprehension or foreboding. There is much to be anxious about—our health, social relationships, examinations, careers, international relations, and the condition of the environment are but a few sources of possible concern. It is normal, even adaptive, to be somewhat anxious about these aspects of life. Anxiety serves us when it prompts us to seek regular medical checkups or motivates us to study for tests. Anxiety is an appropriate response to threats, but anxiety can be abnormal when its level is out of proportion to a threat, or when it seems to come out of the blue—that is, when it is not in response to environmental changes. In extreme forms, anxiety can impair our daily functioning. Consider the following case:

Panic on the Long Island Railroad

Slowly the trains snake their way through the maze of tunnels that lie beneath the city, carrying the Dashing Dans and Danielles on their way to work each morning. Most commuters pass the time by reading the morning newspapers, sipping coffee, or catching a few last winks. For Dick, the morning commute was an exercise in terror on an ordinary day in July. At first, Dick noticed the perspiration clinging to his shirt. The air-conditioning seemed to be working fine, for a change. How then was he to account for the sweat? As the train entered the tunnel and darkness shrouded the windows, Dick was gripped by sheer terror. He sensed his heart beating faster, the muscles in his neck tightening. Queasiness soured his stomach. He felt as though he might pass out. Other commuters, engrossed in their morning papers or their private thoughts, paid no heed to Dick, nor did they seem concerned about the darkness that enveloped the train.

Dick had known these feelings all too well before. But now the terror was worse. Other days he could bear it. This time, it seemed to start earlier than usual, before the train entered the tunnel. "Just don't think about it," he told himself, hoping it would pass. "I must think of something to distract myself." He tried humming a song, but the panic grew worse. He tried telling himself that it would be all right, that at any moment the train would enter the station and the doors would open. Not this day, however. On this day, the train came to a screeching halt. The conductor announced a "signaling problem." Dick tried to calm himself: "It's only a short delay. We'll be moving soon." But the train did not start moving soon. More apologies from the conductor. A train had broken down further ahead in the tunnel. Dick realized it could be a long delay, hours perhaps. Suddenly, he felt the urgent desire to escape. But how? he wondered. There was barely room for a crawlspace outside the train. Then again, could he even break the window and crawl out of the train, if he had to?

He felt like he was losing control. Wild imaginings flooded his mind. He saw himself bolting down the aisles in a futile attempt to escape, bowling people over, trying vainly to pry open the doors. He was charged with a sense of doom. Something terrible was about to happen to him. "Is this the first sign of a heart attack?" he wondered anxiously. By now, the perspiration had soaked his clothes. His once neat tie hung awry. He felt his breathing become heavy and labored, drawing attention from other passengers. "What do they think of me?" he thought. "Will they help me if I need them?"

The train jerked into motion. He realized he would soon be free. "I'm going to be okay," he told himself, "the feelings will pass. I'm going to be myself again." The train pulled slowly into the station, twenty minutes late. The doors opened and the passengers hurried off. Stepping out himself, Dick adjusted his tie and readied himself to start the day. He felt as though he'd been in combat. Nothing that his boss could dish out could hold a candle to what he had experienced on the 7:30 train.

—*From the Authors' Files*

■

anxiety An emotional state characterized by physiological arousal, unpleasant feelings of tension, and a sense of apprehension or foreboding.

panic disorder A type of anxiety disorder characterized by repeated episodes of intense *anxiety* or panic.

anxiety disorder A type of mental disorder whose most prominent feature is anxiety.

THINK ABOUT IT

Anxiety may be a normal emotional reaction in some situations but not in others. Think of a situation in which anxiety would be a normal reaction and one in which it would be a maladaptive reaction. What are the differences? What criteria would you use to distinguish between the normal and abnormal?

Dick had suffered a panic attack, one of many he had experienced before seeking treatment. The attacks varied in frequency. Sometimes they occurred daily, sometimes once a week or so. He never knew whether an attack would occur on a particular day. He knew, however, that he couldn't go on living like this. He feared that one day he would suffer a heart attack on the train. He pictured some passengers trying vainly to revive him while others stared at him in the detached distant way that people stare at traffic accidents. He pictured emergency workers rushing to the train, bearing him on a stretcher through the darkened tunnels to an ambulance.

For a while he considered changing jobs, accepting a less remunerative job closer to home, one that would free him from the need to take the train. He also considered driving to work, but the roads were too thick with traffic. No choice, he figured; either commute by train or switch jobs. His wife, Jill, was unaware of his panic attacks. She wondered why his shirts were heavily stained with perspiration and why Dick was talking about changing jobs. She worried about making ends meet on a lower income. She had no idea it was the train ride, and not his job, that Dick was desperate to avoid.

Panic attacks, like that suffered by Dick, are a feature of **panic disorder,** a type of **anxiety disorder.** During a panic attack, one's level of anxiety can rise to the level of sheer terror. Panic attacks are an extreme form of anxiety. Anxiety encompasses a myriad of physical features, cognitions, and behaviors as shown in Table 6.1. Although anxious people do not often experience all of them, it is easy to see why anxiety is distressing.

TABLE 6.1 Some Features of Anxiety

Physical Features of Anxiety

Jumpiness, jitteriness
Trembling or shaking of the hands or limbs
Sensations of a tight band around the forehead
Tightness in the pit of the stomach or chest
Heavy perspiration
Sweaty palms
Light-headedness or faintness
Dryness in the mouth or throat
Difficulty talking
Difficulty catching one's breath
Shortness of breath or shallow breathing
Heart pounding or racing
Tremulousness in one's voice
Cold fingers or limbs
Dizziness
Weakness or numbness
Difficulty swallowing
A "lump in the throat"
Stiffness of the neck or back
Choking or smothering sensations
Cold, clammy hands
Upset stomach or nausea
Hot or cold spells
Frequent urination
Feeling flushed
Diarrhea
Feeling irritable or "on edge"

Behavioral Features of Anxiety

Avoidance behavior
Clinging, dependent behavior
Agitated behavior

Cognitive Features of Anxiety

Worrying about something
A nagging sense of dread or apprehension about the future
Belief that something dreadful is going to happen, with no clear cause
Preoccupation with bodily sensations
Keen awareness of bodily sensations
Feeling threatened by people or events that are normally of little or no concern
Fear of losing control
Fear of inability to cope with one's problems
Thinking the world is caving in
Thinking things are getting out of hand
Thinking things are swimming by too rapidly to take charge of them
Worrying about every little thing
Thinking the same disturbing thought over and over
Thinking that one must flee crowded places or else pass out
Finding one's thoughts jumbled or confused
Not being able to shake off nagging thoughts
Thinking that one is going to die, even when one's doctor finds nothing medically wrong
Worrying that one is going to be left alone
Difficulty concentrating or focusing one's thoughts

Types of Anxiety Disorders

The anxiety disorders, along with dissociative disorders and somatoform disorders (see Chapter 7), were classified as neuroses throughout most of the 19th century. The term *neurosis* derives from roots meaning "an abnormal or diseased condition of the nervous system." The Scottish physician William Cullen coined it in the 18th century. As the derivation implies, it was assumed neurosis had biological origins. It was seen as an affliction of the nervous system.

At the beginning of the 20th century, Cullen's organic assumptions were largely replaced by Sigmund Freud's psychodynamic views. Freud maintained that neurotic behavior stems from the threatened emergence of unacceptable anxiety-evoking ideas into conscious awareness. Various neurotic behavior patterns—anxiety disorders, somatoform disorders, and dissociative disorders—might look different enough on the surface. According to Freud, however, they all represent ways in which the ego attempts to defend itself against anxiety. Freud's **etiological** assumption, in other words, united the disorders as neuroses. Freud's concepts were so widely accepted in the early 1900s that they formed the basis for the classification systems found in the first two editions of the *Diagnostic and Statistical Manual of Mental Disorders (DSM)*.

Since 1980, the *DSM* has not contained a category termed *neuroses.* The present *DSM* is based on similarities in observable behavior and distinctive features rather than on causal assumptions. Many clinicians continue to use the terms *neurosis* and *neurotic* in the manner in which Freud described them, however. Some clinicians use "neuroses" as a convenient means of grouping milder behavioral problems in which people maintain relatively good contact with reality. "Psychoses," such as schizophrenia, are typified by loss of touch with reality, and by the appearance of bizarre behavior, beliefs, and hallucinations. Anxiety is not limited to the diagnostic categories traditionally termed "neuroses," moreover. People with adjustment problems, depression, and psychotic disorders may also encounter problems with anxiety.

The present version of the *DSM* system, the *DSM-IV*, recognizes the following specific types of anxiety disorders: panic disorder; phobic disorders, such as specific phobia, social phobia, and agoraphobia; generalized anxiety disorder; obsessive-compulsive disorder; and acute and posttraumatic stress disorders. Table 6.2 lists the diagnostic features of anxiety disorders. The anxiety disorders are not mutually exclusive. People frequently meet diagnostic criteria for more than one of them.

Web Link 6.1
wWw NIMH Self-Screening for Anxiety Disorders

etiological Relating to cause or origin.

TABLE 6.2 Diagnostic Features of Anxiety Disorders

Agoraphobia	Fear and avoidance of places or situations in which it would be difficult or embarrassing to escape, or in which help might be unavailable in the event of a panic attack or panic-type symptoms.
Panic Disorder Without Agoraphobia	Occurrence of recurrent, unexpected panic attacks in which there is persistent concern about them but without accompanying agoraphobia.
Panic Disorder with Agoraphobia	Occurrence of recurrent, unexpected panic attacks in which there is persistent concern about them and accompanying agoraphobia.
Generalized Anxiety Disorder	Persistent and excessive levels of anxiety and worry that is not tied to any particular object, situation, or activity.
Specific Phobia	Clinically significant anxiety relating to exposure to specific objects or situations, often accompanied by avoidance of these stimuli.
Social Phobia	Clinically significant anxiety relating to exposure to social situations or performance situations, often accompanied by avoidance of these situations.
Obsessive-Compulsive Disorder	Recurrent obsessions and/or compulsions.
Posttraumatic Stress Disorder	The reexperiencing of a highly traumatic event accompanied by heightened arousal and avoidance of stimuli associated with the event.
Acute Stress Disorder	Features similar to those of posttraumatic stress disorder but limited to the days and weeks following exposure to the trauma.

Note. All of these disorders are coded on Axis I in the *DSM-IV.*
Source. Adapted from *DSM-IV-TR* (APA, 2000).

VIDEO 6.1
Panic Disorder: *The Case of Jerry*

Web Link 6.2 WWW
Q&A: About Panic Disorder

Panic. Panic attacks have stronger physical components—especially cardiovascular symptoms—than other types of anxiety reactions.

Panic Disorder

Panic disorder involves the occurrence of repeated, unexpected panic attacks. Panic attacks involve intense anxiety reactions accompanied by physical symptoms such as a pounding heart; rapid respiration, shortness of breath, or difficulty breathing; heavy perspiration; and weakness or dizziness (Glass, 2000). There is a stronger bodily component to panic attacks than to other forms of anxiety. The attacks are accompanied by feelings of sheer terror and a sense of imminent danger or impending doom and by an urge to escape the situation. They are usually accompanied by thoughts of losing control, going crazy, or dying. People who experience panic attacks tend to be keenly aware of changes in their heart rates (Richards, Edgar, & Gibbon, 1996). They often believe they are having a heart attack even though there is nothing wrong with their hearts. But since the symptoms of panic attacks can mimic those of heart attacks or even severe allergic reactions, a thorough medical evaluation should be performed.

A panic attack occurs suddenly and builds to a peak of intensity within 10 to 15 minutes (USDHHS, 1999a). Attacks usually last for minutes, but can extend to hours, and are associated with a strong urge to escape the situation in which they occur. For a diagnosis of panic disorder to be made, there must be the presence of recurrent unexpected panic attacks—attacks that are not triggered by specific objects or situations. They seem to come out of the blue. Although the first attacks occur spontaneously or unexpectedly, over time they may become associated with certain situations or cues, such as entering a crowded department store, or, like Dick, riding on a train.

In many cases, people who experience panic attacks limit their activities to avoid places in which they fear attacks may occur or they are cut off from their usual supports. Panic disorder often leads to agoraphobia—fear of being in public places in which escape may be difficult or help unavailable (Glass, 2000). After a panic attack, the person may feel exhausted, as if he or she has survived a truly traumatic experience, as in the following case:

A Case of Panic Disorder

"I was inside a very busy shopping precinct and all of a sudden it happened; in a matter of seconds I was like a mad woman. It was like a nightmare, only I was awake; everything went black and sweat poured out of me—my body, my hands, and even my hair got wet through. All of the blood seemed to drain out of me; I went white as a ghost. I felt as if I was going to collapse; it was as if I had no control over my limbs; my back and legs were very weak and I felt as though it were impossible to move. It was as if I had been taken over by some stronger force. I saw all of the people looking at me—just faces, no bodies; all merged into one. My heart started pounding in my head and my ears; I thought that my heart was going to stop. I could see black and yellow lights. I could hear the voices of the people but from a long way off. I could not think of anything except the way that I was feeling and how I had to get out and run quickly or I would die. I must escape and get into fresh air. Outside it subsided a little but I felt limp and weak; my legs were like jelly as though I had run a race and lost; I had a lump in my throat like a golf ball. The incident seemed to me to have lasted hours. I was absolutely drained when I got home and I just broke down and cried; it took until the next day to feel normal again."

—Adapted from Hawkrigg, 1975, pp. 1280–1282

People often describe panic attacks as the worst experiences of their lives. Their coping abilities are overwhelmed. They may feel they must flee. If flight seems useless, they may freeze. There is a tendency to cling to others for help or support. Some people with panic attacks fear going out alone. Recurrent panic attacks may become so difficult to cope with that sufferers become suicidal. A study of community residents who suffered panic attacks found that 12% had attempted suicide (Weissman et al., 1989).

Table 6.3 lists the diagnostic features of panic attacks. Not all of these features need to be present. Not all panic attacks are signs of panic disorder; about 10% of otherwise healthy people in the population may experience an isolated attack in a given year (USDHHS, 1999a). A diagnosis of panic disorder is based on the following criteria: (1) encountering repeated (at least two) unexpected panic attacks; and (2) at least one of the attacks is followed by at least a month of persistent fear of subsequent attacks, or worry about the implications or consequences of the attack (e.g., fear of losing one's mind or "going crazy" or having a heart attack), or significant change in behavior (e.g., refusing to leave the house or venture into public for fear of having another attack) (APA, 2000). An estimated 1% to 4% of the population are affected by panic disorder at some point in their lives (APA, 2000; USDHHS, 1999a).

Panic disorder usually begins in late adolescence through the mid-30s (APA, 2000). Women are about twice as likely to develop panic disorder (USDHHS, 1999a) (see Figure 6.1). What little we know about the long-term course of panic disorder suggests it tends to follow a chronic course that waxes and wanes in severity over time (Ehlers, 1995).

Generalized Anxiety Disorder

Generalized anxiety disorder (GAD) is characterized by persistent feelings of anxiety that are not triggered by any specific object, situation, or activity, but rather seems to be what Freud labeled "free floating." The central feature of GAD is worry (Ruscio, Borkovec, & Ruscio, 2001). People with GAD are chronic worriers. They may worry excessively about their life circumstances, such as their finances, the well-being of their children, and their social relationships. Nine of 10 of them, according to one study, report excessive worrying about even minor things (Sanderson & Barlow, 1990). Children with generalized anxiety are more likely to be worried about academics, athletics, and other social aspects of school life. Other related features include restlessness; feeling tense, "keyed up," or "on edge"; becoming easily fatigued; having difficulty concentrating or finding one's mind going blank; irritability, muscle tension; and disturbances of sleep, such as difficulty falling asleep, staying asleep, or having restless and unsatisfying sleep (APA, 2000).

TABLE 6.3   Diagnostic Features of Panic Attacks

A panic attack involves an episode of intense fear or discomfort in which at least four of the following features develop suddenly and reach a peak within 10 minutes:

1. Heart palpitations, pounding heart, tachycardia (rapid heart rate)
2. Sweating
3. Trembling or shaking
4. Shortness of breath or smothering sensations
5. Choking sensations
6. Chest pains or discomfort
7. Feelings of nausea or other signs of abdominal distress
8. Feelings of dizziness, unsteadiness, light-headedness, or faintness
9. Feelings of strangeness or unreality about one's surroundings (derealization) or detachment from oneself (depersonalization)
10. Fear of losing control or going crazy
11. Fear of dying
12. Numbness or tingling sensations
13. Chills or hot flushes

Source. Adapted from the *DSM-IV-TR* (APA, 2000).

---

generalized anxiety disorder (GAD)   A type of anxiety disorder characterized by general feelings of dread and foreboding and heightened states of bodily arousal.

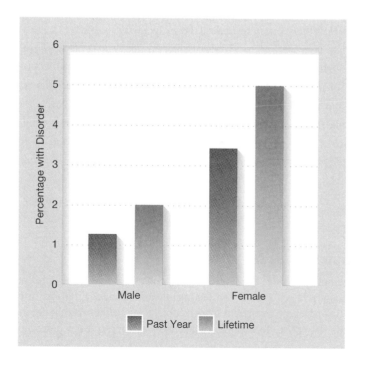

FIGURE 6.1 Prevalence of panic disorder by gender.
Panic disorder affects nearly two times as many women as men.

Source. National Comorbidity Survey (Kessler et al., 1994).

GAD tends to be a stable disorder that initially arises in the mid-teens to mid-20s and then follows a lifelong course (Rapee, 1991). The lifetime prevalence of GAD in the general U.S. population is estimated to be about 5% (APA, 2000). The disorder is believed to be about twice as common in women as in men (APA, 2000; USDHHS, 1999a).

Although GAD typically involves less intense physiological responses than panic disorder, the emotional distress associated with GAD is severe enough to interfere substantially with the person's daily life (Wittchen et al., 1994). GAD frequently occurs together (comorbidly) with other disorders, such as depression or other anxiety disorders like agoraphobia and obsessive-compulsive disorder.

In the following case, we find a number of features of generalized anxiety disorder:

A Case of Generalized Anxiety Disorder

Earl was a 52-year-old supervisor at the automobile plant. His hands trembled as he spoke. His cheeks were pale. His face was somewhat boyish, making his hair seem grayed with worry.

He was reasonably successful in his work, although he noted that he was not a "star." His marriage of nearly three decades was in "reasonably good shape," although sexual relations were "less than exciting—I shake so much that it isn't easy to get involved." The mortgage on the house was not a burden and would be paid off within 5 years, but "I don't know what it is; I think about money all the time." The three children were doing well. One was employed, one was in college, and one was in high school. But "With everything going on these days, how can you help worrying about them? I'm up for hours worrying about them."

"But it's the strangest thing," Earl shook his head. "I swear I'll find myself worrying when there's nothing in my head. I don't know how to describe it. It's like I'm worrying first and then there's something in my head to worry about. It's not like I start thinking about this or that and I see it's bad and then I worry. And then the shakes come, and then, of course, I'm worrying about worrying, if you know what I mean. I want to run away; I don't want anyone to see me. You can't direct workers when you're shaking."

Going to work had become a major chore. "I can't stand the noises of the assembly lines. I just feel jumpy all the time. It's like I expect something awful to happen. When it gets bad like that I'll be out of work for a day or two with shakes."

Earl had been worked up "for everything; my doctor took blood, saliva, urine, you name it. He listened to everything, he put things inside me. He had other people look at me. He told me to stay away from coffee and alcohol. Then from tea. Then from chocolate and Coca-Cola, because there's a little bit of caffeine [in them]. He gave me Valium [a minor tranquilizer] and I thought I was in heaven for a while. Then it stopped working, and he switched me to something else. Then that stopped working, and he switched me back. Then he said he was 'out of chemical miracles' and I better see a shrink or something. Maybe it was something from my childhood."

—*From the Authors' Files*

■

Phobic Disorders

The word *phobia* derives from the Greek *phobos*, meaning "fear." The concepts of fear and anxiety are closely related. *Fear* is the feeling of anxiety and agitation in response to a threat. Phobic disorders are persistent fears of objects or situations that are disproportionate to the threats they pose. To experience a sense of gripping fear when your car is about to go out of control is normal because there is an objective basis to the fear. In phobic disorders, however, the fear exceeds any reasonable appraisal of danger. People with a driving phobia, for example, might become fearful even when they are driving well below the speed limit on a sunny, uncrowded highway. Or they might be so afraid that they will not drive or even ride in a car. People with phobic disorders are not out of touch with reality; they generally recognize their fears are excessive or unreasonable.

A curious thing about phobias is that they usually involve fears of the ordinary events in life, not the extraordinary. People with phobias become fearful of ordinary experiences that most people take for granted, such as taking an elevator or driving on a highway. Phobias can become disabling when they interfere with such daily tasks as taking buses, planes, or trains; driving; shopping; or leaving the house.

Different types of phobias usually appear at different ages, as noted in Table 6.4. The ages of onset appear to reflect levels of cognitive development and life experiences. Fears of animals are frequent subjects of children's fantasies, for example. Agoraphobia, in contrast, often follows the development of panic attacks beginning in adulthood.

Here let us consider three types of phobic disorders classified within the *DSM* system: *specific phobia*, *social phobia*, and *agoraphobia*.

Specific Phobias **Specific phobias** are persistent, excessive fears of specific objects or situations, such as fear of heights (**acrophobia**), fear of enclosed spaces (**claustrophobia**), or fear of small animals such as mice or snakes and various other "creepy-crawlies." The person experiences high levels of fear and physiological arousal when encountering the phobic object, which prompts strong urges to avoid or escape the situation or avoid the feared stimulus, as in the following case:

A Case of Specific Phobia

Passing the bar exam was a significant milestone in Carla's life, but it left her feeling terrified at the thought of entering the county courthouse. She wasn't afraid of encountering a hostile judge or losing a case, but of climbing the stairs leading to a second floor promenade where the courtrooms were located. Carla, 27, suffered from acrophobia, or fear of heights. "It's funny, you know," Carla told her therapist. "I have no problem flying or looking out the window of a plane at 30,000 feet. But the escalator at the mall throws me into a tailspin. It's just any situation where I could possibly fall, like over the side of a balcony or banister." People with anxiety disorders look to avoid situations or objects they fear. Carla scouted out the courthouse before she was scheduled to appear. She was relieved to find a service elevator in the rear of the building she could use instead of climbing the stairs. She told her fellow attorneys with whom she was presenting the case that she suffered from a heart condition and couldn't climb stairs. Not suspecting the real reason she wanted to avoid the stairs, one of the attorneys turned to her and said, "This is great. I never knew this elevator existed. Thanks for finding it."

—*From the Authors' Files*

To rise to the level of a psychological disorder, the phobia must significantly impact the person's lifestyle or functioning, or cause significant distress. You may have a fear of snakes, but unless your fear interferes with your daily life or causes you significant emotional distress it would not warrant a diagnosis of phobic disorder.

Specific phobias often begin in childhood. Many children develop passing fears of specific objects or situations. Some, however, go on to develop chronic clinically significant phobias (Merckelbach et al., 1996). Claustrophobia seems to develop later than most other specific phobias, with a mean age of onset of 20 years (see Table 6.4).

TABLE 6.4 Typical Age of Onset for Various Phobias

	No. of Cases	Mean Age of Onset
Animal phobia	50	7
Blood phobia	40	9
Injection phobia	59	8
Dental phobia	60	12
Social phobia	80	16
Claustrophobia	40	20
Agoraphobia	100	28

Source. Adapted from Öst (1987, 1992).

specific phobia A persistent and excessive fear of a specific object or situation.

acrophobia Excessive, irrational fear of heights.

claustrophobia Excessive, irrational fear of small, enclosed spaces.

(A)

(B)

(C)

Three types of phobic disorder. The man in photo A has a specific phobia for dogs, a common phobia that may have an evolutionary origin. The young woman in photo B would like to join others but keeps to herself because of social phobia, an intense fear of social criticism and rejection. The woman in photo C has a specific phobia for injections. She does not fear the potential pain of the injection; rather, she cannot tolerate the idea of the needle sticking her.

Specific phobias are among the most common psychological disorders, affecting about 7% to 11% of the general population at some point in their lives (APA, 2000). Specific phobias tend to persist for years or decades unless they are treated successfully (USDHHS, 1999a). Women are about twice as likely to develop specific phobias (APA, 2000). This gender difference may to some degree reflect cultural factors that socialize women to be dependent on men for protection from threatening objects in the environment. Examiners also need to be aware of cultural factors when making diagnostic judgments. Fears of magic or spirits are common in some cultures and should not be considered a sign of a phobic disorder unless the fear is excessive in the light of the cultural context in which it occurs and leads to significant emotional distress or impaired functioning (APA, 2000).

Social Phobia It is not abnormal to experience some fear of social situations such as dating, attending parties or social gatherings, or giving a talk or presentation to a class or group. Yet people with **social phobia** (also called *social anxiety disorder*) have such an intense fear of social situations that they may avoid them altogether or endure them only with great distress. Underlying social phobia is an excessive fear of negative evaluations from others. People with social phobia fear doing or saying something humiliating or embarrassing. They may feel as if a thousand eyes are scrutinizing their every move. They tend to be severely critical of their social skills and become absorbed in evaluating their own performance when interacting with others. Some even experience full-fledged panic attacks in social situations.

Stage fright and speech anxiety are common types of social phobias. A random survey of some 500 residents of Winnipeg, Manitoba, found that about 1 in 3 had experienced excessive anxiety when speaking to a large audience that was significant enough to have had a detrimental impact on their lives (Stein, Walker, & Forde, 1996). People with social pho-

social phobia Excessive fear of social interactions or situations.

bias may find excuses for declining social invitations. They may lunch at their desks to avoid socializing with coworkers. Or they may find themselves in social situations and attempt a quick escape at the first sign of anxiety. Relief from anxiety negatively reinforces escape behavior, but escape prevents people with phobias from learning to cope with fear-evoking situations more adaptively. Leaving the scene before the anxiety dissipates only strengthens the association between the social situation and anxiety. Some people with social phobia are unable to order food in a restaurant for fear the server or their companions might make fun of the foods they order or how they pronounce them. Others fear meeting new people and dating.

Social phobias can severely impact daily functioning and the quality of life (Leibowitz et al., 2000; Olfson et al., 2000; Stein & Kean, 2000). They may prevent people from completing educational goals, advancing in their careers, or even holding a job in which they need to interact with others. The greater the number of feared situations, the greater the level of impairment tends to be (Stein, Torgrud, & Walker, 2000). People with social phobias often turn to tranquilizers or try to "medicate" themselves with alcohol when preparing for social interactions (see Figure 6.2). In extreme cases, they may become so fearful of interacting with others that they become essentially housebound.

Estimates of the lifetime prevalence of social phobia range from 3% to 13% (APA, 2000). The disorder appears to be more common among women than men, perhaps because of the greater social or cultural pressures placed on young women to please others and earn their approval.

Social phobia typically begins in childhood or adolescence and is often associated with a history of shyness (USDHHS, 1999a). People with social phobia typically report they were shy as children (Stemberger et al., 1995). Consistent with the *diathesis-stress model*, shyness may represent a diathesis or predisposition that makes one more vulnerable to develop social phobia in the face of stressful experiences, such as traumatic social encounters (e.g., being embarrassed in front of others). Once social phobia develops, it typically follows a chronic and persistent course throughout life.

Agoraphobia The word *agoraphobia* is derived from Greek words meaning "fear of the marketplace," which is suggestive of a fear of being out in open, busy areas. Agoraphobia involves fear of places and situations from which it might be difficult or embarrassing to escape in the event of panicky symptoms or a full-fledged panic attack, or of situations in which help may be unavailable if such problems should occur. People with agoraphobia may fear shopping in crowded stores; walking through crowded streets; crossing a bridge; traveling on a bus, train, or car; eating in restaurants; or even leaving the house. They may

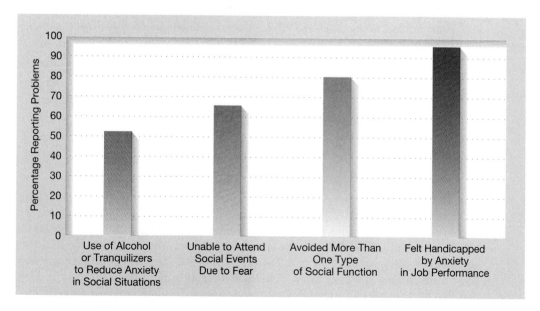

FIGURE 6.2 Percentages of people with social phobia reporting specific difficulties associated with their fears of social situations.
More than 90% of people with social phobia feel handicapped by anxiety in their jobs.

Source. Adapted from Turner & Beidel, 1989.

structure their lives around avoiding exposure to fearful situations and in some cases become housebound for months or even years, even to the extent of being unable to venture outside to mail a letter. Agoraphobia has the potential of becoming the most incapacitating type of phobia.

Agoraphobia is more common in women than men (USDHHS, 1999a). Frequently it begins in late adolescence or early adulthood. Approximately 6% of adult Americans have experienced agoraphobia at some point in their lives (Eaton, Dryman, & Weissman, 1991). Agoraphobia may occur with or without an accompanying panic disorder. In panic disorder with agoraphobia, the person may live in fear of recurrent attacks and avoid public places where attacks have occurred or might occur. Because panic attacks can descend from nowhere, some people restrict their activities for fear of making public spectacles of themselves or finding themselves without help. Others venture outside only with a companion. Still others forge ahead despite intense anxiety.

People with agoraphobia who have no history of panic disorder may experience mild panicky symptoms, such as dizziness, that lead them to avoid venturing away from places where they feel safe or secure. They too tend to become dependent on others for support. There is some evidence that people with agoraphobia without a history of panic disorder tend to function more poorly than do people who have both panic disorder and agoraphobia (Goisman et al., 1994). The following case of agoraphobia without a history of panic disorder illustrates the dependencies often associated with agoraphobia:

A Case of Agoraphobia

Helen, a 59-year-old widow, became increasingly agoraphobic after the death of her husband 3 years earlier. By the time she came for treatment, she was essentially housebound, refusing to leave her home except under the strongest urging of her daughter, Mary, age 32, and only if Mary accompanied her. Her daughter and 36-year-old son, Pete, did her shopping for her and took care of her other needs as best they could. However, the burden of caring for their mother, on top of their other responsibilities, was becoming too great for them to bear. They insisted that Helen begin treatment and Helen begrudgingly acceded to their demands.

Helen was accompanied to her evaluation session by Mary. She was a frail looking woman who entered the office clutching Mary's arm and insisted that Mary stay throughout the interview. Helen recounted that she had lost her husband and mother within 3 months of one another; her father had died 20 years earlier. Although she had never experienced a panic attack, she always considered herself an insecure, fearful person. Even so, she had been able to function in meeting the needs of her family until the deaths of her husband and mother left her feeling abandoned and alone. She had now become afraid of "just about everything" and was terrified of being out on her own, lest something bad would happen and she wouldn't be able to cope with it. Even at home, she was fearful that she might lose Mary and Pete. She needed constant reassurance from them that they too wouldn't abandon her.

—From the Authors' Files

Obsessive-Compulsive Disorder

An **obsession** is an intrusive and recurrent thought, idea, or urge that seems beyond the person's ability to control. Obsessions can be potent and persistent enough to interfere with daily life and can engender significant distress and anxiety. They include doubts, impulses, and mental images. One may wonder endlessly whether or not one has locked the doors and shut the windows, for example. One may be obsessed with the impulse to do harm to

obsession A recurring thought or image that the individual cannot control.

one's spouse. One can harbor images, such as the recurrent fantasy of a young mother that her children had been run over by traffic on the way home from school.

A **compulsion** is a repetitive behavior (such as hand-washing or checking door locks) or mental acts (such as praying, repeating certain words, or counting) that the person feels compelled or driven to perform (APA, 2000). Compulsions often occur in response to obsessional thoughts and are frequent and forceful enough to interfere with daily life or cause significant distress. A compulsive hand-washer, Corinne, engaged in elaborate hand-washing rituals. She spent 3 to 4 hours daily at the sink and complained, "My hands look like lobster claws." Some people literally take hours checking and rechecking that all the appliances are off before they leave home, and then doubts still remain.

Most compulsions fall into two categories: checking rituals and cleaning rituals. Rituals can become the focal point of life. Checking rituals, such as repeatedly checking that the gas jets are turned off or the doors are securely locked before leaving the house, cause delays and annoy companions; cleaning can occupy several hours a day. Table 6.5 shows some relatively common obsessions and compulsions.

Compulsions often accompany obsessions and appear to at least partially relieve the anxiety created by obsessional thinking. By washing one's hands 40 or 50 times in a row each time a public doorknob is touched, the compulsive hand-washer may experience some relief from the anxiety engendered by the obsessive thought that germs or dirt still linger in the folds of skin. The person may believe the compulsive act will help prevent some dreaded event from occurring, even though there is no realistic basis to the belief or the behavior far exceeds what is reasonable under the circumstances. Compulsive rituals apparently also reduce the anxiety that would occur if they were prevented from being carried out (Foa, 1990).

Obsessive-compulsive disorder (OCD) affects between 2% and 3% of the general population at some point in their lives (APA, 2000; Taylor, 1995). A Swedish study found that while most OCD patients eventually showed some improvement, most also continued to have some symptoms of the disorder over the course of their lifetimes (Skoog & Skoog, 1999). The disorder occurs about equally often in men and women (APA, 2000; USDHHS, 1999a). The *DSM* diagnoses obsessive-compulsive disorder

An obsessive thought? One type of obsession involves recurrent, intrusive images of a calamity occurring as the result of one's own carelessness. For example, a person may not be able to shake the image of his or her house catching fire due to an electrical short in an appliance inadvertently left on.

VIDEO 6.2

Obsessive-Compulsive Disorder: *The Case of Ed*

TABLE **6.5** **Examples of Obsessive Thoughts and Compulsive Behaviors**	
Obsessive Thought Patterns	**Compulsive Behavior Patterns**
Thinking that one's hands remain dirty despite repeated washing.	Rechecking one's work time and time again.
Difficulty shaking the thought that a loved one has been hurt or killed.	Rechecking the doors or gas jets before leaving home.
Repeatedly thinking that one has left the door to the house unlocked.	Constantly washing one's hands to keep them clean and germ free.
Worrying constantly that the gas jets in the house were not turned off.	
Repeatedly thinking that one has done terrible things to loved ones.	

Truth OR Fiction? REVISITED

It may take an hour or more for people with obsessive-compulsive disorder to leave the house.

TRUE. People with obsessive-compulsive disorder may be delayed in leaving the house for an hour or more as they carry out their checking rituals.

compulsion A repetitive or ritualistic behavior that the person feels compelled to perform.

Lady Macbeth. In Shakespeare's tragedy *Macbeth,* after spurring her husband on to murder the king and usurp the throne, Lady Macbeth obsessively washes her hands in an effort to cleanse herself of her crime.

when people are troubled by recurrent obsessions, compulsions, or both such that they cause marked distress, occupy more than an hour a day, or significantly interfere with normal routines or occupational or social functioning (APA, 2000). Many people with OCD, especially those who developed the disorder during childhood, also have a history of tic disorders. Investigators suspect there may be a genetic link between tic disorders and OCD, or at least child-onset OCD (Eichstedt & Arnold, 2001).

The line between obsessions and the firmly held but patently false beliefs that are labeled *delusions,* which are found in schizophrenia, is sometimes less than clear. Obsessions, such as the belief that one is contaminating other people, can, like delusions, become almost unshakable. Although adults with OCD may be uncertain at a given time about whether their obsessions or compulsions are unreasonable or excessive (Foa & Kozak, 1995), they will eventually concede that their concerns are groundless or excessive. True delusions fail to be shaken. Children with OCD may not come to recognize their concerns are groundless, however. The following case illustrates a checking compulsion:

A Case of Obsesssive-Compulsive Disorder

Jack, a successful chemical engineer, was urged by his wife Mary, a pharmacist, to seek help for "his little behavioral quirks," which she had found increasingly annoying. Jack was a compulsive checker. When they left the apartment, he would insist on returning to check that the lights or gas jets were off, or that the refrigerator doors were shut. Sometimes he would apologize at the elevator and return to the apartment to carry out his rituals. Sometimes the compulsion to check struck him in the garage. He would return to the apartment, leaving Mary fuming. Going on vacation was especially difficult for Jack. The rituals occupied the better part of the morning of their departure. Even then, he remained plagued by doubts.

Mary had also tried to adjust to Jack's nightly routine of bolting out of bed to recheck the doors and windows. Her patience was running thin. Jack realized that his behavior was impairing their relationship as well as causing himself distress. Yet he was reluctant to enter treatment. He gave lip service to wanting to be rid of his compulsive habits, but he also feared that surrendering his compulsions would leave him defenseless against the anxieties they helped ease.

—From the Authors' Files

■

Acute and Posttraumatic Stress Disorders

In adjustment disorders (discussed in Chapter 5), people have difficulty adjusting to life stressors, such as business or marital problems, chronic illness, or bereavement over a loss. Here we focus on stress-related disorders that arise from exposure to *traumatic* events. **Acute stress disorder (ASD)** is a maladaptive reaction that occurs during the initial month following the traumatic experience. **Posttraumatic stress disorder (PTSD)** is a prolonged maladaptive reaction to a traumatic experience. ASD is a major risk factor for PTSD, as many people with ASD later develop PTSD (Harvey & Bryant, 1999, 2000; Sharp & Harvey, 2001). In contrast to ASD, PTSD may persist for months, years, or even decades and may not develop until many months or years after exposure to the traumatic event (Zlotnick et al., 2001).

Both types of stress disorders have occurred among soldiers exposed to combat, rape survivors, victims of motor vehicle and other accidents, and people who have witnessed the

acute stress disorder (ASD) A traumatic stress reaction occurring in the days and weeks following exposure to a traumatic event.

posttraumatic stress disorder (PTSD) A prolonged maladaptive reaction to a traumatic event.

destruction of their homes and communities by natural disasters such as floods, earth-quakes, or tornadoes, or technological disasters such as railroad or airplane crashes.

In ASD and PTSD, the traumatic event involves either actual or threatened death or serious physical injury, or threat to one's own or another's physical safety. The person's response to the threat involves feelings of intense fear, helplessness, or a sense of horror. Children with PTSD may have experienced the threat differently, such as by showing confused or agitated behavior.

Exposure to trauma is quite common in the general population ("What Is PTSD?" 1996). A recent random sample of Americans showed that 72% reported some traumatic experience, such as exposure to natural disasters, death of a child, serious motor vehicle accidents, witnessing violence, or experiencing physical assault, rape, or physical or sexual abuse (Elliott, 1997).

Though most people who suffer trauma experience some degree of psychological distress (Sharp & Harvey, 2001), not all trauma survivors go on to develop ASD or PTSD. Yet many do. The prevalence of PTSD among trauma survivors remains an open question. In recent studies, investigators found that about 1 in 3 survivors of motor vehicle accidents developed PTSD within a year of the accident (Koren, Arnon, & Klein, 1999; Ursano et al., 1999). Yet some investigators find lower rates of PTSD among severely injured accident victims (e.g., Schnyder et al., 2000). A study of 255 adult survivors of the 1995 Oklahoma City bombing showed a prevalence rate for PTSD of 34% within 6 months of the disaster (North et al., 1999). Though we don't yet know how many people will develop PTSD in the aftermath of the 2001 terrorist attack on the World Trade Center in New York, we can expect the emotional toll to be staggering.

Overall, investigators believe that about 8% of U.S. adults are affected by PTSD at some point in their lives (Kessler et al., 1995). About 2% of American adults currently show evidence of diagnosable PTSD. The prevalence of ASD in the general population is not known.

Vulnerability to PTSD may depend on such factors as resiliency and vulnerability to the effects of trauma, prior history of childhood sexual abuse, severity of the trauma and degree of exposure, availability of social support, use of active coping responses in dealing with the traumatic stressor, and feelings of shame (Andrews et al., 2000; Brewin, Andrews, & Valentine, 2000; Nishith, Mechanic, & Resick, 2000; Prigerson et al., 2001; Regehr, Hill, & Glancy, 2000; Sharkansky et al., 2000; Silva et al., 2000). Finding a sense of purpose or meaning in the traumatic experience, such as believing that the war one is fighting is just, may also bolster the person's ability to cope with the stressful circumstances and reduce the risk of traumatic stress reactions (Sutker et al., 1995).

Although men more often encounter traumatic experiences, women are more likely to develop PTSD in response to trauma (Ehlers, Mayou, & Bryant, 1998; Michaud, 2000). Overall, women are about twice as likely to develop the disorder during their lifetimes than are men. The risk of PTSD in women is also linked to a history of battering in marriage and childhood sexual abuse (Astin et al., 1995; Rodriguez et al., 1997). Researchers find that women who develop PTSD also tend to have an increased risk of suffering major depression and alcohol use disorders (Breslau et al., 1997b). PTSD may also occur among children exposed to traumatic experiences (Silva et al., 2000).

The *DSM-IV* loosened the criteria for PTSD to include reactions to a wider range of traumatic stressors, including receiving a diagnosis of a life-threatening illness. In breast cancer survivors, PTSD symptoms appear to be more common than would be expected in the general population (Cordova et al., 1995). A recent study of patients who had experienced severe traumatic brain injuries showed a 27% rate of PTSD (Harvey et al., 2000).

PTSD entered the popular vocabulary after the Vietnam conflict of the 1960s. Veterans with PTSD have a greater likelihood than other veterans to have problems at home; about 60% report a high level of marital problems (Jordan et al., 1992). They are also more likely to commit suicide (Bullman & Kang, 1994). Many veterans with PTSD also abuse alcohol and drugs and become violent or socially withdrawn (Chemtob et al., 1997). They also have high rates of other psychological disorders, including major depression, panic disorder, and social phobias (Orsillo et al., 1996).

Web Link 6.3
wWw **Coping with the Aftermath of a Disaster**

Truth OR Fiction? REVISITED

Men are more than twice as likely as women to develop posttraumatic stress disorder (PTSD).

FALSE. Women are about twice as likely as men to develop PTSD.

Features of Traumatic Stress Reactions ASD and PTSD share many of the same features or symptoms (Bryant, 2001). Some common features are reexperiencing the traumatic event; avoidance of cues or stimuli associated with the event; a numbing of general or emotional responsiveness; heightened states of bodily arousal; and critical emotional distress or impairment of functioning. The major difference in the features of the two disorders is the emphasis in ASD on *dissociation*—feelings of detachment from oneself or one's environment (Bryant, 2001; USDHHS, 1999a). People with acute stress disorder may feel they are "in a daze" or that the world seems like a dreamlike or unreal place. In acute stress disorder, people may also be unable to perform necessary tasks, such as obtaining needed medical or legal assistance (APA, 2000).

Acute stress disorder frequently occurs in the context of combat or exposure to natural or technological disasters. A soldier may come through a horrific battle not remembering important features of the battle, and feeling numb and detached from the environment. People who are injured or who nearly lose their lives in a hurricane may walk around "in a fog" for days or weeks afterward; be bothered by intrusive images, flashbacks, and dreams of the disaster; or relive the experience as though it were happening again.

In acute and posttraumatic stress disorders, the traumatic event may be reexperienced in various ways. There can be intrusive memories, recurrent disturbing dreams, and the feeling the event is indeed recurring (as in "flashbacks" to the event). Exposure to events that resemble the traumatic experience can cause intense psychological distress. People with traumatic stress reactions tend to avoid stimuli that evoke recollections of the trauma. For example, they may not be able to handle a television account of it or a friend's wish to talk about it. They may have feelings of detachment or estrangement from other people. They may show less responsiveness to the external world after the traumatic event, losing the ability to enjoy previously preferred activities or to have loving feelings (Litz, 1992).

Have you ever been awakened by a nightmare and been reluctant to return to sleep for fear of reentering the orb of the dream? Nightmares in traumatic stress reactions often involve the reexperiencing of the traumatic event, which can lead to abrupt awakenings and difficulty going back to sleep—because of fear associated with the nightmare and elevated levels of arousal. Other features of heightened arousal include difficulty falling or staying asleep, irritability or angry outbursts, hypervigilance (being continuously on guard), difficulty concentrating, and an exaggerated startle response (jumping in response to sudden noises or other stimuli) (APA, 2000).

Trauma. Trauma may result from experiences in combat (left) or from terrorist violence (right), as in these survivors fleeing the World Trade Center disaster of September 11, 2001. In either case, stress-related problems may not develop until long after the experience, but may linger for years afterward in the form of posttraumatic stress disorder (PTSD).

Although PTSD often remits within a period of 6 months (USDHHS, 1999a), it can last for years, even decades (Bremmer et al., 1996; Kessler et al., 1995). Many World War II and Korean War veterans, for example, are found to meet diagnostic criteria for PTSD when evaluated four or five decades after their combat experience ended (Engdahl et al., 1997; Schnurr, Ford, & Friedman, 2000). Veterans with PTSD often present with a range of other problem behaviors, including substance abuse, marital problems, and poor work histories (Calhoun et al., 2000). Yet there is some good news to report: People who obtain treatment for PTSD typically recover sooner from the symptoms of PTSD than those who do not (Kessler et al., 1995). We can't say whether treatment shortens the duration of PTSD symptoms because it is possible that people who seek out treatment may differ in important ways from those who do not. Still, it suggests treatment has a positive influence.

Ethnic Differences in Anxiety Disorders

Although anxiety disorders have been the subject of extensive study, little attention has been directed toward examining ethnic differences in the prevalence of these disorders. Are anxiety disorders more common in certain racial/ethnic groups? We might think that stressors that African Americans in our society are more likely to encounter, such as racism and economic hardship, might contribute to a higher rates of anxiety disorders in this population group (Neal & Turner, 1991). On the other hand, it is possible that African Americans, by dint of having to cope with these hardships in early life, may have developed a resiliency in the face of stress that shields them from anxiety disorders.

The National Comorbidity Survey (NCS), which was based on a sample that closely represented the general U.S. adult population, found that anxiety disorders overall and specific anxiety disorders in particular were no more common among African Americans than among non-Hispanic White Americans (Eaton et al., 1994). Moreover, panic disorder was actually less common among African Americans in the 45- to 54-year age range than among non-Hispanic White Americans. Panic disorder was also less common among Hispanics than non-Hispanic Whites among people in the 35- to 44-year age range. Trivial differences were found among younger people across racial/ethnic lines. All in all, it appears that the rates of anxiety disorders are generally comparable across racial and ethnic groupings.

Anxiety disorders are not unique to our culture. Panic disorder, for example, is known to occur in many countries in the world, perhaps even universally (Amering & Katschnig, 1990). A multinational study of more than 40,000 people in 10 countries (Canada, Puerto Rico, France, United States, West Germany, Italy, Lebanon, Taiwan, Korea, and New Zealand) showed that rates of panic disorder were relatively consistent, ranging between 1% and 3% in all of these countries except Taiwan, where the rate was under 1%. However, the specific features of panic attacks, such as shortness of breath or fear of dying, may vary from culture to culture (Amering & Katschnig, 1990). Some culture-bound syndromes have features similar to panic attacks, such as *ataque de nervios* (see Chapter 3).

PTSD is also found in other cultures. High rates of PTSD were found in a southwestern U.S. Indian tribe, and among earthquake survivors in China, hurricane survivors in Nicaragua, Khmer refugees who survived the "killing fields" of the 1970s Pol Pot war in Cambodia, tortured Bhutanese refugees (van Ommeren et al., 2001), and survivors of the Balkan conflicts of the 1990s (Cardozo et al., 2000; Goenjian et al., 2001; Mitka, 2000; Mutler, 2000; Sack, Clarke, & Seeley, 1996; Wang et al., 2000; Weine et al., 2000). Cultural factors may play a role in determining how people manage and cope with trauma as well as their vulnerability to traumatic stress reactions and the specific form such a disorder might take (de Silva, 1993).

Theoretical Perspectives

The anxiety disorders offer something of a theoretical laboratory. Many theories of abnormal behavior were developed with these disorders in mind. Here we consider the contributions of these theoretical perspectives to our understanding of anxiety disorders.

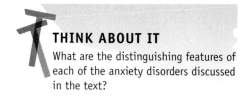

THINK ABOUT IT
What are the distinguishing features of each of the anxiety disorders discussed in the text?

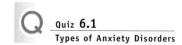

Quiz **6.1**
Types of Anxiety Disorders

Unconscious defense mechanisms? For psychodynamic theorists, phobias represent the operation of unconscious defense mechanisms such as projection and displacement. In their view, a fear of heights may represent the ego's attempt to defend itself against the emergence of threatening self-destructive impulses, such as an impulse to jump from a dangerous height. By avoiding heights, the person can maintain a safe distance from such threatening impulses. Because this process occurs unconsciously, the person may be aware of the phobia, not of the unconscious impulses that it symbolizes.

projection A defense mechanism in which one's own sexual or aggressive impulses are attributed to another person.

displacement A defense mechanism in which one transfers sexual or aggressive impulses toward less threatening or safer objects or persons.

two-factor model A theoretical model that accounts for the development of phobic reactions on the basis of classical and operant conditioning.

Psychodynamic Perspectives

From the psychodynamic perspective, anxiety is a danger signal that threatening impulses of a sexual or aggressive (murderous) nature are nearing the level of awareness. To fend off these threatening impulses, the ego tries to stem or divert the tide by mobilizing its defense mechanisms. For example, with phobias, the defense mechanisms of **projection** and **displacement** come into play. A phobic reaction is believed to involve the projection of the person's own threatening impulses onto the phobic object. For instance, a fear of knives or other sharp instruments may represent the projection of one's own destructive impulses onto the phobic object. The phobia serves a useful function. Avoiding contact with sharp instruments prevents these destructive wishes from becoming consciously realized or acted upon. The threatening impulses remain safely repressed. Similarly, people with acrophobia may harbor unconscious wishes to jump that are controlled by avoiding heights. The phobic object or situation symbolizes or represents these unconscious wishes or desires. The person is aware of the phobia, but not of the unconscious impulses that it symbolizes.

Freud's (1909/1959) historic case of "Little Hans," a 5-year-old boy who feared he would be bitten by a horse if he left his house, illustrates his principle of displacement. Freud hypothesized that Hans's fear of horses represented the displacement of an unconscious fear of his father. According to Freud's conception of the Oedipus complex, boys have unconscious incestuous desires to possess their mothers and fears of retribution from their fathers, whom they see as rivals in love. Hans's fear of being bitten by horses thus symbolized an underlying fear of castration.

Learning theorists view Hans's childhood fears as a case of classical conditioning (Wolpe & Rachman, 1960). They argue that Hans's fear had been learned from his being frightened by an accident involving a horse and a transport vehicle, which generalized to fears of horses. The story of Little Hans has sparked a spirited debate in the psychological annals.

Applying the psychodynamic model to other anxiety disorders, we might hypothesize that in generalized anxiety disorder, unconscious conflicts remain hidden, but anxiety leaks through to the level of awareness. The person is unable to account for the anxiety because its source remains shrouded in unconsciousness, however. In panic disorder, unacceptable sexual or aggressive impulses approach the boundaries of consciousness and the ego strives desperately to repress them, generating high levels of conflict that bring on a full-fledged panic attack. Panic dissipates when the impulse has been safely repressed.

Obsessions are believed to represent the leakage of unconscious impulses into consciousness, and compulsions are acts that help keep these impulses repressed. Obsessive thoughts about contamination by dirt or germs may represent the threatened emergence of unconscious infantile wishes to soil oneself and play with feces. The compulsion (in this case, cleanliness rituals) helps keep such wishes at bay or partly repressed.

The psychodynamic model remains largely speculative, in large part because of the difficulty (some would say impossibility) of arranging scientific tests to determine the existence of the unconscious impulses and conflicts believed to lie at the root of these disorders.

Learning Perspectives

From a learning perspective, anxiety disorders are acquired through the process of learning, specifically conditioning and observational learning. According to O. Hobart Mowrer's (1948) classic **two-factor model,** both classical and operant conditioning are involved in the development of phobias. The fear component of phobia is believed to be acquired by classical conditioning. It is assumed that previously neutral objects and situations gain the capacity to evoke fear by being paired with noxious or aversive stimuli. A child who is frightened by a barking dog may acquire a phobia for dogs. A child who receives a painful injection may develop a phobia for hypodermic syringes. Consistent with this model, evidence shows that many cases of acrophobia, claustrophobia, and blood and injection phobias involve earlier pairings of the phobic object with aversive experiences (e.g., Kendler et al., 1992c; Merckelbach et al., 1996).

As Mowrer pointed out, the avoidance component of phobias is acquired and maintained by operant conditioning. That is, relief from anxiety negatively reinforces avoiding fear-inducing stimuli. The person with an elevator phobia learns to avoid anxiety over riding the elevator by opting for the stairs instead. Avoiding the phobic stimulus thus lessens anxiety, which negatively reinforces the avoidance behavior. Yet there is a significant cost to avoiding the phobic stimulus. The person is not able to unlearn the fear via exposure to the phobic stimulus in the absence of any aversive consequences.

The development of panic disorder may represent a form of classical conditioning (Bouton, Mineka, & Barlow, 2001). In this view, both external cues (e.g., being in a crowd) and internal cues (e.g., heart palpitations or dizziness) may become conditioned stimuli (CSs) that elicit panicky feelings because they have been associated with the occurrence of panic attacks in the past.

Learning theorists have also noted the role of observational learning in acquiring fears. Modeling (observing parents or others react fearfully to a stimulus) and receiving negative information (hearing from others or reading that a particular stimulus—spiders, for example—are fearful or disgusting) may also lead to phobias (Merckelbach et al., 1996). In one study of 42 people with severe phobias for spiders, observational learning apparently played a more prominent role in fear acquisition than did conditioning (Merckelbach, Arnitz, & de Jong, 1991).

Some investigators suggest that people may be genetically prepared to more readily acquire phobic responses to certain classes of stimuli than others (McNally, 1987; Mineka, 1991; Seligman & Rosenhan, 1984). We're more likely to develop a fear of spiders than rabbits, for example. This model, called **prepared conditioning,** suggests that evolution would have favored the survival of human ancestors who were genetically predisposed to acquire fears of threatening objects, such as large animals, snakes, and other "creepy-crawlers"; heights; enclosed spaces; and even strangers. This model may explain why it is more likely for us to develop fears of spiders or heights than of objects that appeared much later on the evolutionary scene, such as guns or knives, even though these later-appearing objects pose more direct threats today to our survival.

prepared conditioning The belief that people are genetically prepared to acquire fear responses to certain stimuli, such as snakes or large animals.

Truth OR Fiction? REVISITED

Some theorists believe we are genetically programmed to more readily acquire fears of some classes of stimuli, including snakes.

TRUE. Some theorists believe that we are genetically predisposed to acquire certain fears, such as fears of large animals and snakes. The ability to readily acquire these fears may have had survival value to our ancestors.

Snakes and spiders. According to the concept of prepared conditioning, we are genetically predisposed to more readily acquire fears of the types of stimuli that would have threatened the survival of ancestral humans—stimuli such as large animals, snakes, and other creepy-crawlers.

PTSD may also be explained from a conditioning framework. From a classical conditioning perspective, traumatic experiences function as unconditioned stimuli that become paired with neutral (conditioned) stimuli such as the sights, sounds, and smells associated with the trauma scene—for example, the battlefield or the neighborhood in which a person has been raped or assaulted (Foy et al., 1987). Subsequent exposure to similar stimuli evokes the anxiety (a conditioned emotional response) associated with PTSD. The conditioned stimuli that reactivate the conditioned response include memories or dream images of the trauma or visits to the scene of the trauma. Consequently, the person avoids these stimuli. Avoidance is an operant response, which is reinforced by relief from anxiety. However, avoidance prolongs PTSD because sufferers do not have the opportunity to learn to manage their conditioned reactions. Extinction (gradual weakening or elimination) of conditioned anxiety may only occur when conditioned stimuli (e.g., cues associated with the trauma) are presented in a supportive therapeutic setting in the absence of the troubling unconditioned stimuli.

From a learning perspective, generalized anxiety is precisely that: a product of stimulus generalization. People concerned about broad life themes, such as finances, health, and family matters, are likely to experience their apprehensions in a variety of settings. Anxiety would thus become connected with almost any environment or situation. Similarly, agoraphobia would represent a kind of generalized anxiety. Anxiety would become triggered by cues associated with various social or vocational situations outside of the home in which the individual is expected to perform independently, as in traveling, going to work, even shopping. Some learning theorists similarly assume that panic attacks, which appear to descend out of nowhere, are triggered by cues that are subtle and not readily identified.

There are challenges to the learning theory account of phobias. Most specific phobias do not appear to develop from any specific traumatic incident, such as being bitten by a dog (USDHHS, 1999a). Learning theorists might counter that people may not recall traumatic or painful experiences from their early childhood. Yet phobias such as social phobias and agoraphobia develop at later ages and appear to involve cognitive processes usually related to an exaggerated appraisal of threat in social situations (excessive fears of embarrassment or criticism) or public places (perceptions of helplessness or fears of panic attacks) rather than the pairing of these situations with aversive experiences.

From the learning perspective, compulsive behaviors are operant responses that are negatively reinforced by relief of the anxiety engendered by obsessional thoughts. If a person obsesses that dirt or foreign bodies contaminate other people's hands, shaking hands or turning a doorknob may evoke powerful anxiety. Compulsive hand-washing following exposure to a possible contaminant provides some relief from anxiety. They thus become more likely to repeat the obsessive-compulsive cycle the next time they are exposed to anxiety-evoking cues, such as shaking hands or touching doorknobs.

The question remains why some people develop obsessive thoughts whereas others do not. Some theorists look to an interaction of learning and biological factors for answers. Perhaps people who develop obsessive-compulsive disorder are physiologically sensitized to overreact to minor cues of danger (Steketee & Foa, 1985).

Cognitive Factors in Anxiety Disorders

The focus of the cognitive perspective is on the role that distorted or dysfunctional ways of thinking may play in the development of anxiety disorders. Let us consider several styles of thinking that investigators have linked to anxiety disorders.

Overprediction of Fear   People with anxiety disorders often overpredict how much fear or anxiety they will experience in anxiety-evoking situations (Rachman, 1994). The person with a snake phobia, for example, may expect to tremble on exposure to a snake. People with dental phobia tend to hold exaggerated expectations of the pain they will experience during dental visits (Marks & De Silva, 1994). Typically speaking, the actual fear or pain

Web Link 6.4
National Anxiety Disorders   wWw
Screening Day

experienced during exposure to the phobic stimulus is a good deal less than what people had expected. Yet the tendency to expect the worst encourages avoidance of feared situations, which in turn prevents the individual from learning to manage and overcome anxiety. Overprediction of dental pain and fear may also lead people to postpone or cancel regular dental visits, which can contribute to more serious dental problems down the road. On the other hand, actual exposure to fearful situations tends to promote more accurate predictions of actual fear levels (Rachman & Bichard, 1988). A clinical implication is that with repeated exposure, people with anxiety disorders may come to anticipate their responses to fear-inducing stimuli more accurately, leading to reductions of fear expectancies. This in turn may reduce avoidance tendencies.

Self-Defeating or Irrational Beliefs Self-defeating thoughts can heighten and perpetuate anxiety and phobic disorders. When faced with fear-evoking stimuli, the person may think, "I've got to get out of here," or "My heart is going to leap out of my chest" (Meichenbaum & Deffenbacher, 1988). Thoughts like these intensify autonomic arousal, disrupt planning, magnify the aversiveness of stimuli, prompt avoidance behavior, and decrease self-efficacy expectancies concerning one's ability to control the situation.

People with phobias also tend to hold more of the sorts of irrational beliefs catalogued by Albert Ellis than nonfearful people do. Such beliefs often involve exaggerated needs to be approved of by everyone one meets and to avoid any situation in which negative appraisal from others might arise. Consider these beliefs: "What if I have an anxiety attack in front of other people? They might think I was crazy. I couldn't stand it if they looked at me that way." Results of one study may hit close to home: College men who believe it is awful (not just unfortunate) to be turned down when requesting a date show more social anxiety than those who are less likely to catastrophize rejection (Gormally et al., 1981).

Cognitive theorists relate obsessive-compulsive disorder to tendencies to exaggerate the risk of unfortunate events occurring (Bouchard, Rhéaume, & Ladouceur, 1999). Because they expect terrible things to happen, people with OCD engage in rituals to prevent them. An accountant who imagines awful consequences for slight mistakes on a client's tax forms may feel compelled to repeatedly check her or his work. Another cognitive factor linked to the development of OCD is perfectionism, or belief that one must perform flawlessly (Shafran & Mansell, 2001). People who hold perfectionist beliefs exaggerate the consequences of turning in less than perfect work and may feel compelled to redo his or her efforts until every detail is flawless.

Oversensitivity to Threat An oversensitivity to threatening cues is a cardinal feature of anxiety disorders (Beck & Clark, 1997). People with phobias perceive danger in situations that most people consider safe, such as riding on elevators or driving over bridges. We all possess an internal alarm system that is sensitive to cues of threat. This system may have had evolutionary advantages to ancestral humans by increasing the chances of survival in a hostile environment (Beck & Clark, 1997). Ancestral humans who responded quickly to signs of threat, such as a rustling sound in the bush that may have indicated a lurking predator about to pounce, may have been better prepared to take defensive action (to fight or flee) than those with less sensitive alarm systems. The emotion of fear is a key element in this alarm system and may have motivated our ancestors to take defensive action, which in turn may have helped them survive. People today who have anxiety disorders may have inherited an acutely sensitive internal alarm that leads them to be overly responsive to cues of threat. Rather than helping them cope effectively with threats, it may lead to inappropriate anxiety reactions in response to a wide range of cues that actually pose no danger to them.

Anxiety Sensitivity Anxiety sensitivity is usually defined as a fear of anxiety and anxiety-related symptoms (Zinbarg et al., 2001). People with high levels of anxiety sensitivity have a fear of fear itself. They fear their emotions or associated bodily states of arousal will get out of control, leading to harmful consequences, such as having a heart

anxiety sensitivity A fear of anxiety and anxiety-related symptoms.

attack (Williams, Chambless, & Ahrens, 1997). They may be prone to panic whenever they experience bodily signs of anxiety, such as a racing heart or shortness of breath, because they take these symptoms to be signs of an impending catastrophe, such as a heart attack. Evidence suggests that anxiety sensitivity may have an inherited component (Stein, Jang, & Livesley, 1999). Anxiety sensitivity may also vary among cultural groups. Investigators found a higher level of anxiety sensitivity in a sample of American Indian and Alaska Native college students than in college students from the majority Caucasian culture (Zvolensky et al., 2001).

Anxiety sensitivity is an important risk factor for panic disorder (Lilienfeld, 1997). In one study, researchers used an anxiety sensitivity measure to predict which military recruits would be most likely to panic during a highly stressful period of basic training (Schmidt, Lerew, & Jackson, 1997). One in 5 recruits who scored in the top 10% on a measure of anxiety sensitivity experienced a panic attack, as compared to only 6% of the other recruits. As we see next, panic-prone individuals also tend to misattribute changes in their bodily sensations to dire consequences.

Misattributions of Bodily Cues Cognitive theorists point to the role that catastrophic misinterpretations of bodily sensations, such as heart palpitations, dizziness, or light-headedness, play in the escalation of panicky symptoms into full-fledged panic attacks (Clark, 1986; Zoellner, Craske, & Rapee, 1996). People with a proneness to panic disorder tend to attribute bodily cues like heart palpitations, dizziness, or light-headedness to an impending heart attack or other threatening event, such as loss of control or "going crazy." These bodily cues may occur as a consequence of unrecognized hyperventilation, temperature changes, or reactions to certain drugs or medications. Or they may be fleeting, normally occurring changes in bodily states that typically go unnoticed by most people. But in panic-prone individuals, these bodily cues may be misattributed to dire causes, setting in motion a vicious cycle that can bring on panic attacks.

A leading cognitive model of panic disorder focuses on the interaction of cognitive and physiological factors, as depicted in Figure 6.3. The model suggests that people with a proneness to panic disorder may perceive environmental cues or bodily cues as unduly threatening or dangerous, perhaps because they are overly sensitive to these cues or have associated these cues with earlier panic attacks (Clark, 1986; Zoellner, Craske, & Rapee, 1996). This sense of threat induces anxiety or feelings of apprehension, which is accompanied by sympathetic nervous system activation that leads to the release of epinephrine (adrenaline) by the adrenal glands (Wilkinson et al., 1998). Epinephrine intensifies physical sensations by inducing an accelerated heart rate, rapid breathing, and sweating. These changes in bodily sensations, in turn, become misinterpreted as signs of an impending panic attack or worse, as an impending catastrophe ("My God, I'm having a heart attack!"). Misattributions of bodily cues further reinforce perceptions of threat, which further heightens anxiety, leading to yet more anxiety-related bodily symptoms, and so on and so on in a vicious cycle that quickly spirals into a full-fledged panic attack.

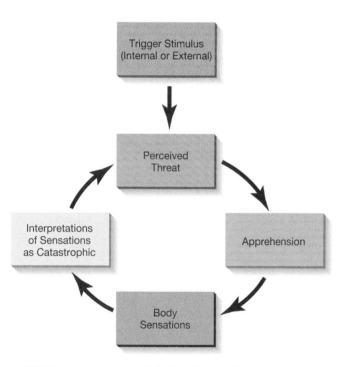

FIGURE 6.3 A cognitive model of panic disorder.
This model depicts the interaction of cognitive and physiological factors. In panic-prone people, perceptions of threat from internal or external cues lead to feelings of apprehension or anxiety, which lead to changes in body sensations (for example, cardiovascular symptoms). These changes lead, in turn, to catastrophic interpretations, thereby intensifying the perception of threat, further heightening anxiety, and so on in a vicious circle that may culminate in a full-blown panic attack.

Source. Adapted from Clark, 1986.

Low Self-Efficacy If you believe you lack the ability to handle the stressful challenges you face in life, the more anxious you are likely to feel in the face of these challenges (Bandura et al., 1985). On the other hand, if you feel capable of performing tasks you undertake, such as playing the piano, giving a speech in public, or riding on a train or driving over bridges without panicking, you are less likely to be troubled by anxiety or fear when you attempt them. People with low levels of self-efficacy (lack of belief in their ability to perform tasks successfully) tend to focus on their perceived inadequacies, as in the following case:

Anxiety and Low Self-Efficacy

Brenda, a 19-year-old sophomore, was plagued by anxiety almost from the moment she began her college studies. She had enrolled in a college several hundred miles away from home. While she had been away from home before—at sleep-away camp and on a teen tour through Europe—college life presented various challenges and stresses, which she felt a lack of ability to handle. She seemed to be most anxious when meeting new friends and when sitting in class, especially the small seminar classes in which she expected to be called on by the professor. She found herself becoming tongue tied and dripping with perspiration whenever she confronted these situations. What was more surprising and perplexing to her was that she had never had any trouble before either making new friends or talking in class.

In both situations, Brenda lost confidence in her ability to express herself. The ideas she wished to express were blocked by anxiety, which impaired her ability to think and speak clearly. The anxiety was maintained by an erroneous perception of herself as not capable of saying the right thing when called upon in class or when meeting new people. Brenda reported that she hadn't had any problems in high school either speaking up in class or making new friends. College, however, was a different experience. At college there were people she hadn't grow up with, and there were professors who had no tolerance, or so she believed, for any student who wasn't a budding genius. Her whole mental set had shifted into a defensive attitude in which self-doubts replaced self-confidence.

Brenda's history of social and academic success couldn't shield her from the nagging self-doubts she began to experience as she confronted the more demanding stresses of college life. She was not any less capable of coping with these challenges in college than she was in high school. She didn't suddenly lose her wits or her social skills when she entered college. What was different was that she began to perceive herself as unable to cope with the demands of a new environment that seemed both unsupportive and threatening. Appraising herself this way, it was little wonder that she experienced anxiety in class and social situations, which impaired her efforts to speak clearly. She then interpreted her speech difficulties as evidence of her inadequacies, feeding the vicious cycle of anxiety in which self-doubt leads to anxiety, which hampers performance, which occasions more self-doubts and anxiety, and so on.

—From the Authors' Files

■

We have increasing evidence of the importance of cognitive factors in anxiety disorders. For example, evidence shows that people with panic disorder do have a greater tendency to misinterpret bodily sensations as signs of impending catastrophe than do people without anxiety disorders or those with other types of anxiety disorders (Clark et al., 1997). Studies also show that panic-prone people have greater awareness of, and sensitivity to, their internal physiological cues, such as heart palpitations (Pauli et al., 1997; Richards, Edgar, & Gibbon, 1996). More research is needed, however, to determine the extent to which cognitive factors play a direct causal role in the development of panic disorder or other anxiety disorders.

Biological Factors in Anxiety Disorders

A growing body of evidence points to the importance of biological factors in anxiety disorders—factors such as heredity and biochemical imbalances in the brain.

Genetic Factors   Genetic factors appear to play important roles in the development of many anxiety disorders, including panic disorder, generalized anxiety disorder, obsessive-compulsive disorder, and phobic disorders (APA, 2000; Gorman et al., 2000; Hettema,

How do self-doubts affect our performance? According to the self-efficacy model, we are likely to feel more anxious in situations in which we doubt our ability to perform competently. Anxiety may hamper our performance, making it more difficult for us to perform successfully. Even accomplished athletes may be seized with anxiety when they are under extreme pressure, as during slumps or when competing in championship games.

Neale, & Kendler, 2001; Kendler et al., 2001). Investigators have also linked a gene to **neuroticism**, a personality trait that may underlie proneness to developing anxiety disorders (Begley, 1998). The trait of neuroticism is characterized by anxiety, a sense of foreboding, and the tendency to avoid fear-inducing stimuli. Researchers estimate that about half of the variability among people in the general population on this underlying trait is due to genetic factors, with environmental factors accounting for the rest (Plomin, Owen, & McGuffin, 1994).

Neurotransmitters A number of neurotransmitters are implicated in anxiety reactions, including **gamma-aminobutyric acid (GABA)**. GABA is an *inhibitory* neurotransmitter, which means that it tones down excess activity in the nervous system and helps quell stress responses (USDHHS, 1999a). When the action of GABA is inadequate, neurons can fire excessively, possibly bringing about seizures. In less dramatic cases, inadequate action of GABA may heighten states of anxiety. This view of the role of GABA is supported by findings that people with panic disorder show lower levels of GABA in some parts of the brain (Goddard et al., 2001). Also, we know that the group of antianxiety drugs called **benzodiazepines,** which include the well-known Valium and Librium, make GABA receptors more sensitive, thus enhancing GABA's calming (inhibitory) effects (Zorumski & Isenberg, 1991).

Irregularities or dysfunctions in serotonin and norepinephrine receptors in the brain are also implicated in anxiety disorders (Southwick et al., 1997). This may explain why antidepressant drugs that affect these neurotransmitter systems often have beneficial effects in treating some types of anxiety disorders, including panic disorder (Glass, 2000) and social phobia (Van Ameringen et al., 2001). Investigators also suspect that genes involved in regulation of serotonin may play a role in determining anxiety-related traits (Lesch et al., 1996).

Biochemical Aspects of Panic Disorder The strong physical components of panic disorder have led some theorists to speculate that panic attacks have biological underpinnings, perhaps involving a dysfunctional alarm system in the brain (Glass, 2000). Psychiatrist Donald Klein (1994) proposed that a defect in the brain's respiratory alarm system leads to a bodily overreaction in panic-prone individuals to cues of suffocation, perhaps involving mild changes in the levels of carbon dioxide in the blood. In Klein's model, cues of suffocation from hyperventilation or other causes trigger a respiratory alarm, which in turn produces the cascading sensations involved in the classic panic attack: shortness of breath, smothering sensations, dizziness, faintness, increased heart rate or palpitations, trembling, sensations of hot or cold flashes, and feelings of nausea. Klein's intriguing proposal has met with some support in the professional community (e.g., McNally et al., 1995; Taylor & Rachman, 1994), as well as some dissenting voices (e.g., Ley, 1997). Other researchers report that episodes of traumatic suffocation (neardrownings or near-chokings) may play a role in the development of panic disorder in some patients (Bouwer & Stein, 1997).

Support for a biological basis of panic disorder is found in studies showing that people with panic disorder are more likely than nonpatient controls to experience more anxious, panicky symptoms in response to biological challenges such as infusion of the chemical *sodium lactate* or manipulation of carbon dioxide (CO_2) levels in the blood either via intentional **hyperventilation** (which reduces levels of CO_2 in the blood) or inhalation of carbon dioxide (which increases CO_2 levels) (e.g., Gorman et al., 2001; Kent et al., 2001; Zvolensky & Eifert, 2001).

Cognitive theorists propose that cognitive factors may be involved in explaining these biological sensitivities. They point out that biological challenges produce intense physical sensations that may be catastrophically misinterpreted by panic-prone people as signs of an impending heart attack or loss of control (McNally & Eke, 1996; Schmidt, Trakowski, & Staab, 1997). Perhaps these misinterpretations—not underlying biological sensitivities—may in turn induce panic.

neuroticism A trait that involves characteristics such as anxious behavior, apprehension about the future, and avoidance behavior.

gamma-aminobutyric acid (GABA) An inhibitory neurotransmitter believed to play a role in anxiety.

benzodiazepines The class of antianxiety drugs that includes Valium and Xanax.

hyperventilation A pattern of overly rapid breathing associated with states of anxiety.

Supportive evidence for the cognitivist perspective comes from a recent study showing that cognitive-behavioral therapy that focused on changing faulty interpretations of bodily sensations eliminated CO_2–induced panic in a majority of panic disorder patients (Schmidt, Trakowski, & Staab, 1997). Moreover, the results of another study showed that panic patients who underwent the CO_2 infusion with a safe person present did not experience more panicky symptoms than normal controls (Carter et al., 1995). Having a supportive person available may lead the person to appraise the situation cognitively as less threatening, which may avert the spiraling of anxiety that can lead to panic attacks. However, simply receiving reassurance about the safety of the CO_2 inhalation procedure does not seem to reduce the rate of panic (Welkowitz et al., 1999).

The fact that panic attacks often seem to come out of the blue also seems to support the belief that the attacks are biologically triggered. However, it is possible that the cues that set off many panic attacks may be internal, involving changes in bodily sensations, rather than external. Changes in physical cues, combined with catastrophic thinking, may lead to a spiraling of anxiety that culminates in a full-blown panic attack.

Biological Aspects of Obsessive-Compulsive Disorder Another biological model receiving attention of late suggests that obsessive-compulsive disorder may involve heightened arousal of a so-called *worry circuit,* a neural network in the brain involved in signaling danger. In OCD, the brain may be constantly sending messages that something is wrong and requires immediate attention, leading to obsessional worrisome thoughts and repetitive compulsive behaviors. This worry circuit incorporates parts of the *limbic system,* a set of structures located below the cerebral cortex that plays a key role in memory formation and processing of emotional responses. One structure in the limbic system, the almond-shaped **amygdala**, works as a kind of "emotional computer" in evaluating stimuli as to whether they represent a threat or danger (Davidson, 2000; Öhman & Mineka, 2001) (see Figure 6.4).

The compulsive aspects of OCD may involve disturbances in brain circuits that normally suppress repetitive behaviors. This disturbance may lead people to feel compelled to perform repetitive behaviors as though they were "stuck in gear" (Leocani et al., 2001). The

amygdala Limbic system structure involved in processing threatening stimuli.

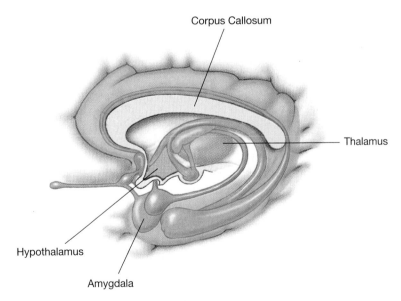

FIGURE 6.4 The amygdala and limbic system.
The amygdala is part of the limbic system, a set of interconnected structures in the brain involved in forming memories and processing emotional responses. The limbic system, which also consists of specific parts of the thalamus and hypothalamus and other nearby structures, is located in the forebrain below the cerebral cortex.

frontal lobes regulate brain centers in the lower brain that control bodily movement. A recent fMRI study showed abnormal patterns of activation in parts of the frontal lobes in OCD patients (Schwartz, 1998). Perhaps a disruption in these neural pathways explains the failure of people with compulsive behavior to inhibit these responses. Changes in frontal activation is also found among patients who respond favorably to cognitive-behavioral treatment, which suggests that CBT may directly affect parts of the brain implicated in OCD (Ingram & Siegle, 2001; Schwartz, 1998).

Tying It Together

Unraveling the complex interactions of environmental, physiological, and psychological factors in explaining how anxiety disorders develop remains a challenge. There may be different causal pathways at work. To illustrate, let us offer some possible causal pathways involved in phobic disorders and panic disorder.

Some people may develop phobias by way of classical conditioning—the pairing of a previously neutral stimulus with an unpleasant or traumatic experience. A person may develop a fear of small animals because of experiences in which they were bitten or nearly bitten. A fear of riding on elevators may arise from experiences of being trapped in elevators or other enclosed spaces.

Bear in mind that not all people who have traumatic experiences develop related phobias. Perhaps some people have a genetic predisposition that sensitizes them to more readily acquire conditioned responses to stimuli associated with aversive situations. Or perhaps people are more sensitized to these experiences because of an inherited predisposition to respond with greater negative arousal to aversive situations. Whatever factors may be involved in the acquisition of the phobia, people with persistent phobias may have learned to avoid any further contact with the phobic stimulus and so do not avail themselves of opportunities to unlearn the phobia through repeated uneventful contacts with the feared object or situation. Then there are people who acquire phobias without any prior aversive experiences with the phobic stimulus, or at least none they can recall. We can conjecture that cognitive factors, such as observing other people's aversive responses, may play a contributing role in these cases.

Possible causal pathways in panic disorder highlight roles for biological, cognitive, and environmental factors. Some people may inherit a genetic predisposition, or *diathesis,* that makes them more likely to panic in response to changes in bodily sensations. This genetic predisposition may involve an overly sensitive suffocation alarm system that is triggered by mild fluctuations in blood levels of carbon dioxide, perhaps resulting from unrecognized hyperventilation. Cognitive factors may also be involved. Cues associated with changing carbon dioxide levels, such as dizziness, tingling, or numbness, may be misconstrued as signs of an impending disaster—suffocation, a heart attack, or loss of control. This in turn may lead, like dominoes falling in line, to an anxiety reaction that quickly spirals into a full-fledged panic attack. Whether the anxiety reaction spirals into a state of panic may depend on another vulnerability factor, the individual's level of anxiety sensitivity. People with a high level of anxiety sensitivity (extreme fear of their own bodily sensations) may be more likely to panic in response to changes in their physical sensations. In some cases, anxiety sensitivity may be so high that panic ensues even in individuals without a genetic predisposition. Panic attacks may come to be triggered by exposure to internal or external cues (conditioned stimuli) that have been associated with panic attacks in the past, such as heart palpitations or boarding a train or elevator.

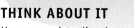

THINK ABOUT IT

How are anxiety disorders conceptualized within the psychodynamic, humanistic, biological, and learning-based perspectives?

Quiz **6.2**
Theoretical Perspectives Q

Treatment of Anxiety Disorders

Each of the major theoretical perspectives has spawned approaches for treating anxiety disorders. Psychological approaches may differ from one another in their techniques and expressed aims, but they seem to have one thing in common: In one way or another, they encourage clients to face rather than avoid the sources of their anxieties. The biological perspective, by contrast, has focused largely on the use of drugs that quell anxiety.

Psychodynamic Approaches

From the psychodynamic perspective, anxieties reflect the energies attached to unconscious conflicts and the ego's efforts to keep them repressed. Traditional psychoanalysis fosters awareness of how clients' anxiety disorders symbolize their inner conflicts, so the ego can be freed from expending its energy on repression. The ego can thus attend to more creative and enhancing tasks.

More modern psychodynamic therapies also foster clients' awareness of inner sources of conflict. They focus more so than traditional approaches on exploring sources of anxiety that arise from current rather than past relationships, however, and they encourage clients to develop more adaptive behaviors. Such therapies are briefer and more directive than traditional psychoanalysis. Though psychodynamic therapies may prove to be helpful in treating anxiety disorders, they lack extensive empirical support documenting their effectiveness (USDHHS, 1999a).

Humanistic Approaches

Humanistic theorists believe that many of our anxieties stem from social repression of our genuine selves. Anxiety occurs when the incongruity between one's true inner self and one's social facade draws closer to the level of awareness. The person senses something bad will happen, but is unable to say what it is because the disowned parts of oneself are not directly expressed in consciousness. Because of the disapproval of others, people may fail to develop their individual talents and recognize their authentic feelings. Humanistic therapies thus aim at helping people get in touch with and express their genuine talents and feelings. As a result, clients become free to discover and accept their true selves, rather than reacting with anxiety whenever their true feelings and needs begin to surface.

Biological Approaches

A variety of drugs are used to treat anxiety disorders. Among the most widely used drugs are mild tranquilizers such as the benzodiazepines Valium (generic name, *diazepam*) and Xanax (*alprazolam*). Though benzodiazepines have calming effects, they can lead to physical dependence (addiction) (USDHHS, 1999a). People who become dependent on them may experience a range of withdrawal symptoms if they stop using the drugs abruptly, including such symptoms as rebound anxiety, insomnia, and restlessness. These unpleasant symptoms may prompt people to resume using the drugs.

Antidepressant drugs have antianxiety and antipanic effects as well as antidepressant effects (Glass, 2000; Roy-Byrne & Cowley, 1998; USDHHS, 1999a). Antidepressants may help counter anxiety by normalizing the activity of neurotransmitters in the brain. Some antidepressants in common use for treating panic disorder include the tricyclics *imipramine* (brand name Tofranil) and *clomipramine* (brand name Anafranil) and the SSRIs *paroxetine* (brand name Paxil) and *sertraline* (brand name Zoloft). However, troublesome side effects may occur, such as heavy sweating and heart palpitations, which leads many patients prematurely to stop using the drugs. The high-potency tranquilizer *alprazolam* (Xanax), which is a type of benzodiazepine, is also helpful in treating panic disorder, social phobia, and generalized anxiety disorder (Barlow et al., 2000; Gould et al., 1997; van Balkom et al., 1997).

Truth OR Fiction? REVISITED

The same drugs used to treat schizophrenia are also used to control panic attacks.

FALSE. Drugs used to treat schizophrenia are not used to treat panic disorder. However, antidepressants have shown therapeutic benefits in helping to control panic attacks.

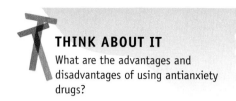

THINK ABOUT IT
What are the advantages and disadvantages of using antianxiety drugs?

Antidepressants may also be helpful in treating other anxiety disorders, including agoraphobia that accompanies panic disorder, social phobia, PTSD, obsessive-compulsive disorder, and generalized anxiety disorder (Brady et al., 2000; Davidson et al., 2001; van Ameringen et al., 2001).

Obsessive-compulsive disorder (OCD) appears to be especially responsive to SSRI-type antidepressants—drugs such as *fluoxetine* (Prozac), *clomipramine* (brand name Anafranil), and *fluvoxamine* (brand name Luvox). These drugs increase the availability in the brain of the neurotransmitter serotonin (Jenike et al., 1997; Riddle et al., 2001; USDHHS, 1999a). The effectiveness of these drugs leads researchers to suspect that problems with serotonin transmission play an important role in the development of OCD, at least in some cases (Hollander et al., 1992). Bear in mind, however, that some people with OCD fail to respond to these drugs, and among those who do respond, a complete remission of symptoms is uncommon (DeVeaugh-Geiss, 1994; Riddle et al., 2001).

A potential problem with drug therapy is that patients may attribute clinical improvement to the drugs and not their own resources. Nor do such drugs produce cures. Relapses are common after patients discontinue the medication (Spiegel & Bruce, 1997). Reemergence of panic is likely unless cognitive-behavioral treatment is provided to help panic patients modify their cognitive overreactions to their bodily sensations (Clark, 1986). Drug therapy is sometimes combined with cognitive-behavioral therapy. Evidence suggests that drug therapy does not interfere with the effectiveness of the cognitive-behavioral treatment (e.g., Bruce, 1996).

Learning-Based Approaches

A substantial body of research demonstrates the effectiveness of learning-based approaches in treating a range of anxiety disorders (USDHHS, 1999a). At the core of these approaches is the effort to help individuals learn to cope more effectively with objects or situations that elicit their fears and anxieties.

Systematic Desensitization

A Fear of Injections

Adam has a phobia for receiving injections. His behavior therapist treats him as he reclines in a comfortable padded chair. In a state of deep muscle relaxation, Adam observes slides projected on a screen. A slide of a nurse holding a needle has just been shown three times, 30 seconds at a time. Each time Adam has shown no anxiety. So now a slightly more discomforting slide is shown: one of the nurse aiming the needle toward someone's bare arm. After 15 seconds, our armchair adventurer notices twinges of discomfort and raises a finger as a signal (speaking might disturb his relaxation). The projector operator turns off the light, and Adam spends two minutes imagining his "safe scene"—lying on a beach beneath the tropical sun. Then the slide is shown again. This time Adam views it for 30 seconds before feeling anxiety.

—From Essentials of psychology *(6th ed.) by S. A. Rathus, p. 537.*

Copyright © 2001. Reprinted with permission of Brooks/Cole, an imprint of Wadsworth Group, a division of Thomson Learning. FAX 800-730-2215.

Adam is undergoing systematic desensitization, a fear-reduction procedure originated by psychiatrist Joseph Wolpe (1958) in the 1950s. Systematic desensitization is a gradual process. Clients learn to handle progressively more disturbing stimuli while they remain relaxed. About 10 to 20 stimuli are arranged in a sequence or hierarchy—called a **fear-stimulus hierarchy**—according to their capacity to evoke anxiety. By using their imagination or by viewing photos, clients are exposed to the items in the hierarchy, gradually imagining them-

fear-stimulus hierarchy An ordered series of increasingly fearful stimuli.

selves approaching the target behavior—be it ability to receive an injection or remain in an enclosed room or elevator—without undue anxiety.

Joseph Wolpe developed systematic desensitization on the assumption that phobias are learned or conditioned responses (Rachman, 2000). He assumed they can be unlearned by counterconditioning. In counterconditioning, a response incompatible with anxiety is made to appear under conditions that usually elicit anxiety. Muscle relaxation is generally used as the incompatible response, and followers of Wolpe usually use the method of progressive relaxation (described in Chapter 5) to help clients acquire relaxation skills. For this reason, Adam's therapist is teaching Adam to experience relaxation in the presence of (otherwise) anxiety-evoking slides of needles.

Behaviorally oriented therapists, like Wolpe, explain the benefits of systematic desensitization and similar therapies in terms of principles of counterconditioning. Cognitively oriented therapists note, however, that remaining in the presence of phobic imagery, rather than running from it, is also likely to enhance self-efficacy expectancies (i.e., self-perceptions of being able to manage the phobic stimuli without anxiety) (Galassi, 1988).

Gradual Exposure This method helps people overcome phobias through a stepwise approach of actual exposure to the phobic stimuli. The effectiveness of exposure therapy is well established, making it the treatment of choice for specific phobias (Barlow, Esler, & Vitali, 1998; G. T. Wilson, 1997). Here exposure therapy was used in treating a patient's case of claustrophobia:

Gradual exposure. In gradual exposure, the client is exposed to a fear-stimulus hierarchy in real-life situations, often with a therapist or companion serving in a supportive role. To encourage the person to accomplish the exposure tasks increasingly on his or her own the therapist or companion gradually withdraws direct support. Gradual exposure is often combined with cognitive techniques that focus on helping the client replace anxiety-producing thoughts and beliefs with calming, rational alternatives.

A Case of Claustrophobia

Claustrophobia (fear of enclosed spaces) is not very unusual, though Kevin's case was. Kevin's claustrophobia took the form of a fear of riding on elevators. What made his case so unusual was his occupation: He worked as an elevator mechanic. Kevin spent his work days repairing elevators. Unless it was absolutely necessary, however, Kevin managed to complete the repairs without riding in the elevator. He would climb the stairs to the floor where an elevator was stuck, make repairs, and hit the down button. He would then race downstairs to see that the elevator had operated correctly. When his work required an elevator ride, panic would seize him as the doors closed. Kevin tried to cope by praying for divine intervention to prevent him from passing out before the doors opened.

Kevin related the origin of his phobia to an accident three years earlier in which he had been pinned in his overturned car for nearly an hour. He remembered feelings of helplessness and suffocation. Kevin developed claustrophobia—a fear of situations from which he could not escape, such as flying on an airplane, driving in a tunnel, taking public transportation, and, of course, riding in an elevator. Kevin's fear had become so incapacitating that he was seriously considering switching careers, although the change would require considerable financial sacrifice. Each night he lay awake wondering whether he would be able to cope the next day if he were required to test-ride an elevator.

Kevin's therapy involved gradual exposure. Gradual exposure, like systematic desensitization, is a step-by-step procedure that involves a fear-stimulus hierarchy. In gradual exposure, however, the target behavior is approached in actuality rather than symbolically. Moreover, the individual is active rather than relaxed in a recliner.

A typical hierarchy for overcoming a fear of riding on an elevator might include the following steps:

1. *Standing outside the elevator.*
2. *Standing in the elevator with the door open.*
3. *Standing in the elevator with the door closed.*
4. *Taking the elevator down one floor.*
5. *Taking the elevator up one floor.*

6. *Taking the elevator down two floors.*
7. *Taking the elevator up two floors.*
8. *Taking the elevator down two floors and then up two floors.*
9. *Taking the elevator down to the basement.*
10. *Taking the elevator up to the highest floor.*
11. *Taking the elevator all the way down and then all the way up.*

Clients begin at step 1 and do not progress to step 2 until they are able to remain calm on the first. If they become bothered by anxiety, they remove themselves from the situation and regain calmness by practicing muscle relaxation or focusing on soothing mental imagery. The encounter is then repeated as often as necessary to reach and sustain feelings of calmness. They then proceed to the next step, repeating the process.

Kevin was also trained to practice self-relaxation and talk calmly and rationally to himself to help himself remain calm during his exposure trials. Whenever he began to feel even slightly anxious, he would tell himself to calm down and relax. He was able to counter the disruptive belief that he was going to fall apart if he was trapped in an elevator with rational self-statements such as, "Just relax. I may experience some anxiety, but it's nothing that I haven't been through before. In a few moments I'll feel relieved."

Kevin slowly overcame his phobia but still occasionally experienced some anxiety, which he interpreted as a reminder of his former phobia. He did not exaggerate the importance of these feelings. Now and then it dawned on him that an elevator he was servicing had once occasioned fear. One day following his treatment, Kevin was repairing an elevator, which serviced a bank vault 100 feet underground. The experience of moving deeper and deeper underground aroused fear, but Kevin did not panic. He repeated to himself, "It's only a couple of seconds and I'll be out." By the time he took his second trip down, he was much calmer.

—From the Authors' Files

Gradual exposure is also widely used in the treatment of agoraphobia (DeRubeis & Crits-Christoph, 1998; Mueser & Liberman, 1995). Treatment is stepwise and gradually exposes the agoraphobic individual to increasingly fearful stimulus situations, such as walking through congested streets or shopping in department stores. A trusted companion or perhaps the therapist may accompany the person during the exposure trials. The eventual goal is for the person to be able to handle each situation alone and without discomfort or an urge to escape. The benefits of gradual exposure are typically enduring. Overall, researchers find that about 6 in 10 people with agoraphobia show clinically meaningful improvement following exposure-based treatment (Jacobson, Wilson, & Tupper, 1988). Fewer than 1 in 3, however, are no longer agoraphobic by the end of treatment.

Flooding The method called **flooding** is a form of exposure therapy in which subjects are exposed to high levels of fear-inducing stimuli either in imagination or real-life situations. Why? The belief is that anxiety represents a conditioned response to a phobic stimulus and should extinguish if the individual remains in the phobic situation for a long enough period of time and no harmful consequences occur. Most individuals with phobias avoid confronting phobic stimuli or beat a hasty retreat at the first opportunity for escape if they cannot avoid them. Consequently, they lack the opportunity to unlearn the fear response through extinction. In one research example, 9 of 10 people with social phobia achieved at least moderate improvement through a flooding technique in which they directly faced fear-inducing situations, such as giving a talk before an expert audience (Turner, Beidel, & Jacob, 1994).

flooding A form of exposure therapy in which subjects are exposed to high levels of fear-inducing stimuli.

Cognitive Therapy Through his rational-emotive behavior therapy approach, Ellis might show people with social phobias how irrational needs for social approval and perfectionism produce unnecessary anxiety in social interactions. Eliminating exaggerated needs for social approval is apparently a key therapeutic factor (Butler, 1989). Beck's cognitive therapy seeks to identify and correct dysfunctional or distorted beliefs. For example, people with social phobias might think no one at a party will want to talk with them and that they will wind up lonely and isolated for the rest of their lives. Cognitive therapists help clients recognize the logical flaws in their thinking and assist them in viewing situations rationally. Clients may be asked to gather evidence to test out their beliefs, which may lead them to alter beliefs they find are not grounded in reality. Therapists may encourage clients with social phobias to test their beliefs that they are bound to be ignored, rejected, or ridiculed by others in social gatherings by attending a party, initiating conversations, and monitoring other people's reactions. Therapists may also help clients develop social skills to improve their interpersonal effectiveness and teach them how to handle social rejection, if it should occur, without catastrophizing.

One example of cognitive techniques is **cognitive restructuring** (also called *rational restructuring*), a process in which therapists help clients pinpoint their self-defeating thoughts and generate rational alternatives so they learn to cope with anxiety-provoking situations. Kevin learned to replace self-defeating thoughts with rational alternatives and to practice speaking rationally and calmly to himself during his exposure trials. Consider the following case:

cognitive restructuring A cognitive therapy method that involves replacing irrational thoughts with rational alternatives.

Getting Stuck on the Elevator

Phyllis, a 32-year-old writer and mother of two sons, had not been on an elevator in 16 years. Her life revolved around finding ways to avoid appointments and social events on high floors. She had suffered from fear of elevators since the age of 8, when she had been stuck between floors with her grandmother.

To help overcome her fear of elevators, Phyllis imagined herself getting stuck in an elevator and countering the self-defeating thoughts she might experience with rational self-statements. She closed her eyes and reported the thoughts that would come to mind. The psychologist encouraged her to create a rational counterpoint to each of them. She then repeated the exercise in imagination and practiced replacing the self-defeating thoughts with rational alternatives, as in the following examples:

Self-Defeating Thought	Rational Alternative
Oh, oh, I'm stuck. I'm going to lose control.	*Relax. Just think coolly, what do I have to do next?*
I can't take it. I'm going to pass out.	*Okay, practice your deep breathing. Help will be coming shortly.*
I'm having a panic attack. I can't stand it.	*You've experienced all these feelings before. Just let them pass through.*
If it takes hours, that would be horrible.	*That would be annoying, but it wouldn't necessarily be horrible. I've gotten stuck in traffic longer than that.*
I've got to get out of here.	*Stay calm. There's no real danger. I can just sit down and imagine I'm somewhere else until someone comes to help.*

—From the Authors' Files

Overcoming fears with virtual reality. Virtual reality is now being used to help people overcome phobias. Using this technique, a person with a fear of heights, as pictured here, can learn to handle exposure to progressively more frightening stimuli in virtual situations. The hope is that this learning will transfer to real-life exposure to such stimuli.

Virtual Therapy for Phobias Virtual reality, the computer-generated simulated environment, has now become a therapeutic tool. By donning a specialized helmet and gloves that are connected to a computer, a person with a fear of heights, for example, can encounter frightening stimuli in this virtual world, such as riding a glass-enclosed elevator to the 49th floor, peering over a railing on a balcony on the 20th floor, or crossing a virtual Golden Gate Bridge (Goleman, 1995b; Steven, 1995). By a process of exposure to a series of increasingly more frightening virtual stimuli, while progressing only when fears at each preceding step diminish, people learn to overcome fears in much the same way they would had they followed a program of graduated exposure to phobic stimuli in real-life situations. The advantage of virtual reality is that it provides an opportunity to experience situations that might be difficult or impossible to arrange in reality (Yancey, 2000). Virtual therapy has been used successfully in helping people overcome phobias, including fears of heights and fear of flying (Rothbaum et al., 1995, 2000; Yancey, 2000). For virtual therapy to be effective, says psychologist Barbara Rothbaum who pioneered the use of the technique, the person must become immersed in the experience and believe at some level it is real and not like watching a videotape (as cited in Goleman, 1995b). "If the first person had put the helmet on and said, 'This isn't scary,' it wouldn't have worked, Dr. Rothbaum said. "But you get the same physiological changes—the racing heart, the sweat—that you would in the actual place" (Goleman, 1995b, p. C11).

We have only begun to explore the potential therapeutic uses of this new technology. Therapists are experimenting with virtual therapy to help people overcome other types of fears, such as fear of public speaking and agoraphobia. It has been used as a form of group therapy in which a group of people who are actually in different places can don virtual reality gear, log on to their computers at the same time, and meet electronically in a simulated therapy office. The virtual group members can see simulated faces of each other and communicate by typing messages directed at the group at large or to individual members (Goleman, 1995b). In other applications, virtual therapy may help clients work through unresolved conflicts with significant figures in their lives by allowing them to confront these "people" in a virtual environment. A family therapist envisions virtual family sessions in which participants can see things from the emotional and physical vantage points of each other member of the family (Steven, 1995). Other potential uses of virtual therapy include treating people with depression, social phobias, and obsessive-compulsive disorder; children with attention-deficit disorders; adults with fears of intimacy or sexual aversion; and people who have problems controlling their anger or aggressive behavior (Glantz et al., 1996; Steven, 1995). Self-help "therapy" modules, consisting of compact disks and virtual reality helmets and gloves, may even begin to appear on the shelves of your neighborhood computer software store in the not-too-distant future. With these self-help modules, people may be able in their own living rooms to confront objects or situations they fear, or learn to stop smoking or lose weight, all with the help and guidance of a "virtual therapist." Virtual therapy has recently been successfully extended to fear of spiders (Carlin, Hoffman, & Weghorst, 1997) and to fear of flying, in which the virtual environment simulates the experience of sitting in an airplane during takeoff and flight (Rothbaum, 1996).

Cognitive-Behavioral Therapy Cognitive-behavioral therapy (CBT) incorporates behavioral techniques, such as exposure, along with cognitive techniques, such as cognitive restructuring. Here we examine the use of CBT in treating several types of anxiety disorders: social phobia, posttraumatic stress disorder, generalized anxiety disorder, obsessive-compulsive disorder, and panic disorder.

Social Phobia Exposure therapy is widely used successfully in treating social phobia (Barlow, Esler, & Vitali, 1998; DeRubeis & Crits-Christoph, 1998; Hoffman, 2000a, 2000b). Clients are instructed to enter increasingly stressful social situations and to remain in those situations until the urge to escape has lessened. The therapist may help guide them during exposure trials, gradually withdrawing direct support so that clients

Truth OR Fiction? REVISITED

Peering over a virtual ledge 20 stories up has helped some people overcome their fear of actual heights.

TRUE. Virtual reality therapy has been used successfully in helping people overcome phobias, including fear of heights.

THINK ABOUT IT
Select a particular anxiety disorder and, using specifics, describe how it would be treated from each of the major treatment approaches discussed in the text.

become capable of handling the situations on their own. The therapist may combine exposure treatment with cognitive techniques that assist clients in replacing maladaptive anxiety-inducing thoughts they may encounter in social situations with more adjustive thoughts. The gains achieved from cognitive-behavioral treatment of social phobia appear to be durable (Gould et al., 1997).

Posttraumatic Stress Disorder Evidence also supports the therapeutic use of cognitive-behavioral therapy in treating PTSD (DeRubeis & Crits-Christoph, 1998; Falsetti & Resnick, 2000; Taylor et al., 2001). A basic treatment component is exposure to cues associated with the trauma. The PTSD patient may be encouraged to talk about the trauma, reexperience parts of the trauma in imagination, view related slides or films, or visit the scene of the traumatic event (Foa et al., 1999; Keane, 1998; Tarrier et al., 2000). For combat-related PTSD, homework assignments may involve visiting war memorials or viewing war movies (Frueh et al., 1996). The person comes to gradually reexperience the traumatic event and accompanying anxiety in a safe setting that is free of negative consequences, which allows extinction to take its course. Exposure therapy may be supplemented with cognitive restructuring that focuses on replacing dysfunctional thoughts with rational alternatives (Marks et al., 1998b). Training in stress management skills, such as self-relaxation, may help enhance the client's ability to cope with the troubling features of PTSD, such as heightened arousal and the desire to run away from trauma-related stimuli. Training in anger management skills may also be helpful, especially with combat veterans with PTSD (Frueh et al., 1996).

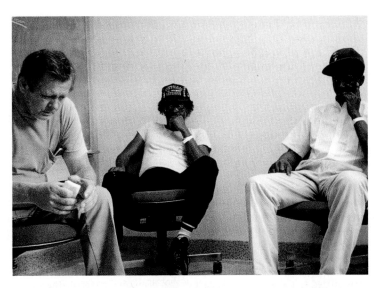

Counseling veterans with posttraumatic stress disorder. Storefront counseling centers have been established across the country to provide supportive services to combat veterans suffering from PTSD.

Generalized Anxiety Disorder Cognitive-behavioral therapists also use a combination of techniques in treating generalized anxiety disorder (GAD). These techniques include training in self-relaxation skills; learning to substitute adaptive thoughts for intrusive, worrisome thoughts; and learning skills of decatastrophizing (avoiding tendencies to think the worst). Cognitive-behavioral approaches in treating GAD have produced greater benefits in controlled studies than either control conditions or alternative therapies in treating GAD (Barlow, Esler, & Vitali, 1998; DeRubeis & Crits-Christoph, 1998; Ladouceur et al., 2000).

Obsessive-Compulsive Disorder Therapists have achieved impressive results in treating obsessive-compulsive disorder with the technique of *exposure with response prevention* (Abramowitz & Foa, 2000; Franklin et al., 2000; McLean et al., 2001). The exposure component involves having clients intentionally place themselves in situations that evoke obsessive thoughts. For many people, such situations are hard to avoid. Leaving the house, for example, may trigger obsessive thoughts about whether or not the gas jets are turned off or the windows and doors are locked. Or clients may be instructed to purposely induce obsessive thoughts by leaving the house messy or rubbing their hands in dirt. Response prevention is the effort to prevent the compulsive behavior from occurring. Clients who rub their hands in dirt must avoid washing them for a designated period of time. The compulsive door-lock checker must avoid checking to see that the door was locked.

Through exposure with response prevention, people with OCD learn to tolerate the anxiety triggered by their obsessive thoughts while they are prevented from performing their compulsive rituals. With repeated trials, the anxiety eventually subsides and the person feels less compelled to perform the ritual. Extinction, or the weakening of the anxiety response following repeated presentation of the obsessional cues in the absence of any aversive consequences, is believed to underlie the treatment effect. Overall, about 4 of 5 people undergoing this therapy show significant improvement (Abramowitz, 1996; Foa, 1996).

Cognitive techniques are often combined with exposure therapy. The therapist focuses on helping the person correct cognitive distortions, such as tendencies to overestimate

A Closer Look

EMDR: A Fad or a Find?

A new and controversial technique has emerged in the treatment of PTSD—eye movement desensitization and reprocessing (EMDR) treatment (Shapiro, 1995). In EMDR, the client is asked to picture in mind an image associated with the trauma while the therapist rapidly moves a finger back and forth in front of the client's eyes for about 15 to 20 seconds. While holding the image in mind, the client is asked to move his or her eyes to follow the therapist's finger. The client then relates to the therapist the images, feelings, and thoughts that were experienced during the procedure. The procedure is then repeated until the client becomes desensitized to the emotional impact of this disturbing material. The technique remains controversial, in large part because we lack a compelling theoretical model to explain its effects (Keane, 1998). We do have evidence showing that EMDR can bring about therapeutic benefits in treating PTSD (e.g., DeBell & Jones, 1997a; Greenwald,

1996; Wilson, Becker, & Tinker, 1997). Yet the benefits produced by EMDR may reflect nonspecific factors common to most forms of therapy (expectancies of improvement, therapist attention) rather than the induction of rapid eye movements (Goldstein et al., 2000; Herbert et al., 2000). It is also conceivable that EMDR is merely a variant of exposure therapy, whereby the repeated presentation of the traumatic image in imagination is responsible for bringing about a reduction in fear (DeRubeis & Crits-Christoph, 1998). In support of this view, investigators who conducted a meta-analysis of research studies in the field reported that EMDR appeared to be no more effective than exposure therapy and that the eye movements that are believed to be an integral element of the technique are unnecessary (Davidson & Parker, 2001). In other words, EMDR may turn out to be but a novel way of conducting exposure-based therapy.

THINK ABOUT IT

John has been experiencing sudden panic attacks on and off for the past few months. During the attacks, he has difficulty breathing and fears that his heart is racing out of control. His personal physician checked him out and told him the problem is with his nerves, not his heart. What treatment alternatives are available to John that might help him deal with this problem?

THINK ABOUT IT

Do you know anyone who has received treatment for an anxiety disorder? What was the outcome? What other treatment alternatives might be available? Which approach to treatment would you seek if you suffered from the same disorder?

Quiz **6.3**
Treatment of Anxiety Disorders

the likelihood and severity of feared consequences. Cognitive-behavioral techniques in treating OCD appear to be at least as effective as drug therapy (use of SSRI-type antidepressants) and may produce more lasting results (Rauch & Jenike, 1998; Stanley & Turner, 1995). Yet some patients may benefit from a combination of psychological and pharmacological treatment (USDHHS, 1999a).

Panic Disorder Cognitive-behavioral therapists also use a variety of techniques in treating panic disorder, including coping skills for handling panic attacks without catastrophizing, breathing retraining and relaxation training to reduce states of heightened bodily arousal, and exposure to situations linked to panic attacks and bodily cues associated with panicky symptoms (Schmidt et al., 2000; Wilson, 1997). The therapist may assist clients with panic disorder to think differently about their bodily cues, such as sensations of dizziness or heart palpitations. By coming to recognize that these cues are fleeting sensations rather than signs of an impending heart attack or other catastrophe, clients learn to cope with them without panicking. Clients learn to replace catastrophizing thoughts and self-statements ("I'm having a heart attack") with calming, rational alternatives ("Calm down. These are panicky feelings that will soon pass."). Panic attack sufferers may also be reassured by having a medical examination to ensure that they are physically healthy and their physical symptoms are not signs of heart disease.

Breathing retraining is a technique that aims at restoring a normal level of carbon dioxide in the blood by having clients breathe slowly and deeply from the abdomen, so as to avoid the shallow, rapid breathing (hyperventilation) that leads to breathing off too much carbon dioxide. In some treatment programs, people with panic disorder purposefully hyperventilate in the controled setting of the treatment clinic in order to discover for themselves the relationship between breathing off too much carbon dioxide and cardiovascular sensations. Through these firsthand experiences, they learn to calm themselves down and cope with these sensations rather than overreacting. Some commonly used elements in cognitive-behavioral therapy for panic disorder are shown in Table 6.6.

Investigators find CBT to be an effective treatment for panic disorder (Barlow et al., 2000; DeRubeis & Crits-Christoph, 1998; Sanderson & Rego, 2000; Overholser, 2000). The results of a recent study show that nearly 90% of panic patients treated with CBT were free

A Closer Look

Coping with a Panic Attack

 People who have panic attacks usually feel their hearts pounding such that they are overwhelmed and unable to cope. They typically feel an urge to flee the situation as quickly as possible. If escape is impossible, however, they may become immobilized and "freeze" until the attack dissipates. What can you do if you suffer a panic attack or an intense anxiety reaction? Let us suggest a few coping responses:

- Don't let your breathing get out of hand. Breathe slowly and deeply.
- Try breathing into a paper bag. The carbon dioxide in the bag may help you calm down by restoring a more optimal balance between oxygen and carbon dioxide.
- "Talk yourself down." Tell yourself to relax. Tell yourself you're not going to die. Tell yourself no matter how painful the attack is, it is likely to pass soon.

- Find someone to help you through the attack. Telephone someone you know and trust. Talk about anything at all until you regain control.
- Don't fall into the trap of making yourself housebound to avert future attacks.
- If you are uncertain about whether or not sensations such as pain or tightness in the chest have physical causes, seek immediate medical assistance. Even if you suspect your attack may "only" be one of anxiety, it is safer to have a medical evaluation than to diagnose yourself.

You need not suffer recurrent panic attacks and fears about loss of control. If your attacks are persistent or frightening, consult a professional. When in doubt, see a professional.

---

of panic attacks when evaluated at a follow-up assessment (Stuart et al., 2000). Despite the common belief that panic disorder is best treated with psychiatric drugs, CBT appears to produce about as good short-term results and even better long-term results after treatment termination than pharmacological approaches (Barlow et al., 2000; Otto, Pollack, & Maki, 2000). People who were treated with CBT may continue to use the skills they acquire even after treatment is completed, whereas those who receive psychiatric drugs may need the drugs to maintain the treatment effect (Glass, 2000). For some individuals, however, the effectiveness of CBT may be enhanced by the addition of antidepressant drugs (van Balkom et al., 1997).

In this chapter we have explored the diagnostic class of anxiety disorders. In the next chapter we examine dissociative and somatoform disorders, which historically have been linked to the anxiety disorders as neuroses.

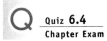
Quiz 6.4
Chapter Exam

Research Update
Chapter 6

TABLE **6.6** **Elements of Cognitive-Behavioral Programs for Treatment of Panic Disorder**

Self-Monitoring	Keeping a log of panic attacks to help determine situational stimuli that might trigger them.
Exposure	A program of gradual exposure to situations in which panic attacks have occurred. During exposure trials, the person engages in self-relaxation and rational self-talk to prevent anxiety from spiraling out of control. In some programs, participants learn to tolerate changes in bodily sensations associated with panic attacks by experiencing these sensations within a controlled setting of the treatment clinic. The person may be spun around in a chair to induce feelings of dizziness, learning in the process that such sensations are not dangerous or signs of imminent harm.
Development of Coping Responses	Developing coping skills to interrupt the vicious cycle in which overreactions to anxiety cues or cardiovascular sensations culminate in panic attacks. Behavioral methods focus on deep, regular breathing and relaxation training. Cognitive methods focus on modifying catastrophic misinterpretations of bodily sensations. Breathing retraining may be used to help the individual avoid hyperventilation during panic attacks.

Sources. Adapted from Craske, Brown, & Barlow, 1991; Rapee, 1987; Turovsky & Barlow, 1995, and other sources.

Overview of Anxiety Disorders

TYPES OF ANXIETY DISORDERS

	Description	Features
Panic Disorder	Occurrence of repeated panic attacks, which are episodes of sheer terror accompanied by strong physiological symptoms, thoughts of imminent danger or impending doom, and an urge to escape	• Fears of recurring attacks may prompt avoidance of situations in which they occur or settings in which help might not be available • Panic attacks begin unexpectedly but may become associated with certain cues or specific situations
Generalized Anxiety Disorder	Persistent anxiety that is not limited to particular situations	• Excessive worrying is the keynote feature • Associated with heightened states of bodily arousal, tenseness, being "on edge"
Phobic Disorders	Excessive fears of particular objects or situations	• Carries a strong avoidance component in which the individual seeks to avoid contact with the phobic stimulus or situation • Subtypes include specific phobia (e.g., acrophobia, claustrophobia, fear of insects or snakes); social phobia (excessive fear of social interactions); and agoraphobia (fear of open, public places)
Obsessive-Compulsive Disorder	Recurrent obsessions (recurrent, intrusive thoughts) and/or compulsions (repetitive behaviors that the person feels compelled to perform)	• Two major types of compulsions: checking rituals and cleaning rituals • Obsessions generate anxiety that may be at least partially relieved by performance of the compulsive rituals
Traumatic Stress Disorders	Acute maladaptive reaction in the immediate aftermath of a traumatic event (acute stress disorder) or prolonged maladaptive reaction to a traumatic event (posttraumatic stress disorder)	• Reexperiencing the traumatic event, avoidance of cues or stimuli associated with the trauma, general or emotional numbing, hyperarousal, emotional distress, and impaired functioning • Vulnerability depends on such factors as severity of the trauma, degree of exposure, coping styles, and availability of social support

CAUSAL FACTORS   Anxiety disorders reflect an interplay of multiple causes

Biological Factors	• Genetic predispositions • Irregularities in neurotransmitter functioning • Abnormalities in brain pathways signaling danger or inhibiting repetitive behaviors • Prepared conditioning
Social-Environmental Factors	• Exposure to threatening or traumatic events • Observing fear responses in others • Lack of social support
Behavioral Factors	• Pairing of aversive stimuli and previously neutral stimuli (classical conditioning) • Anxiety relief from performing compulsive rituals or avoiding phobic stimuli (operant conditioning) • Lack of extinction opportunities due to avoidance of feared objects or situations
Emotional and Cognitive Factors	• Unresolved psychological conflicts (Freudian or psychodynamic theory) • Cognitive factors, such as overprediction of fear, self-defeating or irrational beliefs, oversensitivity to threat, anxiety sensitivity, misattribution of bodily cues, and low self-efficacy

TREATMENT APPROACHES   Treatment may include one or more therapeutic approaches

Drug Therapy	• To control anxiety symptoms
Cognitive-Behavioral Therapy	• To unlearn phobic reactions and develop more adaptive ways of thinking
Psychodynamic Therapy	• To gain insight into underlying conflicts that anxiety symptoms may symbolize
Humanistic Therapy	• To identify and come to accept one's genuine feelings and needs

Summing Up

Types of Anxiety Disorders

What are anxiety disorders? Anxiety, a generalized sense of apprehension or fear, is normal and desirable under some conditions, but it can become abnormal when it is excessive or inappropriate. Disturbed patterns of behavior in which anxiety is the most prominent feature are labeled anxiety disorders.

What is panic disorder? Panic disorder is characterized by often immobilizing, repeated panic attacks, which involve intense physical features, notably cardiovascular symptoms, that may be accompanied by sheer terror and fears of losing control, losing one's mind, or dying. Panic attack sufferers often limit their outside activity in fear of recurrent attacks. This can lead to agoraphobia, the fear of venturing into public places.

What is generalized anxiety disorder? Generalized anxiety disorder is a type of anxiety disorder involving persistent anxiety that seems to be "free floating" or not tied to specific situations.

What are phobic disorders? Phobias are excessive irrational fears of specific objects or situations. Phobias involve a behavioral component, avoidance of the phobic stimulus, in addition to physical and cognitive features. Specific phobias are excessive fears of particular objects or situations, such as mice, spiders, tight places, or heights. Social phobia involves an intense fear of being judged negatively by others. Agoraphobia involves fears of venturing into public places. Agoraphobia may occur with, or in the absence of, panic disorder.

What is obsessive-compulsive disorder? Obsessive-compulsive disorder, or OCD, involves recurrent patterns of obsessions, compulsions, or a combination of the two. Obsessions are nagging, persistent thoughts that create anxiety and seem beyond the person's ability to control. Compulsions are apparently irresistible repetitious urges to perform certain behaviors, such as repeated elaborate washing after using the bathroom.

What are the two types of traumatic stress disorders? There are two types of stress disorders—acute stress disorder and posttraumatic stress disorder. Both involve maladaptive reactions to traumatic stress. Acute stress disorder occurs in the days and weeks following exposure to a traumatic event. Posttraumatic stress disorder persists for months or even years or decades after the traumatic experience and may not begin until months or years after the event.

What relationships exist between ethnicity and the prevalence of anxiety disorders? Evidence from a nationally representative sample of U.S. adults showed that rates of anxiety disorders were generally comparable across racial and ethnic groupings.

Theoretical Perspectives

How are anxiety disorders conceptualized within the psychodynamic perspective? Psychodynamic theorists view anxiety disorders as attempts by the ego to control the conscious emergence of threatening impulses. Feelings of anxiety are warning signals that threatening impulses are nearing awareness. The ego mobilizes defense mechanisms to divert the impulses, thus leading to different anxiety disorders.

How do learning theorists view anxiety disorders? Learning theorists explain anxiety disorders through conditioning and observational learning. Mowrer's two-factor model incorporates classical and operant conditioning in the explanation of phobias. Phobias, however, appear to be moderated by cognitive factors, such as self-efficacy expectancies. The principles of reinforcement may help explain patterns of obsessive-compulsive behavior. People may be genetically predisposed to acquire certain types of phobias that may have had survival value for our prehistoric ancestors.

What cognitive factors are implicated in anxiety disorders? Cognitive factors may also play a role in the anxiety disorders, such as overpredictions of fear, self-defeating or irrational beliefs, oversensitivity to threatening cues and signs of anxiety, low self-efficacy expectations, and misattributions of bodily cues.

How do investigators explore the biological underpinnings of panic disorder? Investigators seek to uncover the biological underpinnings of anxiety disorders by studying the roles of genetic factors, neurotransmitters, and induction of panic by means of biological challenges.

Treatment of Anxiety Disorders

What are the major therapeutic approaches to treating anxiety disorders? Traditional psychoanalysis helps people work through unconscious conflicts that are believed to underlie anxiety disorders. Modern psychodynamic approaches focus more on current disturbed relationships in the client's life and encourage the client to develop more adaptive behavior patterns. Humanistic therapy focuses on helping clients identify and accept their true selves rather than reacting with anxiety whenever their genuine feelings and needs begin to surface. Drug therapy for anxiety disorders focuses on the use of benzodiazepines and antidepressants (which have more than just antidepressant effects). Learning-based approaches to treating anxiety disorders encompass a broad range of behavioral and cognitive-behavioral techniques, including exposure therapy, cognitive restructuring, exposure and response prevention, and relaxation skills training. Cognitive approaches, such as rational-emotive behavior therapy and cognitive therapy, help people identify and correct faulty thinking patterns that may underlie anxiety reactions. The cognitive-behavioral treatment of panic disorder incorporates self-monitoring, exposure, and development of coping responses to anxiety-inducing cues.

CHAPTER SEVEN

Dissociative and Somatoform Disorders

Naoki Okamoto
Untitled

Truth OR Fiction?

- In some reported cases, alternate personalities in people with multiple personalities had their own allergic reactions and eyeglass prescriptions. (p. 197)

- The term *split personality* refers to schizophrenia. (p. 200)

- Very few of us have episodes in which we feel strangely detached from our own bodies or thought processes. (p. 203)

- Most people with multiple personalities do not report any history of physical or sexual abuse during childhood. (p. 206)

- Some people show up repeatedly at hospital emergency rooms, feigning illness and seeking treatment for no apparent reason. (p. 211)

- Some people who have lost their ability to see or move their legs become strangely indifferent toward their physical condition. (p. 213)

- In China in the 1980s, more than 2,000 people fell prey to the belief that their genitals were shrinking and retracting into their bodies. (p. 216)

In the Middle Ages, the clergy used rites of exorcism to bring forth demons from people believed to be possessed. Using curious incantations, exorcists contended for the victims' souls against the demons believed to lurk within.

Curious phrasings were also heard in 20th-century Los Angeles. They were intended to evoke another sort of demon from Kenneth Bianchi, a suspect in a police inquest.

At one point, the question was put to Bianchi, "Part, are you the same thing as Ken or are you different?" The interviewer was not a member of the clergy, but a police psychiatrist. Bianchi had been dubbed the "Hillside strangler" by the press. He had terrorized the city, leaving prostitutes dead in the mountains that bank the metropolis.

Under hypnosis—not religious incantations—Bianchi claimed that a hidden personality, or "part," named "Steve," had committed the murders. He also claimed that "Ken" knew nothing of the murders and that he was suffering from multiple personality disorder (now called *dissociative identity disorder*), one of the intriguing but perplexing psychological disorders we explore in this chapter.

Dissociative identity disorder is classified as a *dissociative disorder,* a type of psychological disorder involving a change or disturbance in the functions of self—identity, memory, or consciousness—that make the personality whole. Normally speaking, we know who we are. We may not be certain of ourselves in an existential, philosophical sense, but we know our names, where we live, and what we do for a living. We also tend to remember the salient events of our lives. We may not recall every detail, and we may confuse what we had for dinner on Tuesday with what we had on Monday, but we generally know what we have been doing for the past days, weeks, and years. Normally speaking, there is a unity to consciousness that gives rise to a sense of self. We perceive ourselves as progressing through space and time. In the dissociative disorders, one or more of these aspects of daily living is disturbed—sometimes bizarrely so.

This chapter also focuses on *somatoform disorders,* a class of psychological disorders involving complaints of physical symptoms that are believed to reflect underlying psychological conflicts or issues. In some cases there is no apparent medical basis to the physical symptoms, such as in the form of hysterical blindness or numbness (now called *conversion disorder*). In other cases, people may hold an exaggerated view of the meaning of their physical symptoms, believing them to be signs of underlying serious illnesses despite the reassurances of their physicians to the contrary.

In early versions of the *DSM,* the dissociative and conversion disorders were grouped with the anxiety disorders under the general category of neurosis. The common grouping was based on the psychodynamic model, which holds that various disorders involve maladaptive ways of managing anxiety. In the anxiety disorders, the appearance of disturbing levels of anxiety was expressed directly in behavior, such as in a phobic reaction to an object or situation. But the role of anxiety in the dissociative and somatoform disorders was inferred rather than expressed in behavior. Persons with dissociative disorders may show no signs of overt anxiety. However, they manifest other psychological problems, such as loss of memory or changes in identity, that, according to the psychodynamic model, serve the purpose of keeping the underlying sources of anxiety out of awareness. Likewise, people with conversion disorder often show a strange indifference to physical problems (e.g., loss of vision) that would greatly concern most of us. Here, too, it was theorized that the "symptoms" mask unconscious sources of anxiety. Some theorists interpret indifference to symptoms to mean that those symptoms have an underlying benefit; that is, they help prevent anxiety from intruding into consciousness.

The *DSM* now separates the anxiety disorders from the other categories of neuroses—the dissociative and somatoform disorders—with which they were historically linked. Yet many practitioners continue to use the broad conceptualization of neuroses as a useful framework for classifying the anxiety, dissociative, and somatoform disorders.

Dissociative Disorders

The major **dissociative disorders** include *dissociative identity disorder, dissociative amnesia, dissociative fugue,* and *depersonalization disorder.* In each case there is a disruption or

dissociative disorder Any of a group of disorders characterized by a disruption, or dissociation, of the functions of identity, memory, or consciousness.

Kenneth Bianchi, the so-called Hillside Strangler. Bianchi claimed that a hidden personality had committed the murders of which he was accused.

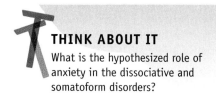

THINK ABOUT IT
What is the hypothesized role of anxiety in the dissociative and somatoform disorders?

dissociation ("splitting off") of the functions of identity, memory, or consciousness that normally make us whole.

Dissociative Identity Disorder

The Ohio State campus dwelled in terror as four college women were seized, coerced to cash checks or get money from automatic teller machines, then raped. A cryptic phone call led to the capture of Billy Milligan, a 23-year-old drifter who had been dishonorably discharged from the navy.

Not the Boy Next Door

Billy wasn't quite the boy next door. He tried twice to commit suicide while he was awaiting trial, so his lawyers requested a psychiatric evaluation. The psychologists and psychiatrists who examined Billy deduced that ten personalities dwelled inside of him. Eight were male and two were female. Billy's personality had been fractured by a brutal childhood. The personalities displayed diverse facial expressions, memories, and vocal patterns. They performed in dissimilar ways on personality and intelligence tests.

Arthur, a sensible but phlegmatic personality, conversed with a British accent. Danny, 14, was a painter of still lifes. Christopher, 13, was normal enough, but somewhat anxious. A 3-year-old English girl went by the name of Christine. Tommy, a 16-year-old, was an antisocial personality and escape artist. It was Tommy who had enlisted in the Navy. Allen was an 18-year-old con artist. Allen also smoked. Adelena was a 19-year-old introverted lesbian. It was she who had committed the rapes. It was probably David who had made the mysterious phone call. David was an anxious 9-year-old who wore the anguish of early childhood trauma on his sleeve. After his second suicide attempt, Billy had been placed in a straitjacket. When the guards checked his cell, however, he was sleeping with the straitjacket as a pillow. Tommy later explained that he was responsible for Billy's escape.

The defense argued that Billy was afflicted with multiple personality disorder. Several alternate personalities resided within him. The alternate personalities knew about Billy, but Billy was unaware of them. Billy, the core or dominant personality, had learned as a child that he could sleep as a way of avoiding the sexual and physical abuse of his father. A psychiatrist claimed that Billy had likewise been "asleep"—in a sort of "psychological coma"—when the crimes were committed. Therefore, Billy should be judged innocent by reason of insanity.

Billy was decreed not guilty by reason of insanity. He was committed to a mental institution. In the institution, 14 additional personalities emerged. Thirteen were rebellious and labeled "undesirables" by Arthur. The fourteenth was the "Teacher," who was competent and supposedly represented the integration of all the other personalities. Billy was released six years later.

—*Adapted from Keyes, 1982*

∎

Billy was diagnosed with multiple personality disorder, which is now called **dissociative identity disorder.** In dissociative identity disorder, sometimes referred to as "split personality," two or more personalities—each with well-defined traits and memories—"occupy" one person. They may or may not be aware of one another. In some isolated cases, alternate personalities (also called *alter personalities*) may even show different EEG records, allergic reactions, responses to medication, and even different eyeglass prescriptions and pupil

dissociative identity disorder A dissociative disorder in which a person has two or more distinct, or alter, personalities.

sizes (Birnbaum, Martin, & Thomann, 1996; S. D. Miller et al., 1991). Or one personality may be color blind, whereas others are not (Braun, 1986). If such patterns stand up to further scientific scrutiny, they would offer a remarkable illustration of the diversity of perceptions and somatic patterns that are possible within the same person.

Celebrated cases of multiple personality have been depicted in the popular media. One became the subject of the 1950s film *The Three Faces of Eve*. In the film, Eve White is a timid housewife who harbors two other personalities: Eve Black, a sexually provocative, antisocial personality, and Jane, a balanced, developing personality who could balance her sexual needs with the demands of social acceptability. The three faces eventually merged into one—Jane, providing a "happy ending." The real-life Eve, whose name was Chris Sizemore, failed to maintain this integrated personality. Her personality reportedly split into 22 subsequent personalities. A second well-known case is that of Sybil. Sybil was played by Sally Field in the film of the same name and reportedly had 16 personalities.

Features In one of the largest studies on multiple personality to date, Ross, Norton, and Wozney (1989) collected 236 case reports of people with the disorder from 203 health professionals in Canada. Unlike reports of multiple personality in the 19th and early 20th centuries, in which most cases involved dual personalities, cases in the Canadian sample averaged 15 to 16 alter personalities each (Ross et al., 1989).

There are many variations. In some cases, the host (main) personality may be unaware of the existence of the other identities, while the other identities are aware of the existence of the host (Dorahy, 2001). In other cases, the different personalities are completely unaware of one another. Sometimes two personalities vie for control of the person. Sometimes there is one dominant or core personality and several subordinate personalities. Some of the more common alternate personalities (or "alter personalities") include children of various ages, adolescents of the opposite gender, prostitutes, and gay males and lesbians (Ross et al., 1989). Some of the personalities may show psychotic symptoms—a break with reality expressed in the form of hallucinations and delusional thinking.

All in all, the clusters of alter personalities serve as a microcosm of conflicting urges and cultural themes. Themes of sexual ambivalence (sexual openness vs. restrictiveness)

wWw   Web Link **7.1**
Overview of Dissociative Disorders

Truth OR Fiction?   REVISITED

In some reported cases, alternate personalities in people with multiple personalities had their own allergic reactions and eyeglass prescriptions.

TRUE. In a few reported cases, alternate personalities were reported to have had their own allergic reactions and eyeglass prescriptions that differed from those of other personalities within the same person.

VIDEO **7.1**
Dissociative Identity Disorder:
The Three Faces of Eve

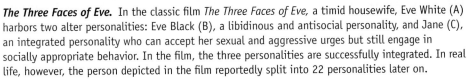
The Three Faces of Eve. In the classic film *The Three Faces of Eve,* a timid housewife, Eve White (A) harbors two alter personalities: Eve Black (B), a libidinous and antisocial personality, and Jane (C), an integrated personality who can accept her sexual and aggressive urges but still engage in socially appropriate behavior. In the film, the three personalities are successfully integrated. In real life, however, the person depicted in the film reportedly split into 22 personalities later on.

and shifting sexual orientations are particularly common. It is as if conflicting internal impulses cannot coexist or achieve dominance. As a result, each is expressed as the cardinal or steering trait of an alternate personality. The clinician can sometimes elicit alternate personalities by inviting them to make themselves known, as in asking, "Is there another part of you that wants to say something to me?" The following case illustrates the emergence of an alternate personality:

Harriet Emerges

[Margaret explained that] she often "heard a voice telling her to say things and do things." It was, she said, "a terrible voice" that sometimes threatened to "take over completely." When it was finally suggested to [Margaret] that she let the voice "take over," she closed her eyes, clenched her fists, and grimaced for a few moments during which she was out of contact with those around her. Suddenly she opened her eyes and one was in the presence of another person. Her name, she said, was "Harriet." Whereas Margaret had been paralyzed, and complained of fatigue, headache and backache, Harriet felt well, and she at once proceeded to walk unaided around the interviewing room. She spoke scornfully of Margaret's religiousness, her invalidism, and her puritanical life, professing that she herself liked to drink and "go partying" but that Margaret was always going to church and reading the Bible. "But," she said impishly and proudly, "I make her miserable—I make her say and do things she doesn't want to." At length, at the interviewer's suggestion, Harriet reluctantly agreed to "bring Margaret back," and after more grimacing and fist clenching, Margaret reappeared, paralyzed, complaining of her headache and backache, and completely amnesiac for the brief period of Harriet's release from prison.

—From Nemiah, 1978, pp. 179–180

As with Billy Milligan, Chris Sizemore, and Margaret, the dominant personality is often unaware of the existence of the alter personalities. It thus seems that the mechanism of dissociation is controlled by unconscious processes. Although the dominant personality lacks insight into the existence of the other personalities, she or he may vaguely sense that something is amiss. There may even be "interpersonality rivalry" in which one personality aspires to do away with another, usually in blissful ignorance of the fact that conferring the *coup de grace* on an alternate would result in the death of all.

Although women constitute the majority of cases of multiple personality (Ross et al., 1989; Schafer, 1986), the proportion of males diagnosed with the disorder has been on the rise (Goff & Summs, 1993). The numbers of reported alternates has also been increasing, rising to an average of 12 alternates during the 1980s from an average of 3 in earlier cases. Women with the disorder tend to have more alternate identities, averaging 15 or more, than do men, who average about 8 identities (APA, 2000). The reasons for this difference remain unknown.

The diagnostic features of dissociative identity disorder are listed in Table 7.1.

Controversies Although multiple personality is generally considered rare, the very existence of the disorder continues to arouse debate. Only a handful of cases worldwide were reported from 1920 to 1970, but since then the number of reported cases has skyrocketed into the thousands (Spanos, 1994). This has led some practitioners to suggest that multiple personality may be more common than was earlier believed (Bliss & Jeppsen, 1985; Schafer, 1986). Others, however, are not so sure. Some professionals believe the disorder is overdiagnosed in highly suggestible people who might simply be following suggestions that they might have the disorder (APA, 2000). Increased public attention paid to the disorder in recent years may also account for the perception that its prevalence is greater than was commonly believed.

TABLE 7.1 Features of Dissociative Identity Disorder (Formerly Multiple Personality Disorder)

1. At least two distinct personalities exist within the person, with each having a relatively enduring and distinct pattern of perceiving, thinking about, and relating to the environment and the self.

2. Two or more of these personalities repeatedly take complete control of the individual's behavior.

3. There is a failure to recall important personal information too substantial to be accounted for by ordinary forgetfulness.

4. The disorder cannot be accounted for by the effects of a psychoactive substance or a general medical condition.

Source. Adapted from the *DSM-IV-TR* (APA, 2000).

The disorder does appear to be culture bound and largely restricted to North America (Spanos, 1994). Relatively few cases have been reported elsewhere, even in such Western countries as Great Britain and France. A recent survey in Japan failed to find even one case, and in Switzerland, 90% of the psychiatrists polled had never seen a case of the disorder (Modestin, 1992; Spanos, 1994). Even in North America, few psychologists and psychiatrists have ever encountered a case of multiple personality. Most cases are reported by a relatively small number of investigators and clinicians who strongly believe in the existence of the disorder. Yet critics wonder, might they be helping to manufacture that which they are seeking?

Some leading authorities, such as the late psychologist Nicholas Spanos, believe so. Spanos and others have challenged the existence of dissociative identity (multiple personality) disorder (Reisner, 1994; Spanos, 1994). To Spanos, multiple personality is not a distinct disorder, but a form of role playing in which individuals first come to construe themselves as having multiple selves and then begin to act in ways that are consistent with their conception of the disorder. Eventually their role playing becomes so ingrained it becomes a reality to them. Perhaps their therapists or counselors unintentionally planted the idea in their minds that their confusing welter of emotions and behaviors may represent different personalities at work. Impressionable people may have learned how to enact the role of persons with the disorder by watching others enacting the role on television and in the movies. Films and TV shows like *The Three Faces of Eve* and *Sybil* have given detailed examples of the behaviors that characterize multiple personalities (Spanos, Weekes, & Bertrand, 1985). Or perhaps therapists provided cues about the features of multiple personality, enough to enact the role convincingly.

Many reinforcers may become contingent on enacting the role of a multiple personality. Receiving attention from others and evading accountability for unacceptable behavior are two possible sources of reinforcement (Spanos et al., 1985). This is not to suggest that people with multiple personalities are "faking," any more than you are faking when you perform different daily roles as student, spouse, or worker. You may enact the role of a student (e.g., sitting attentively in class, raising your hand when you wish to talk, etc.) because you have learned to organize your behavior according to the nature of the role and because you have been rewarded for doing so. People with multiple personalities may have come to identify so closely with the role that it becomes real for them.

In support of his belief that multiple personality represents a form of role playing, Spanos and his colleagues showed that with proper cues, college students in a laboratory simulation of the Bianchi-type interrogation could easily enact a multiple personality role, even attributing the blame to an alternate personality for a murder they were accused of committing (Spanos et al., 1985). Perhaps the manner in which the Bianchi interrogation was conducted had cued Bianchi to enact the multiple personality role in order to evade criminal responsibility. (It didn't work, as he was eventually convicted.)

Relatively few cases of multiple personality involve criminal behavior, in which enactment of a multiple personality role might relieve individuals of criminal responsibility for their behavior. But even in more typical cases, there may be more subtle incentives for enacting the role of a multiple personality, such as a therapist's expression of interest and excitement at discovering a multiple personality. People with multiple personalities were often highly imaginative during childhood. Accustomed to playing games of "make-believe," they may readily adopt alternate identities, especially if they learn how to enact the multiple personality role and there are external sources of validation, such as a clinician's interest and concern.

The social reinforcement model may help to explain why some clinicians seem to "discover" many more cases of multiple personality than others. These clinicians may be "multiple personality magnets." They may unknowingly cue clients to enact the multiple personality role and reinforce the performance with extra attention and concern. With the right set of cues, certain clients may adopt the role of a multiple personality to please their clinicians. The role-playing model has been challenged by some authorities (for example, Gleaves, 1996), and it remains to be seen how many cases of the disorder in clinical practice the model can explain.

VIDEO **7.2**
Dissociative Identity Disorder:
Dr. Holliday Milby

dissociative amnesia A dissociative disorder in which a person experiences memory loss without any identifiable organic cause.

Whether multiple personality is a real phenomenon or a form of role playing, there is no question that people who display this behavior have serious emotional and behavioral difficulties. Moreover, the diagnosis may not be all that unusual among some subgroups in the population, such as psychiatric inpatients. In one study of 484 adult psychiatric inpatients, at least 5% showed evidence of multiple personality (Ross et al., 1991). We have noted a tendency for *claims* of multiple personality to spread on inpatient units. In one case, Susan, a prostitute admitted for depression and suicidal thoughts, claimed that she could only exchange sex for money when "another person" inside her emerged and took control. (Suicidal behavior is common among people with multiple personalities. Seventy-two percent of the cases in the Canadian study [Ross et al., 1989] had attempted suicide, and about 2% had succeeded.) Upon hearing this, another woman, Ginny—a child abuser who had been admitted for depression after her daughter had been removed from her home by social services—claimed that she only abused her daughter when another person inside of her assumed control of her personality. Susan's chart recommended that she be evaluated further for multiple personality disorder (the term used at the time to refer to the disorder), but Ginny was diagnosed with a depressive disorder and a personality disorder, not with multiple personality disorder.

Multiple personality, which often is called "split personality" by laypeople, should not be confused with schizophrenia. The term *split personality* refers to multiple personality, not schizophrenia. Schizophrenia (which comes from roots that mean "split brain") occurs much more commonly than multiple personality and involves the "splitting" of cognition, affect, and behavior. There may thus be little agreement between the thoughts and the emotions, or between the individual's perception of reality and what is truly happening. The person with schizophrenia may become giddy when told of disturbing events, or may experience hallucinations or delusions (see Chapter 13). In people with multiple personalities, the personality apparently divides into two or more personalities, but each of them usually shows more integrated functioning on cognitive, affective, and behavioral levels than is true of people with schizophrenia.

Dissociative Amnesia

Dissociative amnesia is believed to be the most common type of dissociative disorder (Maldonado, Butler, & Speigel, 1998). *Amnesia* derives from the Greek roots *a-*, meaning "not," and *mnasthai*, meaning "to remember." In **dissociative amnesia** (formerly called *psychogenic amnesia*), the person becomes unable to recall important personal information, usually involving traumatic or stressful experiences, in a way that cannot be accounted for by simple forgetfulness. Nor can the memory loss be attributed to a particular organic cause, such as a blow to the head or a particular medical condition, or to the direct effects of drugs or alcohol. Unlike some progressive forms of memory impairment (such as dementia associated with Alzheimer's disease; see Chapter 15), the memory loss in dissociative amnesia is reversible, although it may last for days, weeks, or even years. Recall of dissociated memories may happen gradually but often occurs suddenly and spontaneously, as when the soldier who has no recall of a battle for several days afterward suddenly recalls the experience after being transported to a hospital away from the battlefield.

Amnesia is not ordinary forgetfulness, such as forgetting someone's name or where you left your car keys. Memory loss in amnesia is more profound or wide-ranging. Most cases of dissociative amnesia take the form of *localized amnesia* in which events occurring during a specific time period are lost to memory. For example, the person cannot recall events for a number of hours or days after a stressful or traumatic incident, such as a battle or car accident. Other forms of dissociative amnesia include selective amnesia and generalized amnesia. In *selective amnesia*, people forget only the disturbing particulars that take place during a certain time period. A person may recall the period of life during which he conducted an extramarital affair, but not the guilt-arousing affair itself. A soldier may recall most of the battle, but not the death of his buddy. In *generalized amnesia*, people forget their entire lives—who they are, what they do, where they live, whom they live with. This form of amnesia is very rare, although you wouldn't think so if you watch day-

Truth OR Fiction? REVISITED

The term *split personality* refers to schizophrenia.

FALSE. The term *split personality* refers to multiple personality, not schizophrenia.

THINK ABOUT IT

Why is the diagnosis of dissociative identity disorder controversial? Do you believe that people with dissociative identity disorder are merely playing a role they have learned? Why or why not?

time soap operas. Persons with generalized amnesia cannot recall personal information, but they tend to retain their habits, tastes, and skills. If you had generalized amnesia, you would still know how to read, although you would not recall your elementary school teachers. You would still prefer French fries to baked potatoes—or vice versa.

People with dissociative amnesia usually forget events or periods of life that were traumatic—that generated strong negative emotions such as horror or guilt. Consider this case:

A Case of Dissociative Amnesia

He was brought to the emergency room of a hospital by a stranger. He was dazed and claimed not to know who he was or where he lived, and the stranger had found him wandering in the streets. Despite his confusion, it did not appear that he had been drinking or abusing drugs or that his amnesia could be attributed to physical trauma. After staying in the hospital for a few days, he awoke in distress. His memory had returned. His name was Rutger and he had urgent business to attend to. He wanted to know why he had been hospitalized and demanded to leave. At time of admission, Rutger appeared to be suffering from generalized amnesia: He could not recall his identity or the personal events of his life. But now that he was requesting discharge, Rutger showed localized amnesia for the period between entering the emergency room and the morning he regained his memory for prior events.

Rutger provided information about the events prior to his hospitalization that was confirmed by the police. On the day when his amnesia began, Rutger had killed a pedestrian with his automobile. There had been witnesses, and the police had voiced the opinion that Rutger—although emotionally devastated—was blameless in the incident. Rutger was instructed, however, to fill out an accident report and to appear at the inquest. Still nonplussed, Rutger filled out the form at a friend's home. He accidentally left his wallet and his identification there. After placing the form in a mailbox, Rutger became dazed and lost his memory.

Although Rutger was not responsible for the accident, he felt awful about the pedestrian's death. His amnesia was probably connected with feelings of guilt, the stress of the accident, and concerns about the inquest.

—Adapted from Cameron, 1963, pp. 355–356

■

People sometimes claim they cannot recall certain events of their lives, such as criminal acts, promises made to others, and so forth. Falsely claiming amnesia as a way of escaping responsibility is called **malingering,** which involves the attempt to fake symptoms or make false claims for personal gain. Our research methods cannot guarantee that we can distinguish people with dissociative amnesia from malingerers. But experienced clinicians can make reasonably well-educated guesses.

Dissociative Fugue

Fugue derives from the Latin *fugere,* meaning "flight." The word *fugitive* has the same origin. Fugue is like amnesia "on the run." In **dissociative fugue** (formerly called *psychogenic fugue*), the person travels suddenly and unexpectedly from his or her home or place of work, is unable to recall past personal information, and either becomes confused about his or her identity or assumes a new identity (either partially or completely) (APA, 2000). Despite these odd behaviors, the person may appear "normal" and show no other signs of mental disturbance (Maldonado et al., 1998). The person may not think about the past, or may report a past filled with false memories without recognizing them as false.

Whereas people with amnesia appear to wander aimlessly, people in a fugue state act more purposefully. Some stick close to home. They spend the afternoon in the park

malingering Faking illness.

dissociative fugue A dissociative disorder in which a person suddenly flees from his or her life situation, travels to a new location, assumes a new identity, and has amnesia for personal material.

THINK ABOUT IT
What is the difference between dissociative amnesia and ordinary forgetfulness?

or in a theater, or they spend the night at a hotel under another name, usually having little if any contact with others during the fugue state. But the new identity is incomplete and fleeting and the individual's former sense of self returns in a matter of hours or a few days. Less common is a pattern in which the fugue state lasts for months or years and involves travel to distant places and assumption of a new identity. These individuals may assume an identity that is more spontaneous and sociable than their former selves, which were typically "quiet" and "ordinary." They may establish new families and successful businesses. Although these events may sound rather bizarre, the fugue state is not considered psychotic because people with the disorder can think and behave quite normally—in their new lives, that is. Then one day, quite suddenly, their awareness of their past identity returns to them, and they are flooded with old memories. Now they typically do not recall the events that occurred during the fugue state. The new identity, the new life—including all its involvements and responsibilities—vanish from memory.

Fugue, like amnesia, is relatively rare and is believed to affect only about 2 people in 1,000 within the general population (APA, 2000). It is most likely to occur in wartime (Loewenstein, 1991) or in the wake of another kind of disaster or extremely stressful event. The underlying notion is that dissociation in the fugue state protects one from traumatic memories or other sources of emotionally painful experiences or conflict (Maldonado et al., 1998).

Fugue can also be difficult to distinguish from malingering. That is, a number of persons who were dissatisfied with their former lives could claim to be amnesic when they are uncovered in their new locations and new identities.

Consider the following case, in which the evidence supports a diagnosis of dissociative fugue (Spitzer et al., 1989):

A Case of Dissociative Fugue?

The man told the police that his name was Burt Tate. "Burt," a 42-year-old white male, had gotten into a fight at the diner where he worked. When the police arrived, they found that he carried no identification. He told them he had drifted into town a few weeks earlier, but could not recall where he had lived or worked before arriving in town. While no charges were pressed against him, the police prevailed upon him to come to the emergency room for evaluation. "Burt" knew the town he was in and the current date, and recognized that it was somewhat unusual that he couldn't remember his past, but didn't seem to be concerned about it. There was no evidence of any physical injuries or head trauma, or of drug or alcohol abuse. The police made some inquiries and discovered that "Burt" fit the profile of a missing person, Gene Saunders, who had disappeared a month earlier from a city some 2,000 miles away. Mrs. Saunders was called in and confirmed that "Burt" was indeed her husband. She reported that her husband, who had worked in middle-level management in a manufacturing company, had been having difficulty at work before his disappearance. He was passed over for promotion and his supervisor was highly critical of his work. The job stress apparently affected his behavior at home. Once easygoing and sociable, he withdrew into himself and began to criticize his wife and children. Then, just before his disappearance, he had a violent argument with his 18-year-old son. His son called him a "failure" and stormed out the door. Two days later, the man disappeared. When he came face to face with his wife again, he claimed he didn't recognize her, but appeared visibly nervous.

—Adapted from Spitzer et al., 1994, pp. 254–255

■

Although the presenting evidence supported a diagnosis of dissociative fugue, clinicians can find it difficult to distinguish true amnesia from amnesia that is faked to allow a person to get a new start in life.

Depersonalization Disorder

Depersonalization involves a temporary loss or change in the usual sense of our own reality. In a state of depersonalization, people feel detached from themselves and their surroundings. They may feel as though they were dreaming or acting like a robot (Guralnik, Schmeidler, & Simeon, 2000; Maldonado, Butler, & Speigel, 1998).

Derealization—a sense of unreality about the external world involving strange changes in perception of surroundings, or in the sense of the passage of time—may also be present. People and objects may seem to change in size or shape; they may sound different. All these feelings can be associated with feelings of anxiety, including dizziness and fears of going insane, or with depression.

Although these sensations are strange, people with depersonalization maintain contact with reality. They can distinguish reality from unreality, even during the depersonalization episode. In contrast to generalized amnesia and fugue, they know who they are. Their memories are intact and they know where they are—even if they do not like their present state. Feelings of depersonalization usually come on suddenly and fade gradually.

Note that we have thus far described only normal feelings of depersonalization. According to the *DSM*, single brief episodes of depersonalization are experienced by about half of all adults, usually during times of extreme stress. Estimates are that 80% to 90% of the general population experiences dissociative experiences at one time or another (Gershuny & Thayer, 1999). Consider Richie's experience:

Depersonalization at Disneyworld

"We went to Orlando with the children after school let out. I had also been driving myself hard, and it was time to let go. We spent three days 'doing' Disneyworld, and it got to the point where we were all wearing shirts with mice and ducks on them and singing Disney songs. On the third day I began to feel unreal and ill at ease while we were watching these middle-American Ivory-soap teenagers singing and dancing in front of Cinderella's Castle. The day was finally cooling down, but I broke into a sweat. I became shaky and dizzy and sat down on the cement next to the 4-year-old's stroller without giving [my wife] an explanation. There were strollers and kids and [adults'] legs all around me, and for some strange reason I became fixated on the pieces of popcorn strewn on the ground. All of a sudden it was like the people around me were all silly mechanical creatures, like the dolls in the 'It's a Small World' [exhibit] or the animals on the 'Jungle Cruise.' Things sort of seemed to slow down, the way they do when you've smoked marijuana, and there was this invisible wall of cotton between me and everyone else.

"Then the concert was over and my wife was like 'What's the matter?' and did I want to stay for the Electrical Parade and the fireworks or was I sick? Now I was beginning to wonder if I was going crazy and I said I was sick, that my wife would have to take me by the hand and drive us back to the Sonesta Village [motel]. Somehow we got back to the monorail and turned in the strollers. I waited in the herd [of people] at the station like a dead person, my eyes glazed over, looking out over kids with Mickey Mouse ears and Mickey Mouse balloons. The mechanical voice on the monorail almost did me in and I got really shaky.

"I refused to go back to the Magic Kingdom. I went with the family to Sea World, and on another day I dropped [my wife] and the kids off at the Magic Kingdom and picked them up that night. My wife thought I was goldbricking or something, and we had a helluva fight about it, but we had a life to get back to and my sanity had to come first."

—*From the Authors' Files*

depersonalization Feelings of unreality or detachment from one's self or one's body.

derealization Loss of the sense of reality of one's surroundings, experienced in terms of strange changes in the environment or in the passage of time.

Truth OR Fiction?   REVISITED

Very few of us have episodes in which we feel strangely detached from our own bodies or thought processes.

FALSE. About half of all adults, according to the *DSM*, at some time experience an episode of depersonalization in which they feel detached from their own bodies or mental processes.

TABLE 7.2 Diagnostic Features of Depersonalization Disorder

1. Recurrent or persistent experiences of depersonalization, which are characterized by feelings of detachment from one's mental processes or body, as if one were an outside observer of oneself. The experience may have a dreamlike quality.
2. The individual is able to maintain reality testing (i.e., distinguish reality from unreality) during the depersonalization state.
3. The depersonalization experiences cause significant personal distress or impairment in one or more important areas of functioning, such as social or occupational functioning.
4. Depersonalization experiences cannot be attributed to other disorders or to the direct effects of drugs, alcohol, or medical conditions.

Source. Adapted from the *DSM-IV-TR* (APA, 2000).

depersonalization disorder A disorder characterized by persistent or recurrent episodes of depersonalization.

Richie's depersonalization experience was limited to the one episode and would not qualify for a diagnosis of **depersonalization disorder.** Depersonalization disorder is diagnosed only when such experiences are persistent or recurrent and cause marked distress (Steinberg, 1991). The *DSM* diagnoses depersonalization disorder according to the criteria shown in Table 7.2. Note the following case example:

A Case of Depersonalization Disorder

A 20-year-old college student feared that he was going insane. For two years, he had increasingly frequent experiences of feeling "outside" himself. During these episodes, he experienced a sense of "deadness" in his body, and felt wobbly, frequently bumping into furniture. He was more apt to lose his balance during episodes which occurred when he was out in public, especially when he was feeling anxious. During these episodes, his thoughts seemed "foggy," reminding him of his state of mind when he was given shots of a pain-killing drug for an appendectomy five years earlier. He tried to fight off these episodes when they occurred, by saying "stop" to himself and by shaking his head. This would temporarily clear his head, but the feeling of being outside himself and the sense of deadness would shortly return. The disturbing feelings would gradually fade away over a period of hours. By the time he sought treatment, he was experiencing these episodes about twice a week, each one lasting from three to four hours. His grades remained unimpaired, and had even improved in the past several months, since he was spending more time studying. However, his girlfriend, in whom he had confided his problem, felt that he had become totally absorbed in himself and threatened to break off their relationship if he didn't change. She had also begun to date other men.

—Adapted from Spitzer et al., 1994, pp. 270–271

In terms of observable behavior and associated features, depersonalization may be more closely related to disorders such as phobias and panic than to dissociative disorders. Unlike other forms of dissociative disorders that seem to protect the self from anxiety, depersonalization can lead to anxiety and in turn to avoidance behavior, as we saw in the case of Richie.

Culture-Bound Dissociative Syndromes

Similarities exist between the Western concept of dissociative disorder and certain culture-bound syndromes found in other parts of the world. For example, *amok* is a culture-bound syndrome occurring primarily in southeast Asian and Pacific island cultures that describes a trancelike state in which a person suddenly becomes highly excited and violently attacks other people or destroys objects (see Chapter 3). People who "run amuck" may later claim to have no memory of the episode or recall feeling as if they were acting like a robot. Another example is *zar*, a term used in countries in North Africa and the Middle East to describe spirit possession in people who experience dissociative states. During these states, individuals engage in unusual behavior, ranging from shouting to banging their heads against the wall. The behavior itself is not deemed abnormal, since it is believed to be controlled by spirits.

Depersonalization. Episodes of depersonalization are characterized by feelings of detachment from oneself. During an episode, it may feel as if one were walking through a dream or observing the environment or oneself from outside one's body.

Questionnaire

The Dissociative Experiences Scale

 Brief dissociative experiences, such as momentary feelings of depersonalization, are quite common. The great majority of us experience them at least some of the time (Gershuny & Thayer, 1999). Dissociative disorders, by contrast, involve more persistent and severe dissociative experiences. Researchers have developed a measure, the Dissociative Experiences Scale (DES), to offer clinicians a way of measuring dissociative experiences that occur in both the general population and among people with dissociative disorders (Bernstein & Putnam, 1986; Putnam & Carlson, 1994; Sanders & Green, 1995; Sar et al., 1996). Fleeting dissociative experiences are quite common, but those reported by people with dissociative disorders are more frequent and problematic than those in the general population (Waller & Ross, 1997).

The following is a listing of some of the types of dissociative experiences drawn from the Dissociative Experiences Scale that many people encounter from time to time. Bear in mind that transient experiences like these are reported by both normal and abnormal groups in varying frequencies. Let us also suggest that if these experiences become persistent or commonplace, or cause you concern or distress, then it might be worthwhile to discuss them with a professional.

Have You Ever Experienced the Following?

1. Suddenly realizing, when you are driving the car, that you don't remember what has happened during all or part of the trip.
2. Suddenly realizing, when you are listening to someone talk, that you did not hear part or all of what the person said.
3. Finding yourself in a place and having no idea how you got there.
4. Finding yourself dressed in clothes that you don't remember putting on.
5. Experiencing a feeling that seemed as if you were standing next to yourself or watching yourself do something and actually seeing yourself as if you were looking at another person.
6. Looking in a mirror and not recognizing yourself.
7. Feeling sometimes that other people, objects, and the world around you are not real.
8. Remembering a past event so vividly that it seems like you are reliving it in the present.
9. Having the experience of being in a familiar place but finding it strange and unfamiliar.
10. Becoming so absorbed in watching television or a movie that you are unaware of other events happening around you.
11. Becoming so absorbed in a fantasy or daydream that it feels as though it were really happening to you.
12. Talking out loud to yourself when you are alone.
13. Finding that you act so differently in a particular situation compared with another that it feels almost as if you were two different people.
14. Finding that you cannot remember whether or not you have just done something or perhaps had just thought about doing it (for example, not knowing whether you have just mailed a letter or have just thought about mailing it).
15. Feeling sometimes as if you were looking at the world through a fog such that people and objects appear faraway or unclear.

Source. Bernstein, E. M., & Putnam, F. W. (1986). Development, reliability, and validity of a dissociation scale. *Journal of Nervous and Mental Disease, 174,* 727–735. Copyright © Williams & Wilkins, 1986.

Theoretical Perspectives

The dissociative disorders are fascinating and perplexing phenomena. How can one's sense of personal identity become so distorted that one develops multiple personalities, blots out large chunks of personal memory, or develops a new self-identity? Although these disorders remain in many ways mysterious, clues have emerged that provide insights into their origins.

Psychodynamic Views Dissociative amnesia may serve an adaptive function of disconnecting or dissociating one's conscious from awareness of traumatic experiences or other sources of psychological pain or conflict (Dorahy, 2001). To psychodynamic theorists, dissociative disorders involve the massive use of repression, resulting in the "splitting off" from consciousness of unacceptable impulses and painful memories. In dissociative amnesia and fugue, the ego protects itself from becoming flooded with anxiety by blotting out disturbing memories or by dissociating threatening impulses of a sexual or aggressive nature. In multiple personality, people may express these unacceptable impulses through the development of alternate personalities. In depersonalization, people stand outside themselves—safely distanced from the emotional turmoil within.

Cognitive and Learning Views Learning and cognitive theorists view dissociation as a learned response that involves *not thinking* about disturbing acts or thoughts in order to avoid feelings of guilt and shame evoked by such experiences. The habit of not thinking about these matters is negatively reinforced by relief from anxiety, or by removal of feelings of guilt or shame. Some social cognitive theorists, such as the late Nicholas Spanos, believe that dissociative identity disorder is a form of role playing acquired through observational learning and reinforcement. This is not quite the same as pretending or malingering; people can honestly come to organize their behavior patterns according to particular roles they have observed. They might also become so absorbed in role playing that they "forget" they are enacting a role.

Brain Dysfunction Might dissociative behavior be connected with underlying brain dysfunction? Research along these lines is still in its infancy, but recent evidence showed differences in brain metabolic activity between people with depersonalization disorder and healthy subjects (Simeon et al., 2000). These findings, which point to a possible dysfunction in parts of the brain involved in body perception, may help account for the feeling of being disconnected from one's body that is associated with depersonalization.

Tying It Together

 Although we have different conceptualizations of dissociative phenomena, psychologists recognize that a history of abuse in childhood often plays a pivotal role. The most widely held view of dissociative identity disorder is that it represents a means of coping with and surviving severe, repetitive childhood abuse, generally beginning before the age of 5 (Burton & Lane, 2001). The severely abused child may retreat into alter personalities as a psychological defense against unbearable abuse. The construction of these alter personalities allows such children to psychologically escape or distance themselves from their suffering (Burton & Lane, 2001). Dissociation offers a means of escape when no other means is available (Gershuny & Thayer, 1999). In the face of continued abuse, these alter personalities may become stabilized, making it difficult for the person to maintain a unified personality. In adulthood, people with multiple personalities may use their alter personalities to block out traumatic childhood memories and their emotional reactions to them, thus wiping the slate clean and beginning life anew in the guise of alter personalities (Schafer, 1986). The alter identities or personalities may also help the person cope with stressful situations or express deep-seated resentments that the individual is unable to integrate within his or her primary personality (Spanos, 1994).

Compelling evidence indicates that exposure to childhood trauma, usually by a relative or caretaker, is involved in the development of dissociative disorders, especially dissociative identity disorder. The great majority of people with multiple personalities report being physically or sexually abused as children (Lewis et al., 1997; Weaver & Clum, 1995). In one sample, 83% of people with dissociative identity disorder reported a history of childhood sexual abuse and 2 out of 3 reported both physical and sexual abuse (Putnam et al., 1986). In other samples, rates of childhood physical or sexual abuse have ranged from 76% to 95% of cases (Ross et al., 1990; Scroppo et al., 1998). Evidence of cross-cultural similarity comes from a study in Turkey, which showed that more than 3 out of 4 of 35 dissociative identity disorder patients reported sexual or physical abuse in childhood (Sar et al., 1996). Childhood trauma or abuse is also reported more often in cases of dissociative amnesia and depersonalization disorder than in control groups (Coons, Bowman, & Pellow, 1989; Simeon et al., 1997, 2001).

Truth OR Fiction? **REVISITED**

Most people with multiple personalities do not report any history of physical or sexual abuse during childhood.

FALSE. The great majority of people with multiple personalities do in fact report being physically or sexually abused as children.

Childhood abuse is not the only source of trauma linked to dissociative disorders. Exposure to the trauma of warfare among both civilians and soldiers plays a part in some cases of dissociative fugue and dissociative amnesia. In fugue, the stress of combat and the secondary gain of leaving the battlefield seem to be important contributors (Loewenstein, 1991). The stress of coping with severe financial problems and the wish to avoid punishment for socially unacceptable behavior are other possible antecedents to episodes of fugue (Riether & Stoudemire, 1988). Exposure to high levels of stress may also be linked to depersonalization disorder (Kluft, 1988).

Imaginary friends? Like the child in the photo, it is normal for children to have imaginary playmates. In the case of many multiple personalities, however, games of "make believe" and the invention of imaginary playmates may be used as psychological defenses against abuse. Research suggests that most people who develop multiple personalities were abused as children.

Diathesis-Stress Model Despite widespread evidence of childhood trauma in cases of dissociative identity disorder, very few abused children develop multiple personalities, even among those who suffer severe abuse. Consistent with the diathesis-stress model, certain personality traits, such as proneness to fantasize, high ability to be hypnotized, and openness to altered states of consciousness, may predispose individuals to develop dissociative experiences in the face of extreme stress, such as traumatic abuse. These personality traits themselves do not lead to dissociative disorders (Rauschenberger & Lynn, 1995). They are actually quite common in the population. However, they may increase the risk that people who experience severe trauma will develop dissociative phenomena as a survival mechanism (Butler et al., 1996). People who are low in fantasy proneness or hypnotizability may experience the kinds of anxious, intrusive thoughts characteristic of posttraumatic stress disorder (PTSD) in the aftermath of traumatic stress, rather than dissociative experiences (Kirmayer, Robbins, & Paris, 1994).

Perhaps most of us can divide our consciousness so that we become unaware of—at least temporarily—those events we normally focus on. Perhaps most of us can thrust the unpleasant from our minds and enact various roles—parent, child, lover, businessperson, soldier—that help us meet the requirements of our situations. Perhaps the marvel is *not* that attention can be splintered, but that human consciousness is normally integrated into a meaningful whole.

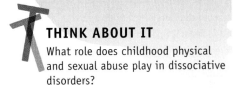

THINK ABOUT IT
What role does childhood physical and sexual abuse play in dissociative disorders?

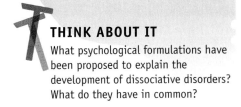

THINK ABOUT IT
What psychological formulations have been proposed to explain the development of dissociative disorders? What do they have in common?

Treatment of Dissociative Disorders

Dissociative amnesia and fugue are usually fleeting experiences that end abruptly. Episodes of depersonalization can be recurrent and persistent, and they are most likely to occur when people are undergoing periods of mild anxiety or depression. In such cases, clinicians usually focus on managing the anxiety or the depression. Much of the attention in the research literature has focused on dissociative identity disorder and specifically on bringing together an integration of the alter personalities into a cohesive personality structure (Burton & Lane, 2001).

Psychoanalysts seek to help people with dissociative identity disorder uncover and learn to cope with early childhood traumas. They often recommend establishing direct contact with alter personalities (Burton & Lane, 2001). For instance, Wilbur (1986) points out that the analyst can work with whatever personality dominates the therapy session. Any and all personalities can be asked to talk about their memories and dreams as best they can. Any and all personalities can be assured that the therapist will help them make sense of their anxieties and to safely "relive" traumatic experiences and make them conscious. Wilbur enjoins therapists to keep in mind that anxiety experienced during a therapy session may lead to a switch in personalities, because alter personalities were presumably developed as a means to cope with intense anxiety. But if therapy is successful, the self will be

A Closer Look

The Recovered Memory Controversy

A high-level business executive's comfortable life fell apart one day when his 19-year-old daughter accused him of having repeatedly molested her throughout her childhood. The executive lost his marriage as well as his $400,000-a-year job. But he fought back against the allegations, which he insisted were untrue. He sued his daughter's therapists, who had assisted her in recovering these memories. A jury sided with the businessman, awarding him $500,000 in damages from the two therapists.

This case is but one of many involving adults who claim to have only recently become aware of memories of childhood sexual abuse. Hundreds of people throughout the country have been brought to trial on the basis of recovered memories of childhood abuse, with many of these cases resulting in convictions and long jail sentences, even in the absence of corroborating evidence. Such recovered memories often occur following suggestive probing by a therapist or hypnotist (Loftus, 1993). The issue of recovered memories continues to be hotly debated in psychology and the broader community. At the heart of the debate is the question, "Are recovered memories believable?" No one doubts that childhood sexual abuse is a major problem confronting our society. But should recovered memories be taken at face value?

Several lines of evidence lead us to question the validity of recovered memories. Experimental evidence shows that false memories can be created, especially under the influence of leading or suggestive questioning (Begley, 2001b; Loftus, 1997; Schacter, 1999; Zoellner et al., 2000). Memory for events that never happened may be induced in people's memories and may seem just as real as memories of events that really did occur (Zola, 1999). Moreover, although people who have

experienced actual abuse in childhood may be somewhat sketchy on the details, total amnesia concerning the trauma is rare (Wakefield & Underwager, 1996). A leading memory expert, psychologist Elizabeth Loftus (1996, p. 356), writes of the dangers of taking recovered memories at face value:

> After developing false memories, innumerable "patients" have torn their families apart, and more than a few innocent people have been sent to prison. This is not to say that people cannot forget horrible things that have happened to them; most certainly they can. But there is virtually no support for the idea that clients presenting for therapy routinely have extensive histories of abuse of which they are completely unaware, and that they can be helped only if the alleged abuse is resurrected from their unconscious.

Should we conclude, then, that recovered memories are bogus? Not necessarily. It is possible for people in adulthood to recover memories of childhood (Melchert, 1996), including memories of abuse (Chu et al., 1999). Some recovered memories may be true; others may not be (Brown, 1997; Reisner, 1996; Rubin, 1996). Unfortunately we don't have the tools to distinguish the true memory from the false one (Loftus, 1993).

We shouldn't think of the brain as a kind of mental camera that stores snapshots of events as they actually happened in the form of memories. Memory is more of a reconstructive process in which bits of information are pieced together in ways that can sometimes lead to a distorted recollection of events, even though the person may be convinced the memory is accurate.

Web Link 7.2 www
Q&A: Memories of Childhood Abuse

able to work through the traumatic memories and will no longer need to escape into alternate "selves" to avoid the anxiety associated with the trauma. Thus, reintegration of the personality becomes possible.

Wilbur describes the formation of another treatment goal in the case of a woman with dissociative identity disorder:

A Case of Dissociative Identity Disorder

A 45-year-old woman had suffered from dissociative identity disorder throughout her life. Her dominant personality was timid and self-conscious, rather reticent about herself. But soon after she entered treatment, a group of "little ones" emerged, who cried profusely. The therapist asked to speak with someone in the personality system who could clarify the personalities that were present. It turned out that they included several children, all of whom were under 9 years of age and had suffered severe, painful sexual abuse at the hands of an uncle, a great-aunt, and a grandmother. The great-aunt was a lesbian with several voyeuristic lesbian friends. They would watch the sexual abuse, generating fear, pain, rage, humiliation, and shame.

It was essential in therapy for the "children" to come to understand that they should not feel ashamed because they had been helpless to resist the abuse.

—*Adapted from Wilbur, 1986, pp. 138–139*

Does therapy work? Coons (1986) followed 20 "multiples" aged from 14 to 47 at time of intake for an average of 3¼ years. Only 5 of the subjects showed a complete reintegration of their personalities. Other therapists report significant improvement in measures of dissociative symptoms and depressive symptoms in treated patients, even in those who failed to achieve integration. However, greater symptom improvement was reported for those who achieved integration (Ellason & Ross, 1997).

Reports of the effectiveness of psychoanalytic or of other forms of therapy, such as behavior therapy, rely on uncontrolled case studies. Controlled studies of treatments of dissociative identity disorder or other forms of dissociative disorder are yet to be reported (Maldonad et al., 1998). The relative infrequency of the disorder has hampered efforts to conduct controlled experiments that compare different forms of treatment with each other and with control groups. Nor do we have evidence showing psychiatric drugs or other biological approaches to be effective in bringing about an integration of various alternate personalities.

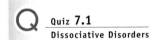
Quiz 7.1
Dissociative Disorders

A Closer Look

The Truth Is Out There

The *X-Files,* one of television's most popular shows in recent years, featured FBI agents who were charged with investigating mysterious phenomena. One of the running themes in the show was the belief in alien abductions. The show picked up on the claims of hundred or thousands of real people who said they had been abducted by space aliens. Though details of alien abductions vary, they usually involve reports of being spirited away to an alien spaceship, whereupon various medical procedures or experiments are performed on them before they are returned to Earth. What are we to make of these reports? Some reports may be fabrications, concocted for publicity or in hopes of achieving fame or securing lucrative Hollywood contract for their stories. Yet many of these claims are difficult to ascribe to either lying or insanity (Newman & Baumeister, 1996).

These reports have not been subjected to formal scientific study, so our beliefs about them rest largely on theoretical speculation. Some psychologists view them as false memories derived from sleep-related hallucinations or nightmares that are pieced together under hypnosis and reinforced by a popular culture that gives credence to alien sightings (Clark & Loftus, 1996; Newman & Baumeister, 1996). Memory is a reconstructive process, not a photographic rendering of events. A number of experiments have shown that under the right circumstances people can be led to believe that they experienced events which did not actually take place (Clark & Loftus, 1996).

Hypnosis is believed to play a part as memories of alien abductions often develop after hypnosis (Orne et al., 1996). However, we cannot simply ascribe memories of alien abductions to effects of hypnotic suggestion on reconstructed memories. Hypnosis doesn't play a part in many cases; in still others hypnosis was used to fill in some details after the person made a report of an alien abduction (Hall, 1996).

Others suggest that memories of alien abductions are individual delusions—false but strongly held beliefs that anyone can develop in the attempt to explain unusual events that happen to them (Banaji & Kihlstrom, 1996). Other avenues of speculation treat alien abduction phenomena as forms of mass delusion supported by a social network of people holding such deviant beliefs (Hall, 1996), or types of dissociative experiences or splitting of consciousness in response to extreme stress (Fisman & Takhar, 1996; Shopper, 1996), or attempts to escape from the self (Newman & Baumeister, 1996). Though speculation abounds, we lack a solid foundation of research evidence on which to judge these theoretical accounts (Arndt & Greenberg, 1996). Perhaps we will learn more as research on this intriguing phenomenon continues. Or perhaps reports of alien abductions will shortly disappear into the trash heap of discarded cultural trends. There is yet another, however unlikely explanation. Perhaps these people were truly abducted by space aliens. On this account, we'd best leave the investigation to the likes of the fictional X-file agents Fox Muldur and Dana Scully.

Overview of Dissociative Disorders

TYPES OF DISSOCIATIVE DISORDERS

	Description	Features
Dissociative Identity Disorder	Emergence of two or more distinct personalities	• Alternates may vie for control • Some cases reported of distinct physiological characteristics of alternates
Dissociative Amnesia	Inability to recall important personal material that cannot be accounted for by medical causes	• Information lost to memory is usually of traumatic or stressful experiences • Subtypes include localized amnesia, selective amnesia, and generalized amnesia
Dissociative Fugue	Amnesia "on the run"; the person travels to a new location and is unable to remember personal information or reports a past filled with false information that is not recognized as false	• Person may be confused about his or her personal identity or assumes a new identity • Person may start a new family or business
Depersonalization Disorder	Episodes of feeling detached from one's self or one's body or having a sense of unreality about one's surroundings (derealization)	• Person may feel as if he or she were living in a dream or acting like a robot • Episodes of depersonalization are persistent or recurrent and cause significant distress

CAUSAL FACTORS   A history of childhood trauma or abuse is implicated in many cases

Biological Factors	• Not known
Social-Environmental Factors	• Childhood sexual or physical abuse (in dissociative identity disorder) • Other traumatic experiences, such as combat trauma (in dissociative amnesia and dissociative fugue)
Behavioral Factors	• Possible reinforcement (attention) for enacting the social role of a multiple personality
Emotional and Cognitive Factors	• Relief from anxiety by psychologically distancing oneself (dissociating) from troubling emotions or memories

TREATMENT APPROACHES
Dissociative identity disorder remains a challenge to treat; dissociative amnesia and dissociative fugue tend to resolve on their own. The relative infrequency of these disorders has limited efforts to mount controlled studies of other therapies

Biomedical Treatment	• Drug therapy (SSRI-type antidepressants) may be helpful in treating depersonalization disorder
Psychodynamic Therapy	• For dissociative identity disorder, psychoanalytic therapy may be used to seek a reintegration of the personality

Somatoform Disorders

The word *somatoform* derives from the Greek *soma*, meaning "body." In the **somatoform disorders,** people have physical symptoms suggestive of physical disorders, but no organic abnormalities can be found to account for them. Moreover, there is evidence, or some reason to believe, that the symptoms reflect psychological factors or conflict. Some people complain of problems in breathing or swallowing, or of a "lump in the throat." Problems such as these can reflect overactivity of the sympathetic branch of the autonomic nervous system, which can be related to anxiety. Sometimes the symptoms take more unusual forms, as in a "paralysis" of a hand or leg that is inconsistent with the workings of the nervous system. In yet other cases, people are preoccupied with the belief that they have a serious disease, yet no evidence of a physical abnormality can be found. We consider several forms of somatoform disorders, including *conversion disorder, hypochondriasis,* and *somatization disorder.*

Somatoform disorders are distinguished from malingering, or purposeful fabrication of symptoms for obvious gain (such as avoiding work). They are also distinguished from a **factitious disorder,** the most common form of which is **Munchausen syndrome.** Munchausen is a form of feigned illness in which the person either fakes being ill or makes him- or herself ill (by ingesting toxic substances, for example). Some Munchausen patients go through unnecessary surgeries, even though they know there is nothing wrong with them. Yet unlike malingering, there is no apparent purpose to the fakery save for the attention the person receives from medical professionals. Because malingering is motivated by external incentives, it is not considered a mental disorder within the *DSM* framework. In factitious disorders, however, the symptoms are not connected with obvious gains. The absence of external incentives in these disorders suggests that they serve a psychological need; hence, they are considered mental disorders.

Why do patients with Munchausen syndrome feign illness or sometimes put themselves at grave risk by causing themselves to be sick or injured? Perhaps enacting the sick role in the protected hospital environment provides a sense of security that was lacking in childhood. Perhaps the hospital becomes a stage on which they can act out resentments against doctors and parents that have been brewing since childhood. Perhaps they are trying to identify with a parent who was often sick. Or perhaps they learned to enact a sick role in childhood to escape from repeated sexual abuse or other traumatic experiences and continue to enact the role to escape stressors in their adult lives (Trask & Sigmon, 1997). No one is really sure, and the disorder remains one of the more puzzling forms of abnormal behavior.

Here let us consider several of the major types of somatoform disorder: conversion disorder, hypochondriasis, body dysmorphic disorder, and somatization disorder.

Conversion Disorder

Conversion disorder is characterized by a major change in or loss of physical functioning, although no medical findings are found to account for the physical symptoms or deficits (see Table 7.3). The symptoms are not intentionally produced. The person is not malingering. The physical symptoms usually come on suddenly in stressful situations. A soldier's hand may become "paralyzed" during intense combat, for example. The fact that conversion symptoms first appear in the context of, or are aggravated by, conflicts or stressors the individual encounters gives credence to the view that they relate to psychological factors (APA, 2000). Reported rates of the disorder in the general population range from as few as 1.1 in 10,000 people to perhaps as many as 1 in 200 people (APA, 2000).

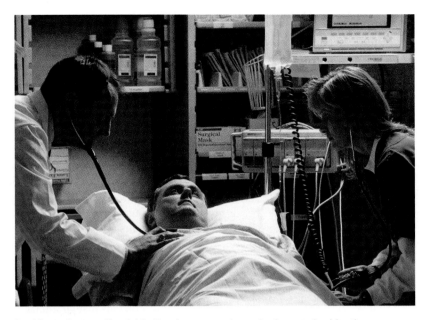

Is this patient really sick? Munchausen syndrome is characterized by the fabrication of medical complaints for no other apparent purpose than to gain admission to hospitals. Some Munchausen patients may produce life-threatening symptoms in their attempts to deceive doctors.

Truth OR Fiction? REVISITED

Some people show up repeatedly at hospital emergency rooms, feigning illness and seeking treatment for no apparent reason.

TRUE. People with Munchausen syndrome may show up repeatedly at emergency rooms, feigning illness and demanding treatment. Their motives remain a mystery.

WWW Web Link **7.3**
About Conversion Disorder

somatoform disorders A group of disorders characterized by complaints of physical problems or symptoms that cannot be explained by physical causes.

factitious disorder A disorder characterized by intentional fabrication of psychological or physical symptoms for no apparent gain.

Munchausen syndrome A type of factitious disorder characterized by the feigning of medical symptoms.

conversion disorder A type of somatoform disorder characterized by loss or impairment of physical function in the absence of any apparent organic cause.

TABLE 7.3 Diagnostic Features of Conversion Disorder

1. At least one symptom or deficit involving voluntary motor or sensory functions that suggests the presence of a physical disorder.

2. Psychological factors are judged to be associated with the disorder because the onset or exacerbation of the physical symptom is linked to the occurrence of psychosocial stressors or conflict situations.

3. The person does not purposefully produce or fake the physical symptom.

4. The symptom cannot be explained as a cultural ritual or response pattern, nor can it be explained by any known physical disorder on the basis of appropriate testing.

5. The symptom causes significant emotional distress, impairment in one or more important areas of functioning, such as social or occupational functioning, or is sufficient to warrant medical attention.

6. The symptom is not restricted to complaints of pain or problems in sexual functioning, nor can it be accounted for by another mental disorder.

Source. Adapted from the *DSM-IV-TR* (APA, 2000).

la belle indifférence A French expression describing the lack of concern over one's symptoms displayed by some people with conversion disorder.

Conversion disorder is so named because of the psychodynamic belief that it represents the channeling, or *conversion,* of repressed sexual or aggressive energies into physical symptoms. Conversion disorder was formerly called *hysteria* or *hysterical neurosis,* and it played an important role in Freud's development of psychoanalysis (see Chapter 1). Hysterical or conversion disorders seem to have been more common in Freud's day than they are today, when they are relatively rare.

According to the *DSM,* conversion symptoms mimic neurological or general medical conditions involving problems with voluntary motor (movement) or sensory functions. Some of the "classic" symptom patterns involve paralysis, epilepsy, problems in coordination, blindness and tunnel vision, loss of the sense of hearing or of smell, or loss of feeling in a limb (anesthesia). The bodily symptoms found in conversion disorders often do not match the medical conditions they suggest. For example, conversion epileptics, unlike true epileptic patients, may maintain control over their bladders during an attack. People whose vision is supposedly impaired may wend their ways through the physician's office without bumping into the furniture. People who become "incapable" of standing or walking may nevertheless perform other leg movements normally. Nonetheless, hysteria may be incorrectly diagnosed in people who turn out to have underlying medical conditions. Perhaps as many as 80% of individuals given the diagnosis of conversion disorder have real neurological problems that go undiagnosed (Gould et al., 1986).

If you suddenly lost your vision, or if you could no longer move your legs, you would probably show understandable concern. But some people with conversion disorders, like those with dissociative amnesia, show a remarkable indifference to their symptoms, a phenomenon termed **la belle indifférence** ("beautiful indifference"). The *DSM* advises against relying on indifference to symptoms as a factor in making the diagnosis, however, because many people cope with real physical disorders by denying their pain or concern, which provides the semblance of indifference and relieves anxieties—at least temporarily.

Hypochondriasis

The core feature of hypochondriasis is a preoccupation or fear that one's physical symptoms are due to an underlying serious illness, such as cancer or a heart problem. The fear persists despite medical reassurances that it is groundless (see Table 7.4).

People with hypochondriasis do not consciously fake their physical symptoms. They generally experience physical discomfort, often involving the digestive system or an assortment of aches and pains. Unlike conversion disorder, hypochondriasis does not involve the loss or distortion of physical function. Unlike the attitude of indifference toward one's symptoms that is sometimes found in conversion disorders, people who develop hypochondriasis are very concerned, indeed unduly concerned, about their symptoms and

TABLE 7.4 Diagnostic Features of Hypochondriasis

1. The person is preoccupied with a fear of having a serious illness, or with the belief that one has a serious illness. The person interprets bodily sensations or physical signs as evidence of physical illness.

2. Fears of physical illness, or beliefs of having a physical illness, persist despite medical reassurances.

3. The preoccupations are not of a delusional intensity (the person recognizes the possibility that these fears and beliefs may be exaggerated or unfounded) and are not restricted to concerns about appearance.

4. The preoccupations cause significant emotional distress or interfere with one or more important areas of functioning, such as social or occupational functioning.

5. The disturbance has persisted for 6 months or longer.

6. The preoccupations do not occur exclusively within the context of another mental disorder.

Source. Adapted from the *DSM-IV-TR* (APA, 2000).

what they fear they may represent. Although the underlying rates of hypochondriasis remain unknown, the disorder appears to be about equally common in men and women. It most often begins between the ages of 20 and 30, although it can begin at any age.

People with hypochondriasis may be overly sensitive to benign changes in physical sensations, such as slight changes in heartbeat and minor aches and pains (Barsky et al., 2001). Anxiety about physical symptoms can produce its own physical sensations, however—for example, heavy sweating and dizziness, even fainting. Thus, a vicious cycle may ensue. People with hypochondriasis may become resentful when their doctors tell them how their own fears may be causing their physical symptoms. They frequently go "doctor shopping" in the hope that a competent and sympathetic physician will heed them before it is too late. Physicians, too, can develop hypochondriasis, as we see in the following case example:

A Case of Hypochondriasis

Robert, a 38-year-old radiologist, has just returned from a 10-day stay at a famous diagnostic center where he has undergone extensive testing of his entire gastrointestinal tract. The evaluation proved negative for any significant physical illness, but rather than feel relieved, the radiologist appeared resentful and disappointed with the findings. The radiologist has been bothered for several months with various physical symptoms, which he describes as symptoms of mild abdominal pain, feelings of "fullness," "bowel rumblings," and a feeling of a "firm abdominal mass." He has become convinced that his symptoms are due to colon cancer and has become accustomed to testing his stool for blood on a weekly basis and carefully palpating his abdomen for "masses" while lying in bed every several days. He has also secretly performed X-ray studies on himself after regular hours. There is a history of a heart murmur that was detected when he was 13 and his younger brother died of congenital heart disease in early childhood. When the evaluation of his murmur proved to be benign, he nonetheless began to worry that something might have been overlooked. He developed a fear that something was actually wrong with his heart, and while the fear eventually subsided, it has never entirely left him. In medical school he worried about the diseases that he learned about in pathology. Since graduating, he has repeatedly experienced concerns about his health that follow a typical pattern: noticing certain symptoms, becoming preoccupied with what the symptoms might mean, and undergoing physical evaluations that proved negative. His decision to seek a psychiatric consultation was prompted by an incident with his 9-year-old son. His son accidentally walked in on him while he was palpating his abdomen and asked, "What do you think it is this time, Dad?" He becomes tearful as he relates this incident, describing his feelings of shame and anger—mostly at himself.

—Adapted from Spitzer et al., 1994, pp. 88–90

People who develop hypochondriasis have more health worries, more psychiatric symptoms, and perceive their health to be worse than do other people (Noyes et al., 1993). They are also more likely than other psychiatric patients to report being sick as children, having missed school because of health reasons, and having experienced childhood trauma, such as sexual abuse or physical violence (Barsky et al., 1994). According to recent studies, most people who meet diagnostic criteria for hypochondriasis continue to show evidence of the disorder when reinterviewed 5 years later (Barsky et al., 1998). Most also have other psychological disorders, especially major depression and anxiety disorders (Barsky, Wyshak, & Klerman, 1992; Noyes et al., 1993).

Hypochondriasis is generally considered to be most common among elderly people. As noted by Paul Costa and Robert McCrae (1985) of the National Institute on Aging,

THINK ABOUT IT
Why is conversion disorder considered a treasure trove in the annals of abnormal psychology? What role did the disorder play in the development of psychological models of abnormal behavior?

WWW **Web Link 7.4**
Facts About Hypochondriasis

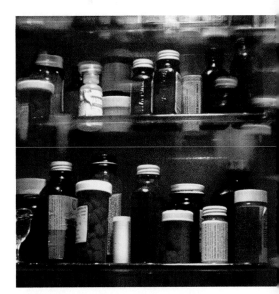

What to take? Hypochondriasis involves persistent concerns or fears that one is seriously ill, although no organic basis can be found to account for one's physical complaints. People with this disorder frequently medicate themselves with over-the-counter medications and find little if any reassurance in doctors' assertions that their health is not in jeopardy.

Can't you see it? A person with body dysmorphic disorder may spend hours in front of a mirror obsessing about an imagined or exaggerated physical defect in appearance.

THINK ABOUT IT
Do you know anyone you would consider to be a "hypochondriac"? What is the basis of your opinion? Did reading the text change your view?

however, authentic age-related health changes do occur, and most "hypochondriacal" complaints probably reflect these changes.

Body Dysmorphic Disorder

People with body dysmorphic disorder (BDD) are preoccupied with an imagined or exaggerated physical defect in their appearance (APA, 2000). They may spend hours examining themselves in the mirror and go to extreme measures to try to correct the perceived defect, even undergoing unnecessary plastic surgery. Others may remove any mirrors from their homes so as not to be reminded of the glaring flaw in their appearance. People with BDD may believe that others view them as ugly or deformed and that their unattractive physical appearance leads others to think negatively of their character or worth as a person (Rosen, 1996). The rates of BDD are not well established, since many people with this disorder fail to seek help or try to keep their symptoms a secret (Cororve & Gleaves, 2001). People with BDD often show a pattern of compulsive grooming or washing, or styling their hair, in an attempt to correct the perceived defect, as in the following case example:

A Case of Body Dysmorphic Disorder

For Claudia, a 24-year-old legal secretary, virtually every day was a bad hair day. She explained to her therapist, "When my hair isn't right, which is like every day, I'm not right." "Can't you see it," she went on to explain, "It's so uneven. This piece should be shorter and this one just lies there. People think I'm crazy but I can't stand looking like this. It makes me look like I'm deformed. It doesn't matter if people can't see what I'm talking about. I see it. That's what counts." Several months earlier Claudia had a haircut she described as a disaster. Shortly thereafter, she had thoughts of killing herself: "I wanted to stab myself in the heart. I just couldn't stand looking at myself."

Claudia checked her hair in the mirror innumerable times during the day. She would spend two hours every morning doing her hair and still wouldn't be satisfied. Her constant pruning and checking had become a compulsive ritual. As she told her therapist, "I want to stop pulling and checking it, but I just can't help myself."

—From the Authors' Files

Having a "bad hair day" for Claudia meant that she would not go out with her friends and would spend every second examining herself in the mirror and fixing her hair. Occasionally she would cut pieces of her hair herself in an attempt to correct the mistakes of her last haircut. But cutting it herself inevitably made it even worse, in her view. Claudia was forever searching for the perfect haircut that would correct defects only she could perceive. Several years earlier she had what she described as a perfect haircut. "It was just right. I was on top of the world. But it began to look crooked when it grew in." Forever in search of the perfect haircut, Claudia had obtained a hard-to-get appointment with a world-renowned hair stylist in Manhattan whose clientele included many celebrities. "People wouldn't understand paying this guy $375 for a haircut, especially on my salary, but they don't realize how important it is to me. I'd pay any amount I could." Unfortunately even this celebrated hair stylist disappointed her: "My $25 haircut from my old stylist on Long Island was better than this."

Claudia reported other fixations about her appearance earlier in life: "In high school, I felt my face was like a plate. It was just too flat. I didn't want any pictures taken of me. I couldn't help thinking what people thought of me. They won't tell you, you know. Even if they say there's nothing wrong, it doesn't mean anything. They were just lying to be polite." Claudia related that she was taught to equate physical beauty with happiness: "I was told that to be successful you had to be beautiful. How can I be happy if I look this way?"

wWw **Web Link 7.5**
Features of Body Dysmorphic Disorder

Somatization Disorder

Somatization disorder, formerly known as Briquet's syndrome, is characterized by multiple and recurrent somatic complaints that begin prior to the age of 30 (but usually during the teen years), persist for at least several years, and result either in the seeking of medical attention or in significant impairment in fulfilling social or occupational roles. Complaints usually involve different organ systems (Spitzer et al., 1989). Seldom a year passes without some physical complaint that prompts a trip to the doctor. People with somatization disorder are heavy users of medical services (G. R. Smith, 1994). Community surveys show that virtually all (95%) of the people with somatization disorder had visited a doctor during the past year and nearly half (45%) had been hospitalized (Swartz et al., 1991). The complaints cannot be explained by physical causes or exceed what would be expected from a known physical problem. Complaints seem vague or exaggerated, and the person frequently receives medical care from a number of physicians, sometimes at the same time.

Somatization disorder usually begins in adolescence or young adulthood and appears to be a chronic or even lifelong disorder (Kirmayer, Robbins, & Paris, 1994; Smith, 1994). It usually occurs in the context of other psychological disorders, especially anxiety disorders and depressive disorders (Swartz et al., 1991). Although not much is known about the childhood backgrounds of people with somatization disorder, one study reported that women with the disorder were significantly more likely to report sexual molestation in childhood than a matched comparison group of women with mood disorders (Morrison, 1989).

The essential feature of hypochondriasis is fear of disease, of what bodily symptoms may portend. Persons with somatization disorder, by contrast, are pestered by the symptoms themselves. Both diagnoses may be given to the same individual if the diagnostic criteria for both disorders are met.

Estimates are that 1 person in 1,000 in the United States is affected by somatization disorder, with 10 times as many cases found among women than men. The disorder is also 4 times more likely to occur among African Americans than other ethnic or racial groups (Swartz et al., 1991). Yet the disorder is controversial. Many patients, especially female patients, are misdiagnosed with psychological disorders, including somatization disorder, because of the failure of modern medicine to identify the underlying medical basis of their physical complaints (Klonoff & Landrine, 1997).

Koro and Dhat Syndromes: Far Eastern Somatoform Disorders?

In the United States, it is common for people who develop hypochondriasis to be troubled by the idea that they have serious illnesses, such as cancer. The koro and dhat syndromes of the Far East share some clinical features with hypochondriasis. Although these syndromes may seem foreign to most American readers, they are each connected with folklore within their Far Eastern cultures.

Koro Syndrome **Koro syndrome** is a culture-bound syndrome found primarily in China and some other Far Eastern countries (Sheung-Tak, 1996). People with koro syndrome fear that their genitals are shrinking and retracting into the body, which they believe will result in death (Fabian, 1991; Goetz & Price, 1994; Tseng et al., 1992). Koro is considered a

somatization disorder A type of somatoform disorder involving recurrent multiple complaints that cannot be explained by any physical cause.

koro syndrome A culture-bound somatoform disorder, found primarily in China, in which people fear that their genitals are shrinking.

dhat syndrome A culture-bound somatoform disorder, found primarily among Asian Indian males, characterized by excessive fears over the loss of seminal fluid.

Truth OR Fiction? REVISITED

In China in the 1980s, more than 2,000 people fell prey to the belief that their genitals were shrinking and retracting into their bodies.

TRUE. An epidemic was reported in China in which some 2,000 people fell prey to the belief that their genitals were shrinking and retracting into their bodies. This condition, called koro, is classified by the *DSM* system as a culture-bound syndrome.

THINK ABOUT IT
Does koro or dhat syndrome seem strange to you? How might your feelings depend on the culture in which you were raised? How might behaviors found in your culture be viewed as strange by members of other cultures?

Dhat syndrome. Found principally in India, dhat syndrome describes men with an intense fear or anxiety over the loss of semen.

culture-bound syndrome, although some cases have been reported outside China and the Far East (e.g., Chowdhury, 1996). The syndrome has been identified mainly in young men, although some cases have also been reported in women (Tseng et al., 1992). Koro syndrome tends to be short-lived and to involve episodes of acute anxiety that one's genitals are retracting. Physiological signs of anxiety that approach panic proportions are common, including profuse sweating, breathlessness, and heart palpitations. Men who suffer from koro have been known to use mechanical devices, such as chopsticks, to try to prevent the penis from retracting into the body (Devan, 1987).

Koro syndrome has been traced within Chinese culture as far back as 3000 B.C.E. (Devan, 1987). Epidemics involving hundreds or thousands of people have been reported in China, Singapore, Thailand, and India (Tseng et al., 1992). In Guangdong Province in China, an epidemic of koro involving more than 2,000 persons occurred during the 1980s (Tseng et al., 1992). Guangdong residents who did not fall victim to koro tended to be less superstitious, higher in intelligence, and less accepting of koro-related folk beliefs (such as the belief that shrinkage of the penis will be lethal) than those who fell victim to the epidemic (Tseng et al., 1992). Medical reassurance that such fears are unfounded often quell koro episodes (Devan, 1987). Medical reassurance generally fails to dent the concerns of Westerners who develop hypochondriasis, however. Koro episodes among those who do not receive corrective information tend to pass with time but may recur.

A number of investigators would like to see the koro syndrome incorporated into the *DSM* as a somatoform disorder (Bernstein & Gaw, 1990; Fishbain, 1991).

Dhat Syndrome **Dhat syndrome** is found among young Asian Indian males and involves excessive fears over the loss of seminal fluid during nocturnal emissions (Akhtar, 1988). Some men with this syndrome also believe (incorrectly) that semen mixes with urine and is excreted through urination. Men with dhat syndrome may roam from physician to physician seeking help to prevent nocturnal emissions or the (imagined) loss of semen mixed with excreted urine. There is a widespread belief within Indian culture (and other Near and Far Eastern cultures) that the loss of semen is harmful because it depletes the body of physical and mental energy (Chadda & Ahuja, 1990). Like other culture-bound syndromes, dhat must be understood within its cultural context:

> In India, attitudes toward semen and its loss constitute an organized, deep-seated belief system that can be traced back to the scriptures of the land ... [even as far back as the classic Indian sex manual, the Kama Sutra, which was believed to be written by the sage Vatsayana between the third and fifth centuries A.D.] ... Semen is considered to be the elixir of life, in both a physical and mystical sense. Its preservation is supposed to guarantee health and longevity.
>
> —*From Akhtar, 1988, p. 71*

It is a commonly held Hindu belief that it takes "forty meals to form one drop of blood; forty drops of blood to fuse and form one drop of bone marrow, and forty drops of this to produce one drop of semen" (Akhtar, 1988, p. 71). Based on the cultural belief in the life-preserving nature of semen, it is not surprising that some Indian males experience extreme anxiety over the involuntary loss of the fluid through nocturnal emissions (Akhtar, 1988). Dhat syndrome has also been associated with difficulty in achieving or maintaining erection, apparently due to excessive concern about loss of seminal fluid through ejaculation (Singh, 1985).

Theoretical Perspectives

Conversion disorder, or "hysteria," was known to Hippocrates, who attributed the strange bodily symptoms to a wandering uterus, which created internal chaos. The term *hysterical* derives from the Greek *hystera*, meaning "uterus." Hippocrates noticed that these complaints were less common among married than unmarried women. He prescribed marriage as a "cure" on the basis of these observations, and also on the theoretical assumption that pregnancy would satisfy uterine needs and fix the organ in place. Pregnancy fosters hormonal and structural changes that are of benefit to some women with menstrual complaints, but Hippocrates's belief in the "wandering uterus" has contributed throughout the centuries to degrading interpretations of complaints by women of physical problems. Despite Hippocrates's belief that hysteria is exclusively a female concern, it also occurs in men.

Modern theoretical accounts of the somatoform disorders, like those of the dissociative disorders, have most often sprung from psychodynamic and learning theories. Although not much is known about biological underpinnings of somatoform disorders, evidence indicates that somatization disorder tends to run in families, primarily among female members (Guze, 1993). This is suggestive of a genetic linkage, although we cannot rule out the possibility that family influences play a part in explaining this familial association.

Psychodynamic Theory Hysterical disorders provided an arena for some of the debate between the psychological and biological theories of the 19th century. The alleviation—albeit often temporarily—of hysterical symptoms through hypnosis by Charcot, Breuer, and Freud contributed to the belief that hysteria was rooted in psychological rather than physical causes and led Freud to the development of a theory of the unconscious mind. Freud held that the ego manages to control unacceptable or threatening sexual and aggressive impulses arising from the id through defense mechanisms such as repression. Such control prevents the outbreak of anxiety that would occur if the person were to become aware of these impulses. In some cases, the leftover emotion or energy that is "strangulated," or cut off, from the threatening impulses becomes *converted* into a physical symptom, such as hysterical paralysis or blindness. Although the early psychodynamic formulation of hysteria is still widely held, empirical evidence has been lacking. One problem with the Freudian view is that it does not explain how energies left over from unconscious conflicts become transformed into physical symptoms (E. Miller, 1987).

According to psychodynamic theory, hysterical symptoms are functional: They allow the person to achieve primary gains and secondary gains. The **primary gains** consist of allowing the individual to keep internal conflicts repressed. The person is aware of the physical symptom but not of the conflict it represents. In such cases, the "symptom" is symbolic of, and provides the person with a "partial solution" for, the underlying conflict. For example, the hysterical paralysis of an arm might symbolize and also prevent the individual from acting out on repressed unacceptable sexual (e.g., masturbatory) or aggressive (e.g., murderous) impulses. Repression occurs automatically, so the individual remains unaware of the underlying conflicts. *La belle indifférence*, first noted by Charcot, is believed to occur because the physical symptoms help relieve rather than cause anxiety. From the psychodynamic perspective, conversion disorders, like dissociative disorders, serve a purpose.

Secondary gains may allow the individual to avoid burdensome responsibilities and to gain the support—rather than condemnation—of those around them. For example, soldiers sometimes experience sudden "paralysis" of their hands, which prevents them from firing their guns in battle. They may then be sent to recuperate at a hospital rather than face enemy fire. The symptoms in such cases are not considered contrived, as would be the case in malingering. A number of bomber pilots during World War II suffered hysterical "night blindness" that prevented them from carrying out dangerous nighttime missions. In the psychodynamic view, their "blindness" may have achieved

primary gains Relief from underlying anxiety gained through the development of neurotic symptoms.

secondary gains Side benefits associated with neurotic or other disorders, such as expressions of sympathy, increased attention, and release from responsibilities.

B-29 bombers on a bombing mission over Japan during World War II. Some World War II pilots were reported to have suffered from hysterical night blindness, which prevented them from carrying out dangerous nighttime missions. Their night blindness may have served the psychological purpose of shielding them from guilt over dropping bombs on civilian areas—a type of primary gain. It may also have served the secondary purpose of helping them avoid dangerous combat missions.

a primary gain of shielding them from guilt associated with dropping bombs on civilian areas. It may also have achieved a secondary purpose of helping them avoid dangerous missions.

Learning Theory Psychodynamic theory and learning theory concur that the symptoms in conversion disorders relieve anxiety. Psychodynamic theorists, however, seek the causes of anxiety in unconscious conflicts. Learning theorists focus on the more direct reinforcing properties of the symptom and its secondary role in helping the individual avoid or escape uncomfortable or anxiety-evoking situations.

From the learning perspective, the symptoms in conversion and other somatoform disorders may also carry the benefits, or reinforcing properties of, the "sick role." Persons with conversion disorders may be relieved of chores and responsibilities such as going to work or performing household tasks (Miller, 1987). Being sick also usually earns sympathy and support. People who received such reinforcers during past illnesses are likely to learn to adopt a sick role even when they are not ill (Kendell, 1983).

Differences in learning experiences may explain why conversion disorders were historically more often reported among women than men. It may be that women in Western culture are more likely than men to have been socialized to cope with stress by enacting a sick role (Miller, 1987). We are not suggesting that people with conversion disorders are fakers. We are merely pointing out that people may learn to adopt roles that lead to reinforcing consequences, regardless of whether they deliberately seek to enact these roles.

Some learning theorists link hypochondriasis and body dysmorphic disorder to obsessive-compulsive disorder (OCD; see Chapter 6) (e.g., Barsky et al., 1992; Cororve & Gleaves, 2001). In hypochondriasis, people are bothered by obsessive, anxiety-inducing thoughts about their health. Running from doctor to doctor may be a form of compulsive behavior that is reinforced by the temporary relief from anxiety they experience when they are reassured by their doctors that their fears are unwarranted. Yet the troublesome thoughts eventually return, prompting repeated consultations. The cycle then repeats. Similarly, with body dysmorphic disorder, the constant grooming and pruning in the attempt to "fix" the perceived physical defect may offer partial relief from anxiety, but the "fix" is never quite good enough to completely erase the underlying concerns. One possibility is that hypochondriasis and body dysmorphic disorder fall within a spectrum of OCD-type disorders.

Cognitive Theory Cognitive theorists have speculated that some cases of hypochondriasis may represent a type of self-handicapping strategy, a way of blaming poor performance on failing health (Smith, Snyder, & Perkins, 1983). In other cases, diverting attention to physical complaints can serve as a means of avoiding thinking about other life problems.

Another cognitive explanation focuses on the role of distorted thinking. People who develop hypochondriasis have a tendency to "make mountains out of molehills" by exaggerating the significance of minor physical complaints (Barsky et al., 2001). They misinterpret benign symptoms as signs of a serious illness, which creates anxiety that leads them to chase down one doctor after another in an attempt to uncover the dreaded disease they fear they have. The anxiety itself may lead to unpleasant physical symptoms, which are likewise exaggerated in importance, leading to more worrisome cognitions.

Cognitive theorists speculate that hypochondriasis and panic disorder, which often occur concurrently, may share a common cause: a distorted way of thinking that leads the person to misinterpret minor changes in bodily sensations as signs of pending catastrophe (Salkovskis & Clark, 1993). Differences between the two disorders may hinge on whether the misinterpretation of bodily cues carries a perception of imminent threat leading to a rapid spiraling of anxiety (panic disorder) or of a longer range threat in the form of an underlying disease process (hypochondriasis). Research into cognitive processes involved in hypochondriasis deserves further study. Given the linkages that may exist between hypochondriasis and anxiety disorders such as panic disorder and OCD, it remains unclear whether hypochondriasis should be classified as a somatoform disorder or an anxiety disorder (Barsky et al., 1992).

Treatment of Somatoform Disorders

The treatment approach that Freud pioneered, psychoanalysis, began with the treatment of hysteria, which is now termed conversion disorder. Psychoanalysis seeks to uncover and bring unconscious conflicts that originated in childhood into conscious awareness. Once the conflict is aired and worked through, the symptom is no longer needed as a "partial solution" and should disappear. The psychoanalytic method is supported by case studies, some reported by Freud and others by his followers. However, the infrequency of conversion disorders in contemporary times has made it difficult to mount controlled studies of the psychoanalytic technique.

The behavioral approach to treating conversion disorders and other somatoform disorders focuses on removing sources of secondary reinforcement (or secondary gain) that may become connected with physical complaints. Family members and others, for example, often perceive individuals with somatization disorder as sickly and infirm and as incapable of carrying normal responsibilities. Other people may be unaware of how they reinforce dependent and complaining behaviors when they relieve the sick person of responsibilities. The behavior therapist may teach family members to reward attempts to assume responsibility and ignore nagging and complaining. The behavior therapist may also work more directly with the person with a somatoform disorder, helping the person learn more adaptive ways of handling stress or anxiety (through relaxation and cognitive restructuring, for example). Exposure with response prevention (ERP, discussed in Chapter 6) and cognitive therapy have also achieved good success in treating hypochondriasis in recent trials (Clark et al., 1998; Visser & Bouman, 2001). Cognitive techniques, such as cognitive restructuring, are used to modify the patient's exaggerated illness-related beliefs, while exposure with response prevention is used to break the cycle of running to doctors for reassurance whenever minor physical complaints occur.

Cognitive-behavioral techniques, most often exposure with response prevention and cognitive restructuring, have also achieved encouraging results in treating body dysmorphic disorder (BDD) (Cororve & Gleaves, 2001). Exposure may take the form of purposefully revealing the perceived defect in public, rather than concealing it through use of make-up or clothing. Response prevention focuses on breaking compulsive rituals, such as mirror checking (for example, by covering mirrors at home) and excessive grooming. In cognitive restructuring, the therapist challenges clients' distorted beliefs about their physical appearance by encouraging them to evaluate their beliefs in the light of evidence.

Attention has recently turned to the use of antidepressants, especially fluoxetine (Prozac), in treating some types of somatoform disorder. Although we lack specific drug therapies for conversion disorder (Simon, 1998), a study of 16 patients with hypochondriasis showed significant reductions in hypochondriacal complaints over the course of a 12-week trial with Prozac (Fallon et al., 1993). Here, too, the lack of controlled drug-placebo studies prevents firm conclusions regarding the efficacy of drug therapy. We also lack any systematic studies of approaches to treating factitious disorder (Münchausen syndrome) and are limited to a few isolated case examples (Simon, 1998).

The dissociative and somatoform disorders remain among the most intriguing and least understood patterns of abnormal behavior.

Quiz **7.2**
Somatoform Disorders

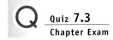

Quiz **7.3**
Chapter Exam

Research Update
Chapter 7

Overview of Somatoform Disorders

TYPES OF SOMATOFORM DISORDERS

	Description	Features
Conversion Disorder	Change or loss of a physical function without medical cause	• Emerges in context of conflicts or stressful experiences, which lends credence to its psychological origins • May be associated with la belle indifférence (indifference to symptoms)
Hypochondriasis	Preoccupation with the belief that one is seriously ill	• Fear persists despite medical reassurance • Tendency to interpret physical sensations or minor aches and pains as signs of serious illness
Somatization Disorder	Recurrent, multiple complaint about physical symptoms that have no clear organic basis	• Symptoms prompt frequent medical visits or cause significant impairment of functioning
Body Dysmorphic Disorder	Preoccupation with an imagined or exaggerated physical defect	• Person may believe that others think less of them as a person because of the perceived defect • Person may engage in compulsive behaviors, such as excessive grooming, that aim to correct the perceived defect

CAUSAL FACTORS Multiple causes are involved

Biological Factors	• Possible genetic influences (somatization disorder)
Social-Environmental Factors	• Socialization of women into more dependent roles, such as the "sick role," that may be expressed in the form of somatoform disorders
Behavioral Factors	• Relief from ordinary responsibilities or escape or avoidance of uncomfortable or anxiety-laden situations (secondary gain) • Reinforcing properties of enacting a "sick role" • Compulsive behaviors associated with hypochondriasis or body dysmorphic disorder may partially relieve anxiety associated with preoccupation with health concerns or perceived physical defects
Emotional and Cognitive Factors	• Misinterpretations of bodily changes or physical symptoms as signs of serious illness (hypochondriasis) • In traditional Freudian theory, psychic energy that becomes cut off from unacceptable impulses is converted into physical symptoms (conversion disorder) • Blaming poor performance on failing health may be a self-handicapping strategy (hypochondriasis)

TREATMENT APPROACHES Treatment typically involves psychodynamic or cognitive-behavioral therapy

Biomedical Treatment	• Limited use of antidepressants in treating hypochondriasis
Cognitive-Behavioral Therapy	• May focus on removing sources of secondary reinforcement (secondary gain), promoting development of coping skills for handling stress, and correcting exaggerated or distorted beliefs about one's health or appearance
Psychodynamic Therapy	• Psychodynamic or insight-oriented therapy may be aimed at identifying and working through underlying unconscious conflicts

Summing Up

Dissociative Disorders

What are dissociative disorders? Dissociative disorders involve changes or disturbances in identity, memory, or consciousness that affect the ability to maintain an integrated sense of self. Thus, the symptoms are theorized to reflect psychological rather than organic factors.

What is dissociative identity disorder? In dissociative identity disorder, two or more distinct personalities, each possessing well-defined traits and memories, exist within the person and repeatedly take control of the person's behavior.

What is dissociative amnesia? In dissociative amnesia, the person experiences a loss of memory for personal information that cannot be accounted for by organic causes.

What is dissociative fugue? In dissociative fugue, the person travels suddenly away from home or place of work, shows a loss of memory for his or her personal past, and experiences identity confusion or takes on a new identity.

What is depersonalization disorder? In depersonalization disorder, the person experiences persistent or recurrent episodes of depersonalization of sufficient severity to cause significant distress or impairment in functioning.

How do theorists explain the development of dissociative disorders? Psychodynamic theorists view dissociative disorders as involving a form of psychological defense by which the ego defends itself against troubling memories and unacceptable impulses by blotting them out of consciousness. There is increasing documentation of a link between dissociative disorders and early childhood trauma, which lends support to the view that dissociation may serve to protect the self from troubling memories. To learning and cognitive theorists, dissociative experiences involve ways of learning not to think about certain troubling behaviors or thoughts that might lead to feelings of guilt or shame. Relief from anxiety negatively reinforces this pattern of dissociation. Some social-cognitive theorists suggest that multiple personality may represent a form of role-playing behavior.

What are the major treatment approaches for dissociative identity disorder? Psychotherapy seeks a reintegration of the personality by focusing on helping persons with dissociative identity disorder uncover and integrate dissociated painful experiences from childhood. Drug therapy may help treat the anxiety and depression often associated with the disorder, but cannot bring about reintegration of the personality.

Somatoform Disorders

What are somatoform disorders? In somatoform disorders, there are physical complaints that cannot be accounted for by organic causes. Thus, the symptoms are theorized to reflect psychological rather than organic factors. Three major types of somatoform disorders are conversion disorder, hypochondriasis, and somatization disorder.

What is conversion disorder? In conversion disorder, symptoms or deficits in voluntary motor or sensory functions occur that suggest an underlying physical disorder, but no apparent medical basis for the condition can be found to account for the condition.

What is hypochondriasis? Hypochondriasis is a preoccupation with the fear of having, or the belief that one has, a serious medical illness, although no medical basis for the complaints can be found and fears of illness persist despite medical reassurances.

What is body dysmorphic disorder? In body dysmorphic disorder, people are preoccupied with an imagined or exaggerated defect in their physical appearance.

What is somatization disorder? Somatization disorder involves multiple and recurrent complaints of physical symptoms that have persisted for many years and that cannot be accounted for by organic causes.

How are somatoform disorders conceptualized within the major theoretical perspectives? The psychodynamic view holds that conversion disorders represent the conversion into physical symptoms of the leftover emotion or energy cut off from unacceptable or threatening impulses that the ego has prevented from reaching awareness. The symptom is functional, allowing the person to achieve both primary gains and secondary gains. Learning theorists focus on reinforcements that are associated with conversion disorders, such as the reinforcing effects of adopting a "sick role." One learning theory model likens hypochondriasis to obsessive-compulsive behavior. Cognitive factors in hypochondriasis include possible self-handicapping strategies and cognitive distortions.

What are the major approaches to treating somatoform disorders? Psychodynamic therapists attempt to uncover and bring to the level of awareness the unconscious conflicts, originating in childhood, believed to be at the root of the problem. Once the conflict is uncovered and worked through, the symptoms should disappear because they are no longer needed as a partial solution to the underlying conflict. Behavioral approaches focus on removing underlying sources of reinforcement that may be maintaining the abnormal behavior pattern. More generally, behavior therapists assist people with somatoform disorders to learn to handle stressful or anxiety-arousing situations more effectively. In addition, a combination of cognitive-behavioral techniques, such as exposure with response prevention and cognitive restructuring, may be used in treating hypochondriasis and body dysmorphic disorder.

CHAPTER EIGHT

Mood Disorders and Suicide

Alexej von Jawlensky
Evening, 1929

Truth OR Fiction?

- Feeling sad or depressed is abnormal. (p. 223)

- Most people who experience a major depressive episode never have another one. (p. 226)

- The bleak light of winter casts some people into a diagnosable state of depression. (p. 228)

- For no apparent cause, some people experience dramatic mood swings from the depths of depression to the heights of elation. (p. 231)

- In some ways, many "mentally healthy" people see things *less* realistically than people who are depressed. (p. 243)

- The most widely used remedy for depression in Germany is not a drug, but an herb. (p. 254)

- The ancient Greeks and Romans used a chemical to curb turbulent mood swings that is still used today. (p. 254)

- People who threaten suicide are basically attention-seekers. (p. 259)

Life has its ups and downs. Most of us feel elated when we have earned high grades, a promotion, or the affections of Ms. or Mr. Right. Most of us feel down or depressed when we are rejected by a date, flunk a test, or suffer financial reverses. It is normal and appropriate to be happy about uplifting events. It is just as normal, just as appropriate, to feel depressed by dismal events. It might very well be "abnormal" if we were *not* depressed by life's miseries.

Moods are enduring states of feeling that color our psychological lives. Feeling down or depressed is not abnormal in the context of depressing events or circumstances. But people with **mood disorders** experience disturbances in mood that are unusually severe or prolonged and impair their ability to function in meeting their normal responsibilities. In any given year, about 7% of Americans suffer from mood disorders (USDHHS, 1999a). Some people become severely depressed even when things appear to be going well, or when they encounter mildly upsetting events that others take in stride. Still others experience extreme mood swings. They ride an emotional roller coaster with dizzying heights and abysmal depths when the world around them remains largely on an even keel.

Types of Mood Disorders

In this chapter we focus on several kinds of mood disorders, including two kinds of depressive disorders, major depressive disorder and dysthymic disorder, and two kinds of mood swing disorders, bipolar disorder and cyclothymic disorder (see Table 8.1). Table 8.2 lists some of the common features of depression. The depressive disorders are considered

---

TABLE 8.1 Types of Mood Disorders

Depressive Disorders (Unipolar Disorders)

Major Depressive Disorder	Occurrence of one or more periods or episodes of depression (called major depressive episodes) without a history of naturally occurring manic or hypomanic episodes. People may have one major depressive episode, followed by a return to their usual state of functioning. The majority of people with a major depressive episode have recurrences that are separated by periods of normal or perhaps somewhat impaired functioning.
Dysthymic Disorder	A pattern of mild depression (but perhaps an irritable mood in children or adolescents) that occurs for an extended period of time—in adults, typically for many years.

Mood Swing Disorders (Bipolar Disorders)

Bipolar Disorder	Disorders with one or more manic or hypomanic episodes (episodes of inflated mood and hyperactivity in which judgment and behavior are often impaired). Manic or hypomanic episodes often alternate with major depressive episodes with intervening periods of normal mood.
Cyclothymic Disorder	A chronic mood disturbance involving numerous hypomanic episodes (episodes with manic features of a lesser degree of severity than manic episodes) and numerous periods of depressed mood or loss of interest or pleasure in activities, but not of the severity to meet the criteria for a major depressive episode.

Source. Adapted from the *DSM-IV-TR* (APA, 2000).

Truth OR Fiction?   REVISITED

Feeling sad or depressed is abnormal.

FALSE. Feeling depressed is not abnormal in the context of depressing events or circumstances.

mood The pervasive quality of an individual's emotional experience.

mood disorder A type of disorder characterized by disturbances of mood.

TABLE 8.2 Common Features of Depression

Changes in Emotional States	Changes in mood (persistent periods of feeling down, depressed, sad or blue)
	Tearfulness or crying
	Increased irritability, jumpiness, or loss of temper
Changes in Motivation	Feeling unmotivated, or having difficulty getting going in the morning or even getting out of bed
	Reduced level of social participation or interest in social activities
	Loss of enjoyment or interest in pleasurable activities
	Reduced interest in sex
	Failure to respond to praise or rewards
Changes in Functioning and Motor Behavior	Moving about or talking more slowly than usual
	Changes in sleep habits (sleeping too much or too little, awakening earlier than usual and having trouble getting back to sleep in early morning hours—so-called early morning awakening)
	Changes in appetite (eating too much or too little)
	Changes in weight (gaining or losing weight)
	Functioning less effectively than usual at work or school
Cognitive Changes	Difficulty concentrating or thinking clearly
	Thinking negatively about oneself and one's future
	Feeling guilty or remorseful about past misdeeds
	Lack of self-esteem or feelings of inadequacy
	Thinking of death or suicide

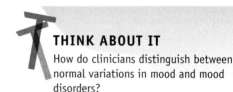

THINK ABOUT IT

How do clinicians distinguish between normal variations in mood and mood disorders?

unipolar Pertaining to a single pole, or direction.

bipolar Characterized by opposite ends of a dimension or continuum, as in bipolar disorder.

major depressive disorder A severe mood disorder characterized by major depressive episodes.

manic Relating to mania, as in the manic phase of bipolar disorder.

hypomanic Referring to a mild state of mania, or elation.

unipolar because the disturbance lies in only one emotional direction or pole—down. Disorders that involve mood swings are **bipolar.** They involve excesses of both depression and elation, usually in an alternating pattern.

Many of us, probably most of us, have periods of sadness from time to time. We may feel down in the dumps, cry, lose interest in things, find it hard to concentrate, expect the worst to happen, or even consider suicide. A survey of a sample of college students at the University of North Iowa showed that about 30% of the students reported feeling at least mildly depressed (Wong & Whitaker, 1993). Downcast mood was greater among freshman than among seniors or graduate students, which may reflect the difficulties that many freshmen have adjusting to college life

For most of us, mood changes pass quickly or are not severe enough to interfere with our lifestyle or ability to function. Among people with mood disorders, including depressive disorders and bipolar disorders, mood changes are more severe or prolonged and affect daily functioning.

Major Depressive Disorder

The diagnosis of **major depressive disorder** (also called *major depression*) is based on the occurrence of one or more *major depressive episodes* in the absence of a history of **manic** or **hypomanic** episodes. In a major depressive episode, the person experiences either a depressed mood (feeling sad, hopeless, or "down in the dumps") or loss of interest or pleasure in all or virtually all activities for a period of at least 2 weeks (APA, 2000). The diagnostic features of a major depressive episode are listed in Table 8.3.

People with major depressive disorder may also have poor appetite, lose or gain substantial amounts of weight, have trouble sleeping or sleep too much, and become physically agitated or—at the other extreme—show a marked slowing down in their motor activity. Major depression impairs people's ability to meet the ordinary responsibility of everyday life (Judd et al., 2000a). People with major depression may lose interest in most of their usual activities and pursuits, have difficulty concentrating and making decisions, have pressing thoughts of death, and attempt suicide. Although depression is a diagnosable psychological disorder, more than 40% of Americans polled in recent surveys perceive it to be a sign of personal weakness (Brody, 1992c). Many people don't seem to understand that people who are clinically depressed can't simply "shake it off" or "snap out of it." This attitude may explain why, despite the availability of safe and effective treatments, most people who are clinically depressed remain undiagnosed and untreated or fail to receive appropriate treatment (Gilbert, 1997a; Hirschfeld et al., 1997). Many people with untreated depression believe they can handle the problem themselves (Blumenthal & Endicott, 1997). Even for those who receive treatment, most receive inadequate or inappropriate care (Hirschfeld et al., 1997; Young et al., 2001).

Major depressive disorder is the most common type of diagnosable mood disorder, with estimates of lifetime prevalence ranging from 10% to 25% for women and from 5% to 12% for men (APA, 2000). An estimated 120 million people worldwide suffer from depression (E. Olson, 2001). About 1 in 20 people in the United States can be diagnosed with major depression at any given time (Blazer et al., 1994). Depression is so common that it has been dubbed the "common cold" of psychological problems (Seligman, 1973). The costs of depression incurred by employers, especially lost workdays, are as great if not greater than the costs of major medical illnesses such as heart disease and diabetes (Druss, Rosenheck, & Sledge, 2000). On the other hand, effective treatment for depression leads not only to psychological improvement but also to more stable employment and increased income, as people are able to return to a more productive level of functioning (Wells et al., 2000).

Major depression, particularly in more severe episodes, may be accompanied by psychotic features, such as delusions that one's body is rotting from illness (Coryell et al., 1996). People with severe depression may also experience hallucinations, such as "hearing" the voices of others, or of demons, condemning them for perceived misdeeds.

When are changes in mood considered abnormal? Although changes in mood in response to the ups and downs of everyday life may be quite normal, persistent or severe changes in mood, or cycles of extreme elation and depression, may suggest the presence of a mood disorder.

TABLE 8.3   Diagnostic Features of a Major Depressive Episode

A major depressive episode is denoted by the occurrence of five or more of the following features or symptoms during a 2-week period, which represents a change from previous functioning. At least one of the features must involve either (1) depressed mood, or (2) loss of interest or pleasure in activities. Moreover, the symptoms must cause either clinically significant levels of distress or impairment in at least one important area of functioning, such as social or occupational functioning, and must not be due directly to the use of drugs or medications, to a medical condition, or be accounted for by another psychological disorder.* Further, the episode must not represent a normal grief reaction to the death of a loved one—that is, **bereavement**.

1. Depressed mood during most of the day, nearly every day. Can be irritable mood in children or adolescents.

2. Greatly reduced sense of pleasure or interest in all or almost all activities, nearly every day for most of the day.

3. A significant loss or gain of weight (more than 5% of body weight in a month) without any attempt to diet, or an increase or decrease in appetite.

4. Daily (or nearly daily) insomnia or hypersomnia (oversleeping).

5. Excessive agitation or slowing down of movement responses nearly every day.

6. Feelings of fatigue or loss of energy nearly every day.

7. Feelings of worthlessness or misplaced or excessive or inappropriate guilt nearly every day.

8. Reduced ability to concentrate or think clearly or make decisions nearly every day.

9. Recurrent thoughts of death or suicide without a specific plan, or occurrence of a suicidal attempt or specific plan for committing suicide.

*The *DSM* includes separate diagnostic categories for mood disorders due to medical conditions or use of substances such as drugs of abuse.
Source. Adapted from the *DSM-IV-TR* (APA, 2000).

---

bereavement The experience of grief suffering following the death of a loved one.

The following case illustrates the range of features connected with major depressive disorder:

A Case of Major Depressive Disorder

A 38-year-old female clerical worker has suffered from recurrent bouts of depression since she was about 13 years of age. Most recently, she has been troubled by crying spells at work, sometimes occurring so suddenly she wouldn't have enough time to run to the ladies room to hide her tears from others. She has difficulty concentrating at work and feels a lack of enjoyment from work she used to enjoy. She harbors severe pessimistic and angry feelings, which have been more severe lately since she has been recently putting on weight and has been neglectful in taking care of her diabetes. She feels guilty that she may be slowly killing herself by not taking better care of her health. She sometimes feels that she deserves to be dead. She has been bothered by excessive sleepiness for the past year and a half, and her driving license has been suspended due to an incident the previous month in which she fell asleep while driving, causing her car to hit a telephone pole. She wakes up most days feeling groggy and just "out of it," and remains sleepy throughout the day. She has never had a steady boyfriend, and lives quietly at home with her mother, with no close friends outside of her family. During the interview, she cried frequently and answered questions in a low monotone, staring downward continuously.

—*Adapted from Spitzer et al., 1989, pp. 59–62*

Major depressive episodes may remit in a matter of months or last for a year or more (APA, 2000; USDHHS, 1999a). Some people experience a single episode with a full return to previous levels of functioning. However, the great majority of people with major depression, perhaps as many as 85%, have repeated occurrences (Mueller et al., 1999). The average person with major depression can expect to have four episodes during his or her lifetime (Judd, 1997). Relapses tend to be more frequent in people who continue to have some leftover depressive symptoms following a first depressive episode (Judd et al., 2000b). Given a pattern of repeated occurrences of major depressive episodes and prolonged symptomatology, many professionals have come to view major depression as a chronic, indeed lifelong disorder. On the positive side, the longer the period of recovery from major depression, the lower the risk of eventual relapse (Solomon et al., 2000).

Risk Factors in Major Depression Factors that place people at increased risk of developing major depression include age (initial onset is more common among younger adults than older adults); socioeconomic status (people lower down the socioeconomic ladder are at greater risk than those who are better off); and marital status (people who are separated or divorced have higher rates than married or never-married people).

Women are nearly twice as likely as men to develop major depression (APA, 2000; Blazer et al., 1994; Kessler et al., 1994) (see Figure 8.1). The difference in relative risk between males and females begins in early adolescence and persists through at least the mid-50s (Barefoot et al., 2001; Kessler et al., 1993). Although hormonal or other biologically linked gender differences may be involved, a panel convened by the American Psychological Association (APA) attributed the gender difference largely to the greater amount of stress that women encounter in contemporary life (Goleman, 1990b; McGrath et al., 1990). The panel concluded that women are more likely than men to encounter such stressful life factors as physical and sexual abuse, poverty, single parenthood, and sexism. Despite the gender difference in prevalence, the course of major depression is similar for both genders: Men and women with the disorder do not differ significantly in the likelihood of having recurrences, the frequency of recurrences, the severity or duration of recurrences, or the time to first recurrence (Eaton et al., 1997).

Major depression versus bereavement.
Major depression is distinguished from a normal grief reaction to the death of a loved one, which is termed bereavement. Major depression may occur in people whose bereavement becomes prolonged or seriously interferes with normal functioning.

Differences in coping styles may also help explain women's greater proneness toward depression. Regardless of whether the factors that precipitate depression are biological, psychological, or social, one's coping responses may exacerbate or reduce the severity and duration of depressive episodes. Nolen-Hoeksema and her colleagues (1991; Nolen-Hoeksema, Morrow, & Fredrickson, 1993) propose that men are more likely to distract themselves when they are depressed, whereas women are more likely to amplify depression by ruminating about their feelings and their possible causes. Women may be more likely to sit at home when they are depressed and think about how they feel or try to understand the reasons they feel the way they do, whereas men may try to distract themselves by doing something they enjoy, such as going to a favorite hangout to get their mind off their feelings. On the other hand, men often turn to alcohol as a form of self-medication, which can lead to another set of psychological and social problems (Nolen-Hoeksema et al., 1993). Rumination is not limited to women, however. Both men and women who ruminate more following the loss of loved ones or when feeling down or sad are more likely to become depressed and to suffer longer and more severe depression than those who ruminate less (Just & Alloy, 1997; Nolen-Hoeksema, 2000).

Although the gender gap in depression continues, it appears to be narrowing as more men are coming forward seeking help for depression. The male ego also seems to be battered by assaults from corporate downsizing and growing financial insecurity. Although long viewed by men as a sign of personal weakness, the stigma associated with depression shows signs of lessening, although not disappearing (*NBC Nightly News*, 1996).

Major depression typically develops in young adulthood, with an average age of onset in the mid-20s (APA, 2000). However, the disorder may affect even young children, although the risks are very low through age 14 (Lewinsohn et al., 1986). A multinational study of nine countries[1] showed that the rates of major depression have been rising in the United States and elsewhere (Cross-National Collaborative Group, 1992). In some countries, young people born after 1955 stood about three times greater likelihood of suffering a major depression than did their grandparents when they were the same age (Goleman, 1992b). The greatest increases were found in Florence, Italy; the least in Christchurch, New Zealand. In all countries, rates for depression were higher among women than men.

No one knows why depression has been on the rise in many cultures, but speculation focuses on social and environmental changes, such as increasing fragmentation of families due to relocations, exposure to wars and internal conflicts, and increased rates of violent crimes, as well as possible exposure to toxins or infectious agents in the environment that might affect mental as well as physical health (Cross-National Collaborative Group, 1992). One example is the dramatic increase in depression that occurred in the period 1950 to 1960 in Beirut, Lebanon. This was a period of chaotic political and demographic changes in the country. Depression dropped sharply in the following period, 1960 to 1970, a time of relative prosperity and stability in the country, but increased again between 1970 and 1980 during a time of social upheaval and internal warfare.

Seasonal Affective Disorder Are you glum on gloomy days? Is your temper short during the brief days of winter? Are you dismal during the dark of long winter nights? Are you feeling up when the long sunny days of spring and summer return?

Many people report that their moods do vary with the weather. For some people, the changing of the seasons from summer into fall and winter leads to a type of depression called *seasonal affective (mood) disorder*—SAD.[2] The features of SAD include fatigue, excessive sleep,

FIGURE 8.1 Prevalence of major depressive episodes by gender.
Major depressive episodes affect about twice as many women as men.

Source. Kessler et al. (1994) National Comorbidity Survey (Kessler et al., 1994).

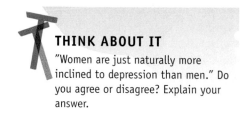

VIDEO 8.1
Depression: *The Case of Helen*

THINK ABOUT IT
"Women are just naturally more inclined to depression than men." Do you agree or disagree? Explain your answer.

Web Link 8.1
Facts About Depression

---

[1]United States, Canada, Puerto Rico, Italy, France, Germany, Lebanon, Taiwan, and New Zealand

[2]Seasonal affective disorder is not classified as a diagnostic category in its own right in the *DSM-IV* but is designated as a specifier of mood disorders in which major depressive episodes occur. For example, major depressive disorder that occurs seasonally would be given a diagnosis of major depressive disorder with seasonal pattern.

postpartum depression (PPD) Persistent and severe mood changes that occur after childbirth.

Light therapy. Exposure to bright artificial light for a few hours a day during the fall and winter months can often bring relief from seasonal affective disorder.

Truth OR Fiction?   REVISITED

The bleak light of winter casts some people into a diagnosable state of depression.

TRUE. The changing of the seasons does lead to a depressive disorder in some people.

Women and depression. Women are more likely to suffer from major depression than men. A panel convened by the APA attributed the higher rates of depression among women to factors such as unhappy marriages, physical and sexual abuse, impoverishment, single parenthood, sexism, hormonal changes, childbirth, and excessive caregiving burdens. APA panel member Bonnie Strickland expressed surprise that even more women were not clinically depressed, since they are treated as second-class citizens.

craving for carbohydrates, and weight gain. SAD tends to lift with the early buds of spring. It affects women more often than men and is most common among young adults.

Although the causes of SAD remain unknown, one possibility is that seasonal changes in light may alter the body's underlying biological rhythms that regulate such processes as body temperature and sleep-wake cycles (Lee et al., 1998). Another possibility is that some parts of the central nervous system may have deficiencies in transmission of the mood-regulating neurotransmitter serotonin during the winter months (Schwartz et al., 1997). Whatever the underlying cause, a trial of intense light therapy, called *phototherapy*, often helps relieve depression. Phototherapy typically consists of exposure to several hours of bright artificial light a day (e.g., Terman et al., 2001). The artificial light apparently supplements the meager sunlight the person otherwise receives. Patients can generally carry out some of their daily activities (for example, eating, reading, writing) during their phototherapy sessions. Improvement typically occurs within several days of phototherapy, but treatment is apparently required throughout the course of the winter season. Light directed at the eyes tends to be more successful than light directed at the skin (Sato, 1997).

Postpartum Depression Many, perhaps even most, new mothers experience mood changes, periods of tearfulness, and irritability following the birth of a child. These mood changes are commonly called the "maternity blues," "postpartum blues," or "baby blues." They usually last for a couple of days and are believed to be a normal response to hormonal changes that attend childbirth. Given these turbulent hormonal shifts, it would be "abnormal" for most women *not* to experience some changes in feeling states shortly following childbirth.

Some mothers, however, undergo severe mood changes that may persist for months or even a year or more. These problems in mood are referred to as **postpartum depression (PPD)**. *Postpartum* derives from the Latin roots *post*, meaning "after," and *papere*, meaning "to bring forth." PPD is often accompanied by disturbances in appetite and sleep, low self-esteem, and difficulties in maintaining concentration or attention. Between 8% and 15% of mothers experience a diagnosable postpartum depressive disorder of at least moderate severity (Campbell & Cohn, 1991; Gitlin & Pasnau, 1989). Postpartum depression is not unique to the United States; evidence from a study in an urban area in Portugal reported a similar prevalence rate (13%) (Augusto et al., 1996).

Questionnaire

Are You Depressed?

 This test, offered by the organizers of the National Depression Screening Day, can help you assess whether you are suffering from a depression. It is not intended for you to diagnose yourself, but rather to raise your awareness of concerns you may want to discuss with a professional.

	YES	NO
1. I feel downhearted, blue, and sad.	___	___
2. I don't enjoy the things that I used to.	___	___
3. I feel that others would be better off if I were dead.	___	___
4. I feel that I am not useful or needed.	___	___
5. I notice that I am losing weight.	___	___
6. I have trouble sleeping through the night.	___	___

	YES	NO
7. I am restless and can't keep still.	___	___
8. My mind isn't as clear as it used to be.	___	___
9. I get tired for no reason.	___	___
10. I feel hopeless about the future.	___	___

Rating your responses: If you agree with at least five of the statements, including either item 1 or 2, and if you have had these complaints for at least 2 weeks, professional help is strongly recommended. If you answered "yes" to statement 3, seek consultation with a professional immediately. If you don't know whom to turn to, contact your college counseling center, neighborhood mental health center, or health provider.

Source. Adapted from J. E. Brody, "Myriad masks hide an epidemic of depression," *The New York Times,* September 30, 1992, p. C12.

Postpartum depression is considered a form of major depression in which the onset of the depressive episode begins within 4 weeks after childbirth (APA, 2000). Investigators find that postpartum depression typically is less severe than other forms of major depression and lifts relatively sooner than most (Whiffen & Gotlib, 1993). Yet some suicides are linked to postpartum depression (McQuiston, 1997). Although PPD may involve chemical or hormonal imbalances brought on by childbirth, factors associated with an increased risk include stress, single or first-time motherhood, financial problems, a troubled marriage, social isolation, lack of support from partners and family members, a history of depression, or having an unwanted, sick, or temperamentally difficult infant (Forman et al., 2000; Ritter et al., 2000; Swendsen & Mazure, 2000). Having PPD also increases the risk that the woman will suffer future depressive episodes (Philipps & O'Hara, 1991).

Postpartum depression is not limited to our culture. Recent reports find high rates of PPD among South African women (Cooper et al., 1999) and Chinese women from Hong Kong (D. T. S. Lee et al., 2001). In the South African sample, a lack of psychological and financial support from the baby's father was associated with an increased risk of the disorder in this sample, mirroring findings with U.S. samples.

Dysthymic Disorder

Major depressive disorder is severe and marked by a relatively abrupt change from one's preexisting state. A milder form of depression seems to follow a chronic course of development that often begins in childhood or adolescence (Klein et al., 2000a, 2000b). Earlier diagnostic formulations of this type of chronic sadness were labeled "depressive neurosis" or "depressive personality" (Brody, 1995a). It was so labeled in an effort to account for several features that are traditionally connected with neurosis, such as early childhood origins, a chronic course, and generally mild levels of severity. The *DSM* labels this form of depression **dysthymic disorder,** or *dysthymia,* which derives from Greek roots *dys-,* meaning "bad" or "hard" and *thymos,* meaning "spirit."

Persons with dysthymic disorder do feel "bad spirited" or "down in the dumps" most of the time, but they are not so severely depressed as those with major depressive disorder. Whereas major depressive disorder tends to be severe and time limited, dysthymic disorder

wWw   **Web Link 8.2**
Facts About Dysthymic Disorder

dysthymic disorder A mild but chronic type of depressive disorder.

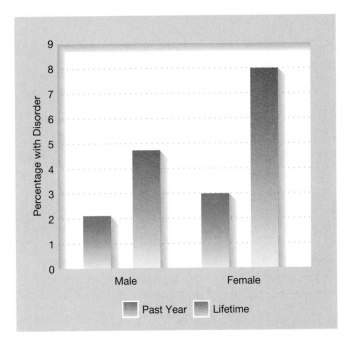

FIGURE 8.2 Prevalence of dysthymic disorder by gender.
Like major depression, dysthymic disorder occurs in about twice as many women as men.

Source. Kessler et al. (1994) National Comorbidity Survey (Kessler et al., 1994).

is relatively mild and nagging, typically lasting for years (Klein et al., 2000b). Feelings of depression and social difficulties continue even after the person makes an apparent recovery (USDHHS, 1999a). The risk of relapse is also quite high (Klein et al., 2000a).

Dysthymia affects about 6% of the general population at some point in their lifetimes (APA, 2000). Like major depressive disorder, dysthymic disorder is more common in women than men (see Figure 8.2).

In dysthymic disorder, complaints of depression may become such a fixture of people's lives that they seem to be intertwined with their personality structures. The persistence of complaints may lead others to perceive them as whining and complaining (Akiskal, 1983). Although dysthymic disorder is less severe than major depressive disorder, persistent depressed mood and low self-esteem can affect the person's occupational and social functioning, as we see in the following case:

A Case of Dysthymic Disorder

The woman, a 28-year-old junior executive, complained of chronic feelings of depression since the age of 16 or 17. Despite doing well in college, she brooded about how other people were "genuinely intelligent." She felt she could never pursue a man she might be interested in dating because she felt inferior and intimidated. While she had extensive therapy through college and graduate school, she could never recall a time during those years when she did not feel somewhat depressed. She got married shortly after college graduation to the man she was dating at the time, although she didn't think that he was anything "special." She just felt she needed to have a husband for companionship and he was available. But they soon began to quarrel and she's lately begun to feel that marrying him was a mistake. She has had difficulties at work, turning in "slipshod" work and never seeking anything more than what was basically required of her and showing little initiative. While she dreams of acquiring status and money, she doesn't expect that she or her husband will rise in their professions because they lack "connections." Her social life is dominated by her husband's friends and their spouses and she doesn't think that other women would find her interesting or impressive. She lacks interest in life in general and expresses dissatisfaction with all facets of her life—her marriage, her job, her social life.

—Adapted from Spitzer et al., 1994, pp. 110–112

Some people are affected by both dysthymic disorder and major depression at the same time. The term **double depression** applies to those who have a major depressive episode superimposed upon a longer-standing dysthymic disorder (Keller, Hirschfeld, & Hanks, 1997). People suffering from double depression generally have more severe depressive episodes than do people with major depression alone (Klein et al., 2000b). Recent evidence suggests that virtually all people with dysthymia eventually develop double depression (Klein et al., 2000a).

We have noted that major depressive disorder and dysthymic disorder are depressive disorders in the sense that the disturbance of mood is only in one direction—down. Yet people with mood disorders may have fluctuations in mood in both directions that exceed the usual ups and downs of everyday life. These types of disorders are called bipolar disorders. Here we focus on the two types of these mood-swing disorders: (1) bipolar disorder, and (2) cyclothymic disorder.

double depression A diagnosis of both major depressive disorder and dysthymic disorder.

Bipolar Disorder

People with **bipolar disorder** ride an emotional roller coaster, swinging from the heights of elation to the depths of depression without external cause. The first episode may be either manic or depressive. Manic episodes, typically lasting from a few weeks to several months, are generally shorter in duration and end more abruptly than major depressive episodes. Some people with recurring bipolar disorder attempt suicide "on the way down" from the manic phase. They report that they would do nearly anything to escape the depths of depression they know lie ahead.

The *DSM* distinguishes between two general types of bipolar disorder, *bipolar I disorder* and *bipolar II disorder* (APA, 2000). In bipolar I disorder, the person experiences at least one full manic episode. In many cases, the person experiences mood swings between elation and depression with intervening periods of normal mood. Some cases present with no evidence of major depressive episodes, but it is assumed that such episodes may either develop in the future or have been overlooked in the past. In a few cases, called the mixed type, both a manic episode and a major depressive episode occur simultaneously.

Bipolar II disorder is associated with a milder form of mania. In bipolar II disorder, the person has experienced one or more major depressive episodes and at least one hypomanic episode. But the person has never had a full-blown manic episode. Whether bipolar I and bipolar II disorders represent qualitatively different disorders or different points along a continuum of severity of bipolar disorder remains to be determined.

Bipolar disorder is relatively uncommon, with reported lifetime prevalence rates from community surveys ranging from 0.4% to 1.6% for bipolar I disorder and about 0.5% for bipolar II disorder (APA, 2000; USDHHS, 1999a). Bipolar disorder typically develops around age 20 in both men and women. Only about 1 in 3 people with bipolar disorder receive any treatment (Goleman, 1994c). Sadly, about 1 in 5 of the people who go untreated eventually commit suicide (Hilts, 1994).

Unlike major depression, rates of bipolar I disorder appear about equal in men and women. In men, however, the onset of bipolar I disorder typically begins with a manic episode, whereas with women, it usually begins with a major depressive episode. The underlying reason for this gender difference remains unknown. Bipolar II disorder appears to be more common in women (APA, 2000).

Sometimes cases involve periods of "rapid cycling" in which the individual experiences two or more full cycles of mania and depression within a year without any intervening normal periods. Rapid cycling is relatively uncommon, but occurs more often among women than men (Leibenluft, 1996). It is usually limited to a year or less, but is associated with poorer social and job functioning (Coryell, Endicott, & Keller, 1992b) and a higher rate of relapse (Keller et al., 1993).

Manic Episode

Manic episodes, or periods of mania, typically begin abruptly, gathering force within days. During a manic episode, the person experiences a sudden elevation or expansion of mood and feels unusually cheerful, euphoric, or optimistic. The person seems to have boundless energy and is extremely sociable, although perhaps to the point of becoming overly demanding and overbearing toward others. Other people recognize the sudden shift in mood to be excessive in the light of the person's circumstances. It is one thing to feel elated if one has just won the state lottery. It is another to feel euphoric because it's Wednesday.

People in a manic episode or phase are excited and may strike others as silly, by carrying jokes too far, for example. They tend to show poor judgment and to become argumentative, sometimes going so far as destroying property. Roommates may find them abrasive and avoid them. They tend to speak very rapidly (with **pressured speech**). Their thoughts and speech may jump from topic to topic (in a **rapid flight of ideas**). Others find it difficult to get a word in edgewise. They may also become extremely generous and make large charitable contributions they can ill afford or give away costly possessions. They may not be able to sit still or sleep restfully. They almost always show decreased need for sleep. They tend to awaken early yet feel well rested and

bipolar disorder A disorder characterized by mood swings between states of extreme elation and severe depression.

manic episode A period of unrealistically heightened euphoria, extreme restlessness, and excessive activity characterized by disorganized behavior and impaired judgment.

pressured speech An outpouring of speech in which words seem to surge urgently for expression.

rapid flight of ideas A characteristic of manic behavior involving rapid speech and changes of topics.

Truth OR Fiction? REVISITED

For no apparent cause, some people experience dramatic mood swings from the depths of depression to the heights of elation.

TRUE. Some people with bipolar disorder do ride an emotional roller coaster between periods of extreme elation and periods of extreme depression, without external cause.

Patty Duke The actress Patty Duke, who won an academy award for her performance as Helen Keller in the movie *The Miracle Worker*, was diagnosed with bipolar disorder as a young adult.

full of energy. They sometimes go for days without sleep and without feeling tired. Although they may have abundant stores of energy, they seem unable to organize their efforts constructively. Their elation impairs their ability to work and to maintain normal relationships.

Curiously, many observers have noted connections between mood disorders and creativity (Jamison, 1993; McDermott, 2001; Richards, 1994). Many distinguished writers, artists, and composers seemed to have suffered from mood disorders, especially bipolar disorder, including such luminaries as the artists Michelangelo and Vincent Van Gogh, the composers William Schumann and Peter Tchaikovsky, the novelists Virginia Woolf and Ernest Hemingway, and the poets Alfred Lord Tennyson, Emily Dickinson, Walt Whitman, and Sylvia Plath. Perhaps some creative people are able to channel the seemingly boundless energy and rapid stream of thoughts associated with manic periods to enhance their productivity and ability to express themselves in novel ways.

People in a manic episode generally experience an inflated sense of self-esteem that may range from extreme self-confidence to wholesale delusions of grandeur. They may feel capable of solving the world's problems or of composing symphonies, despite a lack of any special knowledge or talent. They may spout off about matters on which they know little, such as how to eliminate world hunger or create a new world order. It soon becomes clear that they are disorganized and incapable of completing their projects. They become highly distractible. Their attention is easily diverted by irrelevant stimuli like the sounds of a ticking clock or of people talking in the next room. They tend to take on multiple tasks, more than they can handle. They may suddenly quit their jobs to enroll in law school, wait tables at night, organize charity drives on weekends, and work on the great American novel in their "spare time." They tend to exercise poor judgment and fail to weigh the consequences of their actions. They may get into trouble as a result of lavish spending, reckless driving, or sexual escapades. In severe cases, they may experience disorders of thinking similar to those of people with schizophrenia. They may experience hallucinations or become grossly delusional, believing, for example, that they have a special relationship with God.

The following case provides a firsthand account of a manic episode. The early stages are dominated by euphoria, boundless energy, and an inflated sense of self. As mania intensifies, the individual may become confused:

Web Link **8.3**
National Depressive
and Manic-Depressive
Association wWw

VIDEO **8.2**
Bipolar Disorder: *The Case of Craig*

A Case of Bipolar Disorder

When I start going into a high, I no longer feel like an ordinary housewife. Instead I feel organized and accomplished and I begin to feel I am my most creative self. I can write poetry easily. I can compose melodies without effort. I can paint. My mind feels facile and absorbs everything. I have countless ideas about improving the conditions of mentally retarded children, of how a hospital for these children should be run, what they should have around them to keep them happy and calm and unafraid. I see myself as being able to accomplish a great deal for the good of people. I have countless ideas about how the environment problem could inspire a crusade for the health and betterment of everyone. I feel able to accomplish a great deal for the good of my family and others. I feel pleasure, a sense of euphoria or elation. I want it to last forever. I don't seem to need much sleep. I've lost weight and feel healthy and I like myself. I've just bought six new dresses, in fact, and they look quite good on me. I feel sexy and men stare at me. Maybe I'll have an affair, or perhaps several. I feel capable of speaking and doing good in politics. I would like to help people with problems similar to mine so they won't feel hopeless.

It's wonderful when you feel like this. . . . The feeling of exhilaration—the high mood—makes me feel light and full of the joy of living. However, when I go beyond this stage, I become manic, and the creativeness becomes so magnified I begin to see things in my mind that aren't real. For instance, one night I created an entire movie, complete with cast, that I still think would be terrific. I saw the people as clearly as if watching them in real life. I also experienced complete terror, as if it were actually happening, when I knew that an assassination scene was about to take place. I cowered under the covers and became a complete shaking wreck. As you know, I went into a manic psychosis at that point. My screams awakened my husband, who tried to reassure me that we were in our bedroom and everything was the same. There was nothing to be afraid of. Nevertheless, I was admitted to the hospital the next day.

—From Fieve, 1975, pp. 12–18

Cyclothymic Disorder

Cyclothymia is derived from the Greek *kyklos*, which means "circle," and *thymos* ("spirit"). The notion of a circular-moving spirit is an apt description because this disorder involves a chronic cyclical pattern of mood disturbance characterized by mild mood swings of at least 2 years (1 year for children and adolescents). **Cyclothymic disorder** usually begins in late adolescence or early adulthood and persists for years. Few, if any, periods of normal mood last for more than a month or two. Neither the periods of elevated or depressed mood are severe enough to warrant a diagnosis of bipolar disorder, however. Estimates from community studies indicate lifetime prevalence rates for cyclothymic disorder of between 0.4% to 1% (4 to 10 people in 1,000), with men and women about equally likely to be affected (APA, 2000).

The periods of elevated mood are called hypomanic episodes, from the Greek prefix *hypo-*, meaning "under" or "less than." *Hypo*manic episodes are less severe than manic episodes and are not accompanied by the severe social or occupational problems associated with full-blown manic episodes. During hypomanic episodes, people may have an inflated sense of self-esteem, feel unusually charged with energy and alert, and may be more restless and irritable than usual. They may be able to work long hours with little fatigue or need for sleep. Their projects may be left unfinished when their moods reverse, however. Then they enter a mildly depressed mood state and find it difficult to summon the energy or interest to persevere. They feel lethargic and depressed, but not to the extent typical of a major depressive episode.

Social relationships may become strained by shifting moods, and work may suffer. Social invitations, eagerly sought during hypomanic periods, may be declined during depressed periods. Phone calls may not be returned as the mood slumps. Sexual interest waxes and wanes with the person's moods.

The boundaries between bipolar disorder and cyclothymic disorder are not yet clearly established. Some forms of cyclothymic disorder may represent a mild, early type of bipolar disorder. Approximately 33% of people with cyclothymic disorder eventually develop bipolar disorder, a figure that is about 33 times higher than the general population (USDHHS, 1999a). We presently lack the ability to distinguish persons with cyclothymia who are likely to eventually develop bipolar disorder (Howland & Thase, 1993). The following case presents an example of the mild mood swings that typify cyclothymic disorder:

A Case of Cyclothymic Disorder

The man, a 29-year-old car salesman, reports that since the age of 14 he has experienced alternating periods of "good times and bad times." During his "bad" periods, which generally last between 4 and 7 days, he sleeps excessively and feels a lack of confidence, energy, and motivation, as if he were "just vegetating." Then his moods abruptly shift for a period of three or four days, usually upon awakening in the morning, and he feels

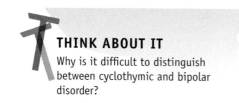

THINK ABOUT IT

Why is it difficult to distinguish between cyclothymic and bipolar disorder?

cyclothymic disorder A mood disorder characterized by a chronic pattern of mild mood swings that is not sufficiently severe to be classified as bipolar disorder.

aflush with confidence and sharpened mental ability. During these "good periods" he engages in promiscuous sex and uses alcohol, in part to enhance his good feelings and in part to help him sleep at night. The good periods may last upwards of 7–10 days at times, before shifting back into the "bad" periods, generally following a hostile or irritable outburst.

—Adapted from Spitzer et al., 1994, pp. 155–157

Quiz **8.1**
Types of Mood Disorders Q

Theoretical Perspectives on Mood Disorders

Mood disorders involve a complex interaction of biological and psychosocial influences (Cui & Vaillant, 1997). Though a full understanding of the causes of mood disorders presently lies beyond our grasp, we have begun to identify many of the important contributors to mood disorders, and in particular depression, the type of mood disorder studied most extensively by investigators. Here we begin with relationships between stress and the mood disorders and then consider the psychological and biological perspectives on mood disorders.

Stress and Mood Disorders

Stressful life events such as the loss of a loved one, the breakup of a romantic relationship, prolonged unemployment, physical illness, marital or relationship problems, economic hardship, pressure at work, or racism and discrimination increase the risks of developing a mood disorder or experiencing a recurrence of a mood disorder, especially major depression (Greenberger et al., 2000; Kendler, Thornton, & Gardner, 2000; Monroe et al., 2001). In one research example, investigators found that in about four of five cases, major depression was preceded by stressful life events (Mazure, 1998). People are also more likely to become depressed when they hold themselves responsible for undesirable events, such as school problems, financial difficulties, unwanted pregnancy, interpersonal problems, and problems with the law (Hammen & de Mayo, 1982).

Yet the relationship between stress and depression may cut both ways: Stressful life events may contribute to depression, and depressive symptoms in themselves may be stressful or lead to additional sources of stress, such as divorce or loss of employment (Cui & Vaillant, 1997; Daley et al., 1997). When you're depressed, for example, you may find it more difficult to keep up with your work at school or on the job, which can lead to more stress as your work backs up. The closer the stressful event taps the person's core concerns (failing at work or school, for instance), the more likely it is to precipitate a relapse in people who have a history of depression (Segal et al., 1992). Traumatic stressful events may play important roles in the cycling of bipolar disorder, although perhaps not in the onset of the disorder (Hammen & Gitlin, 1997; Miklowitz & Alloy, 1999).

Though stress is often implicated in depression, not everyone who encounters stress becomes depressed. Factors such as coping skills, genetic endowment, and availability of social support contribute to the likelihood of depression in the face of stressful events (US-DHHS, 1999a). The development of depression may also be influenced by prior abuse or trauma. Consistent with the diathesis-stress model, researchers find that young women are more likely to develop depression in the face of stressful life events if they possessed a diathesis in the form of exposure to childhood adversities such as family violence or parental mental disorders or alcoholism (Hammen, Henry, & Daley, 2000). Moreover, physical or sexual abuse in childhood can disrupt the development of early attachment bonds to parents, setting the stage for later relationship problems and emotional disorders involving depression and anxiety (USDHHS, 1999a).

A strong marital relationship may provide a source of support during times of stress. Not surprisingly, people who are divorced or separated have higher rates of

Stress and depression. Depression is strongly associated with major stressors, such as prolonged unemployment and economic hardship. However, whether people consider themselves responsible for the hardship affects their likelihood of becoming depressed. In addition, it may be difficult to determine whether a person becomes depressed over losing a job or loses a job because of suffering from depression.

depression and suicide attempts than married people (Weissman et al., 1991). The availability of social support is also associated with quicker recoveries from episodes of both major depression and bipolar disorder (Johnson et al., 1999; Moos, Cronkite, & Moos, 1998).

People with major depression often lack skills needed to solve interpersonal problems with friends, coworkers, or supervisors (Marx, Williams, & Claridge, 1992). But those who take a more active approach to solving their interpersonal problems tend to have better clinical outcomes than depressed people who assume a more passive style of coping (Sherbourne, Hays, & Wells, 1995).

Psychodynamic Theories

The classic psychodynamic theory of depression of Freud (1917/1957) and his followers (e.g., Abraham, 1916/1948) holds that depression represents anger directed inward rather than against significant others. Anger may become directed against the self following either the actual or threatened loss of these important others.

Freud believed that **mourning,** or normal bereavement, is a healthy process by which one eventually comes to separate oneself psychologically from a person who is lost through death, separation, divorce, or other reason. Pathological mourning, however, does not promote healthy separation. Rather, it fosters lingering depression. Pathological mourning is likely to occur in people who hold powerful **ambivalent** feelings—a combination of positive (love) and negative (anger, hostility) feelings—toward the person who has departed or whose departure is feared. Freud theorized that when people lose, or even if they fear losing, an important figure about whom they feel ambivalent, their feelings of anger toward the other person turn to rage. Yet rage triggers guilt, which in turn prevents the person from venting anger directly at the lost person (called an "object").

mourning Normal feelings of grief following a loss.

ambivalent Holding conflicting feelings toward another person or a goal.

Social support as a buffer against depression. Social support appears to buffer the effects of stress and may reduce the risk of depression. People who lack important relationships and who rarely join in social activities are more likely to suffer from depression.

To preserve a psychological connection to the lost object, people *introject*, or bring inward, a mental representation of the object. They thus incorporate the other person into the self. Now anger is turned inward, against the part of the self that represents the inward representation of the lost person. This produces self-hatred, which in turn leads to depression.

From the psychodynamic viewpoint, bipolar disorder represents shifting dominance of the individual's personality between the ego and superego. In the depressive phase, the superego is dominant, producing exaggerated notions of wrongdoing and flooding the individual with feelings of guilt and worthlessness. After a time, the ego rebounds and asserts supremacy, producing feelings of elation and self-confidence that characterize the manic phase. The excessive display of ego eventually triggers a return of guilt, once again plunging the individual into depression.

While also emphasizing the importance of loss, more recent psychodynamic models focus more on issues relating to the individual's sense of self-worth or self-esteem. One model, called the *self-focusing model*, considers how people allocate their attentional processes after a loss (death of a loved one, a personal failure, etc.) (Pyszczynski & Greenberg, 1987). According to this model, depression-prone people experience a period of intense self-examination (self-focusing) following a major loss or disappointment. They become preoccupied with thoughts about the lost object (loved one) or important goal and remain unable to surrender hope of somehow regaining it.

Consider a person who must cope with the termination of a failed romantic relationship. It may be clear to all concerned that the relationship is beyond hope of revival. The self-focusing model proposes, however, that the depression-prone individual persists in focusing attention on restoring the relationship, rather than recognizing the futility of the effort and getting on with life. Moreover, the lost partner was a source of emotional support and someone upon whom the depression-prone individual had relied to maintain feelings of self-esteem. Following the loss, the depression-prone individual feels stripped of hope and optimism because these positive feelings had depended on the other person, now lost. The loss of self-esteem and feelings of security, not of the relationship per se, precipitates depression. If depression-prone people peg their self-worth to a specific occupational goal, such as success in a modeling career, failure triggers self-focusing and consequent depression. Only by surrendering the object or lost goal and fostering alternate sources of identity and self-worth can the cycle be broken.

Research Evidence Psychodynamic theorists focus on the role of loss in depression. Research does show that the losses of significant others (through death or divorce, for example) are often associated with the onset of depression (Paykel, 1982). Such losses may also lead to other psychological disorders, however. There is yet a lack of research to support Freud's view that repressed anger toward the departed loved one is turned inward in depression.

Research supporting the self-focusing model is mixed. On one hand, people who are depressed have been shown to engage in more self-focusing following failure experiences than do nondepressed people, and in relatively lower levels of self-focusing following successes (Pyszczynski & Greenberg, 1985, 1986). Also supporting the model is evidence from a laboratory study that diverting attention away from the self can reduce depressed affect in depressed subjects (Nix et al., 1995). On the other hand, self-focused attention is linked to disorders other than depression, including anxiety disorders, alcoholism, mania, and schizophrenia (Ingram, 1991). The general linkage between self-focused attention and psychopathology may limit the model's value as an explanation of depression.

Humanistic Theories

From the humanistic framework, people become depressed when they cannot imbue their existence with meaning and make authentic choices that lead to self-fulfillment. The world is then a drab place. People's search for meaning gives color and substance to their lives. Guilt may arise when people believe they have not lived up to their potentials. Humanistic psychologists challenge us to take a long hard look at our lives. Are they worthwhile and enriching? Or are they drab and routine? If the latter, it may be we have frustrated our needs for self-actualization. We may be settling, coasting through life. Settling can give rise to a sense of dreariness that becomes expressed in depressive behavior—lethargy, sullen mood, and withdrawal.

Like psychodynamic theorists, humanistic theorists also focus on the loss of self-esteem that can arise when people lose friends or family members, or suffer occupational setbacks or losses. We tend to connect our personal identity and sense of self-worth with our social roles as parents, spouses, students, or workers. When these role identities are lost, through the death of a spouse, the departure of children to college, or loss of a job, our sense of purpose and self-worth can be shattered. Depression is a frequent consequence of such losses. It is especially likely when we base our self-esteem on our occupational role or success. The loss of a job, a demotion, or a failure to achieve a promotion are common precipitants of depression, especially when we are reared to value ourselves on the basis of occupational success.

Learning Theories

Whereas the psychodynamic perspectives focus on inner, often unconscious, determinants of mood disorders, learning theorists dwell more on situational factors, such as the loss of positive reinforcement. We perform best when levels of reinforcement are commensurate with our efforts. Changes in the frequency or effectiveness of reinforcement can shift the balance so that life becomes unrewarding.

Reinforcement and Depression Learning theorist Peter Lewinsohn (1974) proposed that depression results from an imbalance between behavioral output and reinforcement input from the environment. A lack of reinforcement for one's efforts can sap motivation and induce feelings of depression. A vicious cycle may ensue: Inactivity and social withdrawal deplete opportunities for reinforcement; lesser reinforcement exacerbates withdrawal. The low rate of activity typical of depression may also be a source of secondary

What happens when we lose our sense of direction? According to the humanistic-existential perspective, depression may result from the inability to find meaning and purpose in one's life.

gain or secondary reinforcement. Family members and other people may rally around people suffering from depression and release them from their responsibilities. Rather than help people who are struggling with depression regain normal levels of productive behavior, sympathy may thus backfire and maintain depressed behavior.

Reduction in reinforcement levels can occur for many reasons. A person who is recuperating at home from a serious illness or injury may find little that is reinforcing to do. Social reinforcement may plummet when people close to us, who were suppliers of reinforcement, die or leave us. People who suffer social losses are more likely to become depressed when they lack the social skills to form new relationships. Some first-year college students are homesick and depressed because they lack the skills to form rewarding new relationships. Widows and widowers may be at a loss as to how to ask someone for a date or start a new relationship.

Changes in life circumstances may also alter the balance of effort and reinforcement. A prolonged layoff may reduce financial reinforcements, which may in turn force painful cutbacks in lifestyle. A disability or an extended illness may also impair one's ability to ensure a steady flow of reinforcements.

Lewinsohn's model is supported by research findings that connect depression to a low level of positive reinforcement. In early work, Lewinsohn and Libet (1972) noted a correspondence between depressed moods and lower rates of participation in potentially reinforcing activities. People with depressive disorders were also found to report fewer pleasant activities than nondepressed people (MacPhillamy & Lewinsohn, 1974). However, it is conceivable that depression precedes rather than follows a reduction in reinforcement (J. M. Williams, 1984). In other words, depression may lead people to withdraw from socially reinforcing activities. Regardless of the root causes of depression, a behavioral treatment approach that encourages depressed people to increase their levels of pleasant activities and provides them with the skills to do so is often helpful in alleviating depression (DeRubeis & Crits-Christoph, 1998; Jacobson et al., 1996).

Interactional Theory The interactions between depressed persons and other people may help explain the former group's shortfall in positive reinforcement. Interactional theory, developed by psychologist James Coyne (1976), proposes that the adjustment to living

Strained relationships. Depressed people may encounter rejection in long-term relationships as the result of the stressful demands they place on others.

with a depressed person can become so stressful that the partner or family member becomes progressively less reinforcing toward the depressed person.

Interactional theory is based on the concept of reciprocal interaction. People's behavior influences, and in turn, is influenced by, the behavior of other. The theory holds that depression-prone people react to stress by demanding greater reassurance and social support. At first people who become depressed may succeed in garnering support. Over time, however, their demands and behavior begin to elicit anger or annoyance. Although loved ones may keep their negative feelings to themselves, so as not to further upset the depressed person, these feelings may surface in subtle ways that spell rejection. Depressed people may react to rejection with deeper depression and greater demands, triggering a vicious cycle of further rejection and more profound depression. They may also feel guilty about distressing their family members, which can exacerbate negative feelings about themselves.

Evidence shows that people who become depressed tend to encounter rejection in long-term relationships (Marcus & Nardone, 1992). Family members may find it stressful to adjust to the behavior of the person who is depressed, especially to such behaviors as withdrawal, lethargy, despair, and constant requests for reassurance. A recent study finds that people whose spouses are being treated for depression tend to report higher than average levels of emotional distress (Benazon, 2000).

All in all, research evidence generally supports Coyne's belief that people who suffer from depression elicit rejection from others, but there remains a lack of evidence to show that this rejection is mediated by negative emotions (anger and annoyance) that the depressed person induces in others (Segrin & Dillard, 1992). Rather, a growing body of literature suggests that depressed people may lack effective social skills, which may account for the fact that others often reject them (Segrin & Abramson, 1994). They tend to be unresponsive, uninvolved, and even impolite when they interact with others. For example, they tend to gaze very little at the other person, to take an excessive amount of time to respond, to show very little approval or validation of the other person, and to dwell on their problems and negative feelings (Segrin & Abramson, 1994). They even dwell on negative feelings when interacting with strangers. In effect, they turn other people off, setting the stage for rejection.

Whether social skills deficits are a cause or a symptom of depression remains to be determined. Whatever the case, impaired social behavior likely may play an important role in determining the persistence or recurrence of depression. As we shall see, some psychological approaches to treating depression (e.g., interpersonal psychotherapy and Lewinsohn's social skills training approach—discussed later) focus on helping people with depression better understand and overcome their interpersonal problems. This may help, in turn, alleviate depression or perhaps prevent future recurrences.

Cognitive Theories

Cognitive theorists relate the origin and maintenance of depression to the ways in which people see themselves and the world around them.

Aaron Beck's Cognitive Theory One of the most influential cognitive theorists, psychiatrist Aaron Beck (Beck, 1976; Beck et al., 1979), relates the development of depression to the adoption early in life of a negatively biased or distorted way of thinking—the **cognitive triad of depression** (see Table 8.4). The cognitive triad includes negative beliefs about oneself (e.g., "I'm no good"), the environment or the world at large (e.g., "This school is awful"), and the future (e.g., "Nothing will ever turn out right for me"). Cognitive theory holds that people who adopt this negative way of thinking are at greater risk of becoming depressed in the face of stressful or disappointing life experiences, such as getting a poor grade or losing a job.

Beck views these negative concepts of the self and the world as mental templates or *cognitive schemes* that are adopted in childhood on the basis of early learning experiences. Children may find that nothing they do is good enough to please their parents or teachers. As a result, they may come to regard themselves as basically incompetent and to perceive their future prospects as dim. These beliefs may sensitize them later in life to interpret any

cognitive triad of depression The view that depression derives from adopting negative views of oneself, the environment or world at large, and the future.

TABLE 8.4 The Cognitive Triad of Depression

Negative View of Oneself	Perceiving oneself as worthless, deficient, inadequate, unlovable, and as lacking the skills necessary to achieve happiness.
Negative View of the Environment	Perceiving the environment as imposing excessive demands and/or presenting obstacles that are impossible to overcome, leading continually to failure and loss.
Negative View of the Future	Perceiving the future as hopeless and believing that one is powerless to change things for the better. One expects of the future only continuing failure and unrelenting misery and hardship.

Note. According to Aaron Beck, depression-prone people adopt a habitual style of negative thinking—the so-called cognitive triad of depression.
Source. Adapted from Beck & Young, 1985; Beck et al., 1979.

failure or disappointment as a reflection of something basically wrong or inadequate about themselves. Minor disappointments and personal shortcomings become "blown out of proportion." Even a minor disappointment becomes a crushing blow or a total defeat, which can lead to depression.

The tendency to magnify the importance of minor failures is an example of an error in thinking that Beck labels a *cognitive distortion*. He believes cognitive distortions set the stage for depression in the face of personal losses or negative life events. Psychiatrist David Burns (1980) enumerated a number of the cognitive distortions associated with depression:

1. *All-or-Nothing Thinking.* Seeing events in black and white, as either all good or all bad. For example, one may perceive a relationship that ended in disappointment as a totally negative experience, despite any positive feelings or experiences that may have occurred along the way. Perfectionism is an example of all-or-nothing thinking. Perfectionists judge any outcome other than perfect success to be complete failure. They may consider a grade of B or even A− to be tantamount to an F. They may feel like abject failures if they fall a few dollars short of their sales quotas or receive a very fine (but less than perfect) performance evaluation. Perfectionism is connected with an increased vulnerability to depression as well as poor outcomes in treatment, whether the treatment involves antidepressant medication or psychological approaches such as cognitive therapy or interpersonal psychotherapy (Blatt et al., 1998; Minarik & Ahrens, 1996).

2. *Overgeneralization.* Believing that if a negative event occurs, it is likely to occur again in similar situations in the future. One may come to interpret a single negative event as foreshadowing an endless series of negative events. For example, receiving a letter of rejection from a potential employer leads one to assume that all other job applications will similarly be rejected.

3. *Mental Filter.* Focusing only on negative details of events, thereby rejecting the positive features of one's experiences. Like a droplet of ink that spreads to discolor an entire beaker of water, focusing only on a single negative detail can darken one's vision of reality. Beck called this cognitive distortion **selective abstraction,** meaning the individual selectively abstracts the negative details from events and ignores their positive features. One thus bases one's self-esteem on perceived weaknesses and failures, rather than on positive features, or on a balance of accomplishments and shortcomings. For example, a person receives a job evaluation that contains positive and negative comments but focuses only on the negative.

selective abstraction A cognitive distortion involving the tendency to focus only on the negative parts of experiences or events.

4. *Disqualifying the Positive.* This refers to the tendency to snatch defeat from the jaws of victory by neutralizing or denying your accomplishments. An example is dismissal of congratulations for a job well done by thinking and saying, "Oh, it's no big deal. Anyone could have done it." By contrast, taking credit where credit is due may help people overcome depression by increasing their belief they can make changes that will lead to a positive future (Needles & Abramson, 1990).

5. *Jumping to Conclusions.* Forming a negative interpretation of events, despite a lack of evidence. Two examples of this style of thinking are "mind reading" and "the fortune teller error." In *mind reading,* you arbitrarily jump to the conclusion that others don't like or respect you, as in interpreting a friend's not calling for a while as a rejection. The *fortune teller error* involves the prediction that something bad is always about to happen to oneself. The person believes the prediction of calamity is factually based even though there is an absence of evidence to support it. For example, the person concludes that a passing tightness in the chest *must* be a sign of heart disease, discounting the possibility of more benign causes.

6. *Magnification and Minimization.* Magnification, or *catastrophizing,* refers to the tendency to make mountains out of molehills—to exaggerate the importance of negative events, personal flaws, fears, or mistakes. Minimization is the mirror image, a type of cognitive distortion in which one minimizes or underestimates one's good points.

7. *Emotional Reasoning.* Basing reasoning on emotions—thinking, for example, "If I feel guilty, it must be because I've done something really wrong." One interprets feelings and events based on emotions rather than on fair consideration of evidence.

8. *Should Statements.* Creating personal imperatives or self-commandments— "shoulds" or "musts." For example, "I *should* always get my first serve in!" or, "I *must* make Chris like me!" By creating unrealistic expectations, **musterbation**—the label given this form of thinking by Albert Ellis—can lead one to become depressed when one falls short.

9. *Labeling and Mislabeling.* Explaining behavior by attaching negative labels to oneself and others. You may explain a poor grade on a test by thinking you were "lazy" or "stupid" rather than simply unprepared for the specific exam or, perhaps, ill. Labeling other people as "stupid" or "insensitive" can engender hostility toward them. Mislabeling involves the use of labels that are emotionally charged and inaccurate, such as calling yourself a "pig" because of a minor deviation from your usual diet.

10. *Personalization.* This refers to the tendency to assume you are responsible for other people's problems and behavior. You may assume your partner or spouse is crying because of something you have done (or not done) rather than recognizing that other causes may be involved.

Consider the errors in thinking illustrated in the following case example:

Errors in Thinking in a Case of Depression

Christie was a 33-year-old real estate sales agent who suffered from frequent episodes of depression. Whenever a deal fell through, she would blame herself: "If only I had worked harder . . . negotiated better . . . talked more persuasively . . . the deal would have been done." After several successive disappointments, each one followed by self-recriminations, she felt like quitting altogether. Her thinking became increasingly dominated by negative thoughts, which further depressed her mood and lowered her self-esteem: "I'm a loser . . . I'll never succeed . . . It's all my fault . . . I'm no good and I'm never going to succeed at anything."

  Christie's thinking included cognitive errors such as the following:
(1) personalization (believing herself to be the sole cause of negative events);

musterbation A rigid thought pattern characterized by the tendency to impose excessive, unrealistic demands on oneself or personal imperatives.

automatic thoughts Thoughts that seem to pop into one's mind.

cognitive-specificity hypothesis The belief that different emotional disorders are linked to particular kinds of automatic thoughts.

(2) labeling and mislabeling *(labeling herself to be a loser); (3)* overgeneralization *(predicting a dismal future on the basis of a present disappointment); and (4)* mental filter *(judging her personality entirely on the basis of her disappointments). In therapy, Christie was helped to think more realistically about events and not to jump to conclusions that she was automatically at fault whenever a deal fell through, or to judge her whole personality on the basis of disappointments or perceived flaws in herself. In place of this self-defeating style of thinking, she began to think more realistically when disappointments occurred, like telling herself, "Okay, I'm disappointed. I'm frustrated. I feel lousy. So what? It doesn't mean I'll never succeed. Let me discover what went wrong and try to correct it the next time. I have to look ahead, not dwell on disappointments in the past."*

—*From the Authors' Files*

Distorted thinking tends to be experienced as automatic, as if the thoughts had just popped into one's head. These **automatic thoughts** are likely to be accepted as statements of fact rather than as opinions or habitual ways of interpreting events.

Beck and his colleagues formulated a **cognitive-specificity hypothesis,** which proposes that different disorders, anxiety disorders and depressive disorders in particular, are characterized by different types of automatic thoughts. The results of one study (Beck et al., 1987) showed some interesting differences in the types of automatic thoughts people with depressive and anxiety disorders reported (see Table 8.5). People with diagnosable depression more often reported thoughts concerning themes of loss, self-deprecation, and pessimism. People with anxiety disorders more often reported thoughts concerning physical danger and other threats.

Research Evidence on Cognitions and Depression Supporting Beck's model is evidence linking distorted cognitions and negative thinking to depressive symptoms and clinical depression (e.g., Clark, Cook, & Snow, 1998; Stader & Hokanson, 1998). People who are depressed also tend to hold more pessimistic views of the future and are more critical of

---

TABLE 8.5   Automatic Thoughts Associated with Depression and Anxiety

Common Automatic Thoughts Associated with Depression	Common Automatic Thoughts Associated with Anxiety
1. I'm worthless.	1. What if I get sick and become an invalid?
2. I'm not worthy of other people's attention or affection.	2. I am going to be injured.
3. I'll never be as good as other people are.	3. What if no one reaches me in time to help?
4. I'm a social failure.	4. I might be trapped.
5. I don't deserve to be loved.	5. I am not a healthy person.
6. People don't respect me anymore.	6. I'm going to have an accident.
7. I will never overcome my problems.	7. Something will happen that will ruin my appearance.
8. I've lost the only friends I've had.	8. I am going to have a heart attack.
9. Life isn't worth living.	9. Something awful is going to happen.
10. I'm worse off than they are.	10. Something will happen to someone I care about.
11. There's no one left to help me.	11. I'm losing my mind.
12. No one cares whether I live or die.	
13. Nothing ever works out for me anymore.	
14. I have become physically unattractive.	

Source. Adapted from Beck et al., 1987.

A Closer Look

On Positive Illusions and Mental Health: Is It Adaptive to See Things As They Truly Are?

 A common assumption exists that there is an objective reality "out there" and that the ability to perceive reality accurately is a basic feature of psychological adjustment. Individuals who perceive the world for what it is may be better able to adapt to their physical and social environments and avoid harm (Colvin & Block, 1994). Yet might it be more adaptive under some circumstances to hold certain positive biases or optimistic illusions about oneself and one's place in the world? Although we usually equate mental health with good reality testing, and mental illness with distorted perceptions and cognitions, the negative perceptions held by many depressed people may not be distorted at all but rather may be quite realistic. Perhaps it is the rest of us who tend to see the world through "rose-colored lenses" that cast too rosy a tint on our perceptions of our abilities and our likelihood of success. Normal human thought, investigators find, is characterized by mild distortions or illusions, such as inflated beliefs about ourselves, exaggerated perceptions about our ability to control events, and unrealistic optimism (Taylor et al., 2000). Mentally healthy people may manage to keep themselves out of the dumps by maintaining these illusions despite evidence to the contrary. In effect, we may need to maintain some positive illusions to maintain our spirits in coping with the "ups and downs" of life (Goode, 2001e). They may also help us keep our chins up and maintain expectancies of success in the future rather than accept negative outcomes as somehow fated for us.

Researchers devised a research project to test the hypothesis that depressed people view their own abilities to control events more realistically than nondepressed people. In essence, they created a laboratory situation in which subjects had no control over a laboratory task so they could assess which subjects nevertheless managed to maintain an *illusion of control*. The results showed that subjects who maintained an illusion of control showed less evidence of depression

following exposure to stressful experiences afterward (Alloy & Clements, 1992). Perhaps the tendency to think we are in charge of our destinies, even incorrectly, reduces our susceptibility to depression. We should caution that more evidence is needed to support the link between positive illusions and psychological adjustment. Let us also note that holding extremely positive illusions, such as delusions of grandeur, is clearly associated with psychological problems such as schizophrenia and mania (Taylor & Brown, 1994).

Truth OR Fiction?   REVISITED

In some ways, many "mentally healthy" people see things *less* realistically than people who are depressed.

TRUE. Researchers find that mentally healthy people may in some ways view the world less realistically than people who are depressed. Many people with depression, however, may be more accurate in their assessment of the extent to which they actually can exercise control over events.

Depressed people may see the proverbial glass not only as half empty but as both half empty and half full, as compared to nondepressed people, who may see the glass only as hall full. In a recent study, researchers found that depressed women attended equally to positive and negative stimuli in a laboratory task (the stimuli were either positive, neutral, or negative words presented on a computer display). Nondepressed women showed a positive bias by attending more to the positive or neutral stimuli (McCabe & Gotlib, 1995). This suggests that depressed individuals are not necessarily biased toward perceiving only the negative. Rather, what seems to set them apart from nondepressed people is their failure to maintain a positive bias.

themselves and others (Glara et al., 1993). Other findings indicate that dysfunctional attitudes (above a certain threshold) increase vulnerability to depression in the face of negative life events (Lewinsohn, Joiner, & Rohde, 2001).

The relationship between negative thinking and depression may depend more on the balance between negative and positive thoughts than on the presence of negative thoughts alone. Research using a thought-counting method showed that people who functioned well psychologically experienced both positive and negative thoughts, but the positive thoughts occurred one and a half to two times as often as the negative thoughts (R. M. Schwartz, 1986). People with a mild level of psychological dysfunction, by contrast, produced about equal numbers of positive and negative thoughts. Thinking positive thoughts may serve as a kind of buffer or shock absorber in helping people cope with negative life events without becoming depressed (Bruch, 1997; Lightsey, 1994a, 1994b).

learned helplessness A behavior pattern characterized by passivity and perceptions of lack of control.

Research also supports Beck's view that people who are depressed tend to magnify their shortcomings. In one study, college students were given a test that supposedly measured the presence of a personality trait and were asked to indicate the value of the trait to them. Students who weren't depressed tended to inflate the value of the trait when they were told they possessed a great deal of it. Students who were depressed, however, exaggerated the importance of the trait when they were informed they had done poorly on the test (Wenzlaff & Grozier, 1988). Whereas students who were depressed accentuated the negative, other students were more self-enhancing; they emphasized the importance of a quality they believed themselves to have.

All in all, there is broad research support for many aspects of the theory, including Beck's concept of the cognitive triad of depression and his view that people with depression think more negatively than nondepressed people about themselves, the future, and the world in general (Haaga, Dyck, & Ernst, 1991). Although dysfunctional cognitions (negative, distorted, or pessimistic thoughts) are more common among people who are depressed, the causal pathways remain unclear. We can't yet say whether dysfunctional or negative thinking causes depression or is merely a feature of depression. Thus the central theme of cognitive theory, that negative, distorted thoughts are causally related to depression, remains to be confirmed (Cole et al., 1998; Stader & Hokanson, 1998).

Perhaps the causal linkages go both ways. Our thoughts may affect our moods and our moods may affect our thoughts (Kwon & Oei, 1994). Think in terms of a vicious cycle. People who feel depressed may begin thinking in more negative, distorted ways. The more negative and distorted their thinking becomes, the more depressed they feel, and the more depressed they feel, the more dysfunctional their thinking becomes. Alternatively, dysfunctional thinking may come first in the cycle, perhaps in response to a disappointing life experience, which then leads to a downcast mood. This in turn may accentuate negative thinking, and so on. We are still faced with the old "chicken or the egg" dilemma of determining which comes first in the causal sequence, distorted thinking or depression. Future research may help tease out these causal pathways. Even if it should become clear that distorted cognitions play no direct causal role in the initial onset of depression, the reciprocal interaction between thoughts and moods may play a role in maintaining depression and in determining the likelihood of recurrence (Kwon & Oei, 1994). We know, for example, that people who recover from depression but continue to hold distorted cognitions tend to be at greater risk of recurrence of depression (Rush & Weissenburger, 1994). Fortunately, evidence shows that dysfunctional attitudes tend to decrease with effective treatment for depression (Fava et al., 1994).

THINK ABOUT IT

Which of the cognitive distortions, if any, that are listed in the text characterize your way of thinking about disappointing experiences in your life? What were the effects of these thought patterns on your mood? How did they affect your feelings about yourself? How might you change these ways of thinking in the future?

Learned Helplessness (Attributional) Theory The **learned helplessness** model proposes that people may become depressed because they learn to view themselves as helpless to control the reinforcements in their environments—or to change their lives for the better. The originator of the learned helplessness concept, Martin Seligman (1973, 1975), suggests that people learn to perceive themselves as helpless because of their experiences. The learned helplessness model therefore straddles the behavioral and the cognitive: Situational factors foster attitudes that lead to depression.

Seligman and his colleagues based the learned helplessness model on early laboratory studies of animals. In these studies, dogs exposed to an inescapable electric shock showed the "learned helplessness effect" by failing to learn to escape when the shock was later made escapable (Overmier & Seligman, 1967; Seligman & Maier, 1967). Exposure to uncontrollable forces apparently taught the animals they were helpless to change their situation. Animals who developed learned helplessness showed behaviors that were similar to

How could he have missed that tackle? This football player missed a crucial tackle and is rehashing it. He is putting himself down and telling himself that there is nothing he can do to improve his performance. Cognitive theorists believe that a person's self-defeating or distorted interpretations of negative events can set the stage for depression.

those of people with depression, including lethargy, lack of motivation, and difficulty acquiring new skills (Maier & Seligman, 1976).

Seligman (1975, 1991) proposed that some forms of depression in humans might result from exposure to apparently uncontrollable situations. Such experiences can instill the expectation that future reinforcements will also be beyond the individual's control. A cruel vicious cycle may come into play in many cases of depression. A few failures may produce feelings of helplessness and expectations of further failure. Perhaps you know people who have failed certain subjects, such as mathematics. They may come to believe themselves incapable of succeeding in math. They may thus decide that studying for the quantitative section of the Graduate Record Exam is a waste of time. They then perform poorly, completing the self-fulfilling prophecy by confirming their expectations, which further intensifies feelings of helplessness, leading to lowered expectations, and so on, in a vicious cycle.

Although it stimulated much interest, Seligman's model failed to account for the low self-esteem typical of people who are depressed. Nor did it explain variations in the persistence of depression. Seligman and his colleagues (Abramson, Seligman, & Teasdale, 1978) offered a reformulation of the theory to meet such shortcomings. The revised theory held that perception of lack of control over reinforcement alone did not explain the persistence and severity of depression. It was also necessary to consider cognitive factors, especially the ways in which people explain their failures and disappointments to themselves.

Seligman and his colleagues recast helplessness theory in terms of the social psychology concept of **attributional style.** An attributional style is a personal style of explanation. When disappointments or failures occur, we may explain them in various characteristic ways. We may blame ourselves (an **internal attribution**), or we may blame the circumstances we face (an **external attribution**). We may see bad experiences as typical events (a **stable attribution**) or as isolated events (an **unstable attribution**). We may see them as evidence of broader problems (a **global attribution**) or as evidence of precise and limited shortcomings (a **specific attribution**). The revised helplessness theory—called the reformulated helplessness theory—holds that people who explain the causes of negative events (like failure in work, school, or romantic relationships) according to these three types of attributions are most vulnerable to depression:

1. Internal factors, or beliefs that failures reflect their personal inadequacies, rather than external factors, or beliefs that failures are caused by environmental factors;
2. Global factors, or beliefs that failures reflect sweeping flaws in personality rather than specific factors, or beliefs that failures reflect limited areas of functioning; and
3. Stable factors, or beliefs that failures reflect fixed personality factors rather than unstable factors, or beliefs that the factors leading to failures are changeable.

Let us illustrate these attributional styles with the example of a college student who goes on a disastrous date. Afterward he shakes his head in wonder and tries to make sense of his experience. An internal attribution for the calamity would involve self-blame, as in "I really messed it up." An external attribution would place the blame elsewhere, as in "Some couples just don't hit it off," or "She must have been in a bad mood." A stable attribution would suggest a problem that cannot be changed, as in "It's my personality." An unstable attribution, on the other hand, would suggest a transient condition, as in "It was probably the head cold." A global attribution for failure magnifies the extent of the problem, as in "I really have no idea what I'm doing when I'm with people." A specific attribution, in contrast, chops the problem down to size, as in "My problem is how to make small talk to get a relationship going."

The revised theory holds that each attributional dimension makes a specific contribution to feelings of helplessness. Internal attributions for negative events are linked to lower self-esteem. Stable attributions help explain the persistence—or, in medical terms, the chronicity—of helplessness cognitions. Global attributions are associated with the generality or pervasiveness of feelings of helplessness following negative events. Attributional style should be distinguished from negative thinking (Gotlib et al., 1993). You may think

attributional style A personal style for explaining cause-and-effect relationships between events.

internal attribution A belief that the cause of an event involved factors within oneself.

external attribution A belief that the cause of an event involved factors outside oneself.

stable attribution A belief that the cause of an event involved stable, rather than changeable, factors.

unstable attribution A belief that the cause of an event involved changeable, rather than stable, factors.

global attribution A belief that the cause of an event involved generalized, rather than specific, factors.

specific attribution A belief that the cause of an event involved specific, rather than generalized, factors.

Is it me? According to reformulated helplessness theory, the kinds of attributions we make concerning negative events can make us more or less vulnerable to depression. Attributing the breakup of a relationship to internalizing ("It's me"), globalizing ("I'm totally worthless"), and stabilizing ("Things are always going to turn out badly for me") causes can lead to depression.

negatively (pessimistically) or positively (optimistically), but still hold yourself to blame for your perceived failures.

Research generally supports the reformulated helplessness (attributional) model. As the model would predict, depressed people are generally more likely than others to attribute the causes of failures to internal, stable, and global factors (e.g., Seligman et al., 1988; Sweeney, Anderson, & Bailey, 1986). A depressive attributional style also predicts responsiveness to antidepressant medication in depressed patients (Levitan, Rector, & Bagby, 1998). Also supporting the model are findings that negative attributional styles and dysfunctional attitudes predict higher lifetime rates of major depression (Alloy et al., 2000). Attributional style may have a stronger relationship to depression in people who tend to think more about the causes of events, however (Haaga, 1995).

Biological Factors

Evidence has accumulated pointing to the important role of biological factors, especially genetics and neurotransmitter functioning, in the development of mood disorders. Recent investigations are examining the biological roots of depression at the neurotransmitter level as well as the genetic, molecular, and even cellular level.

Genetic Factors A growing body of knowledge implicates genetic factors in mood disorders. We know that mood disorders, including major depression and especially bipolar disorder, tend to run in families (Klein et al., 2001; USDHHS, 1999a). Families, however, share environmental similarities as well as genes. Family members may share blue eyes (an inherited attribute) but also a common religion (a cultural attribute). Yet evidence pointing to a genetic basis for mood disorders comes from studies showing that the closer the genetic relationship one shares with a person with a major mood disorder (major depression or bipolar disorder), the greater the likelihood that one will also suffer from a major mood disorder (e.g., Vincent et al., 1999).

Twin studies and adoptee studies provide additional evidence of a genetic contribution. A higher concordance (agreement) rate among monozygotic (MZ) twins than dizygotic (DZ) twins for a given disorder is taken as supportive evidence of genetic factors. Both types of twins share common environments, but MZ twins share 100% of their genes as compared to 50% for DZ twins. The concordance rate for major mood disorders (unipolar and bipolar disorders) between MZ twins ranges from 45% to 70%, which is more than double the rate between DZ twins (Kendler et al., 1992a, 1993b). This provides strong support for a genetic component, but is short of the 100% concordance we would expect if genetics were solely responsible for these disorders. Adoptee studies, which might provide corroborating evidence of genetic factors in mood disorders, are sparse.

All in all, researchers believe that heredity plays an important role in major depression (Kendler & Prescott, 1999; Sullivan, Neale, & Kendler, 2000). However, genetics isn't the only determinant of major depression, nor is it necessarily the most important determinant. Environmental factors, such as exposure to stressful life events, appear to play at least as great a role—if not a greater role—than genetics (Kendler & Prescott, 1999). It appears that major depression is a complex disorder that is caused by a combination of genetic and environmental factors (Sullivan, Neale, & Kendler, 2000).

Genetic factors may play a greater role in explaining bipolar disorder than unipolar depression (major depressive disorder) (Krehbiel, 2000). As for dysthymic disorder, data from twin studies indicates that the disorder may be relatively less influenced by genetic factors than either major depression or bipolar disorder (Torgersen, 1986).

Biochemical Factors and Brain Abnormalities in Depression Early research on the biological underpinnings of depression focused on deficits in neurotransmitter levels in the brain. Neurotransmitters were first suspected of playing a role in depression back in the 1950s. Findings were reported then that hypertensive patients who were taking the drug *reserpine* often became depressed. Reserpine depletes the supplies of various neuro-

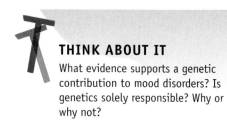

THINK ABOUT IT

What evidence supports a genetic contribution to mood disorders? Is genetics solely responsible? Why or why not?

transmitters in the brain, including norepinephrine and serotonin (USDHHS, 1999a). Then came the discovery that drugs that increase the brain levels of neurotransmitters such as norepinephrine and serotonin can relieve depression. These drugs, called antidepressants, include *tricyclics*, such as imipramine (trade name Tofranil) and amitriptyline (trade name Elavil); *monoamine oxidase* (MAO) inhibitors, such as phenelzine (trade name Nardil); and *selective serotonin-reuptake inhibitors* (SSRIs), such as fluoxetine (trade name Prozac) and sertraline (trade name Zoloft). But later research cast doubt on the belief that depression is caused simply by a lack of particular neurotransmitters in the brain. For example, while antidepressants increase the availability of neurotransmitters in the brain within hours, depressed patients do not usually begin to show a response to treatment for several weeks (Nierenberg et al., 2000). Therefore, it is unlikely that these drugs work by simply boosting levels of neurotransmitters in the brain (Duman, Heninger, & Nestler, 1997).

More complex views of the role of neurotransmitters in depression are evolving (Cravchik & Goldman, 2000). A widely held view today is that depression involves irregularities in (1) the numbers of receptors on receiving neurons where neurotransmitters dock (having either too many or too few); or (2) in the sensitivity of receptors to particular neurotransmitters (Yatham et al., 2000). Antidepressants may work by affecting either the number or sensitivity of receptors. Deficiencies of certain neurotransmitters may also play a role (Lambert et al., 2000). Complicating matters further, there are several different types of receptors for each neurotransmitter. There may also be many subtypes for each type (USDHHS, 1999a). The actions of particular antidepressants may be specific to certain types or subtypes of receptors.

Another avenue of research focuses on possible abnormalities in the *prefrontal cortex*, the area of the frontal lobes lying in front of the motor areas. Investigators find evidence of lower metabolic activity and size of the prefrontal cortex in clinically depressed people as compared to healthy controls (e.g., Damasio, 1997). The prefrontal cortex is involved in regulating neurotransmitters believed to be involved in mood disorders, including serotonin and norepinephrine, so it is not surprising that evidence points to irregularities in this region of the brain. Other investigators find that MRI scans of the brains of people with bipolar disorder show evidence of structural abnormalities in parts of the brain involved in regulating mood states (Strakowski et al., 1999).

We also find evidence of other biochemical pathways to depression, including roles for proteins that help nerve cells communicate (Kramer et al., 1998) and endocrine system activity involving the thyroid gland, the adrenal glands, and in women, fluctuations of the female sex hormones estrogen and progesterone (Marangell et al., 1997; Seeman, 1997; Stahl, 2001).

Tying It Together

 Depression and other mood disorders involve interplay of multiple factors. Consistent with the *diathesis-stress model*, depression may reflect an interaction of biological factors (such as genetic factors, neurotransmitter irregularities, or brain abnormalities), psychological factors (such as cognitive distortions or learned helplessness), and social and environmental stressors (such as divorce or loss of a job).

Let us consider a possible causal pathway based on the diathesis-stress model (see Figure 8.3). Stressful life events, such as prolonged unemployment or a divorce, may have a depressing effect by reducing neurotransmitter activity in the brain. These biochemical effects may be more likely to occur or be more pronounced in people with a certain genetic predisposition or *diathesis* for depression. However, a depressive disorder may not develop, or may develop in a milder form, in people with more effective coping resources for handling stressful situations. For example, people who

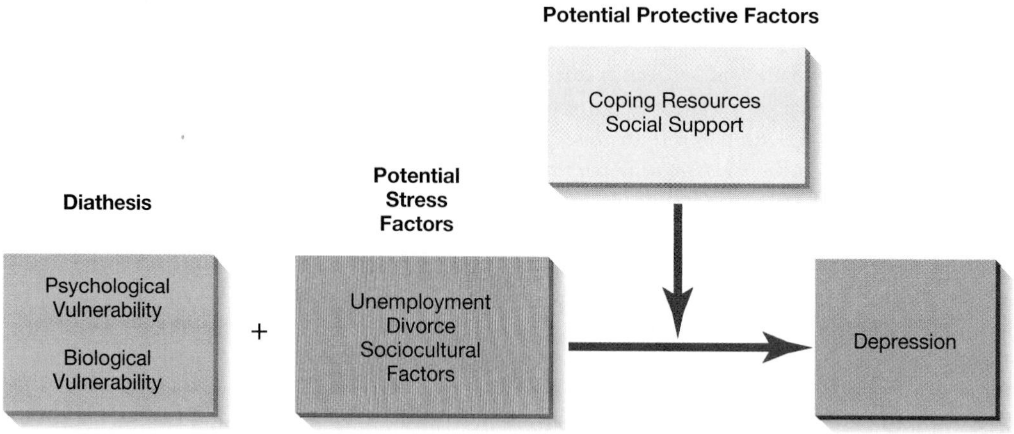

FIGURE 8.3 Diathesis-stress model of depression.

THINK ABOUT IT

Jonathan becomes clinically depressed after losing his job and his girlfriend. Based on your review of the different theoretical perspectives on depression, explain how these losses may have figured in Jonathan's depression.

Quiz **8.2**
Theoretical Perspectives on Mood Disorders

receive emotional support from others may be better able to withstand the effects of stress than those who have to go it alone. So too for people who make active coping efforts to meet the challenges they face in life.

Sociocultural factors may be major sources of stress that influence the development of mood disorders (Ostler et al., 2001). These factors include poverty; overcrowding; exposure to racism, sexism, and prejudice; violence in the home or community; unequal stressful burdens placed on women; and family disintegration. These factors may figure prominently in either precipitating mood disorders or accounting for their recurrence. Other sources of stress include negative life events such as the loss of a job, the development of a serious illness, the breakup of a romantic relationship, and the loss of a loved one.

The diathesis for depression may take the form of a psychological vulnerability involving a depressive thinking style, one characterized by tendencies to exaggerate the consequences of negative events, to heap blame on oneself, and to perceive oneself as helpless to effect positive change. This cognitive diathesis may increase the risk of depression in the face of negative life events. These cognitive influences may also interact with a genetically based diathesis to further increase the risk of depression following stressful life events. Then too, the availability of social support from others may help bolster a person's resistance to stress during difficult times. People with more effective social skills may be better able to garner and maintain social reinforcement from others and thus be better able to resist depression than people lacking social skills. But biochemical changes in the brain might make it more difficult for the person to cope effectively and bounce back from stressful life events. Lingering biochemical changes and feelings of depression may exacerbate feelings of helplessness, compound the effects of the initial stressor, and so on.

Gender-related differences in coping styles may also come into play. Men and women may respond differently to feelings of depression. According to Nolen-Hoeksema, women are more likely to ruminate when facing emotional problems, and men are more likely to seek refuge in a bottle. These or other differences in coping styles may propel women into longer and more severe bouts of depression while setting the stage for the development of alcohol-related problems in men. As you can see, a complex web of contributing factors may be involved in the development of mood disorders.

Treatment of Mood Disorders

Just as theoretical perspectives suggest that many factors may be involved in the development of mood disorders, there are various approaches to treatment that derive from psychological and biological models. Here we focus on several of the leading contemporary approaches.

Psychodynamic Approaches

Traditional psychoanalysis aims to help people who become depressed understand their ambivalent feelings toward important people (objects) in their lives they have lost or whose loss was threatened. By working through feelings of anger toward these lost objects, they can turn anger outward—through verbal expression of feelings, for example—rather than leave it to fester and turn inward.

Traditional psychoanalysis can take years to uncover and deal with unconscious conflicts. Modern psychoanalytic approaches also focus on unconscious conflicts, but they are more direct, relatively brief, and focus on present as well as past conflicted relationships. A recent study supported the efficacy of structured, short-term dynamic therapy (Luborsky et al., 1996). Eclectic psychodynamic therapists may use behavioral methods to help clients acquire the social skills needed to develop a broader social network.

Interpersonal psychotherapy (IPT). IPT is usually a brief, psychodynamically oriented therapy that focuses on issues in the person's current interpersonal relationships. Like traditional psychodynamic approaches, IPT assumes that early life experiences are key issues in adjustment, but IPT focuses on the present—the here and now.

Newer models of psychotherapy for depression have emerged from the interpersonal school of psychodynamic therapy derived initially from the work of Harry Stack Sullivan (see Chapter 2) and other neo-Freudians, such as Karen Horney. One contemporary example is **interpersonal psychotherapy (IPT)** (Klerman et al., 1984). IPT is a brief form of therapy (usually no more than 9 to 12 months) that focuses on the client's current interpersonal relationships. The developers of ITP believe that depression occurs within an interpersonal context and that relationship issues need to be emphasized in treatment. IPT has been shown to be an effective treatment for major depression and shows promise in treating other psychological disorders, including dysthymic disorder and bulimia (DeRubeis & Crits-Christoph, 1998; Leichsenring, 2001).

Although IPT shares some features with traditional psychodynamic approaches (principally the belief that early life experiences and persistent personality features are important issues in psychological adjustment), it differs from traditional psychodynamic therapy by focusing primarily on clients' current relationships rather than on helping them acquire insight into unconscious internal conflicts of childhood origins. Although unconscious factors and early childhood experiences are recognized, therapy focuses on the present—the here and now.

IPT helps clients deal with unresolved or delayed grief reactions following the death of a loved one as well as role conflicts in present relationships (Weissman & Markowitz, 1994). The therapist helps clients express grief and come to terms with their loss while assisting them in developing new activities and relationships to help renew their lives. The therapist also helps clients identify areas of conflict in their present relationships, understand the issues that underlie them, and consider ways of resolving them. If the problems in a relationship are beyond repair, the therapist helps the client consider ways of ending it and establishing new relationships. In the case of Sal D., a 31-year-old TV repairman's assistant, depression was associated with marital conflict:

Interpersonal Psychotherapy in a Case of Depression

Sal began to explore his marital problems in the fifth therapy session, becoming tearful as he recounted his difficulty expressing his feelings to his wife because of feelings of being "numb." He felt that he had been "holding on" to his feelings, which was causing him to become estranged from his wife. The next session zeroed in on the similarities between himself and his father, in particular how he was distancing himself from his wife in a similar way to how his father had kept a distance from him. By session 7, a turning point had been reached. Sal expressed how he and his wife had become

interpersonal psychotherapy (IPT) A brief form of psychodynamic therapy that focuses on the client's current interpersonal relationships.

"emotional" and closer to one another during the previous week and how he was able to talk more openly about his feelings, and how he and his wife had been able to make a joint decision concerning a financial matter that had been worrying them for some time. When later he was laid off from his job, he sought his wife's opinion, rather than picking a fight with her as a way of thrusting his job problems on her. To his surprise he found that his wife responded positively—not "violently" as he had expected—to times when he expressed his feelings. In his last therapy session (session 12), Sal expressed how therapy had led to a "reawakening" within himself with respect to the feelings he had been keeping to himself—an openness that he hoped to create in his relationship with his wife.

—Adapted from Klerman et al., 1984, pp. 111–113

∎

Behavioral Approaches

Behavioral treatment approaches presume that depressive behaviors are learned and can be unlearned. Behavior therapists aim to directly modify behaviors rather than to foster awareness of possible unconscious causes of these behaviors. Behavior therapy has been shown to produce substantial benefits in treating depression both in adults and adolescents (Craighead, Craighead, & Ilardi, 1998).

One illustrative behavioral program was developed by Lewinsohn and his colleagues (Lewinsohn et al., 1996). It consists of a 12-session, 8-week group therapy program organized as a course—the *Coping With Depression (CWD) Course*. The course helps clients acquire relaxation skills, increase pleasant activities, and build social skills that enable them to obtain social reinforcement. For example, students learn how to accept rather than deny compliments and how to ask friends to join them in activities to raise the frequency and quality of their social interactions. Participants are taught to generate a self-change plan, to think more constructively, and to develop a lifetime plan for maintaining treatment gains and preventing recurrent depression. The therapist is considered a teacher; the client, a student; the session, a class. Each participant is treated as a responsible adult who is capable of learning. The structure involves lectures, activities, and homework and each session follows a structured lesson plan. Depressed adolescents who received the CWD treatment showed lower rates of depression and increased activity levels compared to control subjects (Lewinsohn et al., 1996).

Cognitive Approaches

Cognitive theorists believe that distorted thinking plays a key role in the development of depression. Aaron Beck and his colleagues have developed a multicomponent treatment approach, called **cognitive therapy**, which focuses on helping people with depression learn to recognize and change their dysfunctional thinking patterns. Depressed people tend to focus on how they are feeling rather than on the thoughts that may underlie their feeling states. That is, they usually pay more attention to how bad they feel than to the thoughts that may trigger or maintain their depressed moods.

Cognitive therapy, like behavior therapy, involves a relatively brief therapy format, frequently 14 to 16 weekly sessions (Butler & Beck, 1995). Therapists use a combination of behavioral and cognitive techniques to help clients identify and change dysfunctional thoughts and develop more adaptive behaviors. For example, they assist clients in connecting thought patterns to negative moods by having them monitor the automatic negative thoughts they experience throughout the day by means of a thought diary or daily record. They note when and where negative thoughts occur and how they feel at the time. Once these disruptive thoughts are identified, the therapist helps the client challenge their validity and replace them with more adaptive thoughts. The following case example shows how a cognitive therapist works with a client to dispute the validity of

cognitive therapy Aaron Beck's form of therapy that helps clients recognize and correct distorted patterns of thinking.

thoughts that reflect the cognitive distortion called *selective abstraction* (the tendency to judge oneself entirely on the basis of specific weaknesses or flaws in character). The client judged herself to be totally lacking in self-control because she ate a single piece of candy while she was on a diet.

A Case Vignette of Cognitive Therapy

CLIENT: *I don't have any self-control at all.*

THERAPIST: *On what basis do you say that?*

C: *Somebody offered me candy and I couldn't refuse it.*

T: *Were you eating candy every day?*

C: *No, I just ate it this once.*

T: *Did you do anything constructive during the past week to adhere to your diet?*

C: *Well, I didn't give in to the temptation to buy candy every time I saw it at the store. . . . Also, I did not eat any candy except that one time when it was offered to me and I felt I couldn't refuse it.*

T: *If you counted up the number of times you controlled yourself versus the number of times you gave in, what ratio would you get?*

C: *About 100 to 1.*

T: *So if you controlled yourself 100 times and did not control yourself just once, would that be a sign that you are weak through and through?*

C: *I guess not—not through and through (smiles).*

—Adapted from Beck et al., 1979, p. 68

■

Ample evidence supports the effectiveness of cognitive therapy in treating major depression and reducing risks of recurrent episodes (DeRubeis et al., 1999, 2001; Jarrett et al., 2001; Leichsenring, 2001). The benefits achieved from cognitive therapy appear to be at least equal to those achieved from antidepressant medication in treating depression (DeRubeis et al., 1999, 2001; Jarrett et al., 1999). However, it remains an open question as to whether a combination approach of antidepressant medication and psychotherapy works better than either approach alone (Murray, 2000b). However, a combination of antidepressant medications and psychotherapy appears to be more effective than psychotherapy alone in treating the more severe, recurrent forms of depression (USDHHS, 1999a). Cognitive therapy, or cognitive behavioral therapy, also appears to produce about the same level of benefit as interpersonal psychotherapy, the most widely studied form of brief, psychodynamically oriented therapy for depression (Elkin et al., 1989; Leichsenring, 2001; Shapiro et al., 1995).

We have little research yet on the psychological treatment of dysthymia, although techniques used in treating major depression, such as cognitive therapy and interpersonal psychotherapy, have shown some promising results (Thase et al., 1997). Large-scale investigations of the effects of psychological treatments for bipolar disorder are underway. Early studies suggest that psychosocial treatments, such as cognitive-behavioral therapy and forms of interpersonal therapy and family therapy, may be effective adjuncts to drug therapy in the treatment of bipolar disorder (Lam et al., 2000; Otto, 2001).

Cognitive theorists suggest that cognitive errors can lead to depression if they are left to rummage around unchallenged in the individual's mind. Cognitive therapists help clients to recognize cognitive distortions and replace them with more rational alternative thoughts.

Table 8.6 shows some common examples of automatic thoughts, the types of cognitive distortions they represent, and some rational alternative responses.

TABLE 8.6   Cognitive Distortions and Rational Responses

Automatic Thought	Kind of Cognitive Distortion	Rational Response
I'm all alone in the world.	All-or-Nothing Thinking	It may feel like I'm all alone, but there are some people who care about me.
Nothing will ever work out for me.	Overgeneralization	No one can look into the future. Concentrate on the present.
My looks are hopeless.	Magnification	I may not be perfect looking, but I'm far from hopeless.
I'm falling apart. I can't handle this.	Magnification	Sometimes I just feel overwhelmed. But I've handled things like this before. Just take it a step at a time and I'll be okay.
I guess I'm just a born loser.	Labeling and Mislabeling	Nobody is destined to be a loser. Stop talking yourself down.
I've only lost 8 pounds on this diet. I should just forget it. I can't succeed.	Negative Focusing/Minimization/ Disqualifying the Positive/Jumping to Conclusions/All-or-Nothing Thinking	Eight pounds is a good start. I didn't gain all this weight overnight, and I have to expect that it will take time to lose it.
I know things must really be bad for me to feel this awful.	Emotional Reasoning	Feeling something doesn't make it so. If I'm not seeing things clearly, my emotions will be distorted too.
I know I'm going to flunk this course.	Fortune Teller Error	Give me a break! Just focus on getting through this course, not on jumping to negative conclusions.
I know John's problems are really my fault.	Personalization	Stop blaming yourself for everyone else's problems. There are many reasons why John's problems have nothing to do with me.
Someone my age should be doing better than I am.	Should Statements	Stop comparing yourself to others. All anyone can be expected to do is their best. What good does it do to compare myself to others? It only leads me to get down on myself rather than get motivated.
I just don't have the brains for college.	Labeling and Mislabeling	Stop calling yourself names like "stupid." I can accomplish a lot more than I give myself credit for.
Everything is my fault.	Personalization	There you go again. Stop playing this game of pointing blame at yourself. There's enough blame to go around. Better yet, forget placing blame and try to think through how to solve this problem.
It would be awful if Sue turns me down.	Magnification	It might be upsetting, but it needn't be awful unless I make it so.
If people really knew me, they would hate me.	Mind Reader	What evidence is there for that? More people who get to know me like me than don't like me.
If something doesn't get better soon, I'll go crazy.	Jumping to Conclusions/ Magnification	I've dealt with these problems this long without falling apart. I just have to hang in there. Things are not as bad as they seem.
I can't believe I have another pimple on my face. This is going to ruin my whole weekend.	Mental Filter	Take it easy. A pimple is not the end of the world. It doesn't have to spoil my whole weekend. Other people get pimples and seem to have a good time.

Biological Approaches

The most common biological approaches to treating mood disorders involve the use of antidepressant drugs and electroconvulsive therapy for depression and lithium carbonate for bipolar disorder.

Antidepressant Drugs   Drugs used to treat depression include several classes of antidepressants: tricyclic antidepressants (TCAs), monoamine oxidase (MAO) inhibitors, and selective serotonin-reuptake inhibitors (SSRIs). All of these drugs increase brain levels and, perhaps, the actions of neurotransmitters. The increased availability of key neurotransmitters in the synaptic cleft may alter the sensitivity of postsynaptic neurons to these chemical messengers. Yet no one is exactly sure how antidepressants work in relieving depression (Januzzi & DeSanctis, 1999; Kupfer, 1999). Antidepressants tend to have a delayed effect, typically requiring several weeks of treatment before a therapeutic benefit is achieved. SSRIs not only lift mood, but in many cases also eliminate delusions that may accompany severe depression (Zanardi et al., 1996). Antidepressant medication is clearly effective in helping relieve major depression in many cases (Kupfer, 1999; Thase et al., 2000; USDHHS, 1999a). Antidepressants are also helpful in treating dysthymia (Hellerstein et al., 2000).

The different classes of antidepressants increase the availability of neurotransmitters, but in different ways (see Figure 8.4). The tricyclics, which include *imipramine* (trade name Tofranil), *amitriptyline* (Elavil), *desipramine* (Norpramin), and *doxepin* (Sinequan), are so named because of their three-ringed molecular structure. They increase levels in the brain of the neurotransmitters norepinephrine and serotonin by interfering with the reuptake (reabsorption by the transmitting cell) of these chemical messengers. The SSRIs (*fluoxextine*, trade name Prozac, is one) work in a similar fashion but have more specific effects on raising the levels of serotonin in the brain. The MAO inhibitors increase the availability of neurotransmitters by inhibiting the action of monoamine oxidase, an enzyme that normally breaks down or degrades neurotransmitters in the synaptic cleft. MAO inhibitors are used less widely than other antidepressants because of potentially serious interactions with certain foods and alcoholic beverages.

Though antidepressants increase the availability of neurotransmitters at the synaptic level in the brain, we still have much to learn about how they work to relieve depression. Most probably, the antidepressant effects of these drugs involve multiple therapeutic actions on more than one neurotransmitter system (Feighner, 1999; USDHHS, 1999a).

The potential side effects of tricyclics and MAO inhibitors include dry mouth, psychomotor retardation, constipation, blurred vision, and, less frequently, urinary retention, paralytic ileus (a paralysis of the intestines, which impairs the passage of intestinal contents), confusion, delirium, and cardiovascular complications, such as reduced blood

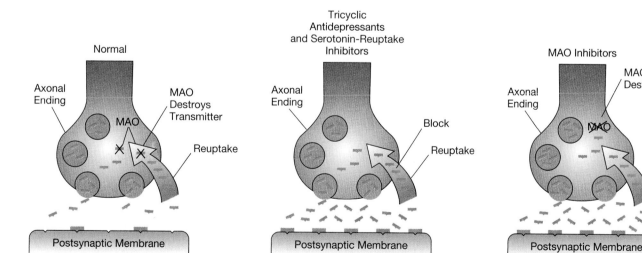

FIGURE 8.4 The actions of various types of antidepressants at the synapse.
Tricyclic antidepressants and serotonin-reuptake inhibitors both increase the availability of neurotransmitters by preventing their reuptake by the presynaptic neuron. Tricyclic antidepressants impede the reuptake of both norepinephrine and serotonin. MAO inhibitors work by inhibiting the action of monoamine oxidase, an enzyme that normally breaks down neurotransmitters in the synaptic cleft.

A Closer Look

St. John's Wort—A Natural "Prozac"?

 Might a humble herb be a remedy for depression? The herb, called St. John's wort, or *Hypericum perforatum*, has been used for centuries to help heal wounds. Now, people are using it to relieve depression (Andrews, 1997). Nowhere is it more popular than Germany, where high-strength versions of the herb became the most widely used antidepressant on the market, outselling Prozac, its nearest competitor, by a margin of 4 to 1. Early small-scale studies in Europe provided preliminary support for the benefits of St. John's wort, with few reported side effects, in treating mild to moderate depression (Carey, 1998). The herb appears to increase the levels of serotonin in the brain by interfering with its reabsorption, the same mechanism believed to account for Prozac's benefits. Although people seeking help for depression may be attracted to the idea of using a natural product such as St. John's wort, more definitive studies are needed to establish its safety and effectiveness (Siegel, 2001). Hopes were lowered by the results of a 2001 study showing that St. John's wort worked no better than a placebo in treating major depression (Shelton et al., 2001; "St. John's Wort," 2001a). Whether or not it might help alleviate less severe forms of depression remains undetermined ("St. John's Wort," 2001b).

Truth OR Fiction?   REVISITED

The most widely used remedy for depression in Germany is not a drug, but an herb.

TRUE. The most widely used remedy for depression in Germany is an herb, St. John's wort. Clinical trials are underway to evaluate its effectiveness.

---

pressure. Tricyclics are also highly toxic, which raises the prospect of suicidal overdoses if the drugs are used without close supervision.

The SSRIs such as Prozac and Zoloft are about equal in effectiveness to the older generation of tricyclics (Kupfer, 1999; McGrath et al., 2000; Noonan, 2000). Yet because they hold two major advantages, they have largely replaced the earlier generation of TCAs. The first advantage is that they are less toxic and so are less dangerous in overdose. Secondly, they have fewer of the common side effects (such as dry mouth, constipation, and weight gain) associated with the tricyclics and MAO inhibitors. Still, Prozac and other SSRIs may produce side effects such as upset stomach, headaches, agitation, insomnia, lack of sexual drive, and delayed orgasm ("Antidepressants Linked," 2000; Michelson et al., 2000).

One issue we need to address in discussing drug therapy is the high rate of relapse following discontinuation of medication (Kocsis et al., 1996). Psychologically based therapies may provide greater protection against relapse, presumably because the learning that occurs during therapy carries past the end of active treatment (Butler & Beck, 1995; Persaud, 2000).

Overall, about 50% to 70% of depressed patients treated on an outpatient basis respond favorably to either psychotherapy or antidepressant medication alone (USDHHS, 1999a). Some people who fail to respond to psychotherapy may respond to antidepressants. Recognize, too, that some people who fail to respond to drug therapy may respond favorably to psychotherapy.

Drug Treatments for Bipolar Disorder The drug lithium carbonate, a powdered form of the metallic element lithium, is the most widely used and recommended treatment for bipolar disorder. It could be said that the ancient Greeks and Romans were among the first to use lithium as a form of chemotherapy. They prescribed mineral water that contained lithium for people with turbulent mood swings.

Lithium is effective in stabilizing moods in people with bipolar disorder and reducing recurrent episodes of mania and depression (Baldessarini & Tondo, 2000; Grof & Alda, 2000). Yet lithium is generally more effective in treating manic than depressive symptoms (Sachs et al., 1994). People with bipolar disorder may need to use lithium indefinitely to control their mood swings, just as diabetics use insulin continuously to control their ill-

Truth OR Fiction?   REVISITED

The ancient Greeks and Romans used a chemical to curb turbulent mood swings that is still used today.

TRUE. The ancient Greeks and Romans did use a chemical substance to control mood swings that is still widely used today. It is called lithium.

ness. Lithium is given orally in the form of a natural mineral salt, lithium carbonate. Despite more than 40 years of use as a therapeutic drug, we still can't say how lithium works (Price & Heninger, 1994).

Yet lithium treatment is no panacea. At least 30% to 40% of patients with mania either fail to respond to the drug or cannot tolerate it (Dubovsky, 2000; Duffy et al., 1998). Among responders, about 6 in 10 eventually relapse (Goleman, 1994c).

Lithium treatment must be closely monitored because of potential toxic effects and other side effects. Lithium can produce a mild impairment in memory, "the kind of thing that might make a productive person stop taking it," as one expert put it (Goleman, 1994c). The drug can also lead to weight gain, lethargy, and grogginess, and to a general slowing down of motor functioning. It can also produce gastrointestinal distress and lead to liver problems over the long term. For a number of reasons, many patients discontinue using lithium or fail to take it reliably (Johnson & McFarland, 1996).

Anticonvulsant drugs used in the treatment of epilepsy, such as *carbamazepine* (brand name Tegretol) and *divalproex* (brand name Depakote), are also used to stabilize moods and relieve manic symptoms in people with bipolar disorder (Alao & Dewan, 2001; Baldessarini, Tohen, & Tondo, 2000; Bowden et al., 2000). Anticonvulsant drugs may be of benefit in treating people with bipolar disorder who either do not respond to lithium or cannot tolerate the drug because of side effects. Anticonvulsant drugs usually cause fewer or less severe side effects than lithium. However, some patients have only a partial response to lithium or anticonvulsant drugs and some fail to respond at all. Thus there remains the need for alternative treatments or drug strategies to be developed, perhaps involving a combination of these or other drugs (Bowden et al., 2000; Tohen et al., 2000).

Electroconvulsive Therapy **Electroconvulsive therapy (ECT),** more commonly called *shock therapy,* continues to evoke controversy. The idea of passing an electric current through someone's brain may seem barbaric. Yet ECT is a generally safe and effective treatment for severe depression, and it can help relieve depression in many cases in which alternative treatments have failed.

ECT involves the administration of an electrical current to the head. A current of between 70 to 130 volts is used to induce a convulsion that is similar to a grand mal epileptic seizure. ECT is usually administered in a series of 6 to 12 treatments distributed in a series of three per week, over a period of several weeks (USDHHS, 1999a). The patient is put to sleep with a brief-acting general anesthetic and given a muscle relaxant to avoid wild convulsions that might result in injury. As a result, spasms may be barely perceptible to onlookers. The patient awakens soon after the procedure and generally remembers nothing. Although ECT had earlier been used in the treatment of a wide variety of psychological disorders, including schizophrenia and bipolar disorder, the American Psychiatric Association recommended in 1990 that ECT be used only to treat major depressive disorder in people who do not respond to antidepressant medication.

ECT leads to significant improvement in about 50% to 60% of people with major depression who have failed to respond to antidepressant medication (Prudic et al., 1996; Sackeim, Prudic, & Devanand, 1990). ECT also results in shorter and less costly hospitalizations for major depression (Olfson et al., 1998). Although it often produces dramatic relief of symptoms of depression, no one knows exactly how ECT works. ECT produces such mammoth chemical and electrical changes in the body that it is difficult to pinpoint the mechanism of therapeutic action. One possibility is that ECT works by normalizing brain levels of certain neurotransmitters. Although ECT can be an effective short-term treatment of severe depression, it too is no panacea. Depression often returns at some later point, even among people who continue to be treated with antidepressant medication (Sackeim et al., 1994).

ECT may be administered to either both sides of the head (*bilateral ECT*) or to only one side of the head (*unilateral ECT*). Unilateral ECT is applied to the nondominant hemisphere of the brain, which, for most people, is the right side. High-dosage

WWW **Web Link 8.4**
Task Force Report on ECT

electroconvulsive therapy (ECT) A method of treating severe depression by means of administering an electric current to the head.

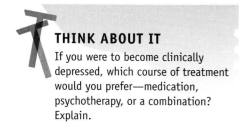

THINK ABOUT IT

If you were to become clinically depressed, which course of treatment would you prefer—medication, psychotherapy, or a combination? Explain.

unilateral ECT appears to be as effective as bilateral ECT, but produces less severe and persistent memory impairment (Lisanby et al., 2000; Sackeim et al., 2000; Sackeim & Vaughn McCall, 2001).

There is an understandable concern among patients, relatives, and professionals themselves about the possible risks of ECT, especially concerning memory loss for events occurring around the time of treatment (Weiner, 2000). As noted in Chapter 4, another nagging problem with ECT is a high rate of relapse following treatment (Sackeim, 2001; Sackeim et al., 2001). All in all, many professionals view ECT as a treatment of last resort, to be considered only after other treatment approaches have been tried and failed.

Clinical Practice Guidelines for Depression

In summing up, let us note the recommendations of a government-sponsored expert panel for the treatment of depression. The guidelines were based on evidence from controlled studies showing the following treatments to be effective in treating depression (Depression Guideline Panel, 1993b):

- Antidepressant medication (tricyclics or selective serotonin-reuptake inhibitors)
- Three specific forms of psychotherapy: cognitive therapy, behavior therapy, and interpersonal psychotherapy
- A combination of one of the recommended forms of psychotherapy and antidepressant medication
- Other specified forms of treatment, including ECT and phototherapy for seasonal depression

Quiz **8.3**
Treatment of Mood Disorders   Q

Suicide

Suicidal thoughts are common enough. Under great stress, many, if not most, people have considered suicide. A recent nationally representative survey found that 13% of U.S. adults reported having experienced suicidal thoughts and 4.6% reported making a suicide attempt (Kessler, Borges, & Walters, 1999). More than half (54%) of one sample of 694 first-year college students reported they had contemplated suicide on at least one occasion (Meehan et al., 1991). In a large sample of adolescents in Oregon, nearly 1 in 5 (19%) reported having suicidal thoughts at some point in their lives (Lewinsohn, Rohde, & Seeley, 1996). It is fortunate that most people who have suicidal thoughts do not act on them. Among the first-year college students who had considered suicide, fewer than 1 in 5 had attempted suicide (Meehan et al., 1991). Still, each year in the United States some 500,000 people are treated in hospital emergency rooms for attempted suicide and more than 30,000 "succeed" in taking their lives (Foxhall, 2001a; National Strategy for Suicide Prevention, 2001). Suicide exacts a heavy toll on the nation, as you can see in statistics reported in a recent report from the U.S. Surgeon General (see Table 8.7).

Suicidal behavior is not a psychological disorder in itself. But it is often a feature or symptom of an underlying psychological disorder, usually a mood disorder, which is the reason we discuss it in this chapter. The federal government estimates that about 60% of people who commit suicide have suffered from a mood disorder (National Strategy for Suicide Prevention, 2001).

Who Commits Suicide?

Suicide is the third leading cause of death among 15 to 24 year olds in the United States, following unintentional injuries and homicide. The suicide rate among adolescents and younger adults nearly tripled in the period 1952 to 1995 (Centers for Disease Control, 2001c). Yet suicide rates increase with age and are highest among adults age 65 and older,

---

TABLE **8.7**   **U.S. Surgeon General's Report on Suicide: Cost to the Nation**

- Every 17 minutes another life is lost to suicide. Every day, 86 Americans take their own life and over 1,500 attempt suicide.
- Suicide is now the eighth leading cause of death in Americans.
- For every two victims of homicide in the United States, there are three deaths from suicide.
- There are now twice as many deaths due to suicide than due to HIV/AIDS.
- Between 1952 and 1995, the incidence of suicide among adolescents and young adults nearly tripled.
- In the month prior to their suicide, 75% of elderly persons had visited a physician.
- Over half of all suicides occur in adult men, ages 25 to 65.
- Many who make suicide attempts never seek professional care immediately after the attempt.
- Males are four times more likely to die from suicide than are females.
- More teenagers and young adults die from suicide than from cancer, heart disease, AIDS, birth defects, stroke, pneumonia and influenza, and chronic lung disease, combined.
- Suicide takes the lives of more than 30,000 Americans every year.

Source. Center for Mental Health Services, 2001.

---

especially older White males (USDHHS, 1999a; National Strategy for Suicide Prevention, 2001; Pearson & Brown, 2000; see Figure 8.5).

Despite life-extending advances in medical care, some older adults may find the quality of their lives is less than satisfactory. With longer life, older people are more susceptible to diseases such as cancer and Alzheimer's, which can leave them with feelings of helplessness and hopelessness that, in turn, can give rise to suicidal thinking. Many older adults also suffer a mounting accumulation of losses of friends and loved ones as time progresses, leading to social isolation. These losses, as well as the loss of good health and of a responsible role in the community, may wear down the will to live. Not surprisingly, the highest suicide rates in older men are among those who are widowed or lead socially isolated lives. Society's increased acceptance of suicide in older people may also play a part. Whatever the causes, suicide has become an increased risk for elderly people. Perhaps society should focus its attention as much on the quality of life that is afforded our elderly and not simply on providing them the medical care that helps make longer life possible.

More women attempt suicide, but more men "succeed" (National Strategy for Suicide Prevention, 2001; USDHHS, 1999a). More males succeed, in large part, because they tend to choose quicker acting and more lethal means, such as handguns. Gender differences in suicide risk may mask the underlying factors. The common finding that men are more likely to take their own lives may be due to the fact that men are also more likely to have a history of alcohol and drug abuse and less likely to have children in the home. When these two factors were taken into account in a recent study, gender differences in suicide risk disappeared (Young et al., 1994).

Overall, Whites are about twice as likely as Blacks to commit suicide. Suicide rates among adolescents are highest among White males, but they are rising at a faster rate among Black males (CDC, 2001c). Native Americans are at much greater than average risk

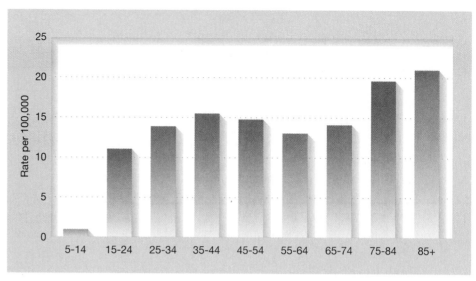

FIGURE 8.5
Suicide rates according to age.
Although adolescent suicides may be more highly publicized, adults, especially older adults, have higher suicide rates.

Source. Murphy, S. L. (2000). Deaths: Final data for 1998. *National vital statistics report*, 48 (11). Hyattsville, MD: National Center for Health Statistics. DHHS Publication No. (PHS) 20000-1120.

of suicide attempts and completed suicides. Overall, Native Americans (American Indians and Alaskan Natives) have a suicide rate that is 50% higher than other groups (Stinson, 2001). As noted in Chapter 2, male Native American adolescents and young adults have the highest suicide rates in the nation (USDHHS, 1999a).

Hopelessness and exposure to others who have attempted or completed suicide may contribute to the increased risk of suicide among Native American youth. Native American youth at greatest risk tend to be reared in communities that are largely isolated from the benefits of U.S. society at large. They perceive themselves as having relatively few opportunities to gain the skills necessary to join the work force in the larger society and are also relatively more prone to substance abuse, including alcohol abuse. Knowledge that peers have attempted or completed suicide renders suicide a highly visible escape from psychological pain.

Why Do People Commit Suicide?

To many lay observers, suicide seems so extreme an act that they believe only "insane" people (meaning people who are out of touch with reality) would commit suicide. However, suicidal thinking does not necessarily imply loss of touch with reality, deep-seated unconscious conflict, or a personality disorder. Having thoughts about suicide generally reflects a narrowing of the range of options people think are available to them to deal with their problems (Rotheram-Borus et al., 1990). That is, they are discouraged by their problems and see no other way out.

The risk of suicide is much greater among people with severe mood disorders, such as major depression and bipolar disorder (Bostwick & Pankratz, 2000). Major depression accounts for about 20% to 35% of suicide deaths in the United States (Angst, Angst, & Stassen, 1999). As many as one in five people with bipolar disorder eventually commit suicide (Cowan & Kandel, 2001). Experts believe that greater efforts toward diagnosing and treating mood disorders may result in lower suicide rates (Isacsson, 2000). Attempted or completed suicide is also linked to other psychological disorders, such as alcoholism and drug dependence, schizophrenia, panic disorder, antisocial personality disorder, posttraumatic stress disorders, borderline personality disorder, and a family history of suicide (e.g.,

Heikkinen et al., 1997; Hufford, 2001; Kotler et al., 2001; Roy, 2000). Suicide is also the leading cause of premature death among people with schizophrenia (Fenton et al., 1997). More than half the suicide attempters in a recent study had two or more psychological disorders (Beautrais et al., 1996).

Not all suicides are connected with psychological disorders. Some people suffering from painful and hopeless physical illness seek to escape further suffering by taking their own lives. These suicides are sometimes labeled "rational suicides" in the belief that they are based on a rational decision that life is no longer worth living in the light of continual suffering. However, in perhaps many of these cases the person's judgment and reasoning ability may be colored by an underlying and potentially treatable psychological disorder, such as depression. Other suicides are motivated by deep-seated religious or political convictions, as in the case of people who sacrifice themselves in acts of protest against their governments. A yet more horrific example is that of terrorists who kill others as well as themselves in the belief that their acts will be rewarded in an afterlife.

Suicide attempts often occur in response to highly stressful life events, especially "exit events" such as the death of a spouse, close friend, or relative; divorce or separation; a family member's leaving home; or the loss of a close friend. People who consider suicide in times of stress may lack problem-solving skills and be less able to find alternative ways of coping with the stressors they face. Underscoring the psychological impact of severe stress, researchers find suicides to be more common among survivors of natural disasters, especially severe floods (Krug et al., 1998).

Theoretical Perspectives on Suicide

The classic psychodynamic model views depression as the turning inward of anger against the internal representation of a lost love object. Suicide then represents inward-directed anger that turns murderous. Suicidal people, then, do not seek to destroy themselves. Instead, they seek to vent their rage against the internalized representation of the love object. In so doing, they destroy themselves as well, of course. In his later writings, Freud speculated that suicide may be motivated by the "death instinct," a tendency to return to the tension-free state that preceded birth. Existential and humanistic theorists relate suicide to the perception that life is meaningless and hopeless. Suicidal people report they find life duller, emptier, and more boring than nonsuicidal people (Mehrabian & Weinstein, 1985).

In the nineteenth century, social thinker Emile Durkheim (1958) noted that people who experienced **anomie**—who feel lost, without identity, rootless—are more likely to commit suicide. Sociocultural theorists likewise believe that alienation in today's society may play a role in suicide. In our modern, mobile society, people frequently move hundreds or thousands of miles to schools and jobs. Executives and their families may be relocated every 2 years or so. Military personnel and their families may be shifted about yet more rapidly. Many people are thereby socially isolated or cut off from their support groups. Moreover, city dwellers tend to limit or discourage informal social contacts because of crowding, overstimulation, and fear of crime. It is thus understandable that many people find few sources of support in times of crisis. In some cases, the availability of family support may not be helpful. Family members may be perceived as part of the problem, not part of the solution.

Learning theorists focus largely on the lack of problem-solving skills for handling significant life stress. According to Shneidman (1985), suicide attempters wish to escape unbearable psychological pain and may perceive no other way out. People who threaten or attempt suicide may also receive sympathy and support from loved ones and others, perhaps making future—and more lethal—attempts more likely. This is not to suggest that suicide attempts or gestures should be ignored. It is not the case that people who threaten suicide are merely seeking attention. Although those who have threatened suicide may not carry out the act, their threats should be taken seriously. People who commit suicide often tell others of their intentions or leave clues beforehand. Moreover, many people make

Truth OR Fiction? REVISITED

People who threaten suicide are basically attention seekers.

FALSE. Although people who threaten suicide may not carry out the act, their threats should be taken seriously. Most people who do commit suicide had told others of their intentions or had left clues.

anomie A feeling of rootlessness.

aborted suicide attempts in which they stop just before inflicting harm on themselves before they go on to make actual suicide attempts (Barber et al., 1998).

Social-cognitive theorists suggest that suicide may be motivated by positive expectancies and by approving attitudes toward the legitimacy of suicide (D. Stein et al., 1998). People who kill themselves may expect that they will be missed or eulogized after death, or that survivors will feel guilty for mistreating them. Suicidal psychiatric patients hold more positive expectancies concerning suicide than do nonsuicidal psychiatric samples. They more often expressed the belief that suicide would solve their problems, for example (Linehan et al., 1987). Suicide may represent a desperate attempt to deal with one's problems in one fell swoop rather than piecemeal.

Social-cognitive theorists also focus on the potential modeling effects of observing suicidal behavior in others, especially among teenagers who feel overwhelmed by academic and social stressors. A *social contagion*, or spreading of suicide in a community, may occur in the wake of suicides that receive widespread publicity. Teenagers, who seem to be especially vulnerable to these modeling effects, may even romanticize the suicidal act as one of heroic courage. The incidence of suicide among teenagers sometimes rises markedly in the period following news reports about suicide (Kessler et al., 1990). In the Oregon study, suicidal behavior of a friend was a risk factor in suicide attempts among adolescents (Lewinsohn, Rohde, & Seeley, 1996). Copycat suicides may be more likely to occur when reports of suicides are sensationalized such that other teenagers expect their demises to have broad impacts on their communities (Kessler et al., 1990).

Biological factors are also implicated in suicide. Reduced serotonin activity is found in many people who attempt or commit suicide (Ghanshyam et al., 1995; Mann & Malone, 1997). Since reduced availability of serotonin is linked to depression, the relationship with suicide is not surprising. Yet serotonin acts to curb or inhibit nervous system activity, so perhaps decreased serotonin activity leads to a *disinhibition* or release of impulsive behavior that takes the form of a suicidal act in vulnerable individuals. Suicide also tends to run in families, which hints of genetic factors. Evidence from a recent twin study showed that among nine twin pairs in which both twins committed suicide, seven were MZ twins and two were DZ twins (Roy et al., 1991). All in all, about one suicide attempter in four has a family member who has committed suicide (Sorensen & Rutter, 1991).

The presence of psychological disorders among other family members may be connected with suicide (Sorensen & Rutter, 1991). But what are the causal connections? Do people who attempt suicide inherit vulnerabilities to disorders that are connected with suicide? Does the family atmosphere subject its members to feelings of hopelessness? Does the suicide of one family member give others the idea of doing the same thing? Does one suicide create the impression that other family members are destined to kill themselves? These are all questions researchers need to address.

Suicide is connected with a complex web of factors, and its prediction is no simpler. Yet it is clear that many suicides could be prevented if people with suicidal feelings would receive treatment for disorders underlying suicidal behavior, including depression, schizophrenia, and alcohol and substance abuse ("Many Suicides Could Be Prevented," 1998). We also need strategies that emphasize the maintenance of hope during times of severe stress (Malone et al., 2000).

Predicting Suicide

"I don't believe it. I just saw him last week and he looked fine."

"She sat here just the other day, laughing with the rest of us. How were we to know what was going on inside her?"

"I knew he was depressed, but I never thought he'd do something like this. I didn't have a clue."

"Why didn't she just call me?"

THINK ABOUT IT

What factors are related to suicide and suicide prevention? Did your reading of the text change your ideas about how you might deal with a suicidal threat by a friend or loved one? If so, how?

A Closer Look

Suicide Prevention

Imagine yourself having an intimate conversation with a close campus friend, Chris. You know that things have not been good. Chris's grandfather died 6 weeks ago, and the two were very close. Chris's grades have been going downhill, and Chris's romantic relationship also seems to be coming apart at the seams. Still, you are unprepared when Chris says very deliberately, "I just can't take it anymore. Life is just too painful. I don't feel like I want to live anymore. I've decided that the only thing I can do is to kill myself."

When somebody discloses that he or she is contemplating suicide, you may feel bewildered and frightened, as if a great burden has been placed on your shoulders. It has. If someone confides suicidal thoughts to you, your goal should be to persuade him or her to see a professional, or to get the advice of a professional yourself as soon as you can. But if the suicidal person declines to talk to another person and you sense you can't break away for such a conference, there are some things you can do then and there:

1. *Draw the person out.* Shneidman advises framing questions like, "What's going on?" "Where do you hurt?" "What would you like to see happen?" (1985, p. 11). Such questions may prompt people to verbalize thwarted psychological needs and offer some relief. They also grant you the time to appraise the risk and contemplate your next move.

2. *Be sympathetic.* Show that you fathom how troubled the person is. Don't say something like, "You're just being silly. You don't really mean it."

3. *Suggest that means other than suicide can be discovered to work out the person's problems,* even if they are not apparent at the time. Shneidman (1985) notes that suicidal people can usually see only two solutions to their predicaments—either suicide or some kind of magical resolution. Professionals try to broaden the available alternatives of people who are suicidal.

4. *Inquire as to how the person expects to commit suicide.* People with explicit methods who also possess the means (for example, a gun or drugs) are at greater risk. Ask if you may hold on to the gun, drugs, or whatever, for a while. Sometimes the person agrees.

5. *Propose that the person accompany you to consult a professional right now.* Many campuses have hot lines that you or the suicidal individual can call. Many towns and cities have such hot lines

Teen suicide. Suicidal teenagers may see no other way of handling their life problems. The availability of counseling and support services may help prevent suicide by assisting troubled teens in learning alternate ways of reducing stress and resolving conflicts with others.

and they can be called anonymously. Other possibilities include the emergency room of a general hospital, a campus health center or counseling center, or the campus or local police. If you are unable to maintain contact with the suicidal person, get professional assistance as soon as you separate.

6. *Don't say something like "You're talking crazy."* Such comments are degrading and injurious to the individual's self-esteem. Don't press the suicidal person to contact specific people, such as parents or a spouse. Conflict with them may have given rise to the suicidal thoughts.

Above all, keep in mind that your primary goal is to confer with a helping professional. Don't go it alone any longer than you have to.

Friends and family members often respond to news of a suicide with disbelief or guilt that they failed to pick up signs of the impending act. Yet even trained professionals find it difficult to predict who is likely to commit suicide.

Evidence points to the pivotal role of hopelessness in predicting suicidal thinking and suicide attempts (Brown et al., 2000; Malone et al., 2000). In one study, psychiatric

Web Link 8.5
WWW   Surgeon General's Call to Action to Prevent Suicide

Quiz **8.4**
Suicide

Quiz **8.5**
Chapter Exam

Research Update
Chapter 8

outpatients with hopelessness scores above a certain cutoff were 11 times more likely to commit suicide than those with scores below the cutoff (Beck et al., 1990). But *when* does hopelessness lead to suicide?

People who commit suicide tend to signal their intentions, often quite explicitly, such as by telling others about their suicidal thoughts (Denneby et al., 1996). Some attempt to cloak their intentions. Behavioral clues may still reveal suicidal intent, however. Edwin Shneidman, a leading researcher on suicide, found that 90% of the people who committed suicide had left clear clues, such as disposing of their possessions (Gelman, 1994). People contemplating suicide may also suddenly try to sort out their affairs, as in drafting a will or buying a cemetery plot. They may purchase guns despite lack of prior interest in firearms. When troubled people decide to commit suicide, they may seem to be suddenly at peace; they feel relieved of having to contend with life problems. This sudden calm may be misinterpreted as a sign of hope.

The prediction of suicide is not an exact science, even for experienced professionals. Many observable factors, such as hopelessness, do seem to be connected with suicide, but we cannot predict *when* a hopeless person will attempt suicide, if at all.

Overview of Mood Disorders

TYPES OF MOOD DISORDERS

	Description	Features
Major Depressive Disorder	Episodes of severe depression	• A range of features may be present, from downcast mood to appetite and sleep disturbance, to lack of interest and motivation • Seasonal affective disorder and postpartum depression are subtypes of major depression
Dysthymic Disorder	Long-standing mild depression	• Feeling "down in the dumps" most of the time, but not as severely depressed as people with major depressive disorder • Double depression is characterized by major depressive episodes occurring during the course of dysthymia
Bipolar Disorder	Mood swings between elation and depression	• The two general subtypes are bipolar I disorder and bipolar II disorder • In rapid cycling, mania and major depression alternate without intervening periods of normal mood
Cyclothymia	Milder mood swings than bipolar disorder	• Chronic, cyclical pattern of shifting mood states from hypomanic episodes to states of mild depression • Frequent periods of depressed mood or loss of interest or pleasure in activities, but not at the level of severity of a major depressive episode

CAUSAL FACTORS Multiple causes are involved, interacting with each other in complex ways

Biological Factors	• Genetic predispositions • Disturbed neurotransmitter functioning • Abnormalities in parts of the brain regulating mood states • Possible endocrine system involvement in mood states
Social-Environmental Factors	• Stressful life events, such as the loss of a loved one or prolonged unemployment
Behavioral Factors	• Lack of reinforcement • Negative interactions with others, leading to rejection
Emotional and Cognitive Factors	• In classic psychoanalytic theory, anger turned inward • Emotional difficulties coping with the loss of significant others • Lack of meaning or purpose in life • Negatively biased or distorted ways of thinking, or a depressive attributional style

TREATMENT APPROACHES Treatment may include one or more therapeutic approaches

Biomedical Treatment	• Antidepressant drugs (tricyclics, MAO inhibitors, SSRIs) to control depressive symptoms by influencing the availability of neurotransmitters in the brain • Lithium or anticonvulsant drugs to stabilize moods in bipolar patients • Electroconvulsive therapy (ECT) in severe cases of depression • Phototherapy for seasonal affective disorder
Cognitive-Behavioral Therapy	• To help clients correct distorted ways of thinking, develop more effective coping responses, and increase levels of positive reinforcement
Interpersonal Therapy	• To resolve interpersonal problems and lingering grief reactions

Summing Up

Types of Mood Disorders

What are mood disorders? Mood disorders are disturbances in mood that are unusually prolonged or severe and serious enough to impair daily functioning.

What are the major types of mood disorders? There are various kinds of mood disorders, including depressive (unipolar) disorders, such as major depressive disorder and dysthymic disorder, and disorders involving mood swings, such as bipolar disorder and cyclothymic disorder.

What is major depressive disorder? In major depression, people experience a profound change in mood that impairs their ability to function. There are many associated features of major depressive disorder, including downcast mood; changes in appetite; difficulty sleeping; reduced sense of pleasure in formerly enjoyable activities; feelings of fatigue or loss of energy; sense of worthlessness; excessive or misplaced guilt; difficulties concentrating, thinking clearly, or making decisions; repeated thoughts of death or suicide; attempts at suicide; and even psychotic behaviors (hallucinations and delusions).

What is dysthymic disorder? Dysthymic disorder is a form of chronic depression that is milder than major depressive disorder but may nevertheless be associated with impaired functioning in social and occupational roles.

What is bipolar disorder? In bipolar disorder, people experience fluctuating mood states that interfere with the ability to function. Bipolar I disorder is identified by one or more manic episodes. Bipolar II is characterized by the occurrence of at least one major depressive episode and one hypomanic episode, but without any full-blown manic episodes.

What are the features of a manic episode? Manic episodes are characterized by sudden elevation or expansion of mood and sense of self-importance, feelings of almost boundless energy, hyperactivity, and extreme sociability, which often takes a demanding and overbearing form. People in manic episodes tend to exhibit pressured or rapid speech, rapid "flight of ideas," and decreased need for sleep.

What is cyclothymic disorder? Cyclothymic disorder is a type of bipolar disorder characterized by a chronic pattern of mild mood swings that sometimes progresses to bipolar disorder.

Theoretical Perspectives on Mood Disorders

How is stress related to mood disorders? Exposure to life stress in associated with an increased risk of development and recurrence of mood disorders, especially major depression. Yet some people are more resilient in the face of stress, perhaps because of psychosocial factors such as social support and coping styles.

How do psychodynamic theorists conceptualize mood disorders? In classic psychodynamic theory, depression is viewed in terms of inward-directed anger. People who hold strongly ambivalent feelings toward people they have lost, or whose loss is threatened, may direct unresolved anger toward the inward representations of these people that they have incorporated or introjected within themselves, producing self-loathing and depression. Bipolar disorder is understood within psychodynamic theory in terms of the shifting balances between the ego and superego. More recent psychodynamic models, such as the self-focusing model, incorporate both psychodynamic and cognitive aspects in explaining depression in terms of the continued pursuit of lost love objects or goals that it would be more adaptive to surrender.

How do humanistic theorists view depression? Theorists working within the humanistic framework view depression as reflecting a lack of meaning and authenticity in a person's life.

How do learning theorists view depression? Learning perspectives focus on situational factors in explaining depression, such as changes in the level of reinforcement. When reinforcement is reduced, the person may feel unmotivated and depressed, which can occasion inactivity and further reduce opportunities for reinforcement. Coyne's interactional theory focuses on the negative family interactions that can lead the family members of people with depression to become less reinforcing toward them.

What are two major cognitive models of depression? Beck's cognitive model focuses on the role of negative or distorted thinking in depression. Depression-prone people hold negative beliefs toward themselves, the environment, and the future. This cognitive triad of depression leads to specific errors in thinking, or cognitive distortions, in response to negative events, which, in turn, lead to depression.

The learned helplessness model is based on the belief that people may become depressed when they come to view themselves as helpless to control the reinforcements in their environment or to change their lives for the better. A reformulated version of the theory held that the ways in which a people explain events—their attributions—determine their proneness toward depression in the face of negative events. The combination of internal, global, and stable attributions for negative events renders one most vulnerable to depression.

What role do biological factors play in mood disorders? Genetics appears to play a role in mood disorders, especially in explaining major depressive disorder and bipolar disorder. Imbalances in the neurotransmitter activity in the brain appear to be involved in depression and mania. The diathesis-stress model is used as an explanatory framework to illustrate how biological or psychological diatheses may interact with stress in the development of depression.

Treatment of Mood Disorders

What approaches to treatment are represented by each of the major theoretical perspectives? Psychodynamic treatment of depression has traditionally focused on helping the depressed person uncover and work through ambivalent feelings toward the lost object, thereby lessening the anger directed inward. Modern psychodynamic approaches tend to be more direct and briefer and focus more on developing adaptive means of achieving self-worth and resolving interpersonal conflicts. Learning theory approaches have focused on helping people with depression increase the frequency of reinforcement in their lives through such means as increasing the rates of pleasant activities in which they participate and assisting them in developing more effective social skills to increase their ability to obtain social reinforcements from others. Cognitive therapists focus on helping the person identify and correct distorted or dysfunctional thoughts and learn more adaptive behaviors. Biological approaches have focused on the use of antidepressant drugs and other biological treatments, such as electroconvulsive therapy (ECT). Antidepressant drugs may help normalize neurotransmitter functioning in the brain. Bipolar disorder is commonly treated with lithium.

Suicide

What factors are linked to suicide? Mood disorders are often linked to suicide. Although women are more likely to attempt suicide, more men actually succeed, probably because they select more lethal means. The elderly—not the young—are more likely to commit suicide, and the rate of suicide among the elderly appears to be increasing. People who attempt suicide are often depressed, but they are generally in touch with reality. They may, however, lack effective problem-solving skills and see no other way of dealing with life stress than suicide. A sense of hopelessness also figures prominently in suicides.

What are the major theoretical approaches to understanding suicide? These draw upon the classic psychodynamic model of anger turned inward; Durkeim's theory of social alienation; and learning, social-cognitive, and biologically based perspectives.

Why should you never ignore a person's threat to commit suicide? Although certainly not all people who threaten suicide go on to commit the act, many do. People who commit suicide often signal their intentions, such as by telling others about their suicidal thoughts.

CHAPTER NINE

Personality
Disorders

Paul Klee
Beware of Red, 1940

All of us have particular styles of behavior and ways of relating to others. Some of us are orderly, others sloppy. Some of us prefer solitary pursuits; others are more social. Some of us are followers; others are leaders. Some of us seem immune to rejection by others, whereas others avoid social initiatives for fear of getting shot down. When behavior patterns become so inflexible or maladaptive that they cause significant personal distress or impair people's social or occupational functioning, they may be diagnosed as personality disorders.

Types of Personality Disorders

In most of us by the age of thirty, the character has set like plaster, and will never soften again.

—William James

Personality disorders are excessively rigid patterns of behavior or ways of relating to others. Their rigidity prevents people from adjusting to external demands; thus the patterns ultimately become self-defeating. The disordered personality traits become evident by adolescence or early adulthood and continue through much of adult life, becoming so deeply ingrained that they are highly resistant to change. The warning signs of personality disorders may be detected during childhood, even in the troubled behavior of preschoolers. Children with psychological disorders or problem behaviors in childhood, such as conduct disorder, depression, anxiety, and immaturity, are at greater than average risk of later developing personality disorders (Bernstein et al., 1996; Kasen et al., 2001). Personality disorders appear to be quite common; a recent community survey of adults in Oslo, Norway, found that 13.4% of community residents showed evidence of one or more personality disorders (Torgersen, Kringlen, & Cramer, 2001).

Despite the self-defeating consequences of their behavior, people with personality disorders do not generally perceive a need to change. Using psychodynamic terms, the *DSM* notes that people with personality disorders tend to perceive their traits as **ego syntonic**—as natural parts of themselves. Consequently, people with personality disorders are more likely to be brought to the attention of mental health professionals by others than to seek services themselves. In contrast, people with anxiety disorders (Chapter 6) or mood disorders (Chapter 8) tend to view their disturbed behaviors as **ego dystonic.** They do not see their behaviors as parts of their self-identities and are thus more likely to seek help to relieve the distress caused by them.

The *DSM* groups clinical syndromes on Axis I and personality disorders on Axis II. Both clinical syndromes and personality disorders may thus be diagnosed in clients whose behavior meets the criteria for both classes of disorders. A person may have an Axis I mood disorder, for example, such as major depression, and also show the more enduring characteristics associated with an Axis II personality disorder.

The *DSM* groups personality disorders into three clusters:

Cluster A: People who are perceived as odd or eccentric. This cluster includes paranoid, schizoid, and schizotypal personality disorders.

Cluster B: People whose behavior is overly dramatic, emotional, or erratic. This grouping consists of antisocial, borderline, histrionic, and narcissistic personality disorders.

Cluster C: People who often appear anxious or fearful. This cluster includes avoidant, dependent, and obsessive-compulsive personality disorders.

Personality Disorders Characterized by Odd or Eccentric Behavior

This group of personality disorders includes paranoid, schizoid, and schizotypal disorders. People with these disorders often have difficulty relating to others, or they may show little or no interest in developing social relationships.

Truth OR Fiction? REVISITED

Warning signs of personality disorders may appear in early childhood.

TRUE. Warning signs of personality disorder may be found in problem behaviors observed in young children, even preschoolers.

wWw **Web Link 9.1**
   Fact Sheet on Personality Disorders

personality disorders Excessively rigid behavior patterns, or ways of relating to others, that ultimately become self-defeating.

ego syntonic Referring to behaviors or feelings that are perceived as natural parts of the self.

ego dystonic Referring to behaviors or feelings that are perceived to be alien to one's self-identity.

THINK ABOUT IT

Which behaviors or ways of relating to others do you view as intrinsic parts of yourself, or ego syntonic? Do you believe they are changeable? Why or why not?

Paranoid Personality Disorder The defining trait of the **paranoid personality disorder** is pervasive suspiciousness—the tendency to interpret other people's behavior as deliberately threatening or demeaning. People with the disorder are excessively mistrustful of others, and their relationships suffer for it. Though they may be suspicious of coworkers and supervisors, they can generally maintain employment.

The following case illustrates the unwarranted suspicion and reluctance to confide in others that typifies people with paranoid personalities:

A Case of Paranoid Personality Disorder

An 85-year-old retired businessman was interviewed by a social worker to determine the health care needs for himself and his infirm wife. The man had no history of treatment for a mental disorder. He appeared to be in good health and mentally alert. He and his wife had been married for 60 years, and it appeared that his wife was the only person he'd ever really trusted. He had always been suspicious of others. He would not reveal personal information to anyone but his wife, believing that others were out to take advantage of him. He had refused offers of help from other acquaintances because he suspected their motives. When called on the telephone, he would refuse to give out his name until he determined the nature of the caller's business. He'd always involved himself in "useful work" to occupy his time, even during the 20 years of his retirement. He spent a good deal of time monitoring his investments and had altercations with his stockbroker when errors on his monthly statement prompted suspicion that his broker was attempting to cover up fraudulent transactions.

—Adapted from Spitzer et al., 1994, pp. 211–213

■

Web Link **9.2** www
Specific Types of Personality Disorders

People who have paranoid personalities tend to be overly sensitive to criticism, whether real or imagined. They take offense at the smallest slight. They are readily angered and hold grudges when they think they have been mistreated. They are unlikely to confide in others because they believe that personal information may be used against them. They question the sincerity and trustworthiness of friends and associates. A smile or a glance may be viewed with suspicion. As a result, they have few friends and intimate relationships. When they do form an intimate relationship, they may suspect infidelity, although there is no evidence to back up their suspicions. They tend to remain hypervigilant, as if they must be on the lookout against harm. They deny blame for misdeeds, even when warranted, and are perceived by others as cold, aloof, scheming, devious, and humorless. They tend to be argumentative and may launch repeated lawsuits against those who they believe have mistreated them.

Clinicians need to weigh cultural and sociopolitical factors when arriving at a diagnosis of paranoid personality disorder. They may find members of immigrant or ethnic minority groups, political refugees, or people from other cultures to be guarded or defensive in their behavior. This behavior may reflect unfamiliarity with the language, customs, or rules and regulations of the majority culture; it may also reflect a cultural mistrust arising from a history of neglect or oppression against the individual's cultural or ethnic group. Such behavior should not be confused with paranoid personality disorder.

Although the suspicions of people with paranoid personality disorder are exaggerated and unwarranted, there is an absence of the outright paranoid delusions that characterize the thought patterns of people with paranoid schizophrenia (for example, believing the FBI is out to get them). People who have paranoid personalities are unlikely to seek treatment for themselves; they see others as causing their problems. The reported prevalence of paranoid personality disorder in the general population ranges from 0.5% to 2.5% (APA, 2000). The disorder is diagnosed in people receiving mental health treatment more often in men than women.

paranoid personality disorder A personality disorder characterized by suspiciousness of others' motives, but not to the point of delusion.

Schizoid Personality Disorder Social isolation is the cardinal feature of **schizoid personality disorder**. Often described as a loner or an eccentric, the person with a schizoid personality lacks interest in social relationships. The emotions of persons with schizoid personalities appear shallow or blunted, but not to the degree found in schizophrenia (see Chapter 13). People with this disorder seem rarely, if ever, to experience strong anger, joy, or sadness. They look distant and aloof. Their faces tend to show no emotional expression, and they rarely exchange social smiles or nods. They seem indifferent to criticism or praise and appear to be wrapped up in abstract ideas rather than in thoughts about people. Although they prefer to remain distant from others, they maintain better contact with reality than people with schizophrenia do. The prevalence of the disorder in the general population remains unknown.

The schizoid personality pattern is usually recognized by early adulthood. Men with this disorder rarely date or marry. Women with the disorder are more likely to accept romantic advances passively and marry, but they seldom initiate relationships or develop strong attachments to their partners.

Akhtar (1987) claims that there may be discrepancies between outer appearances and the inner lives of people with schizoid personalities. Although they may appear to have little appetite for sex, for example, they may harbor voyeuristic wishes and become attracted to pornography. Akhtar also suggests that the distance and social aloofness of people with schizoid personalities may be somewhat superficial. They may also harbor exquisite sensitivity, deep curiosities about people, and wishes for love that they cannot express. In some cases, sensitivity is expressed in deep feelings for animals rather than people:

Schizoid personality. It is normal to be reserved about displaying one's feelings, especially when one is among strangers. But people with schizoid personalities rarely express emotions and are distant and aloof. Yet the emotions of people with schizoid personalities are not as shallow or blunted as they are in people with schizophrenia.

A Case of Schizoid Personality Disorder

John, a 50-year-old retired police officer, sought treatment a few weeks after his dog was hit by a car and died. Since the dog's death, John has felt sad and tired. He has had difficulty concentrating and sleeping. He lives alone and prefers to be by himself, limiting his contacts with others to a passing "Hello" or "How are you?" He feels that social conversation is a waste of time and feels awkward when others try to initiate a friendship. Though he avidly reads newspapers and keeps abreast of current events, he has no real interest in people. He works as a security guard and is described by his coworkers as a "loner" and a "cold fish." The only relationship he had was with his dog, with which he felt he could exchange more sensitive and loving feelings than he could share with people. At Christmas, he would "exchange gifts" with his dog, buying presents for the dog and wrapping a bottle of Scotch for himself as a gift from the animal. The only event that ever saddened him was the loss of his dog. In contrast, the loss of his parents failed to evoke an emotional response. He considers himself to be different from other people and is bewildered by the displays of emotionality that he sees in others.

—Adapted from Spitzer et al., 1989, pp. 249–250

Schizotypal Personality Disorder **Schizotypal personality disorder** usually becomes evident by early adulthood. The diagnosis applies to people who have difficulties forming close relationships and whose behavior, mannerisms, and thought patterns are peculiar or odd, but not disturbed enough to merit a diagnosis of schizophrenia. They may be especially anxious in social situations, even when interacting with familiar people. Their social

Truth OR Fiction? REVISITED

People with schizoid personalities may have deeper feelings for animals than they do for people.

TRUE. People with a schizoid personality may show little or no interest in people but develop strong feelings for animals.

schizoid personality disorder A personality disorder characterized by persistent lack of interest in social relationships, flattened affect, and social withdrawal.

schizotypal personality disorder A personality disorder characterized by eccentricities of thought and behavior, but without clearly psychotic features.

ideas of reference A form of delusional thinking in which a person reads personal meaning into the behavior of others or external events.

anxieties seem to be associated with paranoid thinking (e.g., fears that others mean them harm) rather than with concerns about being rejected or evaluated negatively by others (APA, 2000).

Schizotypal personality disorder may be slightly more common in males than in females and is believed to affect about 3% of the general population (APA, 2000). Clinicians need to be careful not to label as schizotypal certain behavior patterns that reflect culturally determined beliefs or religious rituals, such as beliefs in voodoo and other magical beliefs.

The eccentricity associated with the schizoid personality is limited to a lack of interest in social relationships. Schizotypal personality disorder refers to a wider range of odd behaviors, beliefs, and perceptions. Persons with the disorder may experience unusual perceptions or illusions, such as feeling the presence of a deceased family member in the room. They realize, however, that the person is not actually there. They may become unduly suspicious of others or paranoid in their thinking. They may develop **ideas of reference,** such as the belief that other people are talking about them. They may engage in "magical thinking," such as believing they possess a "sixth sense" (i.e., can foretell the future) or that others can sense their feelings. They may attach unusual meanings to words. Their own speech may be vague or unusually abstract, but it is not incoherent or filled with the loose associations that characterize schizophrenia. They may appear unkempt, display unusual mannerisms, and engage in unusual behaviors, such as talking to themselves in the presence of others. Their faces may register little emotion. Like people with schizoid personalities, they may fail to exchange smiles with, or nod at, others. Or they may appear silly and smile and laugh at the wrong times. They tend to be socially withdrawn and aloof, with few if any close friends or confidants. They seem to be especially anxious around unfamiliar people. We can see evidence of the social aloofness and illusions that are often associated with schizotypal personality disorder in this case:

A Case of Schizotypal Personality Disorder

Jonathan, a 27-year-old auto mechanic, had few friends and preferred science fiction novels to socializing with other people. He seldom joined in conversations. At times, he seemed to be lost in his thoughts, and his coworkers would have to whistle to get his attention when he was working on a car. He often showed a "queer" expression on his face. Perhaps the most unusual feature of his behavior was his reported intermittent experience of "feeling" his deceased mother standing nearby. These illusions were reassuring to him, and he looked forward to their occurrence. Jonathan realized they were not real. He never tried to reach out to touch the apparition, knowing it would disappear as soon as he drew closer. It was enough, he said, to feel her presence.

—From the Authors' Files

■

THINK ABOUT IT

Distinguish between schizoid and schizotypal personality disorder by giving examples of some ways in which a person with each disorder might behave.

Despite the *DSM*'s grouping of "schizotypal" behaviors with personality disorders, the schizotypal behavior pattern may fall within a spectrum of schizophrenia-related disorders that also includes paranoid and schizoid personality disorders, as well as schizoaffective disorder (discussed in Chapter 13) and schizophrenia itself. Schizotypal personality disorder may actually share a common genetic basis with schizophrenia (Kendler & Walsh, 1995). Biological relatives of people with schizotypal personality disorder are more likely than relatives of people with non-schizophrenia-related personality disorders (for example, histrionic, borderline, or narcissistic disorders) to be diagnosed as suffering from schizophrenia or a related disorder (Siever et al., 1990).

Let us note, however, that schizotypal personality disorder tends to follow a chronic course, and relatively few people diagnosed with the disorder go on to develop schizophrenia or other psychotic disorders (APA, 2000). Perhaps the emergence of schizophrenia in persons with this shared genetic predisposition is determined by such factors as stressful early family relationships.

Personality Disorders Characterized by Dramatic, Emotional, or Erratic Behavior

This cluster of personality disorders includes the antisocial, borderline, histrionic, and narcissistic types. The behavior patterns of these types are excessive, unpredictable, or self-centered. People with these disorders have difficulty forming and maintaining relationships.

Antisocial Personality Disorder People with **antisocial personality disorder** persistently violate the rights of others and often break the law. They disregard social norms and conventions, are impulsive, and fail to live up to interpersonal and vocational commitments. Yet they often show a superficial charm and are at least average in intelligence (Cleckley, 1976). Perhaps the features that are most striking about them are their low levels of anxiety in threatening situations and lack of guilt or remorse following wrongdoing. Punishment seems to have little if any effect on their behavior. Although parents and others have usually punished them for their misdeeds, they persist in leading irresponsible and impulsive lives.

Although women are more likely than men to develop anxiety and depressive disorders, men are more likely than women to receive diagnoses of antisocial personality disorder (Robins, Locke, & Reiger, 1991). The prevalence rates for the disorder in community samples range from about 3% to 6% in men and about 1% in women (APA, 2000; Kessler et al., 1994; see Figure 9.1). For the diagnosis of antisocial personality disorder to be applied, the person must be at least 18 years of age. The alternative diagnosis of conduct disorder is used with younger people (see Chapter 14). Many children with conduct disorders do not continue to show antisocial behavior as adults.

We once used terms like *psychopath* and *sociopath* to refer to the type of people who today are classified as having antisocial personalities, people whose behavior is amoral and asocial, impulsive, and lacking in remorse and shame. Some clinicians continue to use these terms interchangeably with *antisocial personality*. The roots of the word *psychopath* focus on the idea that there is something amiss (pathological) in the individual's psychological functioning. The roots of *sociopathy* center on the person's social deviance.

The pattern of behavior that characterizes antisocial personality disorder begins in childhood or adolescence and extends into adulthood. However, the antisocial and criminal behavior associated with the disorder tends to decline with age, and may actually disappear by the time the person reaches the age of 40. Not so for the underlying personality traits associated with the disorder—traits such as egocentricity; manipulativeness; lack of empathy, guilt, or remorse; and callousness toward others. These appear to be relatively stable even with increasing age (Harpur & Hare, 1994).

Much of our attention in this chapter focuses on antisocial personality disorder. Historically it is the personality disorder that has been most extensively studied by scholars and researchers.

Sociocultural Factors and Antisocial Personality Disorder

Antisocial personality disorder cuts across all racial and ethnic groups. Researchers find no evidence of ethnic or racial differences in the rates of the disorder (Robins, Tipp, & Przybeck, 1991). The disorder is more common, however, among people in lower socioeconomic groups. One explanation is that people with antisocial personality disorder may drift downward occupationally, perhaps because their antisocial behavior makes it difficult for them to hold steady jobs or progress upward. It is possible too that people from lower socioeconomic levels are more likely to have been reared by parents who themselves modeled antisocial behavior. However, it is also possible that the diagnosis is misapplied to people living in hard-pressed communities who may engage in seemingly antisocial behaviors as a type of survival strategy (APA, 2000).

antisocial personality disorder
A personality disorder characterized by antisocial and irresponsible behavior and lack of remorse for misdeeds.

Antisocial personality. Serial killer Ted Bundy, shown here shortly before his execution, killed without feeling or remorse but also displayed some of the superficial charm seen in some people with antisocial personality disorder.

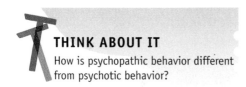

THINK ABOUT IT
How is psychopathic behavior different from psychotic behavior?

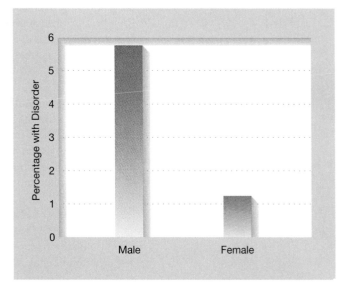

FIGURE 9.1 Lifetime prevalences of antisocial personality disorder by gender.
Antisocial personality disorder is more than five times as common among men than women. However, the disorder has been rising more rapidly among women in recent years.

Source. National Comorbidity Survey (Kessler et al, 1994).

Criminality or antisocial personality disorder? It is likely that many prison inmates could be diagnosed with antisocial personality disorder; however, people may become criminals or delinquents not because of a disordered personality but because they were raised in environments or exposed to subcultures that both encouraged and rewarded criminal behavior.

Truth OR Fiction? REVISITED

People with psychopathic personalities inevitably run afoul of the law.

FALSE. Not all criminals show signs of psychopathy and not all people with psychopathic personalities become criminals.

VIDEO **9.1**

Antisocial Personality Disorder:
The Case of Paul

Antisocial Behavior and Criminality We may tend to think of antisocial behavior as synonymous with criminal behavior. Although a strong relationship does exist between the two, not all criminals show signs of psychopathy and not all people with psychopathic personalities become criminals (Lilienfeld & Andrews, 1996). Many are law-abiding and quite successful in their chosen occupations. Yet they possess a personality style characterized by a callous disregard of the interests and feelings of others.

Investigators have begun to view psychopathic personality as composed of two somewhat independent dimensions. The first is a personality dimension. It consists of such traits as superficial charm, selfishness, lack of empathy, callous and remorseless use of others, and disregard for their feelings and welfare. This type of psychopathic personality applies to people who have these kinds of psychopathic traits but don't become lawbreakers.

The second dimension is considered a behavioral dimension. It is characterized by the adoption of a generally unstable and antisocial lifestyle, including frequent problems with the law, poor employment history, and unstable relationships (Brown & Forth, 1997; Cooke & Michie, 1997). These two dimensions are not entirely separate; many psychopathic individuals show evidence of both sets of traits.

We should also note that people may become criminals or delinquents not because of a disordered personality but because they were reared in environments or subcultures that encouraged and rewarded criminal behavior. Although the behavior of criminals is deviant to society at large, it may be normal by the standards of their subcultures. We should also recognize that lack of remorse, which is a cardinal feature of antisocial personality disorder, does not characterize all criminals. Some criminals regret their crimes, and evidence of remorse is considered when a sentence is passed.

Only about half of prison inmates could be diagnosed with antisocial personality disorder (Robins et al., 1991). Conversely, fewer than half of the people with antisocial personality disorder run afoul of the law (Robins et al., 1991). Many fewer still fit (thankfully!) the stereotype of the psychopathic killer popularized in such films as *The Silence of the Lambs.*

Profile of the Antisocial Personality Hervey Cleckley (1941) showed that the characteristics that define the psychopathic (antisocial) personality—self-centeredness, irresponsibility, impulsivity, and insensitivity to the needs of others—exist not only among criminals but also among many respected members of the community, including doctors, lawyers, politicians, and business executives.

Common features of people with antisocial personality disorder include failure to conform to social norms, irresponsibility, aimlessness and lack of long-term goals or plans, impulsive behavior, outright lawlessness, violence, chronic unemployment, marital problems, lack of remorse or empathy, substance abuse, a history of alcoholism, and a disregard for the truth and for the feelings and needs of others (Patrick, Cuthbert, & Lang, 1994; Robins et al., 1991). Irresponsibility may be seen in a personal history dotted by repeated, unexplained absences from work, abandonment of jobs without having other job opportunities to fall back on, or long stretches of unemployment despite available job opportunities. Irresponsibility extends to financial matters, where there may be repeated failure to repay debts, to pay child support, or to meet other financial responsibilities to one's family and dependents. The diagnostic features of antisocial personality disorder, as defined in the *DSM,* are shown in Table 9.1.

The following case represents a number of antisocial characteristics:

A Case of Antisocial Behavior

The 19-year-old male is brought by ambulance to the hospital emergency room in a state of cocaine intoxication. He's wearing a T-shirt with the imprint "Twisted Sister" on the front, and he sports a punk-style haircut. His mother is called and sounds groggy and confused on the phone; the doctors must coax her to come to the hospital. She later tells the doctors that her son has arrests for shoplifting and for driving while intoxicated. She suspects that he takes drugs, although she has no direct evidence. She believes that he is performing fairly well at school and has been a star member of the basketball team.

It turns out that her son has been lying to her. In actuality, he never completed high school and never played on the basketball team. A day later, his head cleared, the patient tells his doctors, almost boastfully, that his drug and alcohol use started at the age of 13, and that by the time he was 17, he was regularly using a variety of psychoactive substances, including alcohol, speed, marijuana, and cocaine. Lately, however, he has preferred cocaine. He and his friends frequently participate in drug and alcohol binges. At times they each drink a case of beer in a day along with downing other drugs. He steals car radios from parked cars and money from his mother to support his drug habit, which he justifies by adopting a (partial) "Robin Hood" attitude—that is, taking money only from people who have lots of it.

—Adapted from Spitzer et al., 1994, pp. 81–83

Although this case is suggestive of antisocial personality disorder, the diagnosis was maintained as provisional because the interviewer could not determine that the deviant behavior (lying, stealing, skipping school) began before the age of 15.

Borderline Personality Disorder Borderline **personality disorder** (BPD) is characterized by a range of behavioral, emotional, and personality features (Sanislow, Grilo, & McGlashan, 2000). At the core is a pervasive pattern of instability in relationships, self-image, and mood, and a lack of control over impulses. People with borderline personality disorder

borderline personality disorder (BPD)
A personality disorder characterized by abrupt shifts in mood, lack of a coherent sense of self, and unpredictable, impulsive behavior.

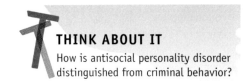

THINK ABOUT IT
How is antisocial personality disorder distinguished from criminal behavior?

TABLE **9.1** **Diagnostic Features of Antisocial Personality Disorder**

(a) The person is at least 18 years old.

(b) There is evidence of a conduct disorder prior to the age of 15, as shown by such behavior patterns as truancy, running away, initiating physical fights, use of weapons, forcing someone into sexual activities, physical cruelty to people or animals, deliberate destruction of property or fire setting, lying, stealing, or mugging.

(c) Since the age of 15, there has been general indifference to and violation of the rights of other people, as shown by several of the following:

  (1) Lack of conformity to social norms and legal codes, as shown by law-breaking behavior that may or may not result in arrest, such as destruction of property, engaging in unlawful occupations, stealing, or harassing others.

  (2) Aggressive and highly irritable style of relating to others, as shown by repeated physical fights and assaults with others, possibly involving abuse of one's spouse or children.

  (3) Consistent irresponsibility, as shown by failure to maintain employment due to chronic absences, lateness, abandonment of job opportunities or extended periods of unemployment despite available work; and/or by failure to honor financial obligations, such as failing to maintain child support or defaulting on debts; and/or by lack of a sustained monogamous relationship.

  (4) Failure to plan ahead or impulsivity, as shown by traveling around without prearranged employment or clear goals.

  (5) Disregard for the truth, evidenced by repeated lying, conning others, or use of aliases for personal gain or pleasure.

  (6) Recklessness with regard to personal safety or the safety of other people, as shown by driving while intoxicated or repeated speeding.

  (7) Lack of remorse for misdeeds, as shown by indifference to the harm done to others, and/or by rationalizing that harm.

Source. Adapted from the *DSM-IV-TR* (APA, 2000).

A Closer Look

Did Samson Have Antisocial Personality Disorder?

Did Samson, the biblical figure who fought the Philistines but lost his great strength when his long hair was shorn by the wily Delilah, have antisocial personality disorder? We noted in Chapter 1 how case studies have been reported on deceased individuals, even historical figures who died several hundred years ago. But applying modern diagnostic criteria to individuals from biblical times requires quite a leap of faith. Yet four psychiatrists writing in a respected professional journal argue that Samson's behavior nearly 3,000 years ago clearly meets many of the criteria for antisocial personality disorder (Altschuler et al., 2001). The biblical account of his behavior shows him to have broken the law, to have lied repeatedly, to have acted impulsively and without regard for the safety of himself and others, to have initiated many physical fights, and to have lacked remorse for his actions—patterns of behavior that today would likely be recognized as signs of antisocial personality disorder (Goode, 2001b). As an example of his reckless disregard of his own safety, the authors point to Samson's revelation to Delilah that the secret of his strength lay in his uncut locks, even after she had made three unsuccessful attempts to pry the secret from him. The biblical account also relates that 3,000 Israelites—Samson's own people!—captured him and turned him over the Philistines. This indicates that his brutal behavior was not viewed as acceptable conduct in the time in which he lived. However, it cannot be determined based on the biblical record whether Samson showed evidence of conduct disorder prior to the age of 15, as the diagnostic criteria for antisocial personality disorder require. On a broader level, the

Samson: A case of antisocial personality disorder? The actor Victor Mature portrayed Samson in the 1949 film *Samson and Delilah*. Recently, several psychiatrists have claimed that the biblical record of Samson's behavior indicates that he met many of the criteria for antisocial personality disorder.

authors argue that modern diagnostic concepts may help us form better understandings of behavior of historical figures that have long seemed puzzling and in need of explanation.

tend to be uncertain about their personal identities—their values, goals, careers, and perhaps even their sexual orientations. This instability in self-image or personal identity leaves them with nagging feelings of emptiness and boredom. They cannot tolerate being alone and will make desperate attempts to avoid feelings of abandonment (Gunderson, 1996). Fear of abandonment renders them clinging and demanding in their social relationships, but their clinging often pushes away the people on whom they depend. Signs of rejection may enrage them, straining their relationships further. Their feelings toward others are consequently intense and shifting. They alternate between extremes of adulation (when their needs are met) and loathing (when they feel scorned). They tend to view other people as all good or all bad, shifting abruptly from one extreme to the other. As a result, they may flit from partner to partner in a series of brief and stormy relationships. People they had idealized are treated with contempt when relationships end or when they feel the other person fails to meet their needs (Gunderson & Singer, 1986).

Many notable figures have been described as having personality features associated with borderline personality disorder, including Marilyn Monroe, Lawrence of Arabia, Adolf Hitler, and the philosopher Sören Kierkegaard (Sass, 1982). Some theorists believe we live in highly fragmented and alienating times that tend to create the problems in forming cohesive identities and stable relationships that characterize people with borderline personalities (Sass, 1982). "Living on the edge," or border, can be seen as a metaphor for an unstable society. Borderline personality disorder is believed to occur in about 2% of the general population (APA, 2000). Although it is diagnosed more often (about 75% of the time) in women, gender differences in prevalence rates for BPD in the general population remain undetermined.

The term *borderline personality* was originally used to refer to individuals whose behavior appeared on the border between neuroses and psychoses. People with borderline personality disorder generally maintain better contact with reality than people with psychoses, although they may show transient psychotic behaviors during times of stress. Generally speaking, they seem to be more severely impaired than most people with neuroses but not as dysfunctional as those with psychotic disorders.

Instability of moods is a central characteristic of borderline personality disorder (Sanislow et al., 2000). Moods run the gamut from anger and irritability to depression and anxiety, with each lasting from a few hours to a few days. People with BPD have difficulty controlling anger and are prone to fights or smashing things. They often act on impulse, such as eloping with someone they have just met. This impulsive and unpredictable behavior is often self-destructive, involving such behaviors as self-mutilation and suicidal gestures and actual attempts (e.g., Sanislow et al., 2000). It may also involve spending sprees, gambling, drug abuse, engaging in unsafe sexual activity, reckless driving, binge eating, or shoplifting. Impulsive acts of self-mutilation may involve such acts as scratching the wrists or burning cigarettes on the arms, as exemplified in the following dialogue:

CLIENT: I've got such repressed anger in me; what happens is . . . I can't *feel* it; I get anxiety attacks. I get very nervous, smoke too many cigarettes. So what happens to me is I tend to *explode*. Into tears or hurting myself or whatever . . . because I don't know how to contend with all those mixed up feelings.

INTERVIEWER: What was the more recent example of such an "explosion"?

CLIENT: I was alone at home a few months ago; I was frightened! I was trying to get in touch with my boyfriend and I couldn't . . . He was nowhere to be found. All my friends seemed to be busy that night and I had no one to talk to . . . I just got more and more nervous and more and more agitated. Finally, *bang!* . . . I took out a cigarette and lit it and stuck it into my forearm. I don't know why I did it because I didn't really care for him all that much. I guess I felt I had to do something dramatic . . ."

—Adapted from Stone, 1980, p. 400

Self-mutilation is sometimes carried out as an expression of anger or a means of manipulating others. Such acts may be intended to counteract self-reported feelings of "numbness," particularly in times of stress. Not surprisingly, frequent self-mutilation among people with BPD is associated with an increased risk of suicidal thinking (Dulit et al., 1994).

Individuals with BPD tend to have very troubled relationships with their families of origin and with others. They often have histories of traumatic experiences in childhood, such as parental losses or separations, abuse, neglect, or witnessing violence (Liotti et al., 2000). They tend to view their relationships as rife with hostility and to perceive others as rejecting and abandoning (Benjamin & Wonderlich, 1994). They also tend to be difficult to work with in psychotherapy, demanding a great deal of support from therapists, calling them at all hours or acting suicidally to elicit support, or dropping out of therapy prematurely. Their feelings toward therapists, as toward other people, undergo rapid alterations between idealization and outrage. These abrupt shifts in feelings are interpreted by psychoanalysts as signs of "splitting," or inability to reconcile the positive and negative aspects of one's experience of oneself and others.

From the modern psychodynamic perspective, borderline individuals cannot synthesize positive and negative elements of personality into complete wholes. They therefore fail to achieve fixed self-identities or images of others. Rather than viewing important figures in their lives as sometimes loving and as sometimes rejecting, they shift back and forth between

wWw **Web Link 9.3**
BPD Sanctuary

Borderline personality. In the movie *Fatal Attraction*, the actress Glenn Close played a character who exhibited many of the characteristics associated with borderline personality disorder, including impulsivity, extreme mood swings, and unstable relationships.

Over the top? Not all people who dress outrageously or flamboyantly have histrionic personalities. What other personality features characterize people with histrionic personality disorder?

viewing them as all good or all bad, between idealization and abhorrence. The psychoanalyst Otto Kernberg, a leading authority on borderline personality, tells of a woman in her 30s whose attitude toward him vacillated in such a way. According to Kernberg, the woman would respond to him in one session as the most wonderful therapist and feel that all her problems were solved. But several sessions later she would turn against him and accuse him of being unfeeling and manipulative, become very dissatisfied with the treatment she was receiving, and threaten to drop out and never come back (Sass, 1982). Borderline personality disorder remains in many ways a perplexing and frustrating problem.

Histrionic Personality Disorder Histrionic personality disorder involves excessive emotionality and an overwhelming need to be the center of attention. The term is derived from the Latin *histrio*, which means "actor." People with histrionic personality disorder tend to be dramatic and emotional, but their emotions seem shallow, exaggerated, and volatile. The disorder was formerly called *hysterical personality*. The following case example illustrates the excessively dramatic behaviors that are typical of someone with histrionic personality disorder:

A Case of Histrionic Personality Disorder

Marcella was a 36-year-old, attractive, but overly made up woman who was dressed in tight pants and high heels. Her hair was in a bird's nest of the type that had been popular when she was a teenager. Her social life seemed to bounce from relationship to relationship, from crisis to crisis. Marcella sought help from the psychologist at this time because her 17-year-old daughter, Nancy, had just been hospitalized for cutting her wrists. Nancy lived with Marcella and Marcella's current boyfriend, Morris, and there were constant arguments in the apartment. Marcella recounted the disputes that took place with high drama, waving her hands, clanging the bangles that hung from her bracelets, and then clutching her breast. It was difficult having Nancy live at home because Nancy had expensive tastes, was "always looking for attention," and flirted with Morris as a way of "flaunting her youth." Marcella saw herself as a doting mother and denied any possibility that she was in competition with her daughter.

Marcella came for a handful of sessions, during which she basically ventilated her feelings and was encouraged to make decisions that might lead to a reduction of some of the pressures on her and her daughter. At the end of each session she said, "I feel so much better" and thanked the psychologist profusely. At termination of "therapy," she took the psychologist's hand and squeezed it endearingly. "Thank you so much, Doctor," she said and made her exit.

—From the Authors' Files

The supplanting of *hysterical* with *histrionic* and the associated exchange of the roots *hystera* (meaning "uterus") and *histrio* allow professionals to distance themselves from the notion that the disorder is intricately bound up with being female. The disorder is diagnosed more frequently in women than men (Hartung & Widiger, 1998), although some studies using structured interview methods find similar rates of occurrence among men and women (APA, 2000). Whether the gender discrepancy in clinical practice reflects true differences in the underlying rates of the disorder, or diagnostic biases or other unseen factors, remains something of an open question (Corbitt & Widiger, 1995).

Despite a long-standing belief among clinicians that histrionic personality is closely related to conversion disorder (see Chapter 7), research has not borne out this connection (Kellner, 1992). People with conversion disorder are actually more likely to show features of dependent personality disorder than histrionic personality disorder.

histrionic personality disorder A personality disorder characterized by excessive need for attention, praise, reassurance, and approval.

People with histrionic personalities may become unusually upset by news of a sad event and cancel plans for the evening, inconveniencing their friends. They may exude exaggerated delight when they meet someone or become enraged when someone fails to notice their new hairstyle. They may faint at the sight of blood or blush at a slight faux pas. They tend to demand that others meet their needs for attention and play the victim when others fall short. If they feel a touch of fever, they may insist that others drop everything to rush them to the doctor. They tend to be self-centered and intolerant of delays of gratification; they want what they want when they want it. They grow quickly restless with routine and crave novelty and stimulation. They are drawn to fads. Others may see them as putting on airs or playacting, although they may evince a certain charm. They may enter a room with a flourish and embellish their experiences with flair. When pressed for details, however, they fail to color in the specifics of their tales. They tend to be flirtatious and seductive but are too wrapped up in themselves to develop intimate relationships or have deep feelings toward others. As a result, their associations tend be stormy and ultimately ungratifying. They tend to use their physical appearance as a means of drawing attention to themselves. Men with the disorder may act and dress in an overly "macho" manner to draw attention to themselves; women may choose very frilly, feminine clothing. Glitter supercedes substance.

People with histrionic personalities may be attracted to professions like modeling or acting, where they can hog the spotlight. Despite outward successes, they may lack self-esteem and strive to impress others to boost their self-worth. If they suffer setbacks or lose their place in the limelight, depressing inner doubts may emerge.

Narcissistic Personality Disorder *Narkissos* was a handsome youth who, according to Greek myth, fell in love with his reflection in a spring. Because of his excessive self-love, in one version of the myth, he was transformed by the gods into the flower we know as the narcissus.

Persons with **narcissistic personality disorder** have an inflated or grandiose sense of themselves and an extreme need for admiration. They brag about their accomplishments and expect others to shower them with praise. They expect others to notice their special qualities, even when their accomplishments are ordinary, and they enjoy basking in the light of adulation. They are self-absorbed and lack empathy for others. Although they share certain features with histrionic personalities, such as demanding to be the center of attention, they have a much more inflated view of themselves and are less melodramatic than people with histrionic personality disorder. The label of borderline personality disorder (BPD) is sometimes applied to them, but people with narcissistic personality disorder are generally better able to organize their thoughts and actions. They tend to be more successful in their careers and are better able to rise to positions of status and power. Their relationships also tend to be more stable than those of people with BPD.

Narcissistic personality disorder is found among less than 1% of people in the general population (APA, 2000). Although more than half of the people diagnosed with the disorder are men, we cannot say whether there is an underlying gender difference in prevalence rates in the general population. A certain degree of narcissism may represent a healthful adjustment to insecurity, a shield from criticism and failure, or a motive for achievement (Goleman, 1988b). Excessive narcissistic qualities can become unhealthful, especially when the cravings for adulation are insatiable. Table 9.2 compares "normal" self-interest with self-defeating extremes of narcissism. Up to a point, self-interest fosters success and happiness. In more extreme cases, as with narcissism, it can compromise relationships and careers.

People with narcissistic personalities tend to be preoccupied with fantasies of success and power, ideal love, or recognition for brilliance or beauty. They, like people with

Narkissos. According to one version of the Greek myth, *Narkissos* fell in love with his reflection in a spring. Because of his excessive self-love, the gods transformed him into a flower—the narcissus.

narcissistic personality disorder A personality disorder characterized by adoption of an inflated self-image and demands for attention and admiration.

TABLE 9.2 Features of Normal Self-Interest Compared with Self-Defeating Narcissism

Normal Self-Interest	Self-Defeating Narcissism
Appreciating acclaim, but not requiring it in order to maintain self-esteem.	Craving adoration insatiably; requiring acclaim in order to feel momentarily good about oneself.
Being temporarily wounded by criticism.	Being inflamed or crushed by criticism and brooding about it extensively.
Feeling unhappy but not worthless following failure.	Having enduring feelings of mortification and worthlessness triggered by failure.
Feeling "special" or uncommonly talented in some way.	Feeling incomparably better than other people, and insisting upon acknowledgment of that preeminence.
Feeling good about oneself, even when other people are being critical.	Needing constant support from other people in order to maintain one's feelings of well-being.
Being reasonably accepting of life's setbacks, even though they can be painful and temporarily destabilizing.	Responding to life's wounds with depression or fury.
Maintaining self-esteem in the face of disapproval or denigration.	Responding to disapproval or denigration with loss of self-esteem.
Maintaining emotional equilibrium despite lack of special treatment.	Feeling entitled to special treatment and becoming terribly upset when one is treated in an ordinary manner.
Being empathic and caring about the feelings of others.	Being insensitive to other people's needs and feelings; exploiting others until they become fed up.

Source. Based on Goleman, 1988b, p. C1.

histrionic personalities, may gravitate toward careers in which they can receive adulation, such as modeling, acting, or politics. Although they tend to exaggerate their accomplishments and abilities, many people with narcissistic personalities are quite successful in their occupations. But they envy those who achieve even greater success. Insatiable ambition may prompt them to devote themselves tirelessly to work. They are driven to succeed, not so much for money as for the adulation that attends success.

Interpersonal relationships are invariably strained by the demands that people with narcissistic personality impose on others and by their lack of empathy with, and concern for, other people. They seek the company of flatterers and are often superficially charming and friendly and able to draw people to them. But their interest in people is one-sided: They seek people who will serve their interests and nourish their sense of self-importance (Goleman, 1988b). They have feelings of entitlement that lead them to exploit others. They treat sex partners as devices for their own pleasure or to brace their self-esteem, as in the case of Bill:

A Case of Narcissistic Personality Disorder

Most people agreed that Bill, a 35-year-old investment banker, had a certain charm. He was bright, articulate, and attractive. He possessed a keen sense of humor that drew people to him at social gatherings. He would always position himself in the middle of the room, where he could be the center of attention. The topics of conversation invariably focused on his "deals," the "rich and famous" people he had met, and his outmaneuvering of opponents. His next project was always bigger and more daring than the last. Bill loved an audience. His face would light up when others responded to him with praise or admiration for his business successes, which were always inflated beyond their true measure. But when the conversation shifted to other people, he would lose interest and

THINK ABOUT IT
We have referred to characters in movies in our illustrations of personality disorders characterized by emotional and erratic behavior. You can probably think of other examples of characters who manifest the traits of these disorders. Why are these characters so frequently encountered in entertainment media? What is the attraction for dramatists, actors, and viewers?

excuse himself to make a drink or to call his answering machine. When hosting a party, he would urge guests to stay late and feel hurt if they had to leave early; he showed no sensitivity to, or awareness of, the needs of his friends.

The few friends he had maintained over the years had come to accept Bill on his own terms. They recognized that he needed to have his ego fed or that he would become cool and detached.

Bill had also had a series of romantic relationships with women who were willing to play the adoring admirer and make the sacrifices that he demanded—for a time. But they inevitably tired of the one-sided relationship or grew frustrated by Bill's inability to make a commitment or feel deeply toward them. Lacking empathy, Bill was unable to recognize other people's feelings and needs. His demands for constant attention from willing admirers did not derive from selfishness, but from a need to ward off underlying feelings of inadequacy and diminished self-esteem. It was sad, his friends thought, that Bill needed so much attention and adulation from others and that his many achievements were never enough to calm his inner doubts.

—From the Authors' Files

■

A person with a narcissistic personality? People with narcissistic personalities are often preoccupied with fantasies of success and power, ideal love, or recognition for their brilliance or beauty. They may pursue careers that provide opportunities for public recognition and adulation, such as acting, modeling, or politics. They may become deeply wounded by any hint that they are not as special as they believe themselves to be.

Personality Disorders Characterized by Anxious or Fearful Behavior

This cluster of personality disorders includes the avoidant, dependent, and obsessive-compulsive types. Although the features of these disorders differ, they share a component of fear or anxiety.

Avoidant Personality Disorder Persons with **avoidant personality disorder** are so terrified of rejection and criticism that they are generally unwilling to enter relationships without ardent reassurances of acceptance. As a result, they may have few close relationships outside their immediate families. They also tend to avoid group occupational or recreational activities for fear of rejection. They prefer to lunch alone at their desks. They shun company picnics and parties, unless they are perfectly sure of acceptance. Avoidant personality disorder, which appears to be equally common in men and women, is believed to affect between 0.5% and 1.0% of the general population (APA, 2000).

avoidant personality disorder A personality disorder characterized by avoidance of social relationships due to fears of rejection.

Unlike people with schizoid qualities, with whom they share the feature of social withdrawal, individuals with avoidant personalities have interest in, and feelings of warmth toward, other people. However, fear of rejection prevents them from striving to meet their needs for affection and acceptance. In social situations, they tend to hug the walls and avoid conversing with others. They fear public embarrassment, the thought that others might see them blush, cry, or act nervously. They tend to stick to their routines and exaggerate the risks or effort involved in trying new things. They may refuse to attend a party that is an hour away on the pretext that the late drive home would be too taxing. Consider the following case example:

A person with an avoidant personality? People with avoidant personalities often keep to themselves because of fear of rejection.

A Case of Avoidant Personality Disorder

Harold, a 24-year-old accounting clerk, had dated but a few women, and he had met them through family introductions. He never felt confident enough to approach a woman on his own. Perhaps it was his shyness that first attracted Stacy. Stacy, a 22-year-old secretary, worked alongside Harold and asked him if he would like to get together sometime after work. At first Harold declined, claiming some excuse, but when Stacy asked again a week later, Harold agreed, thinking she must really like him if she were willing to pursue him. The relationship developed quickly, and soon they were dating virtually every night. The relationship was strained, however. Harold interpreted any slight hesitation in her voice as a lack of interest. He repeatedly requested reassurance that she cared about him, and he evaluated every word and gesture for evidence of her feelings. If Stacy said that she could not see him because of fatigue or illness, he assumed she was rejecting him and sought further reassurance. After several months, Stacy decided she could no longer accept Harold's nagging, and the relationship ended. Harold assumed that Stacy had never truly cared for him.

—From the Authors' Files

■

There is a good deal of overlap between avoidant personality disorder and social phobia, particularly with a severe subtype of social phobia that involves a generalized pattern of social phobia (excessive, irrational fear of most social situations) (Turner, Beidel, & Townsley, 1992; Widiger, 1992). Although research evidence shows that many cases of generalized social phobia occur in the absence of avoidant personality disorder (Holt, Heimberg, & Hope, 1992), relatively fewer cases of avoidant personality occur in the absence of generalized social phobia (Widiger, 1992). Thus avoidant personality disorder may represent a more severe form of social phobia (Hoffman et al., 1995). Still, the scientific jury is out on the question of whether avoidant personality disorder should be considered a severe form of generalized social phobia or a distinct diagnostic category as it is presently classified.

Dependent Personality Disorder **Dependent personality disorder** describes people who have an excessive need to be taken care of by others. This leads them to be overly submissive and clinging in their relationships and extremely fearful of separation. People with this disorder find it very difficult to do things on their own. They seek advice in making even the smallest decision. Children or adolescents with the problem may look to their parents to select their clothes, diets, schools or colleges, even their friends. Adults with the disorder allow others to make important decisions for them. Sometimes they are so dependent on others for making decisions that they allow their parents to determine whom they will marry, as in the case of Matthew:

A Case of Dependent Personality Disorder

Matthew, a 34-year-old single accountant who lives with his mother, sought treatment when his relationship with his girlfriend came to an end. His mother had objected to marriage because his girlfriend was of a different religion, and—because "blood is thicker than water"—Matthew acceded to his mother's wishes and ended the relationship. Yet he is angry with himself and at his mother because he feels that she is too possessive to ever grant him permission to get married. He describes his mother as a domineering woman who "wears the pants" in the family and is accustomed to having things her way. Matthew alternates between resenting his mother and thinking that perhaps she knows what's best for him.

Matthew's position at work is several levels below what would be expected of someone of his talent and educational level. Several times he has declined promotions in

dependent personality disorder
A personality disorder characterized by difficulty making independent decisions and overly dependent behavior.

order to avoid increased responsibilities that would require him to supervise others and make independent decisions. He has maintained close relationships with two friends since early childhood and has lunch with one of them on every working day. On days his friend calls in sick, Matthew feels lost. Matthew has lived his whole life at home, except for one year away at college. He returned home because of homesickness.

—Adapted from Spitzer et al., 1994, pp. 179–180

After marriage, people with dependent personality disorder may rely on their spouses to make decisions such as where they should live, which neighbors they should cultivate, how they should discipline the children, what jobs they should take, how they should budget money, and where they should vacation. Like Matthew, individuals with dependent personality disorder avoid positions of responsibility. They turn down challenges and promotions and work beneath their potential. They tend to be overly sensitive to criticism and are preoccupied with fears of rejection and abandonment. They may be devastated by the end of a close relationship or by the prospect of living on their own. Because of fear of rejection, they often subordinate their wants and needs to those of others. They may agree with outlandish statements about themselves and do degrading things in order to please others.

Although dependent personality disorder is diagnosed more frequently in women (APA, 2000; Bornstein, 1997), it is not clear that there is any underlying difference in the prevalence of the disorder between men and women (Corbitt & Widiger, 1995). The diagnosis is often applied to women who, for fear of abandonment, tolerate husbands who openly cheat on them, abuse them, or gamble away the family's resources. Underlying feelings of inadequacy and helplessness discourage them from taking effective action. In a vicious cycle, their passivity encourages further abuse, leading them to feel yet more inadequate and helpless. The diagnosis of women with this pattern is controversial and may be seen as unfairly "blaming the victim," because women in our society are often socialized to dependent roles. A panel convened by the American Psychological Association noted that women also encounter greater stress than men in contemporary life (Goleman, 1990b). Moreover, since women generally encounter greater social pressures to be passive, demure, or deferential than men, dependent behaviors in women may reflect cultural influences rather than an underlying personality disorder.

Dependent personality disorder has been linked to other psychological disorders, including major depression, bipolar disorder, and social phobia, and to physical problems, such as hypertension, cancer, and gastrointestinal disorders like ulcers and colitis (Bornstein, 1999; Loranger, 1996; Reich, 1996). There also appears to be a link between dependent personality and what psychodynamic theorists refer to as "oral" behavior problems, such as smoking, eating disorders, and alcoholism (Bornstein, 1993, 1999). Psychodynamic writers trace dependent behaviors to the utter dependence of the newborn baby and the baby's seeking of nourishment through oral means (suckling). From infancy, they suggest, people associate the provision of food with love. Food may come to symbolize love, and persons with dependent personalities may overeat to ingest love symbolically. Research shows that people with dependent personalities are more reliant on others for support and guidance than is the average person (Greenberg & Bornstein, 1988a). People with dependent personalities often attribute their problems to physical rather than emotional causes and seek support and advice from medical experts rather than psychologists or counselors (Greenberg & Bornstein, 1988b).

Obsessive-Compulsive Personality Disorder The defining features of **obsessive-compulsive personality disorder** involve an excessive degree of orderliness, perfectionism, rigidity, difficulty coping with ambiguity, difficulties expressing feelings, and meticulousness in work habits. About 1% of people in community samples are diagnosed with the disorder (APA, 2000). The disorder is about twice as common in men than women. Unlike obsessive-compulsive anxiety disorder, people with obsessive-compulsive

obsessive-compulsive personality disorder A personality disorder characterized by rigid ways of relating to others, perfectionistic tendencies, lack of spontaneity, and excessive attention to detail.

"A place for everything, and everything in its place"? People with obsessive-compulsive personalities may have invented this maxim. Many such people have excessive needs for orderliness in their environment, as suggested in this Laurie Simmons photograph, *Red Library #2*.

personality disorder do not necessarily experience outright obsessions or compulsions. If they do, both diagnoses may be deemed appropriate.

Persons with obsessive-compulsive personality disorder are so preoccupied with the need for perfection that they cannot complete things in a timely fashion. Their efforts inevitably fall short of their expectations, and they force themselves to redo their work. Or they may ruminate about how to prioritize their assignments and never seem to get started working. They focus on details that others perceive as trivial. As the saying goes, they often fail to see the forest for the trees. Their rigidity impairs their social relationships; they insist on doing things their way rather than compromising. Their zeal for work keeps them from participating in, or enjoying, social and leisure activities. They tend to be stingy with money. They find it difficult to make decisions and postpone or avoid them for fear of making the wrong choice. They tend to be overly rigid in issues of morality and ethics because of inflexibility in personality rather than deeply held convictions. They tend to be overly formal in relationships and find it difficult to express feelings. It is hard for them to relax and enjoy pleasant activities; they worry about the costs of such diversions. Consider the following case example:

A Case of Obsessive-Compulsive Personality Disorder

Jerry, a 34-year-old systems analyst, was perfectionistic, overly concerned with details, and rigid in his behavior. Jerry was married to Marcia, a graphics artist. He insisted on scheduling their free time hour by hour and became unnerved when they deviated from his agenda. He would circle a parking lot repeatedly in search of just the right parking spot to ensure that another car would not scrape his car. He refused to have the apartment painted for over a year because he couldn't decide on the color. He had arranged all the books in their bookshelf alphabetically and insisted that every book be placed in its proper position.

Jerry never seemed to be able to relax. Even on vacation, he was bothered by thoughts of work that he had left behind and by fears that he might lose his job. He couldn't understand how people could lie on the beach and let all their worries evaporate in the summer air. Something can always go wrong, he figured, so how can people let themselves go?

—From the Authors' Files

Problems with the Classification of Personality Disorders

Questions remain about the reliability and validity of the diagnostic categories for personality disorders (Farmer, 2000). There may be too much overlap among the diagnoses to justify so many different categories. Agreement between raters on personality disorder diagnoses remains modest at best (Coolidge & Segal, 1998). The classification system also seems to blur the distinctions between normal and abnormal variations in personality. Some categories of personality disorder, moreover, may be based on sexist presumptions. Finally, there is concern that the diagnoses may confuse labels with explanations.

Undetermined Reliability and Validity The present *DSM* system sought to remove ambiguities in the diagnostic criteria of personality disorders by providing descriptive criteria that more tightly define particular disorders. The reliability and validity of the definitions used in the *DSM-IV* remains to be fully tested, however.

Problems Distinguishing Axis I from Axis II Disorders Some reviewers question whether Axis II personality disorders can be reliably differentiated from Axis I clinical syndromes such as anxiety or mood disorders (Farmer, 2000; Livesley et al., 1994). For example, clinicians may have difficulty distinguishing between obsessive-compulsive disorder and obsessive-compulsive personality disorder. Clinical syndromes are believed to be variable over time, whereas personality disorders are held to be generally more enduring patterns of disturbance. Yet evidence indicates that features of personality disorders may vary over time with changes in circumstances. On the other hand, some Axis I clinical syndromes (dysthymia, for example) follow a more or less chronic course.

Overlap Among Disorders There is also a high degree of overlap among the personality disorders (Westen & Shedler, 1999). Overlap undermines the *DSM*'s conceptual clarity or purity by increasing the number of cases that seem to fit two or more diagnostic categories (Livesley, 1985). Although some personality disorders have distinct features, many appear to share common traits, such as problems in romantic relationships (Daley, Burge, & Hammen, 2000). Moreover, the same person may have traits suggestive of dependent personality disorder (inability to make decisions or initiate activities independently) and of avoidant personality disorder (extreme social anxiety and heightened sensitivity to criticism). Overall, about two in three people with personality disorders meet diagnostic criteria for more than one type of personality disorder (Widiger, 1991). The high degree of overlap suggests that the personality disorders included in the *DSM* system may not be sufficiently distinct from one another (Westen & Schedler, 1999). Some so-called disorders may thus represent different aspects of the same disorder, not separate diagnostic categories.

Difficulty in Distinguishing Between Variations in Normal Behavior and in Abnormal Behavior Another problem with the diagnosis of personality disorders is that they involve traits which, in lesser degrees, describe the behavior of most normal individuals. Feeling suspicious now and then does not mean you have a paranoid personality disorder. The tendency to exaggerate your own importance does not mean you are narcissistic. You may avoid social interactions for fear of embarrassment or rejection without having an avoidant personality disorder, and you may be especially conscientious in your work without having an obsessive-compulsive personality disorder. Because the defining attributes of these disorders are commonly occurring personality traits, clinicians should only apply these diagnostic labels when the patterns are so pervasive that they interfere with the individual's functioning or cause significant personal distress. Yet it can be difficult to know where to draw the line between normal variations in behavior and personality disorders. We continue to lack data to guide us more precisely in determining the point at which a trait becomes sufficiently inflexible or maladaptive to justify a personality disorder diagnosis (Widiger & Costa, 1994).

Sexist Biases The construction of certain personality disorders may have sexist underpinnings. For example, diagnostic criteria for personality disorders label stereotypical feminine behaviors as pathological with greater frequency than is the case with stereotypical masculine behaviors. The concept of the histrionic personality, for example, seems a caricature of the traditional stereotype of the feminine personality: flighty, emotional, shallow, seductive, attention seeking. But if the feminine stereotype corresponds to a mental disorder, shouldn't we also have a diagnostic category that reflects the masculine stereotype of the "macho male"? It may be possible to show that overly masculinized traits are associated with significant distress or impairment in social or occupational functioning in certain males: Highly masculinized males often get into fights and experience difficulties working

Truth OR Fiction? REVISITED

It may be difficult to draw a clear line between normal variations in behavior and personality disorders.

TRUE. The boundaries between normal variations in behavior and personality disorders can be blurry.

Truth OR Fiction? REVISITED

The diagnosis of some personality disorders may reflect sexist biases.

TRUE. The concepts of histrionic and dependent personality disorders may indeed be sexist. It could be argued that the descriptions of these disorders are parodies of the traditional feminine gender-role stereotype.

Are there sexist biases in the conception of personality disorders? The concept of the histrionic personality disorder seems to be a caricature of the highly stereotyped feminine personality. Why, then, is there not also something akin to a macho male personality disorder, which caricatures the highly stereotyped masculine personality?

for female bosses. There is no personality disorder that corresponds to the "macho male" stereotype, however.

The diagnosis of dependent personality disorder may also unfairly stigmatize women who are socialized into dependent roles as having a "mental disorder." Women may be at greater risk of receiving diagnoses of histrionic or dependent personality disorders because clinicians perceive these patterns as more common among women or because women are more likely than men to be socialized into these behavior patterns.

Clinicians may also be biased in favor of perceiving women as having histrionic personality disorder and men as having antisocial personality disorder, even when they do not differ in symptomatology (Garb, 1997). Clinicians may also have a gender bias when it comes to diagnosing borderline personality disorder. In one study, researchers presented a hypothetical case example to a sample of 311 psychologists, social workers, and psychiatrists (Becker & Lamb, 1994). Half of the sample was presented with a case identified as a female; the other half read the identical case, except that it was identified as male. Clinicians more often diagnosed the case identified as female as having borderline personality disorder.

THINK ABOUT IT

Are some personality disorders more likely to be diagnosed in men or in women because of societal expectations rather than because of real underlying pathology? Have you ever assumed, for example, that women are "just dependent or hysterical" or that men are "just narcissists or antisocial"? What kinds of problems do these underlying assumptions pose for clinicians and researchers?

THINK ABOUT IT

What are the major points of controversy concerning the classification of personality disorders? Explain the problems that result from using labels as explanations of behavior? Have you ever been "labeled" in this way? What kinds of real-life problems can this cause?

Confusing Labels with Explanations It may seem obvious that we should not confuse diagnostic labels with explanations, but in practice the distinction is sometimes clouded. If we confuse labeling with explanation, we may fall into the trap of circular reasoning. What is wrong, for example, with the logic of the following statements?

1. John's behavior is antisocial.
2. Therefore, John has an antisocial personality disorder.
3. John's behavior is antisocial because he has an antisocial personality disorder.

The statements are circular in reasoning because they (1) use behavior to make a diagnosis, and then (2) use the diagnosis as an explanation for the behavior. We may be guilty of circular reasoning in our everyday speech. Consider: "John never gets his work in on time; therefore, he is lazy. John doesn't get his work in because he's lazy." The label may be acceptable and useful in everyday conversation, but it lacks scientific rigor. For a construct such as *laziness* to have scientific rigor, we need to understand the causes of laziness and the factors that help maintain it. We should not confuse the label we attach to behavior with the cause of the behavior.

Moreover, labeling people with disturbing behavior as personality disordered tends to overlook the social and environmental contexts in which the behavior occurs. We need to attend to the impact of specific traumatic life events, which may occur with a greater range or intensity among members of one gender or cultural group, as important factors underlying patterns of maladaptive behavior. The conceptual underpinnings of the personality disorders lack such a perspective. Moreover, conceptualizations of personality disorders fail to account for the social inequalities in society and the differences in power between the genders or between dominant and minority cultures that may give rise to the types of problems identified as personality disorders. For example, Brown (1992) and Walker (1988) document the significant prevalence of a history of childhood physical and sexual abuse among women diagnosed with personality disorders. The ways in which people cope with abuse may come to be viewed as flaws in their character rather than as reflections of the dysfunctional societal factors that underlie abusive relationships.

All in all, personality disorders are convenient labels for identifying common patterns of ineffective and ultimately self-defeating behavior, but labels do not explain their causes. Still, the development of an accurate descriptive system is an important step toward scientific explanation. The establishment of reliable diagnostic categories sets the stage for valid research into causation and treatment.

Quiz **9.1**
Types of Personality Disorders

Theoretical Perspectives

In this section we consider theoretical perspectives on the personality disorders. Many of the theoretical accounts of disturbed personality derive from the psychodynamic model. We thus begin with a review of traditional and modern psychodynamic models.

Psychodynamic Perspectives

Traditional Freudian theory focused on problems arising from the Oedipus complex as the foundation for many abnormal behaviors, including personality disorders. Freud believed that children normally resolve the Oedipus complex by forsaking incestuous wishes for the parent of the opposite gender and identifying with the parent of the same gender. As a result, they incorporate the parent's moral principles in the form of a personality structure called the superego. Many factors may interfere with appropriate identification, however, such as having a weak or absent father or an antisocial parent. These factors may sidetrack the normal developmental process, preventing children from developing the moral constraints that prevent antisocial behavior and the feelings of guilt or remorse that normally follow behavior that is hurtful to others. Freud's account of moral development focused mainly on the development of males. He has been criticized for failing to account for the moral development of females.

More recent psychodynamic theories have generally focused on the earlier, pre-Oedipal period of about 18 months to 3 years, during which infants are theorized to begin to develop their identities as separate from those of their parents. These recent advances in psychodynamic theory focus on the development of the sense of self in explaining such disorders as narcissistic and borderline personality disorders.

Hans Kohut One of the principal shapers of modern psychodynamic concepts is Hans Kohut, whose views are labeled **self psychology.** Kohut focused much of his attention on the development of the narcissistic personality.

Kohut (1966) believed that people with narcissistic personalities might mount a façade of self-importance to cover up deep feelings of inadequacy. The narcissist's self-esteem is like a reservoir that needs to be constantly replenished lest it run dry. A steady stream of praise and attention prevents the narcissist from withering with insecurity. A sense of grandiosity helps people with a narcissistic personality mask their underlying feelings of worthlessness. Failures or disappointments threaten to expose these feelings and drive the person into a state of depression. As a defense against despair, the person attempts to diminish the importance of disappointments or failures. People with narcissistic personalities may become enraged by others whom they perceive have failed to protect them from disappointment or have declined to shower them with reassurance, praise, and admiration. They may become infuriated by even the slightest criticism, no matter how well intentioned. They may mask feelings of rage and humiliation by adopting a facade of cool indifference. They can make difficult psychotherapy clients because they may become enraged when therapists puncture their inflated self-images to help them develop more realistic self-concepts.

Kohut believed that early childhood is characterized by a normal stage of "healthful narcissism." Infants feel powerful, as though the world revolves around them. Infants also normally perceive their parents as idealized towers of strength and wish to be one with them and to share their power (Edmundson, 2001; Strozier, 2001). Empathic parents reflect their children's inflated perceptions by making them feel that anything is possible and by nourishing their self-esteem (e.g., telling them how terrific and precious they are). Even empathic parents are critical from time to time, however, and puncture their children's grandiose sense of self. Or they fail to measure up to their children's idealized views of them. Gradually, unrealistic expectations dissolve and are replaced by more realistic appraisals. This process of childhood narcissism that eventually gives way to more realistic appraisals of self and others is perfectly normal. Earlier grandiose self-images form the basis for assertiveness later in childhood and set the stage for ambitious striving in adulthood. In adolescence, childhood idealization is transformed into realistic admiration for parents, teachers, and friends. In adulthood, these ideas develop into a set of internal ideals, values, and goals.

self psychology A theory that describes processes that normally lead to achievement of a cohesive sense of self.

Truth OR Fiction?   REVISITED

Despite a veneer of self-importance, people with narcissistic personalities may harbor deep feelings of insecurity.

TRUE. Theorists such as Hans Kohut believe that people with narcissistic personalities might mount a facade of self-importance to cover up deep feelings of inadequacy.

splitting An inability to reconcile the positive and negative aspects of the self and others, resulting in sudden shifts between positive and negative feelings.

symbiotic The state of oneness that normally exists between mother and infant.

separation-individuation The process by which an infant develops a separate identity from that of the mother.

Separation-individuation. According to the influential psychodynamic theorist Margaret Mahler, young children undergo a process of separation-individuation by which they learn to differentiate their own identities from their mothers. She believed that a failure to successfully master this developmental challenge may lead to the development of a borderline personality.

Lack of parental empathy and support, however, sets the stage for pathological narcissism in adulthood. Children who are not prized by their parents may fail to develop a sturdy sense of self-esteem. They may be unable to tolerate even slight blows to their self-worth. They develop damaged self-concepts and feel incapable of being loved and admired because of perceived inadequacies or flaws. Pathological narcissism involves the construction of a grandiose facade of self-perfection that is merely a shell to cloak perceived inadequacies. The facade always remains on the brink of crumbling, however, and it must be continually shored up by a constant flow of reassurance that one is special and unique. This leaves the person vulnerable to painful blows to self-esteem following failure to achieve social or occupational goals. So needy of constant approval, the person with a narcissistic personality may fly into a rage when he or she feels slighted in any way.

Kohut's approach to therapy provides clients who have a narcissistic personality with an initial opportunity to express their grandiose self-images and to idealize the therapist. Over time, however, the therapist helps them explore the childhood roots of their narcissism and gently points out imperfections in both client and therapist to encourage clients to form more realistic images of the self and others.

Otto Kernberg Modern psychodynamic views of the borderline personality also trace the disorder to difficulties in the development of the self in early childhood. Otto Kernberg (1975), a leading psychodynamic theorist, views borderline personality in terms of a pre-Oedipal failure to develop a sense of constancy and unity in one's image of the self and others. Kernberg proposes that childhood failure to synthesize these contradictory images of good and bad results in a failure to develop a consistent self-image and in tendencies toward **splitting**—shifting back and forth between viewing oneself and other people as "all good" or "all bad."

In Kernberg's view, parents, even excellent parents, invariably fail to meet all their children's needs. Infants therefore face the early developmental challenge of reconciling images of the nurturing, comforting "good mother" with those of the withholding, frustrating "bad mother." Failure to reconcile these opposing images into a realistic, unified, and stable parental image may fixate children in the pre-Oedipal period. As adults, then, they may retain these rapidly shifting attitudes toward their therapists and others.

Margaret Mahler Margaret Mahler, another influential modern psychodynamic theorist, explained borderline personality disorder in terms of childhood separation from the mother figure. Mahler and her colleagues (Mahler & Kaplan, 1977; Mahler, Pine, & Bergman, 1975) believed that during the first year infants develop a **symbiotic** attachment to their mothers. *Symbiosis* is a biological term derived from Greek roots meaning "to live together" and describes life patterns in which two species lead interdependent lives. In psychology, symbiosis is likened to a state of oneness in which the child's identity is fused with the mother's. Normally, children gradually differentiate their own identities or senses of self from their mothers. The process is called **separation-individuation.** Separation is the developing of a separate psychological and biological identity from the mother. Individuation involves recognizing the personal characteristics that define one's self-identity. Separation-individuation may be a stormy process. Children may vacillate between seeking greater independence and moving closer to, or "shadowing," the mother, which is seen as a wish for reunion. The mother may disrupt normal separation-individuation by refusing to let go of the child or by too quickly pushing the child toward independence. The tendencies of people with borderline personalities to react to others with ambivalence, to alternate between love and hate, are suggestive to Mahler of earlier ambivalences during the separation-individuation process. Borderline personality disorder may arise from the failure to master this developmental challenge.

All in all, psychodynamic theory provides a rich theoretical mine for the understanding of the development of several personality disorders. But some critics contend that theories of disorders such as borderline personality disorder and narcissistic personality disorder are based largely on inferences drawn from behavior and retrospective accounts of adults rather than on observations of children (Sass, 1982). Mahler's theory has been challenged by evidence that even infants show a certain degree of psychological differentiation from others (Klein, 1981). We may also question whether direct comparisons should be made between normal childhood experiences and abnormal behaviors in adulthood. For example, the ambivalences that characterize the adult borderline personality may bear only a superficial relationship, if any, to children's vacillations between closeness and separation with maternal figures during separation-individuation.

Later we underscore the links between abuse in childhood and later development of personality disorders. These linkages suggest that failure to form close-bonding relationships with parental caretakers in childhood plays a critical role in developing many of the maladaptive personality patterns classified as personality disorders.

Learning Perspectives

Learning theorists tend to focus more on the acquisition of behaviors than on the notion of enduring personality traits. Similarly, they think more in terms of maladaptive behaviors than of disorders of "personality" or "personality traits." Trait theorists believe that personality traits steer behavior, providing a framework for consistent behavior in diverse situations. Many critics (e.g., Mischel, 1993), however, argue that behavior is actually less consistent across situations than trait theorists would suggest. Behavior may depend more on situational demands than on inherent traits. For example, we may describe a person as lazy and unmotivated. But is this person always lazy and unmotivated? Aren't there some situations in which the person may be energetic and ambitious? What differences in these situations may explain differences in behavior? Learning theorists are interested in defining the learning histories and situational factors that give rise to maladaptive behaviors and the reinforcers that maintain them.

Learning theorists suggest it is in childhood that many important experiences occur that shape the development of the maladaptive habits of relating to others that constitute personality disorders. For example, children who are regularly discouraged from speaking their minds or exploring their environments may develop a dependent personality behavior pattern. Obsessive-compulsive personality disorder may be connected with excessive parental discipline or overcontrol in childhood. Theodore Millon (1981) suggests that children whose behavior is rigidly controlled and punished by parents, even for slight transgressions, may develop inflexible, perfectionistic standards. As these children mature, they may strive to develop themselves in an area in which they excel, such as schoolwork or athletics, as a way of avoiding parental criticism or punishment. But overattention to a single area of development may prevent them from becoming well rounded. They may thus squelch spontaneity and avoid new challenges or risks. They may also place perfectionistic demands on themselves, so as to avoid any risk of punishment or rebuke, and develop other behaviors associated with the obsessive-compulsive personality pattern.

Millon suggests that histrionic personality disorder may be rooted in childhood experiences in which social reinforcers, such as parental attention, are connected to the child's appearance and willingness to perform for others, especially in cases where reinforcers are dispensed inconsistently. Inconsistent attention teaches children not to take approval for granted and to strive for it continually. People with histrionic personalities may also have identified with parents who are dramatic, emotional, and attention-seeking. Extreme sibling rivalry would further heighten motivation to perform for attention from others.

Social-cognitive theories emphasize the role of reinforcement in explaining the origins of antisocial behaviors. Ullmann and Krasner (1975) proposed, for example, that people with antisocial personalities might have failed to learn to respond to other people as potential reinforcers. Most children learn to treat others as reinforcing agents because others reinforce them with praise when they behave appropriately and punish them for misbehavior. Reinforcement and punishment provide feedback (information about social expectations) that helps children modify their behavior to maximize the chances of future rewards and minimize the risks of future punishment. As a consequence, children become socialized. They become sensitive to the demands of powerful others, usually parents and teachers, and learn to regulate their behavior accordingly. They thus adapt to social expectations. They learn what to do and what to say, how to dress and how to act to obtain social reinforcement or approval from others.

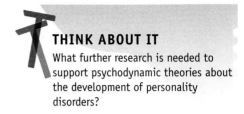

THINK ABOUT IT
What further research is needed to support psychodynamic theories about the development of personality disorders?

wWw **Web Link 9.4**
Personality Disorders Foundation

What are the origins of antisocial personality disorder? Are youth who develop antisocial personalities largely "unsocialized" because their early learning experiences lack the consistency and predictability that help other children connect their behavior with rewards and punishments? Or are they very "socialized," but socialized to imitate the behavior of other antisocial youth? To what extent does criminal behavior or membership in gangs overlap with antisocial personality disorder?

People with antisocial personalities, by contrast, may not have become socialized in this way because their early learning experiences lacked the consistency and predictability that helped other children connect their behavior with rewards and punishments. Perhaps they were sometimes rewarded for doing the "right thing," but just as often not. They may have borne the brunt of harsh physical punishments that depended more on parental whims than on their own conduct. As adults, they may not place much value on what other people expect because there was no clear connection between their own behavior and reinforcement in childhood. They may have learned as children that there was little they could do to prevent punishment and so perhaps lost the motivation to try. Although Ullmann and Krasner's views may account for some features of antisocial personality disorder, they may not adequately address the development of the "charming" type of antisocial personality; people in this group are skillful at reading the social cues of others and in using them for personal advantage.

Social-cognitive theorist Albert Bandura (1973, 1986) has studied the role of observational learning in aggressive behavior, which is one of the common components of antisocial behavior. He and his colleagues (e.g., Bandura, Ross, & Ross, 1963) have shown that children acquire skills, including aggressive skills, by observing the behavior of others. Exposure to aggression may come from watching violent television programs or in observing parents who act violently toward each other. Bandura does not believe children and adults display aggressive behaviors in a mechanical way, however. Rather, people usually do not imitate aggressive behavior unless they are provoked and believe they are more likely to be rewarded than punished for it. When models get their way with others by acting aggressively, children may be more likely to imitate them. Children may also acquire antisocial behaviors such as cheating, bullying, or lying by direct reinforcement if they find that those behaviors help them avoid blame or manipulate others.

Social-cognitive psychologists have also shown that the ways in which people with personality disorders interpret their social experiences influence their behavior. Antisocial adolescents, for example, tend to incorrectly interpret other people's behavior as threatening (Dodge, 1985). Often, perhaps because of their family and community experiences, they presume that others intend them ill when they do not. In a promising cognitive therapy method based on such findings, called **problem-solving therapy,** antisocial adolescent boys have been encouraged to reconceptualize their social interactions as problems to be solved rather than as threats to their "manhood" (Lochman, 1992). They then generate nonviolent solutions to social confrontations and, like scientists, test the most promising ones. In the section on biological perspectives we also see that the antisocial personality's failure to profit from punishment is connected with a cognitive factor: the *meaning* of the aversive stimulus.

All in all, learning approaches to personality disorders, like the psychodynamic approaches, have their limitations. They are grounded in theory rather than in observations of family interactions that presage the development of personality disorders. Research is needed to determine whether childhood experiences proposed by psychodynamic and learning theorists actually lead to the development of particular personality disorders as hypothesized.

Family Perspectives

Many theorists have argued that disturbances in family relationships underlie the development of personality disorders. Consistent with psychodynamic formulations, researchers find that people with borderline personality disorder (BPD) *remember* their parents as having been more controlling and less caring than do reference subjects with other psychological disorders (Zweig-Frank & Paris, 1991). When people with BPD recall their earliest memories, they are more likely than other people to paint significant others as malevolent or evil. They portray their parents and others close to them as having been likely to injure them deliberately or to fail to help them escape injuries by others (Nigg et al., 1992).

A number of researchers have linked a history of physical or sexual abuse or neglect in childhood to the development of personality disorders, including BPD, in adulthood (e.g., Johnson et al., 1999; Trull, 2001; Wilkinson-Ryan & Westen, 2000). Perhaps the "splitting" observed in people with the disorder is a function of having learned to cope with unpredictable and harsh behavior from parental figures or other caregivers.

problem-solving therapy A form of therapy that focuses on helping people develop more effective problem-solving skills.

Again consistent with psychodynamic theory, family factors such as parental over-protection and authoritarianism have been implicated in the development of dependent personality traits that may hamper the development of independent behavior (Bornstein, 1992). Extreme fears of abandonment may also be involved, perhaps resulting from a failure to develop secure bonds with parental attachment figures in childhood due to parental neglect, rejection, or death. Subsequently, a chronic fear of being abandoned by other people with whom one has close relationships may develop, leading to the clinginess that typifies dependent personality disorder. Theorists also suggest that obsessive-compulsive personality disorder may emerge within a strongly moralistic and rigid family environment, which does not permit even minor deviations from expected roles or behavior (e.g., Oldham, 1994).

As with BPD, researchers find that childhood abuse or neglect is a risk factor in the development of antisocial personality disorder (APD) in adulthood (Luntz & Widom, 1994). In a view that straddles the psychodynamic and learning theories, the McCords (McCord & McCord, 1964) focus on the role of parental rejection or neglect in the development of APD. They suggest that children normally learn to associate parental approval with conformity to parental practices and values, and disapproval with disobedience. When tempted to transgress, children feel anxious for fear of losing parental love. Anxiety serves as a signal that encourages the child to inhibit antisocial behavior. Eventually, the child identifies with parents and internalizes these social controls in the form of a conscience. When parents do not show love for their children, this identification does not occur. Children do not fear loss of love because they have never had it. The anxiety that might have served to restrain antisocial and criminal behavior is absent.

Children who are rejected or neglected by their parents may not develop warm feelings of attachment to others. They may lack the ability to empathize with the feelings and needs of others, developing instead an attitude of indifference toward others. Or perhaps they retain a wish to develop loving relationships but lack the ability to experience genuine feelings.

Although family factors may be implicated in some cases of antisocial personality disorder, many neglected children do not later show antisocial or other abnormal behaviors. We are left to develop other explanations to predict which deprived children will develop antisocial personalities or other abnormal behaviors, and which will not.

Biological Perspectives

Little is known about biological factors in most personality disorders. Although many theorists see personality disorders as the expression of maladaptive personality traits, the potential biological facets of such traits remain for the most part unknown.

Genetic Factors We have little direct evidence of genetic transmission of personality disorders (Carey & DiLalla, 1994). We do have suggestive evidence of genetic factors, based in part on findings that the first-degree biological relatives (parents and siblings) of people with certain personality disorders, especially antisocial, schizotypal, and borderline types, are more likely to be diagnosed with these disorders than are members of the general population (APA, 2000; Battaglia et al., 1995; Nigg & Goldsmith, 1994).

Studies of familial transmission are limited because family members share common environments as well as genes. Hence researchers have turned to twin and adoptee studies to tease out genetic and environmental effects. Evidence from twin studies suggests that the dimensions of personality associated with particular personality disorders may have an inherited component (Livesley et al., 1993). Researchers examined the genetic contribution to 18 dimensions that underlie various personality disorders, including callousness, identity problems, anxiousness, insecure attachment, narcissism, social avoidance, self-harm, and oppositionality (negativity) (Livesley et al., 1993). Genetic influences were suggested by findings of greater correlations on a given trait among identical (monozygotic, or MZ) twins than among fraternal (dizygotic, or DZ) twins. A statistical measure of heritability, reflecting the percentage of variability on a given trait that is accounted for by genetics, was computed for each personality dimension. The results showed that 12 of the 18 dimensions

THINK ABOUT IT
What features do the psychodynamic and family perspectives on personality disorders have in common? How do they differ?

had heritabilities in the 40% to 60% range, indicating a substantial genetic contribution to these characteristics. The highest heritabilities were for narcissism (64%) and identity problems (59%) and the lowest for conduct problems (0%) and submissiveness (25%). Bear in mind that these twins were selected from the general population, not from a sample of people with diagnosed personality disorders. Therefore, the results may not be generalizable to people with diagnosable disorders. Still, the findings suggest that genetics plays a role in varying degrees to the development of traits that underlie personality disorders. Certainly not all people possessing these traits develop personality disorders. It is possible, however, that people with a genetic predisposition for these traits may be more vulnerable to developing personality disorders if they encounter certain environmental influences, such as being reared in a dysfunctional family.

Evidence from adoption studies suggests that both genetic and environmental factors affect the risk of developing antisocial personality disorder. Adopted-away children of biological parents with antisocial personality disorder stand a greater than average risk of developing the disorder themselves, but their risk level also depends on the family environment of their adoptive families (APA, 2000). Providing further evidence of the role of heredity, investigators find striking similarities among identical twins who were reared apart on antisocial or psychopathic personality traits (DiLalla et al., 1996).

Lack of Emotional Responsiveness According to a leading theorist, Hervey Cleckley (1976), people with antisocial personalities can maintain their composure in stressful situations that would induce anxiety in most people. Lack of anxiety in response to threatening situations may help explain the failure of punishment to induce antisocial people to relinquish antisocial behavior. For most of us, the fear of getting caught and being punished are sufficient to inhibit antisocial impulses. People with antisocial personalities, however, often fail to inhibit behavior that has led to punishment in the past (Arnett, Smith, & Newman, 1997). They may not learn to inhibit antisocial or aggressive behavior because they experience little if any fear or anticipatory anxiety about being caught and punished.

In an early classic study, Lykken (1957) showed that prison inmates with antisocial personalities performed more poorly than normal controls on a shock-avoidance task, although their general learning ability did not differ from that of normals. The shock-avoidance task involved learning responses to avoid getting a mild electric shock. Lykken reasoned that the inmates who had antisocial personalities were less able to learn avoidance responses because they experienced unusually low levels of anxiety in anticipation of the shock.

Schachter and Latané (1964) found that prisoners with antisocial personalities performed significantly better on the Lykken avoidance-learning task when they were administered epinephrine (adrenaline), a hormone that increases heart rate and other indices of arousal of the autonomic nervous system. Their performance apparently improved because the epinephrine had heightened their anticipatory anxiety. Other researchers (Chesno & Kilmann, 1975) showed similar results after raising antisocial subjects' levels of autonomic arousal through bursts of aversive noise rather than injections of epinephrine.

Cognitive theorists can point to research showing that the effects of aversive stimuli on people with antisocial personality disorder may depend on the *meaning* or *value* of the stimuli. Anticipation of aversive stimulation in the form of electric shock may not foster avoidance learning in persons with antisocial personalities, but the threat of punishment in the form of loss of money may do so. In another classic study, Schmauk (1970) had subjects perform a maze-learning task under three different forms of punishment for incorrect responses: electric shock, loss of money (losing a quarter for each error from an initial "bankroll" of 40 quarters), and social disapproval (the experimenter said "Wrong" following each incorrect response). Under the shock and social punishment conditions, people with antisocial personalities performed more poorly than normal controls. They outperformed normal controls, however, when they were threatened with forfeiture of money. Though people with antisocial personalities may not be deterred from misconduct by the threat of physical punishment, they may be keenly sensitive to the loss of money. Perhaps they learn better from their mistakes when the cost is meaningful to them.

Truth OR Fiction? REVISITED

People with antisocial personalities tend to remain unduly calm in the face of impending pain.

TRUE. People with antisocial personalities tend to show little anxiety in anticipation of impending pain. This lack of emotional responsivity may help explain why the threat of punishment seems to have so little effect on deterring their antisocial behavior.

When people get anxious, their palms tend to sweat. This skin response, called the *galvanic skin response* (GSR), is a sign of activation of the sympathetic branch of the autonomic nervous system (ANS). In an early study, Hare (1965) showed that people with antisocial personalities had lower GSR levels when they were expecting painful stimuli than did normal controls. Apparently, the people with antisocial personalities experienced little anxiety in anticipation of impending pain.

Hare's findings of a weaker GSR response in people with antisocial personalities has been replicated a number of times (e.g., Arnett, 1997; Patrick, Cuthbert, & Lang, 1994). Other research generally supports the view that people with antisocial personalities are generally less aroused than others, both at times of rest and in situations in which they are faced with stress (Fowles, 1993). This lack of emotional responsivity may help explain why the threat of punishment seems to have so little effect on deterring their antisocial behavior. It is conceivable that the autonomic nervous system (ANS) of people with antisocial personalities is underresponsive to threatening stimuli.

The Craving-for-Stimulation Model Other investigators have attempted to explain the antisocial personality's lack of emotional response in terms of the levels of stimulation necessary to maintain an **optimum level of arousal.** Our optimum levels of arousal are the degrees of arousal at which we feel best and function most efficiently.

Psychopathic individuals appear to have exaggerated cravings for stimulation (Arnett et al., 1997). Perhaps they require a higher-than-normal threshold of stimulation to maintain an optimum state of arousal (Quay, 1965). That is, they may need more stimulation than other people to maintain interest or function normally.

A need for higher levels of stimulation may explain why people with psychopathic traits tend to become bored more easily than other people and more often gravitate to more stimulating but potentially dangerous activities, like the use of intoxicants such as drugs or alcohol, motorcycling, skydiving, high-stakes gambling, or sexual adventures. A higher-than-normal threshold for stimulation would not directly cause antisocial or criminal behavior; after all, part of the "right stuff" of the nation's respected astronauts includes sensation seeking. However, the threat of boredom and inability to tolerate monotony may influence some sensation seekers to drift into crime or reckless behavior (R. J. Smith, 1978).

Brain Abnormalities Studies utilizing sophisticated brain-imaging techniques link antisocial personality disorder to abnormalities in the prefrontal cortex of the frontal lobes (Damasio, 2000; Raine et al., 2000). The prefrontal cortex is the part of the brain responsible for inhibiting impulsive behavior, weighing the consequences of our actions, solving problems, and planning for the future (Angier, 2000a; Duncan et al., 2000). Brain abnormalities could help account for many features of APD, including lack of conscience, failure to inhibit impulsive behavior, low arousal states, poor problem-solving efforts, and failure to think about the consequences of one's behavior before acting (Raine et al., 2000). Nevertheless, the question of just how many people with APD are affected by underlying brain abnormalities remains to be determined.

Sociocultural Perspectives

The sociocultural perspective leads us to examine the social conditions that may contribute to the development of the behavior patterns identified as personality disorders. Because antisocial personality disorder is reported most frequently among people from lower socioeconomic classes, we might examine the role that the kinds of stressors encountered by disadvantaged families play in developing these behavior patterns. Many inner city neighborhoods are beset by social problems such as alcohol and drug abuse, teenage pregnancy, and disorganized and disintegrating families. These stressors are associated with an increased likelihood of child abuse and neglect, which may in turn contribute to lower self-esteem and breed feelings of anger and resentment in children. Neglect and abuse may become translated into the lack of empathy and a callous disregard for the welfare of others that are associated with antisocial personalities.

THINK ABOUT IT
Consider the current state of knowledge about biological causes of antisocial personality disorder. What social-policy issues does this information raise, if it is confirmed by further research?

optimum level of arousal The level of arousal associated with peak performance and optimal feelings of well-being.

Questionnaire

The Sensation-Seeking Scale

 Do you crave stimulation or seek sensation? Are you satisfied by reading or in watching television, or must you ride the big wave or bounce your motorbike over desert dunes? Zuckerman (1980) finds four factors related to sensation seeking: (1) pursuit of thrill and adventure, (2) disinhibition (that is, proclivity to express impulses), (3) pursuit of experience, and (4) susceptibility to boredom. Although some sensation seekers get involved with drugs or encounter trouble with the law, many are law abiding and limit their sensation seeking to sanctioned activities. Thus sensation seeking should not be interpreted as criminal or antisocial in itself.

Zuckerman developed several sensation-seeking scales that assess the levels of stimulation people seek to feel at their best and function efficiently. A brief form of one of them follows. To assess your own sensation-seeking tendencies, pick the choice, A or B, that best depicts you. Then compare your responses to those in the key at the end of the chapter.

1. A. I would like a job that requires a lot of traveling.
   B. I would prefer a job in one location.
2. A. I am invigorated by a brisk, cold day.
   B. I can't wait to get indoors on a cold day.
3. A. I get bored seeing the same old faces.
   B. I like the comfortable familiarity of everyday friends.
4. A. I would prefer living in an ideal society in which everyone is safe, secure, and happy.
   B. I would have preferred living in the unsettled days of our history.
5. A. I sometimes like to do things that are a little frightening.
   B. A sensible person avoids activities that are dangerous.
6. A. I would not like to be hypnotized.
   B. I would like to have the experience of being hypnotized.
7. A. The most important goal in life is to live it to the fullest and experience as much as possible.
   B. The most important goal in life is to find peace and happiness.
8. A. I would like to try parachute jumping.
   B. I would never want to try jumping out of a plane, with or without a parachute.

Sensation! Is there a connection between sensation seeking and antisocial personality disorder? Not all people who crave excitement have antisocial personalities. Yet people with antisocial personalities may have an excessive need for stimulation that makes them more likely to engage in antisocial or reckless behavior.

9. A. I enter cold water gradually, giving myself time to get used to it.
   B. I like to dive or jump right into the ocean or a cold pool.
10. A. When I go on a vacation, I prefer the change of camping out.
    B. When I go on a vacation, I prefer the comfort of a good room and bed.
11. A. I prefer people who are emotionally expressive even if they are a bit unstable.
    B. I prefer people who are calm and even-tempered.
12. A. A good painting should shock or jolt the senses.
    B. A good painting should give one a feeling of peace and security.
13. A. People who ride motorcycles must have some kind of unconscious need to hurt themselves.
    B. I would like to drive or ride a motorcycle.

Source. From Zuckerman, M. Sensation seeking. In H. London & J. Exner (Eds.), *Dimensions of personality.* New York: John Wiley & Sons. Copyright © 1980 by John Wiley & Sons. This material is used by permission of John Wiley & Sons, Inc.

Children reared in poverty are also more likely to be exposed to deviant role models, such as neighborhood drug dealers. Maladjustment in school may lead to alienation and frustration with the larger society, leading to antisocial behavior (Siegel, 1992). Addressing the problem of antisocial personality may involve attempts at a societal level to redress social injustice and improve social conditions.

Little information is available about the rates of personality disorders in other cultures. One initiative in this direction involved a joint program sponsored by the World Health Organization (WHO) and the Alcohol, Drug Abuse, and Mental Health Administration (ADAMHA) of the U.S. government. The goal of the program was to develop and standardize diagnostic instruments that could be used to arrive at psychiatric diagnoses worldwide. One result of this effort was the development of the International Personality Disorder Examination (IPDE), a semistructured interview protocol for diagnosing personality disorders (Loranger et al., 1994). The IPDE was pilot-tested by psychiatrists and clinical psychologists in 11 different countries (India, Switzerland, the Netherlands, Great Britain, Luxembourg, Germany, Kenya, Norway, Japan, Austria, and the United States). The interview protocol had reasonably good reliability for diagnosing personality disorders among the different languages and cultures that were sampled. Although more research is needed to determine the rates of particular personality disorders in other countries, investigators found the borderline and avoidant types to be the most frequently diagnosed. Perhaps the characteristics associated with these personality disorders reflect some dimensions of personality disturbance that are commonly encountered throughout the world.

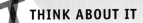

THINK ABOUT IT
Have you known anyone who you believe might fit the profile of the antisocial personality? What factors do you believe may have shaped this particular individual's personality development? How did the individual's personality affect his or her relationships with others?

Quiz 9.2
Theoretical Perspectives

Treatment of Personality Disorders

We began the chapter with a quote from the eminent psychologist William James, who suggested that people's personalities seem to be "set in plaster" by a certain age. His view may seem to be especially applicable to many people with personality disorders, who are typically highly resistant to change.

People with personality disorders usually see their behaviors, even maladaptive, self-defeating behaviors, as natural parts of themselves. Although they may be unhappy and distressed, they are unlikely to perceive their own behavior as causative. Like Marcella, whom we described as showing features of a histrionic personality disorder, they may condemn others for their problems and believe others, not they, need to change. Thus they usually do not seek help on their own. Or they begrudgingly acquiesce to treatment at the urging of others but drop out or fail to cooperate with the therapist. Or they may go for help when they feel overwhelmed by anxiety or depression and terminate treatment as soon as they find some relief rather than probe more deeply for the underlying causes of their problems. People with personality disorders also tend to respond more poorly to treatment of problems like depression than do others, perhaps because of the negative influence of their maladaptive behavioral patterns (Shea, Widiger, & Klein, 1992).

Psychodynamic Approaches

Psychodynamic approaches are often used to help people diagnosed with personality disorders become more aware of the roots of their self-defeating behavior patterns and learn more adaptive ways of relating to others. Progress in therapy may be hampered by difficulties in working therapeutically with people with personality disorders, especially clients with borderline and narcissistic personality disorders. Psychodynamic therapists often report that people with borderline personality disorder tend to have turbulent relationships with them, sometimes idealizing them, sometimes denouncing them as uncaring.

Despite problems in treating people with personality disorders in psychotherapy, some promising results have been reported using psychodynamically oriented therapies (e.g., Bateman & Fonagy, 2001). One example involves a brief, structured form of psychodynamic therapy pioneered at New York's Beth Israel Medical Center (Winston et al., 1991). There, researchers reported that a relatively brief form of therapy that averaged 40 weeks of treatment resulted in significant improvement both in symptom complaints and the social adjustment of people with personality disorders (Winston et al., 1994). The treatment emphasized interpersonal behavior and used a more active, confrontational style in addressing the client's defenses than is the case in traditional psychoanalysis.

Web Link 9.5
Online Screening for Personality Disorders (NYU School of Medicine)

THINK ABOUT IT
What factors make it difficult to treat people with personality disorders? If you were a therapist, how might you attempt to overcome these difficulties?

Behavioral Approaches

Behavior therapists see their task as changing clients' behaviors rather than their personality structures. Many behavioral theorists do not think in terms of clients' "personalities" at all, but rather in terms of acquired maladaptive behaviors that are maintained by reinforcement contingencies. Behavior therapists therefore focus on attempting to replace maladaptive behaviors with adaptive behaviors through techniques such as extinction, modeling, and reinforcement. If clients are taught behaviors likely to be reinforced by other people, the new behaviors may well be maintained.

Despite difficulties in treating borderline personality disorder (BPD), two groups of therapists headed by Aaron Beck (e.g., Arntz, 1994; Beck, Freeman, & Associates, 1990) and Marsha Linehan (Linehan, 1993; Linehan et al., 1991, 1994) report promising results using cognitive-behavioral techniques. Beck's approach focuses on helping the individual correct cognitive distortions that underlie tendencies to see oneself and others as either all good or all bad. Linehan's technique, called *dialectical behavior therapy* (DBT), combines behavior therapy and supportive psychotherapy. Behavioral techniques are used to help clients develop more effective social skills and problem-solving skills, which can help improve their relationships with others and ability to cope with negative events. Because people with BPD tend to be overly sensitive to even the slightest cues of rejection, therapists provide continuing acceptance and support, even when clients push the limits by becoming manipulative or overly demanding. While early results in using DBT are promising, researchers recognize that more research support is needed to support its efficacy in treating this challenging disorder (Scheel, 2000; Swenson, 2000; Turner, 2000).

Some antisocial adolescents have been placed, often by court order, in residential and foster-care programs that contain numerous behavioral treatment components. These residential programs have concrete rules and clear rewards for obeying them. At Achievement Place, for example, which was founded in Kansas in the 1960s and has been reproduced elsewhere, prosocial behaviors such as completing homework are systematically reinforced; antisocial behaviors, such as using profanity, are extinguished (Kirigin & Wolf, 1998). Some residential programs rely on *token economies,* in which prosocial behaviors are rewarded with tokens such as plastic chips that can be exchanged for privileges. Although participants in such programs may show improved behavior, it remains unclear whether such programs reduce the risk that adolescent antisocial behavior will continue into adulthood.

Biological Approaches

Drug therapy does not directly treat personality disorders. Antidepressants or antianxiety drugs are sometimes used to treat the emotional distress that individuals with personality disorders may encounter, however. Drugs do not alter the long-standing patterns of maladaptive behavior that may give rise to distress. However, a study indicates that the antidepressant Prozac can reduce aggressive behavior and irritability in impulsive and aggressive individuals with personality disorders (Coccaro & Kavoussi, 1997). Researchers suspect that impulsive and aggressive behavior may be related to serotonin deficiencies. Prozac and similar drugs act to increase the availability of serotonin in the synaptic connections in the brain.

Much remains to be learned about working with people who have personality disorders. The major challenges involve recruiting people who do not see themselves as being disordered into treatment and prompting them to develop insight into their self-defeating or injurious behaviors. Current efforts to help such people are too often reminiscent of the old couplet:

> He that complies against his will,
> Is of his own opinion still.
>
> —Samuel Butler, *Hudibras*

In this chapter we have considered a number of problems in which people act out on maladaptive impulses yet fail to see how their behaviors are disrupting their lives. In the next chapter we explore other maladaptive behaviors that are frequently connected with lack of self-insight: behaviors involving substance abuse.

 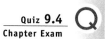

Overview of Personality Disorders

TYPES OF PERSONALITY DISORDERS

Personality Disorders Characterized by Odd or Eccentric Behavior

Paranoid Personality Disorder
- Pervasive suspiciousness of the motives of others but without outright paranoid delusions

Schizoid Personality Disorder
- Social aloofness and shallow or blunted emotions

Schizotypal Personality Disorder
- Persistent difficulty forming close social relationships and odd or peculiar beliefs and behaviors without clear psychotic features

Personality Disorders Characterized by Dramatic, Emotional, or Erratic Behavior

Antisocial Personality Disorder
- Chronic antisocial behavior, callous treatment of others, irresponsible behavior, and lack of remorse for wrongdoing

Borderline Personality Disorder
- Tumultuous moods and stormy relationships with others, unstable self-image, and lack of impulse control

Histrionic Personality Disorder
- Overly dramatic and emotional behavior; demands to be the center of attention; excessive needs for reassurance, praise, and approval

Narcissistic Personality Disorder
- Grandiose sense of self; extreme needs for admiration

Personality Disorders Characterized by Anxious or Fearful Behavior

Avoidant Personality Disorder
- Chronic pattern of avoiding social relationships due to fears of rejection

Dependent Personality Disorder
- Excessive dependence on others and difficulty making independent decisions

Obsessive-Compulsive Personality Disorder
- Excessive needs for orderliness and perfectionism, excessive attention to detail, rigid ways of relating to others

THEORETICAL PERSPECTIVES

Psychodynamic Perspectives
- To Kohut, the failure to replace childhood narcissism with more realistic appraisals of self and others underlies the development of narcissistic personality
- To Kernberg, the failure in early childhood to develop a cohesive sense of self and others leads to the development of borderline personality
- To Mahler, the failure to master the developmental challenge of separation-individuation early in life underlies the development of borderline personality

Learning Perspectives
- Behavioral features of personality disorders relate to learning experiences in childhood, including observational learning of deviant or aggressive behavior
- Lack of opportunity in childhood to learn explorative or independent behaviors may lead to dependent personality traits
- Excessive parental discipline or overcontrol may lead to obsessive-compulsive personality traits
- Inconsistent attention and reinforcement for attention-getting behaviors may lead to histrionic personality traits
- Lack of predictable and consistent reinforcement for socially approved behavior may lead to antisocial personality traits

Family Perspectives
- For antisocial personality disorder, parental rejection or neglect may lead to a failure to internalize parental values and failure to develop empathy
- Parental overprotection and authoritarianism may lead to the development of dependent personality traits

Sociocultural Perspectives
- Social or economic disadvantage and exposure to deviant role models may lead to the failure to develop properly socialized behaviors
- Physical or sexual abuse may underlie the development of borderline personality traits

Biological Perspectives
- Possible genetic influences on personality traits underlying personality disorders
- Possible inherited component of antisocial personality disorder
- For antisocial personality disorder, possible lack of emotional responsiveness in threatening situations
- For antisocial personality disorder, possible needs for higher levels of stimulation to maintain optimum levels of arousal
- For antisocial personality disorder, reduced activity in brain centers controlling impulsive behavior

▶

Overview of Personality Disorders (continued)

TREATMENT APPROACHES	Despite difficulties working therapeutically with individuals with personality disorders, promising results are emerging based on psychodynamic and cognitive-behavioral approaches
Drug Therapy	• Antidepressants or antianxiety drugs may be used to control symptoms but do not alter underlying patterns of behavior
Cognitive-Behavioral Therapy	• To help foster more adaptive behavior, to develop more effective social skills and problem-solving skills, and to replace faulty thinking with rational alternatives
Psychodynamic Therapy	• To help people understand the childhood roots of their problems and learn more effective ways of relating to others

Summing Up

Types of Personality Disorders

What are personality disorders? Personality disorders are maladaptive or rigid behavior patterns or personality traits associated with states of personal distress that impair the person's ability to function in social or occupational roles. People with personality disorders do not generally recognize a need to change themselves.

What are the classes of personality disorders within the DSM *system?* The *DSM* classifies personality disorders on Axis II and categorizes them according to the following clusters of characteristics: odd or eccentric behavior; dramatic, emotional, or erratic behavior; or anxious or fearful behavior.

What are the features associated with personality disorders characterized by odd or eccentric behavior? People with paranoid personality disorder are unduly suspicious and mistrustful of others, to the point that their relationships suffer. But they do not hold the more flagrant paranoid delusions typical of schizophrenia. Schizoid personality disorder describes people who have little if any interest in social relationships, show a restricted range of emotional expression, and appear distant and aloof. People with schizotypal personalities appear odd or eccentric in their thoughts, mannerisms, and behavior, but not to the degree found in schizophrenia.

What are the features associated with personality disorders characterized by dramatic, emotional, or erratic behavior? Antisocial personality disorder describes people who persistently engage in behavior that violates social norms and the rights of others and who tend to show no remorse for their misdeeds. Borderline personality disorder is defined in terms of instability in self-image, relationships, and mood. People with borderline personality disorder often engage in impulsive acts, which are frequently self-destructive. People with histrionic personality disorder tend to be highly dramatic and emotional in their behavior, whereas people

diagnosed with narcissistic personality disorder have an inflated or grandiose sense of self, and like those with histrionic personalities, they demand to be the center of attention.

What are the features associated with personality disorders characterized by anxious or fearful behavior? Avoidant personality disorder describes people who are so terrified of rejection and criticism that they are generally unwilling to enter relationships without unusually strong reassurances of acceptance. People with dependent personality disorder are overly dependent on others and have extreme difficulty acting independently or making even the smallest decisions on their own. People with obsessive-compulsive personality disorder have various traits such as orderliness, perfectionism, rigidity, and overattention to detail, but are without the true obsessions and compulsions associated with obsessive-compulsive (anxiety) disorder.

What are some problems associated with the classification of personality disorders? Various controversies and problems attend the classification of personality disorders, including lack of demonstrated reliability and validity, too much overlap among the categories, difficulty in distinguishing between variations in normal behavior and abnormal behavior, underlying sexist biases in certain categories, and confusion of labels with explanations.

Theoretical Perspectives

How do traditional Freudian concepts of disturbed personality development compare with more recent psychodynamic approaches? Earlier Freudian theory focused on unresolved Oedipal conflicts in explaining normal and abnormal personality development. More recent psychodynamic theorists have focused on the pre-Oedipal period in explaining the development of such personality disorders as narcissistic and borderline personality.

How do learning theorists view personality disorders? Learning theorists view personality disorders in terms of maladaptive patterns of behavior rather than personality traits. Learning theorists seek to identify the early learning experiences and present reinforcement patterns that may explain the development and maintenance of personality disorders.

What is the role of family relationships in personality disorders? Many theorists argue that disturbed family relationships play formative roles in the development of personality disorders. For example, theorists have connected antisocial personality to parental rejection or neglect and parental modeling of antisocial behavior.

How do encoding strategies of antisocial adolescents differ from those of their peers? Antisocial adolescents are more likely to interpret social cues as provocations or intentions of ill will. This cognitive bias may lead them to be confrontative in their relationships with peers.

What roles might biological factors play in antisocial personality disorder? Research suggests that people with antisocial personalities may lack emotional responsiveness to physically threatening stimuli and have reduced levels of autonomic reactivity. People with antisocial personalities may also require higher levels of stimulation to maintain optimal levels of arousal.

What role do sociocultural factors play in the development of personality disorders? The effects of poverty, urban blight, and drug abuse can lead to family disorganization and disintegration, making it less likely that children will receive the nurturance and support they need to develop more socially adaptive behavior patterns. Sociocultural theorists believe that such factors may underlie the development of personality disorders, especially antisocial personality disorder.

Treatment of Personality Disorders

How do therapists approach the treatment of personality disorders? Therapists from different schools of therapy try to assist people with personality disorders to gain better awareness of their self-defeating behavior patterns and learn more adaptive ways of relating to others. Despite difficulties in working therapeutically with people with personality disorders, promising results have emerged from the use of relatively short-term psychodynamic therapy and cognitive-behavioral treatment approaches.

Key for Sensation-Seeking Scale

Because this is an abbreviated version of a questionnaire, no norms are applicable. However, answers that agree with the following key are suggestive of sensation seeking:

1. A
2. A
3. A
4. B
5. A
6. B
7. A
8. A
9. B
10. A
11. A
12. A
13. B

CHAPTER TEN

Substance Abuse and Dependence

Christopher Richard Wynne Nevinson
A Bursting Shell, 1915

Truth OR Fiction?

- More deaths are caused by illicit drugs, especially cocaine and heroin, than by legally available drugs. (p. 299)

- You cannot become psychologically dependent on a drug without first being physically addicted to it. (p. 303)

- Alcohol "goes to women's heads" more rapidly than to men's. (p. 308)

- Alcohol use at any level increases the risk of heart attacks. (p. 312)

- Heroin was developed during the search for a nonaddictive drug that would relieve pain as effectively as morphine. (p. 314)

- Coca-Cola originally contained cocaine. (p. 314)

- Habitual smoking is just a bad habit, not a physical addiction. (p. 317)

- Breast cancer is the leading cause of cancer deaths among U.S. women. (p. 317)

- Being able to "hold your liquor" better than most people helps prevent the development of problem drinking. (p. 322)

- A widely used treatment for addiction to heroin is based on the substitution of another addictive drug. (p. 331)

Our society is flooded with **psychoactive** substances, or drugs, that alter the mood and twist perceptions—substances that lift you up, calm you down, and turn you upside down. Many young people start using these substances because of peer pressure or because their parents and other authority figures tell them not to.

The old standby alcohol is the most popular drug on campus—whether the campus is a high school or college (Johnston, Bachman, & O'Malley, 1992). In fact, nearly 9 of 10 college students report using alcohol within the past year, as compared to 1 student in 3 who reports using any illicit drug. Under certain conditions, the use of substances that affect mood and behavior is normal enough, at least as gauged by statistical frequency and social standards. It is normal to start the day with caffeine in the form of coffee or tea, to take wine or coffee with meals, to meet friends for a drink after work, and to end the day with a nightcap. Many of us take prescription drugs that calm us down or ease our pain. Flooding the bloodstream with nicotine by means of smoking is normal in the sense that about 1 in 4 Americans smoke. Some psychoactive substances are illegal and are used illicitly, such as cocaine, marijuana, and heroin. Others are available by prescription, such as minor tranquilizers and amphetamines. Still others are available without prescription or over the counter, such as tobacco (which contains nicotine, a mild stimulant) and alcohol (which is a depressant). Ironically, the most widely and easily accessible substances—tobacco and alcohol—cause more deaths through sickness and accidents than all illicit drugs combined.

After falling steadily during the 1980s, use of illicit drugs, such as marijuana, among adolescents rose sharply during the early 1990s, before beginning to decline by the end of the decade (Machan, 2000; "Teen Drug Use," 2000). Still, nearly 1 in 10 (9%) 12- to 17-year-olds reports using illicit drugs, such as marijuana and heroin, during the past month (Stout, 2000). By the time young people get to their senior year in high school, about half have used an illicit drug (Johnston, O'Malley, & Bachman, 1996). Two in 5 have tried marijuana. Among college students, about half have smoked marijuana at least once. After declining for a number of years, cocaine abuse began creeping upwards in many U.S. cities during the late 1990s (LeDuff, 2000; Mathias, 2000).

Table 10.1 shows data on reported drug use compiled from a continuing government survey of young people in the United States. The results shown here focus on college students. Respondents are asked whether they have ever used a substance or used it during the past 30 days. Note the recent increase in cocaine use, after a period of steady decline. The use of marijuana also climbed sharply during the 1990s, partially reversing an earlier decline. The most dramatic increase, however, occurred with the use of ecstasy (MDMA).

The most widely used drugs on campus (excepting caffeine) remain alcohol and nicotine (in the form of cigarette smoking). Cigarette smoking is rising not only among college students but also among high school students. By 1999, nearly 3 of 10 high school students (28%) were lighting up (Centers for Disease Control, 2000). For every person who smokes marijuana for the first time each year, there are about 250 people who start smoking cigarettes (Stout, 2000).

Binge drinking has emerged as a major problem on college campuses. *Binge drinking* is usually defined as having five or more drinks (for men) or four or more drinks (for women) on one occasion. Nearly half of the nation's college students report they have engaged in binge drinking during the past 2 weeks (McGinn, 2000). The president of Pennsylvania State University claimed that binge drinking was a bigger problem on college campuses than the use of illicit drugs ("College Binge Drinking Worries," 1999). Nationally, alcohol dependence has been on the rise, due largely to increases in adolescent alcohol abuse leading eventually to outright dependence (Hill et al., 2000; Nelson, Heath, & Kessler, 1998).

Truth OR Fiction? REVISITED

More deaths are caused by illicit drugs, especially cocaine and heroin, than by legally available drugs.

FALSE. Two legally available substances, alcohol and tobacco, cause more deaths.

wWw **Web Link 10.1**
Binge Drinking

psychoactive Referring to chemical substances that have psychological effects.

substance use disorders Disorders that involve maladaptive use of psychoactive substances (e.g., substance dependence).

Classification of Substance-Related Disorders

The *DSM-IV* classifies substance-related disorders into two major categories: substance use disorders and substance-induced disorders. **Substance use disorders** involve maladaptive use of psychoactive substances. These types of disorders include substance abuse and

TABLE 10.1	Trends in Drug Use Among College Students During Lifetime and During Last 30 Days (in percentages)					
Drug	**Used . . .**	**1984**	**1988**	**1992**	**1996**	**2000**
Marijuana	Ever	59.0	51.3	44.1	45.1	51.2
	Last 30 days	23.0	16.3	14.6	17.5	20.0
Inhalants	Ever	10.4	12.6	14.2	11.4	12.9
	Last 30 days	0.7	1.3	1.1	0.8	0.9
Hallucinogens (includes LSD)	Ever	12.9	10.2	12.0	12.6	14.4
	Last 30 days	1.8	1.7	2.3	1.9	1.4
Cocaine (includes crack)	Ever	21.7	15.8	7.9	5.0	9.1
	Last 30 days	7.6	4.2	1.0	0.8	1.4
MDMA ("ecstasy")	Ever	NA	NA	2.9	4.3	13.1
	Last 30 days	NA	NA	0.4	0.7	2.5
Heroin	Ever	0.5	0.3	0.5	0.7	1.7
	Last 30 days	0.0	0.1	0.0	0.0	0.2
Stimulants (other than cocaine and crystal meth)	Ever	27.8	17.7	10.5	9.5	12.3
	Last 30 days	5.5	1.8	1.1	0.9	2.9
Barbiturates	Ever	6.4	3.6	3.8	4.6	6.9
	Last 30 days	0.7	0.5	0.7	0.8	1.1
Alcohol	Ever	94.2	94.9	91.8	88.4	86.6
	Last 30 days	71.1	77.0	71.4	67.0	67.4
Cigarettes	Ever	NA	NA	NA	NA	NA
	Last 30 days	21.5	22.6	23.5	27.9	28.2

Source. Johnston, L. D., O'Malley, P. M., & Bachman, J. G. *National survey results on drug use* from *The Monitoring the Future Study* 1975–2000. Volume II., *College students and young adults, ages 19–40.* U.S. Department of Health and Human Services, Public Health Service, National Institutes of Health: National Institute on Drug Abuse, 2001, Tables 9-1 (p. 213) and 9-3 (p. 215).

substance-induced disorders Disorders that can be induced by using psychoactive substances, such as intoxication.

intoxication A state of drunkenness.

substance abuse The continued used of a psychoactive drug despite the knowledge that it is causing a social, occupational, psychological, or physical problem.

substance dependence Impaired control over the use of a psychoactive substance; often characterized by physiological dependence.

tolerance Physical habituation to a drug such that with frequent use, higher doses are needed to achieve the same effects.

substance dependence. **Substance-induced disorders** are those that can be induced by using psychoactive substances, such as intoxication, withdrawal syndromes, mood disorders, delirium, dementia, amnesia, psychotic disorders, anxiety disorders, sexual dysfunctions, and sleep disorders. Different substances have different effects, so some of these disorders apply to one, to a few, or to nearly all substances.

Substance **intoxication** refers to a state of drunkenness or "being high." These effects largely reflect the chemical actions of the psychoactive substances. The particular features of intoxication depend on which drug is ingested, the dose, the user's biological reactivity, and—to some degree—the user's expectations. Signs of intoxication often include confusion, belligerence, impaired judgment, inattention, and impaired motor and spatial skills. Extreme intoxication from use of alcohol, cocaine, opioids, and PCP can even result in death (yes, you can die from alcohol overdoses), either because of the substance's biochemical effects or because of behavior patterns—such as suicide—that are connected with psychological pain or impaired judgment brought on by use of the drug.

Substance Abuse and Dependence

Where does substance use end and abuse begin? According to the *DSM*, substance abuse involves a pattern of recurrent use that leads to damaging consequences. Damaging consequences may involve failure to meet one's major role responsibilities (e.g., as student, worker, or parent), putting oneself in situations where substance use is physically dangerous (e.g., mixing driving and substance use), encountering repeated problems with the law arising from substance use (e.g., multiple arrests for substance-related behavior), or having recurring social or interpersonal problems because of substance use (e.g., repeatedly getting into fights when drinking).

VIDEO 10.1

Substance Abuse:
Therapist Jean Obert

Two of the many faces of alcohol use—and abuse. Alcohol is our most widely used—and abused—drug. Many people use alcohol to celebrate achievements and happy occasions, as in the photograph on the left. Unfortunately, like the man in the photograph on the right, some people use alcohol to drown their sorrows, which may only compound their problems. Where exactly does substance use end and abuse begin? According to the *DSM,* use becomes abuse when it leads to damaging consequences.

When people repeatedly miss school or work because they are drunk or "sleeping it off," their behavior may fit the definition of **substance abuse.** A single incident of excessive drinking at a friend's wedding would not qualify. Nor would regular consumption of low to moderate amounts of alcohol be considered abusive so long as it is not connected with any impairment in functioning. Neither the amount nor the type of drug ingested, nor whether or not the drug is illicit, is the key to defining substance abuse according to the *DSM.* Rather, the determining feature of substance abuse is whether a pattern of drug-using behavior becomes repeatedly linked to damaging consequences.

Substance abuse may continue for a long period of time or progress to **substance dependence,** a more severe type of substance use disorder in which abuse is associated with physiological signs of dependence (tolerance or withdrawal) *or* compulsive use of a substance. People who become compulsive users lack control over their drug use. They may be aware of how their drug use is disrupting their lives or damaging their health, but feel helpless or powerless to stop using drugs, even though they may want to. By the time they become dependent on a given drug, they've given over much of their lives to obtaining and using it. The diagnostic features associated with substance dependence are listed in Table 10.2.

Repeated use of a substance may alter the body's physiological reactions, leading to the development of tolerance or a physical withdrawal syndrome (see Table 10.2). **Tolerance** is a state of physical habituation to a drug such that with frequent use, higher doses are needed to achieve the same effect. A **withdrawal syndrome** (also called an *abstinence syndrome*) involves a characteristic cluster of withdrawal symptoms that occur when a dependent person abruptly stops using a particular substance following a period of heavy, prolonged use. People who experience a withdrawal syndrome often return to using the substance in order to relieve the discomfort associated with withdrawal, which serves to maintain the addictive pattern. Withdrawal symptoms vary with the particular type of drug. With alcohol dependence, typical withdrawal symptoms include dryness in the mouth, nausea or vomiting, weakness, **tachycardia,** anxiety and depression, headaches, insomnia, elevated blood pressure, and fleeting hallucinations.

withdrawal syndrome A characteristic cluster of symptoms following the sudden reduction or cessation of use of a psychoactive substance after physiological dependence has developed.

tachycardia Abnormally rapid heartbeat.

Throes of withdrawal. Withdrawal symptoms are characteristic of the abstinence syndrome that develops when a person who is physiologically dependent on a drug abruptly suspends use of the drug.

delirium tremens A withdrawal syndrome that occurs following sudden decrease of drinking in people with chronic alcoholism.

delirium A state of mental confusion, disorientation, and extreme difficulty focusing attention.

disorientation A state of mental confusion and lack of awareness of time, place, or the identity of oneself or others.

TABLE 10.2 Diagnostic Features of Substance Dependence

Substance dependence is defined as a maladaptive pattern of use that results in significant impairment or distress, as shown by the following features occurring within the same year:

1. Tolerance for the substance, as shown by either
   (a) the need for increased amounts of the substance to achieve the desired effect or intoxication, or
   (b) marked reduction in the effects of continuing to ingest the same amounts.
2. Withdrawal symptoms, as shown by either
   (a) the withdrawal syndrome that is considered characteristic for the substance, or
   (b) the taking of the same substance (or a closely related substance, as when methadone is substituted for heroin) to relieve or to prevent withdrawal symptoms.
3. Taking larger amounts of the substance, or for longer periods of time than the individual intended (e.g., person had desired to take only one drink, but after taking the first, continues drinking until severely intoxicated).
4. Persistent desire to cut down or control intake of substance or lack of success in trying to exercise self-control.
5. Spending a good deal of time in activities directed toward obtaining the substance (e.g., visiting several physicians to obtain prescriptions or engaging in theft), in actually ingesting the substance, or in recovering from its use. In severe cases, the individual's daily life revolves around substance use.
6. The individual has reduced or given up important social, occupational, or recreational activities due to substance use (e.g., person withdraws from family events in order to indulge in drug use).
7. Substance use is continued despite evidence of persistent or recurrent psychological or physical problems either caused or exacerbated by its use (e.g., repeated arrests for driving while intoxicated).

Note. Not all of these features need be present for a diagnosis to be made.
Source. Adapted from the *DSM-IV-TR* (APA, 2000).

In some cases of chronic alcoholism, withdrawal produces a state of **delirium tremens,** or DTs. The DTs are usually limited to chronic, heavy users of alcohol who dramatically lower their intake of alcohol after many years of heavy drinking. The DTs involve intense autonomic hyperactivity (profuse sweating and tachycardia) and **delirium**—a state of mental confusion characterized by incoherent speech, **disorientation,** and extreme restlessness. Terrifying hallucinations—frequently of creepy, crawling animals—may also be present.

Substances that may lead to withdrawal syndromes include, in addition to alcohol, opioids, cocaine, amphetamines, sedatives and barbiturates, nicotine, and antianxiety agents (minor tranquilizers). Marijuana and hallucinogens like LSD are not recognized as producing a withdrawal syndrome, because of a lack of evidence that abrupt withdrawal from these substances reliably produces clinically significant withdrawal effects (APA, 2000).

In the *DSM* system, substance dependence is often, but not always, associated with the development of physiological dependence (Langenbucher et al., 2000). In some cases it involves a pattern of compulsive use without physiological dependence. For example, people may become compulsive users of marijuana, especially when they come to rely on the drug to help them cope with the stresses of daily life. Yet they may not require larger amounts of the substance to get "high" or experience distressing withdrawal symptoms when they cease using it. In most cases, however, substance dependence and physiological features of dependence occur together. Despite the fact that the *DSM* considers substance abuse and dependence to be distinct diagnostic categories, the borderline between the two is not always clear.

THINK ABOUT IT

What is the basis for determining when drug use becomes abuse or dependence? Have you or someone you know crossed the line between use and abuse?

An estimated 15 million people in the United States suffer from substance dependence (Cowan & Kandel, 2001). Alcohol dependence alone affects about 1 in 7 (14%) U.S. adults (Anthony, Warner, & Kessler, 1994; Warner et al., 1995). About 1 in 4 U.S. adults suffer from nicotine dependence resulting from regular use of tobacco products, most usually cigarettes (Breslau et al., 2001). About 1 in 13 (7.5%) have developed a dependence on an illicit drug, inhalant, or nonprescription use of tranquilizers or other psychiatric (psychotropic) drugs. Figure 10.1 gives the lifetime prevalence of drug dependence for various types of drugs.

People may abuse or become dependent on more than one psychoactive substance at the same time. People who abuse or become dependent on heroin, for instance, may also abuse or become dependent on other drugs, such as alcohol, cocaine, or stimulants—either simultaneously or successively. People who engage in these patterns of polydrug abuse face increased risk of harmful overdoses. Moreover, the "successful" treatment of one form of abuse may not affect, or in some cases may even exacerbate, abuse of other drugs.

Addiction, Physiological Dependence, and Psychological Dependence

The *DSM* uses the terms *substance abuse* and *substance dependence* to classify people whose use of these substances impairs their functioning. It does not use the term *addiction* to describe these problems. Yet the concept of addiction is widespread among professionals and laypeople alike. But what is meant by addiction?

People define addiction in different ways. For our purposes, we define **addiction** as the habitual or compulsive use of a drug accompanied by evidence of physiological dependence. **Physiological dependence** means that one's body has changed as a result of the regular use of a psychoactive drug in such a way that it depends on a steady supply of the substance. The major signs of physiological dependence involve the development of tolerance and/or an abstinence syndrome. **Psychological dependence** involves the compulsive use of a drug to meet a psychological need, such as relying on a drug to cope with stress. As we noted earlier, you can become psychologically dependent on a drug without developing a physiological dependence or addiction.

On the other hand, people may become physiologically dependent on a drug but not become a compulsive user or psychologically dependent. For example, people recuperating from surgery are often given narcotics derived from opium as painkillers. Some may develop signs of physiological dependence, such as tolerance and a withdrawal syndrome, but not become habitual users or show a lack of control over the use of these drugs.

In recent years, the concept of addiction has also extended beyond the abuse of chemical substances to apply to many habitual forms of maladaptive behavior, such as pathological gambling. In the vernacular, we hear of people being addicted to love or shopping or to almost anything. The concept of addiction has even been extended to excessive use of the Internet (Griffiths, 1999; Young, 1999). Research evidence is accumulating that suggests that excessive Internet use carries similar risks as gambling (Jamison, 2000). Investigators find that it can lead to social isolation, depression, and problems at work or school. Many heavy Internet users show evidence of compulsive use, especially those who are drawn to the anonymous social contacts available through Internet chat rooms. They may feel a building up of tension prior to engaging in Internet activity, which is followed by a sudden relief when they log on. Many heavy users sacrifice sleep or forego family or work responsibilities to satisfy their compulsive needs. Internet chat rooms may also pose dangers of spreading sexually transmitted disease. Investigators found that seeking sexual partners through the Internet was a common practice among a

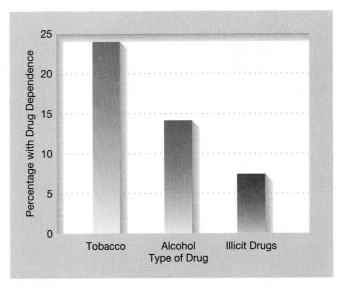

FIGURE 10.1 Lifetime prevalence of drug dependence by type of drug.
One in 4 adults in the United States suffers from tobacco dependence at some point. About 1 in 7 experiences alcohol dependence and about 1 in 13 develops a drug dependence on an illicit drug.
Source. National Comorbidity Survey (Anthony, Warner, & Kessler, 1994).

Truth OR Fiction? REVISITED

You cannot become psychologically dependent on a drug without first being physically addicted to it.

FALSE. You can become psychologically dependent on a drug without developing a physiological dependence.

addiction Impaired control over the use of a chemical substance, accompanied by physiological dependence.

physiological dependence A condition in which the drug user's body comes to depend on a steady supply of the substance.

psychological dependence Compulsive use of a substance to meet a psychological need.

Internet addiction? Compulsive, dependent use of the Internet and other forms of compulsive behavior, such as compulsive gambling or shopping, have been likened to forms of nonchemical addiction. Whether we label such maladaptive patterns of behavior as "addictions" depends on how we define the concept of addiction.

THINK ABOUT IT

Do you or someone you know show evidence of any nonchemical forms of addiction, such as compulsive shopping, gambling, or sexual behavior? How is this behavior affecting your (his or her) life? What can you (he or she) do about overcoming it?

sample of people seeking HIV testing and counseling (McFarlane et al., 2000). In another study, an outbreak of syphilis was linked to a group of people who had met through an Internet chat room (Klausner et al., 2000).

Whether compulsive gambling or shopping or excessive Internet use constitute addictions depends on how we define our terms. For our purposes, we limit the term *addiction* to compulsive use of substances that produce physiological dependence. Although these other behaviors may be forms of compulsive behavior, we are reluctant to call them addictions because they do not involve physiological dependence on a chemical substance.

Racial/Ethnic Differences in Substance Dependence

Despite the popular stereotype that drug dependence is more frequent among ethnic minorities, this belief is not supported by evidence. The National Comorbidity Survey (NCS) shows that drug dependence is actually less common among African Americans than non-Hispanic White Americans and no more common among Hispanic Americans than among non-Hispanic White Americans (Anthony et al., 1994). Moreover, African American adolescents are much less likely than non-Hispanic White adolescents to develop substance abuse or dependence problems (Kilpatrick et al., 2000). In a later section we shall examine evidence on racial/ethnic group differences in alcohol use and abuse.

Pathways to Drug Dependence

Although the progression to substance dependence varies from person to person, some common pathways can be described according to the following stages (Weiss & Mirin, 1987):

1. *Experimentation.* During the stage of experimentation, or occasional use, the drug temporarily makes users feel good, even euphoric. Users feel in control and believe they can stop at any time.

2. *Routine use.* During the next stage, a period of routine use, people begin to structure their lives around the pursuit and use of drugs. Denial plays a major role at this stage, as users mask the negative consequences of their behavior to themselves and others. Values change. What had formerly been important, such as family and work, comes to matter less than the drugs.

   The following clinical interview illustrates how denial can mask reality. This 48-year-old executive was brought for a consultation by his wife. She complained his once-successful business was jeopardized by his erratic behavior, he was grouchy and moody, and he had spent $7,000 in the previous month on cocaine.

   CLINICIAN: Have you missed many days at work recently?
   EXECUTIVE: Yes, but I can afford to, since I own the business. Nobody checks up on me.
   CLINICIAN: It sounds like that's precisely the problem. When you don't go to work, the company stays open, but it doesn't do very well.
   EXECUTIVE: My employees are well trained. They can run the company without me.
   CLINICIAN: But that's not happening.
   EXECUTIVE: Then there's something wrong with them. I'll have to look into it.
   CLINICIAN: It sounds as if there's something wrong with you, but you don't want to look into it.
   EXECUTIVE: Now you're on my case. I don't know why you listen to everything my wife says.
   CLINICIAN: How many days of work did you miss in the last two months?
   EXECUTIVE: A couple.
   CLINICIAN: Are you saying that you missed only two days of work?

EXECUTIVE:	Maybe a few.
CLINICIAN:	Only three or four days?
EXECUTIVE:	Maybe a little more.
CLINICIAN:	Ten? Fifteen?
EXECUTIVE:	Fifteen.
CLINICIAN:	All because of cocaine?
EXECUTIVE:	No.
CLINICIAN:	How many were because of cocaine?
EXECUTIVE:	Less than fifteen.
CLINICIAN:	Fourteen? Thirteen?
EXECUTIVE:	Maybe thirteen.
CLINICIAN:	So you missed thirteen days of work in the last two months because of cocaine. That's almost two days a week.
EXECUTIVE:	That sounds like a lot but it's no big deal. Like I say, the company can run itself.
CLINICIAN:	How long have you been using cocaine?
EXECUTIVE:	About three years.
CLINICIAN:	Did you ever use drugs or alcohol before that in any kind of quantity?
EXECUTIVE:	No.
CLINICIAN:	Then let's think back five years. Five years ago, if you had imagined yourself missing over a third of your workdays because of a drug, and if you had imagined yourself spending the equivalent of $84,000 a year on that same drug, and if you saw your once-successful business collapsing all around you, wouldn't you have thought that that was indicative of a pretty serious problem?
EXECUTIVE:	Yes, I would have.
CLINICIAN:	So what's different now?
EXECUTIVE:	I guess I just don't want to think about it.

—From Weiss & Mirin, 1987, pp. 79–80

As routine drug use continues, problems mount. Users devote more resources to their drugs. Family bank accounts are ravaged, "temporary" loans are sought from friends and family for trumped-up reasons, and family heirlooms and jewelry are sold to pawnbrokers for a fraction of their value. Lying and manipulation become a way of life to cover up the drug use. The husband sells the TV set to a pawnbroker and forces the front door open to make it look like a burglary. The wife claims to have been robbed at knifepoint to explain the disappearance of a gold chain or engagement ring. Family relationships become strained as the mask of denial shatters and the consequences of drug abuse become apparent: days lost from work, unexplained absences from home, rapid mood shifts, depletion of family finances, failure to pay bills, stealing from family members, and missing family gatherings or children's birthday parties.

VIDEO **10.2**

Substance Abuse:
Therapist Louise Roberts

3. *Addiction or dependence.* Routine use becomes addiction or dependence when users feel powerless to resist drugs, either because they want to experience their effects or to avoid the consequences of withdrawal. Little or nothing else matters at this stage, as seen in the case of a 41-year-old architect, who related the following conversation with his wife:

A Case of Cocaine Dependence

She had just caught me with cocaine again after I had managed to convince her that I hadn't used in over a month. Of course I had been tooting (snorting) almost every day, but I had managed to cover my tracks a little better than usual. So she said to me that I was going to have to make a choice—either cocaine or her. Before she finished the

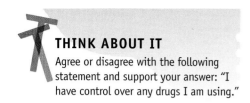

THINK ABOUT IT

Agree or disagree with the following statement and support your answer: "I have control over any drugs I am using."

Quiz **10.1**
Classification of Substance-Related Disorders

sentence, I knew what was coming, so I told her to think carefully about what she was going to say. It was clear to me that there wasn't a choice. I love my wife, but I'm not going to choose anything over cocaine. It's sick, but that's what things have come to. Nothing and nobody comes before my coke.

—*From Weiss & Mirin, 1987, p. 55*

Now let us examine the effects of different types of drugs of abuse and the consequences associated with their use and abuse.

Drugs of Abuse

Drugs of abuse are generally classified within three major groupings: (1) depressants, such as alcohol and opioids; (2) stimulants, such as amphetamines and cocaine; and (3) hallucinogens.

Depressants

A **depressant** is a drug that slows down or curbs the activity of the central nervous system. It reduces feelings of tension and anxiety, causes our movements to become sluggish, and impairs our cognitive processes. In high doses, depressants can arrest vital functions and cause death. The most widely used depressant, alcohol, can lead to death when taken in large amounts because of its depressant effects on respiration (breathing). Other effects are specific to the particular kind of depressant. For example, some depressants, such as heroin, produce a "rush" of pleasure. Here let us consider several of the major types of depressants.

Alcohol You may not have thought of alcohol as a drug, perhaps because it is so popular, or perhaps because it is ingested by drinking rather than by smoking or injection. But alcoholic beverages—such as wine, beer, and hard liquor—contain a depressant called *ethyl alcohol* (or *ethanol*). The concentration of the drug varies with the type of beverage (wine and beer have less pure alcohol per ounce than distilled spirits such as rye, gin, or vodka). Alcohol is classified as a depressant drug because it has biochemical effects similar to those of a class of minor tranquilizers, the benzodiazepines, which includes the well-known drugs *diazepam* (Valium) and *chlordiazepoxide* (Librium). We can think of alcohol as a type of over-the-counter tranquilizer.

Alcohol is used in many ways. It is our mealtime relaxant, our party social facilitator, our bedtime sedative. We observe holy days, laud our achievements, and express joyful wishes with alcohol. Adolescents assert their maturity with alcohol. Pediatricians have swabbed the painful gums of teething babies with alcohol. Alcohol even deals the death-blow to germs on surface wounds and is the active ingredient in antiseptic mouthwashes.

Most American adults drink alcohol at least occasionally. Most people who drink do so in moderation, but many develop significant problems with alcohol use (Garbutt et al., 1999; Miller & Brown, 1997). Alcohol is the most widely abused substance in the United States and worldwide. Alcohol dependence affects an estimated 14 million Americans, about 14% of the adult population. Alcohol abuse without dependence is believed to affect about 9% of adult Americans (Kessler et al., 1994). Many lay and professional people use the term **alcoholism** to refer to alcohol dependence. Though definitions of alcoholism vary, we use the term to refer to a physical dependence on, or addiction to, alcohol that is characterized by impaired control over the use of the drug.

The personal and social costs of alcoholism exceed those of all illicit drugs combined. Alcohol abuse is connected with lower productivity, loss of jobs, and downward movement in socioeconomic status. Estimates are that perhaps 30% to 40% of homeless people in the United States suffer from alcoholism (McCarty et al., 1991). About one in three suicides in this country and about the same proportion of deaths due to unintentional injury (such as from motor vehicle accidents) are believed to be alcohol-related (Hingson et al., 2000).

depressant A drug that lowers the level of activity of the central nervous system.

alcoholism An alcohol dependence disorder or addiction that results in serious personal, social, occupational, or health problems.

Questionnaire

Are You Hooked?

 Are you dependent on alcohol? If you shake and shiver and undergo the tortures of the darned (our editor insisted on changing this word to maintain the decorum of a textbook) when you go without a drink for a while, the answer is clear enough. Sometimes the clues are more subtle, however.

The following questions, adapted from the National Council on Alcoholism's self-test, can shed some light on the question. Simply place a check mark in the yes or no column for each item. Then check the key at the end of the chapter.

	YES	NO
1. Do you sometimes go on drinking binges?	___	___
2. Do you tend to keep away from your family or friends when you are drinking?	___	___
3. Do you become irritated when your family or friends talk about your drinking?	___	___

	YES	NO
4. Do you feel guilty now and then about your drinking?	___	___
5. Do you often regret the things you have said or done when you have been drinking?	___	___
6. Do you find that you fail to keep the promises you make about controlling or cutting down on your drinking?	___	___
7. Do you eat irregularly or not at all when you are drinking?	___	___
8. Do you feel low after drinking?	___	___
9. Do you sometimes miss work or appointments because of drinking?	___	___
10. Do you use more and more to get drunk or high?	___	___

Source. Adapted from *Newsweek*, February 20, 1989, p. 52.

More teenagers die from alcohol-related motor vehicle accidents than from any other cause (National Highway Traffic Safety Administration, 1988). All told, an estimated 100,000 people in the United States die from alcohol-related causes each year, mostly from alcohol-related motor vehicle crashes and diseases (Kalb, 2001b; Wood, Vinson, & Sher, 2001).

Alcohol, not cocaine or other drugs, is the drug of choice among young people today and the leading drug of abuse (Johnston et al., 1992). Drinking has become so integrated into college life that it has become essentially normative, as much a part of the college experience as attending a weekend football or basketball game. Despite the popular image of the person who develops alcoholism as a skid-row drunk, only a small minority of people with alcoholism fit the stereotype. The great majority of people with alcoholism are the type of people you're likely to see every day—your neighbors, coworkers, friends, and members of your own family. They are found in all walks of life and from every social and economic class. Many have families, hold good jobs, and live fairly comfortably. Yet alcoholism can have just as devastating an effect on the well-to-do as the indigent, leading to wrecked careers and marriages, to motor vehicle and other accidents, and to severe, life-threatening physical disorders, as well as exacting an enormous emotional toll.

No one drinking pattern is exclusively associated with alcoholism. Some people with alcoholism drink heavily every day; others binge only on weekends. Others can abstain for lengthy periods of time but periodically "go off the wagon" and engage in episodes of binge drinking that may last for weeks or months.

wWw **Web Link 10.2**
How to Cut Down on Your Drinking

wWw **Web Link 10.3**
Self-Screening for Alcoholism

Risk Factors for Alcoholism Investigators have identified a number of factors that place people at increased risk for developing alcoholism and alcohol-related problems. These include the following:

1. *Gender.* Men are more than twice as likely as women (20% vs. 8%, respectively) to develop alcohol dependence disorder (Grant, 1997). One possible reason for this gender difference is sociocultural; perhaps tighter cultural constraints are placed on women. Yet it may also be that alcohol hits women harder, and not only because women usually weigh less than men. Alcohol seems to "go to women's heads" more rapidly than men's. This is apparently because women metabolize less alcohol in the

stomach than men do. Why is this? It appears that women have less of an enzyme that metabolizes alcohol in the stomach than men do (Lieber, 1990). Consequently, ounce for ounce women absorb more alcohol into their bloodstreams than do men. As a result, they are likely to become inebriated on less alcohol than men.

2. *Age.* The great majority of cases of alcohol dependence develop in young adulthood, typically before age 40 (Langenbucher & Chung, 1995). Although alcohol use disorders tend to develop somewhat later in women than in men, women who develop these problems experience similar health, social, and occupational problems by middle age as their male counterparts.

3. *Antisocial personality disorder.* Antisocial behavior in adolescence or adulthood increases the risk of later alcoholism. On the other hand, many people with alcoholism showed no antisocial tendencies in adolescence, and many antisocial adolescents do not abuse alcohol or other drugs as adults (Nathan, 1988).

4. *Family history.* The best predictor of problem drinking in adulthood appears to be a family history of alcohol abuse. Family members who drink may act as models ("set a poor example"). Moreover, the biological relatives of people with alcohol dependence may also inherit a predisposition that makes them more likely to develop problems with alcohol.

5. *Sociodemographic factors.* A lifetime history of alcohol dependence is more common among people of lower income and educational levels and among people living alone (Anthony et al., 1994).

Ethnicity and Alcohol Use and Abuse Higher rates of alcohol use and alcoholism are found to vary among American ethnic and racial groups (Beauvais, 1998; Lex, 1987; Moncher, Holden, & Trimble, 1990; Schinke, 1999). Jewish Americans, for example, have relatively low rates of alcoholism (Yeung & Greenwald, 1992), perhaps because Jews tend to expose children to the ritual use of wine within a religious context and to impose strong cultural restraints on excessive and underage drinking. Asian Americans also tend to drink less heavily than most other groups (Schinke, 1999). They too also place strong cultural constraints on excessive drinking. But a biological factor may also be involved. Asian Americans are more likely than other groups to show a flushing response to alcohol. Flushing is characterized by redness and feelings of warmth on the face, and, at higher doses, nausea, heart palpitations, dizziness, and headaches (Ellickson, Hays, & Bell, 1992). Genes that control the metabolism of alcohol are responsible for the flushing response (Begley, 2001b). Since people like to avoid these unpleasant experiences, flushing may serve as a natural defense against alcoholism by curbing excessive alcohol intake.

Hispanic American men and non-Hispanic White men have similar rates of alcohol consumption and alcohol-related physical problems (Caetano, 1987; Kessler et al., 1994). Hispanic American women, however, are much less likely to use alcohol and to develop alcohol use disorders than non-Hispanic White women. Why this difference? An important factor may be cultural expectations. Traditional Hispanic American cultures place severe restrictions on the use of alcohol by women, especially heavy drinking. However, with increasing acculturation, Hispanic American women in the United States apparently are becoming more similar to Euro-American women with respect to

Women and alcohol. Women are less likely to develop alcoholism, in part because of greater cultural constraints on excessive drinking by women and perhaps because women absorb more pure alcohol into the bloodstream than men; thus women become more affected by the alcohol they consume than men who drink the same amount.

Alcohol and ethnic diversity. The damaging effects of alcohol abuse appear to be taking the heaviest toll on African Americans and Native Americans. The prevalence of alcohol-related cirrhosis of the liver is nearly twice as high among African Americans than among White Americans, even though African Americans are less likely to develop alcohol abuse or dependence disorders. Jewish Americans have relatively low incidences of alcohol-related problems, perhaps because they tend to expose children to the ritual use of wine in childhood and impose strong cultural restraints on excessive drinking. Asian Americans tend to drink less heavily than most other Americans, in part because of cultural constraints and possibly because they have less biological tolerance of alcohol, as shown by a greater flushing response to alcohol.

alcohol use and abuse. Drinking rates among more acculturated Asian American groups are also comparable to those of the general population (Schinke, 1999).

Alcohol abuse is taking a heavy toll on African Americans. The prevalence of *cirrhosis* a degenerative, potentially fatal liver disease, is nearly twice as high in African Americans as in non-Hispanic White Americans. African Americans are also much more likely to develop alcohol-related coronary heart disease and oral and throat cancers (Rogan, 1986). Yet African Americans are much less likely than non-Hispanic White Americans to develop alcohol abuse or dependence (Anthony et al., 1994; Grant et al., 1994). Why, then, do African Americans suffer more from alcohol-related problems?

Socioeconomic factors may help explain these differences. African Americans are more likely to encounter the stresses of unemployment and economic hardship, and stress may compound the damage to the body caused by heavy alcohol consumption. African Americans also tend to have poorer access to medical services and may be less likely to receive early treatment for the medical problems caused by alcohol abuse.

American Indians are perhaps the American ethnic group that suffers most from alcohol-related problems. Though rates of drinking vary from tribe to tribe, the American Indian population has very high rates of problem drinking and alcohol-related consequences, such as cirrhosis of the liver, fetal abnormalities, and automobile and other accident fatalities (Beauvais, 1998; Rabasca, 2000a; Schinke, 1999).

Many Indian people believe the loss of their culture is largely responsible for their high rates of drinking-related problems (Beauvais, 1998). The disruption of traditional Indian culture caused by the appropriation of Indian lands and by attempts by European American society to sever Native Americans from their cultural traditions while denying them full access to the dominant culture resulted in severe cultural and social disorganization that may account for their high rates of depression and substance abuse (Kahn, 1982). Beset by such problems, Native American adults are also prone to child abuse and neglect. Abuse and neglect contribute to feelings of hopelessness and depression among adolescents, who then seek to escape their feelings through alcohol and other drugs (Berlin, 1987).

Conceptions of Alcoholism: Disease, Moral Defect, or Behavior Pattern? According to the medical perspective, alcoholism is a disease. E. M. Jellinek (1960), a leading proponent of the disease model, believed that alcoholism is a permanent, irreversible condition. Jellinek believed that once a person with alcoholism takes a drink, the biochemical effects of the drug on the brain create an irresistible physical craving for more. Jellinek's ideas have contributed to the view that, "Once an alcoholic, always an alcoholic." Alcoholics Anonymous (AA), which has adopted Jellinek's concepts, views people who suffer from alcoholism as either drinking or "recovering." In other words, alcoholism is never cured. Jellinek's concepts have also supported the idea that "just one drink" will cause the person with alcoholism to "fall off the wagon." In this view, the sole path to recovery is abstinence.

Yet not all professionals regard alcoholism as a disease in the medical sense. To some, the term is used as a label to describe a harmful pattern of alcohol ingestion and related behaviors. In this view, the "just-one-drink" hypothesis is not a biochemical inevitability. It is, instead, a common self-fulfilling prophecy, as we see later in the chapter.

Psychological Effects of Alcohol The effects of alcohol or other drugs vary from person to person. By and large they reflect the interaction of (1) the physiological effects of the substances, and (2) our interpretations of those effects. What do most people expect from alcohol? People frequently hold stereotypical expectations that alcohol will reduce states of tension, enhance pleasurable experiences, wash away their worries, and enhance their social skills. But what *does* alcohol actually do?

At a physiological level, alcohol, like the benzodiazepines (a family of antianxiety drugs; see Chapter 6), appears to heighten the sensitivity of GABA receptor sites. Because GABA is an inhibitory neurotransmitter, increasing the action of GABA reduces overall nervous system activity, producing feelings of relaxation. As people drink, their senses become clouded, and balance and coordination suffer. Still higher doses act on the parts of the brain that regulate involuntary vital functions, such as heart rate, respiration rate, and body temperature.

People may do many things when drinking that they would not do when sober, in part because of expectations concerning the drug, in part because of the drug's effects on the brain. For example, they may become more flirtatious or sexually aggressive or say or do things they later regret. Their behavior may reflect their expectation that alcohol has liberating effects and provides an external excuse for questionable behavior. Later, they can claim, "It was the alcohol, not me." The drug may impair the brain's ability to curb impulsive, risk-taking, or violent behavior (Curtin et al., 2001) (discussed further in Chapter 16), perhaps by interfering with information-processing functions. Although alcohol may make them feel more relaxed and self-confident, it may prevent them from exercising good judgment, which can lead them to make choices they would ordinarily reject, such as engaging in risky sex (Gordon & Carey, 1996). One of the lures of alcohol is that it induces short-term feelings of euphoria and elation that can drown self-doubts and self-criticism. Alcohol may also make people less capable of perceiving the unfortunate consequences of their behavior.

Alcohol in increasing amounts can dampen sexual arousal or excitement and impair our ability to perform sexually. As an intoxicant, alcohol also hampers coordination and motor ability, and slurs speech. These effects help explain why alcohol use is implicated in nearly 50% of the nation's fatal auto accidents, about 25% of fatal falls, and 30% to 50% of fatal fires and drownings (see Miller & Brown, 1997; Ravenholt, 1984). Figure 10.2 shows the relationship between alcohol dosage and impaired driving.

Alcohol and driving. Nearly half of the nation's fatal motor vehicle accidents, and about 25% of fatal falls, involve the use of alcohol.

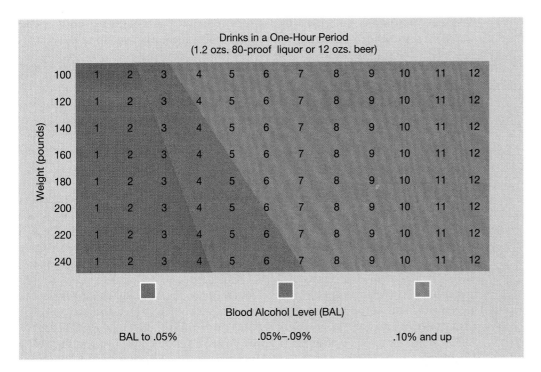

FIGURE 10.2 Alcohol intake and blood alcohol level.
Using this chart, you can estimate your blood alcohol level (BAL) as a function of your alcohol intake.
For example, if you weigh 180 pounds and consume six beers in a 1-hour period, your BAL would be
over .10%—a level beyond the 0.08% legal limit for driving in many states. But any amount of
drinking may impair driving ability.

Source. Adapted from National Highway Traffic Safety Administration.

Physical Health and Alcohol Chronic, heavy alcohol use affects virtually every
organ and body system, either directly or indirectly. Heavy alcohol use is linked to a
higher risk of some forms of cancer, including cancer of the throat, esophagus, larynx,
stomach, colon, liver, and possibly the bowels and breasts (e.g., Fuchs et al., 1995; Reichman, 1994). Heavy drinking is also linked to a wide range of other serious health concerns, including coronary heart disease, neurological disorders, and other forms of liver
disease (Gordis, 1999). Two of the major forms of alcohol-related liver disease are
alcoholic hepatitis, a serious and potentially life-threatening inflammation of the liver, and
cirrhosis of the liver, a potentially fatal disease in which healthy liver cells are replaced with
scar tissue.

Habitual drinkers tend to be malnourished, which can put them at risk of complications arising from nutritional deficiencies. Chronic drinking is thus associated with such
nutritionally linked disorders such as cirrhosis of the liver (linked to protein deficiency)
and **alcohol-induced persisting amnestic disorder** (connected with vitamin B deficiency).
This condition, also known as *Korsakoff's syndrome,* is characterized by glaring confusion,
disorientation, and memory loss for recent events (see Chapter 15).

All told, about 100,000 deaths annually in the United States result from various
alcohol-related diseases and motor vehicle and other accidents (Potter, 1997). After tobacco, alcohol is the second leading cause of premature death in our society. Men who
drink heavily stand nearly twice the risk of dying before the age of 65 as men who abstain;
women who drink heavily are more than three times as likely to die before age 65 as are
women who abstain ("NIAAA Report," 1990).

Mothers who drink during pregnancy place their fetuses at risk for infant mortality, birth defects, central nervous system dysfunctions, and later academic problems.
Children whose mothers drink during pregnancy may develop fetal alcohol syndrome

THINK ABOUT IT
Do you use alcohol? How does it affect
you physically and mentally? Have you
drunk alcohol and driven? How do you
feel about that? Have you ever done
anything under the influence of alcohol
that you later regretted? What? Why?

**alcohol-induced persisting amnestic
disorder** A form of brain damage associated
with chronic thiamine deficiency and
alcoholism; characterized by memory loss,
disorientation, and confabulations.

THINK ABOUT IT
Do you think it is wise to use alcohol in moderation to reduce the risk of cardiovascular disease? Why or why not?

barbiturates Types of depressants that are used to reduce anxiety or to induce sleep but that are highly addictive.

sedatives Types of depressants that reduce states of tension and restlessness and induce sleep.

(FAS), a syndrome characterized by facial features such as a flattened nose, widely spaced eyes, and underdeveloped upper jaw, as well as mental retardation (Wood et al., 2001). FAS affects from one to three of every 1,000 live births.

We don't know whether a minimum amount of alcohol is needed to produce FAS (Wood et al., 2001). Though the risk is greater among women who drank heavily during pregnancy, FAS has been found among children of mothers who drank as little as 2 ounces of alcohol a day during the first trimester (Astley et al., 1992). Although the question of whether there is any safe dose of alcohol during pregnancy continues to be debated, the fact remains that FAS is an entirely preventable birth defect. The safest course for women who know or suspect they are pregnant is not to drink. Period.

Moderate Drinking: Is There a Health Benefit? Despite this list of adverse effects associated with heavy drinking, evidence shows that moderate use of alcohol (1 to 2 drinks per day) is linked to lower risks of heart attacks, lower death rates, and lower risk of heart failure in older adults (Abramson et al., 2001; Goldberg et al., 2001; Gronbaek et al., 2000; "New Research," 2000). It remains unclear whether wine, especially red wine, is more beneficial than other forms of alcohol (Goldberg et al., 2001). Researchers suspect that alcohol may help prevent blood clots from forming that can clog arteries and lead to heart attacks. Alcohol also appears to increase the levels of HDL cholesterol, the so-called good cholesterol that sweeps away fatty deposits along artery walls (Goldberg et al., 2001). Although moderate use of alcohol may have a protective effect on the heart, public health officials caution that promoting the possible health benefits of alcohol may backfire by increasing the risks of alcohol abuse and dependence (Brody, 1994d). Health promotion efforts might be better directed toward finding safer ways of achieving the health benefits associated with moderate drinking than by encouraging alcohol consumption, such as by quitting smoking, lowering dietary fat and cholesterol, and exercising more regularly (Gaziano, 1993).

Barbiturates Estimates indicate that about 1% of the adult population meet criteria for a substance abuse or dependence disorder involving the use of barbiturates, sleep medication (hypnotics), or antianxiety agents at some point in their lives (Anthony & Helzer, 1991). **Barbiturates** such as amobarbital, pentobarbital, phenobarbital, and secobarbital are depressants, or **sedatives.** These drugs have several medical uses, including alleviation of anxiety and tension, anesthetizing of pain, and treatment of epilepsy and high blood pressure. Barbiturate use quickly leads to psychological dependence and physiological dependence in the form of both tolerance and development of a withdrawal syndrome.

Barbiturates are also popular street drugs because they are relaxing and produce a mild state of euphoria, or "high." High doses of barbiturates, like alcohol, produce drowsiness, slurred speech, motor impairment, irritability, and poor judgment—a particularly deadly combination of effects when their use is combined with operation of a motor vehicle. The effects of barbiturates last from 3 to 6 hours.

Because of synergistic effects, a mixture of barbiturates and alcohol is about four times as powerful as either drug used by itself. A combination of barbiturates and alcohol is implicated in the deaths of the entertainers Marilyn Monroe and Judy Garland. Even such widely used antianxiety drugs as Valium and Librium, which have a wide margin of safety when used alone, can be dangerous and lead to overdoses when their use is combined with alcohol (APA, 2000).

Physiologically dependent people need to be withdrawn carefully, and only under medical supervision, from sedatives, barbiturates, and antianxiety agents. Abrupt withdrawal can produce states of delirium that may involve visual, tactile, or auditory hallucinations and disturbances in thinking processes and consciousness. The longer the period of use and the higher the doses used, the greater the risk of severe withdrawal effects. Epileptic (grand mal) seizures and even death may occur if the individual undergoes untreated, abrupt withdrawal.

Opioids. **Opioids** are **narcotics,** a term used for addictive drugs that have pain-relieving and sleep-inducing properties. Opioids include both naturally occurring opiates (morphine, heroin, codeine) derived from the juice of the poppy plant and synthetic drugs (Demerol, Percodan, Darvon) manufactured in the laboratory to have opiate-like effects. The ancient Sumerians named the poppy plant *opium,* meaning "plant of joy."

Opioids produce a rush or intense feelings of pleasure, which is the primary reason for their popularity as street drugs. They also dull awareness of one's personal problems, which is attractive to people seeking a mental escape from stress.

The major medical application of opioids—natural or synthetic—is the relief of pain, or **analgesia.** Medical use of opioids, however, is carefully regulated because overdoses can lead to coma and even death. Yet some prescription opioids, especially the drug OxyContin, become drugs of abuse when they are used illicitly as street drugs (Tough, 2001). Street use of opioids is associated with many fatal overdoses and accidents. In a number of American cities, young men are more likely to die of a heroin overdose than in an automobile accident (Alter, 2001).

Estimates are that about 0.7% of the adult population (7 people in 1,000) currently have or have had an opiate abuse or dependence disorder (Anthony & Helzer, 1991). Once dependence sets in, it usually follows a chronic course, although brief periods of abstinence are frequent (APA, 2000).

Opiates become drugs of abuse because they produce euphoric states of pleasure, or a "rush." Their pleasurable effects derive from their ability to directly stimulate the brain's pleasure circuits—the same brain networks responsible for feelings of sexual pleasure or pleasure from eating a satisfying meal (Begley, 2001b).

Two revealing discoveries, made in the 1970s, showed that the brain produces chemicals of its own that have opiate-like effects. One was that neurons in the brain had receptor sites into which opiates fit—like a key in a lock. The second was that the human body produces its own opiate-like substances that dock at the same receptor sites as opiates do. These natural substances are labeled **endorphins,** which is short for "endogenous morphine"—that is, morphine coming from within. Endorphins play important roles in regulating natural states of pleasure and pain. Opioids mimic the actions of endorphins by docking at receptor sites intended for them, which in turn stimulates the brain centers that produce pleasurable sensations.

The withdrawal syndrome associated with opioids can be severe. It begins within 4 to 6 hours of the last dose. Flulike symptoms are accompanied by anxiety, feelings of restlessness, irritability, and cravings for the drug. Within a few days, symptoms progress to rapid pulse, high blood pressure, cramps, tremors, hot and cold flashes, fever, vomiting, insomnia, and diarrhea, among other symptoms. Although these symptoms can be uncomfortable, they are usually not devastating, especially when other drugs are prescribed to relieve them. Moreover, unlike withdrawal from barbiturates, the withdrawal syndrome rarely results in death.

Morphine Morphine—which receives its name from Morpheus, the Greek god of dreams—was introduced at about the time of the United States Civil War. Morphine, a powerful opium derivative, was used liberally to deaden pain from wounds. Physiological dependence on morphine became known as the "soldier's disease." There was little stigma attached to dependence until morphine became a restricted substance.

Heroin Heroin, the most widely used opiate, is a powerful depressant that can create a euphoric rush. Users of heroin claim that it is so pleasurable it can eradicate any thought of food or sex. Heroin was developed in 1875 during a search for a drug that would relieve

opioids Natural or synthetic drugs with strong addictive properties; natural opioids, referred to as opiates, are derived from the opium poppy.

narcotics Drugs that are used for pain relief and treatment of insomnia but that have strong addictive potential.

analgesia Relief from pain without loss of consciousness.

endorphins Natural substances that function as neurotransmitters in the brain and are similar in their effects to morphine.

morphine A strongly addictive narcotic derived from the opium poppy that relieves pain and induces feelings of well-being.

heroin A narcotic derived from morphine that has strong addictive properties.

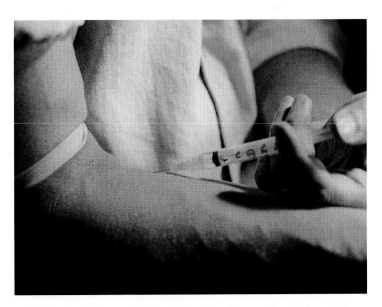

Shooting up. Heroin users often inject the substance directly into their veins. Heroin is a powerful depressant that provides a euphoric rush. Users often claim that heroin is so pleasurable that it obliterates any thought of food or sex.

pain as effectively as morphine, but without causing addiction. Chemist Heinrich Dreser transformed morphine into a new and stronger miracle drug, heroin, by means of a minor chemical change. He believed, erroneously, that heroin did not create physiological dependence.

Heroin is usually injected either directly beneath the skin (skin popping) or into a vein (mainlining). The positive effects are immediate. There is a powerful rush that lasts from 5 to 15 minutes and a state of satisfaction, euphoria, and well-being that lasts from 3 to 5 hours. In this state, all positive drives seem satisfied. All negative feelings of guilt, tension, and anxiety disappear. With prolonged usage, addiction can develop. Many physiologically dependent people support their habits through dealing (selling heroin), prostitution, or selling stolen goods. Heroin is a depressant, however, and its chemical effects do not directly stimulate criminal or aggressive behavior.

Stimulants

Stimulants such as amphetamines and cocaine are psychoactive substances that increase the activity of the nervous system. Effects vary somewhat from drug to drug, but some stimulants contribute to feelings of euphoria and self-confidence. Stimulants such as amphetamines, cocaine, and even caffeine (the stimulant found in coffee) increase the availability in the brain of the neurotransmitters norepinephrine and dopamine. High levels of these neurotransmitters therefore remain available in the synaptic gaps between neurons, maintaining high levels of nervous system activity and states of high arousal.

Amphetamines The **amphetamines** are a class of synthetic stimulants. Street names for stimulants include speed, uppers, bennies (for *amphetamine sulfate*; trade name Benzedrine), "meth" (for *methamphetamine*; trade name Methedrine), and dexies (for *dextroamphetamine*; trade name Dexedrine).

Amphetamines are used in high doses for their euphoric rush. They are often taken in pill form, or smoked in a relatively pure form called "ice" or "crystal meth." The most potent form of amphetamine, liquid methamphetamine, is injected directly into the veins and produces an intense and immediate rush. Some users inject methamphetamine for days on end to maintain an extended high. Eventually such highs come to an end. People who have been on extended highs sometimes "crash" and fall into a deep sleep or depression. Some people commit suicide on the way down. High doses can cause restlessness, irritability, hallucinations, paranoid delusions, loss of appetite, and insomnia.

More than 1 million people in the United States use "meth," almost three times as many as use heroin (Bonné, 2001). Physiological dependence can develop from using amphetamines, leading to an abstinence syndrome characterized most often by depression and fatigue, as well as by unpleasant, vivid dreams, insomnia or hypersomnia (excessive sleeping), increased appetite, and either a slowing down of motor behavior or agitation (APA, 2000). Psychological dependence is seen most often in people who use amphetamines as a way of coping with stress or depression.

Methamphetamine abuse can cause brain damage, producing deficits in learning and memory in addition to other effects (Blakeslee, 2001; Ernst et al., 2000; Volkow et al., 2001; Zickler, 2000). Violent behavior may also occur, especially when the drug is smoked or injected intravenously (APA, 2000). The hallucinations and delusions of **amphetamine psychosis** mimic the features of paranoid schizophrenia, which has encouraged researchers to study the chemical changes induced by amphetamines as possible causes of schizophrenia.

Ecstasy The drug *ecstasy*, or MDMA (3,4-methylenedioxymethamphetamine) is a designer drug, a chemical knockoff similar in chemical structure to amphetamine (Braun, 2001). It produces mild euphoria and hallucinations and has attracted a growing user base among young people, especially on college campuses and in clubs and "raves" in many cities (Hernandez, 2000; Mathias, 2000; "Dip in Youth Killing," 2000). Ecstasy is fast becoming the nation's most popular illicit drug (Kuhn & Wilson, 2001). Use by high school seniors nearly doubled during the latter half of the 1990s (Butterfield, 2001). The drug can produce adverse psychological effects, including depression, anxiety, insomnia, and even paranoia and

amphetamines Types of stimulants, such as Benzedrine or Dexedrine.

amphetamine psychosis A psychotic state induced by ingestion of amphetamines.

psychosis. The drug may also impair cognitive functioning, including learning ability and attention and may have long-lasting effects on memory (Gouzoulis-Mayfrank et al., 2000; Reneman, et al., 2001). The drug may also deplete levels of serotonin in the brain, a neurotransmitter linked to regulation of mood and appetite. This may explain why users of the drug can experience feelings of depression when they go off the drug ("Ecstasy Use," 2000). Physical side effects include higher heart rate and blood pressure, a tense or chattering jaw, and body warmth and/or chills (Braun, 2001). The drug can be lethal when taken in high doses (Kuhn & Wilson, 2001).

Cocaine It might surprise you to learn that the original formula for Coca-Cola contained an extract of **cocaine.** In 1906, however, the company withdrew cocaine from its secret formula. The beverage was originally described as a "brain tonic and intellectual beverage," in part because of its cocaine content. Cocaine is a natural stimulant extracted from the leaves of the coca plant—the plant from which the soft drink obtained its name. Coca-Cola is still flavored with an extract from the coca plant, one that is not known to be psychoactive.

Ecstasy. Recreational use of the drug ecstasy has become popular in many clubs catering to young people. Yet even occasional use of the drug may affect cognitive functioning, such as learning, memory, and attention. High doses can be lethal.

It was long believed that cocaine was not physically addicting. However, evidence supports the addictive properties of the drug in producing a tolerance effect and an identifiable withdrawal syndrome, which is characterized by depressed mood and disturbances in sleep and appetite (APA, 2000). Intense cravings for the drug and loss of ability to experience pleasure may also be present. Withdrawal symptoms are usually brief in duration and may involve a "crash," or period of intense depression and exhaustion following abrupt withdrawal.

cocaine A stimulant derived from the leaves of the coca plant.

crack The hardened, smokable form of cocaine.

freebasing A method of ingesting cocaine by heating it with ether to separate its most potent component (its "free base") and then smoking the extract.

Cocaine is usually snorted in powder form or smoked in the form of **crack,** a hardened form of cocaine that may contain more than 75% pure cocaine. Crack "rocks"—so called because they look like small white pebbles—are available in small ready-to-smoke amounts and considered to be the most habit-forming street drug available. Crack produces a prompt and potent rush that wears off in a few minutes. The rush from snorting is milder and takes a while to develop, but it tends to linger longer than the rush of crack.

Freebasing also intensifies the effects of cocaine. Cocaine in powder form is heated with ether, freeing the psychoactive chemical base of the drug, and then smoked. Ether, however, is highly flammable.

Next to marijuana, cocaine is the most widely used illicit drug in the United States. Nearly 3% (2.7%) of adults in the United States in the 15- to 54-year age range have a history of cocaine dependence (Anthony et al., 1994). Cocaine abuse is characterized by periodic binges lasting perhaps 12 to 36 hours, which are then followed by 2 to 5 days of abstinence, during which time the abuser may experience cravings that prompt another binge (Gawin et al., 1989). According to one estimate, between 10% and 15% of people who try snorting cocaine eventually develop cocaine abuse or dependence (Gawin, 1991).

The cocaine epidemic may have peaked in some respects (see Table 10.1 showing declining use among college students). Although the numbers of casual users of cocaine have greatly declined, there has been no corresponding reduction in the numbers of hard-core users.

Crack. Crack "rocks" resemble small, white pebbles. Crack produces a powerful, prompt rush when smoked. Small, ready-to-smoke doses are available at prices that have made them affordable to adolescents.

Effects of Cocaine Like heroin, cocaine directly stimulates the brain's reward or pleasure circuits (Volkow et al., 1997). It also produces a sudden rise in blood pressure, constricts blood vessels (with associated reduction of the oxygen supply to the heart), and accelerates the heart rate. Overdoses can produce restlessness, insomnia, headaches, nausea, convulsions, tremors, hallucinations, delusions, and even sudden death. Such a death usually results from respiratory or cardiovascular collapse. Although intravenous use of cocaine carries the greatest risk of a lethal overdose, other forms of use can also cause fatal overdoses. Table 10.3 summarizes a number of the health risks of cocaine use.

TABLE 10.3 Health Risks of Cocaine Use

Physical Effects and Risks

Effects	Risks
Increased heart rate	Accelerated heart rate may give rise to heart irregularities that can be fatal, such as ventricular tachycardia (extremely rapid contractions) or ventricular fibrillation (irregular, weakened contractions).
Increased blood pressure	Rapid or large changes in blood pressure may place too much stress on a weak-walled blood vessel in the brain, which can cause it to burst, producing cerebral hemorrhage or stroke.
Increased body temperature	Can be dangerous to some individuals.
Possible grand mal seizures (epileptic convulsions)	Some grand mal seizures are fatal, particularly when they occur in rapid succession or while driving a car.
Respiratory effects	Overdoses can produce gasping or shallow, irregular breathing that can lead to respiratory arrest.
Dangerous effects in special populations	Various special populations are at greater risk from cocaine use or overdose. People with coronary heart disease have died because their heart muscles were taxed beyond the capacity of their arteries to supply oxygen.

Medical Complications of Cocaine Use

Nasal Problems	When cocaine is administered intranasally (snorted), it constricts the blood vessels serving the nose, decreasing the supply of oxygen to these tissues, leading to irritation and inflammation of the mucous membranes, ulcers in the nostrils, frequent nosebleeds, and chronic sneezing and nasal congestion. Chronic use may lead to tissue death of the nasal septum, the part of the nose that separates the nostrils, requiring plastic surgery.
Lung Problems	Freebase smoking may lead to serious lung problems within 3 months of initial use.
Malnutrition	Cocaine suppresses the appetite so that weight loss, malnutrition, and vitamin deficiencies may accompany regular use.
Seizures	Grand mal seizures, typical of epileptics, may occur due to irregularities in the electrical activity of the brain. Repeated use may lower the seizure threshold, described as a type of "kindling" effect.
Sexual Problems	Despite the popular belief that cocaine is an aphrodisiac, frequent use can lead to sexual dysfunctions, such as impotence and failure to ejaculate among males, and decreased sexual interest in both sexes. Although some people report initial increased sexual pleasure with cocaine use, they may become dependent on cocaine for sexual arousal or lose the ability to enjoy sex for extended periods following long-term use.
Other Effects	Cocaine use may increase the risk of miscarriage among pregnant women. Sharing of infected needles is associated with transmission of hepatitis, endocarditis (infection of the heart valve), and HIV. Repeated injections often lead to skin infections as bacteria are introduced into the deeper levels of the skin.

Source. Adapted from Weiss & Mirin (1987).

Repeated use and high-dose use of cocaine can lead to depression and anxiety (Weiss & Mirin, 1987). Depression may be severe enough to prompt suicidal behavior. Both initial and routine users report episodes of "crashing" (feelings of depression after a binge), although crashing is more common among long-term high-dose users. Psychotic behaviors, which can be induced by cocaine use as well as by use of amphetamines, tend to become more severe with continued use. Cocaine psychosis is usually preceded by a period of heightened suspiciousness, depressed mood, compulsive behavior, fault finding, irritability, and increasing paranoia (Weiss & Mirin, 1987). The psychosis may also include intense visual and auditory hallucinations and delusions of persecution.

Nicotine Habitual smoking is not merely a bad habit: It is also a form of physical addiction to a stimulant drug, nicotine, found in tobacco products including cigarettes, cigars, and smokeless tobacco (Kessler et al., 1997b). Smoking (or other tobacco uses) is the means of administering the drug to the body.

More than 400,000 lives in the United States are lost each year from smoking-related causes, mostly from lung cancer, cardiovascular disease, and chronic obstructive lung disease (Fried et al., 1998). This figure is nearly eight times the number that dies from motor vehicle accidents and about equal to the population of a city the size of Atlanta, Georgia. Smoking is implicated in 1 in 3 cancer deaths, including more than 100,000 deaths due to lung cancer (Boyle, 1993). Smokers overall stand twice the risk of dying from cancer as nonsmokers; among heavy smokers, the risk is four times as great (Bartecchi, MacKenzie, & Schrier, 1994).

The World Health Organization estimates that 1 billion people worldwide smoke, and more than 3 million die each year from smoking-related causes. Smoking is expected to become the world's leading cause of death by the year 2020 ("Smoking," 1996). Smoking may also pose risks to one's mental health. A recent study reported that cigarette smoking among adolescents may increase the risk of anxiety disorders in late adolescence and early adulthood (J. G. Johnson et al., 2000).

Largely because of health concerns, the percentage of Americans who smoke declined from 42% in 1966 to about 25% today (Miller & Brown, 1997). On the other hand, we are losing the battle against teenage smoking, which increased sharply during the early to late 1990s (Feder, 1996; Stolberg, 1998b). The greatest increase in teenage cigarette smoking was among African Americans, up by 80%.

Lung cancer, which in 90% of cases is caused by smoking, has now surpassed breast cancer as the leading killer of women. Although quitting smoking clearly has health benefits, it unfortunately does not reduce the risks to normal (nonsmoking) levels. The lesson is clear: If you don't smoke, don't start; but if you do smoke, quit.

Ethnic differences in smoking rates are shown in Figure 10.3. With the exception of Native Americans (American Indian/Alaskan Native), women in each ethnic group are less likely to smoke than their male counterparts. Figure 10.4 shows relationships between

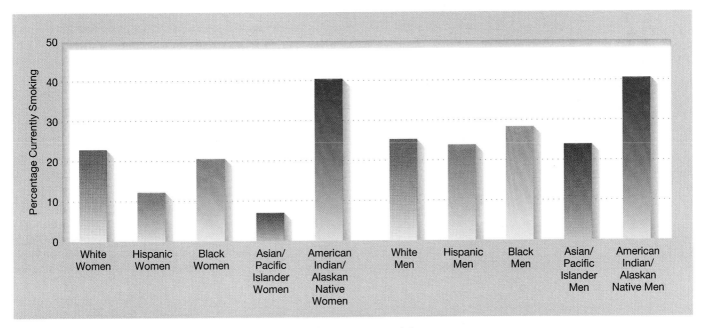

FIGURE 10.3 Gender and racial breakdown of cigarette smokers among U.S. adults.
Smoking rates are highest for Native American men and women. Women in each ethnic group (with the exception of Native Americans) are less likely to smoke than their male counterparts. The rates for non-Hispanic White American men and women are comparable.

Source. Centers for Disease Control (2001b).

FIGURE 10.4 Cigarette smokers in the United States in relation to poverty status and level of education.
Smoking is becoming increasingly more prevalent among the poorer and less educated members of society.

Source. Centers for Disease Control (2001b).

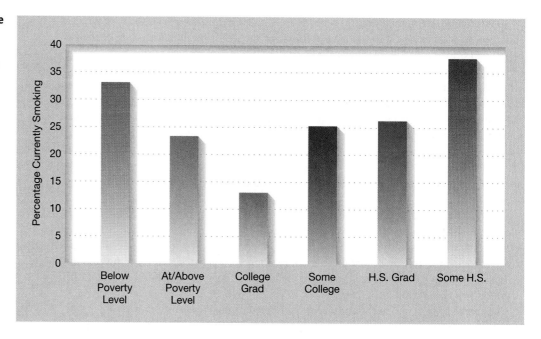

smoking rates and income and educational levels. Note how smoking is disproportionately represented among the poorer and less educated segments of the population.

Nicotine is delivered to the body through the use of tobacco products. As a stimulant it increases alertness but can also give rise to cold, clammy skin, nausea and vomiting, dizziness and faintness, and diarrhea—all of which account for the discomforts of novice smokers. Nicotine also stimulates the release of epinephrine, a hormone that generates a rush of autonomic activity, including rapid heartbeat and release of stores of sugar into the blood. Nicotine quells the appetite and provides a sort of psychological "kick." Nicotine also leads to the release of endorphins, the opiate-like hormones produced in the brain. This may account for the pleasurable feelings associated with tobacco use.

Habitual use of nicotine leads to a physiological dependence on the drug (Lichtenstein & Glasgow, 1992). Nicotine dependence is associated with both tolerance (intake rises to a level of a pack or two a day before leveling off) and a characteristic withdrawal syndrome. The withdrawal syndrome for nicotine includes such features as lack of energy, depressed mood, irritability, frustration, nervousness, impaired concentration, lightheadedness and dizziness, drowsiness, headaches, fatigue, irregular bowels, insomnia, cramps, lowered heart rate, heart palpitations, increased appetite, weight gain, sweating, tremors, and craving for cigarettes (APA, 2000; Klesges et al., 1997). It is nicotine dependence, not cigarette smoking per se, that is classifiable as a mental disorder in the *DSM* system. The great majority of regular smokers (80% to 90%) meet diagnostic criteria for nicotine dependence (APA, 2000).

Hallucinogens

Hallucinogens, also known as *psychedelics,* are a class of drugs that produce sensory distortions or hallucinations, including major alterations in color perception and hearing. Hallucinogens may also have additional effects, such as relaxation and euphoria, or, in some cases, panic.

The hallucinogens include such drugs as lysergic acid diethylamide (LSD), psilocybin, and mescaline. Psychoactive substances that are similar in effect to psychedelic drugs are marijuana (cannabis) and phencyclidine (PCP). Mescaline is derived from the peyote cactus and has been used for centuries by Native Americans in the Southwest, Mexico, and Central America in religious ceremonies, as has psilocybin, which is derived from certain mushrooms. LSD, PCP, and marijuana are more commonly used in the United States.

THINK ABOUT IT
Speculate on the reasons that smoking is more prevalent among poorer and less educated segments of the U.S. population and on why smoking is on the rise among teenagers. What kinds of public health messages might be effective at reaching these at-risk groups?

hallucinogens Substances that cause hallucinations.

Although tolerance to hallucinogens may develop, we lack evidence of a consistent or clinically significant withdrawal syndrome associated with their use (APA, 2000). Cravings following withdrawal may occur, however.

LSD LSD is the acronym for **lysergic acid diethylamide,** a synthetic hallucinogenic drug. In addition to the vivid parade of colors and visual distortions produced by LSD, users have claimed it "expands consciousness" and opens new worlds—as if they were looking into some reality beyond the usual reality. Sometimes they believe they have achieved great insights during the LSD "trip," but when it wears off they usually cannot follow through or even summon up these discoveries.

The effects of LSD are unpredictable and depend on the amount taken as well as the user's expectations, personality, mood, and surroundings (USDHHS, 1992). The user's prior experiences with the drug may also play a role, as users who have learned to handle the effects of the drug through past experience may be better prepared than new users.

Some users have unpleasant experiences with the drug, or "bad trips." Feelings of intense fear or panic may occur (USDHHS, 1992). Users may fear losing control or sanity. Some experience terrifying fears of death. Fatal accidents have sometimes occurred during LSD trips. **Flashbacks,** typically involving a reexperiencing of some of the perceptual distortions of the "trip," may occur days, weeks, or even years afterward. Flashbacks tend to occur suddenly and often without warning. Perceptual distortions may involve geometric forms, flashes of color, intensified colors, afterimages, or appearances of halos around objects, among others (APA, 2000). They may stem from chemical changes in the brain caused by the prior use of the drug. Triggers for flashbacks include entry into darkened environments, use of various drugs, anxiety or fatigue states, or stress (APA, 2000). Psychological factors, such as underlying personality problems, may also be involved in explaining why some users experience flashbacks. In some cases, a flashback may involve an imagined reenactment of the LSD experience.

Phencyclidine (PCP) Phencyclidine, or PCP—which is referred to as "angel dust" on the streets—was developed as an anesthetic in the 1950s but was discontinued as such when the hallucinatory side effects of the drug were discovered. A smokable form of PCP became popular as a street drug in the 1970s. By the mid-1980s, more than one in five young people in the 18 to 25 age range had used PCP (USDHHS, 1986b). However, its popularity has since waned, largely because of its unpredictable effects.

The effects of PCP, like most drugs, are dose related. In addition to causing hallucinations, PCP accelerates the heart rate and blood pressure and causes sweating, flushing, and numbness. PCP is classified as a *deliriant*—a drug capable of producing states of delirium. It also has dissociating effects, causing users to feel as if there is some sort of invisible barrier or wall between themselves and their environments. Dissociation can be experienced as pleasant, engrossing, or frightening, depending on the user's expectations, mood, setting, and so on. Overdoses can give rise to drowsiness and a blank stare, convulsions, and, now and then, coma; paranoia and aggressive behavior; and tragic accidents resulting from perceptual distortion or impaired judgment during states of intoxication.

Marijuana Marijuana is derived from the *Cannabis sativa* plant. Marijuana sometimes produces mild hallucinations, so it is regarded as a minor hallucinogen. The psychoactive substance in marijuana is **delta-9-tetrahydrocannabinol,** or THC. THC is found in branches and leaves of the plant but is highly concentrated in the resin of the female plant. **Hashish,** or "hash," is also derived from the resin. Although it is more potent than marijuana, hashish has similar effects.

Use of marijuana exploded throughout the so-called swinging 1960s and the 1970s, but the drug then lost some (but not all) of its cachet. Still, marijuana remains our most widely used illegal drug, although its prevalence doesn't compare with alcohol's. Approximately 33% of people in the United States age 12 or older, nearly 70 million people, have tried marijuana at least once in their lives, and 5% are current users (USDHHS, 1993).

lysergic acid diethylamide (LSD) A type of hallucinogen.

flashbacks The experience of sensory distortions or hallucinations occurring after use of LSD or other hallucinogenic drugs.

marijuana A hallucinogenic drug derived from the leaves and stems of the plant *Cannabis sativa*.

delta-9-tetrahydrocannabinol (THC) The active ingredient in marijuana.

hashish A drug derived from the resin of the plant *Cannabis sativa*.

WWW **Web Link 10.5**
Marijuana Facts

Cannabis (or marijuana) dependence is the most common form of illicit-drug dependence in the United States, affecting an estimated 4.2% of the adult population at some point in their lives (Anthony et al., 1994). Males are more likely than females to develop a cannabis use disorder (either abuse or dependence), and the rates of these disorders is greatest among young people age 18 to 30 (APA, 2000).

Low doses of the drug can produce relaxing feelings similar to drinking alcohol. Some users report that at low doses the drug makes them feel more comfortable in social gatherings. Higher doses, however, often lead users to withdraw into themselves. Some users believe the drug increases their capacity for self-insight or creative thinking, although the insights achieved under its influence may not seem so insightful once the drug's effects have passed. People may turn to marijuana, as to other drugs, to help them cope with life problems or to help them function when they are under stress. Strongly intoxicated people perceive time as passing more slowly. A song of a few minutes may seem to last an hour. There is increased awareness of bodily sensations, such as heartbeat. Smokers also report that strong intoxication heightens sexual sensations. Visual hallucinations may occur.

Strong intoxication can cause smokers to become disoriented. If their moods are euphoric, disorientation may be construed as harmony with the universe. Yet some smokers find strong intoxication disturbing. An accelerated heart rate and sharpened awareness of bodily sensations cause some smokers to fear their hearts will "run away" with them. Some smokers are frightened by disorientation and fear they will not "come back." High levels of intoxication now and then induce nausea and vomiting.

Cannabis dependence is associated more with patterns of compulsive use or psychological dependence than with physiological dependence. Although tolerance to many of the drug's effects may occur with chronic use, some users report reverse tolerance, or *sensitization*. A withdrawal syndrome has not been reliably demonstrated (APA, 2000). However, new research with animals points to some disturbing similarities between marijuana and addictive drugs like heroin and cocaine (Wickelgren, 1997). In one study researchers found that withdrawal from marijuana activated the same brain circuits involved in withdrawal from opioids, alcohol, and cocaine (Rodríguez de Fonseca et al., 1997). These brain circuits are also involved in producing feelings of anxiety when an animal or person is under stress (Blakeslee, 1997a). In another study, researchers determined that marijuana activated the same reward circuits in the brain as heroin (Tanda, Pontien, & Chiara, 1997). Although these studies were conducted with animals, researchers believe the underlying biological mechanisms may apply to humans as well (Blakeslee, 1997a).

College students who are heavy users of marijuana show evidence of intellectual impairment, including diminished ability in tasks requiring attention, abstraction, and mental flexibility (Pope & Yurgelun-Todd, 1996). However, it is unclear whether these deficits are due to the drug or to characteristics of people who become heavy users (Lee, 1996). We do know that marijuana impairs perception and motor coordination and thus makes driving and the operation of other machines dangerous. It also impairs short-term memory and retards learning ability. Although it induces positive mood changes in many users, some people report anxiety and confusion; there are also occasional reports of psychotic reactions. Marijuana elevates heart rate and blood pressure and is linked to an increased risk of heart attacks in people with heart disease ("Another Worry," 2000). Finally, marijuana smoke contains carcinogenic hydrocarbons, so chronic users risk lung cancer and other respiratory diseases.

THINK ABOUT IT

Do you believe that illicit drugs should be legalized or decriminalized? Why or why not?

Quiz **10.2**
Drugs of Abuse

Theoretical Perspectives

People begin using psychoactive substances for various reasons. Some adolescents may start using drugs because of peer pressure or because they believe drugs make them seem more sophisticated or grown up. Some use drugs as a way of rebelling against their parents or society at large. Regardless of why people get started with drugs, they continue to use them because drugs produce pleasurable effects or because they find it difficult to stop. Most adolescents drink alcohol to "get high," not to establish that they are adults. Many people smoke cigarettes for the pleasure they provide. Others smoke to help them relax when they are tense and, paradoxically, to give them a kick or a lift when they are tired. Yet many would like to quit but find it difficult to break their addiction.

People who are anxious about their jobs or social lives may be drawn to the calming effects of alcohol, marijuana (in certain doses), tranquilizers, and sedatives. People with low self-confidence and self-esteem may be drawn to the ego-bolstering effects of amphetamines and cocaine. Many poor young people attempt to escape the poverty, anguish, and tedium of inner city life through using heroin and similar drugs. More well-to-do adolescents may rely on drugs to manage the transition from dependence to independence and major life changes concerning jobs, college, and lifestyles.

In the next sections we consider several major theoretical perspectives on substance abuse and dependence.

Biological Perspectives

We are beginning to learn more about the biological underpinnings of addiction. Much of the recent research has focused on neurotransmitters, especially dopamine, and on the role of genetic factors.

WWW **Web Link 10.6**
The Brain's Response to Drugs

Neurotransmitters Drugs such as nicotine, alcohol, amphetamines, heroin, cocaine, and even marijuana produce pleasurable effects by increasing the concentration of dopamine in the brain's pleasure or reward circuits—the network of neurons responsible for the pleasurable feelings we experience from sexual stimulation, or winning a sporting event, or even eating a scrumptious dessert (Begley, 2001b; O'Brien & McLellan, 1997; Volkow et al., 1997). The feelings of pleasure from using these drugs may range from mild happiness to euphoria.

But what of long-term use? Investigators suspect that chronic drug use reduces the numbers of receptors on the receiving neurons where dopamine docks (Begley, 2001b). It may also reduce the brain's ability to produce dopamine on its own (Blakeslee, 1997a). Consequently, the ability to derive pleasure from activities of everyday life, such as having a good meal, attending an enjoyable movie, and the like, wanes. The chronic drug user comes to rely on drugs to produce feelings of pleasure that the brain may no longer be able to produce on its own, and to avert depression, anxiety, and other disturbing feelings. Without drugs, life may not seem to be worth living. These changes in the dopamine system may explain the intense cravings and anxiety that accompany drug withdrawal and the difficulty people with chemical dependencies have maintaining abstinence.

The biochemical bases of drug use and abuse are complex and appear to involve other neurotransmitters besides dopamine. For example, researchers suspect that serotonin may also activate the brain's pleasure or reward circuits in response to cocaine, alcohol, and other drug use (Begley, 2001b; Rocha et al., 1998).

We also know that a group of neurotransmitters called endorphins have pain-blocking properties similar to those of opioids such as heroin. Endorphins and opiates dock at the same receptor sites in the brain. Normally, the brain produces a certain level of endorphins that maintains a sort of psychological steady state of comfort and potential to experience pleasure. However, when the body becomes habituated to a supply of opioids, it may stop producing endorphins. This makes the user dependent on opiates for feelings of comfort, relief from pain, and feelings of pleasure. When the habitual user stops using heroin or other opiates, feelings of discomfort and little aches and pains may be magnified until the body resumes adequate production of endorphins. This discomfort may account, at least in part, for the unpleasant withdrawal symptoms that opiate addicts experience. However, this model remains speculative, and more research is needed to document direct relationships between endorphin production and withdrawal symptoms.

Genetic Factors Evidence links genetic factors to various forms of substance use and abuse, including alcoholism, opiate addiction, and even cigarette smoking (Kendler Thornton, & Pederson, 2000; McLellan et al., 2000; Nurnberger et al., 2001; Wall et al., 2001). We focus our discussion on alcohol dependence, because this has been the area of the greatest research interest.

Alcoholism tends to run in families (APA, 2000; Wood et al., 2001). The closer the genetic relationship, the greater the risk. Familial patterns provide only suggestive evidence of genetic factors, because families share common environment as well as common genes. More definitive evidence comes from twin and adoptee studies.

Monozygotic (MZ) twins have identical genes, whereas fraternal or dizygotic (DZ) twins share only half of their genes. If genetic factors are involved, we would expect MZ twins to have higher concordance (agreement) rates for alcoholism than DZ twins. Evidence of higher concordance rates for alcoholism is found among MZ twins than DZ twins, although the results are more consistent for male samples than female samples (Wood et al., 2001).

A limitation of twin studies is that MZ twins may share more environmental as well as genetic similarity. That is, they may be treated more alike than DZ twins. However, evidence also shows that male adoptees whose biological parents suffered from alcoholism have an increased risk of developing alcoholism themselves, even if they are raised in nondrinking homes (Gordis, 1995; Schuckit, 1987). Among women, however, the rate of alcoholism in adopted-away daughters of parents with alcoholism is only slightly higher than that for adopted-away daughters of nonalcoholics, thus casting doubt on a strong genetic linkage to alcoholism in women (Svikis, Velez, & Pickens, 1994). All in all, genetic factors are believed to play a moderate role in male alcoholism and a modest role in female alcoholism (McGue, 1993). Other evidence points to a genetic contribution in other forms of substance abuse, including opioid, marijuana, cocaine, and nicotine dependence (Lerman et al., 1999; Sabol et al., 1999; Tsuang et al., 1998).

If alcoholism or other forms of substance abuse and dependence are influenced by genetic factors, what is it that is inherited? Some clues have begun to emerge. Researchers have linked alcoholism, nicotine dependence, and opioid addiction to genes involved in determining the structure of dopamine receptors in the brain (Kotler, 1997). We've mentioned that dopamine is involved in regulating states of pleasure, which leads researchers to suspect that genetic factors enhance feelings of pleasure derived from alcohol, which in turn may increase cravings for the drug (Altman, 1990a). In all likelihood there is no one "alcoholism gene" but rather a set of genes that interact with each other and with environmental factors to increase the risk of alcoholism (Devor, 1994). Other evidence suggests that a genetic vulnerability to alcoholism may involve a combination of factors, such as reaping greater pleasure from alcohol and a capacity for greater biological tolerance for the drug (Pihl, Peterson, & Finn, 1990; Pollock, 1992).

Other research has shown that men who have immediate biological relatives (parents or siblings) with a history of alcoholism tend to metabolize alcohol more rapidly than do men without a history of alcoholism in their immediate families (Schuckit & Rayes, 1979). People who metabolize alcohol relatively quickly can tolerate larger doses and are less likely to develop upset stomachs, dizziness, and headaches when they drink. Unfortunately, a lower sensitivity to the unpleasant effects of alcohol may make it difficult to know when to say when. Thus people who are better able to "hold their liquor" may be at greater risk of developing drinking problems. They may need to rely on other cues, such as counting their drinks, to learn to limit their drinking. People whose bodies more readily "put the brakes" on excess drinking may be less likely to develop problems in moderating their drinking than those with better tolerance.

Other research suggests that men with a family history of alcoholism may be genetically predisposed to be unusually tense or nervous because of deficiencies of certain neurotransmitters in the brain (Goleman, 1990a, 1992b). Perhaps they turn to alcohol to help them relax.

Whatever the role of heredity in alcoholism, there is ample "room" for other factors, which is highlighted by the finding that at least one-third of people with alcoholism have no family history of the disorder (Schuckit, 1983). Most researchers today believe that alcoholism and other forms of substance dependence involve the actions of multiple genes together with social, cultural, and psychological factors (Devor, 1994; Dick et al., 2001).

Truth OR Fiction? REVISITED

Being able to "hold your liquor" better than most people helps prevent the development of problem drinking.

FALSE. Being able to "hold you liquor" may encourage you to drink more, which may set the stage for the development of problem drinking.

Learning Perspectives

Learning theorists propose that substance-related behaviors are largely learned and can, in principle, be unlearned. They focus on the roles of operant and classical conditioning and observational learning. Substance abuse problems are not regarded as symptoms of diseases but rather as problem habits. Although learning theorists do not deny that genetic or biological factors may be involved in the genesis of substance abuse problems, they place a greater emphasis on the role of learning in the development and maintenance of these problem behaviors (McCrady, 1993, 1994). They also recognize that people who suffer from depression or anxiety may turn to alcohol as a way of relieving these troubling emotional states, however briefly. Evidence shows that emotional stress, such as anxiety or depression, often sets the stage for the development of substance abuse (Dixit & Crum, 2000; McGue, Slutske, & Iaono, 1999).

Drug use may become habitual because of the pleasure or positive reinforcement, or temporary relief from negative emotions like anxiety and depression, that drugs can produce. With drugs like cocaine, which appear capable of directly stimulating pleasure mechanisms in the brain, the positive reinforcement is direct and powerful.

Operant Conditioning People may initially use a drug because of social influence, trial and error, or social observation. In the case of alcohol, they learn that the drug can produce reinforcing effects, such as feelings of euphoria, and reductions in states of anxiety and tension. Alcohol may also release behavioral inhibitions. Alcohol can thus be reinforcing when it is used to combat depression (by producing euphoric feelings, even if short-lived), to combat tension (by functioning as a tranquilizer), or to help people sidestep moral conflicts (for example, by dulling awareness of moral prohibitions against sexual behavior or aggression). Social reinforcers are also made available by substance abuse, such as the approval of drug-abusing companions and, in the cases of alcohol and stimulants, the (temporary) overcoming of social shyness.

Alcohol and Tension Reduction Learning theorists have long maintained that one of the primary reinforcers for using alcohol is relief from states of tension or unpleasant states of arousal (Hussong et al., 2001; Wood et al., 2001). The *tension-reduction theory* proposes that the more often one drinks to reduce tension or anxiety, the stronger or more habitual the habit becomes. Viewed in this way, alcohol use can be likened to a form of self-medication, a way of easing psychological pain, at least temporarily, as in the following case example:

A Case of Self-Medication

"I use them (the pills and alcohol) to take away the hurt I feel inside." Joceyln, a 36-year-old mother of two, was physically abused by her husband, Phil. "I have no self-esteem. I just don't feel I can do anything," she told her therapist. Jocelyn had escaped from an abusive family background by getting married at age 17, hoping that it would offer her a better life. The first few years of marriage were free of abuse but things changed when Phil lost his job and began to drink heavily. By then, Jocelyn had two young children and felt trapped. She blamed herself for her unhappy family life, for Phil's drinking, for her son's learning disability. "The only thing I can do is drink or do pills. At least then I don't have to think about things for awhile."

—*From the Authors' Files*

Self-medication? People who turn to other drugs or alcohol as a form of self-medication for anxiety or depression may only compound their problems by developing a substance use disorder.

Drugs, including nicotine from cigarette smoking, may be used as a form of self-medication for depression (Breslau et al., 1998). Stimulants like nicotine temporarily elevate the mood, whereas depressants like alcohol quell anxiety. Although nicotine, alcohol, and other drugs may temporarily alleviate emotional distress, they cannot resolve underlying personal or emotional problems. Rather than learning to resolve these problems, people who use drugs as forms of self-medication often find themselves facing additional substance-related problems.

Negative Reinforcement and Withdrawal Once people become physiologically dependent, *negative reinforcement* comes into play in maintaining the drug habit. In other words, people may resume using drugs to gain relief from unpleasant withdrawal symptoms. In operant conditioning terms, the resumption of drug use is negatively reinforced by relief from unpleasant withdrawal symptoms. For example, the addicted smoker who quits cold turkey may shortly return to smoking to fend off the discomfort of withdrawal. Smokers who are able to quit and maintain abstinence are occasionally bothered by urges to smoke but have learned to manage them.

The Conditioning Model of Cravings Classical conditioning may help explain drug cravings experienced by people with drug dependency. Drug cravings may have a biological basis, reflecting a bodily need to restore levels of the addictive substance. But they also come to be triggered by environmental cues associated with prior use of the substance (Kilts et al., 2001). These drug-related cues, such as the sight or aroma of an alcoholic beverage or the sight of a needle and syringe, may become conditioned stimuli that elicit a conditioned response in the form of strong desires or cravings for the drug (Drummond & Glautier, 1994). For example, socializing with certain companions ("drinking buddies") or even passing a liquor store may elicit conditioned cravings for alcohol. In recent research, alcoholic subjects showed distinctive changes in brain activity in areas of the brain that regulate emotion, attention, and appetitive behavior when they were shown pictures of alcoholic beverages (George et al., 2001). Social drinkers, by comparison, did not show this pattern of brain activation.

Sensations of anxiety or depression that were paired with the use of alcohol or drugs may also elicit cravings. The following case illustrates conditioned cravings to environmental cues:

A Case of Conditioned Drug Cravings

A 29-year-old man was hospitalized for the treatment of heroin addiction. After four weeks of treatment, he returned to his former job, which required him to ride the subway past the stop at which he had previously bought his drugs. Each day, when the subway doors opened at this location, [he] experienced enormous craving for heroin, accompanied by tearing, a runny nose, abdominal cramps, and gooseflesh. After the doors closed, his symptoms disappeared, and he went on to work.

—From Weiss & Mirin, 1987, p. 71

Similarly, some people are primarily "stimulus smokers." They reach for a cigarette in the presence of smoking-related stimuli, such as seeing someone smoke or smelling smoke. Smoking becomes a strongly conditioned habit because it is paired repeatedly with many situational cues—watching TV, finishing dinner, driving in the car, studying, drinking or socializing with friends, sex, and, for some, using the bathroom.

The conditioning model of craving is strengthened by research showing that people with alcoholism tend to salivate more than others at the sight and smell of alcohol (Monti et al., 1987). In Pavlov's classic experiment, a salivation response was conditioned in dogs by repeatedly pairing the sound of a bell (a neutral or conditioned stimulus) with the presentation of food powder (an unconditioned stimulus). Salivation among people who develop alcoholism can also be viewed as a conditioned response to alcohol-related cues. Whereas salivating to a bell may be harmless, salivating at a bottle of Scotch, or at a picture of a bottle in a magazine ad, can throw the person who suffers from alcoholism and is trying to remain abstinent into a tailspin. People with drinking problems who show the greatest salivary response to alcohol cues may be at highest risk of relapse. They may also profit from treatments designed to extinguish their responses to alcohol-related cues.

One such treatment, called *cue exposure training,* holds promise in the treatment of alcohol dependence and other forms of addictive behavior (Drummond & Glautier, 1994). In cue exposure treatment, the person is repeatedly seated in front of the drug or alcohol-related cues, such as open alcoholic beverages, while prevented from using the drug. This pairing of the cue (alcohol bottle) with nonreinforcement (by dint of preventing drinking) may lead to extinction of the conditioned craving. Cue exposure treatment may be combined with coping skills training to help people with substance abuse problems learn to cope with drug use urges without resorting to drug use (Monti et al., 1994). It has also been used to help nondependent problem drinkers learn to stop drinking after two or three drinks (Sitharthan et al., 1997).

Observational Learning The role of modeling or observational learning may at least partly explain the increased risk of substance abuse problems in adolescents in families with a history of a substance abuse or dependence (Kilpatrick et al., 2000). For example, parents who model inappropriate or excessive drinking may set the stage for alcohol use and abuse in their children. In one study, teens who said their fathers drank more than two drinks a day had about a 75% greater risk of developing substance abuse problems than did teens with fathers who were described as light drinkers or abstainers ("Teens Who Have Problems," 1999). Researchers also find that young men from families with a history of alcoholism were more strongly affected by exposure to others who modeled excessive drinking than were men without familial alcoholism (Chipperfield & Vogel-Sprott, 1988). Perhaps their parents had modeled excessive drinking and they had learned to regulate their own intake by observing the drinking behavior of others. When their drinking companions drink to excess, they may be more likely to follow their lead.

Cognitive Perspectives

Evidence supports the role of various cognitive factors in substance abuse and dependence, including expectancies and beliefs.

Outcome Expectancies, and Substance Abuse The beliefs and expectancies you hold concerning the effects of alcohol and other drugs clearly influence your decision to use them or not. People who hold positive expectancies about the effects of a drug are not only more likely to use the drug (Schafer & Brown, 1991) but also more likely to use larger quantities of the drug (Baldwin, Oei, & Young, 1994). One of the key factors in predicting alcohol use and misuse in adolescents is the degree to which their friends hold positive attitudes toward alcohol use (Scheier, Botvin, & Baker, 1997; Wood et al., 2001). Similarly, fifth and seventh graders who hold more positive impressions of smokers (for example, seeing them as cool, independent, or good looking) were more likely than their peers to become smokers by the time they reach the ninth grade (Dinh et al., 1995). Smoking prevention programs may need to focus on changing the image that young people hold of smokers long before they ever light up a cigarette themselves. Positive alcohol expectancies also appear in children even before drinking begins.

Among the most widely held positive expectancies concerning alcohol are that it reduces tension, helps divert attention from one's problems, heightens pleasure, and lessens anxiety in social situations and makes one more socially adept. The belief that alcohol helps make a person more socially adept (more relaxed, outgoing, assertive, and carefree in social interactions) appears to be an especially important factor in prompting drinking in adolescents and college students (Burke & Stephens, 1999; Smith et al., 1995).

Self-Efficacy Expectancies Part of the appeal of substances such as alcohol lies in their ability to enhance self-efficacy expectancies (beliefs in our ability to accomplish tasks) either directly (by enhancing feelings of energy, power, and well-being) or indirectly (by reducing stressful states of arousal, such as anxiety) (G. T. Wilson, 1987). Cocaine also enhances self-efficacy expectancies, an outcome sought in particular by performance-conscious athletes. People may therefore come to rely on substances in challenging situations where they doubt their abilities. Alcohol can also help protect one's sense of self-efficacy by shunting criticism for socially unacceptable behavior from the self to the alcohol. People who "screw up" while drinking can maintain their self-esteem by attributing their shortcomings to the alcohol.

Does One "Slip" Cause People with Substance Abuse or Dependence to Go on Binges? Perhaps What You Believe Is What You Get

According to the disease model of alcoholism, abstainers who binge after just one drink do so largely for biochemical reasons. Experimental research, however, suggests that cognitive factors may be more important. In fact, the one-drink hypothesis may be explained by the drinker's expectancies rather than by the biochemical properties of alcohol.

Studies of the one-drink hypothesis, like many other studies on alcohol, are made possible by the fact that the taste of vodka can be cloaked by tonic water. In a classic study by Marlatt and his colleagues (1973), subjects were led to believe they were participating in a taste test. Alcohol-dependent subjects and social drinkers who were informed they were sampling an alcoholic beverage (vodka) drank significantly more than counterparts who were informed they were sampling a nonalcoholic beverage. The expectations of the alcohol-dependent subjects and the social drinkers alike were the crucial factors that predicted the amount consumed (see Figure 10.5). *The actual content of the beverages was immaterial.*

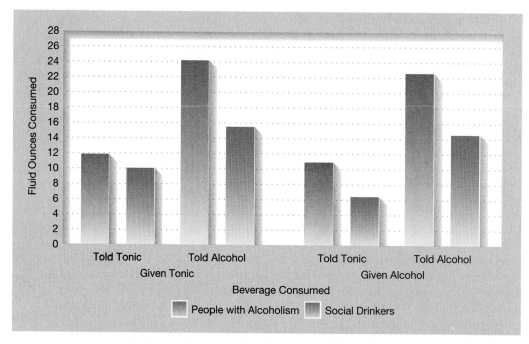

FIGURE 10.5 Must people who develop alcoholism fall off the wagon if they have one drink? It is widely believed that people who develop alcoholism will lose control if they have just one drink. Will they? If so, why? Laboratory research by Marlatt and his colleagues suggests that the tendency of people who suffer from alcoholism to drink to excess following a first drink may be the result of a self-fulfilling prophecy rather than a craving. Like the dieter who eats a piece of chocolate, people who develop alcoholism may assume that they have lost control because they have fallen off the wagon and then go on a binge. This figure shows that people with alcoholism who participated in the Marlatt study drank more when they were led to believe that the beverage contained alcohol, regardless of its actual content. It remains unclear, however, whether binge drinking by people with alcohol-related problems in real-life settings can be explained as a self-fulfilling prophecy.

Source. Adapted from Marlatt et al. (1973).

Marlatt (1978) explained the one-drink effect as a self-fulfilling prophecy. If people with alcohol-related problems believe that just one drink will cause a loss of control, they perceive the outcome as predetermined when they drink. Their drinking—even taking one drink—may thus escalate into a binge. When individuals who were formerly physiologically dependent on alcohol share this belief—which is propounded by many groups, including AA—they may interpret "just one drink" as "falling off the wagon." Marlatt's point is that the "mechanism" of falling off the wagon due to the consumption of one drink is cognitive, reflecting one's expectations about the effects of the drink, and not physiological. This expectation is an example of what Aaron Beck refers to as *absolutist thinking*. When we insist on seeing the world in black and white rather than shades of gray, we may interpret one bite of dessert as proof we are off our diets, or one cigarette as proof we are hooked again. Rather than telling ourselves, "Okay, I goofed, but that's it. I don't have to have more," we encode our lapses as catastrophes and transform them into relapses. Still, alcohol-dependent people who believe they may go on a drinking binge if they have just one drink are well advised to abstain rather than place themselves in a situation they feel they may not be able to manage.

Psychodynamic Perspectives

According to traditional psychodynamic theory, alcoholism reflects certain features of what is termed an *oral-dependent personality*. Alcoholism is, by definition, an oral behavior pattern. Psychodynamic theory also associates excessive alcohol use with other oral traits, such as dependence and depression, and traces the origins of these traits to fixation in the oral stage of psychosexual development. Excessive drinking in adulthood symbolizes an individual's efforts to attain oral gratification.

Psychodynamic theorists also view smoking as an oral fixation, although they have not been able to predict who will or will not smoke. Sigmund Freud smoked upward of 20 cigars a day despite several vain attempts to desist. Although he contracted oral cancer and had to have his jaw replaced, he would still not surrender his "oral fixation." He eventually succumbed to cancer of the mouth in 1939 at the age of 83, after years of agony.

Research support for these psychodynamic concepts is mixed. Although people who develop alcoholism often show dependent traits, it is unclear whether dependence contributes to or stems from problem drinking. Chronic drinking, for example, is connected with loss of employment and downward movement in social status, both of which would render drinkers more reliant on others for support. Moreover, an empirical connection between dependence and alcoholism does not establish that alcoholism represents an oral fixation that can be traced to early development.

Then too, many—but certainly not all—people who suffer from alcoholism have antisocial personalities characterized by independence seeking as expressed through rebelliousness and rejection of social and legal codes (Graham & Strenger, 1988). All in all, there doesn't appear to be a single alcoholic personality (Wood et al., 2001).

Sociocultural Perspectives

Drinking is determined, in part, by where we live, whom we worship with, and the social or cultural norms that regulate our behavior. Cultural attitudes can encourage or discourage problem drinking. As we have already

Peer pressure. Peer pressure is a major influence on alcohol and drug use among adolescents.

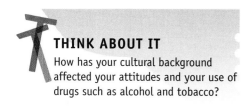

THINK ABOUT IT

How has your cultural background affected your attitudes and your use of drugs such as alcohol and tobacco?

seen, rates of alcohol abuse vary across ethnic and religious groups. Let us note some other sociocultural factors. Church attendance, for example, is generally connected with abstinence from alcohol. Perhaps people who are more willing to engage in culturally sanctioned activities, such as churchgoing, are also more likely to adopt culturally sanctioned prohibitions against excessive drinking. Rates of alcohol use also vary across cultures. For example, alcohol use is greater in Germany than in the United States, apparently because of a cultural tradition that makes the consumption of alcohol, especially beer, normative within German society (Cockerham, Kunz, & Lueschen, 1989).

Drug use by peers and peer pressure to use drugs are important influences in determining alcohol and drug use among adolescents ("Peers Sway," 2001; Simons-Morton et al., 2001; Wills & Cleary, 1999). Kids who start drinking before age 15 stand a fivefold higher risk of developing alcohol dependence in adulthood than do teens who began drinking at a later age (Kluger, 2001). Yet studies of Hispanic and African American adolescents show that support from family members can reduce the negative influence of drug-using peers on the adolescent's use of tobacco and other drugs (Farrell & White, 1998; Frauenglass et al., 1997).

Tying It Together

Substance abuse and dependence are complex patterns of behavior that involve an interplay of biological, psychological, and environmental factors. Genetic factors and the early home environment may give rise to predispositions (diatheses) to abuse and dependence. In adolescence and adulthood, positive expectations concerning drug use, together with social pressures and a lack of cultural constraints, affect drug use decisions and tendencies toward abuse. When physiological dependence occurs, people may use a substance to avoid withdrawal symptoms.

Genetic factors may create an inborn tolerance for certain drugs, such as alcohol, which can make it difficult to regulate usage, to know "when to say when." Some individuals may have genetic tendencies that lead them to become unusually tense or anxious. Perhaps they turn to alcohol or other drugs to quell their nervousness. Genetic predispositions may interact with environmental factors that increase the potential for drug abuse and dependence—factors such as pressure from peers to use drugs, parental modeling of excessive drinking or drug use, and family disruption that results in a lack of effective guidance or support. Cognitive factors, especially positive drug expectancies (e.g., beliefs that using drugs will enhance one's social skills or sexual prowess), may also raise the potential for alcohol or drug problems.

Sociocultural factors need to be taken into account in this matrix of factors, such as the availability of alcohol and other drugs, presence or absence of cultural constraints that might curb excessive or underage drinking, the glamorizing of drug use in popular media, and inborn tendencies (such as among Asians) to flush more readily following alcohol intake.

Learning factors also play important roles. Drug use may be *positively* reinforced by the pleasurable effects associated with the use of the drug (mediated perhaps by release of dopamine in the brain or by activation of endorphin receptors). It may also be *negatively* reinforced by the reduction of states of tension and anxiety that depressant drugs such as alcohol, heroin, and tranquilizers can produce. In a sad but ironic twist, people who become dependent on drugs may continue to use them solely because of the relief from withdrawal symptoms and cravings they encounter when they go without the drug.

Problems of substance abuse and dependence are best approached by investigating the distinctive constellation of factors that apply to each individual case. No single model or set of factors will explain each case, which is why we need to understand each individual's unique characteristics and personal history.

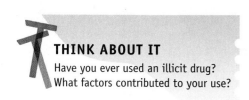

THINK ABOUT IT

Have you ever used an illicit drug? What factors contributed to your use?

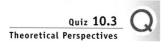

Quiz **10.3**
Theoretical Perspectives

Treatment of Substance Abuse and Dependence

There have been and remain a vast array of nonprofessional, biological, and psychological approaches to substance abuse and dependence. However, treatment has often been a frustrating endeavor. In many, perhaps most, cases, people with drug dependencies really do not want to discontinue the substances they are abusing. Most people who abuse cocaine, for example, like most abusers of alcohol and other drugs, do not seek treatment on their own. Those who do not seek treatment tend to be heavy abusers who deny the negative impact of cocaine on their lives and dwell within a social milieu that fails to encourage them to get help. When people do come for treatment, helping them through a withdrawal syndrome is usually straightforward enough, as we shall see. However, helping them pursue a life devoid of their preferred substances is more problematic. Moreover, treatment takes place in a setting—such as the therapist's office, a support group, a residential center, or a hospital—in which abstinence is valued and encouraged. Then the individual returns to the work, family, or street settings in which abuse and dependence were instigated and maintained. The problem of returning to abuse and dependence following treatment—that is, of *relapse*—can thus be more troublesome than the problems involved in initial treatment.

Another complication is that many people with substance abuse problems also have psychological disorders, and vice versa (McCrady & Langenbucher, 1996; Miller & Brown, 1997). Most clinics and treatment programs focus on the drug or alcohol problem, or the other psychological disorders, rather than treating all these problems simultaneously, however. This narrow focus results in poorer treatment outcomes, including more frequent rehospitalizations among those with these *dual diagnoses*. It has been estimated that 20% to 70% of people who have other psychological disorders—and 50% to 70% of the young adults with other psychological disorders—merit a dual diagnosis that includes substance abuse (Polcin, 1992).

Biological Approaches

An increasing range of biological approaches is used in treating problems of substance abuse and dependence. For people with chemical dependencies, biological treatment typically begins with **detoxification**—that is, helping them through withdrawal from addictive substances.

Detoxification Detoxification is often carried out in a hospital setting to provide the support needed to help the person withdraw safely from the addictive substance. In the case of addiction to alcohol or barbiturates, hospitalization allows medical personnel to monitor the development of potentially dangerous withdrawal symptoms, such as convulsions. Antianxiety drugs, such as the benzodiazepines Librium and Valium, may help block more severe withdrawal symptoms such as seizures and delirium tremens (Mayo-Smith, 1997). Behavioral treatment using monetary rewards for abstinent behavior (judged by clean urine samples) may help improve outcomes during detoxification from opioids (Bickel et al., 1997). Detoxification to alcohol takes about a week. Detoxification is an important step toward staying clean, but it is only a start. Approximately half of all drug abusers relapse within a year of detoxification (Cowley, 2001a). Continuing support and use of structured forms of therapy, such as behavioral counseling and possible use of therapeutic drugs, may hopefully increase the chances of long-term success.

A number of therapeutic drugs are used in treating people with chemical dependencies, and more chemical compounds are in the testing stage (Kranzler, 2000). Here we survey some of the major drugs in use today.

Disulfiram The drug *disulfiram* (brand name Antabuse) discourages alcohol consumption because the combination of the two produces a violent response consisting of nausea, headache, heart palpitations, and vomiting (Kalb, 2001b). In some extreme cases, combining

THINK ABOUT IT
Do you know anyone who has received treatment for a drug abuse problem? What was the outcome?

detoxification The process of ridding the system of alcohol or other drugs under supervised conditions.

methadone An artificial narcotic that is used to help people who are addicted to heroin to abstain from it without a withdrawal syndrome.

Web Link **10.7** wWw
A Guide to Quitting Smoking

Is the path to abstinence from smoking skin deep? Forms of nicotine replacement therapy—such as nicotine transdermal (skin) patches and chewing gum that contains nicotine—allow people to continue to take in nicotine when they quit smoking. Though nicotine replacement therapy is more effective than a placebo in helping people quit smoking, it does not address the behavioral components of addiction to nicotine, such as the habit of smoking while drinking alcohol. For this reason, nicotine replacement therapy may be more effective if it is combined with behavior therapy that focuses on changing smoking habits.

disulfiram and alcohol can produce such a dramatic drop in blood pressure that the individual goes into shock and may even die. Although disulfiram has been used widely in alcoholism treatment, its effectiveness is limited because many patients who want to continue drinking simply stop using the drug. Others stop taking the drug because they believe that they can maintain abstinence without it. Unfortunately, many return to uncontrolled drinking. Another drawback is that the drug has toxic effects in people with liver disease, a frequent ailment of people who suffer from alcoholism. Little evidence supports the efficacy of the drug in the long run (Garbutt et al., 1999; Schuckit, 1996).

Antidepressants Antidepressants show promise in reducing cravings for cocaine following withdrawal. These drugs stimulate neural processes that regulate feelings of pleasure derived in everyday experiences. If pleasure can be more readily derived from non-drug-related activities, cocaine users may be less likely to return to using cocaine to induce pleasurable feelings. However, antidepressants have not yet produced consistent results in reducing relapse rates for cocaine dependence, so it is best to withhold judgment concerning their efficacy (O'Brien, 1996).

Deficiencies of the neurotransmitter serotonin may play a role in producing desires or cravings for alcohol (Anton, 1994). Research is underway on whether alcohol cravings and consumption can be curbed by using serotonin-reuptake inhibitors (Prozac is one) and other drugs that help normalize serotonin activity in the brain (B. A. Johnson et al., 2000b; Kranzler, 2000). The actions of another neurotransmitter, dopamine, may account for the pleasurable or euphoric effects of alcohol. Drugs that mimic dopamine may be helpful in blocking the pleasurably reinforcing effects of alcohol.

Nicotine Replacement Therapy Most regular smokers, perhaps the great majority, are nicotine dependent. The use of nicotine replacements in the form of prescription gum (brand name Nicorette), transdermal (skin) patches, and a recently approved nasal spray may help smokers avoid the unpleasant withdrawal symptoms and cravings for cigarettes that may occur following smoking cessation (Tiffany, Cox, & Elash, 2000). After quitting smoking, ex-smokers can gradually wean themselves from the nicotine replacement.

Evidence shows that nicotine chewing gum and the nicotine patch are effective aids in quitting smoking (e.g., O'Brien & McKay, 1998; Skaar et al., 1997). The jury is still out on nicotine nasal sprays. Though nicotine replacement may help quell the physiological components of withdrawal, they have no effect on the behavioral patterns of addiction, such as the habit of smoking while drinking alcohol or socializing. As a result, nicotine replacement may be ineffective in promoting long-term changes unless it is combined with behavioral therapy that focuses on changing smoking habits ("Last Draw for Smokers," 1996).

In 1997, the government approved the use of the first non-nicotine-based antismoking drug, an antidepressant called *bupropion* (trade name Zyban). The drug has been shown to be more effective than placebo in helping smokers quit (Hurt et al., 1997). It is the first drug that works on reducing cravings for nicotine, in much the same way that other antidepressants are being used to reduce cocaine cravings.

Methadone Maintenance Programs **Methadone** is a synthetic opiate that has been used for more than 30 years in treating heroin addiction ("Beyond Methadone," 2000). It blunts cravings for heroin and helps curb the unpleasant symptoms that accompany withdrawal (P. G. O'Connor, 2000; Sees, 2000). Because methadone in normal doses does not produce a high or leave the user feeling drugged, it can help heroin addicts hold jobs and get their lives back on track (Cowley, 2001a; Fiellin et al., 2001; R. E. Johnson et al., 2000). However, like other opioids, methadone is highly addictive. For this reason, people treated with methadone can be conceptualized as swapping dependence on one drug for dependence on another. Yet because most methadone programs are publicly financed, they relieve people who are addicted to heroin of the need to engage in criminal activity to support their dependence on methadone.

Approximately 120,000 people in the United States participate in methadone programs. Although methadone can be taken indefinitely, individuals may be weaned from it without returning to using heroin. Although methadone treatment produces clear benefits in improved daily functioning, not everyone succeeds with methadone, even with counseling. Some addicts turn to other drugs such as cocaine to get high or return to using heroin. Others drop out of methadone programs (Goode, 2001c).

Recently, another type of synthetic narcotic, *buprenorphine,* has been brought to market. Many treatment providers prefer buprenorphine to methadone because it produces less of a sedative effective and can be taken in pill form only three times a week, whereas methadone is given in liquid form on a daily basis (O'Connor, 2001a). For maximum effectiveness, methadone or buprenorphine treatment should be combined with psychological counseling and psychosocial rehabilitation (P. G. O'Connor, 2000; E. O'Connor, 2001a; Rounsaville & Kosten, 2000).

Naloxone and Naltrexone **Naloxone** and **naltrexone** are sister drugs that block the high produced by heroin and other opioids. By blocking the opioid's effects, they may be useful in helping addicts avoid relapsing following opiate withdrawal (Anton et al., 2001; Dettmer et al., 2001).

Naltrexone (brand name ReVia) blocks the high from alcohol as well as from opiates. In a double-blind placebo-control study, naltrexone in combination with behavioral treatment cut the relapse rates in people treated for alcoholism by more than half (Volpicelli et al., 1994). Naltrexone doesn't prevent the person from taking a drink, but seems to blunt cravings for the drug (Kalb, 2001b). By blocking the pleasure produced by alcohol, the drug can help break the vicious cycle in which one drink creates a desire for another, leading to episodes of binge drinking.

A nagging problem with drugs such as naltrexone, naloxone, disulfiram, and methadone is that people with substance abuse problems may simply stop using them and return to their substance-abusing behavior. Nor do such drugs provide alternative sources of positive reinforcement that can replace the pleasurable states produced by drugs of abuse. Drugs such as these are only effective in the context of a broader treatment program, consisting of psychological counseling and other treatment components, such as job training, and stress management training—treatments designed to provide people with substance abuse problems the skills they need to embark on a life in the mainstream culture (Miller & Brown, 1997).

Culturally Sensitive Treatment of Alcoholism

Members of ethnic minority groups may resist traditional treatment approaches because they feel excluded from full participation in society. Native American women, for example, tend to respond less favorably to traditional alcoholism counseling than White women (Rogan, 1986). Hurlburt and Gade (1984) attribute this difference to the resistance of Native American women to "White man's" authority. They suggest that the early stages of intervention might be more successful in overcoming this resistance if treatment was provided by Native American counselors.

The use of counselors from the client's own ethnic group is an example of a culturally sensitive treatment approach. Culturally sensitive programs also address all facets of the human being, including racial and cultural identity, that nurture ethnic pride and help people resist the temptation to cope with stress through chemicals (Rogan, 1986). Culturally sensitive treatment approaches have been extended to other forms of drug dependence, including programs for smoking cessation (Nevid & Javier, 1997; Nevid, Javier, & Moulton, 1996).

Treatment providers may also be more successful if they recognize and incorporate indigenous forms of healing into the treatment process. For example, spirituality is an important aspect of traditional Native American culture, and spiritualists have played important roles as natural healers. Seeking the assistance of a spiritualist may help improve the counseling relationship.

THINK ABOUT IT
What do you think of the concept of using methadone, a narcotic drug, to treat addiction to another narcotic drug, heroin? What are the advantages and disadvantages of this approach? Do you believe the government should support methadone maintenance programs? Why or why not?

naloxone A drug that prevents users from becoming high if they take heroin.

naltrexone A drug related to naloxone that blocks the high from alcohol as well as from opiates.

Culturally sensitive treatment. Culturally sensitive therapy or treatment addresses all aspects of the person, including ethnic factors and the nurturance of pride in one's cultural identity. Ethnic pride may help people resist the temptation to cope with stress through alcohol and other substances.

Web Link **10.8**
Alcoholics Anonymous (AA) wWw
World Services

Web Link **10.9**
National Association for Children wWw
of Alcoholics

Likewise, given the importance of the church in African American and Hispanic American culture, counselors working with people with alcohol use disorders from these groups may be more successful when they draw on clergy and church members as resources in the treatment process.

Nonprofessional Support Groups

Despite the complexity of the factors contributing to substance abuse and dependence, these problems are frequently handled by laypeople or nonprofessionals. Such people often have or had the same problems themselves. For example, self-help group meetings are sponsored by organizations such as Alcoholics Anonymous, Narcotics Anonymous, and Cocaine Anonymous. These groups promote abstinence and provide members an opportunity to discuss their feelings and experiences in a supportive group setting. More experienced group members (sponsors) support newer members during periods of crisis or potential relapse. The meetings are sustained by nominal voluntary contributions.

The most widely used nonprofessional program, Alcoholics Anonymous (AA), is based on the belief that alcoholism is a disease, not a sin. AA assumes that people who suffer from alcoholism are never cured, regardless of how long they abstain from alcohol or how well they control their drinking. Instead of being "cured," people who suffer from alcoholism are seen as "recovering." It is also assumed that people who suffer from alcoholism cannot control their drinking and need help to stop drinking. AA has more than 50,000 chapters in North America. AA is so deeply embedded in the consciousness of helping professionals that many of them automatically refer newly detoxified people to AA as the follow-up agency. About half of AA members have problems with illicit drugs as well as alcohol.

The AA experience is in part spiritual, in part group supportive, in part cognitive. AA follows a 12-step approach that focuses on accepting one's powerlessness over alcohol and turning one's will and life over to a higher power (Cowley, 2001a). This spiritual component may be helpful to some participants but not to others, who prefer not to appeal for divine support. (Other lay organizations, such as Rational Recovery, do not adopt a spiritual approach.) The later steps focus on examining one's character flaws, admitting one's wrongdoings, being open to a higher power (or God) for help to overcome one's character defects, making amends to others, and, in step 12, bringing the AA message to other people suffering from alcoholism (McCrady, 1994). Prayer and or meditation are urged upon members to help them get in touch with their higher power. The meetings themselves provide group support. So does the buddy, or sponsoring, system, which encourages members to call each other for support when they feel tempted to drink.

AA claims to have a high success rate, one in the neighborhood of 75% (Wallace, 1985). Critics note that percentages this high are based on personal testimonies rather than on careful surveys or experiments. Moreover, such estimates include only persons who attend meetings for extended periods. The dropout rate is high, with as many as 70% of members dropping out within 10 meetings, according to one survey. Even AA estimates that 50% of members drop out after 3 months ("Treatment of Alcoholism—Part II," 1996). It has been difficult to conduct controlled studies because AA does not keep records of its members in order to protect their anonymity and also because of an inability to conduct randomized clinical trials in AA settings (McCaul & Furst, 1994). On the other hand, the greater a person's involvement with AA, researchers find, the better the outcome in terms of days not drinking or using drugs (Morgenstern et al., 1997). We cannot say for certain whether regular participation in AA is responsible for better outcomes, or whether personal motivation may account for both greater AA participation and change in substance-using behavior. In all likelihood success is due to both factors. Nor can we say who is likely to succeed in AA and who is not.

Al-Anon, begun in 1951, is a spinoff of AA that supports the families and friends of people suffering from alcoholism. There are some 26,000 Al-Anon groups nationwide (Desmond, 1987). Another spin-off of AA, Alateen, provides support to children whose parents have alcoholism, helping them see they are not to blame for their parents' drinking and are thus undeserving of the guilt they may feel.

Al-Anon An organization that sponsors support groups for family members of people with alcoholism.

Residential Approaches

A residential approach to treatment involves a stay in a hospital or therapeutic residence. Hospitalization may be recommended when substance abusers cannot exercise self-control in their usual environments, or cannot tolerate withdrawal symptoms, and when their behavior is self-destructive or dangerous to others. Outpatient treatment is less costly and often indicated when withdrawal symptoms are less severe, clients are committed to changing their behavior, and environmental support systems, such as families, strive to help clients make the transition to a drug-free lifestyle. The great majority (nearly 90%) of people treated for alcoholism are treated on an outpatient basis (McCaul & Furst, 1994).

Most inpatient programs use an extended 28-day detoxification, or drying-out, period. Clients are helped through withdrawal symptoms in a few days. Then the emphasis shifts to counseling about the destructive effects of alcohol and combating distorted ideas or rationalizations. Consistent with the disease model, the goal of abstinence is urged.

Despite their popularity, researchers find that most people with alcohol use disorders do not require hospitalization (some certainly do). Studies comparing outpatient and inpatient programs reveal no overall difference in relapse rates (Miller & Hester, 1986). However, medical insurance may not cover outpatient treatment, which may encourage many people who may benefit from outpatient treatment to admit themselves for inpatient treatment.

A number of residential therapeutic communities are also in use. Some of them have part- or full-time professional staffs. Others are run entirely by laypeople. Residents are expected to remain free of drugs and take responsibility for their actions. They are often confronted about their excuses for failing to take responsibility for themselves and about their denial of the damage being done by their drug abuse. They share their life experiences to help one another develop productive ways of handling stress.

As with AA, we lack evidence from controlled studies demonstrating the efficacy of residential treatment programs. Also like AA, therapeutic communities have high numbers of early dropouts. Moreover, many former members of residential treatment programs who remain substance free during their time in residence relapse upon returning to the world outside. A recent study suggests that a day treatment therapeutic community may be as effective as a residential treatment facility (Guydish et al., 1998).

Psychodynamic Approaches

Psychoanalysts view substance abuse and dependence as symptomatic of conflicts that are rooted in childhood experiences. Focusing on substance abuse or dependence per se is seen to offer, at most, a superficial type of therapy. It is assumed that if the underlying conflicts are resolved, abusive behavior will also subside as more mature forms of gratification are sought. Traditional psychoanalysts also assume that programs directed solely at abusive behavior will be of limited benefit because they fail to address the underlying psychological causes of abuse. Although there are many reports of successful psychodynamic case studies of people with substance abuse problems, there is a dearth of controlled and replicable research studies. The effectiveness of psychodynamic methods for treating substance abuse and dependence thus remains unsubstantiated.

Behavioral Approaches

The use of behavior therapy or behavior modification in treating substance abuse and dependence focuses on modifying abusive and dependent behavior patterns. The issue to many behaviorally oriented therapists is not whether substance abuse and dependence are diseases but whether abusers can learn to change their behavior when they are faced with temptation.

Self-Control Strategies Self-control training focuses on helping abusers develop skills they can use to change their abusive behavior. Behavior therapists focus on three components of substance abuse:

1. The *antecedent* cues or stimuli (A's) that prompt or trigger abuse,
2. The abusive *behaviors* (B's) themselves, and
3. The reinforcing or punishing *consequences* (C's) that maintain or discourage abuse.

Table 10.5 shows the kinds of strategies used to modify the "ABC's" of substance abuse.

Aversive Conditioning In **aversive conditioning,** painful or aversive stimuli are paired with substance abuse or abuse-related stimuli to make abuse less appealing. In the case of problem drinking, tastes of different alcoholic beverages are usually paired with chemically induced nausea and vomiting or with electric shock (G. T. Wilson, 1991). As a consequence, alcohol may come to elicit an aversive conditioned response, such as fear or nausea that inhibits drinking. Relief from aversive responses then negatively reinforces avoidance of alcohol.

Social Skills Training Social skills training helps people develop effective interpersonal responses in social situations that prompt substance abuse. Assertiveness training, for example, may be used to teach people with alcohol-related problems how to fend off social pressures to drink. Behavioral marital therapy seeks to improve marital communication and a couple's problem-solving skills to relieve marital stresses that can trigger abuse. Couples may learn how to use written behavioral contracts. One such contract might stipulate that the person with a substance abuse problem agrees to abstain from drinking or to take Antabuse, and his or her spouse agrees to refrain from comments about past drinking and the probability of future lapses. The available evidence supports the utility of social skills training and behavioral marital therapy approaches in treating alcoholism (Finney & Monahan, 1996; O'Farrell et al., 1996).

Relapse-Prevention Training

The word **relapse** derives from Latin roots meaning "to slide back." From 50% to 90% of people who are successfully treated for substance abuse problems eventually relapse (Leary, 1996b). Because of the prevalence of relapse, behaviorally oriented therapists have devised a number of methods referred to as **relapse-prevention training.** Such training helps people with substance abuse problems cope with high-risk situations and to prevent *lapses,* (slips)—from becoming full-blown relapses (Marlatt & Gordon, 1985). High-risk situations include negative mood states, such as depression, anger, or anxiety; interpersonal conflict (e.g., marital problems or conflicts with employers); and socially conducive situations such as "the guys getting together." Participants learn to cope with these situations, for example, by learning self-relaxation skills to counter anxiety and learning to resist social pressures to resume use of the substance. Trainees are also taught to avoid practices that might prompt a relapse, such as keeping alcohol on hand for friends.

Although it contains many behavioral strategies, relapse-prevention training is a cognitive-behavioral technique in that it also focuses on the person's *interpretations* of any lapses or slips that may occur, such as smoking a first cigarette or taking a first drink following quitting. Clients are taught how to avoid the so-called **abstinence violation effect (AVE)**—the tendency to overreact to a lapse—by learning to reorient their thinking about lapses and slips. People who have a slip may be more likely to relapse if they attribute their slip to personal weakness, and experience shame and guilt, than if they attribute the slip to an external or transient event (Curry, Marlatt, & Gordon, 1987). For example, consider a skater who slips on the ice (Marlatt & Gordon, 1985). Whether or not the skater gets back up and continues to perform depends largely on whether the skater sees the slip as an isolated and correctable event or as a sign of complete failure. Evidence shows that the best predictor of progression from a first to a second lapse among ex-smokers was the feeling of giving up after the first lapse (Shiffman et al., 1996). But those who responded to a first lapse by using coping strategies were more likely to succeed in averting a subsequent lapse on the same day.

Participants in relapse-prevention training programs are encouraged to view lapses as temporary setbacks that provide opportunities to learn what kinds of situations lead to temptation and how they can avoid or cope with such situations. If they can learn to think,

aversive conditioning A behavior therapy technique in which a maladaptive response is paired with exposure to an aversive stimulus to develop a conditioned aversion.

relapse A recurrence of a problem behavior or disorder.

relapse-prevention training A cognitive-behavioral technique involving the use of behavioral and cognitive strategies for resisting temptations and preventing relapses.

abstinence violation effect (AVE) The tendency to overreact to a minor lapse with feelings of guilt and resignation that may trigger a relapse.

TABLE 10.5   Self-Control Strategies for Modifying the "ABC's" of Substance Abuse

1. Controlling the A's (Antecedents) of Substance Abuse

People who abuse or become dependent on psychoactive substances become conditioned to a wide range of external (environmental) and internal stimuli (bodily states). They may begin to break these stimulus-response connections by:

- Removing drinking and smoking paraphernalia from the home—all alcoholic beverages, beer mugs, carafes, ashtrays, matches, cigarette packs, lighters, etc.
- Restricting the stimulus environment in which drinking or smoking is permitted. Use the substance only in a stimulus-deprived area of their homes, such as the garage, bathroom, or basement. All other stimuli that might be connected to using the substance are removed—there is no TV, reading materials, radio, or telephone. In this way, substance abuse becomes detached from many controlling stimuli.
- Not socializing with others with substance abuse problems, by avoiding situations linked to abuse—bars, the street, bowling alleys, etc.
- Frequenting substance-free environments—lectures or concerts, a gym, museums, evening classes; and by socializing with nonabusers, sitting in nonsmoking cars of trains, eating in restaurants without liquor licenses.
- Managing the internal triggers for abuse. This can be done by practicing self-relaxation or meditation and not taking the substance when tense; by expressing angry feelings by writing them down or self-assertion, not by taking the substance; by seeking counseling for prolonged feelings of depression, not alcohol, pills, or cigarettes.

2. Controlling the B's (Behaviors) of Substance Abuse

People can prevent and interrupt substance abuse by:

- Using response prevention—breaking abusive habits by physically preventing them from occurring or making them more difficult (e.g., by not bringing alcohol home or cigarettes to the office).
- Using competing responses when tempted; by being prepared to handle substance-related situations with appropriate ammunition—mints, sugarless chewing gum, etc; by taking a bath or shower, walking the dog, walking around the block, taking a drive, calling a friend, spending time in a substance-free environment, practicing meditation or relaxation, or exercising when tempted, rather than using the substance.
- Making abuse more laborious—buying one can of beer at a time; storing matches, ashtrays, and cigarettes far apart; wrapping cigarettes in foil to make smoking more cumbersome; pausing for 10 minutes when struck by the urge to drink, smoke, or use another substance and asking oneself, "Do I really need *this* one?"

3. Controlling the C's (Consequences) of Substance Abuse

Substance abuse has immediate positive consequences such as pleasure, relief from anxiety and withdrawal symptoms, and stimulation. People can counter these intrinsic rewards and alter the balance of power in favor of nonabuse by:

- Rewarding themselves for nonabuse and punishing themselves for abuse.
- Switching to brands of beer and cigarettes they don't like.
- Setting gradual substance-reduction schedules and rewarding themselves for sticking to them.
- Punishing themselves for failing to meet substance-reduction goals. People with substance abuse problems can assess themselves, say, 10 cents for each slip and donate the cash to an unpalatable cause, such as a brother-in-law's birthday present.
- Rehearsing motivating thoughts or self-statements—such as writing reasons for quitting smoking on index cards. For example:

    Each day I don't smoke adds another day to my life.
    Quitting smoking will help me breathe deeply again.
    Foods will smell and taste better when I quit smoking.
    Think how much money I'll save by not smoking.
    Think how much cleaner my teeth and fingers will be by not smoking.
    I'll be proud to tell others that I kicked the habit.
    My lungs will become clearer each and every day I don't smoke.

Smokers can carry a list of 20 to 25 such statements and read several of them at various times throughout the day. They can become parts of one's daily routine, a constant reminder of one's goals.

A Closer Look

The Controlled Drinking Controversy

The disease model of alcoholism contends that people who suffer from the disease who have just one drink will lose control and go on a binge. Some professionals, however, like Linda and Mark Sobell (1973, 1984), have argued that behavior modification self-control techniques can teach many people with alcohol abuse or dependence to engage in **controlled drinking**—to have a drink or two without necessarily falling off the wagon.

The contention that people who develop alcoholism can learn to drink moderately remains controversial. The proponents of the disease model of alcoholism, who have wielded considerable political strength, stand strongly opposed to attempts to teach controlled social drinking.

Investigators have found that controlled social drinking may be a reasonable treatment goal for younger people with problem drinking who are less alcohol dependent but are headed on the road toward chronic alcoholism (e.g., Adamson & Sellman, 2001; Larimer et al., 1993 Miller & Muñoz, 1983; Sanchez-Craig & Wilkinson, 1986/1987). Evidence supporting controlled social drinking programs for people with chronic alcoholism, however, remains lacking. Yet interest in controlled drinking programs has waned, largely because of strong opposition from professionals and lay organizations committed to the abstinence model.

Controlled drinking programs may be best suited for younger persons with early-stage alcoholism or problem drinking, for those who reject goals of total abstinence or who have failed in programs requiring abstinence, and for those who do not show severe withdrawal symptoms (Marlatt et al., 1993; Rosenberg, 1993). Researchers also find that women tend to do better than men in controlled drinking programs (Marlatt et al., 1993).

Controlled drinking programs may actually represent a pathway to abstinence for people who would not otherwise enter abstinence-only treatment programs (Marlatt et al., 1993). That is, treatment in a controlled drinking program may be the first step toward giving up drinking completely. A large percentage (about one in four in one study; Miller et al., 1993) enters with the goal of achieving controlled drinking but become abstinent by the end of treatment. On the other hand, controlled social drinking may not be appropriate for people with established alcohol dependence and those who are taking medications that interact with alcohol or have other medical risks that might be aggravated by alcohol ("Treatment of Alcoholism—Part II," 1996).

THINK ABOUT IT

Many teenagers today have parents who themselves smoked marijuana or used other drugs when they were younger. If you were one of those parents, what would you tell your kids about drugs?

---

controlled drinking An approach to treating problem drinkers whose goal is moderate social drinking rather than abstinence.

Quiz **10.4**
Treatment of Substance Abuse and Dependence

Quiz **10.5**
Chapter Exam

Research Update
Chapter 10

"Okay, I had a slip, but that doesn't mean all is lost unless I believe it is," they are less likely to catastrophize lapses and subsequently relapse.

All in all, efforts to treat people with substance abuse and dependence problems have been mixed at best. Many abusers really do not want to discontinue use of these substances, although they would prefer, if possible, to avoid their negative consequences. The more effective substance abuse treatments programs involve multiple treatment approaches that match the needs of substance abusers and the range of problems they often encounter, including co-occurring (comorbid) psychiatric problems like depression (Brown et al., 1997; Kessler et al., 1997b; Rychtarik et al., 2000). *Comorbidity* (co-occurrence) of substance use disorders and other psychological disorders has become the rule in treatment facilities rather than the exception (Brems & Johnson, 1997). Substance abusers who have comorbid disorders or more severe psychological problems typically fare more poorly in treatment for their drug or alcohol problems (Simpson et al., 1999). For people with alcoholism and other substance abuse problems, a number of different therapies, including 12-step and cognitive-behavioral approaches, seem to work well if they are well delivered (Miller & Brown, 1997; Project MATCH Research Group, 1997).

The major problem is that as many as 80% of people in the United States with alcohol use disorders have no contact whatsoever with alcohol treatment programs or self-help organizations (Institute of Medicine, 1990). Clearly more needs to be done to help people whose use of alcohol and other drugs puts them at risk.

In the case of inner city youth who have become trapped within a milieu of street drugs and hopelessness, the availability of culturally sensitive drug counseling and job training opportunities would be of considerable benefit in helping them assume more productive social roles. The challenge is clear: to develop cost-effective ways of helping people recognize the negative effects of substances and forgo the powerful and immediate reinforcements they provide.

Overview of Substance-Related Disorders

TYPES OF SUBSTANCE-RELATED DISORDERS

Substance Use Disorders	Maladaptive use of a psychoactive substance	• **Substance Abuse Disorder:** Pattern of drug-using behavior leading to negative consequences, such as repeatedly losing time from work or aggravating an underlying physical problem • **Substance Dependence Disorder:** A more severe form of substance use disorder, it is associated with physiological dependence or compulsive use of a substance
Substance-Induced Disorders	Physiological or psychological disorders induced by the use of a psychoactive substance	• Intoxication • Dementia • Drug withdrawal syndromes • Amnesia • Mood disorders • Psychotic disorders • Delirium

CAUSAL FACTORS   Multiple factors interact in leading to problems of substance abuse and dependence

Biological Factors	• Pleasurable effects and addictive properties of drugs may depend on their effects on neurotransmitter systems in the brain • Genetic factors may create predispositions for substance-related disorders
Psychosocial Factors	• Positive reinforcement (pleasure inducing) and negative reinforcement (relief from states of tension or anxiety and avoidance or escape from unpleasant withdrawal symptoms) contribute to initiation and maintenance of drug use • Modeling of excessive drinking by family members and friends • Cravings may be conditioned responses to cues associated with prior drug use • In psychodynamic theory, alcohol and drug abuse represent forms of oral fixation and are linked to dependent personality traits
Cognitive Factors	• Positive outcome expectancies linked to drug use • Effects of drugs in boosting self-efficacy expectations • "Falling off the wagon" as a self-fulfilling prophecy
Sociocultural Factors	• Peer pressure from drug-using peers • Exposure to deviant subcultures (e.g., gang culture) in which drug use is commonplace or encouraged

TREATMENT APPROACHES   Intensive, multicomponent treatment approaches generally work best

Biological Approaches	• Detoxification to help substance abusers withdraw safely from addictive drugs • Use of drugs that cause extreme nausea when combined with alcohol (Antabuse) • Use of antidepressants to control drug cravings • Use of chemical substitutes, such as nicotine replacement in place of cigarettes, or methadone in place of heroin • Use of drugs that block the high produced by opioids or alcohol (naloxone and naltrexone)
Behavioral Approaches	• To break drug-abusing patterns of behavior and strengthen more adaptive behaviors
Psychodynamic Approaches	• To help individuals with substance abuse problems identify and resolve underlying psychological conflicts
Other Treatment Approaches	• **Residential treatment approaches** and **nonprofessional support groups,** such as AA, to help individuals regain control over their lives and maintain abstinence in the community • **Relapse prevention training** to help individuals learn to resist drug temptations, to cope effectively with high-risk situations, and to prevent lapses from becoming relapses

Summing Up

Classification of Substance-Related Disorders

How does the* DSM *distinguish between substance abuse disorders and substance dependence disorders? According to the *DSM*, substance abuse disorders involve a pattern of recurrent use of a substance that repeatedly leads to damaging consequences. Substance dependence disorders involves impaired control over use of a substance and often include features of physiological dependence on the substance, as manifest by the development of tolerance or an abstinence syndrome.

What do we mean by the terms* addiction *and* psychological dependence? Although different people use the term *addiction* differently, it is used here to refer to the habitual or compulsive use of a substance combined with the development of physiological dependence. Psychological dependence involves compulsive use of a substance, with or without the development of physiological dependence.

Drugs of Abuse

What are depressants? Depressants are drugs that depress or slow down nervous system activity. They include alcohol, sedatives and minor tranquilizers, and opioids. Their effects include intoxication, impaired coordination, slurred speech, and impaired intellectual functioning. Chronic alcohol abuse is linked to alcohol-induced persisting amnestic disorder (Korsakoff's syndrome), cirrhosis of the liver, fetal alcohol syndrome, and other physical health problems. Barbiturates are depressants or sedatives that have been used medically for relief of anxiety and short-term insomnia, among other uses. Opioids such as morphine and heroin are derived from the opium poppy. Others are synthesized. Used medically for relief of pain, they are strongly addictive.

What are stimulants? Stimulants increase the activity of the nervous system. Amphetamines and cocaine are stimulants that increase the availability of neurotransmitters in the brain, leading to heightened states of arousal and pleasurable feelings. High doses can produce psychotic reactions that mimic features of paranoid schizophrenia. Habitual cocaine use can lead to a variety of health prob-

lems, and an overdose can cause sudden death. Repeated use of nicotine, a mild stimulant found in cigarette smoking, leads to physiological dependence.

What are hallucinogens? Hallucinogens are drugs that distort sensory perceptions and can induce hallucinations. They include LSD, psilocybin, and mescaline. Other drugs with similar effects are cannabis (marijuana) and phencyclidine (PCP). There is little evidence that these drugs induce physiological dependence, although psychological dependence may occur.

Theoretical Perspectives

How do the major theoretical perspectives view the causes of substance abuse and dependence? The biological perspective focuses on uncovering the biological pathways that may explain mechanisms of physiological dependence. The biological perspective spawns the disease model, which posits that alcoholism and other forms of substance dependence are disease processes. Learning perspectives view substance abuse disorders as learned patterns of behavior, with roles for classical and operant conditioning and observational learning. Cognitive perspectives focus on roles of attitudes, beliefs, and expectancies in accounting for substance use and abuse. Sociocultural perspectives emphasize the cultural, group, and social factors that underlie drug use patterns, including the role of peer pressure in determining adolescent drug use. Psychodynamic theorists view problems of substance abuse, such as excessive drinking and habitual smoking, as signs of an oral fixation.

Treatment

What treatments approaches are used to help people overcome problems of substance abuse and dependence? Biological approaches to substance abuse disorders include detoxification; the use of drugs such as disulfiram, methadone, naloxone, naltrexone, and antidepressants; and nicotine replacement therapy. Residential treatment approaches include hospitals and therapeutic residences. Nonprofessional support groups, such as Alcoholics Anonymous, promote abstinence within a supportive group setting.

Psychodynamic therapists focus on uncovering the inner conflicts originating in childhood that they believe lie at the root of substance abuse problems. Behavior therapists focus on helping people with substance-related problems change problem behaviors through such techniques as self-control training, aversive conditioning, and skills training approaches. Regardless of the initial success of a treatment technique, relapse remains a pressing problem in treating people with substance abuse problems. Relapse-prevention training employs cognitive-behavioral techniques to help recovering substance abusers cope with high-risk situations and to prevent lapses from becoming relapses by helping participants interpret lapses in less damaging ways.

Key for "Are You Hooked?" Questionnaire

Any yes answer suggests you may be dependent on alcohol. If you have answered any of these questions in the affirmative, we suggest you seriously examine what your drinking means to you.

CHAPTER ELEVEN

Eating Disorders, Obesity, and Sleep Disorders

Pablo Picasso
Girl Before a Mirror

Truth OR Fiction?

- Though others see them as but "skin and bones," young women with anorexia nervosa still see themselves as too fat. (p. 343)

- Dieting represents an abnormal eating pattern among American women. (p. 346)

- Bulimic women induce vomiting only after binges. (p. 347)

- Drugs used to treat depression may also help curb bulimic binges. (p. 349)

- The excess calories consumed by Americans each day could feed a country of 80 million people. (p. 353)

- Obesity is one of the most common psychological disorders in the United States. (p. 353)

- When you lose weight, your body starts putting the brakes on the rate at which it burns calories. (p. 355)

- Obese people lose fat cells when they diet. (p. 355)

- Most dieters eventually gain back the weight they lose. (p. 358)

- Many people suffer from sleep attacks in which they suddenly fall asleep without any warning. (p. 362)

- Some people literally gasp for breath hundreds of times during sleep without realizing it. (p. 363)

Jessica was a 20-year-old communications major when she consulted a psychologist for the first time. For years she had kept a secret from everyone, including her fiancé, Ken. She and Ken were planning to get married in 3 months. She had decided that it was time to finally confront the problem. She told the psychologist she didn't want to bring the problem into the marriage with her, that it wouldn't be fair to Ken. She said, "I don't want him to have to deal with this. I want to stop this before the marriage. I have to stop bingeing and throwing up." Jessica went on to describe her problem: "I go on binges and then throw it all up. It makes me feel like I am in control, but really I'm not." To conceal her secret, she would lock herself in the bathroom, run the water in the sink to mask the sounds, and induce vomiting. She would then clean up after herself and spray an air deodorant to mask any telltale odors. "The only one who suspects," she said with embarrassment, "is my dentist. He said my teeth are beginning to decay from stomach acid."

Jessica had *bulimia nervosa*, an eating disorder characterized by recurrent cycles of bingeing and purging. Eating disorders like *bulimia nervosa* and *anorexia nervosa* often affect young people of high school or college age, especially young women. Although rates of diagnosable eating disorders in college students are not as high as you might think, chances are you have known people with anorexia or bulimia or with disturbed eating patterns that fall within a spectrum of disturbed eating behaviors, such as repeated binge eating or excessive dieting. You probably also know people who suffer from obesity, a major health problem for increasing numbers of Americans. Other psychological disorders that commonly affect young adults are sleep disorders. The most common form of sleep disorder, chronic insomnia, affects many young people who are making their way in the world and tend to bring their worries and concerns to bed with them.

Eating Disorders

In a nation of plenty, some people literally starve themselves—sometimes to death. They are obsessed with their weight and desire to achieve an exaggerated image of thinness. Others engage in repeated cycles in which they binge on food and then attempt to purge their excess eating, such as by inducing vomiting. These dysfunctional patterns are, respectively, the two major types of eating disorders, **anorexia nervosa** and **bulimia nervosa. Eating disorders** are characterized by disturbed patterns of eating and maladaptive ways of controlling body weight. Like many other psychological disorders, anorexia and bulimia are often accompanied by other forms of psychopathology, including depression, anxiety disorders, and substance abuse disorders.

Anorexia nervosa and bulimia nervosa were once considered very rare, but they are becoming increasingly common in the United States and other developed countries. The great majority of cases occur among women, especially young women. Although these disorders may develop in middle or even late adulthood, they typically begin during adolescence or early adulthood when the pressures to be thin are the strongest (Beck, Casper, & Andersen, 1996). As these social pressures have increased, so too have rates of eating disorders. Approximately 0.5% (1 in 200) females in our society develop anorexia nervosa (APA, 2000). The prevalence rate of bulimia nervosa among women is estimated to range between 1% and 3% (APA, 2000). A much larger percentage of young women show anorexic or bulimic behaviors, but not to the point that they would warrant a diagnosis of an eating disorder. Studies of college women indicate that perhaps 1 in 2 have binged and purged at least once (Fairburn & Wilson, 1993). Rates of anorexia and bulimia among males are about one-tenth those among females (APA, 2000).

Anorexia Nervosa

The Case of Karen

Karen was the 22-year-old daughter of a renowned English professor. She had begun her college career full of promise at the age of 17, but two years ago, after "social problems" occurred, she had returned to live at home and taken progressively lighter course loads at

 **VIDEO 11.1**
Eating Disorders:
Nutritionist Alise Thresh

anorexia nervosa An eating disorder characterized by maintenance of an abnormally low body weight, distortions of body image, intense fears of gaining weight, and, in females, amenorrhea.

bulimia nervosa An eating disorder characterized by recurrent binge eating followed by self-induced purging, accompanied by overconcern with body weight and shape.

eating disorder A psychological disorder characterized by disturbed patterns of eating and maladaptive ways of controlling body weight.

Web Link **11.1** wWw
Facts About Eating Disorders

a local college. Karen had never been overweight, but about a year ago her mother noticed that she seemed to be gradually "turning into a skeleton."

Karen spent literally hours every day shopping at the supermarket, butcher, and bakeries conjuring up gourmet treats for her parents and younger siblings. Arguments over her lifestyle and eating habits had divided the family into two camps. The camp led by her father called for patience; that headed by her mother demanded confrontation. Her mother feared that Karen's father would "protect her right into her grave" and wanted Karen placed in residential treatment "for her own good." The parents finally compromised on an outpatient evaluation.

At an even 5 feet, Karen looked like a prepubescent 11-year-old. Her nose and cheekbones protruded crisply. Her lips were full, but the redness of the lipstick was unnatural, as if too much paint had been dabbed on a corpse for the funeral. Karen weighed only 78 pounds, but she had dressed in a stylish silk blouse, scarf, and baggy pants so that not one inch of her body was revealed.

Karen vehemently denied that she had a problem. Her figure was "just about where I want it to be" and she engaged in aerobic exercise daily. A deal was struck in which outpatient treatment would be tried as long as Karen lost no more weight and showed steady gains back to at least 90 pounds. Treatment included a day hospital with group therapy and two meals a day. But word came back that Karen was artfully toying with her food—cutting it up, sort of licking it, and moving it about her plate—rather than eating it. After 3 weeks Karen had lost another pound. At that point, her parents were able to persuade her to enter a residential treatment program, where her eating behavior could be more carefully monitored.

—From the Authors' Files

At risk? Anorexia is most common among young women involved in ballet and modeling, in which a great emphasis is put upon achieving an ultrathin body image.

Anorexia derives from the Greek roots *an-*, meaning "without," and *orexis*, meaning "a desire for." *Anorexia* thus means "without desire for [food]," which is something of a misnomer, because loss of appetite among people with anorexia nervosa is rare. However, they may be repelled by food and refuse to eat more than is absolutely necessary to maintain a minimal weight for their ages and heights. Often, they starve themselves to the point where they become dangerously emaciated. By and large, anorexia nervosa develops in early to late adolescence, between the ages of 12 and 18, although earlier and later onsets are sometimes found.

The clinical features listed in Table 11.1 are used to diagnose anorexia nervosa. Although reduced body weight is the most obvious sign, the most prominent clinical feature is an intense fear of obesity. One common pattern of anorexia begins after menarche when the girl notices added weight and insists it must come off. The addition of body fat is normal in adolescent females: in an evolutionary sense, fat is added in preparation for childbearing and nursing (Angier, 1999). But anorexic women seek to rid their bodies of any additional weight and so turn to extreme dieting and, often, excessive exercise. These efforts continue unabated after the initial weight-loss goal is achieved, however—even after their families and others express concern. Another common pattern occurs among young women when they leave home to attend college and encounter difficulties ad-

TABLE 11.1 Diagnostic Features of Anorexia Nervosa

A. Refusal to maintain weight at or above the minimal normal weight for one's age and height; for example, a weight more than 15% below normal.

B. Strong fear of putting on weight or becoming fat, despite being thin.

C. A distorted body image in which one's body—or part of one's body—is perceived as fat, although others perceive the person as thin.

D. In case of females who have had menarche, absence of three or more consecutive menstrual periods.

Source. Adapted from the *DSM-IV-TR* (APA, 2000).

justing to the demands of college life and independent living. Anorexia is also more common among young women involved in ballet or modeling in which there is often a strong emphasis on maintaining an unrealistically thin body shape.

Although anorexia in women is far more common than in men, an increasing number of young men are presenting with anorexia. Many are involved in sporting activities, such as wrestling, in which they have experienced pressure to maintain a lower weight classification.

Adolescent girls and women with anorexia almost always deny that they are losing too much weight or wasting away. They may argue that their ability to engage in stressful exercise demonstrates their fitness. Women with eating disorders are more likely than normal women to view themselves as heavier than they are (Horne, Van Vactor, & Emerson, 1991). Others may see them as nothing but "skin and bones," but anorexic women have a distorted body image and may still see themselves as too fat. Although they literally starve themselves, they may spend much of the day thinking and talking about food, and even preparing elaborate meals for others (Rock & Curran-Celentano, 1996).

How do I see myself? A distorted body image is a key component of eating disorders.

Subtypes of Anorexia There are two general subtypes of anorexia, a *binge-eating/ purging type* and a *restrictive type.* The first type is characterized by frequent episodes of binge eating and purging; the second type is not. Although repeated cycles of binge eating and purging occur in bulimia, bulimic individuals do not reduce their weight to anorexic levels. The distinction between the subtypes of anorexia is supported by differences in personality patterns. Individuals with the eating/purging type tend to have problems relating to impulse control, which in addition to binge-eating episodes may involve substance abuse or stealing (Garner, 1993). They tend to alternate between periods of rigid control and impulsive behavior. Those with the restrictive type tend to rigidly, even obsessively, control their diet and appearance.

VIDEO 11.2
Anorexia:
The Case of Tamora

Medical Complications of Anorexia Anorexia can lead to serious medical complications that in extreme cases can be fatal. Losses of as much as 35% of body weight may occur and anemia may develop. Females suffering from anorexia are also likely to encounter dermatological problems such as dry, cracking skin; fine, downy hair; even a yellowish discoloration that may persist for years after weight is regained. Cardiovascular complications include heart irregularities, hypotension (low blood pressure), and associated dizziness upon standing, sometimes causing blackouts. Decreased food ingestion can cause gastrointestinal problems such as constipation, abdominal pain, and obstruction or paralysis of the bowels or intestines. Menstrual irregularities are common, and **amenorrhea** (absence or suppression of menstruation) is part of the clinical definition of anorexia in females. Muscular weakness and abnormal growth of bones may occur, causing loss of height and **osteoporosis.**

The death rate from anorexia is estimated at 5% to 8% over a 10-year period, with most deaths due to suicide or medical complications associated with severe weight loss (Goleman, 1995g).

Truth OR Fiction? REVISITED

Though others see them as but "skin and bones," young women with anorexia nervosa still see themselves as too fat.

TRUE. Others may see them as nothing but "skin and bones," but anorexic women have a distorted body image and may still see themselves as too fat.

amenorrhea Absence of menstruation.

osteoporosis A physical disorder caused by calcium deficiency and characterized by brittle bones.

Bingeing. People with bulimia nervosa may cram thousands of calories during a single binge and then attempt to purge what they have consumed by forcing themselves to vomit.

Bulimia Nervosa

The Case of Nicole

Nicole has only opened her eyes, but already she wishes it was time for bed. She dreads going through the day, which threatens to turn out like so many other days of her recent past. Each morning she wonders, is this the day that she will be able to get by without being obsessed by thoughts of food? Or will she "blow it again" and spend the day gorging herself? Today is the day she will get off to a new start, she promises herself. Today she will begin to live like a normal person. Yet she is not convinced that it is really up to her.

Nicole starts the day with eggs and toast. Then she goes to work on cookies; doughnuts; bagels smothered with butter, cream cheese, and jelly; granola; candy bars; and bowls of cereal and milk—all within 45 minutes. Then she cannot take in any more food and turns her attention to purging what she has eaten. She goes to the bathroom, ties back her hair, turns on the shower to mask any noise she will make, drinks a glass of water, and makes herself vomit. Afterward she vows, "Starting tomorrow, I'm going to change." But she suspects that tomorrow may be just another chapter of the same story.

—Adapted from Boskind-White & White, 1983, p. 29

■

TABLE 11.2 Diagnostic Features of Bulimia Nervosa

A. Recurrent episodes of binge eating (gorging) as shown by both:
  (1) Eating an unusually high quantity of food during a 2-hour period, and
  (2) Sense of loss of control over food intake during the episode.

B. Regular inappropriate behavior to prevent weight gain such as self-induced vomiting, abuse of laxatives, diuretics or enemas, or by fasting or excessive exercise.

C. A minimum average of two episodes a week of binge eating and inappropriate compensatory behavior to prevent weight gain over a period of at least 3 months.

D. Persistent overconcern with the shape and weight of one's body.

Source. Adapted from the *DSM-IV* (APA, 2000).

Nicole suffers from bulimia nervosa. *Bulimia* derives from the Greek roots *bous,* meaning "ox" or "cow," and *limos,* meaning "hunger." The unpretty picture inspired by the origin of the term is one of continuous eating, like a cow chewing its cud. Bulimia nervosa is an eating disorder characterized by recurrent episodes of gorging on large quantities of food, followed by use of inappropriate ways to prevent weight gain. These may include purging by means of self-induced vomiting; use of laxatives, diuretics, or enemas; or fasting or engaging in excessive exercise (see Table 11.2). A woman with bulimia may use two or more strategies for purging, such as vomiting and laxatives (Tobin, Johnson, & Dennis, 1992). Although people with anorexia are extremely thin, bulimic individuals are usually of normal weight. However, they have an excessive concern about their shapes and weight.

Bulimic individuals typically gag themselves to induce vomiting. Most attempt to conceal their behavior. Fear of gaining weight is a constant factor. Although an overconcern with body shape and weight is a cardinal feature of bulimia and anorexia, bulimic individuals do not pursue the extreme thinness characteristic of anorexia. Their ideal weights are similar to those of women who do not suffer from eating disorders.

The binge itself usually occurs in secret, most commonly at home during unstructured afternoon or evening hours (Drewnowski, 1997; Guertin, 1999). A binge typically lasts from 30 to 60 minutes and involves consumption of forbidden foods that are generally sweet and rich in fat. Binge eaters typically feel they lack control over their bingeing and may consume 5,000 to 10,000 calories at a sitting. One young woman described eating everything available in the refrigerator, even to the point of scooping out margarine from its container with her finger. The episode continues until the binger is spent or exhausted, suffers painful stomach distension, induces vomiting, or runs out of food. Drowsiness, guilt, and depression usually ensue, but bingeing is initially pleasant because of release from dietary constraints.

The average age for onset of bulimia is the late teens, when concerns about dieting and dissatisfaction with bodily shape or weight are at their height. Bulimia nervosa typically affects (non-Hispanic) White women in late adolescence or early adulthood (APA,

2000). Despite the widespread belief that eating disorders, especially anorexia nervosa, are more common among affluent people, the available evidence shows no strong linkage between socioeconomic status and eating disorders (Wakeling, 1996). Beliefs that eating disorders are associated with high socioeconomic status may reflect the tendency for affluent patients to obtain treatment. Alternatively, it may be that the social pressures on young women to strive to achieve an ultrathin ideal have now generalized across all socioeconomic levels.

Medical Complications of Bulimia Bulimia is also associated with many medical complications. Many of these stem from repeated vomiting. There may be irritations of the skin around the mouth due to frequent contact with stomach acid, blockage of salivary ducts, decay of tooth enamel, and dental cavities. The acid from the vomit may damage taste receptors on the palate, making the person less sensitive to the taste of vomit with repeated purgings (Rodin et al., 1990). Decreased sensitivity to the aversive taste of vomit may play a role in maintaining the purging behavior. Cycles of bingeing and vomiting may cause abdominal pain, hiatal hernia, and other abdominal complaints. Stress on the pancreas may produce pancreatitis (inflammation), which is a medical emergency. Disturbed menstrual function is found in as many as 50% of normal weight women with bulimia (Weltzin et al., 1994). Excessive use of laxatives may cause bloody diarrhea and laxative dependency, so the person cannot have normal bowel movements without laxatives. In extreme cases, the bowel can lose its reflexive eliminatory response to pressure from waste material. Bingeing on large quantities of salty food may cause convulsions and swelling. Repeated vomiting or abuse of laxatives can lead to potassium deficiency, producing muscular weakness, cardiac irregularities, even sudden death—especially when diuretics are used. As with anorexia, menstruation may come to a halt.

THINK ABOUT IT
Why do you think that people with anorexia and bulimia continue their destructive behaviors in spite of the medical complications of these conditions?

VIDEO 11.3
Bulimia: *The Case of Ann*

Causes of Anorexia and Bulimia

Like other psychological disorders, anorexia and bulimia involve a complex interplay of factors. But most significant of all are the social pressures felt by young women that lead them to base their self-worth on their physical appearance, especially their weight.

Sociocultural Factors Sociocultural theorists point to societal pressures and expectations placed on young women in our society as contributing to the development of eating disorders (Bemporad, 1996; Stice, 1994). The pressure to achieve an unrealistic standard of thinness, combined with the importance attached to appearance in defining the female role in our society, can lead young women to become dissatisfied with their bodies (Stice, 2001). Even in children as young as eight, girls express more dissatisfaction with their bodies than do boys (Ricciardelli & McCabe, 2001). Body dissatisfaction in young women may lead to excessive dieting and to the development of disturbed eating behaviors. The idealization of thinness in women can be illustrated in the changes in the body mass index (BMI) of winners of the Miss America pageant (Rubinstein & Caballero, 2000) (see Figure 11.1). Body mass index is a measure of height-adjusted weight.

The pressure to be thin falls most heavily on women. This pressure is so prevalent that dieting has become the normative pattern of eating among young

To be like Barbie. The Barbie doll has long represented a symbol of the buxom but thin feminine form that has become idealized in our culture. If women were to be proportioned like the classic Barbie doll, they would resemble the woman in the photograph on the right. To achieve this idealized form, the average woman would need to grow nearly a foot in height, reduce her waist by 5 inches, and add 4 inches to her bustline. What message do you think the Barbie-doll figure conveys to young girls?

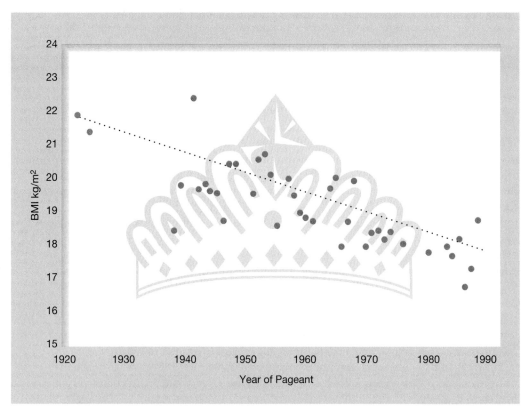

FIGURE 11.1 Thinner and Thinner.
Note the downward trend in the body mass index levels (BMIs) of Miss America contest winners over time. What might these data suggest about changes in society's view of the ideal female form?
Source. Rubinstein & Caballero (2000).

Truth OR Fiction? REVISITED

Dieting represents an abnormal eating pattern among American women.

FALSE. Dieting is so pervasive that it has essentially become a normative pattern of eating among American women.

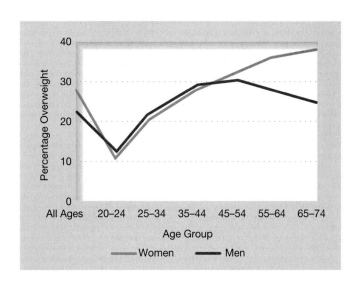

FIGURE 11.2 Prevalence of overweight by gender and age.
Source. National Heart, Lung, and Blood Institute (NHLBI), National Institutes of Health. (1993, March). *Data fact sheet: Obesity and cardiovascular disease.* Bethesda, MD: Author.

American women. Four of five young women in the United States have gone on a diet by the time they reach their 18th birthdays. In actuality, the gender gap in obesity is quite small—27% of women versus 24% of men (see Figure 11.2). Moreover, gender differences in obesity do not arise until midlife.

In support of the sociocultural model, evidence shows that eating disorders are less common, even rare, in non-Western countries (Stice, 1994; Wakeling, 1996). Even in Western cultures, eating disorders are more prevalent in the weight-obsessed United States than in other Western countries for which data is available, such as Greece and Spain, or in the most technologically advanced nation in the Far East, Japan (Stice, 1994). Rates of disordered eating behaviors and eating disorders also vary in the United States among ethnic groups, with higher rates in Euro American adolescents than in African American and other ethnic minority adolescents (Leon et al., 1995; Stice, 1994). One likely reason for this discrepancy is that body image and body dissatisfaction are less closely tied to body weight among minority women (Angier, 2000b). Yet disordered eating behaviors that may give rise to eating disorders are more common among African American women who identify more closely with the dominant White culture (Abrams, Allen, & Gray, 1993). Disturbed eating behaviors may also be more common among Native American adolescents than is commonly believed (Smith & Krejci, 1991). Investigators also caution that body dissatisfaction may be more prevalent among Hispanic and Asian girls than is generally recognized and may set the stage for distorted eating behaviors in these groups (Robinson et al., 1996). There are also signs that eating disorders may increase in the future in developing countries (Grange, Telch, & Tibbs, 1998).

Psychosocial Factors Although cultural pressures to conform to an ultrathin female ideal play a major role in eating disorders, the great majority of young women exposed to these pressures do not develop eating disorders. Other factors must be involved. One likely factor with bulimia at least is a history of rigid dieting (Patton et al., 1999; Rock & Curran-Celentano, 1996). Women with bulimia typically engage in extreme dieting characterized by very strict rules about what they can eat, how much they can eat, and how often they can eat (Drewnowski et al., 1994). Not surprisingly, they tend to spend more time thinking about their weight than do nonbulimic women (Zotter & Crowther, 1991).

Bulimic women tend to have been slightly overweight preceding the development of bulimia, and the initiation of the binge-purge cycle usually follows a period of strict dieting to lose weight. In a typical scenario, the rigid dietary controls fail, which prompts initial bingeing. This sets in motion a chain reaction in which bingeing leads to fear of weight gain, which prompts self-induced vomiting or excessive exercise to reduce any added weight. Some bulimic women become so concerned about possible weight gain that they resort to vomiting after every meal (Lowe, Golaves, & Murphy-Eberenz, 1998). Purging is negatively reinforced because it produces relief, or at least partial relief, from anxiety over gaining weight.

Body dissatisfaction is another important factor in eating disorders (Heatherton et al., 1997). Body dissatisfaction may lead to maladaptive attempts—through self-starvation and purging—to attain a desired body weight or shape. Bulimic and anorexic women tend to be extremely concerned about their body weight and shape (Fairburn et al., 1997). Even many normal weight children express concerns about their weight ("Nutrition, Obesity and Perception," 2001).

Cognitive factors are also involved. Young women with anorexia often have perfectionistic attitudes and high achievement strivings (Halmi et al., 2000). They may get down on themselves whenever they fail to meet their impossibly high standards. Their extreme dieting may give them a sense of control and independence that they may feel they lack in other aspects of their lives (Shafran & Mansell, 2001). Bulimic women tend to be both perfectionistic and dichotomous ("black or white") in their thinking patterns (Fairburn et al., 1997). Thus, they expect themselves to adhere perfectly to their rigid dietary rules and judge themselves as complete failures when they deviate even slightly. They also judge themselves harshly for episodes of binge eating and purging. These cognitive factors influence each other, as illustrated in Figure 11.3. In addition, women with bulimic tendencies

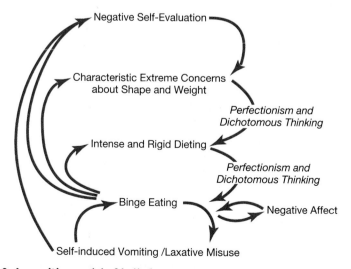

FIGURE 11.3 A cognitive model of bulimia nervosa.

Source. Fairburn, C. G. (1997). Eating disorders. In D. M. Clark & C. G. Fairburn, Eds., *Science and practice of cognitive behaviour therapy.* Oxford: Oxford University Press. Reprinted with permission of Oxford University Press.

tend to have a dysfunctional type of cognitive style that may lead to exaggerated beliefs about the negative consequences of gaining weight (Poulakis & Wertheim, 1993).

Psychodynamically oriented writers believe that girls with anorexia may have difficulties separating from their families and consolidating separate, individuated identities (Bruch, 1973; Minuchin, Rosman, & Baker, 1978). Perhaps anorexia represents the girl's unconscious effort to remain a prepubescent child. By maintaining the veneer of childhood, pubescent girls may avoid dealing with such adult issues as increased independence and separation from their families, sexual maturation, and assumption of personal responsibilities.

Some learning theorists view anorexia as a type of weight phobia. Excessive, irrational fears of putting on weight may reflect the tendencies in our culture to idealize the slender female form. Learning theorists also suggest that purging may be a type of compulsive ritual reinforced by the reduction of the fear of gaining weight that follows a binge-eating episode, just as compulsive hand washing in people with obsessive-compulsive may be reinforced by relief from disorder anxiety induced by obsessive thoughts.

A number of investigators have linked bulimia to problems in interpersonal relationships. Bulimic women tend to be shy and to have few if any close friends (Fairburn et al., 1997). One study of 21 college women with bulimia and a matched control group of 21 nonbulimic women found that those with bulimia had more social problems. They believed that less social support was available to them and reported more social conflict, especially with family members (Grissett & Norvell, 1992). They also rated themselves, and were judged by others, as less socially skillful than the control group. Although causal links between a lack of social skills and eating disorders remain to be elaborated, it is possible that enhancing the social skills of women with bulimia may increase the quality of their relationships and perhaps reduce their tendencies to use food in maladaptive ways.

Young women with bulimia also tend to have more emotional problems and lower self-esteem than other dieters (Fairburn et al., 1997). Bulimia often occurs together with many kinds of psychological disorders, including alcoholism, major depression, and anxiety disorders such as panic disorder, phobia, and generalized anxiety disorder (Kendler et al., 1991). Perhaps some forms of binge eating involve attempts at coping with emotional distress (Sherwood et al., 2000). Unfortunately, cycles of bingeing and purging serve to exacerbate emotional problems rather than relieve them. Bulimic women are also more likely than other women to have experienced childhood sexual and physical abuse (Kent & Waller, 2000; Wonderlich et al., 1997). Bulimia may develop in some cases as an ineffective means of coping with abuse.

What we have gained from this research is the understanding that bulimia often develops within a context of extreme, rigid dieting overlaying interpersonal, emotional, and cognitive factors.

Family Factors Eating disorders frequently develop against a backdrop of family conflicts (Fairburn et al., 1997; Wonderlich et al., 1997). Some theorists focus on the brutal effect of self-starvation on parents. They suggest that some adolescents use refusal to eat to punish their parents for feelings of loneliness and alienation they experience in the home. One related study compared the mothers of adolescent girls with eating disorders to the mothers of other girls. Mothers of the adolescents with eating disorders were more likely to be unhappy about their families' functioning, to have their own problems with eating and dieting, to believe their daughters ought to lose weight, and to regard their daughters as unattractive (Pike & Rodin, 1991). Is binge eating, as suggested by Humphrey (1986), a metaphoric effort to gain the nurturance and comfort that the mother is denying her daughter? Does purging represent the symbolic upheaval of negative feelings toward the family?

Families of young women with eating disorders tend to be more often conflicted, less cohesive and nurturing, yet more overprotective and critical than those of reference groups (Fairburn et al., 1997). The parents seem less capable of promoting independence in their

Questionnaire

The Fear of Fat Scale

 The fear of becoming fat is a prime factor underlying eating disorders like anorexia and bulimia. The Goldfarb Fear of Fat scale (Goldfarb, Dykens, & Gerrard, 1985) measures the degree to which people fear becoming fat. The scale may help identify individuals at risk of developing eating disorders. It differentiates between anorexic and normal women, and between bulimic and nonbulimic women. Dieters, however, also score higher on the scale than nondieters.

To complete the Fear of Fat scale, read each of the following statements and write in the number that best represents your own feelings and beliefs. Then check the key at the end of the chapter.

1 = very untrue
2 = somewhat untrue
3 = somewhat true
4 = very true

_____ **1.** My biggest fear is of becoming fat.
_____ **2.** I am afraid to gain even a little weight.

_____ **3.** I believe there is a real risk that I will become overweight someday.

_____ **4.** I don't understand how overweight people can live with themselves.

_____ **5.** Becoming fat would be the worst thing that could happen to me.

_____ **6.** If I stopped concentrating on controlling my weight, chances are I would become very fat.

_____ **7.** There is nothing that I can do to make the thought of gaining weight less painful and frightening.

_____ **8.** I feel like all my energy goes into controlling my weight.

_____ **9.** If I can eat even a little, I may lose control and not stop eating.

_____ **10.** Staying hungry is the only way I can guard against losing control and becoming fat.

Source. Goldfarb, L. A., Dykens, E. M., & Gerrard, M. (1985). The Goldfarb Fear of Fat scale. *Journal of Personality Assessment, 49,* 329–332. Reprinted with permission.

---

daughters. Conflicts with parents over issues of autonomy are often implicated in the development of both anorexia nervosa and bulimia (Ratti, Humphrey, & Lyons, 1996). Yet it remains uncertain whether these family patterns contribute to the initiation of eating disorders or whether eating disorders go on to disrupt family life. The truth probably lies in an interaction between the two.

From the **systems perspective,** families are systems that regulate themselves in ways that minimize the open expression of conflict and reduce the immediate need for overt change. Within this perspective, girls who develop anorexia may be seen as helping maintain the shaky balances and harmonies found in dysfunctional families by displacing attention from family conflicts and marital tensions onto themselves (Minuchin et al., 1978). The girl may become the *identified patient,* although the family unit is actually dysfunctional.

Regardless of the factors that initiate eating disorders, social reinforcers may maintain them. Children with eating disorders may quickly become the focus of attention of their families, and receive attention from their parents that might otherwise be lacking.

Biological Factors Scientists suspect that abnormalities in brain mechanisms controlling hunger and satiety are involved in bulimia, most probably involving the brain chemical serotonin (Goode, 2000a). Serotonin plays a key role in regulating mood and appetite, especially appetite for carbohydrates. Low levels of the chemical, or lack of sensitivity of serotonin receptors in the brain, may prompt binge-eating episodes, especially carbohydrate bingeing (Levitan et al., 1997). This line of thinking is buttressed by evidence that antidepressants, such as Prozac, which increases serotonin activity, can decrease binge-eating episodes in bulimic women (Jimerson et al., 1997). We also know that many women with eating disorders are depressed or have a history of depression, and imbalances of serotonin are implicated in depressive disorders.

THINK ABOUT IT
How do sociocultural and psychosocial issues interact to cause eating disorders? How might we as a society change the social influences that lead many young women to develop disordered eating habits?

Truth OR Fiction? REVISITED

Drugs used to treat depression may also help curb bulimic binges.

TRUE. Antidepressants have been shown to be helpful in curbing binge eating among bulimic women.

systems perspective The view that problems reflect the systems (family, social, school, ecological, etc.) in which they occur.

Evidence also points to a role for genetic factors in eating disorders (Wade et al., 2000). Eating disorders also tend to run in families, which is suggestive of a genetic component (Goode, 2000a). Stronger evidence comes from a study of more than 2,000 female twins, which showed a much higher concordance rate for bulimia, 23% versus 9%, among monozygotic (MZ) twins than dizygotic (DZ) twins (Kendler et al., 1991). A greater concordance for anorexia was also found among MZ than DZ twins, 50% versus 5% (Holland, Sicotte, & Treasure, 1988). Nonetheless, genetic factors cannot fully account for the development of eating disorders. Perhaps in the manner of the diathesis-stress model, a genetic predisposition involving a dysfunction of neurotransmitter activity interacts with family, social, cultural, and environmental pressures in leading to the development of eating disorders (Strober & Humphrey, 1987).

Treatment of Anorexia Nervosa and Bulimia Nervosa

Eating disorders are difficult to treat. People with anorexia may be hospitalized, especially when weight loss is severe or body weight is falling rapidly. In the hospital they are usually placed on a closely monitored refeeding regimen. Behavior therapy is also commonly used, with rewards made contingent on adherence to the refeeding protocol (Rock & Curran-Celentano, 1996). Commonly used reinforcers include ward privileges and social opportunities.

Web Link **11.2** wWw
Prevention of Eating Disorders

Psychodynamic therapy is sometimes combined with behavior therapy to probe for deeper psychological conflicts. Family therapy may also be employed to help resolve underlying family conflicts. Behavior therapy has been shown to be effective in promoting weight gain of anorexic patients during hospitalization (Johnson, Tsoh, & Varnado, 1996). Individual or family therapy following hospitalization has also shown favorable long-term benefits (Eisler et al., 1997). Hospitalization may be helpful in breaking the binge-purge cycle in bulimia, but appears to be necessary only where eating behaviors are clearly out of control and outpatient treatment has failed, or where there is evidence of severe medical complications, suicidal thoughts or attempts, or substance abuse.

Cognitive-behavioral therapy (CBT) is useful in helping bulimic individuals challenge self-defeating thoughts and beliefs, such as unrealistic, perfectionistic expectations regarding dieting and body weight. Another common dysfunctional thinking pattern is dichotomous (all-or-nothing) thinking that predisposes them to purge when they slip even a little from their rigid diets. CBT also challenges tendencies to overemphasize appearance in determining self-worth. To eliminate self-induced vomiting, therapists may use the behavioral technique of *exposure with response prevention* that was developed for treatment of people with obsessive-compulsive disorder. In this technique, the bulimic patient is exposed to eating forbidden foods while the therapist stands by to prevent vomiting until the urge to purge passes. Bulimic individuals thus learn to tolerate violations of their dietary rules without resorting to purging. Cognitive-behavioral therapy (CBT) has been shown to reduce binge-eating and purging episodes in people with bulimia (Agras et al., 2000a; Anderson & Maloney, 2001; Goode, 2000a; Tuschen-Caffier, Pook, & Frank, 2001). Another form of psychotherapy, interpersonal therapy (IPT), has also been used effectively in treating bulimia. Interpersonal therapy focuses on resolving interpersonal problems in the belief that more effective interpersonal functioning will lead to healthier food habits and attitudes. Although IPT did not produce as good results as CBT in a recent trial (Agras et al., 2000b), it may be used as an alternative treatment in cases where CBT proves unsuccessful (Wilson & Fairburn, 1998).

Antidepressant drugs have also shown therapeutic benefits in treating bulimia (Goode, 2000a; Wilson & Fairburn, 1998). They are believed to work by decreasing the urge to binge through normalizing serotonin—the brain chemical involved in regulating appetite. Antidepressant medication, especially Prozac, also appears promising in treating anorexia, perhaps because it helps relieve underlying depression (Johnson, Tsoh, & Varnado, 1996).

A review of the available evidence suggests that cognitive-behavioral therapy is more effective than antidepressant medication in treating bulimia nervosa and carries a lower rate of relapse (Johnson, Tsoh, & Varnado, 1996; Wilson & Fairburn, 1998). CBT may be considered a treatment of first choice for bulimia, followed by the use of antidepressant medication if psychological treatment is not successful (Compas et al., 1997). In a recent study, antidepressant medication showed therapeutic benefits in treating patients who had failed to respond to cognitive-behavioral treatment (Walsh et al., 2000). Studies examining whether a combination CBT/medication treatment approach is more effective than either treatment component alone have thus far produced inconsistent results (Johnson, Tsoh, & Varnado, 1996; Walsh et al., 1997).

Although progress has been made in treating eating disorders, there is considerable room for improvement. Even in CBT, about half of treated patients show continued evidence of bulimic behavior (Compas et al., 1997; Wilson & Fairburn, 1998). Eating disorders can be tenacious and enduring problems, especially when excessive fears of body weight and distortions in body image continue beyond active treatment. A recent study reported that 10 years after an initial presentation with bulimia, approximately 30% of women still showed recurrent binge-eating or purging behaviors (Keel et al., 1999). Recovery from anorexia also tends to be a long process. A recent study of 88 German patients with anorexia showed that 50% of the patients did not recover sooner than 6 years after their first hospitalization (Herzog, Schellberg, & Deter, 1997).

Difficulties in treating eating disorders only buttresses the need for effective prevention programs that target young women at risk. Recently, investigators showed positive results from an Internet-based intervention that focused on changing disordered eating behaviors and attitudes and reducing body dissatisfaction in a sample of college women (Celio et al., 2000). The intervention had a significant impact on reducing risk factors for eating disorders (i.e., disordered attitudes and behaviors) as compared to a waiting list control condition.

Binge-Eating Disorder

People with **binge-eating disorder (BED)** have recurrent eating binges but do not purge themselves of the excess food afterwards. Binge-eating disorder is classified in the *DSM* manual as a potential disorder requiring further study. We presently know too little about the characteristics of people with BED to warrant its inclusion as an official diagnostic category. The criteria used for diagnosing the disorder also need further evaluation. Presently, persons who qualify for the diagnosis show evidence of bingeing at least 2 days a week for a period of 3 months (Stotland, 2000). During a binge, they continue to eat despite feeling uncomfortably full. They are embarrassed to be seen during a binge and feel guilty afterwards.

The available evidence indicates that unlike bulimia, BED is more commonly found among obese individuals (Spitzer et al., 1992). It is believed to affect about 2% of the population (Goode, 2000a). BED is frequently associated with depression and with a history of unsuccessful attempts at losing excess weight and keeping it off. People with BED tend to be older than those with anorexia or bulimia (Arnow, Kenardy, & Agras, 1992). Like other eating disorders, it is found more frequently among women.

People with BED are often described as "compulsive overeaters." During a binge they feel a loss of control over their eating. BED may fall within a broader domain of compulsive behaviors characterized by impaired control over maladaptive behaviors, such as pathological gambling and substance abuse disorders. A history of dieting may play a role in some cases of BED, although it appears to be a less important factor in BED than in bulimia (Howard & Porzelius, 1999).

Cognitive-behavioral techniques have shown positive effects in treating binge-eating disorder (Wilson & Fairburn, 1998). Antidepressants, especially antidepressants of the SSRI family, may also reduce the frequency of binge-eating episodes by helping regulate serotonin levels in the brain (McElroy et al., 2000; Stotland, 2000).

binge-eating disorder (BED) A disorder characterized by recurrent eating binges without purging; classified as a potential disorder requiring further study.

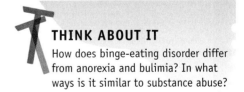

THINK ABOUT IT
Do you know anyone who has suffered from an eating disorder? What factors discussed in the text might help you to better understand the causes of the person's problem?

THINK ABOUT IT
How does binge-eating disorder differ from anorexia and bulimia? In what ways is it similar to substance abuse?

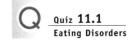

Quiz **11.1**
Eating Disorders

Overview of Eating Disorders

TYPES OF EATING DISORDERS

	Description	Features
Anorexia Nervosa	Self-starvation, resulting in a minimal weight for one's age and height or dangerously unhealthy weight	• Strong fears of gaining weight or becoming fat • Distorted self-image (perceiving oneself as fat despite extreme thinness) • Two general subtypes: binge-eating/purging type and restrictive type • Potentially serious, even fatal medical complications • Typically affects young, Euro-American women
Bulimia Nervosa	Recurrent episodes of binge eating followed by purging	• Weight is usually maintained within a normal range • Overconcern about body shape and weight • Binge-purge episodes may result in serious medical complications • Typically affects young, Euro-American women
Binge-Eating Disorder (a proposed disorder requiring further study)	Recurrent binge eating without compensatory purging	• Individuals with BED frequently are described as compulsive overeaters • Typically affects obese women who are older than those affected by anorexia or bulimia

CAUSAL FACTORS An interplay of multiple factors are at work in eating disorders

Sociocultural Factors	• Excessive pressures on young women to adhere to unrealistic standards of thinness
Psychological Factors	• Rigid or highly restrictive dieting may set the stage for loss of control following dietary transgressions, resulting in bulimic binges • Body dissatisfaction may prompt unhealthy ways of achieving desired body weight • Perceived lack of control over other aspects of life apart from dieting • Difficulties separating from one's family and establishing an individuated identity • Psychological needs for perfectionism and tendencies to think in dichotomous or black-and-white terms
Family Factors	• Families of eating disorder patients are often characterized by conflict, lack of cohesion and nurturing, and failure to foster independence and autonomy in their daughters • From a family systems perspective, a daughter's eating disorder may serve to maintain a shaky balance within a dysfunctional family by diverting attention away from family or marital problems
Biological Factors	• Possible imbalances in neurotransmitter systems in the brain regulating mood and appetite • Possible genetic influences

TREATMENT APPROACHES Often difficult to treat but a range of therapeutic approaches is available

Biomedical Treatment	• Hospitalization may be needed to help anorexic patients restore a healthy body weight or bulimic patients break binge-purge cycles in cases where outpatient therapy has failed • Antidepressant medication may be used to regulate appetite by altering brain chemistry or to relieve underlying depression
Psychotherapy	• Psychodynamic therapy aims at exploring and resolving underlying psychological conflicts
Cognitive-Behavioral Therapy	• To help individuals with an eating disorder challenge self-defeating thoughts and beliefs and develop healthier eating habits and thinking patterns • Behavior modification helps hospitalized anorexic patients regain weight by means of linking desired rewards to appropriate eating behaviors • Exposure with response prevention helps bulimic individuals tolerate eating forbidden foods without bingeing and purging
Family Therapy	• May be used to resolve family conflicts and improve communication among family members

Obesity: A National Epidemic

obesity A condition of excess body fat; generally defined by a BMI above 30.

Obesity has become a national epidemic. Consider some statistics:

- More Americans are overweight today than at any time since the government started tracking obesity in the 1960s. According to recent estimates, 61% of American adults are overweight and more than a quarter (26%) are obese ("CDC Says," 2000). The prevalence of obesity in the United States skyrocketed by about 50% during the 1990s (Mokdad et al., 1999, 2000).

- Obesity in children and adolescents is also on the upswing. About one in three children are overweight or at risk of becoming overweight (Cowley, 2000a). Obese children stand a better than 75% chance of becoming obese adults (Begley, 2000).

- Americans consume 815 billion calories of food each day, which is 200 billion calories more than necessary to maintain their weight at moderate levels of activity (C. D. Jenkins, 1988). The extra calories are enough to sustain a country of 80 million people.

- Some 65 million Americans diet every year and use nearly 30,000 approaches (Blumenthal, 1988). As many as one in four Americans are on a diet on any given day (French & Jeffery, 1994).

- More than 90% of dieters fail to keep pounds off permanently (Wilson, 1994). Whether they drop 15 pounds or 50, most dieters put almost all the pounds back on within a year (Brody, 1992a).

Despite all the money and effort spent on weight-loss products and programs, our collective waistlines are getting larger—a result, government health experts believe, of consuming too many calories and exercising too little ("CDC Says," 2000). The increased use of laborsaving devices (driving more, walking less) eventually translates into added inches to our waistlines (Bouchard, 1997). We are fast becoming a nation of couch potatoes and cyberslugs who are glued to the TV or computer screen (*"Did someone say supersize it?"*).

Obesity is classified as a chronic medical disorder, not a psychological disorder (Atkinson, 1997). It is also a major risk factor in such chronic, potentially life-threatening diseases as heart disease, diabetes, and some forms of cancer (Devlin, Yanovski, & Wilson, 2000; "Diabetes," 2001; Michaud et al., 2001; Pinel, Assanand, & Lehman, 2000; "Third of Some Cancers," 2001). Experts estimate that 300,000 people in the United States die prematurely because of obesity-linked diseases (Mokdad et al., 2000; Must et al., 1999). Though obesity is a medical condition, it involves psychological factors in both its development and treatment. This reminds us of the complex interrelationships between the mind and body.

Are You Obese?

The most widely used standard for determining obesity is the body mass index, or BMI. The BMI takes into account a person's body weight and height. It is calculated by dividing body weight (in kilograms) by the square of the person's height (in meters).

The National Institutes of Health has set a level of 25 as the cutoff for determining whether a person is overweight (see Figure 11.4) (Brody, 1998; Shapiro, 1998). This level is associated with a weight level about 20% above the recommended weight for a person's age and height. People in the range of 25 to 27 are considered slightly overweight. People with a BMI greater than 30 are considered obese.

What Causes Obesity?

What causes obesity? Body weight varies as a function of energy balance. When caloric intake exceeds energy output, the excess calories are stored in the body in the form of fat, leading to obesity (Esparza et al., 2000). The key to preventing obesity is to bring energy expenditure in line with energy (caloric) intake. Unfortunately, this is easier said than done.

Truth OR Fiction?   REVISITED

The excess calories consumed by Americans each day could feed a country of 80 million people.

TRUE. The excess calories consumed daily by Americans could feed a country of 80 million people. We, however, are paying the penalty of excess caloric intake in the form of obesity.

Truth OR Fiction?   REVISITED

Obesity is one of the most common psychological disorders in the United States.

FALSE. Obesity is a medical disorder, not a psychological disorder.

Hazardous waist. Obesity is indeed a hazard to health and longevity.

The Body Mass Index

Federal health authorities are using this index to determine who is overweight. Under new guidelines, a body mass of **25** or more is considered overweight. To use the table, find the appropriate height in the left-hand column. Move across to a given weight. The number at the top of the column is the BMI at that height and weight. Pounds have been rounded off.

BMI

HEIGHT (inches)	19	20	21	22	23	24	25	26	27	28	29	30	31	32	33	34	35
								Body Weight (pounds)									
58	91	96	100	105	110	115	119	124	129	134	138	143	148	153	158	162	167
59	94	99	104	109	114	119	124	128	133	138	143	148	153	158	163	168	173
60	97	102	107	112	118	123	128	133	138	143	148	153	158	163	168	174	179
61	100	106	111	116	122	127	132	137	143	148	153	158	164	169	174	180	185
62	104	109	115	120	126	131	136	142	147	153	158	164	169	175	180	186	191
63	107	113	118	124	130	135	141	146	152	158	163	169	175	180	186	191	197
64	110	116	122	128	134	140	145	151	157	163	169	174	180	186	192	197	204
65	114	120	126	132	138	144	150	156	162	168	174	180	186	192	198	204	210
66	118	124	130	136	142	148	155	161	167	173	179	186	192	198	204	210	216
67	121	127	134	140	146	153	159	166	172	178	185	191	198	204	211	217	223
68	125	131	138	144	151	158	164	171	177	184	190	197	203	210	216	223	230
69	128	135	142	149	155	162	169	176	182	189	196	203	209	216	223	230	236
70	132	139	146	153	160	167	174	181	188	195	202	209	216	222	229	236	243
71	136	143	150	157	165	172	179	186	193	200	208	215	222	229	236	243	250
72	140	147	154	162	169	177	184	191	199	206	213	221	228	235	242	250	258
73	144	151	159	166	174	182	189	197	204	212	219	227	235	242	250	257	265
74	148	155	163	171	179	186	194	202	210	218	225	233	241	249	256	264	272
75	152	160	168	176	184	192	200	208	216	224	232	240	248	256	264	272	279
76	156	164	172	180	189	197	205	213	221	230	238	246	254	263	271	279	287

FIGURE 11.4 The body mass index.

Source. Adapted from G.A. Bray & D.S. Gray (1998). Obesity. Part I-Pathogenesis. *Western Journal of Medicine, 149,* 429–441. Reprinted from *Clinical guidelines on the identification, evaluation, and treatment of overweight and obesity in adults.* National Heart, Lung, and Blood Institute, 1998, Bethesda, MD.

Research suggests that a number of factors contribute to the imbalance between energy intake and expenditure that underlies obesity, including genetics, metabolic factors, lifestyle factors, and psychological factors.

Genetic Factors We know that obesity clearly runs in families (Bouchard, 1997). It was once assumed that obese parents encouraged their children to become heavy by setting poor examples. A study of Scandinavian adoptees strongly suggests a key role for heredity, however (Stunkard et al., 1986). It revealed that children's weight is more closely related to the weight of their biological parents than to that of their adoptive parents. Perhaps the strongest evidence for the role of genetics comes from a study of identical twins that showed that regard-

Web Link **11.3**
Guidelines on Overweight wWw
and Obesity

less of whether the twins were reared together or apart, they wound up weighing virtually the same when they became adults (Stunkard et al., 1990). Consistent with a genetic explanation, fraternal twins varied much more in body weight (corrected for height) than did MZ twins.

Most experts in the field believe that genetics plays an important role in determining the risk of obesity (Devlin et al., 2000). But genetics doesn't tell the whole story. Obesity experts recognize that both genetics and environmental factors (diet and exercise patterns) contribute to obesity (Wing & Polley, 2001).

Metabolic Factors When we lose weight, especially significant amounts of weight, the body reacts as if it were starving. It responds to falling weight by slowing the **metabolic rate,** the rate at which it burns calories (Kolata, 1995c; Leibel, Rosenbaum, & Hirsch, 1995). This makes it difficult to continue losing more weight or even maintain the weight loss. Some theorists believe that mechanisms in the brain control the body's metabolism to keep body weight around a genetically determined **set point** (Keesey, 1980). You may be able to offset this metabolic adjustment by following a more vigorous exercise regimen. Vigorous exercise burns calories directly and may increase the metabolic rate by replacing fat tissue with muscle, especially if the exercise program involves weight-bearing activity. Also, ounce for ounce, muscle burns more calories than fat. Before starting an exercise regimen, check with your physician to determine which types of activity are best suited to your overall health condition.

Fat Cells The efforts of heavy people to keep a slender profile may be sabotaged by cells within their own bodies termed **fat cells.** No, fat cells are not cells that are fat. They are cells that store fat. Fat cells comprise fatty tissue in the body (also called *adipose tissue*). Obese people have more fat cells (Brownell & Wadden, 1992) than people who are not obese. Severely obese people may have some 200 billion fat cells, as compared to 25 or 30 billion in normal weight individuals. Why does this matter? As time passes after eating, the blood sugar level declines, drawing out fat from these cells to supply more nourishment to the body. The hypothalamus in the brain detects the depletion of fat in these cells. The hypothalamus then signals the cerebral cortex, triggering the hunger drive, which motivates eating and thereby replenishes the fat cells.

People with more fatty tissue send more signals of fat depletion to the brain than people who are equal in weight but who have fewer fat cells. As a result, they feel food deprived sooner. Sad to say, dieters do not expel fat cells; instead, they shrink them. Many dieters who are markedly obese, even successful dieters, thus complain they are constantly hungry as they struggle to maintain normal weights. People with high levels of adipose tissue are doubly beset, because fatty tissue metabolizes food more slowly than muscle.

How is the number of fat cells in our bodies determined? Unfortunately, heredity seems to play a role. Excessive food intake in early childhood may also have an influence, however (Brownell & Wadden, 1992).

Lifestyle Factors Obese people are typically less physically active than people of normal weight (Brownell & Wadden, 1992; "The Sedentary Society," 1996). Although correlational evidence is insufficient to establish causality, it is reasonable to assume that inactivity and overweight may interact with each other. In other words, inactivity may lead to weight gain, and weight gain may in turn lead people to become less active.

Other lifestyle factors, such as adopting a high-fat diet and eating larger portions, also contribute to obesity (Wing & Polley, 2001). Exposure to a constant bombardment of food-related cues in television commercials, print advertising, and the like, may also play a part. Even though evidence does not show obese people to be more sensitive to food cues than normal weight individuals, overresponsivity to these cues can lead to inappropriate food consumption in people of any weight class.

metabolic rate The rate at which energy is used in the body.

set point A value, such as body weight, that the body's regulatory mechanisms attempt to maintain.

fat cells Body cells specialized to store fat.

Truth OR Fiction? REVISITED

When you lose weight, your body starts putting the brakes on the rate at which it burns calories.

TRUE. Unfortunately, the body reacts to falling weight by slowing the metabolic rate, the rate at which it burns calories. This makes it difficult to continue losing weight or even maintain the weight loss.

Truth OR Fiction? REVISITED

Obese people lose fat cells when they diet.

FALSE. So far as we know, people do not lose fat cells as they lose weight.

All in the family? Obesity tends to run in families. The question is, *Why?*

Psychological Factors According to psychodynamic theory, eating is the cardinal oral activity. Psychodynamic theorists believe that people who were fixated in the oral stage by conflicts concerning dependence and independence are likely to regress in times of stress to excessive oral activities such as overeating. Other psychological factors connected with overeating and obesity include low self-esteem, lack of self-efficacy expectancies, family conflicts, and negative emotions. Although the connections between these factors and obesity affect both men and women, women most frequently seek treatment for obesity, largely because of the greater pressures they experience to adhere to social expectations of thinness. Consider the cases of Joan and Terry:

The Case of Joan

Joan was trapped in the yo-yo syndrome, repeatedly dropping 20 pounds, then regaining it. Whenever Joan got stuck at a certain weight plateau, or started to regain weight, her self-esteem plummeted. She'd hear herself muttering, "Who am I kidding? I'm not worthy of being thin. I should just accept being fat."

An incident with her mother revealed how her negative thinking was often triggered. Joan had lost 24 pounds from an original weight of 174 and was beginning to feel good about herself. Most other people reinforced her by complimenting her on her weight loss. She called her mother, who lived in another state, to share the good news. Instead of jumping on the bandwagon, her mother cautioned her not to expect too much from her success. After all, her mother pointed out, she had been repeatedly disappointed in the past. The message came through loud and clear: Don't get your hopes up because you will only be more disappointed in the end. Joan's mother may have only meant to protect Joan from eventual disappointment, but the message she conveyed reinforced the negative view that Joan held of herself: You're a loser. Don't expect too much of yourself. Accept your reality. Don't try to change. You're a hopeless case.

As soon as she hung up the receiver, Joan rushed to the pantry. Without hesitation, she devoured three packages of chocolate chip cookies in a frenzied binge on the stairway. The next day she told her psychologist that the binge had reactivated childhood memories of bingeing on Oreo cookies while hiding in the stairwell.

The Case of Terry

For years Terry's husband had scrutinized every morsel she consumed. "Haven't you had enough?" he would ask derisively. The more he harped on her weight, the more anger she felt, although she did not express her feelings directly. The criticism did not apply only to her weight. She also heard "You're not smart enough . . . Why don't you take better care of yourself? . . . How come you're not sexy?" After years of assault on her self-esteem, Terry petitioned for divorce, convinced the single life could be no worse than her marriage.

While separated and awaiting the final divorce decree, Terry felt free to be herself for the first time in her adult life. However, she had not expected the effect freedom would have on her weight. She ballooned from 155 pounds to 186 pounds within a few months. She identified leftover resentment from her marriage as the driving factor. "There's no one to make me diet anymore," she said. Her overeating was like saying, "See, I can eat if I want to." Without her husband, she could express her anger and outrage toward him by eating to excess. Unfortunately, her mode of expressing anger was self-defeating. Terry's lingering resentment encouraged her to act spitefully rather than constructively.

—From the Authors' Files

Ethnic and Socioeconomic Differences in Obesity

Obesity does not affect ethnic/racial groups in our society in equal proportions. It is more prevalent among people of color, especially among women of color (see Figure 11.5) (National Institutes of Health, 1998, 1999). The question is, why?

Socioeconomic Factors Obesity is more prevalent among poorer people (Stunkard & Sørensen, 1993). Since people of color in our society are as a group lower in socioeconomic status than (non-Hispanic) White Americans, we should not be surprised that rates of obesity are higher among people of color, at least among women of color.

Why are people on the lower rungs of the socioeconomic ladder at greater risk of obesity? For one thing, more affluent people have greater access to information about nutrition and health. They are more likely to take health education courses. They have greater access to health care providers. Poorer people also exercise less regularly than more affluent people do. The fitness boom has been largely limited to more affluent people. They have the time and income to participate in organized fitness programs. Many poor people in the inner city also turn to food as a way of coping with the stresses of poverty, discrimination, crowding, and crime.

Acculturation Though acculturation may help immigrant people adapt more successfully to their new culture, it can become a double-edged sword if it involves adoption of unhealthful dietary practices of the host culture. Consider that Japanese American men living in California and Hawaii eat a higher-fat diet than Japanese men do. Not surprisingly, the prevalence of obesity is two to three times higher among Japanese American men than among men living in Japan (Curb & Marcus, 1991).

Acculturation may also contribute to high rates of obesity among Native Americans, who are more likely than White Americans to have diseases linked to obesity, such as cardiovascular disease and diabetes (Broussard et al., 1991). A study of several hundred Cree and Ojibwa Indians in Canada found that nearly 90% of the women in the 45- to 54-year-old age group were obese (Young & Sevenhuyser, 1989). The adoption of a high-fat Western-style

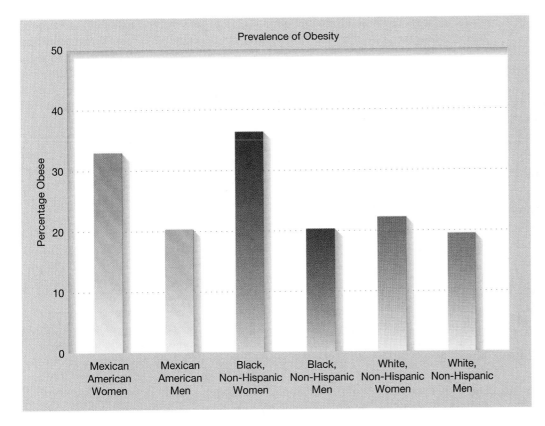

FIGURE 11.5 Rates of obesity (age 20 or higher).
This figure shows the rates of obesity among U.S. adults in relation to race and ethnicity.

Source. National Institutes of Health, National Heart, Lung, and Blood Institute. (1998). *Clinical guidelines on the identification, evaluation, and treatment of overweight and obesity in adults.* Bethesda, MD: Author.

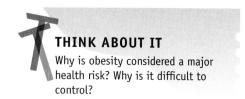

THINK ABOUT IT

Why is obesity considered a major health risk? Why is it difficult to control?

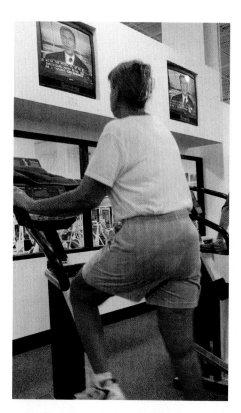

Taking it off and keeping it off. Health experts recognize that losing excess weight and keeping if off requires a lifelong commitment to adopting a sensible diet and engaging in regular exercise.

diet, the destruction of physically demanding native industries, and chronic unemployment combined with low levels of physical activity are cited as factors contributing to obesity among Native Americans in the United States and Canada.

Metabolic Factors Biological factors, such as genetic differences in metabolic rates, may also be involved. Researchers report that Black women had lower resting metabolic rates (rate at which calories or food energy is burned while at rest) than did a sample of White women (Brody, 1997a).

Whatever the underlying reasons accounting for racial/ethnic differences in obesity may be, evidence shows that these differences may be narrowing. Though rates of obesity rose for men and women in all racial/ethnic groups during the 1980s, they rose most sharply among Whites (Burros, 1994; McMurtrie, 1994).

What Can Be Done? Preventing obesity calls for strategies that apply regardless of ethnicity or income level, such as cutting back on fat intake and sugar consumption and adopting regular exercise habits. But certain health initiatives need to be specifically targeted toward the needs of the socially and economically disadvantaged groups, including the following (Jeffery, 1991):

- Increased access to health education;
- Requirements for health education curricula in all public schools;
- Guarantees of universal access to treatment of obesity;
- Increased access to healthful foods and recreational opportunities.

Facing the Challenge of Obesity

The goal of weight-loss programs should be to help people who are overweight achieve and maintain a healthy weight, not a cosmetically desirable weight that is the product of a thinness-obsessed society. Yet, for people who are overweight or obese, various treatment alternatives are available to help them reduce excess weight. Some people turn to diet drugs, but unfortunately the track record for these drugs in the long run is not very encouraging (Winter, 2000). Moreover, they may cause adverse and possibly harmful side effects (Chase, 1998). The problem with drug therapy is that long-term weight management involves lifestyle changes in diet and exercise. Even people whose heredity may work against them can control their weight within some broad limits through adopting a sensible diet, increasing activity and exercise levels, and changing problem eating habits (Brownell & Wadden, 1992; Foster et al., 1997; Ross et al., 2000). A modest weight loss on the order of 10% or 15% of body weight can reduce the health risks associated with obesity (Lane, 1994).

Behavior modification programs focus on helping individuals change problem eating habits by altering the "ABC's" of eating. The A's are the *antecedents* of eating—cues or stimuli that trigger eating. These include environmental stimuli such as the sight and aromas of food, internal stimuli such as sensations of hunger, and emotional states such as anxiety, fatigue, anger, depression, and boredom. Controlling the A's of eating involves redesigning the environment so people are not continuously bombarded by food-related cues.

The B's refer to eating *behaviors* themselves. People who eat too quickly prevent their brains from "catching up" to their stomachs, because it takes about 15 minutes or so for feelings of satiety to register in the brain after food reaches the stomach. Therefore, they do not realize that they are full, and they keep eating. The B's of eating extend to preparatory behaviors such as shopping, food storage habits, and so on.

The C's are the *consequences* of overeating. The immediate pleasure of overeating often overshadows the long-term negative consequences of obesity and risk to health. Food is also connected to other reward systems. Food can become a substitute friend or lover. When people feel depressed, they can lift their spirits with food, if only temporarily. Because food activates the parasympathetic branch of the autonomic nervous system (through digestive processes), food also acts as a natural sedative or tranquilizer, quelling feelings of anxiety or tension and helping people relax or get to sleep. In helping people cope with the C's of eating, behavior therapists make the long-term benefits of sensible eating more immediate. Methods commonly used to address the ABCs of eating are shown in Table 11.3.

Behavior modification leads to modest weight losses that are generally well maintained through at least a year after treatment (Brownell & Wadden, 1992). However, long-term outcomes reveal a dimmer picture (Devlin et al., 2000). As many as 90% to 95% of people who lose weight by dieting or behavior modification return to their baseline weight levels within 5 years (Kolata, 2000a; Wilson, 1994). The problem is that changes in diet, eating habits, and exercise patterns that led to initial weight loss are not carried over into changes in lifestyles that would promote long-term maintenance of weight loss. The lesson here is clear-cut: People seeking to lose excess weight and keep it off need to make a lifelong commitment to following a sensible, calorie-sparing diet and engaging in regular exercise (Brody, 2000; Fogelholm et al., 2000; Kolata, 2000b; Wing & Polley, 2001).

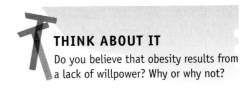

THINK ABOUT IT
Do you believe that obesity results from a lack of willpower? Why or why not?

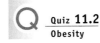

Q **Quiz 11.2**
Obesity

Sleep Disorders

Sleep is a biological function that remains in many ways a mystery. We know that sleep is restorative and that most of us need at least 7 or more hours of sleep a night to function at our best. Yet we cannot identify the specific biochemical changes occurring during sleep that account for its restorative function. We also know that many of us are troubled by sleep problems, although the causes of some of these problems remain obscure. Sleep problems of sufficient severity and frequency that they lead to significant personal distress or impaired functioning in social, occupational, or other roles are classified in the *DSM* system as **sleep disorders.**

Highly specialized diagnostic facilities, called sleep disorders centers, have been established throughout the United States and Canada to provide a more comprehensive assessment of sleep problems than is possible in the typical office setting. People with sleep disorders typically spend a few nights at a sleep center, where they are wired to devices that track their physiological responses during sleep or attempted sleep—brain waves, heart and respiration rates, and so on. This form of assessment is termed **polysomnographic (PSG) recording,** because it involves simultaneous measurement of diverse physiological response patterns, including brain waves, eye movements, muscle movements, and respiration. Information obtained from physiological monitoring of sleep patterns is combined with that obtained from medical and psychological evaluations, subjective reports of sleep disturbance, and sleep diaries (i.e., daily logs compiled by the problem sleeper that track the length of time between retiring to bed and falling asleep, number of hours slept, nightly awakenings, daytime naps, and so on). Multidisciplinary teams of physicians and psychologists sift through this information to arrive at a diagnosis and suggest treatment approaches to address the presenting problem.

The *DSM* groups sleep disorders within two major categories: *dyssomnias* and *parasomnias.*

WWW **Web Link 11.4**
What Is Your Sleep IQ?

sleep disorders Persistent or recurrent sleep-related problems that cause distress or impaired functioning.

polysomnographic (PSG) recording Simultaneous measurement of multiple physiological responses during sleep or attempted sleep.

dyssomnias Sleep disorders involving disturbances in the amount, quality, or timing of sleep.

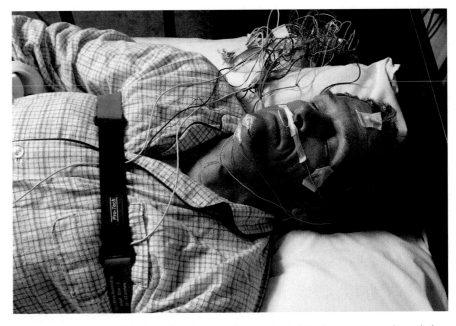

Sleep center. People with sleep disorders are often evaluated in sleep centers, where their physiological responses can be monitored as they sleep.

Dyssomnias

Dyssomnias are sleep disorders that are characterized by disturbances in the amount, quality, or timing of sleep. There are five specific types of

TABLE 11.3   Behavioral Techniques of Modifying the ABC's of Eating to Foster Weight Loss

Changing the A's of Overeating

Change the Environmental A's	Avoid settings that trigger overeating. (Eat at The Celery Stalk, not The Chocolate Gourmet.) Don't leave tempting treats around the house. Serve food on smaller plates. Use a lunch plate rather than a dinner plate. Don't leave seconds on the table. Serve preplanned portions. Do not leave open casseroles on the table. Immediately freeze leftovers. Don't keep them warm on the stove. Avoid the kitchen as much as possible. Disconnect eating from other stimuli, such as watching television, talking on the telephone, or reading. Establish food-free zones in your home. Imagine there is a barrier at the entrance to your bedroom that prevents the passage of food.
Control the Internal A's	Don't bury disturbing feelings in a box of cookies or a carton of mocha delight ice cream. Relabel feelings of hunger as signals that you're burning calories. Say to yourself, "It's okay to feel hungry. It doesn't mean I'm going to die or pass out. Each minute I delay eating, more calories are burned."

Changing the B's of Overeating

Slow Down the Pace of Eating	Put down utensils between bites. Take smaller bites. Chew thoroughly. Savor each bite. Don't wolf bites down to make room for the next. Take a break during the meal. Put down your utensils and converse with your family or guests for a few minutes. (Give your rising blood sugar level a chance to signal your brain.) When you resume eating, ask yourself whether you need to finish every bite. Leave something over to be thrown away or enjoyed later.
Modify Shopping Behavior	Shop from a list. Don't browse through the supermarket. Shop quickly. Don't make shopping the high point of your day. Treat the supermarket like enemy territory. Avoid the aisles containing junk food and snacks. If you must walk down these aisles, put on mental blinders and look straight ahead. Never shop when hungry. Shop after meals, not before.
Practice Competing Responses	Substitute nonfood activities for food-related activities. When tempted to overeat, leave the house, take a bath, walk the dog, call a friend, or walk around the block. Substitute low-calorie foods for high-calorie foods. Keep lettuce, celery, or carrots in the middle of the refrigerator so they are available when you want a snack. Fill spare time with non-food-related activities: volunteer at the local hospital, play golf or tennis, join exercise groups, read in the library (rather than the kitchen), take long walks.
Break the Chain	Stretch the overeating chain. Before allowing yourself to snack, wait 10 minutes. Next time wait 15 minutes, and so on. Break the eating chain at its weakest link. It's easier to interrupt the eating chain by taking a route home that bypasses the bakery than to exercise self-control when you're placing your order.

Changing the C's of Overeating

Reward Yourself for Meeting Calorie/Diet Goals	One pound of body weight is equivalent to 3,500 calories. To lose 1 pound per week, you need to cut 3,500 calories per week, or 500 calories per day, from your typical calorie intake level, assuming your weight has been stable. Reward yourself for meeting weekly calorie goals. Reward yourself with gifts you would not otherwise purchase for yourself, such as a special gift for yourself, like a cashmere sweater or tickets to a show. Repeat the reward program from week to week. If during some weeks you miss your calorie goals, don't lose heart. Get back on track next week.
Use Self-Punishment	Charge yourself for deviating from your diet. Send one dollar to a political candidate you despise, or to a hated cause, each time the chocolate cake wins.

dyssomnias: primary insomnia, primary hypersomnia, narcolepsy, breathing-related sleep disorder, and circadian rhythm sleep disorder.

Insomnia The term **insomnia** derives from the Latin *in-*, meaning "not" or "without," and, of course, *somnus*, meaning "sleep." Occasional bouts of insomnia, especially during times of stress, are not abnormal. But persistent insomnia characterized by recurrent difficulty getting to sleep or remaining asleep is an abnormal behavior pattern. (Pallesen et al., 2001). About one in three adult Americans experience chronic or persistent insomnia in any given year (Gillin, 1991). Chronic insomnia lasting a month or longer is often a sign of an underlying physical problem or a psychological disorder such as depression. If the underlying problem is treated successfully, chances are that normal sleep patterns will be restored. Chronic insomnia that cannot be accounted for by another psychological or physical disorder, or by the effects of drugs or medications, is classified as a sleep disorder called *primary insomnia.*

wWw __Web Link 11.5__
__Facts About Insomnia__

An estimated 14 million people in the United States, most of them over the age of 40, have primary insomnia (Nagourney, 2001b). People with primary insomnia have persistent difficulty falling asleep, remaining asleep, or achieving restorative sleep (sleep that leaves the person feeling refreshed and alert) for a period of a month or longer. Young people with primary insomnia usually complain it takes too long to get to sleep. Older people with insomnia are more likely to complain of waking frequently during the night, or of waking too early in the morning.

Primary insomnia leads to daytime fatigue and causes significant levels of personal distress or difficulties performing usual social, occupational, student, or other roles. Not surprisingly, there is a high rate of comorbidity (co-occurrence) between insomnia and other psychological problems, especially anxiety and depression (Breslau et al., 1996; Morin & Ware, 1996). Although the prevalence of primary insomnia is unknown, it is considered the most common form of sleep disturbance.

Psychological factors play a prominent role in primary insomnia. People troubled by primary insomnia tend to bring their anxieties and worries to bed with them, which raises their bodily arousal to a level that prevents natural sleep. Then they worry about not getting enough sleep, which only compounds their sleep difficulties. They may try to force themselves to sleep, which tends to backfire by creating more anxiety and tension, making sleep even less likely to occur. Sleep cannot be forced. Trying to make yourself fall asleep is likely to backfire. We can only set the scene for sleep by retiring when we are tired and relaxed and allowing sleep to occur naturally.

Hypersomnia The word *hypersomnia* is derived from the Greek *hyper*, meaning "over" or "more than normal," and the Latin *somnus*, meaning "sleep." Primary **hypersomnia** involves a pattern of excessive sleepiness during the day that continues for a month or longer. The excessive sleepiness (sometimes referred to as "sleep drunkenness") may take the form of difficulty awakening following a prolonged sleep period (typically 8 to 12 hours of sleep). Or there may be a pattern of daytime sleep episodes, occurring virtually every day, in the form of intended or unintended napping (such as inadvertently falling asleep while watching TV). Despite the fact that daytime naps often last an hour or more, the person does not feel refreshed upon awakening. The disorder is considered primary because it cannot be accounted for by inadequate amounts of sleep during the night due to insomnia or other factors (such as loud neighbors keeping the person up), by another psychological or physical disorder, or by drug or medication use.

Although many of us feel sleepy during the day from time to time, and may even drift off occasionally while reading or watching TV, the person with primary hypersomnia has more persistent and severe periods of sleepiness that typically lead to difficulties in daily functioning, such as missing important meetings because of difficulty awakening. Although the prevalence of the disorder is unknown, surveys of the general population show complaints relating to daytime sleepiness affecting between 0.5% to 5% of the adult population (APA, 2000).

insomnia Difficulties falling asleep, remaining asleep, or achieving restorative sleep.

hypersomnia A pattern of excessive sleepiness during the day.

narcolepsy A sleep disorder characterized by sudden, irresistible episodes of sleep.

cataplexy A brief, sudden loss of muscle control.

REM sleep The stage of sleep associated with dreaming and characterized by rapid eye movements under the closed eyelids.

breathing-related sleep disorder A sleep disorder in which sleep is repeatedly disrupted by difficulty with breathing normally.

apnea Temporary cessation of breathing.

Web Link **11.6** WWW
Facts About Narcolepsy

Truth OR Fiction?   REVISITED

Many people suffer from sleep attacks in which they suddenly fall asleep without any warning.

FALSE. Sleep attacks are relatively uncommon. They are characteristic of a disorder called narcolepsy that affects between 2 and 16 persons in 10,000.

Web Link **11.7** WWW
Facts About Sleep Apnea

Narcolepsy The word **narcolepsy** derives from the Greek *narke,* meaning "stupor" and *lepsis,* meaning "an attack." People with narcolepsy experience sleep attacks in which they suddenly fall asleep without any warning at various times during the day. They remain asleep for a period of about 15 minutes on the average. The person can be in the midst of a conversation at one moment and slump to the floor fast asleep a moment later. The diagnosis is made when sleep attacks occur daily for a period of 3 months or longer and are combined with the presence of one or both of the following conditions: (1) **cataplexy** (a sudden loss of muscular control); and (2) intrusions of **REM sleep** in the transitional state between wakefulness and sleep (APA, 2000). REM, or rapid eye movement, sleep is the stage of sleep associated with dreaming. It is so named because the sleeper's eyes tend to dart about rapidly under the closed lids. Narcoleptic attacks are associated with an almost immediate transition into REM sleep from a state of wakefulness. In normal sleep, REM typically follows several stages of non-REM sleep.

Cataplexy typically follows a strong emotional reaction such as joy or anger. It can range from a mild weakness in the legs to a complete loss of muscle control that results in the person suddenly collapsing (Dahl, 1992). People with narcolepsy may also experience *sleep paralysis,* a temporary state following awakening in which the person feels incapable of moving or talking. The person may also report frightening hallucinations, called *hypnagogic hallucinations,* which occur just before the onset of sleep and tend to involve visual, auditory, tactile, and kinesthetic (body movement) sensations.

Narcolepsy affects men and women equally and is a relatively uncommon disorder, affecting an estimated 0.02% (2 in 10,000) to 0.16% (16 in 10,000) people within the general adult population (APA, 1994). Unlike hypersomnia in which daytime sleep episodes follow a period of increasing sleepiness, narcoleptic attacks occur abruptly and are experienced as refreshing upon awakening. The attacks can be dangerous and frightening, especially if they occur when the person is driving or using heavy equipment or sharp implements. About 2 of 3 people with narcolepsy have fallen asleep while driving, and 4 of 5 have fallen asleep on the job (Aldrich, 1992). Household accidents resulting from falls are also common (Cohen, Ferrans, & Eshler, 1992). Not surprisingly, the disorder is associated with a lower quality of life in terms of general health and daily functioning (Ferrans, Cohen, & Smith, 1992). The cause or causes of narcolepsy remain unknown, but suspicion focuses on the loss of brain cells in the hypothalamus that produce a sleep-regulating chemical (Bazell, 2000; Mignot & Thorsby, 2001; Peyron et al., 2000; Thannickal et al., 2000).

Breathing-Related Sleep Disorder People with a **breathing-related sleep disorder** experience repeated disruptions of sleep due to respiratory problems (APA, 2000). These frequent disruptions of sleep result in insomnia or excessive daytime sleepiness.

The subtypes of the disorder are distinguished in terms of the underlying causes of the breathing problem. The most common type is *obstructive sleep apnea,* which involves repeated episodes of either complete or partial obstruction of breathing during sleep (Zwilich, 2000). The disorder affects as many as 18 million Americans (Smith, 2001a). The word **apnea** derives from the Greek prefix *a-,* meaning "not, without," and *pneuma,* meaning "breath." The breathing difficulty results from the blockage of airflow in the upper airways, which is often caused by a structural defect, such as an overly thick palate or enlarged tonsils or adenoids. In cases of complete obstruction, the sleeper may literally stop breathing for periods of from 15 to 90 seconds as many as 500 times during the night! When these lapses of breathing occur, the sleeper may suddenly sit up, gasp for air, take a few deep breaths, and fall back asleep without awakening or realizing that breathing was interrupted.

Although a biological reflex kicks in to force a gasping breath after these brief interruptions of breathing, the frequent disruptions of normal sleep resulting from apneas can leave people feeling sleepy the following day, making it difficult for them to function effectively. Obstructive sleep apnea is a relatively common problem, with estimates indicating that the disorder affects approximately 1% to 10% of the adult population and perhaps an even higher percentage of older adults (APA, 2000). The disorder is most common in middle-aged men. Although men with apnea outnumber women by about a

2:1 ratio, the disorder often goes undiagnosed in women (Young et al., 1996). It is also more common among people who are obese, apparently because of a narrowing of the upper airways due to an enlargement of soft tissue (APA, 2000).

Not surprisingly, people who have sleep apnea report a poorer quality of life than unaffected people (Gall, Isaac, & Kryger, 1993). Sleep apnea is also a health concern because of its association with an increased risk of hypertension, a major risk factor for heart attacks and strokes (Nieto et al., 2000; Peppard et al., 2000; Zwilich, 2000).

Circadian Rhythm Sleep Disorder Most bodily functions follow a cycle or an internal rhythm—called a circadian rhythm—that lasts about 24 hours. Even when people are relieved of scheduled activities and work duties and placed in environments that screen the time of day, they usually follow relatively normal sleep-wake schedules.

In **circadian rhythm sleep disorder,** this rhythm becomes grossly disturbed because of a mismatch between the sleep schedule demands imposed on the person and the person's internal sleep-wake cycle. The disruption in normal sleep patterns caused by the mismatch can lead to insomnia or hypersomnia. Like other sleep disorders, the mismatch must be persistent and severe enough to cause significant levels of distress or impair one's ability to function in social, occupational, or other roles. The jet lag that can accompany travel between time zones does not qualify because it is usually transient. However, frequent changes of time zones and frequent changes of work shifts (as encountered, for example, by nursing personnel) can induce more persistent or recurrent problems adjusting sleep patterns to scheduling demands, resulting in a circadian rhythm sleep disorder. Treatment may involve a program of making gradual adjustments in the sleep schedule to allow the person's circadian system to become aligned with changes in the sleep-wake schedule (Dahl, 1992).

Parasomnias

The **parasomnias** involve abnormal behaviors or physiological events taking place during sleep or at the threshold between wakefulness and sleep. Among the more common parasomnias are nightmare disorder, sleep terror disorder, and sleepwalking disorder.

Nightmare Disorder **Nightmare disorder** involves recurrent awakenings from sleep because of frightening dreams (nightmares). The nightmares typically involve lengthy story-like dreams that include threats of imminent physical danger to the individual, such as being chased, attacked, or injured. The person usually recalls the nightmare vividly upon awakening. Although alertness is regained quickly after awakening, anxiety and fear may linger and prevent a return to sleep. Perhaps half the adult population occasionally experiences nightmares, although the percentages of people having the intense, recurrent nightmares that produce the kind of emotional distress or difficulties in functioning that would lead to a diagnosis of nightmare disorder remains unknown.

Nightmares are often associated with traumatic experiences and are generally more frequent when the individual is under stress. Supporting the general link between trauma and nightmares, researchers report that the incidence of nightmares was greater among survivors of the 1989 San Francisco earthquake in the weeks following the quake than among comparison groups (Wood et al., 1992). An increased frequency of nightmares was also observed among children who were exposed to the 1994 Los Angeles earthquake (Kolbert, 1994).

Sleep apnea. Loud snoring may be a sign of obstructive sleep apnea, a breathing-related sleep disorder in which the person may temporarily stop breathing as many as 500 times during a night's sleep. Loud snoring, described by bed partners as reaching levels of industrial noise pollution, may alternate with momentary silences when breathing is suspended.

Truth OR Fiction? REVISITED

Some people literally gasp for breath hundreds of times during sleep without realizing it.

TRUE. People with sleep apnea may gasp for breath hundreds of times during the night without realizing it.

circadian rhythm sleep disorder A sleep disorder characterized by a mismatch between the body's normal sleep-wake cycle and the demands of the environment.

parasomnias Sleep disorders involving abnormal behaviors or physiological events that occur during sleep or while falling asleep.

nightmare disorder A sleep disorder characterized by recurrent awakenings due to frightening nightmares.

sleep terror disorder A sleep disorder characterized by recurrent episodes of sleep terror resulting in abrupt awakenings.

sleepwalking disorder A sleep disorder involving repeated episodes of sleepwalking.

Nightmares generally occur during REM sleep. REM periods tend to become longer and the dreams occurring during REM more intense in the latter half of sleep, so nightmares usually occur late at night or toward morning. Although nightmares may contain great motor activity, as in fleeing from an assailant, dreamers show little muscle activity. The same biological processes that activate dreams—including nightmares—inhibit body movement, causing a type of paralysis. This is indeed fortunate, as it prevents the dreamer from jumping out of bed and running into a dresser or a wall in the attempt to elude the pursuing assailants from the dream.

Sleep Terror Disorder It typically begins with a loud, piercing cry or scream in the night. Even the most soundly asleep parent will be summoned to the child's bedroom as if shot from a cannon. The child (most cases involve children) may be sitting up, appearing frightened and showing signs of extreme arousal—profuse sweating with rapid heartbeat and respiration. The child may start talking incoherently or thrash about wildly, but remain asleep. If the child awakens fully, he or she may not recognize the parent or may attempt to push the parent away. After a few minutes the child falls back into a deep sleep and upon awakening in the morning remembers nothing of the experience. These terrifying attacks, called *sleep terrors*, are more intense than ordinary nightmares. Unlike nightmares, sleep terrors tend to occur during the first third of nightly sleep and during deep, non-REM sleep (Dahl, 1992).

A **sleep terror disorder** involves repeated episodes of sleep terrors resulting in abrupt awakenings that begin with a panicky scream (APA, 2000). If awakening occurs during a sleep terror episode, the person will usually appear confused and disoriented for a few minutes. The person may feel a vague sense of terror and be able to report some fragmentary dream images, but not the sort of detailed dreams typical of nightmares. Most of the time the person falls back asleep and remembers nothing of the experience the following morning.

Sleep terror disorder in children is typically outgrown during adolescence. More boys than girls are affected by the disorder, but among adults the gender ratio is about even. In adults, the disorder tends to follow a chronic course during which the frequency and intensity of the episodes waxes and wanes over time. Prevalence data on the disorder are lacking, but episodes of sleep terror are estimated to occur in 1% to 6% of children and in less than 1% of adults (APA, 2000). The cause of sleep terror disorder remains a mystery.

Sleepwalking Disorder **Sleepwalking disorder** involves repeated episodes in which the sleeper arises from bed and walks about the house while remaining fully asleep. Because these episodes tend to occur during the deeper stages of sleep in which there is an absence of dreaming, sleepwalking episodes do not seem to involve the enactment of a dream. In sleepwalking disorder, the occurrence of repeated episodes of sleepwalking are of sufficient severity to cause significant levels of personal distress or impaired functioning. Sleepwalking disorder is most common in children, affecting between 1% and 5% of children according to some estimates (APA, 2000). Between 10% and 30% of children are believed to have had at least one episode of sleepwalking. The prevalence of the disorder among adults is unknown, as are its causes. However, perhaps as many as 7% of adults have experienced occasional sleepwalking episodes (APA, 2000). The causes of sleepwalking remain obscure, although both genetic and environmental factors are believed to be involved (Hublin et al., 1997).

Although sleepwalkers typically avoid walking into things, accidents occasionally happen. Sleepwalkers tend to have a blank stare on their faces during these episodes. They are generally unresponsive to others and difficult to awaken. When they do awaken the following morning, they typically have little if any recall of the experience. If they are awakened during the episode, they may be disoriented or confused for a few minutes (as is the case with sleep terrors), but full alertness is soon restored. There is no basis to the belief that it is harmful to sleepwalkers to awaken them during episodes. Isolated incidents of violent behavior have been associated with sleepwalking, but these are rare occurrences and may well involve other forms of psychopathology.

THINK ABOUT IT

What are the distinguishing features of the major types of sleep disorders? Why are they categorized as psychological problem in the *DSM*?

Treatment of Sleep Disorders

The most common method for treating sleep disorders in the United States is the use of sleep medications called **hypnotics.** However, because of problems associated with these drugs, nonpharmacological treatment approaches, principally cognitive-behavioral therapy, have come to the fore.

Biological Approaches Antianxiety drugs are often used to treat insomnia, including a class of minor tranquilizers called benzodiazepines (for example, Valium, Librium, and Ativan) (Pallesen et al., 2001). (These drugs are also widely used in the treatment of anxiety disorders, as we saw in Chapter 6.) Another widely used drug, *zolpidem* (trade name Ambien), appears to be about as effective as the benzodiazepines but may produce fewer side effects and possibly fewer withdrawal effects (Kupfer & Reynolds, 1997). Nonetheless, all these drugs can produce chemical dependence if used regularly over time.

When used for the short-term treatment of insomnia, antianxiety drugs are generally effective in reducing the time it takes to get to sleep, increasing total length of sleep and reducing nightly awakenings (Nowell et al., 1998). They work by reducing arousal and inducing feelings of calmness, thereby making the person more receptive to sleep.

A number of problems are associated with using drugs to combat insomnia (Kryger, Roth, & Dement, 2000). Sleep-inducing drugs tend to suppress REM sleep, which may interfere with some of the restorative functions of sleep. They can also lead to a carryover or "hangover" the following day, which is associated with daytime sleepiness and reduced performance. Rebound insomnia can also follow discontinuation of the drug, causing worse insomnia than was originally the case. Rebound insomnia may be lessened, however, by tapering off the drug rather than abruptly discontinuing it. These drugs quickly lose their effectiveness at a given dosage level, so progressively larger doses must be used to achieve the same effect. High doses can be dangerous, especially if they are mixed with alcoholic beverages at bedtime. Regular use can also lead to physical dependence (addiction). Once dependence is established, withdrawal symptoms following cessation of use may occur, including agitation, tremors, nausea, headaches, and in severe cases, delusions or hallucinations.

Users can also become *psychologically* dependent on sleeping pills. That is, they can develop a psychological need for the medication and assume they will not be able to get to sleep without them. Because worry about going without drugs heightens bodily arousal, such self-doubts are likely to become self-fulfilling prophecies. Moreover, users may attribute their success in falling asleep to the pill and not to themselves, which strengthens reliance on the drugs and makes it harder to forgo using them.

Not surprisingly, there is little evidence of long-term benefits of drug therapy after withdrawal (Morin & Wooten, 1996). Relying on sleeping pills does nothing to resolve the underlying cause of the problem or help the person learn more effective ways of coping with it. If hypnotic drugs like benzodiazepines are to be prescribed at all for sleep problems, they should only be used for a brief time (a few weeks at most) and at the lowest possible dose (Dement, 1992; Kupfer & Reynolds, 1997). The aim should be to provide a temporary respite so the clinician can help the client find effective ways of handling the sources of stress and anxiety that contribute to insomnia.

Minor tranquilizers of the benzodiazepine family and tricyclic antidepressants are also used to treat the deep-sleep disorders—sleep terrors and sleepwalking. They seem to have a beneficial effect by decreasing the length of deep sleep and reducing partial arousals between sleep stages (Dahl, 1992). Use of sleep medications for these disorders, like primary insomnia, also incurs the risk of physiological and psychological dependence and thus should be used only in severe cases and only as a temporary means of "breaking the cycle." Other psychoactive drugs, such as stimulants, are sometimes used to help maintain wakefulness in people with narcolepsy and to combat daytime sleepiness in people with hypersomnia. Daily naps of 10 to 60 minutes, and coping support from mental health professionals or self-help groups, may also be of help to people with narcolepsy (Aldrich, 1992). Sleep apnea is sometimes treated with drugs that act on brain

WWW **Web Link 11.8**
National Sleep Foundation

Does going to bed mean going to sleep? People who use their beds for many other activities, including eating, reading, and watching television, may find that lying in bed loses its value as a cue for sleeping. Behavior therapists use stimulus control techniques to help people with insomnia create a stimulus environment associated with sleeping.

THINK ABOUT IT

What are the drawbacks of relying on sleep medications to combat chronic insomnia?

THINK ABOUT IT

Do your sleep habits help or hinder your sleeping patterns? Explain.

Quiz **11.3**
Sleep Disorders

Quiz **11.4**
Chapter Exam

Research Update
Chapter 11

centers that stimulate breathing. Surgery may also be used to widen the upper airways. Mechanical devices may help maintain breathing during sleep, such as a nose mask that exerts pressure to keep the upper airway passages open or a battery-powered device that continuously blows air through the nose to prevent the airways from collapsing (e.g., Ballester et al., 1999).

Psychological Approaches Psychological approaches have by and large been limited to treatment of primary insomnia. Overall, cognitive-behavioral treatment approaches have produced substantial benefits in treating chronic insomnia, as measured by both substantial reductions in the time it takes to get to asleep and wakefulness during the night, as well as improved ratings of sleep quality (Currie et al., 2000; Edinger et al., 2001; Espie et al., 2001). In one recent study, two of three treatment participants were able to fall asleep within 30 minutes of retiring (Espie, Inglis, & Harvey, 2001). Sleep experts believe that CBT is just as effective as sleep medication in treating insomnia in the short-term and more effective in the long-term (Smith, 2001a).

Cognitive-behavioral techniques are short term in emphasis and focus on directly lowering states of physiological arousal, modifying maladaptive sleeping habits, and changing dysfunctional thoughts. Cognitive-behavioral therapists typically use a combination of techniques, including stimulus control, establishment of a regular sleep-wake cycle, relaxation training, and rational restructuring. Stimulus control involves changing the stimulus environment associated with sleeping. Under normal conditions, we learn to associate stimuli relating to lying down in bed with sleeping, so that exposure to these stimuli comes to induce feelings of sleepiness. But when people use their beds for many other activities—such as eating, reading, and watching television—the bed may lose its association with sleepiness. Moreover, the longer the person with insomnia lies in bed tossing and turning, the more the bed becomes associated with cues related to anxiety and frustration. Stimulus control techniques attempt to strengthen the connection between the bed and sleep by restricting as much as possible the activities spent in bed to sleeping. Typically, the person is instructed to limit the time spent in bed trying to fall sleep to 10 or 20 minutes at a time. If sleep does not occur within the designated time, the person is instructed to leave the bed and go to another room to restore a relaxed frame of mind before returning to bed, such as by sitting quietly, reading, watching TV, or practicing relaxation exercises. Moreover, the person is encouraged to establish a regular sleep-wake cycle by adopting more consistent sleeping and waking times (Riedel & Lichstein, 2001). Relaxation techniques, such as the Jacobson progressive relaxation approach, may also be practiced before bedtime to help reduce the level of physiological arousal. Based on a meta-analysis of outcome studies, it does not appear that the combination of stimulus control and relaxation training produces any larger benefit than either approach alone (Murtagh & Greenwood, 1995).

Rational restructuring involves substituting rational alternatives for self-defeating, maladaptive thoughts or beliefs (see accompanying "Closer Look" section for examples). The belief that failing to get a good night's sleep will lead to unfortunate, even disastrous, consequences the next day reduces the chances of falling asleep because it raises the level of anxiety and can lead the person to try unsuccessfully to force sleep to happen. Most of us do reasonably well if we lose sleep or even miss a night of sleep, even though we might like more.

A Closer Look

To Sleep, Perchance to Dream

 Many of us have difficulty from time to time falling asleep or remaining asleep. Although sleep is a natural function and cannot be forced, we can develop more adaptive sleep habits that help us become more receptive to sleep. However, if insomnia or other sleep-related problems persist or become associated with difficulties functioning during the day, it would be worthwhile to have the problem checked out with a professional. Here are some techniques to help you acquire more adaptive sleep habits:

1. Retire to bed only when you feel sleepy.

2. Limit as much as possible your activities in bed to sleeping. Avoid watching TV or reading in bed.

3. If after 10 to 20 minutes of lying in bed you are unable to fall asleep, get out of bed, leave the bedroom, and put yourself in a relaxed mood by reading, listening to calming music, or practicing self-relaxation.

4. Establish a regular routine. Sleeping late to make up for lost sleep can throw off your body clock. Set your alarm for the same time each morning and get up, regardless of how many hours you have slept.

5. Avoid naps during the daytime. You'll feel less sleepy at bedtime if you catch *z*'s during the afternoon.

6. Avoid ruminating in bed. Don't focus on solving your problems or organizing the rest of your life as you're attempting to sleep. Tell yourself that you'll think about tomorrow, tomorrow. Help yourself enter a more sleepful frame of mind by engaging in a mental fantasy or mind trip, or just let all thoughts slip away from consciousness. If an important idea comes to you, don't rehearse it in your mind. Jot it down on a handy pad so you won't lose it. But if thoughts persist, get up and follow them elsewhere.

7. Put yourself in a relaxed frame of mind before sleep. Some people unwind before bed by reading; others prefer watching TV or just resting quietly. Do whatever you find most relaxing. You may find it helpful to incorporate within your regular bedtime routine the techniques for lowering your level of arousal discussed earlier in this chapter, such as meditation or progressive relaxation.

8. Establish a regular daytime exercise schedule. Regular exercise during the day (not directly before bedtime) can help induce sleepiness upon retiring.

9. Avoid use of caffeinated beverages, such as coffee and tea, in the evening or late afternoon. Also, avoid drinking alcoholic beverages. Alcohol can interfere with normal sleep patterns (reduced total sleep, REM sleep, and sleep efficiency) even when consumed 6 hours before bedtime (Landolt et al., 1996).

10. Practice rational restructuring. Substitute rational alternatives for self-defeating thoughts. Here are some examples:

Self-Defeating Thoughts	Rational Alternatives
"I must fall asleep right now or I'll be a wreck tomorrow."	"I may feel tired, but I've been able to get by with little sleep before. I can make up for it tomorrow by getting to bed early."
"What's the matter with me that I can't seem to fall sleep?"	"Stop blaming yourself. You can't control sleep. Just let whatever happens, happen."
"If I don't get to sleep right now, I won't be able to concentrate tomorrow on the exam (conference, meeting, etc.)."	"My concentration may be off a bit, but I'm not going to fall apart. There's no point blowing things out of proportion. I might as well get up for a while and watch a little TV rather than lie here ruminating."

Overview of Sleep Disorders

TYPES OF SLEEP DISORDERS	Sleep disorders are often evaluated in specialized sleep centers where multiple physiological responses during sleep can be measured simultaneously in the form of polysomnographic (PSG) recording	
	Description	**Subtypes/Features**
Dyssomnias	Disturbances in the amount, quality, or timing of sleep	• **Insomnia:** Difficulty falling asleep, remaining asleep, or getting enough restful sleep • **Hypersomnia:** Excessive daytime sleepiness • **Narcolepsy:** Sudden attacks of sleep during the day • **Breathing-Related Sleep Disorder:** Sleep repeatedly interrupted due to difficulties breathing • **Circadian Rhythm Sleep Disorder:** Disruption of the internal sleep-wake cycle due to time changes in sleep patterns
Parasomnias	Disturbances occurring either during sleep or at the threshold between sleep and wakefulness	• **Nightmare Disorder:** Repeated awakenings due to nightmares • **Sleep Terror Disorder:** Repeated experiences of sleep terrors resulting in abrupt awakenings • **Sleepwalking Disorder:** Repeated episodes of sleepwalking

CAUSAL FACTORS	Many causes remain unspecified, but biological and psychosocial factors are prominent contributors
Biological Factors	• Underlying physical problems (in insomnia, apnea, and narcolepsy) • Possible genetic defects disrupting brain mechanisms controlling sleep (in narcolepsy) • Drug use interfering with normal sleep
Psychological Factors	• Psychological factors, such as anxiety or depression, that interfere with getting to sleep or remaining asleep • Frequent time shifting of sleep and waking times (in circadian rhythm sleep disorder) • Exposure to trauma (in nightmare disorder)

TREATMENT APPROACHES	Sleep medication may offer short-term relief for insomnia, but cognitive-behavioral therapy helps people change unhealthy sleep habits
Drug Therapy	• May be used for short-term relief of insomnia and to treat deep-sleep disorders (sleep terrors and sleepwalking), narcolepsy, and sleep apnea
Biomedical Treatment	• Surgery or mechanical devices may be used to open airways in apnea patients
Cognitive-Behavioral Therapy	• May be used to change maladaptive sleep habits and dysfunctional thoughts or beliefs about sleep

Summing Up

Eating Disorders

What are the major types of eating disorders? Two major types of eating disorders are included in the *DSM*: anorexia nervosa and bulimia nervosa. Anorexia nervosa involves maintenance of weight more than 15% below normal levels, intense fears of becoming overweight, distorted body image, and in females, amenorrhea. Bulimia nervosa involves preoccupation with weight control and body shape, repeated binges, and regular purging to keep weight down, which is characterized by self-starvation and failure to maintain normal body weight. Another type of eating disorder, binge-eating disorder (BED), is presently classified as a potential disorder requiring further study.

What factors are implicated in the development of eating disorders? Eating disorders typically begin in adolescence and affect many more females than males. Anorexia and bulimia are linked to preoccupations with weight control and maladaptive ways of trying to keep weight down. Many other factors are implicated in their development, including social pressures on young women to adhere to unrealistic standards of thinness, issues of control, underlying psychological problems, and conflict within the family, especially over issues of autonomy. People with BED tend to be older than those with anorexia or bulimia and to suffer from obesity.

What are the major forms of treatment for eating disorders? Severe cases of anorexia are often treated in an inpatient setting where a refeeding regimen can be closely monitored. Behavior modification and other psychological interventions, including psychotherapy and family therapy, may also be helpful. Most cases of bulimia are treated on an outpatient basis, with evidence supporting the therapeutic benefits of cognitive-behavioral therapy, interpersonal therapy, and antidepressant medication. Cognitive-behavioral therapy and antidepressant medication have shown positive effects in treating binge-eating disorder.

Obesity

Is obesity a psychological disorder? No, obesity is classified as a chronic disease, not a psychological disorder. It is a major risk factor linked to many serious chronic diseases, including heart disease and diabetes. Rates of obesity in the United States have been rising. The causes of obesity include genetic factors, metabolic factors, fat cells, lifestyle factors, and psychological factors.

Why is obesity difficult to treat? Quickie diets and diet pills don't work because long-term success in losing weight and keeping it off depends on making lasting changes in eating habits and exercise patterns.

Sleep Disorders

What are the major types of sleep disorders? Sleep disorders are classified in two major categories, dyssomnias and parasomnias. Dyssomnias are disturbances in the amount, quality, or timing of sleep. They include five specific types: primary insomnia, primary hypersomnia, narcolepsy, breathing-related sleep disorder, and circadian rhythm sleep disorder. Parasomnias are disturbed behaviors or abnormal physiological responses occurring either during sleep or at the threshold between wakefulness and sleep. Parasomnias include three major types: nightmare disorder, sleep terror disorder, and sleepwalking disorder.

What are the major forms of treatment for sleep disorders? The most common form of treatment of sleep disorders involves the use of antianxiety drugs. However, use of these drugs should be time limited because of the potential for psychological and/or physical dependence, among other problems associated with their use. Cognitive-behavioral interventions have produced substantial benefits in helping people with chronic insomnia.

Norms for the Fear of Fat Scale

Comparative scores are available for women only. You may compare your own score on the Fear of Fat scale to those obtained by the following groups:

Group	N	Mean
Nondieting college women (women satisfied with their weight)	49	17.30
General female college population	73	18.33
College women who are dissatisfied with their weight and have been on three or more diets during the past year	40	23.90
Bulimic college women (actively bingeing and purging)	32	30.00
Anorexic women in treatment	7	35.00

Source. Goldfarb, L.A., Dykens, E.M., & Gerrard, M. (1985). The Goldfarb Fear of Fat scale. *Journal of Personality Assessment, 49,* 329–332.

Keep the following in mind as you interpret your score:

1. The Goldfarb samples are quite small.
2. A score at a certain level does not place you in that group; it merely means that you report an equivalent fear of fat. In other words, a score of 33.00 does not indicate you have bulimia or anorexia. It means that your self-reported fear of fat approximates those reported by bulimic and anorexic women in the Goldfarb study.

CHAPTER TWELVE

Gender Identity Disorder, Paraphilias, and Sexual Dysfunctions

Bharati Chaudhuri
Invisible Tension, 1992

Truth OR Fiction?

- Despite changes in societal attitudes toward homosexuality, it is still classified as a mental disorder within the DSM system. (p. 372)

- Gay males and lesbians have a gender identity of the opposite sex. (p. 373)

- Wearing revealing bathing suits is a form of exhibitionism, according to clinical criteria. (p. 378)

- Becoming aroused while watching your partner disrobe or viewing an explicit movie falls within the clinical definition of voyeurism. (p. 380)

- Some people cannot become sexually aroused without pain or humiliation. (p. 381)

- Orgasm is a reflex. (p. 386)

- Premature ejaculation affects a relatively small proportion of men. (p. 387)

- The male sex hormone testosterone is produced by the body in both women and men. (p. 389)

- Though it is used mostly by men, Viagra can also help women overcome sexual dysfunctions. (p. 397)

Off the fog-bound shore of Ireland lies the isle of Inis Beag.[1] From the air, it is a verdant jewel, warm and enticing. From the ground, the perspective is different.

For example, the inhabitants of Inis Beag believe that normal women do not have orgasms and those who do must be deviant (Messenger, 1971). Premarital sex is virtually unknown. Women participate in sexual relations in order to conceive children and pacify their husbands' lustful urges. They need not be concerned about being called on for frequent performances, because the men of Inis Beag believe, groundlessly, that sex saps their strength. Relations on Inis Beag take place in the dark—literally and figuratively, and with nightclothes on. Consistent with local standards of masculinity, the man ejaculates as quickly as he can. Then he rolls over and goes to sleep, without concern for his partner's satisfaction. Women do not complain, however, as they are reared to believe it is abnormal for them to experience sexual pleasure.

If Inis Beag is not your cup of tea, perhaps the ambience of Mangaia will strike you as more congenial. Mangaia is a Polynesian pearl. Languidly, Mangaia lifts out of the azure waters of the Pacific. Inis Beag and Mangaia are on opposite sides of the world—literally and figuratively.

From childhood, Mangaian children are expected to explore their sexuality through masturbation (Marshall, 1971). Mangaian teenagers are encouraged by their elders to engage in sexual relations. They will be found on hidden beaches or beneath the sheltering fronds of palms, industriously practicing skills acquired from their elders. Mangaian women usually reach orgasm numerous times before their partners do. Young men vie to see who is more skillful in helping their partners attain multiple orgasms.

The inhabitants of Mangaia and Inis Beag have like anatomic features, and the same hormones pulse through their bodies. Their attitudes and cultural values about what is normal and abnormal differ vastly, however. Their attitudes affect their sexual behavior and the enjoyment they attain—or do not attain—from sex. In sex, as in other areas of behavior, the lines between the normal and the abnormal are not always drawn precisely. Sex, like eating, is a natural function. Yet this natural function has been profoundly affected by custom, folklore, superstition, and cultural, religious, and moral beliefs.

Even in the United States today, we find attitudes as diverse as those on Inis Beag and Mangaia. Some people feel guilty about any form of sexual activity and thus reap little if any pleasure from sex. Others, who see themselves as the children of the sexual revolution of the 1960s and 1970s, may worry about whether they have become free enough or skillful enough in their sexual activity.

Normal and Abnormal in Sexual Behavior

In the realm of sexual behavior, our conceptions of what is normal and what is not are clearly influenced by sociocultural factors. Various patterns of sexual behavior that might be considered abnormal in Inis Beag, such as masturbation, premarital intercourse, and oral-genital sex, are normal in American society from the standpoint of statistical frequency. For example, a recent national survey, based on a representative sample of 3,432 males and females between the ages of 18 and 59, found that 63% of the adult men and 42% of the adult women surveyed reported that they had masturbated during the previous year (Laumann et al., 1994). It is likely that many more practiced masturbation but were hesitant to admit so to interviewers.

Attitudes toward **homosexuality** vary widely from culture to culture and from time to time. Studies of tribal societies show societal attitudes ranging from condemnation to tolerance and acceptability (Ford & Beach, 1951). In our society, homosexuality was once considered a form of mental illness, but in 1973 the American Psychiatric Association decided to remove homosexuality from its listing of mental disorders. Though homosexuality

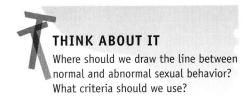

THINK ABOUT IT
Where should we draw the line between normal and abnormal sexual behavior? What criteria should we use?

homosexuality A sexual orientation characterized by erotic interest in, and development of romantic relationships with, members of one's own gender.

---

[1]Inis Beag is actually a pseudonym for an Irish folk community.

What is normal and what is abnormal in the realm of sexual and sexually related behavior patterns? The cultural context must be considered in defining what is normal and what is abnormal. The people in these photographs—and the ways in which they cloak or expose their bodies—would be quite out of place in one another's societies.

Truth OR Fiction? REVISITED

Despite changes in societal attitudes toward homosexuality, it is still classified as a mental disorder within the *DSM* system.

FALSE. Homosexuality is no longer classified as a mental disorder.

 Quiz 12.1
Normal and Abnormal
in Sexual Behavior

 VIDEO 12.1
Gender Identity Disorder:
The Case of Denise

gender identity One's psychological sense of being female or male.

gender identity disorder A disorder in which the individual believes that her or his anatomical gender is inconsistent with her or his gender identity.

is no longer considered a mental disorder, lesbians and gay males continue to be targets of extreme hostility, fear, and prejudice (see nearby *Closer Look* feature).[2]

Sexual behavior may be considered abnormal if it is self-defeating, deviates from social norms, harms others, causes personal distress, or interferes with one's ability to function. The disorders we feature in this chapter—gender identity disorder, paraphilias, and sexual dysfunctions—meet one or more of the criteria of abnormality. In exploring these disorders, we touch on questions that probe the boundaries between abnormality and normality. Are some instances of voyeurism or exhibitionism normal and others abnormal? When is it considered abnormal to have difficulty becoming sexually aroused or reaching orgasm?

Gender Identity Disorder

Our **gender identity** is our sense of being male or female. Gender identity is normally based on anatomic gender. In the normal run of things, our gender identity is consistent with our anatomic gender. In **gender identity disorder,** however, there is a conflict between one's anatomic gender and one's gender identity.

Gender identity disorder may begin in childhood. Children with the disorder find their anatomic gender to be a source of persistent and intense distress. The diagnosis is not used simply to label "tomboyish" girls and "sissyish" boys. It is applied to children who persistently repudiate their anatomic traits (girls might insist on urinating standing up or assert they do not want to grow breasts; boys may find their penis and testes revolting) or who are preoccupied with clothing or activities that are stereotypic of the other gender (see Table 12.1).

The diagnosis of gender identity disorder (formerly called *transsexualism*) applies to both children and adults who perceive themselves psychologically as members of the opposite gender and who show persistent discomfort with their anatomic gender.

Though the overall rate of gender identity disorder is not known, the disorder is believed to occur about five times more often in boys than girls (Zucker & Green, 1992). The disorder takes many paths. It can come to an end or abate markedly by adolescence, with

[2]In keeping with the suggestions of the American Psychological Association's (1991) Committee on Lesbian and Gay Concerns, we refer to *gay males* and *lesbians* rather than *homosexuals*. As noted by the Committee, there are several problems with the label *homosexual:* One, because it has been historically associated with concepts of deviance and mental illness, it may perpetuate negative stereotypes of gay men and lesbians. Two, the term is often used to refer to men only, thus rendering lesbians invisible. Third, it is often ambiguous in meaning—that is, does it refer to sexual behavior or sexual orientation?

the child becoming more accepting of her or his gender identity. Or it may persist into adolescence or adulthood, leading to a transsexual identity (Cohen-Kettenis et al., 2001). Or the child may also develop a gay male or lesbian sexual orientation at about the time of adolescence (Zucker & Green, 1992).

Many transexual adults undergo gender reassignment surgery. In these procedures, surgeons attempt to construct external genitalia that are close as possible to those of the opposite gender. People who undergo these operations can engage in sexual activity, even achieve orgasm, yet they are incapable of conceiving or bearing children because they lack the internal reproductive organs of their reconstructed gender. Investigators generally find favorable psychological outcomes following gender reassignment surgery (e.g., Cohen-Kettenis & van Goozen, 1997), especially when safeguards are taken to restrict surgical treatment to the most appropriate candidates. In one recent study, 14 male-to-female and 5 female-to-male patients were found to be functioning well socially and psychologically postoperatively, with none expressing regrets about the procedure (Cohen-Kettenis & van Goozen, 1997). In other research, none of 20 adolescent patients who underwent gender reassignment surgery later expressed regrets about their decision (Smith et al., 2001).

Men seeking gender reassignment outnumber women applicants by perhaps 3 or 4 to 1, but outcomes are generally more favorable for female-to-male cases. One reason may be society's greater acceptance of women who desire to live as men. Another reason appears to be that females with gender identity disorder are generally better adjusted than their male counterparts before surgery (Kockott & Fahrner, 1988). Male-to-female patients whose surgery left no telltale signs (such as scarring of the breasts or leftover erectile tissue) were found to be better adjusted than those whose surgery was less successful in allowing them to "pass" as female (Ross & Need, 1989).

Gender identity should not be confused with sexual orientation. Gay males and lesbians have erotic interests in members of their own gender, but their gender identity (sense

WWW   Web Link **12.1**
Transgender Forum

Truth OR Fiction?   REVISITED

Gay males and lesbians have a gender identity of the opposite sex.

FALSE. Gender identity should not be confused with sexual orientation. Gay males and lesbians have erotic interest in members of their own gender, but their gender identity is consistent with their anatomic sex.

WWW   Web Link **12.2**
Q&A: About Sexual Orientation

TABLE 12.1   Clinical Features of Gender Identity Disorder

(**a**) A strong, persistent identification with the other gender.

At least four of the following features are required to make the diagnosis in children:

   (1) Repeated expression of the desire to be a member of the other gender (or expression of the belief that the child does belong to the other gender)

   (2) Preference for wearing clothing stereotypical of members of the other gender

   (3) Presence of persistent fantasies about being a member of the other gender, or assumption of parts played by members of the other gender in make-believe play

   (4) Desire to participate in leisure activities and games considered stereotypical of the other gender

   (5) Strong preference for playmates that belong to the other gender (at ages when children typically prefer playmates of their own gender).

   Adolescents and adults typically express the wish to be of the other gender, frequently "pass" as a member of the other gender, and wish to live as a member of the other gender, or believe that their emotions and behavior typify the other gender.

(**b**) A strong, persistent sense of discomfort with one's anatomic gender or with the behaviors that typify the gender role of that gender.

   In children, these features are commonly present: Boys state that their external genitals are repugnant or that it would be better not to have them, show aversion to "masculine" toys, games, and rough-and-tumble play. Girls prefer not to urinate while sitting, express the wishes not to grow breasts or to menstruate, or show an aversion to "feminine" clothing.

   Adolescents and adults typically state that they were born the wrong gender and express the wish for medical intervention (e.g., hormone treatments or surgery) to rid them of their own sex characteristics and simulate the characteristics of the other gender.

(**c**) There is no "intersex condition," such as ambiguous sexual anatomy, that might give rise to such feelings.

(**d**) The features cause serious distress or impair key areas of occupational, social, or other functioning.

Source. Adapted from the *DSM-IV-TR* (APA, 2000).

A Closer Look

Homophobia: Social Prejudice or Personal Psychopathology?

Conceptions of abnormal behavior are societally constructed beliefs as to what behaviors are deemed normal or abnormal within a given culture and at a particular time. Mental health professionals base judgments of abnormality on evidence showing that a particular pattern of behavior either causes personal distress or interferes significantly with a person's ability to function in meeting social and occupational roles. Yet evidence does not support the view that lesbians, gay males, and bisexuals are any more psychologically disturbed than comparison heterosexual groups, despite the ostracism, prejudice, and discrimination they face in society (Coleman, 1987; Reiss, 1980).

George Weinberg (1972) coined the term **homophobia** to describe the persistent, irrational fear of lesbians and gay men. Fear and anxiety about lesbians and gay men or lesbian/gay sexual orientations has been deemed irrational because such fears are usually based on beliefs that are of questionable validity or have been overwhelmingly disputed. Examples of false beliefs about lesbians and gay men are that gay men are more likely to become child molesters than heterosexual men, that lesbians and gay men wish to be members of the other gender, that they do not make good parents, that their children will become lesbian or gay, that they are sexually promiscuous or indiscriminate in their sexual attractions, that their relationships are transitory and focused only on sexual interactions, and that they are responsible for the AIDS epidemic (Jenny, Roesler, & Poyer, 1994; Peplau, 1991). Many people who hold these beliefs feel justified in engaging in prejudice against lesbians and gay men that may range from personal rudeness or hostility to vandalism, harassment and even violent physical attacks (Freiberg, 1995; Katz, 1995).

As these attacks are commonplace in many parts of the United States, they create a climate of terror for lesbians and gay men and make their lives more difficult. The fact that these beliefs persist among many otherwise intelligent people, despite evidence to the contrary, and that they are often connected to expressions of violence that harms others makes their understanding an important social issue. It also raises important questions for behavioral scientists about what purpose these beliefs serve, what they mean to those who hold them, and how to alter them.

Many theoreticians use the term **heterosexism** (Herek, 1996) to describe a broader cultural ideology and resulting pattern of institutional discrimination against lesbians and gay men. They suggest that the antigay feelings of individuals are only a part of a broader institutional pattern that is embedded in our culture and is based on the cultural assumption that reproductive sexuality is the only outcome of psychosexual development that is psychologically healthy and morally correct. They go on to suggest that antigay sentiments are rewarded in our society more than they are punished and are not considered to be abnormal or pathological.

Still, others believe that homophobia represents a form of clinical pathology in that it is an irrational belief or belief system that persists in the face of evidence to the contrary. Marvin Kantor (1998) views homophobia as an emotional disorder in which the false beliefs about lesbians and gay men and the anxiety associated with them represents a symptom that is similar to that of a paranoid delusion. In this view, homophobic beliefs may represent people's underlying fears or anxieties about their own latent homosexual attractions or strivings or insecurity about their own masculinity or femininity.

Gay bashing. In a heinous case that brought gay bashing into the national spotlight in 1998, a gay 21-year-old University of Wyoming student, Matthew Shepard, was pistol-whipped, tied to a fencepost, and left to die by a group of assailants.

Violent physical and verbal attacks against lesbians and gay men are referred to as gay bashing and are considered a hate crime. According to Kantor, many people who feel the need to bash lesbians and gay men and/or those who actually do so are really attempting to reassure themselves that they do not have such feelings or attractions. By punishing those who express these forbidden wishes, the gay basher may be seeking to prove to himself and others that he is not one of them.

Research on people who are homophobic suggests that they tend to have rigid personalities and are intolerant of anything that deviates from their personal view of appropriate behavior (Kantor, 1998). Other research suggests that they are people who have not, to their knowledge, had direct contact with lesbians or gay men (Herek, 1996). Their beliefs are selectively drawn from a larger culture that has historically put forth in the media demeaning images of lesbians and gay men by depicting them as dangerous, perverted, depressed, or so much the focus of comic relief that they would not be taken seriously. Ignorance about lesbians and gay men, maintained by their invisibility, fuels homophobic attitudes.

Because of the harm that homophobia and heterosexism does to lesbians and gay men and because of its adverse effects on their mental health, these phenomena are worthy of our serious attention and understanding. Do heterosexism and homophobia constitute some form of social or personal pathology, or both?

of being male or female) is consistent with their anatomic sex. They do not desire to become members of the opposite gender or despise their own genitalia, as we may find in people with gender identity disorder.

Unlike a gay male or lesbian sexual orientation, gender identity disorder is very rare. People with gender identity disorder who are sexually attracted to members of their own anatomic gender are unlikely to consider themselves gay males or lesbians, however. Nature's gender assignment is a mistake in their eyes. From their perspective, they are trapped in the body of the wrong gender.

Theoretical Perspectives

No one knows what causes gender identity disorder (Money, 1994). Psychodynamic theorists point to extremely close mother–son relationships, empty relationships between the mothers and fathers, and fathers who were absent or detached (Stoller, 1969). These family factors may foster strong identification with the mother in young males, leading to a reversal of expected gender roles and identity. Girls with weak, ineffectual mothers and strong, masculine fathers may overly identify with their fathers and develop a psychological sense of themselves as "little men."

Learning theorists similarly point to father absence in the case of boys—to the unavailability of a strong male role model. Socialization patterns might have affected children who were reared by parents who had wanted children of the other gender and who strongly encouraged cross-gender dressing and patterns of play.

Nonetheless, the great majority of people with the types of family histories described by psychodynamic and learning theorists do not develop gender identity disorder. Perhaps these family factors play a role in combination with a biological predisposition. We know that people with gender identity disorder often showed cross-gender preferences in toys, games, and clothing very early in childhood. If there are critical early learning experiences in gender identity disorder, they may occur very early in life. Prenatal hormonal imbalances may also be involved. Perhaps the brain is "masculinized" or "feminized" by sex hormones during certain stages of prenatal development. The brain could become differentiated as to gender identity in one direction while the genitals develop in the other direction (Money, 1987). All in all, researchers suspect that gender identity disorders may develop as the result of an interaction in utero between the developing brain and the release of sex hormones (Zhou et al., 1995). Yet speculations about the origins of gender identity disorder remain unsubstantiated by hard evidence. But whatever the biological contributions to gender identity turn out to be, are people who are different by virtue of their gender identities necessarily suffering from a disease or disorder? The answer may depend on how the society or culture in which they live regards them, as we explore further in the accompanying "Closer Look" feature.

Paraphilias

The word *paraphilia* was coined from the Greek roots *para*, meaning "to the side of," and *philos*, meaning "loving." In the **paraphilias,** people show sexual arousal ("loving") in response to atypical stimuli ("to the side of" normally arousing stimuli). According to the *DSM-IV*, paraphilias involve recurrent, powerful sexual urges and fantasies lasting 6 months or longer that center on (1) nonhuman objects such as underwear, shoes, leather, or silk, (2) humiliation or experience of pain in oneself or one's partner, or (3) children and other persons who do not or cannot grant consent. Although acting out on paraphilic urges is not required for a diagnosis (the person might be distressed by the urges but not act on them), people with paraphilias often engage in overt paraphilic behaviors such as exhibitionism and voyeurism.

Some persons who receive the diagnosis can function sexually in the absence of paraphilic stimuli or fantasies. Others resort to paraphilic stimuli under stress. Still others cannot become sexually aroused unless these stimuli are used, in actuality or in fantasy. For

homophobia Hatred and fear of lesbians and gay males.

heterosexism The culturally based belief system that holds that only reproductive sexuality is psychologically healthy and morally correct.

paraphilias Sexual disorders in which the person experiences recurrent sexual urges and fantasies involving nonhuman objects, inappropriate or nonconsenting partners, or painful or humiliating situations.

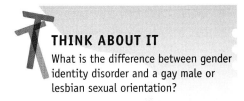

THINK ABOUT IT
What is the difference between gender identity disorder and a gay male or lesbian sexual orientation?

Q Quiz **12.2**
    Gender Identity Disorder

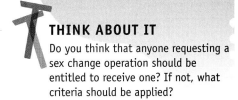

THINK ABOUT IT
Do you think that anyone requesting a sex change operation should be entitled to receive one? If not, what criteria should be applied?

A Closer Look

Gender Identity Disorder: A Disorder or Culture-Specific Creation?

Though our concept of gender, or maleness and femaleness, reflects the biological division of the sexes, it is also a social construction. It is a culturally based concept for designating the roles, attributes, responsibilities, privileges, and traits that a given culture assigns to men and women. Gender roles embody the behaviors a specific culture considers appropriate and fundamental to being a man or a woman. Gender identity, however, is a psychological construct that reflects an individual's psychological sense of their own gender, of who and what they are. Most of the assumptions we make about gender identity are based on the construction of gender as a dichotomous, mutually exclusive category—either male or female. We also assume that people's concept of their own gender should be consistent with their biological (anatomic) sex. People whose gender is at odds with their biological sex may be classified as having gender identity disorder. We assume people should be satisfied with the gender assigned by nature. As gender is also a social construction—a concept society creates and uses to assign people to different categories and statuses—it is also embedded in a socio-political context in which a person's gender not only defines them personally but also designates their place in a social hierarchy that determines their access to gender-based privileges. For example, men in our society have traditionally been accorded greater access than women to high prestige occupations in business, medicine, law, and engineering. Though gender roles today are less rigid than they were a few generations ago, differences in social expectations continue. Certainly more women are working today, but by and large they earn less than men and are still expected to shoulder the lion's share of household and child-care responsibilities.

Just as traditional gender roles have been challenged, so too have traditional concepts of gender identity been challenged by people who are dissatisfied with their biological sex and/or wish to adopt the gender roles of the other sex. The assumptions we make about the fixed dichotomy of gender into maleness and femaleness are further challenged by cross-cultural studies that reveal the presence of cultures that have a socially sanctioned identity for persons who are regarded as neither male or female. In these cultures, individuals who adopt the gender roles and identity of the other biological sex are not considered pathological or undesirable. They are simply regarded as having a third or other gender.

Into the late 1800s, the Plains Indians and many other Western tribes responded with understanding when a young member of the tribe crossed traditional gender roles (Wade & Tavris, 1994). Crossing traditional gender roles was not merely allowed but was accorded a respectable status in these societies. More than half of the surviving native languages have words that describe people who were neither male nor female but something else. Their presence and their roles are depicted in ways that indicated they were socially acceptable and even desirable members of the tribe. Native tribal members believed that human beings contained male and female elements. In many tribes, "two spirit" was the term used for persons who were believed to embody a higher level of integration of their male and female spirit. Sometimes a *two spirit* person was a biological male who took on the tribe's female gender roles but was not considered a male or a female (Tafoya, 1996). On the other hand, a female could take on the role and behaviors associated with tribal males. She could be initiated into puberty as a male and could adopt male roles and activities thereafter, including marrying a female.

Native Americans are not the only cultural group that has categories for people who do not fit contemporary U.S. gender dichotomies. These societies highlight social contexts and cultures in which dichotomous categories of gender were not presumed to be the norm and in which inconsistencies between biological sex, gender identities, and gender roles were not considered a psychological problem. Given the variability of gender roles and identities that we observe across cultures, we may question the validity of the concept of what has been described as a "disorder."

Califia (1997) and others (Israel & Tarver, 1997; K. K. Wilson, 1997) argue that although people who are dissatisfied with their biological sex or who wish to adopt the gender role that is inconsistent with their biological sex are perhaps atypical, their conditions should neither constitute nor function as a marker of psychopathology. Rather, their dysphoria can be attributed to living in a society that insists that people fit into either of two arbitrarily designated categories and subjects them to ill treatment if they do not. Their plight may be compared to that of lesbians and gay men. We understand that the distress that lesbians and gay men often experience in reference to their sexual orientation is a function of the hostility and abuse they receive because of it. Their distress is not an inevitable consequence of their sexual orientation, but rather an appropriate response to the negative treatment they receive.

It could be argued that dissatisfaction with one's biological sex or an inconsistency between one's biological sex and desired gender role or identity is not a problem unless you live in a society that says it is and is intolerant of it. If the society you live in were intolerant of you for being different, it is understandable you would become distressed by it. The ill treatment that people with *transgender* identities (identities that cross traditional gender lines) in our society receive can be a significant source of personal distress (Reid & Whitehead, 1992). Looked at in this way, our concept of gender identity disorder may be understood as a social construction that reflects our culture's definition of gender and treatment of people who are different, rather than a diseased or disordered condition residing within the person. In other cultures in which concepts of mutually exclusive gender categories do not apply, the disorder is not held to exist. Just as beliefs about sexual orientation have changed over time, perhaps greater tolerance and a greater appreciation for the diversity of gender expression in human beings will lead us to conceptualize gender identity with greater flexibility.

some individuals, the paraphilia is their exclusive means of attaining sexual gratification. With the exceptions of sexual masochism and some isolated cases of other disorders, paraphilias are almost never diagnosed in women (Seligman & Hardenburg, 2000). Even with masochism, it is estimated that men receiving the diagnosis outnumber women by a ratio of 20 to 1 (APA, 2000).

Some paraphilias are relatively harmless and victimless. Among these are fetishism and transvestic fetishism. Others, such as exhibitionism and pedophilia, have unwilling victims. A most harmful paraphilia is sexual sadism when acted out with a nonconsenting partner. Voyeurism falls somewhere in between, because the "victim" does not typically know he or she is being watched.

Exhibitionism

Exhibitionism involves recurrent, powerful urges to expose one's genitals to an unsuspecting stranger in order to surprise, shock, or sexually arouse the victim. The person may masturbate while fantasizing about or actually exposing himself (almost all cases involve men). The victims are almost always females.

Exhibitionism. Exhibitionism is a type of paraphilia that characterizes people who seek sexual arousal or gratification through exposing themselves to unsuspecting victims. People with this disorder are usually not interested in actual sexual contact with their victims.

The person diagnosed with exhibitionism is typically not interested in actual sexual contact with the victim and therefore not usually dangerous. Nevertheless, victims may believe themselves in great danger and may be traumatized by the act. Victims are probably best advised to show no reaction to people who expose themselves but to just continue on their way, if possible. It would be unwise to insult the person who exposed himself, lest it provoke a violent reaction. Nor do we recommend an exaggerated show of shock or fear; it tends to reinforce the person for the act of exposing himself.

Some researchers view exhibitionism as a means of indirectly expressing hostility toward women, perhaps because of perceptions of having been wronged by women in the past or of not being noticed or taken seriously by them (Geer, Heiman, & Leitenberg, 1984). Men with this disorder tend to be shy, dependent, and lacking in social and sexual skills, even socially inhibited (Dwyer, 1988). Some doubt their masculinity and harbor feelings of inferiority. Their victims' revulsion or fear boosts their sense of mastery of the situation and heightens their sexual arousal. Consider the following case example of exhibitionism:

A Case of Exhibitionism

Michael was a 26-year-old, handsome, boyish-looking married male with a 3-year-old daughter. He had spent about one-quarter of his life in reform schools and in prison. As an adolescent, he had been a fire-setter. As a young adult, he had begun to expose himself. He came to the clinic without his wife's knowledge because he was exposing himself more and more often—up to three times a day—and he was afraid that he would eventually be arrested and thrown into prison again.

Michael said he liked sex with his wife, but it wasn't as exciting as exposing himself. He couldn't prevent his exhibitionism, especially now, when he was between jobs and worried about where the family's next month's rent was coming from. He loved his daughter more than anything and couldn't stand the thought of being separated from her.

Michael's method of operation was as follows: He would look for slender adolescent females, usually near the junior high school and the senior high school. He would take his penis out of his pants and play with it while he drove up to a girl or a small group of girls. He would lower the car window, continuing to play with himself, and ask them for

exhibitionism A paraphilia in which one is sexually aroused by exposing one's genitals to a stranger.

fetishism A paraphilia in which one uses an inanimate object or body part as a focus of sexual interest and arousal.

transvestic fetishism A paraphilia in heterosexual males characterized by recurrent sexual urges involving dressing in female clothing.

Truth OR Fiction? REVISITED

Wearing revealing bathing suits is a form of exhibitionism, according to clinical criteria.

FALSE. Wearing revealing bathing suits is not a form of exhibitionism in the clinical sense of the term. Virtually all people diagnosed with the disorder are men, and they are motivated by the wish to shock and dismay unsuspecting observers, not to show off the attractiveness of their bodies.

Origins of fetishism? The conditioning model of the origins of fetishism suggests that men who develop fetishisms involving women's undergarments may have had experiences in childhood in which sexual arousal was repeatedly paired with exposure to their mother's undergarments. The developing fetish may have been strengthened by eroticizing the meaning of these stimuli by incorporating them within erotic fantasies or masturbatory activity.

directions. Sometimes the girls didn't see his penis. That was okay. Sometimes they saw it and didn't react. That was okay, too. When they saw it and became flustered and afraid, that was best of all. He would start to masturbate harder, and now and then he managed to ejaculate before the girls had departed.

Michael's history was unsettled. His father had left home before he was born, and his mother had drunk heavily. He was in and out of foster homes throughout his childhood, "all over" the capital district area of New York State. Before he was 10 years old, he was involved in sexual activities with neighborhood boys. Now and then, the boys also forced neighborhood girls into petting, and Michael had mixed feelings when the girls got upset. He felt bad for them, but he also enjoyed it. A couple of times girls seemed horrified at the sight of his penis, and it made him "really feel like a man. To see that look, you know, with a girl, not a woman, but a girl—a slender girl, that's what I'm after."

—From the Authors' Files

Wearing revealing bathing suits is not a form of exhibitionism in the clinical sense of the term. Virtually all people diagnosed with the disorder are men, and they are motivated by the wish to shock and dismay unsuspecting observers, not to show off the attractiveness of their bodies. Nor do professional strippers typically meet the clinical criteria for exhibitionism. Although they may seek to show off the attractiveness of their bodies, they are generally not motivated by the desire to expose themselves to unsuspecting strangers in order to arouse them or shock them. The chief motive of the stripteaser, of course, may simply be to earn a living.

Fetishism

The French word *fétiche* is thought to derive from the Portuguese *feitico,* referring to a "magic charm." In this case, the "magic" lies in the object's ability to arouse sexually. The chief feature of **fetishism** is recurrent, powerful sexual urges and arousing fantasies involving inanimate objects, such as an article of clothing (bras, panties, hosiery, boots, shoes, leather, silk, and the like). It is normal for men to like the sight, feel, and smell of their lovers' undergarments. Men with fetishism, however, may prefer the object to the person and may not be able to become sexually aroused without it. They often experience sexual gratification by masturbating while fondling the object, rubbing it, or smelling it; or by having their partners wear it during sexual activity.

The origins of fetishism may be traced to early childhood in many cases. Most individuals with a rubber fetish in one research sample were able to recall first experiencing a fetishistic attraction to rubber sometime between the age of 4 and 10 (Gosselin & Wilson, 1980).

Transvestic Fetishism

The chief feature of **transvestic fetishism** is recurrent, powerful urges and related fantasies involving cross-dressing for purposes of sexual arousal. Other people with fetishisms can be satisfied by handling objects such as women's clothing while they masturbate; people with transvestic fetishism want to wear them. They may wear full feminine attire and makeup or favor one particular article of clothing, such as women's stockings. Transvestic fetishism is reported only among heterosexual men. Typically, the man cross-dresses in private and imagines himself to be a woman who he is stroking as he masturbates. Some frequent transvestite clubs or become involved in a transvestic subculture.

Gay men may cross-dress to attract other men or because it is fashionable to masquerade as women in some social circles, not because they are sexually aroused by cross-dressing. Males with gender identity disorder cross-dress because of gender discomfort associated with wearing men's clothing. Because cross-dressing among gay men and men with gender identity disorder is performed for other reasons than sexual arousal or gratification, it is not considered a form of transvestic fetishism. Nor are female impersonators who cross-dress for theatrical purposes considered to have a form of transvestism. For reasons such as these, the diagnosis is limited to heterosexuals.

Most men with transvestism are married and engage in sexual activity with their wives, but they seek additional sexual gratification through dressing as women, as in the following case example:

Web Link **12.3**
National Council of Sexual Addiction and Compulsivity

A Case of Transvestic Fetishism

Archie was a 55-year-old plumber who had been cross-dressing for many years. There was a time when he would go out in public as a woman, but as his prominence in the community grew, he became more afraid of being discovered in public. His wife Myrna knew of his "peccadillo," especially since he borrowed many of her clothes, and she also encouraged him to stay at home, offering to help him with his "weirdness." For many years, his paraphilia had been restricted to the home. The couple came to the clinic at the urging of the wife. Myrna described how Archie had imposed his will on her for 20 years. Archie would wear her undergarments and masturbate while she told him how disgusting he was. (The couple also regularly engaged in "normal" sexual intercourse, which Myrna enjoyed.) The cross-dressing situation had come to a head because a teenaged daughter had almost walked into the couple's bedroom while they were acting out Archie's fantasies.

With Myrna out of the consulting room, Archie explained how he grew up in a family with several older sisters. He described how underwear had been perpetually hanging all around the one bathroom to dry. As an adolescent, Archie experimented with rubbing against articles of underwear, then with trying them on. On one occasion a sister walked in while he was modeling panties before the mirror. She told him he was a "dredge to society" and he straightaway experienced unparalleled sexual excitement. He masturbated when she left the room, and his orgasm was the strongest of his young life.

Archie did not think that there was anything wrong with wearing women's undergarments and masturbating. He was not about to give it up, regardless of whether his marriage was destroyed as a result. Myrna's main concern was finally separating herself from Archie's "sickness." She didn't care what he did anymore, so long as he did it by himself. "Enough is enough," she said.

That was the compromise the couple worked out in marital therapy. Archie would engage in his fantasies by himself. He would choose times when Myrna was not at home, and she would not be informed of his activities. He would also be very, very careful to choose times when the children would not be around.

Six months later the couple were together and content. Archie had replaced Myrna's input into his fantasies with transvestic-sadomasochistic magazines. Myrna said, "I see no evil, hear no evil, smell no evil." They continued to have sexual intercourse. After a while, Myrna even forgot to check to see which underwear had been used.

—From the Authors' Files

Voyeurism

The chief feature of **voyeurism** is either acting on or being strongly distressed by recurrent, powerful sexual urges and related fantasies involving watching unsuspecting people, generally strangers, who are undressed, disrobing, or engaging in sexual activity. The purpose of

voyeurism A paraphilia characterized by recurrent sexual urges involving watching unsuspecting others in sexual situations.

watching, or "peeping," is to attain sexual excitement. The person who engages in voyeurism does not typically seek sexual activity with the person or persons being observed.

Are the acts of watching one's partner disrobe or viewing sexually explicit films forms of voyeurism? The answer is no. The people who are observed know they are being observed by their partners or will be observed by film audiences. Voyeuristic acts involve watching unsuspecting persons disrobing or engaging in sexual activities. Note that feelings of sexual arousal while watching our partners undress or observing sex scenes in R- and X-rated films fall within the normal spectrum of human sexuality.

During voyeuristic acts, the person usually masturbates while watching or while fantasizing about watching. Peeping may be the person's exclusive sexual outlet. Some people engage in voyeuristic acts in which they place themselves in risky situations. The prospect of being found out or injured apparently heightens the excitement.

Frotteurism

The French word *frottage* refers to the artistic technique of making a drawing by rubbing against a raised object. The chief feature of the paraphilia of **frotteurism** is recurrent, powerful sexual urges and related fantasies involving rubbing against or touching a nonconsenting person. Frotteurism or "mashing" generally occurs in crowded places, such as subway cars, buses, or elevators. It is the rubbing or touching, not the coercive aspect of the act, that is sexually arousing to the man. He may imagine himself enjoying an exclusive, affectionate sexual relationship with the victim. Because the physical contact is brief and furtive, people who commit frotteuristic acts stand only a small chance of being caught by authorities. Even the victims may not realize at the time what has happened or register much protest (Spitzer et al., 1989). In the following case example, a man victimized about 1,000 women over a period of years but was arrested only twice:

A Case of Frotteurism

A 45-year-old man was seen by a psychiatrist following his second arrest for rubbing against a woman in the subway. He would select as his target a woman in her 20s as she entered the subway station. He would then position himself behind her on the platform and wait for the train to arrive. He would then follow her into the subway car and when the doors closed would begin bumping against her buttocks, while fantasizing that they were enjoying having intercourse in a loving and consensual manner. About half of the time he would reach orgasm. He would then continue on his way to work. Sometimes when he hadn't reached orgasm, he would change trains and seek another victim. While he felt guilty for a time after each episode, he would soon become preoccupied with thoughts about his next encounter. He never gave any thought to the feelings his victims might have about what he had done to them. While he was married to the same woman for 25 years, he appears to be rather socially inept and unassertive, especially with women.

—Adapted from Spitzer et al., 1994, pp. 164–165; reprinted from Nevid, Fichner-Rathus, & Rathus, 1995, p. 570

frotteurism A paraphilia characterized by recurrent sexual urges involving bumping or rubbing against nonconsenting others for sexual gratification.

pedophilia A paraphilia involving recurrent, powerful sexual urges and related fantasies involving sexual activity with prepubescent children.

Pedophilia

Pedophilia derives from the Greek *paidos*, meaning "child." The chief feature of pedophilia is recurrent, powerful sexual urges and related fantasies involving sexual activity with prepubescent children (typically 13 years old or younger). Molestation of children may or may not occur. To be diagnosed with pedophilia, the person must be at least 16 years of age and at least 5 years older than the child or children toward whom the person is sexually attracted or has victimized. In some cases of pedophilia, the person is attracted only to children. In other cases, the person is attracted to adults as well.

Although some persons with pedophilia restrict their pedophilic activity to looking at or undressing children, others engage in exhibitionism, kissing, fondling, oral sex, and anal intercourse and, in the case of girls, vaginal intercourse (Knudsen, 1991). Not being worldly wise, children are often taken advantage of by molesters who inform them they are "educating" them, "showing them something," or doing something they will "like." Some men with pedophilia limit their sexual activity with children to incestuous relations with family members; others only molest children outside the family. Not all child molesters have pedophilia, however. The clinical definition of pedophilia is brought to bear only when sexual attraction to children is recurrent and persistent. Some molesters engage in these acts or experience pedophilic urges only occasionally or during times of opportunity.

Despite the stereotype, most cases of pedophilia do not involve "dirty old men" who hang around schoolyards in raincoats. Men with this disorder (virtually all cases involve men) are usually (otherwise) law-abiding, respected citizens in their 30s or 40s. Most are married or divorced and have children of their own. They are usually well acquainted with their victims, who are typically either relatives or friends of the family. Many cases of pedophilia are not isolated incidents. They may be a series of acts that begin when children are very young and continue for many years until they are discovered or the relationship is broken off (Finkelhor et al., 1990).

The origins of pedophilia are complex and varied. Some cases fit the stereotype of the weak, shy, socially inept, and isolated man who is threatened by mature relationships and turns to children for sexual gratification because children are less critical and demanding (Ames & Houston, 1990). In other cases, it may be that childhood sexual experiences with other children were so enjoyable that the man, as an adult, is attempting to recapture the excitement of earlier years. Or perhaps in some cases of pedophilia, men who were sexually abused in childhood by adults may now be reversing the situation in an effort to establish feelings of mastery. Men whose pedophilic acts involve incestuous relationships with their own children tend to fall at one extreme or the other on the dominance spectrum, either being very dominant or passive (Ames & Houston, 1990).

Sexual Masochism

Sexual masochism derives its name from the Austrian novelist Leopold Ritter von Sacher-Masoch (1836–1895), who wrote stories and novels about men who sought sexual gratification from women inflicting pain on them, often in the form of flagellation (being beaten or whipped). Sexual masochism involves strong, recurrent urges and fantasies relating to sexual acts that involve being humiliated, bound, flogged, or made to suffer in other ways. The urges are either acted on or cause significant personal distress. In some cases of sexual masochism, the person cannot attain sexual gratification in the absence of pain or humiliation.

In some cases, sexual masochism involves binding or mutilating oneself during masturbation or sexual fantasies. In others, a partner is engaged to restrain (bondage), blindfold (sensory bondage), paddle, or whip the person. Some partners are prostitutes; others are consensual partners who are asked to perform the sadistic role. In some cases, the person may desire, for purposes of sexual gratification, to be urinated or defecated upon or subjected to verbal abuse.

A most dangerous expression of masochism is **hypoxyphilia,** in which participants are sexually aroused by being deprived of oxygen—for example by using a noose, plastic bag, chemical, or pressure on the chest during a sexual act, such as masturbation. The oxygen deprivation is usually accompanied by fantasies of asphyxiating or being asphyxiated by a lover. People who engage in this activity generally discontinue it before they lose consciousness, but occasional deaths due to suffocation have resulted from miscalculations (Blanchard & Hucker, 1991).

THINK ABOUT IT
Do you believe exhibitionists, voyeurs, and pedophiles should be punished, treated, or both? Do you think that people with these different types of paraphilias should be treated differently by society? Explain.

Truth OR Fiction? REVISITED

Some people cannot become sexually aroused without pain or humiliation.

TRUE. Some people with sexual masochism cannot become sexually aroused unless they are subjected to pain or humiliation by others.

sexual masochism A paraphilia characterized by recurrent, powerful sexual urges and fantasies involving receiving humiliation or pain.

hypoxyphilia A form of sexual masochism in which a person seeks sexual gratification by being deprived of oxygen.

sexual sadism A paraphilia characterized by recurrent, powerful sexual urges and fantasies involving inflicting humiliation or pain.

sadomasochism Sexual activities involving the attainment or gratification by means of inflicting and receiving pain and humiliation

Sexual Sadism

Sexual sadism is named after the infamous Marquis de Sade, the 18th-century Frenchman who wrote stories about the pleasures of achieving sexual gratification by inflicting pain or humiliation on others. Sexual sadism is the flip side of sexual masochism. It involves recurrent, powerful urges and related fantasies to engage in acts in which the person is sexually aroused by inflicting physical suffering or humiliation on another person. People with this paraphilia either act out their fantasies or are disturbed by them. They may recruit consenting partners, who may be lovers or wives with a masochistic streak, or prostitutes. Still others stalk and assault nonconsenting victims and become aroused by inflicting pain or suffering on their victims. Sadistic rapists fall into this last group. Most rapists, however, do not seek to become sexually aroused by inflicting pain on their victims; they may even lose sexual interest when they see their victims in pain.

Many people have occasional sadistic or masochistic fantasies or engage in sex play involving simulated or mild forms of **sadomasochism** with their partners. Sadomasochism describes a mutually gratifying sexual interaction involving both sadistic and masochistic acts. Simulation may take the form of using a feather brush to strike one's partner, so that no actual pain is administered. People who engage in sadomasochism frequently switch roles during their encounters or from one encounter to another. The clinical diagnosis of sexual masochism or sadism is not usually brought to bear unless such people become distressed by their behavior or fantasies, or act them out in ways that are harmful to themselves or others.

Other Paraphilias

There are many other paraphilias. These include making obscene phone calls ("telephone scatologia"), necrophilia (sexual urges or fantasies involving sexual contact with corpses), partialism (sole focus on part of the body), zoophilia (sexual urges or fantasies involving sexual contact with animals), and sexual arousal associated with feces (coprophilia), enemas (klismaphilia), and urine (urophilia).

Theoretical Perspectives

Psychodynamic theorists see many paraphilias as defenses against leftover castration anxiety from the Oedipal period. The thought of the penis disappearing within the vagina is unconsciously equated with castration. The man who develops a paraphilia may avoid this threat of castration anxiety by displacing sexual arousal into safer activities—for example, undergarments, children, or watching others. By sequestering his penis under women's clothes, the man with transvestic fetishism engages in a symbolic act of denial that women do not have penises, which eases castration anxiety by unconsciously providing evidence of women's (and his own) safety. The shock and dismay shown by the victim of a man who exposes himself provides unconscious reassurance that he does, after all, have a penis. Sadism involves an unconscious identification with the man's father—the "aggressor" of his Oedipal fantasies—and relieves anxiety by giving him the opportunity to enact the role of the castrator. Some psychoanalytic theorists see masochism as a way of coping with conflicting feelings about sex. Basically, the man feels guilty about sex, but is able to enjoy it so long as he is being punished for it. Others view masochism as the redirection inward of aggressive impulses originally aimed at the powerful, threatening father. Like the child who is relieved when his inevitable punishment is over, the man gladly accepts humiliation and punishment in place of castration. These views remain speculative and controversial. We lack any direct evidence that men with paraphilias are handicapped by unresolved castration anxiety.

Learning theorists explain paraphilias in terms of conditioning and observational learning. Some object or activity becomes inadvertently associated with sexual arousal. The object or activity then gains the capacity to elicit sexual arousal. For example, a boy who glimpses his mother's stockings on the towel rack while he is masturbating may go on to develop a fetish for stockings (Breslow, 1989). Orgasm in the presence of the object reinforces the erotic connection, especially when it occurs repeatedly. Yet if fetishes were acquired by mechanical association, we might expect people to develop fetishes to stimuli that are inadvertently and repeatedly connected with sexual activity, such as bedsheets, pillows, even ceilings. But they do not. The *meaning* of the stimulus plays a primary role. The development of fetishes may depend on eroticizing certain types of stimuli (such as women's undergarments) by incorporating them within sexual fantasies and masturbation rituals.

Fetishes can often be traced to early childhood. Consider the development of rubber fetishes. Reinisch (1990) speculates that the earliest awareness of sexual arousal or response (such as erection) may have been connected with rubber pants or diapers such that an association was made between the two, setting the stage for the development of the fetish.

Like other patterns of abnormal behavior, paraphilias may involve multiple biological, psychological, and sociocultural factors. Money and Lamacz (1990) hypothesize a multifactorial model that traces the development of paraphilias to childhood. They suggest that childhood experiences etch a pattern, or "lovemap," which can be likened to a software program in the brain that determines the kinds of stimuli and behaviors that come to arouse people sexually. In the case of paraphilias, lovemaps become "vandalized" by early traumatic experiences, such as incest, physical abuse, neglect, or excessively harsh antisexual child rearing. Yet not all children who undergo such experiences develop paraphilias. Nor do all people with paraphilias have such traumatic experiences. Perhaps some children are more vulnerable to developing distorted lovemaps than others. The precise nature of such vulnerability remains to be defined.

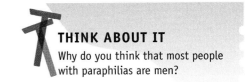

THINK ABOUT IT
Why do you think that most people with paraphilias are men?

Treatment of Paraphilias

People with paraphilia don't typically seek treatment on their own. They usually receive treatment in prison after they have been convicted of a sexual offense. Or they may be referred to a treatment provider by the courts. Under these circumstances, it is not surprising that sex offenders are often resistant or recalcitrant to treatment. Therapists recognize that treatment may be futile when clients lack the motivation to change their behavior. Nonetheless, evidence suggests that some forms of treatment, principally behavior therapy and cognitive behavioral therapy, may be helpful to sex offenders who seek to change their behavior.

One behavioral technique used in treating paraphilias is aversive conditioning. The goal of treatment is to induce a negative emotional response to inappropriate stimuli or fantasies. In this technique, a stimulus that elicits sexual arousal (for example, panties) is paired repeatedly with an aversive stimulus (for example, electric shock) in the hope that the stimulus will acquire aversive properties. A basic limitation of aversive conditioning is that it does not help the individual acquire more adaptive behaviors in place of maladaptive response patterns. This may explain why researchers find that a broad-based, cognitive-behavioral program for treating exhibitionism that emphasized the development of adaptive thoughts, the building of social skills, and the development of stress management skills was more effective than an alternative program based on aversion therapy (Marshall, Eccles, & Barbaree, 1991). *Covert sensitization* is a variation of aversive conditioning in which the pairing of an aversive stimulus and the problem behavior occurs in imagination.

Maletzky (1991, 1998) reported on the success rates of the largest treatment program study to date, based on more than 7,000 cases of rapists and sex offenders with paraphilias. Treatment incorporated a variety of behavioral techniques, including aversive conditioning and nonaversive methods, to help individuals acquire more adaptive behaviors. Though success rates exceeding 80% were reported, the criteria for success depended on part on self-reports of an absence of deviant sexual interests or behavior. As we know, self-reports may be biased, especially in offender groups. Secondly, lacking a control group, we cannot discount the possibility that other factors, such as fears of legal consequences, influenced the outcome.

Some promising results are also reported in using the antidepressant Prozac in treating voyeurism and fetishism (Lorefice, 1991; Perilstein, Lipper, & Friedman, 1991). Why Prozac? Prozac has been used effectively in treating obsessive-compulsive disorder (see Chapter 6). Researchers speculate that paraphilias may fall within an obsessive-compulsive spectrum. Many people with paraphilias report feeling compelled to carry out paraphilic acts, in much the same way that people with obsessive-compulsive disorder feel driven to perform compulsive acts. Paraphilias also tend to have an obsessional quality. The person experiences intrusive, repetitive urges to engage in paraphilic acts or thoughts that relate to the paraphilic object or situation. However, Maletzky (1998) cautions that these drugs may act to reduce sexual drives, rather than specifically target deviant sexual fantasies.

Quiz **12.3**
Paraphilias

Overview of Paraphilias

MAJOR TYPES OF PARAPHILIAS	Atypical or deviant patterns of sexual gratification; excepting masochism, these disorders occur almost exclusively among males
Exhibitionism	Sexual gratification from exposing one's genitals in public
Voyeurism	Sexual gratification from observing unsuspecting others who are naked, undressing, or engaging in sexual arousal
Sexual masochism	Sexual gratification associated with the receipt of humiliation or pain
Fetishism	Sexual attraction to inanimate objects or particular body parts
Frotteurism	Sexual gratification associated with acts of bumping or rubbing against nonconsenting strangers
Sexual sadism	Sexual gratification associated with inflicting humiliation or pain on others
Transvestic fetishism	Sexual gratification associated with cross-dressing
Pedophilia	Sexual attraction to children

CAUSAL FACTORS	Multiple causes may be involved
Learning Perspective	• Atypical stimuli become conditioned stimuli for sexual arousal as the result of prior pairing with sexual activity • Atypical stimuli may become eroticized by incorporating them within erotic and masturbatory fantasies
Psychodynamic Perspective	• Unresolved castration anxiety from childhood leads to sexual arousal being displaced onto safer objects or activities
Multifactorial Perspective	• Sexual or physical abuse in childhood may corrupt normal sexual arousal patterns

TREATMENT APPROACHES	Results remain questionable
Biomedical Treatment	• Antidepressants to help individuals control deviant sexual urges or reduce sexual drives
Cognitive-Behavioral Therapy	• Including aversive conditioning (pairing deviant stimuli with aversive stimuli), covert sensitization (pairing the undesirable behavior with an aversive stimulus in imagination), and nonaversive methods that help individuals acquire more adaptive behaviors

Sexual Dysfunctions

Sexual dysfunctions involve problems with sexual interest, arousal, or response. Sexual dysfunctions are widespread in our society, affecting 43% of women and 31% of men, according to a recent national survey (Laumann, Paik, & Rosen, 1999). They are often significant sources of distress to the affected person and his or her partner. There are various types of sexual dysfunctions, but they tend to share some common features, as outlined in Table 12.2. Table 12.3 shows the estimated rates of several major types of sexual dysfunction based on recent community samples.

Some cases of sexual dysfunction have existed throughout the individual's lifetime, and are thus labeled *lifelong dysfunctions.* In the case of an *acquired dysfunction,* the problem begins following a period (or at least one occurrence) of normal functioning. In the case of a *situational dysfunction,* the problem occurs in some situations (for example, with one's spouse), but not in others (for example, with a lover or when masturbating), or at some times but not others. In the case of a *generalized dysfunction,* the problem occurs in all situations and at all times the individual engages in sexual activity.

To provide perspective on the sexual dysfunctions, we first describe normal patterns of sexual response. Then we explore the various types of sexual dysfunctions and the methods used to treat them.

sexual dysfunctions Persistent problems with sexual interest, arousal, or response.

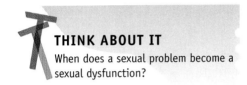

THINK ABOUT IT
When does a sexual problem become a sexual dysfunction?

TABLE 12.2 Common Features of Sexual Dysfunctions

Feature	Description
Fear of failure	Fears relating to failure to achieve or maintain erection or failure to reach orgasm.
Assumption of a spectator role rather than a performer role	Monitoring and evaluating your body's reactions during sex.
Diminished self-esteem	Thinking less of yourself for failure to meet your standard of normality.
Emotional effects	Guilt, shame, frustration, depression, anxiety.
Avoidance behavior	Avoiding sexual contacts for fear of failure to perform adequately; making excuses to your partner.

Source. From Nevid, Fichner-Rathus, & Rathus (1995), p. 445. Reprinted with permission.

TABLE 12.3 Estimated Prevalence of Various Current Sexual Dysfunctions (percentage of respondents reporting any problem)

Premature ejaculation	36–38
Erectile dysfunction	4–9
Male orgasmic disorder	4–10
Female orgasmic disorder	5–10

Source. Adapted from Spector, I. M., & Carey, M. P. (1990). Incidence and prevalence of the sexual dysfunctions: A critical review of the empirical evidence. *Archives of Sexual Behavior, 19,* 389–408.

When a source of pleasure becomes a source of anxiety. Sexual dysfunctions can be a source of intense personal distress and lead to friction between partners. Problems in communication can give rise to or exacerbate sexual dysfunctions.

The Sexual Response Cycle

Sexual dysfunctions interfere with the initiation or completion of the sexual response cycle. Much of our understanding of the sexual response cycle is based on the pioneering work of sex researchers William Masters and Virginia Johnson. Elaborating on their work and others, such as the sex therapist Helen Singer Kaplan, the *DSM* describes the sexual response cycle in terms of four distinct phases:

1. *Appetitive Phase.* This phase involves sexual fantasies and the desire to engage in sexual activity. The occurrence of sexual fantasies and desires are quite normal; the question is, "How much (or how little) sexual interest is normal?"

2. *Excitement Phase.* This phase involves the physical changes and feelings of pleasure that occur during the process of sexual arousal. In response to sexual stimulation, the heart rate, respiration rate, and blood pressure increase. Sexual excitement involves two essential sexual reflexes—erection in the man and vaginal lubrication ("wetness") in the woman. In men, erection occurs as blood vessels in chambers of loose tissue within the penis dilate to permit an increased blood flow to expand the tissues. In women, the breasts swell and the nipples become erect. Blood engorges the genitals, causing the clitoris to expand. The vagina lengthens and dilates, and lubrication appears as the engorgement of the blood vessels in the vagina forces moisture through capillary membranes.

3. *Orgasm Phase.* In both men and women, the building up of sexual tension reaches a peak and is released through involuntary rhythmic contractions of the pelvic muscles that are accompanied by feelings of pleasure. Orgasm, like erection and lubrication, is a reflex. In men, the contraction of the pelvic muscles forces semen to be expelled through the tip of the penis during ejaculation. In women, the pelvic muscles surrounding the outer third of the vagina contract reflexively. In men and women, the first contractions are strongest and spaced at 0.8-second intervals (five contractions in 4 seconds). Subsequent contractions are weaker and spread farther apart.

    People cannot will or force an orgasm. Nor can they will or force other sexual reflexes, such as erection and vaginal lubrication. We can only set the stage for these sexual responses and let them happen. Setting the stage for orgasm involves receiving adequate sexual stimulation and having an accepting attitude toward sexual pleasure. But trying to force an orgasm is likely to prevent it from happening.

4. *Resolution Phase.* Relaxation and a sense of well-being occur. During this phase, men are physiologically incapable of achieving erection and orgasm for a period of time. Women, however, may be able to maintain a high level of sexual excitement with continued stimulation, and experience multiple orgasms in swift succession. During the sexual revolution of the 1960s and 1970s, awareness of this capacity for multiple orgasm caused some women to think they ought not to be satisfied with just one orgasm. This is the flip side of the old saw that sexual enjoyment is appropriate for men only. In sex, as in other areas of life, oughts and shoulds are often arbitrary demands that elicit feelings of anxiety and inadequacy.

Types of Sexual Dysfunctions

The *DSM-IV* groups most sexual dysfunctions within the following categories:

1. Sexual desire disorders
2. Sexual arousal disorders

3. Orgasm disorders

4. Sexual pain disorders

The first three categories correspond to the first three phases of the sexual response cycle.

Sexual Desire Disorders Sexual desire disorders involve disturbances in sexual appetite or an aversion to genital sexual activity. People with **hypoactive sexual desire disorder** have an absence or lack of sexual interest or desire. Typically there is either a complete or virtual absence of sexual fantasies. However, clinicians have not reached any universally agreed-upon criteria for determining the level of sexual desire that is considered normal (J. G. Beck, 1995). Individual clinicians must weigh various factors in reaching a diagnosis in cases of low sexual desire, such as the client's lifestyle (for example, in parents contending with the demands of infants or young children, lack of sexual energy or interest is to be expected), sociocultural factors (for example, culturally restrictive attitudes may restrain sexual desire or interest), the quality of the relationship between the client and her or his partner (declining sexual interest or activity may reflect relationship problems rather than diminished drive), and the client's age (desire normally declines but does not disappear with increasing age). Couples usually seek help when one or both partners recognize that the level of sexual activity in the relationship is deficient or has waned to the point that little desire or interest remains. Sometimes the lack of desire is limited to one partner. In other cases, both partners may feel sexual urges, but anger and conflict concerning other issues inhibit sexual interaction. Giving lie to the myth that men are always ready for sex, the numbers of men presenting with hypoactive sexual desire disorder appears to be on the rise (Letourneau & O'Donohue, 1993).

People with **sexual aversion disorder** have a strong aversion to genital sexual contact and avoid all or nearly all genital contact with a partner. They may, however, desire and enjoy affectionate contact or nongenital sexual contact. Their disgust with any form of genital contact may stem from childhood sexual abuse, rape, or other traumatic experiences. In other cases, deep-seated feelings of sexual guilt or shame may impair sexual response. In men, the diagnosis is often connected with a history of erectile failure (Spark, 1991). Such men may associate sexual opportunities with failure and shame. Their partners may also develop aversions to sexual contact because their sexual contacts have been so frustrating or emotionally painful.

Sexual Arousal Disorders Disorders of sexual arousal involve an inability to achieve or maintain the physiological responses involved in sexual arousal or excitement—vaginal lubrication in the woman or penile erection in the man—that are needed to allow completion of sexual activity.

In women, sexual arousal is characterized by lubrication of the vaginal walls that makes entry by the penis possible. In men, sexual arousal is characterized by erection. Almost all women now and then have difficulty becoming or remaining lubricated. Almost all men have occasional difficulty attaining or maintaining an erection through intercourse. The diagnoses of **female sexual arousal disorder** and **male erectile disorder** (also called *sexual impotence* or *erectile dysfunction*) are reserved for persistent or recurrent problems in becoming genitally aroused.

Orgasm Disorders Orgasm or sexual climax is an involuntary reflex that results in rhythmic contractions of the pelvic muscles and is usually accompanied by feelings of intense pleasure. In men, these contractions are accompanied by expulsion of semen. There are three specific types of orgasm disorders: **female orgasmic disorder, male orgasmic disorder,** and **premature ejaculation.**

Orgasmic disorders are seen as a pattern of difficulty reaching orgasm, or inability to reach orgasm following a normal level of sexual interest and arousal. The clinician needs to make a judgment about whether there is an "adequate" amount and type of stimulation to achieve an orgasmic response. A broad range of normal variation in sexual response needs to be considered. Many women, for example, require direct clitoral stimulation (by means

hypoactive sexual desire disorder Persistent or recurring lack of sexual interest or sexual fantasies.

sexual aversion disorder A type of sexual dysfunction characterized by aversion to and avoidance of genital sexual contact.

female sexual arousal disorder A sexual dysfunction in women involving difficulty becoming sexually aroused or lack of sexual excitement or pleasure during sexual activity.

male orgasmic disorder A sexual dysfunction in males involving difficulty achieving orgasm following a normal pattern of sexual interest and excitement.

female orgasmic disorder A sexual dysfunction in women involving difficulty reaching orgasm or inability to reach orgasm following a normal level of sexual interest and arousal.

male erectile disorder A sexual dysfunction in men characterized by difficulty achieving or maintaining erection during sexual activity.

premature ejaculation A sexual dysfunction in men characterized by ejaculation following minimal sexual stimulation.

Truth OR Fiction? REVISITED

Premature ejaculation affects a relatively small proportion of men.

FALSE. Premature ejaculation is extremely common, affecting about one in three men.

Web Link 12.4
wWw Online Sexual Disorders Screening for Women (NYU School of Medicine)

Web Link 12.5
wWw Online Sexual Disorders Screening for Men (NYU School of Medicine)

dyspareunia Persistent or recurrent pain experienced during or following sexual intercourse.

vaginismus A sexual dysfunction characterized by persistent or recurring contraction of the muscles surrounding the vaginal opening, making intercourse difficult or impossible.

of stimulation by her own hand or her partner's) in order to achieve orgasm during vaginal intercourse. This should not be considered abnormal, since the clitoris, not the vagina, is the woman's most erotically sensitive organ.

In men, a pattern of difficulty achieving orgasm following a normal pattern of sexual interest and excitement is termed *male orgasmic disorder*. This disorder is relatively rare and has received very little attention in the clinical literature (Dekker, 1993; Rosen & Leiblum, 1995). Men with this problem can usually reach orgasm through masturbation but not through intercourse. Because of its infrequency, there are only a few isolated case studies on the problem (Rathus, 1978).

Premature ejaculation refers to a pattern of ejaculating with minimal sexual stimulation. It can occur prior to, upon, or shortly after penetration, but before the man desires it. Note the subjective elements. In making the diagnosis, the clinician weighs the man's age, the novelty of the partner, and the frequency of sexual activity. Occasional experiences of rapid ejaculation, such as when the man is with a new partner, has had infrequent sexual contacts, or is very highly aroused, fall within the normal spectrum. More persistent patterns of premature ejaculation would occasion a diagnosis of the disorder. About one in three men experience premature ejaculation (Spector & Carey, 1990).

Sexual Pain Disorders In **dyspareunia**, sexual intercourse is associated with recurrent pain in the genital region. The pain cannot be explained fully by an underlying medical condition and so is believed to have a psychological component. However, many, perhaps even most, cases of pain during intercourse are traceable to an underlying medical condition, such as insufficient lubrication or a urinary tract infection. The *DSM* classifies these cases under a different diagnostic label, "Sexual Dysfunction Due to Medical Condition."

Vaginismus involves an involuntary spasm of the muscles surrounding the vagina when vaginal penetration is attempted, making sexual intercourse painful or impossible.

Theoretical Perspectives

Like most psychological disorders, sexual dysfunctions reflect the interplay of biological, psychological, and other factors.

Biological Perspectives Many cases of sexual dysfunction stem from underlying biological factors or from a combination of biological and psychological factors (Carey, Wincze & Meisler, 1998). Deficient testosterone production and thyroid overactivity or underactivity are among the many biological conditions that can lead to impaired sexual desire (Kresin, 1993). Medical conditions can also impair sexual arousal in both men and women. Diabetes, for instance, is the most common organic cause of erectile dysfunction, with estimates indicating that half of diabetic men eventually suffer some degree of erectile dysfunction (Thomas & LoPiccolo, 1994). Diabetes may also impair sexual response in women, with decreased vaginal lubrication being the most common consequence.

Biological factors may play a prominent role in as many as 70% to 80% of cases of erectile dysfunction (Brody, 1995b). Other biological factors that can impair sexual desire, arousal, and orgasm include nerve-damaging conditions such as multiple sclerosis; lung disorders; kidney disease; circulatory problems; damage caused by sexually transmitted diseases; and side effects of various drugs (Brody, 1995b; Segraves, 1988; Spark, 1991). Yet, even in cases of sexual dysfunction that are traced to physical causes, emotional problems such as anxiety and depression and marital conflict can compound the problem.

The male sex hormone testosterone plays a pivotal role in energizing sexual desire and sexual activity in both men and women (Tuiten et al., 2000; Yates, 2000). Both men and women produce testosterone in their bodies, although women produce smaller amounts. Men with deficient production of testosterone may lose sexual interest and the capacity for erections (Kresin, 1993; Spark, 1991). The adrenal glands and ovaries are the sites where testosterone is produced in women. Women who have these organs surgically removed because of invasive disease no longer produce testosterone and may gradually lose sexual interest and the capacity for sexual response. Recent evidence shows that replacement testosterone can improve sexual functioning in such cases (Shifren et al., 2000). We should recognize, however, that most men and women with sexual dysfunctions have normal hormone levels (Spark, 1991).

Psychodynamic Perspectives Psychodynamic hypotheses generally revolve around presumed conflicts of the phallic stage (Fenichel, 1945). Mature genital sexuality is believed to require successful resolution of the Oedipus and Electra complexes. Men with sexual dysfunctions are presumed to suffer from unconscious castration anxiety. Sexual intercourse elicits an unconscious fear of retaliation by the father, rendering the vagina unsafe. Erectile dysfunction "saves" the man from having to enter the vagina. Premature ejaculation allows him to "escape" rapidly and may also represent unconscious hatred of women (Kaplan, 1974). Orgasmic disorder prevents him from completing the act and unconsciously minimizes his guilt and fear. Rapid ejaculation serves the unconscious purpose of expressing hatred through soiling the woman and denying her sexual pleasure.

In women, unresolved penis envy engenders hostility toward men. The woman who remains fixated in the phallic stage punishes her partner for having a penis by not permitting the organ to bring her pleasure, as in female sexual arousal disorder. The clamping down of the vaginal muscles in vaginismus may express an unconscious wish to castrate her partner (Kaplan, 1974). In orgasmic disorder, she has failed to overcome penis envy and to develop mature sexuality, which involves transferring erotic feelings from the clitoris to the vagina. She thus prevents orgasm from occurring through intercourse. It is difficult to test the validity of the psychoanalytic concepts because they involve unconscious conflicts, like castration anxiety and penis envy, which cannot be scientifically observed. Evidence for these views relies on case studies that involve interpretation of patients' histories. Case study accounts are open to rival interpretations, however. We can say with certainty, however, that despite the traditional psychoanalytic conception, clitoral stimulation remains a key part of the woman's erotic response as she matures and is not a sign of an immature fixation.

Learning Perspectives Learning theorists focus on the role of conditioned anxiety in the development of sexual dysfunctions. The occurrence of physically or psychologically painful experiences associated with sexual activity may cause a person to respond to sexual encounters with anxiety that is strong enough to counteract sexual pleasure and performance. A history of sexual abuse or rape plays a role in many cases in women of sexual arousal disorder, sexual aversion disorder, orgasmic disorder, and vaginismus. People who have been sexually traumatized earlier in life may find it difficult to respond sexually when they develop intimate relationships. They may be flooded with feelings of helplessness, unresolved anger, or misplaced guilt, or experience flashbacks of the abusive experiences when they engage in sexual relations with their partners, preventing them from becoming sexually aroused or achieving orgasm (see Chapter 16 for a discussion of the psychological effects of rape).

Sexual fulfillment is also based on learning sexual skills. Sexual skills or competencies, like other types of skills, are acquired through opportunities for new learning. We learn about how our bodies and our partners respond sexually in various ways, including trial and error with our partners, by learning about our own sexual response through self-exploration (as in masturbation), by reading about sexual techniques, and perhaps by talking to others or viewing sex films or videotapes. Yet children who are raised to feel guilty or anxious about sex may have lacked such opportunities to develop sexual knowledge and skills. Consequently, they may respond to sexual opportunities with feelings of anxiety and shame rather than arousal and pleasure.

Cognitive Perspectives Albert Ellis (1977b) points out that irrational beliefs and attitudes may contribute to sexual dysfunctions. Consider the irrational beliefs that we must have the approval at all times of everyone who is important to us and that we must be thoroughly competent at everything we do. If we cannot accept the occasional disappointment of others, we may catastrophize the significance of a single frustrating sexual episode. If we insist that every sexual experience be perfect, we set the stage for inevitable failure.

Truth OR Fiction? REVISITED

The male sex hormone testosterone is produced by the body in both women and men.

TRUE. Both men and women produce testosterone in their bodies, although women produce smaller amounts than men.

Evidence also points to a role for personal attributions, or perceived causes of events. Attributing the cause for erectile difficulty to oneself rather than to the situation may play an important role in determining future sexual functioning (Weisberg et al., 2001).

The prominent sex therapist Helen Singer Kaplan (1974) noted problems that can occur with our ability to regulate our levels of sexual arousal. Men who ejaculate prematurely, for example, may have difficulty gauging their level of sexual arousal. As a consequence, they may not be able to temporarily suspend stimulation in time to delay ejaculation.

Most men respond to sexual arousal with positive emotions, such as joy and warmth. But for men with sexual dysfunctions, sexual arousal becomes disconnected from positive emotions (Rowland, Cooper, & Slob, 1996). Psychologist David Barlow (1986) proposed that anxiety may have inhibiting or arousing effects on sexual response depending on the man's thought processes (see Figure 12.1). For men with sexual dysfunctions, anxiety has inhibiting effects. Perhaps because they expect to fail in sexual encounters, their thoughts are focused on anticipated feelings of shame and embarrassment rather than on erotic stimuli. Concerns about failing increase autonomic arousal or anxiety, which leads them to focus even more attention on the consequences of failure, which in turn leads to dysfunctional performance. Failure experiences in turn lead to avoidance of sexual encounters because these situations have become encoded as opportunities for repeated failure, frustration, and self-defeat. Functional men, by contrast, expect to succeed and focus their attention on erotic stimuli, not on fears of failure. Their erotic attentional focus increases autonomic arousal or anxiety, but not to the point that it interferes with their sexual response. Mild anxiety may actually enhance their sexual arousal. By focusing on erotic cues, functional men become more aroused, successfully engage in sexual activity, and heighten their expectations of future successful performance—all leading to increased approach tendencies.

The cognitive model formulated by Barlow highlights the role of interfering cognitions in sexual dysfunctions. Interfering cognitions include expectancies of failure that are evoked by performance demands. They heighten anxiety to the point of impairing sexual performance. In a vicious cycle, the more people focus on these interfering cognitions, the more difficult it will be for them to perform sexually—and the more likely they will be to focus on interfering cognitions in the future. Although the model was derived from research on men, Barlow believes it may also help explain sexual dysfunctions in women.

Problems in Relationships As the saying goes, "It takes two to tango." Sexual relations are usually no better than other facets of relationships or marriages (Perlman & Abramson, 1982). Couples who harbor resentments toward one another may choose the sexual arena for combat. Communication problems, moreover, are linked to general marital dissatisfaction. Couples who find it difficult to communicate their sexual desires may lack the means to help their partners become more effective lovers.

The following case illustrates how sexual arousal disorder may be connected with problems in the relationship:

The Case of Paul and Petula

After living together for six months, Paul and Petula are contemplating marriage. But a problem has brought them to a sex therapy clinic. As Petula puts it, "For the last two months he hasn't been able to keep his erection after he enters me." Paul is 26 years old, a lawyer; Petula, 24, is a buyer for a large department store. They both grew up in middle-class, suburban families, were introduced through mutual friends and began having intercourse, without difficulty, a few months into their relationship. At Petula's urging, Paul moved into her apartment, although he wasn't sure he was ready for such a step. A week later he began to have difficulty maintaining his erection during intercourse, although he felt strong desire for his partner. When his erection waned, he would try again, but would lose his desire and be unable to achieve another erection. After a few times like this, Petula would become so angry that she

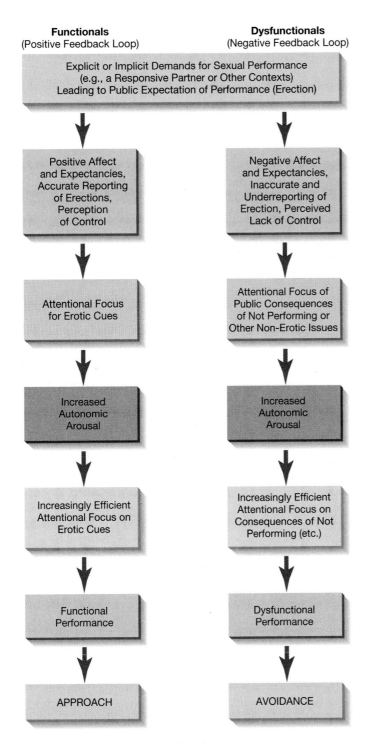

FIGURE 12.1 Barlow's model of erectile dysfunction.
In this model, past experience with erectile dysfunction leads men to expect that they will fail again. They consequently focus on anticipated feelings of shame and embarrassment when they engage in sexual relations rather than on erotic stimuli. These concerns heighten their anxiety, impairing their performance and distracting them from erotic cues. Functional men, by contrast, expect to succeed and focus more of their attention on erotic stimuli, which heightens their sexual response. Though they too may experience anxiety, it is not severe enough to distract them from erotic cues or impair their performance.

Source. Barlow, D. H. (1986), Causes of sexual dysfunction: The role of anxiety and cognitive interference. *Journal of Consulting and Clinical Psychology,* *54,* p. 146. Copyright © 2001 by the American Psychiatric Association. Reprinted with permission.

began striking Paul in the chest and screaming at him. Paul, who at 200 pounds weighed more than twice as much as Petula, would just walk away, which angered Petula even more. It became clear that sex was not the only trouble spot in their relationship. Petula complained that Paul preferred to spend time with his friends and go to baseball games than to spend time with her. When together at home, he would become absorbed in watching sports events on television, and showed no interest in activities she enjoyed—attending the theater, visiting museums, etc. Since there was no evidence that the sexual difficulty was due to either organic problems or depression, a diagnosis of male erectile disorder was given. Neither Paul nor Petula was willing to discuss their nonsexual problems with a therapist. While the sexual problem was treated successfully with a form of sex therapy modeled after techniques developed by Masters and Johnson, and the couple later married, Paul's ambivalences continued, even well into their marriage, and there were future recurrences of sexual problems as well.

—Adapted from Spitzer et al., 1994, pp. 198–200

Sociocultural Perspectives Around the turn of the 20th century, an Englishwoman was quoted as saying she would "close her eyes and think of England" when her husband approached her for sexual relations. This old-fashioned stereotype suggests how sexual pleasure was once considered exclusively a male preserve—that sex, for women, was primarily a duty. Mothers usually informed their daughters of the conjugal duties before the wedding, and girls encoded sex as just one of the ways in which women serviced the needs of others. Women who harbor such stereotypical attitudes toward female sexuality may be unlikely to become aware of their sexual potentials. In addition, sexual anxieties may transform negative expectations into self-fulfilling prophecies. Sexual dysfunctions in men, too, may be linked to severely restricted sociocultural beliefs and sexual taboos.

Modern psychodynamic theorists recognize that anger and other negative feelings that women may hold toward men can lead to sexual dysfunctions. Yet they believe that these negative emotions stem from sociocultural factors rather than from penis envy. Women in our society are often socialized to sacrifice for and submit to their husbands, which may engender rebellion that finds expression through sexual dysfunctions.

Javier (1993) notes, for example, the idealization within many Hispanic cultures of the *marianismo* stereotype, which derives its name from the Virgin Mary. From this sociocultural perspective, the ideal virtuous woman "suffers in silence" as she submerges her needs and desires to those of her husband and children. She is the provider of joy, even in the face of her own pain or frustration. It is not difficult to imagine that some women who adopt these stereotypical expectations may find it difficult to assert their own needs for sexual gratification or may express resistance to this cultural ideal by becoming sexually unresponsive.

Sociocultural factors play an important role in erectile dysfunction as well. Investigators find a greater incidence of erectile dysfunction in cultures with more restrictive sexual attitudes toward premarital sex among females, toward sex in marriage, and toward extramarital sex (Welch & Kartub, 1978). Men in these cultures may be prone to develop sexual anxiety or guilt that may interfere with sexual performance.

In India, cultural beliefs that link the loss of semen to a draining of the man's life energy underlie the development of dhat syndrome, which involves an excessive fear of semen loss (see Chapter 7). Men with this condition sometimes develop erectile dysfunction because their fears about the risks of wasting precious seminal fluid interfere with their ability to perform sexually (Singh, 1985).

Psychological Factors Various psychological factors such as depression, anxiety, guilt, and low self-esteem can impair sexual interest or performance. One principal culprit is **performance anxiety**, a type of anxiety that involves an excessive concern about whether we will be able to perform successfully. People troubled by performance anxiety become

performance anxiety Fear relating to the threat of failure to perform adequately.

spectators during sex rather than performers. Their attention is focused on how their bodies are responding (or not responding) to sexual stimulation and on their concerns about the negative consequences of failing to perform adequately, rather than absorbing themselves in their erotic experiences. Men with performance anxiety may have difficulty achieving or maintaining an erection or may ejaculate prematurely; women may fail to become adequately aroused or have difficulty achieving orgasm. A vicious cycle may ensue in which each failure experience instills deeper doubts, which leads to more anxiety during sexual encounters, which occasions repeated failure, and so on.

In Western cultures, the connection between a man's sexual performance and his sense of manhood is deeply ingrained. The man who repeatedly fails to perform sexually may suffer a loss of self-esteem, become depressed, or feel he is no longer a man (Carey, Wincze, & Meisler, 1998). He may see himself as a total failure, despite other accomplishments in life. Sexual opportunities are construed as tests of his manhood, and he may respond to them by trying to will (force) an erection. Willing an erection may backfire, because erection is a reflex that cannot be forced. With so much of his self-esteem riding on the line whenever he makes love, it is little wonder that anxiety about the quality of his performance—performance anxiety—may mount to a point that it inhibits erection. The erectile reflex is controlled by the parasympathetic branch of the autonomic nervous system. Activation of the sympathetic nervous system, which occurs when we are anxious, can block parasympathetic control, preventing the erectile reflex from occurring. Ejaculation, in contrast, is under sympathetic nervous system control, so heightened levels of arousal, as in the case of performance anxiety, can trigger premature ejaculation.

Eugene, a client who suffered from erectile dysfunction, described his feelings of sexual inadequacy this way:

The Case of Eugene

I always felt inferior, like I was on probation, having to prove myself. I felt like I was up against the wall. You can't imagine how embarrassing this was. It's like you walk out in front of an audience that you think is a nudist convention and it turns out to be a tuxedo convention.

—From the Authors' Files

Another man, Timothy, described how performance anxiety led him to prepare for sexual relations as though he were psyching himself up for a big game:

The Case of Timothy

At work I have control over what I do. With sex, you don't have control over your sex organ. I know that my mind can control what my hands do. But the same is not true of my penis. I had begun to view sex as a basketball game. I used to play in college. When I would prepare for a game, I'd always be thinking, "Who was I guarding that night?" I'd try to psych myself up, sketching out in my mind how to play this guy, thinking through all possible moves and plays. I began to do the same thing with sex. If I were dating someone, I'd be thinking the whole evening about what might happen in bed. I'd always be preparing for the outcome. I'd sketch out in my mind how I was going to touch her, what I'd ask her to do. But all the time, right through dinner or the movies, I'd be worrying that I wouldn't get it up. I kept picturing her face and how disappointed she'd be. By the time we did go to bed, I was paralyzed with anxiety.

—From the Authors' Files

Women, too, may equate their self-esteem with their ability to reach frequent and intense orgasms. Yet when men and women try to bear down to will arousal or lubrication, or to force an orgasm, they may find that the harder they try, the more these responses elude them. Thirty or 40 years ago the pressures concerning sex often revolved around the issue "Should I or shouldn't I?" Today, however, the pressures for both men and women are often based more on achieving performance goals relating to proficiency at reaching orgasm and satisfying one's partner's sexual needs.

Sex Therapy

Until the groundbreaking research of sex researchers William Masters and Virginia Johnson in the 1960s, there was no effective treatment for most sexual dysfunctions. Psychoanalytic forms of therapy approached sexual dysfunctions indirectly, for example. It was assumed that sexual dysfunctions represented underlying conflicts, and the dysfunctions might abate if the underlying conflicts—the presumed causes of the dysfunctions—were resolved through psychoanalysis. A lack of evidence that psychoanalytic approaches reversed sexual dysfunctions led clinicians and researchers to develop other approaches that focus more directly on the sexual problems themselves.

Contemporary sex therapists assume that sexual dysfunctions can be treated by directly modifying the couple's sexual interactions and patterns of communication. Pioneered by Masters and Johnson, sex therapy employs a variety of relatively brief, cognitive-behavioral techniques that center on enhancing self-efficacy expectancies, improving a couple's ability to communicate, fostering sexual competencies (sexual knowledge and skills), and reducing performance anxiety. Therapists may also work with couples to help them iron out problems in the relationship that may impede sexual functioning. When feasible, both sex partners are involved in therapy. In some cases, however, individual therapy may be preferable, as we shall see.

Significant changes have occurred in the treatment of sexual dysfunctions in the past 20 years. There is greater emphasis now on the role of biological or organic factors in the development of sexual problems and greater use of medical treatments, such as the use of the drug *Viagra* in treating male erectile dysfunction (Rosen & Leiblum, 1995). But even men whose erectile problems can be traced to physical causes can benefit from sex therapy along with medical intervention (Carey, Wincze, & Meisler, 1998).

Let us briefly survey some of the more common sex therapy techniques for particular types of disorders.

Sexual Desire Disorders Sex therapists may try to help people with low sexual desire kindle their sexual appetite through the use of self-stimulation (masturbation) exercises together with erotic fantasies. Or in working with couples, the therapist might prescribe mutual pleasuring exercises the couple could perform at home or encourage them to expand their sexual repertoire in order to add novelty and excitement to their sex life. When a lack of sexual desire is connected with depression, the treatment would probably focus on relieving the underlying depression in the hope that sexual interest would rebound when the depression lifts. When problems of low sexual desire or sexual aversion appear to be rooted in deep-seated causes, sex therapist Helen Singer Kaplan (1987) recommended the use of insight-oriented approaches to help uncover and resolve underlying issues. Some cases of hypoactive sexual desire involve hormonal deficiencies, especially lack of testosterone (Rabkin, Wagner, & Rabkin, 2000). Testosterone replacement is effective only in the relatively few cases in which production of the hormone is truly deficient (Spark, 1991). A lack of sexual desire may also reflect relationship problems that may need to be addressed through couples therapy. Couples therapy might also be used when sexual aversion develops from problems in the relationship (Gold & Gold, 1993). In other cases of sexual aversion, a program of mutual pleasuring, beginning with partner stimulation in nongenital areas and gradually progressing to genital stimulation, may help desensitize fears about sexual contact.

Disorders of Arousal Women who have difficulty becoming sexually aroused and men with erectile problems are first educated to the fact that they need not "do" anything to become aroused. As long as their problems are psychological, not organic, they need only

THINK ABOUT IT

Can you think of examples in your own life in which you have been hampered by performance anxiety of one kind or another? What did you do about it?

Masters and Johnson. Sex therapists William Masters and Virginia Johnson.

experience sexual stimulation under relaxed, nonpressured conditions, so that disruptive cognitions and anxiety do not inhibit reflexive responses.

Masters and Johnson have the couple counter performance anxiety by engaging in **sensate focus exercises.** These are nondemand sexual contacts—sensuous exercises that do not demand sexual arousal in the form of vaginal lubrication or erection. Partners begin by massaging one another without touching the genitals. The partners learn to "pleasure" each other and to "be pleasured" by means of following and giving verbal instructions and by guiding each other's hands. The method fosters both communication and sexual skills and countermands anxiety because there is no demand for sexual arousal. After several sessions, direct massage of the genitals is included in the pleasuring exercise. Even when obvious signs of sexual excitement are produced (lubrication or erection), the couple does not straight-away engage in intercourse, because intercourse might create performance demands. After excitement is achieved consistently, the couple engages in a relaxed sequence of other sexual activities, culminating eventually in intercourse. A number of similar sex therapy methods were employed in the following case:

Viagra. Viagra, the first drug approved to treat erectile dysfunction, became the fastest selling new drug in history after its introduction in 1998. Former senator and presidential candidate Bob Dole became a spokesperson for the drug and has appeared in many advertisements for it.

The Case of Victor

Victor P., a 44-year-old concert violinist, was eager to show the therapist reviews of his concert tour. A solo violinist with a distinguished orchestra, Victor's life revolved around practice, performances, and reviews. He dazzled audiences with his technique and the energy of his performance. As a concert musician, Victor had exquisite control over his body, especially his hands. Yet he could not control his erectile response in the same way. Since his divorce seven years earlier, Victor had been troubled by recurrent episodes of erectile failure. Time and time again he had become involved in a new relationship, only to find himself unable to perform sexually. Fearing repetition, he would sever the relationship. He was unable to face an audience of only one. For a while he dated casually, but then he met Michelle.

Michelle was a writer who loved music. They were a perfect match because Victor, the musician, loved literature. Michelle, a 35-year-old divorcée, was exciting, earthy, sensual, and accepting. The couple soon grew inseparable. He would practice while she would write—poetry mostly, but also short magazine pieces. Unlike some women Victor met who did not know Bach from Bartok, Michelle held her own in conversations with Victor's friends and fellow musicians over late night dinner at Sardi's. They kept their own apartments; Victor needed his own space and solitude for practice.

*In the nine months of their relationship, Victor was unable to perform on the stage that mattered most to him—his canopied bed. It was just so frustrating, he said. "I would become erect and then just as I approach her to penetrate, pow! It collapses on me." Victor's history of nocturnal erections and erections during light petting suggested that he was basically suffering from performance anxiety. He was bearing down to force an erection, much as he might try to learn the fingering of a difficult violin piece. Each night became a command performance in which Victor served as his own severest critic. Victor became a spectator to his own performance, a role that Masters and Johnson refer to as **self-spectatoring.** Rather than focus on his partner, his attention was riveted on the size of his penis. As noted by the late great pianist Vladimir Horowitz, the worst thing a pianist can do is watch his fingers. Perhaps the worst thing a man with erectile problems can do is watch his penis.*

To break the vicious cycle of anxiety, erectile failure, and more anxiety, Victor and Michelle followed a sex therapy program (Rathus & Nevid, 1977) modeled after the Masters-and-Johnson-type treatment. The aim was to restore the pleasure of sexual activity, unfettered by anxiety. The couple was initially instructed to abstain from

sensate focus exercises Mutual pleasuring activities focused on the partners taking turns giving and receiving physical pleasure.

self-spectatoring The tendency to observe one's behavior as if one were a spectator.

attempts at intercourse to free Victor from any pressure to perform. The couple progressed through a series of steps:

1. *Relaxing together in the nude without any touching, such as when reading or watching TV together.*
2. *Sensate focus exercises.*
3. *Genital stimulation of each other manually or orally to orgasm.*
4. *Nondemand intercourse (intercourse performed without any pressure on the man to satisfy his partner). The man may afterward help his partner achieve orgasm by using manual or oral stimulation.*
5. *Resumption of vigorous intercourse (intercourse involving more vigorous thrusting and use of alternative positions and techniques that focus on mutual satisfaction). The couple is instructed not to catastrophize occasional problems that may arise.*

The therapy program helped Victor overcome his erectile disorder. Victor was freed of the need to prove himself by achieving erection on command. He surrendered his post as critic. Once the spotlight was off the bed, he became a participant and not a spectator.

—From the Authors' Files

Disorders of Orgasm Women with orgasmic disorder often harbor underlying beliefs that sex is dirty or sinful. They may have been taught not to touch themselves. They are often anxious about sex and have not learned, through trial and error, what kinds of sexual stimulation will arouse them and help them reach orgasm. Treatment in these cases includes modification of negative attitudes toward sex. When orgasmic disorder reflects the woman's feelings about or relationship with her partner, treatment requires working through these feelings or enhancing the relationship.

In either case, Masters and Johnson work with the couple and first use sensate focus exercises to lessen performance anxiety, open channels of communication, and help the couple acquire pleasuring skills. Then during genital massage and, later, during intercourse, the woman directs her partner to use caresses and techniques that stimulate her. By taking charge, the woman becomes psychologically freed from the stereotype of the passive, submissive female role.

Many researchers find that a program of directed masturbation is most effective in helping *preorgasmic* women—women who have never achieved orgasm through any means (Baucom et al., 1998; LoPiccolo & Stock, 1986). Masturbation provides a chance to learn about one's own body and give oneself pleasure without reliance on a partner or need to attend to a partner's needs. Directed masturbation programs educate women about their sexual anatomy and encourage them to experiment with self-caresses in the privacy of their own homes. Women proceed at their own pace and are encouraged to incorporate sexual fantasies and imagery during self-stimulation exercises designed to heighten their level of sexual arousal. They gradually learn to bring themselves to orgasm, sometimes with the help of an electric vibrator. Once women can masturbate to orgasm, additional couples-oriented treatment can facilitate but does not guarantee transference to orgasm with a partner.

Although scant attention in the scientific literature has been focused on male orgasmic disorder, the standard treatment, barring any underlying organic problem, focuses on increasing sexual stimulation and reducing performance anxiety (LoPiccolo, 1990; LoPiccolo & Stock, 1986).

The most widely used approach to treating premature ejaculation, called the *stop-start* or *stop-and-go* technique, was introduced in 1956 by the urologist James Semans. The man and his partner suspend sexual activity just when he is about to ejaculate and then resume stimulation when his sensations subside. Repeated practice enables him to regulate ejaculation by sensitizing him to the cues that precede the ejaculatory reflex (making him more aware of his "point of no return," the point at which the ejaculatory reflex is triggered).

Vaginismus and Dyspareunia Vaginismus is a conditioned reflex involving the involuntary constriction of the vaginal opening. It involves a psychologically based fear of penetration, rather than a physical defect or disorder (LoPiccolo & Stock, 1986). Treatment for vaginismus involves a combination of relaxation techniques and the use of vaginal dilators to gradually desensitize the vaginal musculature. The woman herself regulates the insertion of dilators (plastic rods) of increasing diameter, always proceeding at her own pace to avoid any discomfort (LoPiccolo & Stock, 1986). The method is generally successful as long as it is unhurried. Because many women with vaginismus and dyspareunia have histories of rape or sexual abuse, psychotherapy may be part of the treatment program in order to deal with the psychological consequences of traumatic experiences.

Evaluation of Sex Therapy Success rates for sex therapy have been more impressive for some disorders than for others. High levels of success are reported in treating vaginismus in women and premature ejaculation in men (J. G. Beck, 1993; O'Donohue, Letourneau, & Geer, 1993). Reported success rates in treating vaginismus have ranged as high as 80% (Hawton & Catalan, 1990) to 100% (Masters & Johnson, 1970). Success rates in treating premature ejaculation with the stop-start procedure as high as 95% have been reported, but relapse rates tend to be high (Segraves & Althof, 1998). Success rates in treating erectile dysfunction with sex therapy techniques are more variable (Rosen, 1996), and we still lack methodologically sound studies needed to support the effectiveness of these techniques (O'Donohue et al., 1999). Outcomes of treatment for male orgasmic disorder also vary and are often disappointing (Dekker, 1993).

Although some progress has been made in treating sexual desire disorders, we would benefit from new treatment techniques because present techniques often fail to resolve the problem (J. G. Beck, 1995; Hawton, 1991). Better results are generally reported from directed masturbation programs for preorgasmic women, with success rates (percentage of women achieving orgasm) reported in a range of 70% to 90% (Rosen & Leiblum, 1995). However, much lower rates are reported when measured in terms of percentages of women reporting orgasm during sexual intercourse with their partners (Segraves & Althof, 1998). Some researchers believe that the final determination of the effectiveness of directed masturbation as a treatment alternative remains to be made (O'Donohue, Dopke, & Swingen, 1997).

Biological Treatments of Male Sexual Dysfunction

Biological treatments of erectile disorder have included a wide range of techniques, but are now focused primarily on the use of drugs to either induce erections or delay ejaculation. The most widely known example is *Viagra*, a drug that expands blood vessels in the penis, which has the effect of increasing blood flow to the penis that causes it to become erect (Goldstein et al., 1998; Kolata, 1998). Taken about an hour before sexual relations, the drug has helped 70% to 80% of erectile dysfunction patients achieve erections. Viagra became the fastest selling new drug in history soon after its release. Unfortunately, Viagra has failed to help women with sexual dysfunctions ("Viagra Fails to Help Women," 2000).

Hormone treatments may be helpful to men with abnormally low levels of male sex hormones but not those whose hormone levels are within normal limits (Spark, 1991). Because hormone treatments can have side effects, such as liver damage, they should not be undertaken lightly.

Vascular surgery may be effective in rare cases in which blockage in the blood vessels prevents blood from swelling the penis, or in which the penis is structurally defective (LoPiccolo & Stock, 1986).

Recent evidence indicates that SSRI-type antidepressant drugs may also help delay ejaculation in men with premature ejaculation (Kim & Seo, 1998; Segraves & Althof, 1998). These drugs affect the availability of neurotransmitters that may play a role in the brain's regulation of the ejaculatory reflex.

All in all, the success rates reported for treating sexual dysfunctions through psychological or biological approaches are quite encouraging, especially when we remember that only a few generations ago there were no effective treatments available.

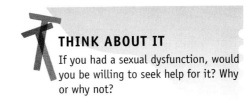

THINK ABOUT IT
If you had a sexual dysfunction, would you be willing to seek help for it? Why or why not?

Truth OR Fiction?   REVISITED

Though it is used mostly by men, Viagra can also help women overcome sexual dysfunctions.

FALSE. We lack evidence that Viagra can help women overcome sexual dysfunctions.

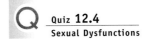

Quiz **12.4**
Sexual Dysfunctions

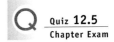

Quiz **12.5**
Chapter Exam

Research Update
Chapter 12

Overview of Sexual Dysfunctions

TYPES OF SEXUAL DYSFUNCTIONS	Problems with sexual interest, arousal, or response that may exist throughout the person's lifetime (lifelong dysfunction) or be acquired at some point after a period of normal functioning (acquired dysfunction)
Sexual Desire Disorders	• **Hypoactive sexual desire disorder:** Lack of sexual interest or desire • **Sexual aversion disorder:** Aversion to, and avoidance of, genital sexual contact
Sexual Arousal Disorders	• **Female sexual arousal disorder:** Difficulty becoming aroused or maintaining sexual arousal or excitement during sexual activity • **Male erectile disorder:** Difficulty achieving or maintaining erection during sexual activity
Orgasm Disorders	• **Female orgasmic disorder:** Difficulty achieving orgasm • **Male orgasmic disorder:** Difficulty achieving orgasm
Sexual Pain Disorders	• **Dyspareunia:** Pain during or following sexual intercourse not explainable by an underlying medical condition • **Vaginismus:** Involuntary contraction of the vaginal musculature, making penile penetration painful or impossible

CAUSAL FACTORS

Biological Factors	• Disease or deficient sex hormone production may disrupt sexual desire, arousal, or response
Psychodynamic Factors	• Psychodynamic theorists speculate that unconscious conflicts dating from childhood may lie at the root of problems with sexual arousal or response
Psychosocial Factors	• Performance anxiety arising from excessive concerns about one's ability to perform sexually • History of sexual trauma or abuse • Lack of opportunity to acquire sexual skills • Exposure to negative attitudes and beliefs toward sexuality, especially female sexuality
Cognitive Factors	• Adoption of irrational beliefs, such as the belief that one should be perfectly competent at all times, may engender performance anxiety • In premature ejaculation, failure to gauge rising levels of sexual tension preceding ejaculation • Interfering cognitions, such as fears of failure, may impair normal sexual response
Relationship Factors	• Relationship problems and failure to communicate sexual needs

TREATMENT APPROACHES — Most cases of sexual dysfunction can be treated successfully

Biomedical Treatment	• Primarily involves use of drugs to treat erectile dysfunction or premature ejaculation
Cognitive-Behavioral Therapy	• Sex therapy—brief, cognitive-behavioral techniques that help individuals and couples develop more satisfying sexual relations and reduce performance anxiety

Summing Up

Normal and Abnormal in Sexual Behavior

Where do we draw the line between normal and abnormal sexual behavior? We may label sexual behavior as abnormal when it deviates from societal norms, or when it is self-defeating, harms others, causes, personal distress, or interferes with one's ability to function. Yet we should recognize that sexual behavior that is considered normal in one culture may be deemed abnormal in another.

Gender Identity Disorder

What is gender identity disorder? People with gender identity disorder find their anatomic gender to be a source of persistent and intense distress. People with the disorder may seek to change their sex organs to resemble those of the opposite gender, and many undergo gender reassignment surgery to accomplish this purpose.

How is gender identity disorder different than sexual orientation? Gender identity disorder involves a mismatch between one's psychological sense of being male or female and one's anatomic sex. Sexual orientation relates to the direction of one's sexual attraction—toward members of one's own gender or the opposite gender. Unlike people with gender identity disorder, people with a gay male or lesbian sexual orientation have a gender identity consistent with their anatomic gender.

Paraphilias

What are paraphilias? Paraphilias are sexual deviations involving patterns of arousal to stimuli such as nonhuman objects (for example, shoes or clothes), humiliation or the experience of pain in oneself or one's partner, or children.

What are the major types of paraphilia? Paraphilias include exhibitionism, fetishism, transvestic fetishism, voyeurism, frotteurism, pedophilia, sexual masochism, and sexual sadism. Although some paraphilias are essentially harmless (such as fetishism), others, such as pedophilia and sexual sadism, often harm nonconsenting victims.

What causes are implicated in paraphilias and what makes these disorders so difficult to treat? Paraphilias may be caused by the interaction of biological, psychological, and social factors. Efforts to treat paraphilias are compromised by the fact that most people with these disorders do not wish to change.

Sexual Dysfunctions

What are the major types of sexual dysfunctions? Sexual dysfunctions include sexual desire disorders (hypoactive sexual desire disorder and sexual aversion disorder), sexual arousal disorders (female sexual arousal disorder and male erectile disorder), orgasm disorders (female and male orgasmic disorders, and premature ejaculation), and sexual pain disorders (dyspareunia and vaginismus).

What causes sexual dysfunctions? Sexual dysfunctions can stem from biological factors (such as disease or the effects of alcohol and other drugs), psychological factors (such as performance anxiety, unresolved conflicts, or lack of sexual competencies), and sociocultural factors (such as sexually restrictive cultural learning).

What are the major goals of sex therapy? Sex therapists help people overcome sexual dysfunctions by enhancing self-efficacy expectancies, teaching sexual competencies, improving sexual communication, and reducing performance anxiety.

What biologically based treatments are available to help treat male sexual dysfunctions? These include hormone treatments, vascular surgery, and most commonly, the use of drugs to help induce erections (Viagra) or delay ejaculation (antidepressants).

CHAPTER THIRTEEN

Schizophrenia and Other Psychotic Disorders

Gino Severini
The Head

Truth OR Fiction?

- Individuals may show all the signs of schizophrenia for several months but still not be diagnosed with the disorder. (p. 404)

- Some people are deluded that they are loved by a famous person. (p. 407)

- The syndrome we identify as schizophrenia is experienced in virtually the same way in every culture that has been available for study. (p. 409)

- Visual hallucinations ("seeing things") are the most common type of hallucination in people with schizophrenia. (p. 413)

- Auditory hallucinations may be a form of inner speech. (p. 415)

- Some people with schizophrenia sustain unusual, uncomfortable positions for hours and will not respond to questions or communicate during these periods. (p. 417)

- A 54-year-old hospitalized woman diagnosed with schizophrenia was conditioned to cling to a broom by being given cigarettes as reinforcers. (p. 419)

- Living in a family that is hostile, critical, and unsupportive can increase the risk of relapse in people with schizophrenia. (p. 426)

- If you have two parents with schizophrenia, it's nearly certain that you will develop schizophrenia yourself. (p. 429)

- Drugs developed in the past few years not only treat schizophrenia, but also can cure it in many cases. (p. 431)

Schizophrenia is perhaps the most puzzling and disabling clinical syndrome. It is the psychological disorder that best corresponds to popular conceptions of madness or lunacy. It often elicits fear, misunderstanding, and condemnation rather than sympathy and concern. Schizophrenia strikes at the heart of the person, stripping the mind of the intimate connections between thoughts and emotions and filling it with distorted perceptions, false ideas, and illogical conceptions, as in the following case example:

Angela's "Hellsmen"

Angela, 19, was brought to the emergency room by her boyfriend Jaime because she had cut her wrists. When she was questioned, her attention wandered. She seemed transfixed by creatures in the air, or by something she might be hearing. It seemed as though she had an invisible earphone.

Angela explained that she had slit her wrists at the command of the "hellsmen." Then she became terrified. Later she related that the hellsmen had cautioned her not to disclose their existence. Angela had been fearful that the hellsmen would punish her for her indiscretion.

Jaime related that Angela and he had been living together for nearly a year. They had initially shared a modest apartment in town. But Angela did not like being around other people and persuaded Jaime to rent a cottage in the country. There Angela spent much of her days making fantastic sketches of goblins and monsters. She occasionally became agitated and behaved as though invisible beings were issuing directions. Her words would begin to become jumbled.

Jaime would try to persuade her to go for help, but she would resist. Then, about nine months ago, the wrist-cutting began. Jaime believed that he had made the bungalow secure by removing all knives and blades. But Angela always found a sharp object.

Then he would bring Angela to the hospital against her protests. Stitches would be put in, she would be held under observation for a while, and she would be medicated. She would recount that she cut her wrists because the hellsmen had informed her that she was bad and had to die. After a few days in the hospital, she would disavow hearing the hellsmen and insist on discharge.

Jaime would take her home. The pattern would repeat itself.

—From the Authors' Files

Schizophrenia touches every facet of the affected person's life. Acute episodes of schizophrenia are characterized by delusions, hallucinations, illogical thinking, incoherent speech, and bizarre behavior. Between acute episodes, people with schizophrenia may still be unable to think clearly and may lack an appropriate emotional response to the people and events in their lives. They may speak in a flat tone and show little if any facial expressiveness (Mandal, Pandey, & Prasad, 1998). Although researchers are immersed in probing the psychological and biological foundations of schizophrenia, the disorder remains in many ways a mystery. Schizophrenia is not the only type of psychotic disorder in which the person experiences a break with reality. In this chapter we also consider other psychotic disorders, including brief psychotic disorder, schizophreniform disorder, schizoaffective disorder, and delusional disorder.

History of the Concept of Schizophrenia

Although various forms of "madness" have afflicted people throughout the course of history, no one knows how long the behavior pattern we now label schizophrenia existed before it was first described as a medical syndrome by Emil Kraepelin in 1893. Modern

schizophrenia An enduring psychotic disorder that involves disturbed behavior, thinking, emotions, and perceptions.

401

dementia praecox The term given by Kraepelin to the disorder we now call schizophrenia.

Emil Kraepelin.

Eugen Bleuler.

conceptualizations of schizophrenia have been largely shaped by the contributions of Kraepelin, Eugen Bleuler, and Kurt Schneider.

Emil Kraepelin

Kraepelin (1856–1926), one of the fathers of modern psychiatry, called the disorder **dementia praecox.** The term derived from the Latin *dementis,* meaning "out" (*de-*) of one's "mind" (*mens*), and the roots that form the word *precocious,* meaning "before" one's level of "maturity." *Dementia praecox* thus refers to premature impairment of mental abilities. Kraepelin believed that dementia praecox was a disease process caused by specific, although unknown, pathology in the body.

Kraepelin wrote that dementia praecox involved the "loss of the inner unity of thought, feeling, and acting." The syndrome begins early in life, and the course of deterioration eventually results in complete "disintegration of the personality" (Kraepelin, 1909–1913, Vol. 2, p. 943). Kraepelin's description of dementia praecox includes behavior patterns such as delusions, hallucinations, and odd motor behaviors—the behavior patterns that typically characterize the disorder today.

Eugen Bleuler

In 1911, the Swiss psychiatrist Eugen Bleuler (1857–1939) renamed dementia praecox *schizophrenia,* from the Greek *schistos,* meaning "cut" or "split," and *phren,* meaning "brain." In doing so, Bleuler focused on the major characteristic of the syndrome, the splitting of the brain functions that give rise to cognition, feelings or affective responses, and behavior. A person with schizophrenia, for example, might giggle inappropriately when discussing an upsetting event, or might show no emotional expressiveness in the face of tragedy.

Although the Greek roots of *schizophrenia* mean "split brain," schizophrenia should not be confused with dissociative identity disorder (formerly multiple personality disorder), which is frequently referred to as "split personality" by laypeople. People with dissociative identity disorder (see Chapter 7) exhibit two or more alter personalities, but the alter personalities typically show better integrated cognitive, affective, and behavioral functioning than is the case in schizophrenia. In schizophrenia, the splitting cleaves cognition, affect, and behavior. There may thus be little agreement between the thoughts and the emotions, or between the individual's perceptions of reality and what is truly happening.

Although Bleuler accepted Kraepelin's description of the symptoms of schizophrenia, he did not accept Kraepelin's views that schizophrenia necessarily begins early in life and inevitably follows a deteriorating course. Bleuler proposed that schizophrenia follows a more variable course. In some cases, acute episodes occur intermittently. In others, there might be limited improvement rather than inevitable deterioration.

Bleuler believed that schizophrenia could be recognized on the basis of four primary features or symptoms. Today, we refer to them as the **four A's:**

1. *Associations.* **Associations,** or relationships among thoughts, become disturbed. We now call this type of disturbance "thought disorder" or "looseness of associations." Looseness of associations means ideas are strung together with little or no relationship among them; nor does the speaker appear to be aware of the lack of connectedness. The person's speech appears to others to be rambling and confused.

2. *Affect.* **Affect,** or emotional response, becomes flattened or inappropriate. The individual may show a lack of response to upsetting events, or burst into laughter upon hearing that a family member or friend has died.

3. *Ambivalence.* People with schizophrenia hold ambivalent or conflicting feelings toward others, such as loving and hating them at the same time.

4. *Autism.* **Autism** is a term that describes withdrawal into a private fantasy world that is not bound by principles of logic.

In Bleuler's view, hallucinations and delusions represent "secondary symptoms," symptoms that accompany the primary symptoms but do not define the disorder. In more recent years, however, other theorists such as Kurt Schneider (1957) have proposed that hallucinations and delusions are key, or primary, features of schizophrenia. Bleuler was strongly influenced by psychodynamic theory. He came to believe that the content of hallucinations and delusions could be explained by the attempt to replace the external world with a world of fantasy.

Bleuler's contributions led to the adoption of a broader definition of schizophrenia and brought the diagnostic category into more common use. Bleuler's ideas were especially influential in the United States. U.S.-trained professionals began to use the diagnosis more freely than their European counterparts, who were more influenced by Kraepelin's narrower definition of the disorder. The diagnosis of schizophrenia was broadened in the United States even beyond Bleuler's criteria to include people who showed combined features of schizophrenia and mood disorders. These cases are now generally classified separately from schizophrenia under the category of schizoaffective disorder. (We will cover this disorder later in this chapter.)

Kurt Schneider

Another influential developer of modern concepts of schizophrenia was the German psychiatrist Kurt Schneider (1887–1967). Schneider believed Bleuler's criteria (his "four A's") were too vague for diagnostic purposes and that they failed to adequately distinguish schizophrenia from other disorders. Schneider's (1957) most notable contribution was to discriminate between the features of schizophrenia that he believed are central to diagnosis, which he termed **first-rank symptoms,** and so-called **second-rank symptoms,** which he believed are found not only in schizophrenia, but also in other psychoses

four A's The primary characteristics of schizophrenia: loose *Associations,* blunted or inappropriate *Affect, Ambivalence,* and *Autism.*

associations Relationships among thoughts.

affect Emotional responsiveness.

autism Withdrawal into a private fantasy world.

first-rank symptoms The primary features of schizophrenia, such as hallucinations and delusions.

second-rank symptoms Symptoms associated with schizophrenia that also occur in other mental disorders.

THINK ABOUT IT
Trace the development of the concept of schizophrenia in your own words. What were the areas of agreement and disagreement? Why is the disorder difficult to define?

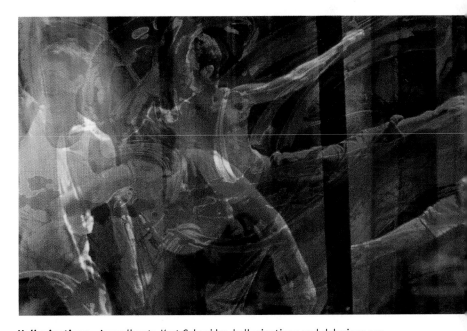

Hallucinations. According to Kurt Schneider, hallucinations and delusions are numbered among the first-rank symptoms of schizophrenia—that is, the symptoms that are central to the diagnosis. So-called second-rank symptoms are found in other disorders as well. Schneider considered confusion and disturbances in mood to be second-rank symptoms.

TABLE **13.1** Major Clinical Features of Schizophrenia

A. Two or more of the following must be present for a significant portion of time over the course of a 1-month period:

(1) delusions

(2) hallucinations

(3) speech that is either incoherent or characterized by marked loosening of associations

(4) disorganized or catatonic behavior

(5) negative features (e.g., flattened affect)

B. Functioning in such areas as social relations, work, or self-care during the course of the disorder is markedly below the level achieved prior to the onset of the disorder. If the onset develops during childhood or adolescence, there is a failure to achieve the expected level of social development.

C. Signs of the disorder have occurred continuously for a period of at least 6 months. This 6-month period must include an active phase lasting at least a month in which psychotic symptoms (listed in A), which are characteristic of schizophrenia, occur.

D. The disorder cannot be attributed to the effects of a substance (e.g., substance abuse or prescribed medication) or to a general medical condition.

Source. Adapted from the *DSM-IV-TR* (APA, 2000).

Truth OR Fiction? REVISITED

Individuals may show all the signs of schizophrenia for several months but still not be diagnosed with the disorder.

TRUE. A diagnosis of schizophrenia requires that signs of the disorder be present for at least 6 months.

Quiz **13.1**
History of the Concept
of Schizophrenia

and in some nonpsychotic disorders, such as personality disorders. In Schneider's view, if first-rank symptoms are present and cannot be accounted for by organic factors, a diagnosis of schizophrenia is justified. Hallucinations and delusions are prominent first-rank symptoms. Disturbances in mood and confused thinking are considered second-rank symptoms. Although Schneider's ranking of disturbed behaviors helped distinguish schizophrenia from other disorders, we now know that first-rank symptoms are sometimes found among people with other disorders, especially bipolar disorder. Although first-rank symptoms are clearly associated with schizophrenia, they are not unique to it.

Contemporary Diagnostic Practices

Today, the contributions of Kraepelin, Bleuler, and Schneider are expressed in modified form in the present *DSM* diagnostic system. However, the diagnostic code for schizophrenia is not limited, as Kraepelin had proposed, to cases where there is a course of progressive deterioration. Today, we recognize that schizophrenia does not necessarily follow a persistent downhill course (USDHHS, 1999a). As many as one-half to two-thirds of schizophrenia patients improve significantly over time, and some patients even recover fully (USDHHS, 1999a).

The present diagnostic code is tighter than earlier conceptualizations. It separates into other diagnostic categories cases in which there are disturbances of mood combined with psychotic behavior and those involving schizophrenic-like thinking but without overt psychotic behavior (schizotypal personality disorder). The *DSM-IV* criteria for schizophrenia also require that psychotic behaviors be present at some point during the course of the disorder and that signs of the disorder be present for at least 6 months. People with briefer forms of psychosis are placed in diagnostic categories that may be connected with more favorable outcomes. Table 13.1 describes the major clinical criteria for schizophrenia.

Other Forms of Psychosis

Although we tend to link psychotic behavior with schizophrenia, the *DSM* recognizes several different types of psychotic disorders.

Brief Psychotic Disorder

Some brief psychotic episodes do not progress to schizophrenia. The *DSM-IV* category of **brief psychotic disorder** applies to a psychotic disorder that lasts from a day to a month and is characterized by at least one of the following features: delusions, hallucinations, disorganized speech, or disorganized or catatonic behavior. Eventually there is a full return to the individual's prior level of functioning. Brief psychotic disorder is often linked to a significant stressor or stressors, such as the loss of a loved one or exposure to brutal traumas in wartime. Some cases in women involve a postpartum onset that begins within the first month after childbirth.

Schizophreniform Disorder

Schizophreniform disorder consists of abnormal behaviors identical to those in schizophrenia that have persisted for at least 1 month but less than 6 months. They thus do not yet justify the diagnosis of schizophrenia. Although some cases have good outcomes, in others the disorder persists beyond 6 months and may be reclassified as schizophrenia or perhaps another form of psychotic disorder, such as schizoaffective disorder. Questions remain about the validity of the diagnosis, however (Strakowski, 1994). It may be more appropriate to diagnose people who show psychotic features of recent origin with a classification such as *psychotic disorder of an unspecified type* until additional information clearly indicates the specific type of disorder involved.

Delusional Disorder

Many of us, perhaps even most of us, feel suspicious of other people's motives at times. We may feel others have it in for us or believe others are talking about us behind our backs. For most of us, however, paranoid thinking does not take the form of outright delusions. The diagnosis of **delusional disorder** applies to people who hold persistent, clearly delusional beliefs, often involving paranoid themes. Delusional disorder is uncommon, affecting an estimated 5 to 10 people in 10,000 during their lifetimes (APA, 2000).

In delusional disorders, the delusional beliefs concern events that may possibly occur, such as the infidelity of a spouse, persecution by others, or attracting the love of a famous person. The apparent plausibility of these beliefs may lead others to take them seriously and check them out before concluding they are unfounded. Apart from the delusion, the individual's behavior does not show evidence of obviously bizarre or odd behavior, as we see in the following case example:

Mr. Polsen's Hit Men

Mr. Polsen, a married 42-year-old postal worker, was brought to the hospital by his wife because he had been insisting that there was a contract out on his life. Mr. Polsen told the doctors that the problem had started some four months ago when he was accused by his supervisor of tampering with a package, an offense that could have cost him his job. When he was exonerated at a formal hearing, his supervisor was "furious" and felt publicly humiliated, according to Mr. Polsen. Shortly afterwards, Mr. Polsen reported, his co-workers began avoiding him, turning away from him when he walked by, as if they didn't want to see him. He then began to think that they were talking about him behind his back, although he could never clearly make out what they were saying. He gradually became convinced that his co-workers were avoiding him because his boss had put a contract on his life. Things remained about the same for two months, when Mr. Polsen began to notice several large white cars cruising up and down the street where he lived. This frightened him and he became convinced there were hit men in these cars. He then refused to leave his home without an escort and would run home in panic when he saw one of these cars approaching. Other than the reports of his belief

brief psychotic disorder A psychotic disorder lasting from a day to a month that often follows exposure to a major stressor.

schizophreniform disorder A psychotic disorder lasting less than six months in duration, with features that resemble schizophrenia.

delusional disorder A type of psychosis characterized by persistent delusions, often of a paranoid nature, that do not have the bizarre quality of the type found in paranoid schizophrenia.

WWW **Web Link 13.1**
Facts About Delusional Disorder

Is someone out to get you? People with delusional disorder often weave paranoid fantasies in their minds such that they confuse with reality.

that his life was in danger, his thinking and behavior appeared entirely normal on interview. He denied experiencing hallucinations and showed no other signs of psychotic behavior, except for the queer beliefs about his life being in danger. The diagnosis of Delusional Disorder, Persecutory type seemed the most appropriate, since there was no evidence that a contract had been taken on his life (hence, a persecutory delusion) and there was an absence of other clear signs of psychosis that might support a diagnosis of a schizophrenic disorder.

—*Adapted from Spitzer et al., 1994, pp. 177–179*

■

Mr. Polsen's delusional belief that "hit teams" were pursuing him was treated with antipsychotic medication in the hospital setting and faded in about 3 weeks. His belief that he had been the subject of an attempted "hit" stuck in his mind, however. A month following admission, he stated, "I guess my boss has called off the contract. He couldn't get away with it now without publicity" (Spitzer et al., 1994, p. 179).

Although delusions frequently occur in schizophrenia, delusional disorder is believed to be distinct from schizophrenia. Persons with delusional disorder do not exhibit the confused or jumbled thinking characteristic of schizophrenia. Hallucinations, when they occur, are not as prominent. Delusions in schizophrenia are embedded within a larger array of disturbed thoughts, perceptions, and behavior. In delusional disorders, the delusion itself may be the only clear sign of abnormality.

Delusional disorder should also be distinguished from another disorder in which paranoid thinking is present—paranoid personality disorder (see Chapter 9). People with paranoid personality disorder may hold exaggerated or unwarranted suspicions of others, but not the outright delusions that are found among people with delusional disorders or paranoid schizophrenia. People with paranoid personality disorder may believe that they were passed over for a promotion because their boss had it in for them, but they would not maintain the unfounded belief that their boss had put a contract on their life.

Various types of delusional disorder are described in Table 13.2. Delusional disorders are relatively uncommon. Once a delusion is established, it may persevere, although the individual's concern about it may wax and wane over the years. In other cases, the delusion

TABLE 13.2 Types of Delusional Disorder

Type	Description
Erotomanic Type	Delusional beliefs that someone else, usually someone of higher social status, such as movie star or political figure, is in love with you; also called *erotomania*.
Grandiose Type	Inflated beliefs about your worth, importance, power, knowledge, or identity, or beliefs that you hold a special relationship to a deity or a famous person. Cult leaders who believe they have special mystical powers of enlightenment may have delusional disorders of this type.
Jealous Type	Delusions of jealousy in which the person may become convinced, without due cause, that his or her lover is unfaithful. The delusional person may misinterpret certain clues as signs of unfaithfulness, such as spots on the bedsheets.
Persecutory Type	The most common type of delusional disorder, persecutory delusions involve themes of being conspired against, followed, cheated, spied upon, poisoned or drugged, or otherwise maligned or mistreated. Persons with such delusions may repeatedly institute court actions, or even commit acts of violence, against those who they perceived are responsible for their mistreatment.
Somatic Type	Delusions involving physical defects, disease, or disorder. Persons with these delusions may believe that foul odors are emanating from their bodies, or that internal parasites are eating away at them, or that certain parts of their body are unusually disfigured or ugly, or not functioning properly despite evidence to the contrary.
Mixed Type	Delusions typify more than one of the other types; no single theme predominates.

Source. Adapted from *DSM-IV-TR* (APA, 2000).

A Closer Look

The Love Delusion

 Erotomania, or the love delusion, is a delusional disorder in which the individual believes he or she is loved by someone else, usually someone famous or of high social status. In reality, the individual has only a passing or nonexistent relationship with the alleged lover (R. L. Goldstein, 1986). Although the love delusion was once thought to be predominantly a female disorder, recent reports suggest it may not be a rarity among men. It has been suggested, for example, that John Hinckley Jr., who attempted to assassinate then-president Ronald Reagan reportedly to impress actress Jodie Foster, could be considered a case of erotomania (Stone, 1984). Although women with erotomania may have a potential for violence when their attentions are rebuffed, men with this condition appear more likely to threaten or commit acts of violence in the pursuit of the objects of their unrequited desires (Goldstein, 1986). Antipsychotic medications may reduce the intensity of the delusion but do not appear to eliminate it (Kelly, Kennedy, & Shanley, 2000; Segal, 1989). Nor is there evidence that psychotherapy helps people with erotomania. The prognosis is thus bleak, and people with erotomania may harass their love objects for many years. Mental health professionals also need to be aware of the potential for violence in the management of people who possess these delusions of love (Mullen, 2000; Segal, 1989). The following cases provide some examples of the love delusion:

Truth OR Fiction? REVISITED

Some people are deluded that they are loved by a famous person.

TRUE. Some people do suffer from the delusion that they are loved by a famous person. They are said to have a delusional disorder, erotomanic type.

Three Cases of Erotomania

Mr. A., a 35-year-old man, was described as a "love-struck" suitor of a daughter of a former President of the United States. He was arrested for repeatedly harassing the woman in an attempt to win her love, although they were actually perfect strangers. Refusing to adhere to the judge's warnings to stop pestering the woman, he placed numerous phone calls to her from prison and was later transferred to a psychiatric facility, still declaring they were very much in love.

Mr. B. was arrested for breaching a court order to stop pestering a famous pop singer. A 44-year-old farmer, Mr. B. had followed his love interest across the country, constantly bombarding her with romantic overtures. He was committed to a psychiatric hospital, but maintained the belief that she'd always wait for him.

Then there was Mr. C., a 32-year-old businessman, who believed a well-known woman lawyer had fallen in love with him following a casual meeting. He constantly called and sent flowers and letters, declaring his love. While she repeatedly rejected his advances and eventually filed criminal charges for harassment, he felt that she was only testing his love by placing obstacles in his path. He abandoned his wife and business and his functioning declined. When the woman continued to reject him, he began sending her threatening letters and was committed to a psychiatric facility.

—Adapted from Goldstein, 1986, p. 802

may disappear entirely for periods of time and then recur. Sometimes the disorder permanently disappears.

Schizophrenia-Spectrum Disorders

Some people have persistent patterns of unusual thinking or emotional responses that seem to lie within the broader spectrum of schizophrenic problems, but may not fit the stringent definition of schizophrenia. The schizophrenia spectrum includes related disorders that vary in severity from milder personality disorders (schizoid, paranoid, and schizotypal types) to schizophrenia itself.

Also classified within the schizophrenia spectrum is **schizoaffective disorder,** which is characterized by a "mixed bag" of symptoms including psychotic features such as hallucinations and delusions, together with major disturbances of mood, such as mania or

wWw Web Link **13.2**
More About Schizoaffective Disorder

erotomania A delusional disorder characterized by the belief that one is loved by someone of high social status.

schizoaffective disorder A type of psychotic disorder in which individuals experience both severe mood disturbance and features associated with schizophrenia.

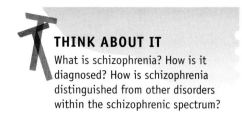

THINK ABOUT IT

What is schizophrenia? How is it diagnosed? How is schizophrenia distinguished from other disorders within the schizophrenic spectrum?

Quiz **13.2**
Other Forms of Psychosis

major depression. Like schizophrenia, schizoaffective disorder tends to follow a chronic course that is characterized by persistent difficulties adjusting to the demands of adult life. A recent 8-year follow-up study showed the same general outcomes between schizophrenia and schizoaffective disorder (Tsuang & Coryell, 1993), underscoring the similar chronic course.

The distinction between schizophrenia and schizophrenia-spectrum disorders may be more a matter of degree than of kind. Differences in genetic vulnerability or environmental stress may lead to the development of milder or more severe forms of a common schizophrenic-type disorder (Andreasen, 1987a).

Research shows that some schizophrenia-spectrum disorders appear to share a common genetic link (Begley, 1998; Fanous et al., 2001). Consistent with a common genetic basis, researchers find a greater than average incidence of schizoaffective disorders among the relatives of people with schizophrenia and a greater than average incidence of schizophrenia among the relatives of people with schizoaffective disorder (Kendler, Gruenberg, & Tsuang, 1985; Maj et al., 1991). Evidence also shows familial linkages between symptomatology in schizophrenia patients and schizotypal personality disorder symptomatology in their relatives (Fanous et al., 2001).

Schizophrenia

Schizophrenia typically develops in late adolescence or early adulthood, at the very time that people are making their way from the family into the outside world (Cowan & Kandel, 2001; Harrop & Trower, 2001). People who develop schizophrenia become increasingly disengaged from society. They fail to function in the expected roles of student, worker, or spouse, and their families and communities grow intolerant of their deviant behavior. The disorder typically develops in the late teens or early 20s, a time at which the brain is reaching full maturation. In about three of four cases, the first signs of schizophrenia appear by the age of 25 (Keith, Regier, & Rae, 1991).

In some cases, the onset of the disorder is acute. It occurs suddenly, within a few weeks or months. The individual may have been well adjusted and shown few if any signs of behavioral disturbance. Then a rapid transformation in personality and behavior leads to an acute psychotic episode.

In most cases, there is a slower, more gradual decline in functioning. It may take years before psychotic behaviors emerge, although early signs of deterioration may be observed. This period of deterioration is called the **prodromal phase.** It is characterized by waning interest in social activities and increasing difficulty in meeting the responsibilities of daily living. At first, such people seem to take less care of their appearance. They fail to bathe regularly or they wear the same clothes repeatedly. Over time, their behavior may become increasingly odd or eccentric. There are lapses in job performance or schoolwork. Their speech may become increasingly vague and rambling. At first these changes in personality may be so gradual that they raise little concern among friends and families. They may be attributed to "a phase" that the person is passing through. But as behavior becomes more bizarre—such as hoarding food, collecting garbage, or talking to oneself on the street—the acute phase of the disorder begins. Frankly psychotic symptoms develop, such as wild hallucinations, delusions, and increasingly bizarre behavior.

Following acute episodes, people who develop schizophrenia may enter the **residual phase,** in which their behavior returns to the level that was characteristic of the prodromal phase. Although flagrant psychotic behaviors may be absent during the residual phase, the person may continue to be impaired by a deep sense of apathy, by difficulties in thinking or speaking clearly, and by the harboring of unusual ideas, such as beliefs in telepathy or clairvoyance. Such patterns of behavior make it difficult to meet expected social roles as wage earners, marital partners, or students. Full return to normal behavior is uncommon but does occur in some cases. More commonly, a chronic pattern develops, which is characterized by occasional acutely psychotic episodes and continued cognitive, emotional, and motivational impairment between episodes (Wiersma et al., 1998; USDHHS, 1999a).

prodromal phase In schizophrenia, the period of decline in functioning that precedes the first acute psychotic episode.

residual phase In schizophrenia, the phase that follows an acute phase, characterized by a return to the level of functioning of the prodromal phase.

Prevalence of Schizophrenia

About 1% of the adult population in the United States is affected by schizophrenia, more than 2 million people in total (APA, 2000; Cowan & Kandel, 2001). According to the results of the World Health Organization (WHO) multinational study reported in Chapter 1, the rate of schizophrenia appears to be similar in both developed and developing cultures (Jablensky et al., 1992). The World Health Organization estimates that about 24 million people worldwide suffer from schizophrenia (Olson, 2001). Nearly 1 million people in the United States receive treatment for schizophrenia each year, with about a third of these requiring hospitalization (Grady, 1997a). The costs for treating schizophrenia are estimated at $30 billion annually and account for 75% of all expenditures in the United States for mental health treatment (Cowan & Kandel, 2001; "Schizophrenia Update—Part I," 1995).

Men tend to have a slightly higher risk of developing schizophrenia (APA, 2000). Women tend to develop the disorder somewhat later than men do, with the age of onset occurring most commonly between age 25 and the mid-30s in women and between age 18 and 25 in men (APA, 2000). Women also tend to achieve a higher level of functioning before the onset of the disorder and to have a less severe course of the disorder than do men (Häfner et al., 1998; USDHHS, 1999a).

Though the occurrence of schizophrenia appears to be universal across cultures, the course of the disorder and its symptoms may vary from culture to culture (Thakker & Ward, 1998). For example, visual hallucinations appear to be more common in some non-Western cultures (Ndetei & Singh, 1983; Ndetei & Vadher, 1984). In a study conducted in an English hospital in Kenya, researchers found that people of African, Asian, or Jamaican background with schizophrenia were about twice as likely to experience visual hallucinations as those of European background (Ndetei & Vadher, 1984).

Major Features of Schizophrenia

Schizophrenia is a pervasive disorder that affects a wide range of psychological processes involving cognition, affect, and behavior (Arango, Kirkpatrick, & Buchanan, 2000). People with schizophrenia show a marked decline in occupational and social functioning. They may have difficulty holding a conversation, forming friendships, holding a job, or taking care of their personal hygiene. Yet no one behavior pattern is unique to schizophrenia, nor is any one behavior pattern invariably present among people with schizophrenia. People with schizophrenia may exhibit delusions, problems with associative thinking, and hallucinations at one time or another, but not necessarily all at once. There are also different kinds or types of schizophrenia, characterized by different behavior patterns.

Men with schizophrenia appear to differ from women with the disorder in several ways. They tend to show an earlier age of onset, have a poorer level of adjustment prior to showing signs of the disorder, and have more cognitive impairment, behavioral deficits, and a poorer response to drug therapy than do women with schizophrenia (Gorwood et al., 1995; Ragland et al., 1999). These differences have led researchers to speculate that men and women may tend to develop different forms of schizophrenia. Perhaps schizophrenia affects different areas of the brain in men and women, which may explain differences in the form or features of the disorder between the genders.

Here let us consider how schizophrenia affects thinking, speech, attentional and perceptual processes, emotional processes, and voluntary behavior.

Disturbances of Thought and Speech Schizophrenia is characterized by disturbances in thinking and in the expression of thoughts through coherent, meaningful speech. Disturbances in thinking may be found in both the content and form of thought.

Disturbances in the Content of Thought The most prominent disturbance in the content of thought involves *delusions*, or false beliefs that remain fixed in the person's mind despite their illogical bases and lack of evidence to support them. They tend to remain unshakable even in the face of disconfirming evidence. Delusions may take many forms.

THINK ABOUT IT
Do the prevalence data for schizophrenia suggest that it is or is not a biologically based disorder? Explain your answer.

 Web Link 13.3
Facts About Schizophrenia

 VIDEO 13.1
Schizophrenia:
The Case of Georgiana

Some of the most common are:

- *Delusions of persecution* (e.g., "The CIA is out to get me")
- Delusions of reference ("People on the bus are talking about me," or "People on TV are making fun of me")
- *Delusions of being controlled* (believing that one's thoughts, feelings, impulses, or actions are controlled by external forces, such as agents of the devil)
- *Delusions of grandeur* (believing oneself to be Jesus or believing one is on a special mission, or having grand but illogical plans for saving the world)

People with delusions of persecution may think they are being pursued by the Mafia, FBI, CIA, or some other group. A woman we treated who had delusions of reference believed that television news correspondents were broadcasting coded information about her. A man with delusions of this type expressed the belief that his neighbors had bugged the walls of his house. Other delusions include beliefs that one has committed unpardonable sins, is rotting away from a horrible disease, or that the world or oneself does not really exist.

The Hospital at the North Pole

Though people with schizophrenia may feel hounded by demons or earthly conspiracies, Mario's delusions had a messianic quality. "I need to get out of here," he said to his psychiatrist. "Why do you need to leave?" the psychiatrist asked. Mario responded, "My hospital. I need to get back to my hospital." "Which hospital?" he was asked. "I have this hospital. It's all white and we find cures for everything wrong with people." Mario was asked where his hospital was located. "It's all the way up at the North Pole," he responded. His psychiatrist asked, "But how do you get there?" Mario responded, "I just get there. I don't know how. I just get there. I have to do my work. When will you let me go so I can help the people?"

—From the Authors' Files

Other commonly occurring delusions include *thought broadcasting* (believing one's thoughts are somehow transmitted to the external world so that others can overhear them), *thought insertion* (believing one's thoughts have been planted in one's mind by an external source), and *thought withdrawal* (believing that thoughts have been removed from one's mind). Mellor (1970) offers the following examples of thought broadcasting, thought insertion, and thought withdrawal:

- *Thought Broadcasting*: A 21-year-old student reported, "As I think, my thoughts leave my head on a type of mental ticker-tape. Everyone around has only to pass the tape through their mind and they know my thoughts." (p. 17)
- *Thought Insertion*: A 29-year-old housewife reported that when she looks out of the window, she thinks, "The garden looks nice and the grass looks cool, but the thoughts of [a man's name] come into my mind. There are no other thoughts there, only his. . . . He treats my mind like a screen and flashes his thoughts on it like you flash a picture." (p. 17)
- *Thought Withdrawal*: A 22-year-old woman experienced the following: "I am thinking about my mother, and suddenly my thoughts are sucked out of my mind by a phrenological vacuum extractor, and there is nothing in my mind, it is empty." (pp. 16–17)

Disturbances in the Form of Thought Unless we are engaged in daydreaming or purposefully letting our thoughts wander, our thoughts tend to be tightly knit together. The connections (or associations) between our thoughts tend to be logical and coherent.

People with schizophrenia tend to think in a disorganized, illogical fashion, however. In schizophrenia, the form or structure of thought processes as well as their content is often disturbed. Clinicians label this type of disturbance a **thought disorder.**

Thought disorder is recognized by the breakdown in the organization, processing, and control of thoughts. Looseness of associations, which we now regard as a cardinal sign of thought disorder, was one of Bleuler's four A's. The speech pattern of people with schizophrenia is often disorganized or jumbled, with parts of words combined incoherently or words strung together to make meaningless rhymes. Their speech may jump from one topic to another, but show little interconnectivity between the ideas or thoughts that are expressed. People with thought disorder are usually unaware that their thoughts and behavior appear abnormal. In severe cases their speech may become completely incoherent or incomprehensible.

Another common sign of thought disorder is poverty of speech (that is, speech that is coherent but so slow, limited in production, or vague that little informational value is conveyed). Less commonly occurring signs include **neologisms** (words made up by the speaker that have little or no meaning to others), **perseveration** (inappropriate but persistent repetition of the same words or train of thought), **clanging** (stringing together of words or sounds on the basis of rhyming, such as, "I know who I am but I don't know Sam"), and **blocking** (involuntary, abrupt interruption of speech or thought). Disconnected speech is more common and more severe among younger patients, while poverty of speech is found more often and is more severe among older patients (Harvey et al., 1997).

Many but not all people with schizophrenia show evidence of thought disorder. Some appear to think and speak coherently but have disordered content of thought, as seen by the presence of delusions. Nor is disordered thought unique to schizophrenia; it has even been found in milder form among people without psychological disorders (Andreasen & Grove, 1986), especially when they are tired or under stress. Disordered thought is also found among other diagnostic groups, such as persons with mania. Thought disorders in people experiencing a manic episode tend to be short-lived and reversible, however. In those with schizophrenia, thought disorder tends to be more persistent or recurrent.

Thought disorder occurs most often during acute episodes, but may linger into residual phases. Thought disorders that persist beyond acute episodes are connected with poorer prognoses, perhaps because lingering thought disorders reflect more severe disorders (Marengo & Harrow, 1987).

Attentional Deficiencies To read this book you must screen out background noises and other environmental stimuli. Attention, the ability to focus on relevant stimuli, is basic to learning and thinking. Kraepelin and Bleuler suggested that schizophrenia involves a breakdown in the processes of attention. People with schizophrenia appear to have difficulty filtering out irrelevant distracting stimuli, a deficit that makes it nearly impossible to focus their attention and organize their thoughts (Asarnow et al., 1991). They may become easily distracted because of a brain abnormality that makes it difficult for them to allocate their attention to relevant tasks and filter out unessential information (Braff, 1993). Scientists have discovered a genetic defect tied to a brain abnormality that may explain this filtering deficit (Grady, 1997a). The mother of a son who had schizophrenia described her son's difficulties in filtering out extraneous sounds:

> His hearing is different when he's ill. One of the first things we notice when he's deteriorating is his heightened sense of hearing. He cannot filter out anything. He hears each and every sound around him with equal intensity. He hears the sounds from the street, in the yard, and in the house, and they are all much louder than normal. (Anonymous, 1985, p. 1; as cited in Freedman et al., 1987, p. 670)

People with schizophrenia also appear to be *hypervigilant*, or acutely sensitive to extraneous sounds, especially during the early stages of the disorder. During acute episodes, they may become flooded by these stimuli, overwhelming their ability to make sense of their environments. Through measuring the brain's involuntary brain wave responses to auditory stimuli, researchers find that the brains of people with schizophrenia are less able

thought disorder A disturbance in thinking characterized by the breakdown of logical associations between thoughts.

neologisms New words.

perseveration The persistent repetition of the same thought or response.

clanging The tendency to string words together because they rhyme or sound alike.

blocking An involuntary interruption of speech.

wWw **Web Link 13.4**
The Schizophrenia Home Page

Filtering out extraneous stimuli. You probably have little difficulty filtering out unimportant stimuli, such as street sounds. But people with schizophrenia may be distracted by irrelevant stimuli and be unable to filter them out. Consequently, they may have difficulty focusing their attention and organizing their thoughts.

than those of other people to inhibit or screen out responses to distracting sounds (Braff, 1993; Freedman et al., 1987).

Investigators suspect that attentional deficits associated with schizophrenia are inherited to a certain extent (Finkelstein et al., 1997; Grady, 1997a). Although the underlying mechanism is not entirely clear, attentional deficits may be related to dysfunction in the subcortical parts of the brain that regulate attention to external stimuli, such as the basal ganglia (Cornblatt & Kelip, 1994). Scientists suspect there may be a "gating" mechanism in the brain responsible for filtering extraneous stimuli, much like closing a gate in a road can stem the flow of traffic (Freedman et al., 1987).

Links between attentional deficits and schizophrenia are supported by various studies focusing on the psychophysiological aspects of attention (Carter et al., 1997). Let us briefly review some of this research.

Eye Movement Dysfunction About one in three chronic schizophrenia patients show evidence of eye movement dysfunctions (Ross, 2000). *Eye movement dysfunction* (also called *eye tracking dysfunction*) involves abnormal movements of the eyes as they track a target that moves across the field of vision. Rather than steadily tracking the target, the eyes fall back and then catch up in a kind of jerky movement. Eye movement dysfunctions appear to involve a defect in the brain's involuntary attentional processes responsible for visual attention.

Eye movement dysfunctions are common among people with schizophrenia and among their first-degree relatives (parents and siblings), which suggests it might be a genetically transmitted trait, or *marker,* that is associated with genes involved in the development of schizophrenia (Holzman et al., 1997; Ross, 2000).

The role of eye movement dysfunction as a biological marker for schizophrenia is clouded, however, because it is not unique to schizophrenia; many people with bipolar disorder show similar types of dysfunction (Sweeney et al., 1994). Research is needed to identify markers that are more specific to schizophrenia. We should also note that not all people with schizophrenia or their family members show eye movement dysfunctions. This suggests there may be different underlying genetic pathways associated with schizophrenia.

Deficiencies in Event-Related Potentials Researchers have also studied brain wave patterns, called event-related potentials, or ERPs, that occur in response to external stimuli. ERPs can be broken down into components that emerge at various intervals following the presentation of a stimulus such as a flash of light or an auditory tone. Early components (brain wave patterns occurring within the first 250 milliseconds [ms], or one quarter of a second, of exposure to a stimulus) may be involved in registering the stimulus in the brain. Later components, such as the P300 component (a brain wave pattern that typically occurs about 300 ms, or three-tenths of a second, after a stimulus) may be involved in focusing attention on the stimulus.

People with schizophrenia often have early ERP components (less than 250 ms) of greater than expected magnitude in response to touch (Holzman, 1987). This pattern of brain wave activity suggests that abnormally high levels of sensory information are reaching higher brain centers in people with schizophrenia, producing a condition called *sensory overload.* This may help explain the difficulty that people with schizophrenia have in filtering out distracting stimuli. We also have evidence of lower than expected levels of P300 brain wave patterns in response to auditory tones (e.g., Salisbury et al., 1998). This evidence points to attentional deficits that may at least partly explain why people with schizophrenia have difficulty extracting meaningful information from stimuli (lights, sounds, touch) that impinge upon them. Studies of ERPs are thus consistent with the view that people with schizophrenia may be flooded with high levels of sensory information but have greater difficulty extracting useful information from it. As a result, they may be confused and find it difficult to filter out irrelevant stimuli such as extraneous noises. Although ERP research is promising, the meaning of ERP abnormalities in schizophrenia is not fully resolved (Tracy, Josiassen, & Bellack, 1995).

In sum, several lines of evidence point to underlying physiological deficits in the ability to attend to relevant stimuli and ignore distracting stimuli among people with schizophrenia (O'Leary et al., 1996). Although the search continues for biological markers for schizophrenia, no definitive biological pattern unique to schizophrenia has yet been found. Recent evidence indicates that training in attention skills may help reduce attentional deficits in schizophrenia patients (Medalia et al., 1998).

Perceptual Disturbances

Voices, Devils, and Angels

Every so often during the interview, Sally would look over her right shoulder in the direction of the office door and smile gently. When asked why she kept looking at the door, she said that the voices were talking about the two of us just outside the door and she wanted to hear what they were saying. "Why the smile?" Sally was asked. "They were saying funny things," she replied, "like maybe you thought I was cute or something."

Tom was flailing his arms wildly in the hall of the psychiatric unit. Sweat seemed to pour from his brow, and his eyes darted about with agitation. He was subdued and injected with haloperidol (brand name Haldol) to reduce his agitation. When he was about to be injected he started shouting, "Father, forgive them for they know not ... forgive them ... father ..." His words became jumbled. Later, after he had calmed down, he reported that the ward attendants had looked to him like devils or evil angels. They were red and burning, and steam issued from their mouths.

—From the Authors' Files

■

Hallucinations, the most common form of perceptual disturbance in schizophrenia, are images perceived in the absence of external stimulation. They are difficult to distinguish from reality. For Sally, the voices coming from outside the consulting room were real enough, even though no one was there. Hallucinations may involve any of the senses. Auditory hallucinations ("hearing voices") are most common. Tactile hallucinations (such as tingling, electrical, or burning sensations) and somatic hallucinations (such as feeling like snakes are crawling inside one's belly) are also common. Visual hallucinations (seeing things that are not there), gustatory hallucinations (tasting things that are not present), and olfactory hallucinations (sensing odors that are not present) are rarer.

Auditory hallucinations occur in about 70% of cases of schizophrenia (Cleghorn et al., 1992). In auditory hallucinations, the voices may be experienced as female or male and as originating inside or outside one's head (Asaad & Shapiro, 1986). Hallucinators may hear voices conversing about them in the third person, debating their virtues or faults.

Some people with schizophrenia experience *command hallucinations,* voices that instruct them to perform certain acts, such as harming themselves or others (Rogers et al., 1990). Angela, for example, was instructed by the "hellsmen" to commit suicide. People with schizophrenia who experience command hallucinations are often hospitalized for fear they may harm themselves or others. There is a good reason for this. A recent study found that four of five people with command hallucinations reported obeying them, with nearly

Truth OR Fiction? REVISITED

Visual hallucinations ("seeing things") are the most common type of hallucinations in people with schizophrenia.

FALSE. Auditory, not visual, hallucinations are the most common type of hallucinations among people with schizophrenia.

half reporting they had obeyed commands to harm themselves during the past month (Kasper, Rogers, & Adams, 1996). Yet command hallucinations often go undetected by professionals, because patients deny them or are unwilling to discuss them.

Hallucinations are not unique to schizophrenia. People with major depression and mania sometimes experience hallucinations. Nor are hallucinations invariably a sign of psychopathology. Cross-cultural evidence shows they are common and socially valued in some developing countries (Bentall, 1990). Even in developed countries like the United States, about 5% of respondents in nonpatient samples report experiencing hallucinations during the preceding year, mostly auditory hallucinations (Honig et al., 1998). Hallucinations in people without psychiatric conditions are often triggered by unusually low levels of sensory stimulation (lying in the dark in a soundproof room for extended time) or low levels of arousal (Teunisse et al., 1996). Unlike psychotic individuals, these people realize that their hallucinations are not real and feel in control of them.

People who are free of psychological disorders sometimes experience hallucinations during the course of a religious experience or ritual (Asaad & Shapiro, 1986). Participants in such experiences may report fleeting trancelike states with visions or other perceptual aberrations. All of us hallucinate nightly, if we consider dreams to be a form of hallucination (perceptual experience in the absence of external stimuli).

Hallucinations may also occur in response to hallucinogenic drugs, such as LSD. Hallucinations may also occur during grief reactions, when images of the deceased may appear, and in other stressful conditions. In most cases, grief-induced hallucinations can be differentiated from psychotic hallucinations in that the individual can distinguish them from reality. Bentall (1990) views the hallucinations of psychiatric patients as involving the lack of ability to distinguish between real and imaginary events. They tend to confuse real and imaginary (hallucinatory) events, that is.

Drug-induced hallucinations tend to be visual and often involve abstract shapes such as circles or stars, or flashes of light. Schizophrenic hallucinations, in contrast, tend to be more fully formed and complex. Hallucinations (for example, of bugs crawling on one's skin) may also occur during delirium tremens (the DTs), which often occur as part of the withdrawal syndrome for chronic alcoholism. Hallucinations may also occur as side effects of medications or in neurological disorders, such as Parkinson's disease.

The causes of psychotic hallucinations remain unknown, but speculations abound (Asaad & Shapiro, 1986). Disturbances in brain chemistry are suspected as playing a causal role. The neurotransmitter dopamine has been implicated, because antipsychotic drugs that block dopamine activity also tend to reduce hallucinations. Conversely, drugs that lead to increased production of dopamine tend to induce hallucinations. Because hallucinations resemble dreamlike states, it is also possible that hallucinations are connected to a failure of brain mechanisms that normally prevent dream images from intruding on waking experiences.

Hallucinations may also represent a type of subvocal inner speech (Cleghorn et al., 1992). Many of us talk to ourselves from time to time, although we usually keep our mutterings beneath our breaths (subvocal) and recognize the voice as our own. Might auditory hallucinations that occur among people with schizophrenia be projections of their own internal voices, or self-speech, onto external sources? In one experiment, 14 of 18 hallucinators who suffered from schizophrenia reported that the voices disappeared when they engaged in a procedure that prevented them from talking to themselves under their breath (Bick & Kinsbourne, 1987). Similar results were obtained for 18 of 21 normal subjects who reportedly experienced hallucinations in response to hypnotic suggestions.

Researchers find that brain activity in Broca's area, a part of the brain involved in controlling speech, was greater in men with schizophrenia when they were hearing voices than at a later time when they were no longer hallucinating (McGuire, Shah, & Murray, 1993). This same area is known to become active when people engage in inner speech (Paulesu, Frith, & Frackowisk, 1993). Researchers also find evidence of similar electrical activity in the auditory cortex of the brain during auditory hallucinations and in response to hearing real sounds (Tiihonen et al., 1992). This evidence supports the view that auditory hallucinations may be a form of inner speech (silent self-talk) that for some unknown rea-

A painting by a man with schizophrenia.
This picture was painted by a young man who reported monsters—apparent hallucinations—like the one pictured here crawling on the floor. He also reported that the chairs next to his bed had turned into devils.

son is attributed to external sources rather than to one's own thoughts (Ford et al., 2001; Hoffman et al., 1999). This line of research has led to treatment applications in which behavior therapists attempt to teach hallucinators to reattribute their voices to themselves (Bentall, Haddock, & Slade, 1994). Hallucinators are also trained to recognize the situational cues associated with their hallucinations. For example,

> ... one patient ... recognized that her voices tended to become worse following family arguments. She became aware that the content of her voices reflected the things that she was feeling and thinking about her family but that she was unable to express. Specific targets and goals were then set to allow her to address these difficulties with her family, and techniques such as rehearsal, problem solving and cognitive restructuring were employed to help her work towards these goals. (Bentall, Haddock, & Slade, 1994, p. 58)

Although cognitive-behavioral approaches to treating hallucinations are still in their infancy, the early results are promising (e.g., Bentall, Haddock, & Slade, 1994; Wiersma et al., 2001). But let us note that even if theories linking subvocal speech to auditory hallucinations stand up to further scientific inquiry, they cannot account for hallucinations in other sensory modalities, such as visual, tactile, or olfactory hallucinations.

The brain mechanisms responsible for hallucinations are likely to involve a number of interconnected systems. One intriguing possibility is that defects in deeper brain structures may lead the brain to create its own reality. This alternative reality goes unchecked because the higher thinking centers in the brain, located in the frontal lobes of the cerebral cortex, fail to perform a reality check on these images to determine whether they are real, imagined, or hallucinated (Begley, 1995). Consequently, people may misattribute their own internally generated voices to outside sources. As we'll see later, evidence from other brain-imaging studies points to abnormalities in the frontal lobes in people with schizophrenia.

Emotional Disturbances Disturbances of affect or emotional response in schizophrenia are typified by blunted affect—also called *flat affect*—and by inappropriate affect. Flat affect is inferred from the absence of emotional expression in the face and voice. People with schizophrenia may speak in a monotone and maintain an expressionless face, or "mask." They may not experience a normal range of emotional response to people and events. Or their emotional responses may be inappropriate, such as giggling at bad news.

It is not fully clear, however, whether emotional blunting in people with schizophrenia is a disturbance in their ability to express emotions, to report the presence of emotions, or to actually experience emotions (Berenbaum & Oltmanns, 1990). Recent laboratory-based evidence shows that schizophrenia patients experience more intense negative emotions, but less intense positive emotions, than controls (Myin-Germeys, Delespaul, & deVries, 2000). In other words, schizophrenia patients may experience strong emotions (especially negative emotions), even if their experiences are not communicated to the world outside through their facial expressions or behavior. People with schizophrenia may lack the capacity to express their emotions outwardly (Kring & Neale, 1996).

Other Types of Impairment People who suffer from schizophrenia may become confused about their personal identities—the cluster of attributes and characteristics that define themselves as individuals and give meaning and direction to their lives. They may fail to recognize themselves as unique individuals and be unclear as to how much of what they experience are parts of themselves. In psychodynamic terms, this phenomenon is sometimes referred to as loss of *ego boundaries*. They may also have difficulty adopting a third-party perspective and fail to perceive their own behavior and verbalizations as socially inappropriate in a given situation because they are unable to see things from another person's point of view (Carini & Nevid, 1992). They also have difficulty recognizing or perceiving emotions in others (Penn et al., 2000).

Disturbances of volition are most often seen in the residual or chronic state. These disturbances are characterized by loss of initiative to pursue goal-directed activities. People with schizophrenia may be unable to carry out plans and may lack interest or drive. Apparent ambivalence toward choosing courses of action may block goal-directed activities.

Truth OR Fiction? REVISITED

Auditory hallucinations may be a form of inner speech.

TRUE. Recent research suggests that auditory hallucinations may be a form of inner speech, which, for unknown reasons, becomes misattributed to external sources.

stupor A state of relative or complete unconsciousness in which a person is not aware of, or responsive to, the environment.

disorganized type The subtype of schizophrenia characterized by disorganized behavior, bizarre delusions, and vivid hallucinations.

THINK ABOUT IT
The authors make the statement that schizophrenia is perhaps the most disabling type of psychological or mental disorder. What makes it so?

A young man diagnosed with disorganized schizophrenia. One of the characteristic features of disorganized schizophrenia is grossly inappropriate affect, as shown by this patient who continually giggles and laughs for no apparent reason.

People with schizophrenia may show highly excited or wild behavior, or slow to a state of **stupor.** They may exhibit odd gestures and bizarre facial expressions, or become unresponsive and curtail spontaneous movement. In extreme cases, as in catatonic schizophrenia, the person may seem unaware of the environment or maintain a rigid posture. Or the person may move about in an excited but seemingly purposeless manner.

People with schizophrenia also tend to show significant impairment in their interpersonal relationships. They tend to withdraw from social interactions and become absorbed in private thoughts and fantasies. Or they cling so desperately to others that they make them uncomfortable. They may become so dominated by their own fantasies that they essentially lose touch with the outside world. They also tend to have been introverted and peculiar even before the appearance of psychotic behavior (Berenbaum & Fujita, 1994). These early signs may be associated with a vulnerability to schizophrenia, at least in people with a genetic risk of developing the disorder.

Subtypes of Schizophrenia

The belief that there are different forms or types of schizophrenia traces back to Kraepelin, who listed three types of schizophrenia: paranoid, catatonic, and hebephrenic (now called disorganized type). The *DSM-IV* lists three specific types of schizophrenia: *disorganized, catatonic,* and *paranoid*. People with schizophrenia who display active psychotic features, such as hallucinations, delusions, incoherent speech, or confused or disorganized behavior, but who do not meet the specifications of the other types are considered to be of an *undifferentiated type*. Others who have no prominent psychotic features at the time of evaluation but have some residual features (for example, social withdrawal, peculiar behavior, blunted or inappropriate affect, strange beliefs or thoughts) would be classified as having a *residual type* of schizophrenia.

Here let us consider the specific types of schizophrenia recognized by the *DSM* system.

Disorganized Type The **disorganized type** of schizophrenia is associated with such features as confused behavior, incoherent speech, vivid and frequent hallucinations, flattened or inappropriate affect, and disorganized delusions that often involve sexual or religious themes. Social impairment is frequent among people with disorganized schizophrenia. They also display silliness and giddiness of mood, giggling and talking nonsensically. They often neglect their appearance and hygiene and lose control of their bladders and bowels. Consider the following case example:

A Case of Schizophrenia, Disorganized Type

A 40-year-old man who looks more like 30 is brought to the hospital by his mother, who reports that she is afraid of him. It is his twelfth hospitalization. He is dressed in a tattered overcoat, baseball cap, and bedroom slippers, and sports several medals around his neck. His affect ranges from anger (hurling obscenities at his mother) to giggling. He speaks with a childlike quality and walks with exaggerated hip movements and seems to measure each step very carefully. Since stopping his medication about a month ago, his mother reports, he had been hearing voices and looking and acting more bizarrely. He tells the interviewer he has been "eating wires" and lighting fires. His speech is generally incoherent and frequently falls into rhyme and clanging associations. His history reveals a series of hospitalizations since the age of 16. Between hospitalizations, he lives with his mother, who is now elderly, and often disappears for months at a time, but is eventually picked up by the police for wandering in the streets.

—Adapted from Spitzer et al., 1994, pp. 189–190

Catatonic Type The **catatonic type** is a subtype of schizophrenia characterized by markedly impaired motor behavior and a slowing down of activity that progresses to a stupor but may switch abruptly into an agitated phase. People with catatonic schizophrenia may show unusual mannerisms or grimacing, or maintain bizarre, apparently strenuous postures for hours, even though their limbs become stiff or swollen. A striking but less common feature is **waxy flexibility,** which involves the adoption of a fixed posture into which they have been positioned by others. They will not respond to questions or comments during these periods, which can last for hours. Later they may report they heard what others were saying at the time, however.

A Case of Schizophrenia, Catatonic Type

A 24-year-old man had been brooding about his life. He professed that he did not feel well, but could not explain his bad feelings. While hospitalized, he initially sought contact with people but a few days later was found in a statuesque position, his legs contorted in an awkward-looking position. He refused to talk to anyone and acted as if he couldn't see or hear anything. His face was an expressionless mask. A few days later, he began to talk, but in an echolalic or mimicking way. For example, he would respond to the question, "What is your name?" by saying, "What is your name?" He could not care for his needs and required to be fed by spoon.

—Adapted from Arieti, 1974, p. 40

Although catatonia is associated with schizophrenia, it may also occur in other physical and psychological disorders, including brain disorders, states of drug intoxication, metabolic disorders, and mood disorders ("What Is Catatonia?," 1995).

Paranoid Type The **paranoid type** of schizophrenia is characterized by preoccupations with one or more delusions or with the presence of frequent auditory hallucinations (APA, 2000). The behavior and speech of someone with paranoid schizophrenia does not show the marked disorganization typical of the disorganized type, nor is there a prominent display of flattened or inappropriate affect or catatonic behavior. Their delusions often involve themes of grandeur, persecution, or jealousy. They may believe, for example, that their spouse or lover is unfaithful despite a lack of evidence. They may also become highly agitated, confused, and fearful.

A Case of Schizophrenia, Paranoid Type

The 25-year-old woman was visibly frightened. She was shaking badly and had the look of someone who feared that she might be attacked at any moment. The night before she had been found cowering in a corner of the local bus station, mumbling incoherently, to herself having arrived in town minutes earlier on a bus from Philadelphia. The station manager had called the police, who took her to the hospital. She told the interviewer that she had to escape Philadelphia because the Mafia was closing in on her. She was a schoolteacher, she explained, at least until the voices started bothering her. The voices would tell her she was bad and had to be punished. Sometimes the voices were in her head, sometimes they spoke to her through the electrical wires in her apartment. The voices told her how someone

A person diagnosed with catatonic schizophrenia. People with catatonic schizophrenia may remain in unusual, difficult positions for hours, even though their limbs become stiff or swollen. They may seem oblivious to their environment, even to people who are talking about them. Yet they may later say that they heard what was being said. Periods of stupor may alternate with periods of agitation.

catatonic type The subtype of schizophrenia characterized by gross disturbances in motor activity, such as catatonic stupor.

waxy flexibility A less common feature of catatonic schizophrenia, in which a person's limbs are moved into a certain posture or position by others and which the person then rigidly maintains.

paranoid type The subtype of schizophrenia characterized by hallucinations and systematized delusions, commonly involving themes of persecution.

from the Mafia would come to kill her. She felt that one of her neighbors, a shy man who lived down the hall, was in league with the Mafia. She felt the only hope she had was to escape. To go somewhere, anywhere. So she hopped on the first bus leaving town, heading nowhere in particular, except away from home.

—*From the Authors' Files*

Type I versus Type II Schizophrenia Some investigators have gone beyond the *DSM* topology in proposing other ways of typing schizophrenia. One alternative typology distinguishes between two basic types of schizophrenia, Type 1 and Type II (Crow, 1980a, 1980b, 1980c). Type I schizophrenia is characterized by the more flagrant symptoms, called **positive symptoms,** such as hallucinations, delusions, and looseness of associations, as well as by an abrupt onset, preserved intellectual ability, and a more favorable response to antipsychotic medication (Penn, 1998). Type II schizophrenia corresponds to a pattern consisting largely of the deficit or **negative symptoms** of schizophrenia. These involve a loss or reduction of normal functions, as shown by such features as lack of emotional expression, low or absent levels of motivation, loss of pleasure in activities, social withdrawal, and poverty of speech, as well as by a more gradual onset, intellectual impairment, and poorer response to antipsychotic drugs (USDHHS, 1999a).

One intriguing possibility is that Type I and Type II schizophrenia represent different pathological processes. The Type I pattern may involve a defect in the inhibitory (blocking) mechanisms in the brain that would normally control excessive or distorted behaviors. Underlying this malfunction may be a disturbance in the supply or regulation of dopamine in the brain, because antipsychotic drugs that regulate dopamine function generally have a favorable impact on positive symptoms. The negative symptoms associated with Type II schizophrenia represent the more enduring or persistent characteristics of schizophrenia. The Type II pattern is associated with poorer functioning before the person developed schizophrenia, or **premorbid functioning,** and with a more progressive decline in functioning leading to enduring disability (Earnst & Kring, 1997; McGlashan & Fenton, 1992). One possibility is that the negative symptoms associated with Type II schizophrenia are caused by structural damage in the brain.

The Type I–Type II distinction remains controversial, as evidence does not clearly support the existence of two distinct behavior patterns in schizophrenia. Some investigators (e.g., Kay, 1990) find that only a minority of people with schizophrenia can be classified as exhibiting either predominantly positive or negative symptoms. Positive and negative symptoms may not define distinct subtypes of schizophrenia but rather separate dimensions that can coexist in the same individual.

Perhaps, as recent research suggests, a three-dimensional model is most appropriate for grouping schizophrenic symptoms (Arango et al., 2000; USDHHS, 1999a). One dimension, a *psychotic dimension,* consists of delusional thinking and hallucinations. A *negative dimension* comprises negative symptoms, such as flat affect and poverty of speech and thought. The third dimension, labeled a *disorganized dimension,* includes inappropriate affect and thought disorder (disordered thought and speech). Although schizophrenic symptoms seem to cluster into these three dimensions, there is considerable overlap among the dimensions. Thus, while the three-factor model may have clinical value in representing particular clusters of symptoms, these dimensions do not appear to represent distinct subtypes of schizophrenia.

Theoretical Perspectives on Schizophrenia

The understanding of schizophrenia has been approached from each of the major theoretical perspectives. Though the underlying causes of schizophrenia remain elusive, they are presumed to involve biological abnormalities in combination with psychosocial and environmental influences (USDHHS, 1999a).

On the run? People with paranoid schizophrenia hold systematized delusions that commonly involve themes of persecution and grandeur. They usually do not show the degree of confusion, disorganization, or disturbed motor behavior seen in people with catatonic or disorganized schizophrenia. Unless they are discussing the areas in which they are delusional, their thought processes can appear to be relatively intact.

THINK ABOUT IT

Why do professionals have several different ways to classify the types of schizophrenia?

positive symptoms Flagrant symptoms of schizophrenia, such as hallucinations, delusions, bizarre behavior, and thought disorder.

negative symptoms Behavioral deficiencies associated with schizophrenia, such as social skills deficits, social withdrawal, flattened affect, poverty of speech and thought, psychomotor retardation, and failure to experience pleasure.

premorbid functioning The level of functioning before the person developed schizophrenia.

Psychodynamic Perspectives According to the psychodynamic perspective, schizophrenia represents the overwhelming of the ego by primitive sexual or aggressive drives or impulses arising from the id. These impulses threaten the ego and give rise to intense intrapsychic conflict. Under such a threat, the person regresses to an early period in the oral stage, referred to as *primary narcissism.* In this period, the infant has not yet learned that the world and it are distinct entities. Because the ego mediates the relationship between the self and the outer world, this breakdown in ego functioning accounts for the detachment from reality that is typical of schizophrenia. Input from the id causes fantasies to become mistaken for reality, giving rise to hallucinations and delusions. Primitive impulses may also carry more weight than social norms and be expressed in bizarre, socially inappropriate behavior.

Freud's followers, such as Erik Erikson and Harry Stack Sullivan, placed more emphasis on interpersonal than intrapsychic factors. Sullivan (1962), for example, who devoted much of his life's work to schizophrenia, emphasized the importance of impaired mother–child relationships, arguing that they can set the stage for gradual withdrawal from other people. In early childhood, anxious and hostile interactions between the child and parent lead the child to take refuge in a private fantasy world. A vicious cycle ensues: The more the child withdraws, the less opportunity there is to develop a sense of trust in others and the social skills necessary to establish intimacy. Then the weak bonds between the child and others prompt social anxiety and further withdrawal. This cycle continues until young adulthood. Then, faced with increasing demands at school or work and in intimate relationships, the person becomes overwhelmed with anxiety and withdraws completely into a world of fantasy.

Critics of Freud's views point out that schizophrenic behavior and infantile behavior are not much alike, so that schizophrenia cannot be explained by regression. Critics of Freud and modern psychodynamic theorists note that psychodynamic explanations are *post hoc,* or retrospective. Early child–adult relationships are recalled from the vantage point of adulthood rather than observed longitudinally. Psychoanalysts have not been able to demonstrate that hypothesized early childhood experiences or family patterns lead to schizophrenia.

Learning Perspectives Although learning theory may not account for schizophrenia, the principles of conditioning and observational learning may play a role in the development of some forms of schizophrenic behavior. From this perspective, people may learn to "emit" schizophrenic behaviors when these are more likely to be reinforced than normal behaviors.

Support for this view is found in operant conditioning studies in which bizarre behavior is shaped by reinforcement. Experiments involving individuals with schizophrenia show, for example, that reinforcement affects the frequency of bizarre versus normal verbalizations and that hospital patients can be shaped into performing odd behaviors. In a classic case example, Haughton and Ayllon (1965) conditioned a 54-year-old woman with chronic schizophrenia to cling to a broom. A staff member gave her the broom to hold and, when she did, another staff member gave her a cigarette. This pattern was repeated several times. Soon the woman could not be parted from the broom. But the fact that reinforcement can influence people to engage in peculiar behavior does not demonstrate that bizarre behaviors characterizing schizophrenia are learned behaviors determined by reinforcement.

Social-cognitive theorists suggest that modeling of schizophrenic behavior can occur within the mental hospital. In that setting, patients may begin to model themselves after fellow patients who act strangely. Hospital staff may inadvertently reinforce schizophrenic behavior by paying more attention to those patients who exhibit more bizarre behavior.

Withdrawing into oneself? Harry Stack Sullivan and some other psychodynamic theorists see individuals with schizophrenia as withdrawing into private fantasy worlds, largely because of severely disturbed relationships with their mothers.

This understanding is consistent with the observation that schoolchildren who disrupt the class garner more attention from their teachers than well-behaved children do.

Perhaps some forms of schizophrenic behavior can be explained by the principles of modeling and reinforcement. However, many people come to display schizophrenic behavior patterns without prior exposure to other people with schizophrenia. In fact, the onset of schizophrenic behavior patterns is more likely to lead to hospitalization than to result from hospitalization.

Biological Perspectives Although we still have much to learn about the biological underpinnings of schizophrenia, most investigators today recognize that biological factors play a determining role.

Genetic Factors We now have compelling evidence that schizophrenia is strongly influenced by genetic factors (Charney, Nestler, & Bunney, 1999; Gottesman, 2001; USDHHS, 1999a). One source of evidence of genetic factors is based on familial studies. Schizophrenia, like many other disorders, tends to run in families (Erlenmeyer-Kimling et al., 1997). Cross-cultural evidence from studies in such countries as Sweden, Iceland, Ireland, as well as the United States, shows an increased risk of schizophrenia in people who have biological relatives with the disorder (Erlenmeyer-Kimling et al., 1997; Kendler & Diehl, 1993). Overall, first-degree relatives of people with schizophrenia (parents or siblings) have about a tenfold greater risk of developing schizophrenia than do members of the general population (APA, 2000; Kendler & Diehl, 1993).

Further supporting a genetic linkage, the closer the genetic relationship between people diagnosed with schizophrenia and their family members, the greater the likelihood (or *concordance rate*) of schizophrenia in their relatives (Gottesman, 2001). Figure 13.1 shows the pooled results of European studies on family incidence of schizophrenia conducted from 1920 to 1987. However, the fact that families share common environments as well as common genes requires that we dig deeper to examine the genetic underpinnings of schizophrenia.

More support for a genetic contribution to schizophrenia is found in twin studies, which show concordance rates for the disorder among identical or monozygotic (MZ) twins of about 48% on the average, which is more than twice the rate found among fraternal or dizygotic (DZ) twins (about 17%) (Gottesman, 1991; Plomin et al., 1994). A twins study in Norway found an even greater spread: 48% concordance in MZ twins versus 3.6% in DZ twins (Onstad et al., 1991).

We should be cautious, however, not to overinterpret the results of twin studies. MZ twins not only share 100% genetic similarity, but they may also be treated more alike than DZ twins. Thus environmental factors may play a role in explaining the higher concordance rates found among MZ twins. To help sort out environmental from genetic factors, investigators have turned to adoption studies in which high-risk (HR) children (children of

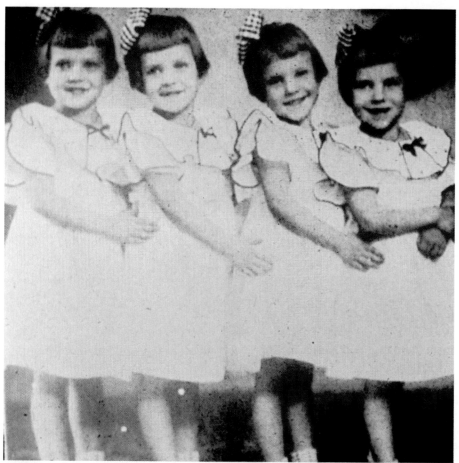

The Genain quadruplets. Schizophrenia is more likely to affect individuals who have family members with the disorder. Here we see a photo of the Genain quadruplets, each of whom developed schizophrenia.

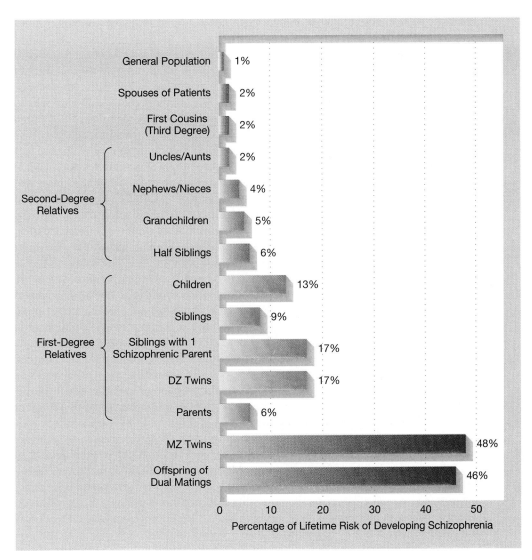

FIGURE 13.1 The familial risk of schizophrenia.
Generally speaking, the more closely one is related to people who have developed schizophrenia, the greater the risk of developing schizophrenia for oneself. Monozygotic (MZ) twins, whose genetic heritages overlap fully, are much more likely than dizygotic (DZ) twins, whose genes overlap by 50%, to be concordant for schizophrenia.

Source. Adapted from Gottesman et al. (1987).

one or more biological parents with schizophrenia) were adopted away shortly after birth and reared apart from their biological parents.

Adoption studies provide the strongest evidence to date for a genetic contribution to schizophrenia. In perhaps the best known example, researchers in Denmark examined official registers and found 39 HR adoptees who had been reared apart from their biological mothers who had schizophrenia (Rosenthal et al., 1968, 1975). Three of the 39 HR adoptees (8%) were diagnosed with schizophrenia, as compared to 0% of a reference group of 47 adoptees whose biological parents had no psychiatric history.

Other investigators have approached the question of heredity in schizophrenia from the opposite direction. U.S. researcher Seymour Kety and Danish colleagues (Kety et al., 1975, 1978) used official records to find 33 index cases of children in Copenhagen, Denmark, who had been adopted early in life and were later diagnosed with schizophrenia. They compared the rates of diagnosed schizophrenia in the biological and adoptive relatives of the index cases with those of the relatives of a matched reference group that consisted of adoptees with no psychiatric history. The results strongly supported the genetic explanation. The incidence of diagnosed schizophrenia was greater among the biological relatives of the adoptees who had schizophrenia than among the biological relatives of the control adoptees. Adoptive relatives of both the index cases and control cases showed similar, *low* rates of schizophrenia. Similar results were found in later research that extended the scope of the investigation to the rest of Denmark (Kety et al., 1994). It thus appears that

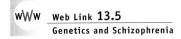

Web Link **13.5**
Genetics and Schizophrenia

cross-fostering study A method of determining heritability of a trait or disorder by examining differences in prevalence among adoptees reared by either adoptive or biological parents who possessed the trait or disorder in question.

dopamine theory The theory that proposes that schizophrenia involves overactivity of dopamine receptors in the brain.

neuroleptics A group of antipsychotic drugs (the "major tranquilizers") used in the treatment of schizophrenia, such as the phenothiazines (Thorazine, Mellaril, etc.).

THINK ABOUT IT

Summarize briefly the evidence that supports a genetic component to the development of schizophrenia. How strong is the genetic component? What other factors might be involved? Is the evidence that having a father over age 50 is a risk factor an argument for or against a genetic component?

family linkages in schizophrenia follow shared genes, not shared environments (Kinney et al., 1997; Moldin, 1994).

Still another approach, the **cross-fostering study,** has yielded additional evidence of genetic factors in schizophrenia. In this approach, investigators compare the incidence of schizophrenia among children whose biological parents either had or didn't have schizophrenia and who were reared by adoptive parents who either had or didn't have schizophrenia. Another Danish study by Wender and his colleagues (Wender et al., 1974) found the incidence of schizophrenia related to the presence of schizophrenia in the children's biological parents, but not in their adoptive parents. High-risk children (children whose biological parents had schizophrenia) were almost twice as likely to develop schizophrenia as those of nonschizophrenic biological parents, regardless of whether or not they were reared by a parent with schizophrenia. It is also notable that adoptees whose biological parents did not suffer from schizophrenia were placed at no greater risk of developing schizophrenia by being reared by an adoptive parent with schizophrenia than by a nonschizophrenic parent. In sum, a genetic relationship with a person with schizophrenia seems to be the most prominent risk factor for developing the disorder.

Though genetic factors are clearly implicated in schizophrenia, scientists have yet to discover any of the particular genes that may be involved (USDHHS, 1999a). The present understanding is that multiple genes are responsible (Buchsbaum & Hazlett, 1998; Cowan & Kandel, 2001). In sum, the evidence to date strongly supports a genetic component in schizophrenia. However, genetics alone does not determine risk of schizophrenia. For one thing, people may carry a high genetic risk of schizophrenia and not develop the disorder. For another, the rate of concordance among MZ twins, as noted earlier, is well below 100%, even though identical twins carry identical genes. The prevailing view today, which we discuss later, is the diathesis-stress model, which holds that schizophrenia involves a complex interplay of genetic and environmental factors.

Some cases of schizophrenia appear to be linked to paternal age. Fathers over the age of 50 in one study had three times the chances of having a child develop schizophrenia than did fathers under the age of 25 (Lewin, 2001; Malaspina et al., 2001; "Father's Age," 2001). Though scientists remain skeptical of the link to paternal age until more data is gathered, the existence of such a link raises the possibility that men too may have a biological clock. Though older men may be capable of siring children, their advancing biological clock may put them at greater risk of transmitting genetic defects to their offspring, including perhaps schizophrenia.

Biochemical Factors Contemporary biological investigations of schizophrenia have focused on the role of the neurotransmitter dopamine. The **dopamine theory** posits that schizophrenia involves an overreactivity of dopamine receptors in the brain—the receptor sites on postsynaptic neurons into which molecules of dopamine lock (Haber & Fudge, 1997).

The major source of evidence for the dopamine model is found in the effects of antipsychotic drugs called major tranquilizers or **neuroleptics.** The most widely used neuroleptics belong to a class of drugs called *phenothiazines,* which includes such drugs as Thorazine, Mellaril, and Prolixin. Neuroleptic drugs block dopamine receptors, thereby reducing the level of dopamine activity (Kane, 1996). As a consequence, neuroleptics inhibit excessive transmission of neural impulses that may give rise to schizophrenic behavior.

Another source of evidence supporting the role of dopamine in schizophrenia is based on the actions of amphetamines, a class of stimulant drugs. These drugs increase the concentration of dopamine in the synaptic cleft by blocking its reuptake by presynaptic neurons. When given in large doses to normal people, these drugs can lead to abnormal behavior states that mimic paranoid schizophrenia.

Overall, evidence points to irregularities in schizophrenia patients in the neural pathways in the brain that utilize dopamine (Meador-Woodruff et al., 1997). The specific nature of this abnormality remains unclear. We can't yet say whether the abnormality involves overreactivity of particular dopamine pathways or more complex interactions among dopamine systems. One possibility is that overreactivity of dopamine receptors may be involved in producing more flagrant behavior patterns (positive symptoms) but not the negative symptoms or deficits associated with schizophrenia. Decreased, rather than increased, dopamine reactivity may be connected with some of the negative symptoms of schizophrenia (Earnst & Kring, 1997; Okubo et al., 1997). We should also note that other neurotransmitters, such as norepinephrine, serotonin, and GABA, also appear to be involved in schizophrenia (Busatto et al., 1997).

Viral Infections Might schizophrenia be caused by a slow-acting virus that attacks the developing brain of a fetus or newborn child? Prenatal rubella (German measles), a viral infection, is a cause of later mental retardation. Could another virus give rise to schizophrenia?

Viral infections are most prevalent in the winter months. The viral theory could account for findings of an excess number of people who later develop schizophrenia being born in the winter (Mortensen et al., 1999; Tam & Sewell, 1995). However, we have yet to find an identified viral agent we can link to schizophrenia. Thus we must consider the viral theory of schizophrenia to be intriguing but inconclusive. Even if a viral basis for schizophrenia were discovered, it would probably account for but a small fraction of cases.

Brain Abnormalities Despite the widespread belief among professionals that schizophrenia is a brain disease, we are still asking the question, "Where is the pathology?" (Stevens, 1997). Researchers are trying to answer this question by using modern brain-imaging techniques, including PET scans, EEGs, CT scans, and MRIs, that probe the inner workings of the brain. Evidence from brain-imaging studies point to various abnormalities in the brains of many people with schizophrenia (e.g., Gur et al., 1998; Ettinger et al., 2001).

The clearest finding of structural damage in the brain is evidence of enlarged brain ventricles (hollow spaces in the brain) occurring in perhaps three of four schizophrenia patients (Coursey, Alford, & Safarjan, 1997) (see Figure 13.2). Enlarged ventricles are signs of loss of brain tissue (cell loss). Investigators also find that brains of schizophrenia patients are about 5% smaller, on average, in total volume than those of normal individuals, with the greatest volume reductions in the cerebral cortex (Cowan & Kandel, 2001).

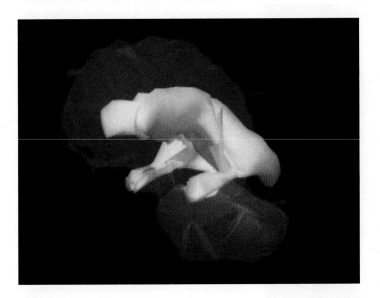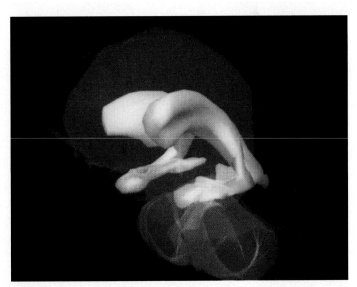

FIGURE 13.2 Structural changes in the brain of a person with schizophrenia as compared with that of a normal subject.
The magnetic resonance imaging (MRI) of the brain of a person with schizophrenia (left) shows a relatively shrunken hippocampus (yellow) and relatively enlarged, fluid-filled ventricles (gray) when compared to the structures of the normal subject (right). The MRI was conducted by schizophrenia researcher Nancy C. Andreasen.

Source: Gershon, E. S., & Rieder, R. O. (1992). Major disorders of mind and brain. *Scientific American, 267*(No. 3), p. 128.

Bear in mind, however, that not all people with schizophrenia show any evidence of enlarged ventricles or other signs of structural damage to brain tissue. This finding leads researchers to suspect that there may be several forms of schizophrenia that have different causal processes. One form may involve a degenerative loss of brain tissue (Knoll et al., 1998). Scientists suspect that some cases of schizophrenia may be associated with a progressive loss of brain tissue or perhaps the failure of the brain to have developed normally in the first place. They suspect that brain abnormalities may be the result of prenatal viral infections, inadequate fetal nutrition, genetic defects, or birth traumas or complications (McGlashan & Hoffman, 2000; McNeil, Cantor-Graae, & Weinberger, 2000; Rosso et al., 2000; Wahlbeck et al., 2001). Still, not all people with schizophrenia show signs of brain damage or abnormal brain development. Some forms of schizophrenia may involve reduced brain growth or degenerative loss of brain tissue early in life whereas others may not (Baaré et al., 2001; Knoll et al., 1998).

A considerable body of evidence points to abnormalities in the prefrontal cortex in schizophrenia patients (Glantz & Lewis, 2000; Gur et al., 2000a; Sanfilipo et al., 2000). Some of this evidence shows reduced brain wave activity in the prefrontal cortex of many schizophrenia patients (Kim et al., 2000; Ragland et al., 2001) (see Figure 13.3). Other evidence shows a loss of brain tissue in the prefrontal cortex in some schizophrenia patients (Fannon et al., 2000; Karp et al., 2001; Mathalno et al.. 2001; Staal et al., 2000).

The prefrontal cortex is the thinking and organizing center of the brain. It is the area of the frontal lobes of the cerebral cortex that lies in front of the motor cortex (the part of the brain that controls voluntary body movements). The prefrontal cortex is involved in controlling many cognitive and emotional functions, the kinds of functions that are often impaired in people with schizophrenia. The prefrontal cortex serves as a kind of mental clipboard for holding information needed to guide organized behavior (Casanova, 1997). Prefrontal abnormalities may explain why people with schizophrenia have difficulty organizing their thoughts and behavior and performing higher level cognitive tasks, such as formulating concepts, prioritizing information, and formulating goals and plans (Barch et al., 2001; Bertolino et al., 2000; Callicott et al., 2000). The prefrontal cortex is also involved in regulating attention, so findings of prefrontal abnormalities coincide with research evidence of deficits in attention among people with schizophrenia. These are intriguing findings that may provide clues as to the biological bases of schizophrenia.

We have yet other evidence of structural differences in the brains of schizophrenia patients in subcortical regions of the brain—structures in the brain lying beneath the cortex that are involved in regulating emotions, attention, and memory formation (e.g., Byrne et al., 2001; Ettinger et al., 2001; Gur et al., 2000b; Wright et al., 2000). Disturbances in brain physiology in subcortical regions, perhaps involving neurotransmitter imbalances or faulty connections (wiring) between neurons, may contribute to disturbances in thinking, attention, and emotions associated with schizophrenia.

Family Theories Disturbed family relationships have long been regarded as playing a role in the development and course of schizophrenia (Miklowitz, 1994). Early family theories of schizophrenia focused on the role of a "pathogenic" family mem-

THINK ABOUT IT

What have we learned about the biological bases of schizophrenia? What don't we know? What might you say to critics who claim that schizophrenia is not a disease because no one has yet found any specific disease process in the brain that accounts for it?

CONTROLS

SCHIZOPHRENICS

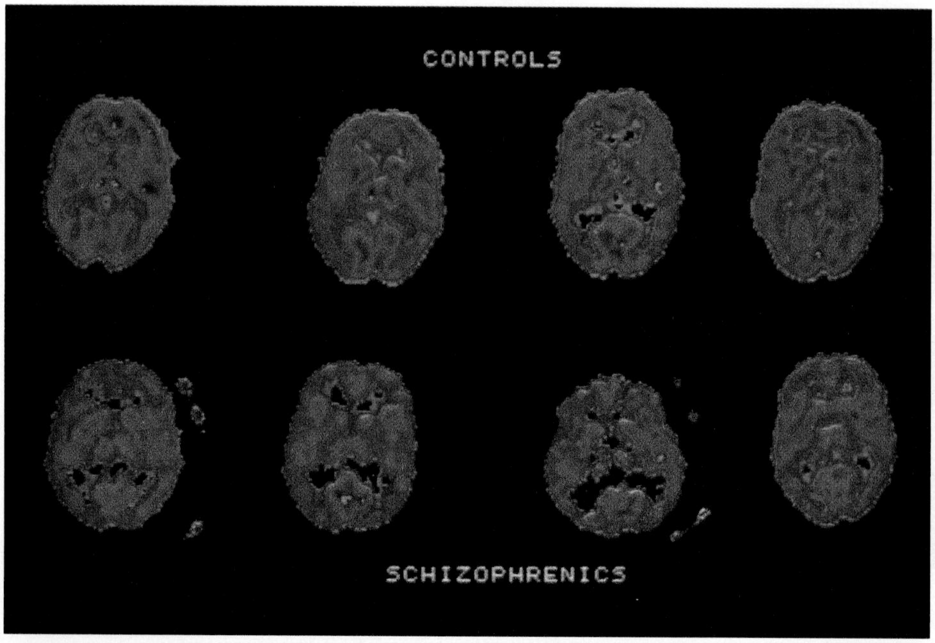

FIGURE 13.3 PET scans of people with schizophrenia versus normals.
Positron emission tomography (PET scan) evidence of the metabolic processes of the brain show relatively less metabolic activity (indicated by less yellow and red) in the frontal lobes of the brains of people with schizophrenia. PET scans of the brains of four normal people are shown in the top row, and PET scans of the brains of four people with schizophrenia are shown below.

ber, such as the **schizophrenogenic mother** (Fromm-Reichmann, 1948, 1950). In what some feminists view as historic psychiatric sexism, the schizophrenogenic mother was described as cold, aloof, overprotective, and domineering. She was characterized as stripping her children of self-esteem, stifling their independence, and forcing them into dependency on her. Children reared by such mothers were believed to be at special risk for developing schizophrenia if their fathers were passive and failed to counteract the pathogenic influences of the mother. Despite extensive research, however, mothers of people who develop schizophrenia do not fit the stereotypical picture of the schizophrenogenic mother (Hirsch & Leff, 1975).

In the 1950s, family theorists began to focus on the role of disturbed communications in the family. One of the more prominent theories, put forth by Gregory Bateson and his colleagues (1956), was that **double-bind communications** contribute to the development of schizophrenia. A double-bind communication transmits two mutually incompatible messages. In a double-bind communication with a child, a mother might freeze up when the child approaches her and then scold the child for keeping a distance. Whatever the child does, she or he is wrong. With repeated exposure to such double binds, the child's thinking may become disorganized and chaotic. The double-binding mother prevents discussion of her inconsistencies, because she cannot admit to herself that she is unable to tolerate closeness. Note this vignette:

A Case Example of Double-Bind Communication

A young man who had fairly well recovered from an acute schizophrenic episode was visited in the hospital by his mother. He was glad to see her and impulsively put his arm around her shoulders whereupon she stiffened. He withdrew his arm and she asked, "Don't you love me anymore?" He then blushed and she said, "Dear, you must not be so easily embarrassed and afraid of your feelings." The patient was able to stay with her only a few minutes more and following her departure he assaulted an aide.

—From Bateson et al., 1956, p. 251

Perhaps double-bind communications serve as a source of family stress that increases the risk of schizophrenia in genetically vulnerable individuals. In more recent years, investigators have broadened the investigation of family factors in schizophrenia by viewing the family in terms of a system of relationships among the members rather than singling out mother–child or father–child interactions. Research has begun to identify stressful factors in the family that may interact with a genetic vulnerability in leading to the development of schizophrenia. Two principal sources of family stress that have been studied are patterns of deviant communications and negative emotional expression in the family.

Communication Deviance Communication deviance (CD) is a pattern of unclear, vague, disruptive, or fragmented communication that is often found among parents and family members of schizophrenia patients. CD is characterized by speech that is hard to follow and from which it is difficult to extract any shared meaning (Wahlberg et al., 2001). High CD parents also have difficulty focusing on what their children are saying (Miklowitz, 1994). They tend to verbally attack their children rather than offer constructive criticism and may subject them to double-bind communications. They also tend to interrupt the child with intrusive, negative comments. They are prone to telling the child what she or he "really" thinks rather than allowing the child to formulate her or his own thoughts and feelings. Parents of people with schizophrenia show higher levels of communication deviance than parents of people without schizophrenia (Miklowitz, 1994).

Communication deviance may be one of the stress-related factors that increase the risk of development of schizophrenia in genetically vulnerable individuals (Goldstein, 1987).

schizophrenogenic mother A since-discarded concept of a cold but overprotective mother who, it was believed, was capable of causing schizophrenia in her children.

double-bind communications A communication pattern involving contradictory or mixed messages without acknowledging the inherent conflict.

Then too, the causal pathway may work in the opposite direction. Perhaps communication deviance is a parental reaction to the behavior of disturbed children. Parents may learn to use odd language as a way of coping with children who continually interrupt and confront them. Or perhaps parents and children share genetic traits that become expressed as disturbed communications and increased vulnerability toward schizophrenia, without there being a casual link between the two.

Expressed Emotion Another measure of disturbed family communications is called expressed emotion (EE). EE involves the tendency of family members to be hostile, critical, and unsupportive of their schizophrenic family members. People with schizophrenia whose families are high in EE tend to show poorer adjustment and have higher rates of relapse following release from the hospital than those with more supportive families (Cutting & Docherty, 2000; King & Dixon, 1999). Assessment of personality functioning shows high EE relatives to possess less empathy, tolerance, and flexibility than low EE relatives (Hooley & Hiller, 2000). High EE relatives also tend to believe that schizophrenia patients can exercise greater control over their behavior than do low EE relatives of the same patients (Weisman et al., 2000). Expressed emotion in relatives is also associated with a greater risk of relapse from other disorders, such as major depression and eating disorders (Butzlaff & Hooley, 1998).

Truth OR Fiction? REVISITED

Living in a family that is hostile, critical, and unsupportive can increase the risk of relapse in people with schizophrenia.

TRUE. Schizophrenia patients in families with hostile, critical, and unsupportive family members who are at greater risk of relapse than those from more supportive families.

Low EE families may actually serve to protect, or buffer, the family member with schizophrenia from the adverse impact of outside stressors and help prevent recurrent episodes (see Figure 13.4). Yet family interactions are a two-way street. Family members and patients influence each other and are influenced in turn. Disruptive behaviors by the schizophrenic family member frustrate other members of the family, prompting them to respond to the person in a less supportive and more critical and hostile way. This in turn can exacerbate the schizophrenia patient's disruptive behavior (Bellack & Mueser, 1993).

Relationships between expressed emotion and rates of recurrence of schizophrenia have been drawn largely from research with non-Hispanic White samples in England and the United States (Karno et al., 1987). Because family patterns are often influenced by cultural factors, researchers have begun to explore whether the EE construct has value in predicting recurrence of schizophrenia in other cultures. Some cross-cultural support for the prognostic value of the construct comes from a study of low-income, relatively unacculturated Mexican American family members of people with schizophrenia (Karno et al., 1987). Paralleling findings with the non-Hispanic White British and American families, high levels of EE (that is, critical, hostile, and emotionally overinvolved attitudes and behaviors) among key family members in the Mexican American sample were associated with an increased risk of relapse among schizophrenia patients living with their families after hospitalization. Evidence from samples of both Mexican American families and Anglo American families with high levels of expressed emotion show them to be more likely than low EE families to view the psychotic behavior of a schizophrenic family member to lie within the person's control (Weisman et al., 1993, 1998). The anger and criticism of high EE family members may stem from the perception that patients can and should exert greater control over their aberrant behavior.

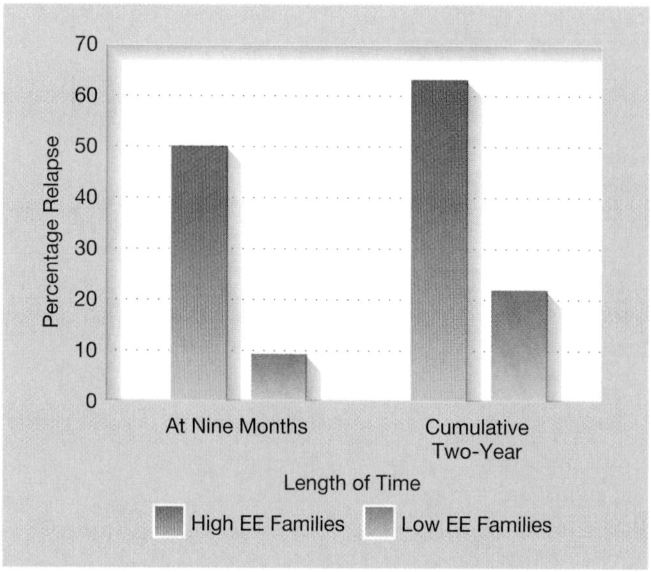

FIGURE 13.4 Relapse rates of people with schizophrenia in high and low EE families.
People with schizophrenia whose families are high in expressed emotion (EE) are at greater risk of relapse than those whose families are low in EE. Whereas low-EE families may help protect the family member with schizophrenia from environmental stressors, high-EE families may impose additional stress.

Source. Adapted from Leff & Vaughn (1981).

We also have evidence for cultural variations in expressed emotion. Much lower prevalences of high EE behaviors, as compared with the (non-Hispanic) White British and American families, were found among a sample of Mexican American families and families from northern India who had family members with schizophrenia (Wig et al., 1987). The (non-Hispanic) White families thus tended to be more openly critical of the members of their families who had schizophrenia than were family members from these other cultural backgrounds. The specific components of EE may also vary across cultures (Martins, de Lemos, & Bebbington, 1992).

Other researchers find that the extended family structure often found in traditional cultures may offer an emotional and financial buffer against the hardships imposed by the behavioral excesses and deficiencies of people with schizophrenia. In Western cultures, these burdens are more likely to be borne by the nuclear family (Lefley, 1990). Such differences remind us of the need to take cultural factors into account when examining relationships between family factors and schizophrenia.

Families of people with schizophrenia tend to have little if any preparation or training for coping with the stressful demands of caring for them (Winefield & Harvey, 1994). Rather than focusing so much attention on the negative influence of high EE family members, perhaps we should seek to help family members learn more constructive ways of relating to one another. Evidence shows that families can be helped to reduce their level of expressed emotion (Penn & Mueser, 1996).

Family Factors in Schizophrenia: Causes or Sources of Stress? No evidence supports the belief that family factors, such as negative family interactions, lead to schizophrenia in children who do not have a genetic vulnerability. What then is the role of family factors in schizophrenia? Within the diathesis-stress model, disturbed patterns of emotional interaction and communication in the family represent a source of potential stress that may increase the risks of developing schizophrenia among people with a genetic predisposition for the disorder. Perhaps these increased risks could be minimized or eliminated if families are taught to handle stress and to be less critical and more supportive of the members of their families with schizophrenia. Counseling programs that help family members of people with chronic schizophrenia learn to express their feelings without attacking or criticizing the person with schizophrenia may prevent family conflicts that damage the person's adjustment. The family member with schizophrenia may also benefit from efforts to reduce the level of contact with relatives who fail to respond to family interventions.

How families conceptualize mental disorders also has a bearing on how they relate to relatives who suffer from them. For example, the term *schizophrenia* is connected with a stigma in our society and with the expectation that the disorder is enduring (Jenkins & Karno, 1992). In contrast, to many Mexican Americans, a person with schizophrenia is perceived as suffering from *nervios* ("nerves"), a cultural label attached to a wide range of troubled behaviors, including anxiety, schizophrenia, and depression, and one that carries less stigmata and more positive expectations than the label of schizophrenia (Jenkins, 1988; Jenkins & Karno, 1992). Researchers believe the label *nervios* may have the effect of destigmatizing the person with schizophrenia:

> Since severe cases of *nervios* are not considered blameworthy or under an individual's control, the person who suffers its effects is deserving of sympathy, support, and special treatment. Moreover, severe cases of *nervios* are potentially curable. It is interesting to note that Mexican-descent relatives do not adopt another possible cultural label for craziness, *loco.* As a *loco,* the individual would be much more severely stigmatized and considered to be out of control with little chance for recovery....
>
> Defining the problem as *nervios,* a common condition that in its milder forms afflicts nearly everyone, provides them a way of identifying with and minimizing the problem by claiming that the ill relative is "just like me, only more so." (Jenkins & Karno, 1992, pp. 17–18)

Family members may respond differently to relatives who have schizophrenia if they ascribe aspects of their behavior to a temporary or curable condition, which they believe can be altered by willpower, than if they believe the behavior is caused by a permanent brain abnormality. The degree to which relatives perceive family members with schizophrenia as having control over their disorders may be a critical factor in how they respond to them. Families may cope better with a family member with schizophrenia if they take a balanced view, believing on the one hand that people with schizophrenia can maintain some control

THINK ABOUT IT
Have you known anyone diagnosed with schizophrenia? What information do you have about the person's family history, family relationships, and stressful life events that might shed light on the development of the disorder?

over their behavior, while allowing that some of their odd or disruptive behavior is a product of their underlying disorder (Weisman et al., 1993). It remains to be seen whether these different ways in which family members conceptualize schizophrenia are connected with differences in the rates of recurrence of the disorder among affected family members.

Tying It Together: The Diathesis-Stress Model

 In 1962, psychologist Paul Meehl proposed an integrative model that led to the development of the diathesis-stress model. Meehl suggested that certain people possess a genetic predisposition to schizophrenia that is expressed behaviorally only if they are reared in stressful environments (Meehl, 1962, 1972).

Later, Zubin and Spring (1977) formulated the diathesis-stress model, which views schizophrenia in terms of the interaction or combination of a *diathesis*, in the form of a genetic predisposition to develop the disorder, with environmental stress that exceeds the individual's stress threshold or coping resources. Environmental stressors may include psychological factors, such as family conflict, child abuse, emotional deprivation, or loss of supportive figures, as well as physical environmental influences, such as early brain trauma or injury. On the other hand, if environmental stress remains below the person's stress threshold, schizophrenia may never develop, even in persons at genetic risk (see Figure 13.5).

But what is the biological basis for the diathesis? No one has yet been able to find any specific brain abnormality present in all individuals who receive a schizophrenia diagnosis (Powchik et al., 1998; Stevens, 1997). Perhaps it shouldn't surprise us that a "one-size-fits-all" model doesn't apply. Schizophrenia is a complex disorder characterized by different subtypes and symptom complexes. There may be different causal processes in the brain explaining different forms of schizophrenia. What we now call *schizophrenia* may turn out to be more than one disorder (Buchanan & Carpenter, 1997; Knoll et al., 1998).

We noted two possible causal processes, one involving structural damage to brain tissue, the other involving disturbed neurotransmitter functioning. These factors, or perhaps a combination of the two, result in disrupted brain circuits involving the prefrontal cortex and its connections to lower brain regions responsible for organizing our thoughts, perceptions, emotions, and attentional processes. These neural networks are involved in processing information efficiently and turning it into meaningful thoughts and behavior. Defect in this circuitry may be involved in explaining the more flagrant, positive features of schizophrenia such as hallucinations, delusions, and thought disorder.

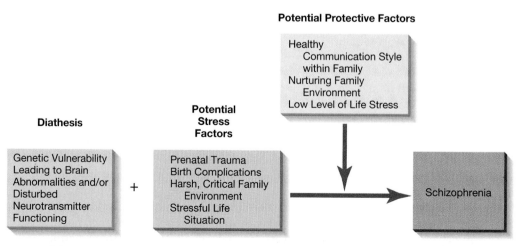

FIGURE 13.5 Diathesis-stress model of schizophrenia.

Research Evidence Supporting the Diathesis-Stress Model Several lines of evidence support the diathesis-stress model. One source of support is the fact that schizophrenia tends to develop in late adolescence or early adulthood, around the time that young people typically face the increased stress associated with developmental challenges relating to establishing independence and finding a role in life. Other evidence shows that psychosocial stress, such as harping criticisms from family members, worsens symptoms in people with schizophrenia, increasing risks of relapse (King & Dixon, 1995). However, the question of whether stress directly triggers the initial onset of schizophrenia in genetically vulnerable individuals still remains open to debate (Walker & Diforio, 1997).

Other sources of stress that may contribute to the development of schizophrenia in genetically vulnerable individuals involve sociocultural factors associated with poverty, such as overcrowding, poor diet and sanitation, impoverished housing, and inadequate health care (Kety, 1980). Other support for the diathesis-stress model comes from longitudinal studies of high-risk (HR) children who are at increased genetic risk of developing the disorder by virtue of having one or both parents with schizophrenia. Longitudinal studies of HR children (offspring of parents with schizophrenia) support the central tenet of the diathesis-stress model that heredity interacts with environmental influences in determining vulnerability to schizophrenia. Longitudinal studies track individuals over extended periods of time. Ideally they begin before the emergence of the disorder or behavior pattern in question and follow its course. In this way, investigators may identify early characteristics that predict the later development of a particular disorder, such as schizophrenia. These studies require a commitment of many years and substantial cost. Because schizophrenia occurs in only about 1% of the general population, researchers have focused on HR children because they are more likely to develop the disorder. Children with one parent with schizophrenia have about a 10% to 25% chance of developing schizophrenia, and those with two parents have about a 45% risk (Erlenmeyer-Kimling et al., 1997; Gottesman, 1991). Still, even children with two biological parents with schizophrenia stand a slightly better than even chance of not developing the disorder themselves.

The best known longitudinal study of HR children was undertaken by Sarnoff Mednick and his colleagues in Denmark. In 1962, the Mednick group identified 207 HR children (children whose mothers had schizophrenia) and 104 reference subjects who were matched for such factors as gender, social class, age, and education but whose mothers did not have schizophrenia (Mednick, Parnas, & Schulsinger, 1987). The children from both groups ranged in age from 10 to 20 years, with a mean of 15 years. None showed signs of disturbance when first interviewed.

Five years later, at an average age of 20, the children were reexamined. By then 20 of the HR children were found to have demonstrated abnormal behavior, although not necessarily a schizophrenic episode (Mednick & Schulsinger, 1968). The children who showed abnormal behavior, referred to as the HR "sick" group, were then compared with a matched group of 20 HR children from the original sample who remained well functioning (an HR "well" group) and a matched group of 20 low-risk (LR) subjects. It turned out that the mothers of the HR "well" offspring had experienced easier pregnancies and deliveries than those of the HR "sick" group or the LR group. Seventy percent of the mothers of the HR "sick" children had serious complications during pregnancy or delivery. Perhaps, consistent with the diathesis-stress model, complications during pregnancy, childbirth, or shortly after birth cause brain damage (a stress factor) that in combination with a genetic vulnerability leads to severe mental disorders in later life. Finnish researchers also find links between fetal and postnatal abnormalities and the development of schizophrenia in adulthood (Jones et al., 1998). The low rate of complications during pregnancy and birth in the HR "well" group in the Danish study suggests that normal pregnancies and births may actually help protect HR children from developing abnormal behavior patterns (Mednick et al., 1987).

Evaluation of these same HR subjects in the late 1980s, when they averaged 42 years of age and had passed through the period of greatest risk for development of schizophrenia, showed a significantly higher percentage of schizophrenia in the HR group than the LR comparison group, 16% versus 2%, respectively (Parnas et al., 1993).

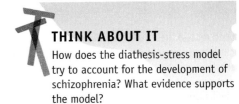

THINK ABOUT IT

How does the diathesis-stress model try to account for the development of schizophrenia? What evidence supports the model?

Protective factors in high-risk children. A supportive and nurturing environment may reduce the likelihood of developing schizophrenia among high-risk children.

Certain environmental factors, such as good parenting, may actually have a protective role in preventing the development of the disorder in people at increased genetic risk. In support of the role of early environmental influences, Mednick and his colleagues found that HR children who developed schizophrenia had poorer relationships with their parents than did HR children who did not go on to develop the disorder (Mednick et al., 1987). The presence of childhood behavior problems may also be a marker for the later development of schizophrenia-related disorders in HR children (Amminger et al., 1999).

Treatment Approaches

There is no cure for schizophrenia. Treatment is generally multifaceted, incorporating pharmacological, psychological, and rehabilitative approaches. Most people treated for schizophrenia in organized mental health settings receive some form of antipsychotic medication, which is intended to control the more flagrant behavior patterns, such as hallucinations and delusions, and decrease the risk of recurrent episodes.

Biological Approaches The advent in the 1950s of antipsychotic drugs—also referred to as major tranquilizers or neuroleptics—revolutionized the treatment of schizophrenia and provided the impetus for large-scale releases of mental patients to the community (deinstitutionalization). Antipsychotic medication helped control the more flagrant behavior patterns of schizophrenia and reduced the need for long-term hospitalization when taken on a maintenance or continuing basis after an acute episode (Kane, 1996; Sheitman et al., 1998). Yet for many patients with chronic schizophrenia, entering a hospital is like going through a revolving door. That is, they are repeatedly admitted and discharged within a relatively brief time frame. Many are simply discharged to the streets once they are stabilized on medication and receive little if any follow-up care or available housing. This often leads to a pattern of chronic homelessness punctuated by brief stays in the hospital. Only a small proportion of people with schizophrenia who are discharged from long-term care facilities are successfully reintegrated into the community (Bellack & Mueser, 1990).

Commonly used antipsychotic drugs include the phenothiazines *chlorpromazine* (Thorazine), *thioridazine* (Mellaril), *trifluoperazine* (Stelazine), and *fluphenazine* (Prolixin). *Haloperidol* (Haldol), which is chemically distinct from the phenothiazines, produces similar effects.

Though we can't say with certainty how these drugs work, it appears they derive their therapeutic effect from blocking dopamine receptors in the brain. This reduces dopamine activity, which seems to quell the more flagrant signs of schizophrenia, such as hallucinations and delusions. The effectiveness of antipsychotic drugs has been repeatedly demonstrated in double-blind, placebo-controlled studies (Kane, 1996). Yet a substantial minority of people with schizophrenia receive little benefit from traditional neuroleptics, and no clear-cut factors determine who will best respond (Kane & Marder, 1993).

The major risk of long-term treatment with neuroleptic drugs (possibly excluding clozapine) is a potentially disabling side effect called **tardive dyskinesia (TD)**. TD is an involuntary movement disorder that can affect any body part (Hansen, Casey, & Hoffman, 1997). It is irreversible in many cases, even when the neuroleptic medication is withdrawn. It occurs most often in patients who are treated with neuroleptics for 6 months or longer. TD can take different forms, the most common of which is frequent eye blinking. Common signs of the disorder include involuntary chewing and eye movements, lip smacking

Web Link **13.6** wWw
Treatment Guidelines for Schizophrenia

tardive dyskinesia (TD) A disorder characterized by involuntary movements of the face, mouth, neck, trunk, or extremities and caused by long-term use of antipsychotic medication.

and puckering, facial grimacing, and involuntary movements of the limbs and trunk. In some cases, the movement disorder is so severe that patients have difficulty breathing, talking, or eating. Overall, about one in four people receiving long-term treatment with neuroleptics eventually develops TD (Jeste & Caligiuri, 1993).

TD is most common among older people and among women (Hansen et al., 1997). Unfortunately, we lack a safe and effective treatment for TD (Egan, Apud, & Wyatt, 1997; Sheitman et al., 1998). Although TD tends to improve gradually or stabilize over a period of years, many people with TD remain persistently and severely disabled.

The risk of this potentially disabling side effect requires physicians to weigh carefully the risks and benefits of long-term treatment with these drugs. Investigators have altered drug regimens in the attempt to reduce the risk of TD, such as by stopping medication in stable outpatients and starting it again when early symptoms reappear. However, intermittent medication schedules are associated with a twofold increase in the risk of relapse and have not been shown to lower the risk of TD (Kane, 1996).

A new generation of drugs, commonly referred to as atypical antipsychotic drugs (*clozapine, risperidone,* and *olanzapine* are examples), are as effective as the older drugs but carry fewer neurological side effects than conventional antipsychotics (Arranz et al., 2000; Kapur & Remington, 2000). They may help schizophrenia patients who have failed to respond to more conventional antipsychotics (Essock et al., 2000; Geddes et al., 2000; Wahlbeck et al., 1999). They also hold promise of providing more effective treatment of negative symptoms than do conventional antipsychotics.

One of these atypical antipsychotics, clozapine, is the only known drug that carries a minimal risk of TD (Conley & Buchanan, 1997; Kane, 1996). However, other side effects limit its use, especially the risk of a potentially lethal disorder in which the body produces inadequate supplies of white blood cells. Because of this risk, patients receiving the drug must receive frequent blood monitoring (USDHHS, 1999a). There are also promising findings that olanzapine may reduce the risk of TD relative to conventional antipsychotics (Tollefson et al., 1997), but more research is needed to reach a more definitive conclusion (Egan et al., 1997).

Antipsychotic drugs help control the more flagrant or bizarre features of schizophrenia, but are not a cure. People with chronic schizophrenia typically receive maintenance doses of antipsychotic drugs once their flagrant symptoms abate. Continued medication reduces the rate of relapse but is no panacea. Many patients, perhaps 15% to 20% per year, relapse even if they are maintained on continued medication (Kane, 1996). Yet estimates are that 75% of patients with schizophrenia who have been in remission for a year or more will relapse within 12 to 18 months if their medication is withdrawn (Kane, 1996). Still, not all people with schizophrenia require antipsychotic medication to maintain themselves in the community. Unfortunately, no one can yet predict which patients can manage effectively without continued medication.

Medication alone is insufficient to meet the multifaceted needs of people with schizophrenia. Drug therapy needs to be supplemented with psychoeducational programs that help schizophrenia patients develop better social skills and adjust to demands of community living. A wide array of treatment components are needed within a comprehensive model of care, including such elements as antipsychotic medication, medical care, family therapy, social skills training, crisis intervention, rehabilitation services, and housing and other social services (Penn & Mueser, 1996; USDHHS, 1999a). Treatment programs also need to ensure a continuity of care between the hospital and the community.

Sociocultural Factors in Treatment

Investigators find that response to psychiatric medications and dosage levels varies with patient ethnicity (USDHHS, 1999a). Asians and Hispanics, for example, may require lower doses of neuroleptics than do Caucasians. Asians also tend to experience more side effects from the same dosage.

Ethnicity may also play a role in the family's involvement in the treatment process. In a study of 26 Asian Americans and 26 non-Hispanic White Americans with schizophrenia, family members of the Asian American patients were more frequently involved in the treatment program (Lin et al., 1991). For example, the Asian American

---

Truth OR Fiction? REVISITED

Drugs developed in the past few years not only treat schizophrenia, but also can cure it in many cases.

FALSE. Antipsychotic drugs help control the symptoms of schizophrenia but cannot cure the disorder.

THINK ABOUT IT

What are the relative risks and benefits of antipsychotic medication? Why is medication alone not sufficient to treat schizophrenia? Do you believe that people with schizophrenia should be treated indefinitely with antipsychotic drugs? Why or why not?

patients were more likely to be accompanied to their medication evaluation sessions by family members. The authors believe that the greater family involvement among Asian Americans represents the relatively stronger sense of family responsibility in Asian cultures. Non-Hispanic White Americans are more likely to emphasize individualism and self-responsibility.

Maintaining connections between the person with schizophrenia and the family and larger community is part of the cultural tradition in many Asian cultures, as well as in other parts of the world, such as Africa. The seriously mentally ill of China, for instance, retain strong supportive links to their families and workplaces, which helps increase their chances of being reintegrated into community life (Liberman, 1994). In traditional healing centers for the treatment of schizophrenia in Africa, the strong support that patients receive from the family and community members, together with a community centered lifestyle, are important elements of successful care (Peltzer & Machleidt, 1992).

There is clear value in working with the family in treating schizophrenia in Asian Americans, as well as in other groups. Researchers find that failure to include the family often compromises the value of therapy for Asian Americans and causes many of them to drop out of therapy prematurely (Lin et al., 1978). Researchers in a hospital in Great Britain reported that living with family members was among the factors that might explain the lower relapse and rehospitalization rates found among Asian people with schizophrenia as compared to White or Afro-Caribbean people (Birchwood et al., 1992). Family interactions are not necessarily harmonious or conducive of better outcomes, however, as research on expressed emotion makes clear. Neglect or rejection of the person with schizophrenia within the family may play an important role in premature treatment termination and poorer outcomes.

Psychodynamic Therapy Freud did not believe that traditional psychoanalysis was well suited to the treatment of schizophrenia. The withdrawal into a fantasy world that typifies schizophrenia prevents the individual with schizophrenia from forming a meaningful relationship with the psychoanalyst. The techniques of classical psychoanalysis, Freud wrote, must "be replaced by others; and we do not know yet whether we shall succeed in finding a substitute" (as cited in Arieti, 1974, p. 532).

Other psychoanalysts, such as Harry Stack Sullivan and Frieda Fromm-Reichmann, adapted psychoanalytic techniques specifically for the treatment of schizophrenia. However, research has failed to demonstrate the effectiveness of psychoanalytic or psychodynamic therapy for schizophrenia. In the light of negative findings, some critics have argued that further research on the use of psychodynamic therapies for treating schizophrenia is not warranted (e.g., Klerman, 1984). However, promising results are reported for a form of individual psychotherapy called *personal therapy* that is grounded in the diathesis-stress model. Personal therapy helps patients cope more effectively with stress and helps them build social skills, such as learning how to deal with criticism from others. Preliminary evidence suggests that personal therapy may reduce relapse rates and improve social functioning, at least among schizophrenia patients living with their families (Bustillo et al., 2001; Hogarty et al., 1997a, 1997b).

Learning-Based Therapies Although few behavior therapists believe that faulty learning causes schizophrenia, learning-based interventions have been shown to be effective in modifying schizophrenic behavior and assisting people with the disorder to develop more adaptive behaviors that can help them adjust more effectively to living in the community. Therapy methods include techniques such as (1) selective reinforcement of behavior (like providing attention for appropriate behavior and extinguishing bizarre verbalizations through withdrawal of attention); (2) the token economy, in which individuals on inpatient units are rewarded for appropriate behavior with tokens, such as plastic chips, that can be exchanged for tangible reinforcers such as desirable goods or privileges; and (3) social skills training, in which clients are taught conversational skills and other appropriate social behaviors through coaching, modeling, behavior rehearsal, and feedback.

Web Link 13.7 wWw
When Someone Has Schizophrenia

Promising results have emerged from studies that apply intensive learning-based approaches in hospital settings. A classic study by Paul and Lentz (1977) showed that a psychosocial treatment program based on a token-economy system improved adaptive behavior in the hospital, decreased need for medication, and lengthened community tenure following release in relation to a traditional, custodial-type treatment condition and a milieu approach that emphasized patient participation in decision making.

Overall, token economies have proven to be more effective than intensive milieu treatment and traditional custodial treatment in improving social functioning and reducing psychotic behavior (Glynn & Mueser, 1992; Mueser & Liberman, 1995). However, the many prerequisites may limit the applicability of this approach. Such programs require strong administrative support, skilled treatment leaders, extensive staff training, and continuous quality control (Glynn & Mueser, 1986).

Recently, investigators have shown promising results in using cognitive-behavioral approaches in reducing or even eliminating hallucinations or delusions in patients with schizophrenia (Bouchard et al., 1996; Bustillo et al., 2001). More research is needed to demonstrate the clinical utility of using CBT to treat psychotic symptoms in general clinical practice.

Social skills training (SST) involves programs that help individuals acquire a range of social and vocational skills. People with schizophrenia are often deficient in basic social skills involving assertiveness, interviewing skills, and general conversational skills, skills that may be needed to adjust successfully to community living. Controlled studies have shown that SST improves social skills and adaptive functioning of schizophrenia patients in the community (Hunter, Bedell, & Corrigan, 1997; Penn, 1998). The effectiveness of SST in enhancing patients' social skills is not limited to our culture; it was recently demonstrated in a sample of Chinese schizophrenia patients in Hong Kong (Tsang, 2001). However, SST has not yet shown clear benefits in reducing either relapse rate or improving employment status (Bustillo et al., 2001).

Although different approaches to skills training have been developed, the basic model uses role-playing exercises within a group format. Participants practice skills such as starting or maintaining conversations with new acquaintances and receive feedback and reinforcement from the therapist and other group members. The first step might be a dry run in which the participant role-plays the targeted behavior, such as asking strangers for bus directions. The therapist and other group members then praise the effort and provide constructive feedback. Role-playing is augmented by techniques such as modeling (observation of the therapist or other group members enacting the desired behavior), direct instruction (specific directions for enacting the desired behavior), shaping (reinforcement for successive approximations to the target behavior), and coaching (therapist use of verbal or nonverbal prompts to elicit a particular desired behavior in the role play). Participants are given homework assignments to practice the behaviors in the settings in which they live, such as on the hospital ward or in the community. The aim is to enhance generalization or transfer of training to other settings. Training sessions may also be run in stores, restaurants, schools, and other real-life settings.

Psychosocial Rehabilitation People with schizophrenia typically have difficulties functioning in social and occupational roles. These problems limit their ability to adjust to community life even in the absence of overt psychotic behavior.

A number of self-help clubs (commonly called clubhouses) and more structured psychosocial rehabilitation centers have sprung up to help people with schizophrenia find a place in society. Many centers were launched by nonprofessionals or by people with schizophrenia themselves, largely because mental health agencies often failed to provide comparable services (Anthony & Liberman, 1986). The clubhouse movement began in 1948 with the founding of Fountain House by a group of formerly hospitalized people with schizophrenia (Foderaro, 1994). There are now more than 200 clubhouses modeled after Fountain House across the country, and some 50 or more in other countries including Sweden, Japan, and Australia. Although no one actually lives in the clubhouse, it serves as a kind of

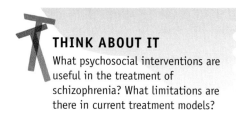

THINK ABOUT IT

What psychosocial interventions are useful in the treatment of schizophrenia? What limitations are there in current treatment models?

self-contained community that provides members with social support and help in finding educational opportunities and paid employment.

Multiservice rehabilitation centers typically offer housing as well as job and educational opportunities. These centers often make use of skills training approaches to help clients learn how to handle money, resolve disputes with family members, develop friendships, take buses, cook their own meals, shop, and so on.

Family Intervention Programs Family conflicts and negative family interactions can heap stress on family members with schizophrenia, increasing the risk of recurrent episodes (Marsh & Johnson, 1997). Researchers and clinicians have worked with families of people with schizophrenia to help them cope with the burdens of care and assist them in developing more cooperative, less confrontational ways of relating to others. The specific components of family interventions vary from program to program, but they usually share some common features, such as a focus on the practical aspects of everyday living, educating family members about schizophrenia, teaching them how to relate in a less hostile way to family members with schizophrenia, improving communication in the family, and fostering effective problem-solving and coping skills for handling family problems and disputes. Evidence shows that structured family intervention programs can reduce friction in the family, improve social functioning in schizophrenia patients, and even reduce relapse rates (Bustillo et al., 2001; Mueser et al., 2001; Penn & Mueser, 1996). However, the benefits appear to be modest, and questions remain about whether relapses are prevented or merely delayed.

In sum, no single treatment approach meets all the needs of people with schizophrenia. The conceptualization of schizophrenia as a lifelong disability underscores the need for long-term treatment interventions that incorporate antipsychotic medication, family therapy, supportive or cognitive-behavioral forms of therapy, vocational training, and provision of decent housing and other social support services (Bustillo et al., 2001; Huxley, Rendall, & Sederer, 2000; Sensky et al., 2000; Tarrier et al., 2000). These interventions should be coordinated and integrated within a comprehensive model of treatment to be most effective in helping the individual achieve maximal social adjustment (Coursey et al., 1997). Treatment services are also more likely to improve client functioning in certain areas, such as improving work or independent living, when they are specifically targeted toward those areas (Brekke et al., 1997). This model may consist of drug therapy, hospitalization as needed, inpatient learning-based programs, family intervention programs, skills training programs, social self-help clubs, and structured rehabilitation programs.

Quiz **13.3**
Schizophrenia

Quiz **13.4**
Chapter Exam

Research Update
Chapter 13

Overview of Schizophrenia

CLINICAL FEATURES OF SCHIZOPHRENIA

Disturbed Thought Processes	• Delusions (fixed false ideas) and thought disorder (disorganized thinking and incoherent speech)
Attentional Deficiencies	• Difficulty attending to relevant stimuli and screening out irrelevant stimuli
Perceptual Disturbances	• Hallucinations (sensory perceptions in the absence of external stimulation)
Emotional Disturbances	• Flat (blunted) or inappropriate emotions
Other Impairments	• Confusion about personal identity, lack of volition, excitable behavior or states of stupor, odd gestures or bizarre facial expressions, and impaired ability to relate to others

MAJOR SUBTYPES OF SCHIZOPHRENIA*

Disorganized Type	• Confused and bizarre behavior, incoherent speech, vivid hallucinations, flat or inappropriate affect, and disorganized delusions
Catatonic Type	• Gross disturbances in motor activity in which behavior may slow to a stupor but abruptly shift to a highly agitated state
Paranoid Type	• Delusions (typically of themes of grandeur, persecution, or jealousy) and frequent auditory hallucinations

*Variations of schizophrenia distinguished in terms of specific subtypes. Another way of subtyping schizophrenia is based on distinguishing between Type I schizophrenia, characterized by more flagrant symptoms (positive symptoms), and Type II schizophrenia, characterized by deficit symptoms (negative symptoms).

CAUSAL FACTORS*

Biological Factors	• Strong evidence of a major genetic contribution • Irregularities in neurotransmitter systems in the brain, especially in brain circuits that utilize the neurotransmitter dopamine • Underlying brain abnormalities in many cases, such as structural damage or deterioration of brain tissue or disturbed brain circuitry in parts of the brain regulating cognitive and emotional functioning • Possible role of viral infections affecting the developing brain prenatally or during early life
Psychosocial Factors	• Stressful experiences may contribute to the development of schizophrenia in genetically vulnerable individuals.

*The specific causes remain unknown, but most researchers believe they reflect an interaction of genetic and stress-related factors, as represented by the diathesis-stress model.

TREATMENT APPROACHES — **A comprehensive treatment approach incorporating biomedical, psychosocial, and family interventions is recommended.**

Biomedical Treatment	• Antipsychotic drugs are used to control psychotic symptoms.
Psychosocial Treatment	• Learning-based approaches, such as the token economy system and social skills training, can help schizophrenia patients develop more adaptive behaviors.
Psychosocial Rehabilitation	• Self-help clubs and structured residential programs can help schizophrenia patients adjust to community living.
Family Intervention Programs	• Family interventions are used to improve communication in the family and reduce levels of family conflict and stress.

Summing Up

History of the Concept of Schizophrenia

What is schizophrenia and how prevalent is it? Schizophrenia is a chronic psychotic disorder characterized by acute episodes involving a break with reality, as manifest by such features as delusions, hallucinations, illogical thinking, incoherent speech, and bizarre behavior. Residual deficits in cognitive, emotional, and social areas of functioning persist between acute episodes. Schizophrenia is believed to affect about 1% of the population.

What key historical figures in psychiatry influenced our conceptions of schizophrenia? Emil Kraepelin was the first to describe the syndrome we identify as schizophrenia. He labeled the disorder *dementia praecox* and believed it was a disease that develops early in life and follows a progressively deteriorating course. Eugen Bleuler renamed the disorder *schizophrenia* and believed its course is more variable. He also distinguished between primary symptoms (the four A's) and secondary symptoms. Kurt Schneider distinguished between first-rank symptoms that define the disorder and second-rank symptoms that occur in schizophrenia and other disorders.

Other Forms of Psychosis

What are other forms of psychotic disorders besides schizophrenia? These include brief psychotic disorder (a psychotic disorder lasting less than a week that may be reactive to a significant stressor), schizophreniform disorder (symptoms identical to those of schizophrenia that lasting for a month to less than 6 months), delusional disorder (denoted by delusions that are apparently plausible and less bizarre than those in schizophrenia), and schizoaffective disorder (combination of psychotic symptoms and significant mood disturbance).

What are schizophrenia-spectrum disorders? The term encompasses the schizophrenic-type disorders that range in severity from milder personality disorders, such as schizotypal and schizoid types, to frankly psychotic disorders, such as schizophrenia itself and schizoaffective disorder.

Schizophrenia

What are the major phases of schizophrenia? Schizophrenia usually develops in late adolescence or early adulthood. Its onset may be abrupt or gradual. Gradual onset is preceded by a prodromal phase, a period of gradual deterioration that precedes the onset of acute symptoms. Acute episodes, which may occur periodically throughout life, are typified by clear psychotic symptoms, such as hallucinations and delusions. Between acute episodes the disorder is characterized by a residual phase in which the person's level of functioning is similar to that which was present during the prodromal phase.

What are the most prominent features of schizophrenia? Among the more prominent features of schizophrenia are disorders in the content of thought (delusions) and the form of thought (thoughtdisorder), as well as the presence of often severe perceptual distortions

(hallucinations) and emotional disturbances (flattened or inappropriate affect). There are also dysfunctions in brain processes regulating attention to the external world.

What are the specific subtypes of schizophrenia? The disorganized type is associated with grossly disorganized behavior and thought processes. The catatonic type is associated with grossly impaired motor behaviors, such as maintenance of fixed postures and muteness for long periods. The paranoid type is characterized by paranoid delusions and frequent auditory hallucinations. The undifferentiated type is a catchall category applying to cases in which schizophrenic episodes don't clearly fit the other types. The residual type applies to individuals with schizophrenia who do not have prominent psychotic behaviors at the time of evaluation. Researchers have also distinguished between two general types of schizophrenia: Type I, characterized by positive symptomatology, more abrupt onset, better response to antipsychotic medication, and better preserved intellectual ability, and Type II, characterized by negative symptomatology, more gradual onset, poorer response to antipsychotic medication, and greater cognitive impairment.

How is schizophrenia conceptualized within traditional psychodynamic theory and learning perspectives? In the traditional psychodynamic model, schizophrenia represents a regression to a psychological state corresponding to early infancy in which the proddings of the id produce bizarre, socially deviant behavior and give rise to hallucinations and delusions. Learning theorists propose that some form of schizophrenic behavior may result from lack of social reinforcement, which leads to gradual detachment from the social environment and increased attention to an inner world of fantasy. Modeling and selective reinforcement of bizarre behavior may explain some schizophrenic behaviors in the hospital setting.

What do we know about the biological bases of schizophrenia? Compelling evidence for a strong genetic component in schizophrenia comes from studies of family patterns of schizophrenia, twin studies, and adoption studies. The mode of genetic transmission remains unknown. Most researchers believe the neurotransmitter dopamine plays a role in schizophrenia, especially in the more flagrant features of the disorder. Viral factors may also be involved, but definite proof of viral involvement is lacking. Evidence of brain dysfunctions and structural damage in schizophrenia is accumulating, but researchers are uncertain about causal pathways.

How is schizophrenia conceptualized within the diathesis-stress model? The diathesis-stress model posits that schizophrenia results from an interaction of a genetic predisposition (the diathesis) and environmental stressors (e.g., family conflict, child abuse, emotional deprivation, loss of supportive figures, early brain trauma).

How are family factors related to the development and course of schizophrenia? Family factors such as communication deviance and expressed emotion may act as sources of stress that increase the risk of development or recurrence of schizophrenia among people with a genetic predisposition.

How does the treatment of schizophrenia involve a multifaceted approach? Contemporary treatment approaches tend to be multifaceted, incorporating pharmacological and psychosocial approaches. Antipsychotic medication is not a cure but tends to stem the more flagrant aspects of the disorder and to reduce the need for hospitalization and the risk of recurrent episodes.

What types of psychosocial interventions have shown promising results? These are principally learning-based approaches, such as token economy systems and social skills training. They help increase adaptive behavior of schizophrenia patients. Psychosocial-rehabilitation approaches help people with schizophrenia adapt more successfully to occupational and social roles in the community. Family intervention programs help families cope with the burdens of care, communicate more clearly, and learn more helpful ways of relating to the patient.

CHAPTER FOURTEEN

Abnormal Behavior in Childhood and Adolescence

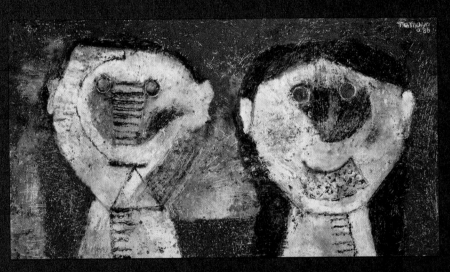

Rufino Tamayo
Dos Caras

Truth OR Fiction?

- Many behavior patterns considered normal for children would be considered abnormal in adults. (p. 439)

- Therapists have used Puerto Rican folktales to help Puerto Rican children adjust to the demands of living in mainstream U.S. society. (p. 440)

- Some people can recall verbatim every story they read in a newspaper. (p. 453)

- Maternal smoking during pregnancy may put children at increased risk of attention-deficit hyperactivity disorder (ADHD). (p. 461)

- Children who are hyperactive are often given depressants to help calm them down. (p. 461)

- Major depression rarely occurs before adulthood. (p. 466)

- Some children refuse to go to school because they believe that terrible things may happen to their parents while they are away. (p. 467)

- Problems of persistent bed-wetting in childhood generally persist into adolescence. (p. 472)

psychological problems in childhood and adolescence often have a special poignancy. They affect children at ages when they have little capacity to cope. Some of these problems, such as autism and mental retardation, prevent children from fulfilling their developmental potentials. Some psychological problems in childhood and adolescents mirror the types of problems found in adults—problems such as mood disorders and anxiety disorders. In some cases, the problems are unique to childhood, such as separation anxiety; in others, such as ADHD or attention-deficit hyperactivity disorder, the problem manifests itself differently in childhood than in adulthood.

Normal and Abnormal Behavior in Childhood and Adolescence

To determine what is normal and abnormal among children and adolescents, we consider, in addition to the criteria outlined in Chapter 1, the child's age and cultural background (USDHHS, 1999a). Many problems are first identified when the child enters school. They may have existed earlier but been tolerated, or unrecognized as problematic, in the home. Sometimes the stress of starting school contributes to their onset. Keep in mind, however, that what is socially acceptable at one age, such as intense fear of strangers at about 9 months, may be socially unacceptable at more advanced ages. Many behavior patterns that would be considered abnormal among adults—such as intense fear of strangers and lack of bladder control—are perfectly normal for children at certain ages.

Cultural Beliefs About What Is Normal and Abnormal

Cultural beliefs help determine whether people view behavior as normal or abnormal. People who base judgments of normality only on standards derived from their own cultures risk being ethnocentric when they view the behavior of people in other cultures as abnormal (Kennedy, Scheirer, & Rogers, 1984). The problem is of special concern regarding child psychopathology. Because children rarely label their own behavior as abnormal, definitions of normality depend largely on how a child's behavior is filtered through the lenses by which parents in a particular culture view that behavior. Cultures may vary with respect to the types of behaviors they classify as unacceptable or abnormal as well as the threshold for labeling child behaviors as deviant or socially unacceptable. Researchers find that parents in different cultures do judge the unusualness of behavior from different perspectives (Lambert et al., 1992).

For example, researchers posed the question, "When a child has psychological problems, what determines whether adults will consider the problem serious or whether they will seek professional help?" (Weisz et al., 1988, p. 601). To explore this question, researchers presented vignettes to Thai and American parents, teachers, and clinical psychologists. The vignettes depicted two children, one with problems characterized by "overcontrol" (for example, shyness and fears) and one with problems characterized by undercontrol (for example, disobedience and fighting). The Thai parents rated *both* sets of problems as less serious and worrisome than American parents (see Figure 14.1), and as more likely to improve without treatment as time passed. Such an interpretation is embedded within traditional Thai-Buddhist beliefs and values, which tolerate broad variations in children's behavior. They assume that change is inevitable and that children's behavior will eventually change for the better. Differences between cultural groups were greater for parents and teachers than for psychologists, which suggests that professional training in a common scientific tradition might offset cultural differences.

Culturally Sensitive Therapy

Psychotherapy with children has been approached from various perspectives and differs in important respects from therapy with adults. Children may not have the verbal skills to express their feelings through speech or the ability to sit in a chair through a therapy

Truth OR Fiction? REVISITED

Many behavior patterns considered normal for children would be considered abnormal in adults.

TRUE. Many behavior patterns that would be considered abnormal among adults—such as intense fear of strangers and lack of bladder control—are perfectly normal for children at certain ages.

play therapy A form of psychodynamic therapy in which play activities and objects are used to help children symbolically enact conflicts or express underlying feelings.

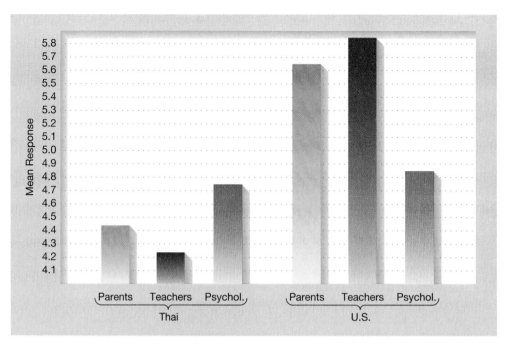

FIGURE 14.1 Ratings by Thai and U.S. parents of the seriousness of children's behavioral problems.
Researchers presented vignettes of children with problems characterized by overcontrol (for example, shyness and fears) and undercontrol (for example, disobedience and fighting) to Thai and American parents. The Thai parents rated both sets of problems as less serious and worrisome than American parents, and as more likely to improve without treatment. The Thai parents apparently assume that people change and that their children's behavior will eventually change for the better.

Source. Weisz, J. R., et al., (1988). Thai and American perspectives on over- and undercontrolled child behavior problem: Exploring the threshold model among parents, teachers, and psychologists. *Journal of Consulting and Clinical Psychology, 56,* 601–609. Copyright © 2001 by the American Psychological Association. Reprinted with permission.

Truth OR Fiction?   REVISITED

Therapists have used Puerto Rican folktales to help Puerto Rican children adjust to the demands of living in mainstream U.S. society.

TRUE. Therapists have used adapted Puerto Rican folktales (*cuentos*) to help Puerto Rican children adjust to the demands of living in mainstream U.S. society.

How serious is this problem? Thai parents might judge the behavior shown by these children to be less serious than American parents would. Thai-Buddhist values tolerate broad variations in children's behavior and assume that it will change for the better.

session. Therapy methods must be tailored to the level of the child's cognitive, physical, social, and emotional development. For example, psychodynamic therapists have developed techniques of **play therapy** in which children enact family conflicts symbolically through their play activities, such as by playacting with dolls or puppets. Or they might be given drawing materials and asked to draw pictures, in the belief that their drawings will reflect their underlying feelings.

Research suggests that culturally sensitive therapies, ones specifically tailored to the cultural backgrounds and needs of children from diverse cultural groups, are important in establishing effective therapeutic relationships with children. Costantino and his colleagues (1986), for example, adapted traditional Puerto Rican folktales, or *cuentos,* as modeling examples in treating Puerto Rican children with behavior problems. The *cuentos* featured child protagonists who served as models for adaptive behavior. The stories were read aloud by the therapists and the children's mothers, and were followed by group discussion of the behavior and feelings of the main character and the moral of the story. The final element in such sessions was role playing, in which children were given the opportunity to imitate the adaptive behavior exemplified by the main character in of the story.

The value of culturally sensitive therapies is not limited to the treatment of Puerto Rican children, of course. Evidence of their value in working with other cultural groups is mounting. For example, researchers find that ethnic-specific treatment programs for Asian American children appear to be more effective in reducing early treatment dropouts and increasing functioning at termination as compared to mainstream outpatient mental health centers (Yeh, Takeuchi, & Sue, 1994).

Prevalence of Mental Health Problems in Children and Adolescents

Just how common are mental health problems among America's children and adolescents? According to a recent report from the U.S. Surgeon General, 1 in 10 children suffer from a mental disorder severe enough to impair their development ("A Children's Mental Illness 'Crisis,'" 2001). More American children suffer from mental disorders than from diabetes, AIDS, and leukemia combined (Chamberlin, 2001). Yet 60% to 80% of children with mental health disorders fail to get the treatment they need (Goldberg, 2001). Children who have *internalized* problems, such as anxiety and depression, are at higher risk of going untreated than are children with *externalized* problems (problems involving acting out or aggressive behavior) that tend to be disruptive or annoying to others.

Boys are at greater risk for developing many childhood problems, ranging from autism to hyperactivity to elimination disorders. Problems of anxiety and depression also affect boys more often than girls. In adolescence, however, anxiety and mood disorders become more common among girls and remain so throughout adulthood (USDHHS, 1999a).

Let us now examine the types of psychological disorders that may affect children and adolescents. We will examine the features of these disorders, their causes, and the treatments used to help children who suffer from them.

Play therapy. In play therapy, children may enact scenes with dolls or puppets that symbolically represent conflicts occurring within their own families.

Quiz 14.1
Normal and Abnormal Behavior in Childhood and Adolescence

Web Link 14.1
Teenage Brain: A Work in Progress

Pervasive Developmental Disorders

Children with **pervasive developmental disorders (PDDs)** show markedly impaired behavior or functioning in multiple areas of development. These disorders generally become evident in the first few years of life and are often associated with mental retardation. They were generally classified as forms of psychoses in early editions of the *DSM*. They were thought to reflect childhood forms of adult psychoses like schizophrenia because they share features such as social and emotional impairment, oddities of communication, and stereotyped motor behaviors. Research has shown that they are distinct from schizophrenia and other psychoses, however. Only very rarely in these children is there evidence of the prominent hallucinations or delusions that would justify a diagnosis of schizophrenia.

The major type of pervasive developmental disorder, which is our focus here, is autistic disorder (autism). **Asperger's disorder,** a milder form of pervasive developmental disorder, is characterized by poor social interactions and stereotyped behavior. However, in contrast to autism, Asperger's disorder does not involve significant language or cognitive deficits (APA, 2000; Szatmari et al., 2000). Other, less common types of pervasive developmental disorder include **Rett's disorder,** a disorder reported only in females; and **childhood disintegrative disorder,** a rare condition that appears to be more common among males.

Though the rate of PDDs remains unclear, a recent community study of preschool children in England showed that 0.6% of the children (6 in 1,000) met criteria for one or another PDD, most commonly autism (Chakrabarti & Fombonne, 2001). The diagnostic features of autistic disorder are found in Table 14.1. Table 14.2 lists the diagnostic features of other types of pervasive developmental disorders.

pervasive developmental disorders (PDDs) A class of developmental disorders characterized by significantly impaired behavior or functioning in multiple areas of development.

Asperger's disorder A pervasive developmental disorder characterized by social deficits and stereotyped behavior but without the significant language or cognitive delays associated with autism.

Rett's disorder A pervasive development disorder characterized by a range of physical, behavioral, motor, and cognitive abnormalities that begin after a few months of apparently normal development.

childhood disintegrative disorder A pervasive developmental disorder involving loss of previously acquired skills and abnormal functioning following a period of apparently normal development during the first two years of life.

TABLE 14.1   Diagnostic Features of Autistic Disorder

A. Diagnosis requires a combination of features from the following groups. Not all of the features from each group need be present for a diagnosis to be made.

Impaired Social Interactions

1. Impairment in the nonverbal behaviors such as facial expressiveness, posture, gestures, and eye contact that normally regulate social interaction
2. Does not develop age-appropriate peer relationships
3. Failure to express pleasure in the happiness of other people
4. Does not show social or emotional reciprocity (give and take)

Impaired Communication

1. Delay in development of spoken language (nor is there an effort to compensate for this lack through gestures)
2. When speech development is adequate, there is nevertheless lack of ability to initiate or sustain conversation
3. Shows abnormalities in form or content of speech (e.g., stereotyped or repetitive speech, as in echolalia; idiosyncratic use of words; speaking about the self in the second or third person—using "you" or "he" to mean "I")
4. Does not show spontaneous social or imaginative (make-believe) play

Restricted, repetitive, and stereotyped behavior patterns

1. Shows restricted range of interests
2. Insists on routines (e.g., always uses same route to go from one place to another)
3. Shows stereotyped movements (e.g., hand flicking, head banging, rocking, spinning)
4. Shows preoccupation with parts of objects (e.g., repetitive spinning of wheels of toy car) or unusual attachments to objects (e.g., carrying a piece of string)

B. Onset occurs prior to the age of 3 through display of abnormal functioning in at least one of the following: social behavior, communication, or imaginative play.

Source. Adapted from the *DSM-IV-TR* (APA, 2000).

Autism

A Case of Autism

Peter nursed eagerly, sat and walked at the expected ages. Yet some of his behavior made us vaguely uneasy. He never put anything in his mouth. Not his fingers nor his toys—nothing. . . .

More troubling was the fact that Peter didn't look at us, or smile, and wouldn't play the games that seemed as much a part of babyhood as diapers. He rarely laughed, and when he did, it was at things that didn't seem funny to us. He didn't cuddle, but sat upright in my lap, even when I rocked him. But children differ and we were content to let Peter be himself. We thought it hilarious when my brother, visiting us when Peter was 8 months old, observed that "That kid has no social instincts, whatsoever." Although Peter was a first child, he was not isolated. I frequently put him in his playpen in front of the house, where the schoolchildren stopped to play with him as they passed. He ignored them, too.

It was Kitty, a personality kid, born two years later, whose responsiveness emphasized the degree of Peter's difference. When I went into her room for the late feeding, her little head bobbed up and she greeted me with a smile that reached from her head to her toes. And the realization of that difference chilled me more than the wintry bedroom.

Peter's babbling had not turned into speech by the time he was 3. His play was solitary and repetitious. He tore paper into long thin strips, bushel baskets of it every day. He spun the lids from my canning jars and became upset if we tried to divert him. Only rarely could I catch his eye, and then saw his focus change from me to the reflection in my glasses. . . .

[Peter's] adventures into our suburban neighborhood had been unhappy. He had disregarded the universal rule that sand is to be kept in sandboxes, and the children themselves had punished him. He walked around a sad and solitary figure, always carrying a toy airplane, a toy he never played with. At that time, I had not heard the word that was to dominate our lives, to hover over every conversation, to sit through every meal beside us. That word was autism.

—Adapted from Eberhardy, 1967

autism A pervasive developmental disorder characterized by failure to relate to others, lack of speech, disturbed motor behaviors, intellectual impairment, and demands for sameness in the environment.

Autism, or *autistic disorder,* is one of the severest disorders of childhood. It is a chronic, lifelong condition. Children with autism, like Peter, seem utterly alone in the world, despite parental efforts to bridge the gulf that divides them.

TABLE 14.2 Diagnostic Features of Other Pervasive Developmental Disorders

Disorder	Diagnostic Features
Asperger's disorder	• Markedly impaired social interactions (e.g., failure to maintain eye contact or to develop age-appropriate peer relationships, or failure to seek out others to share enjoyable activities or interests) • Development of narrow, repetitive, and stereotyped behaviors, interests, and activities (e.g., twisting hands or fingers; rigidly adhering to fixed routines or rituals that lack any clear purpose; fascination with train schedules) • No clinically significant delay in language or cognitive development or in development of self-help skills or adaptive behaviors apart from social interactions
Rett's disorder	After apparently normal development during the first few months of life, the following abnormalities develop: • Slowing of head growth • Deteriorating motor skills (loss of purposeful hand skills) • Development of stereotyped hand movements, typically resembling hand-wringing or hand washing • Development of poorly coordinated gait or movement of whole body • Loss of social interest • Severe deficits in language development • Typically associated with profound or severe mental retardation
Childhood disintegrative disorder	After apparently normal development for at least the first 2 years of life: • Significant loss of previously acquired skills in such areas as understanding or using language, social or adaptive functioning, bowel or bladder control, play, or motor skills • Abnormal functioning as shown by impaired social interactions or communication, and development of narrow, stereotyped, and repetitive behaviors, interests, or activities

Source. Adapted from the *DSM-IV-TR* (APA, 2000).

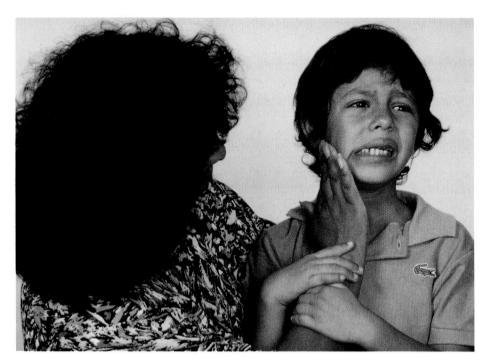

Autism. Autism, one of the most severe childhood disorders, is characterized by pervasive deficits in the ability to relate to and communicate with others, and by a restricted range of activities and interests. Children with autistic disorder lack the ability to relate to others and seem to live in their own private worlds.

Web Link **14.2** wWw
Facts About Autism

The word *autism* derives from the Greek *autos,* meaning "self." The term was first used in 1906 by the Swiss psychiatrist Eugen Bleuler to refer to a peculiar style of thinking among people with schizophrenia (autism is one of Bleuler's "four As"). Autistic thinking is the tendency to view oneself as the center of the universe, to believe that external events somehow refer to oneself. In 1943, another psychiatrist, Leo Kanner, applied the diagnosis "early infantile autism" to a group of disturbed children who seemed unable to relate to others, as if they lived in their own private worlds. Unlike children suffering from mental retardation, these children seemed to shut out any input from the outside world, creating a kind of "autistic aloneness" (Kanner, 1943).

Medical authorities today believe that autism is more common than was previously believed, affecting an estimated 2 to 20 persons in 10,000 in the general population (APA, 2000; Fox, 2000). The disorder, which occurs mostly among boys, generally becomes evident in toddlers between 18 and 30 months of age (Rapin, 1997). However, it is not until about age 6 that the average child is first diagnosed with the disorder (Fox, 2000). Delays in diagnosis can be detrimental, as children with autism generally do better the earlier they are diagnosed and treated (Fox, 2000).

Autism seems always to have been with Peter. In the following case example, the disorder apparently developed between the ages of 12 and 24 months:

The Case of Eric

"People used to say to me they hoped they [would have] a baby just like mine," Sarah said of Eric, 3 years old at the time. As an infant, Eric smiled endearingly, laughed, and hugged. He uttered a dozen words by his first birthday. By 16 months he had memorized the alphabet and could read some signs. "People were very impressed," Sarah said.

Gradually, things changed, but it took months for Sarah to realize that Eric had a problem. At the age of 2, other members of Eric's play group bubbled with conversation. Eric had abandoned words completely. Instead, Eric combined letters and numbers in idiosyncratic ways, such as "B–T–2–4–6–Z–3."

Eric grew increasingly withdrawn. His diet was essentially self-limited to peanut butter and jelly sandwiches. He spent hour after hour arranging letters and numbers on a magnetic board. But the "symptom" that distressed Sarah most was impossible to measure: when she gazed into Eric's eyes, she no longer saw a "sparkle."

—Adapted from Martin, 1989

Children with autism are often described by their parents as having been "good babies" early in infancy. This generally means they were not demanding. As they develop, however, they begin to reject physical affection, such as cuddling, hugging, and kissing. Their speech development begins to fall behind the norm. Although Eric did quite well through his first 16 months, there are often signs of social detachment beginning as early as the first year of life, such as failure to look at other people's faces (Osterling & Dawson, 1994). The clinical features of the disorder appear prior to 3 years of age (APA, 2000). Autism is four to five times more common among males than females (APA, 2000).

Features of Autism Perhaps the most poignant feature of autism is the child's utter aloneness (see Table 14.1). Other features include language and communication problems and ritualistic or stereotyped behavior. The child may also be mute, or if some language skills are present, they may be characterized by peculiar usage, as in echolalia (parroting back what the child has heard in a high-pitched monotone); pronoun reversals (using "you" or "he" instead of "I"); use of words that have meaning only to those who have intimate knowledge of the child; and tendencies to raise the voice at the end of sentences, as if asking a question. Nonverbal communication may also be impaired or absent. For example, children with autistic disorder may not engage in eye contact or display facial expressions. They are also slow to respond to adults who try to grab their attention, if they attend at all (Leekam & López, 2000). Although they may be unresponsive to others, researchers find they are capable of displaying strong emotions, especially strong negative emotions such as anger, sadness, and fear (Capps et al., 1993; Kasari et al., 1993).

A primary feature of autism is repeated purposeless stereotyped movements—interminably twirling, flapping the hands, or rocking back and forth with the arms around the knees. Some children with autism mutilate themselves, even as they cry out in pain. They may bang their heads, slap their faces, bite their hands and shoulders, or pull out their hair. They may also throw sudden tantrums or panics. Another feature of autism is aversion to environmental changes—a feature termed "preservation of sameness." When familiar objects are moved even slightly from their usual places, children with autism may throw tantrums or cry continually until their placement is restored. Like Eric, children with autistic disorder may insist on eating the same food every day.

Children with autism are bound by ritual. The teacher of a 5-year-old girl with autistic disorder learned to greet her every morning by saying, "Good morning, Lily, I am very, very glad to see you" (Diamond, Baldwin, & Diamond, 1963). Although Lily would not respond to the greeting, she would shriek if the teacher omitted even one of the *very*s.

Children who develop autism appear to have failed to develop a differentiated self-concept, a sense of themselves as distinct individuals. Despite their unusual behavior, they are often quite attractive and often have an "intelligent look" about them. However, as measured by scores on standardized tests, their intellectual development tends to lag below the norm. Three of four show evidence of mental retardation (Rapin, 1997). Even those who function at an average level of intelligence show deficits in activities requiring the ability to symbolize, such as recognizing emotions, engaging in symbolic play, and solving problems conceptually. They also display difficulty in attending to tasks that involve interacting with other people. The relationship between autism and intelligence is clouded, however, by difficulties in administering standardized IQ tests to these children. Testing requires cooperation, a skill that is dramatically lacking in children with autism. At best, we can only estimate their intellectual ability.

Theoretical Perspectives The causes of autism remain unknown, but are presumed to involve underlying brain abnormalities. Early, discredited views of autism viewed the child's aloofness as a reaction to parents who were cold and detached—"emotional refrigerators" who lacked the ability to establish warm relationships with their children. Research failed to support the assumption—so devastating to many parents—that they are in fact frosty and remote (Hoffmann & Prior, 1982). Of course there is truth to the notion that children with autism and their parents do not relate to one another very well, but causal connections are clouded. Rather than rejecting their children and thus fostering autism, parents may grow somewhat aloof because their efforts to relate to their children repeatedly meet with failure. Aloofness then becomes a result of autism, not a cause.

Psychologist O. Ivar Lovaas and his colleagues (1979) offered a cognitive-learning perspective on autism. They suggest that children with autism have perceptual deficits that limit them to processing only one stimulus at a time. As a result, they are slow to learn by

VIDEO 14.1

Autism: *Dr. Kathy Pratt*

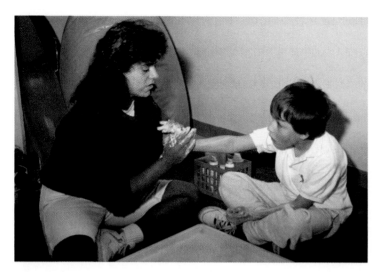

Establishing contact. One of the principal therapeutic tasks in working with children with autism is the establishment of interpersonal contact. Behavior therapists use reinforcers to increase adaptive social behaviors, such as paying attention to the therapist and playing with other children. Behavior therapists may also use punishments to suppress self-mutilative behavior.

means of classical conditioning (association of stimuli). From the learning theory perspective, children become attached to their primary caregivers because they are associated with primary reinforcers such as food and hugging. Children with autism, however, attend either to the food or to the cuddling and do not connect it with the parent.

Cognitive theorists have focused on the kinds of cognitive deficits shown by children with autism and the possible relationships among them. Children with autism appear to have difficulty integrating information from various senses (Rutter, 1983). At times they seem unduly sensitive to stimulation. At other times they become so insensitive that an observer might wonder whether they are deaf. Perceptual and cognitive deficits seem to diminish their capacity to make use of information—to comprehend and apply social rules.

But what is the basis of these perceptual and cognitive deficits? The many impairments associated with autism, including mental retardation, language deficits, bizarre motor behavior, even seizures, suggest an underlying neurological basis involving some form of brain damage or neurochemical imbalance in the brain (Perry et al., 2001; Stokstad, 2001). Evidence from MRI and PET scan studies show abnormalities in the brains of boys and men with autistic disorder, including enlarged ventricles indicative of a loss of brain cells (Haznedar et al., 2000; Piven et al., 1997). But researchers have yet to pinpoint any particular brain disturbance that could account for autism (Rapin, 1997; Zilbovicius et al., 1995). Perhaps autism stems from multiple causes involving more than one type of brain abnormality (Ritvo & Ritvo, 1992). Scientists suspect that the underlying causes of the disorder may involve defective genes or prenatal exposure to toxic agents (O'Connor, 2001b; Stokstad, 2001). Still, the underlying causes of autism remain a mystery.

Treatment Although there is no cure for autism, 30 years of research have supported the efficacy of intensive behavioral treatment programs that apply principles of learning to reduce disturbed behaviors and improve learning and communication skills in autistic children (USDHHS, 1999a). No other treatment approach has yielded comparable results (Gill, 2001). Behavioral approaches are based largely on operant conditioning methods in which rewards and punishments are systematically applied to increase the child's ability to attend to others, to play with other children, to develop academic skills, and to eliminate self-mutilative behavior.

Because children who suffer from autism show behavioral deficits, a central focus of behavior modification is the development of new behavior. New behaviors are maintained by reinforcements, so it is important to teach these children, who often respond to people as they would to a piece of furniture, to accept people as reinforcers. People can be established as reinforcers by pairing praise with such primary reinforcers as food. Then social reinforcement (praise) and primary reinforcers (food) can be used to shape and model toileting behaviors, speech, and social play. The involvement of families and residential treatment personnel in these behavioral programs prompts the maintenance and generalization of behavioral changes (Romanczyk, 1986).

Techniques based on extinction (withholding reinforcement following a response) are sometimes used to eliminate self-mutilative behaviors such as head banging. However, extinction often fails to eliminate the behavior. The problem seems to be that many repetitive behavior patterns—such as rocking and self-injurious behaviors—are maintained by internal reinforcements such as increased stimulation. Therefore, withdrawal of social reinforcers may have little if any effect. Aversive stimulation such as spanking and, in extreme cases, electric shock, may be used in cases when more benign approaches prove ineffective. Brief bursts of mild but painful electrical stimulation can eliminate self-mutilation within a minute of application (Lovaas, 1977). Using electric shock with children raises moral, ethical, and legal concerns, of course. Lovaas has countered that failure to eliminate self-injurious behavior places the child at greater risk of physical harm and denies children the opportunity to participate in other kinds of therapy. The use of aversive stimulation should be combined with positive reinforcement for acceptable alternate behaviors.

The most effective behavioral treatment programs are highly intensive and structured, offering a great deal of individual instruction (Rapin, 1997). The classic example is the program developed by psychologist O. Ivar Lovaas of UCLA. In a classic study by Lovaas (1987), autistic children received more than 40 hours of one-to-one behavior modification each week for at least 2 years. Significant intellectual and educational gains were reported for 9 of the 19 children (47%) in the program. The children who improved achieved normal IQ scores and were able to succeed in the first grade. Only 2% of a control group that did not receive the intensive treatment achieved similar gains. Treatment gains were well maintained at the time of a follow-up when the children were 11 years old (McEachin, Smith, & Lovaas, 1993).

Although intensive behavioral programs may produce impressive gains, longer term follow-ups remain to be reported. We should also note that some children make great progress and others do not (Smith, 1999). Children who are better functioning at the start of treatment typically gain the most.

Biological approaches have had only limited impact in the treatment of autism. This may be changing. One line of research has shown that drugs that enhance serotonin activity, such as SSRIs, can reduce repetitive thoughts and behavior and aggression and lead to some improvement in social relatedness and language use in adults with autism (Mc-Dougle et al., 1996). The effects of these drugs on children with autism remain to be seen. Other research has focused on drugs normally used to treat schizophrenia, such as Haldol, which blocks dopamine activity. Several controlled studies show Haldol to be helpful in many cases in reducing social withdrawal and repetitive motor behavior (such as rocking behavior), aggression, hyperactivity, and self-injurious behavior (McBride et al., 1996). We have not seen drugs lead to consistent improvement in the cognitive and language development in children with autism, however.

Autistic traits generally continue into adulthood to one degree or another. Yet some autistic children do go on to achieve college degrees and are able to function independently (Rapin, 1997). Others need continuing treatment throughout their lives, even institutionalized care. Even the highest functioning adults with the disorder manifest deficient social and communication skills and a highly limited range of interests and activities (APA, 2000).

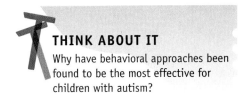

THINK ABOUT IT
Why have behavioral approaches been found to be the most effective for children with autism?

Quiz 14.2
Pervasive Developmental Disorders

Mental Retardation

About 1% of the general population is affected by **mental retardation,** a broad-ranging delay in the development of cognitive and social functioning (APA, 2000). The course of mental retardation is variable. Many children with mental retardation improve over time, especially if they receive support, guidance, and enriched educational opportunities. Those who are reared in impoverished environments may fail to improve or may deteriorate further in relation to other children.

Mental retardation is diagnosed by a combination of three criteria: (1) low scores on formal intelligence tests (an IQ score of approximately 70 or below); (2) evidence of impaired functioning in performing life tasks expected of someone of the same age in a given cultural setting; and (3) development of the disorder before the age of 18 (APA, 2000; Robinson, Zigler, & Gallagher, 2001).

The *DSM* classifies mental retardation according to level of severity, as shown in Table 14.3. Most children with mental retardation (about 85%) fall into the mildly retarded range. These children are generally capable of meeting basic academic demands, such as learning to read simple passages. As adults they are generally capable of independent functioning, although they may require some guidance and support. Table 14.4 provides a description of the deficits and abilities associated with various degrees of mental retardation.

mental retardation A generalized delay or impairment in the development of intellectual and adaptive abilities.

Down syndrome A condition caused by the presence of an extra chromosome on the 21st pair and characterized by mental retardation and various physical anomalies.

TABLE 14.3   Levels of Mental Retardation

Degree of Severity	Approximate IQ Range	Percentage of People with Mental Retardation within the Range
Mild mental retardation	50–55 to approximately 70	Approximately 85%
Moderate mental retardation	35–40 to 50–55	10
Severe mental retardation	20–25 to 35–40	3–4
Profound mental retardation	Below 20 or 25	1–2

Source. Adapted from the *DSM-IV-TR* (APA, 2000).

Causes of Retardation

The causes of mental retardation may be primarily biological in nature, or primarily psychosocial, or a combination of both (APA, 2000). Biological causes include chromosomal and genetic disorders, infectious diseases, and maternal alcohol use during pregnancy. However, more than half of the cases of mental retardation remain unexplained, with most of these falling in the mild range of severity (Flint et al., 1995). These unexplained cases might involve cultural or familial causes, such as being raised in an impoverished home environment. Or perhaps they involve an interaction of psychosocial and genetic factors, the nature of which remains poorly understood (Thaper et al., 1994).

Web Link **14.3**
American Association   wWw
on Mental Retardation

Down Syndrome and Other Chromosomal Abnormalities The most common chromosomal abnormality resulting in mental retardation is **Down syndrome**

TABLE 14.4   Levels of Retardation, Typical Ranges of IQ Scores, and Types of Adaptive Behaviors Shown

Approximate IQ Score Range	Preschool Age 0–5 Maturation and Development	School Age 6–21 Training and Education	Adult 21 and Over Social and Vocational Adequacy
Mild 50–70	Often not noticed as retarded by casual observer, but is slower to walk, feed self, and talk than most children.	Can acquire practical skills and useful reading and arithmetic to a 3rd to 6th grade level with special education. Can be guided toward social conformity.	Can usually achieve social and vocational skills adequate to self-maintenance; may need occasional guidance and support when under unusual social or economic stress.
Moderate 35–49	Noticeable delays in motor development, especially in speech; responds to training in various self-help activities.	Can learn simple communication, elementary health and safety habits, and simple manual skills; does not progress in functional reading or arithmetic.	Can perform simple tasks under sheltered conditions; participates in simple recreation; travels alone in familiar places; usually incapable of self-maintenance.
Severe 20–34	Marked delay in motor development; little or no communication skill; may respond to training in elementary self-help—e.g., self-feeding.	Usually walks, barring specific disability; has some understanding of speech and some response; can profit from systematic habit training.	Can conform to daily routines and repetitive activities; needs continuing direction and supervision in protective environment.
Profound Below 20	Gross retardation; minimal capacity for functioning in sensorimotor areas; needs nursing care.	Obvious delays in all areas of development; shows basic emotional responses; may respond to skillful training in use of legs, hands, and jaws; needs close supervision.	May walk, may need nursing care, may have primitive speech; will usually benefit from regular physical activity; incapable of self-maintenance.

Source. From *Essentials of psychology* (6 ed.) by S.A. Rathus (1996). Copyright © 2001. Reprinted with permission of Brooks/Cole, an imprint of the Wadsworth Group, a division of Thomson Learning. FAX 800-730-2215.

(formerly called Down's syndrome), which is characterized by an extra or third chromosome on the 21st pair of chromosomes, resulting in 47 chromosomes rather than the normal complement of 46 (Wade, 2000). Down syndrome occurs in about 1 in 800 births. It usually occurs when the 21st pair of chromosomes in either the egg or the sperm fails to divide normally, resulting in an extra chromosome. Chromosomal abnormalities become more likely as parents age, so expectant couples in their mid-30s or older often undergo prenatal genetic tests to detect Down syndrome and genetic abnormalities. Down syndrome can be traced to a defect in the mother's chromosomes in about 95% of cases (Antonarakas et al., 1991), with the remainder attributable to defects in the father's sperm.

People with Down syndrome are recognizable by certain physical features, such as a round face, broad, flat nose, and small, downward-sloping folds of skin at the inside corners of the eyes that gives the impression of slanted eyes. A protruding tongue, small, squarish hands and short fingers, a curved fifth finger, and disproportionately small arms and legs in relation to their bodies also characterize children with Down syndrome. Nearly all of these children have mental retardation, and many suffer from physical problems, such as malformations of the heart and respiratory difficulties. Sadly, most die by middle age. In their later years, they tend to suffer memory losses and experience childish emotions that represent a form of senility.

Children with Down syndrome suffer various deficits in learning and development. They tend to be uncoordinated and to lack proper muscle tone, which makes it difficult for them to carry out physical tasks and engage in play activities like other children. Down syndrome children suffer memory deficits, especially for information presented verbally, which makes it difficult for them to learn in school. They also have difficulty following instructions from teachers and expressing their thoughts or needs clearly in speech. Despite their disabilities, most can learn to read, write, and perform simple arithmetic, if they receive appropriate schooling and the right encouragement.

Although less common than Down syndrome, chromosomal abnormalities on the sex chromosome may also result in mental retardation, such as in Klinefelter's syndrome and Turner's syndrome. Klinefelter's syndrome, which only occurs among males, is characterized by the presence of an extra X chromosome, resulting in an XXY chromosomal pattern rather than the XY pattern that men normally have. Estimates of the prevalence of Klinefelter's syndrome range from 1 in 500 to 1 in 1,000 male births (Brody, 1993c). Men with this XXY pattern fail to develop appropriate secondary sex characteristics, resulting in small, underdeveloped testes, low sperm production, enlarged breasts, poor muscular development, and infertility. Mild retardation or learning disabilities frequently occur among these men. Men with Klinefelter's syndrome often don't discover they have the condition until they undergo tests for infertility.

Found only among females is Turner's syndrome, which is characterized by the presence of a single X sex chromosome instead of the normal two. Although such girls develop normal external genitals, their ovaries remain poorly developed, producing reduced amounts of estrogen. As women, they tend to be shorter than average and infertile. They also tend to show evidence of mild retardation, especially in skills relating to math and science.

Fragile X Syndrome and Other Genetic Abnormalities
Fragile X syndrome is the most common type of inherited (genetic) mental retardation (Kwon et al., 2001). It is the second most common form of retardation overall, after Down syndrome (Plomin et al., 1994). The disorder is believed to be caused by a mutated gene on the X chromosome (Hagerman, 1996). The defective gene is located in an area of the chromosome that appears fragile, hence the name **fragile X syndrome.** Fragile X syndrome causes mental retardation in every 1,000 to 1,500 males and (generally less severe) mental handicaps in every 2,000 to 2,500 females (Angier, 1991b; Rousseau et al., 1991). The effects of fragile X syndrome range from mild learning disabilities to retardation so profound that those affected can hardly speak or function.

Females normally have two X chromosomes, whereas males have only one. For females, having two X chromosomes seems to provide some protection against the disorder

fragile X syndrome An inherited form of mental retardation caused by a mutated gene on the X chromosome.

Striving to achieve. Most children with Down syndrome can learn basic academic skills if they are afforded opportunities to learn and provided with the right encouragement.

phenylketonuria (PKU) A genetic disorder that prevents the metabolization of phenylpyruvic acid, leading to mental retardation unless the diet is strictly controlled.

cytomegalovirus A source of infection that, in pregnant women, carries a risk of mental retardation to the unborn child.

if the defective gene turns up on one of the two chromosomes (Angier, 1991b). This may explain why the disorder usually has more profound effects on males than on females. Yet the mutation does not always manifest itself. Many males and females carry the fragile X mutation but show no clinical evidence of it. Yet they can pass along the syndrome to their offspring.

A genetic test can detect the presence of the mutation by direct DNA analysis (Rousseau et al., 1991) and may be of help to prospective parents in genetic counseling. Prenatal testing of the fetus is also possible (Sutherland et al., 1991). Although there is no treatment for fragile X syndrome, identifying the defective gene is the first step toward understanding how the protein produced by the gene functions to produce the disability, which may lead to the development of treatments in the future (Angier, 1991b).

Phenylketonuria (PKU) is a genetic disorder that occurs in 1 in 10,000 births (Plomin et al., 1994). It is caused by a recessive gene that prevents the child from metabolizing the amino acid phenylalanine, which is found in many foods. Consequently, phenylalanine and its derivative, phenylpyruvic acid, accumulate in the body, causing damage to the central nervous system that results in mental retardation and emotional disturbance. The presence of PKU can be detected among newborns by analyzing blood or urine samples. Although there is no cure for PKU, children with the disorder may suffer less damage or develop normally if they are placed on a diet low in phenylalanine soon after birth (Brody, 1990). Such children receive protein supplements that compensate for their nutritional loss.

Today, various prenatal tests can detect the presence of chromosomal abnormalities and genetic disorders. In *amniocentesis,* which is usually conducted about 14 to 15 weeks following conception, a sample of amniotic fluid is drawn with a syringe from the amniotic sac that contains the fetus. Cells from the fetus can then be separated from the fluid, allowed to grow in a culture, and examined for abnormalities, including Down syndrome. Blood tests are used to detect carriers of other disorders.

Prenatal Factors Some cases of mental retardation are caused by maternal infections or substance abuse during pregnancy. Rubella (German measles) in the mother, for example, can be passed along to the unborn child, causing brain damage that results in retardation, and it may play a role in autism. Although the mother may experience mild symptoms or none at all, the effects on the fetus can be tragic. Other maternal diseases that may cause retardation in the child include syphilis, **cytomegalovirus,** and genital herpes.

Widespread programs that immunize women against rubella before pregnancy and tests for syphilis during pregnancy have reduced the risk of transmission of these infections to children. Most children who contract genital herpes from their mothers do so during delivery by coming into contact with the herpes simplex virus in the birth canal. Caesarean sections (C-sections) reduce the risk of the baby's coming into contact with the virus during childbirth.

Drugs that the mother ingests during pregnancy may pass through the placenta to the child. Some can cause severe birth deformities and mental retardation. Children whose mothers drink alcohol during pregnancy are often born with fetal alcohol syndrome (described in Chapter 10). FAS is among the most prominent causes of mental retardation. Maternal smoking during pregnancy has also been linked to the development of attention-deficit hyperactivity disorder in children (Milberger et al., 1996).

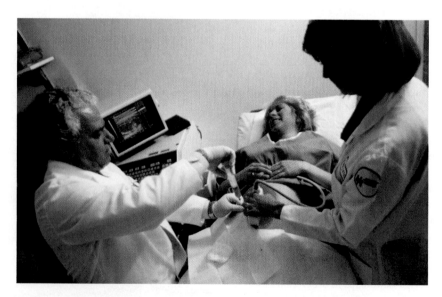

Amniocentesis. In amniocentesis, a physician extracts a sample of amniotic fluid to test for biochemical and chromosomal abnormalities. Here the physician uses ultrasound to determine the location of the fetus to help prevent accidental injury to it while placing the syringe in the mother's abdomen.

Birth complications, such as oxygen deprivation or head injuries, place children at increased risk for neurological disorders, including mental retardation. Prematurity also places children at risk of retardation and other developmental problems. Brain infections, such as encephalitis and meningitis, or traumas during infancy and early childhood can cause mental retardation and other health problems. Children who ingest toxins, such as paint chips containing lead, may also suffer brain damage that produces mental retardation.

Cultural-Familial Causes Most cases of mental retardation fall in the mild range of severity. In most of these cases, there is no apparent biological cause or distinguishing physical feature that sets the child apart from other children. Psychosocial factors, such as an impoverished home or social environment that is intellectually unstimulating, or parental neglect or abuse, may play a causal or contributing role in the development of mental retardation in such children. Supporting a family linkage is evidence from a study in Atlanta in which mothers who failed to finish high school were four times more likely than better educated mothers to have children with mild retardation (Drews et al., 1995).

These cases are considered **cultural-familial retardation.** Children in impoverished families may lack toys, books, or opportunities to interact with adults in intellectually stimulating ways. Consequently, they may fail to develop appropriate language skills or become unmotivated to learn the skills that are valued in contemporary society. Economic burdens, such as the need to hold multiple jobs, may prevent their parents from spending time reading to them, talking to them at length, and exposing them to creative play or trips to museums and parks. They may spend most of their days glued to the TV set. The parents, most of whom were also reared in poverty, may lack the reading or communication skills to help shape the development of these skills in their children. A vicious cycle of poverty and impoverished intellectual development may be repeated from generation to generation.

Children with this form of retardation may respond dramatically when provided with enriched learning experiences, especially at the earlier ages. Social programs like Head Start, for example, have helped children at risk of cultural-familial retardation to function within the normal range of ability (e.g., Barnett & Escobar, 1990).

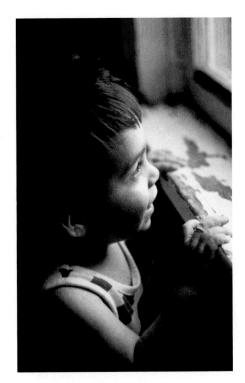

Environmental hazards. Children who are exposed to environmental hazards, such as paint chips containing lead-based paint, may suffer brain damage that can lead to mental retardation.

Intervention

The services that children with mental retardation require to meet the developmental challenges they face depend in part on the level of severity and type of retardation (Dykens & Hodapp, 1997; Snell, 1997). With appropriate training, children with mild retardation may approach a sixth grade level of competence. They can acquire vocational skills that allow them to support themselves minimally through meaningful work. Many such children can be mainstreamed in regular classes. At the other extreme, children with severe or profound mental retardation may need institutional care or placement in a residential care facility in the community, such as a group home. Placement in an institution is often based on the need to control destructive or aggressive behavior, not because of severity of the individual's intellectual impairment. Consider the case of a child with moderate retardation:

A Case of Moderate Mental Retardation

The mother pleaded with the emergency room physician to admit her 15-year-old son, claiming that she couldn't take it anymore. Her son, a Down syndrome patient with an IQ of 45, had alternated since the age of 8 between living in institutions and at home. Each visiting day he pleaded with his mother to take him home, and after about a year at each placement, she would bring him home but find herself unable to control his behavior. During temper tantrums, he would break dishes and destroy furniture and had

cultural-familial retardation A mild form of mental retardation that is influenced by impoverishment of the home environment.

Imparting skills. In 1975, Congress enacted legislation that requires public schools to provide children with disabilities with educational programs that meet their individual needs.

recently become physically assaultive toward his mother, hitting her on the arm and shoulder during a recent scuffle when she attempted to stop him from repeatedly banging a broom on the floor.

—*Adapted from Spitzer et al., 1989, pp. 338–340*

■

Controversy remains concerning whether children with mental retardation should be mainstreamed in regular classes or placed in special education classes. Although some children with mild retardation may achieve better when they are mainstreamed, others may not do so well in regular classes. They may find these classes overwhelming and withdraw from their schoolmates. There has also been a trend toward deinstitutionalization of people with more severe mental retardation, a policy shift motivated in large part by public outrage over the appalling conditions that existed in many institutions serving this population. The Developmentally Disabled Assistance and Bill of Rights Act, which Congress passed in 1975, provided that persons with mental retardation have the right to receive appropriate treatment in the least restrictive treatment setting. Nationwide, the population of institutions for people with mental retardation shrunk by nearly two-thirds from the 1970s to the 1990s.

People with mental retardation who are capable of functioning in the community have the right to receive less restrictive care than is provided in large institutions. Many are capable of living outside the institution and have been placed in supervised group homes. Residents typically share household responsibilities and are encouraged to participate in meaningful daily activities, such as training programs or sheltered workshops. Others live with their families and attend structured day programs. Adults with mild retardation often work in outside jobs and live in their own apartments or share apartments with other persons with mild retardation. Although the large-scale dumping of mental patients in the community from psychiatric institutions resulted in massive social problems and swelled the ranks of America's homeless population, deinstitutionalization of people with mental retardation has largely been a success story that has been achieved with rare dignity (Winerip, 1991).

Children and adults with mental retardation may need psychological counseling to help them adjust to life in the community. Many have difficulty making friends and may become socially isolated. Problems with self-esteem are also common, especially because people who have mental retardation are often demeaned and ridiculed. Supportive counseling may be supplemented with behavioral techniques that help them acquire skills in areas such as personal hygiene, work, and social relationships. More structured behavioral approaches can be used to teach persons with more severe retardation such basic hygienic behaviors as toothbrushing, self-dressing, and hair combing.

Other behavioral treatment techniques include social skills training, which focuses on increasing the individual's ability to relate effectively to others, and anger management training to help individuals develop more effective ways of handling conflicts without aggressive acting out (Huang & Cuvo, 1997; Rose, 1996).

Children with mental retardation stand perhaps a three to four times greater-than-normal chance of developing other psychological disorders, such as attention-deficit hyperactivity disorder (ADHD), depression, or anxiety disorders (Borthwick-Duffy, 1994). As many as three of four boys with fragile X syndrome, for example, develop ADHD (Matson & Sevin, 1994). Mental health professionals have been slow to recognize the prevalence of mental health problems among people with mental retardation, perhaps because of a long-held conceptual distinction between emotional impairment on the one hand and intellectual deficits on the other (Nezu, 1994). Many professionals even assumed (wrongly) that people with mental retardation were somehow immune from psychological problems or that they lacked the necessary verbal ability to benefit from psychotherapy (Bütz, Bowlling, & Bliss, 2000; Nezu, 1994). Given these commonly held beliefs, it is perhaps not surprising that many of the psychological problems of people with mental retardation have gone unrecognized and untreated (Reiss & Valenti-Hein, 1994). However, evidence shows that people with mental retardation can benefit from psychotherapy (Bütz et al., 2000).

A Closer Look

Savant Syndrome

Got a minute? Try the following:

1. Without referring to a calendar, calculate the day of the week that March 15, 2079, will fall on.

2. List the prime numbers between 1 and 1 billion. (Hint: the list starts 1, 2, 3, 5, 7, 11, 13, 17 . . .)

3. Repeat verbatim the newspaper stories you read over coffee this morning.

4. Sing accurately every note played by the first violin in Beethoven's Ninth Symphony.

These tasks are impossible for all but a very few. Ironically, people who are most likely to be able to accomplish these feats suffer from autism, mental retardation, or both. Such a person is commonly called an *idiot savant*. The term *savant* is derived from the French *savoir,* meaning "to know." The label *savant syndrome* is preferable to the pejorative term *idiot savant* to refer to someone with severe mental deficiencies who possesses some remarkable mental abilities. The prevalence of the savant syndrome among people with mental retardation is estimated at about .06%, or about 1 case in 2,000 (Hill, 1977). The emergence of the savant syndrome is also closely linked to infantile autism (Miller, 1999). Most people with savant syndrome, like most people with autism, are male (Treffert, 1988). Among a sample of 5,400 people with autism, 531 (9.8%) were reported by parents to have the savant syndrome (Rimland, 1978). Because they want to think of their children as special, however, parents might overreport the incidence of the savant syndrome.

Several hundred people with the savant syndrome have been described in this century. They are reported to have shown remarkable but circumscribed mental skills, such as calendar calculating, rare musical

Savant syndrome. Dustin Hoffman (left) won the Best Actor Oscar for his portrayal in the film *Rainman* of a man with autism who showed a remarkable capacity for numerical calculation. Tom Cruise (right) played his brother. Hoffman was able to capture the sense of emotional detachment and isolation of his character.

talent, even accomplished poetry (Dowker, Hermelin, & Pring, 1996)—all of which stand in contrast to their limited general intellectual abilities. People with the savant syndrome also have outstanding memories. Just as we learn about health by studying illness, we may be able to learn more about normal mechanisms of memory by studying people in whom memory stands apart from other aspects of mental functioning (e.g., Kelly, Macaruso, & Sokol, 1997).

The savant syndrome phenomenon occurs more frequently in males by a ratio of about 6 to 1. The special skills of people with the savant syndrome tend to appear out of the blue and may disappear as suddenly. Some people with the syndrome engage in lightning calculations. A 19th-century enslaved person in Virginia, Thomas Fuller, "was able to calculate the number of seconds in 70 years, 17 days, and 12 hours in a minute and one half, taking into account the 17 leap years that would have occurred in the period" (S. C. Smith, 1983). There are also cases of persons with the syndrome who were blind but could play back any musical piece, no matter how complex, or repeat long passages of foreign languages without losing a syllable. Some people with the syndrome make exact estimates of elapsed time. One could reportedly repeat verbatim the contents of a newspaper he had just heard; another could repeat backward what he had just read (Tradgold, 1914, cited in Treffert, 1988).

Truth OR Fiction? REVISITED

Some people can recall verbatim every story they read in a newspaper.

TRUE. Ability to recall news stories verbatim is found in some individuals with the savant syndrome.

Various theories have been presented to explain the savant syndrome (Treffert, 1988). Some believe that children with the savant syndrome have unusually well-developed memories that allow them to record and scan vast amounts of information. It has been suggested that people with the savant syndrome may inherit two sets of hereditary factors, one for retardation and the other for special abilities. Perhaps it is coincidental that their special abilities and their mental handicaps were inherited in common. Other theorists suggest that the left and right hemispheres of their cerebral cortexes are organized in an unusual way. This latter belief is supported by research suggesting that the special abilities they possess often involve skills associated with right hemisphere functioning. Still other theorists suggest they learn special skills to compensate for their lack of more general skills, perhaps as a means of coping with their environment, or perhaps as a means of earning social reinforcements. Perhaps their skills in concrete functions, like calculation, compensate for their lack of abstract thinking ability. Linguists like Noam Chomsky (1965) theorize that people are neurologically "prewired" to grasp the deep structure that underlies all human languages. Perhaps, as the neurologist Oliver Sacks speculates (1985b), the

▶

brain circuits of some people with the savant syndrome are wired with a "deep arithmetic"—an innate structure for perceiving mathematical relationships that is analogous to the prewiring that allows people to perceive and produce language.

Recent research has pointed to possible gender-linked left hemisphere damage occurring prenatally or congenitally. Compensatory right hemisphere development might then take place, establishing specialized brain circuitry that processes concrete and narrowly defined kinds of information (Treffert, 1988). An environment that reinforces savant abilities and provides opportunities for practice and concentration would give further impetus to the development of these unusual abilities. Still the savant syndrome remains a mystery.

THINK ABOUT IT
Do you think children with mental retardation should be mainstreamed within regular classes? Why or why not?

Learning Disorders

Nelson Rockefeller served as governor of New York State and as vice president of the United States. He was brilliant and well educated. However, despite the best of tutors, he always had trouble reading. Rockefeller suffered from **dyslexia,** a term derived from the Greek roots *dys-*, meaning "bad," and *lexikon,* meaning "of words." Dyslexia is the most common type of **learning disorder** (also called a *learning disability*) (Shaywitz, 1998). It accounts for perhaps 80% of cases of learning disability and describes individuals who have trouble reading despite possessing at least average intelligence (Miller-Medzon, 2000). Mental retardation involves a general delay in intellectual development. People with learning disorders, by contrast, may be intelligent, even gifted, but show poor development in reading, math, or writing skills to a point that it impairs their school performance or daily functioning. Today, about one in eight children (about 12%) is placed in a program for the learning disabled, and the percentage of children participating in such programs is growing (Levine, 2000).

Learning disorders tend to be chronic disorders that continue to affect development into adulthood. Children with learning disorders tend to perform poorly in school. They are often viewed as failures by their teachers and their families. It is not surprising that most of them develop low expectations and problems with self-esteem.

Types of Learning Disorders

Types of learning disorders include *mathematics disorder, disorder of written expression,* and *reading disorder.*

Mathematics Disorder *Mathematics disorder* describes children with deficiencies in arithmetic skills. They may have problems understanding basic mathematical terms or operations, such as addition or subtraction; decoding mathematical symbols (+, =, etc.); or learning multiplication tables. The problem may become apparent as early as the first grade (age 6) but is not generally recognized until about the second or third grade.

Web Link 14.4 wWw
Facts About Learning Disabilities

Disorder of Written Expression *Disorder of written expression* refers to children with grossly deficient writing skills. The deficiency may be characterized by errors in spelling, grammar, or punctuation, or by difficulty in composing sentences and paragraphs. Severe writing difficulties generally become apparent by age 7 (second grade), although milder cases may not be recognized until the age of 10 (fifth grade) or later.

Reading Disorder Reading disorder—*dyslexia*—characterizes children who have poorly developed skills in recognizing words and comprehending written text. Dyslexia is estimated to affect about 4% of school-age children (APA, 2000). Children with dyslexia may read slowly with difficulty, and distort, omit, or substitute words when reading aloud. They have trouble decoding letters and letter combinations and translating them into the appropriate sounds (Miller-Medzon, 2000). They may also misperceive letters as upside down (for example, confusing *w* for *m*) or in reversed images (*b* for *d*). Dyslexia is usually apparent by the age of 7, coinciding with the second grade, although it is sometimes recognized in 6-year-olds. Children

dyslexia A learning disorder characterized by impaired reading ability.

learning disorder A deficiency in a specific learning ability in the context of normal intelligence and exposure to learning opportunities.

and adolescents with dyslexia tend to be more prone than their peers to depression, to have lower self-worth and feelings of competence in their academic work, and to have signs of attention-deficit hyperactivity disorder (Boetsch, Green, & Pennington, 1996).

More boys are diagnosed with reading disorder than girls, but this difference may have more to do with a bias toward identifying the disorder in males rather than an underlying gender difference in the rate of the disorder (APA, 2000). Boys with dyslexia are more likely than girls to show disruptive behavior in class and so are more likely to be referred for evaluation. Carefully conducted studies find similar rates of the disorder in boys and girls (APA, 2000; Shaywitz, 1998).

Rates of dyslexia vary with respect to native language. Rates of dyslexia are high in English-speaking and French-speaking countries, where the language contains a large number of ways of spelling words containing the same meaningful sounds (e.g., the same "o" sound in the words "toe" and "tow") than in Italy, where the language has a smaller ratio of sounds to letter combinations ("Dyslexia," 2001; Paulesu et al., 2001).

Dyslexia. Children with dyslexia have difficulty decoding words. Note the reversal of the letters *w* and *l* in the word *owl* in this picture of a girl with dyslexia completing a writing exercise.

Theoretical Perspectives

Hypotheses of the origins of learning disorders tend to focus on cognitive-perceptual problems and possible underlying neurological factors. Many children with learning disorders have problems with visual or auditory perception. They may lack the capacity to copy words or to discriminate geometric shapes. Other children have short attention spans or show hyperactivity, which may also be suggestive of an underlying brain abnormality.

Much of the research on learning disorders has focused on dyslexia. Although no one can say with certainty what causes dyslexia, mounting evidence points to underlying deficits in how the brain processes visual and auditory information (e.g., Azar, 2000b; Miller-Medzon, 2000; Murray, 2000a). Evidence of impaired visual processing in the brains of people with dyslexia points to a possible defect in a visual relay station in the brain through which visual information flows from the eye to the visual cortex for processing (Livingstone et al., 1991). As a result, the brains of people with dyslexia may not be able to decipher a rapid succession of visual stimuli needed to decode letters and words. Words may thus become blurry, fuse together, or seem to jump off the page—problems reported by people with dyslexia.

Additional evidence from PET studies shows lower levels of activity in dyslexic people in parts of the brain involved in language processing and reading (Helmuth, 2001; Paulesu et al., 2001). These differences in brain function are observed in dyslexic subjects from England, France, and Italy, which suggest that the disorder has a common biological basis despite the differences in the rates of the disorder across these countries.

Sensory pathways for hearing and even touch are also implicated in dyslexia. Some forms of dyslexia may be traceable to abnormalities in brain circuits responsible for processing the rapid flow of sounds (Blakeslee, 1994b). This flaw in brain circuitry may make it difficult to understand rapidly occurring speech sounds, such as the sounds corresponding to the letters *b* and *p* in syllables like *ba* and *pa*. Problems in discerning the differences between many basic speech sounds can make it difficult for people with dyslexia to learn to speak correctly and later, perhaps, to learn to read. They continue to have problems distinguishing in rapid speech between words like *boy* and *toy* or *pet* and *bet*. If defects in brain circuitry responsible for relaying and processing sensory data are involved in learning disorders, as the evidence now suggests, it may lead the way to the development of specialized treatment programs to help children adjust to their sensory capabilities.

Taken together, evidence points to a neurological basis to the cognitive problems in dyslexia (Paulesu et al., 2001). The underlying dysfunction may have a genetic basis, as evidence connects genetic factors with a greater risk of dyslexia (Shaywitz, 1998; Nagourney, 2001a). As we can see from Figure 14.2, people with dyslexic parents are at increased risk of

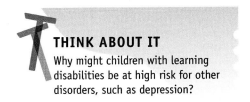

THINK ABOUT IT
Why might children with learning disabilities be at high risk for other disorders, such as depression?

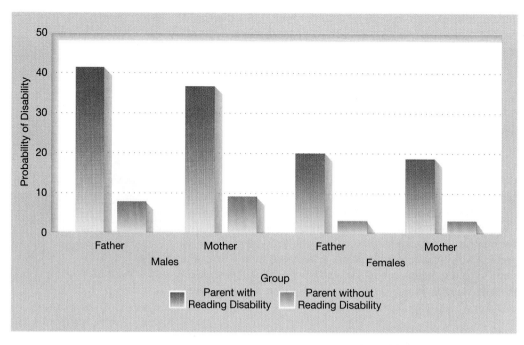

FIGURE 14.2 Familial risk of developmental reading disorder (dyslexia).
Boys are at greater risk than girls of developing dyslexia, and children of both genders whose parents with dyslexia are at relatively greater risk. Although these data are consistent with a genetic explanation of the etiology of dyslexia, it is also possible that parents with dyslexia do not provide their children with the types of stimulation such as books and reading bedtime stories that foster reading skills.

Source. Adapted from Vogler et al. (1985).

having the disorder themselves (Vogler, DeFries, & Decker, 1985). Moreover, higher rates of concordance (agreement) for dyslexia are found between identical (MZ) than fraternal (DZ) twins, 70% versus 40%, respectively (Plomin et al., 1994). Suspicion has focused on the role that particular genes may play in causing subtle defects in brain circuitry involved in reading.

Intervention

Interventions for learning disorders have generally been approached from the following perspectives (Lyon & Moats, 1988):

1. *The psychoeducational model.* Psychoeducational approaches emphasize children's strengths and preferences, rather than attempt to correct assumed underlying deficiencies. For example, a child who retains auditory information better than visual information might be taught verbally, for example, using tape recordings rather than written materials.

2. *The behavioral model.* The behavioral model assumes that academic learning is built on a hierarchy of basic skills, or "enabling behaviors." To read effectively, one must first learn to recognize letters, then attach sounds to letters, then combine letters and sounds into words, and so on. The child's learning competencies are assessed to determine where deficiencies lie in the hierarchy of skills. An individualized program of instruction and reinforcement helps the child acquire the skills needed to perform academic tasks.

3. *The medical model.* This model assumes that learning disorders are symptoms of biologically based deficiencies in cognitive processing. Proponents suggest that remediation should be directed at the underlying pathology rather than the learning disability. If the child has a visual defect that makes it difficult to follow a line of text, treatment should aim to remediate the visual deficit, perhaps through visual-tracking exercises. Improvement in reading ability would be expected to follow.

4. *The neuropsychological model.* This approach borrows from the psychoeducational and medical models. It assumes that learning disorders reflect underlying biologically based deficits in processing information (medical model). It also assumes that educational programs should be adapted to take into account these underlying deficits and individualized to the child's needs (Levine, 2000).

5. *The linguistic model.* The linguistic approach focuses on children's basic language deficiencies, such as failing to recognize how sounds and words are strung together to create meaning, which can give rise to problems in reading, spelling, and finding the words to express themselves. Adherents to this model teach language skills sequentially, helping the student grasp the structure and use of words (Shaywitz, 1998; Wagner & Torgesen, 1987).

6. *The cognitive model.* This model focuses on how children organize their thoughts when they learn academic material. Within this perspective, children are helped to learn by (1) recognizing the nature of the learning task, (2) applying effective problem-solving strategies to complete tasks, and (3) monitoring the success of their strategies. Children with arithmetic problems might be guided to break down a math problem into its component tasks, think through the steps necessary to complete each task, and evaluate their performance at each step to judge how to proceed. Children progress through a systematic approach to problem solving that can be applied to diverse academic tasks.

Evaluation of Treatment Approaches   The medical model is currently limited by lack of evidence that underlying deficiencies are correctable or that such improvements foster academic skills (Hinshaw, 1992; Lyon & Moats, 1988). There is also a lack of evidence for the psychoeducational approach (Brady, 1986; Lyon & Moats, 1988). Although the neuropsychological approach has not yet been fully tested, interventions focused on changing the child's learning strategies in order to circumvent apparent underlying neuropsychological deficits have thus far failed to demonstrate significant gains in children with severe forms of learning disability (Hinshaw, 1992). The interventions showing the most promising results to date are those that provide direct instruction in the academic skills in which the child is deficient, such as oral and written language skills (Hinshaw, 1992). The behavioral model has also shown some promising results in improving the performance of children who are deficient in reading and arithmetic skills (Koorland, 1986). Whether the gains from behavioral training generalize to classroom performance beyond the training setting remains to be seen. The linguistic approach has received some support, but not enough to advocate widespread use in treating children with reading and spelling deficiencies (Lyon & Moats, 1988). The cognitive model, too, has received some support, but many children with learning disorders have not developed enough basic knowledge in their problem areas to use it to think through problems.

Many children who have learning disorders are placed in special education programs or classes. Yet programs for learning-disabled children vary widely in quality and we still lack firm evidence demonstrating their long-term effectiveness (Hinshaw, 1992; Wingert & Kantrowitz, 1997).

communication disorders A class of psychological disorders characterized by difficulties in understanding or using language.

THINK ABOUT IT
Do you think people with learning disorders should be given special consideration when given standardized tests, like the Scholastic Aptitude Test (SAT), such as having extra time? Why or why not?

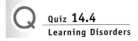
Quiz **14.4**
Learning Disorders

Communication Disorders

Communication disorders involve difficulties in understanding or using language. The categories of communication disorders include *expressive language disorder, mixed receptive/ expressive language disorder, phonological disorder,* and *stuttering.* Each of these disorders interferes with academic or occupational functioning or ability to communicate socially. Table 14.5 lists the *DSM-IV* classification of learning disorders and communication disorders.

Expressive language disorder involves impairment in the use of spoken language, such as slow vocabulary development, errors in tense, difficulties recalling words, and problems producing sentences of appropriate length and complexity for the individual's age. Affected children may also have a phonological (articulation) disorder, compounding their speech problems.

TABLE **14.5**	*DSM-IV* Classification of Learning Disorders and Communication Disorders
Learning Disorders	Reading Disorder
	Mathematics Disorder
	Disorder of Written Expression
Communication Disorders	Expressive Language Disorder
	Mixed Receptive/Expressive Language Disorder
	Phonological Disorder
	Stuttering

Source. Adapted from the *DSM-IV-TR* (APA, 2000).

Mixed receptive/expressive language disorder refers to children who have difficulties both understanding and producing speech. There may be difficulty understanding words or sentences. In some cases, children have difficulty understanding certain word types (such as words expressing differences in quantity—*large, big,* or *huge*), spatial terms (such as *near* or *far*), or sentence types (such as sentences that begin with the word *unlike*). Other cases are marked by difficulties understanding simple words or sentences.

Phonological disorder involves difficulties in articulating the sounds of speech in the absence of defects in the oral speech mechanism or neurological impairment. Children with the disorder may omit, substitute, or mispronounce certain sounds—especially *ch, f, l, r, sh,* and *th* sounds, which are usually articulated properly by the time children reach the early school years. It may sound as if they are uttering "baby talk." In more severe cases, there are problems articulating sounds usually mastered during the preschool years: *b, m, t, d, n,* and *h.* Speech therapy is often helpful, and milder cases often resolve themselves by the age of 8.

Stuttering involves disturbances in the ability to speak fluently with appropriate timing of speech sounds. The lack of normal fluency must be inappropriate for the person's age in order to justify the diagnosis. Stuttering usually begins between 2 and 7 years of age and affects about 1 child in 100 before puberty (APA, 2000). The disorder is characterized by one or more of the following characteristics: (1) repetitions of sounds and syllables; (2) prolongations of certain sounds; (3) interjections of inappropriate sounds; (4) broken words, such as pauses occurring within a spoken word; (5) blocking of speech; (6) circumlocutions (substitutions of alternative words to avoid problematic words); (7) displaying an excess of physical tension when emitting words; and (8) repetitions of monosyllabic whole words (for example, "I-I-I-I am glad to meet you") (APA, 2000). Stuttering occurs predominantly among males by a ratio of about 3 to 1. Stuttering remits in upward of 80% of children, typically before age 16. As many as 60% of cases show remission without any treatment. Stuttering is believed to involve an interaction of genetic and environmental factors (Felsenfeld, 1996; Yairi, Ambrose; & Cox, 1996). Underlying social anxiety or social phobias may be involved in some cases, at least among adults with stuttering problems (De-Carle & Pato, 1996; Schneier, Wexler, & Liebowitz, 1997). Treatment of communication disorders is generally approached with speech therapy and with psychological counseling for social anxiety or other emotional problems.

Quiz **14.5**
Communication Disorders

Attention-Deficit and Disruptive Behavior Disorders

The category of *attention-deficit and disruptive behavior disorders* refers to a diverse range of problem behaviors, including *attention-deficit hyperactivity disorder* (ADHD), *conduct disorder* (CD), and *oppositional defiant disorder* (ODD). These disorders are socially disruptive and usually more upsetting to other people than to the children who receive these diagnoses. Although there are differences among these disorders, the rate of co-morbidity (co-occurrence) among these disorders is very high (Jensen, Martin, & Cantwell, 1997).

Attention-Deficit Hyperactivity Disorder

Many parents believe that their children are not attentive toward them—that they run around on whim and do things in their own way. Some inattention, especially in early childhood, is normal enough. In **attention-deficit hyperactivity disorder (ADHD)**, however, children display impulsivity, inattention, and **hyperactivity** that are considered inappropriate to their developmental levels.

ADHD is divided into three subtypes: a predominantly inattentive type, a predominantly hyperactive or impulsive type, or a combination type characterized by high levels of both inattention and hyperactivity-impulsivity (APA, 2000). The disorder is usually first diagnosed during elementary school, when problems with attention or hyperactivity-impulsivity make it difficult for the child to adjust to school. Although signs of hyperactivity are often observed earlier, many overactive toddlers do not go on to develop ADHD.

ADHD is the most commonly diagnosed psychological disorder in children today (Bradley & Golden, 2001). The disorder is estimated to affect between 3% and 7% of school-age children, or some two million American youngsters in total (Shute, Locy, & Pasternak, 2000; Wingert, 2000; APA, 2000). ADHD is diagnosed two to nine times more often in boys than girls (APA, 2000). Although inattention appears to be the basic problem, associated problems include inability to sit still for more than a few moments, bullying, temper tantrums, stubbornness, and failure to respond to punishment (see Table 14.6).

Activity and restlessness impair the ability of children with ADHD to function in school. They seem incapable of sitting still. They fidget and squirm in their seats, butt into

attention-deficit hyperactivity disorder (ADHD) A behavior disorder characterized by excessive motor activity and inability to focus one's attention.

hyperactivity An abnormal behavior pattern characterized by difficulty in maintaining attention and extreme restlessness.

TABLE 14.6 Diagnostic Features of Attention-Deficit Hyperactivity Disorder (ADHD)

Kind of Problem	Specific Behavior Pattern
Lack of attention	Fails to attend to details or makes careless errors in schoolwork, etc.
	Has difficulty sustaining attention in schoolwork or play
	Doesn't appear to pay attention to what is being said
	Fails to follow through on instructions or to finish work
	Has trouble organizing work and other activities
	Avoids work or activities that require sustained attention
	Loses work tools (e.g., pencils, books, assignments, toys)
	Becomes readily distracted
	Is forgetful in daily activities
Hyperactivity	Fidgets with hands or feet or squirms in his or her seat
	Leaves seat in situations such as the classroom in which remaining seated is required
	Is constantly running around or climbing on things
	Has difficulty playing quietly
Impulsivity	Frequently "calls out" in class
	Fails to wait his/her turn in line, games, etc.

To receive a diagnosis of ADHD, the disorder must begin by the age of 7; must have significantly impaired academic, social, or occupational functioning; and must be characterized by a designated number of clinical features shown in this table occurring over a 6-month period in at least two settings such as at school, at home, or at work.

Source. Adapted from the *DSM-IV-TR* (APA, 2000).

other children's games, have outbursts of temper, and may engage in dangerous behavior, such as running into the street without looking. All in all, they can drive parents and teachers to despair.

Where does "normal" age-appropriate overactivity end and hyperactivity begin? Assessment of the degree of hyperactive behavior is crucial, because many normal children are called "hyper" from time to time. Some critics of the ADHD diagnosis argue that it merely labels children who are difficult to control as mentally disordered or sick. Most children, especially boys, are highly active during the early school years. Proponents of the diagnosis counter that there is a difference in quality between normal overactivity and ADHD. Normally overactive children are usually goal directed and can exert voluntary control over their behavior. But children with ADHD appear hyperactive without reason and do not seem to be able to conform their behavior to the demands of teachers and parents. Put another way: Most children can sit still and concentrate for a while when they want to do so; children who are hyperactive seemingly cannot.

Although children with ADHD tend to be of average or above-average intelligence, they often underachieve in school. They are frequently disruptive in the classroom and tend to get into fights (especially the boys). They may fail to follow or remember instructions or complete assignments. They are more likely to have learning disabilities, to repeat grades, and to be placed in special education classes (Faraone et al., 1993). They also show a higher frequency of physical injuries and hospital admissions than their peers ("Children with Hyperactivity," 2001; Leibson et al., 2001). They also stand a greater risk of mood disorders, anxiety disorders, and problems getting along with family members (Biederman et al., 1996a, b). Compared to their peers, ADHD boys tend to lack empathy, or awareness of other people's feelings (Braaten & Rosén, 2000). Not surprisingly, children with ADHD tend to be unpopular with their classmates. The disorder often persists into adolescence and adulthood. Although ADHD symptoms tend to decline as children age, the disorder often persists in milder form into adolescence and adulthood (Biederman, Mick, & Faraone, 2000; Faraone et al., 2000; Wender et al., 2000). Children with ADHD are more likely than their peers to go on to become delinquents, to be suspended from school, and to require continued interventions during adolescence (Lambert et al., 1987) (see Figure 14.3).

Web Link 14.5
Diagnosis and Treatment WWW
of Attention Deficit
Hyperactivity Disorder

VIDEO 14.2 ⊙
ADHD: *Dr Raun Melmed*

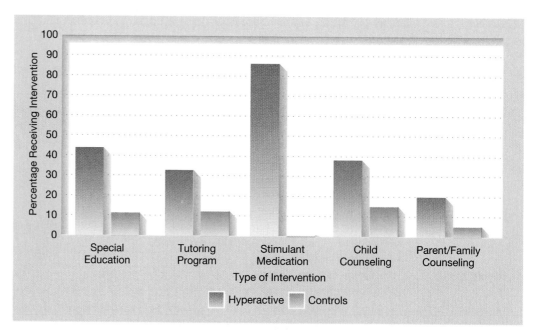

FIGURE 14.3 Interventions received by adolescents who were earlier diagnosed as hyperactive.
Adolescents who were diagnosed as hyperactive during childhood were more likely than other adolescents to receive the kinds of interventions shown in this figure.

Source. Adapted from Lambert et al. (1987).

Theoretical Perspectives Although the causes of ADHD are not known, both biological and environmental influences appear to be involved. Investigators believe that genetic factors make a substantial genetic contribution to ADHD (Bradley & Golden, 2001; Faraone et al., 2001). Evidence of a genetic contribution comes largely from studies showing higher concordance rates for ADHD among monozygotic (MZ) twins than DZ (dizygotic) twins (Sherman et al., 1997). Yet environmental factors and the gene-environment interaction also play important roles (Bradley & Golden, 2001). For example, ADHD is much more common in children whose mothers smoked during pregnancy than in other children (Milberger et al., 1996). Maternal smoking may cause defects in the brain during prenatal development. Investigators continue to track down other possible environmental factors, such as a high level of family conflict, emotional stress during pregnancy, and poor parenting skills in handling children's misbehavior.

Investigators are also seeking to track down the parts of the brain that may be affected in children with ADHD. One prominent view today is that ADHD involves a genetically determined pattern of underactivity of the frontal lobes of the cerebral cortex, the parts of the brain responsible for inhibiting impulses and maintaining self-control (Barkley, 1997, 2001). Neuropsychological testing, EEG studies, and MRI studies point to subtle brain abnormalities in children and adolescents with ADHD in areas of the brain involved in regulating attention, arousal, control of motor (movement) behavior, and communication between the left and right hemispheres (e.g., Castellanos et al., 2001; Murray, 2000; Semrud-Clikeman et al., 2000). Yet different subtypes of ADHD may reflect dysfunctions in different regions of the brain (Bradley & Golden, 2001). Irregularities in nerve pathways in the brain that use the neurotransmitter serotonin may also help explain the impulsive and hyperactive components of ADHD (Quist & Kennedy, 2001).

Treatment It seems odd that drugs used to help many ADHD children calm down and attend better in school belong to a class of stimulants that includes *Ritalin* (methylphenidate), *Cylert* (pemoline), and other long-acting stimulants that can be taken in once-a-day doses (Rugino & Copley, 2001). Stimulant drugs have the paradoxical effect of calming down children with ADHD and increasing their attention spans. Although the use of stimulant medication is not without its critics, it is clear that these drugs can help many children with ADHD calm down and concentrate better on tasks and schoolwork, perhaps for the first times in their lives (Greenhill, 1998). These drugs not only improve attention in ADHD children but also reduce impulsivity, overactivity, and disruptive, annoying, or aggressive behavior (Gillberg et al., 1997; Hinshaw, 1992). Stimulant medication appears to be safe and effective when carefully monitored and successful in helping about three of four children with ADHD (Barkley, 1997). Improvements are noted at home as well as in school. The normal (voluntary) high activity levels shown in physical education classes and on weekends are not disrupted, however.

Use of stimulant medication increased dramatically during the 1990s (Gibbs, 1998; Zito et al., 2000). We do not know what accounts for the seemingly paradoxical effects of stimulants in calming children with ADHD, although it is suspected that these drugs work on neurotransmitter systems in the brain. These drugs heighten dopamine activity in the frontal lobes of the brain, the area regulating attention and control of impulsive behavior. Thus, the drugs may help ADHD children focus their attention and avoid acting out impulsively (Casey et al., 1997).

Although stimulant medication can help reduce restlessness and increase attention in school, these gains may not translate into improved academic performance ("Attention Deficit Disorder—Part II," 1995; Rutter, 1997). However, a recent study showed that combining stimulant medication and behavior modification succeeded in boosting academic performance in teenagers with ADHD, including performance on such measures as quiz scores and daily assignments (Carpenter, 2001a; Evans, Pelham, & Smith, 2001). One problem with stimulant medication, as with many other uses of psychotropic drugs, is a high rate of relapse once the child stops taking the medication (Greenhill, 1998). Also, the range of effectiveness is limited, as in the following case example:

Attention-deficit hyperactivity disorder (ADHD). ADHD is more common in boys than girls and is characterized by attentional difficulties, restlessness, impulsivity, excessive motor behavior (continuous running around or climbing), and temper tantrums.

Truth OR Fiction? REVISITED

Maternal smoking during pregnancy may put children at increased risk of attention-deficit hyperactivity disorder (ADHD).

TRUE. Maternal smoking during pregnancy is associated with an increased risk of ADHD in children.

Truth OR Fiction? REVISITED

Children who are hyperactive are often given depressants to help calm them down.

FALSE. Children with ADHD are often given stimulant drugs like Ritalin, not depressants. These stimulants have a paradoxical effect of calming them down and increasing their attention spans.

Eddie Hardly Ever Sits Still

Nine-year-old Eddie is a problem in class. His teacher complains that he is so restless and fidgety that the rest of the class cannot concentrate on their work. He hardly ever sits still. He is in constant motion, roaming the classroom, talking to other children while they are working. He has been suspended repeatedly for outrageous behavior, most recently swinging from a fluorescent light fixture and unable to get himself down. His mother reports that Eddie has been a problem since he was a toddler. By the age of 3 he had become unbearably restless and demanding. He has never needed much sleep and always awakened before anyone else in the family, making his way downstairs and wrecking things in the living room and kitchen. Once, at the age of 4, he unlocked the front door and wandered into traffic, but was rescued by a passerby.

Psychological testing shows Eddie to be average in academic ability, but to have a "virtually nonexistent" attention span. He shows no interest in television or in games or toys that require some concentration. He is unpopular with peers and prefers to ride his bike alone or to play with his dog. He has become disobedient at home and at school and has stolen small amounts of money from his parents and classmates.

Eddie has been treated with methylphenidate (Ritalin), but it was discontinued because it had no effect on his disobedience and stealing. However, it did seem to reduce his restlessness and increase his attention span at school.

Adapted from Spitzer et al., 1989, pp. 315–317

Then there's the matter of side effects. Although short-term side effects (e.g., loss of appetite or insomnia) usually subside within a few weeks or may be eliminated by lowering the dose, stimulant drugs may lead to other effects, including a slowdown of physical growth (Wingert, 2000). Fortunately, children taking stimulant medication eventually catch up to their peers in physical stature (Gittelman-Klein & Mannuzza, 1990; Gorman, 1998).

With so many children on Ritalin and similar drugs, critics claim we are too ready to seek a "quick fix" for problem behavior in children rather than examine other factors contributing to the child's problem, such as problems in the family (Gibbs, 1998). As one pediatrician put it, "It takes time for parents and teachers to sit down and talk to kids. . . . It takes less time to get a child a pill" (Hancock, 1996, p. 52). Whatever the benefits of stimulant medication, medication alone typically fails to bring the social and academic behavior of children with ADHD into a normal range (Hinshaw, 1992). Drugs cannot teach new skills. So attention has focused on whether a combination of stimulant medication and behavioral or cognitive-behavioral techniques can produce greater benefits than either approach alone. Cognitive-behavioral treatment of ADHD combines behavior modification, typically based on the use of reinforcement (for example, a teacher praising the child with ADHD for sitting quietly) and cognitive modification (for example, training the child to silently talk himself or herself through the steps involved in solving challenging academic problems). Thus far evidence is mixed on the value of combining cognitive-behavioral therapy with medication (Braswell & Kendall, 2001; Hinshaw, Klein, & Abikoff, 1998).

Conduct Disorder

Although it also involves disruptive behavior, **conduct disorder** differs in important ways from ADHD. Whereas children with ADHD seem literally incapable of controlling their behavior, children with conduct disorder purposefully engage in patterns of antisocial behavior that violate social norms and the rights of others. Whereas children with ADHD throw temper tantrums, children diagnosed as conduct disordered are intentionally aggressive and cruel. Like antisocial adults, many conduct-disordered children are callous and apparently do not experience guilt or remorse for their misdeeds. They may steal or de-

THINK ABOUT IT
What are the risks and benefits of using stimulant medication, like Ritalin, in treating ADHD in children? If you had a child with ADHD, would you consider using these drugs? Why or why not?

conduct disorder A psychological disorder in childhood and adolescence characterized by disruptive, antisocial behavior.

stroy property. In adolescence they may commit rape, armed robbery, even homicide. They may cheat in school—when they bother to attend—and lie to cover their tracks. They frequently engage in substance abuse and sexual activity.

Rates of conduct disorder in the general population range from less than 1% to more than 10%, depending on the particular study (APA, 2000). Conduct disorders are much more common among boys than girls, and the disorder typically takes a somewhat different form in boys than girls. In boys, conduct disorder is more likely to be manifested by stealing, fighting, vandalism, or disciplinary problems at school, whereas in girls it is more likely to involve lying, truancy, running away, substance use, and prostitution. Children with conduct disorder often present with other disorders or problem behaviors, including ADHD, social withdrawal, and major depression (Lambert et al., 2001).

Conduct disorder is typically a chronic or persistent disorder (Lahey et al., 1995). Longitudinal studies show that elementary school children with conduct disorder are more likely than other children to engage in delinquent acts as early adolescents (Tremblay et al., 1992). Antisocial behavior in the form of delinquent acts (stealing, truancy, vandalism, fighting or threatening others, and so on) during early adolescence (ages 14 to 15) has also been found to predict alcohol and substance abuse in late adolescence, especially among boys (Boyle et al., 1992). Another form of conduct disorder may involve a cluster of personality traits that have different origins than antisocial behavior (Wootton et al., 1997). These personality traits include callousness (uncaring, mean, cruel) and an unemotional way of relating to others (Barry et al., 2000).

Oppositional Defiant Disorder

Debate continues among professionals over the issue of whether conduct disorder (CD) and **oppositional defiant disorder (ODD)** are separate disorders or variations of a common disruptive behavior disorder (Rey, 1993). Or perhaps ODD is a precursor or milder form of conduct disorder (Abikoff & Klein, 1992; Biederman et al., 1996a). At present, the two disorders are conceptualized as related but separate. ODD is more closely related to nondelinquent (negativistic) conduct disturbance, and conduct disorder involves more outright delinquent behavior in the form of truancy, stealing, lying, and aggression (Rey, 1993). Yet oppositional defiant disorder, which typically develops earlier than CD, may lead to the development of antisocial behavior and conduct disorder at later ages (Loeber, Lahey, & Thomas, 1991).

Children with ODD tend to be negativistic or oppositional. They are defiant of authority, which is exhibited by their tendency to argue with parents and teachers and refuse to follow requests or directives from adults. They may deliberately annoy other people, become easily angered or lose their temper, become touchy or easily annoyed, blame others for their mistakes or misbehavior, feel resentful toward others, or act in spiteful or vindictive ways toward others (Angold & Costello, 1996; APA, 2000). The disorder typically begins before age 8 and develops gradually over a period of months or years. It typically starts in the home environment but may extend to other settings, such as school.

ODD is one of the most common diagnoses among children (Doll, 1996). Studies show that among children diagnosed with a psychological disorder, about one in three are judged to meet criteria for ODD (Rey, 1993). A recent view of epidemiological studies estimated the prevalence of ODD among children in the general community at about 6% (Rey, 1993). ODD is more common overall among boys than girls. However, this overall effect masks a gender shift over age. Among children 12 years of age or younger, ODD appears to be more than twice as common among boys. Yet among adolescents, a higher prevalence is reported in girls (Rey, 1993). By contrast, most studies find conduct disorder to be more common in boys than girls across all age groups.

Theoretical Perspectives on ODD and CD The causal factors in ODD remain obscure. Some theorists believe that oppositionality is an expression of an underlying child temperament described as the "difficult-child" type (Rey, 1993). Others believe that unresolved parent-child conflicts or overly strict parental control may lie at the root of the disorder. Psychodynamic theorists look at ODD as a sign of fixation at the anal stage of psychosexual

oppositional defiant disorder (ODD) A psychological disorder in childhood and adolescence characterized by excessive oppositionality or tendencies to refuse requests from parents and others.

Oppositional defiant disorder (ODD). ODD is characterized by negativistic and oppositional behavior in response to directives from parents, teachers, or other authority figures. Children with ODD may act spitefully or vindictively toward others, but do not typically show the cruelty, aggressivity, and delinquent behavior associated with conduct disorder. Yet questions remain about whether the two disorders are truly distinct or are variations of a common underlying disorder involving disruptive behavior patterns.

development, when conflicts between the parent and child may emerge over toilet training. Leftover conflicts may later become expressed in the form of rebelliousness against parental wishes (Egan, 1991). Learning theorists view oppositional behaviors as arising from parental use of inappropriate reinforcement strategies. In this view, parents may inappropriately reinforce oppositional behavior by "giving in" to the child's demands whenever the child refuses to comply with the parent's wishes, which can become a pattern.

Family factors are also implicated in the development of conduct disorder. Some forms of conduct disorder appear to be linked to ineffective parenting styles, such as failure to provide positive reinforcement for appropriate behavior and use of harsh and inconsistent discipline for misbehavior. Families of children with CD tend to be characterized by negative, coercive interactions (Dadds et al., 1992). Children with CD are often very demanding and noncompliant in relating to their parents and other family members. Family members often reciprocate by using negative behaviors, such as threatening or yelling at the child or using physical means of coercion. Parental aggression against children with conduct behavior problems is common, including pushing, grabbing, slapping, spanking, hitting, or kicking (Jourile et al., 1997). Parents of children with oppositional defiant disorders or severe conduct disorder display high rates of antisocial personality disorder and substance abuse (Frick et al., 1992). It's not too much of a stretch to speculate that parental modeling of antisocial behaviors can lead to antisocial conduct in children.

Conduct disorders often occur in a context of parental distress, such as marital conflict. Another factor is maternal depression. Depressed mothers tend to display poor parenting behaviors—such as vague and interrupted commands—that may foster disruptive behavior in their children (Forehand et al., 1988). Mothers of children with conduct disorders are also more likely than other mothers to be inconsistent in their use of discipline and less able to supervise their children's behavior (Frick et al., 1992). Maternal smoking during pregnancy has also been linked to a greater likelihood of conduct disorder in sons (Wakschlag et al., 1997). Perhaps maternal smoking affects the developing fetus in ways that lead to conduct problems, or perhaps there are other characteristics of mothers who smoke, such as ineffective parenting skills, that set the stage for childhood behavior problems.

Some investigations focus on the ways in which children with disruptive behavior disorders process information. For example, children who are overly aggressive in their behavior tend to be biased in their processing of social information: They may assume that others intend them ill when they do not (Lochman, 1992). They usually blame others for the scrapes they get into. They believe that they are misperceived and treated unfairly. They may believe that aggression leads to favorable results (Dodge et al., 1997). They are also less able than their peers to generate alternative, nonviolent, responses to social conflicts (Lochman & Dodge, 1994).

Genetic factors may interact with family or other psychosocial factors in the development of conduct disorder (APA, 2000; O'Connor et al., 1998; Slutske et al., 1998). Genetic factors may also be involved in the development of oppositional defiant disorder.

Treatment The treatment of conduct disorders remains a challenge. Although there is no established pharmacological treatment approach, a recent study indicates that Ritalin may be effective in reducing antisocial behavior in CD children and adolescents (Klein et al., 1997). Traditional psychotherapy has not generally been shown to help disruptive children change their behavior. Placing children with conduct disorders in residential treatment programs that establish explicit rules and clear rewards for obeying them may offer greater promise (e.g., Henggeler et al., 1986). Such programs usually rely on operant conditioning procedures that involve systematic use of rewards and punishments.

Many children with conduct disorders, especially boys, display aggressive behavior and have problems controlling their anger. Many can benefit from programs designed to help them learn anger coping skills that they can use to handle conflict situations without resorting to violent behavior. Cognitive-behavioral therapy has been used to teach boys who engage in antisocial and aggressive behavior to reconceptualize social provocations as problems to be solved rather than as challenges to their manhood that must be answered with violence. They have been trained to use calming self-talk to inhibit impulsive behavior and control anger whenever they experience social taunts or provocations and to generate and try out nonviolent solutions to social conflicts (Lochman & Lenhart, 1993). Other programs present child models on videotape demonstrating skills of anger control. The results of these programs appear promising (Kazdin & Weisz, 1998; Webster-Stratton & Hammond, 1997). Sometimes the disruptive child's parents are brought into the treatment process (Kazdin, Siegel, & Bass, 1992).

Henggeler and his colleagues (1986) have developed a "family-ecological" approach based on Urie Bronfenbrenner's (1979) ecological theory. Like Bronfenbrenner, Henggeler sees children as embedded within various social systems—family, school, criminal justice, community, and so on. He focuses on how juvenile offenders affect and are affected by the systems with which they interact. The techniques themselves are not unique. Rather, the family-ecological approach tries to change children's relationships with multiple systems to end disruptive interactions. This multiple systems or *multisystemic therapy (MST) approach* has shown promising results in the treatment of juvenile offenders in terms of reducing the frequency of subsequent arrests in comparison with youths who received typical youth services from a county youth services department (Henggeler, Melton, & Smith, 1992; Henggeler et al., 1997; Kazdin, 1998).

The following example illustrates the involvement of the parents in the behavioral treatment of a case of oppositional defiant disorder:

A Case of Oppositional Defiant Disorder

Billy was a 7-year-old second grader referred by his parents. The family was relocated frequently because the father was in the navy. Billy usually behaved when his father was taking care of him, but he was noncompliant with his mother and yelled at her when she gave him instructions. His mother was incurring great stress in the effort to control Billy, especially when her husband was at sea.

Billy had become a problem at home and in school during the first grade. He ignored and violated rules in both settings. Billy failed to carry out his chores and frequently yelled at and hit his younger brother. When he acted up, his parents would restrict him to his room or the yard, take away privileges and toys, and spank him. But all of these measures were used inconsistently. He also played on the railroad tracks near his home and twice the police had brought him home after he had thrown rocks at cars.

A home observation showed that Billy's mother often gave him inappropriate commands. She interacted with him as little as possible and showed no verbal praise, physical closeness, smiles, or positive facial expressions or gestures. She paid attention to him only when he misbehaved. When Billy was noncompliant, she would yell back at him and then try to catch him to force him to comply. Billy would then laugh and run from her.

Billy's parents were informed that the child's behavior was a product of inappropriate cueing techniques (poor directions), a lack of reinforcement for appropriate behavior, and lack of consistent sanctions for misbehavior. They were taught the appropriate use of reinforcement, punishment, and time out. The parents then charted Billy's problem behaviors to gain a clearer idea of what triggered and maintained them. They were shown how to reinforce acceptable behavior and use time out as a contingent punishment for misbehavior. Billy's mother was also taught relaxation training to help desensitize her to Billy's disruptions. Biofeedback was used to enhance the relaxation response.

During a 15-day baseline period, Billy behaved in a noncompliant manner about four times per day. When treatment was begun, Billy showed an immediate drop to about one instance of noncompliance every two days. Follow-up data showed that instances of noncompliance were maintained at a bearable level of about one per day. Fewer behavioral problems in school were also reported, even though they had not been addressed directly.

—*Adapted from Kaplan, 1986, pp. 227–230*

time out A behavioral technique in which a person who behaves in an undesirable way is removed from a reinforcing environment and placed in an unreinforcing environment for a short time.

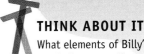

THINK ABOUT IT

What elements of Billy's treatment do you believe contributed to its effectiveness? Would this type of approach be likely to be as effective with a conduct disorder?

Quiz 14.6
Attention-Deficit and Disruptive Behavior Disorders

Social avoidance. Socially avoidant children tend to be excessively shy and withdrawn and have difficulty interacting with other children.

Truth OR Fiction? REVISITED

Major depression rarely occurs before adulthood.

FALSE. Major depression is actually quite common in later childhood and adolescence.

Web Link 14.6 wWw
Depression in Children and Adolescents

---

separation anxiety disorder A childhood disorder characterized by extreme fear of separation from parents or other caretakers.

Anxiety and Depression

Anxieties and fears are a normal feature of childhood, just as they are a normal feature of adult life. Childhood fears—of the dark or of small animals—are commonplace and are usually outgrown naturally. Anxiety is considered abnormal, however, when it is excessive and interferes with normal academic or social functioning or becomes troubling or persistent. Children, like adults, may suffer from different types of diagnosable anxiety disorders, including specific phobias, social phobias, generalized anxiety disorder (GAD), PTSD, and mood disorders, including major depression and bipolar disorder. Although these disorders may develop at any age, we will consider further a type of disorder that typically develops during early childhood: separation anxiety disorder.

Children may also show the more general pattern of avoidance of social interactions that characterizes avoidant personality disorder. Although children who are socially avoidant or have social anxiety disorder (also called social phobia) may have warm relationships with family members, they tend to be shy and withdrawn around others. Their avoidance of people outside the family interferes with their development of social relationships with their peers. Such problems tend to develop after normal fear of strangers fades, at age 2½ or later. Their distress at being around other children at school can also affect their academic progress. Having a social anxiety disorder during adolescence or young adult also increases the likelihood of later developing a depressive disorder (Stein et al., 2001).

We may think of childhood as the happiest time of life. Most children are protected by their parents and are unencumbered by adult responsibilities. From the perspective of aging adults, their bodies seem made of rubber and free of aches. They have apparently boundless energy. Despite the stereotype of a happy childhood, clinical depression is common among children and adolescents. Estimates indicate that perhaps 8% to 9% of children in the 10- to 13-year age range experience major depression during any given 1-year period (Goleman, 1994a). Although rare, major depression has even been found among preschoolers. Although there is no discernible gender difference in the risk of depression in childhood, a prominent gender differences appears after the age of 15, with adolescent girls becoming about twice as likely to become depressed as adolescent boys (Hankin et al., 1998; Lewinsohn, Rohde, & Seeley, 1994).

Separation Anxiety Disorder

It is normal for young children to show anxiety when they are separated from their caregivers. Mary Ainsworth (1989), who has chronicled the development of attachment behaviors, notes that separation anxiety is a normal feature of the child-caregiver relationship and begins during the first year. The sense of security normally provided by bonds of attachment apparently encourages children to explore their environments and become progressively independent of their caregivers (Bowlby, 1988).

Separation anxiety disorder is diagnosed when separation anxiety is persistent and excessive or inappropriate for the child's developmental level. That is, 3-year-olds ought to be able to attend preschool without nausea and vomiting brought on by anxiety. Six-year-olds ought to be able to attend first grade without persistent dread that something awful will happen to themselves or their parents. Children with this disorder tend to cling to their parents and follow them around the house. They may voice concerns about death and dying and insist that someone stay with them while they are falling asleep. Other features of the disorder include nightmares, stomachaches, nausea and vomiting when separation is anticipated (as on school days), pleading with parents not to leave, or throwing tantrums when parents are about to depart. Children may refuse to attend school for fear that something will happen to their parents while they are away. The disorder affects about 4% of children and young adolescents and occurs more frequently, according to community-based studies, among females (APA, 2000). The disorder may persist into adulthood, leading to an exaggerated concern about the well-being of one's children and spouse and difficulty tolerating any separation from them.

In previous years, separation anxiety disorder was usually referred to as *school phobia.* Separation anxiety disorder may occur at preschool ages, however. Today, most cases in which younger children refuse to attend school are viewed as forms of separation anxiety. In adolescence, however, refusal to attend school is also frequently connected with academic and social concerns, in which case the label of separation anxiety disorder would not apply.

The development of separation anxiety disorder frequently follows a stressful life event, such as illness, the death of a relative or pet, or a change of schools or homes. Alison's problems followed the death of her grandmother:

Alison's Fear of Death

Alison's grandmother died when Alison was 7 years old. Her parents decided to permit her request to view her grandmother in the open coffin. Alison took a tentative glance from her father's arms across the room, then asked to be taken out of the room. Her 5-year-old sister took a leisurely close-up look, with no apparent distress.

Alison had been concerned about death for two or three years by this time, but her grandmother's passing brought on a new flurry of questions: "Will I die?", "Does everybody die?", and so on. Her parents tried to reassure her by saying, "Grandma was very, very old, and she also had a heart condition. You are very young and in perfect health. You have many, many years before you have to start thinking about death."

Alison also could not be alone in any room in her house. She pulled one of her parents or her sister along with her everywhere she went. She also reported nightmares about her grandmother and, within a couple of days, insisted on sleeping in the same room with her parents. Fortunately, Alison's fears did not extend to school. Her teacher reported that Alison spent some time talking about her grandmother, but her academic performance was apparently unimpaired.

Alison's parents decided to allow Alison time to "get over" the loss. Alison gradually talked less and less about death, and by the time 3 months had passed, she was able to go into any room in her house by herself. She wanted to continue to sleep in her parents' bedroom, however. So her parents "made a deal" with her. They would put off the return to her own bedroom until the school year had ended (a month away), if Alison would agree to return to her own bed at that time. As a further incentive, a parent would remain with her until she fell asleep for the first month. Alison overcame the anxiety problem in this fashion with no additional delays.

—From the Authors' Files

Perspectives on Anxiety Disorders in Childhood

Theoretical understandings of excessive anxiety in children to some degree parallel explanations of anxiety disorders in adults. Psychoanalytic theorists argue that childhood anxieties and fears, like their adult counterparts, symbolize unconscious conflicts. Cognitive theorists focus on the role of cognitive biases underlying anxiety reactions. In support of the cognitive model, investigators find that highly anxious children show cognitive biases in processing information, such as interpreting ambiguous situations as threatening, expecting negative outcomes, doubting their ability to deal with problem situations, and engaging in negative self-talk (e.g., Bögels & Zigerman, 2000; Weems et al., 2001). Expecting the worst,

THINK ABOUT IT
Where would you draw the line between "normal" childhood fears and specific phobias?

Separation anxiety. In separation anxiety disorder, a child shows persistent anxiety when separated from her or his parents that is inconsistent with her or his developmental level. Such children tend to cling to their parents and resist even brief separations.

combined with having low self-confidence, encourages avoidance of feared activities—with friends, in school, and elsewhere. Negative expectations also heighten feelings of anxiety to the point where they may impair performance in the classroom or the athletic field.

Learning theorists suggest that the occurrence of generalized anxiety may touch on broad themes, such as fears of rejection or failure that carry across situations. Underlying fears of rejection or self-perceptions of inadequacy may generalize to most areas of social interaction and achievement. Genetics may also play a role in separation anxiety and other anxiety disorders (Coyle, 2001).

Whatever the causes, overanxious children may profit from the anxiety-control techniques we discussed in Chapter 6, such as gradual exposure to phobic stimuli and relaxation training. Cognitive techniques such as replacing anxious self-talk with coping self-talk may also be helpful. Cognitive-behavioral approaches have produced impressive results in treating childhood anxiety disorders (Barrett et al., 2001; Beidel, Turner, & Morris, 2000; Braswell & Kendall, 2001). Treatment with the drug fluvoxamine (Luvox), a selective serotonin-reuptake inhibitor, also shows good therapeutic effects in treating children and adolescents with various types of anxiety disorders (Coyle, 2001; Riddle et al., 2001; Walkup et al., 2001).

Depression in Childhood and Adolescence

Children and adolescents may suffer from diagnosable mood disorders, including bipolar disorder and major depression. Like depressed adults, depressed children and adolescents typically have feelings of hopelessness, more distorted thinking patterns and tendencies to blame themselves for negative events, and lower self-esteem, self-confidence, and perceptions of competence than their nondepressed peers (Lewinsohn et al., 1994; Kovacs, 1996). They often report episodes of sadness and crying, feelings of apathy, as well as insomnia, fatigue, and poor appetite. They may also experience suicidal thoughts or even attempt suicide. Yet depression in children may be associated with some distinctive features as well, such as refusal to attend school, fears of parents' dying, and clinging to parents. Depression may also be masked by behaviors that do not appear directly related to depression. Conduct disorders, academic problems, physical complaints, and even hyperactivity may stem, now and then, from unrecognized depression. Among adolescents, aggressive and sexual acting out may also be signs of underlying depression.

One thing we should recognize is that depressed children or adolescents may fail to label what they are feeling as depression. They may not report feeling sad even though they appear sad to others and may be tearful (Goleman, 1994a). Part of the problem is cognitive-developmental. Children are not usually capable of recognizing internal feeling states until about the age of 7. They may not be able to identify negative feeling states in themselves, including depression, until adolescence (Larson et al., 1990). Even adolescents may not recognize what they are experiencing as depression.

The average length of a major depressive episode in childhood or adolescence is about 11 months, but an individual episode may last for as long as 18 months in some cases (Goleman, 1994a). Moderate levels of depression, however, may persist for years, severely impacting school performance and social functioning (Nolen-Hoeksema & Girgus, 1994). Adolescent depression is associated with an increased risk of future major depressive episodes and suicide attempts in adulthood (Weissman, 1999). About three of four children who become depressed from age 8 to 13 have a recurrence later in life (Goleman, 1994a).

Depressed children may also lack various skills, including academic, athletic, and social skills (Seroczynski, Cole, & Maxwell, 1997). They may find it hard to concentrate in school and may suffer from impaired memory, making it difficult for them to keep their grades up (Goleman, 1994a). They often keep their feelings to themselves, which may prevent their parents from recognizing the problem and seeking help for them. Negative feelings may also be expressed in the form of anger, sullenness, or impatience, leading to conflicts with parents that in turn can accentuate and prolong depression in the child.

Childhood depression rarely occurs by itself. Depressed children typically experience other psychological disorders, especially anxiety disorders and conduct or oppositional

Is this child too young to be depressed? Although we tend to think of childhood as the happiest and most carefree time of life, depression is actually quite common among children and adolescents. Depressed children may report feelings of sadness and lack of interest in previously enjoyable activities. Many, however, do not report or are not aware of feelings of depression, even though they may look depressed to observers. Depression may also be masked by other problems, such as conduct or school-related problems, physical complaints, and overactivity.

defiant disorders (Hammen & Compas, 1994). Eating disorders are also common among depressed adolescents, at least among females (Rohde, Lewinsohn, & Seeley, 1991). Overall, childhood depression increases the chances that a child will develop another psychological disorder by at least 20-fold (Angold & Costello, 1993). A sizeable percentage of depressed adolescents (between 20% and 40%) later develop bipolar disorder (USDHHS, 1999a).

THINK ABOUT IT
What behaviors in children might be masking unrecognized depression?

Correlates and Treatment of Depression in Childhood and Adolescence

Depression and suicidal behavior in childhood are frequently related to family problems and conflicts. Children who are exposed to stressful life events affecting the family, such as parental conflict or unemployment, stand an increased risk of depression, especially younger children (Nolen-Hoeksema, Girgus, & Seligman, 1992). Stressful life events and a lack of social support from friends and family also figure into the profile of adolescents who become depressed (Lewinsohn et al., 1994). Depression in adolescents may be triggered by such stressful life events as conflicts with parents and dissatisfaction with school grades. In girls, disturbed eating behaviors and body dissatisfaction after puberty often predict which girls will go on to develop major depression during adolescence (Stice et al., 2000). Interestingly, the relationship between loss of a parent in childhood and later depression during childhood or adolescence is not a consistent finding; some studies show a connection whereas others do not (Lewinsohn et al., 1994).

As children mature and their cognitive abilities increase, however, cognitive factors, such as attributional styles, appear to play a stronger role in the development of depression. Older children (sixth and seventh graders) who adopt a more helpless or pessimistic explanatory style (attributing negative events to internal, stable, and global causes, and attributing positive events to external, unstable, and specific causes) are more likely than children with a more optimistic explanatory style to develop depression (Nolen-Hoeksema et al., 1992). Researchers also find that adolescents who are depressed tend to hold more dysfunctional attitudes and to adopt a more helpless explanatory style than do their non-depressed peers (Lewinsohn et al., 1994). Like their adult counterparts, children and adolescents with depression tend to adopt a cognitive style that is characterized by negative attitudes toward themselves and the future (Garber, Weiss, & Shanley, 1993). All in all, the distorted cognitions of depressed children include the following:

1. Expecting the worst (pessimism)
2. Catastrophizing the consequences of negative events
3. Assuming personal responsibility for negative outcomes, even when it is unwarranted
4. Selectively attending to the negative aspects of events

Although there are links between cognitive factors and depression, it remains to be determined whether children become depressed because of a depressive mindset or whether depression causes changes in thinking patterns (USDHHS, 1999a). Genetic factors also appear to play a role in explaining depressive symptoms, at least among adolescents (O'Connor et al., 1998). The role of genetics in childhood depression requires further study, however (Kovacs et al., 1997).

Adolescent girls face a greater risk of depression than do adolescent boys, perhaps because they typically face more social challenges than boys—challenges such as pressures to narrow their interests and pursue feminine-typed activities (Nolen-Hoeksema & Girgus, 1994). Girls who adopt a more passive, ruminative style of coping may be at greatest risk of becoming depressed. Gender differences in adolescent depression may have a cultural component. A recent study reported that gender differences in depressive symptoms were greater among U.S. adolescents than among Chinese adolescents (Greenberger et al., 2000). The reasons for these cross-cultural differences remain to be explored.

Accumulating evidence supports the effectiveness of cognitive-behavioral therapy (CBT) in treating depressed children and adolescents (Berman et al., 2000; Braswell & Kendall, 2001; Lewinsohn & Clarke, 1999). Although individual approaches vary, CBT usually involves a coping skills model in which children or adolescents receive social skills

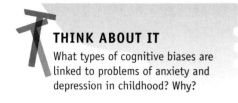

THINK ABOUT IT
What types of cognitive biases are linked to problems of anxiety and depression in childhood? Why?

training (e.g., learning how to start a conversation or make friends) to increase the likelihood of obtaining social reinforcement (Kazdin & Weisz, 1998). CBT typically also includes training in problem-solving skills and ways of increasing the frequency of rewarding activities and countering depressive styles of thinking. In addition, family therapy may be useful in helping families resolve underlying conflicts and reorganize their relationships in ways that members can become more supportive of each other.

We should not assume that because antidepressants are effective in treating depression in adults they will work as well, or be as safe, when used with children (Bitiello & Jensen, 1997). However, SSRI-type antidepressants, such as Prozac, have shown promise in treating depression in children and adolescents (USDHHS, 1999a). Lithium is also used with generally favorable results in treating children and adolescents with bipolar disorder (USDHHS, 1999a).

Suicide Among Children and Adolescents Suicide is relatively uncommon among younger children and adolescents, with statistics showing less than 1 case per 100,000 persons among younger children and fewer than 2 cases per 100,000 among 10- to 14-year-olds (Brody, 1992b; "Report: Adolescent Suicide," 1995). Despite the low frequency, the rate among the 10- to 14-year-olds more than doubled from 1980 to the early 1990s, although it fell slightly for the population under age 25 on the whole (Gelman, 1994). The suicide rate for adolescents in the 15 to 19 age range is considerably higher, some 8 per 100,000 persons (USDHHS, 1991b) and has risen sharply since the mid-20th century. More ready access to guns, together with a rising incidence of family disruption and disintegration, may help explain the rise in adolescent suicides. These official statistics only account for reported suicide; some apparent accidental deaths, such as those due to falling from a window, may be suicides as well.

Despite the commonly held view that children and adolescents who talk about suicide are only venting their feelings, young people who do intend to kill themselves may very well talk about it beforehand (Brody, 1992b). In fact, those who discuss their plans are the ones most likely to carry them out. Moreover, children and adolescents who have survived suicide attempts are most likely to try it again (Brody, 1992b). Unfortunately, parents tend not to take their children's suicidal talk seriously. They often refuse treatment for their children, or terminate treatment prematurely.

Several factors are associated with an increased risk of suicide among children and adolescents (Levy, Jurkovic, & Spirito, 1995; Lewinsohn et al., 1994, 2001; Neiger, 1988):

1. *Gender.* Girls, like women, are three times more likely than boys to attempt suicide. Boys, like men, are more likely to succeed, however, perhaps because boys, like men, are more apt to use lethal means, such as guns. The presence of a loaded handgun in the house turns out to be the greatest risk factor for completed suicide among children, even those as young as 5 (Brody, 1992b).

2. *Age.* Young people in late adolescence or early adulthood (ages 15 to 24) are at greater risk than younger adolescents.

3. *Geography.* Adolescents in less populated areas are more likely to commit suicide. Adolescents in the rural western regions of the United States have the highest suicide rate.

4. *Race.* The suicide rates for African American, Asian American, and Hispanic American youth are about 30% to 60% lower than that of non-Hispanic White youth (USDHHS, 1991a). Among young adults age 15 to 24, Native Americans commit suicide nearly twice as often as do European Americans. Although European American teens are more likely to commit suicide than African American teens, rates of suicide are rising fastest among African American teenage males (Shaffer, Gould, & Hicks, 1994).

5. *Depression and hopelessness.* Major depression with features of hopelessness and low self-esteem are major risk factors for suicide among adolescents, as it is among adults (USDHHS, 1999a).

6. *Previous suicidal behavior.* One quarter of adolescents who attempt suicide are repeaters. More than 80% of adolescents who take their lives have talked about it before doing so. Suicidal teenagers may carry lethal weapons, talk about death, make

suicide plans, or engage in risky or dangerous behavior. A family history of suicide also increases risk of teenage suicide (Mann et al., 1996).

7. *Family problems.* Family problems are present among about 75% of adolescent suicide attempters. The problems include family instability and conflict, physical or sexual abuse, loss of a parent due to death or separation, and poor parent-child communication (Asarnow, Carlson, & Guthrie, 1987; Wagner, 1997).

8. *Stressful life events.* Many suicides among young people are directly preceded by stressful or traumatic events, such as breaking up with a girlfriend or boyfriend, having an unwanted pregnancy, getting arrested, having problems at school, moving to a new school, or having to take an important test.

9. *Substance abuse.* Addiction in the adolescent's family, or by the adolescent, is a factor.

10. *Social contagion.* Adolescent suicides sometimes occur in clusters, especially when a suicide or a group of suicides receives widespread publicity (Kessler et al., 1990; USDHHS, 1999a). Adolescents may romanticize suicide as a heroic act of defiance. There are often suicides or attempts among the siblings, friends, parents, or adult relatives of suicidal adolescents. Adolescent suicides may occur in bunches in a community, especially when adolescents are subjected to mounting academic pressures, such as competing for admission to college. Perhaps the suicide of a family member or schoolmate renders suicide a more "real" option for managing stress or punishing others. Perhaps the other person's suicide gives the adolescent the impression that he or she is "doomed" to commit suicide. Note the case of Pam:

Web Link 14.7
Teen Suicide: American Psychiatic Association

Pam, Kim, and Now Brian

Pam was an exceptionally attractive 17-year-old who was hospitalized after cutting her wrists. "Before we moved to [an upper-middle-class town in Westchester County]," she told the psychologist, "I was the brightest girl in the class. Teachers loved me. If we had had a yearbook, I'd have been the most likely to succeed. Then we moved, and suddenly I was hit with it. Everybody was bright, or tried to be. Suddenly I was just another ordinary student planning to go to college.

"Teachers were good to me, but I was no longer special, and that hurt. Then we all applied to college. Do you know that 90 percent of the kids in the high school go on to college? I mean four-year colleges? And we all knew—or suspected—that the good schools had quotas on kids from here. I mean you can't have 30 kids from our senior class going to Yale or Princeton or Wellesley, can you? You're better off applying from Utah.

"Then Kim got her early-acceptance rejection from Brown. Kim was number one in the class. Nobody could believe it. Her father'd gone to Brown and Kim had almost 1500 SATs. Kim was out of commission for a few days—I mean she didn't come to school or anything—and then, boom, she was gone. She offed herself, kaput, no more, the end. Then Brian was rejected from Cornell. A few days later, he was gone, too. And I'm like, 'These kids were better than me.' I mean their grades and their SATs were higher than mine, and I was going to apply to Brown and Cornell. I'm like, 'What chance do I have? Why bother?' "

—*From the Authors' Files*

■

THINK ABOUT IT
Considering the risk factors presented in the text, do you know anyone who is at high risk? What could be done to lower the risk of that person committing suicide?

You can see how catastrophizing cognitions can play a role in such tragic cases. Consistent with the literature on suicide among adults, suicidal children make little use of active problem-solving strategies in handling stressful situations. They may see no other way out of their perceived failures or stresses. As with adults, one approach to working with suicidal children involves helping them challenge distorted thinking and generate alternate strategies for handling the problems and stressors they face.

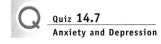

Quiz 14.7
Anxiety and Depression

Truth OR Fiction? REVISITED

Problems of persistent bed-wetting in childhood generally persist into adolescence.

FALSE. Most cases of enuresis usually resolve themselves by adolescence at the latest.

enuresis Failure to control urination after one has reached the "normal" age for attaining such control.

Elimination Disorders

Fetuses and newborn children eliminate waste products reflexively. As children develop, they are trained to inhibit the natural reflexes that govern urination and bowel movements. In the classic *Patterns of Child Rearing,* Robert Sears and his colleagues (1957) reported that American children were toilet trained, on the average, at 18 months. However, nighttime bladder accidents occurred frequently until about 24 months. Today, most children in the United States achieve bladder control between the ages of 2 and 3. Many continue to have nighttime accidents for another year or so, however. Enuresis and encopresis are disorders involving problems with elimination that are not due to organic causes.

Enuresis

Enuresis derives from the Greek roots *en-*, meaning "in," and *ouron,* meaning "urine." **Enuresis** is failure to control urination after one has reached the "normal" age for attaining such control. Conceptions of what age is normal for achieving control can vary among clinicians. *DSM-IV* standards are shown in Table 14.7. Enuresis, like so many other developmental disorders, is more common among boys. Enuresis is estimated to affect 7% of boys and 3% of girls by age 5. The disorder usually resolves itself by adolescence if not earlier, although in about 1% of cases the problem continues into adulthood (APA, 2000).

Enuresis may occur during nighttime sleep only, during waking hours only, or both during nighttime sleep and waking hours. Nighttime-only enuresis is the most common type, and accidents occurring during sleep are referred to as *bed-wetting.* Achieving bladder control at night is more difficult than achieving daytime control. When asleep at night, children must learn to wake up when they feel the pressure of a full bladder and then go to the bathroom to relieve themselves. The younger the "trained" child is, the more likely she or he is to wet the bed at night. It is perfectly normal for children who have acquired daytime control over their bladders to have nighttime accidents for a year or more. Bed-wetting usually occurs during the deepest stage of sleep and may reflect immaturity of the nervous system. The diagnosis of enuresis applies in cases of repeated bed-wetting or daytime wetting of clothes by children of at least 5 years of age.

Theoretical Perspectives Numerous psychological explanations of enuresis have been advanced. Psychodynamic explanations suggest that enuresis may represent the expression of hostility toward children's parents because of harsh toilet training. It may represent regression in response to the birth of a sibling or some other stressor or life change, such as starting school or suffering the death of a parent or relative. Learning theorists point out that enuresis occurs most commonly in children whose parents attempted to train them early. Early failures may have connected anxiety with efforts to control the bladder. Conditioned anxiety, then, induces rather than curbs urination.

Evidence from a 1995 Danish study strongly suggests that *primary enuresis,* the most prevalent form of the disorder, which characterizes children who have persistent bed-wetting and have never established urinary control, is genetically transmitted (Eiberg, Berendt, & Mohr, 1995; Goleman, 1995e). We don't yet understand the genetic mechanism accounting for the transmission of the disorder, but one possibility is that it may involve genes that regulate the rate of development of motor control over eliminatory reflexes by the cerebral cortex. Although genetic factors appear to be involved in the transmission of primary enuresis, it is likely that environmental and behavioral factors also come into play in determining the development and course of the disorder. The other type of enuresis, *secondary enuresis,* characterizes children who develop the problem after having established urinary control and is associated with occasional bed-wetting. Genetic factors are apparently not involved in this type of enuresis (Goleman, 1995e).

Treatment Enuresis usually resolves itself as children mature. Behavioral methods have been shown to be helpful when enuresis endures or causes parents or children great distress, however. Such methods condition children to wake up when their bladders are full. One reasonably dependable example is Mowrer's bell-and-pad method.

The problem in bed-wetting is that children with enuresis continue to sleep despite bladder tension that awakens most other children. As a consequence, they reflexively urinate in bed. Psychologist O. Hobart Mowrer pioneered the bell-and-pad method, in which a special pad is placed beneath the sleeping child. When the pad is wet, an electrical circuit closes, causing a bell to ring and the sleeping child to waken. After several repetitions, most children learn to wake up in response to bladder tension—*before* they wet the pad. The technique is usually explained through principles of classical conditioning. In the bell-and-pad method, tension in children's bladder is paired repeatedly with a stimulus (a bell) that wakes them up. The bladder tension (conditioned stimulus, or CS) comes to elicit the same response (waking up—the conditioned response, or CR) that is elicited by the bell (the unconditioned stimulus, or US). Variations of the bell-and-pad method have also been used successfully with adults who have enuresis (van Son, Mulder, & Londen, 1990).

Both psychological treatment, usually involving the Mowrer urine alarm technique or some variation, or drug therapy, are often helpful in treating enuresis. The drug fluvoxamine, an SSRI-type antidepressant, works on brain systems that control urination (Kano & Arisaka, 2000; Horrigan, & Barnhill, 2000). The available evidence points to better results with psychological treatment, however (Houts, Berman, & Abramson, 1994).

Encopresis

Encopresis derives from the Greek roots *en-* and *kopros,* meaning "feces." **Encopresis** is lack of control over bowel movements that is not caused by an organic problem. The child must have a chronological age of at least 4, or in children with developmental delays, a mental age of at least 4 years (APA, 2000). About 1% of 5-year-olds have encopresis. Soiling, like enuresis, is more common among boys. Encopresis is rare among adolescents in their middle teens, except among teens who are profoundly or severely retarded. Soiling may be voluntary or involuntary and is not caused by an organic problem, except in cases in which constipation is involved (APA, 2000). Among the possible predisposing factors are inconsistent or incomplete toilet training and psychosocial stressors, such as the birth of a sibling or beginning school.

Soiling, unlike enuresis, is more likely to happen during the day than at night. It can thus be keenly embarrassing to the child. Classmates often avoid or ridicule soilers. Because feces have a strong odor, teachers may find it hard to act as though nothing of consequence has happened. Parents, too, are eventually galled by recurrent soiling and may increase their demands for self-control and employ powerful punishments for failure. Because of all this, the child may start to hide soiled underwear. Such children may distance themselves from classmates, or feign sickness to stay at home. Their levels of anxiety concerning soiling increase. Because anxiety (arousal of the sympathetic branch of the autonomic nervous system) promotes bowel movements, control may become yet more elusive.

When soiling is involuntary, it is often associated with constipation, impaction, or retention that results in subsequent overflow. Constipation may be related to psychological factors, such as fears associated with defecating in a particular place or with a more general pattern of negativistic or oppositional behavior. Or constipation may be related to physiological factors, such as complications from an illness or from medication. Much less frequently, encopresis is deliberate or intentional.

Soiling often appears to follow harsh punishment of an accident or two, particularly in children who are already highly stressed or anxious. Harsh punishment may rivet children's attention on soiling. They may then ruminate about soiling, raising their level of anxiety so that self-control is impaired.

Operant conditioning methods may be helpful in dealing with soiling. These employ rewards (by praise and other means) for successful attempts at self-control and mild punishments for continued accidents (for example, gentle reminders to attend more closely to bowel tension and having the child clean her or his own underwear). When encopresis persists, thorough medical and psychological evaluation is recommended to determine possible causes and appropriate treatments.

encopresis Lack of control over bowel movements that is not caused by an organic problem in a child who is at least 4 years old.

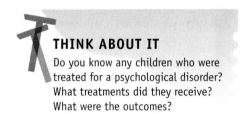
THINK ABOUT IT
Do you know any children who were treated for a psychological disorder? What treatments did they receive? What were the outcomes?

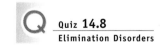
Quiz 14.8
Elimination Disorders

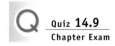
Quiz 14.9
Chapter Exam

Research Update
Chapter 14

Overview of Disorders of Childhood and Adolescence

TYPES OF DISORDERS

	Description	Major Types/Levels of Severity	Features
Pervasive Developmental Disorder	Marked impairment in multiple areas of development	• Autistic Disorder • Asperger's Disorder	• **Autism:** Major deficits in relating to others, impaired language and cognitive functioning, and restricted range of activities and interests • **Asperger's Disorder:** Poor social interactions and stereotyped behavior but without the significant language or cognitive deficits of autism
Mental Retardation	A broad-based delay in the development of cognitive and social functioning	• Deficits vary with level of severity from mild to profound	• Diagnosed on the basis of low IQ score and poor adaptive functioning
Learning Disorders	Deficiencies in specific learning abilities in the context of at least average intelligence and exposure to learning opportunities	• Mathematics Disorder • Disorder of Written Expression • Reading Disorder (Dyslexia)	• **Mathematics Disorder:** Difficulty understanding basic mathematical operations • **Disorder of Written Expression:** Grossly deficient writing skills • **Reading Disorder:** Difficulty recognizing words and comprehending written text
Communication Disorders	Difficulties in understanding or using language	• Expressive Language Disorder • Mixed Receptive/Expressive Language Disorder • Phonological Disorder • Stuttering	• **Expressive Language Disorder:** Difficulty using spoken language • **Mixed Receptive/Expressive Disorder:** Difficulty understanding and producing speech • **Phonological Disorder:** Difficulty articulating the sounds of speech • **Stuttering:** Difficulty speaking fluently without interruption
Attention-Deficit and Disruptive Behavior Disorders	Patterns of disturbed behavior that are generally disruptive to others and to adaptable social functioning	• Attention-Deficit Hyperactivity Disorder (ADHD) • Conduct Disorder (CD) • Oppositional Defiant Disorder (ODD)	• **ADHD:** Problems of impulsivity, inattention, and hyperactivity • **CD:** Antisocial behavior that violates social norms and the rights of others • **ODD:** Pattern of noncompliant, negativistic, or oppositional behavior
Anxiety and Mood Disorders	Emotional disorders affecting children and adolescents	• Separation Anxiety Disorder • Specific Phobia • Social Phobia • Generalized Anxiety Disorder • Major Depression • Bipolar Disorder	• Anxiety and depression often have similar features in children as in adults, but some differences exist • Children may suffer from school phobia as a form of separation anxiety • Depressed children may fail to label their feelings as depression or may show behaviors that mask depression, such as conduct problems and physical complaints
Elimination Disorders	Persistent problems with controlling urination or defecation that cannot be explained by organic causes	• Enuresis (lack of control over urination) • Encopresis (lack of control over defecation)	• **Enuresis:** Nighttime-only enuresis (bed-wetting) is the most common type • **Encopresis:** Occurs most often during daytime hours

CAUSAL FACTORS	TREATMENT APPROACHES
• **Autism:** Causes unknown, but are presumed to involve underlying brain abnormalities, possibly resulting from genetic defects or prenatal exposure to toxic agents	• **Autism:** Intensive, long-term behavioral treatment to improve adaptive behavior and communication skills
• Chromosomal abnormalities, such as Down syndrome • Genetic abnormalities, such as fragile X syndrome • Prenatal infections or maternal substance abuse • Cultural-familial causes	• Psychoeducational interventions to foster development of academic skills and adaptive behaviors; institutional care may be needed in more severe cases
• Causes unclear, but may involve abnormalities in brain circuits for processing visual and auditory information (in dyslexia) • Genetic factors are also implicated in dyslexia	• Interventions based on one or more of the following theoretical models: —Psychoeducational model —Neuropsychological model —Behavioral model —Linguistic model —Medical model —Cognitive model
• **Stuttering:** Causes unclear, but may involve a combination of genetic and environmental influences	• Speech therapy and possible additional psychological counseling for social anxiety associated with speech impairment
• Family factors, such as unresolved parent-child conflict; negative marital conflict; and coercive parent-child interactions • Poor parenting behaviors, such as lack of reinforcement for appropriate behavior • Possible genetic component and subtle brain abnormalities associated with ADHD	• **ADHD:** Drug therapy (Ritalin or other stimulant drug), cognitive-behavioral therapy to help develop more appropriate behaviors and attentional skills • Parent training to assist parents in use of more appropriate reinforcement • **CD:** Residential treatment programs, anger management programs, and more broadly based multisystemic therapy to help develop more appropriate social behaviors
• Cognitive factors, such as dysfunctional thinking patterns, are observed in depressed and anxious children as well as adults • Stressful life events, family conflicts and problems, and lack of social support • Genetic factors may also play a role, especially in adolescent depression	• Cognitive-behavioral therapy to help anxious and depressed children develop healthier thinking patterns and coping skills • SSRI-type antidepressants, such as Prozac, may be helpful, but more research examining their effectiveness is needed
• **Enuresis:** Psychological conflicts, conditioned anxiety, and biological factors (genetic) may be involved • **Encopresis:** Causes may involve a combination of such factors as constipation, inconsistent or incomplete toilet training, psychosocial stressors, and anxiety or other psychological factors	• **Enuresis:** Some variation of the bell-and-pad method is commonly used • **Encopresis:** Operant conditioning methods may be employed (rewards for successful efforts at self-control, mild punishment for continued accidents)

Summing Up

Normal and Abnormal Behavior in Childhood and Adolescence

What factors do we need to consider in distinguishing normal and abnormal behavior in childhood and adolescence? In addition to the criteria described in Chapter 1, we need to take into account the child's age and cultural background.

Pervasive Developmental Disorders

What are pervasive developmental disorders? Pervasive developmental disorders involve marked deficiencies in multiple areas of development. They develop within the first years of life and are often associated with mental retardation. Autistic disorder is the most prominent type of pervasive developmental disorder.

What are the clinical features of autism? Children with autism shun affectionate behavior, engage in stereotyped behavior, attempt to preserve sameness, and tend to have peculiar speech habits such as echolalia, pronoun reversals, and idiosyncratic speech. The causes of autism remain unknown, but gains in academic and social functioning have been obtained through the use of intensive behavior therapy.

Mental Retardation

What is mental retardation and how is it assessed? Mental retardation is a general delay in the development of intellectual and adaptive abilities. It is assessed by intelligence tests and measures of functional ability. Most cases fall in the mildly retarded range.

What are the causes of mental retardation? Mental retardation is caused by chromosomal abnormalities, such as Down syndrome; genetic disorders, such as fragile X syndrome and phenylketonuria; prenatal factors, such as maternal diseases and alcohol use; and familial/cultural factors associated with intellectually impoverished home environments.

Learning Disorders

What are learning disorders? Learning disorders (also called learning disabilities) are specific deficits in the development of arithmetic, writing, or reading skills.

What are the causes of learning disorders and approaches to treatment? The causes remain under study but most probably involve underlying brain dysfunctions that make it difficult to process or decode visual and auditory information. Intervention focuses mainly on attempts to remediate specific skill deficits.

Communication Disorders

What are communications disorders? These disorders are characterized by impaired understanding or use of language. The specific types of communications disorders include expressive language disorder, mixed receptive/expressive language disorder, phonological disorder, and stuttering.

Attention-Deficit and Disruptive Behavior Disorders

What are attention-deficit and disruptive behavior disorders? This category includes attention-deficit hyperactivity disorder, conduct disorder, and oppositional defiant disorder. ADHD is characterized by impulsivity, inattention, and hyperactivity. Children with conduct disorders intentionally engage in antisocial behavior. Children with ODD show negativistic or oppositional behavior but not outright delinquent or antisocial behavior characteristic of conduct disorder. However, ODD may lead to the development of conduct disorder.

How are these disorders treated? Stimulant medication is generally effective in reducing hyperactivity, but it has not led to general academic gains. Behavior therapy may help ADHD children adapt better to school. Behavior therapy may also be helpful in modifying behaviors of children with conduct disorders and oppositional defiant disorder.

Anxiety and Depression

What types of anxiety disorders affect children? Anxiety disorders that occur commonly among children and adolescents include specific phobias, social phobia, and generalized anxiety disorder. Children may also show separation anxiety disorder, which involves excessive anxiety at times when they are separated from their parents. Cognitive biases, such as expecting negative outcomes, negative self-talk, and interpreting ambiguous situations as threatening, figure prominently in anxiety disorders in children and adolescents, as they often do among adults.

What are the distinguishing features of depression in childhood and adolescence? Depressed children, especially younger children, may not report or be aware of feeling depressed. Depression may also be masked by seemingly unrelated behaviors, such as conduct disorders. Depressed children also tend to show cognitive biases associated with depression in adulthood, such as adoption of a pessimistic explanatory style and distorted thinking. Although rare, suicide in children does occur and threats should be taken seriously. Risk factors for adolescent suicide include gender, age, geography, race, depression, past suicidal behavior, strained family relationships, stress, substance abuse, and social contagion.

Elimination Disorders

What are elimination disorders? These are problems of impaired control over urination (enuresis) and bowel movements (encopresis) that cannot be accounted for by organic causes. Both disorders are more common in boys.

What is the bell-and-pad method for treating enuresis? The bell-and-pad method conditions children with enuresis to respond to bladder tension.

CHAPTER FIFTEEN

Cognitive Disorders and Disorders Related to Aging

Paul Klee
Allegorische Figurine

Truth OR Fiction?

- A man with a brain tumor patted the heads of fire hydrants and parking meters in the belief that they were children. (p. 480)

- The most often identified cause of delirium is ingestion of toxic mushrooms. (p. 482)

- After a motorcycle accident, a medical student failed to recognize the woman he had married a few weeks earlier. (p. 484)

- Dementia is a normal part of the aging process. (p. 485)

- People who occasionally become forgetful in middle age are probably suffering from the early stages of Alzheimer's disease. (p. 488)

- A common pain reliever found in most people's medicine cabinets has been found to reduce the risk of Alzheimer's disease when taken regularly. (p. 493)

- A famous folksinger and songwriter was misdiagnosed with alcoholism and spent several years in mental hospitals until the correct diagnosis was made. (p. 496)

- A form of dementia is linked to mad-cow disease. (p. 497)

In *The Man Who Mistook His Wife for a Hat,* neurologist Oliver Sacks (1985a) tells of Dr. P., a distinguished musician and teacher who had lost the ability to recognize objects visually. For example, Dr. P. failed to recognize the faces of his students at the music school. When a student spoke, however, Dr. P. immediately recognized his or her voice. Not only did the professor fail to discriminate faces visually, but sometimes he perceived faces where none existed. He patted the heads of fire hydrants and parking meters, which he took to be children. He warmly addressed the rounded knobs on furniture. These peculiarities were generally dismissed as jokes and laughed off by Dr. P. and his colleagues. After all, Dr. P. was well known for his oddball humor and jests. But Dr. P.'s music remained as accomplished as ever, his general health seemed fine, and so these misperceptions seemed little to be concerned about.

Not until 3 years later did Dr. P. seek a neurological evaluation. His ophthalmologist had found that although Dr. P.'s eyes were healthy, he had problems interpreting visual stimulation. So he made the referral to Dr. Sacks, a neurologist. When Sacks engaged Dr. P. in conversation, Dr. P.'s eyes fixated oddly on miscellaneous features of Dr. Sack's face—his nose, then his right ear, then his chin, sensing parts of his face but apparently not connecting them in a meaningful pattern. When Dr. P. sought to put on his shoe after a physical examination, he confused his foot with the shoe. When preparing to leave, Dr. P. looked around for his hat, and then . . .

> [Dr. P.] reached out his hand, and took hold of his wife's head, tried to lift it off, to put it on. He had apparently mistaken his wife for a hat! His wife looked as if she was used to such things. (Sacks, 1985a, p. 10)

Dr. P.'s peculiar behavior may seem amusing to some, but his loss of visual perception was tragic. Although Dr. P. could identify abstract forms and shapes—a cube, for example—he no longer recognized the faces of his family, or his own. Some features of particular faces would strike a chord of recognition. For example, he could recognize a picture of Einstein from the distinctive hair and mustache, and a picture of his own brother from the square jaw and big teeth. But he was responding to isolated features, not grasping the facial patterns as wholes.

Sacks recounts a final test:

> It was still a cold day, in early spring, and I had thrown my coat and gloves on the sofa.
> "What is this?" I asked, holding up a glove.
> "May I examine it?" he asked, and, taking it from me, he proceeded to examine it as he had examined the geometrical shapes.
> "A continuous surface," he announced at last, "infolded on itself. It appears to have"—he hesitated—"five outpouchings, if this is the word."
> "Yes," I said cautiously. "You have given me a description. Now tell me what it is."
> "A container of some sort?"
> "Yes," I said, "and what would it contain?"
> "It would contain its contents!" said Dr. P., with a laugh. "There are many possibilities. It could be a change-purse, for example, for coins of five sizes. It could . . ."
> I interrupted the blarney flow. "Does it not look familiar? Do you think it might contain, might fit, a part of your body?"
> No light of recognition dawned on his face.
> No child would have the power to see and speak of "a continuous surface . . . infolded on itself," but any child, any infant, would immediately know a glove as a glove, see it as familiar, as going with a hand. Dr. P. didn't. He saw nothing as familiar. Visually, he was lost in a world of lifeless abstractions. (Sacks, 1985a, p. 13)

Later, we might add, Dr. P. accidentally put the glove on his hand, exclaiming, "My God, it's a glove!" (Sacks, 1985a, p. 13). His brain immediately seized the pattern of **tactile** information, although his visual brain centers were powerless to provide a confirmatory interpretation. Dr. P., that is, showed lack of visual knowledge—a symptom referred to as visual **agnosia,** derived from Greek roots meaning "without knowledge." Still, Dr. P.'s musical abilities and verbal skills remained intact. He was able to function, to dress himself, take a

tactile Pertaining to the sense of touch.

agnosia A disturbance of sensory perception, usually affecting visual perception.

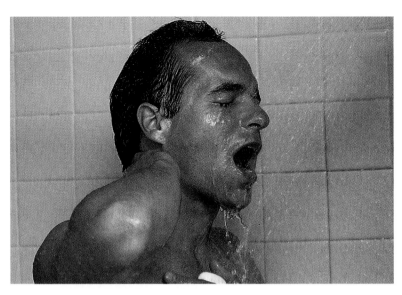

Does this man's singing help him coordinate his actions? In a celebrated case study, Dr. Oliver Sacks discussed the case of "Dr. P.," who was discovered to be suffering from a brain tumor that impaired his ability to interpret visual cues. Yet he could continue to eat meals and wash and dress himself so long as he could sing to himself.

shower, and eat his meals by singing various songs to himself—for example, eating songs and dressing songs—that helped him coordinate his actions. However, if his dressing song was interrupted while he was dressing himself, he would lose his train of thought and be unable to recognize not only the clothes his wife had laid out but also his own body. When the music stopped, so did his ability to make sense of the world. Sacks later learned that Dr. P. had a massive tumor in the area of the brain that processes visual information. Dr. P. was apparently unaware of his deficits, having filled his visually empty world with music in order to function and imbue his life with meaning and purpose.

Dr. P.'s case is unusual in the peculiarity of his symptoms, but it illustrates the universal dependence of psychological functioning on an intact brain. The case also shows how some people adjust—sometimes so gradually that the changes are all but imperceptible—to developing physical or organic problems. Dr. P.'s visual problems might have been relatively more debilitating in a person who was less talented or who had less social support to draw on. In this chapter, we focus on cognitive disorders, which are psychological disorders that arise from injuries or diseases that affect the brain.

Truth OR Fiction? REVISITED

A man with a brain tumor patted the heads of fire hydrants and parking meters in the belief that they were children.

TRUE. A man with a brain tumor patted the heads of fire hydrants and parking meters in the belief that they were children. The tumor caused dysfunction in the parts of his brain that processed visual information.

Web Link **15.1** wWw
Brain Disorders Network

cognitive disorders Mental disorders characterized by impaired cognitive abilities and daily functioning in which biological causation is either known or presumed.

Cognitive Disorders

Cognitive disorders involve disturbances in thinking or memory that represent a marked change from the individual's prior level of functioning (APA, 2000). Cognitive disorders are not psychologically based; they are caused by physical or medical conditions, or drug use or withdrawal, that affect the functioning of the brain. In some cases the specific cause of the cognitive disorder can be identified; in others, it cannot be pinpointed. Although these disorders are biologically based, we can see in the case of Dr. P. that psychological and environmental factors play key roles in determining the impact and range of disabling symptoms as well as the individual's ability to cope with deterioration of cognitive and physical abilities.

Our ability to perform cognitive functions—to think, reason, and store and recall information—is dependent on the functioning of the brain. Cognitive disorders arise when the brain is either damaged or impaired in its ability to function due to injury, illness, exposure to toxins, or use or abuse of psychoactive drugs. When brain damage results from an injury or stroke, deterioration in intellectual, social, and occupational functioning can be rapid and severe. In the case of a progressive form of deterioration, such as Alzheimer's disease (discussed in the next section of this chapter), the decline is more gradual but leads eventually to a state of virtual helplessness. The extent and location of brain damage largely determine the range and severity of impairment. By and large, the more widespread the damage, the greater and more extensive the impairment in functioning. The location of the damage is also critical because many brain structures or regions perform specialized functions. Damage to the temporal lobe, for example, is associated with defects in memory and attention, whereas damage to the occipital lobe may result in visual-spatial deficits, such as Dr. P.'s loss of ability to recognize familiar faces.

People who suffer from cognitive disorders may become completely dependent on others to meet basic needs in feeding, toileting, and grooming. In other cases, although some assistance in meeting the demands of daily living may be required, people are able to function at a level that permits them to live semi-independently.

There are three major types of cognitive disorders: delirium, dementia, and amnestic disorders (see Table 15.1).

TABLE 15.1	Major Types of Delirium, Dementia, and Amnestic Disorder
Delirium	Delirium Due to a General Medical Condition
	Substance Intoxication Delirium
	Substance Withdrawal Delirium
Dementia	Dementia of the Alzheimer's Type
	Vascular Dementia
	Dementia Due to HIV Disease
	Dementia Due to Head Trauma
	Dementia Due to Parkinson's Disease
	Dementia Due to Huntington's Disease
	Dementia Due to Pick's Disease
	Dementia Due to Creutzfeldt-Jakob Disease
	Dementia Due to Other General Medical Conditions (e.g., hypothyroidism or brain tumor)
	Substance-Induced Persisting Dementia
Amnestic disorder	Amnestic Disorder Due to a General Medical Condition
	Substance-Induced Persisting Amnestic Disorder

Source. Adapted from *DSM–IV-TR* (APA, 2000).

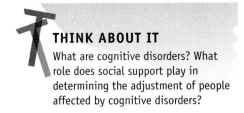

THINK ABOUT IT
What are cognitive disorders? What role does social support play in determining the adjustment of people affected by cognitive disorders?

Delirium

Delirium derives from the Latin roots *de-*, meaning "from," and *lira*, meaning "line" or "furrow." It means straying from the line, or the norm, in perception, cognition, and behavior. **Delirium** involves a state of extreme mental confusion in which people have difficulty concentrating and speaking clearly and coherently (see Table 15.2). People suffering from delirium may find it difficult to tune out irrelevant stimuli or shift their attention to new tasks. They may speak excitedly, but their speech carries little if any meaning. Disorientation as to time (not knowing the current date, day of the week, or time) and place (not knowing where you are) is common. Disorientation to person (the identities of oneself and others) is not. People in a state of delirium may experience terrifying hallucinations, especially visual hallucinations. Disturbances in perceptions often occur, such as misinterpretations of sensory stimuli (for example, confusing an alarm clock for a fire bell) or illusions (for instance, feeling as if the bed has an electrical charge passing through it). There can be a dramatic slowing down of movement into a state resembling catatonia. There may be

TABLE 15.2 Features of Delirium

Domain	Level of Severity		
	Mild	Moderate	Severe
Emotion	Apprehension	Fear	Panic
Cognition and perception	Confusion, racing thoughts	Disorientation, delusions	Meaningless mumbling, vivid hallucinations
Behavior	Tremors	Muscle spasms	Seizures
Autonomic activity	Abnormally fast heartbeat (tachycardia)	Perspiration	Fever

Source. Adapted from Freemon (1981), p. 82.

delirium A state of mental confusion, disorientation, and inability to focus attention.

dementia Profound deterioration of mental functioning, involving impaired memory, thinking, judgment, and language use.

senile dementias Forms of dementia that begin after age 65.

presenile dementias Forms of dementia that begin at or before age 65.

amnestic disorders Disturbances of memory associated with inability to learn new material or recall past events.

Truth OR Fiction? REVISITED

The most often identified cause of delirium is ingestion of toxic mushrooms.

FALSE. Though ingestion of certain types of poisonous mushrooms may result in delirium, the most frequently identified cause of delirium is abrupt withdrawal from alcohol or other drugs.

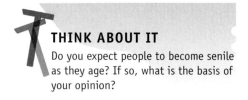

THINK ABOUT IT
Do you expect people to become senile as they age? If so, what is the basis of your opinion?

Web Link **15.2** wWw
Dementia: What Are the Warning Signs?

rapid fluctuations between restlessness and stupor. Restlessness is characterized by insomnia, agitated, aimless movements, even bolting out of bed or striking out at nonexistent objects. This may alternate with periods in which victims have to struggle to stay awake.

Delirium can result from a variety of medical conditions (Lichtenberg & Duffy, 2000). These include head trauma; metabolic disorders, such as hypoglycemia (low blood sugar); fluid or electrolyte imbalances; seizure disorders (epilepsy); deficiencies of the B vitamin thiamine; brain lesions; and various diseases that affect the functioning of the central nervous system, including Parkinson's disease, Alzheimer's disease, viral encephalitis (a type of brain infection), liver disease, and kidney disease (APA, 2000). Delirium may also occur due to exposure to toxic substances (such as eating certain poisonous mushrooms), as a side effect of using certain medications, or during states of drug or alcohol intoxication. Delirium may also result from abrupt cessation of use of psychoactive substances, especially alcohol, usually after periods of chronic, heavy use. Abrupt withdrawal from psychoactive drugs, especially alcohol, is the most common cause of delirium (Freemon, 1981). People with chronic alcoholism who abruptly stop drinking may experience a form of delirium called *delirium tremens* or DTs. During an acute episode of the DTs, the person may be terrorized by wild and frightening hallucinations, such as "bugs crawling down walls" or on the skin. The DTs can last for a week or more and are best treated in a hospital setting, where the patient can be carefully monitored and the symptoms treated with mild tranquilizers and environmental support. Although there are many known causes of delirium, in many cases the specific cause cannot be identified.

Whatever the cause, delirium involves a generalized disturbance of the brain's metabolic processes and imbalances in the levels of neurotransmitters. As a result, the ability to process information is impaired and confusion reigns. The abilities to think and speak clearly, to interpret sensory stimuli accurately, and to attend to the environment decline. Delirium may occur abruptly, as in cases resulting from seizures or head injuries, or gradually over hours or days, as in cases involving infections, fever, or metabolic disorders. During the course of delirium, the person's mental state will often fluctuate between periods of clarity ("lucid intervals"), which are most common in the morning, and periods of confusion and disorientation. Delirium is generally worse in the dark and following sleepless nights.

Unlike dementia, in which there is a steady deterioration of mental ability, states of delirium often clear up spontaneously when the underlying organic or drug-related cause is resolved. The course of delirium is relatively brief, usually lasting about a week, but rarely longer than a month. However, if the underlying cause persists or leads to further deterioration, delirium may progress to coma or death.

Dementia

Dementia involves a profound deterioration in mental functioning characterized by severe problems with memory and by one or more of the cognitive deficits listed in Table 15.3 (APA, 2000). There are more than 70 known causes of dementia, including brain diseases such as Alzheimer's disease and Pick's disease, and infections or disorders that affect the functioning of the brain, such as meningitis, HIV infection, and encephalitis. In some cases, the dementia can be halted or reversed, especially when it is caused by certain types of tumors and treatable infections, or when it results from depression or substance abuse. Most dementias are progressive and irreversible, however, including the most common form, dementia of the Alzheimer's type (Kasl-Godley & Gatz, 2000). Alzheimer's disease accounts for more than half of the cases of dementia.

Dementias usually occur in people over the age of 80. Those that begin after age 65 are called late-onset or **senile dementias.** Those that begin at age 65 or earlier are termed early-onset or **presenile dementias.**

Amnestic Disorders

Amnestic disorders (commonly called amnesias) are characterized by a dramatic decline in memory functioning that is not connected with states of delirium or dementia. Amnesia

TABLE 15.3 Cognitive Deficits in Dementia

Cognitive Deficit	Definition	Description
Aphasia	Impaired ability to comprehend and/or produce speech	There are several types of aphasia. In sensory or receptive aphasia, people have difficulty understanding written or spoken language, but retain the ability to express themselves through speech. In motor aphasia, the ability to express thoughts through speech is impaired, but the person can understand spoken language. A person with a motor aphasia may not be able to summon up the names of familiar objects or may scramble the normal order of words.
Apraxia	Impaired ability to perform purposeful movements despite an absence of any defect in motor functioning.	There may be an inability to tie a shoelace or button a shirt, although the person can describe how these activities should be performed and despite the fact that there is nothing wrong with the person's arm or hand. The person may have difficulty pantomiming the use of an object (e.g., combing one's hair).
Agnosia	Inability to recognize objects despite an intact sensory system.	Agnosias may be limited to specific sensory channels. A person with a visual agnosia may not be able to identify a fork when shown a picture of the object, although he or she has an intact visual system and may be able to identify the object if allowed to touch it and manipulate it by hand. Auditory agnosia is marked by impairment in the ability to recognize sounds; in tactile agnosia, people are unable to identify objects (such as coins or keys) by holding them or touching them.
Disturbance in executive functioning	Deficits in planning, organizing, or sequencing activities or in engaging in abstract thinking.	An office manager who formerly handled budgets and scheduling loses the ability to manage the flow of work in the office or adapt to new demands. An English teacher loses the ability to extract meaning from a poem or story.

Source. Adapted from *DSM-IV-TR* (APA, 2000).

involves an inability to learn new information (deficits in short-term memory) or to recall previously accessible information or past events from one's life (deficits in long-term memory). Problems with short-term memory may be revealed by an inability to remember the names of, or to recognize, people whom the person met 5 or 10 minutes earlier. Immediate memory, as measured by ability to repeat back a series of numbers, seems to be unimpaired in states of amnesia. The number series is unlikely to be recalled later, however, no matter how often it is rehearsed.

Unlike the memory disorders of dissociative amnesia and dissociative fugue discussed in Chapter 7, amnestic disorder results from a physical cause. Amnestic disorders frequently follow a traumatic event, such as a blow to the head, an electric shock, or an operation. A head injury may prevent people from remembering events that occurred shortly before the accident. The victim of an automobile accident or a football player who is knocked unconscious may be unable to remember events that occurred within several minutes of the injury. The automobile accident victim may not remember anything that transpired after getting into the car. The football player who is rendered amnestic from a blow to the head during the game may not remember anything after leaving the locker room. In some cases, memories for the remote past are retained but recent memories are

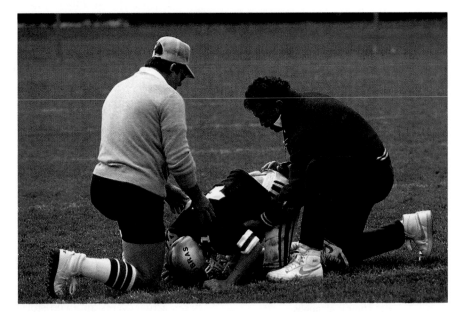

Amnestic disorder. An amnestic disorder syndrome can follow a traumatic injury such as a blow to the head. This football player may not be able to recall the events that happened just prior to his being tackled, nor the collision itself.

lost. People with amnesia may be more likely to remember events from their childhood than last evening's dinner, for example. Consider the following case:

Who Is She?

A medical student was rushed to the hospital after he was thrown from a motorcycle. His parents were with him in his hospital room when he awakened. As his parents were explaining what had happened to him, the door suddenly flew open and his flustered wife, whom he had married a few weeks earlier, rushed into the room, leaped onto his bed, and began to caress him and expressed her great relief that he was not seriously injured. After several minutes of expressing her love and reassurance, his wife departed and the flustered student looked at his mother and asked: "Who is she?"

—Adapted from Freemon, 1981, p. 96

The medical student's long-term memory loss included memories dating not only to the accident but also further back to the time before he was married or had met his wife. Like most victims of posttraumatic amnesia, the medical student recovered his memory fully.

People with an amnestic disorder may experience disorientation, more commonly involving disorientation to place (not knowing where one is at the time) and time (not knowing the day, month, and year) than disorientation as to self (not knowing one's own name). They may also lack insight into their memory loss and attempt to deny or mask their memory deficits even when evidence of their impairment is presented to them (APA, 2000). They may also attempt to fill the gaps in their memories with imaginary events. Or they may admit they have a memory problem but appear apathetic about it, showing a kind of emotional blandness.

Although people with amnestic disorder may suffer profound memory losses, their general intelligence tends to remain within a normal range. Memory loss in pure amnesia may thus be distinguished from that occurring in progressive dementias like Alzheimer's disease, in which memory and intellectual functioning both deteriorate. Early detection and diagnosis of the causes of memory problems are vital to many sufferers, because 20% to 30% of them are correctable (Cohen, 1986).

Other causes of amnesia include brain surgery; **hypoxia,** or sudden loss of oxygen to the brain; brain infection or disease; **infarction,** or blockage of the blood vessels supplying the brain; and chronic, heavy use of certain psychoactive substances, most commonly alcohol.

Alcohol-Induced Persisting Amnestic Disorder (Korsakoff's Syndrome) A common cause of amnestic disorder is thiamine deficiency linked to chronic abuse of alcohol. Alcohol abusers tend to take poor care of their nutritional needs and may not follow a diet rich enough in vitamin B_1, or thiamine. Thiamine deficiencies may produce an irreversible form of memory loss called *alcohol-induced persisting amnestic disorder,* which is more commonly known as **Korsakoff's syndrome.** The word *persisting* is used because the memory deficits persist even years after the person stops drinking (APA, 2000). Korsakoff's syndrome is not limited to people with chronic alcoholism, however. It has been reported in other groups who experience thiamine deficiencies during times of deprivation, such as among prisoners of war.

People with Korsakoff's syndrome have major gaps in their memory of past experiences (Phaf, Geurts, & Eling, 2000). Their memory deficits are believed to result from the loss of brain tissue due to bleeding in the brain. Despite their memory losses, patients with Korsakoff's syndrome may retain their general level of intelligence. They are often described as being superficially friendly but lacking in insight, unable to discriminate between actual events and wild stories they invent to fill the gaps in their memories. They sometimes become grossly disoriented and confused and require custodial care.

Korsakoff's syndrome often follows an acute attack of **Wernicke's disease,** another brain disorder caused by thiamine deficiency. Wernicke's disease is characterized by confu-

hypoxia Decreased supply of oxygen to the brain or other organs.

infarction The development of an infarct, or area of dead or dying tissue, resulting from the blocking of blood vessels normally supplying the tissue.

Korsakoff's syndrome A syndrome associated with chronic alcoholism that is characterized by memory loss and disorientation (also called *alcohol-induced persisting amnestic disorder*).

Wernicke's disease A brain disorder, associated with chronic alcoholism, characterized by confusion, disorientation, and difficulty maintaining balance while walking.

sion and disorientation, difficulty maintaining balance while walking (**ataxia**), and paralysis of the muscles that control eye movements. These symptoms may pass, but the person is often left with Korsakoff's syndrome and enduring memory impairment. If, however, Wernicke's disease is treated promptly with major doses of vitamin B$_1$, Korsakoff's syndrome may not develop. Once Korsakoff's syndrome has set in, it is usually permanent, although slight improvement is possible with treatment.

ataxia Loss of muscle coordination.

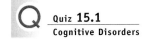

Quiz **15.1**
Cognitive Disorders

Psychological Disorders Related to Aging

Many physical changes occur with aging. Changes in calcium metabolism cause the bones to grow brittle and heighten the risk of breaks from falls. The skin grows less elastic, creating wrinkles and folds. The senses become less keen, so older people see and hear less acutely. Older people need more time (called *reaction time*) to respond to stimuli, whether they are driving or taking intelligence tests. For example, older drivers require more time to react to traffic signals and other cars. The immune system functions less effectively with increasing age, so people become more vulnerable to illness as they age. The skin becomes less elastic and cuts more easily. The sense of hearing declines, as does the elasticity of the lenses of the eyes, which makes it more difficult to focus on close objects or fine print.

Cognitive changes occur as well as we age. It is normal for people in later life to experience some decline in memory functioning and general cognitive ability, as measured by tests of intelligence, or IQ tests. The decline is sharpest on timed items, such as the performance scales of the Wechsler Adult Intelligence Scale. Although some declines in cognitive ability (reading comprehension, spatial ability as in map reading, or basic mathematical reasoning) in later life is common, it is not universal. Studies show that 20% to 30% of people in their 80s perform about as well on intelligence tests as those in their 30s and 40s (Goleman, 1994d). Some abilities, such as vocabulary and accumulated store of knowledge, hold up rather well in later life. However, people typically experience some reduction in memory as they age, especially memory for names or recent events. But apart from the occasional social embarrassment resulting from forgetting a person's name, cognitive declines experienced by most people as they age do not significantly interfere with their ability to meet their social or occupational responsibilities. Declines in cognitive functioning may also be offset to a certain extent by increased knowledge and experience.

The important point here is that dementia, or senility, is not the result of a normal process of aging (USDHHS, 1999a). It is a sign of degenerative brain disease. Screening and testing on neurological and neuropsychological tests can help distinguish dementias from normal aging processes. Generally speaking, the decline in intellectual functioning in dementia is more rapid and severe.

Let us now turn to consider relationships between various psychological disorders and aging, beginning with anxiety disorders.

Anxiety Disorders and Aging

Though anxiety disorders may develop at any point in life, they tend to be less prevalent among older adults than their younger counterparts (Flint, 1994). Still, anxiety disorders are the most common type of mental disorder affecting older adults and are about twice as common as mood disorders, such as depression ("Anxiety," 2000). Approximately 1 in 10 adults over the age of 55 suffers from a diagnosable anxiety disorder (USDHHS, 1999a). Older women are more likely to be affected by anxiety disorders than older men, by a ratio of two to one (Stanley & Beck, 2000). The most frequently occurring anxiety disorders among older adults are generalized anxiety disorder (GAD) and phobic disorders. Panic disorder is rare. Most cases of agoraphobia affecting older adults tend to be of recent origin and may involve the loss of social support systems due to the death of a spouse or close friends. Then again, some older individuals who are frail may have realistic fears of falling on the street and may be misdiagnosed as agoraphobic if they refuse to leave the house alone. Generalized anxiety disorder may arise from the perception that one lacks control

What changes take place as we age? How do they affect our moods? Although some declines in cognitive and physical functioning are connected with aging, older adults who remain active and engage in rewarding activities can be highly satisfied with their lives.

Agoraphobia? Or a need for support? Some older adults may refuse to venture away from home on their own because of realistic fears of falling in the street. They may be in need of social support, not therapy.

Web Link **15.3** wWw
Age Page: Depression

Elder stress. Older people of color may experience similar stresses as other older adults, but they are also more likely to have been exposed to additional social stresses, such as discrimination and poverty.

over one's life, which may develop in later life as the person contends with infirmity, loss of friends and loved ones, and lessened economic opportunities. Mild tranquilizers, such as the benzodiazepines (Valium is one), are commonly used to quell anxiety in older adults. Yet psychological interventions, such as cognitive-behavior therapy, may be an appropriate alternative to the use of psychiatric drugs (Stanley & Beck, 2000).

Depression and Aging

Though the risks of major depression also decline with age, depression is a major problem faced by many older adults (Karel & Hinrichsen, 2000; Unützer et al., 1997). In some cases, depression is a continuation of a lifelong pattern; in other cases, it first arises in later life. Between 8% and 20% of older adults experience some symptoms of depression (USDHHS, 1999a), with perhaps about 3% of them suffering from major depressive disorder (Rimer, 1999; Steffens et al., 2000). Rates of depression are higher still among residents of nursing homes. Though fewer older adults suffer from major depression than do younger adults, suicide is more frequent among older adults, especially older males (Knight & Satre, 1999; USDHHS, 1999a).

Depression in later life is also associated with a faster rate of physical decline and a higher mortality rate (Brenda et al., 1998; Zubenko et al., 1997). Depression may be linked to a higher mortality rate because of coexisting medical conditions or perhaps because of a lack of compliance with taking necessary medications.

Older people of color have many of the same concerns as other older adults, such as reduced opportunities for social participation and loneliness, but they are also likely to have encountered social stresses such as discrimination and poverty, and among immigrant groups, acculturative stress and English language deficiency. A history of discrimination and prejudice may make it difficult for people of color to trust therapists who are not of their own racial or ethnic group (Freed, 1992). The importance of acculturative stress was underscored in a study of Mexican American older adults that showed those who were minimally acculturated to U.S. society to have greater rates of depression than either highly acculturated or bicultural individuals (Zamanian et al., 1992).

Depressive disorders occur commonly in people suffering from various brain disorders, several of which, like Alzheimer's disease and stroke, disproportionately affect older people (Teri & Wagner, 1992). Researchers estimate that depressive disorders occur in as many as half of stroke victims and about a third to a half of people affected by Alzheimer's disease or Parkinson's disease (e.g., Chemerinski et al., 2001; Heun et al., 2001; Lyketsos et al., 2000). In the case of Parkinson's disease, depression may be not only a reaction to coping with the disease, but also result from neurobiological changes in the brain that are caused by the disease (Rao, Huber, & Bornstein, 1992).

The availability of social support appears to buffer the effects of stress, bereavement, and illness, thereby reducing the risk of depression. Social support is especially important to older people who are challenged because of physical disability. However, coping with a depressed spouse can take its toll, leading to an increased risk of depression in the caretaking spouse (Tower & Kasl, 1996).

On the other hand, participation in volunteer organizations and religious institutions is associated with a lower risk of depression among older people (Palinkas, Wingard, & Barrett-Connor, 1990). These forms of social participation may provide not only a sense of meaning and purpose but also a needed social outlet.

Older people may be especially vulnerable to depression because of the stress of coping with life changes associated with the so-called golden years—retirement; physical illness or incapacitation; placement in a residential facility or nursing home; the deaths of a spouse, siblings, lifetime friends, and acquaintances; or the need to care for a spouse whose health is declining. Retirement, whether voluntary or forced, may sap the sense of meaningfulness in life and lead to a loss of role identity. Deaths of relatives and friends induce grief and remind older people of their own advanced age as well as reducing the availability of social support. Older adults may feel incapable of forming new friendships or finding new goals in life.

Evidence suggests that the chronic strain of coping with a family member with dementia can lead to depression in the caregiver, even in the absence of any prior vulnerability to depression. Nearly half of Alzheimer's caregivers become depressed (Small et al., 1997).

Despite the prevalence of depression in older people, physicians often fail to recognize it or to treat it appropriately (Rimer, 1999). In one study of more than 500 elderly people in Ontario who committed suicide, nearly 9 of 10 were found to have gone untreated (Duckworth & McBride, 1996). Health care providers may be less likely to recognize depression among older people than in middle-aged or young people because they tend to focus more on the older patient's physical complaints or because depression in older people is often masked by physical complaints and sleeping problems.

Most older people with memory deficits do not suffer from Alzheimer's disease. They are more likely to have memory losses due to depression or other factors like chronic alcohol use or the effects of small strokes (Bäckman & Forsell, 1994). The good news is that the memory impairment lapses that can accompany depression in many older adults often lift when the underlying depression is resolved.

Evidence indicates that treatments for depression that are effective for younger people, such as antidepressant medication, cognitive-behavioral therapy, and interpersonal psychotherapy, as well as ECT, are also effective in treating geriatric depression (Bondareff et al., 2000; Karel & Hinrichsen, 2000; J. W. Williams et al., 2000; Zeiss & Breckenridge, 1997). In fact, older adults benefit as much, although perhaps more slowly, from pharmacological and psychological interventions as midlife or younger adults (Reynolds et al., 1996; Scogin & McElreath, 1994). These finding should help put to rest the belief that psychotherapy is not appropriate for older people. We lack evidence, however, showing whether any particular form of psychotherapy is clearly superior in treating depression in older people.

Sleep Problems and Aging

Sleep problems, especially insomnia, are common among older people (Lichstein et al., 2001). Insomnia in late adulthood is actually more prevalent than depression (Morgan, 1996). People are likely to experience sleep problems as they age, which may to a certain extent reflect age-related changes in sleep physiology, such as tendencies to wake up earlier in the morning (Martin, Shochat, & Ancoli-Israel, 2000). However, sleep problems may be a feature of other psychological disorders, such as depression, dementia, and anxiety disorders, as well as medical illness (Lamberg, 2000). Psychosocial factors, such as loneliness and the related difficulty of sleeping alone after loss of a spouse, may also be involved. Dysfunctional cognitions, such as excessive concerns about the negative consequences of losing sleep and perceptions of hopelessness and helplessness about controlling sleep, may play a role in perpetuating insomnia in older people (Morin et al., 1993a).

Mild tranquilizers are often used in treating late-life insomnia. However, problems such as dependence and withdrawal symptoms caution against their long-term use. Fortunately, researchers find that behavioral approaches, similar to those described in Chapter 11, are effective in treating insomnia in later life (Lichstein, Wilson, & Johnson, 2000; Martin, Shochat, & Ancoli-Israel, 2000). Moreover, older adults are as capable of benefiting from the treatment as younger adults.

A study of sleep apnea (temporary cessation of breathing during sleep) in a geriatric population showed that between 25% and 42% of the people studied had five or more apneas per hour of sleep (Ancoli-Israel et al., 1991). Apnea may involve more than a sleep problem; it is also linked to an increased risk of dementia and of cardiovascular disorders (Strollo & Rogers, 1996).

THINK ABOUT IT
Why do you suppose that depression is so common among older people? To what extent might it be related to the diminished role expectations placed on older people in our society? In what ways might society provide more meaningful social roles for people as they age?

Alzheimer's disease (AD) A progressive brain disease characterized by gradual loss of memory and intellectual functioning, personality changes, and eventual loss of ability to care for oneself.

Dementia of the Alzheimer's Type

Alzheimer's disease (AD) is a degenerative brain disease that leads to a progressive and irreversible form of dementia, characterized by loss of memory and other cognitive functions. As noted, it accounts for more than half of the cases of dementia in the general population (see Figure 15.1) (Selkoe, 1992; Tune, 1998). Alzheimer's disease affects about 4 million Americans and is the fourth leading cause of death among adults (Cowan & Kandel, 2001).

Although AD is strongly connected with aging, it is a disease and not a consequence of normal aging (Butler, 2001). Alzheimer's affects about 1 in 10 Americans over the age of 65 and about half of those over the age of 85 (Lemonick & Park, 2001). The risk of AD nearly doubles in each 5-year period after age 60 (USDHHS, 1999a). Women are at higher risk of developing the disease than are men, though this may be a consequence of women tending to live longer. As the U.S. population on the whole continues to age, the numbers of Americans with AD is expected to nearly quadruple during the first half of the century,

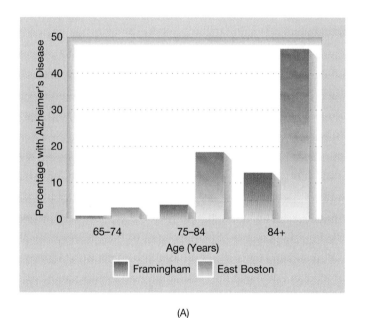

(A)

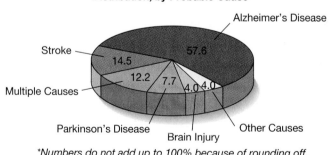

(B)

FIGURE 15.1 Prevalence of Alzheimer's disease among older population of two communities in Massachusetts and distribution of probable causes of dementia. Studies of East Boston and Framingham in Massachusetts show that the prevalence of Alzheimer's disease increases with age among older people. The figures reported for Framingham are lower than those reported in East Boston, most probably because the Framingham study employed narrower criteria in diagnosing the disease. Note in part B that Alzheimer's disease is considered the probable cause in most cases of dementia (57.6%).

Some Treatable Causes of Dementia	
Medications	Certain Tumors or Infections of the Brain
Emotional Depression	Blood Clots Pressing on the Brain
Vitamin B_{12} Deficiency	Metabolic Imbalances (Including Thyroid,
Chronic Alcoholism	Kidney or Liver Disorders)

(C)

rising to nearly 14 million by the year 2000 (Kawas & Brookmeyer, 2001; Lemonick & Park, 2001). Economic costs of AD are estimated at more than $90 billion a year in the United States (Cowan & Kandel, 2001).

The dementia associated with AD involves a progressive deterioration of mental abilities involving memory, language, and problem solving. Occasional memory loss or forgetfulness in middle life (e.g., forgetting where one put one's glasses) is a normal consequence of the aging process and not a sign of the early stages of Alzheimer's disease (Bazell, 2000). People in later life (and some of us not quite that advanced in years) complain of not remembering names as well as they used to, or of forgetting names that were once well known to them. Although mild forgetfulness may concern people, it need not impair their social or occupational functioning.

Suspicions of AD are raised when cognitive impairment is more severe and pervasive, affecting the individual's ability to meet the ordinary responsibilities of daily work and social roles. Over the course of the illness, people with AD may get lost in parking lots or in stores, or even in their own homes (Kolata, 1994b). The wife of an AD patient describes how AD has affected her husband: "With no cure, Alzheimer's robs the person of who he is. It is painful to see Richard walk around the car several times because he can't find the door" (Morrow, 1998a, p. D4). Agitation, wandering behavior, depression, and aggressive behavior become common as the disease progresses (Chen et al., 1999; Slone & Gleason, 1999).

People with AD may become confused or delusional in their thinking and may sense that their mental ability is slipping away but not understand why. Bewilderment and fear may lead to paranoid delusions or beliefs that their loved ones have betrayed them, robbed them, or don't care about them. They may forget the names of their loved ones or fail to recognize them. They may even forget their own names.

Psychotic features such as delusions and hallucinations were found in about one in three people with AD in a recent study (Jeste et al., 1992). The appearance of psychotic symptoms appears to be connected with greater cognitive impairment and more rapid deterioration. People with Alzheimer's disease are frequently depressed or suicidal, but their doctors may overlook the danger signs or disregard them (Teri & Wagner, 1992).

Alzheimer's disease was first described in 1907 by the German physician Alois Alzheimer (1864–1915). During an autopsy of a 56-year-old woman who had suffered from severe dementia, he found two brain abnormalities now regarded as signs of the disease: plaques (portions of degenerative brain tissue) and neurofibrillary tangles (twisted bundles of nerve cells) (Näslund et al., 2000) (see Figure 15.2). The darkly shaded areas in the photo to the right in Figure 15.2 show the diminished brain activity associated with Alzheimer's disease.

Alzheimer's disease. Alzheimer's disease (AD) has struck a number of notable people, including former President Ronald Reagan, here shown with his wife, Nancy, at his first public appearance after being diagnosed with AD.

w\w\w   **Web Link 15.4**
          Facts About Alzheimer's Disease

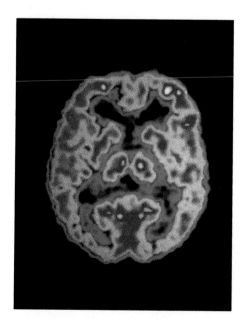
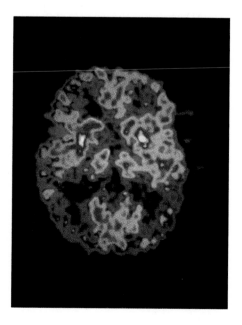

FIGURE 15.2 PET scans of brains from a healthy aged adult (left) and a patient with Alzheimer's disease (right).
The darkly shaded areas in the photo to the right suggest how the neurological changes associated with Alzheimer's disease (as marked by the excess of dark shading) impair brain activity.

Source. Friedland, R. P., Case Western Reserve University, courtesy of *Clinical Neuroimaging.* Copyright © 1988 by John Wiley and Sons, Inc.

Alzheimer's disease. Alzheimer's disease can devastate patients' families. Spouses usually provide the bulk of daily care. This man has been caring for his wife for several years, and he believes that his hugs and kisses sometimes prompt his wife to murmur his name.

Diagnosis There is no clear-cut diagnostic test for AD. The diagnosis of AD is generally based on a process of exclusion and given only when other possible causes of dementia are eliminated. Other medical and psychological conditions may mimic AD, such as severe depression resulting in memory loss and impaired cognitive functioning. Consequently, misdiagnoses may occur, especially in the early stages of the disease. A confirmatory diagnosis of AD can be made only upon inspection of brain tissue by biopsy or autopsy. However, biopsy is rarely performed because of the risk of hemorrhaging or infection, and autopsy, of course, occurs too late to help the patient.

Features of Alzheimer's Disease

Alzheimer's disease develops gradually but progresses steadily, leading to dementia by about 3 years following onset (Cooke, 1994; Skoog, 2000). Earlier age of onset of AD appears to be associated with poorer cognitive functioning, even when the duration of the illness is taken into account. When AD strikes earlier in life, it may involve a more severe form of the disease.

The early stages of the disease are marked by limited memory problems and subtle personality changes ("New Use of Brain Scan," 2000). People may at first have trouble managing their finances; remembering recent events or basic information such as telephone numbers, area codes, zip codes, and the names of their grandchildren; and performing numerical computations (Reisberg et al., 1986). A business executive who once managed millions of dollars may become unable to perform simple arithmetic. There may be subtle personality changes, such as signs of withdrawal in people who had been outgoing or irritability in people who had been gentle. In these early stages, people with AD generally appear neat and well groomed and are generally cooperative and socially appropriate.

As AD progresses to a level of moderate severity, assistance may be required in managing everyday tasks. People with AD in the moderately severe range may be unable to select clothes for the season or the occasion. They may be unable to recall their addresses or names of family members. When they drive, they begin making mistakes, such as failing to stop at stop signs or accelerating when they should be braking.

Families who helplessly watch their loved ones slowly deteriorate have been described as attending a "funeral that never ends" (Aronson, 1988). Living with a person with advanced AD may seem like living with a stranger, so profound are the changes in the person's personality and behavior. The difficulties imposed on the families by the symptoms of advanced AD, such as wandering away, aggressiveness, destructiveness, incontinence, screaming, and remaining awake at night all contribute to the level of stress imposed on caregivers (Gurland & Cross, 1986).

Some people with AD are not aware of their deficits. Others deny them. At first they may attribute their problems to other causes, such as stress or fatigue. Denial may protect people with AD in the early or mild stages of the disease from recognition that their intellectual abilities are in decline (Reisberg et al., 1986). Or the recognition that one's mental abilities are slipping away may lead to depression.

VIDEO **15.1**
Alzheimer's Disease:
The Case of Wilburn "John" Johnson

Cognitive impairment becomes more severe as the disease progresses. At the moderately severe level, people encounter difficulties in various aspects of personal functioning, such as toileting and bathing themselves. There are large gaps in their memories for recent events. They may not be able to recall their complete addresses but may remember parts of them. Or they may forget the name of the president but be able to recall his last name if given the first name. They may fail to recognize familiar people or forget their names. They often make mistakes in recognizing themselves in mirrors. Memory for remote events is also affected. They are generally unable to recall the names of their schools, parents, or birthplaces. They may no longer be able to speak in full sentences. Verbal responses may be limited to a few words.

Movement and coordination functions deteriorate further. People with AD at the moderately severe level may begin walking in shorter, slower steps. They may no longer be able to sign their names, even when assisted by others. They may have difficulty handling a knife and fork. Agitation becomes a prominent feature at this stage, and victims may act out in response to the threat of having to contend with an environment that no longer seems controllable. They may pace or fidget, or display aggressive behavior such as yelling, throwing, or hitting. Patients may wander off because of restlessness and be unable to find their way back.

People with advanced AD may start talking to themselves or experience visual hallucinations or paranoid delusions. They may believe someone is attempting to harm them or is stealing their possessions, or that their spouses are unfaithful to them. They may believe their spouses are actually other people.

At the most severe stage, cognitive functions decline to the point where people become essentially helpless. They may lose the ability to speak or control body movement (Fuchs, 2001). They become incontinent; are unable to communicate, walk, or even sit up; and require assistance in toileting and feeding. In the end state, seizures, coma, and death result.

The major features of Alzheimer's disease, such as memory loss, disorientation, and behavior problems, are illustrated by the following case:

A Case of Dementia of the Alzheimer's Type

A 65-year-old draftsman began to have problems remembering important details at work; at home he began to have difficulty keeping his financial records up-to-date and remembering to pay bills on time. His intellectual abilities progressively declined, forcing him eventually to retire from his job. Behavioral problems began to appear at home, as he grew increasingly stubborn and even verbally and physically abusive toward others when he felt thwarted.

On neurological examination, he displayed disorientation as to place and time, believing that the consultation room was his place of employment and that the year was "1960 or something," when it was actually 1982. He had difficulty with even simple memory tests, failing to remember any of six objects shown to him ten minutes earlier, not recalling the names of his parents or siblings, or the name of the president of the United States. His speech was vague and filled with meaningless phrases. He couldn't perform simple arithmetical computations, but he could interpret proverbs correctly.

Shortly following the neurological consultation, the man was placed in a hospital since his family was no longer able to control his increasingly disruptive behavior. In the hospital, his mental abilities continued to decline, while his aggressive behavior was largely controlled by major tranquilizers (antipsychotic drugs). He was diagnosed as suffering from a primary degenerative dementia of the Alzheimer type. He died at age 74, some 8 years following the onset of his symptoms.

—Adapted from Spitzer et al., 1989, pp. 131–132

THINK ABOUT IT
What is Alzheimer's disease? What have we learned about the biological underpinnings of the disease? What don't we know?

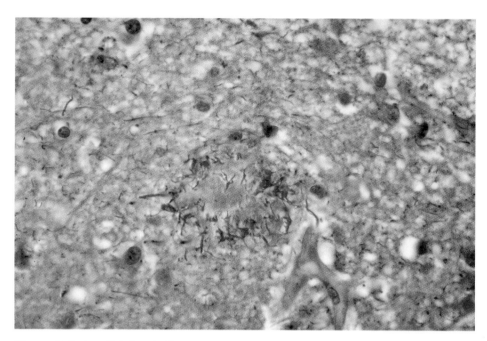

Plaques linked to Alzheimer's disease. In Alzheimer's disease, nerve tissue in the brain degenerates, forming steel-wool-like clumps or plaques composed of beta-amyloid protein fragments.

THINK ABOUT IT

What treatments are available for Alzheimer's disease? What are their limitations?

Causal Factors We don't know either what causes AD or how to prevent it or cure it. AD may involve multiple causes, so we may need to look for different causal pathways. We do know that plaques, the steel-wool-like clumps that form in the brains of people with Alzheimer's disease, are composed of a material called *beta amyloid,* which consists of fibrous protein fragments (Iwata et al., 2001; Skoog, 2000). For some unknown reason, possibly involving a genetic mutation, these fragments break off from a larger protein during metabolism and cluster together in strings that attract remnants of other nerve cells, forming plaques. These plaques may be responsible for destroying adjacent brain tissue, leading to the death of brain cells across a large area of the brain, which in turn may lead to the memory loss, confusion, and other symptoms of the disease.

Genetics plays an important role in AD (Ertekin-Taner et al., 2000; Myers et al., 2000; USDHHS, 1999a). Late-onset AD is linked to genes that regulate production of a protein called *apolipoprotein E* (APOe) (Voelker, 2000). This protein transports cholesterol through the bloodstream. People possessing defects in these genes may begin to show signs of brain deterioration even before memory symptoms appear ("New Use of Brain Scan," 2000). Their brains also appear to work harder when performing a memory task, which suggests that the brain is trying to compensate for underlying abnormalities (Bookheimer et al., 2000). Other genes may also be involved in AD, including genes involved in cell metabolism (the process of converting food into energy), and in the production of beta amyloid (Bertram et al., 2000; Ertekin-Taner et al., 2000; Li, 2000).

Treatment AD patients show reduced levels of the neurotransmitter acetylcholine (ACh), which may result from death of brain cells in an area of the brain (the nucleus basalis of Meynert) that manufactures the chemical. Presently several drugs are available that produce modest results in slowing the cognitive decline in AD ("Agency Approves," 2001; Skoog, 2000; USDHHS, 1999a). These drugs all work by inhibiting the breakdown of ACh, which increases the availability of the chemical in the brain. These drugs may slow the progression of the disease but are far from a cure. Psychosocial interventions, such as memory training programs, may also help AD patients make optimal use of their remaining abilities (Kasl-Godley & Gatz, 2000).

There are some promising leads on the prevention front. Preliminary evidence shows that people who regularly take anti-inflammatory drugs, such as the widely used pain reliever ibuprofen (brand names *Advil, Nuprin,* or *Motrin*), are less likely than others to develop AD (Hager & Peyser, 1997; Veld et al., 2001). Ibuprofen may reduce the risk of AD by curbing brain

Boosting memory. Memory training programs are not a cure, but they may help Alzheimer's patients make the best use of their remaining abilities.

Questionnaire

Examining Your Attitudes Toward Aging

 What are your assumptions about late adulthood? Do you see older people as basically different from the young in their behavior patterns and their outlooks, or just as a few years more mature?

To evaluate the accuracy of your attitudes toward aging, mark each of the following items true (T) or false (F). Then turn to the answer key at the end of the chapter.

TRUE FALSE

1. By age 60 most couples have lost their capacity for satisfying sexual relations. ___ ___

2. Older people cannot wait to retire. ___ ___

3. With advancing age people become more externally oriented, less concerned with the self. ___ ___

4. As individuals age, they become less able to adapt satisfactorily to a changing environment. ___ ___

5. General satisfaction with life tends to decrease as people become older. ___ ___

6. As people age they tend to become more homogeneous—that is, all old people tend to be alike in many ways. ___ ___

TRUE FALSE

7. For the older person, having a stable intimate relationship is no longer highly important. ___ ___

8. The aged are susceptible to a wider variety of psychological disorders than young and middle-aged adults. ___ ___

9. Most older people are depressed much of the time. ___ ___

10. Church attendance increases with age. ___ ___

11. The occupational performance of the older worker istypically less effective than that of the younger adult. ___ ___

12. Most older people are just not able to learn new skills. ___ ___

13. Compared to younger persons, older people tend to think more about the past than the present or the future. ___ ___

14. Most people in later life are unable to live independently and reside in nursing-home-like institutions. ___ ___

Source. Adapted from Rathus, S. A., & Nevid, J. S. (1995)3. *Adjustment and growth: The challenges of life.* (6th ed.), p. 440. Reprinted with permission of Brooks/Cole, an imprint of Wadsworth Group, a division of Thomson Learning. FAX 800-730-2215.

---

inflammation associated with the disease (M. F. Weiner, 1996). But further research is needed to demonstrate conclusively whether anti-inflammatory drugs do in fact reduce the risks of AD (Breitner & Zandi, 2001; Kolata, 2001b).

Researchers report initial success with an experimental vaccine in reducing or preventing buildup of plaques in the brains of laboratory mice ("Alzheimer's Vaccine," 2001). Although tests remain to be done with humans, the vaccine offers hope that we may one day be able to prevent Alzheimer's disease or stem the further progression of the disease in people already affected.

Vascular Dementia

The brain, like other living tissues, depends on the bloodstream to supply it with oxygen and glucose and to carry away its metabolic wastes. A stroke, also called a **cerebrovascular accident (CVA),** occurs when part of the brain becomes damaged because of a disruption in its blood supply, usually as the result of a blood clot that becomes lodged in an artery that services the brain and obstructs circulation. The areas of the brain affected may be damaged or destroyed, leaving the victim with disabilities in motor, speech, and cognitive functions. Death may also occur. Vascular dementia (formerly called *multi-infarct dementia*) is a form of dementia that results from repeated strokes. (An *infarct* refers to the death of tissue caused by insufficient blood supply.) Vascular dementia, the second most common form of dementia, most often affects people in later life but at somewhat earlier ages than dementia due to Alzheimer's disease. It accounts for about 20% of cases of dementia ("Update on Alzheimer's Disease," Part I, 1995) and appears to be more common in men

Truth OR Fiction? REVISITED

A common pain reliever found in most people's medicine cabinets has been found to reduce the risk of Alzheimer's disease when taken regularly.

TRUE. Recent evidence suggests that regular use of the pain reliever ibuprofen may reduce the risk of AD. However, physicians caution against routine use of the drug for this purpose because of the risks of side effects.

cerebrovascular accident (CVA) Damage to part of the brain because of a disruption in its blood supply, usually as the result of a blood clot.

Pick's disease A form of dementia, similar to Alzheimer's disease, but distinguished by specific abnormalities (Pick's bodies) in nerve cells and absence of neurofibrillary tangles and plaques.

Parkinson's disease A progressive disease of the basal ganglia characterized by muscle tremor and shakiness, rigidity, difficulty walking, poor control of fine motor movements, lack of facial muscle tonus, and, in some cases, cognitive impairment.

Quiz **15.2**

Psychological Disorders Related to Aging

Battling Parkinson's disease. Actor Michael J. Fox has been waging a personal battle against Parkinson's disease and has brought national attention to the need to fund research efforts to develop more effective treatments for this degenerative brain disease.

than women (APA, 2000). Unlike AD, heredity does not appear to play a major role in vascular dementia (Bergem et al., 1997).

Single strokes may produce gross impairments in specific functions, such as aphasia, but single strokes do not typically cause the more generalized cognitive declines that characterize dementia. Vascular dementia generally results from multiple strokes that occur at different times and that have cumulative effects on a wide range of mental abilities.

Features of Vascular Dementia The symptoms of vascular dementia are similar to those of dementia of the Alzheimer's type, including impaired memory and language ability, agitation and emotional instability, and loss of ability to care for one's own basic needs. However, AD is characterized by an insidious onset and a gradual decline of mental functioning, whereas vascular dementia typically occurs abruptly and follows a stepwise course of deterioration involving a pattern of rapid declines in cognitive functioning that are believed to reflect the effects of additional strokes (Brinkman et al., 1986; Kasl-Godley & Gatz, 2000). Some cognitive functions in people with vascular dementia may remain relatively intact in the early course of the disorder, leading to a pattern of patchy deterioration in which islands of mental competence remain while other abilities suffer gross impairment, depending on the particular areas of the brain that have been damaged by multiple strokes.

Dementias Due to General Medical Conditions

We have examined relationships between aging and psychological disorders such as dementia and depression. Next we consider a number of physical disorders that affect psychological functioning in various ways.

Dementia Due to Pick's Disease

Pick's disease causes a progressive dementia that is symptomatically similar to AD. Symptoms include memory loss and social inappropriateness, such as a loss of modesty or the display of flagrant sexual behavior. Diagnosis is confirmed only upon autopsy by the *absence* of the neurofibrillary tangles and plaques that are found in AD and by the presence of other abnormal structures—Pick's bodies—in nerve cells. Pick's disease is believed to account for perhaps 5% of dementias. Unlike AD, it becomes evident most often between the ages of 50 and 60, although it can occur at later ages (APA, 2000). The risk declines with advancing age after 70. Men are more likely than women to suffer from Pick's disease.

Pick's disease appears to run in families, and a genetic component is suspected in its etiology (Brun, 1996; Hutton, 2001). It has been estimated that members of the immediate family of victims of Pick's disease have an overall risk of 17% of contracting the disease by age 75 (Heston, White, & Mastri, 1987).

Dementia Due to Parkinson's Disease

Dementia occurs in approximately 20% to 60% of people with **Parkinson's disease** (APA, 2000), a slowly progressing neurological disease that affects between one half million and one million people in the United States, including the former heavyweight champion Muhammad Ali and the actor Michael J. Fox (Cowan & Kandel, 2001; Cowley, 2000b). The disease affects men and women about equally and most often strikes between the ages of 50 and 69.

Parkinson's disease is characterized by uncontrollable shaking or tremors, rigidity, disturbances in posture (leaning forward), and lack of control over body movements. People with Parkinson's disease may be able to exercise control over their shaking or tremors, but only briefly. Some cannot walk at all. Others walk laboriously, in a crouch. Some execute voluntary body movements with difficulty, have poor control over fine motor movements, such as finger control, and have sluggish reflexes. They may look expressionless, as if they are wearing masks, a symptom that apparently reflects the degeneration of brain tissue that controls facial muscles. It is particularly difficult for patients to engage in sequences of complex movements, such as those required to sign their names. People with Parkinson's disease may be unable to coordinate two movements at the same time, as seen in this description of a Parkinson's patient who had difficulty walking and reaching for his wallet at the same time:

Motor Impairment in a Case of Parkinson's Disease

A 58-year-old man was walking across the hotel lobby in order to pay his bill. He reached into his inside jacket pocket for his wallet. He stopped walking instantly as he did so and stood immobile in the lobby in front of strangers. He became aware of his suspended locomotion and resumed his stroll to the cashier; however, his hand remained rooted in his inside pocket, as though he were carrying a weapon he might display once he arrived at the cashier.

—Adapted from Knight, Godfrey, & Shelton, 1988

■

Despite the severity of motor disability, cognitive functions seem to remain intact during the early stages of the disease. Dementia is more common in the later stages of the disease or among those with more severe forms of the disease (APA, 2000). The form of dementia associated with Parkinson's disease typically involves a slowing down of thinking processes, impaired ability to think abstractly or plan or organize a series of actions, and difficulty retrieving memories. Overall, the cognitive impairments associated with Parkinson's disease tend to be more subtle than those associated with Alzheimer's disease (Knight et al., 1988). People with Parkinson's disease often become socially withdrawn and are at greater-than-average risk for depression (Cummings, 1992). Depression may be due to difficulty in coping with the disease or to the biochemical changes that are part and parcel of the disease (Rao et al., 1992).

Parkinson's disease is caused by the destruction or impairment of dopamine-producing nerve cells in an area of the brain called the *substantia nigra* ("black substance") that is involved in regulating body movement (Health Resources, 2000; Kolata, 2001a). The causes of the disease remain unknown, but genetic factors appear to be involved in at least some forms of the disease (Blakeslee, 2000c; Olson, 2000; Sveinbjornsdottir et al., 2000).

Whatever the underlying cause, the symptoms of the disease—the uncontrollable tremors, shaking, rigid muscles, and difficulty walking—are tied to deficiencies in the amount of dopamine in the brain. The drug L-dopa increases levels of dopamine in the brain and brought hope to Parkinson's patients when it was first used in treating the disease in the 1970s. L-dopa is converted in the brain into dopamine.

L-dopa helps control the symptoms of the disease and slows its progression, but it does not cure it (Parkinson Study Group, 2000). About 80% of people with Parkinson's disease show significant improvement in their tremors and motor symptoms following treatment with L-dopa. After a few years, however, L-dopa begins to lose its effectiveness, and the disease continues to progress. Several other drugs are in the experimental stage, offering hope for further advances in treatment. Another source of hope comes from experimental use of electrical stimulation of deep-brain structures (Deep-Brain Stimulation for Parkinson's Disease Study Group, 2001) and from genetic studies that may one day lead to an effective gene therapy for the disease (Kordower et al., 2000; Olson, 2000).

Dementia Due to Huntington's Disease

Huntington's disease, also known as *Huntington's chorea,* was first recognized by the neurologist George Huntington in 1872. Huntington's disease involves a progressive deterioration of the basal ganglia, especially of the caudate nucleus and the putamen, which primarily affects neurons that produce ACh and GABA.

THINK ABOUT IT
How might your underlying attitudes toward older people affect the ways in which you relate to them? How might societal attitudes toward older people affect the allocation of funds for social services and for medical research?

wWw Web Link **15.5**
National Parkinson Foundation, Inc.

Huntington's disease An inherited degenerative disease that is characterized by jerking and twisting movements, paranoia, and mental deterioration.

Woody Guthrie. The folksinger Woody Guthrie died from Huntington's disease in 1967, after 22 years of battling the disease.

Web Link **15.6**
The Huntington's Disease Society wWw
of America

Truth OR Fiction? REVISITED

A famous folksinger and songwriter was misdiagnosed with alcoholism and spent several years in mental hospitals until the correct diagnosis was made.

TRUE. The folksinger and songwriter was Woody Guthrie, whose Huntington's disease went misdiagnosed for years.

THINK ABOUT IT

The availability of a genetic test for Huntington's disease means that a child of someone with Huntington's can find out whether he or she carries the gene that will eventually lead to the disease. If you faced this situation, do you think you would want to know whether you carried the gene? Why or why not?

The most prominent physical symptoms of the disease are involuntary, jerky movements of the face (grimaces), neck, limbs, and trunk—in contrast to the poverty of movement that typifies Parkinson's disease. These twitches are termed *choreiform*, which derives from the Greek *choreia*, meaning "dance." Unstable moods, alternating with states of apathy, anxiety, and depression, are common in the early stages of the disease. As the disease progresses, paranoia may develop and people may become suicidally depressed. Difficulties retrieving memories in the early course of the disease may develop into dementia as the disease progresses. Eventually, there is loss of control of bodily functions, leading to death occurring within about 15 years after onset of the disease.

Huntington's disease, which afflicts about 1 in 10,000 people, typically begins in the prime of adulthood, between the ages of 30 and 45 ("Researchers Gain Insight," 2001). Men and women are equally likely to develop the disease (APA, 2000). One of the victims of the disease was the folksinger Woody Guthrie, who gave us the beloved song "This Land Is Your Land," among many others. He died of Huntington's disease in 1967, after 22 years of battling the malady. Because of the odd, jerky movements associated with the disease, Guthrie, like many other Huntington's victims, was misdiagnosed as suffering from alcoholism. He spent several years in a number of mental hospitals before the correct diagnosis was made.

Huntington's disease is caused by a genetic defect on a single defective gene (Cowan & Kandel, 2001; Nucifora Jr. et al., 2001; Tamminga, 1997). It is transmitted genetically from either parent to children of either gender. People who have a parent with Huntington's disease stand a 50% chance of inheriting the gene. People who inherit the gene eventually contract the disease.

Until recently, children of Huntington's disease victims had to wait until the symptoms developed—usually in midlife—to learn whether they had inherited the disease. A genetic test has been developed that can detect carriers of the defective gene, those who will eventually develop the disease should they live long enough. Eventually, perhaps, genetic engineering may provide a means of modifying the defective gene or its effects. Because researchers have not yet developed ways to cure or control Huntington's disease, some potential carriers, like folksinger Arlo Guthrie, son of Woody Guthrie, preferred not knowing whether they inherited the gene. Meanwhile, research continues. One promising development in experimental work with monkeys involves the use of brain implants that release a substance that protects the kind of brain cells killed off by Huntington's disease ("Tests Suggest," 1997). We don't yet know whether the use of such implants could be used to treat the disease in humans.

Dementia Due to HIV Disease

Human immunodeficiency virus (HIV), the virus that causes AIDS, can invade the central nervous system causing a cognitive disorder—dementia due to HIV disease. The most typical signs of dementia due to HIV disease include forgetfulness and impaired concentration and problem-solving ability (APA, 2000). Common behavioral features of the dementia are apathy and social withdrawal. As AIDS progresses, the dementia grows more severe, taking the form of delusions, disorientation, further impairments in memory and thinking processes, and perhaps even delirium. In its later stages, the dementia may resemble the profound deficiencies found among people with advanced Alzheimer's disease.

Dementia is rare in persons with HIV who have not yet developed full-blown AIDS. Yet one in four people with AIDS develops some form of cognitive impairment that may progress to dementia (Center for Mental Health Services, 1994). Signs of intellectual impairment short of full-blown dementia may also occur earlier than the onset of AIDS (Baldeweg et al., 1997). People with HIV who show early signs of intellectual impairment appear to be at greater risk of early death from AIDS ("Cognitive Impairment," 1996; Wilkie et al., 1998).

Dementia Due to Creutzfeldt-Jakob Disease

Creutzfeldt-Jakob disease is a rare and fatal brain disease (Cowley, 2001b). It is characterized by the formation of small cavities in the brain that resemble the holes in a sponge. Dementia is a common feature of the disease. The disease typically affects people in the 40- to 60-year-old age range, although it may develop in adults at any age (APA, 2000). There are no treatments for the disease and death usually results within months of onset of symptoms. In about 5% to 15% of cases there is evidence of familial transmission, which suggests that a genetic component may be involved in determining susceptibility to the disease. The human form of mad-cow disease, a fatal illness spread by eating infected beef, is a variant of Creutzfeldt-Jakob disease (Cowan & Kandel, 2001; "How Mad-Cow Disease Jumped to Humans," 2001; McNeil, 2001).

Dementia Due to Head Trauma

Head trauma can injure the brain. Jarring, banging, or cutting brain tissues, usually because of accident or assault, are causes of such injuries. Progressive dementia due to head trauma is more likely to result from multiple head traumas (as in the case of boxers who receive multiple blows to the head during their careers) than to a single blow or head trauma (APA, 2000). Yet even a single head trauma can have psychological effects, and if severe enough, can lead to physical disability or death. Specific changes in personality following traumatic injury to the brain vary with the site and extent of the injury, among other factors (Prigatano, 1992). Damage to the frontal lobe, for example, is associated with a range of emotional changes involving alterations of mood and personality.

Heading toward brain damage? Multiple blows to the head may lead to a progressive form of dementia.

Neurosyphilis

General paresis (from the Greek *parienai,* meaning "to relax") is a form of dementia—or "relaxation" of the brain in its most negative connotation—that results from neurosyphilis, a form of syphilis in which the disease organism, in a late stage of infection, directly attacks the brain and central nervous system. General paresis is of historical significance to abnormal psychology. The 19th-century discovery of the connection between this form of dementia and a concrete physical illness, syphilis, strengthened the medical model and held out the promise that organic causes would eventually be found for other abnormal behavior patterns. Syphilis is a sexually transmitted disease caused by the bacterium *Treponema pallidum.*

General paresis is associated with physical symptoms such as tremors, slurred speech, impaired motor coordination, and, eventually, paralysis—all of which are suggestive of relaxed control over the body. Psychological signs include shifts in mood states, blunted emotional responsiveness, and irritability; delusions; changes in personal habits, such as suspension of personal grooming and hygiene; and progressive intellectual deterioration, including impairments of memory, judgment, and comprehension. Some people with general paresis grow euphoric and entertain delusions of grandiosity. Others become lethargic and depressed. Eventually, people with general paresis lapse into a state of apathy and confusion, characterized by the inability to care for themselves or to speak intelligibly. Death eventually ensues, either because of renewed infection or because of the damage caused by the existing infection.

Late-stage syphilis once accounted for 10% to 30% of admissions to psychiatric hospitals. However, advances in detection and the development of antibiotics that cure the infection have sharply reduced the incidence of late-stage syphilis and the development of general paresis. The effectiveness of treatment depends on when antibiotics are introduced and the extent of central nervous system damage. In cases where extensive tissue damage has been done, antibiotics can stem the infection and prevent further damage, thereby producing some improvement in intellectual performance. They cannot restore people to their original levels of functioning, however.

Truth OR Fiction?   REVISITED

A form of dementia is linked to mad-cow disease.

TRUE. A form of dementia is caused by the human form of mad-cow disease.

General paresis A form of dementia resulting from neurosyphilis.

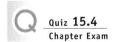

Quiz 15.3
Dementias Due to General Medical Conditions

Quiz 15.4
Chapter Exam

Research Update
Chapter 15

Overview of Cognitive Disorders

TYPES OF COGNITIVE DISORDERS

	Description	Features
Delirium	States of extreme mental confusion interfering with concentration and ability to speak coherently	• Difficulty filtering out irrelevant stimuli or shifting attention • Excited speech that conveys little meaning • Disorientation as to time and place • Frightening hallucinations or other perceptual distortions • Motor behavior may slow to a stupor or fluctuate between states of restlessness and stupor • Mental states may fluctuate between lucid intervals and periods of confusion
Dementia	Profound deterioration of mental functioning, including memory	• Most forms are irreversible and progressive, such as dementia of the Alzheimer's type • Associated with specific cognitive deficits, such as aphasia, apraxia, agnosia, and disturbance in executive functioning • Types of dementias are grouped by age of onset into senile dementias (beginning after age 65) and presenile dementias (beginning at age 65 or earlier)
Amnestic Disorder	Profound deficit in memory not associated with delirium or dementia	• May affect short-term memory and/or long-term memory • Person may be disoriented, especially as to place and time

CAUSAL FACTORS

Delirium
• Medical conditions, such as head trauma, metabolic disorders, low blood sugar, fluid or electrolyte imbalances, epilepsy, vitamin B deficiencies, and brain lesions
• Brain diseases, such as Parkinson's disease and Alzheimer's disease
• Abrupt withdrawal from alcohol in cases of chronic alcoholism (called delirium tremens, or DTs)

Dementia
• Brain diseases, such as Alzheimer's disease, Pick's disease, Parkinson's disease, Huntington's disease, HIV disease, and Creutzfeldt-Jakob disease
• Neurosyphilis
• Multiple strokes (vascular dementia)
• Brain tumors
• Head trauma
• Brain infections such as meningitis and encephalitis
• Causes of Alzheimer's disease remain unknown, but evidence points to a genetic contribution

Amnestic Disorder
• Physical causes such as a blow to the head
• Complications from brain surgery
• Brain infection
• Blockage of blood supply to the brain
• Heavy use of certain psychoactive substances (as in Korsakoff's syndrome)

TREATMENT APPROACHES

Delirium
• May clear up spontaneously or when the underlying medical condition is treated successfully
• Monitoring in hospital setting may be needed, especially for the DTs

Dementia
• Available treatments for dementia of the Alzheimer's type are limited to drugs that may slow the progression of the disease but are not a cure

Amnestic Disorder
• Memory may return spontaneously or with effective treatment of underlying conditions

Summing Up

Cognitive Disorders

What are cognitive disorders? Cognitive disorders involve disturbances of thinking or memory that represent a marked decline in intellectual or memory functioning. They are caused by physical or medical conditions, or drug use or withdrawal, affecting the functioning of the brain.

What is delirium? Delirium is a state of mental confusion characterized by symptoms such as impaired attention, disorientation, disorganized thinking and rambling speech, reduced level of consciousness, and perceptual disturbances. Delirium is most commonly caused by alcohol withdrawal, as in the form of delirium tremens (DTs).

What is dementia? Dementia involves cognitive deterioration or impairment, as evidenced by memory deficits, impaired judgment, personality changes, and disorders of higher cognitive functions such as problem-solving ability and abstract thinking.

Is dementia a normal part of aging? No, dementia is not a normal consequence of aging but a sign of a degenerative brain disorder. There are various causes of dementias, including Alzheimer's disease and Pick's disease, and brain infections or disorders.

What are amnestic disorders? Amnestic disorders involve deficits in short-term or long-term memory. The most common cause of amnestic syndrome is alcohol-induced persisting amnestic disorder, or Korsakoff's syndrome, which involves a thiamine deficiency typically associated with patterns of chronic alcohol abuse.

Psychological Disorders Related to Aging

What types of psychological problems affect people in later life? Generalized anxiety disorder and phobic disorders are the most commonly occurring anxiety disorders among older people. Depression to varying degrees is common among people in later life and may be associated with memory deficits that may lift as the depression clears. Dementia of the Alzheimer's type and vascular dementia primarily affect people in later life. They involve irreversible and progressive memory impairment. Certain sleep disorders, such as insomnia and sleep apnea, are also common among older people.

What are Alzheimer's disease and vascular dementia? Alzheimer's disease (AD) is a progressive brain disease characterized by progressive loss of memory and cognitive ability, as well as deterioration in personality functioning and self-care skills. There is no cure or effective treatment for AD. Research into its causes has focused on genetic factors and imbalances in neurotransmitters, especially acetylcholine. Vascular dementia results from multiple strokes (blood clots that block the supply of blood to parts of the brain, damaging or destroying brain tissue).

Dementias Due to General Medical Conditions

What other general medical conditions can lead to dementia? Various other medical conditions can lead to dementia, including Pick's disease, Parkinson's disease, Huntington's disease, Creutzfeldt-Jakob disease, HIV disease, head trauma, and neurosyphilis.

Scoring Key for Attitudes Toward Aging Scale

1. False. Most healthy couples continue to engage in satisfying sexual activities into their 70s and 80s.
2. False. This is too general a statement. Those who find their work satisfying are less desirous of retiring.
3. False. In late adulthood, we tend to become more concerned with internal matters—our physical functioning and our emotions.
4. False. Adaptability remains reasonably stable throughout adulthood.
5. False. Age itself is not linked to noticeable declines in life satisfaction. Of course, we may respond negatively to disease and losses, such as the death of a spouse.
6. False. Although we can predict some general trends for older adults, we can also do so for younger adults. Older adults, like their younger counterparts, are heterogeneous in personality and behavior patterns.
7. False. Older adults with stable intimate relationships are more satisfied.
8. False. We are susceptible to a wide variety of psychological disorders at all ages.
9. False. Only a minority are depressed.
10. False. Actually, church attendance declines, but not verbally expressed religious beliefs.
11. False. Although reaction time may increase and general learning ability may undergo a slight decline, older adults usually have little or no difficulty at familiar work tasks. In most jobs, experience and motivation are more important than age.
12. False. Learning may just take a bit longer.
13. False. Older adults do not direct a higher proportion of thoughts toward the past than do younger people. Regardless of our age, we may spend more time daydreaming at any age if we have more time on our hands.
14. False. Fewer than 10% of older adults require some form of institutional care.

CHAPTER SIXTEEN

Violence and Abuse

Rufino Tamayo
Title Unknown (Abstract)

Truth OR Fiction?

- Despite all the talk about crime, the United States has a relatively low homicide rate as compared with other industrialized countries. (p. 501)

- A male teen in the United States stands a greater chance of dying from a gunshot wound than from all natural causes of death combined. (p. 501)

- Though alcohol use is linked to aggression, it is rarely involved in homicides. (p. 510)

- Women who remain with men who abuse them suffer from a form of masochism. (p. 517)

- The most common form of child maltreatment is physical abuse. (p. 519)

- Women are more likely to be raped by men they know than by strangers. (p. 522)

- Child molesters typically use physical force to compel children into performing sexual acts. (p. 526)

- In some cases, sexual relations between clients and therapists are therapeutically justified. (p. 533)

There was a time not so long ago when people would leave their doors unlocked, walk through city parks long into the night, and open their front doors to strangers without hesitation. Today, fear of violent crime and the threat of terrorist attacks increasingly govern our behavior. We live behind triple-locked doors, equip our homes and cars with the most sophisticated security systems, and endure long waits at security checkpoints at the nation's airports. Some of us rarely if ever go out at night, even in our own neighborhoods. Yet we are much more likely to be attacked or killed by people we know than by strangers—by our spouses, family members, friends or acquaintances, or people we date.

By international standards, the United States stands out as a violent culture. Homicide is the second leading cause of death, after accidents, among young people in the 15 to 24 age range. It is the leading cause of death among Black males in this age group (Coontz & Franklin, 1997). The murder rate in the United States is nearly 10 times what it is in Japan; the robbery rate is nearly 150 times greater (Kristof, 1995). The homicide rate in the United States is especially high (see Figure 16.1), exceeding by a wide margin the homicide rates of other developed nations (United Nations, 1998).

Although other factors are clearly involved in the high rate of homicides in the United States, a contributing factor is easy access to firearms. About three of four homicides of young people result from the use of firearms, as compared to fewer than one in four in other developed nations (Kristof, 1995). A national survey showed that one in five teenagers in the United States carries a weapon ("One in Five," 1998). More male teens in the United States die from firearms than from all natural causes combined (M. L. Rosenberg, 1993). It is too easy for many young people in the United States to acquire guns, and an alarming number of them carry them (O'Donnell, 1995).

Although the homicide rate in the United States remains high, there is good news. The murder rate overall, and homicides of young persons involving the use of firearms, began dropping in the early 1990s (Fingerhut, Ingram, & Feldman, 1998). Moreover, violent crime overall declined steadily during the 1990s, the longest period of decline in 25 years (Butterfield, 1997a, 1997c).

In this chapter we focus on violent and abusive behavior. We will see that violence and abuse take many forms, from outright physical aggression to sexual harassment. We will also see that the search for the origins of violent and abusive behavior is best approached from a multifactorial model that takes into account sociocultural, psychological, and biological factors.

Violence and Abnormal Behavior

In Chapter 1 we introduced you to the idea that abnormal behavior can be defined in a number of ways, including unusualness, social deviance or unacceptability, faulty perceptions or interpretations of reality, severe personal distress, maladaptiveness, and dangerousness. Given these definitions, is violent behavior abnormal?

The answer largely depends on the context in which the behavior occurs. The behavior of a professional football player or hockey player may indeed be violent, but it is not what we would usually consider to be abnormal, except perhaps if it exceeds the boundaries of what would be considered sporting. (In hockey, it may be difficult to know where to draw the line.) Prizefighters earn their livings in a sport that is by its nature violent. Even though the physical pounding a prizefighter endures in the ring may lead to the development of physical and psychological disorders (see Chapter 15), prizefighting is not classified as abnormal behavior.

Warfare or combat is also inherently violent and certainly dangerous to self and others. Yet we don't typically consider the violent behavior of soldiers who fight wars or the general officers who direct them as abnormal. Perhaps we might consider the behavior of the nations themselves that wage war or their leaders as abnormal. But those who risk their lives and commit violent acts against soldiers of other nations are generally seen as loyal or patriotic, perhaps even heroic, not abnormal.

Where, then, do we draw the line between violent behavior that is deemed normal and that which is deemed abnormal? We adopt the following standard. We consider violent

Truth OR Fiction?   REVISITED

Despite all the talk about crime, the United States has a relatively low homicide rate as compared with other industrialized countries.

FALSE. The United States leads the industrialized world in homicide rates.

Truth OR Fiction?   REVISITED

A male teen in the United States stands a greater chance of dying from a gunshot wound than from all natural causes of death combined.

TRUE. A male teenager is more likely to die from a gunshot wound than from all natural causes combined.

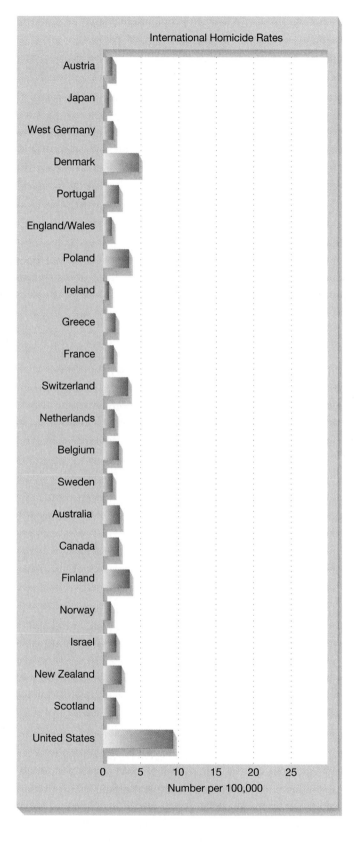

FIGURE 16.1 Homicide rates: U.S. versus other developed countries.
The homicide rate in the United States far exceeds the rates in other developed countries. The easy availability of firearms is clearly a contributing factor to the high rate of homicides in the United States.

Source. United Nations. (1998). *Demographic yearbook.* New York: Author.

behavior to be abnormal if it (1) occurs outside a socially sanctioned context, and (2) is either self-defeating or dangerous (harmful to oneself or others). The football player who slams an opponent into the ground is rewarded with a multimillion-dollar contract; the one who slams his wife against the wall commits a violent act that is abnormal as well as criminal. The spouse abuser's behavior is clearly dangerous (harmful to others and perhaps to self), socially unacceptable, and also maladaptive or self-defeating, because it can lead to arrest, marital dissolution, and retaliation, as well as failing to resolve the underlying conflict. It may also be associated with severe personal distress.

Violence and Psychological Disorders

A common perception exists that people with psychological disorders are especially prone to violence. Some people with psychological disorders do commit violent acts, just as assuredly as do some people without diagnosable psychological disorders. The great majority of people with psychological disorders, however, are nonviolent (Lamberg, 1998). Substance or alcohol abuse, and a history of criminal behavior are much more strongly tied to violent crimes than are mental disorders (Bonta, Law, & Hanson, 1998).

On the other hand, evidence points to an increased risk of violence associated with some mental disorders, such as schizophrenia, especially during times of active hallucinations and delusions (Hodgkins et al., 1998; Link & Stueve, 1998). Most of the violent acts committed by former patients occur within their networks of families and friends (Link & Stueve, 1998; Steadman et al., 1998). Factors such as substance abuse and poor adherence to medication in people with severe mental disorders (schizophrenia or bipolar disorder) are also linked to a higher risk of violent behavior (e.g., Steadman et al., 1998; Swartz et al., 1998; Tiihonen et al., 1997).

As many as one in two people with schizophrenia have either an alcohol or illicit drug dependence disorder (Miller & Brown, 1997; Ziedonis & Trudeau, 1997). People with these dual diagnoses are labeled *MICAs* (mentally ill chemical abusers). They sometimes engage in violent behavior when they stop taking their psychiatric medication and return to using alcohol or drugs. Alcohol and other drugs may contribute to violence by impairing behavioral controls over impulses. We should also note that violent behavior is sometimes a feature of antisocial personality disorder (see Chapter 9) and conduct disorder in children and adolescents (see Chapter 14). All told, however, only a small proportion of aggressive or violent behavior on our streets and in our homes can be attributed to diagnosable psychological disorders. We need to consider other explanations derived from biological, social-cognitive, and sociocultural perspectives to provide a fuller accounting of violent and abusive behavior.

America the violent. The homicide rate in the United States is 10 times what it is in Japan. Young men in the United States are more likely to die as the result of homicide than young men in any of the other developed nations listed in Figure 16.1. These empty shoes of young gunshot victims are a poignant reminder of the many needless deaths caused by homicides.

Quiz **16.1**
Violence and Abnormal Behavior

Explaining Human Aggression

Are human beings basically aggressive by nature? Or is aggression learned behavior? There is no shortage of opinions among observers of the human condition as to the origins of human aggression. We have yet to come to any generally accepted theory of violence and aggression. Here, let us consider how several of the major theoretical perspectives have approached the problem. We also offer our own speculations on what these perspectives may teach us about our capacity to aggress and do violence against others.

Biological Perspectives

The animal world is not a peaceable kingdom. Animals in their natural habitat face a constant struggle to survive as either prey or predator. The classic biological view of

instinct A fixed, inborn pattern of behavior that is specific to members of a particular species.

sociobiology Biological perspective that explains psychological traits as behavioral tendencies that increased our ancestors' chances of survival and were passed down genetically.

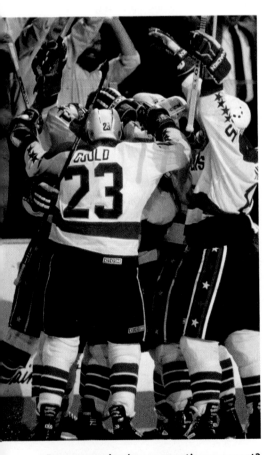

Does aggression have a genetic component? Sociobiologists believe that aggressive tendencies that might have helped ancestral humans to survive might be part of our genetic inheritance.

aggression holds that it is a product of **instinct.** Instincts are fixed, inborn patterns of behavior that are specific to members of a particular species. We say that birds instinctively build nests and salmon instinctively return upstream to spawn. Classic instinct theory holds that predators possess an aggressive instinct that has a survival function. A predator is more likely to survive and be around long enough to pass along its genetic inheritance to its offspring if it responds "instinctively" by attacking its prey. Within species, aggression usually occurs among males and typically involves a way of establishing dominance or access to mates. The more aggressive males may thus have greater access to the most fertile females and be more likely to pass along their genetic inheritance to future generations, presumably including genes controlling aggressive behavior, than would their more placid brethren.

To what extent might human aggression be instinctual? An early proponent of the belief that human aggression is a product of instinct was Sigmund Freud. As he looked upon the destruction and devastation that human beings had wrought in the Great War (as World War I was called at the time), Freud came to believe there must be an underlying instinct that accounts for human aggression, which he dubbed the "death instinct." The "death instinct" was basically self-destructive in its aim, having as its ultimate purpose the return to the tension-free state that preceded birth. The death instinct can give rise to self-destructive behaviors, including suicide. Sometimes it is turned against others in the form of outward aggression, violence, and warfare. In Freud's view, instinctual impulses such as aggression and sex strive for expression and must be released in some form. The ego is responsible for finding socially appropriate outlets for channeling these impulses. Thus, aggressive impulses may be "vented" by participating in rough-and-tumble sports such as football or hockey or by seeking to "trounce" your opponent in tennis or bridge. They may also be expressed vicariously, such as by watching a violent movie or sporting event. The venting of aggressive impulses, which is termed *catharsis*, is believed to act as something of a safety valve, an acceptable way of "letting off steam." Outward aggression arises when the ego is unable to contain these destructive impulses, which can occur if the ego is weak or overtaxed.

Sociobiological Views Today, most scholars reject the instinct theory of human behavior in large part because it fails to account for the diversity that exists among humans and the importance of learning and culture in determining behavior. A newer biological perspective, called **sociobiology,** has emerged. Sociobiologists do not explain human aggression on the basis of instinct. Rather, they believe that we inherit behavioral tendencies or dispositions, including aggressive tendencies, that increased the chances of survival of our early ancestors and were passed down along the genetic highway all the way to us (Gaulin & McBurney, 2001; Goode, 2000b; Thornhill & Palmer, 2000). They believe that we inherit not only physical traits such as hair color or height, but also behavioral traits such as aggression, even though such traits may no longer be adaptive in modern civilization.

The period of time since the dawning of modern civilization is but a brief moment in our history as a species, a mere blink of the eye. Sociobiologists believe that aggressiveness may be a behavioral trait or disposition that had survival value to our earliest ancestors who eked out a bare-bones existence in groups of hunter-gatherers ordered along distinct gender roles in which men hunted and killed animals and women collected edible roots and shrubs. Sociobiologists see contemporary evidence showing that boys and men tend to be more aggressive than girls or women as consistent with this evolutionary perspective (Knight, Fabes, & Higgins, 1996). They may also see attraction to violence in contemporary media and in video games as a by-product of our aggressive inheritance.

Sociobiological or evolutionary viewpoints remain controversial. Critics claim that humans are not marionettes whose strings are pulled by invisible genetic masters. They argue that culture, learning, and personal choice are more important determinants of our behavior than genetics (Eagly & Wood, 1991). On the other hand, contemporary evolutionary models argue for an interactionist approach that posits that biological factors interact with social and environmental factors in creating conditions that lead to aggressive behavior (Buss & Shackelford, 1997). They believe there is ample room for both biology and culture in explaining human behavior. Here, let us consider evidence that may uncover the biological underpinnings of aggressive behavior.

Neurobiological Bases of Aggression Investigations of brain mechanisms in aggression have focused attention on the role of the hypothalamus. If we electrically stimulate certain parts of the hypothalamus of other animals such as rats and monkeys, we can elicit attack behavior or other stereotypical violent responses. This leads us to believe that the hypothalamus may act as a control center in regulating aggressive behavior, at least in other animals. However, the human brain is much more complex than that of other species and our behavior depends more on learning than on neural reflexes. Whatever brain mechanisms may be involved in regulating aggression in humans may be subject to the overriding influences of culture and learning.

Contemporary neurobiological research on aggression has focused largely on the role of neurotransmitters, especially serotonin and the male sex hormone testosterone (e.g., Virkkunen & Linnoila, 1993; Virkkunen et al., 1994).

Serotonin acts as an inhibitory neurotransmitter in some parts of the brain, especially the *limbic system,* a part of the brain involved in regulating primitive drives such as hunger, thirst, and aggression. The limbic system also plays key roles in learning, memory, and the regulation of emotions. Researchers suspect that serotonin helps put the brakes on primitive behaviors, including acts of impulsive aggression (Cowley & Underwood, 1998). In one study, men who had committed crimes involving acts of impulsive violence were found to have abnormally low levels of serotonin in their brains, whereas men who had committed violent criminal acts involving premeditation and planning had normal levels of serotonin (Toufexis, 1993). Serotonin activity has also been implicated in aggressive behavior in young boys (Pine et al., 1997). Dysfunctions in serotonin activity may also have implications for explaining the impulsive, aggressive behavior observed in people with certain personality disorders, such as borderline personality disorder (Siever & Trestman, 1993).

In animal research, investigators find that if you destroy certain parts of the brain involved in serotonin production, the level of aggressive behavior increases (Siever & Trestman, 1993). This can be observed in increased mouse-killing behavior in rats. Other research shows that more dominant male monkeys have higher levels of serotonin than lower-ranking males. A leading investigator, John Mann of Columbia University, calls serotonin a "behavioral seat belt" because of its role as a restraining mechanism in holding back impulsive behavior, including sexual and aggressive impulses (Bjork et al., 2000; Cowley & Underwood, 1998; Davidson, Putnam, & Larson, 2000). Yet other researchers are taking more of a "wait and see" attitude. They believe it is premature to make any definitive statements about the role of serotonin in human aggression (Berman, Tracy, & Coccaro, 1997).

Testosterone is also implicated in aggression, in part because men tend to be more aggressive than women (Buss & Kenrick, 1998; Segell, 2000). Although testosterone is produced in both men and women, the levels in men are much higher. Researchers find that teenage boys with elevated levels of testosterone are more likely to respond aggressively to provocations than their peers (Olweus, 1987). Others report that violent criminals have unusually high levels of testosterone (Virkkunen & Linnoila, 1993). High testosterone levels are also found among female prisoners who are high in aggressive dominance (Dabbs & Hargrove, 1997).

Researchers also find cross-cultural evidence supporting a link between testosterone and aggressive behavior in adult men. A study of men from the !Kung San tribe of Namibia, Africa, showed that men with higher levels of testosterone were more violent than those with lower levels (Christiansen & Winkler, 1992). Because these studies are correlational in nature, we cannot conclude that testosterone plays a causal role in aggression. Yet it gives us reason to believe that high levels of testosterone may be a link in a chain leading to aggressive behavior. The picture is clouded, however, by evidence, admittedly preliminary in nature, linking lowered levels of testosterone to aggressive behavior in men ("Testosterone Wimping Out?," 1995). Although more research is needed on the links

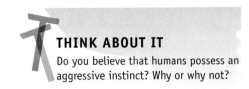

THINK ABOUT IT
Do you believe that humans possess an aggressive instinct? Why or why not?

Web Link **16.1**
www Youth Violence: A Report
of the Surgeon General

between testosterone and aggression in men, it is possible that either excesses or deficits of the hormone may be involved in mediating aggressive behavior in men.

More evidence of biological factors in human aggression comes from genetic studies of criminality and violent behavior. Are propensities toward violent behavior inherited? Evidence from both twin studies and adoptee studies points to a genetic contribution to criminality (Carey, 1992). However, not all criminals are violent; some commit property offenses. The heritability of violent criminality per se is less clear and remains to be more fully explored in future research.

Social-Cognitive Perspectives

Social-cognitive theorists such as Albert Bandura (1973, 1986) propose that aggression is learned behavior acquired in the same way as other behaviors. The roles of modeling and reinforcement are highlighted in the learning of aggressive behavior. Children may learn to imitate violent behavior they observe at home, in the schoolyard, or on television or in other media. If they are then reinforced for acting aggressively, such as by getting their way with their peers or earning peer approval or respect, their tendency to aggress may become stronger over time.

A child's exposure to aggressive models may begin in the home in the form of witnessing spousal violence or suffering violence firsthand in the form of physical abuse or punishment meted out by parents. One lesson the child may draw from such experiences is that violence in the context of interpersonal relationships is an acceptable way of getting others to do what you want them to do, or of punishing them when they fail to comply with your requests. Evidence shows that aggressive or violent children often come from homes where parents and other family members model aggressive behavior ("Risk Factors," 2000).

Childhood exposure to crime and violence is widespread, especially among urban youth. A study of urban high school students showed that 93% reported having witnessed a violent act and 44% had been victimized themselves (Berman et al., 1997). Not surprisingly, young people exposed to violence, or who have been victims themselves, are at greater risk of mental health problems, including PTSD, depression, anxiety, as well as trouble with teachers, than are their nonvictimized peers (Boney-McCoy & Finkelhor, 1996; Freeman, Shaffer, & Smith, 1996).

Psychologist David Lykken (1993) points to a lack of proper socialization as a root cause of violence in our society. He argues that the inability or unwillingness of parents, especially single parents, to socialize their children—to teach them right from wrong—leads children to become overly aggressive.

Social-cognitive theorists also incorporate roles for expectancies and competencies in explaining aggressive behavior. People who expect that aggressive behavior will produce positive outcomes are more likely to act in kind. People who lack competencies for solving interpersonal problems without resorting to aggression may be more likely to act aggressively in conflict situations.

Social-cognitive theorists also focus on the ways in which people interpret confrontational or conflict situations (Berkowitz, 1994). When people see other people's motives as hostile, they are more likely to act aggressively than when they form a more benign interpretation of the other's behavior. Evidence shows that young people who have problems with aggression tend to distort other people's motives. They tend to assume other people intend them harm when they do not (Crick & Dodge, 1994). In a similar way, men who commit date rape may misread the woman's expressed wishes, believing that the woman is merely playing "hard to get" when she resists his sexual overtures. Cognitive theorists also recognize that people are more likely to act aggressively when they magnify the importance of a perceived insult (e.g., Lochman & Dodge, 1994).

Social-cognitive theorists argue against the catharsis view of aggression. The expression of aggression, even in controlled situations such as a sporting event, may not reduce the potential for aggression but actually increase it by providing additional opportunities for reinforcement.

Web Link **16.2**
Raising Children to Resist Violence: **wWw**
What You Can Do

Effects of Prior Abuse and Victimization Violence may also beget violence from one generation to another. Many people who engage in abusive or violent behavior were themselves abused as children. In one recent study, dangerously violent adolescents had higher levels of exposure to violence and victimization than nonviolent matched controls (Flannery, Singer, & Wester, 2001). In another study, teenage boys who were physically abusive toward their dating partners were more likely than nonviolent boys to have been maltreated during childhood (Wolfe et al., 2001).

Physically abused children often begin to show violent behavior early in childhood (Davis & Boster, 1992). Neglected children may be at even greater risk of becoming violent later in life. However, the pathway between child abuse (which includes physical abuse, neglect, and maltreatment) and later violent or abusive behavior is neither direct nor certain. Most studies show that the majority of abused children do not become delinquents or violent offenders (Widom, 1989a, 1989b). Child abuse may lead to other outcomes, such as withdrawal or self-destructive behavior, rather than outward aggression. We need to expand our knowledge of how other factors, such as exposure to violence in media, interact with child abuse to increase the potential for later violent behavior.

The intergenerational transmission of violent behavior may involve a modeling effect. If children are abused, or if they observe one parent battering the other, they may learn that violent behavior is an acceptable means of dealing with interpersonal conflicts. Children who are exposed to violence in the home or were abused themselves may fail to establish secure, loving attachments with their parents and a sense of empathy and respect for the feelings of others, which may set the stage for wanton acts of violent cruelty toward others. It is also conceivable that there is a genetic component underlying the intergenerational transmission of violent behavior.

Effects of Media Violence Another modeling effect is the influence of exposure to violence in the media, especially violence on television. It is estimated that the average child, who watches 2 to 4 hours of TV daily, will have seen on the TV screen some 8,000 murders, and 100,000 other acts of violence, by the time he or she completes elementary school (Eron, 1993). But does exposure to media violence contribute to violent behavior?

Relationships between media exposure to violence and aggressive behavior in children are complex and may cut both ways. More aggressive children may be more inclined to watch violent programming (DeAngelis, 1993). Yet most experts believe that exposure to violent media contributes to aggressive and violent behavior in children and adolescents ("Health Groups," 2000; Huesmann & Miller, 1994). Classic experiments by psychologist Albert Bandura and his colleagues showed that children imitated aggressive behavior they observed on television, even when the models were cartoon characters (e.g., Bandura, Ross, & Ross, 1963). Figure 16.2 illustrates how children imitate aggressive behavior of an adult model that was shown hitting a toy "Bobo" doll. In other laboratory-based studies, both children and adults are found to act more aggressively when exposed to violence on television or other media (DeAngelis, 1993). Evidence also points to increased aggressive behavior in boys and men following exposure to violent video games (Anderson & Dill, 2000).

Exposure to violence in the media may contribute to aggressive behavior in several ways (Eron, 1993; "Health Groups," 2000; Huesmann & Miller, 1994). It may prime or kindle aggressive thoughts or impulses. Repeated exposure to media violence may lessen inhibitions for using violence to resolve conflicts, especially when characters on TV or in the movies are rewarded for acting violently or are shown "getting away with it." Repeated exposure to media violence may also have an emotional numbing or habituating effect, leading viewers to become desensitized to acts of real violence and perhaps less sensitive to the fate of victims. Having said this, evidence suggests that exposure to violence on TV is clearly not as powerful a predictor of aggressive behavior in children as violence observed in the home, the schools, or the community (Gunter & McAleer, 1990).

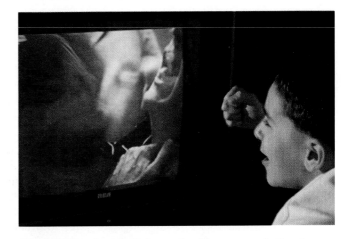

What's Johnny learning? Research evidence supports the view that exposure to violent media contributes to aggressive behavior in children. What mechanisms may account for these effects?

FIGURE 16.2 A classic experiment in the imitation of aggressive models.
Research by Albert Bandura and his colleagues has shown that children frequently imitate the aggressive behavior that they observe. In the top row, an adult model strikes a clown doll. The lower rows show a boy and a girl imitating the aggressive behavior.

THINK ABOUT IT
Given the evidence provided in the text, do you think that a biological or a socio-cognitive explanation for violence is more persuasive? Explain your answer.

Web Link **16.3** wWw
Children and Television Violence

Parents may take a more active role in limiting their children's exposure to violent programming. Television shows carry labels indicating whether violent behavior is present, so parents can screen what their children watch. In addition, new television sets are equipped with V-chips that permit parents to block violent programming (Rutenberg, 2001). Parents can also impress upon children the differences between violence in the media and real violence. They can inform them that media violence is staged and is not real, that television actors, unlike real victims, can simply wipe away fake blood. They can help children understand how the media sensationalizes or glamorizes violent behavior and that most people in real life deal with conflict situations through peaceful means.

Sociocultural Perspectives

From the sociocultural perspective, violent behavior is rooted in underlying social causes, many of which go hand in hand, such as poverty, lack of opportunity, family breakdown, and exposure to deviant role models. Social stressors such as prolonged unemployment also play a role. Data drawn from the Epidemiologic Catchment Area (ECA) study showed that people who were nonviolent and employed when first interviewed but were later laid off were nearly six times more likely to engage in violent behavior than others who remained employed (Catalano et al., 1993). In countries such as Japan that are characterized by social cohesiveness, strong family ties, and a relatively balanced distribution of wealth, violent crime is but a small fraction of what it is in the more fragmented U.S. society (Kristof, 1995). Children in the United States who grow up in economically disadvantaged, inner city neighborhoods show higher levels of aggression than do less disadvantaged children (Guerra et al., 1995). In helping to explain the poverty-aggression connection, let us note that poorer children are generally exposed to greater levels of life stress, including stress associated with exposure to neighborhood violence. They also tend to be more accepting of aggressive behavior (Guerra et al., 1995). Children who are exposed to more life stress and those who adopt more accepting beliefs concerning aggression tend to behave more aggressively than do other children.

Another factor linking poverty and violent behavior is the gang subculture. In America's poorer neighborhoods, a subculture of violence has sprung up, organized around deviant peer groups or gangs, in which protecting "turf" and proving one's manhood by taking up the gun or the knife has become the social norm. To young people who feel alienated from society and who hold little or no hope for their future, the sense of belongingness and acceptance that comes from joining a gang can be a tempting lure that may be difficult to resist, especially for those youngsters from disintegrated or disrupted families that are unable to provide them with support and moral guidance.

Sociocultural theorists also examine the role of violence as a social influence tactic. Violence, or the threat of violence, may be viewed as a form of coercion used to get people to comply with one's wishes, whether it involves strong-arm tactics of organized crime "enforcers" or abusive spouses who demand that their partners accede to their demands.

Sociocultural perspectives on violence also consider how cultural values and methods of child rearing have a way of breeding violence. In other cultures, such as in Thailand and Jamaica, aggression in children is actively discouraged and politeness and deference is fostered (Tharp, 1991). By contrast, our culture socializes children to be competitive and independent. Cultural differences may explain findings that children in Thailand and Jamaica are more likely than U.S. children to be "overcontrolled" and to complain of sleeping problems, fears, and physical problems, whereas children in the United States are more likely to be "undercontrolled" and perceived by others as argumentative, disobedient, and belligerent (Tharp, 1991).

Homicide Rates and Ethnicity Homicide is more prevalent among racial and ethnic minority groups (Council of Economic Advisors, 1998). We shouldn't be surprised by these differences, as homicide and other violent crime is more common among people at lower socioeconomic levels (Parker & Pruitt, 2000). Traditionally disadvantaged minorities in the United States are disproportionately represented at the lower rungs of the economic ladder.

Although African Americans constitute about 13% of the population, about 50% of the murder victims in the United States are African American (U.S. Department of Justice, 1994). Homicides committed by or against young African Americans are especially high. The chances of African American men in the 15 to 34 age range becoming victims of homicide are about nine times greater than the chances of non-Hispanic White American men in the same age range. The proportion of homicides committed by young men is more than seven times greater among African Americans (85.6 per 100,000) than non-Hispanic White Americans (11.2 per 100,000). The odds of becoming a victim of homicide are almost as great among young Hispanic American men as young African American men (Tardiff et al., 1994). In the great majority of homicides in the United States, the victim and the perpetrator were of the same race and knew each other. Blacks tend to kill Blacks; Whites tend to kill Whites.

We need to consider other factors in explaining ethnic differences in homicide rates besides socioeconomic status. Another second factor is the proliferation of firearms, especially in poorer, predominantly minority communities. Yet another factor is illicit drug use, which is often linked to street crime, especially in poorer communities.

Alcohol and Aggression

Alcohol use is implicated in nearly 40% of violent crimes, including more than 60% of homicides, at least 25% of serious assaults, and more than 25% of rapes (Collins & Messerschmidt, 1993; Gordis, 1999; Martin, 1992). The U.S. Justice Department estimates that more than one of three adult offenders had been drinking just preceding the commission of their crimes (Cable News Network, 1998).

A cross-cultural study of violent crime data from 11 countries in different parts of the world showed that in nearly two of three violent crimes overall, the perpetrator had been drinking at the time the crime was committed (Murdoch, Pihl, & Ross, 1990). The risks of homicide, suicide, and violent death are greater among alcohol and illicit drug users than nonusers (Rivara et al., 1997). Even people living with alcohol or drug users who

Sociocultural roots of violence. According to the sociocultural perspective, violent behavior is rooted in social ills, such as poverty, family breakdown, and social decay, that give rise to deviant subcultures, such as gangs.

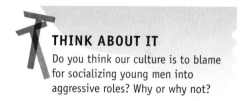

THINK ABOUT IT
Do you think our culture is to blame for socializing young men into aggressive roles? Why or why not?

don't drink or use drugs themselves are at greater risk of being killed than are people living in drug-free households (Wren, 1997a).

Although linkages between alcohol and aggressive behavior are correlational in nature, a growing body of experimental findings points to alcohol playing a causal role in both verbal and physical aggression (e.g., Giancola & Zeichner, 1997; Ito, Miller, & Pollock, 1996). Several factors may be involved in explaining alcohol's effects. For one thing, alcohol has certain cognitive effects, such as impairing decision-making ability. We may be less able to weigh the consequences of our actions when we have been drinking, which in some circumstances may lead us to act aggressively with little if any regard for the consequences that may result. Alcohol use may also loosen inhibitions or restraints (a process called *disinhibition*) that normally curtail impulsive behavior, including acts of impulsive violence. Alcohol also has a relaxing effect and may make the person less sensitive to anxiety-arousing cues relating to potential punishment that might ordinarily serve to inhibit aggressive behavior. Perhaps, too, people may act aggressively when drinking because of their expectations about the effects of alcohol, rather than because of its biochemical properties per se. Alcohol and other drugs may also make it more difficult for people to perceive the motives of others accurately, leading them to perceive a malevolent intent in other's behavior that can trigger a violent response.

Not everyone who drinks becomes aggressive, however. Relationships between violent behavior and alcohol or other drug use are complex and may be moderated by a number of factors, including the dosage level and the user's biological sensitivity to the drug's effects, the user's relationship to the victim, the setting of the encounter, as well as other situational, individual, and sociocultural factors. For example, some people become more violent when they drink than do others, and violent behavior tends to occur more often when people drink in some situations, such as sporting events, than in others. Differences in the levels or actions of the neurotransmitter serotonin may also be involved. Researchers have linked tendencies to become violent under the influence of alcohol to low levels of serotonin in the brain, which suggests a deficiency of serotonin may lower the threshold for violent behavior following alcohol use (Virkkunen & Linnoila, 1993). All in all, it appears that the interplay of alcohol and violent behavior involves complex relationships between the chemical effects of alcohol on the brain and environmental cues, which under certain circumstances may lead to violent behavior.

Emotional Factors in Violent Behavior

Emotional factors, especially frustration and anger, often figure prominently in aggressive behavior. Frustration is the emotional state associated with the thwarting or blocking of one's attempt to achieve a goal. According to the classic *frustration-aggression* hypothesis, frustration always produces aggression, and aggression is always a consequence of frustration. Consider the following example. Let's say you attend a movie but are unable to enjoy it because someone sitting in front of you is constantly talking and says you should be the one to move if it bothers you so much. You may feel frustrated because your goal of enjoying the movie is thwarted, but will you attack the person you hold responsible? Perhaps, but perhaps not. We've come to recognize that although frustration often plays a role in aggression, it may lead to other responses than aggression. In the preceding example, you might leave the theater or complain to the manager rather than instigating a fight. Moreover, aggression often has other causes than frustration. For example, aggression may involve a response to a direct provocation or retaliation for perceived wrongdoing. Aggression in response to frustration is more likely when it induces anger and when the person blames the other person for being responsible for the situation.

Anger is often a catalyst or instigator of violent or aggressive behavior. A husband strikes his wife in a "fit of anger" when he feels frustrated that dinner is not waiting for him when he returns from work. The child abuser lashes out in anger when the child fails to comply quickly enough with his or her demands. In the schoolyard, a slight provocation is blown out of proportion, eliciting an angry response that quickly escalates into a physical confrontation. Problems with controlling anger figure prominently in personality disorders, especially borderline and antisocial personality disorders. People with borderline personality disorder often show a lack of control over their anger, having frequent temper outbursts or displays of impulsive, aggressive behavior directed at themselves or others. People with anti-social personalities may channel feelings of resentment and anger against family or society in general into violent or aggressive behavior. But anger management is not only a problem for people with personality disorders. In Chapter 5, we noted how problems related to anger and hostility are implicated as risk factors in cardiovascular disorders. We saw in Chapter 14 how children and adolescents with conduct disorders often have problems controlling their anger and need to learn anger coping skills, such as calming self-talk, to handle conflict situations without resorting to violent behavior. Cognitive-behavior therapists have made important inroads in helping people with anger management problems, as we discuss further in the nearby "A Closer Look" section.

Tying It Together

Human aggression is a complex behavior that cannot be explained by any single cause. Although some aggressive displays in other animals may be a product of "instinct," instinct theories fail to account for the variation in aggressive behavior in humans. A terrorist bombing, a mugging on a street corner, organized warfare, and a husband slamming his wife against the wall are all considered forms of aggression, but the motives that underlie them reflect different political, social, and psychological factors.

Although we cannot reduce human aggression to the level of instinct, increasing evidence points to roles for biological factors in human aggression. Biology may have more to teach us about the more impulsive forms of violent behavior, such as explosive acts of rage, than the more calculated forms of violence, such as reprisals for perceived wrongdoing or premeditated, violent crimes. Biological factors may also play a more direct role in lowering the threshold for violence in people who use alcohol or other drugs.

We also need to consider roles for culture and learning. Violent behavior is practically unknown in some cultures, but all too common in others, including unfortunately our own. Children are exposed to cultural attitudes that legitimize certain forms of violence. Young boys learn from peer influences and from television and movie role models that conflicts are settled with fists or weapons rather than words. Cognitive factors such as ways of interpreting provocations, expectations that violence will lead to positive outcomes, and tendencies to practice angering self-statements in conflict situations help account for individual differences in aggressive behavior.

Consider one possible causal pathway involving multiple factors leading to impulsive violence. Young people who are exposed to aggressive role models in the home and the community may learn that violent behavior is an acceptable way to respond to conflict, perhaps even the expected way. They may lack resources for handling stress or channeling anger in more constructive ways. We can further speculate that a biological predisposition for impulsive, violent behavior, perhaps mediated by a serotonin imbalance, may further increase the potential for violence in people exposed to these learning experiences. Alcohol use may also enter the mix of factors that raise the potential for violence, perhaps even to a greater extent in people with these biological vulnerabilities.

What can be done to prevent violence? One illustrative example comes from the state of Washington, where school children are exposed to nonaggressive ways of handling problem situations. The curriculum focuses on the following skills:

1. *Empathy training,* which helps children identify their own feelings and become more aware of other children's feelings;

2. *Anger management training,* in which children are taught coping skills to control anger;

3. *Impulse control training,* in which students learn problem-solving skills to handle problem situations.

The program has had some success in reducing physically aggressive behavior and fostering more appropriate social behavior. What can each of us do in our own lives to counter violence?

THINK ABOUT IT

How prone to anger are you? To violence? What factors make it more or less likely that you will act out aggressively or violently in a given situation?

 Quiz 16.2

Explaining Human Aggression

A Closer Look

Anger Management

Cognitive-behavioral therapists assist people with anger control problems by helping them identify and correct anger-inducing thoughts they experience in situations in which they are provoked by others. Clients are taught to scrutinize the fleeting thoughts they have in confrontative situations and to recognize the cognitive distortions underlying these thoughts, such as tendencies to personalize a stranger's rudeness as a personal affront and demanding that others live up to their expectations.

Psychologist Ray Novaco (1974, 1977) developed a treatment program for anger control based on stress inoculation therapy, a type of cognitive-behavioral treatment that helps people manage anticipated stressors by developing new coping skills, such as self-relaxation, and by countering disruptive thoughts that occur in confrontative situations (e.g., "Who does he think he is? I'll show him!") with more adaptive self-statements (e.g., "Relax, don't get steamed up. The guy's just a jerk."). Like a vaccine that inoculates you against a virus by exposing you to an inert variant of the microbe, stress inoculation therapy exposes participants to a managed "dose" of the stressor by having them imagine themselves keeping their "cool" in confrontative situations by practicing coping responses and adaptive self-statements. Other cognitive-behavioral approaches, such as problem-solving therapy, are also used to help people with anger management problems generate alternative, nonviolent solutions to conflict situations. A key facet in these treatment programs is helping people rethink provocations as problems to be solved rather than as threats demanding an aggressive response.

Anger management training programs have been used with a number of different groups, including adults with anger control problems and violent youth. Treatment programs for violent youth often require a broader, multifaceted approach that involves cognitive, behavioral, and emotional components (Davis & Boster, 1993; Deffenbacher et al., 1996). The cognitive component helps participants rethink minor provocations so they don't flare out of control and to use calming self-talk in angering situations. The behavioral component may include training in relaxation skills to help participants calm themselves down in angering situations and in social problem-solving skills, which helps them develop alternative ways of coping with confrontative situations. The emotional component may involve the opportunity to receive emotional support within the context of supportive group therapy sessions.

Anger and aggression. Anger is often an instigator of aggressive behavior. What techniques do cognitive-behavioral therapists use to help people control anger and manage frustrating or confrontative situations without resorting to violence?

Coping with Frustrating or Confrontational Situations

What we tell ourselves about the motives that underlie other people's behavior can increase our arousal and prompt an aggressive response. Let us suggest a few coping responses that may help you tone down your response to frustrating or confrontational situations:

1. *Attend to your internal states of arousal.* When you feel yourself getting "hot under the collar," tell yourself, "Stop and think." Take stock of any angering thoughts you may have.

2. *Pause for a moment to consider the evidence.* Are you taking the situation too personally? Are you overreacting to it? Are you jumping to conclusions about the other person's motives? Are there other ways of viewing the person's behavior, other than as a personal affront?

3. *Practice adaptive self-statements,* such as "I can deal with this. Easy does it."

4. *Practice a competing response to anger, such as calming mental imagery, or meditative or self-relaxation exercises.* Or disrupt an anger response by taking a walk around the block, watching TV, or reading. Or, to paraphrase Mark Twain, count to 10 when you're feeling angry. If that doesn't work, count to 100. The time-honored

Domestic Violence

Web Link **16.4**
Controlling Anger—Before WWW
It Controls You

More than 2 million women in the United States are severely beaten by their husbands each year (Koss et al., 1994). About one in eight husbands has committed an act of spousal violence (Holtzworth-Munroe, 1995). More than 1,000 women annually in the United States

technique of counting to 10 interrupts the tendency to respond impulsively to provocations. It gives you extra time to collect your thoughts, and even more importantly, to diffuse any self-angering thoughts with some rational counters: "Hey, calm down. This is not worth getting bent out of shape. Stay cool."

5. *Counter anger with empathy.* Rather than saying, "What a despicable person he is to act that way," think, "Maybe he's having a rough day," or, "She's just jealous of me and is acting out like a child." Or, "He must be a very unhappy person to act that way." Or, "She may

have reasons—or thinks she has reasons—for acting this way. Anyway, that's her problem, not mine. Don't take it so personally. Better to focus on solving this problem rather than getting steamed."

6. *Think through alternative, nonviolent solutions to the problem or situation and formulate a plan of action.*

7. *Give yourself a mental pat on the back for coping assertively, not aggressively, in the situation.*

Table 16.1 offers examples of angering self-statements and rational alternatives for some common confrontational situations.

TABLE 16.1 Anger Management: Substituting Rational Responses for Angering Self-Statements

Situation	Angering Self-Statement	Rational Alternative
A provocateur says, "So what are you going to do about it?"	"That jerk. Who does he think he is? I'll teach him a lesson he won't forget!"	"He must really have a problem if he acts this way. But that's his problem. I don't have to act at his level."
You get caught in a monster traffic jam.	"Why does this always happen to me? I can't stand this."	"This may be inconvenient, but it's not the end of the world. Don't blow it out of proportion. Everyone gets caught in traffic every now and then. Just relax and listen to some music."
You're waiting behind someone in the checkout line at the supermarket who has to cash a check. It seems like it's taking hours.	"He (she) has some nerve holding up the line. It's so unfair for someone to make other people wait. I'd like to tell him off!"	"It will only take a few minutes. People have a right to cash their checks in the market. Just relax and read a magazine off the rack while you wait."
You're cruising looking for a parking spot when suddenly another car cuts you off and seizes a vacant parking space.	"No one should be allowed to treat me like this. I'd like to punch him out."	"Don't expect other people to always be considerate of your interests. Stop personalizing things." "Relax, there's no sense going to war over this."
Your spouse or partner comes home several hours later than expected, without calling ahead.	"It's so unfair. I can't let him (her) treat me like this."	"Make it fair. Explain how you feel without putting him (her) down."
You're watching a movie at the theater and someone sitting next to you is talking throughout the picture.	"Don't they have any regard for other people's rights? I'm so angry with these people I could tear their heads off."	"Even if they're inconsiderate it doesn't mean I have to get angry about it or ruin my enjoyment of the movie. If they don't quiet down when I ask them, I'll just change my seat or call the manager."
A person insults you or treats you disrespectfully.	"I just can't walk away from this like nothing happened."	"Of course you can. When did anger ever settle anything? There are better ways of handling this than getting steamed."

---

die as the result of beatings by partners in intimate relationships (Rennison, 2001). Women stand a greater chance of being attacked, raped, injured, or killed by their current or former male partners than by other types of assailants (Koss et al., 1994). Yet it may surprise you to learn that evidence from community samples in the United States and other countries, such as New Zealand, show that women are as likely as men are, if not more likely, to

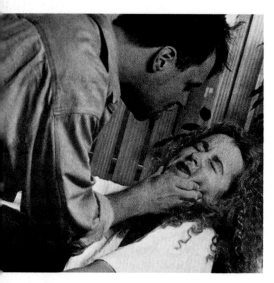

Spouse abuse. About one in four couples in the United States report incidences of domestic violence. Though both spouses may abuse one another, women suffer a much greater incidence of severe abuse at the hands of their partners and resulting physical injury and psychological effects.

THINK ABOUT IT
Relate what you learned about causes of violence in the previous section to the information just presented about psychological patterns of spouse abusers. Which causes seem most important?

commit acts of violence against their partner (Magdol et al., 1997; Margolin & Burman, 1993). In about half of the couples in which partner abuse occurs, both partners engage in acts of physical abuse against one another. However, the sheer frequency of battering does not take into account differences in the severity of the abuse. Women are much more likely than men to suffer severe abuse and to sustain physical injuries, including severe injuries such as broken bones and damage to internal organs (O'Leary, 1995). For this reason, our focus is on the male batterer.

Different motivations may be involved in accounting for partner violence in men and women. One hypothesis gaining interest is that men tend to attack while women tend to react. That is, male violence toward women may stem from factors that threaten their traditional position of dominance in relationships, such as unemployment and drug abuse. Violence perpetrated by women may arise from the stress of coping with an abusive partner (Magdol et al., 1997).

Although domestic violence cuts across all strata of our society, it is most commonly reported among people of lower socioeconomic levels. This may reflect a greater level of stress experienced by people who are struggling financially. It may also reflect a reporting bias, a tendency for upper income groups to use personal physicians who may be less inclined to report incidents of domestic violence than health care providers in public facilities who tend to serve less affluent groups (Margolin & Burman, 1993). Some evidence suggests that it is income disparity between husband and wife, with the wife earning more than the husband, that contributes to wife abuse, not poverty per se (McCloskey, 1996).

Ethnic or racial group differences appear unrelated to the risk of domestic violence when we take into account socioeconomic level and other sociodemographic factors (Margolin & Burman, 1993). The lack of opportunity and alienation from the larger society experienced by many economically disadvantaged people, including many ethnic minority group members, increases the potential for mental health problems and violence and abuse within domestic relationships (Nelson et al., 1992).

Psychological Characteristics of Male Batterers

Although there is no one psychological profile of male batterers, they tend to show higher levels of anger, hostility, impulsivity, verbal aggression, early problem behavior, and antisocial and borderline personality traits than nonbatterers (e.g., Holtzworth-Munroe, Rehman, & Herron, 2000; Murphy et al., 2001). Male batterers also tend to externalize or minimize blame for their actions and feel inadequate or dissatisfied with themselves (Flournoy & Wilson, 1991). Other characteristics associated with increased risk of battering include youthful age, lower income and occupational and educational status, high levels of stress, problem behaviors during adolescence, lack of assertive self-expression, exposure to parental violence in childhood, being the victim of physical abuse by one's mother during teenage years, and alcohol use, especially heavy use (e.g., Feldman, 1997; Magdol et al., 1998).

Patterns of Abuse

Battering typically occurs within a larger pattern of abuse involving physical abuse of children and sexual abuse of spouses. Battering often starts before marriage vows are taken, and although it may involve milder forms of aggression at first, such as pushing and grabbing, it may escalate if nothing is done to stop it (Holtzworth-Munroe, 1995).

Relationship factors, especially marital conflict, also play a role in initiating and maintaining spousal abuse. Moreover, as compared to nonviolent couples, physically aggressive couples show poorer problem-solving skills (Anglin & Holtzworth-Munroe, 1997). They also focus less of their efforts on solving their problems while showing more negative interactions in which angry responses from one spouse beget angry responses from the other (Margolin & Burman, 1993).

Spousal violence often follows an event that serves as a trigger for the abuser to lose control (Ryan, 1993). The triggering event may involve criticism or rejection from the spouse or incidents that lead the man to feel trapped, insecure, or threatened (Bitler, Linnoila, & George, 1994). The use of alcohol or other drugs further raises the risk that such events will lead to a battering episode. An analysis of some 62 episodes of domestic violence showed that about 90% of the assailants reported using alcohol or other drugs on the day of the assault (Brookoff et al., 1997).

Male batterers often have low self-esteem and a sense of personal inadequacy (Murphy, Meyer, & O'Leary, 1994). They may become excessively dependent on their wives for emotional support and feel threatened if they perceive their partners becoming more independent or developing separate interests from their own. Spousal violence may represent an inappropriate way of responding to this emotional threat. Abusers also tend to have poor problem-solving skills in handling conflict situations with their spouses (Else et al., 1993), which may explain (although not condone) why they turn to the use of physical force when a triggering event occurs.

Sociocultural Viewpoints

Writing from a sociocultural perspective, feminist theorists consider domestic violence to be a product of the differential power relationships that exist between men and women in our society. Men are socialized into dominant roles in which they expect women to be subordinate to their wishes (Koss et al., 1994). Cross-cultural evidence shows that the husband's need for control is an underlying contributor to wife abuse (Wilson & Daly, 1996). Men also learn that aggressive displays of masculine power are socially sanctioned and are even glorified in some settings, such as on the athletic field. These role expectations, together with a willingness to accept interpersonal violence as an appropriate means of resolving differences, creates a context for spousal abuse in situations in which the man's sense of control is threatened when he perceives his partner as failing to meet his needs or respect his wishes. Men who batter may also have less power in their relationships and may attempt to make up for their lack of power by using physical force.

Feminist theorists further point out that domestic violence exists because our society condones it (Gardiner, 1992). The man who beats his wife may be taken aside and "talked to" by a police officer rather than arrested on the spot. Even if he is arrested and convicted, his punishment is likely to be less severe (sometimes just a "slap on the wrist") than if he had assaulted a stranger.

Effects of Domestic Violence

In addition to the risk of physical injury, domestic violence can lead to posttraumatic stress disorder (PTSD) and other psychological effects, especially depression and low self-esteem (Cascardi et al., 1995; O'Leary, 1995; Shalev, Yehuda, & McFarlane, 2000; Watson et al., 1997). In one study, more than three fourths of battered women presented with evidence of diagnosable PTSD (Watson et al., 1997). Typically, the more severe the abuse, the greater the level of psychological distress. Battering may also be a contributing factor to alcohol or substance use disorders. Domestic violence may also lead the abused woman to flee the abusive situation, which in the absence of other resources may lead to homelessness. For the male abuser, battering may lead to a severing of family ties that may also ultimately lead to homelessness.

Exposure to domestic violence also takes an emotional toll on the children (Graham-Bermann, & Edleson, 2001; Rossman, 2001). More than 3 million children in the United States witness violence between their parents each year (DeAngelis, 1995b). In a study of 62 incidents of domestic violence in Memphis, Tennessee, children witnessed 85% of the assaults (Brookoff et al., 1997). Witnessing interparental violence has direct negative effects on the child's emotional health and behavior, leading in many cases to depression and behavior problems. Even nonphysical forms of parental aggression, such as insults, threats, or kicking furniture, is associated with more behavioral and emotional problems in children (Jouriles et al., 1996). Parental modeling of spouse abuse may also set the stage for perpetuating an intergenerational pattern of abuse from generation to

What about the children? Children too are affected by spousal abuse. Children exposed to interparental abuse may become depressed or develop behavioral problems. Childhood exposure may also set the stage for the perpetuation of spousal abuse from one generation to another. Many children are also beaten by the abusers.

generation. Clearly, it sets a poor example by modeling the use of violence as an acceptable means of resolving interpersonal conflicts. Many abusers, as well as many battered spouses, also have histories of being emotionally or physically abused during childhood. Moreover, domestic violence often occurs in a context in which children are physically abused by the offender as well (O'Leary et al., 2000). The greater the frequency of domestic violence, the more likely that children too will suffer physical abuse at the hands of the violent father or mother (Ross, 1996).

Why Don't Battered Women Just Leave?

About half of the abused women who seek professional assistance return to their abusive husbands or partners (Strube, 1988). Why do women remain in abusive relationships or take back abusive partners after a separation? Are they driven by unconscious, masochistic needs to punish themselves?

Professionals who work with abused women argue that women in abusive relationships are better understood as trauma survivors than as masochists (Strube, 1988). Battered women have much in common with other trauma survivors, such as former political hostages and victims of kidnapping. Leonore Walker (1979) coined the term *battered woman syndrome* to describe the traumatizing effects of battering, which includes feelings of helplessness and impaired coping ability that can make it difficult for the battered woman to leave the abuser and establish a new life on her own. Compounding their problems, many battered wives lack the economic means to establish an independent household of their own for themselves and their children. Consequently, many fear becoming destitute if they leave the batterer.

Spousal violence may exact a greater emotional toll than other forms of trauma because the agent of abuse is someone whom the woman trusted and loved and with whom she may need to continue a relationship, especially if children are involved. Betrayal of trust may intensify the woman's emotional reactions and further impair her ability to cope.

A review of the literature on the effects of spousal violence identifies several psychological factors that may affect the battered woman's ability to cope effectively (Follingstad, Neckerman, & Vormbrock, 1988):

1. *Shattering the myth of personal invulnerability.* Many people maintain an illusion that they are somehow immune to the traumas or tragic events that befall others, such as violent crime, crippling traffic accidents, or fatal cancers. This illusion, which helps maintain a sense of personal security, may be shattered in women exposed to spousal abuse, leaving them feeling vulnerable. If a woman is brutalized by the man in whom she placed her trust, she may come to think that other bad things will also befall her. The shield of invulnerability cracks. Her sense of safety and security in her own home that most of us take for granted may be destroyed.

2. *Reduced problem-solving ability.* Trauma may hamper the woman's ability to weigh alternative solutions to her problems. Survivors may become so preoccupied with the immediate problem of preventing recurrent beatings that they cannot focus on ways of making the larger life changes that will extricate them and their children from the marriages. Women may even come to believe that they cannot take control of events and that submission is the only realistic way of preventing further abuse. Some abused women sink to a state of despair in which they essentially "give up" trying and decide to return to the abuser rather than seek alternatives (Newman, 1993).

3. *Stress-related reactions.* Battered women may experience a form of posttraumatic stress disorder that can further impair their coping ability. Like soldiers who have had traumatic combat experiences, battered women may reexperience beatings in the form of nightmares, flashbacks, and intrusive images of abuse. They may become numbed to their environment, have sleep disturbances, feel anxious in the presence of cues or reminders of beatings, and avoid situations or stimuli connected with beatings. Anxiety and feelings of dread may lead the battered woman to withdraw from the outside world and cut off support from other people. Feelings of pessimism,

anger, guilt, and depression are also common, along with suicidal thoughts and attempts. Problems with alcohol or drug abuse may also develop, further impairing the woman's ability to function effectively.

4. *Thought conversion.* Hostages and kidnap victims who are held for a lengthy period of time sometimes experience a conversion in attitudes and come to regard their captors with positive or sympathetic feelings, at the same time developing negative feelings toward potential rescuers. In a similar way, battered women who are subjected to chronic abuse may come to view their tormenters in more sympathetic terms.

5. *Finding meaning in the abuse.* According to existential psychiatrist Viktor Frankl (1959), people have a basic psychological need to find meaning in their experiences, even in brutal abuse. Some battered women may try to find meaning in the abuse, or even justify it, by using rationalization. Rationalizations (e.g., "He didn't really mean it . . . it was really the alcohol . . . it was really my fault.") as well as the use of denial (e.g., "It wasn't really that bad.") tend to perpetuate abusive relationships.

6. *Learned helplessness.* Domestic violence can lead to feelings of helplessness, which can sap the woman's motivation to seek to overcome the trauma and make it less likely she will seek help to extricate herself from the abusive relationship (Walker, 1979; Wilson et al., 1992). Helplessness may develop as the abused woman finds that her repeated attempts to make changes in the relationship fail or when her requests for external help are met with frustrating "run-arounds" or lack of concern from criminal justice or mental health personnel. She may come to believe that nothing she can do will prevent the battering or extricate herself from the situation.

7. *Difficulties handling troubling emotions.* Battered women may have difficulty handling their anger toward the abuser, perhaps because they have learned, from his example, that anger is a dangerous or uncontrollable emotion (Carmen, Rieker, & Mills, 1984). Unexpressed anger may become redirected inward in the form of self-blame and self-loathing, which, in turn, can lead to feelings of resignation and depression and to self-destructive behaviors ranging from substance abuse to suicide attempts. Depression may further hamper the woman's ability to change her life.

We also need to take into account the cultural expectations placed on women. Women in many cultures are expected to adhere to a self-sacrificial ideal that a woman's role is to sacrifice her needs for the sake of her children and family. If she is abused, she may see her role as "suffering in silence" lest her response to the situation threaten family stability. Yet she may face a conflict between two conflicting moral values: (1) that "good women provide a strong family base for their children," and (2) that "people should not harm those they love" (Pilowsky, 1993). The turning point to taking effective action may come when she asserts as a stronger moral imperative the belief that self-respect and self-care are the moral rights of every woman.

In sum, battered women are trauma survivors, not masochists. Labeling them as masochists has the unfortunate effect of blaming the victim for the abuse. When we see battered women as survivors, rather than masochists, we supplant blaming them with an effort to understand the psychological factors that may lead them to feel trapped in their relationships. Such understanding may facilitate the development of programs to help abused women make hard decisions and counteract tendencies toward rationalization, self-hatred, and denial. Viewing the woman who suffers abuse as a survivor also shifts blame away from her and onto the batterer where it belongs.

Treatment of Batterers and Abused Partners

Before treatment can begin, the battering must stop. Only then can any therapeutic attempt at healing or reconciliation begin. Couples therapy or family therapy may be useful in treating couples and families with a history of domestic violence (O'Leary, 1995). In some cases, each spouse receives individual therapy along with marital or couples therapy. The therapist may help the couple understand rage as an expression of a sense of inner powerlessness and assist them to better understand each other's emotional pain and learn

Truth OR Fiction?   REVISITED

Women who remain with men who abuse them suffer from a form of masochism.

FALSE. Battered women are trauma survivors, not masochists. Labeling them as masochists has the unfortunate effect of blaming the victim for the abuse.

more productive ways of handling anger and resolving conflicts without resorting to violence (Mones & Panitz, 1994). In some cases, the relationship cannot be saved and the couple may need help in coping with the consequences of divorce.

Group therapy for male batterers may allow batterers to feel secure enough to express their inner feelings and be confronted by other group members if they avoid taking responsibility for their abusive behavior. Support groups for battered women are also available in many communities, often led by women who were formerly abused themselves. They provide mutual support and help battered women recognize the cycle of violence, develop escape strategies, weigh alternatives to marriage, enhance self-esteem, and decrease self-blame.

Abusers may be mandated by the courts to receive treatment as an alternative to incarceration. Unfortunately, evidence casts doubt on whether court-mandated treatment reduces future acts of domestic violence as compared to the deterrent effects of traditional criminal justice penalties (Rosenfeld, 1992). Another problem is that many abusers simply stop attending therapy, despite a court order requiring their attendance.

Quiz **16.3** Ⓠ
Domestic Violence

Child Abuse

Each year about one million children in the United States are identified as victims of child abuse (Eckenrode et al., 2000; Golden, 2000). More than 1,000 children in the United States die each year as the result of abuse or neglect. As horrific as these numbers are, they greatly understate the problem, as most incidents of child maltreatment are never publicly identified.

Child abuse cuts across all ethnic, racial, and national boundaries. A random sample of households in Ontario, Canada, showed that 31% of the adult men and 21% of the adult women reported a history of physical abuse in childhood (MacMillan et al., 1997). Although reliable statistics in less developed countries are often hard to come by, a survey in the African nation of Nigeria revealed a large percentage of children and adolescents reported having seen an abused or neglected child and believed that child abuse and neglect was widespread in their country (Ebigbo, 1993). Sad to say, child abuse may be universal, although particular rates of child abuse may vary across countries.

The child's own parents are the perpetrators of abuse in the great majority of cases. Although the mother is identified as the abuser in about 60% of cases of physical abuse (DeAngelis, 1995b), it's known that mothers assume a disproportionate share of child-care responsibilities and constitute the great majority of single-parent heads of households.

Child abuse does not arise out of a vacuum, but may be seen as progressing through a series of increasingly coercive behaviors by the abusive parent. Cognitive factors, such as blaming the child for the abuse (e.g., "If he didn't want to get hit, he should not have left his clothes lying around"), serve to justify the abuse and may contribute to the progression to more abusive behaviors. Abusive parents tend to see their children's misbehavior as intentional, even when it is not. They also rely more heavily on physical punishment and less on reasoning as a means of controlling their children than do nonabusive parents (Belsky, 1993). They often lack appropriate parenting and problem-solving skills for dealing with child behavior problems and have a low tolerance for demands made by children (Milner, 1993; Pogge, 1992). Yet, it does not appear that parents who physically abuse their children are more likely than nonabusers to have diagnosable psychological disorders (Pogge, 1992). Nor do they have any clearly identifiable psychological traits that set them apart.

Modeling of excessive use of physical punishment by parents may help explain intergenerational transmission of child abuse. When children are abused, or when they observe their parents resorting to violence against one another when stressed or angry, they may come to view violence as an acceptable response for handling conflict and child disobedience.

Child abuse. About 1 million children in the U.S. are identified as victims of child abuse each year. More than 1,000 die each year as the result of abuse or neglect at the hands of their parents or caretakers. Here we see a memorial organized by community residents in New York City after the death of a 6-year-old victim of child abuse.

TABLE 16.2   Types of Child Abuse

Type of Abuse	Definition
Physical abuse	Nonaccidental physical injury of a child caused by a parent or caretaker. The injuries may range from superficial bruises to broken bones, burns, and serious internal injuries and may result in death in some cases.
Physical neglect	Failing to provide children with, or withholding from them, adequate food, shelter, clothing, hygiene, medical care, or supervision needed to promote their growth and development.
Sexual abuse	The sexual exploitation of children involving acts ranging from nontouching offenses, such as exhibitionism, to genital fondling, sexual intercourse, or involving them in the production of pornography.
Emotional maltreatment	The use of constant harsh criticism of the child involving the use of verbally abusive language, or emotional neglect, which is characterized by the withholding of physical and emotional contact needed to promote normal emotional development and, in some extreme cases, physical development.

Source. Adapted from Alpert & Green (1992), pp. 228–229.

Types of Child Abuse

Child abuse includes several types of physical, sexual, and emotional maltreatment or neglect. A widely used set of definitions of the different types of maltreatment was developed by the New York State Federation on Child Abuse and Neglect (New York City Board of Education, 1984) (see Table 16.2). Despite these definitions, it can be difficult to determine where to draw the line between "acceptable" spanking or hitting and child abuse. Neglect is the most common form of abuse, representing nearly half (49%) of substantiated cases (Daro & Wiese, 1995). Physical abuse accounts for 21% of cases, sexual abuse for 11%, emotional maltreatment for 3%, and other forms for 16% (see Figure 16.3).

Mandatory reporting laws in all 50 states require mental health professionals, including psychologists, social workers, and marriage and family counselors, to notify child protective officials if they come to know of child abuse or have reasonable suspicions that abuse is occurring. Despite mandatory reporting laws, a great many cases of child abuse go unreported.

Risk Factors in Child Abuse

A number of parental factors are associated with an increased risk of child abuse, including stress, witnessing family violence in one's family of origin, being abused during one's own childhood, failure to develop an appropriate attachment to one's children, poor anger

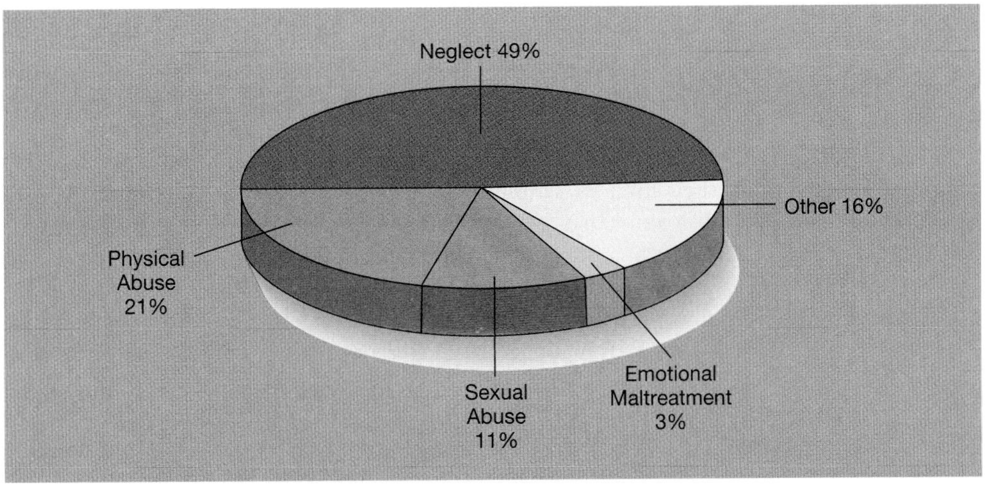

Truth OR Fiction?   REVISITED

The most common form of child maltreatment is physical abuse.

FALSE. Neglect, not physical abuse, is the most common form of child abuse.

FIGURE 16.3 Substantiated cases of child maltreatment by type.
This figure shows the breakdown of substantiated cases of child maltreatment reported by child protective agencies in 36 states in the United States for 1993 and 1994. Child neglect was the most frequent type of child maltreatment, followed by physical abuse.

Source. National Committee to Prevent Child Abuse (NCPCA); Daro & Wiese (1995).

management skills, alcohol or substance abuse, holding rigid rules concerning child rearing, and acceptance of violence as a means of resolving conflicts and controlling children's behavior (Belsky, 1993; Pogge, 1992). Moreover, teenage parents, undereducated parents, and single parents are more likely than other parents to physically abuse their children (Christmas, Wodarski, & Smokowski, 1996; DeAngelis, 1995b). Investigators find no discernible difference in the risk of child abuse across ethnic groups or socioeconomic levels of parents when the parent's level of stress is taken into account (Pogge, 1992).

Stress, a major risk factor in child abuse in its own right, also underlies other risk factors such as poverty and single parenthood. Sources of parental stress include unemployment or job-related problems, medical problems, financial pressures, marital conflict, and living in an unstable and unsafe environment.

The stress of adapting to changing family structures is another risk factor in child maltreatment. A great many families in our society have disintegrated or are in the process of coming apart at the seams. For some parents, stressful demands of changes in family structure lead to feelings of powerlessness and lower self-esteem that, in turn, may lead to child neglect or to irrational, impulsive acts of physical abuse of children.

Effects of Child Abuse

The physical injuries suffered by physically abused children are disturbing and often tragic, ranging from welts and bruises to broken bones and massive internal injuries, which sometimes result in death. The emotional wounds of abuse and neglect may run even deeper and be longer lasting. Abused or neglected children often have difficulties forming healthy peer relationships and healthy attachments to others. They may lack the capacity for empathy or fail to develop a sense of conscience or concern about the welfare of others. They may act out in ways that mirror the cruelty they've experienced in their lives, such as by torturing or killing animals, setting fires, or aggressing against smaller, more vulnerable children.

Other common psychological effects of neglect and abuse include lowered self-esteem, depression, immature behaviors such as bed-wetting or thumb-sucking, suicide attempts and suicidal thinking, poor school performance, behavior problems, and failure to venture beyond the home to explore the outside world (Golden, 2000; Saywitz et al., 2000; Shonk & Cicchetti, 2001; Wolfe et al., 2001). Child abuse is also associated with an increased risk in later life of such psychological disorders as bulimia, dissociative identity disorder (multiple personality), PTSD, depression, substance abuse, and borderline personality disorder (e.g., Lipman, MacMillan, & Boyle, 2001; McCauley et al., 1997). In adulthood, abused or maltreated children are more likely to engage in criminal behavior, to be unemployed or to hold lower paying jobs, to have completed fewer years of education, and to have higher suicide rates as compared to nonabused controls (Widom, 1991).

Child Abuse Treatment

Given the scope of the problem, child maltreatment clearly represents a national emergency. Government efforts at the federal and state levels to deal with the problem have thus far been largely unsuccessful, despite the expenditures of billions of dollars annually (Alpert & Green, 1992). Nonetheless, some progress has been made in treating physically abusive parents and their children, with most gains reported in the use of behavioral and cognitive-behavioral programs that focus on training the parents in various skills relating to stress management, anger control, and parenting techniques (Wekerle & Wolfe, 1993). Parent training programs aim at helping the abusive parents learn to cope better with stress and improve their interactions with their children (DeAngelis, 1995b). Yet we still lack long-term follow-ups to determine whether such programs have lasting benefits in preventing recurrent episodes of child abuse.

Although therapists who work with abusive families recognize the importance of ethnic and cultural issues in planning treatment programs, research exploring the development of culturally sensitive treatment interventions remains lacking. We also know little about the effects of child abuse treatment programs that target the children themselves, in part because virtually all programs are geared toward treating the abusive parents (DeAngelis, 1995a). Also lacking are studies specifically targeting child neglect as distinguished from physical or emotional abuse, despite evidence that neglect can have even more damaging consequences than physical abuse (DeAngelis, 1995b). In fact, nearly half of the child fatalities due to maltreatment are the result of neglect, not physical abuse (Daro & Wiese, 1995).

Preventing Child Abuse

Much of the focus in preventing child abuse has centered on training new and expectant parents, and especially teen parents, in parenting skills. Although skills training approaches have been shown to increase parenting knowledge and to enhance child-rearing skills, we still await evidence from large well-controlled studies that such programs succeed in reducing the rates of child abuse in at-risk families (Wekerle & Wolfe, 1993). A major limitation in the research to date is that virtually all participants in these parenting programs are women; the needs of men who are potentially at risk of becoming abusive parents have yet to be addressed on any widespread basis.

Because stress associated with poverty is a major risk factor in child abuse, significant progress in the battle against child abuse and neglect may come only when we deter young people from having children until they are financially and psychologically prepared to raise children (Belsky, 1993; Christmas, Wodarski, & Smokowski, 1996). Yet child abuse is not limited to young parents or the poor. Finding solutions to the problems of child abuse will likely involve ways of helping people acquire the parenting and communication skills they need to be caring, effective parents, as well as adhering to a national policy of zero tolerance for child abuse. Parenting programs may need to be integrated within the high school curriculum, as driving education programs are today.

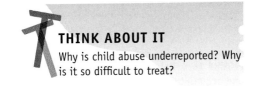

THINK ABOUT IT
Why is child abuse underreported? Why is it so difficult to treat?

Quiz 16.4
Child Abuse

Sexual Aggression

We use the term *sexual aggression* to include both acts of outright sexual violence, such as rape or sexual assault, as well as sexual harassment, in which one person aggresses against another sexually by subjecting the other person to unwanted sexual overtures, demands, or lewd comments. Sexual molestation of children is also by definition a form of sexual aggression, even if no direct force is used to obtain sexual favors, because children by virtue of their developmental level are deemed incapable of providing informed consent.

Rape

Although rape is not a diagnosable mental disorder, it certainly meets several of the criteria used to define abnormal behavior. It is socially unacceptable, violates social norms, and is grievously harmful to its victims. Rape may also be associated with some clinical syndromes, especially some forms of sexual sadism.

Forcible rape is the use of force, violence, or threats of violence to coerce someone into sexual intercourse. **Statutory rape** is sexual intercourse with a person who is unable to give consent, either because of being under the age of consent or because of mental disability, even though the person may cooperate with the rapist.

Incidence of Rape The federal government reports about 153,000 completed rapes and about 67,000 attempted rapes are committed each year in the United States (U.S. Bureau of Justice Statistics, 1999). Yet most rapes go unreported to police. The prevalence of rapes reported to authorities in the United States is 20 times greater than the rate in Japan and 13 times greater than the rate in Great Britain ("Women Under Assault," 1990).

There is some good news to report, however. The numbers of reported rapes began declining during the mid-1990s. Unreported rapes also appear to be on the decline. Whether this decline represents an ebbing of sexual crimes against women remains to be seen.

forcible rape Forced sexual intercourse with a nonconsenting person.

statutory rape Sexual intercourse with a minor, even with the minor's cooperation.

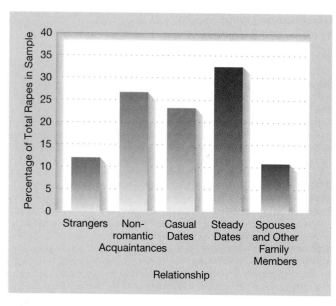

FIGURE 16.4 Relative percentages of stranger rapes and acquaintance rapes.
According to a large-scale survey of more than 3,000 college women at 32 colleges, the great majority of rapes of college women were committed by men whom the women were acquainted with, including dates, nonromantic acquaintances, and family members.
Source. Adapted from Koss (1988).

Web Link **16.5** WWW
Rape Fact Sheet

Truth OR Fiction? REVISITED

Women are more likely to be raped by men they know than by strangers.

TRUE. Most rapes are not committed by strangers, but by men with whom the women were acquainted.

Based on a compilation of official records and large-scale surveys of victims, researchers estimate that between 14% and 25% of U.S. women have been raped or will be raped at some point during their lifetimes (Brener et al., 1999; Calhoun & Atkeson, 1991; Polaschek, Ward, & Hudson, 1997). In about four of five cases of rape overall the woman was acquainted with the assailant (Gibbs, 1991), though typically they were not intimate acquaintances or lovers. Figure 16.4 shows the relationship patterns of rapist and victim based on a large, national survey of college women (Koss, Gidycz, & Wisniewski, 1987). This survey revealed a disturbingly high percentage of the women reporting they had experienced rape (15.4%) or attempted rape (12.1%) (Koss et al., 1987). In nearly 90% of the rapes in the college sample, the woman was acquainted with the assailant (Koss, 1988). In any given year, about 3% of college women in the United States suffer a rape or attempted rape (Fisher, Cullen, & Turner, 2000).

Any woman is at risk of rape, including women and girls of all ages, races, and socioeconomic levels.[1] However, younger women are most at risk, especially adolescent girls. In a recent survey of 9th-through 12th-grade female students in Massachusetts, about one in five students reported either being physically or sexually abused by a dating partner (Silverman et al., 2001). More than half of the reported rapes in the United States are committed against girls under the age of 18; about one in six rapes are committed against girls under the age of 12 ("U. S. Finds," 1994). The younger the woman, the more likely she is to be acquainted with the assailant.

Theoretical Perspectives on Rape There is no single kind of rape or rapist. Rape has more to do with violent impulses and issues of power and control than sexual gratification. Rapists are no more likely than other offenders to have the kinds of psychological disorders coded on Axis I of the *DSM-IV* (Polaschek et al., 1997). Some rapists have such feelings of shyness and inadequacy that they report being unable to find willing partners; others are basically antisocial and tend to act out on their impulses regardless of the cost to the victim. Many of these antisocial rapists have long records as violent offenders (Siegel, 1992). Many were sexually abused themselves as children (Dhawan & Marshall, 1996). For still other rapists, violent cues appear to enhance sexual arousal, so they are motivated to combine sex with aggression (Barbaree & Marshall, 1991). College men who report having used force or threat of force to gain sexual favors showed greater penile arousal in a laboratory study in response to depictions of rape scenes than did noncoercive men (Lohr, Adams, & Davis, 1997). Some rapists who were abused as children may humiliate women as a way of expressing anger and power over women, and of taking revenge.

On the basis of clinical experience with more than 1,000 rapists, Groth and Hobson (1983) hypothesize the existence of three basic kinds of rape: anger rape, power rape, and sadistic rape. The anger rape is a savage, unpremeditated attack triggered by feelings of hatred and resentment. Anger rapists often use more force than necessary to gain compliance to take revenge for humiliations they have suffered—or believe they have suffered—at the hands of women. The power rapist is basically motivated by the desire to control another person. Groth and Hobson (1983) suggest that power rapists use rape to try "to resolve disturbing doubts about [their] masculine identity and worth, [or] to combat deep-seated feelings of insecurity and vulnerability" (p. 165). Sadistic rapes frequently employ torture and bondage, merging sex and aggression. Sadistic rapists are most likely to mutilate their victims.

Sociocultural factors also need to be considered. Although some rapists show evidence of psychopathology on psychological tests, especially psychopathic traits, many do not (Brown & Forth, 1997; Herkov et al., 1996). The very normality of many rapists on psychological instruments suggests that socialization factors play an important role. Some

---

[1]Although male rapes do occur, the great majority of cases involve women who are raped.

sociocultural theorists argue that our culture actually breeds rapists by socializing men into sexually dominant and aggressive roles associated with stereotypical concepts of masculinity (e.g., Hall & Barongan, 1997). For example, consider the aggressive competitiveness expressed by this male college student in his views about dating relationships:

> A man is supposed to view a date with a woman as a premeditated scheme for getting the most sex out of her. Everything he does, he judges in terms of one criterion—"getting laid." He's supposed to constantly pressure her to see how far he can get. She is his adversary, his opponent in a battle, and he begins to view her as a prize, an object, not a person. While she's dreaming about love, he's thinking about how to conquer her. (Powell, 1991, p. 55)

Evidence shows that sexually coercive college men tend to have an excessively masculinized personality orientation, adhere more strictly to traditional gender roles, view women as adversaries in the "mating game," and hold more accepting attitudes toward the use of violence against women than do noncoercive men (e.g., O'Donohue, McKay, & Schewe, 1996; Polaschek et al., 1997). They are also more prone to blame rape survivors than rapists and to become more sexually aroused by portrayals of rape than are men who hold less rigid stereotypes. Sociocultural influences also reinforce themes that may underlie rape, such as the cultural belief that a masculine man is expected to be sexually assertive and overcome a woman's resistance until she "melts" in his arms (Stock, 1991).

Date rape is a form of acquaintance rape. According to recent surveys of high school girls in Massachusetts and Minnesota, between 1 in 10 and 1 in 5 report a history of being physically or sexually assaulted by a dating partner (Goode, 2001f; Stenson, 2001b). College men on dates frequently perceive their dates' protests as part of an adversarial sex game. One male undergraduate said, "Hell, no" when asked whether a date had consented to sex. He added, "But she didn't say no, so she must have wanted it, too. It's the way it works" (Celis, 1991). Consider the comments of Jim, a man who raped a woman he had just met at a party:

A Case of Date Rape

She looked really hot, wearing a sexy dress that showed off her great body. We started talking right away. I knew that she liked me by the way she kept smiling and touching my arm while she was speaking. She seemed pretty relaxed so I asked her back to my place for a drink . . . When she said yes, I knew that I was going to be lucky!

When we got to my place, we sat on the bed kissing. At first, everything was great. Then, when I started to lay her down on the bed, she started twisting and saying she didn't want to. Most women don't like to appear too easy, so I knew that she was just going through the motions. When she stopped struggling, I knew that she would have to throw in some tears before we did it.

She was still very upset afterwards, and I just don't understand it! If she didn't want to have sex, why did she come back to the room with me? You could tell by the way she dressed and acted that she was no virgin, so why she had to put up such a big struggle I don't know.

—*From Trenton State College, 1991*

Date rape. Many rape awareness workshops, like the one depicted here, have been held on college campuses in order to combat the problem of date rape on campus.

Rape crisis counseling. Rape crisis centers help rape survivors cope with the trauma of rape. They provide them with emotional support and help them obtain medical, psychological, and legal services.

Web Link **16.6** wWw
FYI: Acquaintance Rape

THINK ABOUT IT
Do you believe a woman who flirts with men in a bar is looking for sex, whether or not she says "no"? Why or why not?

THINK ABOUT IT
Did you ever attempt to coerce someone into sexual activity? Did you feel justified at the time? How do you feel about it now?

Let us rebut these beliefs. Accepting a date is not the equivalent of consenting to intercourse. Accompanying a man to his room or apartment is not the equivalent of consenting to intercourse. Kissing and petting are not the equivalent of consenting to intercourse. When a woman fails to consent or says no, the man must take no for an answer.

Effects of Rape Women who are raped suffer more than the rape itself. They report loss of appetite, headaches, irritability, anxiety and depression, and menstrual irregularity in the wake of a rape. Some become sullen, withdrawn, and mistrustful. In some cases, women show an unrealistic composure, which often gives way to venting of feelings later on. Because of society's tendency to blame the victim for the assault, some survivors also have misplaced feelings of guilt, shame, and self-blame. Survivors often develop sexual dysfunctions such as lack of sexual desire and difficulty becoming sexually aroused. Survivors show signs of posttraumatic stress disorder (PTSD), including intrusive memories of the rape, nightmares, emotional numbing, and heightened autonomic arousal (Gilboa-Schechtman & Foa, 2001; Nishith, Mechanic, & Resick, 2000). Psychological problems experienced by rape survivors, such as depression and anxiety, often continue for years after the assault (Sadler et al., 2000).

Treatment of Rape Survivors Treatment of rape survivors is often a two-phase process that first assists women in coping with the immediate aftermath of rape and then helps them with their long-term adjustment. Crisis intervention provides women with emotional support and information to help them see to their immediate needs as well as to help them develop strategies for coping with the trauma. Longer-term treatment may be designed to help rape survivors cope with undeserved feelings of guilt and shame, lingering feelings of anxiety and depression, and the interpersonal and sexual problems they may develop with the men in their lives. Unfortunately, most rape survivors do not seek help from mental health professionals, rape crisis centers, or rape survivor assistance programs (Kimerling & Calhoun, 1994). The cultural stigma associated with seeking help for mental health problems may discourage a fuller utilization of psychological services.

Child Sexual Abuse

Few crimes are as heinous as sexual abuse of children. The consequences of sexual abuse can be severe and long lasting, leading to emotional problems and difficulties developing intimate relationships that last long into the future. Estimates suggest that at least 20% or 25% of women have a history of childhood sexual abuse (Bradley & Follingstad, 2001). As shocking as these figures may be, surveys may undershoot the mark, as people may not be willing to report abuse. Although girls are more likely than boys to be sexually abused, estimates are that boys constitute perhaps one-fifth to one-third of sexually abused children (DeAngelis, 1995b; Finkelhor, 1990).

Sexual abuse, like other forms of violence and abuse, cuts across all socioeconomic and family background characteristics (Finkelhor, 1993). Neither social class nor ethnicity appears to be associated with relative risk. However, children from less cohesive or disintegrating families appear more likely to be victimized than children from intact families. The average age at which children are first sexually abused ranges between 7 and 10 for boys and 6 and 12 for girls (Knudsen, 1991).

Patterns of Child Sexual Abuse Sexual abuse of children includes a range of sexual acts such as fondling, kissing, exhibitionism, touching of genitals, oral sex, anal intercourse, and

A Closer Look

Rape Prevention

 Given the incidence of rape, it is important to be aware of strategies that may prevent it. By listing strategies for rape prevention, we do not mean to imply that rape survivors are somehow responsible for falling prey to an attack. The responsibility for any act of sexual violence lies with the perpetrator, not with the person who is assaulted, and perhaps with society for fostering attitudes that underlie sexual violence. On a societal level, we need to do a better job of socializing young men to acquire prosocial and respectful attitudes toward women. Exposure to feminist, egalitarian, and multicultural education may help promote more respectful attitudes in young men (Hall & Barongan, 1997; Kershner, 1996).

Preventing Stranger Rape

- Establish signals and plans with other women in the building or neighborhood.
- List first initials only in the phone directory and on the mailbox.
- Use dead-bolt locks.
- Lock windows and install iron grids on first-floor windows.
- Keep doorways and entries well lit.
- Have keys handy for the car or the front door.
- Do not walk by yourself after dark.
- Avoid deserted areas.
- Do not allow strange men into the apartment or the house without checking their credentials.
- Keep the car door locked and the windows up.
- Check out the backseat of the car before getting in.
- Don't live in a risky building.
- Don't give rides to hitchhikers (that includes women hitchhikers).
- Don't converse with strange men on the street.

- Shout "Fire!" not "Rape!" People flock to fires but circumvent scenes of violence.

Preventing Date Rape

- Avoid getting into secluded situations until you know your date very well.
- Be wary when a date attempts to control you in any way, such as frightening you by driving rapidly or taking you some place you would rather not go.
- Stay sober. We often do things we would not otherwise do—including sexual activity with people we might otherwise reject—when we have had too many drinks. Be aware of your limits.
- Be very assertive and clear concerning your sexual intentions. Some rapists, particularly date rapists, tend to misinterpret women's wishes. If their dates begin to implore them to stop during kissing or petting, they construe pleading as "female game playing." So if kissing or petting is leading where you don't want it to go, speak up.
- When dating a person for the first time, try to date in a group.
- Encourage your college or university to offer educational programs about date rape. The University of Washington, for example, offers students lectures and seminars on date rape and provides women with escorts to get home. Many universities require all incoming students to attend orientation sessions on rape prevention.
- Talk to your date about his attitudes toward women. If you get the feeling that he believes that men are in a war with women, or that women try to "play games" with men, you may be better off dating someone else.

Sources. Adapted from Boston Women's Health Book Collective, 1984; Rathus & Fichner-Rathus, 1994.

among girls, vaginal intercourse (Knudsen, 1991). Because children are not deemed capable of giving voluntary consent, any sexual act between an adult and a child is considered a form of sexual abuse, even if there is no force or physical threat used or the child gives consent.

Sexual abuse of children is more likely to be committed by family members than by strangers, but girls are even more likely than boys to be abused by a family member or acquaintance (Faller, 1989). Boys are more often threatened or suffer physical injuries during a sexual assault than is the case with girls (Knudsen, 1991). A study at the University of New Mexico found that while the frequency of childhood sexual abuse (about 30% overall) was similar between Hispanic and non-Hispanic White college women, Hispanic women reported that perpetrators were more likely to be extended family members and less likely to be members of the immediate family or non-family members than did non-Hispanic White women (Arroyo, Simpson, & Aragon, 1997).

It may surprise you to learn that the abuser seldom uses physical force. Most of the time the abuser is able to use manipulation, deception, or threat of force to obtain the

Former teacher sent to prison for child rape. Mary Kay LeTourneau is shown here being led away from the courtroom after the judge revoked her suspended sentence and ordered her to be sent to prison for having continued contact with the boy whom she was convicted of raping.

child's compliance rather than direct force. Children are not worldly wise and are typically submissive to adult authority. They may be easily misled or manipulated by an unscrupulous adult, especially when the abuser is someone with whom the child has had a trusting relationship. Threat of force may be used if guile and deception fail to achieve compliance. Although most abused children suffer one incident of abuse, in some cases a pattern of abuse occurs that continues for a period of months or even years. Children who are abused by family members are most likely to suffer repeated incidents of abuse.

The most common type of abuse of girls or boys involves genital fondling (Knudsen, 1991). In one female sample, intercourse occurred in only 4% of cases, as compared to genital fondling that occurred in 38% and exhibitionism that occurred in 20% (Knudsen, 1991). However, in cases of sexual abuse of girls by family members, a common pattern involves a gradual progression of abuse that begins with affectionate fondling during the preschool years, progresses to oral sex or mutual masturbation during middle childhood, and then to vaginal or anal intercourse in preadolescence or adolescence.

Characteristics of Abusers The great majority of abusers of both boys and girls are men. Authorities in the field estimate that men perpetrate perhaps 95% of cases of abuse involving young girls and 80% involving young boys (Finkelhor & Russell, 1984). But not all sex offenders are men, as the case of a Seattle woman, Mary Kay LeTourneau, illustrates:

The Case of Mary Kay LeTourneau

She wore red coveralls—the uniform of the female prisoner. She looked exhausted and disheveled as she stood for sentencing. She is Mary Kay LeTourneau, a 35-year-old former grade school teacher in suburban Seattle. She is the woman who had sexual relations, and a baby, with a former student—a 13-year-old boy. LeTourneau wept as her lawyer pleaded for mercy and made no comment when the judge offered her a chance to speak. She was sentenced to seven years and five months in prison and denounced by the judge who had been lenient some months earlier, in a case that has raised questions as to whether female sex offenders can be held to different standards than men. In November of 1997, she had pleaded guilty to raping the boy and promised King County Superior Court Judge Linda Lau that she would have no further contact with him.

"I give you my word," LeTourneau had said. "It will not happen again." LeTourneau is the mother of four children by her ex-husband. She had no previous criminal record and was given a suspended prison sentence and ordered to undergo treatment. But in February of 1998, after hearing testimony that LeTourneau had again seen the boy, and possibly planned to flee with him, Judge Lau revoked the suspension and sent LeTourneau to prison. Prosecutors, state legislators and professionals who treat sex offenders note that LeTourneau had escaped an earlier prison sentence largely because she was attractive and presented herself as being in love with an emotionally mature boy.

The victim? The boy repeatedly protested to the media that he was not a victim, that he was in love with his former teacher and deeply saddened by her conviction. LeTourneau had claimed that the boy is emotionally mature beyond his years. But people who treat sex offenders say that they often justify sex with underage people by saying that the victim is emotionally mature.

The saga apparently continues. In April 2000 the boy, 16 at the time, filed law suits against the city of Des Moines, Washington, and his local school district for emotional suffering, lost income and the cost of raising his two children, who were in the custody of his mother ("Boy to Sue," 2000).

—Adapted from Rathus, Nevid, & Fichner-Rathus, 2002

Although most abusers are adult males, some are adolescent males, many of whom were abused themselves as young boys and may be imitating their own victimization (Muster, 1992). Gay males and lesbians account for only a small percentage of abusers of either boys or girls.

Despite the popular stereotype, most abusers do not fit the profile of the proverbial stranger hanging around the schoolyard. Most cases of child sexual abuse, perhaps as many as 75% to 80%, involve assailants who have some kind of relationship with the child or the child's family, typically a relative or step-relative, a family friend, or a neighbor (Zielbauer, 2000). In many cases (estimates range from 10% to 50% of cases), the molester is a family member, typically a father, uncle, or stepfather.

Family members who discover that a child has been abused are less likely to report the abuse to authorities when the offender is a family member, perhaps because to do so might shame the family and out of concern that they might be held accountable for failing to protect the child. In a Boston study, none of the parents whose children were abused by family members notified the authorities, as compared to about one in four parents whose children were abused by acquaintances and about three of four whose children were abused by strangers (Finkelhor, 1984).

In an early study, Gebhard and his colleagues (1965) found that many fathers who had sexually abused their daughters were religiously devout, fundamentalistic, and moralistic. Such men, when sexually frustrated, may be less likely to find extramarital and extrafamilial sexual outlets. The father may be under stress but fails to find adequate emotional and sexual support from his wife. He may turn to a daughter as a wife surrogate. The girl is often mature enough to have assumed household chores and may become, in her father's eyes, the "woman of the house." The wife may be surprised by revelations of incest, despite obvious clues and even the daughter's repeated complaints. Sometimes the wife seems involved in a tacit conspiracy to allow the abuse to continue to preserve the family or because of fear of the abuser.

Banning (1989) offers a sociocultural explanation of why a disproportionate number of molesters are men. Banning argues that men are socialized in our culture to seek younger and weaker partners they can more easily dominate. In the extreme, this pattern can lead to sexual interest in young girls, who because of their age can be more easily dominated than adult women. Yet child molestation may also be motivated by pedophilia, an unusual pattern of sexual arousal characterized by a sexual interest in children, sometimes to the exclusion of more appropriate (adult) stimuli (see Chapter 12). A cycle of sexual abuse and other forms of sexual violence is a common finding, with children who suffer sexual abuse engaging in sexual abuse against their own children or committing other types of sexual offenses as adults (McCloskey & Bailey, 2000; Romano & De-Luca, 1996).

VIDEO **16.1**
Child Sexual Abuse: *The Case of Karen*

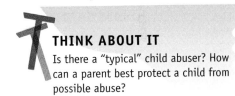

THINK ABOUT IT
Is there a "typical" child abuser? How can a parent best protect a child from possible abuse?

Effects of Child Sexual Abuse The effects of child sexual abuse are variable and no one pattern applies in all cases (Price et al., 2001). Though some sexually abused children may show no clear psychological effects, most exhibit some types of psychological problems, most commonly anxiety, depression, aggressive behavior, poor self-esteem, eating disorders, premature sexual behavior or promiscuity, suicidal thinking, and substance abuse (e.g., Kisiel & Lyons, 2001; Meston & Heiman, 2000; Saywitz et al., 2000). Regressive behavior in the form of thumb sucking, or recurrences of childhood fears, such as fear of the dark or of strangers, are common. Psychological problems may continue into adulthood in the form of PTSD, anxiety, depression, substance abuse and relationship problems (Bradley & Follingstad, 2001; Kendler et al., 2000b; Read et al., 2001). Late adolescence and early adulthood are particularly difficult times for survivors of child sexual abuse because unresolved feelings of anger and guilt and a deep sense of mistrust can prevent the expected development of intimate relationships (Jackson et al., 1990). Although much of the research on effects of childhood sexual abuse has focused on female survivors, a significant proportion of male survivors also suffer adverse psychological effects into adulthood (Dhaliwal et al., 1996). It is a myth to believe that sexual abuse has little effect on boys.

Some child survivors retreat into a personal fantasy world or refuse to leave the house. We noted in Chapter 7 how many cases of dissociative identity disorder (multiple

So there really was a monster in her bedroom.

For many kids, there's a real reason to be afraid of the dark.

Last year in Indiana, there were 6,912 substantiated cases of sexual abuse. The trauma can be devastating for the child and for the family. So listen closely to the children around you.

If you hear something you don't want to believe, perhaps you should. For helpful information on child abuse prevention, contact the LaPorte County Child Abuse Prevention Council, 7451 Johnson Road, Michigan City, IN 46360. (219) 874-0007

LaPorte County Child Abuse Prevention Council

So there really was a monster in her bedroom. Not all monsters are imagined. Some, like incest perpetrators, are family members.

Web Link **16.7** wWw
FYI: Child Sexual Abuse

personality) have been linked to a history in childhood of retreating into fantasy to cope with sexual abuse. Childhood sexual abuse is also linked to the later development of borderline personality disorder (Murray, 1993; Weaver & Clum, 1995).

Although the effects of child sexual abuse are more similar than not between boys and girls (e.g., both genders tend to experience fears and sleep disturbances), there are some important differences. The clearest gender difference is that boys tend to develop "externalized" behavior problems such as excessive aggressive behavior, whereas girls tend to experience "internalized" problems, such as depression (Finkelhor et al., 1990).

Although long-term effects of child sexual abuse are common, they appear to be greater among survivors who were abused by their fathers or stepfathers, who were abused at an earlier age, who were subjected to penetration, who suffered more prolonged and severe abuse, or who were forced to submit or threatened with physical force (DeAngelis, 1995b). Adult survivors of childhood sexual abuse who blame themselves for the abuse tend to have more psychological problems than those who blame the perpetrator (Feinauer & Stuart, 1996). The use of cognitive coping skills in adulthood, such as disclosing and discussing the abuse but not dwelling on it, appears to differentiate well-adjusted and poorly adjusted college women who suffered sexual abuse as children (Himelein & McElrath, 1996).

When the offender is a father or other family member, the effects of abuse are amplified by the deep feeling of the betrayal of trust by the offender as well as by their mothers or other family members whom they perceive as having failed to protect them. They may have felt powerless to control their bodies or their lives and may find it difficult to ever develop a trusting relationship in adulthood.

Researchers have begun to examine ethnic group differences in the effects of child sexual abuse. In one example, investigators at a child sex abuse clinic compared samples of Asian American, African American, Hispanic American, and non-Hispanic White American child survivors (Rao, DiClemente, & Ponton, 1992). The results showed that Asian American children were more likely to develop suicidal thoughts and less likely to overtly display anger or engage in sexual acting out than were children from the other groups.

Gail Wyatt (1990) investigated childhood sexual abuse in a sample of 126 African American women and 122 Euro-American (non-Hispanic White) women in Los Angeles County. The subjects were matched on such variables as marital status, number of children, and education. The operational definition of childhood sexual abuse was broad, including acts such as exhibitionism, fondling, oral sex, and sexual intercourse. The prevalence of abuse was similar in both groups. Nearly one woman in two had suffered at least one incident of abuse, and nearly 40% of these incidences had gone unreported to authorities. The African American women were somewhat less likely to report abuse to their immediate family members or to the police. However, they were nearly twice as likely to have informed extended family members than were the Euro-American women, a finding that underscores the importance of the extended family among African Americans. African American women were more likely than Euro-American women (35% versus 22%) to avoid reporting abuse for fear of repercussions. The African American women may have felt more vulnerable to the financial adversity that their families would have had to endure if the abuser—often their mothers' boyfriends or their stepfathers on whom the family was financially dependent—had been forced to leave the home. Euro-American women more often expressed fear of being blamed for the abuse as a reason for nonreporting (36%) than did African American women (23%). Other investigators report that Mexican American women, raised in a culture in which women are often expected to "suffer in silence," are also less likely than Euro-American women to report rape and sexual abuse (Lira, Koss, & Russo, 1999).

The psychological impact of abuse in the Gail Wyatt study was similar for both groups. Women from both groups were likely to have felt violated and to harbor feelings of fear, disgust, and anger. Sexual problems in adulthood were also common in both groups. However, the African American women were more prone to report that the abusive experiences from childhood affected their general attitudes toward men and led them to avoid men who in some ways reminded them of their abusers.

Treating Survivors of Child Sexual Abuse Because most cases of child sexual abuse go unreported, survivors of abuse may not receive psychotherapy for overcoming trauma-related feelings of anger and (misplaced) guilt until adulthood. Sex therapy may help adult survivors overcome sexual dysfunctions and fears. Group therapy may help them face their feelings in a supportive setting with people who have undergone similar trauma.

When sexual abuse is uncovered in childhood, a multicomponent treatment approach may be recommended, including individual therapy for the child survivor, joint therapy with the child and nonoffending parent, and family therapy (Celano et al., 1996; Cohen & Mannarino, 1997). Therapy with the child survivor typically focuses on providing support, addressing issues of betrayal and powerlessness, and helping the child see that he or she is not to blame.

Treating the Offenders Convicted rapists and child molesters are criminals and typically sentenced to prison as a form of punishment, not treatment. They may receive psychological treatment during their incarceration in the hope that it will help prepare them for their eventual release and deter them from committing future offenses when they do reenter society. Treatment programs are more likely to be successful when they address the long-term adjustment of the sex offender and do not expect a permanent "cure" to result from a single round of prison-based treatment sessions (Hanson, Steffy, & Gauthier, 1993). The most widely used form of treatment for incarcerated sex offenders is group therapy, predicated on the belief that although sex offenders may trick counselors, they cannot so readily fool each another (Kaplan, 1993).

Group therapy may be supplemented by cognitive-behavior therapy techniques such as covert sensitization, which we discussed in Chapter 12. Also coming into greater use is *empathy training,* which attempts to increase the offender's sensitivity toward his victim by having him write about his crime from what he imagines would be the victim's perspective. The fact remains, however, that the great majority of incarcerated sex offenders receive little or nothing in the way of psychological treatment in prison (Goleman, 1992a).

A biologically based treatment involves the use of antiandrogen (testosterone-reducing) drugs such as Depo-Provera. These drugs lower the sex drive, which may help offenders control their urges to offend, at least so long as they continue using the drug (Roesler & Witztum, 2000). The effects of antiandrogens are reversible when the drugs are discontinued. However, problems with compliance with taking the drugs consistently present a major obstacle to their widespread use. Moreover, taking antiandrogens does not help rapists resolve the psychological factors underlying their sexual attacks, particularly resentment and anger toward women and needs for dominance and power. Nor does it assist men with pedophilia to learn to respond to more adaptive erotic cues, rather than to images of children. Nor do drugs provide offenders with opportunities to develop social skills they need to develop consensual sexual relationships. Despite these drawbacks, the use of antiandrogens appears to be about equal in effectiveness to cognitive-behavioral treatments in preventing recidivism of sex offenders, with both treatment approaches producing medium-sized treatment effects in reducing recidivism in relation to an absence of treatment (Hall, 1995). Antiandrogens may also be helpful when they are used in conjunction with psychological counseling (Leary, 1998).

Overall, efficacy studies of treatment of sex offenders show a modest benefit in reducing recidivism rates associated with comprehensive cognitive-behavioral treatment, or psychological treatment combined with antiandrogen therapy (Hall, 1995; Polaschek et al., 1997). Generally speaking, better outcomes are achieved with child molesters and exhibitionists than with rapists. Not surprisingly, recidivism rates are higher among sex offenders who fail to complete treatment and who show deviant sexual interest, such as penile arousal to child pornography (Hanson & Bussiére, 1998). More extreme measures, such as surgical castration (removal of the testes), have been used in some European countries but not as yet in the United States. The effects of surgical castration on recidivism are not clear.

One treatment alternative that remains largely unexplored is targeting men who are sexually attracted to children or who have a predisposition to rape *before* they commit abusive acts. Perhaps early intervention can prevent sexual violence from occurring.

Survivors of child sexual abuse. Most cases of child sexual abuse go unreported. This means that survivors of abuse may not receive any psychological counseling to help them deal with their traumatic experiences until adulthood, if then.

THINK ABOUT IT
Do you know anyone who was sexually abused during childhood? What were the effects? Are there any lingering effects? Was the abuser reported to authorities? Why or why not?

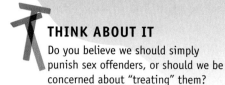

THINK ABOUT IT
Do you believe we should simply punish sex offenders, or should we be concerned about "treating" them? Explain your opinion.

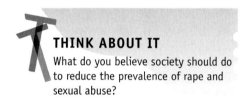

THINK ABOUT IT
What do you believe society should do to reduce the prevalence of rape and sexual abuse?

Unfortunately, most men who would likely be good candidates for early intervention do not come forward for treatment until they are convicted of a sexual crime.

Preventing Child Sexual Abuse Sexual abuse prevention includes community efforts, such as enactment and enforcement of laws requiring teachers and helping professionals to report cases of suspected child sexual or physical abuse to child protective services. Many states have enacted laws that require convicted sex offenders to register with the local police. These laws, called "Megan's laws," after a 7-year-old New Jersey girl who was killed by a neighbor with a history of sexual assault, are intended to let members of the community know of the presence of sex offenders (Weber, 1996).

At the individual level, school-based sexual abuse prevention programs reach about two of three children in the United States (Goleman, 1993c). Although these programs vary in their content, most teach children to avoid contact with strangers and to distinguish between acceptable touching (a member of their family embracing them affectionately or patting them on the head) and "bad" or unacceptable touching. However, evidence attesting to the efficacy of child sexual abuse prevention programs remains limited.

Children are more likely to report incidents of sexual abuse if they are reassured that they will be believed and not be blamed, that their parents will continue to love them, and that they and their families will be protected from the abuser. Ensuring the credibility of children's reports of sexual abuse remains a thorny issue, however, as children are easily suggestible and can be led to believe that abuse occurred even when it did not, especially if investigators direct the inquiry in ways that plant ideas in the children's minds. Recall too (see Chapter 7) the controversy that has swirled around the issue of recovered memories of childhood sexual or physical abuse that the individual only becomes aware of at some point in adulthood, often during therapy or hypnosis. The judicial system is faced with the daunting challenge of distinguishing between true and faulty memories, especially when there is an absence of independent verification of abuse.

Sexual Harassment

Sexual harassment is a form of sexual coercion in which one person subjects another to unwanted sexual comments, overtures, gestures, physical contact, or direct demands for sexual favors as a condition of employment, retention, or advancement (see Table 16.3). Women tend to perceive a wider ranger of behaviors as harassing than do men (Rotundo, Nguyen, & Sackett, 2001). For example, women are more likely to perceive behaviors involving expression of derogatory attitudes, dating pressures, and physical sexual contact (e.g., fondling or kissing) as forms of harassment than do men. Men and women are in stronger agreement in classifying such extreme behaviors as rape, requests

sexual harassment Speech, gestures, demands, or physical contact of a sexual nature that is unwelcomed by the person to whom it is directed.

TABLE 16.3 Examples of Sexual Harassment

Verbal harassment or abuse
Subtle pressure for sexual activity
Remarks about a person's clothing, body, or sexual activities
Leering or ogling at a person's body
Unwelcome touching, patting, or pinching
Brushing against a person's body
Demands for sexual favors accompanied by implied or overt threats concerning one's job or student status
Physical assault

Source. Adapted from Powell (1991).

for sexual involvement as a condition of employment or promotion, and unwanted pressure or requests for sexual involvement as forms of sexual harassment.

Sexual harassment can occur in many settings, including the workplace, school, or therapist's consulting room. The great majority of cases of sexual harassment involve men harassing women. Sexual harassment in the workplace is considered a form of sex discrimination, and employers can be held accountable if sexual harassment creates a hostile or abusive work environment or interferes with an employee's work performance. A 1998 decision by the U.S. Supreme Court held that persons can bring a sexual harassment action even if they did not suffer any career setback, such as a dismissal or loss of a promotion, as the result of the harassment (Greenhouse, 1998). Employers can be accountable if they either *knew* that harassment was occurring or *should have known* and failed to promptly correct the situation (McKinney & Maroules, 1991).

Although sexual harassment may involve many motives, it typically has more to do with the abuse of power than with sexual motivation (Goleman, 1991). Harassers usually hold a dominant position in relation to the person who is harassed and abuse their authority by taking advantage of the other person's vulnerability. Resentment and hostility directed at women who venture beyond the traditional gender boundaries and enter traditional male occupations may be expressed in the form of sexual taunts and overtures by men as a way of "keeping women in their place" (Fitzgerald, 1993a).

Sexual harassment? Sexual harassment is behavior of a sexual nature that is unwelcome by the recipient. Sexual harassment on the job creates a work environment that is hostile or abusive to the person on the receiving end. It may also interfere with the person's ability to perform his or her job. Would you say that the man's behavior here could be interpreted as harassment? What would you do if you were sexually harassed?

Although laws prohibit sexual harassment, and people subjected to harassment can sue to have the harassment stopped or can obtain monetary awards for emotional damages they suffer, relatively few formal complaints are filed. Why? For one thing, harassment may be difficult to prove because it usually occurs without corroborating witnesses or evidence. Like survivors of rape, people who are harassed may fear that they will not be believed or will suffer retaliation by the harasser, lose their jobs, or have their reputations soured in the industries in which they work.

What should you do if you are sexually harassed? The accompanying "A Closer Look" section discusses some options for you to consider.

Prevalence of Sexual Harassment Sexual harassment is the most frequently occurring form of sexual victimization in the United States (Fitzgerald, 1993a). Overall, estimates indicate that at least 33% of women, and 15% of men, encounter sexual harassment in a work or academic setting (Choi et al., 1998; Stawar, 1999). Sexual harassment even extends downward to teenage workers. A recent survey of 16- and 17-year-old girls with jobs found that nearly half (49%) said they had been victims of sexual harassment (Goodstein & Connelly, 1998). Moreover, a recent national survey of high school students showed that about 80% of the boys and girls reported being sexually harassed by their peers (Smith, 2001b).

Sexual harassment directed at women is especially common in worksites that are traditional male preserves, such as the construction site, the shipyard, and the firehouse (Fitzgerald, 1993a). Despite the increased attention to the problem of sexual harassment in the military, studies actually show a decline in the prevalence of harassment in these settings (Seppa, 1997). Cross-cultural research, though limited, shows high frequencies of sexual harassment in other developed countries that have been studied; in Japan, about 70% of women report incidents of harassment; in Europe, about 50% (Castro, 1992).

A Closer Look

How to Resist Sexual Harassment

 What would you do if an employer or a professor sexually harassed you? How would you handle it? Would you try to ignore it and hope it would stop? What actions might you take? We offer some suggestions, adapted from Powell (1991), that might be helpful. Recognize, however, that responsibility for sexual harassment always lies with the perpetrator and the organization that permits sexual harassment to take place, not with the person subjected to the harassment.

1. *Convey a professional attitude.* Harassment may be stopped cold by responding to the harasser with a businesslike, professional attitude. If a harassing professor suggests that you come back after school to review your term paper so the two of you will be undisturbed, set limits assertively. Tell the professor that you'd feel more comfortable discussing the paper during regular office hours. The harasser should quickly get the message that you wish to maintain a strictly professional relationship. If the harasser persists, do not blame yourself. You are only responsible for your own actions. When the harasser persists, a more direct response may be appropriate: "Professor Jones, I'd like to keep our relationship on a purely professional basis, okay?"

2. *Avoid being alone with the harasser.* If you are being harassed by your professor but need some advice about preparing your term paper, approach him or her after class when other students are milling about, not privately during office hours. Or bring a friend to wait outside the office while you consult the professor.

3. *Maintain a record.* Keep a record of all incidents of harassment as documentation in the event you decide to lodge an official complaint. The record should include the following: (1) where the incident took place; (2) the date and time; (3) what happened, including the exact words that were used, if you can recall them; (4) how you felt; and (5) the names of any witnesses. Some people who have been subjected to sexual harassment have carried a hidden tape recorder during contacts with the harasser. Such recordings may not be admissible in a court of law, but they are persuasive in organizational grievance procedures. A hidden tape recorder may be illegal in your state, however. It is thus advisable to check the law.

4. *Talk with the harasser.* It may be uncomfortable to address the issue directly with a harasser, but doing so puts the offender on notice that you are aware of the harassment and want it to stop. It may be helpful to frame your approach in terms of a description of the specific offending actions (e.g., "When we were alone in the office, you repeatedly attempted to touch me or brush up against me"); your feelings about the offending behavior ("It

made me feel like my privacy was being violated. I'm very upset about this and haven't been sleeping well"); and what you would like the offender to do ("So I'd like you to agree never to attempt to touch me again, okay?"). Having a talk with the harasser may stop the harassment. If the harasser denies the accusations, it may be necessary to take further action.

5. *Write a letter to the harasser.* Set down on paper a record of the offending behavior, and put the harasser on notice that the harassment must stop. Your letter might (1) describe what happened ("Several times you have made sexist comments about my body"); (2) describe how you feel ("It made me feel like a sexual object when you talked to me that way"); and (3) describe what you would like the harasser to do ("I want you to stop making sexist comments to me").

6. *Seek support.* Support from people you trust can help you through the often-trying process of resisting sexual harassment. Talking with others allows you to express your feelings and receive emotional support, encouragement, and advice. In addition, it may strengthen your case if you have the opportunity to identify and talk with other people who have been harassed by the offender.

7. *Consider filing a complaint.* Companies and organizations, such as universities and colleges, are required by law to respond reasonably to complaints of sexual harassment. In large organizations, a designated official (sometimes an ombudsman, affirmative action officer, or sexual harassment adviser) is usually charged to handle such complaints. Set up an appointment with this official to discuss your experiences. Ask about the grievance procedures in the organization and your right to confidentiality. Have available a record of the dates of the incidents, what happened, how you felt about it, and so on.

   The two major government agencies that handle charges of sexual harassment are the Equal Employment Opportunity Commission (look under the government section of your phone book for the telephone number of the nearest office) and your state Human Rights Commission (listed in your phone book under state or municipal government). These agencies may offer advice on how you can protect your legal rights and proceed with a formal complaint.

8. *Consider legal remedies.* Sexual harassment is illegal and actionable. If you are considering legal action, consult an attorney familiar with this area of law. You may be entitled to back pay (if you were fired for reasons arising from the sexual harassment), job reinstatement, and punitive damages.

Source. Adapted from Nevid et al., 1995. Reprinted with permission.

Sexual harassment on college campuses is also common. A survey of 2,000 college women showed that about half had been subjected to sexual harassment from professors, most commonly in the form of crude or degrading remarks (Fitzgerald et al., 1988). Nearly 1 in 3 reported unwanted sexual attention and 1 in 10 reported unwanted sexual contact, including fondling and outright sexual assaults. A compilation of results from various studies showed that 7% to 27% of men also reported some exposure to sexual harassment on campus (McKinney & Maroules, 1991).

Sexual harassment may also occur between doctor and patient, or between therapist and client. Professionals may use their power and influence to pressure patients or clients into having sexual relations. In some cases, harassment is disguised by unscrupulous therapists who make it seem that sexual contact would be therapeutically beneficial. Clients tend to perceive therapists as experts whose suggestions carry great authority. Thus, they may be vulnerable to exploitation by therapists who abuse the trust that clients place in their hands. Let's be absolutely clear here: There is no therapeutic justification for a therapist to have sex with a client. The ethical codes of psychologists and other mental health professionals specifically prohibit any kind of sexual contact between therapists and clients. There is no therapeutic justification for sexual relations between client and therapist. Any therapist who makes a sexual overture toward a client, or tries to persuade a client to have sexual relations, is acting unethically. Professionals too may be sexually harassed. Surveys show that more than one-third of female doctors (Frank, Brogan, & Schiffman, 1998) and more than one-half of female psychologists (deMayo, 1997) report they have been sexually harassed by patients.

Effects of Sexual Harassment Sexual harassment, like other forms of sexual abuse, can have damaging psychological effects, including anxiety and lowered self-esteem (e.g., Koss et al., 1994). Women subjected to sexual taunts or outright demands for sexual favors in the workplace may feel forced to resign. Women attending college who are unable to stop sexual harassment by professors may drop courses, switch majors, or even transfer to other schools, often at great personal sacrifice (Fitzgerald, 1993a, 1993b). Forms of sexual harassment such as verbal taunts, sexual teasing, and staring may even have similar effects as sexual abuse, leading to disturbances in body image and eating behavior (Weiner & Thompson, 1997).

The effects of sexual harassment are compounded by the attitude held by many in our society that people who complain of harassment or rape are somehow to blame for their difficulties (Powell, 1991). People who bring harassment complaints may be perceived as exaggerating the incident or taking things too seriously. Women, especially, are subjected to stereotypical expectations that they are to be nice and demure—to be passive and never to "make a scene." A woman who seeks to protect her rights by filing a complaint may be labeled as a "troublemaker." "Women are damned if they assert themselves and victimized if they don't" (Powell, 1991, p. 114).

We focused in this chapter on interpersonal aggression, acts in which one person does violence to another. Yet, throughout history, human aggression in the form of organized conflict and warfare has claimed far more lives than individual aggression and has left widespread devastation in its wake. With the terrorist attack on America on September 11, 2001, the horrific effects of organized violence came to our shores. As we look ahead in this new millenium, we might wonder whether psychologists and other social scientists might use their skills in conflict resolution to help people mediate conflicts that give rise to war and acts of terrorism. Can psychologists succeed where leaders of government, kings and queens, philosophers, and great historic figures have failed? Certainly the causes of organized warfare are complex, which belies any attempt at finding a simple solution. Yet, perhaps psychologists can use their unique perspectives to help people learn nonaggressive ways of resolving conflicts. For example, the cognitive perspective might give us insights into ways in which leaders of nations interpret situations that might set the stage for a warlike response to international conflicts. Efforts toward developing a "peace psychology" are still in their infancy (see Feshbach, 1994). We cannot say whether such efforts will succeed, but we can say it would be a far greater shame not to try.

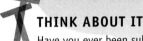

Truth OR Fiction? REVISITED

In some cases, sexual relations between clients and therapists are therapeutically justified.

FALSE. There is no therapeutic justification for sexual relations between a client and therapist. It is unethical conduct on the part of the therapist.

THINK ABOUT IT
Have you ever been subjected to sexual harassment? What was the outcome? Would you do anything differently if it were to happen again?

THINK ABOUT IT
Suppose you were to be subject to sexual harassment and confided in a friend who tells you, "Forget it. It's no big deal. It happens to everyone sooner or later." How would you respond?

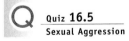
Quiz **16.5**
Sexual Aggression

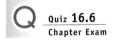
Quiz **16.6**
Chapter Exam

Research Update
Chapter 16

Summing Up

Violence and Abnormal Behavior

Is violent or aggressive behavior abnormal? Applying the criteria discussed in Chapter 1, we may consider violent or aggressive behavior to be abnormal when it is not socially sanctioned and is either self-defeating or results in harm to self or others.

What is the relationship between violent behavior and psychological disorders? Most people with psychological disorders are nonviolent. However, evidence shows an increased rate of violent behavior is associated with some abnormal behavior patterns, such as acute episodes of schizophrenia, or when severe mental disorders are compounded by problems of alcohol or substance abuse or poor adherence to medication.

Explaining Human Aggression

What are the major biological perspectives on human aggression? The instinct model of human aggression does not hold favor today largely because of criticism that it fails to account for diversity in aggressive behavior in humans and the importance of learning and culture. Contemporary biological models focus on the neurobiological underpinnings of aggression, including brain mechanisms involved in regulating aggressive behavior, the role of neurotransmitters, especially serotonin, and the role of the male sex hormone testosterone.

How do social-cognitive theorists view human aggression? Social-cognitive theorists view aggressive behavior as learned behavior that is influenced by modeling (exposure to aggressive models), expectancies (expectations of positive outcomes of aggressive behavior), competencies (skills needed to handle conflict situations through nonviolent means), and interpretation of social cues in confrontative situations (e.g., misreading other people's motives or intentions).

How do sociocultural theorists view human aggression? Sociocultural theorists believe that violent behavior is rooted in underlying social causes, such as poverty, lack of opportunity, family breakdown, exposure to deviant role models, and social stressors such as unemployment. They also focus on the role of violence as a social influence tactic.

How might alcohol use contribute to aggressive behavior? Alcohol use may make it difficult to weigh the consequences of one's behavior, loosen inhibitions, and decrease sensitivity to anxiety-arousing cues that might otherwise serve to inhibit aggressive impulses.

How are emotional factors implicated in aggression? Emotional states such as frustration and anger may act as catalysts for aggressive behavior, especially when the person blames someone else for being responsible for the frustrating or angering situation.

What general conclusion might we reach about the underlying causes of human aggression? Most theorists recognize that human aggression is a complex form of behavior that cannot be explained by any single cause. We may come to a better understanding of human aggression by adopting a multiple causation model that takes into account the contributions and interactions of biological, psychological, and sociocultural factors.

Domestic Violence

What factors are linked to domestic violence? Relationship problems, alcohol use, and feelings of inadequacy and low self-esteem on the part of the batterer often figure prominently in battering relationships. Spousal battering typically occurs within a larger pattern of abuse that may also involve child abuse and sexual aggression against the spouse. Battering incidents often follow a triggering event that leads the abuser to lose control.

How do feminist theorists view domestic violence? Feminist theorists believe that domestic violence arises from the differential power relationships that exist between men and women in our society. They point out that domestic violence occurs within a larger social context in which men are socialized into dominant roles while women are expected to be subordinate to their interests.

What are the effects of domestic violence? The effects range from physical injury to PTSD and other emotional problems, especially depression and self-esteem. Women who remain in abusive relationships should be viewed as survivors of trauma, not as masochists.

Child Abuse

What are the different forms of child abuse and maltreatment? There are several different forms of child abuse and maltreatment, including neglect, physical abuse, sexual abuse, and emotional maltreatment. Neglect is the most frequently occurring form of abuse.

What factors are linked to child abuse? Stress, poor parenting and anger management skills, and a history of being physically abused during childhood or witnessing family violence are implicated among various risk factors for predicting which parents are at increased risk of abusing their children.

What are the effects of child abuse? The effects of child abuse range from physical injuries, even death, to emotional consequences, such as difficulties forming healthy attachments, low self-esteem, suicidal thinking, depression, and failure to explore the outside world, among other problems. The emotional and behavioral consequences of child abuse and neglect often extend into adulthood.

Sexual Aggression

What factors underlie rape? Rape has more to do with violent impulses and issues of power than with pursuit of sexual gratification. The desires to dominate women or express hatred toward them are prominent motives for rape. Although some rapists show clear evidence of underlying psychopathology, many do not. Sociocultural theorists argue that cultural attitudes and practices may socialize young men into sexually aggressive or dominant roles.

What effects does rape have on survivors? Although the effects are variable, rape survivors often suffer a range of immediate and long-term psychological effects.

What is child sexual abuse? Any sexual act involving children is a form of sexual abuse, even if no direct force or threat of force is used, or the child consents. The great majority of assailants have had some prior relationship with the child or child's family.

What are the effects of child sexual abuse? Although the effects vary, survivors typically experience a range of emotional and behavioral problems in childhood and adolescence. Survivors may also have difficulty forming or maintaining intimate relationships in adulthood.

What is sexual harassment? Sexual harassment involves unwelcome sexual comments, overtures, gestures, physical contact, or direct demands for sexual favors as a condition of employment, retention, or advancement. Sexual harassment may occur in many places, including the workplace, school, or doctor's or therapist's office. Like other forms of abuse, sexual harassment can have damaging psychological consequences.

What factors underlie sexual harassment? Sexual harassment typically has more to do with the abuse of power than sexual motivation. It is often used by men as a tactic to "keep women in their place," especially in situations that have been traditional male preserves.

CHAPTER SEVENTEEN

Abnormal Psychology and Society

P. Filonov
Man in the World

Truth OR Fiction?

- People can be committed to psychiatric facilities because of eccentric behavior. (p. 538)

- Psychologists and other mental health professionals can accurately predict the dangerousness of people they evaluate. (p. 540)

- Therapists are not obligated to breach client confidentiality even to warn intended victims of threats of violence made against them by their clients. (p. 542)

- A ruling in a legal case in Alabama established that patients in mental hospitals in the state may be required to perform general housekeeping duties in the facility. (p. 545)

- An attempt to assassinate the president of the United States was seen by millions of television viewers, but the would-be assassin was found not guilty by a court of law. (p. 547)

- The insanity defense is used in a large number of trials, usually successfully. (p. 548)

- People who are found not guilty of a crime by reason of insanity may remain confined to a mental hospital indefinitely—for many years longer than they would have been sentenced to prison, if they had been found guilty. (p. 550)

- It is possible for a defendant to be held to be competent to stand trial but still be judged not guilty of a crime by reason of insanity. (p. 552)

arry Hogue—the "wild man" of West 96th Street. Hogue, a homeless veteran of the Vietnam War who dwells in the alleyways and doorways of Manhattan's Upper West Side. Hogue, a middle-aged man who goes barefoot in winter, eats from garbage cans, and mutters to himself (Dugger, 1992). Hogue, who reportedly stalked a teacher and threatened to cook and eat her fawn-colored Akita. Hogue, who reportedly becomes violent when he smokes crack and was once arrested for pushing a schoolgirl in front of a school bus (Shapiro, 1992). (Miraculously, she escaped injury.) Hogue, who had been shuttled in and out of state psychiatric hospitals and prisons more than 40 times (Wickenhaver, 1992). Hogue, for whom the criminal justice systems and mental health systems are nothing but revolving doors. Hogue, whom many regard as the living embodiment of the cracks in our mental health, criminal justice, and social services systems.

Typically, Hogue would improve during a brief hospital stay and be released, only to return to using crack instead of his psychiatric medication. His behavior would then deteriorate (Dugger, 1994).

What does society do about Larry Hogue? What does society do about Joyce Brown?

Joyce Brown? Joyce Brown was a middle-aged woman who also lived on the streets of New York. At one time she slept above a hot air vent on the sidewalk on the Upper East Side of Manhattan, in the midst of some of the most expensive real estate in the world. Sometimes she was observed defecating in her clothes or on the sidewalk. She hurled insults at strangers and refused to go to a shelter, preferring to live in the streets, despite the obvious dangers of potential attack and the risks of exposure to the elements.

In New York, a program was begun to provide outreach services to homeless people in need of psychological treatment. Teams of specialists, each consisting of a nurse, a social worker, and a psychiatrist, were charged with the task of identifying and monitoring behaviorally disordered homeless people, helping them obtain services, bringing them soup and sandwiches, and taking them to the hospital if they were deemed to represent an immediate threat to themselves or others under the authority provided by state laws governing psychiatric commitment, even if it was against the individual's will.

Brown had been picked up and brought against her will to a city hospital for evaluation, where she was diagnosed with paranoid schizophrenia and judged to be in need of treatment. She resisted treatment and claimed that she had a right to live her life as she saw fit, even if it offended other people. As long as she committed no crime, what right did society have to deprive her of her liberty? Yes, she admitted, she had defecated in the streets. But there were no public rest rooms available, and establishments such as restaurants had refused her access.

Brown sued for her release, and while her case meandered through the courts, she remained in the hospital, although her doctors were prevented from medicating her against her will. Because she refused medication, the doctors released her, claiming there was little they could do for her. Although we've lost track of Joyce Brown, Larry Hogue turned up a few years later in his old haunts on the Upper West Side of Manhattan, where he was seen panhandling. Local residents expressed fears that he would return to terrorizing them (Holloway, 1998).

The cases of Larry Hogue and Joyce Brown touch on the more general issue of how to balance the rights of the individual with the rights of society. Do people, for example, have the right to live on the streets under unsanitary conditions? There are those who argue that a just and humane society has the right and responsibility to care for people who are perceived incapable of protecting their own best interests, even if "care" means involuntarily committing them to a psychiatric institution. Do people who are obviously mentally disturbed have the right to refuse treatment? Do psychiatric institutions have the right to inject them with antipsychotic and other drugs against their will? Should mental patients with a history of disruptive or violent behavior be hospitalized indefinitely or permitted to live in supervised residences in the community once their conditions are stabilized? When severely disturbed people break the law, should society respond to them with the criminal justice system or with the mental health system?

"The Wild Man of West 96th Street." Larry Hogue, the so-called "Wild Man of West 96th Street" in New York City, has become a symbol of the cracks in the mental health, criminal justice, and social services systems.

In this chapter we consider psychiatric commitment and other issues that arise from society's response to abnormal behavior, such as the rights of patients in institutions, the use of the insanity defense in criminal cases, and the responsibility of professionals to warn individuals who may be placed at risk by the dangerous behavior of their clients.

Psychiatric Commitment and Patient's Rights

Legal placement of people in psychiatric institutions against their will is called **civil,** or psychiatric, **commitment.** Through civil commitment, individuals deemed to be mentally disordered and to be a threat to themselves or others may be involuntarily confined to psychiatric institutions to provide them with treatment and help ensure their own safety and that of others. Civil commitment should be distinguished from *legal* or *criminal commitment,* in which an individual who has been acquitted of a crime by reason of insanity is placed in a psychiatric institution for treatment. In **legal commitment,** a criminal's unlawful act is judged by a court of law to result from a mental disorder or defect, and the person is committed to a psychiatric hospital where treatment can be provided rather than incarcerated in a prison.

Civil commitment should also be distinguished from *voluntary hospitalization,* in which an individual voluntarily seeks treatment in a psychiatric institution, and can, with adequate notice, leave the institution when she or he so desires. Even in such cases, however, when the hospital staff believes that a voluntary patient presents a threat to her or his own welfare or to others, they may petition the court to change the patient's legal status from voluntary to involuntary.

Civil commitment in a psychiatric hospital usually requires that a petition be filed by a relative or a professional. Psychiatric examiners may be empowered by the court to evaluate the person in a timely fashion, after which a judge hears psychiatric testimony and decides whether or not to commit the individual. In the event of commitment, the law usually requires periodic legal review and recertification of the patient's involuntary status. The legal process is intended to ensure that people are not indefinitely "warehoused" in psychiatric hospitals. Hospital staff must demonstrate the need for continued inpatient treatment.

Legal safeguards are usually in place to protect people's civil rights in commitment proceedings. Defendants have the right to due process and to be assisted by an attorney, for example. But when individuals are deemed to present a clear and imminent threat to themselves or others, the court may order immediate hospitalization until a more formal commitment hearing can be held. Such emergency powers are usually limited to a specific period, usually 72 hours. During this time a formal commitment petition must be filed with the court, or the individual has a right to be discharged.

Standards for psychiatric commitment have been tightened over the past generation, and the rights of individuals who are subject to commitment proceedings are more strictly protected. In the past, psychiatric abuses were more commonplace. People were often committed without clear evidence that they posed a threat. Not until 1979, in fact, did the U.S. Supreme Court rule, in *Addington* v. *Texas,* that in order for individuals to be hospitalized involuntarily, they must be judged both to be "mentally ill" and to present a clear and present danger to themselves or others. Thus people cannot be committed because of their eccentricity.

Few would argue that contemporary tightening of civil commitment laws provides greater protection of the rights of the individual. Even so, some critics of the psychiatric system have called for the complete abolition of psychiatric commitment on the grounds that commitment deprives the individual of liberty in the name of therapy, and that such a loss of liberty cannot be justified in a free society. Perhaps the most vocal and persistent critic of the civil commitment statutes is psychiatrist Thomas Szasz (Szasz, 1970). Szasz argued that the label of *mental illness* is a societal invention that transforms social deviance into medical illness. In Szasz's view, people should not be deprived of their liberty because their behavior is perceived to be socially deviant or disruptive. According to Szasz, people who violate the law should be prosecuted for criminal behavior, not confined to a psychiatric hospital.

Truth OR Fiction? REVISITED

People can be committed to psychiatric facilities because of eccentric behavior.

FALSE. People cannot be committed because they are eccentric. The U.S. Supreme Court has determined that people must be judged mentally ill and present a clear and present danger to themselves or others to be psychiatrically committed.

civil commitment The legal process of placing a person in a mental institution, even against his or her will.

legal commitment The legal process of confining a person found not guilty by reason of insanity in a mental institution.

Although psychiatric commitment may prevent some individuals from acting violently, it does violence to many more by depriving them of liberty:

> The mental patient, we say, *may be* dangerous: he may harm himself or someone else. But we, society, *are* dangerous: we rob him of his good name and of his liberty, and subject him to tortures called "treatments." (Szasz, 1970, p. 279)

Szasz's strident opposition to institutional psychiatry and his condemnation of psychiatric commitment focused attention on abuses in the mental health system. Szasz also persuaded many professionals to question the legal, ethical, and moral bases of coercive psychiatric treatment in the forms of involuntary hospitalization and forced medication. Many caring and concerned professionals draw the line at abolishing psychiatric commitment, however. They argue that people may not be acting in their considered best interests when they threaten suicide or harm to others, or when their behavior becomes so disorganized that they cannot meet their basic needs.

Predicting Dangerousness

To be psychiatrically committed, people must be judged to be dangerous to themselves or others. Professionals are thus responsible for making accurate predictions of dangerousness to determine whether people should be involuntarily hospitalized or maintained involuntarily in the hospital. But how accurate are professionals in predicting dangerousness? Do professionals have special skills or clinical wisdom that renders their predictions accurate, or are their predictions no more accurate than those of laypeople?

Unfortunately, psychologists and other mental health professionals who rely on their clinical judgments are not very accurate when it comes to predicting dangerousness of the people they treat. Mental health professionals tend to overpredict dangerousness—that is, to label many individuals as dangerous when they are not (Monahan, 1981). Clinicians tend to err on the side of caution in overpredicting the potential for dangerous behavior, perhaps because they believe that failure to predict violence may have more serious consequences than overprediction. Overprediction of dangerousness does deprive many people of liberty on the basis of fears that turn out to be groundless. According to Szasz and other critics of the practice of psychiatric commitment, the commitment of the many to prevent the violence of the few is a form of preventive detention that violates the basic principles on which the United States was founded.

The leading professional organizations, the American Psychological Association (1978) and the American Psychiatric Association (1998), have both gone on record as stating that neither psychologists nor psychiatrists, respectively, can reliably predict violent behavior. As a leading authority in the field, John Monahan of the University of Virginia, put

THINK ABOUT IT
Do you believe we should abolish psychiatric commitment? Why or why not?

Should she be committed to a psychiatric institution? People must be judged as dangerous in order to be psychiatrically hospitalized against their wills. This photograph of emergency workers pulling a woman away from a ledge after she threatened to jump leaves little doubt about the dangerousness of her behavior. But professionals have not demonstrated that they can reliably predict future dangerousness.

the issue, "When it comes to predicting violence, our crystal balls are terribly cloudy" (Rosenthal, 1993, p. A1).

The accuracy of clinician predictions of dangerousness is significantly better than predictions based on chance alone, but is still often inaccurate (Kaplan, 2000). Clinician predictions are generally also less accurate than predictions based on evidence of past violent behavior (Gardner et al., 1996; Mossman, 1994). Basically, clinicians do not possess any special knowledge or ability for predicting violence beyond that of the average person. In fact, a layperson supplied with information concerning an individual's past violent behavior may be more accurate in predicting the individual's potential for future violence than the clinician who bases a prediction solely on information obtained from a clinical interview (Mossman, 1994). Unfortunately, although past violent behavior may be the best predictor of future violence, hospital staff may not be permitted access to criminal records or may lack the time or resources to track down these records (Rosenthal, 1993). The prediction problem has been cited by some as grounds for the abandonment of dangerousness as a criterion for civil commitment.

Although their crystal balls may be cloudy, mental health professionals who work in institutional settings continue to be called on to make these predictions—deciding whom to commit and whom to discharge based largely on how they appraise the potential for violence. Clinicians may be more successful in predicting violence by basing predictions on a composite of factors, including evidence of past violent behavior, than on any single factor (Shaffer, Waters, & Adams, 1994). Not surprisingly, the accuracy of clinician predictions of violence tends to be greater when clinicians agree with one another than when they disagree (McNiel, Lam, & Binder, 2000). Accuracy is also improved when clinicians make short-term predictions of dangerousness, such as predictions of imminent violence (Binder, 1999). Another variable that may increase predictability is substance abuse. The potential for violence is heightened in people with serious psychiatric disorders when they use alcohol, crack, or other drugs (Rosenthal, 1993; Tardiff et al., 1997). It is also heightened among schizophrenia patients who experience command hallucinations—voices commanding them to harm themselves or others (McNiel, Lam, & Binder, 2000).

Various factors may lead to inaccurate predictions of dangerousness, including the following.

The *Post Hoc* Problem Recognizing violent tendencies after a violent incident occurs (*post hoc*) is easier than predicting it (*ad hoc*). It is often said that hindsight is 20/20. Like Monday morning quarterbacking, it is easier to piece together fragments of people's prior behaviors as evidence of their violent tendencies *after* they have committed acts of violence. Predicting a violent act before the fact is a more difficult task, however.

The Problem in Leaping from the General to the Specific Generalized perceptions of violent tendencies may not predict specific acts of violence. Most people who have "general tendencies" toward violence may never act on them. Nor is classification within a diagnostic category associated with aggressive or dangerous behavior, such as antisocial personality disorder, a sufficient basis for predicting specific violent acts in individuals (Bloom & Rogers, 1987).

Problems in Defining Dangerousness One difficulty in assessing the predictability of dangerousness is the lack of agreement in defining the criteria for labeling behavior as violent or dangerous. There is no universal agreement on the definition of violence or dangerousness. Most people would agree that crimes such as murder, rape, and assault are acts of violence. There is less agreement, even among authorities, for labeling other acts—for example, driving recklessly, harshly criticizing one's spouse or children, destroying property, selling drugs, shoving into people at a tavern, or stealing cars—as violent or dangerous. Consider, also, the "dangerous behavior" of business owners and corporate executives who produce and market cigarettes despite widespread knowledge of the death and disease caused by these substances. Clearly, the determination of which behaviors are regarded as dangerous involves moral and political judgments within a given social context (Monahan, 1981).

Base-Rate Problems The prediction of dangerousness is complicated by the fact that violent acts such as murder, assault, or suicide are infrequent or rare events at the individual level within the general population, even if newspaper headlines sensationalize them regularly. Other rare events—such as earthquakes—are also difficult to predict with any degree of certainty concerning when or where they will strike.

The relative difficulty of making predictions of infrequent or rare events is known as the *base-rate problem.* Consider as an example the problem of suicide prediction. If the suicide rate in a given year has a low base rate of about 1% of a clinical population, the likelihood of accurately predicting that any given person in this population will commit suicide is not very favorable. You would be correct 99% of the time if you predicted that any given individual in this population would *not* commit suicide in a given year. But to predict the nonoccurrence of suicide in every case would mean you would fail to predict the relatively few cases in which suicide does occur, even though virtually all of your predictions would likely be correct. Yet predicting the one likely case of suicide among each 100 people in the population is likely to be tricky. You are likely to be wrong more often than not if you made predictions of suicide in a given year in only 3 cases out of 100 (even if 1 of the 3 did commit suicide).

When clinicians make predictions, they weigh the relative risks of incorrectly failing to predict the occurrence of a behavior (a *false negative*) against the consequences of incorrectly predicting it (a *false positive*). Clinicians often err on the side of caution by overpredicting dangerousness. From the clinician's perspective, erring on the side of caution might seem like a no-lose situation. Yet many people committed to an institution under such circumstances are denied their liberty when they would not actually have acted violently against themselves or others.

The Unlikelihood of Disclosure of Direct Threats of Violence How likely is it that truly dangerous people will disclose their intentions to a health professional who is evaluating them or to their own therapist? The client in therapy is not likely to inform a therapist of a clear threat, such as "I'm going to kill _____ next Wednesday morning." Threats are more likely to be vague and nonspecific, as in "I'm so sick of _____; I could kill her," or "I swear he's driving me to murder." In such cases, therapists must infer dangerousness from hostile gestures and veiled threats. Vague, indirect threats of violence are less reliable indicators of dangerousness than specific, direct threats.

The Difficulty of Predicting Behavior in the Community from Behavior in the Hospital Mental health professionals fall well short of the mark when making long-term predictions of dangerousness (Buchanan, 1999). They are often wrong when making predictions of dangerousness of hospitalized patients following their release from the hospital. One reason is that they often base their predictions on patients' behavior in the hospital. But violent or dangerous behavior may be situation specific. A model patient who is able to adapt to a structured environment like that of a psychiatric hospital may be unable to cope with pressures of independent communal life. Clinicians are generally more accurate when their predictions are based on the patient's past behavior in the community, such as a history of violent incidents, rather than on behavior in the hospital setting (Klassen & O'Connor, 1988).

As we explore in the nearby "A Closer Look" section, the problem of predicting dangerousness also arises when therapists need to evaluate the seriousness of threats made by their patients against others.

Patients' Rights

We have considered society's right to hospitalize involuntarily people who are judged to be mentally ill and to pose a threat to themselves or others. What happens following commitment, however? Do involuntarily committed patients have the right to receive or demand treatment? Or can society just warehouse them in psychiatric facilities indefinitely without treating them? Consider the opposite side of the coin as well: May people who are involuntarily committed refuse treatment? Such issues—which have been brought into public light

Is he suicidal? One reason clinicians have difficulty predicting violent behaviors such as suicide or murder is that they are relatively infrequent acts. Clinicians often err on the side of caution and so have a tendency toward overpredicting dangerousness.

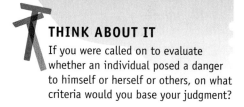

THINK ABOUT IT
If you were called on to evaluate whether an individual posed a danger to himself or herself or others, on what criteria would you base your judgment?

wWw   **Web Link 17.2**
      Confidentiality Issues

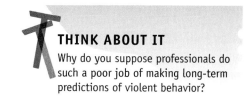

THINK ABOUT IT
Why do you suppose professionals do such a poor job of making long-term predictions of violent behavior?

A Closer Look

The Duty to Warn

One of the most difficult dilemmas a therapist may face is whether to disclose confidential information that may protect third parties from harm. Part of the difficulty lies in determining whether the client has made a bona fide threat against another person. The other part of the dilemma is that information a client discloses in psychotherapy is generally protected as privileged communication, which carries a right to confidentiality. But this right is not absolute. Courts in some states have determined that a therapist is obliged to breach confidentiality under certain conditions, such as when there is clear and compelling evidence that an individual poses a serious threat to others.

Truth OR Fiction?   REVISITED

Therapists are not obligated to breach client confidentiality even to warn intended victims of threats of violence made against them by their clients.

FALSE. Therapists are obligated under some state laws to breach client confidentiality in order to warn people when threats of violence are made against them by their clients.

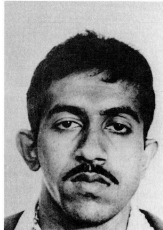

Tatiana Tarasoff and Prosenjit Poddar. Poddar, Tatiana's killer, was a rejected suitor who had made threats against her to his therapist at a university health center. Poddar was subsequently convicted of voluntary manslaughter in her death. A suit brought by Tatiana's parents against the university led to a landmark court ruling that established an obligation on therapists to warn third parties of threats made against them by their clients.

A California case, *Tarasoff* v. *the Regents of the University of California,* established the legal basis for the therapist's **duty to warn.** In 1969, a graduate student at the University of California at Berkeley, Prosenjit Poddar, a native of India, became depressed when his romantic overtures toward a young woman, Tatiana Tarasoff, were rebuffed. Poddar entered psychotherapy with a psychologist at a student health facility, during the course of which he informed the psychologist that he intended to kill Tatiana when she returned from her summer vacation. The psychologist, concerned about Poddar's potential for violence, first consulted with his colleagues and then notified the campus police. He informed them that Poddar was dangerous and recommended he be taken to a facility for psychiatric treatment.

Poddar was subsequently interviewed by the campus police. They believed he was rational and released him after he promised to keep his distance from Tatiana. Poddar then terminated treatment with the psychologist, and shortly afterward killed Tatiana. He shot her with a pellet gun when she refused to allow him entry to her home and then repeatedly stabbed her as she fled into the street. Poddar was found guilty of the lesser sentence of voluntary manslaughter rather than murder based on testimony of three psychiatrists that Poddar suffered from diminished mental capacity and paranoid schizophrenia. Under California law, his diminished capacity prevented the finding of malice that was necessary for conviction on a charge of first- or second-degree murder. Following a prison term, Poddar returned to India, where he reportedly made a new life for himself (Schwitzgebel & Schwitzgebel, 1980).

Tatiana's parents, however, sued the university. They claimed that the university health center had failed in its responsibility to warn Tatiana of the threat made against her by Poddar. The Supreme Court of

---

by landmark court cases—fall under the umbrella of *patients' rights.* Generally speaking, the history of abuses in the mental health system, as highlighted in such popular books and movies as *One Flew Over the Cuckoo's Nest,* have led to a tightening of standards of care and adoption of legal guarantees to protect patients' rights. The legal status of some issues, such as the right to treatment, remains unsettled, however.

Right to Treatment We might assume that mental health institutions that accept people for treatment would provide them with treatment. Not until the 1972 landmark federal court case of *Wyatt* v. *Stickney,* however, did a federal court establish a minimum standard of care to

duty to warn The therapist's obligation to warn third parties of threats made against them by clients.

the State of California agreed with the parents. They ruled that a therapist who has reason to believe that a client poses a serious threat to another person is obligated to warn the potential victim. This obligation is not met by notifying police. This ruling imposed on therapists a duty-to-warn obligation when their clients show the potential for violence by making threats against others.

The ruling recognized that the rights of the intended victim outweigh the rights of confidentiality. Under *Tarasoff*, the therapist does not merely have a *right* to breach confidentiality and warn potential victims of danger, but is *obligated* by law to divulge such confidences to the victim.

The duty-to-warn provision poses ethical and practical dilemmas for psychologists and other psychotherapists. Psychotherapists, in states that apply the *Tarasoff* obligation, have a duty to assess the potential violence of their clients, even though professionals are not generally able to predict dangerousness with a high degree of accuracy. Under *Tarasoff*, then, therapists may actually feel obliged to protect their personal interests and those of others by breaching confidentiality on the mere suspicion that their clients harbor violent intentions toward third parties. Because there are very few cases in which clients' threats are carried out, the *Tarasoff* ruling may deny many clients their rights to confidentiality in order to prevent such rare instances. Although some clinicians may "overreact" to *Tarasoff* and breach confidentiality without sufficient cause, it can be argued that the interests of the few potential victims outweigh the interests of the many who may suffer a loss of confidentiality.

Although therapists apparently possess no special ability to predict dangerousness, the *Tarasoff* ruling obliges them to judge whether or not their clients' disclosures indicate a clear intent to harm others. In the *Tarasoff* case, the threat was obvious enough to prompt the therapist to breach confidentiality by requesting the help of campus police. In most cases, however, threats are not so clear-cut. There remains a lack of clear criteria for determining whether or not a therapist "should have known" that a client was dangerous before a violent act occurs (Fulero, 1988). In the absence of guidelines that specify the criteria therapists should use to fulfill their duty to warn, they must rely on their best subjective judgments.

Although the intent of the *Tarasoff* decision was to protect potential victims, it may inadvertently increase the risks of violence when applied to clinical practice (Stone, 1976). For example,

1. *Clients may be less willing to confide in their therapists.* Under the obligations imposed on therapists by *Tarasoff*, clients may be less willing to confide violent urges to their therapists, making it more difficult for therapists to help them diffuse these feelings before they are acted on.

2. *Potentially violent people may be less likely to enter therapy.* People with violent tendencies may be less willing to enter therapy for fear that disclosures made to a therapist may be revealed.

3. *Therapists may be less likely to probe violent tendencies for fear of legal complications.* To protect themselves and their careers, therapists may avoid asking clients questions concerning potential violence in the belief that they are legally protected if they remain ignorant of them (Wise, 1978). Therapists might also avoid accepting patients for treatment who are believed to have violent tendencies.

It is unclear whether *Tarasoff* has protected lives or endangered lives. It is clear, however, that *Tarasoff* has raised concerns for clinicians who are trying to meet their legal responsibilities under *Tarasoff* and their clinical responsibilities to their clients.

A survey of psychiatric residents in San Francisco showed that nearly half had issued Tarasoff-type warnings (Binder & McNiel, 1996). In most cases, the intended victim had already been aware of the threat. Most of the patients were told by their therapists that warnings had been issued. Though issuing a warning produced no clear effects on the therapeutic relationship in most cases, negative effects were reported in some cases.

The *Tarasoff* case was brought in California, and the decision applied only to that state (DeBell & Jones, 1997b). Other states vary in their statutes that apply in duty-to-warn cases (Schaffer, 2000). In most states, therapists are granted discretion in deciding whether or not to notify a threatened person or law enforcement officials when threats are made by their clients in the therapeutic context (USDHHS, 1999a). Therapists must be aware of the statutes and legal precedents that exist in the particular states in which they practice. Therapists must also not lose sight of the primary therapeutic responsibility to their clients when legal issues arise. They must balance the obligation to meet their responsibilities under duty-to-warn provisions with the need to help their clients resolve the feelings of rage and anger that give rise to violent threats.

be provided by hospitals. The case was a class action suit against Stickney, the commissioner of mental health for the State of Alabama, brought on behalf of Ricky Wyatt, a mentally retarded young man, and other patients at a state hospital and school in Tuscaloosa.

The federal district court in Alabama held both that the hospital had failed to provide treatment to Wyatt and others and that living conditions at the hospital were inadequate and dehumanizing. The court described the hospital dormitories as "barnlike structures" that afforded no privacy to the residents. The bathrooms had no partitions between stalls, the patients were outfitted with shoddy clothes, the wards were filthy and crowded, the kitchens were unsanitary, and the food was substandard. In addition, the staff

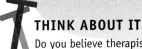

THINK ABOUT IT
Do you believe therapists should be obligated to breach confidentiality in cases in which their patients make threats against others? Why or why not? What concerns have therapists raised about the duty to warn? Do you believe their concerns are warranted?

What are the rights of mental patients?
Popular books and films such as *One Flew Over the Cuckoo's Nest* starring Jack Nicholson have highlighted many of the abuses of mental hospitals. In recent years, a tightening of standards of care and the adoption of legal safeguards have led to better protection of the rights of patients in mental hospitals.

Web Link **17.3** wWw
National Alliance for the Mentally Ill

was inadequate in numbers and poorly trained. The case of *Wyatt* v. *Stickney* established certain patient rights, including the right not to be required to perform work that is performed for the sake of maintaining the facility. The court held that mental hospitals must, at a minimum, provide the following:

1. A humane psychological and physical environment,
2. Qualified staff in numbers sufficient to administer adequate treatment, and
3. Individualized treatment plans (*Wyatt* v. *Stickney*, 334 Supp., p. 1343, 1972).

The court established that the state was obliged to provide adequate treatment for people who were involuntarily confined to psychiatric hospitals. The court further ruled that to commit people to hospitals for treatment involuntarily, and then not to provide treatment, violated their rights to due process under the law.

A listing of some of the rights granted institutionalized patients under the court's ruling is shown in Table 17.1. Although the ruling of the court was limited to Alabama, many other states have followed suit and revised their mental hospital standards to ensure that involuntarily committed patients are not denied basic rights.

Other court cases have further clarified patients' rights.

O'Connor* v. *Donaldson The 1975 case of Kenneth Donaldson is another landmark in patients' rights. Donaldson, a former patient at a state hospital in Florida, sued two hospital doctors on the grounds that he had been involuntarily confined without receiving treatment for 14 years, despite the fact that he posed no serious threat to himself or others. Donaldson had been originally committed on the basis of a petition filed by his father, who had perceived him as delusional. Despite the fact that Donaldson received no treatment during his confinement and was denied grounds privileges and occupational training, his repeated requests for discharge were denied by the hospital staff. He was finally released when he threatened to sue the hospital. Once discharged, Donaldson did sue his doctors and was awarded damages of $38,500 from O'Connor, the superintendent of the hospital. The case was eventually argued before the U.S. Supreme Court.

TABLE 17.1 Partial Listing of the Patient's Bill of Rights Under *Wyatt* v. *Stickney*

1. Patients have rights to privacy and to be treated with dignity.
2. Patients shall be treated under the least restrictive conditions that can be provided to meet the purposes that commitment was intended to serve.
3. Patients shall have rights to visitation and telephone privileges unless special restrictions apply.
4. Patients have the right to refuse excessive or unnecessary medication. In addition, medication may not be used as a form of punishment.
5. Patients shall not be kept in restraints or isolation except in emergency conditions in which their behavior is likely to pose a threat to themselves or others and less restrictive restraints are not feasible.
6. Patients shall not be subject to experimental research unless their rights to informed consent are protected.
7. Patients have the right to refuse potentially hazardous or unusual treatments, such as lobotomy, electroconvulsive shock, or aversive behavioral treatments.
8. Unless it is dangerous or inappropriate to the treatment program, patients shall have the right to wear their own clothing and keep possessions.
9. Patients have rights to regular exercise and to opportunities to spend time outdoors.
10. Patients have rights to suitable opportunities to interact with the opposite gender.
11. Patients have rights to humane and decent living conditions.
12. No more than six patients shall be housed in a room and screen or curtains must be provided to afford a sense of privacy.
13. No more than eight patients shall share one toilet facility, with separate stalls provided for privacy.
14. Patients have a right to nutritionally balanced diets.
15. Patients shall not be required to perform work that is performed for the sake of maintenance of the facility.

Court testimony established that although the hospital staff had not perceived Donaldson to be dangerous during his hospitalization, they had refused to release him. The hospital doctors argued that continued hospitalization had been necessary because they had believed Donaldson was unlikely to adapt successfully to community living. The doctors had prescribed antipsychotic medications as a course of treatment, but Donaldson had refused to take them because of his Christian Science beliefs. As a result, he received only custodial care.

The Supreme Court held that "mental illness [alone] cannot justify a State's locking a person up against his will and keeping him indefinitely in simple custodial confinement. There is still no constitutional basis for confining such persons involuntarily if they are dangerous to no one and can live safely in freedom" (p. 2493). The ruling addressed patients who are not considered dangerous. It is not yet clear whether the same constitutional rights would be applied to committed patients who are judged to be dangerous.

In its ruling in *O'Connor* v. *Donaldson,* the Supreme Court did not deal with the larger issue of the rights of patients to receive treatment. The ruling does not directly obligate state institutions to treat involuntarily committed, nondangerous people because the institutions may elect to release them instead.

The Supreme Court did touch on the larger issue of society's rights to protect itself from individuals who are perceived as offensive. In delivering the opinion of the Court, Justice Potter Stewart wrote,

> May the State fence in the harmless mentally ill solely to save its citizens from exposure to those whose ways are different? One might as well ask if the State, to avoid public uneasiness, could incarcerate all who are physically unattractive or socially eccentric. Mere public intolerance or animosity cannot constitutionally justify the deprivation of a person's physical liberty. (*O'Connor* v. *Donaldson,* 95 S. Ct. 2486, 1975)

Youngberg* v. *Romeo In a 1982 case, *Youngberg* v. *Romeo,* the U.S. Supreme Court more directly addressed the issue of the patient's right to treatment. Even so, it seemed to retreat somewhat from the patients' rights standards established in *Wyatt* v. *Stickney.* Nicholas Romeo, a 33-year-old man with profound retardation who was unable to talk or care for himself, had been institutionalized in a state hospital and school in Pennsylvania. While in the state facility he had a history of injuring himself through his violent behavior and was often kept in restraints. The case was brought by the patient's mother, who alleged that the hospital was negligent in not preventing his injuries and in routinely using physical restraints for prolonged periods while not providing adequate treatment.

The Supreme Court ruled that involuntarily committed patients, like Nicholas, have a right to be confined in less restrictive conditions, such as being freed from physical restraints whenever it is reasonable to do so. The Supreme Court ruling also included a limited recognition of the committed patient's right to treatment. The Court held that institutionalized patients have a right to minimally adequate training to help them function free of physical restraints, but only to the extent that such training can be provided in reasonable safety. The determination of reasonableness, the Court held, should be made on the basis of the judgment of the qualified professionals in the facility. The federal courts should not interfere with the internal operations of the facility, the Court held, because "there's no reason to think judges or juries are better qualified than appropriate professionals in making such decisions" (p. 2462). The courts should only second-guess the judgments of qualified professionals, the Supreme Court held, when such judgments are determined to depart from professional standards of practice. But the Supreme Court did not address the broader issues of the rights of committed patients to receive training that might eventually enable them to function independently outside the hospital.

Kenneth Donaldson. Donaldson points to the U.S. Supreme Court decision that ruled that people who are considered mentally ill but not dangerous cannot be confined against their will if they can be maintained safely in the community.

WWW   **Web Link 17.4**
Mental Health Bill of Rights

Truth OR Fiction?   **REVISITED**

A ruling in a legal case in Alabama established that patients in mental hospitals in the state may be required to perform general housekeeping duties in the facility.

FALSE. The Alabama case of *Wyatt* v. *Stickney* established certain patient rights, including the right not to be required to perform work that is performed for the sake of maintaining the facility.

Quiz **17.1**
Psychiatric Commitment
and Patient's Rights

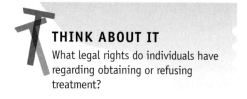

THINK ABOUT IT

Under what circumstances do you think someone should be confined to a mental hospital? What rights should patients have under such circumstances?

THINK ABOUT IT

What legal rights do individuals have regarding obtaining or refusing treatment?

The related issue of whether people with severe psychological disorders who reside in the community have a constitutional right to receive mental health services (and whether states are obliged to provide these services) continues to be argued in the courts at both the state and federal levels (Perlin, 1994).

Right to Refuse Treatment Consider the following scenario. A person, John Citizen, is involuntarily committed to a mental hospital for treatment. The hospital staff determines that John suffers from a psychotic disorder, paranoid schizophrenia, and should be treated with antipsychotic medication. John, however, decides not to comply with treatment. He claims that the hospital has no right to treat him against his will. The hospital staff seeks a court order to mandate treatment, arguing it makes little sense to commit people involuntarily unless the hospital is empowered to treat them as the staff deems fit.

Does an involuntary patient, like John, have the right to refuse treatment? If so, does this right conflict with states' rights to commit people to mental institutions to receive treatment for their disorders? One might also wonder whether people who are judged in need of involuntary hospitalization are competent to make decisions about which treatments are in their best interests.

The rights of committed patients to refuse psychotropic medications was tested in the 1979 case *Rogers* v. *Okin,* in which a Massachusetts federal district court imposed an injunction on a Boston state hospital that prohibited the forced medication of patients except in emergency situations. The court ruled that committed patients could not be forcibly medicated, except in the case of emergency—for example, when patients' behaviors pose a significant threat to themselves or others. The court recognized that a patient may be unwise to refuse medication, but it held that a patient with or without a mental disorder has the right to exercise bad judgment so long as the effects of the "error" do not impose "a danger of physical harm to himself, fellow patients, or hospital staff" (p. 1367).

Despite the concerns some mental health professionals raised that patients who refused medications would be "rotting with their rights on" (Gutheil, 1980), legal protections ensuring patients' rights to refuse psychiatric treatments do not appear to have had seriously damaging or disruptive effects on mental health services or on the people receiving these services (Kapp, 1994).

Although statutes and regulations vary from state to state, cases in which hospitalized patients refuse medications are often first brought before an independent review panel. If the panel rules against the patient, the case may then be brought before a judge, who makes the final decision about whether or not the patient is to be forcibly medicated. In actual practice, the number of refusals of medication is generally low, about 10% overall. Furthermore, between 70% and 90% of refusals that reach the review process are eventually overridden. Hospitalized patients in a recent study who refused medication tended to be more assaultive, were more likely to require seclusion and restraint, and had longer hospitalizations than did compliant patients (Kasper et al., 1997). However, the refusal episodes tended to be brief, about 3 days on the average, and all initial refusers were eventually treated.

Our discussion of legal issues and abnormal behavior now turns to the controversy concerning the insanity defense.

The Insanity Defense

As President Ronald Reagan stepped out of the Washington Hilton on March 31, 1981, gunshots rang out. Secret Service agents formed a human

Not guilty by reason of insanity. In 1981, John Hinckley Jr. attempted to assassinate President Ronald Reagan outside the Washington Hilton Hotel. Here Reagan winces as he was shot in the upper left side. Hinckley was later found not guilty by reason of insanity. The public outrage over the Hinckley verdict led to a reexamination of the insanity plea in many states.

shield around the president as another agent shoved him into a waiting limousine, which then sped away to a hospital. At first, the president did not know he had been wounded. He said later that it sounded like firecrackers. Agents seized the gunman, John Hinckley, a 25-year-old drifter. Not only the president had been wounded. James Brady, his press secretary, was hit by a stray bullet that shattered his spine, leaving him partially paralyzed. A Secret Service agent was also shot.

Hinckley had left a letter in his hotel room revealing his hope that his assassination of the president would impress a young actress, Jodie Foster. Hinckley had never met Foster but had a crush on her.

There was never any question at the trial that Hinckley had fired the wounding bullets, but the prosecutor was burdened to demonstrate beyond a reasonable doubt that at the time of the assassination attempt, Hinckley had the capacity to control his behavior and appreciate its wrongfulness. The defense presented testimony that portrayed Hinckley as an incompetent schizophrenic who suffered under the delusion that he would achieve a "magic union" with Foster as a result of killing the president. The prosecutor portrayed Hinckley as making a conscious and willful choice to kill the president. The prosecution further argued that whatever mental disorder Hinckley might have had did not prevent him from controlling his behavior.

The jury sided with the defense. A man who was seen by millions of TV viewers attempting to assassinate President Reagan was found "not guilty by reason of insanity." The verdict led to a public outcry across the country, with many calling for the abolition of the insanity defense. Public opinion polls taken several days after the Hinckley verdict was returned showed the public had little confidence in the psychiatric testimony that had been offered at the trial (Slater & Hans, 1984). One objection focused on the fact that once the defense presented evidence to support a plea of insanity, the federal prosecutor had the responsibility of proving *beyond a reasonable doubt* that the defendant was sane. It can be difficult enough to demonstrate that someone is sane or insane in the present, so imagine the problems that attend proving someone was sane at the time a criminal act was committed.

In the aftermath of the Hinckley verdict, the federal government and many states changed their statutes to shift the burden of proof to the defense to prove insanity (Ogloff, Roberts, & Roesch, 1993). Even the American Psychiatric Association went on record as stating that psychiatric expert witnesses should not be called on to render opinions about whether defendants can control their behavior. In the opinion of the psychiatric association, these are not medical judgments that psychiatrists are trained to provide.

Perceptions of the use of the **insanity defense** tend to stray far from the facts. The public grossly overestimates the number of cases in which the insanity defense is used and how often it succeeds. The public estimates that the insanity defense is used in about 1 in 3 felony cases, but in actuality it is used in fewer than 1% of cases (Silver, Cirincione, & Steadman, 1994; Steadman et al., 1993). A study in Baltimore showed that the insanity defense plea was used in a minuscule 1/100th of 1% of indictments brought to trial (Janofsky et al., 1996). Whereas the public believes that 44% of defendants who claim insanity are acquitted, the actual figure (based on a review of the records in eight states) was 26% (Silver et al., 1994; Steadman et al., 1993). In actual practice, out of 1,000 felony cases, there are fewer than 10 in which the insanity defense is used, and only about 2 or 3 in which it is used successfully. Thus despite public perceptions to the contrary, the use of the insanity defense is actually rather rare, and the rate of acquittals is rarer still ("Insanity," 1992).

The public also overestimates the proportion of defendants acquitted on the basis of insanity who are set free rather than confined to mental health institutions and underestimates the length of hospitalization of those who are confined (Silver et al., 1994). The facts show that people found not guilty on the basis of insanity are often confined to mental hospitals for longer periods of time than they would have served in prison (Lymburner & Roesch, 1999). The net result is that although changes in the insanity defense, or its abolition, may prevent some few flagrant cases of abuse, they are not likely to afford the public much broader protection.

In the wake of the Hinckley acquittal, a number of states adopted a new type of verdict, the "guilty-but-mentally-ill" (GBMI) verdict (Boudouris, 2000; Maeder, 1985). The

Jodie Foster. John Hinckley reportedly attempted to assassinate President Reagan in order to impress Ms. Foster, whom he had seen in the film *Taxi Driver* but never met. In the film, Robert DeNiro, who portrayed a person with paranoid schizophrenia, rescued Foster's character from a life of prostitution. Hinckley's attorneys claimed that their client experienced similar rescue fantasies.

Truth OR Fiction? REVISITED

An attempt to assassinate the president of the United States was seen by millions of television viewers, but the would-be assassin was found not guilty by a court of law.

TRUE. A man who was seen by millions of TV viewers attempting to assassinate President Reagan was found "not guilty by reason of insanity" by a court of law.

insanity defense A legal defense in which a defendant in a criminal case pleads innocent on the basis of insanity.

Guilty but mentally ill? John du Pont, an heir to the du Pont family fortune, was tried for the 1996 murder of Olympic gold medalist wrestler David Schultz. Du Pont was found guilty but mentally ill, a verdict that remains controversial in part because it is seen by some people as merely a way of stigmatizing defendants who are found guilty as also being mentally ill.

GBMI verdict offers juries the option of finding a defendant both guilty and mentally ill, if they determine that the defendant is mentally ill but that the mental illness did not cause the defendant to commit the crime. The GBMI verdict provides that people so convicted may be imprisoned but also receive treatment while in prison. The GBMI verdict has now been adopted in many states as a supplement to, not a replacement of, the insanity defense (Ogloff et al., 1993).

The GBMI verdict is something of an in-between determination, in that the defendant is neither acquitted nor found guilty in the traditional sense of the term. The verdict has sparked a great deal of controversy. Although GBMI was intended to reduce the number of NGRI (not guilty by reason of insanity) verdicts, this outcome has apparently not occurred. All in all, the GBMI verdict appears to be a social experiment that has not yet proved its usefulness and is seen by some as merely a means of stigmatizing defendants who are found guilty as also being mentally ill (Maeder, 1985).

In a celebrated case, John E. du Pont, an heir to the du Pont family fortune, was found guilty but mentally ill following trial for the 1996 murder of Olympic gold medalist wrestler David Schultz ("Du Pont Heir Found Guilty," 1997). Du Pont was subsequently remanded to a state psychiatric hospital for treatment rather than to prison. At trial, it was reported that du Pont exhibited bizarre behavior and suffered from delusions of being spied on by Nazis and of having his body inhabited by bugs.

Although the public outrage over the Hinckley and other celebrated insanity verdicts has led to a reexamination of the insanity defense, society has long held to the doctrine of free will as a basis for determining responsibility for wrongdoing. The doctrine of free will, as applied to criminal responsibility, requires that people can be held guilty of a crime only if they are judged to have been in control of their actions at the time of commission of the crime. Not only must it be determined by a court of law that a defendant had committed a crime beyond a reasonable doubt, but the issue of the individual's state of mind must be considered as well in determining guilt. The court must thus rule not only on whether a crime was committed but also on whether an individual is held morally responsible and deserving of punishment. The insanity defense is based on the belief that when a criminal act derives from a distorted state of mind, and not from the exercise of free will, the individual should not be punished but rather treated for the underlying mental disorder. The insanity defense has a long legal history.

Legal Bases of the Insanity Defense

We can find in modern law three major court rulings that bear on the insanity defense. The first involved a case in Ohio in 1834 in which it was ruled that people could not be held responsible if they are compelled to commit criminal actions because of impulses they are unable to resist.

The second major legal test of the insanity defense is referred to as the M'Naghten rule, based on a case in England in 1843 of a Scotsman, Daniel M'Naghten, who had intended to assassinate the prime minister of England, Sir Robert Peel. Instead, he killed Peel's secretary, whom he had mistaken for the prime minister. M'Naghten claimed that the voice of God had commanded him to kill Peel. The English court acquitted M'Naghten on the basis of insanity, finding that the defendant had been " … labouring under such a defect of reason, from disease of the mind, as not to know the nature and quality of the act he was doing; or, if he did know it, that he did not know he was doing what was wrong." The M'Naghten rule holds that people do not bear criminal responsibility if, by reason of a mental disease or defect, they either have no knowledge of their actions or are unable to tell right from wrong.

To find the third major case that helped lay the foundation for the modern insanity defense we must jump more than 100 years to 1954 and the case of *Durham* v. *United States*. In this case, the presiding judge, David Bazelon, held that the "accused [person] is not criminally responsible if his unlawful act was the product of mental disease or mental defect" (pp. 874–875). Under the Durham rule, juries were expected to decide not only whether the accused suffered from a mental disease or defect but also whether this mental condition was causally connected to the criminal act. The court recognized that criminal intent is a precondition of criminal responsibility:

> The legal and moral traditions of the western world require that those who, of their own free will and with evil intent . . . commit acts which violate the law, shall be criminally responsible for those acts. Our traditions also require that where such acts stem from and are the product of a mental disease or defect . . . moral blame shall not attach, and hence there will not be criminal responsibility. (*Durham* v. *United States,* 214 F2d 862, D.C. circ. 1954)

The intent of the Durham rule was to reject as outmoded the two earlier standards of legal insanity, the irresistible impulse rule and the "right–wrong" principle under the M'Naghten rule. Judge Bazelon argued that the "right–wrong test" was outmoded because the concept of "mental disease" is broader than the ability to recognize right from wrong. The legal basis of insanity should thus not be judged on just one feature of a mental disorder, such as deficient reasoning ability. The irresistible impulse test was denied because the court recognized that in certain cases, criminal acts arising from "mental disease or defect" might occur in a cool and calculating manner rather than in the manner of a sudden, irresistible impulse.

The Durham rule, however, has proved to be unworkable for several reasons, such as a lack of precise definitions of such terms as *mental disease* or *mental defect* (Maeder, 1985). Courts were confused, for example, about issues such as whether a personality disorder (e.g., antisocial personality disorder) constituted a "disease." It also proved difficult for juries to draw conclusions about whether an individual's "mental disease" was causally connected to the criminal act. Without clear or precise definitions of terms, juries came to rely increasingly on expert psychiatric testimony, often serving as little more than rubber stamps as their verdicts endorsed the testimony of expert witnesses (Maeder, 1985).

By 1972, the Durham rule had failed and was replaced in many jurisdictions by a set of legal guidelines formulated by the American Law Institute (ALI) to define the legal basis of insanity, or some variation of these standards (Ogloff et al., 1993). These guidelines, which essentially combine the M'Naghten principle with the irresistible impulse principle, include the following provisions:

1. A person is not responsible for criminal conduct if at the time of such conduct as a result of mental disease or defect he lacks substantial capacity either to appreciate the criminality (wrongfulness) of his conduct or to conform his conduct to the requirements of law.

2. . . . the terms "mental disease or defect" do not include an abnormality manifested only by repeated criminal or otherwise antisocial conduct. (American Law Institute, 1962, p. 66)

The first guideline incorporates aspects of the M'Naghten test (being unable to appreciate right from wrong) and the irresistible impulse test (being unable to conform one's behavior to the requirements of law) of insanity. The second guideline asserts that repeated criminal behavior (such as a pattern of drug dealing) is not sufficient in itself to establish a mental disease or defect that might relieve the individual of criminal responsibility. Although many legal authorities believe the ALI guidelines are an improvement over earlier tests, questions remain as to whether a jury composed of ordinary citizens can be expected to make complex judgments about the defendant's state of mind, even on the basis of expert testimony. Under the ALI guidelines, juries must determine whether defendants lack substantial capacity to be aware of, or capable of, conforming their behavior to the law. By adding the term *substantial capacity* to the legal test, the ALI guidelines may also broaden the legal basis of the insanity defense because this may imply that defendants need not be completely incapable of controlling their criminal actions in order to meet the legal test of not guilty by reason of insanity.

Under our system of justice, juries must struggle with the complex question of determining criminal responsibility, not merely criminal actions. But what of those individuals who successfully plead not guilty by reason of insanity? Should they be committed to a

THINK ABOUT IT

Describe how the test for legal insanity has changed over time. How does this reflect changing ideas about mental illness and abnormal behavior?

Truth OR Fiction? REVISITED

People who are found not guilty of a crime by reason of insanity may remain confined to a mental hospital indefinitely—for many years longer than they would have been sentenced to prison, if they had been found guilty.

TRUE. People who are found not guilty of a crime by reason of insanity may remain confined to a mental hospital indefinitely.

mental institution for a fixed sentence, as they might have been had they been incarcerated in a penal institution? Or should their commitments be of an indeterminate term and their release depend on their mental status? The legal basis for answering such questions was decided in the following case of a man, Michael Jones, whose acquittal by reason of insanity resulted in involuntary commitment to a mental hospital for a period that turned out to be seven times longer than the maximum prison sentence for the crime.

Determining the Length of Criminal Commitment

The issue of determinate versus indeterminate commitment was addressed in the case of Michael Jones (*Jones* v. *United States*), who was arrested in 1975 and charged with petty larceny for attempting to steal a jacket from a Washington, D.C., department store. Jones was first committed to a public mental hospital, St. Elizabeth's Hospital (which, incidentally, is the hospital where John Hinckley remains committed as of this writing). Jones was diagnosed by a hospital psychologist as suffering from paranoid schizophrenia and was kept hospitalized until he was judged competent to stand trial, about 6 months later. Jones offered a plea of not guilty by reason of insanity, which the court accepted without challenge, remanding him to St. Elizabeth's. Despite the fact that Jones's crime carried a maximum sentence of 1 year in prison, Jones's repeated attempts to obtain release were denied in subsequent court hearings.

The U.S. Supreme Court eventually heard his appeal *7 years* after he was hospitalized. The Supreme Court reached its decision in 1983. It ruled against Jones's appeal and affirmed the decision of the lower courts that he was to remain in the hospital. The Supreme Court thereby established a principle that individuals who are acquitted by reason of insanity "constitute a special class that should be treated differently" than civilly committed individuals. They may be committed for an indefinite period to a mental institution under criteria that require a less stringent level of proof of dangerousness than would ordinarily be applied in cases of civil commitment. Thus people found not guilty by reason of insanity may remain confined to a mental hospital for many years longer than they would have been sentenced to prison had they been found guilty.

Among other things, the Supreme Court ruling in *Jones* v. *United States* provides that the usual and customary sentences that the law provides for particular crimes have no bearing on criminal commitment. In the words of the Court,

> different considerations underlie commitment of an insanity acquittee. As he was not convicted, he may not be punished. His confinement rests on his continuing illness and dangerousness. There simply is no necessary correlation between severity of the offense and length of time necessary for recovery. (*Jones* v. *United States*, 103 S.Ct. 3043, 1983)

The ruling held that a person who is criminally committed may be confined "to a mental institution until such time as he has regained his sanity or is no longer a danger to society" (p. 3053). As in the case of Michael Jones, people who are acquitted on the basis of insanity may remain confined in a mental institution for longer periods of time than they would have been sentenced to prison. It is also possible, however, that such persons could be released earlier than they might have been released from prison, if their "mental condition" is found to have improved. A person acquitted of a serious crime by virtue of the insanity defense may even be released within a few weeks or months, although, practically speaking, it is doubtful that improvement would be established so quickly. Public outrage over a speedy release, especially for a major crime, might also prevent rapid release.

The indeterminateness of legal or criminal commitment raises various questions. Is it reasonable to deny people like Michael Jones their liberty for an indefinite and possibly lifelong term for a relatively minor crime, such as petty larceny? On the other hand, is justice served by acquitting perpetrators of heinous crimes by reason of insanity and then allowing them the opportunity for an early release if they are deemed by professionals to be able to rejoin society?

The Supreme Court's ruling in *Jones* v. *United States* seems to imply that we must separate the notion of legal sentencing from that of legal or criminal commitment. The former, in which sentences are scaled according to the seriousness of the crime, rests on the principle that the punishment should fit the crime. In legal or criminal commitment, however, persons acquitted of their crimes by reason of insanity are guiltless in the eyes of the law. They must be treated, not punished, until such time that their mental status has improved to the point that permits them to safely reenter society.

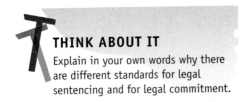

THINK ABOUT IT
Explain in your own words why there are different standards for legal sentencing and for legal commitment.

Perspectives on the Insanity Defense

The insanity defense places special burdens on juries. In assessing criminal responsibility, the jury is expected to determine not only that a crime was committed by the accused, but also the defendant's state of mind at the time of commission of the crime. In rejecting the Durham decision, courts have relieved psychiatrists and other expert witnesses from bearing the burden of responsibility for determining whether or not the defendant's behavior is a product of a "mental disease or defect." But is it reasonable to assume that juries of people from all walks of life are better able to assess defendants' states of mind than mental health professionals? In particular, how can a jury evaluate the testimony of expert conflicting witnesses? The task imposed on the jury is made even more difficult by the mandate to decide whether or not the defendant was mentally incapacitated *at the time of the crime.* The defendant's courtroom behavior may bear little resemblance to his or her behavior during the crime.

Thomas Szasz and others who deny the existence of mental illness itself have raised another challenge to the insanity defense. If mental illness does not exist, then the insanity defense becomes groundless. Szasz argues that the insanity defense is ultimately degrading because it strips people of personal responsibility for their behavior. People who break laws are criminals, Szasz argues, and should be prosecuted and sentenced accordingly. Acquittal of defendants by reason of insanity treats them as nonpersons, as unfortunates who are not deemed to possess the basic human qualities of free choice, self-determination, and personal responsibility. We are each responsible for our behavior, Szasz contends, and we should each be held accountable for our misdeeds.

Szasz argues that the insanity defense has historically been invoked in crimes that were particularly heinous or perpetrated against persons of high social rank. When persons of low social rank commit crimes against persons of higher status, Szasz argues, the effect of the insanity defense is to direct attention away from the social ills that may have motivated the crime. Despite Szasz's contention, however, the insanity defense is invoked in many cases of less shocking crimes or in cases involving persons from similar social classes.

How, then, are we to evaluate the insanity defense? To abolish the insanity defense in all forms would be to reverse hundreds of years of a legal tradition that has recognized that people are not to be held responsible for their criminal behavior when their ability to control themselves is impaired by a mental disorder or defect.

Consider a hypothetical example. John Citizen commits a crime, say a heinous crime like murder, while acting on a delusional belief that the victim was intent on assassinating him. The accused claims that voices from his TV set informed him of the identity of the assailant and commanded him to kill the assailant to save himself and other potential victims. Cases like this are thankfully rare. Few mentally disturbed persons, even few people with psychotic features, commit violent crimes, and even fewer commit murder.

In reaching a judgment on the insanity plea, we need to consider whether we believe the law should allow special standards to apply in cases such as our hypothetical case, or whether one standard of criminal responsibility should apply to all. If we assert the legitimacy of the insanity defense in some cases, we still need a standard of insanity that can be interpreted and applied by juries of ordinary citizens. The furor over the Hinckley verdict suggests that issues concerning the insanity plea remain unsettled.

THINK ABOUT IT
Do you believe the insanity verdict should be abolished? Should it be replaced with another type of verdict, such as the guilty-but-mentally-ill verdict? Why or why not?

Competency to Stand Trial

There is a basic rule of law that those who stand accused of crimes must be able to understand the charges and proceedings brought against them and be able to participate in their own defense. The concept of *competency to stand trial* should not be confused with the legal

Truth OR Fiction? REVISITED

It is possible for a defendant to be held to be competent to stand trial but still be judged not guilty of a crime by reason of insanity.

TRUE. A defendant can be held competent to stand trial but still be judged not guilty of a crime by reason of insanity.

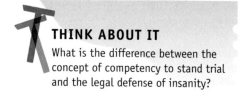

THINK ABOUT IT

What is the difference between the concept of competency to stand trial and the legal defense of insanity?

Quiz **17.2** Q
The Insanity Defense

Quiz **17.3** Q
Chapter Exam

defense of insanity. A defendant can be held competent to stand trial but still be judged not guilty of a crime by reason of insanity. A clearly delusional person, for example, may understand the court proceedings and be able to confer with defense counsel, but still be acquitted by reason of insanity. On the other hand, a person may be incapable of standing trial at a particular time, but be tried and acquitted or convicted at a later time when competency is restored.

Far more people are confined to mental institutions on the basis of a determination that they lack the mental competence to stand trial than on the basis of the insanity verdict (Roesch et al., 1999). There may be 45 people committed under the mental competency to stand trial criteria for every one committed following a verdict of not guilty by reason of insanity (Steadman, 1979).

People declared incompetent to stand trial are generally confined to a mental institution until they are deemed competent or a determination is made that they are unlikely to ever regain competency. Abuses may occur, however, if the accused are kept incarcerated for indefinite periods awaiting trial. In earlier years, it was not uncommon for people who were declared incompetent to have their trials delayed for months or years until they were judged ready to stand trial, if indeed they were ever judged to be competent. In 1972, however, the U.S. Supreme Court ruled, in the case of *Jackson* v. *Indiana,* that a person could not be kept in a mental hospital awaiting trial longer than it would take to determine whether treatment was likely to restore competency. If it did not seem the person would ever become competent, even with treatment, the individual would have to be either released or committed under the procedures for civil commitment.

A 1992 ruling by the U.S. Supreme Court, in the case of *Medina* v. *California,* held that the burden of proof for determining competency to stand trial lies with the defendant, not the state (Greenhouse, 1992). This decision may speed the trials of many people who commit crimes and whose competency is in question.

We opened this book by noting that despite the public impression that abnormal behavior affects only the few, it actually affects nearly every one of us in one way or another. Let us close by suggesting that if we all work together to foster research into the causes, treatment, and prevention of abnormal behavior, perhaps we can meet the multifaceted challenges that abnormal behavior poses to so many of us and to our society at large.

Summing Up

Psychiatric Commitment and Patient's Rights

What is the difference between civil commitment and legal commitment? The legal process by which people are placed in psychiatric institutions against their will is called civil or psychiatric commitment. Civil commitment is intended to provide treatment to people who are deemed to suffer from mental disorders and to pose a threat to themselves or others. Legal or criminal commitment, by comparison, involves the placement of a person in a psychiatric institution for treatment who has been acquitted of a crime by reason of insanity. In voluntary hospitalization, people voluntarily seek treatment in a psychiatric facility and can leave of their own accord unless a court rules otherwise.

How successful are mental health professionals in predicting the dangerousness of patients they evaluate? Although people must be judged dangerous to be placed involuntarily in a psychiatric facility, mental health professionals have not demonstrated any special ability to predict dangerousness. Factors that may account for the failure to predict dangerousness include (1) recognizing violent tendencies post hoc is easier than predicting it; (2) generalized perceptions of violent tendencies may not predict specific acts of violence; (3) lack of agreement in defining violence or dangerousness; (4) base-rate problems; (5) unlikelihood of direct threats of violence; and (6) predictions based on hospital behavior may not generalize to community settings.

What is meant by the duty to warn? Although information disclosed by a client to a therapist generally carries a right to confidentiality, the California *Tarasoff* ruling held that therapists have a duty or obligation to warn third parties of threats made against them by their clients.

What landmark court cases dealt with the rights of patients in psychiatric facilities? In *Wyatt* v. *Stickney*, a court in Alabama imposed a minimum standard of care. In *O'Connor* v. *Donaldson,* the U.S. Supreme Court ruled that nondangerous mentally ill people could not be held in psychiatric facilities against their will if such people could be maintained safely in the community. In *Youngberg* v. *Romeo,* the Supreme Court ruled that involuntarily confined patients have a right to less restrictive types of treatment and to receive training to help them function. Court rulings, such as that of *Rogers* v. *Okin* in Massachusetts, have established that patients have a right to refuse medication, except in case of emergency.

The Insanity Defense

What are the legal bases of the insanity defense? Three court cases established legal precedents for the insanity defense. In 1834, a court in Ohio applied a principle of irresistible impulse as the basis of an insanity defense. The M'Naghten rule, based on a case in England in 1843, treated the failure to appreciate the wrongfulness of one's action as the basis of legal insanity. The Durham rule was based on a case in the United States in 1954 in which it was held that persons did not bear criminal responsibility if their criminal behavior was the product of "mental disease or mental defect." Another set of standards developed by the American Law Institute that combines the M'Naghten and irresistible impulse principles has been adopted in some form in 22 states. People who are criminally committed may be hospitalized for an indefinite period of time, with their eventual release dependent on a determination of their mental status.

What is meant by the legal concept of competency to stand trial? People who are accused of crimes but are incapable of understanding the charges against them or assisting in their own defense can be found incompetent to stand trial and remanded to a psychiatric facility. In the case of *Jackson* v. *Indiana,* the U.S. Supreme Court placed restrictions on the length of time a person judged incompetent to stand trial could be held in a psychiatric facility.

GLOSSARY

A

Abnormal psychology. The branch of psychology that deals with the description, causes, and treatment of abnormal behavior patterns.

Abstinence violation effect (AVE). The tendency to overreact to a minor lapse with feelings of guilt and resignation that may trigger a relapse.

Acculturation. The process of adapting to a new culture.

Acquired immunodeficiency syndrome (AIDS). An immunological disease caused by HIV.

Acrophobia. Excessive, irrational fear of heights.

Acute stress disorder (ASD). A traumatic stress reaction occurring in the days and weeks following exposure to a traumatic event.

Addiction. Impaired control over the use of a chemical substance, accompanied by physiological dependence.

Adjustment disorder. A maladaptive reaction to an identified stressor, which is characterized by impaired functioning or signs of emotional distress that exceed what would normally be expected.

Adoptee studies. Studies that compare the traits and behavior patterns of adopted children to those of their biological parents and their adoptive parents.

Affect. Emotional responsiveness.

Agnosia. A disturbance of sensory perception, usually affecting visual perception.

Agoraphobic. Relating to excessive, irrational fear of open places.

Al-Anon. An organization that sponsors support groups for family members of people with alcoholism.

Alarm reaction. The first stage of the GAS, characterized by heightened sympathetic activity.

Alcoholism. An alcohol dependence disorder or addiction that results in serious personal, social, occupational, or health problems.

Alcohol-induced persisting amnestic disorder. A form of brain damage associated with chronic thiamine deficiency and alcoholism; characterized by memory loss, disorientation, and confabulation.

Alzheimer's disease (AD). A progressive brain disease characterized by gradual loss of memory and intellectual functioning, personality changes, and eventual loss of ability to care for oneself.

Ambivalent. Holding conflicting feelings toward another person or a goal.

Amenorrhea. Absence of menstruation.

Amnestic disorders. Disturbances of memory associated with inability to learn new material or recall past events.

Amphetamine psychosis. A psychotic state induced by ingestion of amphetamines.

Amphetamines. Types of stimulants, such as Benzedrine or Dexedrine.

Amygdala. Limbic system structure involved in processing threatening stimuli.

Anal expulsive. A loosening of restraint, as seen in extreme sloppiness or messiness.

Anal fixation. Attachment to objects and behaviors characteristic of the anal stage.

Anal retentive. Excessive need for self-control and orderliness.

Anal stage. The psychosexual stage during toddlerhood in which pleasure is sought primarily through anal activities.

Analgesia. Relief from pain without loss of consciousness.

Analogue measure. A measure taken in a contrived situation meant to simulate a real-life situation.

Analogue. Something that resembles something else.

Analytical psychology. Jung's theory, emphasizing the collective unconscious, archetypes, and the self as the unifying force of personality.

Anomie. A feeling of rootlessness.

Anorexia nervosa. An eating disorder characterized by maintenance of an abnormally low body weight, distortions of body image, intense fears of gaining weight, and, in females, amenorrhea.

Antianxiety drugs. Drugs that combat anxiety and reduce states of muscle tension.

Antibodies. Substances produced by white blood cells that identify and target antigens for destruction.

Antidepressants. Drugs used to treat depression.

Antigens. Substances that trigger an immune response.

Antipsychotic drugs. Drugs used to treat schizophrenia or other psychotic disorders.

Antisocial personality disorder. A personality disorder characterized by antisocial and irresponsible behavior and lack of remorse for misdeeds.

Anxiety. An emotional state characterized by physiological arousal, unpleasant feelings of tension, and a sense of apprehension or foreboding.

Anxiety disorder. A type of mental disorder whose most prominent feature is anxiety.

Anxiety sensitivity. A fear of anxiety and anxiety-related symptoms.

Apnea. Temporary cessation of breathing.

Archetypes. Primitive images or concepts that reside in the collective unconscious.

Arteriosclerosis. A disease involving thickening and hardening of the arteries.

Asperger's disorder. A pervasive developmental disorder characterized by social deficits and stereotyped behavior but without the significant language or cognitive delays associated with autism.

Associations. Relationships among thoughts.

Ataxia. Loss of muscle coordination.

Atherosclerosis. The buildup of fatty deposits along artery walls that leads to the formation of artery-clogging plaque.

Attention-deficit hyperactivity disorder (ADHD). A behavior disorder characterized by excessive motor activity and inability to focus one's attention.

Attributional style. A personal style for explaining cause-and-effect relationships between events.

Autism. A pervasive developmental disorder characterized by failure to relate to others, lack of speech, disturbed motor behaviors, intellectual impairment, and demands for sameness in the environment.

Autism. Withdrawal into a private fantasy world.

Automatic thoughts. Thoughts that seem to pop into one's mind.

Autonomic nervous system. The division of the peripheral nervous system that regulates the activities of the glands and involuntary functions.

Aversive conditioning. A behavior therapy technique in which a maladaptive response is paired with exposure to an aversive stimulus to develop a conditioned aversion.

Avoidant personality disorder. A personality disorder characterized by avoidance of social relationships due to fears of rejection.

Axon. The long, thin part of a neuron along which nerve impulses travel.

B

Barbiturates. Types of depressants that are used to reduce anxiety or to induce sleep but that are highly addictive.

Basal ganglia. An assemblage of neurons located between the thalamus and cerebrum, involved in coordinating motor (movement) processes.

Baseline. The rate at which a behavior occurs before treatment.

Behavior therapy. The therapeutic application of learning-based techniques.

Behavioral assessment. The approach to clinical assessment that focuses on the objective recording and description of the problem behavior.

Behavioral interview. Clinical interview that focuses on relating the problem behavior to antecedent stimuli and reinforcement consequences.

Behavioral rating scale. A scale used to record the frequency of occurrence of target behaviors.

Behaviorism. The school of psychology that defines psychology as the study of observable behavior.

Benzodiazepines. The class of antianxiety drugs that includes Valium and Xanax.

Bereavement. The experience of grief suffering following the death of a loved one.

Binge-eating disorder (BED). A disorder characterized by recurrent eating binges without purging; classified as a potential disorder requiring further study.

Biofeedback training (BFT). A method of feeding back to the individual information about bodily functions so that the person can gain some degree of control over these functions.

Bipolar. Characterized by opposite ends of a dimension or continuum, as in bipolar disorder.

Bipolar disorder. A disorder characterized by mood swings between states of extreme elation and severe depression.

Blind. A state of being unaware of whether one has received an experimental treatment.

Blocking. An involuntary interruption of speech.

Borderline personality disorder (BPD). A personality disorder characterized by abrupt shifts in mood, lack of a coherent sense of self, and unpredictable, impulsive behavior.

Brain electrical activity mapping (BEAM). Imaging technique involving computer analysis of data from multiple electrodes to reveal areas of the brain with relatively high or low levels of activity.

Breathing-related sleep disorder. A sleep disorder in which sleep is repeatedly disrupted by difficulty with breathing normally.

Brief psychotic disorder. A psychotic disorder lasting from a day to a month that often follows exposure to a major stressor.

Bulimia nervosa. An eating disorder characterized by recurrent binge eating followed by self-induced purging, accompanied by over-concern with body weight and shape.

C

Cardiovascular disease. A disease or disorder of the cardiovascular system, such as coronary heart disease or hypertension.

Case study. A carefully drawn biography based on clinical interviews, observations, and psychological tests.

Castration anxiety. The young boy's unconscious fear that he will be castrated as punishment for his incestuous desire for his mother.

Cataplexy. A brief, sudden loss of muscle control.

Catastrophize. To exaggerate the negative consequences of events.

Catatonic type. The subtype of schizophrenia characterized by gross disturbances in motor activity, such as catatonic stupor.

Catecholamines. A group of substances that includes neurotransmitters (dopamine and norepinephrine) and hormones (epinephrine and norepinephrine).

Catharsis. The discharge of states of tension associated with repression of threatening impulses or material; the purging or free expression of feelings.

Central nervous system. The brain and spinal cord.

Cerebellum. A structure in the hindbrain involved in coordination and balance.

Cerebral cortex. The wrinkled surface area of the cerebrum, it is responsible for processing sensory stimuli and controlling higher mental functions, such as thinking and use of language.

Cerebrovascular accident (CVA). Damage to part of the brain because of a disruption in its blood supply, usually as the result of a blood clot.

Cerebrum. The large mass of the forebrain, consisting of the two cerebral hemispheres.

Childhood disintegrative disorder. A pervasive developmental disorder involving loss of previously acquired skills and abnormal functioning following a period of apparently normal development during the first two years of life.

Choleric. Having or showing bad temper.

Chromosomes. The structures found in the nuclei of cells that carry the units of heredity, or genes.

Circadian rhythm sleep disorder. A sleep disorder characterized by a mismatch between the body's normal sleep-wake cycle and the demands of the environment.

Civil commitment. The legal process of placing a person in a mental institution, even against his or her will.

Clanging. The tendency to string words together because they rhyme or sound alike.

Claustrophobia. Excessive, irrational fear of small, enclosed spaces.

Client-centered therapy. Another term for *person-centered therapy.*

Closed-ended questions. Questionnaire or test items with a limited range of response options.

Cocaine. A stimulant derived from the leaves of the coca plant.

Cognitive disorders. Mental disorders characterized by impaired cognitive abilities and daily functioning in which biological causation is either known or presumed.

Cognitive restructuring. A cognitive therapy method that involves replacing irrational thoughts with rational alternatives.

Cognitive therapy. Aaron Beck's form of therapy that helps clients recognize and correct distorted patterns of thinking.

Cognitive triad of depression. The view that depression derives from adopting negative views of oneself, the environment or world at large, and the future.

Cognitive-behavioral therapy (CBT). A learning-based approach to therapy incorporating cognitive and behavioral techniques.

Cognitive-specificity hypothesis. The belief that different emotional disorders are linked to particular kinds of automatic thoughts.

Collective unconscious. The storehouse of archetypes and racial memories.

Comatose. In a coma, a state of deep, prolonged unconsciousness.

Communication disorders. A class of psychological disorders characterized by difficulties in understanding or using language.

Compulsion. A repetitive or ritualistic behavior that the person feels compelled to perform.

Compulsion to utter. The urge to verbally express repressed material.

Computed tomography (CT scan). Computer-enhanced imaging of the internal structures of the brain by passing a narrow X-ray beam through the head.

Concordance. Agreement.

Concurrent validity. A type of test validity based on the statistical relationship between the test and a criterion measure taken at the same time.

Conditional positive regard. Valuing other people on the basis of whether their behavior meets one's approval.

Conditioned response. In classical conditioning, a learned response to a previously neutral stimulus.

Conditioned stimulus. A previously neutral stimulus that evokes a conditioned response after repeated pairings with an unconditioned stimulus that had previously evoked that response.

Conditions of worth. Standards by which one judges the worth or value of oneself or others.

Conduct disorder. A psychological disorder in childhood and adolescence characterized by disruptive, antisocial behavior.

Confidentiality. Protection of the identity of participants by keeping records secure and not disclosing their identities.

Congruence. The fit between one's thoughts, behaviors, and feelings.

Conscious. To Freud, the part of the mind that corresponds to our present awareness.

Construct validity. The degree to which treatment effects can be accounted for by the theoretical mechanisms (constructs) represented in the independent variables; the degree to which a test measures the hypothetical construct that it purports to measure.

Content validity. The degree to which the content of a test covers a representative sample of the content it is designed to measure.

Contrasted groups approach. A method of determining concurrent validity that uses a test's ability to differentiate between members of two or more comparison groups.

Control subjects. In an experiment, subjects who do not receive the experimental treatment.

Controlled drinking. An approach to treating problem drinkers that has as its goal to moderate social drinking rather than abstinence.

Conversion disorder. A type of somatoform disorder characterized by loss or impairment of physical function in the absence of any apparent organic cause.

Corpus callosum. A thick bundle of fibers that connects the two cerebral hemispheres.

Correlation. A relationship or association between variables.

Countertransference. The transfer of feelings or attitudes that the analyst holds toward other persons onto the client.

Couples therapy. Therapy that focuses on resolving conflicts in distressed couples.

Crack. The hardened, smokable form of cocaine.

Creative self. To Adler, the self-aware part of the personality that strives to achieve its potential.

Criterion validity. The degree to which a test correlates with an independent, external criterion or standard.

Critical thinking. Adoption of a questioning attitude and careful scrutiny of claims and arguments in the light of evidence.

Cross-fostering study. A method of determining heritability of a trait or disorder by examining differences in prevalence among adoptees reared by either adoptive or biological parents who possessed the trait or disorder in question.

Cultural-familial retardation. A mild form of mental retardation that is influenced by impoverishment of the home environment.

Culture-bound syndrome. A pattern of abnormal behavior that is found within only one or a few cultures.

Cyclothymic disorder. A mood disorder characterized by a chronic pattern of mild mood swings that is not sufficiently severe to be classified as bipolar disorder.

Cytomegalovirus. A source of infection that, in pregnant women, carries a risk of mental retardation to the unborn child.

D

Debriefed. To be fully informed about an experiment after it takes place.

Defense mechanisms. The reality-distorting strategies used by the ego to shield the self from awareness of anxiety-provoking materials.

Deinstitutionalization. The policy of shifting care for patients with severe or chronic mental health problems from inpatient facilities to community-based facilities; the practice of discharging hospitalized mental patients into the community and of reducing the need for new admissions through alternative treatment approaches.

Delirium. A state of mental confusion, disorientation, and extreme difficulty focusing attention.

Delirium tremens. A withdrawal syndrome that occurs following sudden decrease of drinking in people with chronic alcoholism.

Delta-9-tetrahydrocannabinol (THC). The active ingredient in marijuana.

Delusion. A firmly held but inaccurate belief that persists despite evidence that it has no basis in reality.

Delusional disorder. A type of psychosis characterized by persistent delusions, often of a paranoid nature, that do not have the bizarre quality of the type often found in paranoid schizophrenia.

Dementia. Deterioration of mental functioning, involving impaired memory, thinking, judgment, and language use.

Dementia praecox. The term given by Kraepelin to the disorder now called schizophrenia.

Demonological model. The model that explains abnormal behavior in terms of supernatural forces.

Demonology. The idea that abnormal behavior is caused by supernatural forces.

Dendrites. The rootlike structures at the ends of neurons that receive nerve impulses from other neurons.

Dependent personality disorder. A personality disorder characterized by difficulty making independent decisions and overly dependent behavior.

Dependent variables. Outcomes of an experiment believed to be dependent on the effects of an independent variable.

Depersonalization disorder. A disorder characterized by persistent or recurrent episodes of depersonalization.

Depersonalization. Feelings of unreality or detachment from one's self or one's body.

Depressant. A drug that lowers the level of activity of the central nervous system.

Derealization. Loss of the sense of reality of one's surroundings, experienced in terms of strange changes in the environment or in the passage of time.

Description. The representation of observations without making interpretations or drawing inferences.

Detoxification. The process of ridding the system of alcohol or other drugs under supervised conditions.

Deviation IQ. An intelligence quotient obtained by determining the deviation between the person's score and the norm (mean).

Dhat syndrome. A culture-bound somatoform disorder, found primarily among Asian Indian males, characterized by excessive fears over the loss of seminal fluid.

Diathesis. A vulnerability or predisposition to a particular disorder.

Diathesis-stress model. A model that posits that abnormal behavior problems involve the interaction of a vulnerability or predisposition and stressful life events or experiences.

Disorganized type. The subtype of schizophrenia characterized by disorganized behavior, bizarre delusions, and vivid hallucinations.

Disorientation. A state of mental confusion and lack of awareness of time, place, or the identity of oneself or others.

Displacement. A defense mechanism in which one transfers sexual or aggressive impulses toward less threatening or safer objects or persons.

Displacing. Transferring impulses toward threatening or unacceptable objects onto more acceptable or safer objects.

Dissociative amnesia. A dissociative disorder in which a person experiences memory loss without any identifiable organic cause.

Dissociative disorder. Any of a group of disorders characterized by a disruption, or dissociation, of the functions of identity, memory, or consciousness.

Dissociative fugue. A dissociative disorder in which a person suddenly flees from his or her life situation, travels to a new location, assumes a new identity, and has amnesia for personal material.

Dissociative identity disorder. A dissociative disorder in which a person has two or more distinct, or alter, personalities.

Distress. A state of physical or emotional pain or suffering.

Dizygotic (DZ) twins. Twins that develop from separate fertilized eggs.

Dopamine theory. The theory that proposes that schizophrenia involves overactivity of dopamine receptors in the brain.

Double depression. A diagnosis of both major depressive disorder and dysthymic disorder.

Double-bind communications. A communication pattern involving contradictory or mixed messages without acknowledging the inherent conflict.

Down syndrome. A condition caused by the presence of an extra chromosome on the 21st pair and characterized by mental retardation and various physical anomalies.

Downward drift hypothesis. The theory that explains the linkage between low socioeconomic status and behavior problems by suggesting that problem behaviors lead people to drift downward in social status.

Duty to warn. The therapist's obligation to warn third parties of threats made against them by clients.

Dyslexia. A learning disorder characterized by impaired reading ability.

Dyspareunia. Persistent or recurrent pain experienced during or following sexual intercourse.

Dyssomnias. Sleep disorders involving disturbances in the amount, quality, or timing of sleep.

Dysthymic disorder. A mild but chronic type of depressive disorder.

E

Eating disorder. A psychological disorder characterized by disturbed patterns of eating and maladaptive ways of controlling body weight.

Eclectic therapy. An approach to psychotherapy that incorporates principles or techniques from various systems or theories.

Ego. The psychic structure that corresponds to the concept of the self, governed by the reality principle and characterized by the ability to tolerate frustration.

Ego analysts. Psychodynamically oriented therapists who are influenced by ego psychology.

Ego dystonic. Referring to behaviors or feelings that are perceived to be alien to one's self-identity.

Ego ideal. The set of higher social values and moral ideals embodied in the superego.

Ego identity. The achievement of a firm sense of personal identity.

Ego psychology. Modern psychodynamic approach that focuses more on the conscious strivings of the ego than on the hypothesized unconscious functions of the id.

Ego syntonic. Referring to behaviors or feelings that are perceived as natural parts of the self.

Electra complex. The conflict that occurs during the phallic stage of development, in which the young girl desires her father and perceives her mother as a rival.

Electroconvulsive therapy (ECT). A method of treating severe depression by administering electrical shock to the head.

Electroencephalograph (EEG). An instrument for measuring the electrical activity of the brain.

Electromyograph (EMG). An instrument for measuring muscle tension.

Emotion-focused coping. A coping style that attempts to minimize emotional responsiveness rather than deal with the stressor directly.

Empathy. The ability to understand someone's experiences and feelings from that person's point of view.

Encopresis. Lack of control over bowel movements that is not caused by an organic problem in a child who is at least 4 years old.

Endocrine system. The system of ductless glands that secrete hormones directly into the bloodstream.

Endorphins. Natural substances that function as neurotransmitters in the brain and are similar in their effects to morphine.

Enuresis. Failure to control urination after one has reached the "normal" age for attaining such control.

Epidemiological method. A method of research that involves tracking the rates of occurrence of a disorder among different groups.

Erogenous zone. A part of the body that is sensitive to sexual stimulation.

Eros. Freud's concept of the basic life instinct that seeks to preserve and perpetuate life.

Erotomania. A delusional disorder characterized by the belief that one is loved by someone of high social status.

Etiological. Relating to cause or origin.

Exhaustion stage. The third stage of the GAS, characterized by lowered resistance, increased parasympathetic activity, and possible physical deterioration.

Exhibitionism. A paraphilia in which one is sexually aroused by exposing one's genitals to a stranger.

Exorcism. A ritual intended to expel demons from a person believed to be possessed.

Expectancies. Beliefs about expected outcomes.

Experimental method. A scientific method that aims to discover cause-and-effect relationships by manipulating independent variables and observing the effects on the dependent variables.

Experimental subjects. In an experiment, subjects who receive the experimental treatment.

External attribution. A belief that the cause of an event involved factors outside oneself.

External validity. The degree to which experimental results can be generalized to other settings and conditions.

F

Face validity. The degree to which the content of a test bears an apparent relationship to the constructs it is designed to measure.

Factitious disorder. A disorder characterized by intentional fabrication of psychological or physical symptoms for no apparent gain.

False negative. An incorrect appraisal that a person is free of a disorder, when in fact he or she has the disorder.

False positive. An incorrect appraisal that a person has a particular disorder.

Family therapy. Therapy in which the family, not the individual, is the unit of treatment.

Fat cells. Body cells specialized to store fat.

Fear-stimulus hierarchy. An ordered series of increasingly fearful stimuli.

Female orgasmic disorder. A sexual dysfunction in women involving difficulty reaching orgasm or inability to reach orgasm following a normal level of sexual interest and arousal.

Female sexual arousal disorder. A sexual dysfunction in women involving difficulty becoming sexually aroused or lack of sexual excitement or pleasure during sexual activity.

Fetishism. A paraphilia in which one uses an inanimate object or body part as a focus of sexual interest and arousal.

Fight-or-flight reaction. The inborn tendency to respond to a threat by either fighting or fleeing.

First-rank symptoms. The primary features of schizophrenia, such as hallucinations and delusions.

Fixation. Arrested development in the form of attachment to objects of an earlier developmental stage.

Flashbacks. The experience of sensory distortions or hallucinations occurring after use of LSD or other hallucinogenic drugs.

Flooding. A form of exposure therapy in which subjects are exposed to high levels of fear-inducing stimuli.

Forced-choice formats. Test questions that require respondents to select from among a limited number of choices.

Forcible rape. Forced sexual intercourse with a nonconsenting person.

Four A's. The primary characteristics of schizophrenia: loose Associations, blunted or inappropriate Affect, Ambivalence, and Autism.

Fragile X syndrome. An inherited form of mental retardation caused by a mutated gene on the X chromosome.

Free association. The method of verbalizing thoughts as they occur without a conscious attempt to edit or censure them.

Freebasing. A method of ingesting cocaine by heating it with ether to separate its most potent component (its "free base") and then smoking the extract.

Frotteurism. A paraphilia characterized by recurrent sexual urges involving bumping or rubbing against nonconsenting others for sexual gratification.

Functional analysis. Analysis of behavior in terms of antecedent stimuli and reinforcement consequences.

Functional magnetic resonance imaging (fMRI). Type of MRI used to identify parts of the brain that become active when people engage in particular tasks.

G

Galvanic skin response (GSR). A measure of the change in electrical activity of the skin that accompanies sympathetic nervous system arousal.

Gamma-aminobutyric acid (GABA). An inhibitory neurotransmitter believed to play a role in anxiety.

Gender identity disorder. A disorder in which the individual believes that her or his anatomical gender is inconsistent with her or his gender identity.

Gender identity. One's psychological sense of being female or male.

Gender roles. The characteristic ways in which males and females are expected to behave in a given culture.

General adaptation syndrome (GAS). The body's three-stage response to states of prolonged or intense stress.

Generalized anxiety disorder (GAD). A type of anxiety disorder characterized by general feelings of dread and foreboding and heightened states of bodily arousal.

Genes. The units, found on chromosomes, that carry heredity.

Genetics. The science of heredity.

Genital stage. The final stage of psychosexual development, characterized by expression of libido through sexual intercourse with an adult of the opposite sex.

Genotype. The set of traits specified by an individual's genetic code.

Genuineness. The ability to recognize and express one's true feelings.

Global attribution. A belief that the cause of an event involved generalized, rather than specific, factors.

Gradual exposure. A behavior therapy technique for overcoming fears through direct exposure to increasingly fearful stimuli.

Group therapy. Therapy method in which a group of clients meet together with a therapist.

H

Halfway houses Supervised community residences that provide a bridge between institutional facilities and independent community living.

Hallucination. A perception that occurs in the absence of an external stimulus and that is confused with reality.

Hallucinogens. Substances that cause hallucinations.

Hashish. A drug derived from the resin of the plant *Cannabis sativa.*

Health psychologist. A psychologist who studies the relationships between psychological factors and physical illness.

Heroin. A narcotic derived from morphine that has strong addictive properties.

Heterosexism. The culturally based belief system that holds that only reproductive sexuality is psychologically healthy and morally correct.

Histrionic personality disorder. A personality disorder characterized by excessive need for attention, praise, reassurance, and approval.

Homophobia. Hatred and fear of lesbians and gay males.

Homosexuality. A sexual orientation characterized by erotic interest in, and development of romantic relationships with, members of one's own gender.

Hormones. Substances secreted by endocrine glands that regulate body functions and promote growth and development.

Human immunodeficiency virus (HIV). The virus that causes AIDS.

Humors. According to the ancient Hippocratic belief system, the vital bodily fluids (phlegm, black bile, blood, yellow bile).

Huntington's disease. An inherited degenerative disease that is characterized by jerking and twisting movements, psychotic behavior, and mental deterioration.

Hyperactivity. An abnormal behavior pattern characterized by difficulty in maintaining attention and extreme restlessness.

Hypersomnia. A pattern of excessive sleepiness during the day.

Hyperventilation. A pattern of overly rapid breathing associated with states of anxiety.

Hypnosis. A trancelike state, induced by suggestion, in which the individual responds to the commands of the hypnotist.

Hypnotics. Drugs, including anesthetics and sedatives, that induce partial or complete unconsciousness and are used to treat sleep disorders.

Hypoactive sexual desire disorder. Persistent or recurring lack of sexual interest or sexual fantasies.

Hypomanic. Referring to a mild state of mania, or elation.

Hypothalamus. A structure in the forebrain involved in regulating body temperature, emotion, and motivation.

Hypothesis. An assumption that is tested through experimentation.

Hypothyroidism. A physical condition, caused by deficiency of the hormone thyroxin, characterized by sluggishness and lowered metabolism.

Hypoxia. Decreased supply of oxygen to the brain or other organs.

Hypoxyphilia. A paraphilia in which a person seeks sexual gratification by being deprived of oxygen.

I

Id. The unconscious psychic structure, present at birth, that contains primitive instincts and is regulated by the pleasure principle.

Ideas of persecution. A form of delusional thinking characterized by false beliefs that one is being persecuted or victimized by others.

Ideas of reference. A form of delusional thinking in which a person reads personal meaning into the behavior of others or external events.

Identification. The process of incorporating the personality or behavior of others.

Immune system. The body's system of defense against disease.

Incidence. The number of new cases of a disorder that occurs within a specific period of time.

Independent variables. Factors that are manipulated in experiments.

Individual psychology. Adler's psychodynamic theory.

Individual response specificity. The belief that people respond to the same stressor in different ways.

Infarction. The development of an infarct, or area of dead or dying tissue, resulting from the blocking of blood vessels normally supplying the tissue.

Inference. A conclusion that is drawn from data.

Inferiority complex. The feelings of inferiority that Adler believed to be a central source of motivation.

Informed consent. The principle that subjects should receive enough information about an experiment beforehand to decide freely whether to participate.

Insanity defense. A legal defense in which a defendant in a criminal case pleads innocent on the basis of insanity.

Insight. The attainment of awareness and understanding of one's true motives and feelings.

Insomnia. Difficulties falling asleep, remaining asleep, or achieving restorative sleep.

Instinct. A fixed, inborn pattern of behavior that is specific to members of a particular species.

Intelligence. (1) The capacity to understand the world and respond to its challenges; (2) the trait measured by intelligence tests.

Intelligence quotient (IQ). A measure of intelligence based on scores on an intelligence test; the ratio between a respondent's mental age and actual age.

Internal attribution. A belief that the cause of an event involved factors within oneself.

Internal consistency. Cohesiveness or interrelationships of items on a test or scales.

Internal locus of control. Perception of one's ability to control reinforcements or affect outcomes.

Internal validity. The degree to which manipulation of the independent variables can be causally related to changes in the dependent variables.

Interpersonal psychotherapy (IPT). A brief form of psychodynamic therapy that focuses on the client's current interpersonal relationships.

Interrater reliability. Consistency of or agreement between raters.

Intoxication. A state of drunkenness.

Introject. To unconsciously incorporate features of another person's personality into one's own ego structure.

Involuntary. Automatic or without conscious direction.

K

Knobs. The swollen endings of axon terminals.

Koro syndrome. A culture-bound somatoform disorder, found primarily in China, in which people fear that their genitals are shrinking.

Korsakoff's syndrome. A syndrome associated with chronic alcoholism that is characterized by memory loss and disorientation (also called alcohol persisting amnestic disorder).

L

La belle indifférence A French expression ("beautiful indifference" in English) describing the lack of concern over one's symptoms displayed by some people with conversion disorder.

Latency stage. The psychosexual stage in middle childhood characterized by repression of sexual impulses.

Latent content. The underlying or symbolic content of dreams.

Learned helplessness. A behavior pattern characterized by passivity and perceptions of lack of control.

Learning disorder. A deficiency in a specific learning ability in the context of normal intelligence and exposure to learning opportunities.

Legal commitment. The legal process of confining a person found not guilty by reason of insanity in a mental institution.

Leukocytes. White blood cells.

Libido. The energy of Eros; sexual drive or energy.

Limbic system. A group of forebrain structures involved in learning, memory, and basic drives.

Longitudinal study. A research study in which subjects are followed over time.

Lysergic acid diethylamide (LSD). A type of hallucinogen.

M

Magnetic resonance imaging (MRI). A computer-generated image of the brain formed by measuring the signals emitted when the head is placed in a strong magnetic field.

Maintaining ethnic identity. Some studies point to psychological benefits in immigrant groups that adapt to the host culture while maintaining ethnic identity.

Major depressive disorder. A severe mood disorder characterized by major depressive episodes.

Male erectile disorder. A sexual dysfunction in men characterized by difficulty achieving or maintaining erection during sexual activity.

Male orgasmic disorder. A sexual dysfunction in males involving difficulty achieving orgasm following a normal pattern of sexual interest and excitement.

Malingering. Faking illness.

Managed care systems. Health care delivery systems that impose limits on the number of treatment sessions they will approve for payment and the fees they will allow for reimbursement.

Manic episode. A period of unrealistically heightened euphoria, extreme restlessness, and excessive activity characterized by disorganized behavior and impaired judgment.

Manic. Relating to mania, as in the manic phase of bipolar disorder.

Manifest content. The reported content or apparent meaning of dreams.

Mantra. A word or phrase that is repeated to induce a state of relaxation and narrowing of consciousness.

Marijuana. A hallucinogenic drug derived from the leaves and stems of the plant *Cannabis sativa.*

Medical model. A biological perspective in which abnormal behavior is viewed as symptomatic of underlying illness.

Medulla. An area of the hindbrain involved in regulation of heartbeat and respiration.

Melancholia. A state of severe depression.

Mental age. The age equivalent that corresponds to a person's level of intelligence as measured by the Stanford-Binet Intelligence Scale.

Mental retardation. A generalized delay or impairment in the development of intellectual and adaptive abilities.

Mental status examination. A structured clinical assessment to determine various aspects of the client's mental functioning.

Meta-analysis. A statistical technique for combining the results of different studies into an overall average.

Metabolic rate. The rate at which energy is used in the body.

Methadone. An artificial narcotic that is used to help people who are addicted to heroin to abstain from it without a withdrawal syndrome.

Modeling. Learning by observing and imitating the behavior of others; a behavior therapy technique for helping an individual acquire a new behavior by means of having a therapist or another individual demonstrate a target behavior that is then imitated by the client

Monoamine oxidase (MAO) inhibitors. A group of antidepressant drugs that increase the availability of neurotransmitters in the brain by inhibiting the actions of an enzyme that breaks down neurotransmitters.

Monozygotic (MZ) twins. Twins that develop from the same fertilized egg and therefore share identical genes.

Mood disorder. A type of disorder characterized by disturbances of mood.

Mood. The pervasive quality of an individual's emotional experience.

Moral principle. The principle that governs the superego to set and enforce moral standards.

Moral therapy. A 19th-century treatment approach that emphasized treating hospitalized patients with care and understanding.

Morphine. A strongly addictive narcotic derived from the opium poppy that relieves pain and induces feelings of well-being.

Mourning. Normal feelings of grief following a loss.

Munchausen syndrome. A type of factitious disorder characterized by the feigning of medical symptoms.

Musterbation. A rigid thought pattern characterized by the tendency to impose excessive, unrealistic demands on oneself or personal imperatives.

Myocardial infarction. A breakdown of heart tissue due to an obstruction in the blood vessels that supply blood to the heart.

N

Naloxone. A drug that prevents users from becoming high if they take heroin.

Naltrexone. A drug related to naloxone that blocks the high from alcohol as well as from opiates.

Narcissistic personality disorder. A personality disorder characterized by adoption of an inflated self-image and demands for attention and admiration.

Narcolepsy. A sleep disorder characterized by sudden, irresistible episodes of sleep.

Narcotics. Drugs that are used for pain relief and treatment of insomnia but that have strong addictive potential.

Naturalistic-observation method. A research method in which subjects' behavior is observed and measured in their natural environments.

Negative correlation. A statistical relationship between two variables such that increases in one are associated with decreases in the other.

Negative reinforcers. Reinforcers that on removal increase the frequency of behavior.

Negative symptoms. Behavioral deficiencies associated with schizophrenia, such as social skills deficits, social withdrawal, flattened affect, poverty of speech and thought, psychomotor retardation, and failure to experience pleasure.

Neo-Freudians. Theorists, such as Jung, Adler, Horney, and Sullivan, who, in comparison with Freud, placed greater emphasis on the importance of cultural and social influences and lesser emphasis on sexual impulses.

Neologisms. New words.

Neuroleptics. A group of antipsychotic drugs (the "major tranquilizers") used in the treatment of schizophrenia, such as the phenothiazines (Thorazine, Mellaril, etc.).

Neurons. Nerve cells.

Neuropsychological. Pertaining to the relationships between the brain and behavior.

Neurosis. A nonpsychotic form of disturbed behavior characterized by problems involving anxiety.

Neuroticism. A trait that involves characteristics such as anxious behavior, apprehension about the future, and avoidance behavior.

Neurotransmitters. Chemical substances that transmit messages from one neuron to another.

Nightmare disorder. A sleep disorder characterized by recurrent awakenings due to frightening nightmares.

Nonspecific factors. Factors not specific to any one form of psychotherapy, such as therapist attention and support, and the engendering of positive expectancies of change.

O

Obesity. A condition of excessive body fat; generally defined by a body mass index (BMI) above 30.

Object relations. The person's relationships to the internalized representations, or "objects," of others' personalities that have been introjected within the person's ego structure.

Object-relations theory. The psychodynamic viewpoint that focuses on the influences of internalized representations of the personalities of parents and other strong attachment figures (called "objects").

Objective tests. Tests that allow a limited range of response options and can therefore be scored objectively.

Obsession. A recurrring thought or image that the individual cannot control.

Obsessive-compulsive personality disorder. A personality disorder characterized by rigid ways of relating to others, perfectionistic tendencies, lack of spontaneity, and excessive attention to detail.

Oedipus complex. The conflict that occurs during the phallic stage of development, in which the young boy desires his mother and perceives his father as a rival.

Open-ended questions. Questions that provide an unlimited range of response options.

Opioids. Natural or synthetic drugs with strong addictive properties; natural opioids, referred to as opiates, are derived from the opium poppy.

Oppositional defiant disorder (ODD). A psychological disorder in childhood and adolescence characterized by excessive oppositionality, or tendencies to refuse requests from parents and others.

Optimum level of arousal. The level of arousal associated with peak performance and optimal feelings of well-being.

Oral stage. The psychosexual stage during infancy in which pleasure is sought primarily through oral activities.

Osteoporosis. A physical disorder caused by calcium deficiency and characterized by brittle bones.

P

Panic disorder. A type of anxiety disorder characterized by repeated episodes of intense anxiety or panic.

Paranoid personality disorder. A personality disorder characterized by suspiciousness of others' motives, but not to the point of delusion.

Paranoid. Referring to irrational suspicions.

Paranoid type. The subtype of schizophrenia characterized by hallucinations and systematized delusions, commonly involving themes of persecution.

Paraphilias. Sexual disorders in which the person experiences recurrent sexual urges and fantasies involving nonhuman objects, inappropriate or nonconsenting partners, or painful or humiliating situations.

Parasomnias. Sleep disorders involving abnormal behaviors or physiological events that occur during sleep or while falling asleep.

Parasympathetic. Pertaining to the division of the autonomic nervous system whose activity reduces states of arousal and regulates bodily processes that replenish energy reserves.

Parkinson's disease. A progressive disease of the basal ganglia characterized by muscle tremor and shakiness, rigidity, difficulty walking, poor control of fine motor movements, lack of facial muscle tonus, and, in some cases, cognitive impairment.

Pathogens. Disease-causing organisms.

Pedophilia. A paraphilia involving recurrent, powerful sexual urges and related fantasies involving sexual activity with prepubescent children.

Performance anxiety. Fear relating to the threat of failure to perform adequately.

Peripheral nervous system. The somatic and autonomic nervous systems.

Perseveration. The persistent repetition of the same thought or response.

Person-centered therapy. The establishment of a warm, accepting therapeutic relationship that frees clients to engage in self-exploration and achieve self-acceptance.

Personality disorders. Excessively rigid behavior patterns, or ways of relating to others, that ultimately become self-defeating.

Pervasive developmental disorders. A class of developmental disorders characterized by significantly impaired behavior or functioning in multiple areas of development.

Phallic stage. A psychosexual stage in early childhood during which pleasure is sought primarily through the phallic region and the child develops incestuous desires for the parent of the opposite sex.

Phenothiazines. A group of antipsychotic drugs ("major tranquilizers") used to treat schizophrenia.

Phenotype. An individual's actual or expressed traits.

Phenylketonuria (PKU). A genetic disorder that prevents the metabolization of phenylpyruvic acid, leading to mental retardation unless the diet is strictly controlled.

Phlegmatic. Slow and solid.

Phrenologist. Someone who studies the bumps on a person's head to determine the person's underlying traits.

Physiological dependence. A condition in which the drug user's body comes to depend on a steady supply of the substance.

Pick's disease. A form of dementia, similar to Alzheimer's disease, but distinguished by specific abnormalities (Pick's bodies) in nerve cells and absence of neurofibrillary tangles and plaques.

Placebo. An inert medication or bogus treatment that is intended to control for expectancy effects.

Play therapy. A form of psychodynamic therapy in which play activities and objects are used to help children symbolically enact conflicts or express underlying feelings.

Pleasure principle. The governing principle of the id, involving demands for immediate gratification of needs.

Polysomnographic (PSG) recording. Simultaneous measurement of multiple physiological responses during sleep or attempted sleep.

Pons. A structure in the hindbrain involved in respiration.

Population. A total group of people, other organisms, or events.

Positive correlation. A statistical relationship between two variables such that increases in one are associated with increases in the other.

Positive reinforcers. Reinforcers that, introduced, increase when the frequency of behavior.

Positive symptoms. Flagrant symptoms of schizophrenia, such as hallucinations, delusions, bizarre behavior, and thought disorder.

Positron emission tomography (PET scan). An imaging technique that forms a computer-generated image by tracing the amount of glucose used in various regions of the brain.

Possession. A superstitious belief in which abnormal behavior is taken as a sign that the person is possessed by demons or the devil.

Postpartum depression (PPD). Persistent and severe mood changes that occur after childbirth.

Posttraumatic stress disorder (PTSD). A prolonged maladaptive reaction to a traumatic event.

Powerful drive for superiority. Complex of feelings that motivates us to achieve prominence and social dominance.

Preconscious. To Freud, the part of the mind whose contents lie outside of present awareness but can be brought into awareness by focusing attention.

Predictive validity. The degree to which a test score is predictive of some future behavior or outcome.

Prefrontal lobotomy. A form of psychosurgery, no longer in use, in which certain neural pathways in the brain are severed in order to control disturbed behavior.

Pregenital. Referring to characteristics typical of psychosexual stages that precede the genital stage.

Premature ejaculation. A sexual dysfunction in men characterized by ejaculation following minimal sexual stimulation.

Premorbid functioning. The level of functioning before the person developed schizophrenia.

Prepared conditioning. The belief that people are genetically prepared to acquire fear responses to certain stimuli, such as snakes or large animals.

Presenile dementias. Forms of dementia that begin before age 65.

Pressured speech. An outpouring of speech in which words seem to surge urgently for expression.

Prevalence. The overall number of cases of a disorder in a population within a specific period of time.

Primary gains. Relief from underlying anxiety gained through the development of neurotic symptoms.

Primary prevention. Efforts designed to prevent problems from arising.

Primary process thinking. In infancy, the mental process by which the id seeks gratification by imagining that it possesses what it desires; thinking that is illogical or magical.

Primary reinforcers. Reinforcers that fulfill basic needs, such as water, food, warmth, and relief from pain.

Proband. The case first diagnosed of a given disorder.

Problem-focused coping. A coping style that attempts to confront the stressor directly.

Problem-solving therapy. A form of therapy that focuses on helping people develop more effective problem-solving skills.

Prodromal phase. In schizophrenia, the period of decline in functioning that precedes the first acute psychotic episode.

Projection. A defense mechanism in which one's own sexual or aggressive impulses are attributed to another person.

Projective tests. Psychological tests that present ambiguous stimuli onto which the examinee is thought to project his or her personality and unconscious motives.

Psychiatrist. A physician who specializes in the diagnosis and treatment of emotional disorders.

Psychic. Relating to mental phenomena.

Psychoactive. Referring to chemical substances that have psychological effects.

Psychoanalysis. The method of psychotherapy developed by Sigmund Freud.

Psychoanalytic theory. The theoretical model of personality developed by Sigmund Freud; also called psychoanalysis.

Psychodynamic model. The theoretical model of Freud and his followers, in which abnormal behavior is viewed as the product of clashing forces within the personality.

Psychodynamic therapy. Therapy that helps individuals gain insight into, and resolve, unconscious conflicts.

Psychological dependence. Compulsive use of a substance to meet a psychological need.

Psychological disorders. Abnormal behavior patterns that involve a disturbance of psychological functioning or behavior.

Psychological hardiness. A cluster of stress-buffering traits characterized by commitment, challenge, and control.

Psychologist. A person with advanced graduate training in psychology.

Psychometric approach. An assessment method that relies on psychological tests to identify and measure the traits that compose an individual's personality.

Psychoneuroimmunology. The study of relationships between psychological factors and immunological functioning.

Psychopharmacology. The field of study that examines the effects of therapeutic or psychiatric drugs.

Psychosexual. Pertaining to Freud's stages of development, in which libido becomes expressed through different erogenous zones during different stages.

Psychosis. A severe form of disturbed behavior characterized by impaired ability to interpret reality and difficulty meeting the demands of daily life.

Psychosomatic. Pertaining to a physical disorder in which psychological factors play a causal or contributing role.

Psychotherapy. A structured form of treatment derived from a psychological framework which consists of one or more verbal interactions or treatment sessions between a client and a therapist.

Punishments. Unpleasant stimuli that reduce the frequency of the behaviors they follow.

R

Random sample. A sample that is drawn in such a way that every member of a population has an equal chance of being included.

Rapid flight of ideas. A characteristic of manic behavior involving rapid speech and changes of topics.

Rational-emotive behavior therapy (REBT). A therapeutic approach that focuses on helping clients replace irrational, maladaptive beliefs with alternative, more adaptive beliefs.

Reactivity. The tendency for the behavior being observed to be influenced by the way in which it is measured.

Reality principle. The governing principle of the ego, which involves considerations of social acceptability and practicality.

Reality testing. The ability to perceive the world accurately and to distinguish between reality and fantasy.

Rebound anxiety. The experiencing of strong anxiety following withdrawal from a tranquilizer.

Receptor site. A part of a dendrite on a receiving neuron that is structured to receive a neurotransmitter.

Reinforcement. A stimulus or event that increases the frequency of the response that it follows.

Relapse. A recurrence of a problem behavior or disorder.

Relapse-prevention training. A cognitive-behavioral technique involving the use of behavioral and cognitive strategies for resisting temptations and preventing relapses.

Reliable. In psychological assessment, the consistency of a measure or diagnostic instrument or system.

REM sleep. The stage of sleep associated with dreaming and characterized by rapid eye movements under the closed eyelids.

Repression. A defense mechanism involving the unconscious ejection of anxiety-provoking ideas, images, or impulses.

Residual phase. In schizophrenia, the phase that follows an acute phase, characterized by a return to the level of functioning of the prodromal phase.

Resistance stage. The second stage of the GAS, involving the body's attempt to withstand prolonged stress and preserve resources.

Resistance. The blocking of thoughts or feelings that would evoke anxiety if they were consciously experienced.

Reticular activating system. Brain structure involved in processes of attention, sleep, and arousal.

Rett's disorder. A pervasive development disorder characterized by a range of physical, behavioral, motor, and cognitive abnormalities that begin after a few months of apparently normal development.

Reversal design. An experimental design that consists of repeated measurement of a subject's behavior through a sequence of alternating baseline and treatment phases.

Reward. A pleasant stimulus or event that increases the frequency of the response that it follows.

Role diffusion. A state of confusion, aimlessness, and heightened susceptibility to the suggestions of others, associated with failure to acquire a firm sense of identity during adolescence.

S

Sadomasochism. Sexual activities involving the attainment or gratification by means of inflicting and receiving pain and humiliation.

Sample. Part of a population.

Sanguine. Having a cheerful disposition.

Sanism. The negative stereotyping of people who are identified as mentally ill.

Schizoaffective disorder. A type of psychotic disorder in which individuals experience both severe mood disturbance and features associated with schizophrenia.

Schizoid personality disorder. A personality disorder characterized by persistent lack of interest in social relationships, flattened affect, and social withdrawal.

Schizophrenia. An enduring psychotic disorder that involves disturbed behavior, thinking, emotions and perceptions.

Schizophreniform disorder. A psychotic disorder lasting less than six months in duration with features that resemble schizophrenia.

Schizophrenogenic mother. The since-discarded concept of a cold but overprotective mother who it was believed was capable of causing schizophrenia in her children.

Schizotypal personality disorder. A personality disorder characterized by eccentricities of thought and behavior, but without clearly psychotic features.

Scientific method. A method of conducting scientific research in which theories or assumptions are examined in the light of evidence.

Second-rank symptoms. Symptoms associated with schizophrenia that also occur in other mental disorders.

Secondary gains. Side benefits associated with neurotic or other disorders, such as expressions of sympathy, increased attention, and release from responsibilities.

Secondary prevention. Efforts to ameliorate existing problems at an early stage.

Secondary process thinking. The reality-based thinking processes and problem-solving activities of the ego.

Secondary reinforcers. Stimuli that gain reinforcement value through their association with established reinforcers, such as money and social approval.

Sedatives. Types of depressants that reduce states of tension and restlessness and induce sleep.

Selection factor. A type of bias in which differences between experimental and control groups result from differences in the subjects placed in the groups, not from the independent variable.

Selective abstraction. A cognitive distortion involving the tendency to focus only on the negative parts of experiences or events.

Selective serotonin-reuptake inhibitors (SSRIs). A group of antidepressant drugs that increase the availability of serotonin in the brain by interfering with its reuptake by the transmitting neuron.

Self psychology. A theory that describes processes that normally lead to achievement of a cohesive sense of self.

Self-actualization. In humanistic psychology, the tendency to strive to become all that one is capable of being. The motive that drives one to reach one's full potential and express one's unique capabilities.

Self-monitoring. The process of observing or recording one's own behaviors, thoughts, or emotions.

Self-report personality test. A structured personality test in which individuals give information about themselves by responding to items that require a limited type of response, such as "yes-no" or "agree-disagree."

Self-spectatoring. The tendency to observe one's behavior as if one were a spectator.

Semi-structured interview. Interview in which the clinician follows a general outline of questions designed to gather essential information but is free to ask them in any order and to branch off in other directions.

Senile dementias. Forms of dementia that begin after age 65.

Sensate focus exercises. Mutual pleasuring activities focused on the partners taking turns giving and receiving physical pleasure.

Sensitivity. The ability of a diagnostic instrument to correctly identify people who have the disorder the test is intended to detect.

Separation anxiety disorder. A childhood disorder characterized by extreme fear of separation from parents or other caretakers.

Separation-individuation. The process by which an infant develops a separate identity from that of the mother.

Set point. A value, such as body weight, that the body's regulatory mechanisms attempt to maintain.

Sexual aversion disorder. A type of sexual dysfunction characterized by aversion to and avoidance of genital sexual contact.

Sexual dysfunctions. Persistent problems with sexual interest, arousal, or response.

Sexual harassment. Speech, gestures, demands, or physical contact of a sexual nature that is unwelcomed by the person to whom such actions are directed.

Sexual masochism. A paraphilia characterized by recurrent, powerful sexual urges and fantasies involving receiving humiliation or pain.

Sexual sadism. A paraphilia characterized by recurrent, powerful sexual urges and fantasies involving inflicting humiliation or pain.

Significant. In statistics, a magnitude of difference that is taken as indicating meaningful differences between groups.

Single-case experimental design. A type of case study in which the subject is used as his or her own control.

Sleep disorders. Persistent or recurrent sleep-related problems that cause distress or impaired functioning.

Sleep terror disorder. A sleep disorder characterized by recurrent episodes of sleep terror resulting in abrupt awakenings.

Sleepwalking disorder. A sleep disorder involving repeated episodes of sleepwalking.

Social phobia. Excessive fear of social interactions or situations.

Social-cognitive theory. A learning-based theory that emphasizes observational learning and incorporates roles for both situational and cognitive variables in determining behavior.

Sociobiology. Biological perspective that explains psychological traits as behavioral tendencies that increased our ancestors' chances of survival and were passed down genetically.

Soma. A cell body.

Somatic nervous system. The division of the peripheral nervous system that relays information from the sense organs to the brain and transmits messages from the brain to the skeletal muscles.

Somatization disorder. A type of somatoform disorder involving recurrent multiple complaints that cannot be explained by any physical cause.

Somatoform disorders. A group of disorders characterized by complaints of physical problems or symptoms that cannot be explained by physical causes.

Specific attribution. A belief that the cause of an event involved specific, rather than generalized, factors.

Specific phobia. A persistent and excessive fear of a specific object or situation.

Specificity. The ability of a diagnostic instrument to avoid classifying people as having a characteristic or disorder when they truly do not have the characteristic or disorder.

Splitting. An inability to reconcile the positive and negative aspects of the self and others, resulting in sudden shifts between positive and negative feelings.

Stable attribution. A belief that the cause of an event involved stable, rather than changeable, factors.

Standard scores. Scores that indicate the relative standing of raw scores in relation to the distribution of normative scores.

Statutory rape. Sexual intercourse with a minor, even with the minor's consent.

Steroids. A group of hormones that includes testosterone, estrogen, progesterone, and corticosteroids.

Stress. A demand made on an organism to adapt or adjust.

Stressor. A source of stress.

Stroke. Blocking of a blood vessel that supplies the brain due to a blood clot.

Structural hypothesis. The belief that the clashing forces within the personality can be divided into three structures: id, ego, and superego.

Structured interview. Interview that follows a preset series of questions in a particular order.

Stupor. A state of relative or complete unconsciousness in which a person is not aware of or responsive to the environment.

Substance abuse. The continued used of a psychoactive drug despite the knowledge that it is causing a social, occupational, psychological, or physical problem.

Substance dependence. Impaired control over the use of a psychoactive substance; often characterized by physiological dependence.

Substance use disorders. Disorders that involve maladaptive use of psychoactive substances, such as substance abuse and substance dependence.

Substance-induced disorders. Disorders that can be induced by using psychoactive substances, such as intoxication.

Superego. The psychic structure that incorporates the values of the parents and important others and that is governed by the moral principle; consists of two parts, the conscience and the ego ideal.

Survey method. A research method in which large samples of people are questioned by means of a survey instrument.

Symbiotic. The state of oneness that normally exists between mother and infant.

Sympathetic. Pertaining to the division of the autonomic nervous system whose activity leads to heightened states of arousal.

Synapse. The junction between the terminal knob of one neuron and the dendrite or soma of another through which nerve impulses pass.

Syndromes. Clusters of symptoms that are characteristic of particular disorders.

Systematic desensitization. A behavior therapy technique for overcoming phobias by means of exposure to progressively more fearful stimuli while one remains deeply relaxed.

Systems perspective. The view that problems reflect the systems (family, social, school ecological, etc.) in which they occur.

T

Tachycardia. Abnormally rapid heartbeat.

Tactile. Pertaining to the sense of touch.

Taijin-kyofu-sho. A psychiatric syndrome, found in Japan, involving excessive fear of offending or embarrassing others.

Tardive dyskinesia (TD). A disorder characterized by involuntary movements of the face, mouth, neck, trunk, or extremities and caused by long-term used of antipsychotic medication.

Temporal stability. The consistency of test responses over time, as measured by test-retest reliability.

Terminals. The small branching structures at the tips of axons.

Test-retest reliability. A method of measuring the reliability of a test by means of comparing the scores of the same subjects on different occasions.

Thalamus. A structure in the forebrain involved in relaying sensory information to the cortex and in processes related to sleep and attention.

Theory. A formulation of the relationships underlying observed events.

Thermistor. A device for registering body temperature.

Thought disorder. A disturbance in thinking characterized by the breakdown of logical associations between thoughts.

Time out. A behavioral technique in which a person who behaves in an undesirable way is removed from a reinforcing environment and placed in an unreinforcing environment for a short time.

Token economy. Behavioral treatment program in which a controlled environment is constructed such that people are reinforced for desired behaviors by receiving tokens that may be exchanged for desired rewards.

Tolerance. Physical habituation to use of a drug; habituation to a drug such that, with frequent use, higher doses are needed to achieve the same effects.

Transcendental meditation (TM). A form of meditation that focuses on repeating a mantra to induce a meditative state.

Transference relationship. The client's transfer onto the analyst of feelings or attitudes the client holds toward important figures in his or her life.

Transvestic fetishism. A paraphilia in heterosexual males characterized by recurrent sexual urges involving dressing in female clothing.

Trephination. A harsh, prehistoric practice of cutting a hole in a person's skull, possibly in an attempt to release demons.

Tricyclics. A group of antidepressant drugs that increase the activity of norepinephrine and serotonin by interfering with the reuptake of these neurotransmitters.

Two-factor model. A theoretical model that accounts for the development of phobic reactions on the basis of classical and operant conditioning.

Type A behavior pattern (TABP). A behavior pattern characterized by a sense of time urgency, competitiveness, and hostility.

U

Unconditional positive regard. The expression of unconditional acceptance of another person's basic worth as a person.

Unconditioned response. An unlearned response.

Unconditioned stimulus. A stimulus that elicits an unlearned response.

Unconscious. To Freud, the part of the mind that lies outside the range of ordinary awareness and that contains instinctual urges.

Unipolar. Pertaining to a single pole, or direction.

Unobtrusive. Not interfering or conspicuous.

Unstable attribution. A belief that the cause of an event involved changeable, rather than stable, factors.

Unstructured interview. Interview in which the clinician adopts his or her own style of questioning rather than following any standard format.

V

Vaginismus. A sexual dysfunction characterized by persistent or recurring contraction of the muscles surrounding the vaginal opening, making intercourse difficult or impossible.

Validity scales. Groups of test items that are used to detect whether the results of a test are valid.

Validity. The degree to which a test or diagnostic system measures the traits or constructs it purports to measure.

Variables. Conditions that are measured (dependent variables) or manipulated (independent variables) in experiments.

Voyeurism. A paraphilia characterized by recurrent sexual urges involving watching unsuspecting others in sexual situations.

W

Waxy flexibility. A feature of catatonic schizophrenia in which a person's limbs are moved into a certain posture or position, which the person then rigidly maintains.

Weaning. The process of accustoming a child to eat solid food.

Wernicke's disease. A brain disorder, associated with chronic alcoholism, characterized by confusion, disorientation, and difficulty maintaining balance while walking.

Withdrawal syndrome. A characteristic cluster of symptoms following the sudden reduction or cessation of use of a psychoactive substance after physiological dependence has developed.

Worldview. The prevailing view of the times (English translation of German term *Weltanschaung*).

REFERENCES

A

Achenbach, T. M., & Edelbrock, C. S. (1979). The Child Behavior Profile: I. Boys aged 12–16 and girls aged 6–11 and 12–16. *Journal of Consulting and Clinical Psychology, 47,* 223–233.

A children's mental illness 'crisis': Report: 1 in 10 children suffers enough to impair development. (2001, January 3). *Associated Press Web Posting.* Retrieved January 5, 2001, from http://www.msnbc.com/news/510934.asp.

Acklin, M. W., et al. (2000). Interobserver agreement, intraobserver reliability, and the Rorschach comprehensive system. *Journal of Personality Assessment, 74,* 15–47.

Adamson, S. J., & Sellman, J. D. (2001). Drinking goal selection and treatment outcome in out-patients with mild-moderate alcohol dependence. *Drug and Alcohol Review, 20,* 351–359.

Adler, J. (1999, June 14). Stress. *Newsweek,* pp. 58–63.

Affleck, G., Tennen, H., Croog, S., & Levine, S. (1987). Causal attribution, perceived benefits, and morbidity after a heart attack: An 8-year study. *Journal of Consulting and Clinical Psychology, 55,* 29–35.

Agency approves fourth Alzheimer's treatment. (2001, March 1). *CNN Web Posting.* Retrieved March 8, 2001, from http://www.cnn.com/2001/HEALTH/conditions/03/01/alzheimers.drug.ap/index.html.

Agras, W. S., et al. (2000a). Outcome predictors for the cognitive behavior treatment of bulimia nervosa: Data from a multisite study. *American Journal of Psychiatry, 157,* 1302–1308.

Agras, W. S., et al. (2000b). A multicenter comparison of cognitive-behavioral therapy and interpersonal psychotherapy for bulimia nervosa. *Archives of General Psychiatry, 57,* 459–466.

Ainsworth, M. D. S. (1989). Attachments beyond infancy. *American Psychologist, 44,* 709–716.

Akhtar, A. (1987). Schizoid personality disorder: A synthesis of developmental, dynamic, and descriptive features. *American Journal of Psychotherapy, 41,* 499–517.

Akhtar, S. (1988). Four culture-bound psychiatric syndromes in India. *The International Journal of Social Psychiatry, 34,* 70–74.

Akiskal, H. S. (1983). Dysthymic disorder: Psychopathology of proposed chronic depressive subtypes. *American Journal of Psychiatry, 140,* 11–20.

Alao, A. O., & Dewan, M. J. (2001). Evaluating the tolerability of the newer mood stabilizers. *Journal of Nervous & Mental Disease, 189,* 60–63.

Aldarondo, E. (1996). Risk marker analysis of the cessation and persistence of wife assault. *Journal of Consulting and Clinical Psychology, 64,* 1010–1019.

Aldrich, M. S. (1992). Narcolepsy. *Neurology, 42* (7, Suppl. 6), 34–43.

Allderidge, P. (1979). Hospitals, madhouses and asylums: Cycles in the care of the insane. *British Journal of Psychiatry, 134,* 1476–1478.

Alloy, L. B., & Clements, C. M. (1992). Illusion of control: Invulnerability to negative affect and depressive symptoms after laboratory and natural stressors. *Journal of Abnormal Psychology, 101,* 2234–2245.

Alloy, L. B., et al. (2000). The Temple-Wisconsin cognitive vulnerability to depression project: Lifetime history of Axis I psychopathology in individuals at high and low cognitive risk for depression. *Journal of Abnormal Psychology, 109,* 403–418.

Alpert, J. L., & Green, D. (1992). Child abuse and neglect: Perspectives on a national emergency. *Journal of Social Distress and the Homeless, 1,* 223–236.

Alter, J. (2001, February 12). The war on addiction. *Newsweek,* pp. 36–39.

Altman, L. K. (1990a, April 18). Scientists see a link between alcoholism and a specific gene. *The New York Times,* pp. A1, A18.

Altman, L. K. (1994a, February 22). Stomach microbe offers clues to cancer as well as ulcers. *The New York Times,* p. C3.

Altman, L. K. (2001, January 30). The AIDS questions that linger. *The New York Times,* pp. F1, F6.

Altshuler, E. L., et al. (2001). Did Samson have antisocial personality disorder? *Archives of General Psychiatry, 58,* 202.

Alzheimer's vaccine passes key test. (2001, July 23). *CNN Web Posting.* Retrieved July 25, 2001, from http://www.cnn.com/2001/HEALTH/07/23/alzheimers.vaccine/index.html.

American Association of Mental Retardation (AAMR). (1992). *Mental retardation: Definition, classification, and systems of supports* (9th ed.). Washington, DC: Author.

American Law Institute. (1962). Model penal code: Proposed official draft. Philadelphia: Author.

American Psychiatric Association. (1991). The APA task force report on benzodiazepine dependence, toxicity, and abuse [Editorial]. *American Journal of Psychiatry, 148,* 151–152.

American Psychiatric Association. (1994). *DSM-IV: Diagnostic and statistical manual of mental disorders* (4th ed.). Washington, DC: Author.

American Psychiatric Association. (1998). *Fact sheet: Violence and mental illness.* Washington, DC: Author.

American Psychiatric Association. (2000). *DSM-IV-TR: Diagnostic and statistical manual of mental disorders* (4th ed., Text Revision). Washington, DC: Author.

American Psychological Association. (1978). Report of the Task Force on the Role of Psychology in the Criminal Justice System. *American Psychologist, 33,* 1099–1113.

American Psychological Association. (1992). Rules and Procedures. *American Psychologist, 47,* 1612–1628.

American Psychological Association. (1992). *Big world, small screen: The role of television in American society.* Washington, DC: Author.

Amering, M., & Katschnig, H. (1990). Panic attacks and panic disorder in cross-cultural perspective. *Psychiatric Annals, 20,* 511–516.

Ames, M. A., & Houston, D. A. (1990). Legal, social, and biological definitions of pedophilia. *Archives of Sexual Behavior, 19,* 333–342.

Amminger, G. P., et al. (1999). Relationship between childhood behavioral disturbance and later schizophrenia in the New York High-Risk Project. *American Journal of Psychiatry, 156,* 525–530.

Ancoli-Israel, S., et al. (1991). Dementia in institutionalized elderly: Relation to sleep apnea. *Journal of the American Geriatrics Society, 39,* 258–263.

Andersen, B. L. (1992). Psychological interventions for cancer patients to enhance the quality of life. *Journal of Consulting and Clinical Psychology, 60,* 552–568.

Andersen, B. L., & Golden-Kreutz, D. M. (2001). Cancer. In D. W. Johnston & M. Johnston (Eds.), *Health psychology, Vol. 8. Comprehensive clinical psychology* (pp. 217–236). Amsterdam, Netherlands: Elsevier Science Publishers.

Andersen, B. L., Golden-Kreutz, D. M., & DiLillo, V. (2001). Cancer. In A. Baum, T. A. Revenson, & J. E. Singer (Eds.), *Handbook of health psychology* (pp. 709–726). Mahwah, NJ: Lawrence Erlbaum Associates.

Anderson, C. A., & Dill, K. E. (2000). Video games and aggressive thoughts, feelings, and behavior in the laboratory and in life. *Journal of Personality and Social Psychology, 78,* 772–790.

Anderson, D. Q., & Maloney, K. C. (2001). The efficacy of cognitive-behavioral therapy on the core symptoms of bulimia nervosa. *Clinical Psychology Review, 21,* 971–988.

Anderson, E. M., & Lambert, M. J. (1995). Short-term dynamically oriented psychotherapy: A review and meta-analysis. *Clinical Psychology Review, 15,* 503–514.

Anderson, E. M., & Lambert, M. J. (2001). A survival analysis of clinically significant change in outpatient psychotherapy. *Journal of Clinical Psychology, 57,* 875–888.

Anderson, L. P. (1991). Acculturative stress: A theory of relevance to Black Americans. *Clinical Psychology Review, 11,* 685–702.

Andreasen, N. C. (1987a). The diagnosis of schizophrenia. *Schizophrenia Bulletin, 13,* 1–8.

Andreasen, N. C. (1999). Understanding the causes of schizophrenia. *New England Journal of Medicine, 340,* 645–647.

Andreasen, N. C., & Grove, W. M. (1986). Thought, language, and communication in schizophrenia: Diagnosis and prognosis. *Schizophrenia Bulletin, 12,* 348–359.

Andreasen, N. C., et al. (1997). Hypofrontality in schizophrenia: Distributed dysfunctional circuits in neuroleptic-naive patients. *The Lancet, 349,* 1730–1734.

Andrews, B., et al. (2000). Predicting PTSD symptoms in victims of violent crime: The role of shame, anger, and childhood abuse. *Journal of Abnormal Psychology, 109,* 69–73.

Andrews, E. L. (1997, September 9). In Germany, humble herb is a rival to Prozac. *The New York Times,* pp. C1, C7.

Angier, N. (1991a, May 30). Gene causing common type of retardation is discovered. *The New York Times,* pp. A1, B11.

Angier, N. (1991b, August 4). Kids who can't sit still. *The New York Times,* Section 4A, pp. 30–33.

Angier, N. (1999). *Woman: An intimate geography.* Boston: Houghton Mifflin.

Angier, N. (2000a, July 21). Study finds region of brain may be key problem solver. *The New York Times,* pp. C1, C4.

Angier, N. (2000b, November 7). Who is fat? It depends on culture. *The New York Times,* pp. F1–F2.

Anglin, K., & Holtzworth-Munroe, A. (1997). Comparing the responses of maritally violent and nonviolent spouses to problematic marital and nonmarital situations: Are the skills deficits of physically aggressive husbands and wives global? *Journal of Family Psychology, 11,* 301–313.

Angold, A., & Costello, E. J. (1993). Depressive comorbidity in children and adolescents: Empirical, theoretical, and methodological issues. *American Journal of Psychiatry, 150,* 1779–1791.

Angold, A., & Costello, J. (1996). Toward establishing an empirical basis for the diagnosis of oppositional defiant disorder. *Journal of the American Academy of Child and Adolescent Psychiatry, 35,* 1205–1212.

Angst, J., Angst, F., & Stassen, H. H. (1999). Suicide risk in patients with major depressive disorder. *The Journal of Clinical Psychiatry, 60,* 57–62.

Antonarakas, S. E., et al. (1991). Prenatal origin of the extra chromosomein trisomy 21 as indicated by analysis of DNA polymorphisms. *The New England Journal of Medicine, 324,* 872–876.

Anonymous. (1985, June 13). Schizophrenia—A mother's agony over her son's pain. *Chicago Tribune*, Section 5, pp. 1–3.

Another worry for aging baby boomers—pot and their hearts. (2000, March 3). *CNN Web Posting*. Retrieved March 13, 2000, from www.canoe.ca/Health0003/03_pot.html.

Ansell, B. J. (2001, January 9). Fearing one fate, women ignore a killer. *The New York Times*, p. F8.

Anthony, J. C., & Helzer, J. E. (1991). Syndromes of drug abuse and dependence. In L. N. Robins & D. A. Regier (Eds.), *Psychiatric disorders in America: The Epidemiologic Catchment Area Study* (pp. 116–154). New York: The Free Press.

Anthony, J. C., Warner, L. A., & Kessler, R. C. (1994). Comparative epidemiology of dependence on tobacco, alcohol, controlled substances, and inhalants: Basic findings from the National Comorbidity Survey. *Experimental and Clinical Psychopharmacology, 2*, 244–268.

Anthony, W. A., Cohen, M., & Kennard, W. (1990). Understanding the current facts and principles of mental health systems planning. *American Psychologist, 45*, 1249–1256.

Anthony, W. A., & Liberman, R. P. (1986). The practice of psychiatric rehabilitation: Historical, conceptual, and research base. *Schizophrenia Bulletin, 12*, 542–559.

Antidepressants linked to sexual side effects. (2000, February 7). *CNN Web Posting*. Retrieved February 8, 2000, from www.cnn.com/2000/HEALTH/02/07/antidepressant.sex.wmd/.

Anton, R. F. (1994). Medications for treating alcoholism. *Alcohol Health and Research World, 18*, 265–271.

Anton, R. F., et al. (2001). Posttreatment results of combining naltrexone with cognitive-behavior therapy for the treatment of alcoholism. *Journal of Clinical Psychopharmacology, 21*, 72–77.

Antoni, M. H., Levine, J., Tischer, P., Green, C., & Millon, T. (1986). Refining personality assessments by combining MCMI high-point profiles and MMPI codes: IV. MMPI 89/98. *Journal of Personality Assessment, 50*, 65–72.

Anxiety: Most common mental health problem. (2000, February 2). *CNN Web Posting*. Retrieved February 4, 2000, from www.cnn.com/2000/HEALTH/02/02/mental.health.wmd/.

Arango, C., Kirkpatrick, B., &. Buchanan, R. W. (2000). Neurological signs and the heterogeneity of schizophrenia. *American Journal of Psychiatry, 157*, 566–572.

Arieti, S. (1974). *Interpretation of schizophrenia* (2nd ed.). New York: Basic Books.

Arndt, A., & Greenberg, J. (1996). Fantastic accounts can take many forms: False memory construction? Yes. Escape from self? We don't think so. *Psychological Inquiry, 7*, 127–132.

Arnett, P. A. (1997). Autonomic responsivity in psychopaths: A critical review and theoretical proposal. *Clinical Psychology Review, 17*, 903–936.

Arnett, P. A., Smith, S. S., & Newman, J. P. (1997). Approach and avoidance motivation in psychopathic criminal offenders during passive avoidance. *Journal of Personality and Social Psychology, 72*, 1413–1428.

Arnow, B., Kenardy, J., & Agras, W. S. (1992). Binge eating among the obese: A descriptive study. *Journal of Behavioral Medicine, 15*, 155–170.

Arntz, A. (1994). Treatment of borderline personality disorder: A challenge for cognitive-behavioral therapy. *Behaviour Research and Therapy, 32*, 419–430.

Aronson, M. K. (1988). Patients and families: Impact and long-term-management implications. In M. K. Aronson (Ed.), *Understanding Alzheimer's disease* (pp. 74–78). New York: Charles Scribners & Sons.

Arranz, M. J., et al. (2000). Pharmacogenetic prediction of clozapine response. *Lancet, 355*, 1615–1616.

Arroyo, J. A., Simpson, T. L., & Aragon, A. S. (1997). Childhood sexual abuse among Hispanic and non-Hispanic White college women. *Hispanic Journal of Behavioral Sciences, 19*, 57–68.

Asaad, G., & Shapiro, B. (1986). Hallucinations: Theoretical and clinical overview. *American Journal of Psychiatry, 143*, 1088–1097.

Asarnow, J. R., Carlson, G. A., & Guthrie, D. (1987). Coping strategies, self-perceptions, hopelessness, and perceived family environments in depressed and suicidal children. *Journal of Consulting and Clinical Psychology, 55*, 361–366.

Asarnow, R. F., et al. (1991). Span of apprehension in schizophrenia. In J. Zubin, S. Steinhauer, & J. Gruzelier (Eds.), *Handbook of schizophrenia: Vol. 5. Neuropsychology, psychophysiology, and information-processing* (pp. 353–370). Amsterdam: Elsevier Science.

Asthma affects 15 million U.S. adults. (2001, August 16). *MSNBC Web Posting, Associated Press*. Retrieved August 16, 2001, from http://www.msnbc.com/news/615104.asp?0dm=H16MH.

Astley, S. J., et al. (1992). Analysis of facial shape in children gestationally exposed to marijuana, alcohol, and/or cocaine. *Pediatrics, 89*, 67–77.

Atkinson, R. L. (1997). Use of drugs in the treatment of obesity. *Annual Review of Nutrition, 17*, 383–403.

Attention Deficit Disorder—Part II. (1995, May). *The Harvard Mental Health Letter, 11*(11), 1–3.

Augusto, A., et al. (1996). Post-natal depression in an urban area of Portugal: Comparison of childbearing women and matched controls. *Psychological Medicine, 26*, 135–141.

Azar, B. (2000a). The debate over child care isn't over yet. *Monitor on Psychology, 31*, pp. 32–34.

Azar, B. (2000b). Brain studies point to inefficient connections in people with dyslexia. *Monitor on Psychology, 31*, pp. 32–34.

Azrin, N. H., & Peterson, A. L. (1989). Reduction of an eye tick by controlled blinking. *Behavior Therapy, 20*, 467–473.

B

Baaré, W. F. C., et al. (2001). Volumes of brain structures in twins discordant for schizophrenia. *Archives of General Psychiatry, 58*, 33–40.

Bäckman, L., & Forsell, Y. (1994). Episodic memory functioning in a community-based sample of old adults with major depression: Utilization of cognitive support. *Journal of Abnormal Psychology, 103*, 361–370.

Baer, L., et al. (1995). Cingulotomy for intractable obsessive-compulsive disorder: Prospective long-term follow-up of 18 patients. *Archives of General Psychiatry, 52*, 384–392.

Bagby, R. M., Nicholson, R., & Buis, T. (1998). Effectiveness of the MMPI-2 validity indicators. *Journal of Personality Assessment, 70*, 405–415.

Bailar, J. C., III. (2001). The powerful placebo and the wizard of Oz. *The New England Journal of Medicine, 344*, 1630–1632.

Baker, R. C., & Kirschenbaum, D. S. (1993). Self-monitoring may be necessary for successful weight control. *Behavior Therapy, 24*, 377–394.

Baldessarini, R. J., Tohen, M., & Tondo, L. (2000). Maintenance treatment in bipolar disorder. *Archives of General Psychiatry, 57*, 490–492.

Baldessarini, R. J., & Tondo, L. (2000). Does lithium treatment still work? Evidence of stable responses over three decades. *Archives of General Psychiatry, 57*, 187–190.

Baldeweg, T., et al. (1997). Neurophysiological changes associated with psychiatric symptoms in HIV-infected individuals without AIDS. *Biological Psychiatry, 41*, 474–487.

Baldwin, A. R., Oei, T. P., & Young, R. (1994). To drink or not to drink: The differential role of alcohol expectancies and drinking refusal self-efficacy in quantity and frequency of alcohol consumption. *Cognitive Therapy & Research, 17*, 511–530.

Ballester, E., et al. (1999). Evidence of the effectiveness of continuous positive airway pressure in the treatment of sleep apnea/hypopnea syndrome. *American Journal of Respiratory and Critical Care Medicine, 159*, 495–501.

Banaji, M. R., & Kihlstrom, J. F. (1996). The ordinary nature of alien abduction memories. *Psychological Inquiry, 7*, 132–135.

Bandura, A. (1973). *Aggression: A social learning analysis.* Englewood Cliffs, NJ: Prentice-Hall.

Bandura, A. (1982). Self-efficacy mechanism in human agency. *American Psychologist, 37*, 122–147.

Bandura, A. (1986). *Social foundations of thought and action: A social-cognitive theory.* Englewood Cliffs, NJ: Prentice-Hall.

Bandura, A. (2001). Social cognitive theory: An agentic perspective. *Annual Review of Psychology, 52*, 1–26.

Bandura, A., Barr-Taylor, C., Williams, S. L., Mefford, I. N., & Barchas, J. D. (1985). Catecholamine secretion as a function of perceived coping self-efficacy. *Journal of Consulting and Clinical Psychology, 53*, 406–414.

Bandura, A., Jeffery, R. W., & Wright, C. L. (1974). Efficacy of participant modeling as a function of response induction aids. *Journal of Abnormal Psychology, 83*, 56–64.

Bandura, A., Ross, S. A., & Ross, D. (1963). Imitation of film-mediated aggressive models. *Journal of Abnormal and Social Psychology, 66*, 3–11.

Banning, A. (1989). Mother-son incest: Confronting a prejudice. *Child Abuse and Neglect, 13*, 563–570.

Barbaree, H. E., & Marshall, W. L. (1991). The role of male sexual arousal in rape: Six models. *Journal of Consulting and Clinical Psychology, 59*, 621–631.

Barber, J., et al. (2000). Alliance predicts patients' outcome beyond in-treatment change in symptoms. *Journal of Consulting and Clinical Psychology, 68*, 1027–1032.

Barber, M. E., et al. (1998). Aborted suicide attempts: A new classification of suicidal behavior. *American Journal of Psychiatry, 155*, 385–389.

Barch, D. M., et al. (2001). Selective deficits in prefrontal cortex function in medication-naive patients with schizophrenia. *Archives of General Psychiatry, 58*, 280–288.

Barefoot, J. C., et al. (2001). A longitudinal study of gender differences in depressive symptoms from age 50 to 80. *Psychology and Aging, 16*, 342–345.

Barkham, M., et al. (1996). Dose-effect relations in time-limited psychotherapy for depression. *Journal of Consulting and Clinical Psychology, 64*, 927–935.

Barkley, R. A. (1997). *ADHD and the nature of self-control.* New York: Guilford Press.

Barkley, R. A. (2001). Executive function and ADHD: A reply. *Journal of the American Academy of Child & Adolescent Psychiatry, 40*, 501–502.

Barkley, R. A., et al. (1976). Evaluation of a token system for juvenile delinquents in a residential setting. *Journal of Behavior Therapy and Experimental Psychiatry, 7*, 227–230.

Barksy, A. J., et al. (2001). Hypochondriacal patients' appraisal of health and physical risks. *American Journal of Psychiatry, 158*, 783–794.

Barlow, D. H. (1986). Causes of sexual dysfunction: The role of anxiety and cognitive interference. *Journal of Abnormal Psychology, 54*, 140–148.

Barlow, D. H., Esler, J. L., & Vitali, A. E. (1998). Psychosocial treatments for panic disorders, phobias, and generalized anxiety disorder. In P. E. Nathan & J. M. Gorman (Eds.), *A guide to treatments that work* (pp. 288–318). New York: Oxford University Press.

Barlow, D. H., Gorman, J. M., Shear, M. K., & Woods, S. W. (2000). Cognitive-behavioral therapy, imipramine, or their combination for panic disorder: A randomized controlled trial. *Journal of the American Medical Association, 283*, 2529–2536.

Barnett, W. S., & Escobar, C. M. (1990). Economic costs and benefits of early intervention. In S. J. Meisels & J. P. Shonkoff (Eds.), *Handbook of early childhood intervention*. New York: Cambridge University Press.

Barrett, P. M., et al. (2001). Cognitive-behavioral treatment of anxiety disorders in children: Long-term (6-year) follow-up. *Journal of Consulting and Clinical Psychology, 69*, 135–141.

Barry, C. T., et al. (2000). The importance of callous–unemotional traits for extending the concept of psychopathy to children. *Journal of Abnormal Psychology, 109*, 335–340.

Barsky, A. J., Wyshak, G., & Klerman, G. L. (1992). Psychiatric comorbidity in *DSM-III-R* hypochondriasis. *Archives of General Psychiatry, 49*, 101–108.

Barsky, A. J., et al. (1994). Histories of childhood trauma in adult hypochondriacal patients. *American Journal of Psychiatry, 151*, 397–401.

Barsky, A. J., et al. (1998). A prospective 4- to 5-year study of *DSM-III-R* hypochondriasis. *Archives of General Psychiatry, 55*, 737–744.

Bartecchi, C. E., MacKenzie, T. D., & Schrier, R. W. (1994). The human costs of tobacco use (First of two parts). *New England Journal of Medicine, 330*, 907–912.

Basch, M. F. (1980). *Doing psychotherapy*. New York: Basic Books.

Basoglu, M., et al. (1997). Double-blindness procedures, rater blindness, and ratings of outcome. *Archives of General Psychiatry, 54*, 744–748.

Bateman, A. B., & Fonagy, P. (2001). Treatment of borderline personality disorder with psychoanalytically oriented partial hospitalization: An 18-month follow-up. *American Journal of Psychiatry, 158*, 36–42.

Bateson, G. D., Jackson, D., Haley, J., & Weakland, J. (1956). Toward a theory of schizophrenia. *Behavioral Science, 1*, 251–264.

Battaglia, M., et al. (1995). A family study of schizotypal disorder. *Schizophrenia Bulletin, 21*, 33–45.

Baucom, D. H., et al. (1998). Empirically supported couple and family interventions for marital distress and adult mental health problems. *Journal of Consulting and Clinical Psychology, 66*, 53–88.

Bazell, R. (2000, August 29). Cause of narcolepsy pinpointed. *MSNBC Web Posting*. Retrieved August 29, 2000, from http://www.msnbc.com/news/452884.asp.

Beautrais, A. L., et al. (1996). Prevalence and comorbidity of mental disorders in persons making serious suicide attempts: A case-control study. *American Journal of Psychiatry, 153*, 1009–1014.

Beauvais, F. (1998). American Indians and alcohol. *Alcohol Health and Research World, 22*, 253–259.

Bebbington, P. (1993). Transcultural aspects of affective disorders. *International Review of Psychiatry, 5*, 145–156.

Bechtoldt, H., Norcross, J. C., Wyckoff, L. A., Pokrywa, M. L., & Campbell, L. F. (2001). Theoretical orientations and employment settings of clinical and counseling psychologists: A comparative study. *The Clinical Psychologist, 54*(1), 3–6.

Beck, A. T. (1976). *Cognitive therapy and the emotional disorders*. New York: International Universities Press.

Beck, A. T., Brown, G., Steer, R. A., Eidelson, J. I., & Riskind, J. H. (1987). Differentiating anxiety and depression: A test of the cognitive content-specificity hypothesis. *Journal of Abnormal Psychology, 96*, 179–183.

Beck, A. T., & Clark, D. A. (1997). An information processing model of anxiety: Automatic and strategic processes. *Behaviour Research and Therapy, 35*, 49–58.

Beck, A. T., Freeman, A., & Associates. (1990). *Cognitive therapy of personality disorders*. New York: Guilford Press.

Beck, A. T., Rush, A. J., Shaw, B. F., & Emery, G. (1979). *Cognitive therapy of depression*. New York: Guilford Press.

Beck, A. T., Ward, C. H., Mendelson, M., Mock, J., & Erbaugh, J. (1961). An inventory for measuring depression. *Archives of General Psychiatry, 4*, 561–571.

Beck, A. T., & Young, J. E. (1985). Depression. In D. H. Barlow (Ed.), *Clinical handbook of psychosocial disorders* (pp. 206–244). New York: Guilford Press.

Beck, A. T., et al. (1990). Relationship between hopelessness and ultimate suicide: A replication with psychiatric outpatients. *American Journal of Psychiatry, 147*, 190–195.

Beck, D., Casper, R., & Andersen, A. (1996). Truly late onset of eating disorders: A study of 11 cases averaging 60 years of age at presentation. *International Journal of Eating Disorders, 20*, 389–395.

Beck, J. G. (1993). Vaginismus. In W. O'Donohue & J. H. Geer (Eds.), *Handbook of sexual dysfunctions: Assessment and treatment* (pp. 381–397). Boston: Allyn & Bacon.

Beck, J. G. (1995). Hypoactive sexual desire disorder: An overview. *Journal of Consulting and Clinical Psychology, 63*, 919–927.

Becker, D., & Lamb, S. (1994). Sex bias in the diagnosis of borderline personality disorder and posttraumatic stress disorder. *Professional Psychology: Research and Practice, 25*, 55–61.

Begley, S. (1995, November 20). Lights of madness. *Newsweek*, pp. 76–77.

Begley, S. (1998, January 26). Is everybody crazy? *Newsweek*, pp. 48–56.

Begley, S. (2000, July 3). What families should do. *Newsweek*, pp. 44–47.

Begley, S. (2001a) Fall. AIDS at 20. *Newsweek*, pp. 35–37.

Begley, S. (2001b), June 11. How it all starts inside your brain. *Newsweek*, pp. 40–42.

Beidel, D. C., Turner, S. M., & Morris, T. L. (2000). Behavioral treatment of childhood social phobia. *Journal of Consulting and Clinical Psychology, 68*, 1072–1080.

Beitman, B. D., Goldfried, M. R., & Norcross, J. C. (1989). The movement toward integrating the psychotherapies: An overview. *American Journal of Psychiatry, 146*, 138–147.

Bellack, A. S., & Mueser, K. T. (1990). Schizophrenia. In A. S. Bellack, M. Hersen, & A. E. Kazdin (Eds.), *International handbook of behavior modification and therapy* (2nd ed., pp. 353–370). New York: Plenum Press.

Bellack, A. S., & Mueser, K. T. (1993). Psychosocial treatment for schizophrenia. *Schizophrenia Bulletin, 19*, 317–336.

Belsky, J. (1993). Etiology of child maltreatment: A developmental-ecological analysis. *Psychological Bulletin, 114*, 413–434.

Bemporad, J. R. (1996). Self-starvation through the ages: Reflections on the pre-history of anorexia nervosa. *International Journal of Eating Disorders, 19*, 217–237.

Benazon, N. R. (2000). Predicting negative spousal attitudes toward depressed persons: A test of Coyne's interpersonal model. *Journal of Abnormal Psychology, 109*, 500–554.

Bender, L. (1938). A visual motor gestalt test and its clinical use. *Research Monograph of the American Orthopsychiatric Association, 3, XI*, 176.

Benet, S. (1974). *Abkhasians: The long living people of the Caucasus*. New York: Holt, Rinehart & Winston.

Benjamin, L., & Wonderlich, S. A. (1994). Social perceptions and borderline personality disorder: The relation to mood disorders. *Journal of Abnormal Psychology, 103*, 610–624.

Bennett, D. (1985). Rogers: More intuition in therapy. *APA Monitor, 16*, p. 3.

Benson, H. (1975). *The relaxation response*. New York: Morrow.

Benson, H., Manzetta, B. R., & Rosner, B. (1973). Decreased systolic blood pressure in hypertensive subjects who practiced meditation. *Journal of Clinical Investigation, 52*, 8.

Bentall, R. P. (1990). The illusion of reality: A review and integration of psychological research on hallucinations. *Psychological Bulletin, 107*, 82–95.

Bentall, R. P., Haddock, G., & Slade, P. (1994). Cognitive behavior therapy for persistent auditory hallucinations: From theory to therapy. *Behavior Therapy, 25*, 51–66.

Berenbaum, H., & Fujita, F. (1994). Schizophrenia and personality: Exploring the boundaries and connections between vulnerability and outcome. *Journal of Abnormal Psychology, 103*, 148–158.

Berenbaum, H., & Oltmanns, T. F. (1990). Emotional experience and expression in schizophrenia and depression. *Journal of Abnormal Psychology, 101*, 37–44.

Bergem, A. L. M., et al. (1997). Heredity in late-onset Alzheimer's disease and vascular dementia. *Archives of General Psychiatry, 54*, 264–270.

Bergner, R. M. (1997). What is psychopathology? And so what? *Clinical Psychology: Science and Practice, 4*, 235–248.

Berkowitz, L. (1994). Is something missing? Some observations prompted by the cognitive-neoassociationist view of anger and emotional aggression. In L. R. Huesmann (Ed.), *Aggressive behavior: Current perspectives*. New York: Plenum Press.

Berlin, I. N. (1987). Effects of changing Native American cultures on child development. *Journal of Community Psychology, 15*, 299–306.

Berman, M. E., Tracy, J. I., & Coccaro, E. F. (1997). The serotonin hypothesis of aggression revisited. *Clinical Psychology Review, 17*, 651–665.

Berman, S. L., et al. (1997). The impact of exposure to crime and violence on urban youth. *American Journal of Orthopsychiatry, 66*, 329–336.

Berman, S. L., et al. (2000). Predictors of outcome in exposure-based cognitive and behavioral treatments for phobic and anxiety disorders in children. *Behavior Therapy, 31*, 713–731.

Bernstein, A. S. (1987). Orienting response research in schizophrenia: Where we have come and where we might go. *Schizophrenia Bulletin, 13*, 623–641.

Bernstein, A. S., et al. (1988). Schizophrenia is associated with altered orienting activity: Depression with electrodermal (cholinergic?) deficit and normal orienting response. *Journal of Abnormal Psychology, 97*, 3–12.

Bernstein, D. P., et al. (1996). Childhood antecedents of adolescent personality disorders. *American Journal of Psychiatry, 153*, 907–913.

Bernstein, E. M., & Putnam, F. W. (1986). Development, reliability, and validity of a dissociation scale. *The Journal of Nervous and Mental Disease, 174*, 727–735.

Bernstein, R. L., & Gaw, A. C. (1990). Koro: Proposed classification for *DSM-IV*. *American Journal of Psychiatry, 147*, 1670–1674.

Bertolino, A., et al. (2000). Specific relationship between prefrontal neuronal-acetyl aspartate and activation of the working memory cortical network in schizophrenia. *American Journal of Psychiatry, 157*, 16–25.

Bertram, L., et al. (2000). Evidence for genetic linkage of Alzheimer's disease to chromosome 10q. *Science, 290*, 2302–2303.

Beutler, L. E. (1995). Common factors and specific effects. *Clinical Psychology: Science and Practice, 2*, 79–82.

Beutler, L. E., Harwood, T. M., & Caldwell, R. (2001). Cognitive-behavioral therapy and psychotherapy integration. In K. S. Dobson (Ed.), *Handbook of cognitive-behavioral therapies* (2nd ed., pp. 138–170). New York: Guilford Press.

Beyond methadone: More options for treating heroin addiction. (2000, November 1). *MSNBC Web Posting*. Retrieved November 7, 2000, from http://www.msnbc.com/news/484097.asp.

Bick, P. A., & Kinsbourne, M. (1987). Auditory hallucinations and subvocal speech in schizophrenic patients. *American Journal of Psychiatry, 144*, 222–225.

Bickel, W. K., et al. (1997). Effects of adding behavioral treatment to opioid detoxification with buprenorphine. *Journal of Consulting and Clinical Psychology, 65*, 803–810.

Biederman, J., Mick, E., & Faraone, S. V. (2000). Age-dependent decline of symptoms of attention-deficit hyperactivity disorder: Impact of remission definition and symptom type. *American Journal of Psychiatry, 157*, 816–818.

Biederman, J., et al. (1996a). Is childhood oppositional defiant disorder a precursor to adolescent conduct disorder? Findings from a four-year follow-up study of children with ADHD. *Journal of the American Academy of Child and Adolescent Psychiatry, 35*, 1193–1204.

Biederman, J. S., et al. (1996b). A prospective 4-year follow-up study of attention-deficit hyperactivity and related disorders. *Archives of General Psychiatry, 53*, 437–446.

Bigler, E. D., & Ehrenfurth, J. W. (1981). The continued inappropriate singular use of the Bender Visual Motor Gestalt Test. *Professional Psychology, 12*, 562–569.

Binder, J. L., & Strupp, H. H. (1997). Negative process: A recurrently discovered and underestimated facet of therapeutic process and outcome in the individual psychotherapy of adults. *Clinical Psychology: Science and Practice, 4*, 121–139.

Binder, R. L. (1999). Are the mentally ill dangerous? *Journal of the American Academy of Psychiatry and the Law, 27*, 189–201.

Binder, R. L., & McNiel, D. E. (1996). Application of the Tarasoff ruling and its effect on the victim and the therapeutic relationship. *Psychiatric Services, 47*, 1212–1215.

Biofeedback applications as central or adjunctive treatment. (1997, April). *Clinician's Research Digest, 15*(4), 5.

Biran, M. (1988). Cognitive and exposure treatment for agoraphobia: Re-examination of the outcome research. *Journal of Cognitive Psychotherapy: An International Quarterly, 2*, 165–178.

Birchwood, M., et al. (1992). The influence of ethnicity and family structure on relapse in first-episode schizophrenia: A comparison of Asian, Afro-Caribbean, and White patients. *British Journal of Psychiatry, 161*, 783–790.

Birnbaum, M. H., Martin, H., & Thomann, K. (1996). Visual function in multiple personality disorder. *Journal of the American Optometric Association, 67*, 327–334.

Bitiello, B., & Jensen, P. S. (1997). Medication development, testing in children and adolescents. *Archives of General Psychiatry, 54*, 871–876.

Bitler, D. A., Linnoila, M., & George, D. T. (1994). Psychosocial and diagnostic characteristics of individual initiating domestic violence. *Journal of Nervous and Mental Disease, 182*, 583–585.

Bjork, J. M., et al. (2000). Differential behavioral effects of plasma tryptophan depletion and loading in aggressive and nonaggressive men. *Neuropsychopharmacology, 22*, 357–359.

Blackman, S. J. (1996). Has drug culture become an inevitable part of youth culture? A critical assessment of drug education. *Educational Review, 48*, 131–142.

Blackwood, H. R., et al. (1996). A locus for bipolar affective disorder on chromosome 4p. *Nature Genetics, 12*, 427–430.

Blais, M. A., et al. (2001). Predicting *DSM-IV* cluster B personality disorder criteria from MMPI-2 and Rorschach data: A test of incremental validity. *Journal of Personality Assessment, 76*, 150–168.

Blakeslee, S. (1994b, August 16). New clue to cause of dyslexia seen in mishearing of fast sounds. *The New York Times*, pp. C1, C10.

Blakeslee, S. (1997a, June 27). Brain studies tie marijuana to other drugs. *The New York Times*, p. A16.

Blakeslee, S. (1997b, December 16). Suicide rate higher in 3 gambling cities, study says. *The New York Times*, p. A16.

Blakeslee, S. (2000, November 5). Pesticide found to produce Parkinson's symptoms in rats. *The New York Times*, p. A38.

Blakeslee, S. (2001, March 6). Drug's effect on brain is extensive, study finds. *The New York Times*, p. F3.

Blanchard, E. B., & Diamond, S. (1996). Psychological treatment of benign headache disorders. *Professional Psychology, 27*, 541–547.

Blanchard, E. B., et al. (1990). A controlled evaluation of thermal biofeedback and thermal feedback combined with cognitive therapy in the treatment of vascular headache. *Journal of Consulting and Clinical Psychology, 58*, 216–224.

Blanchard, R., & Hucker, S. J. (1991). Age, transvestism, bondage, and concurrent paraphilic activities in 117 fatal cases of autoerotic asphyxia. *British Journal of Psychiatry, 159*, 371–377.

Blankstein, K. R., & Segal, Z. V. (2001). Cognitive assessment: Issues and methods. In K. S. Dobson (Ed.), *Handbook of cognitive-behavioral therapies* (2nd ed., pp. 40–85). New York: Guilford Press.

Blatt, S. J., et al. (1998). When and how perfectionism impedes the brief treatment of depression: Further analyses of the National Institute of Mental Health Treatment of Depression Collaborative Research Program. *Journal of Consulting and Clinical Psychology, 66*, 423–428.

Blazer, D. G., et al. (1994). The prevalence and distribution of major depression in a National Comorbidity Survey. *American Journal of Psychiatry, 151*, 979–986.

Bliss, E. L., & Jeppsen, E. A. (1985). Prevalence of multiple personality among inpatients and outpatients. *American Journal of Psychiatry, 142*, 250–251.

Bloom, B. L. (1992). Computer-assisted psychological intervention: A review and commentary. *Clinical Psychology Review, 12*, 169–197.

Bloom, J. D., & Rogers, J. L. (1987). The legal basis of forensic psychiatry: Statutorily mandated psychiatric diagnosis. *American Journal of Psychiatry, 144*, 847–853.

Blumenthal, D. (1988, October 9). Dieting reassessed. *The New York Times Magazine, Part 2: The Good Health Magazine*, pp. 24–25, 53–54.

Blumenthal, R., & Endicott, J. (1997). Barriers to seeking treatment for major depression. *Depression and Anxiety, 4*, 273–278.

Boetsch, E. A., Green, P. A., & Pennington, B. F. (1996). Psychosocial correlates of dyslexia across the life span. *Development and Psychopathology, 8*, 539–562.

Bögels, S. M., & Zigerman, D. (2000). Dysfunctional cognitions in children with social phobia, separation anxiety disorders, and generalized anxiety disorder. *Journal of Abnormal Child Psychology, 28*, 205–211.

Bolton, P. (2001). Cross-cultural validity and reliability testing of a standard psychiatric assessment instrument without a gold standard. *Journal of Nervous & Mental Disease, 189*, 238–242.

Bondareff, W., et al. (2000). Comparison of sertraline and nortriptyline in the treatment of major depressive disorder in late life. *American Journal of Psychiatry, 157*, 745–750.

Boney-McCoy, S., & Finkelhor, D. (1996). Is youth victimization related to trauma symptoms and depression after controlling for prior symptoms and family relationships? A longitudinal, prospective study. *Journal of Consulting and Clinical Psychology, 64*, 1406–1416.

Bonné, J. (2001, February 6). Meth's deadly buzz. *MSNBC.com Special Report*. Retrieved February 8, 2001, from http://www.msnbc.com/news/510835.asp?bt=nm&btu=http://www.msnbc.com/tools/newstools/d/news_menu.asp&cp1=1.

Bonta, J., Law, M., & Hanson, K. (1998). The prediction of criminal and violent recidivism among mentally disordered offenders: A meta-analysis. *Psychological Bulletin, 123*, 123–142.

Bookheimer, S. Y., et al. (2000). Patterns of brain activation in people at risk for Alzheimer's disease. *The New England Journal of Medicine, 343*, 450–456.

Boren, T., Faulk, P., Roth, K. A., Larson, G., & Normark, S. (1993). Attachment of *Helicobacter pylori* to human gastric epithelium mediated by blood group antigens. *Science, 262*, 1892–1895.

Bornstein, M. R., Bellack, A. S., & Hersen, M. (1977). Social-skills training for unassertive children: A multiple-baseline analysis. *Journal of Applied Behavior Analysis, 10*, 183–195.

Bornstein, R. F. (1992). The dependent personality: Developmental, social, and clinical perspectives. *Psychological Bulletin, 112*, 3–23.

Bornstein, R. F. (1993). *The dependent personality*. New York: The Guilford Press.

Bornstein, R. F. (1997). Dependent personality disorder in the *DSM-IV* and beyond. *Clinical Psychology: Science and Practice, 4*, 175–187.

Bornstein, R. F. (1999). Criterion validity of objective and projective dependency tests: A meta-analytic assessment of behavioral prediction. *Psychological Assessment, 11*, 48–57.

Bornstein, R. F. (1999). Dependent and histrionic personality disorders. In T. Millon et al. (Eds.), *Oxford textbook of psychopathology. Oxford textbooks in clinical psychology, Vol. 4* (pp. 535–554). New York: Oxford University Press.

Borthwick-Duffy, S. A. (1994). Epidemiology and prevalence of psychopathology in individuals with dual diagnoses. *Journal of Consulting and Clinical Psychology, 62*, 17–27.

Boskind-White, M., & White, W. C. (1983). *Bulimarexia: The binge-purge cycle*. New York: W. W. Norton.

Boston Women's Health Book Collective. (1984). *The new our bodies, ourselves*. New York: Simon & Schuster.

Bostwick, J. M., & Pankratz, V. S. (2000). Affective disorders and suicide risk: A reexamination. *American Journal of Psychiatry, 157*, 1925–1932.

Botelho, R. J., & Richmond, R. (1996). Secondary prevention of excessive alcohol use: Assessing the prospects of implementation. *Family Practice, 13*, 182–193.

Bouchard, C. (1997). Obesity in adulthood—The importance of childhood and parental obesity. *The New England Journal of Medicine, 337*, 926–927.

Bouchard, C., Rhéaume, J., & Ladouceur, R. (1999). Responsibility and perfectionism in OCD: An experimental study. *Behaviour Research & Therapy, 37*, 239–248.

Bouchard, S., et al. (1996). Cognitive restructuring in the treatment of psychotic symptoms in schizophrenia: A critical analysis. *Behavior Therapy, 27*, 257–277.

Boudouris, J. (2000). The insanity defense in Polk County, Iowa. *American Journal of Forensic Psychology, 18*, 41–79.

Bouton, M. E., Mineka, S., & Barlow, D. H. (2001). A modern learning theory perspective on the etiology of panic disorder. *Psychological Review, 108*, 4–32.

Bouwer, C., & Stein, D. J. (1997). Association of panic disorder with a history of traumatic suffocation. *American Journal of Psychiatry, 154*, 1566–1570.

Bowden, C. L., et al. (2000). A randomized, placebo-controlled 12-month trial of divalproex and lithium in treatment of outpatients with bipolar I disorder. *Archives of General Psychiatry, 57*, 481–489.

Bowers, T. G., & Clum, G. A. (1988). Relative contribution of specific and nonspecific treatment effects: Meta-analysis of placebo-controlled behavior therapy research. *Psychological Bulletin, 103*, 315–323.

Bowlby, J. (1988). *A secure base*. New York: Basic Books.

Boy to sue city over tryst with teacher. (2000, April 14). *Reuters News Agency*.

Boyd-Franklin, N. (1989). *Black families in therapy: A multisystems approach*. New York: Guilford Press.

Boyle, M. H., et al. (1992). Predicting substance use in late adolescence: Results from the Ontario Child Health Study Follow-up. *American Journal of Psychiatry, 149*, 761–767.

Boyle, P. (1993). The hazards of passive—and active—smoking. *New England Journal of Medicine, 328,* 1708–1709.

Braaten, E. B., & Rosén, L. E. (2000). Self-regulation of affect in attention deficit–hyperactivity disorder (ADHD) and non-ADHD boys: Differences in empathic responding. *Journal of Consulting and Clinical Psychology, 68,* 313–321.

Braddock, D. (1992). Community mental health and mental retardation services in the United States: A comparative study of resource allocation. *American Journal of Psychiatry, 149,* 175–183.

Bradley, J. D. D., & Golden, C. J. (2001). Biological contributions to the presentation and understanding of attention-deficit/hyperactivity disorder: A review. *Clinical Psychology Review, 21,* 907–929.

Bradley, R. G., & Follingstad, D. R. (2001). Utilizing disclosure in the treatment of the sequelae of childhood sexual abuse. A theoretical and empirical review. *Clinical Psychology Review, 21,* 1–32.

Brady, K., et al. (2000). Efficacy and safety of sertraline treatment of posttraumatic stress disorder: A randomized controlled trial. *Journal of the American Medical Association, 283,* 1837–1844.

Brady, S. (1986). Short-term memory, phonological processing, and reading ability. *Annals of Dyslexia, 36,* 138–153.

Braff, D. L. (1993). Information processing and attention dysfunction in schizophrenia. *Schizophrenia Bulletin, 19,* 233–259.

Braswell, L., & Kendall, P. C. (2001). Cognitive-behavioral therapy with youth. In K. S. Dobson (Ed.), *Handbook of cognitive-behavioral therapies* (2nd ed., pp. 246–294). New York: The Guilford Press.

Braun, B. G. (Ed.). (1986). *Treatment of multiple personality disorder.* Washington, DC: American Psychiatric Press.

Braun, S. (2001, Spring). Seeking insight by prescription. *Cerebrum,* pp. 10–21.

Breaux, C., Matsuoka, J. K., & Ryujin, D. H. (1995, August). *National utilization of mental health services by Asian/Pacific Islanders.* Paper presented at the meeting of the American Psychological Association, New York, NY.

Breitner, J. C. S., & Zandi, P. P. (2001). Do nonsteroidal anti-inflammatory drugs reduce the risk of Alzheimer's disease? *New England Journal of Medicine, 345,* 1567–1568.

Brekke, J. S., et al. (1997). The impact of service characteristics on functional outcomes from community support programs for persons with schizophrenia: A growth curve analysis. *Journal of Consulting and Clinical Psychology, 65,* 464–475.

Bremmer, J. D., et al. (1996). Chronic PTSD in Vietnam combat veterans: Course of illness and substance abuse. *American Journal of Psychiatry, 153,* 369–375.

Brems, C., & Johnson, M. E. (1997). Clinical implications of the co-occurrence of substance use and other psychiatric disorders. *Professional Psychology: Research and Practice, 28,* 437–447.

Brenda, W. J. H., et al. (1998). Depressive symptoms and physical decline in community-dwelling older persons. *Journal of the American Medical Association, 279,* 1720–1726.

Brener, N. D., McMahon, P. M., Warren, C. W., & Douglas, K. A. (1999). Forced sexual intercourse and associated health-risk behaviors among female college students in the United States. *Journal of Consulting and Clinical Psychology, 67,* 252–259.

Breslow, N. (1989). Sources of confusion in the study and treatment of sadomasochism. *Journal of Social Behavior and Personality, 4,* 263–274.

Breslau, N., et al. (1996). Sleep disturbance and psychiatric disorders: A longitudinal epidemiological study of young adults. *Biological Psychiatry, 39,* 411–418.

Breslau, N., et al. (1997a). Sex differences in posttraumatic stress disorder. *Archives of General Psychiatry, 54,* 1044–1048.

Breslau, N., et al. (1997b). Psychiatric sequelae of posttraumatic stress disorder in women. *Archives of General Psychiatry, 54,* 81–87.

Breslau, N., et al. (1998). Major depression and stages of smoking: A longitudinal investigation. *Archives of General Psychiatry, 55,* 161–166.

Breslau, N., et al., (2001). Nicotine dependence in the United States: Prevalence, trends, and smoking persistence. *Archives of General Psychiatry, 58,* 810–816.

Brewin, C. R., Andrews, B., & Valentine, J. D. (2000). Meta-analysis of risk factors for posttraumatic stress disorder in trauma-exposed adults. *Journal of Consulting and Clinical Psychology, 68,* 748–766.

Brinkman, S. D., Largen, J. W., Jr., Cushman, L., Braun, P. R., & Block, R. (1986). Clinical validators: Alzheimer's disease and multi-infarct dementia. In L. W. Poon (Ed.), *Handbook for clinical memory assessment of older adults* (pp. 307–313). Washington, DC: American Psychological Association.

Brody, J. E. (1988a, May 5). Sifting fact from myth in the face of asthma's growing threat to American children. *The New York Times,* p. B19.

Brody, J. E. (1990, June 7). A search to bar retardation in a new generation. *The New York Times,* p. B9.

Brody, J. E. (1992a, May 15). Study finds liquid diet works (but not for the 50% who quit). *The New York Times,* p. B7.

Brody, J. E. (1992b, June 16). Suicide myths cloud efforts to save children. *The New York Times,* pp. C1, C3.

Brody, J. E. (1992c, September 30). Myriad masks hide an epidemic of depression. *The New York Times,* p. C12.

Brody, J. E. (1993c, December 15). Living with a common genetic abnormality. *The New York Times,* p. C17.

Brody, J. E. (1994b, February 9). Depression in the elderly: Old notions hinder help. *The New York Times,* p. C13.

Brody, J. E. (1994d, December 28). Wine for the heart: Over all, risks may outweigh benefits. *The New York Times,* p. C10.

Brody, J. E. (1995a, January 18). Dysthymia: Help for chronic sadness. *The New York Times,* p. C8.

Brody, J. E. (1995b, August 2). With more help available for impotence, few men seek it. *The New York Times,* p. C9.

Brody, J. E. (1996a, August 7). Relaxation method may aid health. *The New York Times,* p. C10.

Brody, J. E. (1996b, November 14). Decline seen in death rates from cancer as a whole. *The New York Times,* p. A21.

Brody, J. E. (1996c, November 20). Controlling anger is good medicine for the heart. *The New York Times,* p. C15.

Brody, J. E. (1997a, March 26). Race and weight. *The New York Times,* p. C8.

Brody, J. E. (1998, June 16). Gaining weight on sugar-free, fat-free diets. *The New York Times,* p. F7.

Brody, J. E. (2000, October 17). One-two punch for losing pounds: Exercise and careful diet. *The New York Times,* p. F6.

Bronfrenbrenner, U. (1979). *The ecology of human development: Experiments by nature and design.* Cambridge, MA: Harvard University Press.

Brookoff, D., et al. (1997). Characteristics of participants in domestic violence: Assessment at the scene of domestic assault. *Journal of the American Medical Association, 277,* 1369–1373.

Broussard, B. A., et al. (1991). Prevalence of obesity in American Indians and Alaska Natives. *American Journal of Clinical Nutrition, 53* (6 Suppl.), 1535S–1542S.

Brown, D. R., Ahmed, F., Gary, L. E., & Milburn, N. G. (1995). Major depression in a community sample of African Americans. *American Journal of Psychiatry,* 373–378.

Brown, G. K., Beck, A. T., Steer, R. A., & Grisham, J. R. (2000). Risk factors for suicide in psychiatric outpatients: A 20-year prospective study. *Journal of Consulting and Clinical Psychology, 68,* 371–377.

Brown, L. S. (1992). A feminist critique of the personality disorders. In L. Brown & M. Balou (Eds.), *Personality and psychopathology: Feminist reappraisals* (pp. 206–228). New York: Guilford Press.

Brown, L. S. (1997, November). Recovered memories of abuse: Research and clinical update. *Clinician's Research Digest, Supplemental Bulletin, 17,* 1–2.

Brown, R. A., et al. (1997). Cognitive-behavioral treatment for depression in alcoholism. *Journal of Consulting and Clinical Psychology, 65,* 715–726.

Brown, S. L., & Forth, A. E. (1997). Psychopathy and sexual assault: Static risk factors, emotional precursors, and rapist subtypes. *Journal of Consulting and Clinical Psychology, 65,* 848–857.

Brown, T. A., et al. (2001). Reliability of *DSM–IV* anxiety and mood disorders: Implications for the classification of emotional disorders. *Journal of Abnormal Psychology, 110,* 49–58.

Brownell, K. D., & Wadden, T. A. (1992). Etiology and treatment of obesity: Understanding a serious, prevalent, and refractory disorder. *Journal of Consulting and Clinical Psychology, 60,* 505–517.

Bruce, T. J. (1996). Predictors of alprazolam discontinuation with and without cognitive behavior therapy for panic disorder: A reply. *American Journal of Psychiatry, 153,* 1109–1110.

Bruch, H. (1973). *Eating disorders: Obesity, anorexia and the person within.* New York: Basic Books.

Bruch, M. A. (1997). Positive thoughts or cognitive balance as a moderator of the negative life events–dysphoria relationship: A reexamination. *Cognitive Therapy and Research, 21,* 25–38.

Brun, A. (1996). Frontal lobe degeneration of non-Alzheimer type. *Acta Neurologica Scandinavica Supplementum, 168,* 28–30.

Bryant, R. A. (2001). Posttraumatic stress disorder and traumatic brain injury: Can they co-exist *Clinical Psychology Review, 21,* 931–948.

Buchanan, A. (1999). Risk and dangerousness. *Psychological Medicine, 29,* 465–473.

Buchanan, R. W., & Carpenter, W. T., Jr. (1997). The neuroanatomies of schizophrenia. *Schizophrenia Bulletin, 23,* 367–372.

Buchsbaum, M. S., & Hazlett, E. A. (1998). Positron emission tomography studies of abnormal glucose metabolism in schizophrenia. *Schizophrenia Bulletin, 24,* 343–364.

Bullman, T. A., & Kang, H. K. (1994). Posttraumatic stress disorder and the risk of traumatic deaths among Vietnam veterans. *Journal of Nervous and Mental Disease, 182,* 604–610.

Buriel, R., Calzada, S., & Vazquez, R. (1982). The relationship of traditional Mexican American culture to adjustment and delinquency among three generations of Mexican American male adolescents. *Hispanic Journal of Behavioral Sciences, 4,* 41–55.

Burke, R. S., & Stephens, R. S. (1999). Social anxiety and drinking in college students: A social cognitive theory analysis. *Clinical Psychology Review, 19,* 513–530.

Burnam, M. A., Hough, R. L., Karno, M., Escobar, J. I., & Telles, C. A. (1987). Acculturation and lifetime prevalence of psychiatric disorders among Mexican Americans in Los Angeles. *Journal of Health and Social Behavior, 28,* 89–102.

Burns, D. D. (1980). *Feeling good: The new mood therapy.* New York: Morris.

Burns, D. D., & Beck, A. T. (1978). Modification of mood disorders. In J. P. Foreyt & D. P. Rathjen (Eds.), *Cognitive behavior therapy: Research and application* (pp. 109–134). New York: Plenum Press.

Burns, D. D., & Nolen-Hoeksema, S. (1992). Therapeutic empathy and recovery from depression in cognitive-behavioral therapy: A structural equation model. *Journal of Consulting and Clinical Psychology, 60,* 441–449.

Burros, M. (1994, July 17). Despite awareness of risks, more in U.S. are getting fat. *The New York Times,* pp. A1, A8.

Burton, N., & Lane, R. C. (2001). The relational treatment of dissociative identity disorder. *Clinical Psychology Review, 21,* 301–320.

Busatto, G. F., et al. (1997). Correlation between reduced in vivo benzodiazepine receptor binding and severity of psychotic symptoms in schizophrenia. *American Journal of Psychiatry, 154,* 56–63.

Buss, D. M., & Kenrick, D. T. (1998). Evolutionary social psychology. In D. T. Gilbert, S. T. Fiske, & G. Lindzey (Eds.), *The handbook of social psychology* (4th ed., Vol. 2, pp. 982–1026). Boston, MA: McGraw-Hill, Inc.

Buss, D. M., & Shackelford, T. K. (1997). Human aggression in evolutionary psychological perspective. *Clinical Psychology Review, 17,* 605–619.

Bustillo, J. R., et al. (2001). The psychosocial treatment of schizophrenia: An update. *American Journal of Psychiatry, 158,* 163–175.

Butler, A. C., & Beck, A. T. (1995, Summer). Cognitive therapy for depression. *The Clinical Psychologist, 48,* 3–5.

Butler, G. (1989). Issues in the application of cognitive and behavioral strategies to the treatment of social phobia. *Clinical Psychology Review, 9,* 91–106.

Butler, L. D., et al. (1996). Hypnotizability and traumatic experience: A diathesis-stress model of dissociative symptomatology. *American Journal of Psychiatry, 153*(Suppl.), 42–63.

Butler, R. N. (2001, Fall/Winter). The myth of old age. *Newsweek Special Issue,* p. 33.

Butterfield, F. (1997a, January 5). Serious crime decreased for fifth year in a row. *The New York Times,* p. A10.

Butterfield, F. (1997c, June 2). Homicides plunge 11 percent in U.S., F.B.I. report says. *The New York Times,* pp. A1, B10.

Butterfield, F. (2001). Violence rises as club drug spreads out into the streets. *The New York Times,* pp. A1, A14.

Bütz, M. R., Bowlling, J. B., & Bliss, C. A. (2000). Psychotherapy with the mentally retarded: A review of the literature and the implications. *Professional Psychology: Research and Practice, 31,* 42–47.

Butzlaff, R. L., & Hooley, J. M. (1998). Expressed emotion and psychiatric relapse. *Archives of General Psychiatry, 55,* 547–552.

Byne, W., et al. (2001). Magnetic resonance imaging of the thalamic mediodorsal nucleus and pulvinar in schizophrenia and schizotypal personality disorder. *Archives of General Psychiatry, 58,* 133–140.

C

Cable News Network. (1998a, April 6). Alcohol remains large factor in violent crime. *CNN Interactive* [Online].

Cable News Network. (1998b, May 20). New studies show a genetic link to the complex disease of alcoholism, *Cable News Network Web Posting.* Retrieved May 23, 1998, from www.cnn.com/HEALTH/9805/20/genetic.alcoholism/.

Caetano, R. (1987). Acculturation and drinking patterns among U.S. Hispanics. *British Journal of Addiction, 82,* 789–799.

Calhoon, S. K. (1996). Confirmatory factor analysis of the Dysfunctional Attitude Scale in a student sample. *Cognitive Therapy and Research, 20,* 81–91.

Calhoun, K. S., & Atkeson, B. M. (1991). *Treatment of rape victims: Facilitating social adjustment.* New York: Pergamon Press.

Calhoun, P. S., et al. (2000). Drug use and validity of substance use self-reports in veterans seeking help for posttraumatic stress disorder. *Journal of Consulting and Clinical Psychology, 68,* 923–927.

Califia, P. (1997). *Sex changes: The politics of transgenderism.* San Francisco: Cleis.

Callicott, J. H., et al. (2000). Selective relationship between prefrontal n-acetylaspartate measures and negative symptoms in schizophrenia. *American Journal of Psychiatry, 157,* 1646–1651.

Cameron, N. (1963). *Personality development and psychopathology: A dynamic approach.* Boston: Houghton Mifflin.

Campbell, S. B., & Cohn, J. F. (1991). Prevalence and correlates of postpartum depression in first-time mothers. *Journal of Abnormal Psychology, 100,* 594–599.

Can stress make you sick? (1998). *Harvard Health Letter, 23*(6), pp. 1–3.

Cancer rates inch down, mostly for men. (1999, April 20). *Cable News Network.* Retrieved April 23, 1999, from http://www.cnn.com.

Capps, L., et al. (1993). Parental perception of emotional expressiveness in children with autism. *Journal of Consulting and Clinical Psychology, 61,* 475–484.

Cardno, A. G., et al. (1999). Heritability estimates for psychotic disorders in the Maudsley twin psychosis series. *Archives of General Psychiatry, 56,* 162–168.

Cardozo, B. L., et al. (2000). Mental health, social functioning, and attitudes of Kosovar Albanians following the war in Kosovo. *Journal of the American Medical Association, 284,* 569–577.

Carey, B. (1998, January/February). The sunshine supplement. *Health,* pp. 52–55.

Carey, G. (1992). Twin imitation for antisocial behavior: Implications for genetic and family environment research. *Journal of Abnormal Psychology, 101,* 18–25.

Carey, G., & DiLalla, D. L. (1994). Personality and psychopathology: Genetic perspectives. *Journal of Abnormal Psychology, 103,* 32–43.

Carey, M. P., Wincze, J. P., & Meisler, A. W. (1998). Sexual dysfunction: Male erectile disorder. In D. H. Barlow (Ed.), *Clinical handbook for psychological disorders* (pp. 442–480). New York: Guilford Publication.

Carini, M. A., & Nevid, J. S. (1992). Social appropriateness and impaired perspective in schizophrenia. *Journal of Clinical Psychology, 48,* 170–177.

Carlin, A. S., Hoffman, H. G., & Weghorst, S. (1997). Virtual reality and tactile augmentation in the treatment of spider phobia. *Behaviour Research and Therapy, 35,* 1153–1158.

Carmen, E. H., Rieker, P. P., & Mills, T. (1984). Victims of violence and psychiatric illness. *American Journal of Psychiatry, 141,* 378–383.

Carney, R. M., Freedland, K. E., & Jaffe, A. S. (2001). Depression as a risk factor for coronary heart disease mortality. *Archives of General Psychiatry, 58.*

Carpenter, S. (2000, September). Psychologists tackle neuroimaging at APA-sponsored Advanced Training Institute. *Monitor on Psychology,* pp. 42–43.

Carpenter, S. (2001a, May). Stimulants boost achievement in ADHD teens. *Monitor on Psychology,* pp. 26–27.

Carpenter, S. (2001b, September). A new reason for keeping a diary. *Monitor on Psychology,* pp. 68–70.

Carter, C. S., et al. (1997). Anterior cingulate gyrus dysfunction and selective attention deficits in schizophrenia: H2O PET study during single-trial Stroop task performance. *American Journal of Psychiatry, 154,* 1670–1675.

Carter, M. M., et al. (1995). Effects of a safe person on induced distress following a biological challenge in panic disorder with agoraphobia. *Journal of Abnormal Psychology, 104,* 156–163.

Carver, C. S., & Gaines, J. G. (1987). Optimism, pessimism, and postpartum depression. *Cognitive Therapy & Research, 11,* 449–462.

Casanova, M. R. (1997). Functional and anatomical aspects of prefrontal pathology in schizophrenia. *Schizophrenia Bulletin, 23,* 517–519.

Cascardi, M., et al. (1995). Characteristics of women physically abused by their spouses and who seek treatment regarding marital conflict. *Journal of Consulting and Clinical Psychology, 63,* 616–623.

Casey, B. J., et al. (1997). Implication of right frontostriatal circuitry in response inhibition and attention-deficit hyperactivity disorder. *Journal of the American Academy of Child and Adolescent Psychiatry, 36,* 374–383.

Castellanos, F. X., et al. (2001). Quantitative brain magnetic resonance imaging in girls with attention-deficit/hyperactivity disorder. *Archives of General Psychiatry, 58,* 289–295.

Castro, J. (1992, January 20). Sexual harassment: A guide. *Time Magazine,* p. 37.

Catalano, R., et al. (1993). Using ECA survey data to examine the effect of job layoffs on violent behavior. *Hospital and Community Psychiatry, 44,* 874–879.

Catz, S. L., & Kelly, J. A. (2001). Living with HIV disease. In A. Baum, T. A. Revenson, & J. E. Singer (Eds.), *Handbook of health psychology* (pp. 841–850). Mahwah, NJ: Erlbaum.

CDC says 61 percent of U.S. adults overweight. (2000, December 15). *CNN Web Posting.* Retrieved December 19, 2000, from http://www.cnn.com/2000/HEALTH/diet.fitness/12/15/fat.america.ap/index.html.

Celano, M., et al. (1996). Treatment of traumagenic beliefs among sexually abused girls and their mothers: An evaluation study. *Journal of Abnormal Child Psychology, 24,* 1–17.

Celio, A. A., et al. (2000). Reducing risk factors for eating disorders: comparison of an Internet- and a classroom-delivered psychoeducational program. *Journal of Consulting and Clinical Psychology, 68,* 650–657.

Celis, W. (1991, January 2). Students trying to draw line between sex and an assault. *The New York Times,* pp. 1, B8.

Center for Mental Health Services (CMHS). (1994). *Mental health statistics.* Office of Consumer, Family and Public Information, Center for Mental Health Services, U.S. Department of Health and Human Services. Rockville, MD: Author.

Center for Mental Health Services (2001, May). *National Strategy for Suicide Prevention: Goals and objectives for action: Summary. A joint effort of SAMHS, CDC, NIH, and HRSA.* Washington, DC: Author.

Centers for Disease Control (CDC). (2000). Tobacco use among middle and high school students—United States, 1999. *Morbidity and Mortality Weekly Report, 49,* 49–53.

Centers for Disease Control (CDC). (2001a). Self-reported asthma prevalence among adults: United States, 2000. *Morbidity and Mortality Weekly Report, 50,* 682–686.

Centers for Disease Control (CDC). (2001b, October 12). Cigarette smoking among adults—United States, 1999. *Morbidity and Mortality Weekly Report, 50*(40). Retrieved November 15, 2001, from http://www.cdc.gov/tobacco/research_data/adults_prev/mm5040.htm.

Centers for Disease Control (CDC). (2001c). *Suicide in the United States.* National Center for Injury Prevention and Control, Centers for Disease Control. Atlanta: Author.

Chadda, R. K., & Ahuja, N. (1990). Dhat syndrome: A sex neurosis of the Indian subcontinent. *British Journal of Psychiatry, 156,* 577–579.

Chakrabarti, S., & Fombonne, E. (2001). Pervasive developmental disorders in preschool children. *Journal of the American Medical Association, 285,* 3093–3099.

Chamberlin, J. (2001, July/August). Putting a face on child mental illness. *Monitor on Psychology,* pp. 28–29.

Chambless, D. L., &. Ollendick, T. H. (2001). Empirically supported psychological interventions: Controversies and evidence. *Annual Review of Psychology, 52,* 685–716.

Chambless, D. L., et al. (1998, Winter). Update on empirically validated therapies, II. *The Clinical Psychologist, 51,* 3–16.

Chan, D. W. (1991). The Beck Depression Inventory: What difference does the Chinese version make? *Psychological Assessment, 3,* 616–622.

Chang, S. C. (1984). Review of I. Yamashita "Taijin-kyofu." *Transcultural Psychiatric Research Review, 21*, 283–288.

Charney, D. S., Nestler, E. J., & Bunney, B. S. (1999). *Neurobiology of mental illness.* New York: Oxford University Press.

Chase, M. (1998, March 2). A new diet drug hits the marketplace, with potential risks. *The Wall Street Journal*, p. B1.

Chemerinski, E., et al. (2001). The specificity of depressive symptoms in patients with Alzheimer's Disease. *American Journal of Psychiatry, 158*, 68–72.

Chemtob, C. M., et al. (1997). Cognitive-behavioral treatment for severe anger in posttraumatic stress disorder. *Journal of Consulting and Clinical Psychology, 65*, 184–189.

Chen, J., et al. (2001). Racial differences in the use of cardiac catheterization after acute myocardial infarction. *The New England Journal of Medicine, 344*, 1443–1449.

Chen, P., Ganguli, M., Mulsant, B. H., & DeKosky, S. T. (1999). The temporal relationship between depressive symptoms and dementia: A community-based prospective study. *Archives of General Psychiatry, 56*, 261–266.

Chermack, S. T., & Giancola, P. R. (1997). The relation between alcohol and aggression: An integrated biopsychosocial conceptualization. *Clinical Psychology Review, 17*, 621–649.

Chesno, F. A., & Kilmann, P. R. (1975). Effects of stimulation intensity on sociopathic avoidance learning. *Journal of Abnormal Psychology, 84*, 144–151.

Cheung, F. (1991). The use of mental health services by ethnic minorities. In H. F. Myers et al. (Eds.), *Ethnic minority perspectives on clinical training and services in psychology* (pp. 23–31). Washington, DC: American Psychological Association.

Cheung, F. M., & Ho, R. M. (1997). Standardization of the Chinese MMPI-A in Hong Kong: A preliminary study. *Psychological Assessment, 9*, 499–502.

Cheung, F., Song, W., & Butcher, J. N. (1991). An infrequency scale for the Chinese MMPI. *Psychological Assessment, 3*, 648–653.

Children with hyperactivity disorder prone to injury. (2001, January 2). *CNN Web Posting.* Retrieved January 4, 2001, from http://www.cnn.com/2001/HEALTH/children/01/02/bc.health.hyperactive.reut/index.html.

Ching, J. W. J., et al. (1995). Perceptions of family values and roles among Japanese Americans: Clinical considerations. *American Journal of Orthopsychiatry, 65*, 216–224.

Chipperfield, B., & Vogel-Sprott, M. (1988). Family history of problem drinking among young male social drinkers: Modeling effects on alcohol consumption. *Journal of Abnormal Psychology, 97*, 423–428.

Chobanian, A. V. (2001). Control of hypertension: An important national priority. *The New England Journal of Medicine, 345*, 534–535.

Choi, K. H., Binson, D., Adelson, M., & Catania, J. A. (1998). Sexual harassment, sexual coercion, and HIV risk among U.S. adults 18–49 years. *AIDS and Behavior, 2*(1), 33–40.

Chowdhury, A. N. (1996). The definition and classification of Koro. *Culture, Medicine and Psychiatry, 20*, 41–65.

Christiansen, B. A., & Goldman, M. S. (1983). Alcohol-related expectancies versus demographic/background variables in the prediction of adolescent drinking. *Journal of Consulting and Clinical Psychology, 52*, 249–257.

Christiansen, K., & Winkler, E. M. (1992). Hormonal, anthropometrical, and behavioral correlates of physical aggression in Kung San men of Namibia. *Aggressive Behavior, 18*, 271–280.

Christmas, A. L., Wodarski, J. S., & Smokowski, P. R. (1996). Risk factors for physical child abuse: A practice theoretical paradigm. *Family Therapy, 23*, 233–248.

Chu, J. A., et al. (1999). Memories of childhood abuse: Dissociation, amnesia, and corroboration. *American Journal of Psychiatry, 156*, 749–755.

Ciesla, J. A., & Roberts, J. E. (2001). Meta-analysis of the relationship between HIV infection and risk for depressive disorders. *American Journal of Psychiatry, 158*, 725–730.

Clark, D. A., Cook, A., & Snow, D. (1998). Depressive symptom differences in hospitalized, medically ill, depressed psychiatric inpatients and nonmedical controls. *Journal of Abnormal Psychology, 107*, 38–48.

Clark, D. M. (1986). A cognitive approach to panic. *Behaviour Research and Therapy, 24*, 461–470.

Clark, D. M., et al. (1997). Misinterpretation of body sensations in panic disorder. *Journal of Consulting and Clinical Psychology, 65*, 203–213.

Clark, S. E., & Loftus, E. F. (1996). The construction of space alien abduction memories. *Psychological Inquiry, 7*, 140–143.

Clay, R. A. (2001a, January). To the heart of the matter. *Monitor on Psychology*, pp. 42–45.

Clay, R. A. (2001b, January). Bringing psychology to cardiac care. *Monitor on Psychology*, pp. 46–49.

Cleckley, H. (1976). *The mask of sanity* (5th ed.). St. Louis: Mosby.

Cleghorn, J. M., et al. (1992). Toward a brain map of auditory hallucinations. *American Journal of Psychiatry, 149*, 1062–1069.

Clemence, A., & Handler, L. O. (2001). Psychological assessment on internship: A survey of training directors and their expectations for students. *Journal of Personality Assessment, 76*, 18–47.

Clemetson, L. (2000, November 6). The new victims of hate. *Newsweek*, p. 61.

Coccaro, E. F., & Kavoussi, R. J. (1997). Fluoxetine and impulsive aggressive behavior in personality-disordered subjects. *Archives of General Psychiatry, 54*, 1081–1088.

Cockerham, W. C., Kunz, G., & Lueschen, G. (1989). Alcohol use and psychological distress: A comparison of Americans and West Germans. *The International Journal of the Addictions, 24*, 951–961.

Cognitive impairment linked to early death in HIV-infected patients. (1996, March 29). *Reuters News Service.*

Cohen, A. C., et al. (1993). Factors determining the decision to institutionalize dementing individuals: A prospective study. *The Gerontologist, 22*, 714–720.

Cohen, D. (1986). Psychopathological perspectives: Differential diagnosis of Alzheimer's disease and related disorders. In L. W. Poon (Ed.), *Handbook for clinical memory assessment of older adults* (pp. 81–88). Washington, DC: American Psychological Association.

Cohen, F. L., Ferrans, C. E., & Eshler, B. (1992). Reported accidents in narcolepsy. *Loss, Grief and Care, 5*, 71–80.

Cohen, J. A., & Mannarino, A. P. (1997). A treatment study for sexually abused preschool children: Outcome during a one-year follow-up. *Journal of the American Academy of Child & Adolescent Psychiatry, 36*, 1228–1235.

Cohen, S., Tyrrell, D. A. J., & Smith, A. P. (1991). Psychological stress and susceptibility to the common cold. *The New England Journal of Medicine, 325*, 606–612.

Cohen, S., et al. (1998). Types of stressors that increase susceptibility to the common cold in healthy adults. *Health Psychology, 17*, 214–223.

Cohen-Kettensi, P. T. (2001). Gender identity disorder in DSM? *Journal of American Academy of Child & Adolescent Psychiatry, 40*, 391.

Cohen-Kettenis, P. T., & van Goozen, S. H. M. (1997). Sex reassignment of adolescent transsexuals: A follow-up study. *Journal of the American Academy of Child and Adolescent Psychiatry, 36*, 263–271.

Cole, D. A., et al. (1998). A longitudinal look at the relation between depression and anxiety in children and adolescents. *Journal of Consulting and Clinical Psychology, 66*, 451–460.

Coleman, D., & Baker, F. M. (1994). Misdiagnosis of schizophrenia in older, Black veterans. *Journal of Nervous and Mental Disease, 182*, 527–528.

Coleman, E. (1987). Bisexuality: Challenging our understanding of sexual orientation. *Sexuality and Medicine, 1*, 225–242.

College binge drinking worries (1999, August 27). *Associated Press, NewsReal, Inc.*

Collins, J. J., & Messerschmidt, P. M. (1993). Epidemiology of alcohol-related violence. *Alcohol Health and Research World, 17*, 93–100.

Collins, P. H. (1990). *Black feminist thought: Knowledge, consciousness, and the politics of empowerment.* Boston: Unwin Hyman.

Colvin, C. R., & Block, J. (1994). Do positive illusions foster mental health? An examination of the Taylor and Brown formulation. *Psychological Bulletin, 16*, 3–20.

Comas-Diaz, L., & Griffith, E. (1988). Introduction: On culture and psychotherapeutic care. In L. Comas-Diaz & E. Griffith (Eds.), *Clinical guidelines in cross-cultural mental health.* New York: Wiley.

Combs, B. J., Hales, D. R., & Williams, B. K. (1980). *An invitation to health.* Menlo Park, CA: Benjamin/Cummings.

Comings, D. E. (1997). Genetic aspects of childhood behavioral disorders. *Child Psychiatry and Human Development, 27*, 139–150.

Compas, B. E., et al. (1998). Sampling of empirically supported psychological treatments from health psychology: Smoking, chronic pain, cancer, and bulimia nervosa. *Journal of Consulting and Clinical Psychology, 66*, 89–112.

Cone, J. D. (1999). Introduction to the special section on self-monitoring: A major assessment method in clinical psychology. *Psychological Assessment, 11*, 411–414.

Conley, R. R., & Buchanan, R. W. (1997). Evaluation of treatment-resistant schizophrenia. *Schizophrenia Bulletin, 23*, 663–674.

Connors, G. J., et al. (1997). The therapeutic alliance and its relationship to alcoholism treatment participation and outcome. *Journal of Consulting and Clinical Psychology, 65*, 588–598.

Cooke, D. J., & Michie, C. (1997). An item response theory analysis of the Hare Psychopathy Checklist—Revised. *Psychological Assessment, 9*, 3–14.

Cooke, R. (1994, November 8). Memory's foe: Progress seen in battle vs. brain killer. *New York Newsday*, p. A16.

Cookson, W. O. C. M., & Moffatt, M. R. (1997). Asthma—An epidemic in the absence of infection? *Science, 275*, 41–42.

Coolidge, F. L., & Segal, D. L. (1998). Evolution of personality disorder diagnosis in the *Diagnostic and Statistical Manual of Mental Disorders. Clinical Psychology Review, 18*, 585–599.

Cooney, N. L., et al. (1997). Alcohol cue reactivity, negative-mood reactivity, and relapse in treated alcoholic men. *Journal of Abnormal Psychology, 106*, 243–250.

Coons, P. M. (1986). Treatment progress in 20 patients with multiple personality disorder. *Journal of Nervous and Mental Disease, 174*, 715–721.

Coons, P. M., Bowman, E. S., & Pellow, T. A. (1989). Post-traumatic aspects of the treatment of victims of sexual abuse and incest. *Psychiatric Clinics of North America, 12*, 325–327.

Coontz, S., & Franklin, D. (1997, October 28). When the marriage penalty is marriage. *The New York Times*, p. A23.

Cooper, P. J., et al. (1999). Post-partum depression and the mother-infant relationship in a South African peri-urban settlement. *British Journal of Psychiary, 175*, 554–558.

Corbitt, E. M., & Widiger, T. A. (1995). Sex differences among the personality disorders: An exploration of the data. *Clinical Psychology: Science and Practice, 2*, 225–238.

Cordes, C. (1985). Common threads found in suicide. *APA Monitor, 16* (10), 11.

Cordova, M. J., et al. (1995). Frequency and correlates of posttraumatic-stress-disorder-like symptoms after treatment for breast cancer. *Journal of Consulting and Clinical Psychology, 63,* 981–986.

Cornblatt, B. A., & Kilep, J. G. (1994). Impaired attention, genetics, and the pathophysiology of schizophrenia. *Schizophrenia Bulletin, 20,* 31–46.

Coronado, S. F., & Peake, T. H. (1992). Culturally sensitive therapy: Sensitive principles. *Journal of College Student Psychotherapy, 7,* 63–72.

Cororve, M. B., & Gleaves, D. H. (2001). Body dysmorphic disorder: A review of conceptualizations, assessment, and treatment strategies. *Clinical Psychology Review, 21,* 949–970.

Coryell, W., Endicott, J., & Keller, M. (1992b). Rapidly cycling affective disorder: Demographics, diagnosis, family history, and course. *Archives of General Psychiatry, 49,* 126–131.

Coryell, W., et al. (1996). Importance of psychotic features to long-term course in major depressive disorder. *American Journal of Psychiatry, 153,* 483–489.

Costa, P. T., Jr., & McCrae, R. R. (1985). Hypochondriasis, neuroticism, and aging: When are somatic complaints unfounded? *American Psychologist, 40,* 19–28.

Costantino, G., et al. (1986). Cuento therapy: A culturally sensitive modality for Puerto Rican children. *Journal of Consulting and Clinical Psychology, 54,* 639–645.

Council of Economic Advisers for the President's Initiative on Race. (1998). *Changing America: Indicators of social and economic well-being by race and Hispanic origin.* Washington, DC: U.S. Government Printing Office.

Coursey, R. D., Alford, J., & Safarjan, B. (1997). Significant advances in understanding and treating serious mental illness. *Professional Psychology: Research and Practice, 28,* 205–216.

Cowan, W. M., & Kandel, E. R. (2001). Prospects for neurology and psychiatry. *Journal of the American Medical Association, 285,* 594–600.

Cowley, G. (2000a, July 3). Generation XXL. *Newsweek,* pp. 40–44.

Cowley, G. (2000b, May 22). The new war on Parkinson's. *Newsweek,* pp. 52–58.

Cowley, G. (2001a, February 12). New ways to stay clean. *Newsweek,* pp. 45–47.

Cowley, G. (2001b, March 12). Cannibals to cows: The path of a deadly disease. *Newsweek,* pp. 53–61.

Cowley, G. (2001c, June 11). Can he find a cure? *Newsweek,* pp. 39–41.

Cowley, G., & Underwood, A. (1998, January 5). A little help from serotonin. *Newsweek,* pp. 78–81.

Cox, W. M., & Klinger, E. (1988). A motivational model of alcohol use. *Journal of Abnormal Psychology, 97,* 168–180.

Coyle, J. T. (2001). Drug treatment of anxiety disorders in children. *The New England Journal of Medicine, 344,* 1326–1327.

Coyne, J. C. (1976). Toward an interactional description of depression. *Psychiatry, 39,* 14–27.

Craighead, W. E., Craighead, L. W., & Ilardi, S. S. (1998). Psychosocial treatments for major depressive disorder. In P. E. Nathan & J. M. Gorman (Eds.), *A guide to treatments that work* (pp. 226–239). New York: Oxford University Press.

Craske, M. G., Brown, T. A., & Barlow, D. H. (1991). Behavioral treatment of panic disorder: A two-year follow-up. *Behavior Therapy, 22,* 289–304.

Cravchik, A., & Goldman, D. (2000). Neurochemical individuality: Genetic diversity among human dopamine and serotonin receptors and transporters. *Archives of General Psychiatry, 57,* 1105–1114.

Crick, N. R., & Dodge, K. A. (1994). A review and reformulation of social information-processing mechanisms in children's social adjustment. *Psychological Bulletin, 115,* 74–101.

Crits-Christoph, P. (1992). The efficacy of brief dynamic psychotherapy: A meta-analysis. *American Journal of Psychiatry, 149,* 151–158.

Cross-National Collaborative Group. (1992). The changing rate of major depression: Cross-national comparisons. *Journal of the American Medical Association, 268,* 3098–3105.

Crow, T. J. (1980a). Molecular pathology of schizophrenia: More than one disease process? *British Medical Journal, 280,* 66–68.

Crow, T. J. (1980b). Positive and negative schizophrenic symptoms and the role of dopamine. *British Journal of Psychiatry, 137,* 383–386.

Crow, T. J. (1980c). Positive and negative schizophrenic symptoms and the role of dopamine: A debate. *British Journal of Psychiatry, 137,* 379–383.

Cuéllar, I., & Roberts, R. E. (1997). Relations of depression, acculturation, and socioeconomic status in a Latino sample. *Hispanic Journal of Behavioral Sciences, 19,* 230–238.

Cui, X-J., & Vaillant, G. E. (1997). Does depression generate negative life events? *Journal of Nervous and Mental Disease, 185,* 145–150.

Cummings, J. L. (1992). Depression and Parkinson's disease: A review. *American Journal of Psychiatry, 149,* 443–454.

Curb, J. D., & Marcus, E. B. (1991). Body fat and obesity in Japanese-Americans. *American Journal of Clinical Nutrition, 53,* 1552S–1555S.

Currie, S. R., et al. (2000). Cognitive-behavioral treatment of insomnia secondary to chronic pain. *Journal of Consulting and Clinical Psychology, 68,* 407–416.

Curry, S., Marlatt, G. A., Gordon, J. R. (1987). Abstinence violation effect: Validation of an attributional construct with smoking cessation. *Journal of Consulting and Clinical Psychology, 55,* 145–149.

Cutrona, C. E., et al. (2000). Direct and moderating effects of community context on the psychological well-being of African American women. *Journal of Personality and Social Psychology, 79,* 1088–1101.

Cutting, L. P., & Docherty, N. M. (2000). Schizophrenia outpatients' perceptions of their parents: Is expressed emotion a factor? *Journal of Abnormal Psychology, 109,* 266–272.

D

Dabbs, J. M., & Hargrove, M. F. (1997). Age, testosterone, and behavior among female prison inmates. *Psychosomatic Medicine, 59,* 477–480.

Dadds, M. R., et al. (1992). Childhood depression and conduct disorder: II. An analysis of family interaction patterns in the home. *Journal of Abnormal Psychology, 101,* 505–513.

Dahl, R. E. (1992). The pharmacologic treatment of sleep disorders. *Psychiatric Clinics of North America, 15,* 161–178.

Daley, S. E., Burge, D., & Hammen, C. (2000). Borderline personality disorder symptoms as predictors of 4-year romantic relationship dysfunction in young women: Addressing issues of specificity. *Journal of Abnormal Psychology, 109,* 451–460.

Daley, S. E., et al. (1997). Predictors of the generation of episodic stress: A longitudinal study of late adolescent women. *Journal of Abnormal Psychology, 106,* 251–259.

Damasio, A. R. (1997). Towards a neuropathology of emotion and mood. *Nature, 386,* 769–770.

Damasio, R. (2000). A neural basis for sociopathy. *Archives of General Psychiatry, 57,* 128–129.

Daro, D., & Wiese, D. (1995). *Current trends in child abuse reporting and fatalities: NCPCA's 1994 annual fifty state survey.* Chicago, IL: National Committee to Prevent Child Abuse.

Davidson, J. R. T., et al. (2001). Multicenter, double-blind comparison of sertraline and placebo in the treatment of posttraumatic stress disorder. *Archives of General Psychiatry, 58,* 485–492.

Davidson, P. R., & Parker, K. C. H. (2001). Eye movement desensitization and reprocessing (EMDR): A meta-analysis. *Journal of Consulting and Clinical Psychology, 69,* 305–316.

Davidson, R. J. (2000). Affective style, psychopathology, and resilience: Brain mechanisms and plasticity. *American Psychologist, 55,* 1196–1214.

Davidson, R. J., Putnam, K. M., & Larson, C. L. (2000). Dysfunction in the neural circuitry of emotion regulation—A possible prelude to violence. *Science, 289,* 591–594.

Davis, D. L., & Boster, L. H. (1992). Cognitive-behavioral-expressive interventions with aggressive and resistant youths. *Child Welfare, 71,* 557–573.

Davis, D. L., & Boster, L. H. (1993). Cognitive-behavioral-expressive interventions with aggressive and resistant youth. *Residential-Treatment for Children and Youth, 10,* 55–68.

Daw, J. (2001, April). Survey uncovers communication breakdown in the treatment of depression. *Monitor on Psychology,* p. 69.

DeAngelis, T. (1993, August). It's back: TV violence, concern for kid viewers. *APA Monitor, 24*(8), p. 16.

DeAngelis, T. (1994b, November). Ethnic-minority issues recognized in DSM-IV. *APA Monitor,* p. 36.

DeAngelis, T. (1995a, April). New threat associated with child abuse. *APA Monitor, 26*(4), pp. 1, 38.

DeAngelis, T. (1995b, April). Research documents trauma of abuse. *APA Monitor, 26*(4), p. 34.

DeBell, C., & Jones, R. D. (1997a). As good as it seems? A review of EMDR experimental research. *Professional Psychology: Research and Practice, 28,* 153–163.

DeBell, C., & Jones, R. D. (1997b). Privileged communication at last? An overview of *Jaffee v. Redmond. Professional Psychology: Research and Practice, 28,* 559–566.

De-Carle, A. J., & Pato, M. T. (1996). Social phobia and stuttering. *American Journal of Psychiatry, 153,* 1367–1368.

Deep-Brain Stimulation for Parkinson's Disease Study Group. (2001). Deep-brain stimulation of the subthalamic nucleus or the pars interna of the globus pallidus in Parkinson's disease. *New England Journal of Medicine, 345,* 956–963.

Deffenbacher, J. L., et al. (2000). An application of Beck's cognitive therapy to general anger reduction. *Cognitive Therapy & Research, 24,* 689–697.

Dekker, J. (1993). Inhibited male orgasm. In W. O'Donohue & J. H. Geer (Eds.), *Handbook of sexual dysfunctions: Assessment and treatment* (pp. 279–301). Boston: Allyn & Bacon.

De La Cancela, V., & Guzman, L. P. (1991). Latino mental health service needs: Implications for training psychologists. In H. F. Myers et al. (Eds.), *Ethnic minority perspectives on clinical training and services in psychology* (pp. 59–64). Washington, DC: American Psychological Association.

Delahanty, D. L., & Baum, A. (2001). Stress and breast cancer. In A. Baum, T. A. Revenson, & J. E. Singer (Eds.), *Handbook of health psychology* (pp. 747–756). Mahwah, NJ: Erlbaum.

deMayo, R. A. (1997). Patient sexual behavior and sexual harassment: A national survey of female psychologists. *Professional Psychology: Research and Practice, 28,* 58–62.

Dement, W. C. (1992). The proper use of sleeping pills in the primary care setting. *Journal of Clinical Psychiatry, 53*(12, Suppl.), 50–56.

Denneby, J. A., et al. (1996). Case-control study of suicide by discharged psychiatry patients. *British Medical Journal, 312,* 1580.

Denollet, J., et al. (1996). Personality as independent predictor of long-term mortality in patients with coronary heart disease. *Lancet, 347,* 417–421.

Depression Guideline Panel. (1993a). *Depression in primary care: Vol. 1. Detection and diagnosis.* Clinical Practice Guideline No. 5. Rockville, MD: U.S. Department of Health and Human Services, Public Health Service, Agency for Health Care Policy and Research (AHCPR Pub. No. 93–0550).

Depression Guideline Panel. (1993b). *Depression in primary care: Vol. 2. Treatment of major depression.* Clinical Practice Guideline No. 5. Rockville, MD: U.S. Department of Health and Human Services, Public Health Service, Agency for Health Care Policy and Research (AHCPR Pub. No. 93–0551).

DeRubeis, R. J., & Crits-Christoph, P. (1998). Empirically supported individual and group psychological treatments for adult mental disorders. *Journal of Consulting and Clinical Psychology, 66,* 37–52.

DeRubeis, R. J., Tang, T. Z., & Beck, A. T. (2001). Cognitive therapy. In K. S. Dobson (Ed.), *Handbook of cognitive-behavioral therapies* (2nd ed., pp. 349–392). New York: Guilford Press.

DeRubeis, R. J., et al. (1999). Medications versus cognitive behavior therapy for severely depressed outpatients: Meta-analysis of four randomized comparisons. *American Journal of Psychiatry, 156,* 1007–1013.

De Silva, P. (1993). Post-traumatic stress disorder: Cross-cultural aspects. *International Review of Psychiatry, 5,* 217–229.

Desmond, E. W. (1987, November). Out in the open: Changing attitudes and new research give fresh hope to alcoholics. *Time Magazine,* pp. 80–90.

Dettmer, K., et al. (2001). Take home naloxone and the prevention of deaths from opiate overdose: Two pilot schemes. *British Medical Journal, 322,* 895–896.

Devan, G. S. (1987). Koro and schizophrenia in Singapore. *British Journal of Psychiatry, 150,* 106–107.

DeVeaugh-Geiss J. (1994). Pharmacologic therapy of obsessive compulsive disorder. *Advances in Pharmacology, 30,* 35–52.

Devlin, M. J., Yanovski, S. Z., & Wilson, G. T. (2000). Obesity: What mental health professionals need to know. *American Journal of Psychiatry, 157,* 854–866.

Devor, E. J. (1994). A developmental-genetic model of alcoholism: Implications for genetic research. *Journal of Consulting and Clinical Psychology, 62,* 1108–1115.

Dhaliwal, G. K., et al. (1996). Adult male survivors of childhood sexual abuse: Prevalence, sexual abuse characteristics, and long-term effects. *Clinical Psychology Review, 16,* 619–639.

Dhawan, S., & Marshall, W. L. (1996). Sexual abuse histories of sexual offenders. *Sexual Abuse Journal of Research and Treatment, 8,* 7–15.

Diabetes as looming epidemic. (2001, January 30). *The New York Times,* p. F8.

Diamond, S., Baldwin, R., & Diamond, R. (1963). *Inhibition and choice.* New York: Harper & Row.

Dick, D. M., Rose, R. J., Viken, R. J., Kaprio, J., & Koskenvuo, M. (2001). Exploring gene-environment interactions: Socioregional moderation of alcohol use. *Journal of Abnormal Psychology, 110,* 625–632.

DiLalla, D. L., Carey, G., Gottesman, I. I., & Bouchard, T. J., Jr. (1996). Heritability of MMPI personality indicators of psychopathology in twins reared apart. *Journal of Abnormal Psychology, 105,* 491–499.

Dinh, K. T., et al. (1995). Children's perceptions of smokers and nonsmokers: A longitudinal study. *Health Psychology, 14,* 32–40.

Dip in youth killing, but not in youth drug use. (2000, December 15). *The New York Times,* p. A 28.

Dixit, A. R., & Crum, R. M. (2000). Prospective study of depression and the risk of heavy alcohol use in women. *American Journal of Psychiatry, 157,* 801–807.

Dixon, L., et al. (1997). Assertive community treatment and medication compliance in the homeless mentally ill. *American Journal of Psychiatry, 154,* 1302–1304.

Dobson, K. S., & Dozois, D. J. A. (2001). Historical and philosophical bases of the cognitive-behavioral therapies. In K. S. Dobson (Ed.), *Handbook of cognitive-behavioral therapies* (2nd ed., pp. 3–40). New York: Guilford Press.

Dodge, K. A. (1985). Attributional bias in aggressive children. *Advances in Cognitive Behavioral Research and Therapy, 4,* 73–110.

Dodge, K. A., et al. (1997). Reactive and proactive aggression in school children and psychiatrically impaired chronically assaultive youth. *Journal of Abnormal Psychology, 106,* 37–51.

Doleys, D. M. (1977). Behavioral treatments for nocturnal enuresis in children: A review of the literature. *Psychological Bulletin, 8,* 30–54.

Doll, B. (1996). Prevalence of psychiatric disorders in children and youth: An agenda for advocacy by school psychology. *School Psychology Quarterly, 11,* 20–46.

Donker, F. J. S. (2000). Cardiac rehabilitation: A review of current developments. *Clinical Psychology Review, 20,* 923–943.

Dorahy, M. J. (2001). Dissociative identity disorder and memory dysfunction: The current state of experimental research and its future directions. *Clinical Psychology Review, 21,* 771–795.

Doubt cast on power of placebos: Study finds sham treatment less effective than once thought. (2001, May 23). *MSNBC Web Posting.* Retrieved May 24, 2001, from http://www.msnbc.com/news/577411.asp.

Dougall, A. L., & Baum, A. (2001). Stress, health, and illness. In A. Baum, T. A. Revenson, & J. E. Singer (Eds.), *Handbook of health psychology* (pp. 339–348). Mahwah, NJ: Erlbaum.

Dowker, A., Hermelin, B., & Pring, L. (1996). A savant poet. *Psychological Medicine, 26,* 913–924.

Drake, R. E., et al. (1991). Housing instability and homelessness among rural schizophrenic patients. *American Journal of Psychiatry, 148,* 211–215.

Drewnowski, A. (1997). Taste preferences and food intake. *Annual Review of Nutrition, 17,* 237–253.

Drewnowski, A., et al. (1994). Eating pathology and *DSM-III-R* bulimia nervosa: A continuum of behavior. *American Journal of Psychiatry, 151,* 1217–1219.

Drews, C. D., et al. (1995). Variation in the influence of selected sociodemographic risk factors for mental retardation. *American Journal of Public Health, 85,* 329–334.

Drummond, D. C., & Glautier, S. (1994). A controlled trial of cue exposure treatment in alcohol dependence. *Journal of Consulting and Clinical Psychology, 62,* 809–817.

Druss, B. G., Rosenheck, R. A., & Sledge, W. H. (2000). Health and disability costs of depressive illness in a major U.S. corporation. *American Journal of Psychiatry, 157,* 1274–1278.

Dryden, W. (1984). *Rational-emotive therapy: Fundamentals and innovations.* London: Croom Helm.

Dryden, W., & Ellis, A. (2001). Rational emotive behavior therapy. In K. S. Dobson (Ed.), *Handbook of cognitive-behavioral therapies* (2nd ed., pp. 295–348). New York: Guilford Press.

Du Pont heir found guilty of murder but mentally ill. (1997, February 26). *The New York Times,* p. A10.

Dubovsky, S. (2000, September). Lithium: The oldest specific psychotropic medication. *Journal Watch for Psychiatry,* pp. 73, 76.

Duckworth, G., & McBride, H. (1996). Suicide in old age: A tragedy of neglect. *Canadian Journal of Psychiatry, 41,* 217–222.

Duffy, A., et al. (1998). Psychiatric symptoms and syndromes among adolescent children of parents with lithium-responsive or lithium-nonresponsive bipolar disorder. *American Journal of Psychiatry, 155,* 431–433.

Duffy, F. H. (1994). The role of quantified electroencephalography in psychological research. In G. Dawson & K. W. Fischer (Eds.), *Human behavior and the developing brain* (pp. 93–132). New York: Guilford Press.

Dugger, C. W. (1992, September 3). Threat only when on crack, homeless man foils system. *The New York Times,* pp. A1, B4.

Dugger, C. W. (1994, July 15). Larry Hogue is arrested in Westchester. *The New York Times,* pp. B1, B2.

Dugger, C. W. (1995, January 23). Slipping through cracks and out the door. *The New York Times,* pp. B1, B2.

Dulit, R. A., et al. (1994). Clinical correlates of self-mutilation in borderline personality disorder. *American Journal of Psychiatry, 151,* 1305–1311.

Duman, R. S., Heninger, G. R., & Nestler, E. J. (1997). A molecular and cellular theory of depression. *Archives of General Psychiatry, 54,* 597–606.

Dumas, J. E., Serketich, W. J., & LaFreniere, P. J. (1995). "Balance of power": A transactional analysis of control in mother-child dyads involving socially competent, aggressive, and anxious children. *Journal of Abnormal Psychology, 104,* 104–113.

Duncan, J., et al. (2000). A neural basis for general intelligence. *Science, 289,* 457–460.

Duncan, R. D., et al. (1996). Childhood physical assault as a risk factor for PTSD, depression, and substance abuse: Findings from a national survey. *American Journal of Orthopsychiatry, 66,* 437–447.

Durham v. United States, 214 F. 2d 862 (DC Circ 1954).

Durkheim, E. (1958). *Suicide.* (J. A. Spaulding & G. Simpson, Trans.). New York: Free Press. (Original work published 1897).

Dwyer, M. (1988). Exhibitionism/voyeurism. *Journal of Social Work and Human Sexuality, 7,* 101–112.

Dykens, E. M., & Hodapp, R. M. (1997). Treatment issues in genetic mental retardation syndromes. *Professional Psychology: Research and Practice, 28,* 263–270.

Dyslexia: The interaction of culture and biology. (2001, March 15). *CNN Web Posting.* Retrieved March 16, 2001, from http://www.cnn.com/2001/fyi/teachers.ednews/03/15/dyslexia.reading.ap.

E

Eagly, A. H., & Wood, W. (1991). Explaining sex differences in social behavior: A meta-analytic perspective. *Personality and Social Psychology Bulletin, 17,* 306–315.

Earnst, K .S., & Kring, A. M. (1997). Construct validity of negative symptoms: An empirical and conceptual review. *Clinical Psychology Review, 17,* 167–189.

Eaton, W. W., Dryman, A., & Weissman, M. M. (1991). Panic and phobia. In L. N. Robins & D. A. Regier (Eds.), *Psychiatric disorders in America: The Epidemiologic Catchment Area Study* (pp. 155–179). New York: Free Press.

Eaton, W. W., et al. (1994). Panic and panic disorder in the United States. *American Journal of Psychiatry, 151,* 413–420.

Eaton, W. W., et al. (1997). Natural history of diagnostic interview schedule/*DSM-IV* major depression: The Baltimore Epidemiologic Catchment Area follow-up. *Archives of General Psychiatry, 54,* 993–999.

Eberhardy, F. (1967). The view from "the couch." *Journal of Child Psychological Psychiatry, 8,* 257–263.

Ebigbo, P. O. (1993). Situation analysis of child abuse and neglect in Nigeria. *Journal of Psychology in Africa, 1,* 159–178.

Eckenrode, J., et al. (2000). Preventing child abuse and neglect with a program of nurse home visitation: The limiting effects of domestic violence. *Journal of the American Medical Association, 284,* 1385–1391.

Eckhardt, C. I., Barbour, K. A., & Stuart, G. L. (1997). Anger and hostility in maritally violent men: Conceptual distinctions, measurement issues, and literature review. *Clinical Psychology Review, 17,* 333–358.

Ecstasy use depletes brain chemical, study finds. (2000, July 25). *CNN Web Posting.* Retrieved July 26, 2000, from http://www.cnn.com/2000/HEALTH/07/25/ecstasy.brain.reut/index.html.

Edelson, E. (1998, March 9). Migraines come into focus. *Newsday*, p. C7.

Edinger, J. D., et al. (2001). Cognitive behavioral therapy for treatment of chronic primary insomnia: A randomized controlled trial. *Journal of the American Medical Association, 285*, 1856–1864.

Edman, J. L., & Johnson, R. C. (1999). Filipino American and Caucasian American beliefs about the causes and treatment of mental problems. *Cultural Diversity and Ethnic Minority Psychology, 5*, 380–386.

Edmundson, M. (2001, June 3). I'm O.K, and then some. *The New York Times Book Review*, p. 33.

Edwards, E. D., & Egbert-Edwards, M. (1990). American Indian adolescents: Combating problems of substance use and abuse through a community model. In A. R. Stiffman & L. E. Davis (Eds.), *Ethnic issues in adolescent mental health* (pp. 285–302). Newbury Park, CA: Sage Publications.

Egan, J. (1991). Oppositional defiant disorder. In J. M. Wiener (Ed.), *Textbook of child and adolescent psychiatry*. Washington, DC: American Psychiatric Press.

Egan, M. F., Apud, J., & Wyatt, R. J. (1997). Treatment of tardive dyskinesia. *Schizophrenia Bulletin, 23*, 583–609.

Ehlers, A. (1995). A 1-year prospective study of panic attacks: Clinical course and factors associated with maintenance. *Journal of Abnormal Psychology, 104*, 164–172.

Ehlers, A., Mayou, R. A., & Bryant, B. (1998). Psychological predictors of chronic posttraumatic stress disorder after motor vehicle accidents. *Journal of Abnormal Psychology, 107*, 508–519.

Eiberg, H., Berendt, I., & Mohr, J. (1995). Assignment of dominant inherited nocturnal euresis (ENUR1) to chromosome 13q. *Nature Genetics, 10*, 354–356.

Eichstedt, J. A., & Arnold, S. L. (2001). Childhood-onset obsessive-compulsive disorder. A tic-related subtype of OCD? *Clinical Psychology Review, 21*, 137–157.

Eisenbruch, M. (1992). Toward a culturally sensitive DSM: Cultural bereavement in Cambodian refugees and the traditional healer as taxonomist. *Journal of Nervous and Mental Disease, 180*, 8–10.

Eisler, I., et al. (1997). Family and individual therapy in anorexia nervosa: A 5-year follow-up. *Archives of General Psychiatry, 54*, 1025–1030.

Elkin, I., et al. (1989). National Institute of Mental Health treatment of depression collaborative research program: General effectiveness of treatments. *Archives of General Psychiatry, 46*, 971–982.

Ellason, J. W., & Ross, C. A. (1997). Two-year follow-up of inpatients with dissociative identity disorder. *American Journal of Psychiatry, 154*, 832–839.

Ellickson, P. L., Hays, R. D., & Bell, R. M. (1992). Stepping through the drug use sequence: Longitudinal scalogram analysis of initiation and regular use. *Journal of Abnormal Psychology, 101*, 441–451.

Elliott, A. J., et al. (1998). Randomized, placebo-controlled trial of paroxetine versus imipramine in depressed HIV-positive outpatients. *American Journal of Psychiatry, 155*, 367–372.

Elliott, D. M. (1997). Traumatic events: Prevalence and delayed recall in the general population. *Journal of Consulting and Clinical Psychology*, 811–820.

Ellis, A. (1977a). *Anger: How to live with and without it*. Secaucus, NJ: Citadel Press.

Ellis, A. (1977b). The basic clinical theory of rational-emotive therapy. In A. Ellis & R. Grieger (Eds.), *Handbook of rational-emotive therapy*. New York: Springer.

Ellis, A. (1993). Reflections on rational-emotive therapy. *Journal of Consulting and Clinical Psychology, 61*, 199–201.

Ellis, A. (1997). Using rational emotive behavior therapy techniques to cope with disability. *Professional Psychology: Research and Practice, 28*, 17–22.

Ellis, A. (2001, January). "Intellectual" and "emotional" insight revisited. *NYS Psychologist, 13*, 2–6.

Ellis, A., & Dryden, W. (1987). *The practice of rational emotional therapy*. New York: Springer.

Ellis, A., Young, J., & Lockwood, G. (1989). Cognitive therapy and rational-emotive therapy: A dialogue. *Journal of Cognitive Psychotherapy, 1*, 205–256.

Else, L., et al. (1993). Personality characteristics of men who physically abuse women. *Hospital and Community Psychiatry, 44*, 54–58.

Engdahl, B., et al. (1997). Posttraumatic stress disorder in a community group of former prisoners of war: A normative response to severe trauma. *American Journal of Psychiatry, 154*, 1576–1581.

Epping-Jordan, J. E., Compas, B. E., & Howell, D. C. (1994). Predictors of cancer progression in young adult men and women: Avoidance, intrusive thoughts, and psychological symptoms. *Health Psychology, 13*, 539–547.

Epping-Jordan, J. E., et al. (1999). Psychological adjustment in breast cancer: Processes of emotional distress. *Health Psychology, 18*, 315–326.

Erlenmeyer-Kimling, L., et al. (1997). The New York high-risk project: Prevalence and comorbidity of Axis I disorders in offspring of schizophrenic parents at 25-year follow-up. *Archives of General Psychiatry, 54*, 1096–1102.

Ernst, T., et al. (2000). Evidence for long-term neurotoxicity associated with methamphetamine abuse: A 1HMRS study. *Neurology, 54*, 1344–1349.

Eron, L. D. (1993, August). Cited in DeAngelis, T. (1993b). It's back: TV violence, concern for kid viewers. *APA Monitor, 24*(8), p. 16.

Ertekin-Taner, N., et al. (2000). Linkage of plasma A-42 to a quantitative locus on chromosome 10 in late-onset Alzheimer's disease pedigrees. *Science, 290*, 2303–2304.

Escobar, J. I. (1998). Immigration and mental health: Why are immigrants better off? *Archives of General Psychiatry, 55*, 781–782.

Escobar, J. I., Hoyos Nervi, C., & Gara, M. (2000). Immigration and mental health: Mexican-Americans in the United States. *Harvard Review of Psychiatry, 8*, 64–72.

Escobar, J. I., & Vega, W. A. (2000). Commentary: Mental health and immigration's AAAs: Where are we and where do we go from here? *Journal of Nervous & Mental Disease, 188*, 736–740.

Esparza, J., et al. (2000). Daily energy expenditure in Mexican and USA Pima Indians: Low physical activity as a possible cause of obesity. *International Journal of Obesity and Related Metabolic Disorders, 24*, 55–59.

Espie, C. A., Inglis, S. J., & Harvey, L. (2001). Predicting clinically significant response to cognitive behavior therapy for chronic insomnia in general medical practice: Analyses of outcome data at 12 months posttreatment. *Journal of Consulting and Clinical Psychology, 69*, 58–66.

Espie, C. A., et al. (2001). The clinical effectiveness of cognitive behaviour therapy for chronic insomnia: Implementation and evaluation of a sleep clinic in general medical practice. *Behaviour Research and Therapy, 39*, 45–60.

Essock, S. M., et al. (2000). Cost-effectiveness of clozapine compared with conventional antipsychotic medication for patients in state hospitals. *Archives of General Psychiatry, 57*, 987–994.

Esterling, B. A., L'Abate, L., Murray, E. J., & Pennebaker, J. W. (1999). Empirical foundations for writing in prevention and psychotherapy: Mental and physical health outcomes. *Clinical Psychology Review, 19*, 79–96.

Ettinger, U., et al. (2001). Magnetic resonance imaging of the thalamus in first-episode psychosis. *American Journal of Psychiatry, 158*, 116–118.

Evans, S. W., et al. (2001). Dose-response effects of methylphenidate on ecologically valid measures of academic performance and classroom behavior in adolescents with ADHD. *Experimental and Clinical Psychopharmacology, 9*, 163–175.

Exner, J. E. (1991). *The Rorschach: A comprehensive system: Vol. 2. Interpretation*. New York: Wiley.

Exner, J. E. (1993). *The Rorschach: A comprehensive system: Vol. 1. Basic foundations* (3rd ed.). New York: Wiley.

Extinguishing Alzheimer's. (1998, June 23). *The New York Times*, p. F7.

F

Fabian, J. L. (1991). "Koro: Proposed classification for DSM-IV": Comment. *American Journal of Psychiatry, 148*, 1766.

Fabrega, H. (1990). Hispanic mental health research: A case for cultural psychiatry. *Journal of Behavioral Sciences, 12*, 339–365.

Fabrega, H., Jr. (1992). Diagnosis interminable: Toward a culturally sensitive DSM-IV. *Journal of Nervous and Mental Disease, 180*, 5–7.

Fairburn, C. G., & Wilson, G. T. (Eds.). (1993). *Binge eating: Nature, assessment, and treatment*. New York: Guilford Press.

Fairburn, C. G., et al. (1997). Risk factors for bulimia nervosa: A community-based case-control study. *Archives of General Psychiatry, 54*, 509–517.

Faller, K. C. (1989). Characteristics of a clinical sample of sexually abused children: How boy and girl victims differ. *Child Abuse and Neglect, 13*, 281–291.

Fallon, B. A., et al. (1993). Fluoxetine for hypochondriacal patients without major depression. *Journal of Clinical Psychopharmacology, 13*, 438–441.

Falsetti, S., & Resnick, H. S. (2000). Treatment of PTSD using cognitive and cognitive behavioral therapies. *Journal of Cognitive Psychotherapy, 14*, 261–285.

Fannon, D., et al. (2000). Features of structural brain abnormality detected in first-episode psychosis. *American Journal of Psychiatry, 157*, 1829–1834.

Fanous, A., et al. (2001). Relationship between positive and negative symptoms of schizophrenia and schizotypal symptoms in nonpsychotic relatives. *Archives of General Psychiatry, 58*, 669–673.

Faraone, S. V., Kremen, W. S., & Tsuang, M. T. (1990). Genetic transmission of major affective disorders: Quantitative models and linkage analyses. *Psychological Bulletin, 108*, 109–127.

Faraone, S. V., et al. (1993). Intellectual performance and school failure in children with attention deficit hyperactivity disorders and their siblings. *Journal of Abnormal Psychology, 102*, 616–623.

Faraone, S. V., et al. (2000). Assessing symptoms of attention deficit hyperactivity disorder in children and adults: Which is more valid? *Journal of Consulting and Clinical Psychology, 68*, 830–842.

Faraone, S. V., et al. (2001). Meta-analysis of the association between the 7-repeat allele of the dopamine d4 receptor gene and attention deficit hyperactivity disorder. *American Journal of Psychiatry, 158*, 1052–1057.

Farber, B. A., Brink, D. C., & Raskin, P. M. (1996). *The psychotherapy of Carl Rogers: Cases and commentary* (pp. 74–75). New York: The Guilford Press.

Farberman, R. K. (1997). Public attitudes about psychologists and mental health care: Research to guide the American Psychological Association Public Education Campaign. *Professional Psychology: Research and Practice, 28*, 128–136.

Farmer, R. F. (2000). Issues in the assessment and conceptualization of personality disorders. *Clinical Psychology Review, 20*, 823–851.

Farr, C. B. (1994). Benjamin Rush and American psychiatry. *American Journal of Psychiatry, 151*(Suppl.), 65–73.

Farrell, A. D., Camplair, P. S., & McCullough, L. (1987). Identification of target complaints by computer interview: Evaluation of the Computerized Assessment System for Psychotherapy Evaluation and Research. *Journal of Consulting and Clinical Psychology, 55*, 691–700.

Farrell, A. D., & White, K. S. (1998). Peer influences and drug use among urban adolescents: Family structure and parent/adolescent relationship as protective factors. *Journal of Consulting and Clinical Psychology, 66,* 248–258.

Father's age tied to schizophrenia. (2001, April 12). *MSNBC News Service, Web Posting.* Retrieved April 13, 2001, from http://www.msnbc.com/news/558493.asp.

Fava, M., et al. (1994). Dysfunctional attitudes in major depression: Changes with pharmacotherapy. *Journal of Nervous and Mental Disease, 182,* 45–49.

Fawzy, F. I., & Fawzy, N. W. (1994). A structured psychoeducational intervention for cancer patients. *General Hospital Psychiatry, 16,* 149–192.

Feder, B. J. (1996, May 24). Increase in teen-age smoking sharpest among black males. *The New York Times,* p. A20.

Feinauer, L. L., & Stuart, D. A. (1996). Blame and resilience in women sexually abused as children. *American Journal of Family Therapy, 24,* 31–40.

Feldman, C. M. (1997). Childhood precursors of adult interpartner violence. *Clinical Psychology: Science and Practice, 4,* 307–333.

Felsenfeld, S. (1996). Progress and needs in the genetics of stuttering. *Journal of Fluency Disorders, 21,* 77–103.

Fenichel, O. (1945). *The psychoanalytic theory of neurosis.* New York: Norton.

Fenton, W. S., et al. (1997). Symptoms, subtype, and suicidality in patients with schizophrenia spectrum disorders. *American Journal of Psychiatry, 154,* 199–204.

Ferguson-Peters, M. (1985). Racial socialization of young Black children. In H. & J. L. McAdoo (Eds.), *Black children* (pp. 159–173). Beverly Hills, CA: Sage Publications.

Ferketich, A. K., et al. (2000). Depression as an antecedent to heart disease among women and men in the NHANES I Study. *Archives of Internal Medicine, 160,* 1261–1268.

Ferrans, C. E., Cohen, F. L., & Smith, K. M. (1992). The quality of life of persons with narcolepsy. *Loss, Grief and Care, 5,* 23–32.

Feshbach, S. (1994). Nationalism, patriotism, and aggression: A clarification of functional differences. In L. R. Huesmann (Ed.), *Aggressive behavior: Current perspectives* (pp. 275–291). New York: Plenum Press.

Fiellin, D. A., et al. (2001). Methadone maintenance in primary care: A randomized controlled trial. *Journal of the American Medical Association, 286,* 1724–1731.

Fieve, R. R. (1975). *Moodswings: The third revolution in psychiatry.* New York: Morrow.

Fiez, J. A. (2001). Bridging the gap between neuroimaging and neuropsychology: Using working memory as a case-study. *Journal of Clinical & Experimental Neuropsychology, 23,* 19–31.

Fingerhut, L. A., Ingram, D. D., & Feldman, J. J. (1998). Homicide rates among U.S. teenagers and young adults: Differences by mechanism, level of urbanization, race, and sex, 1987 through 1995. *Journal of the American Medical Association, 280,* 423–427.

Finkelhor, D. (1984). *Child sexual abuse: Theory and research.* New York: Free Press.

Finkelhor, D. (1990). Early and long-term effects of child sexual abuse: An update. *Professional Psychology: Research and Practice, 21,* 325–330.

Finkelhor, D. (1993). Epidemiological factors in the identification of child abuse. Special issue: Clinical recognition of sexually abused children. *Child Abuse and Neglect, 17,* 67–70.

Finkelhor, D., & Russell, D. (1984). Women as perpetrators: Review of the evidence. In D. Finkelhor (Ed.), *Child sexual abuse: Theory and research.* New York: Free Press.

Finkelhor, D., et al. (1990). Sexual abuse in a national survey of adult men and women: Prevalence, characteristics, and risk factors. *Child Abuse and Neglect, 14,* 19–28.

Finkelstein, J. R. J., et al. (1997). Attentional dysfunctions in neuroleptic-naive and neuroleptic-withdrawn

schizophrenic patients and their siblings. *Journal of Abnormal Psychology, 106,* 203–212.

Finney, J. W., & Monahan, S. C. (1996). The cost-effectiveness of treatment for alcoholism: A second approximation. *Journal of Studies on Alcohol, 57,* 229–243.

Fishbain, D. A. (1991). "Koro: Proposed classification for DSM-IV": Comment. *American Journal of Psychiatry, 148,* 1765–1766.

Fisher, B. S., Cullen, F. T., & Turner, M. (2000). *The sexual victimization of college women.* Washington, DC: U.S. Bureau of Justice Statistics.

Fisman, S., & Takhar, J. (1996). "Fear of alien abduction": Reply. *Journal of the American Academy of Child and Adolescent Psychiatry, 35,* 556–557.

Fitzgerald, L. F. (1993a). Sexual harassment: Violence against women in the workplace. *American Psychologist, 48,* 1070–1076.

Fitzgerald, L. F. (1993b). *Sexual harassment in higher education: Concepts and issues.* Washington, DC: National Education Association.

Fitzgerald, L. F., et al. (1988). The incidence and dimensions of sexual harassment in academia and the workplace. *Journal of Vocational Behavior, 32,* 152–175.

Flannery, D. J., Singer, M. I., & Wester, K. (2001). Violence exposure, psychological trauma, and suicide risk in a community sample of dangerously violent adolescents. *Journal of American Academy of Child & Adolescent Psychiatry, 40,* 435–442.

Flint, A. J. (1994). Epidemiology and comorbidity of anxiety disorders in the elderly. *American Journal of Psychiatry, 151,* 640–649.

Flint, J., et al. (1995). The detection of subtelomeric chromosomal rearrangements in idiopathic mental retardation. *Nature Genetics, 9,* 132–140.

Flournoy, P. S., & Wilson, G. L. (1991). Assessment of MMPI profiles of male batterers. *Violence and Victims, 6,* 309–320.

Foa, E. B. (1990, August/September). Obsessive-compulsive disorder. In *American Psychiatric Association, DSM-IV Update.* Washington, DC: American Psychiatric Association.

Foa, E. B. (1996). The efficacy of behavioral therapy with obsessive-compulsives. *The Clinical Psychologist, 49,* 19–21.

Foa, E. B., & Kozak, M. J. (1995). *DSM-IV* field trial: Obsessive-compulsive disorder. *American Journal of Psychiatry, 152,* 90–96.

Foa, E. B., et al. (1999). A comparison of exposure therapy, stress inoculation training, and their combination for reducing posttraumatic stress disorder in female assault victims. *Journal of Consulting and Clinical Psychology, 67,* 194–200.

Foderaro, L. W. (1994, November 8). "Clubhouse" helps mentally ill find the way back. *The New York Times,* p. B1.

Fogelholm, M., Kukkonen-Harjual, K., Nenonen, A., & Pasenen, M. (2000). Effects of walking training on weight maintenance after a very-low-energy diet in premenopausal obese women: A randomized controlled trial. *Archives of Internal Medicine, 160,* 2177–2184.

Follette, W. C., & Houts, A. C. (1996). Models of scientific progress and the role of theory and taxonomy development: A case study of the *DSM. Journal of Consulting and Clinical Psychology, 64,* 1120–1132.

Follingstad, D. R., Neckerman, A. P., & Vormbrock, J. (1988). Reactions to victimization and coping strategies of battered women: The ties that bind. *Clinical Psychology Review, 8,* 373–390.

Ford, C. S., & Beach, F. A. (1951). *Patterns of sexual behavior.* New York: Harper & Row.

Ford, J. M., et al. (2001). Cortical responsiveness during inner speech in schizophrenia: An event-related potential study. *American Journal of Psychiatry, 158,* 1914–1916.

Forehand, R., Brody, G., Slotkin, J., Fauber, R., McCombs, A., & Long, N. (1988). Young adolescent and maternal

depression: Assessment, interrelations, and family predictors. *Journal of Consulting and Clinical Psychology, 56,* 422–426.

Forman, D. N., et al. (2000). Postpartum depression: Identification of women at risk. *British Journal of Obstetrics and Gynaecology, 107,* 1210–1217.

Foster, G. D., et al. (1997). What is a reasonable weight loss? Patients' expectations and evaluations of obesity treatment outcomes. *Journal of Consulting and Clinical Psychology, 65,* 79–85.

Foster, S. L., & Cone, J. D. (1986). Design and use of direct observation procedures. In A. R. Ciminiero, K. S. Calhoun, & H. E. Adams (Eds.), *Handbook of behavioral assessment* (2nd ed., pp. 253–324). New York: Wiley.

Fowles, D. C. (1993). Electrodermal activity and antisocial behavior: Empirical findings and theoretical issues. In J. C. Roy et al. (Eds.), *Psychological theories of drinking and alcoholism* (pp. 181–226). New York: Guilford Press.

Fox, J. A., & Zawitz, M. W. (2000). *Homicide trends in the United States: 1998 Update.* Washington, DC: U.S. Department of Justice, Bureau of Justice Statistics.

Fox, M. (2000, August 21). Autism checks urged for all babies. *Reuters Limited, MSNBC Web Posting.* Retrieved August 23, 2000, from http://www. msnbc. com/news/449244.asp.

Fox, M. (2001, January 29). Strong family-heart disease tie found. *Reuters Web Posting.* Retrieved January 31, 2001, from http://www.msnbc.com/news/523336.asp.

Foxhall, K. (2000a, October). Platform for a long-term push. *Monitor on Psychology,* p. 30.

Foxhall, K. (2000b, October). Dispatches from the prescription privileges fronts. *Monitor on Psychology,* pp. 30–31.

Foxhall, K. (2001a, January). Suicide by profession: Lots of confusion, inconclusive data. *Monitor on Psychology,* p. 19.

Foxhall, K. (2001b, March). Study finds marital stress can triple women's risk of recurrent coronary event. *Monitor on Psychology, 32,* p. 14.

Foy, D. W., Resnick, H. S., Sipprele, R. C., & Carroll, E. M. (1987). Premilitary, military, and postmilitary factors in the development of combat-related posttraumatic stress disorder. *The Behavior Therapist, 10,* 3–9.

Frackiewicz, E. J., Sramek, J. J., Herrera, J. M., & Cutler, N. R. (1999). Review of neuroleptic dosage in different ethnic groups. In J. M. Herrera et al. (Eds.), *Cross cultural psychiatry* (pp. 107–130). Chichester, England: Wiley.

Frank, E., Brogan, D., & Schiffman, M. (1998). Harassment among U.S. women physicians. *Archives of Internal Medicine, 158,* 352–358.

Frankl, V. E. (1959). *Man's search for meaning.* Boston: Beacon Press.

Franklin, M. E., et al. (2000). Effectiveness of exposure and ritual prevention for obsessive-compulsive disorder: Randomized compared with nonrandomized samples. *Journal of Consulting and Clinical Psychology, 68,* 594–602.

Fraser, J. S. (1996). All that glitters is not always gold: Medical offset effects and managed behavioral health care. *Professional Psychology: Research & Practice, 27,* 335–344.

Frauenglass, S., et al. (1997). Family support decreases influence of deviant peers on Hispanic adolescent's substance use. *Journal of Clinical Child Psychology, 26,* 15–23.

Freed, A. O. (1992). Discussion: Minority elderly. *Journal of Geriatric Psychiatry, 25,* 105–111.

Freedman, R., et al. (1987). Neurobiological studies of sensory gating in schizophrenia. *Schizophrenia Bulletin, 13,* 669–678.

Freeman, L. N., Shaffer, D., & Smith, H. (1996). The neglected victims of homicide: The needs of young siblings of murder victims. *American Journal of Orthopsychiatry, 66,* 337–345.

Freemon, F. R. (1981). *Organic mental disease.* Jamaica, NY: Spectrum.

Freiberg, P. (1995, June). Psychologists examine attacks on homosexuals. *APA Monitor, 26*(6), pp. 30–31.

French, S. A., & Jeffery, R. W. (1994). Consequences of dieting to lose weight: Effects on physical and mental health. *Health Psychology, 13,* 195–212.

Freud, S. (1957). Mourning and melancholia (1917). In J. Rickman (Ed.), *A general selection from the works of Sigmund Freud.* Garden City, NY: Doubleday.

Freud, S. (1959a). Analysis of a phobia in a 5-year-old boy. In A. J. Strachey (Ed. & Trans.), *Collected papers. Vol. 3.* New York: Basic Books. (Original work published 1909)

Freud, S. (1964). New introductory lectures. In *Standard edition of the complete psychological works of Sigmund Freud (Vol. 22).* London: Hogarth. (Original work published in 1933)

Freund, K., & Blanchard, R. (1986). The concept of courtship disorder. *Journal of Sex and Marital Therapy, 12,* 79–92.

Frick, P. J., et al. (1992). Familial risk factors to oppositional defiant disorder and conduct disorder: Parental psychopathology and maternal parenting. *Journal of Consulting and Clinical Psychology, 60,* 49–55.

Fried, L. P., et al. (1998). Risk factors for 5 year mortality in older adults: The Cardiovascular Health Study. *Journal of the American Medical Association, 279,* 585–592.

Friedman, M., & Rosenman, R. H. (1974). *Type A behavior and your heart.* New York: Harper & Row.

Friedman, M., & Ulmer, D. (1984). *Treating Type A behavior and your heart.* New York: Fawcett Crest.

Friedman, M., et al. (1986). Alteration of type A behavior and its effect on cardiac recurrences in postmyocardial infarction patients: Summary results of the recurrent coronary prevention project. *American Heart Journal, 112,* 653–665.

Fromm-Reichmann, F. (1948). Notes on the development of treatment of schizophrenics by psychoanalytic psychotherapy. *Psychiatry, 11,* 263–273.

Fromm-Reichmann, F. (1950). *Principles of intensive psychotherapy.* Chicago: University of Chicago Press.

Frueh, B. C., et al. (1996). Trauma management therapy: A preliminary evaluation of a multicomponent behavioral treatment for chronic combat-related PTSD. *Behaviour Research and Therapy, 34,* 533–543.

Fuchs, C. S., et al. (1995). Alcohol consumption and mortality among women. *The New England Journal of Medicine, 332,* 1245–1250.

Fuchs, M. (2001, June 9). For Alzheimer's patients, some solace, if not hope. *The New York Times,* pp. B1, B6.

Fulero, S. M. (1988). Tarasoff: 10 years later. *Professional Psychology: Research and Practice, 19,* 184–190.

G

Gabbard, G. O., et al. (1997). The economic impact of psychotherapy: A review. *American Journal of Psychiatry, 154,* 147–155.

Galassi, J. P. (1988). Four cognitive-behavioral approaches: Additional considerations. *The Counseling Psychologist, 16*(1), 102–105.

Gall, R., Isaac, L., & Kryger, M. (1993). Quality of life in mild obstructive sleep apnea. *Sleep, 16*(Suppl.), S59–S61.

Gallant, J. E. (2000). Strategies for long-term success in the treatment of HIV infection. *Journal of the American Medical Association, 283,* 1329–1334.

Ganellen, R. J. (1996). Comparing the diagnostic efficiency of the MMPI, MCMI-II, and Rorschach: A review. *Journal of Personality Assessment, 67,* 219–243.

Garb, H. N. (1997). Race bias, social class bias, and gender bias in clinical judgment. *Clinical Psychology: Science and Practice, 4,* 99–120.

Garb, H. N. (2000). Computers will become increasingly important for psychological assessment: Not that there's anything wrong with that! *Psychological Assessment, 12,* 31–39.

Garber, J., Weiss, B., & Shanley, N. (1993). Cognitions, depressive symptoms, and development in adolescents. *Journal of Abnormal Psychology, 102,* 47–57.

Garbutt, J. C., et al. (1999). Pharmacological treatment of alcohol dependence. *Journal of the American Medical Association, 281,* 1318–1325.

Garcia, M., & Marks, G. (1989). Depressive symptomatology among Mexican-American adults: An examination with the CES-D scale. *Psychiatry Research, 27,* 137–148.

Gardiner, S. (1992). Out of harm's way: Intervention with children in shelters. Special issue: Feminist perspectives in child and youth care practices. *Journal of Child and Youth Care, 7,* 41–48.

Gardner, W., et al. (1996). Clinical versus actuarial predictions of violence in patients with mental illnesses. *Journal of Consulting and Clinical Psychology, 64,* 602–609.

Garfield, S. L. (1994). Eclecticism and integration in psychotherapy: Developments and issues. *Clinical Psychology: Science and Practice, 1,* 123–137.

Garner, D. M. (1993). Binge eating in anorexia nervosa. In C. G. Fairburn & G. T. Wilson (Eds.), *Binge eating: Nature, assessment, and treatment* (pp. 50–76). New York: Guilford.

Gatchel, R. J. (2001). Biofeedback and self-regulation of physiological activity: A major adjunctive treatment modality in health psychology. In A. Baum, T. A. Revenson, & J. E. Singer (Eds.), *Handbook of health psychology* (pp. 95–104). Mahwah, NJ: Erlbaum.

Gaulin, S. J. C., & McBurney, D. H. (2001). *Psychology: An evolutionary approach.* Upper Saddle River, NJ: Prentice-Hall.

Gauthier, J. G., Ivers, H., & Carrier, S. (1996). Nonpharmacological approaches in the management of recurrent headache disorders and their comparison and combination with pharmacotherapy. *Clinical Psychology Review, 16,* 543–571.

Gawin, F. H. (1991). Cocaine addiction: Psychology and neurophysiology. *Science, 251,* 1581.

Gawin, F. H., et al. (1989). Desipramine facilitation of initial cocaine abstinence. *Archives of General Psychiatry, 46,* 117–121.

Gaziano, J. M. (1993). Moderate alcohol intake, increased levels of high-density lipoprotein and its subfractions, and decreased risk of myocardial infarction. *New England Journal of Medicine, 329,* 1829–1834.

Ge, X., et al. (1994). Parents' stressful life events and adolescent depressed mood. *Journal of Health and Social Behavior, 35,* 28–44.

Gebhard, P. H., Gagnon, J. H., Pomeroy, W. B., & Christenson, C. V. (1965). *Sex offenders: An analysis of types.* New York: Harper & Row.

Geddes, J., et al. (2000). Atypical antipsychotics in the treatment of schizophrenia: Systematic overview and meta-regression analysis. *British Medical Journal, 321,* 1371–1376.

Geer, J., Heiman, J., & Leitenberg, H. (1984). *Human sexuality.* Englewood Cliffs, NJ: Prentice-Hall.

Gelman, D. (1994, April 18). The mystery of suicide. *Newsweek,* pp. 44–49.

George, M. S., et al. (2001). Activation of prefrontal cortex and anterior thalamus in alcoholic subjects on exposure to alcohol-specific cues. *Archives of General Psychiatry, 58,* 345–352.

Gershon, E. S., & Rieder, R. O. (1992). Major disorders of mind and brain. *Scientific American, 267*(3), 126–133.

Gershuny, B. S., & Thayer, J. F. (1999). Relations among psychological trauma, dissociative phenomena, and trauma-related distress: A review and integration. *Clinical Psychology Review, 19,* 631–657.

Ghanshyam, N., et al. (1995). Platelet serotonin-2A receptors: A potential biological marker for suicidal behavior. *American Journal of Psychiatry, 152,* 850–855.

Giancola, P. R., & Zeichner, A. (1997). The biphasic effects of alcohol on human physical aggression. *Journal of Abnormal Psychology, 106,* 598–607.

Gibbs, N. (1991, June 3). When is it rape? *Time Magazine,* pp. 48–54.

Gibbs, N. (1998, November 30). The age of Ritalin. *Time,* pp. 84–94.

Gidron, Y., & Davidson, K. (1996). Development and preliminary testing of a brief intervention for modifying CHD-predictive hostility components. *Journal of Behavioral Medicine, 19,* 203–220.

Gidron, Y., Davidson, K., & Bata, I. (1999). The short-term effects of a hostility-reduction intervention on male coronary heart disease patients. *Health Psychology, 18,* 416–420.

Giembycz, M. A., & O'Connor, B. J. (2000). *Asthma: Epidemiology, anti-inflammatory therapy and future trends.* Boston: Birkhauser.

Gil, K. M., et al. (1990). The relationship of negative thoughts to pain and psychological distress. *Behavior Therapy, 21,* 349–362.

Gilbert, S. (1997a, January 22). Lag seen in aid for depression. *The New York Times,* p. C9.

Gilbert, S. (1997b, June 25). Social ties reduce risk of a cold. *The New York Times,* p. C11.

Gilboa-Schechtman, E., & Foa, E. B. (2001). Patterns of recovery from trauma: The use of intraindividual analysis. *Journal of Abnormal Psychology, 110,* 392–400.

Gill, A. R. (2001). Interventions for autism. In reply. *Journal of the American Medical Association, 286,* 670–671. [Letter]

Gillberg, C., et al. (1997). Long-term stimulant treatment of children with attention-deficit hyperactivity disorder symptoms: A randomized, double-blind, placebo-controlled trial. *Archives of General Psychiatry, 54,* 857–864.

Gillin, J. C. (1991). The long and the short of sleeping pills. *The New England Journal of Medicine, 324,* 1735–1736.

Gilroy, L., et al. (2000). Controlled comparison of computer-raided vicarious exposure versus live exposure in the treatment of spider phobia. *Behavior Therapy, 31,* 733–744.

Gitlin, M. J., & Pasnau, R. O. (1989). Psychiatric syndromes linked to reproductive function in women: A review of current knowledge. *American Journal of Psychiatry, 146,* 1413–1422.

Gittelman-Klein, R., & Mannuzza, S. (1990). Hyperactive boys almost grown up. *Archives of General Psychiatry, 45,* 1131–1134.

Glantz, K., et al. (1996). Virtual reality (VR) for psychotherapy: From the physical to the social environment. *Psychotherapy, 33,* 464–473.

Glantz, L. A., & Lewis, D. A. (2000). Decreased dendritic spine density on prefrontal cortical pyramidal neurons in schizophrenia. *Archives of General Psychiatry, 57,* 65–73.

Glara, M. A., et al. (1993). Perceptions of self and other in major depression. *Journal of Abnormal Psychology, 102,* 93–100.

Glaser, R., et al. (1987). Stress-related immune suppression: Health implications. *Brain, Behavior, and Immunity, 1,* 7–20.

Glaser, R., Kiecolt-Glaser, J. K., Speicher, C. E., & Holliday, J. E. (1985). Stress, loneliness, and changes in herpes virus latency. *Journal of Behavioral Medicine, 8,* 249–260.

Glass, R. M. (2000). Panic disorder—It's real and it's treatable. *Journal of the American Medical Association, 283,* 2573–2574. [Editorial]

Glass, R. M. (2001). Electroconvulsive therapy: Time to bring it out of the shadows. *Journal of the American Medical Association, 285,* 1346–1348. [Editorial]

Gleaves, D. H. (1996). The sociocognitive model of disso-ciative identity disorder: A reexamination of the evi-dence. *Psychological Bulletin, 120,* 42–59.

Glynn, S., & Mueser, K. T. (1986). Social learning for chronic mental inpatients. *Schizophrenia Bulletin, 12,* 648–668.

Glynn, S., & Mueser, K. T. (1992). Social learning. In R. P. Liberman (Ed.), *Handbook of psychiatric rehabilitation* (pp. 127–152). New York: Macmillan.

Goddard, A. W., et al. (2001). Reductions in occipital cor-tex GABA levels in panic disorder detected with 1h-magnetic spectroscopy. *Archives of General Psychiatry, 58,* 556–561.

Goenjian, A. K., et al. (2001). Posttraumatic stress and depressive reactions among Nicaraguan adolescents after Hurricane Mitch. *American Journal of Psychiatry, 158,* 788–794.

Goetz, K. L., & Price, T. R. P. (1994). The case of koro: Treatment response and implications for diagnostic classification. *Journal of Nervous and Mental Disease, 182,* 590–591.

Goff, D, C., & Summs, C. A. (1993). Has multiple person-ality disorder remained consistent over time? A com-parison of past and recent cases. *Journal of Nervous and Mental Disease, 181,* 595–600.

Goisman, R. M., et al. (1994). Panic, agoraphobia, and panic disorder with agoraphobia: Data from a multi-center anxiety disorders study. *Journal of Nervous and Mental Disease, 182,* 72–79.

Gold, S. R., & Gold, R. G. (1993). Sexual aversions: A hid-den disorder. In W. O'Donohue & J. H. Geer (Eds.), *Handbook of sexual dysfunctions: Assessment and treat-ment* (pp. 83–102). Boston: Allyn & Bacon.

Goldberg, C. (2001, July 9). Children trapped by mental illness. *The New York Times,* pp. A1, A11.

Goldberg, I. J., et al. (2001). Wine and your heart: A sci-ence advisory for healthcare professionals from the Nutrition Committee, Council on Epidemiology and Prevention, and Council on Cardiovascular Nursing of the American Heart Association. *Circulation, 103,* 472–475.

Golden, C. J., Hammeke, T. A., & Purisch, A. D. (1980). *The Luria-Nebraska Neuropsychological Battery: Man-ual.* Los Angeles: Western Psychological Services.

Golden, O. (2000). The federal response to child abuse and neglect. *American Psychologist, 55,* 1050–1053.

Goldfarb, L. A., Dynens, E. M., & Gerrard, M. (1985). The Goldfarb fear of fat scale. *Journal of Personality Assess-ment, 49,* 329–332.

Goldstein, A. J., et al. (2000). EMDR for panic disorder with agoraphobia: Comparison with waiting list and credible attention-placebo control conditions. *Journal of Consulting and Clinical Psychology, 68,* 947–956.

Goldstein, I., et al. (1998). Oral sildenafil in the treatment of erectile dysfunction. *The New England Journal of Medicine, 338,* 1397–1404.

Goldstein, M. J. (1987). The UCLA high-risk project. *Schizophrenia Bulletin, 13,* 505–514.

Goldstein, R. L. (1986). Erotomania. *American Journal of Psychiatry, 143,* 802.

Goleman, D. (1988b, November 1). Narcissism looming larger as root of personality woes. *The New York Times,* pp. C1, C16.

Goleman, D. (1990a, June 26). Scientists pinpoint brain irregularities in drug addicts. *The New York Times,* pp. C1, C7.

Goleman, D. (1990b, December 6). Women's depression is higher. *The New York Times.*

Goleman, D. (1991, October 22). Sexual harassment: It's about power, not lust. *The New York Times,* pp. C1, C12.

Goleman, D. (1992a, April 14). Therapies offer hope for sex offenders. *The New York Times,* pp. C1, C11.

Goleman, D. (1992b, October 14). Study ties genes to drinking in women as much as in men. *The New York Times,* p. C14.

Goleman, D. (1993c, October 6). Abuse-prevention efforts aid children. *The New York Times,* p. C13.

Goleman, D. (1993e, December 7). Stress and isolation tied to a reduced life span. *The New York Times,* p. C5.

Goleman, D. (1994a, January 11). Childhood depression may herald adult ills. *The New York Times,* pp. C1, C10.

Goleman, D. (1994c, April 19). Revamping psychiatrists' bible. *The New York Times,* pp. C1, C11.

Goleman, D. (1994d, April 26). Mental decline in aging need not be inevitable. *The New York Times,* p. C1, C10.

Goleman, D. (1995b, May 2). Biologists find site of work-ing memory. *The New York Times,* pp. C 1, C9.

Goleman, D. (1995e, July 1). A genetic clue to bed-wetting is located. *The New York Times,* p. A8.

Goleman, D. (1995g, October 4). Eating disorder rates surprise experts. *The New York Times,* p. C11.

Goode, E. (2000a, October 24). Watching volunteers, experts seek clues to eating disorders. *The New York Times,* pp. F1, F6.

Goode, E. (2000b, March 14). Human nature: Born or made? *The New York Times,* pp. F1, F9.

Goode, E. (2001a, February 20). What's in an inkblot? Some say, not much. *The New York Times,* pp. F1, F4.

Goode, E. (2001b, February 20). Samson diagnosis: Anti-social personality disorder, with muscles. *The New York Times,* p. F7.

Goode, E. (2001c, May 22). For users of heroin, decades of despair. *The New York Times,* p. F5.

Goode, E. (2001d, August 27). Disparities seen in mental care for minorities. *The New York Times,* pp. A1, A12.

Goode, E. (2001e, April 10). "A new improved me": Now appearing everywhere. *The New York Times,* p. F7.

Goode, E. (2001f, August 1). Study says 20% of girls reported abuse by a date. *The New York Times,* p. A10.

Goodstein, L., & Connelly, M. (1998, April 30). Teen-age poll finds a turn to the traditional. *The New York Times,* p. A20.

Gordis, E. (1995). The National Institute on Alcohol Abuse and Alcoholism. *Alcohol Health & Research World, 19,* 5–11.

Gordis, E. (1999, May 5). *What we know: Conceptual advances in alcohol research.* National Institute on Alco-hol Abuse and Alcoholism (NIAAA). Retrieved July 13, from http://www.niaaa.nih.gov/about/conceptual.htm.

Gordon, C. M., & Carey, M. P. (1996). Alcohol's effects on requisites for sexual risk reduction in men: An initial experimental investigation. *Health Psychology, 15,* 56–60.

Gormally, J., Sipps, G., Raphael, R., Edwin, D., & Varvil-Weld, D. (1981). The relationship between maladap-tive cognitions and social anxiety. *Journal of Consulting and Clinical Psychology, 49,* 300–301.

Gorman, C. (1998, November 30). How does it work? *Time,* p. 92.

Gorman, J. M., Kent, J. M., Sullivan, G. M., & Coplan, J. D. (2000). Neuroanatomical hypothesis of panic disorder, revised. *American Journal of Psychiatry, 57,* 493–505.

Gorman, J. M., et al. (2001). Physiological changes during carbon dioxide inhalation in patients with panic disor-der, major depression, and premenstrual dysphoric disorder: Evidence for a central fear mechanism. *Archives of General Psychiatry, 58,* 125–131.

Gorwood, P., et al. (1995). Gender and age at onset in schizophrenia: Impact of family history. *American Journal of Psychiatry, 152,* 208–212.

Gosselin, C., & Wilson, G. (1980). *Sexual variations.* New York: Simon & Schuster.

Gotlib, I. H., et al. (1993). Negative cognitions and attri-butional style in depressed adolescents: An examina-tion of stability and specificity. *Journal of Abnormal Psychology, 102,* 607–615.

Gottesman, I. I. (1991). *Schizophrenia genetics: The origins of madness.* New York: Freeman.

Gottesman, I. I., McGuffin, P., & Farmer, A. E. (1987). Clinical genetics as clues to the "real" genetics of schiz-ophrenia. *Schizophrenia Bulletin, 13,* 23–47.

Gould, R., Miller, B. L., Goldberg, M. A., & Benson, D. F. (1986). The validity of hysterical signs and symptoms. *The Journal of Nervous and Mental Disease, 174,* 593–597.

Gould, R. A., et al. (1997). Cognitive-behavioral and pharmacological treatment for social phobia: A meta-analysis. *Clinical Psychology: Science and Practice, 4,* 291–306.

Gouzoulis-Mayfrank, E., et al. (2000). Impaired cognitive performance in drug free users of recreational ecstasy (MDMA). *Journal of Neurology, Neurosurgery, & Psy-chiatry, 68,* 719–725.

Grady, D. (1997a, January 21). Brain-tied gene defect may explain why schizophrenics hear voices. *The New York Times,* pp. C1, C3.

Graham, J. R. (2000). *MMPI-2: Assessing personality and psychopathology.* New York: Oxford University Press.

Graham, J. R., & Strenger, V. E. (1988). MMPI characteris-tics of alcoholics: A review. *Journal of Consulting and Clinical Psychology, 56,* 197–205.

Graham-Bermann, S. A., & Edleson, J. L. (Eds.). (2001). *Domestic violence in the lives of children: The future of research, intervention, and social policy* (pp. 35–65). Washington, DC: American Psychological Association.

Grange, D., Telch, C. F., & Tibbs, J. (1998). Eating attitudes and behaviors in 1,435 South African caucasian and non-caucasian college students. *American Journal of Psychiatry, 155,* 250–254.

Grant, B. F. (1997). Prevalence and correlates of alcohol use and *DSM-IV* alcohol dependence in the United States: Results of the National Longitudinal Alcohol Epidemiologic Survey. *Journal of Studies on Alcohol, 58,* 464–473.

Grant, B. F., et al. (1994). Prevalence of *DSM-IV* alcohol abuse and dependence: United States, 1992. *Alcohol Health & Research World, 18,* 243–248.

Gray-Little, B., & Hafdahl, A. R. (2000). Factors influenc-ing racial comparisons of self-esteem: A quantitative review. *Psychological Bulletin, 126,* 26–54.

Greenberg, R. P., & Bornstein, R. F. (1988a). The depen-dent personality: I. Risk for physical disorders. *Journal of Personality Disorders, 2,* 126–135.

Greenberg, R. P., & Bornstein, R. F. (1988b). The depen-dent personality: II. Risk for psychological disorders. *Journal of Personality Disorders, 2,* 136–143.

Greenberg, R. P., Bornstein, R. F., Greenberg, M. D., & Fisher, S. (1992). A meta-analysis of antidepressant outcome under "blinder" conditions. *Journal of Con-sulting and Clinical Psychology, 60,* 664–669.

Greenberg, R. P., et al. (1994). A meta-analysis of fluoxe-tine outcome in the treatment of depression. *Journal of Nervous and Mental Disease, 182,* 547–551.

Greenberger, E., Chen, C., &. Tally, S. R. (2000). Family, peer, and individual correlates of depressive sympto-matology among U.S. and Chinese adolescents. *Journal of Consulting and Clinical Psychology, 68,* 209–219.

Greene, B. (2000). Gender, sex and culture: Gender and culture. In A. Kazdin (Ed.), *Encyclopedia of psychology.* Washington, DC: American Psychological Association Press.

Greene, B. A. (1985). Considerations in the treatment of Black patients by White therapists. *Psychotherapy, 22,* 389–393.

Greene, B. A. (1986). When the therapist is White and the patient is Black: Considerations for psychotherapy in the feminist heterosexual and lesbian communities. *Women & Therapy, 5,* 41–65.

Greene, B. A. (1990). Sturdy bridges: The role of African American mothers in the socialization of African American children. *Women & Therapy, 10,* 205–225.

Greene, B. A. (1992b). Black feminist psychotherapy. In E. Wright (Ed.), *Psychoanalysis and feminism: A critical dictionary* (pp. 34–35). Oxford, U.K.: Basil Blackwell.

Greene, B. A. (1992c). Still here: A perspective on psychotherapy with African American women. In J. Chrisler & D. Howard (Eds.), *New directions in feminist psychology*. New York: Springer.

Greene, B. A. (1993a, Spring). Psychotherapy with African American women: The integration of feminist and psychodynamic approaches. *Journal of Training and Practice in Professional Psychology, 7*, 49–66.

Greene, B. A. (1993b). African American women. In L. Comas-Diaz & B. Greene (Eds.), *Women of color and mental health*. New York: Guilford Press.

Greenhill, L. L. (1998). Childhood attention deficit hyperactivity disorder: Pharmacological treatments. In P. E. Nathan & J. M. Gorman (Eds.), *A guide to treatments that work* (pp. 42–64). New York: Oxford University Press.

Greenhouse, C. J. (1998). Tuning to a key of gladness. *Law and Society Review, 32*, 5–21.

Greenhouse, L. (1992, June 23). Defendants must prove incompetency. *The New York Times*, p. A17.

Greenwald, R. (1996). The information gap in the EMDR controversy. *Professional Psychology: Research & Practice, 27*, 67–72.

Griffith, J. (1983). Relationship between acculturation and psychological impairment in adult Mexican-Americans. *Hispanic Journal of Behavioral Sciences, 5*, 431–459.

Griffiths, K. M., & Christensen, H. (2000). Quality of web-based information on treatment of depression: Cross sectional survey. *British Medical Journal, 16*, 1511–1515.

Griffiths, M. (1999). Internet addiction: Fact or fiction? *Psychologist, 12*, 246–250.

Grissett, N. I., & Norvell, N. K. (1992). Perceived social support, social skills and quality of relationships in bulimic women. *Journal of Consulting and Clinical Psychology, 60*, 293–299.

Grissom, R. J. (1996). The magical number .7 + -.2: Meta-meta-analysis of the probability of superior outcome in comparisons involving therapy, placebo, and control. *Journal of Consulting and Clinical Psychology, 64*, 973–982.

Grob, G. N. (1983). *Mental illness and American society, 1875–1940*. Princeton, NJ: Princeton University Press.

Grob, G. N. (1994). *The mad among us: A history of the care of America's mentally ill*. New York: Free Press.

Grof, P., & Alda, M. (2000). Discrepancies in the efficacy of lithium. *Archives of General Psychiatry, 57*, 191.

Gronbaek, M., et al. (2000). Type of alcohol consumed and mortality from all causes, coronary hear disease, and cancer. *Annals of Internal Medicine, 133*, 411–419.

Groth, A., & Hobson, W. (1983). The dynamics of sexual assault. In L. Schlesinger & E. Revitch (Eds.), *Sexual dynamics of antisocial behavior*. Springfield, IL: Thomas.

Guarnaccia, P. J., Angel, R., & Worobey, J. L. (1991). The impact of marital status and employment status on depressive affect for Hispanic Americans. *Journal of Community Psychology, 19*, 136–149.

Guarnaccia, P. J., & Rodriguez, O. (1996). Concepts of culture and their role in the development of culturally competent mental health services. *Hispanic Journal of Behavioral Sciences, 18*, 419–443.

Guerra, N. G., et al. (1995). Stressful events and individual beliefs as correlates of economic disadvantage and aggression among urban children. *Journal of Consulting and Clinical Psychology, 63*, 518–528.

Guertin, T. L. (1999). Eating behavior of bulimics, self-identified binge eaters, and noon-eating disordered individuals: What differentiates these populations? *Clinical Psychology Review, 19*, 1–24.

Gullette, E. C. D., et al. (1997). Effects of mental stress on myocardial ischemia during daily life. *Journal of the American Medical Association, 277*, 1521–1526.

Gunderson, J. G. (1996). The borderline patient's intolerance of aloneness: Insecure attachments and therapist

availability. *American Journal of Psychiatry, 153*, 752–758.

Gunderson, J. G., & Phillips, K. A. (1991). A current view of the interface between borderline personality disorder and depression. *American Journal of Psychiatry, 148*, 967–975.

Gunderson, J. G., & Singer, M. T. (1986). Defining borderline patients: An overview. In M. H. Stone (Ed.), *Essential papers on borderline disorders* (pp. 453–474). New York: New York University Press.

Gunter, B., & McAleer, J. L. (1990). *Children and television: The one eyed monster?* Florence, KY: Taylor and Francis/Routledge.

Gur, R. E., & Pearlson, G. D. (1993). Neuroimaging in schizophrenia research. *Schizophrenia Bulletin, 19*, 337–353.

Gur, R. E., et al. (1998). A follow-up magnetic resonance imaging study of schizophrenia: Relationship of neuroanatomical changes to clinical and neurobehavioral measures. *Archives of General Psychiatry, 55*, 145–152.

Gur, R. E., et al. (2000a). Reduced dorsal and orbital prefrontal gray matter volumes in schizophrenia. *Archives of General Psychiatry, 57*, 761–768.

Gur, R. E., et al. (2000b). Temporolimbic volume reductions in schizophrenia. *Archives of General Psychiatry, 57*, 769–775.

Guralnik, O., Schmeidler, J., & Simeon, D. (2000). Feeling unreal: Cognitive processes in depersonalization. *American Journal of Psychiatry, 157*, 103–109.

Gurland, B. J., & Cross, P. S. (1986). Public health perspectives on clinical memory testing of Alzheimer's disease and related disorders. In L. W. Poon (Ed.), *Handbook for clinical memory assessment of older adults* (pp. 11–20). Washington, DC: American Psychological Association.

Gutheil, T. G. (1980). In search of true freedom: Drug refusal, involuntary medication, and "rotting with your rights on." *American Journal of Psychiatry, 137*, 327–328.

Guthrie, P. C., & Mobley, B. D. (1994). A comparison of the differential diagnostic efficiency of three personality disorder inventories. *Journal of Clinical Psychology, 50*, 656–665.

Gutierrez, P. M., & Silk, K. R. (1998). Prescription privileges for psychologists: A review of the psychological literature. *Professional Psychology: Research and Practice, 29*, 213–222.

Guydish, J., et al. (1998). Drug abuse day treatment: A randomized clinical trial comparing day and residential treatment programs. *Journal of Consulting and Clinical Psychology, 66*, 280–289.

Guze, S. B. (1993). Genetics of Briquet's syndrome and somatization disorder: A review of family, adoption, and twin studies. *Annals of Clinical Psychiatry, 5*, 225–230.

H

Haaga, D. A. F. (1995). Metatraits and cognitive assessment: Application to attributional style and depressive symptoms. *Cognitive Therapy and Research, 19*, 121–142.

Haaga, D. A. F., Dyck, M. J., & Ernst, D. (1991). Empirical status of cognitive theory of depression. *Psychological Bulletin, 110*, 215–236.

Haber, S. N., & Fudge, J. L. (1997). The interface between dopamine neurons and the amygdala: Implications for schizophrenia. *Schizophrenia Bulletin, 23*, 471–482.

Häfner, H., et al. (1998). Causes and consequences of the gender difference in age at onset of schizophrenia. *Schizophrenia Bulletin, 24*, 99–113.

Hager, M., & Peyser, M. (1997, March 24). Battling Alzheimer's. *Newsweek*, p. 66.

Hagerman, R. J. (1996). Fragile X syndrome. *Child and Adolescent Psychiatric Clinics of North America, 5*, 895–911.

Hall, G. C. (1995). Sexual offender recidivism revisited: A meta-analysis of recent treatment studies. *Journal of Consulting and Clinical Psychology, 63*, 802–809.

Hall, G. C., & Barongan, C. (1997). Prevention of sexual aggression: Sociocultural risk and protective factors. *American Psychologist, 52*, 5–14.

Hall, R. L. (1996). Escaping the self or escaping the anomaly? *Psychological Inquiry, 7*, 143–148.

Halmi, K. A., et al. (2000). Perfectionism in anorexia nervosa: Variation by clinical subtype, obsessionality, and pathological eating behavior. *American Journal of Psychiatry, 157*, 1799–1805.

Hammen, C., & Compas, B. E. (1994). Unmasking unmasked depression in children and adolescents: The problem of comorbidity. *Clinical Psychology Review, 14*, 585–603.

Hammen, C., & de Mayo, R. (1982). Cognitive correlates of teacher stress and depressive symptoms: Implications for attributional models of depression. *Journal of Abnormal Psychology, 91*, 96–101.

Hammen, C., & Gitlin, M. (1997). Stress reactivity in bipolar patients and its relation to prior history of disorder. *American Journal of Psychiatry, 154*, 856–857.

Hammen, C., Henry, R., & Daley, S. E. (2000). Depression and sensitization to stressors among young women as a function of childhood adversity. *Journal of Consulting and Clinical Psychology, 68*, 782–787.

Hancock, L. (1996, March 18). Mother's little helper. *Newsweek*, pp. 51–56.

Hankin, B. L., et al. (1998). Development of depression from preadolescence to young adulthood: Emerging gender differences in a 10-year longitudinal study. *Journal of Abnormal Psychology, 107*, 128–140.

Hansen, T. E., Casey, D. E., & Hoffman, W. F. (1997). Neuroleptic intolerance. *Schizophrenia Bulletin, 23*, 567–582.

Hanson, R. K., & Bussiere, M. T. (1998). Predicting relapse: A meta-analysis of sexual offender recidivism studies. *Journal of Consulting and Clinical Psychology, 66*, 348–362.

Hanson, R. K., Steffy, R. A., & Gauthier, R. (1993). Long-term recidivism of child molesters. *Journal of Consulting and Clinical Psychology, 61*, 646–652.

Hare, R. D. (1965). Temporal gradient of fear arousal in psychopaths. *Journal of Abnormal Psychology, 70*, 442–445.

Hare, R. D. (1986). Criminal psychopaths. In J. C. Yuille (Ed.), *Police selection and training: The role of psychology* (pp. 187–206). Dordrecht, Netherlands: Martinos Nijhoff.

Hare, R. D., Hart, S. D., & Harpur, T. J. (1991). Psychopathy and the *DSM-IV* criteria for antisocial personality disorder. *Journal of Abnormal Psychology, 100*, 391–398.

Harpur, T. J., & Hare, R. D. (1994). Assessment of psychopathy as a function of age. *Journal of Abnormal Psychology, 103*, 604–609.

Harrop, C., & Trower, P. (2001). Why does schizophrenia develop at late adolescence? *Clinical Psychology Review, 21*, 241–266.

Hartung, C. M., & Widiger, T. A. (1998). Gender differences in the diagnosis of mental disorders: Conclusions and controversies of the *DSM-IV*. *Psychological Bulletin, 123*, 260–278.

Harvey, A. G., & Bryant, R. A. (1999). The relationship between acute stress disorder and posttraumatic stress disorder: A 2-year prospective evaluation. *Journal of Consulting and Clinical Psychology, 67*, 985–988.

Harvey, A. G., & Bryant, R. A. (2000). Two-year prospective evaluation of the relationship between acute stress disorder and posttraumatic stress disorder following mild traumatic brain injury. *American Journal of Psychiatry, 157*, 629–631.

Harvey, P. D., et al. (1997). Age-related differences in formal thought disorder in chronically hospitalized schizophrenic patients: A cross-sectional study. *American Journal of Psychiatry, 154*, 205–210.

Haughton, E., & Ayllon, T. (1965). Production and elimination of symptomatic behavior. In L. P. Ullmann & L. Krasner (Eds.), *Case studies in behavior modification.* New York: Holt, Rinehart and Winston.

Havassy, B. E., Hall, S. M., & Wasserman, D. A. (1991). Social support and relapse: Commonalities among alcoholics, opiate users, and cigarette smokers. *Addictive Behaviors, 16,* 235–246.

Hawkrigg, J. J. (1975). Agoraphobia. *Nursing Times, 71,* 1280–1282.

Hawton, K. (1991). Sex therapy. Special issue: The changing face in behavioral psychotherapy. *Behavioral Psychotherapy, 19,* 131–136.

Hawton, K., & Catalan, J. (1990). Sex therapy for vaginismus: Characteristics of couples and treatment outcomes. *Sexual and Marital Therapy, 5,* 39–48.

Haznedar, M. M., et al. (2000). Limbic circuitry in patients with autism spectrum disorders studied with positron emission tomography and magnetic resonance imaging. *American Journal of Psychiatry, 157,* 1994–2001.

Headache coping strategies depend on the cause. (2000, August 14). *CNN Web Posting.* Retrieved August 20, 2000, from http://www.cnn.com/2000/HEALTH/08/14/headache.redux/index.html.

Health groups directly link media to child violence. (2000, July 26). *CNN Web Posting.* Retrieved July 27, 2000, from http://www.cnn.com/2000/HEALTH/children/07/26/children.violence.ap/.

Health Resources: Neurosurgery: //On Call®. (2000, March 16). *Parkinson's disease.* American Association of Neurological Surgeons/Congress of Neurological Surgeons. Retrieved April 4, 2000, from http://www.neurosurgery.org/health/patient/detail.asp?DisorderID=46.

Heatherton, T. F., et al. (1997). A 10-year longitudinal study of body weight, dieting, and eating disorder symptoms. *Journal of Abnormal Psychology, 106,* 117–125.

Heidrich, S. M., Forsthoff, C. A., & Ward, S. E. (1994). Psychological adjustment in adults with cancer: The self as mediator. *Health Psychology, 13,* 346–353.

Heikkinen, M. E., et al. (1997). Psychosocial factors and completed suicide in personality disorders. *Acta Psychiatrica Scandinavica, 95,* 49–57.

Hellerstein, D. J., et al. (2000). Double-blind comparison of sertraline, imipramine, and placebo in the treatment of dysthymia: Effects on personality. *American Journal of* Psychiatry, *157,* 1445–1452.

Helmuth, L. (2001). Commentary: Dyslexia: Same brains, different languages. *Science, 291,* 2064.

Helzer, J. E., Burnam, A., & McEvoy, L. T. (1991). Alcohol abuse and dependence. In L. N. Robins & D. A. Regier (Eds.), *Psychiatric disorders in America: The Epidemiologic Catchment Area Study* (pp. 81–115). New York: Free Press.

Henggeler, S. W., Melton, G. B., & Smith, L. A. (1992). Family preservation using multisystemic therapy: An effective alternative to incarcerating serious juvenile offenders. *Journal of Consulting and Clinical Psychology, 60,* 953–961.

Henggeler, S. W., et al. (1986). Multisystemic treatment of juvenile offenders: Effects on adolescent behavior and family interaction. *Developmental Psychology, 22,* 132–141.

Henggeler, S. W., et al. (1997). Multisystemic therapy with violent and chronic juvenile offenders and their families: The role of treatment fidelity in successful dissemination. *Journal of Consulting and Clinical Psychology, 65,* 821–833.

Henkin, W. A. (1985). Toward counseling the Japanese in America: A cross-cultural primer. *Journal of Counseling and Development, 63,* 500–503.

Herbert, J. D., et al. (2000). Science and pseudoscience in the development of eye movement desensitization and reprocessing. *Clinical Psychology Review, 20,* 945–972.

Herek, G. M. (1996). Heterosexism and homophobia. In R. P. Cabaj & T. S. Stein (Eds.), *Textbook of homosexuality and mental health* (pp. 101–113). Washington, DC: American Psychiatric Association Press.

Herkov, M. J., et al. (1996). MMPI differences among adolescent inpatients, rapists, sodomists, and sexual abusers. *Journal of Personality Assessment, 66,* 81–90.

Hernandez, R. (2000, August 2). In new drug battle, use of ecstasy among young soars. *The New York Times,* p. A21.

Hertz, M. R. (1986). Rorschach bound: A 50-year memoir. *Journal of Personality Assessment, 50,* 396–416.

Herzog, W., Schellberg, D., & Deter, H. C. (1997). First recovery in anorexia nervosa patients in the long-term course: A discrete-time survival analysis. *Journal of Consulting and Clinical Psychology, 65,* 169–177.

Heston, L. L., White, J. A., & Mastri, A. R. (1987). Pick's disease: Clinical genetics and natural history. *Archives of General Psychiatry, 44,* 409–411.

Hettema, J. M., Neale, M. C., & Kendler, K. S. (2001). A review and meta-analysis of the genetic epidemiology of anxiety disorders. *American Journal of Psychiatry, 158,* 1568–1578.

Heun, R., et al. (2001). A family study of Alzheimer disease and early- and late-onset depression in elderly patients. *Archives of General Psychiatry, 58,* 190–196.

Hewitt, P. L., Flett, G. L., & Ediger, E. (1996). Perfectionism and depression: Longitudinal assessment of a specific vulnerability hypothesis. *Journal of Abnormal Psychology, 105,* 276–280.

Hilchey, T. (1994, November 11). High anxiety raises risk of heart failure in men, study finds. *The New York Times,* p. A17.

Hill, A. L. (1977). Idiot savants: Rate of incidence. *Perceptual and Motor Skills, 44,* 161–162.

Hill, J. O., & Peters, J. C. (1998). Environmental contributions to the obesity epidemic. *Science, 280,* 1371–1374.

Hill, K. G., et al. (2000). Early adult outcomes of adolescent binge drinking: Person- and variable-centered analyses of binge drinking trajectories. *Alcohol: Clinical Experimental Research, 24,* 892–901.

Hill, S. Y. (1980). Introduction: The biological consequences. In *Alcoholism and alcohol abuse among women: Research issues.* Rockville, MD: National Institute on Alcohol Abuse and Alcoholism.

Hilts, P. J. (1991, October 9). Report is critical of mental clinics. *The New York Times,* p. L25.

Himelein, M. J., & McElrath, J. V. (1996). Resilient child sexual abuse survivors: Cognitive coping and illusion. *Child Abuse and Neglect, 20,* 747–758.

Hingson, R. W., et al. (2000). Age of drinking onset and unintentional injury involvement after drinking. *Journal of the American Medical Association, 284,* 1527–1533.

Hinshaw, S. P. (1992). Academic underachievement, attention deficits, and aggression: Comorbidity and implications for intervention. *Journal of Consulting and Clinical Psychology, 60,* 893–903.

Hinshaw, S. P., Klein, R. G., & Abikoff, H. (1998). Childhood attention deficit hyperactive disorder: Nonpharmacological and combination treatments. In P. E. Nathan & J. M. Gorman (Eds.), *A guide to treatments that work* (pp. 26–41). New York: Oxford University Press.

Hirsch, S. R., & Leff, J. P. (1975). *Abnormalities in parents of schizophrenics.* Oxford, U.K.: Oxford University Press.

Hirschfield, R. M. A., et al. (1997). The National Depressive and Manic-Depressive Association consensus statement on the undertreatment of depression. *Journal of the American Medical Association, 277,* 333–340.

Hodgins, S., et al. (1998). In reply. *Archives of General Psychiatry, 55,* 87–88.

Hoffman, R. E., et al. (1999). Selective speech perception alterations in schizophrenic patients reporting hallucinated "voices." *American Journal of Psychiatry, 156,* 393–399.

Hoffman, S. G. (2000a). Treatment of social phobia: Potential mediators and moderators. *Clinical Psychology: Science and Practice, 7*(1), 3–16.

Hoffman, S. G. (2000b). Self-focused attention before and after treatment of social phobia. *Behavior Research and Therapy, 38,* 717–725.

Hoffman, S. G., et al. (1995). Psychophysiological differences between subgroups of social phobia. *Journal of Abnormal Psychology, 104,* 224–231.

Hoffman, W., & Prior, M. (1982). Neuropsychological dimensions of autism in children: A test of the hemispheric dysfunction hypothesis. *Journal of Clinical Neuropsychology, 4,* 27–42.

Hogarty, G. E., Schroeder, N. R., Ulrich, R., Mussare, N., Peregino, F., & Herron, E. (1979b). Fluphenazine and social therapy in the aftercare of schizophrenic patients. *Archives of General Psychiatry, 36,* 1283–1294.

Hogarty, G. E., et al. (1997a). Three-year trials of personal therapy among schizophrenic patients living with or independent of family, II: Effects on adjustment of patients. *American Journal of Psychiatry, 154,* 1514–1524.

Holland, A. J., Sicotte, N., & Treasure, J. (1988). Anorexia nervosa: Evidence of a genetic basis. *Journal of Psychosomatic Research, 32,* 561–571.

Hollander, E., et al. (1992). Serotonergic function in obsessive-compulsive disorder: Behavioral and neuroendocrine responses to oral m-chlorophenylpiperazine and fenfluramine in patients and health volunteers. *Archives of General Psychiatry, 49,* 21–28.

Hollingshead, A. B., & Redlich, F. C. (1958). *Social class and mental illness: A community study.* New York: Wiley.

Hollon, S. D., Evans, M. D., & DeRubeis, R. J. (1990). Cognitive mediation of relapse prevention following treatment for depression: Implications of differential risk. In R. E. Ingram (Ed.), *Contemporary psychological approaches to depression: Theory, research, and treatment* (pp. 117–136). New York: Plenum Press.

Hollon, S. D., & Kendall, P. C. (1980). Cognitive self-statements in depression: Development of an automatic thoughts questionnaire. *Cognitive Therapy and Research, 4,* 383–395.

Holloway, L. (1998, February 12). A mental patient skips care and West Siders worry again. *The New York Times,* p. B5.

Holmes, D. S., Solomon, S., Cappo, B. M., & Greenberg, J. L. (1983). Effects of transcendental meditation versus resting on physiological and subjective arousal. *Journal of Personality and Social Psychology, 44,* 1244–1252.

Holmes, G. R., Offen, L., & Waller, G. (1997). See no evil, hear no evil, speak no evil: Why do relatively few male victims of childhood sexual abuse receive help for abuse-related issues in adulthood? *Clinical Psychology Review, 17,* 69–88.

Holroyd, K. A., et al. (2001). Management of chronic tension-type headache with tricyclic antidepressant medication, stress management therapy, and their combination: A randomized controlled trial. *Journal of the American Medical Association, 285,* 2208–2215.

Holt, C. S., Heimberg, R. G., & Hope, D. A. (1992). Avoidant personality disorder and the generalized subtype of social phobia. *Journal of Abnormal Psychology, 101,* 318–325.

Holtzworth-Munroe, A. (1995). Marital violence. *The Harvard Mental Health Letter, 12,* pp. 4–6.

Holtzworth-Munroe, A., Rehman, U., & Herron, K. (2000). General and spouse-specific anger and hostility in subtypes of maritally violent men and nonviolent men. *Behavior Therapy, 31,* 603–630.

Holzman, P. S. (1987). Recent studies of psychophysiology in schizophrenia. *Schizophrenia Bulletin, 13,* 49–75.

Holzman, P. S., et al. (1997). Smooth pursuit eye tracking in twins: A critical commentary. *Archives of General Psychiatry, 54,* 429–431.

Honig, A., et al. (1998). Auditory hallucinations: A comparison between patients and nonpatients. *Journal of Nervous and Mental Disease, 186,* 646–651.

Hooley, J. M., & Hiller, J. B. (2000). Personality and expressed emotion. *Journal of Abnormal Psychology, 109,* 40–44.

Horne, L. R., Van Vactor, J. C., & Emerson, S. (1991). Disturbed body image in patients with eating disorders. *American Journal of Psychiatry, 148,* 211–215.

Horrigan, J. P., & Barnhill, J. L. J. (2000). "Fluvoxamine and enuresis:" Comment. *Journal of the American Academy of Child & Adolescent Psychiatry, 39,* 1465–1466.

Houts, A. C., Berman, J. S., & Abramson, H. (1994). Effectiveness of psychological and pharmacological treatments for nocturnal enuresis. *Journal of Consulting and Clinical Psychology, 62,* 373–745.

How mad-cow disease jumped to humans. (2001, February). *Tufts University Health & Nutrition Letter,* p. 18.

Howard, C. E., & Porzelius, L. K. (1999). The role of dieting in binge eating disorder: Etiology and treatment implications. *Clinical Psychology Review, 19,* 25–44.

Howard, K. I., Kopta, S. M., Krause, M. S., & Orlinksy, D. E. (1986). The dose-effect relationship in psychotherapy. *American Psychologist, 41,* 159–164.

Howland, R. H., & Thase, M. E. (1993). A comprehensive review of cyclothymic disorder. *Journal of Nervous and Mental Disease, 18,* 485–493.

Hrobjartsson, A., & Gotzsche, P. C. (2001). Is the placebo powerless? An analysis of clinical trials comparing placebo with no treatment. *The New England Journal of Medicine, 344,* 1594–1602.

Huang, L. H. (1994). An integrative approach to clinical assessment and intervention with Asian-American adolescents. *Journal of Clinical Child Psychology, 23,* 21–31.

Huang, W., & Cuvo, A. J. (1997). Social skills training for adults with mental retardation in job-related settings. *Behavior Modification, 21,* 3–44.

Hublin, C., et al. (1997). Prevalence and genetics of sleepwalking: A population-based twin study. *Neurology, 48,* 177–181.

Hudziak, J. J., et al. (1996). Clinical study of the relation of borderline personality disorder to Briquet's syndrome (hysteria), somatization disorder, antisocial personality disorder, and substance abuse disorders. *American Journal of Psychiatry, 153,* 1598–1606.

Huesmann, L. R., & Miller, L. S. (1994). Long-term effects of repeated exposure to media violence in childhood. In L. R. Huesmann (Ed.), *Aggressive behavior: Current perspectives.* New York: Plenum Press.

Hufford, M. R. (2001). Alcohol and suicidal behavior. *Clinical Psychology Review, 21,* 797–811.

Humphrey, L. L. (1986). Family dynamics in bulimia. In S. C. Feinstein et al. (Eds.), *Adolescent psychiatry.* Chicago: University of Chicago Press.

Hunsley, J., & Bailey, J. H. (1999). The clinical utility of the Rorschach: Unfulfilled promises and an uncertain future. *Psychological Assessment, 11,* 266–277.

Hunter, R. H., Bedell, J. R., & Corrigan, P. W. (1997). Current approaches to assessment and treatment of persons with serious mental illness. *Professional Psychology: Research & Practice, 28,* 217–228.

Hurlburt, G., & Gade, E. (1984). Personality differences between Native American and Caucasian women alcoholics: Implications for alcoholism counseling. *White Cloud Journal, 3,* 35–39.

Hurt, R. D., et al. (1997). A comparison of sustained-release bupropion and placebo for smoking cessation. *The New England Journal of Medicine, 337,* 1195–1202.

Hussong, A. M., et al. (2001). Specifying the relations between affect and heavy alcohol use among young adults. *Journal of Abnormal Psychology, 110,* 449–461.

Hutton, M. (2001). Missense and splice site mutations in tau associated with FTDP-17: Multiple pathogenic mechanisms. *Neurology, 56*(Suppl. 4), S21–S25.

Huxley, N. A., Rendall, M., & Sederer, L. (2000). Psychosocial treatments in schizophrenia: A review of the past 20 years. *Journal of Nervous & Mental Disease, 188,* 187–201.

Hyman, D. J., & Pavlik, V. N. (2001). Characteristics of patients with uncontrolled hypertension in the United States. *The New England Journal of Medicine, 345,* 479–486.

I

Ickovics, J. R., et al. (2001). Mortality, CD4 cell count decline, and depressive symptoms among HIV-seropositive women: Longitudinal analysis from the HIV Epidemiology Research Study. *Journal of the American Medical Association, 285,* 1466–1474.

Ilardi, S. S., & Craighead, W. E. (1994). The role of non-specific factors in cognitive-behavior therapy for depression. *Clinical Psychology: Science and Practice, 1,* 138–156.

in 't Veld, B. A., et al. (2001). Nonsteroidal antiinflammatory drugs and the risk of Alzheimer's disease. *New England Journal of Medicine, 345,* 1515–1521.

Ingersoll, S. L, & Patton, S. O. (1991). *Treating perpetrators of sexual abuse.* Lexington, MA: Lexington Books.

Ingraham, L. J., et al. (1995). Twenty-five year followup of the Israeli High-Risk Study: Current and lifetime psychopathology. *Schizophrenia Bulletin, 21,* 183–192.

Ingram, R. E. (1991). Tilting at windmills: A response to Pyszczynski, Greenberg, Hamilton, and Nix. *Psychological Bulletin, 110,* 544–550.

Ingram, R. E., Miranda, J., & Segal, Z. V. (1998). *Cognitive vulnerability to depression.* New York: Guilford Press.

Ingram, R. E., & Siegle, G. J. (2001). Cognition and clinical science: From revolution to evolution. In K. S. Dobson (Ed.), *Handbook of cognitive-behavioral therapies* (2nd ed., pp. 111–137). New York: Guilford Press.

Insanity: A defense of last resort. (1992, February 3). *Newsweek,* p. 49

Institute of Medicine. (1990). *Broadening the base of treatment for alcohol problems.* Washington, DC: National Academy Press.

Ioannidis, J. P. A., & Karassa, P. (2001). Comparison of evidence of treatment effects in randomized and non-randomized studies. *Journal of the American Medical Association, 286,* 821–830.

Ioannidis, J. P. A., et al. (2001). Comparison of evidence of treatment effects in randomized and nonrandomized studies. *Journal of the American Medical Association, 286,* 821–830.

Iribarren, C., et al. (2000). Association of hostility with coronary artery calcification in young adults: The CARDIA Study. *Journal of the American Medical Association, 283,* 546–551.

Irle, E., et al. (1998). Obsessive-compulsive disorder and ventromedial frontal lesions: Clinical and neuropsychological findings. *American Journal of Psychiatry, 155,* 255–263.

Ironson, G., et al. (1997). Posttraumatic stress symptoms, intrusive thoughts, loss, and immune function after hurricane Andrew. *Psychosomatic Medicine, 59,* 128–141.

Isacsson, G. (2000). Suicide prevention—A medical breakthrough? *Acta Psychiatrica Scandinavica, 102,* 113–117.

Israel, G. E., & Tarver II, D. E. (1997). *Transgender care: Recommended guidelines, practical information, and personal accounts.* Philadelphia: Temple University Press.

Ito, T. A., Miller, N., & Pollock, V. E. (1996). Alcohol and aggression: A meta-analysis on the moderating effects of inhibitory cues, triggering events, and self-focused attention. *Psychological Bulletin, 120,* 60–82.

Iwata, N., et al. (2001). Metabolic regulation of brain abeta by neprilysin. *Science, 292,* 1550–1552.

J

Jablensky, A., et al. (1992). Schizophrenia: Manifestations, incidence and course in different cultures: A World Health Organization ten-country study. *Psychological Medicine, 20*(Monograph Suppl.), 1–97.

Jackson, J. L. (1999). Psychometric considerations in self-monitoring assessment. *Psychological Assessment, 11,* 439–447.

Jackson, J., et al. (1990). Young adult women who report childhood intrafamilial sexual abuse: Subsequent adjustment. *Archives of Sexual Behavior, 19,* 211–221.

Jacobs, M. K., et al. (2001). A Comparison of computer-based versus traditional individual psychotherapy. *Professional Psychology: Research and Practice, 32,* 92–96.

Jacobs, W., Newman, G. H., & Burns, J. C. (2001). The Homeless Assessment Program: A service-training model for providing disability evaluations for homeless, mentally ill individuals. *Professional Psychology: Research and Practice, 32,* 319–323.

Jacobson, N. S., Wilson, L., & Tupper, C. (1988). The clinical significance of treatment gains resulting from exposure-based interventions for agoraphobia: A reanalysis of outcome data. *Behavior Therapy, 19,* 539–554.

Jacobson, N. S., et al. (1996). A component analysis of cognitive-behavioral treatment for depression. *Journal of Consulting and Clinical Psychology, 64,* 295–304.

Jamison, B. (2000, June 13). Obsessive Internet use poses risk of isolation, depression, researchers say. WebMD.com. Retrieved June 29, 2000, from http://www.webmd.com.

Jamison, K. R. (1993). *Touched with fire.* New York: Free Press.

Janofsky, J. S., et al. (1996). Insanity defense pleas in Baltimore City: An analysis of outcome. *American Journal of Psychiatry, 153,* 1464–1468.

Januzzi, J., & DeSanctis, R. (1999). Looking to the brain to save the heart. *Cerebrum, 1,* 31–43.

Jarrett, R. B., et al. (1999). Treatment of atypical depression with cognitive therapy or phenelzine. *Archives of General Psychiatry, 56,* 431–437.

Jarrett, R. B., et al. (2001). Preventing recurrent depression using cognitive therapy with and without a continuation phase: A randomized clinical trial. *Archives of General Psychiatry, 58,* 381–388.

Javier, R. A. (1993). Cited in Rathus, S. A. (1993). *Psychology* (5th ed.). Fort Worth, TX: Harcourt Brace Jovanovich.

Jaycox, L. H., Reivich, K. J., Gillham, J., & Seligman, M. E. P. (1994). Prevention of depressive symptoms in school children. *Behaviour Research and Therapy, 32,* 801–816.

Jeffery, R. W. (1991). Population perspectives on the prevention and treatment of obesity in minority populations. *American Journal of Clinical Nutrition, 53*(6 Suppl.), 1621A–1624S.

Jellinek, E. M. (1960). *The disease concept of alcoholism.* New Haven, CT: College and University Press.

Jemmott, J. B., et al. (1983, June 25). Academic stress, power motivation, and decrease in secretion rate of salivary secretory immunoglobin A. *Lancet,* 1400–1402.

Jenike, M. A., et al. (1997). Placebo-controlled trial of fluoxetine and phenelzine for obsessive-compulsive disorder. *American Journal of Psychiatry, 154,* 1261–1264.

Jenkins, C. D. (1988). Epidemiology of cardiovascular diseases. *Journal of Consulting and Clinical Psychology, 56,* 324–332.

Jenkins, J. H. (1988). Ethnopsychiatric interpretations of schizophrenic illness: The problem of nervios within Mexican-American families. *Culture, Medicine, and Psychiatry, 12,* 301–329.

Jenkins, J. H., & Karno, M. (1992). The meaning of expressed emotion: Theoretical issues raised by cross-cultural research. *American Journal of Psychiatry, 149,* 9–21.

Jenny, C., Roesler, T. A., & Poyer, K. L. (1994). Are children at risk for sexual abuse by homosexuals? *Pediatrics, 94,* 41–44.

Jensen, P. S., Martin, D., & Cantwell, D. P. (1997). Comorbidity in ADHD: Implications for research practice, and *DSM-V. Journal of the American Academy of Child and Adolescent Psychiatry, 36,* 1065–1079.

Jerome, L. W., et al. (2000). The coming of age in telecommunications in psychological research and practice. *American Psychologist, 55,* 507–421.

Jeste, D. V., & Caligiui, M. P. (1993). Tardive dyskinesia. *Schizophrenia Bulletin, 19,* 303–315.

Jeste, D. V., Lindamer, L. A., Evans, J., & Lacro, J. P. (1996). Relationship of ethnicity and gender to schizophrenia and pharmacology of neuroleptics. *Psychopharmacology Bulletin, 32,* 243–251.

Jeste, D. V., et al. (1992). Cognitive deficits of patients with Alzheimer's disease with and without delusions. *American Journal of Psychiatry, 149,* 184–188.

Jian, W., et al. (1996). Mental stress-induced myocardial ischemia and cardiac events. *Journal of the American Medical Association, 275,* 1651–1656.

Jimerson, D. C., et al. (1997). Decreased serotonin function in bulimia nervosa. *Archives of General Psychiatry, 54,* 529–534.

Johnson, B. A., et al. (2000). Ondansetron for reduction of drinking among biologically predisposed alcoholic patients: A randomized controlled trial. *Journal of the American Medical Association, 284,* 963–971.

Johnson, J. G., et al. (1999). A longitudinal investigation of social causation and social selection processes involved in the association between socioeconomic status and psychiatric disorders. *Journal of Abnormal Psychology, 108,* 490–499.

Johnson, J. G., et al. (2000). Association between cigarette smoking and anxiety disorders during adolescence and early adulthood. *Journal of the American Medical Association, 284,* 2348–2351.

Johnson, R. E., et al. (2000). A comparison of levomethadyl acetate, buprenorphine, and methadone for opioid dependence. *The New England Journal of Medicine, 343,* 1290–1297.

Johnson, R. J., & McFarland, B. H. (1996). Lithium use and discontinuation in a health maintenance organization. *American Journal of Psychiatry, 153,* 993–1000.

Johnson, S., et al. (1999). Social support and the course of bipolar disorder. *Journal of Abnormal Psychology, 108,* 558–566.

Johnson, W. G., Tsoh, J. Y., & Varnado, P. J. (1996). Eating disorders: Efficacy of pharmacological and psychological interventions. *Clinical Psychology Review, 16,* 457–478.

Johnston, L. D., Bachman, J. G., & O'Malley, P. M. (1992, January 25). *Monitoring the future: A continuing study of the lifestyles and values of youth.* Ann Arbor, MI: The University of Michigan News and Information Services.

Johnston, L. D., O'Malley, P. M., and Bachman, J. G. (1996). *National Survey Results on Drug Use from the Monitoring the Future Study, 1975–1995. Volume I. Secondary School Students.* Washington, DC: U.S. Department of Health and Human Services, Public Health Service, National Institutes of Health: National Institute on Drug Abuse.

Joiner, T. E., Alfano, M. S., & Metalsky, G. I. (1992). When depression breeds contempt: Reassurance seeking, self-esteem, and rejection of depressed college students by their roommates. *Journal of Abnormal Psychology, 101,* 165–173.

Jones v. United States, 103 S. Ct. 3043 (1983).

Jones, E. (1953). *The life and work of Sigmund Freud.* New York: Basic Books.

Jones, P. B., et al. (1998). Schizophrenia as a long-term outcome of pregnancy, delivery, and perinatal complications: A 28-year follow-up of the 1966 North Finland general population birth cohort. *American Journal of Psychiatry, 155,* 355–364.

Jouriles, E. N., et al. (1996). Physical violence and other forms of marital aggression: Links with children's behavior problems. *Journal of Family Psychology, 10,* 223–234.

Jouriles, E. N., et al. (1997). Psychometric properties of family members' reports of parental physical aggression toward clinic-referred children. *Journal of Consulting and Clinical Psychology, 65,* 309–318.

Judd, L. J. (1997). The clinical course of unipolar major depressive disorders. *Archives of General Psychiatry, 54,* 989–991.

Judd, L. L., et al. (2000a). Psychosocial disability during the long-term course of unipolar major depressive disorder. *Archives of General Psychiatry, 57,* 375–380.

Judd, L. L., et al. (2000b). Does incomplete recovery from first lifetime major depressive episode herald a chronic course of illness? *American Journal of Psychiatry, 157,* 1509–1511.

Just, N., Abramson, L. Y., & Alloy, L. B. (2001). Remitted depression studies as tests of the cognitive vulnerability hypotheses of depression onset. A critique and conceptual analysis. *Clinical Psychology Review, 21,* 63–83.

Just, N., & Alloy, L. B. (1997). The response styles theory of depression: Tests and an extension of the theory. *Journal of Abnormal Psychology, 106,* 221–229.

K

Kahn, M. W. (1982). Cultural clash and psychopathology in three aboriginal cultures. *Academic Psychology Bulletin, 4,* 553–561.

Kalb, C. (2001a, January 22). Seeing a virtual shrink. *Newsweek,* pp. 34–37.

Kalb, C. (2001b). Can this pill stop you from hitting the bottle? *Newsweek,* pp. 46–48.

Kalichman, S. C. (2000). HIV transmission risk behaviors of men and women living with HIV-AIDS: Prevalence, predictors, and emerging clinical intervention. *Clinical Psychology: Science and Practice, 7,* 32–47.

Kammeyer, K. C. W. (1990). *Marriage and family: A foundation for personal decisions* (2nd ed.). Boston: Allyn & Bacon.

Kammeyer, K. C. W., Ritzer, G., & Yetman, N. R. (1990). *Sociology: Experiencing changing societies.* Boston: Allyn & Bacon.

Kane, J. M. (1996). Drug therapy: Schizophrenia. *The New England Journal of Medicine, 334,* 34–41.

Kane, J. M., & Marder, S. R. (1993). Psychopharmalogic treatment of schizophrenia. *Schizophrenia Bulletin, 19,* 287–302.

Kanner, A. D., Coyne, J. C., Schaefer, C., & Lazarus, R. S. (1981). Comparison of two modes of stress measurement: Daily hassles and uplifts versus major life events. *Journal of Behavioral Medicine, 4,* 1–39.

Kanner, L. (1943). Autistic disturbances of affective content. *Nervous Child, 2,* 217–240.

Kano, K., & Arisaka, O. (2000). Fluvoxamine and enuresis. *Journal of the American Academy of Child & Adolescent Psychiatry, 39,* 1464–1465.

Kantor, M. (1998). *Homophobia: Description, development and dynamics of gay bashing.* Westport, CT: Praeger.

Kaplan, D. (1993, January 18). The incorrigibles. *Newsweek,* pp. 48–50.

Kaplan, H. S. (1974). *The new sex therapy: Active treatment of sexual dysfunctions.* New York: Brunner/Mazel.

Kaplan, H. S. (1987). *Sexual aversion, sexual phobias, and panic disorder.* New York: Brunner/Mazel.

Kaplan, R. M. (2000). Two pathways to prevention. *American Psychologist, 55,* 382–396.

Kaplan, S. J. (1986). *The private practice of behavior therapy: A guide for behavioral practitioners.* New York: Plenum Press.

Kapp, M. B. (1994). Treatment and refusal rights in mental health: Therapeutic justice and clinical accommodation. *American Journal of Orthopsychiatry, 64,* 223–234.

Kapur, S., & Remington, G. (2000). Atypical antipsychotics: Patients value the lower incidence of extrapyramidal side effects. *British Medical Journal, 321,* 1360–1361.

Karel, J. J., & Hinrichsen, G. (2000). Treatment of depression in late life: Psychotherapeutic interventions. *Clinical Psychology Review, 20,* 707–729.

Karel, M. J. (1997). Aging and depression: Vulnerability and stress across adulthood. *Clinical Psychology Review, 17,* 847–879.

Karlen, N. (1995, May 29). Greetings from Minnesober. *The New York Times Magazine,* pp. 32–35.

Karno, M., et al. (1987). Expressed emotions and schizophrenic outcome among Mexican-American families. *Journal of Nervous and Mental Disease, 175,* 143–151.

Karp, B. I., et al. (2001). Abnormal neurologic maturation in adolescents with early-onset schizophrenia. *American Journal of Psychiatry, 158,* 118–122.

Kasari, D., et al. (1993). Affective development and communication in children with autism. In A. P. Kaiser & D. B. Gray (Eds.), *Enhancing children's communication: Research foundation for intervention* (pp. 201–222). New York: Brookes.

Kasen, S., et al. (2001). Childhood depression and adult personality disorder: Alternative pathways of continuity. *Archives of General Psychiatry, 58,* 231–236

Kasl-Godley, J., & Gatz, M. (2000). Psychosocial interventions for individuals with dementia: An integration of theory, therapy, and a clinical understanding of dementia. *Clinical Psychology Review, 20,* 755–782.

Kasper, J. A., et al. (1997). Prospective study of patients' refusal of antipsychotic medication under a physician discretion review procedure. *American Journal of Psychiatry, 154,* 483–489.

Kasper, M. E., Rogers, R., & Adams, P. A. (1996). Dangerousness and command hallucinations: An investigation of psychotic inpatients. *Bulletin of the American Academy of Psychiatry and the Law, 24,* 219–224.

Katz, J. N. (1995). *The invention of heterosexuality.* New York: Dutton.

Kawachi, I., et al. (1994). Prospective study of phobic anxiety and risk of coronary heart disease in men. *Circulation, 89,* 1992–1997.

Kawas, C. H., & Brookmeyer, R. (2001). Aging and the Public Health Effects of Dementia. *The New England Journal of Medicine, 344,* 1160–1161. [Editorial]

Kay, S. R. (1990). Significance of the positive-negative distinction in schizophrenia. *Schizophrenia Bulletin, 16,* 635–652.

Kazdin, A. E. (1992). *Research design in clinical psychology* (2nd ed.). Boston: Allyn & Bacon.

Kazdin, A. E. (1998). Psychosocial treatments for conduct disorder in children. In P. E. Nathan & J. M. Gorman (Eds.), *A guide to treatments that work* (pp. 65–89). New York: Oxford University Press.

Kazdin, A. E., Siegel, T. D., & Bass, D. (1992). Cognitive problem-solving skills training and parent management training in the treatment of antisocial behavior in children. *Journal of Consulting and Clinical Psychology,* 733–747.

Kazdin, A. E., & Weisz, J. R. (1998). Identifying and developing empirically supported child and adolescent treatments. *Journal of Consulting and Clinical Psychology, 66,* 19–36.

Keane, T. M. (1998). Psychological and behavioral treatments for post-traumatic stress disorder. In P. E. Nathan & J. M. Gorman (Eds.), *A guide to treatments that work* (pp. 398–407). New York: Oxford University Press.

Kearins, J. M. (1981). Visual spatial memory in Australian aboriginal children in desert regions. *Cognitive Psychology, 13,* 434–460.

Keel, P. K., et al. (1999). Long-term outcome of bulimia nervosa. *Archives of General Psychiatry, 56,* 63–69.

Keesey, R. E. (1980). A set-point analysis of the regulation of body weight. In A. J. Stunkard (Ed.), *Obesity.* Philadelphia: Saunders.

Keith, S. J., Regier, D. A., & Rae, D. S. (1991). Schizophrenic disorders. In L. N. Robins & D. A. Regier (Eds.), *Psychiatric disorders in America: The Epidemiologic Catchment Area Study* (pp. 33–52). New York: Free Press.

Keller, M. B., Hirschfeld, R. M. A., & Hanks, D. L. (1997). Double depression: A distinctive subtype of unipolar depression. *Journal of Affective Disorders, 45,* 65–73.

Keller, M. B., et al. (1993). Bipolar I: A five-year prospective follow-up. *Journal of Nervous and Mental Disease, 181,* 238–245.

Kellner, R. (1992). Diagnosis and treatment of hypochondriacal syndromes. *Psychosomatics, 33,* 278–289.

Kelly, J. A., Brasfield, T. L., & St. Lawrence, J. S. (1991). Predictors of vulnerability to AIDS risk behavior relapse. *Journal of Consulting and Clinical Psychology, 59,* 163–166.

Kelly, J. A., et al. (1995). Factors predicting continued high-risk behavior among gay men in small cities: Psychological, behavioral, and demographic characteristics related to unsafe sex. *Journal of Consulting and Clinical Psychology, 63,* 101–107.

Kelly, J. A., et al. (1998). Implications of HIV treatment advances for behavioral research on AIDS: Protease inhibitors and new challenges in HIV secondary prevention. *Health Psychology, 17,* 310–319.

Kelly, S. J., Macaruso, P., & Sokol, S. M. (1997). Mental calculation in an autistic savant: A case study. *Journal of Clinical and Experimental Neuropsychology, 19,* 172–184.

Kendell, R. E. (1983). Hysteria. In G. F. M. Russell & L. A. Hersov (Eds.), *Handbook of psychiatry (Vol. 4). The neuroses and personality disorders* (pp. 232–246). Cambridge: Cambridge University Press.

Kendler, K. (1992). Cited in Goleman, D. (1992, October 14). Study ties genes to drinking in women as much as in men. *The New York Times,* p. C14.

Kendler, K. S. (1994). Twin studies of psychiatric illness: Current status and future directions. *Archives of General Psychiatry, 50,* 905–918.

Kendler, K. S. (2001). A psychiatric dialogue on the mind-body problem. *American Journal of Psychiatry, 158,* 989–1000.

Kendler, K. S., & Diehl, S. R. (1993). The genetics of schizophrenia: A current, genetic-epidemiologic perspective. *Schizophrenia Bulletin, 19,* 261–295.

Kendler, K. S., & Gardner, C. O. (1998). Boundaries of major depression: An evaluation of *DSM-IV* criteria. *American Journal of Psychiatry, 155,* 172–177.

Kendler, K., S., Gardner, C. O., & Prescott, C. A. (2000). Corrections to 2 prior articles. *Archives of General Psychiatry, 57,* 94–95. [Letter]

Kendler, K. S., Gruenberg, A. M., & Tsuang, M.T. (1985). Psychiatric illness in first-degree relatives of schizophrenic and surgical control patients, a family study using *DSM-III* criteria. *Archives of General Psychiatry, 42,* 770–779.

Kendler, K. S., Myers, J. M., & Neale, M. C. (2000). A multidimensional twin study of mental health in women. *American Journal of Psychiatry, 157,* 521–527.

Kendler, K. S., & Prescott, C. A. (1999). A population-based twin study of lifetime major depression in men and women. *Archives of General Psychiatry, 56,* 39–44.

Kendler, K. S., & Thornton, L. M., & Gardner, C. O. (2000). Stressful life events and previous episodes in the etiology of major depression in women: An evaluation of the "kindling" hypothesis. *American Journal of Psychiatry, 157,* 1243–1251.

Kendler, K. S., Thornton, L. M., & Pedersen, N. L. (2000). Tobacco consumption in Swedish twins reared apart and reared together. *Archives of General Psychiatry, 57,* 886–892.

Kendler, K. S., & Walsh, D. (1995). Schizotypal personality disorder in parents and the risk for schizophrenia in siblings. *Schizophrenia Bulletin, 21,* 47–52.

Kendler, K. S., et al. (1991). The genetic epidemiology of bulimia nervosa. *American Journal of Psychiatry, 148,* 1627–1637.

Kendler, K. S. et al. (1992a). A population-based twin study of major depression in women: The impact of varying definitions of illness. *Archives of General Psychiatry, 49,* 257–266.

Kendler, K. S., et al. (1992c). The genetic epidemiology of phobias in women: The interrelationship of agoraphobia, social phobia, situational phobia, and simple phobia. *Archives of General Psychiatry, 49,* 273–281.

Kendler, K. S., et al. (1993a). A pilot Swedish twin study of affective illness, including hospital- and population-ascertained subsamples. *Archives of General Psychiatry, 50,* 699–706.

Kendler, K. S., et al. (1993b). The lifetime history of major depression in women: Reliability of diagnosis and heritability. *Archives of General Psychiatry, 50,* 863–870.

Kendler, K .S., et al. (1997). Resemblance of psychotic symptoms and syndromes in affected sibling pairs from the Irish study of high-density schizophrenia families: Evidence for possible etiologic heterogeneity. *American Journal of Psychiatry, 154,* 191–198.

Kendler, K. S., et al. (2000a). Clinical features of schizophrenia and linkage to chromosomes 5q, 6p, 8p, and 10p in the Irish study of high-density schizophrenia families. *American Journal of Psychiatry, 157,* 402–408.

Kendler, K. S., et al. (2000b). Childhood sexual abuse and adult psychiatric and substance use disorders in women: An epidemiological and co-twin control analysis. *Archives of General Psychiatry, 57*(10), 953–959.

Kendler, K. S., et al. (2001). The genetic epidemiology of irrational fears and phobias in men. *Archives of General Psychiatry, 58,* 257–265.

Kennedy, S., Scheirer, J., & Rogers, A. (1984). The price of success: Our monocultural science. *American Psychologist, 390,* 966–967.

Kent, A., & Waller, G. (2000). Childhood emotional abuse and eating psychopathology. *Clinical Psychology Review, 20,* 887–903.

Kent, J. M., et al. (2001). Specificity of panic response to CO_2 inhalation in panic disorder: A comparison with major depression and premenstrual dysphoric disorder. *American Journal of Psychiatry, 158,* 58–67.

Kernberg, O. F. (1975). *Borderline conditions and pathological narcissism.* New York: Jason Aronson.

Kershner, R. (1996). Adolescent attitudes about rape. *Adolescence, 31,* 29–33.

Kessler, R. C. (1994). The National Comorbidity Survey: Preliminary results and future directions. *International Journal of Methods in Psychiatric Research, 4,* 114.1–114.13.

Kessler, R. C., Borges, G., & Walters, E. E. (1999). Prevalence and risk factors for lifetime suicide attempts in the National Comorbidity Survey. *Archives of General Psychiatry, 56,* 617–626.

Kessler, R. C., et al. (1990). Clustering of teenage suicides after television news stories about suicides: A reconsideration. *American Journal of Psychiatry, 145,* 1379–1383.

Kessler, R. C., et al. (1993). Sex and depression in the National Comorbidity Survey I: Lifetime prevalence, chronicity and recurrence. *Journal of Affective Disorders, 29,* 85–96.

Kessler, R. C., et al. (1994). Lifetime and 12-month prevalence of *DSM-III-R* psychiatric disorders in the United States: Results from the National Comorbidity Survey. *Archives of General Psychiatry, 51,* 8–19.

Kessler, R. C., et al. (1995). Posttraumatic stress disorder in the National Comorbidity Survey. *Archives of General Psychiatry, 52,* 1048–1060.

Kessler, R. C., et al. (1997a). Differences in the use of psychiatric outpatient services between the United States and Ontario. *The New England Journal of Medicine, 336,* 551–557.

Kessler, R. C., et al. (1997b). Lifetime co-occurrence of *DSM-III-R* alcohol abuse and dependence with other psychiatric disorders in the National Comorbidity Survey. *Archives of General Psychiatry, 54,* 313–321.

Kety, S. S. (1980). The syndrome of schizophrenia: Unresolved questions and opportunities for research. *British Journal of Psychiatry, 136,* 421–436.

Kety, S. S., Rosenthal, D., Wender, P. H., Schulsinger, F., & Jacobsen, B. (1975). Mental illness in the biological and adoptive families of adoptive individuals who have become schizophrenic: A preliminary report based on psychiatric interviews. In R. R. Fieve, D. Rosenthal, & H. Brill (Eds.), *Genetic research in psychiatry.* Baltimore: The Johns Hopkins University Press.

Kety, S. S., Rosenthal, D., Wender, P. H., Schulsinger, F., & Jacobsen, B. (1978). The biological and adoptive families of adopted individuals who become schizophrenic. In C. Wynne, R. L. Cromwell, & S. Mathysse (Eds.), *The nature of schizophrenia* (pp. 25–37). New York: Wiley.

Kety, S., et al. (1994). Mental illness in the biological and adoptive relatives of schizophrenic adoptees: Replication of the Copenhagen study in the rest of Denmark. *Archives of General Psychiatry, 51,* 442–455.

Keyes, D. (1982). *The minds of Billy Milligan.* New York: Bantam Books.

Kiecolt-Glaser, J. K., & Glaser, R. (1992). Psychoneuroimmunology: Can psychological interventions modulate immunity? *Journal of Consulting and Clinical Psychology, 60,* 569–575.

Kiecolt-Glaser, J. K., Speicher, C. E., Holliday, J. E., & Glaser, R. (1984). Stress and the transformation of lymphocytes in Epstein-Barr virus. *Journal of Behavioral Medicine, 7,* 1–12.

Kiecolt-Glaser, J. K., et al. (1987b). Marital quality, marital disruption, and immune function. *Psychosomatic Medicine, 49,* 13–34.

Kiecolt-Glaser, J. K., et al. (1988). Marital discord and immunity in males. *Psychosomatic Medicine, 50,* 213–229.

Kiecolt-Glaser, J., et al. (1995). Slowing of wound healing by psychological stress. *Lancet, 346,* 1194–1196.

Kiesler, C. A., & Sibulkin, A. E. (1987). *Mental hospitalization: Myths and facts about a national crisis.* Newbury Park, CA: Sage.

Kiesler, D. J. (1999). *Beyond the disease model of mental disorders.* Westport, CT: Praeger Publishers.

Kilpatrick, D. G., et al. (2000). Risk factors for adolescent substance abuse and dependence: Data from a national sample. *Journal of Consulting and Clinical Psychology, 68,* 19–30.

Kilts, C. D., et al. (2001). Neural activity related to drug craving in cocaine addiction. *Archives of General Psychiatry, 58,* 334–341.

Kim, J. J., et al. (2000). Regional neural dysfunctions in chronic schizophrenia studied with positron emission tomography. *American Journal of Psychiatry, 157,* 549–559.

Kim, S. C., & Seo, K. K. (1998). Efficacy and safety of fluoxetine, sertraline, and clomipramine in patients with prompter ejaculation: A double-blind, placebo controlled study. *Journal of Urology, 159,* 425–427.

Kimerling, R., & Calhoun, K. S. (1994). Somatic symptoms, social support, and treatment seeking among sexual assault victims. *Journal of Consulting and Clinical Psychology, 62,* 333–340.

King, S., & Dixon, M. J. (1995). Expressed emotion, family dynamics, and symptom severity in a predictive model of social adjustment for schizophrenic young adults. *Schizophrenia Research, 14,* 121–132.

King, S., & Dixon, M. J. (1999). Expressed emotion and relapse in young schizophrenia outpatients. *Schizophrenia Bulletin, 25,* 377–386.

Kinney, D. K., et al. (1997). Thought disorder in schizophrenic and control adoptees and their relatives. *Archives of General Psychiatry, 54,* 475–479.

Kirigin, K. A., & Wolf, M. M. (1998). Application of the teaching-family model to children and adolescents with conduct disorder. In V. B. Van Hasselt & M. Hersen (Eds.), *Handbook of psychological treatment protocols for children and adolescents. The LEA series in personality and clinical psychology* (pp. 359–380). Mahwah, NJ: Erlbaum.

Kirmayer, L. J., Robbins, J. M., & Paris, J. (1994). Somatoform disorders: Personality and the social matrix of somatic distress. *Journal of Abnormal Psychology, 103,* 125–136.

Kisiel, C. L., & Lyons, J. S. (2001). Dissociation as a mediator of psychopathology among sexually abused children and adolescents. *American Journal of Psychiatry, 158,* 1034–1039.

Kissel, R. C., Whitman, T. L., & Reid, D. H. (1983). An institutional staff training and self-management program for developing multiple self-care skills in severely-profoundly retarded individuals. *Journal of Applied Behavior Analysis, 16,* 395–415.

Klassen, D., & O'Connor, W. A. (1988). Predicting violence in schizophrenic and non-schizophrenic patients: A prospective study. *Journal of Community Psychology, 16,* 217–227.

Klausner, J. D., et al. (2000). Tracing a syphilis outbreak through cyberspace. *The Journal of the American Medical Association, 284,* 447–449.

Klein, D. F. (1994). "Klein's suffocation theory of panic": Reply. *Archives of General Psychiatry, 51,* 506.

Klein, D. N., Lewinsohn, P. M., Seeley, J. R., & Rohde, P. (2001). A family study of major depressive disorder in a community sample of adolescents. *Archives of General Psychiatry, 58,* 13–20.

Klein, D. N., Schwartz, J. E., Rose, S., & Leader, J. B. (2000a). Five-year course and outcome of dysthymic disorder: A prospective, naturalistic follow-up study. *American Journal of Psychiatry, 157,* 931–939.

Klein, D. N., Taylor, E. B., Dickstein, S., & Harding, K. (1988). Primary early-onset dysthymia: Comparison with primary nonbipolar nonchronic major depression on demographic, clinical, familial, personality, and socioenvironmental characteristics and short-term outcome. *Journal of Abnormal Psychology, 97,* 387–398.

Klein, D. N., et al. (2000b). Comparison of *DSM-III-R* chronic major depression and major depression superimposed on dysthymia (double depression): Validity of the distinction. *Journal of Abnormal Psychology, 109,* 419–427.

Klein, M. (1981). On Mahler's autistic and symbiotic phases: An exposition and evaluation. *Psychoanalysis and Contemporary Thought, 4,* 69–105.

Klein, R. G., et al. (1997). Clinical efficacy of methylphenidate in conduct disorder with and without attention deficit hyperactivity disorder. *Archives of General Psychiatry, 4,* 1073–1080.

Kleinman, A. (1987). Anthropology and psychiatry: The role of culture in cross-cultural research on illness. *British Journal of Psychiatry, 151,* 447–454.

Klerman, G. L. (1984). Ideology & science in the individual psychotherapy of schizophrenia. *Schizophrenia Bulletin, 10,* 608–612.

Klerman, G. L., Weissman, M. M., Rounsaville, B. J., & Chevron, E. S. (1984). *Interpersonal psychotherapy of depression.* New York: Basic Books.

Klesges, R. C., et al. (1997). How much weight gain occurs following smoking cessation? A comparison of weight gain using both continuous and point prevalence abstinence. *Journal of Consulting and Clinical Psychology, 65,* 286–291.

Klonoff, E. A., & Landrine, H. (1997). *Preventing misdiagnosis of women: A guide to physical disorders that have psychiatric symptoms.* Thousand Oaks, CA: Sage.

Kluft, R. P. (1986). Three high functioning multiples. *Journal of Nervous and Mental Disease, 174,* 722–726.

Kluft, R. P. (1988). The dissociative disorders. In J. Talbott, R. Hales, & S. Yudofsky (Eds.), *Textbook of psychiatry.* Washington, DC: American Psychiatric Press.

Kluger, J. (2001, June 18). How to manage teen drinking (the smart way). *Time,* pp. 42–44.

Knight, B. G., & Satre, D. D. (1999). Cognitive behavioral psychotherapy with older adults. *Clinical Psychology: Science and Practice, 6,* 188–203.

Knight, G. P., Fabes, R. A., & Higgins, D A. (1996). Concerns about drawing causal inferences from meta-analyses: An example in the study of gender differences in aggression. *Psychological Bulletin, 119,* 410–421.

Knight, R. G., Godfrey, H. P. D., & Shelton, E. J. (1988). The psychological deficits associated with Parkinson's disease. *Clinical Psychology Review, 8,* 391–410.

Knoll, J. L., IV, et al. (1998). Heterogeneity of the psychoses: Is there a neurodegenerative psychosis? *Schizophrenia Bulletin, 24,* 365–379.

Knudsen, D. D. (1991). Child sexual coercion. In E. Grauerholz & M. A. Koralewski (Eds.), *Sexual coercion: A sourcebook on its nature, causes, and prevention* (pp. 17–28). Lexington, MA: Lexington Books.

Kobak, K. A., et al. (1996). Computer-administered clinical rating scales: A review. *Psychopharmacology, 127,* 291–301.

Kobak, K. A., et al. (1997). A computer-administered telephone interview to identify mental disorders. *Journal of the American Medical Association, 278,* 905–910.

Kobasa, S. C. (1979). Stressful life events, personality, and health: An inquiry into hardiness. *Journal of Personality and Social Psychology, 37,* 1–11.

Kobasa, S. C., Maddi, S. R., & Kahn, S. (1982). Hardiness and health: A prospective study. *Journal of Personality and Social Psychology, 42,* 168–177.

Kockott, G., & Fahrner, E. (1988). Male-to-female and female-to-male transsexuals: A comparison. *Archives of Sexual Behavior, 17,* 539–545.

Kocsis, J. H., et al. (1996). Maintenance therapy for chronic depression: A controlled clinical trial of desipramine. *Archives of General Psychiatry, 53,* 769–774.

Kogan, A. O., & Guilford, P. M. (1998). Side effects of short-term 10,000-lux light therapy. *American Journal of Psychiatry, 155,* 293–294.

Kogon, M. M., et al. (1997). Effects of medical and psychotherapeutic treatment on the survival of women with metastatic breast carcinoma. *Cancer, 80,* 225–230.

Kohut, H. (1966). Forms and transformations of narcissism. *Journal of the American Psychoanalytic Association, 14,* 243–272.

Kolata, G. (1994a, February 3). Sweeteners-hyperactivity link is discounted. *The New York Times,* p. A19.

Kolata, G. (1994b, November 11). A simpler test for Alzheimer's is reported. *The New York Times,* p. A20.

Kolata, G. (1995b, February 9). Landmark in Alzheimer research: Breeding mice with the disease. *The New York Times,* p. A20.

Kolata, G. (1995c, March 9). Metabolism found to adjust for a body's natural weight. *The New York Times,* pp. A1, A22.

Kolata, G. (1998, March 28). U.S. approves sale of impotence pill; huge market seen. *The New York Times,* pp. A1, A8.

Kolata, G. (2000a, October 18). Days off are not allowed, experts argue. *The New York Times,* pp. A1, A20.

Kolata, G. (2000b, October 17). How the body knows when to gain or lose. *The New York Times,* pp. F1, F8.

Kolata, G. (2001a, March 8). Parkinson's research is set back by failure of fetal cell implants. *The New York Times,* pp. A1, A16.

Kolata, G. (2001b, November 22). Hints of an Alzheimer's aid in anti-inflammatory drugs. *The New York Times,* p. A24.

Kolbert, E. (1994, January 21). Demons replace dolls and bicycles in world of children of the quake. *The New York Times,* p. A19.

Kolko, D. J., & Rickard-Figueroa, J. L. (1985). Effects of video games on the adverse corollaries of chemotherapy in pediatric oncology patients: A single-case analysis. *Journal of Consulting and Clinical Psychology, 53,* 223–228.

Koorland, M. A. (1986). Applied behavior analysis and the correction of learning disabilities. In J. K. Torgesen & B. Y. L. Wong (Eds.), *Psychological and educational perspectives on learning disabilities* (pp. 297–328). Orlando, FL: Academic Press.

Kordower, J. H., et al. (2000). Neurodegeneration prevented by lentiviral vector delivery of GDNF in primate models of Parkinson's disease. *Science, 290,* 767–773.

Koren, D., Arnon, I., & Klein, E. (1999). Acute stress response and posttraumatic stress disorder in traffic accident victims: A one-year prospective, follow-up study. *American Journal of Psychiatry, 156,* 367–373.

Korotitsch, W. J., &. Nelson-Gray, R. O. (1999). An overview of self-monitoring research in assessment and treatment. *Psychological Assessment, 11,* 415–425.

Koss, M. P. (1988). Stranger and acquaintance rape: Are there differences in the victim's experience? *Psychology of Women Quarterly, 12,* 1–24.

Koss, M. P., Gidycz, C. A., & Wisniewski, N. (1987). The scope of rape: Incidence and prevalence of sexual aggression and victimization in a national sample of higher education students. *Journal of Consulting and Clinical Psychology, 55,* 162–170.

Koss, M. P., et al. (1994). *No safe haven: Male violence against women at home, at work, and in the community.* Washington, DC: American Psychological Association.

Kotler, M. (1997). Excess dopamine D4 receptor (D4DR) exon III seven repeat allele in opioid-dependent subjects. *Molecular Psychiatry, 2,* 251–254.

Kotler, M., et al. (2001). Anger, impulsivity, social support, and suicide risk in patients with posttraumatic stress disorder. *Journal of Nervous & Mental Disease, 189,* 162–167.

Kovacs, M. (1996). Presentation and course of major depressive disorder during childhood and later years of the life span. *Journal of the American Academy of Children and Adolescent Psychiatry, 35,* 705–715.

Kovacs, M., et al. (1997). A controlled family history study of childhood-onset depressive disorder. *Archives of General Psychiatry, 54,* 613–623.

Kraepelin, E. (1909–1913). *Psychiatrie* (8th ed.). Leipzig: J. A. Barth.

Kramer, M. S., et al. (1998, September 11). Distinct mechanism for antidepressant activity by blockade of central substance P receptors. *Science,* pp. 1640–1645.

Krantz, D. S., Contrada, R. J., Hills, D. R., & Friedler, E. (1988). Environmental stress and biobehavioral antecedents of coronary heart disease. *Journal of Consulting and Clinical Psychology, 56,* 333–341.

Kranzler, H. R. (2000). Medications for alcohol dependence: New vistas. *Journal of the American Medical Association, 284,* 1016–1017. [Editorial]

Kranzler, H. R., et al. (1996). Comorbid psychiatric diagnosis predicts three year outcomes in alcoholics: A posttreatment natural history study. *Journal of Studies in Alcohol, 57,* 619–626.

Krehbiel, K. (2000, October). Diagnosis and treatment of bipolar disorder. *Monitor on Psychology,* p. 22.

Kresin, D. (1993) Medical aspects of inhibited sexual desire disorder. In W. O'Donohue & J. H. Geer (Eds.), *Handbook of sexual dysfunctions: Assessment and treatment* (pp. 15–52). Boston: Allyn & Bacon.

Kring, A. M., & Neale, J. M. (1996). Do schizophrenic patients show a disjunctive relationship among expressive, experiential, and psychophysiological components of emotion? *Journal of Abnormal Psychology, 105,* 249–257.

Kristof, N. D. (1995, May 14). Japanese say no to crime: Tough methods, at a price. *The New York Times,* pp. A1, A8.

Krug, E., et al. (1998). Suicide after natural disasters. *The New England Journal of Medicine, 338,* 373–378.

Kryger, M. H., Roth, T., & Dement, W. C. (Eds.). (2000). *Principles and practice of sleep medicine* (3rd ed.). Philadelphia: W. B. Saunders.

Kubisyzn, T. W., et al. (2000). Empirical support for psychological assessment in clinical health care settings. *Professional Psychology: Research and Practice, 31,* 119–130.

Kuhn, C. M., & Wilson, W. A. (2001, Spring). Our dangerous love affair with ecstasy. *Cerebrum*, pp. 22–33.

Kuiper, N. A., & Martin, R. A. (1993). Humor and self-concept. *Humor International Journal of Humor Research, 6*, 251–270.

Kupfer, D. J. (1999). Research in affective disorders comes of age. *American Journal of Psychiatry, 156*, 165–167. [Editorial]

Kupfer, D. J., & Reynolds, C. F. (1997). Current concepts: Management of insomnia. *The New England Journal of Medicine, 336*, 341–346.

Kupfersmid, J. (1995). Does the Oedipus complex exist? *Psychotherapy, 32*, 535–547.

Kutchins, H., & Kirk, S. A. (1995, May). *DSM-IV*: Does bigger and newer mean better? *The Harvard Mental Health Letter, 11*(11), 4–6.

Kwon, H., et al. (2001). Functional neuroanatomy of visuospatial working memory in Fragile X syndrome: Relation to behavioral and molecular measures. *American Journal of Psychiatry, 158*, 1040–1051.

Kwon, S., & Oei, T. P. S. (1994). The roles of two levels of cognitions in the development, maintenance, and treatment of depression. *Clinical Psychology Review, 14*, 331–358.

L

Ladouceur, R., et al. (2000). Efficacy of a cognitive–behavioral treatment for generalized anxiety disorder: Evaluation in a controlled clinical trial. *Journal of Consulting and Clinical Psychology, 68*, 957–964.

Lahey, B. B., et al. (1995). Four-year longitudinal study of conduct disorder in boys: Patterns and predictors of persistence. *Journal of Abnormal Psychology, 104*, 83–93.

Lam, D. H., et al. (2000). Cognitive therapy for bipolar illness: A pilot study of relapse prevention. *Cognitive Therapy & Research, 24*, 503–520.

Lamb, H. R., & Lamb, D. M. (1990). Factors contributing to homelessness among the chronically and severely mentally ill. *Hospital and Community Psychiatry, 41*, 301–305.

Lamberg, L. (1998). Mental illness and violent acts: Protecting the patient and the public. *Journal of the American Medical Association, 280*, 407–408.

Lamberg, L. (2000). Sleep disorders, often unrecognized, complicate many physical illnesses. *Journal of the American Medical Association, 284*, 2173–2175.

Lambert, E. W., et al. (2001). Looking for the disorder in conduct disorder. *Journal of Abnormal Psychology, 110*, 110–123.

Lambert, G., et al. (2000). Reduced brain norepinephrine and dopamine release in treatment-refractory depressive illness: Evidence in support of the catecholamine hypothesis of mood disorders. *Archives of General Psychiatry, 57*, 787–793.

Lambert, M. C., et al. (1992). Jamaican and American adult perspectives on child psychopathology: Further exploration of the threshold model. *Journal of Consulting and Clinical Psychology, 60*, 146–149.

Lambert, M. J., & Bergin, A. E. (1994). The effectiveness of psychotherapy. In A. E. Bergin & S. L. Garfield (Eds.), *Handbook of psychotherapy and behavior change* (4th ed., pp. 72–113). New York: Wiley.

Lambert, M. J., & Okiishi, J. C. (1997). The effects of the individual psychotherapist and implications for future research. *Clinical Psychology: Science and Practice, 4*, 66–75.

Lambert, N. M., Hartsough, C. S., Sassone, D., & Sandoval, J. (1987). Persistence of hyperactivity symptoms from childhood to adolescence and associated outcomes. *American Journal of Orthopsychiatry, 57*, 22–32.

Landerman, L. R., et al. (1994). The relationship between insurance coverage and psychiatric disorder in predicting use of mental health services. *American Journal of Psychiatry, 151*, 1785–1790.

Landolt, H. P., et al. (1996). Late-afternoon ethanol intake affects nocturnal sleep and the sleep EEG in middle-aged men. *Journal of Clinical Psychopharmacology, 16*, 428–436.

Lane, E. (1994, December 6). Losing weight isn't enough. *New York Newsday*, p. A6.

Lang, P. J. (1968). Fear reduction and fear behavior: Problems in treating a construct. In J. M. Schlein (Ed.), *Research in psychotherapy, Vol. III* (pp. 90–102). Washington, DC: American Psychological Association.

Lang, P.J., & Lazovik, A. D. (1963). Experimental desensitization of phobia. *Journal of Abnormal and Social Psychology, 66*, 519–525.

Langenbucher, J. W., & Chung, T. (1995). Onset and staging of *DSM-IV* alcohol dependence using mean age and survival-hazard methods. *Journal of Abnormal Psychology, 104*, 346–354.

Langenbucher, J., et al. (2000). Toward the *DSM–V*: The withdrawal-gate model versus the *DSM-IV* in the diagnosis of alcohol abuse and dependence. *Journal of Consulting and Clinical Psychology, 68*, 799–809.

Lara, M. E., Leader, J., & Klein, D. N. (1997). The association between social support and course of depression: Is it confounded with personality? *Journal of Abnormal Psychology, 106*, 478–482.

Larimer, M. E., Marlatt, G. A., Baer, J. S., Quigley, L. A., Blume, A. W., & Hawkins, E. H. (1998). Harm reduction for alcohol problems: Expanding access to and acceptability of prevention and treatment services. In G. Marlatt (Ed.), *Harm reduction: Pragmatic strategies for managing high-risk behaviors* (pp. 69–121). New York: Guilford Press.

Larson, R. W., Raffaelli, M., Richards, M. H., Ham, M., & Jewell, L. (1990). Ecology of depression in late childhood and early adolescence: A profile of daily states and activities. *Journal of Abnormal Psychology, 99*, 92–102.

Last draw for smokers. (1996, October). *UC Berkeley Wellness Letter, 13*, 2–3.

Lauerman, C. (2000, November 7). Psychological counseling is now just a computer click away. Retrieved November 21, 2000, from http://www.psycport.com/news/2000/11/07/Knigt/3822-0076-MEDE-THERAPY.TB.html.

Laughter may be best medicine for heart disease. (2000, November 15) *CNN Web Posting*. Retrieved November 18, 2000, from http://www.cnn.com/2000/HEALTH/11/15/heart.laughter.reut/index.html.

Laumann, E. O., Gagnon, J. H., Michael, R. T., & Michaels, S. (1994). *The social organization of sexuality: Sexual practices in the United States*. Chicago: University of Chicago Press.

Laumann, E. O., Paik, A., & Rosen, R. C. (1999). Sexual dysfunction in the United States: Prevalence and predictors. *Journal of the American Medical Association, 281*, 537–544.

Lawson, D. M. (1983). Alcoholism. In M. Hersen (Ed.), *Outpatient behavior therapy: A clinical guide* (pp. 143–172). New York: Grune & Stratton.

Lawson, W. B. (1986). Racial and ethnic factors in psychiatric research. *Hospital and Community Psychiatry, 37*, 50–54.

Lawson, W. B. (1996). Clinical issues in the pharmacotherapy of African-Americans. *Psychopharmacology Bulletin, 32*, 275–281.

Lawson, W. B. (1999). Psychiatric diagnosis of African Americans. In J. M. Herrera, W. B. Lawson, & J. J. Sramek (Eds.), *Cross cultural psychiatry* (pp. 99–104). Chichester, England: Wiley.

Lazarus, A. A. (1992). Multimodal therapy: Technical eclecticism with minimal integration. In J. C. Norcross & M. R. Goldfried (Eds.), *Handbook of psychotherapy integration* (pp. 231–263). New York: Basic Books.

Lazarus, R. S., & Folkman, S. (1984). *Stress, appraisal, and coping*. New York: Springer.

Leary, W. E. (1996b, December 18). Responses of alcoholics to therapies seem similar. *The New York Times*, p. A17.

Leary, W. E. (1998, Feburary 12). New therapy offers promise in treatment of pedophiles. *The New York Times*, p. A11.

Leavitt, F., & Labott, S. M. (1997). Criterion-related validity of Rorschach analogues of dissociation. *Psychological Assessment, 9*, 244–249.

LeDuff, C. (2000, August 21). Cocaine quietly reclaims its hold as good times return. *The New York Times*, pp. B1, B2.

Lee, C. C., & Richardson, B. L. (1991). *Multicultural issues in counseling: New approaches to diversity*. Alexandria, VA: AACD.

Lee, D. T. S., et al. (2001). A psychiatric epidemiological study of postpartum Chinese women. *American Journal of Psychiatry, 158*, 220–226.

Lee, I-M., et al. (2001). Physical activity and coronary heart disease in women: Is "no pain, no gain" passé? *Journal of the American Medical Association, 285*, 1447–1454.

Lee, T. M. C., et al. (1998). Seasonal affective disorder. *Clinical Psychology: Science and Practice, 5*, 275–290.

Leedham, B., et al. (1995). Positive expectations predict health after heart transplantation. *Health Psychology, 14*, 74–79.

Leekam, S. R, & López, B. (2000). Attention and joint attention in preschool children with autism. *Developmental Psychology, 36*, 261–273.

Lefcourt, H. M., & Martin, R. A. (1986). *Humor and life stress: Antidote to adversity*. New York: Springer-Verlag.

Leff, J., & Vaughn, C. (1981). The role of maintenance therapy and relatives' expressed emotion in relapse of schizophrenia: A two-year follow-up. *British Journal of Psychiatry, 139*, 102–104.

Lefley, H. P. (1990). Culture and chronic mental illness. *Hospital and Community Psychiatry, 41*, 277–286.

Lehrer, M., et al. (1994). Relaxation and music therapies for asthma among patients prestabilized on asthma medication. *Journal of Behavioral Medicine, 17*, 1–24.

Lehrer, P. M., Sargunaraj, D., & Hochron, S. (1992). Psychological approaches to the treatment of asthma. *Journal of Consulting and Clinical Psychology, 60*, 639–643.

Leibel, R. L., Rosenbaum, M., & Hirsch, J. (1995). Changes in energy expenditure resulting from altered body weight. *New England Journal of Medicine, 332*, 621–628.

Leibenluft, E. (1996). Women with bipolar illness: Clinical and research issues. *American Journal of Psychiatry, 153*, 163–173.

Leibson, C. L., et al. (2001). Use and costs of medical care for children and adolescents with and without attention-deficit/hyperactivity disorder. *Journal of the American Medical Association, 285*, 60–66.

Leichsenring, F. (2001). Comparative effects of short-term psychodynamic psychotherapy and cognitive-behavioral therapy in depression: A meta-analytic approach. *Clinical Psychology Review, 21*, 401–419.

Lemonick, M. D., & Park, A. (2001, May 14). Alzheimer's: The Nun study. *Time*, pp. 54–64.

Leocani, L., et al. (2001). Abnormal pattern of cortical activation associated with voluntary movement in obsessive-compulsive disorder: An EEG study. *American Journal of Psychiatry, 158*, 140–142.

Leon, G. R., et al. (1995). Prospective analysis of personality and behavioral vulnerabilities and gender influences in the later development of disordered eating. *Journal of Abnormal Psychology, 104*, 140–149.

Lerman, C., et al. (1999). Evidence suggesting the role of specific genetic factors in cigarette smoking. *Health Psychology, 18*, 14–20.

Lesch, K. P., et al. (1996). Association of anxiety-related traits with a polymorphism in the serotonin transporter gene regulatory region. *Science, 274*, 1527–1531.

Leserman, J., et al. (2000). Impact of stressful life events, depression, social support, coping, and cortisol on progression to AIDS. *American Journal of Psychiatry, 157,* 1221–1228.

Leshner, A. I. (1999). Science is revolutionizing our view of addiction and what to do about it *American Journal of Psychiatry, 156,* 1–3.

Lesser, I. (1992, December). *Ethnic differences in response to psychotropic drugs.* Paper presented at a symposium, Anxiety Disorders in African Americans, presented by the State University of New York Health Science Center at Brooklyn, Brooklyn, NY.

Letourneau, E., & O'Donohue, W. (1993). Sexual desire disorders. In W. O'Donohue & J. H. Geer (Eds.), *Handbook of sexual dysfunctions: Assessment and treatment* (pp. 53–81). Boston: Allyn & Bacon.

Levenson, J. L., & Bemis, C (1991). The role of psychological factors in cancer onset and progression. *Psychosomatics, 32,* 124–132.

Levenstein, S., et al. (1999). Stress and peptic ulcer disease. *Journal of the American Medical Association, 281,* 10–11.

Levine, A. (2000, December 22). Tomorrow's education, made to measure. *The New York Times,* p. A 33.

Levitan, R. D., Rector, N. A., & Bagby, R. M. (1998). Negative attributional style in seasonal and nonseasonal depression. *American Journal of Psychiatry, 155,* 428–430.

Levitan, R. D., et al. (1997). Hormonal and subjective responses to intravenous metachlorophenylpiperazine in bulimia nervosa. *Archives of General Psychiatry, 54,* 521–527.

Levy, S. R., Jurkovic, G. L., & Spirito, A. (1995). A multisystems analysis of adolescent suicide attempters. *Journal of Abnormal Child Psychology, 23,* 221–234.

Lewin, T. (2001, April 15). Ask not for whom the clock ticks. *The New York Times Week in Review,* p. 4.

Lewinsohn, P. M. (1974). A behavioral approach to depression. In R. J. Friedman & M. M. Katz (Eds.), *The psychology of depression: Contemporary theory and research.* Washington, DC: Winston-Wiley.

Lewinsohn, P. M., & Clarke, G. N. (1999). Psychosocial treatments for adolescent depression. *Clinical Psychology Review, 19,* 329–342.

Lewinsohn, P. M., Clarke, G. N., Rhode, P., Hops, H., & Seely, J. (1996). A course in coping: A cognitive-behavioral approach to the treatment of adolescent depression. In D. Hibbs & P. S. Jensen (Eds.), *Psychosocial treatments for child and adolescent disorders: Empirically based strategies for clinical practice* (pp. 109–135). Washington, DC: American Psychological Association.

Lewinsohn, P. M., Duncan, E. M., Stanton, A. K., & Hautzinger, M. (1986). Age at first onset for nonpolar depression. *Journal of Abnormal Psychology, 95,* 378–383.

Lewinsohn, P. M., Joiner, T. E., & Rohde, P. (2001). Evaluation of cognitive diathesis-stress models in predicting major depressive disorder in adolescents. *Journal of Abnormal Psychology, 110,* 203–215.

Lewinsohn, P. M., & Libet, J. M. (1972). Pleasant events, activity schedules and depression. *Journal of Abnormal Psychology, 79,* 291–295.

Lewinsohn, P. M., Rohde, P., & Seeley, J. R. (1994). Psychosocial risk factors for future adolescent suicide attempts. *Journal of Consulting and Clinical Psychology, 62,* 297–305.

Lewinsohn, P. M., Rohde, P., & Seeley, J. R. (1996). Adolescent suicidal ideation and attempts: Prevalence, risk factors, and clinical implications. *Clinical Psychology: Science and Practice, 3,* 25–46.

Lewinsohn, P. M., Teri, L., & Wasserman, D. (1983). Depression. In M. Hersen (Ed.), *Outpatient behavior therapy: A practical guide* (pp. 81–108). New York: Grune & Stratton.

Lewinsohn, P. M., et al. (1994). Adolescent psychopathology: II. Psychosocial risk factors for depression. *Journal of Abnormal Psychology, 103,* 302–315.

Lewinsohn, P. M., et al. (1996). A course in coping: A cognitive-behavioral approach to the treatment of adolescent depression. In D. Hibbs & P. S. Jensen (Eds.), *Psychosocial treatments for child and adolescent disorders: Empirically based strategies for clinical practice* (pp. 109–135). Washington, DC: American Psychological Association.

Lewinsohn, P. M., et al. (2001). Gender differences in suicide attempts from adolescence to young adulthood. *Journal of American Academy of Child & Adolescent Psychiatry, 40,* 427–434.

Lewis, D. O., et al. (1997). Objective documentation of child abuse and dissociation in 12 murderers with dissociative identity disorder. *American Journal of Psychiatry, 154,* 1703–1710.

Lewis, R. J., Dlugokinski, E. L., Caputo, L. M., & Griffin, R. B. (1988). Children at risk for emotional disorders: Risk and resource dimensions. *Clinical Psychology Review, 8,* 417–440.

Lewis-Hall, F. (1992, December). *Overview of DSM-III-R: Focus on panic disorder and obsessive-compulsive disorder.* Paper presented at a symposium, Anxiety Disorders in African Americans, presented by the State University of New York Health Science Center at Brooklyn, Brooklyn, NY.

Lex, B. W. (1987). Review of alcohol problems in ethnic minority groups. *Journal of Consulting and Clinical Psychology, 55,* 293–300.

Ley, R. (1997). The Ondine curse, false suffocation alarms, trait-state suffocation fear, and dyspnea-suffocation fear in panic attacks. *Archives of General Psychiatry, 54,* 677.

Li, Y. M., et al. (2000). Photoactivated-secretase inhibitors directed to the active site covalently label presenilin, 1. *Nature, 405,* 689–694.

Liberman, R. P. (1994). Treatment and rehabilitation of the seriously mentally ill in China: Impressions of a society in transition. *American Journal of Orthopsychiatry, 64,* 68–77.

Lichstein, K. L., Wilson, N. M., & Johnson, C. T. (2000). Psychological treatment of secondary insomnia. *Psychology and Aging, 15,* 232–240.

Lichstein, K. L., et al. (2001). Primary versus secondary insomnia in older adults: Subjective sleep and daytime functioning. *Psychology and Aging, 16,* 264–271.

Lichtenberg, P. A., & Duffy, M. (2000). Psychological assessment and psychotherapy in long-term care. *Clinical Psychology: Science and Practice,* 317–328.

Lichtenstein, E., & Glasgow, R. E. (1992). Smoking cessation: What have we learned over the past decade? *Journal of Consulting and Clinical Psychology, 60,* 518–527.

Lieber, C. S. (1990, January 14). Cited in "Barroom biology: How alcohol goes to a woman's head." *The New York Times,* p. E24.

Liebowitz, M. R., et al. (2000). Social phobia or social anxiety disorder: What's in a name? *Archives of General Psychiatry, 57,* 191–192.

Lightsey, O. W., Jr. (1994a). Positive automatic cognitions as moderators of the negative life event-dysphoria relationship. *Cognitive Therapy and Research, 18,* 353–365.

Lightsey, O. W., Jr. (1994b). "Thinking positive" as a stress buffer: The role of positive automatic cognitions in depression and happiness. *Journal of Counseling Psychology, 41,* 325–334.

Lilienfeld, S. O. (1997). The relation of anxiety sensitivity to higher and lower order personality dimensions: Implications for the etiology of panic attacks. *Journal of Abnormal Psychology, 106,* 539–544.

Lilienfeld, S. O., & Andrews, B. P. (1996). Identifying noncriminal psychopaths. *Journal of Personality Assessment, 66,* 488–524.

Lilienfeld, S. O., & Marino, L. (1995). Mental disorder as a Roschian concept: A critique of Wakefield's "harmful dysfunction" analysis. *Journal of Abnormal Psychology, 104,* 411–420.

Lilienfeld, S. O., Wood, J. M, & Garb, H. N. (2000). The scientific status of projective techniques. *Psychological Science in the Public Interest, 1,* 27–66.

Lin, K., et al. (1991). Ethnicity and family involvement in the treatment of schizophrenic patients. *Journal of Nervous & Mental Disease, 179,* 631–633.

Lin, T. Y., et al. (1978). Ethnicity and patterns of help-seeking. *Culture, Medicine, and Psychiatry, 2,* 3–14.

Lindsey, K. P., & Paul, G. L. (1989). Involuntary commitments to public mental institutions: Issues involving the overrepresentation of blacks and assessment of relevant functioning. *Psychological Bulletin, 106,* 171–183.

Linehan, M. M. (1993). *Cognitive-behavioral treatment of borderline personality disorder.* New York: Guilford Press.

Linehan, M. M., Camper, P., Chiles, J. A., Strosahl, K., & Shearin, E. (1987). Interpersonal problem solving and parasuicide. *Cognitive Therapy and Research, 11,* 1–12.

Linehan, M., et al. (1991). Cognitive-behavioral treatment of chronically parasuicidal borderline patients. *Archives of General Psychiatry, 48,* 1060–1064.

Linehan, M. M., et al. (1994). Interpersonal outcome of cognitive behavioral treatment for chronically suicidal borderline patients. *American Journal of Psychiatry, 151,* 1771–1776.

Link, B. G., & Stueve, A. (1998). New evidence on the violence risk posed by people with mental illness. *Archives of General Psychiatry, 55,* 403–404.

Liotti, G., et al. (2000). Predictive factors for borderline personality disorder. *Acta Psychiatrica Scandinavica, 102,* 282–289.

Lipman, E. L., MacMillan, H. L., & Boyle, M. H. (2001). Childhood abuse and psychiatric disorders among single and married mothers. *American Journal of Psychiatry, 158,* 73–77.

Lipsey, M. W., & Wilson, D. B. (1993). The efficacy of psychology, educational, and behavioral treatment: Confirmation from meta-analysis. *American Psychologist, 48,* 1181–1209.

Lipsey, M. W., & Wilson, D. B. (1995). Reply to comments on Lispey and Wilson (1993). *American Psychologist, 50,* 113–115.

Lipton, R. B., et al. (1998). Efficacy and safety of acetaminophen, aspirin, and caffeine in alleviating migraine headache pain. *Archives of Neurology, 55,* 210–217.

Lipton, R. B, et al. (2000a). Stratified care vs. step care strategies for migraine: The Disability in Strategies of Care (DISC) Study: A randomized trial. *Journal of the American Medical Association, 284,* 2599–2605.

Lipton, R. B., et al. (2000b). Migraine, quality of life, and depression. *Neurology, 55,* 629–635.

Lira, L. R., Koss, M. P., & Russo, N. F. (1999). Mexican American women's definitions of rape and sexual abuse. *Hispanic Journal of Behavioral Sciences, 21*(3), 236–265.

Lisanby, S. H., et al. (2000). The effects of electroconvulsive therapy on memory of autobiographical and public events. *Archives of General Psychiatry, 57,* 581–590.

Litz, B. T. (1992). Emotional numbing in combat-related post-traumatic stress disorder: A critical review and reformulation. *Clinical Psychology Review, 12,* 417–432.

Livesley, W. J. (1985). The classification of personality disorder, II: The problem of criteria. *Canadian Journal of Psychiatry, 30,* 359–362.

Livesley, W. J., et al. (1993). Genetic and environmental contributions to dimensions of personality disorder. *American Journal of Psychiatry, 150,* 1826–1831.

Livesley, W. J., et al. (1994). Categorical distinctions in the study of personality disorder: Implications for classification. *Journal of Abnormal Psychology, 103,* 6–17.

Livingstone, M., et al. (1991). Physiological and anatomical evidence for a magnocellular defect in developmental dyslexia. *Proceedings of the National Academy of Sciences, 88,* 7943–7947.

Lobel, M., et al. (2000). The impact of prenatal maternal stress and optimistic disposition on birth outcomes in medically high-risk women. *Health Psychology, 19*, 544–553.

Lochman, J. E. (1992). Cognitive-behavioral intervention with aggressive boys: Three-year follow-up and preventive effects. *Journal of Consulting and Clinical Psychology, 60*, 426–432

Lochman, J. E., & Dodge, K. A. (1994). Social-cognitive processes of severely violent, moderately aggressive, and nonaggressive boys. *Journal of Consulting and Clinical Psychology, 62*, 366–374.

Lochman, J. E., & Lenhart, L. (1993). Anger coping intervention for aggressive children: Conceptual models and outcome effects. *Clinical Psychology Review, 13*, 785–805.

Loeber, R., Lahey, B. B., & Thomas, C. (1991). Diagnostic conundrum of oppositional defiant disorder and its comorbid conditions: Effects of age and gender. *Journal of Consulting and Clinical Psychology, 59*, 379–390.

Loewenstein, R. J. (1991). Psychogenic amnesia and psychogenic fugue: A comprehensive review. *Annual Review of Psychiatry, 10*, 223–247.

Loftus, E. F. (1993). The reality of repressed memories. *American Psychologist, 48*, 518–537.

Loftus, E. F. (1996). The myth of repressed memory and the realities of science. *Clinical Psychology: Science and Practice, 3*, 356–365.

Loftus, E. F. (1997). Creating childhood memories. *Applied Cognitive Psychology, 11*, S75–S86.

Lohman, J. J. H. M. (2001). Treatment strategies for migraine headache. *Journal of the American Medical Association, 285*, 1014.

Lohr, B. A., Adams, H. E., & Davis, J. M. (1997). Sexual arousal to erotic and aggressive stimuli in sexually coercive and noncoercive men. *Journal of Consulting and Clinical Psychology, 106*, 230–242.

LoPiccolo, J. (1990). Sexual dysfunction. In A. S. Bellack, M. Hersen, & A. E. Kazdin (Eds.), *International handbook of behavior modification therapy* (2nd ed., pp. 557–564). New York: Plenum Press.

LoPiccolo, J., & Stock, W. E. (1986). Treatment of sexual dysfunction. *Journal of Consulting and Clinical Psychology, 54*, 158–167.

Loranger, A. W. (1996). Dependant personality disorder: Age, sex, and Axis I comorbidity. *Journal of Nervous and Mental Disease, 184*, 17–21.

Loranger, A. W., et al. (1994). The international personality disorder examination: The World Health Organization/ Alcohol, Drug, Abuse and Mental Health Administration International Pilot Study of Personality Disorders. *Archives of General Psychiatry, 51*, 215–224.

Lorefice, L. S. (1991). Fluoxetine treatment of a fetish. *Journal of Clinical Psychiatry, 52*, 41.

Lovaas, O. I. (1977). *The autistic child: Language development through behavior modification.* New York: Halstead Press.

Lovaas, O. I. (1987). Behavioral treatment and normal educational and intellectual functioning in young autistic children. *Journal of Consulting and Clinical Psychology, 55*, 3–9.

Lovaas, O. I., Koegel, R. L., & Schreibman, L. (1979). Stimulus overselectivity in autism: A review of the research. *Psychological Bulletin, 86*, 1236–1254.

Lowe, M. R., Gleaves, D. H., Murphy-Eberenz, K. P. (1998). On the relation of dieting and bingeing in bulimia nervosa. *Journal of Abnormal Psychology, 107*, 263–271.

Lubin, B., Larsen, R. M., Matarazzo, J. D., & Seever, M. (1985). Psychological test usage patterns in five professional settings. *American Psychologist, 40*, 857–861.

Luborsky, I., et al. (1996). Factors in outcomes of short-term dynamic psychotherapy for chronic vs. non-chronic major depression. *Journal of Psychotherapy: Practice and Research, 5*, 152–159.

Luborsky, L., et al. (1988). *Who will benefit from psychotherapy? Predicting therapeutic outcomes.* New York: Basic Books.

Luntz, B. K., & Widom, C. S. (1994). Antisocial personality disorder in abused and neglected children grown up. *American Journal of Psychiatry, 151*, 670–674.

Lurigio, A. J., & Lewis, D. A. (1989). Worlds that fail: A longitudinal study of urban mental patients. *Journal of Social Issues, 45*, 79–90.

Lutgendorf, S. K., et al. (1997). Cognitive-behavioral stress management decreases dysphoric mood and herpes simplex virus-type 2 antibody titer in symptomatic HIV-seropositive gay men. *Journal of Consulting and Clinical Psychology, 65*, 31–43.

Lyketsos C. G., et al. (2000). Randomized, placebo-controlled, double-blind clinical trial of sertraline in the treatment of depression complicating Alzheimer's disease: Initial results from the Depression in Alzheimer's Disease Study. *American Journal of Psychiatry, 157*, 1686–1689.

Lykken, D. T. (1957). A study of anxiety in the sociopathic personality. *Journal of Abnormal and Social Psychology, 55*, 6–10.

Lykken, D. T. (1993). Predicting violence in the violent society. *Applied and Preventive Psychology, 2*, 13–20.

Lymburner, J. A., & Roech, R. (1999). The insanity defense: Five years of research (1993–1997). *International Journal of Law and Psychiatry, 22*, 213–240.

Lyon, F. R., & Moats, L. C. (1988). Critical issues in the instruction of the learning disabled. *Journal of Consulting and Clinical Psychology, 56*, 830–835.

M

Machan, D. (2000, December). Forget the champagne. *Forbes*, pp. 118–120.

MacMillan, H. L., et al. (1997). Prevalence of child physical and sexual abuse in the community: Results from the Ontario health supplement. *Journal of the American Medical Association, 278*, 131–135.

MacPhillamy, D. J., & Lewinsohn, P. M. (1974). Depression as a function of levels of desired and obtained pleasure. *Journal of Abnormal Psychology, 83*, 651–657.

Maddi, S. R., & Kobasa, S. C. (1984). *The hardy executive: Health under stress.* Homewood, IL: Dow Jones-Irwin.

Maeder, T. (1985). *Crime and madness: The origins and evolution of the insanity defense.* New York: Harper & Row.

Magdol, L., et al. (1997). Gender differences in partner violence in a birth cohort of 21-year olds: Bridging the gap between clinical and epidemiological approaches. *Journal of Consulting and Clinical Psychology, 65*, 68–78.

Magdol, L., et al. (1998). Developmental antecedents of partner abuse: A prospective longitudinal study. *Journal of Abnormal Psychology, 107*, 375–389.

Maher, W. B., & Maher, B. A. (1985). Psychopathology: I. From ancient times to the eighteenth century. In G. A. Kimble & K. Schlesinger (Eds.), *Topics in the history of psychology* (Vol. 2). Hillsdale, NJ: Erlbaum.

Mahler, M., & Kaplan, L. (1977). Developmental aspects in the assessment of narcissistic and so-called borderline personalities. In P. Hartocollis (Ed.), *Borderline personality disorders: The concept, the syndrome, the patient* (pp. 71–85). New York: International Universities Press.

Mahler, M. S., Pine, F., & Bergman, A. (1975). The borderline syndrome: The role of the mother in the genesis and psychic structure of the borderline personality. *International Journal of Psychoanalysis, 56*, 163–177.

Maier, S. F., & Seligman, M. E. P. (1976). Learned helplessness: Theory and evidence. *Journal of Experimental Psychology (General), 105*, 3–46.

Maier, S. F., Watkins, L. R., & Fleshner, M. (1994). Psychoneuroimmunology; The interface between behavior, brain, and immunity. *American Psychologist, 49*, 1004–1017.

Maier, T. (1995, February 21). Drug hailed as a "magic bullet" has skeptics. *Newsday*, p. B23.

Maj, M., et al. (1991). A family study of DSM–III–R schizoaffective disorder, depressive type, compared with schizophrenia and psychotic and nonpsychotic major depression. *American Journal of Psychiatry, 148*, 612–616.

Malaspina, D., et al. (2001). Advancing paternal age and the risk of schizophrenia. *Archives of General Psychiatry, 58*, 361–367.

Maldonado, J. R., Butler, L. D., & Spiegel, D. (1998). Treatments for dissociative disorders. In P. E. Nathan & J. M. Gorman (Eds.), *A guide to treatments that work* (pp. 423–446). New York: Oxford University Press.

Maletsky, B. M. (1980). Self-referred vs. court-referred sexually deviant patients: Success with assisted covert sensitization. *Behavior Therapy, 11*, 306–314.

Maletsky, B. M. (1991). *Treating the sexual offender.* Newbury Park, CA: Sage.

Maletsky, B. M. (1998). The paraphilias: Research and treatment. In P. E. Nathan & J. M. Gorman (Eds.), *A guide to treatments that work* (pp. 472–500). New York: Oxford University Press.

Malmo, R. B., & Shagass, C. (1949). Physiological study of symptom mechanism in psychiatric patients under stress. *Psychosomatic Medicine, 11*, 25–29.

Malone, K. M., et al. (2000). Protective factors against suicidal acts in major depression: Reasons for living. *American Journal of Psychiatry, 157*, 1084–1088.

Mandal, M. K., Pandey, R., & Prasad, A. B. (1998). Facial expression of emotions and schizophrenia: A review. *Schizophrenia Bulletin, 24*, 399–412.

Mann, J. J., & Malone, K. M. (1997). Cerebrospinal fluid amines and higher-lethality suicide attempts in depressed inpatients. *Biological Psychiatry, 41*, 162–171.

Mann, J. J., et al. (1996). Postmortem studies of suicide victims. In S. J. Watson (Ed.), *Biology of schizophrenia and affective disease* (pp. 179–221). Washington, DC: American Psychiatric Press.

Many suicides could be prevented if people would watch for signs. (1998, June 16). *St. Louis Post-Dispatch*, p. D2.

Marangell, L. B., et al. (1997). Inverse relationship of peripheral thyrotropin-stimulating hormone levels to brain activity in mood disorders. *American Journal of Psychiatry, 154*, 224–230.

Marcus, D. K., & Nardone, M. E. (1992). Depression and interpersonal rejection. *Clinical Psychology Review, 12*, 433–449.

Marengo, J., & Harrow, M. (1987). Schizophrenic thought disorder at follow-up: A persistent or episodic course? *Archives of General Psychiatry, 44*, 651–659.

Margolin, G., & Burman, B. (1993). Wife abuse versus marital violence: Different terminologies, explanations, and solutions. *Clinical Psychology Review, 13*, 59–73.

Mark, D. H. (1998). Editor's Note. *Journal of the American Medical Association, 279*, 151.

Markowitz, J. C., et al. (1998). Treatment of depressive symptoms in human immunodeficiency virus-positive patients. *Archives of General Psychiatry, 55*, 452–457.

Markovitz, J. H., et al. (1993). Psychological predictors of hypertension in the Framingham Study: Is there tension in hypertension? *Journal of the American Medical Association, 270*, 2439–2443.

Marks, I., et al. (1998a). Computer-aided treatments of mental health problems. *Clinical Psychology: Science and Practice, 5*, 151–170.

Marks, I., et al. (1998b). Treatment of posttraumatic stress disorder by exposure and/or cognitive restructuring: A controlled study. *Archives of General Psychiatry, 55*, 317–325.

Marks, M., & De Silva, P. (1994). The "match/mismatch" mode of fear: Empirical status and clinical implications. *Behaviour Research and Therapy, 32*, 759–770.

Marlatt, G. A. (1978). Craving for alcohol, loss of control, and relapse: A cognitive-behavioral analysis. In P. E. Nathan, G. A. Marlatt, & T. Loberg (Eds.), *Alcoholism: New directions in behavioral research and treatment* (pp. 271–314). New York: Plenum Press.

Marlatt, G. A., Demming, B., & Reid, J. B. (1973). Loss of control drinking in alcoholics: An experimental analogue. *Journal of Abnormal Psychology, 81*, 233–241.

Marlatt, G. A., & Gordon, J. R. (1985). *Relapse prevention: Maintenance strategies in the treatment of addictive behaviors.* New York: Guilford Press.

Marlatt, G. A., et al. (1993). Harm reduction for alcohol problems: Moving beyond the controlled drinking controversy. *Behavior Therapy, 24*, 461–504.

Marlatt, G. A., et al. (1998). Screening and brief intervention for high-risk college student drinkers: Results from a 2-year follow-up assessment. *Journal of Consulting and Clinical Psychology, 66*, 604–615.

Marsh, D. T., & Johnson, D. L. (1997). The family experience of mental illness: Implications for intervention. *Professional Psychology: Research & Practice, 28*, 229–237.

Marshall, D. (1971). Sexual behavior on Mangaia. In D. Marshall & R. Suggs (Eds.), *Human sexual behavior: Variations in the ethnographic spectrum.* Englewood Cliffs, NJ: Prentice-Hall.

Marshall, W. L., Eccles, A., & Barbaree, H. E. (1991). The treatment of exhibitionists: A focus on sexual deviance versus cognitive and relationship features. *Behaviour Research and Therapy, 29*, 129–135.

Martin, D. (1989, January 25). Autism: Illness that can steal a child's sparkle. *The New York Times*, p. B1.

Martin, D. J., Garske, J. P., & Davis, M. K. (2000). Relation of the therapeutic alliance with outcome and other variables: A meta-analytic review. *Journal of Consulting and Clinical Psychology, 68*, 438–450.

Martin, J., Shochat, T., & Ancoli-Israel, S. (2000). Assessment and treatment of sleep disturbances in older adults. *Clinical Psychology Review, 20*, 783–805.

Martin, P. R., & Seneviratne, H. M. (1997). Effects of food deprivation and a stressor on head pain. *Health Psychology, 16*, 310–318.

Martin, R. A., & Lefcourt, H. M. (1983). Sense of humor as a moderator of the relation between stressors and moods. *Journal of Personality and Social Psychology, 45*, 1313–1324.

Martin, R. A., et al. (1993). Humor, coping with stress, self-concept, and psychological well-being. *Humor International Journal of Humor Research, 6*, 89–104.

Martin, S. E. (1992). The epidemiology of alcohol-related interpersonal violence. *Alcohol Health and Research World, 16*, 230–237.

Martins, C., de Lemos, A. I., & Bebbington, P. E. (1992). A Portuguese/Brazilian study of expressed emotion. *Social Psychiatry and Psychiatric Epidemiology, 27*, 22–27.

Marx, E. M., Williams, J. M. G., & Claridge, G. C. (1992). Depression and social problem solving. *Journal of Abnormal Psychology, 101*, 78–86.

Mason, M. (1994, September). Why ulcers run in families. *Health*, pp. 44, 48.

Masters, W. H., & Johnson, V. E. (1970). *Human sexual inadequacy.* Boston: Little, Brown.

Mathalno, D. H., et al. (2001). Progressive brain volume changes and the clinical course of schizophrenia in men: A longitudinal magnetic resonance imaging study. *Archives of General Psychiatry, 58*, 148–157.

Mathias, R. (2000). Cocaine, marijuana, and heroin abuse up, methamphetamine abuse down. *NIDA Notes, 15*(3), 4–5.

Matson, J. L., & Sevin, J. A. (1994). Theories of dual diagnosis in mental retardation. *Journal of Consulting and Clinical Psychology, 62*, 6–16.

Mayo-Smith, M. F. (1997). Pharmacological management of alcohol withdrawal. A meta-analysis and evidence-based practice guideline. American Society of Addiction Medicine Working Group on Pharmacological Management of Alcohol Withdrawal. *Journal of the American Medical Association, 278*, 144–151.

Mays, V. M. (1985). The Black American and psychotherapy: The dilemma. *Psychotherapy, 22*, 379–388.

Mazure, C. M. (1998). Life stressors as risk factors in depression. *Clinical Psychology: Science and Practice, 5*, 291–313.

McBride, P. A., Anderson, G. M., & Shapiro, T. (1996). Autism research: Bringing together approaches to pull apart the disorder. *Archives of General Psychiatry, 53*, 980–983.

McCabe, S. B., & Gotlib, I. H. (1995). Selective attention and clinical depression: Performance on a deployment-of-attention task. *Journal of Abnormal Psychology, 104*, 241–245.

McCarty, D., et al. (1991). Alcoholism, drug abuse, and the homeless. *American Psychologist, 46*, 1139–1148.

McCaul, M. E, & Furst, J. (1994). Alcoholism treatment in the United States. *Alcohol Health & Research World, 18*, 253–260.

McCauley, J., et al. (1997). Clinical characteristics of women with a history of childhood abuse: Unhealed wounds. *Journal of the American Medical Association, 277*, 1362–1368.

McClelland, D. C., Alexander, C., & Marks, E. (1982). The need for power, stress, immune functions, and illness among male prisoners. *Journal of Abnormal Psychology, 91*, 61–70.

McCloskey, L. A. (1996). Socioeconomic and coercive power within the family. *Gender and Society, 10*, 449–463.

McCloskey, L. A., & Bailey, J. A. (2000). The intergenerational transmission of risk for child sexual abuse. *Journal of Interpersonal Violence, 15*, 1019–1035.

McConaghy, N. (1990). Sexual deviation. In A. S. Bellack, M. Hersen, & A. E. Kazdin (Eds.), *International handbook of behavior modification and therapy* (2nd ed., pp. 565–580). New York: Plenum Press.

McCord, J. (1983). A 40-year perspective on effects of child abuse and neglect. *Child Abuse and Neglect, 7*, 265–270.

McCord, W., & McCord, J. (1964). *The psychopath: An essay on the criminal mind.* New York: D. Van Nostrand.

McCrady, B. S. (1993). Alcoholism. In D. H. Barlow (Ed.), *Clinical handbook of psychological disorders* (2nd ed., pp. 362–393). New York: Guilford Press.

McCrady, B. S. (1994). Alcoholics Anonymous and behavior therapy: Can habits be treated as diseases? Can diseases be treated as habits? *Journal of Consulting and Clinical Psychology, 62*, 1159–1166.

McCrady, B. S., & Langenbucher, J. W. (1996). Alcohol treatment and health care system reform. *Archives of General Psychiatry, 53*, 737–746.

McDermott, J. F. (2001). Emily Dickinson revisited: A study of periodicity in her work. *American Journal of Psychiatry, 158*, 686–690.

McDermut, W., Miller, I. W., & Brown, R. A. (2001). The efficacy of group psychotherapy for depression: A meta-analysis and review of the empirical research. *Clinical Psychology: Science and Practice, 8*, 98–116.

McDougle, C. J., et al. (1996). A double-blind, placebo-controlled study of fluvoxamine in adults with autistic disorder. *Archives of General Psychiatry, 53*, 1001–1008.

McEachin, J. J., Smith, T., & Lovaas, O. I. (1993). Long-term outcome for children with autism who received early intensive behavioral treatment. *American Journal on Mental Retardation, 97*, 359–372.

McElroy, S., et al. (1996). Placebo-controlled trial of sertraline in the treatment of binge eating disorder. *American Journal of Psychiatry, 157*, 1004–1006.

McFarlane, M., Bull, S. S., & Rietmeijer, C. A. (2000). The Internet as a newly emerging risk environment for sexually transmitted diseases. *Journal of the American Medical Association, 284*, 443–446.

McGinn, D. (2000, November 21). Scouting a dry campus. *Newsweek*, pp. 83–84.

McGinn, L. K., & Sanderson, W. C. (2001). What allows cognitive behavioral therapy to be brief: Overview, efficacy, and crucial factors facilitating brief treatment. *Clinical Psychology: Science and Practice, 8*, 23–37.

McGlashan, T. H., & Fenton, W. S. (1992). The positive-negative distinction in schizophrenia: Review of natural history validators. *Archives of General Psychiatry, 49*, 63–72.

McGlashan, T. H., & Hoffman, R. E. (2000). Schizophrenia as a disorder of developmentally reduced synaptic connectivity. *Archives of General Psychiatry, 57*, 637–648.

McGovern, P. G., et al. (1996). Recent trends in acute coronary heart disease. *The New England Journal of Medicine, 334*, 884–890.

McGovern, T. F. (1991). Ethical Considerations. In L. R. Dippel & T. J. Hutton (Eds.), *Caring for the Alzheimer patient: A practical guide* (2nd ed., pp. 169–177). Amherst, NY: Prometheus Books.

McGrath, E., Keita, G. P., Strickland, B. R., & Russo, N. F. (1990). *Women and depression: Risk factors and treatment issues.* Washington DC: American Psychological Association.

McGrath, P. J., et al. (2000). A placebo-controlled study of fluoxetine versus imipramine in the acute treatment of atypical depression. *American Journal of Psychiatry, 157*, 344–350.

McGue, M. (1993). From proteins to cognitions: The behavioral genetics of alcoholism. In R. Plomin & G. E. McClearn (Eds.), *Nature, nurture & psychology* (pp. 245–268). Washington, DC: American Psychological Association.

McGue, M., Slutske, W., & Iaono, W. G. (1999). Personality and substance use disorders: II. Alcoholism versus drug use disorders. *Journal of Consulting and Clinical Psychology, 67*, 394–404.

McGuire, P. K., Shah, G. M. S., & Murray, R. M. (1993). Increased blood flow in Broca's area during auditory hallucinations in schizophrenia. *The Lancet, 342*, 703–706.

McIntosh, H. (1998, November). Autism is likely to be linked to several genes. *APA Monitor, 29*(11), p. 13.

McKenna, M. C., et al. (1999). Psychosocial factors and the development of breast cancer: A meta-analysis. *Health Psychology, 18*, 520–531.

McKinney, K., & Maroules, N. (1991). Sexual harassment. In E. Grauerholz & M. A. Koralewski (Eds.), *Sexual coercion: A sourcebook on its nature, causes, and prevention* (pp. 29–44). Lexington, MA: Lexington Books.

McLean, P. D., et al. (2001). Cognitive versus behavior therapy in the group treatment of obsessive-compulsive disorder. *Journal of Consulting and Clinical Psychology, 69*, 205–214.

McLellan, A. T., et al. (1994). Similarity of outcome predictors across opiate, cocaine, and alcohol treatments: Role of treatment services. *Journal of Consulting and Clinical Psychology, 62*, 1141–1158.

McLellan, A. T., et al. (2000). Drug dependence, a chronic medical illness: Implications for treatment, insurance, and outcomes evaluation. *Journal of the American Medical Association, 284*, 1689–1695.

McMurtrie, B. (1994, July 19). Overweight fatten ranks. *New York Newsday*, p. A26.

McNally, R. (1987). Preparedness and phobias: A review. *Psychological Bulletin, 101*, 283–303.

McNally, R. J., Cassiday, K. L., & Calamari, J. E. (1990). Taijin-kyofu-sho in a Black American woman: Behavioral treatment of a "culture-bound" anxiety disorder. *Journal of Anxiety Disorders, 4*, 83–87.

McNally, R. J., & Eke, M. (1996). Anxiety sensitivity, suffocation fear, and breath-holding duration as predictors of response to carbon dioxide challenge. *Journal of Abnormal Psychology, 105*, 146–149.

McNally, R. J., et al. (1995). Clinical versus nonclinical panic: A test of suffocation false alarm theory. *Behaviour Research & Therapy, 33,* 127–131.

McNeil, D. G, Jr. (2001, February 4). Epidemic errors. *The New York Times Week in Review,* pp. 1, 5.

McNeil, T. F., Cantor-Graae, E., & Weinberger, D. R. (2000). Relationship of obstetric complications and differences in size of brain structures in monozygotic twin pairs discordant for schizophrenia. *American Journal of Psychiatry, 157,* 203–212.

McNiel, D. E., Lam, J. N., & Binder, R. L. (2000). Relevance of interrater agreement to violence risk assessment. *Journal of Consulting and Clinical Psychology, 68,* 6, 1111–1115.

McNiel, D. E., et al. (2000). The relationship between command hallucinations and violence. *Psychiatric Services, 51,* 1288–1292.

McNulty, J. L., et al. (1997). Comparative validity of MMPI-2 scores of African American and Caucasian mental health center clients. *Psychological Assessment, 9,* 464–470.

McQuiston, J. T. (1997, February 5). New mother on Long Island suffering from depression is found, apparently a suicide. *The New York Times,* p. B5.

Meacham, J. (2000, September 18). The new face of race. *Newsweek,* pp. 38–41.

Mead, M. (1935). *Sex and temperament in three primitive societies.* New York: Morrow.

Meador-Woodruff, J. H., et al. (1997). Dopamine receptor transcript expression in striatum and prefrontal and occipital cortex: Focal abnormalities in orbitofrontal cortex in schizophrenia. *Archives of General Psychiatry, 54,* 1089–1095.

Medalia, A., et al. (1998). Effectiveness of attention training in schizophrenia. *Schizophrenia Bulletin, 24,* 147–152.

Mednick, S. A., Parnas, J., & Schulsinger, F. (1987). The Copenhagen High-Risk project, 1962–86. *Schizophrenia Bulletin, 13,* 485–495.

Mednick, S. A., & Schulsinger, F. (1968). Some premorbid characteristics related to breakdown in children with schizophrenic mothers. In D. Rosenthal & S. S. Kety (Eds.), *The transmission of schizophrenia* (pp. 267–291). New York: Pergamon Press.

Meehan, P. J., et al. (1991). Attempted suicide among young adults: Progress toward a meaningful estimate of prevalence. *American Journal of Psychiatry, 149,* 41–44.

Meehl, P. E. (1962). Schizotaxia, schizotypy, schizophrenia. *American Psychologist, 17,* 827–838.

Meehl, P. E. (1972). A critical afterword. In I. I. Gottesman & J. Shields (Eds.), *Schizophrenia and genetics: A twin study vantage point* (pp. 367–415). New York: Academic Press.

Mehrabian, A., & Weinstein, L. (1985). Temperament characteristics of suicide attempters. *Journal of Consulting and Clinical Psychology, 53,* 544–546.

Meichenbaum, D. (1993). Changing conceptions of cognitive behavior modification: Retrospect and prospect. *Journal of Consulting and Clinical Psychology, 61,* 202–204.

Meichenbaum, D., & Deffenbacher, J. L. (1988). Stress inoculation training. *The Counseling Psychologist, 16*(1), 69–90.

Melani, D. (2001, January 17). Emotions can pull trigger on heart attack. *Evansville Courier & Press, Scripps Howard News Service.* Retrieved January 19, 2001, from http://www.psycport.com/news/2001/01/17/eng-courier press_features/eng-courierpress_features_134435_74_9803814571351.html.

Melchert, T. P. (1996). Childhood memory and a history of different forms of abuse. *Professional Psychology: Research and Practice, 27,* 438–446.

Mellor, C. S. (1970). First rank symptoms of schizophrenia. *British Journal of Psychiatry, 177,* 15–23.

Mental health problems cost North America and EU $120 billion. (2000, October 10). United Press International.

PsycPort News Story, American Psychological Association. Retrieved October 28, 2000, from http://www.psycport.com/news/2000/10/10/up/0000-0148-switzerland-mentalhea.html.

Merckelbach, H., Arntz, A., & de Jong, P. (1991). Conditioning experiences in spider phobics. *Behaviour Research and Therapy, 29,* 301–304.

Merckelbach, H., et al. (1996). The etiology of specific phobias: A review. *Clinical Psychology Review, 16,* 337–361.

Messenger, J. (1971). Sex and repression in an Irish folk community. In D. Marshall & R. Suggs (Eds.), *Human sexual behavior: Variations in the ethnographic spectrum.* Englewood Cliffs, NJ: Prentice-Hall.

Messer, S. B. (2001a). Empirically supported treatments: What's a nonbehaviorist to do? In B. D. Slife & R. N. Williams (Eds.), *Critical issues in psychotherapy: Translating new ideas into practice* (pp. 3–19). Thousand Oaks, CA: Sage.

Messer, S. B. (2001b). What makes brief psychodynamic therapy time efficient? *Clinical Psychology: Science and Practice, 8,* 5–22.

Meston, C. M., & Heiman, J. R. (2000). Sexual abuse and sexual function: An examination of sexually relevant cognitive processes. *Journal of Consulting and Clinical Psychology, 68*(3), 399–406.

Meyer, G. J. (1997). Assessing reliability: Critical corrections for a critical examination of the Rorschach comprehensive system. *Psychological Assessment, 9,* 480–489.

Meyer, G. J. (2000). Incremental validity of the Rorschach Prognostic Rating Scale over the MMPI Ego Strength Scale and IQ. *Journal of Personality Assessment, 74,* 365–370.

Meyer, G. J., et al. (2001). Psychological testing and psychological assessment: A review of evidence and issues. *American Psychologist, 56,* 128–165.

Meyer, T. J., & Mark, M. M. (1995). Effects of psychosocial interventions with adult cancer patients: A meta-analysis of randomized experiments. *Health Psychology, 14,* 101–108.

Michaud, D. S., et al. (2001). Physical activity, obesity, height, and the risk of pancreatic cancer. *Journal of the American Medical Association, 286,* 921–929.

Michaud, E. (2000, October). Women's secret terror. *Prevention,* pp. 118–127.

Michelson, D., Bancroft, J., Targum, S., Kim, Y., & Tepner, R. (2000). Female sexual dysfunction associated with antidepressant administration: A randomized, placebo-controlled study of pharmacologic intervention. *American Journal of Psychiatry, 157,* 239–243.

Mignot, E., & Thorsby, E. (2001). Narcolepsy and the HLA System. *The New England Journal of Medicine, 344,* 692.

Miklowitz, D. J. (1994). Family risk indicators in schizophrenia. *Schizophrenia Bulletin, 20,* 137–149.

Miklowitz, D. J., & Alloy, L. B. (1999). Psychosocial factors in the course and treatment of bipolar disorder: Introduction to the special section. *Journal of Abnormal Psychology, 108,* 555–557.

Milberger, S., et al. (1996). Is maternal smoking during pregnancy a risk factor for attention deficit hyperactivity disorder in children? *American Journal of Psychiatry, 153,* 1138–1142.

Milberger, S., et al. (1997). Pregnancy, delivery, and infancy complications and attention deficit hyperactivity disorder: Issues of gene-environment interaction. *Biological Psychiatry, 41,* 65–75.

Miller, A. (2000, Fall/Winter). Growing up in the new family. *Newsweek Special Issue,* pp. 80–84.

Miller, E. (1987). Hysteria: Its nature and explanation. *British Journal of Clinical Psychology, 26,* 163–173.

Miller, G. E., & Cohen, S. (2001). Psychological interventions and the immune system: A meta-analytic review and critique. *Health Psychology, 20,* 47–63.

Miller, L. K. (1999). The savant syndrome: Intellectual impairment and exceptional skills. *Psychological Bulletin, 125,* 31–46.

Miller, S. D., et al. (1991). Optical differences in multiple personality disorder: A second look. *Journal of Nervous & Mental Disease, 179,* 132–135.

Miller, T. Q., et al. (1991). Reasons for the trend toward null findings in research on Type A behavior. *Psychological Bulletin, 110,* 469–485.

Miller, W. R., & Brown, S. A., (1997). Why psychologists should treat alcohol and drug problems. *American Psychologist, 52,* 1269–1279.

Miller, W. R., & Hester, R. K. (1986). Inpatient alcoholism treatment: Who benefits? *American Psychologist, 41,* 794–805.

Miller, W. R., Leckman, A. L., Delaney, H. D., & Tinkcom, M. (1993). Long-term follow-up of behavioral self-control training. *Journal of Studies on Alcohol, 53,* 249–261.

Miller, W. R., & Muñoz, R. F. (1983). *How to control your drinking* (2nd ed.). Albuquerque: University of New Mexico Press.

Miller-Medzon, K. (2000, August 20). Early dyslexia detection leads to normal learning. *Boston Herald,* pp. 1, 11.

Millon, T. (1981). *Disorders of personality DSM-III: Axis II.* New York: Wiley.

Millon, T. (1982). *Millon Clinical Multiaxial Inventory manual* (3rd ed.). Minneapolis: National Computer Systems.

Milner, J. S. (1993). Social information processing and physical child abuse. *Clinical Psychology Review, 13,* 275–294.

Minarik, M. L., & Ahrens, A. H. (1996). Relations of eating and symptoms of depression and anxiety to the dimensions of perfectionism among undergraduate women. *Cognitive Research & Therapy, 20,* 155–169.

Mineka, S. (1991, August). Paper presented to the annual meeting of the American Psychological Association, San Francisco. (Cited in Turkington, C. [1991]). Evolutionary memories may have phobia role. *APA Monitor, 22*(11), 40.

Minuchin, S., Rosman, B. L., & Baker, L. (1978). *Psychosomatic Families: Anorexia nervosa in context.* Cambridge, MA: Harvard University Press.

Mischel, W. (1993). *Introduction to personality* (5th ed.). Forth Worth, TX: Harcourt Brace Jovanovich.

Mitka, M. (2000). Psychiatrists help survivors in the Balkans. *Journal of the American Medical Association, 283,* 1277–1278.

Modestin, J. (1992). Multiple personality disorder in Switzerland. *American Journal of Psychiatry, 149,* 88–92.

Mokdad, A. H., Serdula, M. K., Dietz, W. H., Bowman, B. A., Marks, J. S., & Kaplan, J. P. (1999). The spread of the obesity epidemic in the United States, 1991–1998. *Journal of the American Medical Association, 282,* 1519–1522.

Mokdad, A. H., et al. (2000). The continuing epidemic of obesity in the United States. *Journal of the American Medical Association, 284,* 1650–1651. [Research Letters]

Mokauu, N. (1990). The impoverishment of native Hawaiians and the social work challenge. *Health and Social Work, 15,* 235–242.

Moldin, S. O. (1994). Indicators of liability to schizophrenia: Perspectives from genetic epidemiology. *Schizophrenia Bulletin, 20,* 169–184.

Monahan, J. (1981). *A clinical prediction of violent behavior.* DHHS Publication, Adm. 81–921. Rockville, MD: National Institutes of Mental Health.

Monahan, J. (1992). Mental disorder and violent behavior: Perceptions and evidence. *American Psychologist, 47,* 511–521.

Moncher, M. S., Holden, G. W., & Trimble, J. E. (1990). Substance abuse among Native-American youth. *Journal of Consulting and Clinical Psychology, 58,* 408–415.

Mones, A. G., & Panitz, P. E. (1994). Marital violence: An integrated systems approach. *Journal of Social Distress and the Homeless, 3*, 39–51.

Money, J. (1987). Sin, sickness, or status? Homosexual gender identity and psychoneuroendocrinology. *American Psychologist, 42*, 384–399.

Money, J. (1994). The concept of gender identity disorder in childhood and adolescence after 39 years. *Journal of Sex and Marital Therapy, 20*, 163–177.

Money, J., & Lamacz, M. (1990). *Vandalized lovemaps.* Buffalo, NY: Prometheus Books.

Monroe, S. M., et al. (1999). Life events and depression in adolescence: Relationship loss as a prospective risk factor for first onset of major depressive disorder. *Journal of Abnormal Psychology, 108*, 606–614.

Monroe, S. M., et al. (2001). Life stress and the symptoms of major depression. *Journal of Nervous & Mental Disease, 189*, 168–175

Monti, P. M., et al. (1987). Reactivity of alcoholics and nonalcoholics to drinking cues. *Journal of Abnormal Psychology, 96*, 122–126.

Monti, P. M., et al. (1994). Cue exposure with coping skills treatment for male alcoholics: A preliminary investigation. *Journal of Consulting and Clinical Psychology, 61*, 1011–1019.

Moos, R. H., Cronkite, R. C., & Moos, B. S. (1998). Family and extrafamily resources and the 10-year course of treated depression. *Journal of Abnormal Psychology, 107*, 450–460.

Moos, R. H., McCoy, L., & Moos, B. S. (2000). Global Assessment of Functioning (GAF) ratings: Determinants and roles as predictors of one-year treatment outcomes. *Journal of Clinical Psychology, 56*, 449–461.

Moran, M. G. (1991). Psychological factors affecting pulmonary and rheumatologic diseases: A review. *Psychosomatics, 32*, 14–23.

Morgan, D. L., & Morgan, R. K. (2001). Single-participant research design: Bringing science to managed care. *American Psychologist, 56*, 119–127.

Morgan, K. (1996). Mental health factors in late-life insomnia. *Reviews in Clinical Gerontology, 6*, 75–83.

Morgenstern, J., et al. (1997). The comorbidity of alcoholism and personality disorders in a clinical population: Prevalence rates and relation to alcohol typology variables. *Journal of Abnormal Psychology, 106*, 74–84.

Morin, C. M., & Ware, J. C. (1996). Sleep and psychopathology. *Applied and Preventive Psychology, 5*, 211–224.

Morin, C. M., & Wooten, V. (1996). Psychological and pharmacological approaches to treating insomnia: Critical issues in assessing their separate and combined effects. *Clinical Psychology Review, 16*, 521–542.

Morin, C. M., et al. (1993a). Dysfunctional beliefs and attitudes about sleep among older adults with and without insomnia complaints. *Psychology and Aging, 8*, 463–467.

Morin, C. M., et al. (1993b). Cognitive-behavior therapy for late-life insomnia. *Journal of Consulting and Clinical Psychology, 61*, 137–146.

Morin, C. M., et al. (1999). Behavioral and pharmacological therapies for late-life insomnia: A randomized controlled trial. *Journal of the American Medical Association, 281*, 991–999.

Morrison, J. (1989). Childhood sexual histories of women with somatization disorder. *American Journal of Psychiatry, 146*, 239–241.

Morrow, D. J. (1998a, March 5). Stumble on the road to market. *The New York Times*, p. D1.

Mortensen, P. B., et al. (1999). Effects of family history and place and season of birth on the risk of schizophrenia. *New England Journal of Medicine, 340*, 603–608.

Mossman, D. (1994). Assessing predictions of violence: Being accurate about accuracy. *Journal of Consulting and Clinical Psychology, 62*, 783–792.

Mowrer, O. H. (1948). Learning theory and the neurotic paradox. *American Journal of Orthopsychiatry, 18*, 571–610.

Mueller, T. I., et al. (1999). Recurrence after recovery from major depressive disorder during 15 years of observational follow-up. *The American Journal of Psychiatry, 156*, 1000–1006.

Mueser, K. T., & Liberman, R. P. (1995). Behavior therapy in practice. In B. Bongar & L. E. Beutler (Eds.), *Comprehensive textbook of psychotherapy: Theory and practice* (pp. 84–110). New York: Oxford.

Mueser, K. T., et al. (2001). Family treatment and medication dosage reduction in schizophrenia: Effects on patient social functioning, family attitudes, and burden. *Journal of Consulting and Clinical Psychology, 69*, 3–12.

Muñoz, R. F., Mrazek, P. J., & Haggerty, R. J. (1996). Institute of Medicine Report on Prevention of Mental Disorders: Summary and commentary. *American Psychologist, 51*, 1116–1121.

Murdoch, D., Pihl, R. O., & Ross, D. (1990). Alcohol and crimes of violence: Present issues. *International Journal of the Addictions, 25*, 1065–1081.

Murphy, C. M., Meyer, S. L., & O'Leary, K. D. (1994). Dependency characteristics of partner assaultive men. *Journal of Abnormal Psychology, 103*, 729–735.

Murphy, C. M., et al. (2001). Correlates of intimate partner violence among male alcoholic patients. *Journal of Consulting and Clinical Psychology, 69*, 528–540.

Murray, B. (2000a). From brain scan to lesson plan. *Monitor on Psychology, 31*, pp. 22–28.

Murray, B. (2000b, July/August). Psychology seeks to replicate groundbreaking research on the success of drug/psychotherapy treatment. *Monitor on Psychology*, p. 13.

Murray, H. A. (1943). *Thematic Apperception Test: Pictures and manual.* Cambridge, MA: Harvard University Press.

Murray, J. B. (1993). Relationship of childhood sexual abuse to borderline personality disorder, posttraumatic stress disorder, and multiple personality disorder. *Journal of Psychology, 127*, 657–676.

Murstein, B. I., & Mathes, S. (1996). Projection on projective techniques & pathology: The problem that is not being addressed. *Journal of Personality Assessment, 66*, 337–349.

Murtagh, D. R. R., & Greenwood, K. M. (1995). Identifying effective psychological treatments for insomnia: A meta-analysis. *Journal of Consulting and Clinical Psychology, 63*, 79–89.

Must, A., et al. (1999). The disease burden associated with overweight and obesity. *Journal of the American Medical Association, 282*, 1523–1529.

Muster, N. J. (1992). Treating the adolescent victim-turned-offender. *Adolescence, 27*, 441–450.

Mutler, A. (2000, August 3). One-fourth of Kosovo's population suffering mental anguish in the aftermath of war. *Associated Press Web Listing*. Copyrighted by Associated Press. Retrieved August 3, 2000, from http://psycport.com/news/2000/08/03/wstm-/2537-2706-Kosovo-StillatWar.html

Myers, A., et al. (2000). Susceptibility locus for Alzheimer's disease on chromosome 10. *Science, 290*, 2304–2305.

Myin-Germeys, I., Delespaul, P. A. E. G., & deVries, M. W. (2000). Schizophrenia patients are more emotionally active than is assumed based on their behavior. *Schizophrenia Bulletin, 26*, 847–853.

N

Nagourney, E. (2001a, April 10). Geography of dyslexia is explored. *The New York Times*, p. F7.

Nagourney, E. (2001b, April 24). A good night's sleep, without the pills. *The New York Times*, p. F8.

Näslund, J., et al. (2000). Correlation between elevated levels of amyloid-peptide in the brain and cognitive decline. *Journal of the American Medical Association, 283*, 1571–1577.

Nathan, P. E. (1988). The addictive personality is the behavior of the addict. *Journal of Consulting and Clinical Psychology, 56*, 183–188.

Nathan, P. E. (1994). DSM-IV: Empirical, accessible, not yet ideal. *Journal of Clinical Psychology, 50*, 103–110.

Nathan, P. E., Stuart, S. P., & Dolan, S. L. (2000). Research on psychotherapy efficacy and effectiveness: Between Scylla and Charybdis? *Psychological Bulletin, 126*, 964–981.

National Center for Health Statistics. (1996b). News releases and fact sheets. *Highlights of a new report from the National Center for Health Statistics (NCHS), Monitoring health care in America: Quarterly fact sheet.* Washington, DC: US Department of Health, Education, and Welfare.

National Highway Traffic Safety Administration. (1988). *Fatal accident reporting system: 1987.* Washington, DC: U.S. Department of Transportation.

National Institute on Alcohol Abuse and Alcoholism. (1990). *7th Special Report to Congress on Alcohol and Health.* Rockville, MD: Author.

National Institutes of Health, National Heart, Lung, and Blood Institute. (1998). *Clinical guidelines on the identification, evaluation, and treatment of overweight and obesity in adults*: Bethesda, MD: Author.

National Institutes of Health, Office of Research on Women's Health, Office of the Director. (1999). *Women of color health data book: Adolescents to seniors.* NIH Publication 99-4247. Bethesda, MD: Author.

National Strategy for Suicide Prevention. (2001, May). *Goals and Objectives for Action: Summary.* A joint effort of SAMHSA, CDC, NIH, and HRSA. The Center for Mental Health Services. Rockville, MD: Author.

NBC Nightly News. (1996, November 11). National Broadcasting Company.

Ndetei, D. M., & Singh, A. (1983). Hallucinations in Kenyan schizophrenic patients. *Acta Psychiatrica Scandinavica, 67*, 144–147.

Ndetei, D. M., & Vadher, A. (1984). A comparative cross-cultural study of the frequencies of hallucination in schizophrenia. *Acta Psychiatrica Scandinavica, 70*, 545–549.

Neal, A. M., & Turner, S. M. (1991). Anxiety disorders research with African Americans: Current status. *Psychological Bulletin, 109*, 400–410.

Needles, D. J., & Abramson, L. Y. (1990). Positive life events, attributional style, and hopefulness: Testing a model of recovery from depression. *Journal of Abnormal Psychology, 99*, 156–165.

Negy, C., & Snyder, D. K. (1997). Ethnicity and acculturation: Assessing Mexican American couples' relationships using the marital satisfaction inventory—revised. *Psychological Assessment, 9*, 414–421.

Neiger, B. L. (1988). Adolescent suicide: Character traits of high-risk teenagers. *Adolescence, 23*, 469–475.

Neighbors, H. (1992, December). *The help seeking behavior of black Americans: A summary of the National Survey of Black Americans.* Paper presented at a symposium, Anxiety Disorders in African Americans, presented by the State University of New York Health Science Center at Brooklyn, Brooklyn, NY.

Nelson, C. B., Heath, A. C., & Kessler, R. C. (1998). Temporal progression of alcohol dependence symptoms in the U.S. household population: Results from the National Comorbidity Survey. *Journal of Consulting and Clinical Psychology, 66*, 474–483.

Nelson, S. H., et. al. (1992). An overview of mental health services for American Indians and Alaska natives in the 1990s. *Hospital and Community Psychiatry, 43*, 257–261.

Nemiah, J. C. (1978). Psychoneurotic disorders. In A. M. Nicholi (Ed.), *Harvard guide to modern psychiatry.* Cambridge, MA: Harvard University Press.

Nestadt, G., Samuels, J., Riddle, M., Bienvienu, O. J. III, Liang, K. Y., LaBuda, M., et al. (2000). A family study of obsessive-compulsive disorder. *Archives of General Psychiatry, 57,* 358–363.

Nestadt, G., et al. (2000). A family study of obsessive-compulsive disorder. *Archives of General Psychiatry, 57,* 358–363.

Neugebauer, R. (1979). Medieval and early modern theories of mental illness. *Archives of General Psychiatry, 36,* 477–484.

Nevid, J. S., Fichner-Rathus, L., & Rathus, S. A. (1995). *Human sexuality in a world of diversity* (2nd ed.). Boston: Allyn & Bacon.

Nevid, J. S., & Javier, R. A. (1997). Preliminary investigation of a culturally-specific smoking cessation intervention for Hispanic smokers. *American Journal of Health Promotion, 11,* 198–207.

Nevid, J. S., Javier, R. A., & Moulton, J. (1996). Factors predicting participant attrition in a community-based culturally-specific smoking cessation program for Hispanic smokers. *Health Psychology, 15,* 226–229.

Neville, H. A., et al. (1996). The impact of multicultural training on white racial identity attitudes and therapy competencies. *Professional Psychology: Research & Practice, 27,* 83–89.

New research could open doors to better migraine treatment. (2000, June 13). *CNN Web Posting.* Retrieved June 15, 2000, from http://www.cnn.com/2000/HEALTH/06/13/migraine/?related.

New research supports health benefits of red wine. (2000, July 3). *Cable News Network.* Retrieved July 5, 2000, from http://www.cnn.com/2000/HEALTH/diet.fitness/07/03/french.paradox/?related.

New use of brain scan may yield delays in Alzheimer's symptoms. (2000, May 15). *CNN Web Posting.* Retrieved May 16, 2000, from http://www.cnn.com/2000/HEALTH/aging/05/15/alzheimers.diagnosis/.

New York City Board of Education. (1984). *Child abuse and neglect prevention training manual: Working together to make a difference.* New York: Office of the Chief Executive for Instruction, Office of Student Progress, and Guidance Services Unit.

Newman, K. D. (1993). Giving up: Shelter experiences of battered women. *Public Health Nursing, 10,* 108–113.

Newman, L. S., & Baumeister, R. F. (1996). Toward an explanation of the UFO abduction phenomenon: Hypnotic elaboration, extraterrestrial sadomasochism, and spurious memories. *Psychological Inquiry, 7,* 99–126.

Nezu, A. M. (1994). Introduction to special section: Mental retardation and mental illness. *Journal of Consulting and Clinical Psychology, 62,* 4–5.

NIAAA report links drinking and early death. (1990, October). *The Addiction Letter, 6,* p. 5.

Niccols, G. A. (1994). Fetal alcohol syndrome: Implications for psychologists. *Clinical Psychology Review, 14,* 91–111.

Nicholson, R. A., et al. (1997). Utility of MMPI-2 indicators of response distortion: Receiver operating characteristic analysis. *Psychological Assessment, 9,* 471–479.

Nickerson, K. J., Helms, J. E., & Terrell, F. (1994). Cultural mistrust, opinions about mental illness, and Black students' attitudes toward seeking psychological help from White counselors. *Journal of Counseling Psychology, 41,* 378–385.

Nierenberg, A. A., et al. (2000). Timing of onset of antidepressant response with fluoxetine treatment. *American Journal of Psychiatry, 157,* 1429–1435.

Nieto, F. J., et al. (2000). Association of sleep-disordered breathing, sleep apnea, and hypertension in a large community-based study. *Journal of the American Medical Association, 283,* 1829–1836.

Nigg, J. T., & Goldsmith, H. H. (1994). Genetics of personality disorders: Perspectives from personality and psychopathology research. *Psychological Bulletin, 115,* 346–380.

Nigg, J. T., et al. (1992). Malevolent object representations in borderline personality disorder and major depression. *Journal of Abnormal Psychology, 101,* 61–67.

Niles, M. A., et al. (1995). Predictors of initial smoking cessation and relapse through the first 2 years of the Lung Health Study. *Journal of Consulting and Clinical Psychology, 63,* 60–69.

Nishith, P., Mechanic, M. B., & Resick, P. A. (2000). Prior interpersonal trauma: The contribution to current PTSD symptoms in female rape victims. *Journal of Abnormal Psychology, 109,* 20–25.

Nix, G., Watson, C., Pyszczynski, T., & Greenberg, J. (1995). Reducing depressive affect through external focus of attention. *Journal of Social and Clinical Psychology, 14,* 36–52.

Nolen-Hoeksema, S. (1991). Responses to depression and their effects on the duration of depressive episodes. *Journal of Abnormal Psychology, 100,* 569–582.

Nolen-Hoeksema, S. (2000). The role of rumination in depressive disorders and mixed anxiety/depressive symptoms. *Journal of Abnormal Psychology, 109,* 504–511.

Nolen-Hoeksema, S., & Girgus, J. S. (1994). The emergence of gender differences in depression during adolescence. *Psychological Bulletin, 115,* 424–443.

Nolen-Hoeksema, S., Girgus, J. S., & Seligman, M. E. P. (1992). Predictors and consequences of childhood depressive symptoms: A 5-year longitudinal study. *Journal of Abnormal Psychology, 101,* 405–422.

Nolen-Hoeksema, S., Morrow, J., & Fredrickson, B. L. (1993). Response styles and the duration of episodes of depressed mood. *Journal of Abnormal Psychology, 102,* 20–28.

Noonan, D. (2000, September 25). Why drugs cost so much. *Newsweek,* pp. 22–30.

North, C. S., et al. (1999). Psychiatric disorders among survivors of the Oklahoma City bombing. *Journal of the American Medical Association, 282,* 755–762.

Novaco, R. W. (1974). *A treatment program for the management of anger through cognitive and relaxation control.* Doctoral Dissertation, Indiana University.

Novaco, R. W. (1977). A stress inoculation approach to anger management in the training of law enforcement officers. *American Journal of Community Psychology, 5,* 327–346.

Nowell, P. D., et al. (1998). Effective treatments for selected sleep disorders. In P. E. Nathan & J. M. Gorman (Eds.), *A guide to treatments that work* (pp. 531–543). New York: Oxford University Press.

Noyes, R., et al. (1993). The validity of *DSM-III-R* hypochondriasis. *Archives of General Psychiatry, 50,* 961–970.

Nucifora Jr., F. C., et al. (2001). Interference by Huntington and atrophin-1 with cbp-mediated transcription leading to cellular toxicity. *Science, 291,* 2423–2428.

Nurnberger, J. I., et al. (2001). Evidence for a locus on chromosome 1 that influences vulnerability to alcoholism and affective disorder. *American Journal of Psychiatry, 158,* 718–724.

Nutrition, obesity and perception. (2001, January 9). *CNN Web Posting.* Retrieved January 11, 2001, from http://www.cnn.com/2001/HEALTH/children/01/09/overweight.kids/index.html.

O

O'Brien, C. P. (1996). Recent developments in the pharmacotherapy of substance abuse. *Journal of Consulting and Clinical Psychology, 64,* 677–686.

O'Brien, C. P., & McKay, J. (1998). Psychopharmacological treatments of substance use disorders. In P. E. Nathan & J. M. Gorman (Eds.), *A guide to treatments that work* (pp. 127–155). New York: Oxford University Press.

O'Brien, C. P., & McLellan, A. T. (1997). Addiction medicine. *Journal of the American Medical Association, 277,* 1840–1841.

O'Connor v. Donaldson, 95 S. Ct. 2486 (1975).

O'Connor, E. (2001a, January). Law sanctions new treatment for heroin addiction—and recommends psychological counseling. *Monitor on Psychology,* p. 18.

O'Connor, E. (2001b, February). Researchers pinpoint potential cause of autism. *Monitor on Psychology,* p. 13.

O'Connor, P. G. (2000). Treating opioid dependence—new data and new opportunities. *The New England Journal of Medicine, 343,* 1332–1334. [Editorial]

O'Connor, T. G., et al. (1998). Co-occurrence of depressive symptoms and antisocial behavior in adolescence: A common genetic liability. *Journal of Abnormal Psychology, 107,* 27–37.

O'Donnell, Clifford R. (1995). Firearm deaths among children and youth. *American Psychologist, 50,* 771–776.

O'Donohue, W., Dopke, C. A., & Swingen, D. N. (1997). Psychotherapy for female sexual dysfunction: A review. *Clinical Psychology Review, 17,* 537–566.

O'Donohue, W., Letourneau, E., & Geer, J. H. (1993). Premature ejaculation. In W. O'Donohue & J. H. Geer (Eds.), *Handbook of sexual dysfunctions: Assessment and treatment* (pp. 303–333). Boston: Allyn & Bacon.

O'Donohue, W., McKay, J. S., & Schewe, P. A. (1996). Rape: The roles of outcome expectancies and hypermasculinity. *Sexual Abuse Journal of Research and Treatment, 8,* 133–141.

O'Donohue, W. T., et al. (1999). Psychotherapy for male sexual dysfunction: A review. *Clinical Psychology Review, 19,* 591–630.

O'Farrell, T. J., et al. (1996). Cost-benefit and cost-effectiveness analyses of behavioral marital therapy as an addition to outpatient alcoholism treatment. *Journal of Substance Abuse, 8,* 145–166.

O'Leary, A. (1990). Stress, emotion, and human immune functions. *Psychological Bulletin, 108,* 382–383.

O'Leary, D. S., et al. (1996). Auditory attentional deficits in patients with schizophrenia: A positron emission tomography study. *Archives of General Psychiatry, 53,* 633–641.

O'Leary, K. D. (1995, July). Assessment and treatment of partner abuse. *Clinician's Research Digest, Supplemental Bulletin 12,* pp. 1–2.

O'Leary, K., et al. (2000). Co-occurrence of partner and parent aggression: Research and treatment implications. *Behavior Therapy, 31,* 631–648.

Oei, T. P. S., & Shuttlewood, G. J. (1996). Specified and nonspecific factors in psychotherapy: A case of cognitive therapy for depression. *Clinical Psychology Review, 16,* 83–103.

Oetting, E. R., Beauvais, F., & Edwards, R. (1988). Alcohol and Indian youth: Social and psychological correlates and prevention. *Journal of Drug Issues, 18,* 87–102.

Ogloff, J. R. P., Roberts, C. F., & Roesch, R. (1993). The insanity defense: Legal standards and clinical assessment. *Applied & Preventive Psychology, 2,* 163–178.

Öhman, A., & Mineka, S. (2001). Fears, phobias, and preparedness: Toward an evolved module of fear and fear learning. *Psychological Review, 108,* 483–522.

Okubo, Y., et al. (1997). Decreased prefrontal dopamine D1 receptors in schizophrenia revealed by PET. *Nature, 385,* 634–636.

Oldham, J. M. (1994). Personality disorders: Current perspectives. *Journal of the American Medical Association, 272,* 213–220.

Olesen, J. (1994). Understanding the biologic basis of migraine. *New England Journal of Medicine, 331,* 1713–1714.

Olfson, M., et al. (1998). Use of ECT for the inpatient treatment of recurrent major depression. *American Journal of Psychiatry, 155,* 22–29.

Olfson, M., et al. (2000). Barriers to the treatment of social anxiety. *American Journal of Psychiatry, 157,* 542–548.

Olson, E. (2001, October 7). Countries lag in treating mental illness, W. H. O. says. *The New York Times*, p. A24.

Olson, L. (2000). Combating Parkinson's disease—Step three. *Science, 290,* 721–724.

Olweus, D. (1987). Testosterone and adrenaline. In S. K. Mednick et al. (Eds.), *The causes of crime: New biological approaches* (pp. 263–282). Cambridge, UK: Cambridge University Press.

One in five teen-agers is armed, a survey finds. (1998). *The New York Times,* p. A19.

Onstad, S., Skre, I., Torgensen, S., & Kringlen, E. (1991). Twin concordance for *DSM-III-R* schizophrenia. *Acta Psychiatrica Scandinavica, 83,* 395–401.

Ormel, J., et al. (2001). The interplay and etiological continuity of neuroticism, difficulties, and life events in the etiology of major and subsyndromal, first and recurrent depressive episodes in later life. *American Journal of Psychiatry, 158,* 885–891.

Orne, M. T., et al. (1996). "Memories" of anomalous and traumatic autobiographical experiences: Validation and consolidation of fantasy through hypnosis. *Psychological Inquiry, 7,* 168–172.

Orsillo, S. M., et al. (1996). Current and lifetime psychiatric disorders among veterans with war zone-related posttraumatic stress disorder. *Journal of Nervous & Mental Disease, 184,* 307–313.

Ortega, A. N., et al. (2000). Acculturation and the lifetime risk of psychiatric and substance use disorders among Hispanics. *Journal of Nervous & Mental Disease, 188,* 728–735.

Orth-Gomér, K., et al. (2000). Marital stress worsens prognosis in women with coronary heart disease: The Stockholm Female Coronary Risk Study. *Journal of the American Medical Association, 284,* 3008–3014.

Osborne, L. (2001, May 6). Regional disturbances. *The New York Times,* p. A17.

Öst, L. (1987). Age of onset in different phobias. *Journal of Abnormal Psychology, 96,* 223–229.

Öst, L. (1992). Blood and injection phobia: Background and cognitive, physiological, and behavioral variables. *Journal of Abnormal Psychology, 101,* 68–74.

Osterling, J., & Dawson, G. (1994). Early recognition of children with autism: A study of first birthday home videotapes. *Journal of Autism and Developmental Disorder, 24,* 247–257.

Ostler, K., et al. (2001). Influence of socio-economic deprivation on the prevalence and outcome of depression in primary care. *British Medical Journal, 178,* 12–17.

Otto, M. W. (2001, February). A pilot study of CBT for bipolar disorders. *Journal Watch Psychiatry, 7,* 9.

Otto, M. W., Pollack, M. H., & Maki, K. M. (2000). Empirically supported treatments for panic disorder: Costs, benefits, and stepped care. *Journal of Consulting and Clinical Psychology, 68,* 556–563.

Ouellette, S. C., & DiPlacido, J (2001). Personality's role in the protection and enhancements of health: Where the research has been, where it is stuck, how it might move. In A. Baum, T. A. Revenson, & J. E. Singer (Eds.), *Handbook of health psychology* (pp 3–318). Mahwah, NJ: Lawrence Erlbaum Associates, Inc.

Ouimette, P. C., Finney, J. W., & Moos, R. H. (1997). Twelve-step and cognitive-behavioral treatment for substance abuse: A comparison of treatment effectiveness. *Journal of Consulting and Clinical Psychology, 65,* 230–240.

Overholser, J. C. (2000). Cognitive-behavioral treatment of panic disorder. *Psychotherapy: Theory, Research, Practice, Training, 37,* 247–256.

Overmier, J. B. L., & Seligman, M. E. P. (1967). Effect of inescapable shock upon subsequent escape and avoidance learning. *Journal of Comparative and Physiological Psychology, 63,* 28–33.

P

Palinkas, L. A., Wingard, D. L., & Barrett-Connor, E. (1990). The biocultural context of social networks and depression among the elderly. *Social Science and Medicine, 4,* 441–447.

Pallesen, S., et al. (2001). Clinical assessment and treatment of insomnia. *Professional Psychology: Research and Practice, 32,* 115–124.

Parker, G., Gladstone, G., & Chee, K. T. (2001). Depression in the planet's largest ethnic group: The Chinese. *American Journal of Psychiatry, 158,* 857–864.

Parker, K. F., & Pruitt, M. V. (2000). Poverty, poverty concentration, and homicide. *Social Science Quarterly, 81,* 555–570.

Parkinson Study Group. (2000). Pramipexole vs. levodopa as initial treatment for Parkinson disease: A randomized controlled trial. *Journal of the American Medical Association, 284,* 1931–1938.

Parnas, J., et al. (1993). Lifetime *DSM-III-R* diagnostic outcomes in the offspring of schizophrenic mothers: Results from the Copenhagen High-Risk Study. *Archives of General Psychiatry, 50,* 707–714.

Patrick, C. J., Cuthbert, B. N., & Lang, P. J. (1994). Emotion in the criminal psychopath: Fear image processing. *Journal of Abnormal Psychology, 103,* 523–534.

Patton, G. C., et al. (1999). Onset of adolescent eating disorders: Population based cohort study over 3 years. *British Medical Journal, 318,* 765–768.

Paul, G. L., & Lentz, R. J. (1977). *Psychosocial treatment of chronic mental patients: Milieu versus social-learning programs.* Cambridge, MA: Harvard University Press.

Paulesu, E., Frith, C. D., & Frackowisk, R. S. J. (1993). The neural correlates of the verbal component of working memory. *Nature, 362,* 342–344.

Paulesu, E., et al. (2001). Dyslexia: Cultural diversity and biological unity. *Science, 291,* 2165–2167.

Pauli, P., et al. (1997). Behavioral and neurophysiological evidence for altered processing of anxiety-related words in panic disorder. *Journal of Abnormal Psychology, 106,* 213–220.

Paykel, E. S. (1982). Life events and early environments. In E. S. Paykel (Ed.), *Handbook of affective disorders.* New York: Guilford Press.

Pearson, J. L., & Brown, G. K. (2000). Suicide prevention in late life: Directions for science and practice. *Clinical Psychology Review, 20,* 685–705.

Peers sway a child's interest in smoking, drinking as early as 6th grade. (2001, January 23). *CNN Web Posting.* Retrieved January 24, 2001, from http://www.cnn.com/2001/HEALTH/01/23/teen.drinking/index.html.

Peltzer, K., & Machleidt, W. (1992). A traditional (African) approach towards the therapy of schizophrenia and its comparison with Western models. *Therapeutic Communities International Journal for Therapeutic and Supportive Organizations, 13,* 229–242.

Pendery, M. L., Maltzman, I. M., & West, L. J. (1982). Controlled drinking by alcoholics? New findings and a re-evaluation of a major affirmative study. *Science, 217,* 169–174.

Pengilly, J. W., & Dowd, E. T. (2000). Hardiness and social support as moderators of stress. *Journal of Clinical Psychology, 56,* 813–820.

Penn, D. L. (1998, June). Assessment and treatment of social dysfunction in schizophrenia. *Clinician's Research Digest, Supplemental Bulletin 18.*

Penn, D. L., & Mueser, K. T. (1996). Research update on the psychosocial treatment of schizophrenia. *American Journal of Psychiatry, 153,* 607–617.

Penn, D. L., et al. (2000). Emotion recognition in schizophrenia: Further investigation of generalized versus specific deficit models. *Journal of Abnormal Psychology, 109,* 555–558.

Penninx, B. W., et al. (2000). The protective effect of emotional vitality on adverse health outcomes in disabled older women. *Journal of the American Geriatrics Society, 48,* 1359–1366.

Penninx, B. W., et al. (2001). Depression and cardiac mortality: Results from a community-based longitudinal study. *Archives of General Psychiatry, 58,* 221–227.

Petrie, K. J., Booth, R. J., & Pennebaker, J. W. (1998). The immunological effects of thought suppression. *Journal of Personality and Social Psychology, 75,* 1264–1272.

Peplau, L. A. (1991). Lesbian and gay relationships. In J. Gonsiorek & J. Weinrich (Eds.), *Homosexuality: research implications for public policy* (pp. 177–196). Newbury Park, CA: Sage.

Peppard, P. E., Young, T., Palta, M., & Skatrud, J. (2000). Prospective study of the association between sleep-disordered breathing and hypertension. *The New England Journal of Medicine, 342,* 1378–1384.

Perilstein, R. D., Lipper, S., & Friedman, L. J. (1991). Three cases of paraphilias responsive to fluoxetine treatment. *Journal of Clinical Psychiatry, 52,* 169–170.

Perlin, M. L. (1994). Law and the delivery of mental health services in the community. *American Journal of Orthopsychiatry, 64,* 194–208.

Perlman, J. D., & Abramson, P. R. (1982). Sexual satisfaction among married & cohabitating individuals. *Journal of Consulting and Clinical Psychology, 50,* 458–460.

Perlman, L. M. (2001). Nonspecific, unintended, and serendipitous effects in psychotherapy. *Professional Psychology: Research and Practice, 32,* 283–288.

Perry, E. K., et al. (2001). Cholinergic activity in autism: Abnormalities in the cerebral cortex and basal forebrain. *American Journal of Psychiatry, 158,* 1058–1066.

Persaud, R. (2000). Recurrent depression and stressful life events: In reply. *Archives of General Psychiatry, 57,* 617. [Letter]

Peterson, E. D., et al. (1997). Racial variation in the use of coronary-revascularization procedures—Are the differences real? Do they matter? *The New England Journal of Medicine, 336,* 480–486.

Pettingale, K. W. (1985). Towards a psychobiological model of cancer: Biological considerations. Special issue: Cancer and the mind. *Social Science and Medicine, 20,* 779–787.

Peyron, C., et al. (2000). A mutation in a case of early onset narcolepsy and a generalized absence of hypocretin peptides in human nacroleptic brains. *Nat Med, 6,* 991–997.

Phaf, R. H., Geurts, H., & Eling, P. A. T. M. (2000). Word frequency and word stem completion in Korsakoff patients. *Journal of Clinical & Experimental Neuropsychology, 22,* 817–829.

Philipps, L. H., & O'Hara, M. W. (1991). Prospective study of postpartum depression: 4½-year follow-up of women and children. *Journal of Abnormal Psychology, 100,* 151–155.

Phinney, J. (1989). Stages of ethnic identity in minority group adolescents. *Journal of Early Adolescence, 9,* 34–49.

Phinney, J., & Alipuria, L. (1990). Ethnic identity in older adolescents from four ethnic groups. *Journal of Adolescence, 13,* 171–183.

Phinney, J., Lochner, B., & Murphy, R. (1990). Ethnic identity development and psychological adjustment in adolescence. In A. Stiffman & L. Davis (Eds.), *Ethnic issues in adolescent mental health.* Newbury Park. CA: Sage.

Pianta, R. C., & Egeland, B. (1994). Relation between depressive symptoms and stressful life events in a sample of disadvantaged mothers. *Journal of Consulting and Clinical Psychology, 62,* 1229–1234.

Pihl, R. O., Peterson, J., & Finn, P. (1990). Inherited predispostion to alcoholism: Characteristics of sons of male alcoholics. *Journal of Abnormal Psychology, 99,* 291–301.

Pike, K. M., & Rodin, J. (1991). Mothers, daughters, and disordered eating. *Journal of Abnormal Psychology, 101,* 198–204.

Pilowsky, J. E. (1993). The courage to leave: An exploration of Spanish-speaking women victims of spousal abuse. *Canadian Journal of Community Mental Health, 12*, 15–29.

Pinderhughes, E. (1989). *Understanding race, ethnicity and power: Keys to efficacy in clinical practice.* New York: Free Press.

Pine, D. S., et al. (1997). Neuroendocrine response to fenfluramine challenge in boys: Associations with aggressive behavior and adverse rearing. *Archives of General Psychiatry, 54*, 839–846.

Pinel, J. P. J., Assanand, S., & Lehman, D. R. (2000). Hunger, eating, and ill health. *American Psychologist, 55*, 1105–1116.

Piven, J., et al. (1997). An MRI study of the corpus callosum in autism. *American Journal of Psychiatry, 154*, 1051–1056.

Plomin, R., DeFries, J., McClearn, G. E., & Rutter, M. (1997). *Behavioral genetics* (3rd ed.). New York: Freeman.

Plomin, R., Owen, M. J., & McGuffin, P. (1994). The genetic basis of complex human behaviors. *Science, 264*, 1733–1739.

Pogge, D. L. (1992). Risk factors in child abuse and neglect. *Journal of Social Distress and the Homeless, 1*, 237–248.

Polaschek, D. L. L., Ward, T., & Hudon, S. M. (1997). Rape and rapists: Theory and treatment. *Clinical Psychology Review, 17*, 117–144.

Polcin, D. L. (1992). Issues in the treatment of dual diagnosis clients who have chronic mental illness. *Professional Psychology: Research and Practice, 23*, 30–37.

Pollock, V. E. (1992). Meta-analysis of subjective sensitivity to alcohol in sons of alcoholics. *American Journal of Psychiatry, 149*, 1534–1538.

Pope, H. G., Jr., & Yurgelun-Todd, D. (1996). The residual cognitive effects of heavy marijuana use in college students. *Journal of the American Medical Association, 275*, 521–527.

Potter, J. D. (1997). Hazards and benefits of alcohol. *The New England Journal of Medicine, 337*, 1763–1764.

Poulakis, Z., & Wertheim, E. H. (1993). Relationships among dysfunctional cognitions, depressive symptoms, and bulimic tendencies. *Cognitive Therapy and Research, 17*, 549–559.

Powchik, P., et al. (1998). Postmortem studies in schizophrenia. *Schizophrenia Bulletin, 24*, 325–341.

Powell, E. (1991). *Talking back to sexual pressure.* Minneapolis: CompCare Publishers.

Price, J. L., Hilsenroth, M. J., Petretic-Jackson, P. A., & Bonge, D. (2001). A review of individual psychotherapy outcomes for adult survivors of childhood sexual abuse. *Clinical Psychology Review, 21*, 1095–1121.

Price, L. H., & Heninger, G. R. (1994). Lithium in the treatment of mood disorders. *New England Journal of Medicine, 331*, 591–598.

Prichard, J. C. (1835). *Treatise on insanity.* London: Gilbert & Piper.

Prigatano, G. P. (1992). Personality disturbances associated with traumatic brain injury. *Journal of Consulting and Clinical Psychology, 60*, 360–368.

Prigerson, H. G., et al. (2001). Combat trauma: Trauma with highest risk of delayed onset and unresolved post-traumatic stress disorder symptoms, unemployment, and abuse among men. *Journal of Nervous & Mental Disease, 189*, 99–108.

Project MATCH Research Group. (1997). Matching alcoholism treatments to client heterogeneity: Project MATCH posttreatment drinking outcomes. *Journal of Studies on Alcohol, 58*, 7–29.

Prudic, J., et al. (1996). Resistance to antidepressant medications and short-term clinical response to ETC. *American Journal of Psychiatry, 153*, 985–992.

Pumariega, A. J. (1986). Acculturation and eating attitudes in adolescent girls: A comparative correlational study. *Journal of the American Academy of Child Psychiatry, 25*, 276–279.

Purdum, T. S. (2001, March 30). Non-Hispanic whites a minority, California census figures show. *The New York Times*, pp. A1, A18.

Putnam, F. W., & Carlson, E. B. (1994). "Screening for multiple personality disorder with the Dissociative Experiences Scale": A reply. *American Journal of Psychiatry, 151*, 1249–1250.

Putnam, F. W., Guroff, J. J., Silberman, E. K., Barban, L., & Post, R. M. (1986). The clinical phenomenology of multiple personality disorder: Review of 100 recent cases. *Journal of Clinical Psychiatry, 47*, 285–293.

Pyszczynski, T., & Greenberg, G. (1985). Depression and preference for self-focusing stimuli after success and failure. *Journal of Personality and Social Psychology, 49*, 1066–1075.

Pyszczynski, T., & Greenberg, G. (1986). Evidence for a depressive self-focusing style. *Journal of Research in Personality, 20*, 95–106.

Pyszczynski, T., & Greenberg, J. (1987). Self-regulatory perseveration and the depressive self-focusing style: A self-awareness theory of reactive depression. *Psychological Bulletin, 102*, 122–138.

Q

Quay, H. C. (1965). Psychopathic personality as pathological stimulation seeking. *American Journal of Psychiatry, 122*, 180–183.

Quist, J., & Kennedy, J. L. (2001). Genetics of childhood disorders: XXIII. ADHD, Part 7: The serotonin system. *Journal of American Academy of Child & Adolescent Psychiatry, 40*, 253–256.

R

Rabasca, L. (2000a, March). Listening instead of preaching. *Monitor on Psychology, 31*, pp. 50–51.

Rabasca, L. (2000b, July/August). Therapy that starts online but aims to continue in the psychologist's office. *Monitor on Psychology*, p. 15.

Rabkin, J. G., Wagner, G. J., & Rabkin R. (2000). A double-blind, placebo-controlled trial of testosterone therapy for HIV-positive men with hypogonadal symptoms. *Archives of General Psychiatry, 57*, 141–147.

Rachman, S. (2000). Joseph Wolpe (1915–1997). *American Psychologist, 55*, 431.

Rachman, S., & Bichard, S. (1988). The overprediction of fear. *Clinical Psychology Review, 8*, 303–311.

Rachman, S. J. (1994). Overprediction of fear: A review. *Behaviour Research and Therapy, 32*, 683–690.

Ragland, J. D., et al. (1999). Neuropsychological laterality indices of schizophrenia: Interactions with gender. *Schizophrenia Bulletin, 25*, 79–89.

Ragland, J. D., et al. (2001). Effect of schizophrenia on frontotemporal activity during word encoding and recognition: A PET cerebral blood flow study. *American Journal of Psychiatry, 158*, 1114–1125.

Räikkönen. K., et al. (1999). Effects of hostility on ambulatory blood pressure and mood during daily living in healthy adults. *Health Psychology, 18*, 44–53.

Raine, A., et al. (2000). Reduced prefrontal gray matter volume and reduced autonomic activity in antisocial personality disorder. *Archives of General Psychiatry, 57*, 119–127.

Rao, K., DiClemente, R. J., & Ponton, L. E. (1992). Child sexual abuse of Asians compared with other populations. *Journal of the American Academy of Child and Adolescent Psychiatry, 31*, 880–886.

Rao, S. M., Huber, S. J., & Bornstein, R. A. (1992). Emotional changes with multiple sclerosis and Parkinson's disease. *Journal of Consulting and Clinical Psychology, 60*, 369–378.

Rapee, R. M. (1987). The psychological treatment of panic attacks: Theoretical conceptualization and review of evidence. *Clinical Psychology Review, 7*, 427–438.

Rapee, R. M. (1991). Generalized anxiety disorder: A review of clinical features and theoretical concepts. *Clinical Psychology Review, 11*, 419–440.

Rapin, I. (1997). Autism. *The New England Journal of Medicine, 337*, 97–104.

Rathus, S. A. (1978). Treatment of recalcitrant ejaculatory incompetence. *Behavior Therapy, 9*, 962.

Rathus, S. A. (1999). *Psychology* (7th ed.). Fort Worth: Harcourt Brace College Publishers.

Rathus, S. A., & Fichner-Rathus, L. (1994). *Making the most of college* (2nd ed.). Englewood Cliffs, NJ: Prentice-Hall.

Rathus, S. A., & Nevid, J. S. (1977). *Behavior therapy.* Garden City, NY: Doubleday.

Rathus, S. A., Nevid, J. S., & Fichner-Rathus, L. (2002). *Human sexuality in a world of diversity* (5th ed.). Boston: Allyn & Bacon.

Ratti, L. A., Humphrey, L. L., & Lyons, J. S. (1996). Structural analysis of families with a polydrug-dependent, bulimic, or normal adolescent daughter. *Journal of Consulting & Clinical Psychology, 64*, 1255–1262.

Rauch, S. L., & Jenike, M. A. (1998). Pharmacological treatment of obsessive compulsive disorder. In P. E. Nathan & J. M. Gorman (Eds.), *A guide to treatments that work* (pp. 358–376). New York: Oxford University Press.

Rauschenberger, S. L., & Lynn, S. J. (1995). Fantasy proneness, *DSM-III-R* Axis I psychopathology, and dissociation. *Journal of Abnormal Psychology, 104*, 373–380.

Ravenholt, R. (1984). Addiction mortality in the United States. 1980: Tobacco, alcohol, and other substances. *Population and Development Review, 10*, 697–724.

Read, J. et al. (2001). Assessing suicidality in adults: Integrating childhood trauma as a major risk factor. *Professional Psychology: Research and Practice, 32*, 367–372.

Ready, T. (2000, June 7). Meditation apparently good for the heart as well as the mind. *CNN Web Posting.* Retrieved June 8, 2000, from http://www.cnn.com/2000/HEALTH/06/07/minding.heart.wmd/.

Redd, W. H. (1995). Behavioral research in cancer as a model for health psychology. *Health Psychology, 14*, 99–100.

Redd, W. H., & Jacobsen, P. (2001). Behavioral intervention in comprehensive cancer care. In A. Baum, T. A. Revenson, & J. E. Singer (Eds.), *Handbook of health psychology* (pp. 757–776). Mahwah, NJ: Erlbaum.

Reed, G. M., McLaughlin, C. J., & Milholland, K. (2000). Ten interdisciplinary principles for professional practice in telehealth: Implications for psychology. *Professional Psychology: Research and Practice, 31*, 170–178.

Regehr, C., Hill, J., & Glancy, G. D. (2000). Individual predictors of traumatic reactions in firefighters. *Journal of Nervous & Mental Disease, 188*, 333–339.

Reich, J. (1996). The morbidity of *DSM-III-R* dependent personality disorder. *Journal of Nervous & Mental Disease, 184*, 22–26.

Reich, J., & Noyes, R. (1986). Letters to the Editor: Differentiating schizoid and avoidant personality disorders. *American Journal of Psychiatry, 143*, 1061–1063.

Reichman, M. E. (1994). Alcohol and breast cancer. *Alcohol Health and Research World, 18*, 182–183.

Reid, B. V., & Whitehead, T. L. (1992). Introduction. In T. L. Whitehead & B. V. Reid (Eds.), *Gender constructs and social issues* (pp. 1–9). Chicago: University of Illinois.

Reinisch, J. M. (1990). *The Kinsey Institute new report on sex: What you must know to be sexually literate.* New York: St. Martin's Press.

Reisberg, B., Ferris, S. H., DeLeon, M. J., & Crook, T. (1982). The Global Deterioration Scale for Assessment of Primary Degenerative Dementia. *American Journal of Psychiatry, 139*, 1136–1139.

Reisberg, B., et al. (1986). Assessment of presenting symptoms. In L. W. Poon (Ed.), *Handbook for clinical memory assessment of older adults* (pp. 108–128). Washington, DC: American Psychological Association.

Reisner, A. D. (1994). Multiple personality disorder diagnosis: A house of cards? *American Journal of Psychiatry, 151,* 629.

Reisner, A. D. (1996). Repressed memories: True and false. *Psychological Record, 46,* 563–579.

Reiss, B. F. (1980). Psychological tests in homosexuality. In J. Marmor (Ed.), *Homosexual behavior* (pp. 296–311). New York: Basic Books.

Reiss, S., & Valenti-Hein, D. (1994). Development of a psychopathology rating scale for children with mental retardation. *Journal of Consulting and Clinical Psychology, 62,* 28–33.

Reneman, L., et al. (2001). Cortical serotonin transporter density and verbal memory in individuals who stopped using 3,4-methylenedioxymethamphetamine (MDMA or "Ecstasy"): Preliminary findings. *Archives of General Psychiatry, 58,* 901–906.

Renfrey, G. S. (1992). Cognitive-behavior therapy and the Native American client. *Behavior Therapy, 23,* 321–340.

Rennison, C. M. (2001). *Intimate partner violence and age of victim, 1993 to 1999.* Washington, DC: U.S. Department of Justice, Bureau of Justice Statistics.

Report: Adolescent suicide rates rise. (1995, April 21). *New York Newsday,* p. A54.

Researchers gain insight into Huntington's. (2001, March 22). *CNN Web Posting.* Retrieved March 24, 2001, from http://www.cnn.com/2001/HEALTH/conditions/03/22/huntingtons.gene/index.html.

Rey, J. M. (1993). Oppositional defiant disorder. *American Journal of Psychiatry, 150,* 1769–1778.

Reynolds, C. F., III, et al. (1996). Treatment outcome in recurrent major depression: A post hoc comparison of elderly ("Young Old") and midlife patients. *American Journal of Psychiatry, 153,* 1288–1292.

Ribisl, K. M., et al. (2000). English language use as a risk factor for smoking initiation among Hispanic and Asian American Adolescents: Evidence for mediation by tobacco-related beliefs and social norms. *Health Psychology, 19,* 403–410.

Ricciardelli, L. A., & McCabe, M. P. (2001). Children's body image concerns and eating disturbance: A review of the literature. *Clinical Psychology Review, 21,* 325–344.

Richards, J. C., Edgar, L. V., & Gibbon, P. (1996). Cardiac acuity in panic disorder. *Cognitive Therapy and Research, 20,* 361–376.

Richards, R. (1994). Creativity and bipolar mood swings: Why the association? In M. P. Shaw & M. A. Runco (Eds.), *Creativity and affect* (pp. 44–72). Norwood: Ablex.

Riddle, M. A., et al. (2001). Fluvoxamine for children and adolescents with obsessive-compulsive disorder: A randomized controlled, multicenter trial. *Journal of the American Academy of Child and Adolescent Psychiatry, 40,* 222–229.

Ridley, C. R. (1984). Clinical treatment of the nondisclosing Black client: A therapeutic paradox. *American Psychologist, 39,* 1234–1244.

Riedel, B. R. W., & Lichstein, K. L. (2001). Strategies for evaluating adherence to sleep restriction treatment for insomnia. *Behaviour Research and Therapy, 39,* 201–212.

Riether, A. M., & Stoudemire, A. (1988). Psychogenic fugue states: A review. *Southern Medical Journal, 81,* 568–571.

Riley, V. (1981). Psychoneuroendocrine influences on immunocompetence and neoplasia. *Science, 212,* 1100–1109.

Rimer, S. (1999, September 5). Gaps seen in treating depression in elderly. *The New York Times,* pp. 1, 18.

Rimland, B. (1978). The savant capabilities of autistic children and their cognitive implications. In G. Serban (Ed.), *Cognitive defects in the development of mental illness.* New York: Brunner-Mazel.

Risk factors help ID violence-prone youths, psychiatrists say. (2000, May 16). *American Heart Association Web Posting.* Retrieved May 19, 2000, from http://www.medicus.clk/AspNyheder/.

Ritter, C., et al. (2000). Stress, psychosocial resources, and depressive symptomatology during pregnancy in low-income, inner-city women. *Health Psychology, 19,* 576–585.

Ritvo, E. R., & Ritvo, R. (1992). "The UCLA-University of Utah Epidemiologic Survey of Autism: The etiologic role of rare diseases": Reply. *American Journal of Psychiatry, 149,* 146–147.

Rivara, F. P., et al. (1997). Alcohol and illicit drug abuse and the risk of violent death in the home. *Journal of the American Medical Association, 278,* 569–575.

Robins, L. N., Locke, B. Z., & Reiger, D. A. (1991). An overview of psychiatric disorders in America. In L. N. Robins & D. A. Regier (Eds.), *Psychiatric disorders in America: The Epidemiologic Catchment Area Study* (pp. 328–366). New York: Free Press.

Robins, L. N., Tipp, J., & Przybeck, T. (1991). Antisocial personality. In L. N. Robins & D. A. Regier (Eds.), *Psychiatric disorders in America: The Epidemiologic Catchment Area Study* (pp. 258–290). New York: Free Press.

Robinson, N. M., Zigler, E., & Gallagher, J. J. (2001). Two tails of the normal curve: Similarities and differences in the study of mental retardation and giftedness. *American Psychologist, 55,* 1413–1424.

Robinson, T., et al. (1996). Ethnicity and body dissatisfaction: Are Hispanic and Asian girls at increased risk of eating disorders. *Journal of Adolescent Health, 19,* 384–393.

Rocha, B. A., et al. (1998). Increased vulnerability to cocaine in mice lacking the serotonin-1 B receptor. [Letter]. *Nature, 393,* 175.

Rock, C. L., & Curran-Celentano. J. (1996). Nutritional management of eating disorders. *The Psychiatric Clinics of North America, 19,* 701–713.

Rodin, J., Bartoshuk, L., Peterson, C., & Schank, D. (1990). Bulimia and taste: Possible interactions. *Journal of Abnormal Psychology, 99,* 32–39.

Rodríguez de Fonseca, F., et al. (1997). Activation of corticotropin-releasing factor in the limbic system during cannabinoid withdrawal. *Science, 276,* 2050–2054.

Rodriguez, G. (2001, February 11). *The New York Times Week in Review,* Section 4, pp. 1, 4.

Rodriguez, N., et al. (1997). Posttraumatic stress disorder in adult female survivors of childhood sexual abuse: A comparison study. *Journal of Consulting and Clinical Psychology, 65,* 53–59.

Roesch, R., Zapf, P. A., Golding, S. L., & Skeem, J. L. (1999). Defining and assessing competence to stand trial. In A. K. Hess, I. B. Weiner, et al. (Eds.), *The handbook of forensic psychology* (2nd ed., pp. 327–349). New York: Wiley.

Roesler, A., & Witztum, E. (2000). Pharmacotherapy of paraphilias in the next millennium. *Behavioral Sciences & the Law, 18*(1), 43–56.

Rogan, A. (1986, Fall). Recovery from alcoholism: Issues for black and Native American alcoholics. *Alcohol Health and Research World, 10,* 42–44.

Rogers, C. R. (1951). *Client-centered therapy.* Boston: Houghton Mifflin.

Rogers, R., et al. (1990). The clinical presentation of command hallucinations in a forensic population. *American Journal of Psychiatry, 147,* 1304–1307.

Rogler, L. H., Cortes, D. E., & Malgady, R. G. (1991). Acculturation and mental health status among Hispanics: Convergence and new directions for research. *American Psychologist, 46,* 584–597.

Rohde, P., Lewinsohn, P. M., & Seeley, J. R. (1991). Comorbidity of unipolar depression: II. Comorbidity with other mental disorders in adolescents and adults. *Journal of Abnormal Psychology, 101,* 214–222.

Romanczyk, R. G. (1986). Some thoughts on future trends in the education of individuals with autism. *The Behavior Therapist, 8,* 162–164.

Romano, E., & De-Luca, R. V. (1996). Characteristics of perpetrators with histories of sexual abuse. *International Journal of Offender Therapy and Comparative Criminology, 40,* 147–156.

Rose, J. (1996). Anger management: A group treatment program for people with mental retardation. *Journal of Developmental and Physical Disabilities, 8,* 133–149.

Rosen, J. C. (1996). Body dysmorphic disorder: Assessment and treatment. In J. K. Thompson (Ed.), *Body image, eating disorders, and obesity* (pp. 149–170). Washington, DC: American Psychological Association.

Rosen, R. C. (1996). Erectile dysfunction: The medicalization of male sexuality. *Clinical Psychology Review, 16,* 497–519.

Rosen, R. C., & Leiblum, S. R. (1995). Treatment of sexual disorders in the 1990s: An integrated approach. *Journal of Consulting and Clinical Psychology, 63,* 877–890.

Rosenberg, H. (1993). Prediction of controlled drinking by alcoholics and problem drinkers. *Psychological Bulletin, 113,* 129–130.

Rosenberg, M. L. (1993). Promoting safety and nonviolent conflict resolution in adolescence. In S. G. Millstein, A. C. Petersen, & E. O. Nightingale (Eds.), *Promoting adolescent health: Third symposium on research opportunities in adolescence.* New York: Carnegie Council on Adolescent Development.

Rosenfeld, B. D. (1992). Court-ordered treatment of spouse abuse. *Clinical Psychology Review, 12,* 205–226.

Rosenheck, R. (2000). Cost-effectiveness of services for mentally ill homeless people: The application of research to policy and practice. *American Journal of Psychiatry, 157,* 1563–1570.

Rosenthal, D., et al. (1968). Schizophrenics' offspring reared in adoptive homes. In D. Rosenthal & S. S. Kety (Eds.), *The transmission of schizophrenia.* Oxford: Pergamon Press.

Rosenthal, D., et al. (1975). Parent-child relationships and psychopathological disorder in the child. *Archives of General Psychiatry, 32,* 466–476.

Rosenthal, E. (1993, April 9). Who will turn violent? Hospitals have to guess. *The New York Times,* pp. A1, C12.

Ross, C. A., Norton, G. R., & Wozney, K. (1989). Multiple personality disorder: An analysis of 236 cases. *Canadian Journal of Psychiatry, 34,* 413–418.

Ross, C. A., et al. (1990). Structured interview data on 102 cases of multiple personality disorder from four centers. *American Journal of Psychiatry, 147,* 596–601.

Ross, C. A., et al. (1991). The frequency of multiple personality disorder among psychiatric inpatients. *American Journal of Psychiatry, 148,* 1717–1720.

Ross, D. E. (2000). The deficit syndrome and eye tracking disorder may reflect a distinct subtype within the syndrome of schizophrenia. *Schizophrenia Bulletin, 26,* 855–866.

Ross, M., & Need, J. (1989). Effects of adequacy of gender reassignment surgery on psychological adjustment: A follow-up of fourteen male-to-female patients. *Archives of Sexual Behavior, 18,* 145–153.

Ross, R., Dagnone, D., Jones, P. J., Smith, H., Paddags, A., & Hudson, R. (2000). Reduction in obesity and related comorbid conditions after diet-induced weight loss or exercise-induced weight loss in men: A randomized, controlled trial. *Annals of Internal Medicine, 133,* 92–103.

Ross, S. M. (1996). Risk of physical abuse to children of spouse-abusing parents. *Child Abuse and Neglect, 20,* 589–598.

Rossman, B. B. R. (2001). Longer term effects of children's exposure to domestic violence. In S. A. Graham-Bermann & J. L. Edleson (Eds.), *Domestic violence in the lives of children: The future of research, intervention, and social policy* (pp. 35–65). Washington, DC: American Psychological Association.

Rosso, I. M., et al. (2000). Obstetric risk factors for early-onset schizophrenia in a Finnish birth cohort. *American Journal of Psychiatry, 157,* 816–818.

Rothbaum, B. O. (1996). Virtual reality exposure therapy in the treatment of fear of flying: A case report. *Behaviour Research and Therapy, 34,* 477–481.

Rothbaum, B. O., et al. (1995). Effectiveness of computer-generated (virtual reality) graded exposure in the treatment of acrophobia. *American Journal of Psychiatry, 152,* 626–628.

Rotheram-Borus, M. J., Trautman, P. D., Dopkins, S. C., & Shrout, P. E. (1990). Cognitive style and pleasant activities among female adolescent suicide attempters. *Journal of Consulting and Clinical Psychology, 58,* 554–561.

Rotter, J. B. (1966). Generalized expectancies for internal vs. external control of reinforcement. *Psychological Monographs, 1,* 210–609.

Rotter, J. B. (1990). Internal versus external control of reinforcement: A case history of a variable. *American Psychologist, 45,* 489–493.

Rotundo, M., Nguyen, D-H., & Sackett, P. R. (2001). A meta-analytic review of gender differences in perceptions of sexual harassment. *Journal of Applied Psychology, 86,* 914–922.

Rounsaville, B. J., & Kosten, T. R. (2000). Treatment for opioid dependence: Quality and access. *Journal of the American Medical Association, 283,* 1337–1339. [Editorial]

Rousseau, F., et al. (1991). Direct diagnosis by DNA analysis of the fragile X syndrome of mental retardation. *New England Journal of Medicine, 325,* 1673–1681.

Rowland, D. L., Cooper, S. E., & Slob, A. K. (1996). Genital and psychoaffective response to erotic stimulation in sexually functional and dysfunctional men. *Journal of Abnormal Psychology, 105,* 194–203.

Roy, A., et al. (1991). Suicide in twins. *Archives of General Psychiatry, 48,* 29–32.

Roy, E. (2000). Relation of family history of suicide to suicide attempts in alcoholics. *American Journal of Psychiatry, 157,* 2050–2051.

Roy-Byrne, P. P., & Cowley, D. S. (1998). Pharmacological treatment of panic, generalized anxiety, and phobic disorders. In P. E. Nathan & J. M. Gorman (Eds.), *A guide to treatments that work* (pp. 319–338). New York: Oxford University Press.

Rubin, L. J. (1996). Childhood sexual abuse: False accusations of "false memory"? *Professional Psychology: Research and Practice, 27,* 447–451.

Rubinstein, S., & Caballero, B. (2000). Is Miss America an undernourished role model? *Journal of the American Medical Association, 283,* 1569.

Rugino, T., & Copley, T. C. (2001). Effects of modafinil in children with attention-deficit/hyperactivity disorder: An open-label study. *Journal of American Academy of Child & Adolescent Psychiatry, 40,* 230–235.

Ruscio, A. M., Borkovec, T. D., & Ruscio, J. (2001). A taxometric investigation of the latent structure of worry. *Journal of Abnormal Psychology, 110,* 413–422.

Rush, A. J., & Weissenburger, J. E. (1994). Do thinking patterns predict depressive symptoms? *Cognitive Therapy and Research, 10,* 225–236.

Rutenberg, J. (2001, July 25). Survey shows few parents use TV V-Chip to limit children's viewing. *The New York Times,* pp. E1, E7.

Rutter, M. (1983). Cognitive deficits in the pathogenesis of autism. *Journal of Child Psychology & Psychiatry, 24,* 513–531.

Rutter, M. (1997). Implications of genetic research for child psychiatry. *Canadian Journal of Psychiatry, 42,* 569–576.

Ryan, G. (1993). Working with perpetrators of sexual abuse and domestic violence. *Pastoral Psychology, 41,* 303–319.

Rychtarik, R. G., et al. (2000). Treatment settings for persons with alcoholism: Evidence for matching clients to inpatient versus outpatient care. *Journal of Consulting and Clinical Psychology, 68,* 277–289.

Ryder, A. G., Alden, L. E., & Paulhus, D. L. (2000). Is acculturation unidimensional or bidimensional? A head-to-head comparison in the prediction of personality, self-identity, and adjustment. *Journal of Personality and Social Psychology, 79*(1), 49–65.

S

Sabol, S. Z.., et al. (1999). A genetic association for cigarette smoking behavior. *Health Psychology, 18,* 7–13.

Sachdev, P., & Hay, P. (1996). Site and size of lesion and psychosurgical outcome in obsessive-compulsive disorder: A magnetic resonance imaging study. *Biological Psychiatry, 39,* 739–742.

Sachs, G. S., Lafer, B., Truman, C., Noeth, M. & Thibault, A. B. (1994). Lithium monotherapy: Miracle, myth and misunderstanding. *Psychiatric Annals, 24,* 299–306.

Sachs, S. (2001, March 11). Redefining minority. *The New York Time, Week in Review,* Section 4, pp. 1, 4.

Sack, W. H., Clarke, G. N., & Seeley, J. (1996). Multiple forms of stress in Cambodian adolescent refugees. *Child Development, 67,* 107–116.

Sackheim, H. A., Prudic, J., & Devanand, D. P. (1990). Treatment of medication-resistant depression with electroconvulsive therapy. In A. Tasman, et al. (Eds.), *Review of psychiatry, Vol. 9.* Washington, DC: American Psychiatric Press.

Sackeim, H. A., & Vaughn McCall, W. (2001). In reply. *Archives of General Psychiatry, 58,* 608–609. [Letter]

Sackeim, H. A., et al. (1994). Effects of stimulus intensity and electrode placement on the efficacy and cognitive effects of electroconvulsive therapy. *New England Journal of Medicine, 328,* 839–846.

Sackeim, H. A., et al. (2000). A prospective, randomized, double-blind comparison of bilateral and right unilateral electroconvulsive therapy at different stimulus intensities. *Archives of General Psychiatry, 57,* 425–434.

Sackeim, H. A., et al. (2001). Continuation pharmacotherapy in the prevention of relapse following electroconvulsive therapy. *Journal of the American Medical Association, 285,* 1299–1307.

Sacks, O. (1985a). *The man who mistook his wife for a hat and other clinical tales.* New York: Summit.

Sadler, A. G., Booth, B. M., Nielson, D., & Doebbeling, B. N. (2000). Health-related consequences of physical and sexual violence: Women in the military. *Obstetrics & Gynecology, 96*(3), 473–480.

Safran, J. D., & Messer, S. B. (1997). Psychotherapy integration: A postmodern critique. *Clinical Psychology: Science and Practice, 4,* 140–152.

Salgado de Snyder, V. N. (1987). Factors associated with acculturative stress and depressive symptomatology among married Mexican immigrant women. *Psychology of Women Quarterly, 11,* 475–488.

Salgado de Snyder, V. N., Cervantes, R. C., & Padilla, A. M. (1990). Gender and ethnic differences in psychosocial stress and generalized distress among Hispanics. *Sex Roles, 22,* 441–453.

Salisbury, D. F., et al. (1998). First-episode schizophrenic psychosis differs from first-episode affective psychosis and controls in P300 amplitude over left temporal lobe. *Archives of General Psychiatry, 55,* 173–180.

Salkovskis, P. M., & Clark, D. M. (1993). Panic disorder and hypochondriasis. Special issue: Panic, cognitions and sensations. *Advances in Behaviour Research and Therapy, 15,* 23–48.

Salokangas, R. K. R., & Saarinen, S. (1998). Deinstitutionalization and schizophrenia in Finland: I. Discharged patients and their care. *Schizophrenia Bulletin, 24,* 457–467.

Sammons, M. T., & Brown, A. B. (1997). The Department of Defense psychopharmacology demonstration project: An evolving program for postdoctoral education in psychology. *Professional Psychology: Research and Practice, 28,* 107–112.

Sanchez, E. G., & Mohl, P. C. (1992). Psychotherapy with Mexican-American patients. *American Journal of Psychiatry, 149,* 626–630.

Sanchez-Craig, M., Annis, H. M., Bornet, A. R., & MacDonald, K. R. (1984). Random assignment to abstinence or controlled drinking: Evaluation of a cognitive-behavioral program for problem drinkers. *Journal of Consulting and Clinical Psychology, 52,* 390–403.

Sanchez-Craig, M., & Wilkinson, D. A. (1986/1987). Treating problem drinkers who are not severely dependent on alcohol. *Drugs and Society, 1,* 39–67.

Sanders, B., & Green, J. A. (1995). The factor structure of the Dissociative Experiences Scale in college students. *Dissociation Progress in the Dissociative Disorders, 7,* 23–27.

Sanderson, W. C., & Barlow, D. H. (1990). A description of patients diagnosed with *DSM-III-R* generalized anxiety disorder. *Journal of Nervous & Mental Disease, 178,* 588–591.

Sanderson, W. C., & Rego, S. A. (2000). Empirically supported treatment for panic disorder: Research, theory, and application of cognitive behavioral therapy. *Journal of Cognitive Psychotherapy, 14,* 219–244.

Sanfilipo, M., et al. (2000). Volumetric measure of the frontal and temporal lobe regions in schizophrenia: Relationship to negative symptoms. *Archives of General Psychiatry, 57,* 471–480.

Sanislow, C. A., Grilo, C. M., & McGlashan, T. H. (2000). Factor analysis of the *DSM-III-R* borderline personality disorder criteria in psychiatric inpatients. *American Journal of Psychiatry, 157,* 1629–1633.

Sar, V., et al. (1996). Structured interview data on 35 cases of dissociative identity disorder in Turkey. *American Journal of Psychiatry, 153,* 1329–1333.

Sass, L. (1982, August 22). The borderline personality. *The New York Times Magazine,* pp. 12–15, 66–67.

Satcher, D. (2000). Mental health: A report of the Surgeon General—Executive summary. *Professional Psychology: Research and Practice, 31,* 5–13.

Satir, V. (1967). *Conjoint family therapy* (rev. ed.). Palo Alto, CA: Science and Behavior Books.

Sato, T. (1997). Seasonal affective disorder and phototherapy: A critical review. *Professional Psychology: Research and Practice, 28,* 164–169.

Saywitz, K. J., Mannarino, A. P., Berliner, L., & Cohen, J. A. (2000). Treatment for sexually abused children and adolescents. *American Psychologist, 55,* 1040–1049.

Schachter, S., & Latané, B. (1964). Crime, cognition, and the autonomic nervous system. In D. Levine (Ed.), *Nebraska symposium on motivation* (Vol. 12, pp. 221–273). Lincoln: University of Nebraska Press.

Schacter, D. L. (1999). The seven sins of memory: Insights from psychology and cognitive neuroscience. *American Psychologist, 54,* 182–203.

Schafer, D. W. (1986). Recognizing multiple personality patients. *American Journal of Psychotherapy, 40,* 500–510.

Schafer, J., & Brown, S. (1991). Marijuana and cocaine effect expectancies and drug use patterns. *Journal of Consulting and Clinical Psychology, 59,* 558–565.

Schaffer, S. J. (2000, November/December). New NY Tarasoff/confidentiality ruling. *NYSPA Notebook,* p. 5.

Scheel, K. R. (2000). The empirical basis of dialectical behavior therapy: Summary, critique, and implications. *Clinical Psychology: Science and Practice, 7,* 68–86.

Scheflin, A. W., & Brown, D. (1996). Repressed memory or dissociative amnesia: What the science says. *Journal of Psychiatry and Law, 24,* 143–188.

Scheier, L. M., Botvin, G. J., & Baker, E. (1997). Risk and protective factors as predictors of adolescent alcohol involvement and transitions in alcohol use: A prospective analysis. *Journal of Studies on Alcohol, 58,* 652–767.

Scheier, M. F., & Carver, C. S. (1985). Optimism, coping, and health: Assessment and implications of generalized outcome expectancies. *Health Psychology, 4,* 219–247.

Scheier, M. F., & Carver, C. S. (1992). Effects of optimism on psychological and physical well-being: Theoretical overview and empirical update. Special issue: Cognitive perspectives in health psychology. *Cognitive Therapy and Research, 16,* 201–228.

Scheier, M. F., et al. (1999). Optimism and rehospitalization after coronary artery bypass graft surgery. *Archives of Internal Medicine, 159,* 829–935.

Schepis, M. R., Reid, D. H., & Fitzgerald, J. R. (1987). Group instruction with profoundly retarded persons: Acquisition, generalization, and maintenance of a remunerative work skill. *Journal of Applied Behavior Analysis, 20,* 97–105.

Schizophrenia Update—Part I (1995, June). *The Harvard Mental Health Letter, 11,* 1–4.

Schmauk, F. J. (1970). Punishment, arousal, and avoidance learning in sociopaths. *Journal of Abnormal Psychology, 76,* 325–335.

Schmidt, N. B., Lerew, D. R., & Jackson, R. J. (1997). The role of anxiety sensitivity in the pathogenesis of panic: Prospective evaluation of spontaneous panic attacks during acute stress. *Journal of Abnormal Psychology, 106,* 355–364.

Schmidt, N. B., Trakowski, J. H., & Staab, J. P. (1997). Extinction of panicogenic effects of a 35% CO_2 challenge in patients with panic disorder. *Journal of Abnormal Psychology, 106,* 630–638.

Schmidt, N. B., et al. (2000). Dismantling cognitive-behavioral treatment for panic disorder: Questioning the utility of breathing retraining. *Journal of Consulting and Clinical Psychology, 68,* 417–424.

Schmitt, E. (2001a, April 1). U.S. now more diverse, ethnically and racially. *The New York Times,* p. A20.

Schmitt, E. (2001b, March 13). For 7 million people in census, one race category isn't enough. *The New York Times,* pp. A1, A14.

Schmitt, E. (2001c, April 1). U.S. now more diverse, ethnically and racially. *The New York Times,* p. A20.

Schneider, K. (1957). Primäre und sekundäre Symptome bei der Schizophrenia. *Fortschritte der Neurologie Psychiatrie, 25,* 487–490.

Schneiderman, N., Antoni, M. H., Saab, P. G., & Ironson, G. (2001). Health psychology: Psychosocial and biobehavioral aspects of chronic disease management. *Annual Review of Psychology, 52,* 555–580.

Schneier, F. R., Wexler, K. B., & Liebowitz, M. R. (1997). Social phobia and stuttering. *American Journal of Psychiatry, 154,* 131.

Schnurr, P. P., Ford, J. D., & Friedman, M. J. (2000). Predictors and outcomes of posttraumatic stress disorder in World War II veterans exposed to mustard gas. *Journal of Consulting and Clinical Psychology, 68,* 258–268.

Schnyder, U., et al. (2001). Incidence and prediction of posttraumatic stress disorder symptoms in severely injured accident victims. *American Journal of Psychiatry, 158,* 594–599.

Schoenman, T. J. (1984). The mentally ill witch in text books of abnormal psychology: Current status and implications of a fallacy. *Professional Psychiatry, 15,* 299–314.

Schteingart, J. S., et al. (1995). Homeless and child functioning in the context of risk and protective factors moderating child outcomes. *Journal of Clinical Child Psychology, 24,* 320–331.

Schuckit, M. A. (1983). Subjective responses to alcohol in sons of alcoholics and control. *Archives of General Psychiatry, 41,* 879–884.

Schuckit, M. A. (1987). Biological vulnerability to alcoholism. *Journal of Consulting and Clinical Psychology, 55,* 301–309.

Schuckit, M. A. (1996). Recent developments in the pharmacotherapy of alcohol dependence. *Journal of Consulting and Clinical Psychology, 64,* 669–676.

Schuckit, M. A., & Rayes, U. (1979). Ethanol ingestion: Differences in blood acetaldehyde concentrations in relatives of alcoholics. *Science, 203,* 54–55.

Schuckit, M. A., et al. (1999). Clinical implications for four drugs of the *DSM-IV* distinction between substance dependence with and without a physiological component. *American Journal of Psychiatry, 156,* 41–49.

Schwartz, B. S., et al. (1998). Epidemiology of tension-type headache. *Journal of the American Medical Association, 279,* 381–383.

Schwartz, J. M. (1998). Neuroanatomical aspects of cognitive-behavior therapy response in obsessive-compulsive disorder. *British Journal of Psychiatry, 173,* 38–44.

Schwartz, R. H., Voth, E. A., Sheridan, M. J. (1997). Marijuana to prevent nausea and vomiting in cancer patients: A survey of clinical oncologists. *Southern Medical Journal, 90,* 167–172.

Schwartz, R. M. (1986). The internal dialogue: On the asymmetry between positive and negative thoughts. *Cognitive Therapy & Research, 10,* 591–605.

Schwitzgebel, R. L., & Schwitzgebel, R. K. (1980). *Law and psychological practice.* New York: Wiley.

Scogin, F., & McElreath, L. K. (1994). Efficacy of psychosocial treatments for geriatric depression: A quantitative review. *Journal of Consulting and Clinical Psychology, 62,* 69–74.

Scroppo, J. C., Drob, S. L., Weinberger, J. L., & Eagle, P. (1998). Identifying dissociative identity disorder: A self-report and projective study. *Journal of Abnormal Psychology, 107,* 272–284.

Sears, R. R., Maccoby, E. E., & Levin, H. (1957). *Patterns of child rearing.* New York: Harper & Row.

The Sedentary Society. (1996, August). *Harvard Heart Letter, 6,* 3–4.

See, L. (1999, November). My face doesn't match my race. *Self,* pp. 60–61.

Seeman, M. V. (1997). Psychopathology in women and men: Focus on female hormones. *American Journal of Psychiatry, 154,* 1641–1647.

Sees, K. L., et al. (2000). Methadone maintenance vs. 180-day psychosocially enriched detoxification for treatment of opioid dependence. *Journal of the American Medical Association, 283,* 1303–1310.

Segal, J. H. (1989). Erotomania revisited: From Kraepelin to *DSM-III-R. American Journal of Psychiatry, 146,* 1261–1266.

Segal, S. P., Bola, J. R., & Watson, M. A. (1996). Race, quality of care, and antipsychotic prescribing practices in psychiatric emergency services. *Psychiatric Services, 47,* 282–286.

Segal, Z.. V., et al. (1992). Cognitive and life stress predictors of relapse in remitted unipolar depressed patients: Test of the congruency hypothesis. *Journal of Abnormal Psychology, 101,* 26–36.

Segell, M. (2000, October 24). Testosterone's not so bad after all. *MSNBC Web Posting.* Retrieved October 28, 2000, from http://www.msnbc.com/news/480175.asp.

Segerstrom, S. C., et al. (1998). Optimism is associated with mood, coping, and immune change in response to stress. *Journal of Personality and Social Psychology, 74,* 1646–1655.

Segraves, R. (1988). Drugs and desire. In S. Leiblum & R. Rosen (Eds.), *Sexual desire disorders.* New York: Guilford Press.

Segraves, R. T., & Althof, S. (1998). Psychotherapy and pharmacotherapy of sexual dysfunctions. In P. E. Nathan & J. M. Gorman (Eds.), *A guide to treatments that work* (pp. 447–471). New York: Oxford University Press.

Segrin, C., & Abramson, L. Y. (1994). Negative reactions to depressive behaviors: A communication theories analysis. *Journal of Abnormal Psychology, 103,* 655–668.

Segrin, C., & Dillard, J. P. (1992). The international theory of depression: A meta-analysis of the research literature. *Journal of Social and Clinical Psychology, 11,* 43–70.

Seligman, L., & Hardenburg, S. A. (2000). Assessment and treatment of paraphilias. *Journal of Counseling & Development, 78,* 107–113.

Seligman, M. E. P. (1973). Fall into helplessness. *Psychology Today, 7,* 43–48.

Seligman, M. E. P. (1975). *Helplessness: On depression, development, and death.* San Francisco: Freeman.

Seligman, M. E. P. (1991). *Learned optimism.* New York: Knopf.

Seligman, M. E. P. (1998, August). *Prevention of depression and positive psychology.* Paper presented at the meeting of the American Psychological Association, San Francisco.

Seligman, M. E. P., & Maier, S. F. (1967). Failure to escape traumatic shock. *Journal of Experimental Psychology, 74,* 1–9.

Seligman, M. E. P., & Rosenhan, D. L. (1984). *Abnormal psychology.* New York: W. W. Norton.

Seligman, M. E. P., et al. (1988). Explanatory style change during cognitive therapy for unipolar depression. *Journal of Abnormal Psychology, 97,* 13–18.

Selkoe, D. J. (1992). Aging brain, aging mind. *Scientific American, 267*(3), 134–142.

Selvin, B. W. (1993, June 1). Transsexuals are coming to terms with themselves and society. *New York Newsday,* pp. 55, 58, 59.

Selye, H. (1976). *The stress of life* (Rev. ed.) New York: McGraw-Hill.

Semrud-Clikeman, M., et al. (2000). Using MRI to examine brain-behavior relationships in males with attention deficit disorder with hyperactivity. *Journal of the American Academy of Child & Adolescent Psychiatry, 39,* 477–484.

Sensky, T., et al. (2000). A randomized controlled trial of cognitive-behavioral therapy for persistent symptoms in schizophrenia resistant to medication. *Archives of General Psychiatry, 57,* 165–172.

Seppa, N. (1997, June). Children's TV remains steeped in violence. *APA Monitor, 28*(6), p. 36.

Seroczynski, A. D., Cole, D. A., & Maxwell, S. E. (1997). Cumulative and compensatory effects of competence and incompetence on depressive symptoms in children. *Journal of Abnormal Psychology, 106,* 586–597.

Shadish, W. R., et al. (2000). The effects of psychological therapies under clinically representative conditions: A meta-analysis. *Psychological Bulletin, 126,* 512–529.

Shadish, W. R., Jr., Lurigio, A. J., & Lewis, D. A. (1989). After deinstitutionalization: The present and future of mental health long-term care policy. *Journal of Social Issues, 45,* 1–15.

Shaffer, C. E., Jr., Waters, W. F., & Adams, S. G., Jr. (1994). Dangerousness: Assessing the risk of violent behavior. *Journal of Consulting and Clinical Psychology, 62,* 1064–1068.

Shaffer, D., Gould, M., & Hicks, R. C. (1994). Worsening suicide rate in black teenagers. *American Journal of Psychiatry, 151,* 1810–1812.

Shafran, R., & Mansell, W. (2001). Perfectionism and psychopathology: A review of research and treatment. *Clinical Psychology Review, 21,* 879–906.

Shalev, A. Y., Yehuda, R., & McFarlane, A. C. (Eds.). (2000). *International handbook of human response to trauma.* New York: Kluwer Academic/Plenum Publishers.

Shapiro, D. A., et al. (1995). Effects of treatment duration and severity of depression on the maintenance of gains after cognitive-behavioral and psychodynamic interpersonal psychotherapy. *Journal of Consulting and Clinical Psychology, 63,* 378–387.

Shapiro, E. (1992, August 22). Fear returns to sidewalks of West 96th Street. *The New York Times,* pp. B3–B4.

Shapiro, F. (1995). *Eye movement desensitization and reprocessing: Basic principles, protocols, and procedures.* New York: Guilford Press.

Shapiro, L. 1998, (June 15). Fat, fatter: But who's counting? *Newsweek,* p. 55.

Sharkansky, E. J., King, D. W., King, L. A., & Wolfe, J. (2000). Coping with Gulf War combat stress: Mediating and moderating effects. *Journal of Abnormal Psychology, 109,* 188–197.

Sharp, T. J., & Harvey, A. G. (2001). Chronic pain and posttraumatic stress disorder: Mutual maintenance? *Clinical Psychology Review, 21,* 857–877.

Shaw, R., Cohen, F., Doyle, B., & Palesky, J. (1985). The impact of denial and repressive style on information gain and rehabilitation outcomes in myocardial infarction patients. *Psychosomatic Medicine, 47,* 262–273.

Shaywitz, S. E. (1998). Dyslexia. *The New England Journal of Medicine, 338,* 307–312.

Shea, M. T., Widiger, T. A., & Klein, M. H. (1992). Comorbidity of personality disorders and depression: Implications for treatment. *Journal of Consulting and Clinical Psychology, 60,* 857–868.

Sheitman, B. B., et al. (1998). Pharmacological treatments of schizophrenia. In P. E. Nathan & J. M. Gorman (Eds.), *A guide to treatments that work* (pp. 167–189). New York: Oxford University Press.

Shelton, R. C., et al. (2001). Effectiveness of St John's Wort in major depression: A randomized controlled trial. *Journal of the American Medical Association, 285,* 1978–1986.

Sherbourne, C. D., Hays, R. D., & Wells, K. B. (1995). Personal and psychosocial risk factors for physical and mental health outcomes and course of depression among depressed patients. *Journal of Consulting and Clinical Psychology, 63,* 345–355.

Sherbourne, C. D., et al. (2000). Impact of psychiatric conditions on health-related quality of life in persons with HIV infection. *American Journal of Psychiatry, 157,* 248–254.

Sherman, D. K., et al. (1997). Twin concordance for attention deficit hyperactivity disorder: A comparison of teachers' and mothers' reports. *American Journal of Psychiatry, 154,* 532–535.

Sherwood, N. E., et al. (2000). The perceived function of eating for bulimic, subclinical bulimic, and non-eating disordered women. *Behavior Therapy, 31,* 777–793.

Sheung-Tak, C. (1996). A critical review of Chinese koro. *Culture, Medicine and Psychiatry, 20,* 67–82.

Shiffman, S., et al. (1996). Progression from a smoking lapse to relapse: Prediction from abstinence violation effects, nicotine dependence, and lapse characteristics. *Journal of Consulting and Clinical Psychology, 64,* 993–1002.

Shifren, J. L., et al. (2000). Transdermal testosterone treatment in women with impaired sexual function after oophorectomy. *The New England Journal of Medicine, 343,* 682–688.

Shneidman, E. S. (1985). *Definition of suicide.* New York: Wiley.

Shnek, Z. M., et al. (2001). Psychological factors and depressive symptoms in ischemic heart disease. *Health Psychology,* 141–145.

Shonk, S. M., & Cicchetti, D. (2001). Maltreatment, competency deficits, and risk for academic and behavioral maladjustment. *Developmental Psychology, 37,* 3–17.

Shopper, M. (1996). Fear of alien abduction. *Journal of the American Academy of Child and Adolescent Psychiatry, 35,* 555–556.

Shute, N., Locy, T., & Pasternak, D. (2000, March 6). The perils of pills. *U.S. News & World Report,* pp. 44–50.

Shweder, R. (1985). Cross-cultural study of emotions. In A. Kleinman & B. Good (Eds.), *Culture and depression.* Berkeley: University of California Press.

Siegel, J. (2001, January 18). St. John's Wort: Nature's antidepressant? *HealthGate Web Posting. NBCI.com.* Retrieved January 28, 2001, from http://healthgate.nbci.com/getcontent.asp?siteid=nbci&docid=/healthy/alternative/2000/johnwort/index

Siegel, L. J. (1992). *Criminology* (4th ed.). St. Paul, MN: West.

Siever, L., & Trestman, R. L. (1993). The serotonin system and aggressive personality disorder. *International Clinical Psychopharmacology, 8*(Suppl. 2), 33–39.

Siever, L. J., et al. (1990). Increased morbid risk for schizophrenia-related disorders in relatives of schizotypal personality disordered patients. *Archives of General Psychiatry, 47,* 634–640.

Silberstein, R. B., et al. (1998). Functional brain electrical activity mapping in boys with attention-deficit/hyperactivity disorder. *Archives of General Psychiatry, 55,* 1105–1112.

Silberstein, S. D., et al. (2000). Rizaptriptan in the treatment of menstrual migraine. *Obstetrics & Gynecology, 96,* 237–242.

Silva, R. R., et al. (2000). Stress and vulnerability to posttraumatic stress disorder in children and adolescents. *American Journal of Psychiatry, 157,* 1229–1235.

Silver, E., Cirincione, C., & Steadman, H. J. (1994). Demythologizing inaccurate perceptions of the insanity defense. *Law and Human Behavior, 18,* 63–70.

Silverman, J. G., et al. (2001). Dating violence against adolescent girls and associated substance use, unhealthy weight control, sexual risk behavior, pregnancy, and suicidality. *Journal of the American Medical Association, 286,* 572–579.

Simeon, D., et al. (1997). Feeling unreal: 30 Cases of *DSM-III-R* depersonalization disorder. *American Journal of Psychiatry, 154,* 1107–1113.

Simeon, D., et al. (2000). Feeling unreal: A PET study of depersonalization disorder. *American Journal of Psychiatry, 157,* 1782–1788.

Simeon, D., et al. (2001). The role of childhood interpersonal trauma in depersonalization disorder. *American Journal of Psychiatry, 158,* 1027–1033.

Simon, G. E. (1998). Management of somatoform and factitious disorders. In P. E. Nathan & J. M. Gorman (Eds.), *A guide to treatments that work* (pp. 408–422). New York: Oxford University Press.

Simons-Morton, B., et al. (2001). Peer and parent influences on smoking and drinking among early adolescents. *Health Education & Behavior, 28,* 95–107.

Simpson, D. D., et al. (1999). A national evaluation of treatment outcomes for cocaine dependence. *Archives of General Psychiatry, 57,* 507–514.

Singh, G. (1985). Dhat syndrome revisited. *Indian Journal of Psychiatry, 27,* 119–122.

Sitharthan, T., et al. (1997). Cue exposure in moderation drinking: A comparison with cognitive-behavior therapy. *Journal of Consulting and Clinical Psychology, 65,* 878–882.

Skaar, K. L., et al. (1997). Smoking cessation 1: An overview of research. *Behavioral Medicine, 23,* 5–13.

Skinner, B. F. (1938). *The behavior of organisms: An experimental analysis.* New York: Appleton.

Skoog, G., & Skoog, I. (1999). A 40-year follow-up of patients with obsessive-compulsive disorder. *Archives of General Psychiatry, 56,* 121–127.

Skoog, I. (2000). Detection of preclinical Alzheimer's disease. *The New England Journal of Medicine, 343,* 502–503.

Slater, D., & Hans, V. P. (1984). Public opinion of forensic psychiatry following the Hinckley verdict. *American Journal of Psychiatry, 141,* 675–679.

Sleek, S. (1994, January). Many methods employed to breach autism's walls. *APA Monitor,* pp. 30–31.

Slone, D. G., & Gleason, C. E. (1999). Behavior management planning for problem behaviors in dementia: A practical model. *Professional Psychology: Research and Practice, 30,* 27–36.

Slutske, W. S., et al. (1998). Common genetic risk factors for conduct disorder and alcohol dependence. *Journal of Abnormal Psychology, 107,* 363–374.

Small, J. G., et al. (1997). Quetiapine in patients with schizophrenia: A high- and low-dose double-blind comparison with placebo. *Archives of General Psychiatry, 54,* 549–557.

Smith, D. (1982). Trends in counseling and psychotherapy. *American Psychologist, 37,* 802–809.

Smith, D. (2001a, October). Sleep psychologists in demand. *Monitor on Psychology,* pp. 36–38.

Smith, D. (2001b, September). Harassment in the hallways. *Monitor on Psychology,* pp. 38–40.

Smith, G. R. (1994). The course of somatization and its effects on utilization of health care resources. *Psychosomatics, 35,* 263–267.

Smith, G. T., et al. (1995). Expectancy for social facilitation from drinking: The divergent paths of high-expectancy and low-expectancy adolescents. *Journal of Abnormal Psychology, 104,* 32–40.

Smith, J. E., & Krejci, J. (1991). Minorities join the majority: Eating disturbances among Hispanic and Native American youth. *International Journal of Eating Disorders, 10,* 179–186.

Smith, M. L., & Glass, G. V. (1977). Meta-analysis of psychotherapy otucome studies. *American Psychologist, 32,* 752–760.

Smith, M. L., Glass, G. V., & Miller, T. I. (1980). *The benefits of psychotherapy.* Baltimore, MD: Johns Hopkins University Press.

Smith, R. E., Smoll, F. L., & Ptacek, J. T. (1990). Conjunctive moderator variables in vulnerability and reliency research: Life stress, social support and coping skills, and adolescent sport injuries. *Journal of Personality and Social Psychology, 58,* 360–370.

Smith, S. C. (1983). *The great mental calculators.* New York: Columbia University Press.

Smith, T. (1999). Outcome of early intervention for children with autism. *Clinical Psychology: Science and Practice, 6,* 33–49.

Smith, T. W., Snyder, C. R., & Perkins, S. C. (1983). The self-serving function of hypochondriacal complaints: Physical symptoms as self-handicapping strategies. *Journal of Personality and Social Psychology, 44,* 787–797.

Smith, Y. L. S., et al. (2001). Adolescents with gender identity disorder who were accepted or rejected for sex reassignment surgery: A prospective follow-up study. *Journal of American Academy of Child & Adolescent Psychiatry, 40,* 472–481.

Smoking will be world's biggest killer. (1996, September 17). *Newsday,* p. A21.

Smyth, J. M. (1998). Written emotional expression: Effect sizes, outcome types, and moderating variables. *Journal of Consulting and Clinical Psychology, 66,* 174–184.

Smyth, J. M., et al. (1999). Effects of writing about stressful experiences on symptom reduction in patients with asthma or rheumatoid arthritis. *Journal of the American Medical Association, 281,* 1304–1309.

Smyth, J. M., & Pennebaker, J. W. (2001). What are the health effects of disclosure? In A. Baum, T. A. Revenson, & J. E. Singer (Eds.), *Handbook of health psychology* (pp. 339–348). Mahwah, NJ: Erlbaum.

Snell, M. E. (1997). Teaching children and young adults with mental retardation in school programs: Current research. *Behaviour Change, 14,* 73–105.

Sobell, L. C., et al. (1990). Behavior therapy. In A. S. Bellack & M. Hersen (Eds.), *Comparative treatment of adult disorders* (pp. 479–505). New York: Wiley.

Sobell, M. B., & Sobell, L. C. (1973). Alcoholics treated by individualized behavior therapy: One year treatment outcome. *Behaviour Research & Therapy, 11,* 599–618.

Sobell, M. B., & Sobell, L. C. (1976). Second year treatment outcome of alcoholics treated by individualized behavior therapy: Results. *Behaviour Research and Therapy, 14,* 195–215.

Sobell, M. B., & Sobell, L. C. (1984). The aftermath of heresy: A response to Pendery et al.'s critique of "Individualized behavior therapy for alcoholics." *Behaviour Research and Therapy, 22,* 413–440.

Solomon, D. A., et al. (1997). Recovery from major depression: A 10-year prospective follow-up across multiple episodes. *Archives of General Psychiatry, 54,* 1001–1006.

Solomon, D. A., et al. (2000). Multiple recurrences of major depressive disorder. *American Journal of Psychiatry, 157,* 229–233.

Sorenson, S. B., & Rutter, C. M. (1991). Transgenerational patterns of suicide attempt. *Journal of Consulting and Clinical Psychology, 59,* 861–866.

Southwick, S. M., et al. (1997). Noradrenergic and serotonergic function in posttraumatic stress disorder. *Archives of General Psychiatry, 54,* 749–758.

Spanos, N. P. (1978). Witchcraft in histories of psychiatry: A critical analysis and an alternative conceptualization. *Psychological Bulletin, 85,* 417–439.

Spanos, N. P. (1994). Multiple identity enactments and multiple personality disorder: A sociocognitive perspective. *Psychological Bulletin, 116,* 143–165.

Spanos, N. P., Weekes, J. R., & Bertrand, L. D. (1985). Multiple personality: A social psychological perspective. *Journal of Abnormal Psychology, 94,* 362–376.

Spark, R. F. (1991). *Male sexual health: A couple's guide.* Mount Vernon, NY: Consumer Reports Books.

Spechler, S. J., Fischbach, L., & Feldman, M. (2000). Clinical aspects of genetic variability in helicobacter pylori. *Journal of the American Medical Association, 283,* 1264–1266.

Spector, I. P., & Carey, M. P. (1990). Incidence and prevalence of the sexual dysfunctions: A critical review of the empirical literature. *Archives of Sexual Behavior, 19,* 389–408.

Spencer, D. J. (1983). Psychiatric dilemmas in Australian aborigines. *International Journal of Social Psychiatry, 29*(3), 208–214.

Spiegel, D., et al. (1989, October 14). Effect of psychosocial treatment on survival of patients with metastatic breast cancer. *Lancet,* pp. 888–891.

Spiegel, D. A., & Bruce, T. J. (1997). Benzodiazepines and exposure-based cognitive behavior therapies for panic disorder: Conclusions from combined treatment trials. *American Journal of Psychiatry, 154,* 773–781.

Spitzer, R. L., Gibbon, M., Skodol, A. E., Williams, J. B. W., & First, M. B. (1989). *DSM-III-R casebook.* Washington, DC: American Psychiatric Press.

Spitzer, R. L., et al. (1992). Binge eating disorder: A multisite field trial of the diagnostic criteria. *International Journal of Eating Disorders, 11,* 191–203.

Spitzer, R. L., et al. (1994). *DSM-IV case book* (4th ed.). Washington, DC: American Psychiatric Press.

Squier, L. H., & Domhoff, G. W. (1998). The presentation of dreaming and dreams in introductory psychology textbooks: A critical examination with suggestions for textbook authors and course instructors. *Dreaming, 8,* 149–168.

St. John's wort doesn't help with major depression. (2001a, June). *Tufts University Health & Nutrition Letter,* p. 2.

St. John's wort ineffective in severe depression. (2001b, April 17). *CNN Web Posting.* Retrieved April 19, 2001, from http://www.cnn.com/2001/HEALTH/conditions/04/17/st.johns.wort/index.html

St. Lawrence, J. S., et al. (1995a). Comparison of education versus behavioral skills training interventions in lowering sexual HIV-risk behavior of substance-dependent adolescents. *Journal of Consulting and Clinical Psychology, 63,* 154–157.

St. Lawrence, J. S., et al. (1995b). Cognitive-behavioral intervention to reduce African American adolescents' risk for HIV infection. *Journal of Consulting and Clinical Psychology, 63,* 221–237.

Staal, W. G., et al. (2000). Structural brain abnormalities in patients with schizophrenia and their healthy siblings. *American Journal of Psychiatry, 157,* 416–421.

Stader, S. R., & Hokanson, J. E. (1998). Psychosocial antecedents of depressive symptoms: An evaluation using daily experiences methodology. *Journal of Abnormal Psychology, 107,* 17–26.

Stahl, S. M. (2001). Sex and psychopharmacology: Is natural estrogen a psychotropic drug in women? *Archives of General Psychiatry, 58,* 537–538. [Letter]

Stamler, J., et al. (1999). Low risk-factor profile and long-term cardiovascular and noncardiovascular mortality and life expectancy: Findings for 5 large cohorts of young adult and middle-aged men and women. *Journal of the American Medical Association, 282,* 2012–2018.

Stamm, B. H., & Perednia, D. A. (2000). Evaluating psychosocial aspects of telemedicine and telehealth systems. *Professional Psychology: Research and Practice, 31,* 184–189.

Stanley, M. A., & Beck, J. G. (2000). Anxiety disorders. *Clinical Psychology Review, 20,* 731–754.

Stanley, M. A., & Turner, S. M. (1995). Current status of pharmacological and behavioral treatment of obsessive-compulsive disorder. *Behavior Therapy, 26,* 163–186.

Stawar, T. (1999). A model for sexual harassment behavior. *Forensic Examiner, 8*(9–10), 30–34.

Steadman, H. J. (1979). *Beating a rap: Defendants found incompetent to stand trial.* Chicago: University of Chicago Press.

Steadman, H. J., et al. (1993). *Before and after Hinckley: Evaluating insanity defense reform.* New York: Guilford Press.

Steadman, H. J., et al. (1998). Violence by people discharged from acute psychiatric inpatient facilities and by others in the same neighborhoods. *Archives of General Psychiatry, 55,* 393–401.

Steer, R. A., et al. (1994). Psychometric properties of the Cognition Checklist with psychiatric outpatients and university students. *Psychological Assessment, 6,* 67–70.

Stefanek, M. E., Ollendick, T. H., Baldock, W. P., Francis, G., & Yaeger, N. J. (1987). Self-statements in aggressive, withdrawn, and popular children. *Cognitive Therapy and Research, 11,* 229–239.

Steffens, D. C., et al. (2000). Prevalence of depression and its treatment in an elderly population: The Cache County Study. *Archives of General Psychiatry, 57,* 601–607.

Stein, D., et al. (1998). The association between attitudes toward suicide and suicidal ideation in adolescents. *Acta Psychiatrica Scandinavia, 97,* 195–201.

Stein, M. B., Baird, A., & Walker, J. R. (1996). Social phobia in adults with stuttering. *American Journal of Psychiatry, 153,* 278–280.

Stein, M. B., Jan, K. L., & Livesley, W. J. (1999). Heritability of anxiety sensitivity: A twin study. *American Journal of Psychiatry, 156,* 246–251.

Stein, M. B., & Kean, Y. M. (2000). Disability and quality of life in social phobia: Epidemiologic findings. *American Journal of Psychiatry, 157,* 1606–1613.

Stein, M. B., Torgrud, L. J., & Walker, J. R. (2000). Social phobia symptoms, subtypes, and severity: Findings from a community survey. *Archives of General Psychiatry, 57,* 1046–1052.

Stein, M. B., Walker, J. R., & Forde, D. R. (1996). Public-speaking fears in a community sample: Prevalence, impact on functioning, and diagnostic classification. *Archives of General Psychiatry, 53,* 169–174.

Stein, M. B., et al. (2001). Social anxiety disorder and the risk of depression: A prospective community study of adolescents and young adults. *Archives of General Psychiatry, 58,* 251–256.

Steinberg, M. (1991). The spectrum of depersonalization: Assessment and treatment. *Annual Review of Psychiatry, 10,* 223–247.

Steketee, G., & Foa, E. B. (1985). Obsessive-compulsive disorder. In D. H. Barlow (Ed.), *Clinical handbook of psychological disorders* (pp. 69–144). New York: Guilford Press.

Stemberger, R. R., et al. (1995). Social phobia: An analysis of possible developmental factors. *Journal of Abnormal Psychology, 194,* 526–531.

Stenson, J. (2001a, August 26). Burden of mental illness in America falls on minorities. *MSNBC Web Posting.* Retrieved August 26, 2001, from http://www.msnbc.com/news/619545.asp.

Stenson, J. (2001b, August 26). Many teens abused by dating partners. *MSNBC Web Posting.* Retrieved August 27, 2001, from http://www.msnbc.com/news/619696.asp.

Stern, E., & Silbersweig, D. A. (2001). Advances in functional neuroimaging methodology for the study of brain system underlying human neuropsychological function and dysfunction. *Journal of Clinical & Experimental Neuropsychology, 23,* 3–18.

Sternberg, E. M. (2000). *The balance within: The science connecting health and emotions.* New York: Freeman.

Steven, J. E. (1995, January 30). Virtual therapy. *The Boston Globe,* pp. 25, 29.

Stevens, J. R. (1997). Anatomy of schizophrenia revisited. *Schizophrenia Bulletin, 23,* 373–383.

Stevens, S. E., Hynan, M. T., & Allen, M. (2000). A meta-analysis of common factor and specific treatment effects across the outcome domains of the phase model of psychotherapy. *Clinical Psychology: Science and Practice, 7,* 273–290.

Stewart, M. W., et al. (1994). Differential relationships between stress and disease activity for immunologically distinct subgroups of people with rheumatoid arthritis. *Journal of Abnormal Psychology, 1103,* 251–258.

Stice, E. (1994). Review of the evidence for a sociocultural model of bulimia nervosa and an exploration of the mechanisms of action. *Clinical Psychology Review, 14,* 633–661.

Stice, E. (2001). A prospective test of the dual-pathway model of bulimic pathology: Mediating effects of dieting and negative affect. *Journal of Abnormal Psychology, 110,* 124–135.

Stice, E., et al. (2000). Body-image and eating disturbances predict onset of depression among female adolescents: A longitudinal study. *Journal of Abnormal Psychology, 109,* 438–444.

Stock, W. E. (1991). Feminist explanations: Male power, hostility, and sexual coercion. In E. Grauerholz & M. A. Koralewski (Eds.), *Sexual coercion: A sourcebook on its nature, causes, and prevention* (pp. 61–73). Lexington, MA: Lexington Books.

Stokstad, E. (2001). New hints into the biological basis of autism. *Science, 294,* pp. 34–37.

Stolberg, S. G. (1998a, March 13). New cancer cases decreasing in U.S. as deaths do, too. *The New York Times,* p. A1, A14.

Stolberg, S. G. (1998b). Rise in smoking by young blacks erodes a success story. *The New York Times,* p. A24.

Stolberg, S. G. (2001, May 10). Blacks found on short end of heart attack procedure. *The New York Times,* p. A20.

Stoller, R. J. (1969). Parental influences in male transsexualism. In R. Green & J. Money (Eds.), *Transsexualism and sex reassignment.* Baltimore: Johns Hopkins University Press.

Stone, A. (1976). The Tarasoff decisions: Suing psychotherapists to safeguard society. *Harvard Law Review, 90,* 358–378.

Stone, A. (1984). *Law, psychiatry and morality.* Washington, DC: American Psychiatric Press.

Stone, A. A., et al. (1994). Daily events are associated with a secretory immune response to an oral antigen in men. *Health Psychology, 13,* 440–446.

Stone, A. A. et al. (2000b). Structured writing about stressful events: Exploring potential psychological mediators of positive health effects. *Health Psychology, 19,* 619–624.

Stone, M. H. (1980). *The borderline syndromes: Constitution, personality, and adaptation.* New York: McGraw-Hill.

Stotland, N. L. (2000, July 26). Sertraline: An effective treatment for binge-eating disorder? *Journal Watch Women's Health,* pp. 1, 4.

Stout, D. (2000, September 1). Use of illegal drugs is down among young, survey finds. *The New York Times*, p. A18.

Stover, E. S., et al. (1996). Perspectives from the National Institute of Mental Health: Preventing or living with AIDS. *Annals of Behavioral Medicine, 18*, 58–60.

Strakowski, S. M. (1994). Diagnostic validity of schizophreniform disorder. *American Journal of Psychiatry, 15*, 815–824.

Strakowski, S. M., et al. (1999). Brain magnetic resonance imaging of structural abnormalities in bipolar disorder. *Archives of General Psychiatry, 56*, 254–260.

Strassberg, D. S. (1997). A cross-national validity study of four MMPI-2 content scales. *Journal of Personality Assessment, 69*, 596–606.

Stricker, G., & Gold, J. R. (1999). The Rorschach: Toward a nomothetically based, idiographically applicable configurational model. *Psychological Assessment, 11*, 240–250.

Stricker, G., & Gold, J. R. (2001, January). An introduction to psychotherapy integration. *NYS Psychologist, 13*, 7–12.

Strober, M., & Humphrey, L. L. (1987). Familial contributions to the etiology and course of anorexia nervosa and bulimia. *Journal of Consulting and Clinical Psychology, 55*, 654–659.

Strollo, P. J., & Rogers, R. M. (1996). Obstructive sleep apnea. *The New England Journal of Medicine, 334*, 99–104.

Strozier, C. B. (2001). *Heinz Kohut: The making of a psychoanalyst.* New York: Farrar, Straus & Giroux.

Strube, M. J. (1988). The decision to leave an abusive relationship: Empirical evidence and theoretical issues. *Psychological Bulletin, 104*, 236–250.

Strupp, H. H. (1992). The future of psychodynamic psychotherapy. *Psychotherapy, 29*, 21–27.

Stuart, G. L., et al. (2000). Effectiveness of an empirically based treatment for panic disorder delivered in a service clinic setting: 1-year follow-up. *Journal of Consulting and Clinical Psychology, 68*, 506–512.

Stunkard, A. J., & Sørensen, T. I. A. (1993). Obesity and socioeconomic status—A complex relation. *New England Journal of Medicine, 329*, 1036–1037.

Stunkard, A. J., et al. (1986). An adoption study of human obesity. *New England Journal of Medicine, 314*, 193, 198.

Stunkard, A. J., et al. (1990). A separated twin study of the body mass index. *New England Journal of Medicine, 322*, 1483–1487.

Stuss, D. T., Gow, C. A., & Hetherington, C. R. (1992). "No longer Gage." Frontal lobe dysfunction and emotional changes. *Journal of Consulting and Clinical Psychology, 60*, 349–359.

Sue, S., et al. (1995). Psychopathology among Asian Americans: A model minority? *Cultural Diversity and Mental Health, 1*, 39–51.

Suinn, R. M. (2001). The terrible twos—Anger and anxiety: Hazardous to your health. *American Psychologist, 56*, 27–36.

Sullivan, H. S. (1962). *Schizophrenia as a human process.* New York: Norton.

Sullivan, P. F., Neale, M. C., & Kendler, K. S. (2000). Genetic epidemiology of major depression: Review and meta-analysis. *American Journal of Psychiatry, 157*, 1552–1562.

Sulloway, F. J. (1983). *Freud: Biologist of the mind.* New York: Basic Books.

Suls, J., Wan, C. K., & Blanchard, E. B. (1994). A multilevel data-analytic approach for evaluation of relationships between daily life stressors and symptomatology: Patients with irritable bowel syndrome. *Health Psychology, 13*, 103–113.

Sutherland, G. R., et al. (1991). Prenatal diagnosis of fragile X syndrome by direct detection of the unstable DNA sequence. *New England Journal of Medicine, 325*, 1720–1722.

Sutker, P. B., et al. (1995). War zone stress, personal resources, and PTSD in Persian Gulf War returnees. *Journal of Abnormal Psychology, 104*, 444–452.

Sveinbjornsdottir, S., et al. (2000). Familial aggregation of Parkinson's disease in Iceland. *New England Journal of Medicine, 343*, 1765–1770.

Svikis, D. S., Velez, M. L., & Pickens, R. W. (1994). Genetic aspects of alcohol use and alcoholism in women. *Alcohol Health & Research World, 18*, 192–196.

Swartz, M., et al. (1991). Somatization disorder. In L. N. Robins & D. A. Regier (Eds.), *Psychiatric disorders in America: The Epidemiologic Catchment Area Study* (pp. 220–257). New York: Free Press.

Swartz, M. S., et al. (1998). Violence and severe mental illness: The effects of substance abuse and nonadherence to medication. *American Journal of Psychiatry, 155*, 226–231.

Sweeney, J. A., et al. (1994). Eye tracking dysfunction in schizophrenia: Characterization of component eye movement abnormalities, diagnostic specificity, and the role of attention. *Journal of Abnormal Psychology, 103*, 222–230.

Sweeney, P. D., Anderson, K., Bailey, S. (1986). Attributional style in depression: A meta-analytic review. *Journal of Personality and Social Psychology, 50*, 974–991.

Swendsen, J. D., & Mazure, C. M. (2000). Life stress as a risk factor for postpartum depression: Current research and methodological issues. *Clinical Psychology: Science and Practice, 7*, 17–31.

Swenson, C. R. (2000). How can we account for DBT's widespread popularity? *Clinical Psychology: Science and Practice*, 87–91.

Szanto, K., et al. (1996). Suicide in elderly depressed patients. Is active vs. passive suicidal ideation a clinically valid distinction? *American Journal of Geriatric Psychiatry, 4*, 197–207.

Szasz, T. S. (1961). *The myth of mental illness.* New York: Harper & Row.

Szasz, T. S. (1970). *Ideology and insanity: Essays on the psychiatric dehumanization of man.* New York: Doubleday Anchor.

Szasz, T. S. (2000). Second commentary on "Aristotle's function argument." *Philosophy, Psychiatry, & Psychology, 7*(1), 3–16.

Szatmari, P., et al. (2000). Two-year outcome of preschool children with autism or Asperger's syndrome. *American Journal of Psychiatry, 157*, 1980–1987.

Szymanski, S., Kane, J. M., & Lieberman, J. A. (1991). A selective review of biological markers in schizophrenia. *Schizophrenia Bulletin, 17*, 99–111.

T

Tafoya, T. N. (1996). Native two-spirit people. In R. P. Cabaj & T. S. Stein (Eds.), *Textbook of homosexuality and mental health* (pp. 603–617). Washington, DC: American Psychiatric Press.

Takahashi, C. (2001, April 8). Selling to Gen Y: A far cry from Betty Crocker. *The New York Times Week in Review*, p. 3.

Tamminga, C. A. (1997). Clinical genetics, II. *American Journal of Psychiatry, 154*, 1046.

Tanda, G., Pontien, & Chiara (1997). Cannabinoid and heroin activation of mesolimbic dopamine transmission by a common opioid receptor mechanism. *Science, 276*, 2048–2050.

Tarasoff v. Regents of the University of California, 131 Cal Rptr. 14, 551 P. 2d 344 (1976).

Tardiff, K., et al. (1994). Homicide in New York City: Cocaine use and firearms. *Journal of the American Medical Association, 272*, 43–46.

Tardiff, K., et al. (1997). Violence by patients admitted to a private psychiatric hospital. *American Journal of Psychiatry, 154*, 88–93.

Tarrier, N., et al. (1999). A randomized trial of cognitive therapy and imaginal exposure in the treatment of chronic posttraumatic stress disorder. *Journal of Consulting and Clinical Psychology, 67*, 13–18.

Tarrier, N., et al. (2000). Two-year follow-up of cognitive-behavioral therapy and supportive counseling in the treatment of persistent symptoms in chronic schizophrenia. *Journal of Consulting and Clinical Psychology, 68*, 917–922.

Task Force on Promotion and Dissemination of Psychological Procedures. (1995). Training in and dissemination of empirically validated psychological treatments: Report and recommendations. *The Clinical Psychologist, 48*(1), 3–24.

Tate, D. F., Wing, R. R., & Winett, R. A. (2001). Internet technology to deliver a behavioral weight loss program. *Journal of the American Medical Association, 285*, 1172–1177.

Taylor, S. (1995). Assessment of obsessions and compulsions: Reliability, validity, and sensitivity to treatment effects. *Clinical Psychology Review, 15*, 261–296.

Taylor, S., & Rachman, S. J. (1994). Klein's suffocation theory of panic. *Archives of General Psychiatry, 51*, 505–506.

Taylor, S., et al. (2001). Posttraumatic stress disorder arising after road traffic collisions: Patterns of response to cognitive–behavior therapy. *Journal of Consulting and Clinical Psychology, 69*, 541–551.

Taylor, S. E., & Brown, J. D. (1994). Positive illusions and well-being revisited: Separating fact from fiction. *Psychological Bulletin, 116*, 21–27.

Taylor, S. E., et al. (2000). Psychological resources, positive illusions, and health. *American Psychologist, 55*, 99–109.

Teen drug use continues to decline. (2000, August 31). *MSNBC Web Posting.* Retrieved September 1, 2000, from http://www.msnbc.com/news/453784.asp.

Teri, L., & Wagner, A. (1992). Alzheimer's disease and depression. *Journal of Consulting and Clinical Psychology, 60*, 379–391.

Terman, J. S., et al. (2001). Circadian time of morning light administration and therapeutic response in winter depression. *Archives of General Psychiatry, 58*, 69–75.

Testosterone wimping out? (1995, July). *Newsweek*, p. 61.

Tests suggest possible protection from Huntington's symptoms. (1997, March 27). *The New York Times*, p. A 20.

Teunisse, R. J., et al. (1996). Visual hallucinations in psychologically normal people: Charles Bonnnet's syndrome. *Lancet, 347*, 794–797.

Thakker, J., & Ward, T. (1998). Culture and classification: The cross-cultural application of the *DSM-IV*. *Clinical Psychology Review, 18*, 501–529.

Thannickal, T. C., et al. (2000). Reduced number of hypocretin neurons in human narcolepsy. *Neuron, 17*, 469–474.

Thaper, A., et al. (1994). The genetics of mental retardation. *British Journal of Psychiatry, 164*, 747–758.

Tharp, R. G. (1991). Cultural diversity and treatment of children. *Journal of Consulting and Clinical Psychology, 59*, 799–812.

Thase, M. E., et al. (1997). Treatment of major depression with psychotherapy or psychotherapy-pharmacotherapy combinations. *Archives of General Psychiatry, 54*, 1009–1015.

Thase, M. E., et al. (2000). Treatment of men with major depression: A comparison of sequential cohorts treated with either cognitive-behavioral therapy or newer generation antidepressants. *Journal of Clinical Psychiatry, 61*, 466–472.

Theorell, T. (1992). Critical life changes: A review of research. *Psychotherapy and Psychosomatics, 57*, 108–117.

Third of some cancers tied to weight: WHO examines impact of obesity, sedentary lifestyle. (2001, April 5). *MSNBC Web Posting.* Retrieved April 7, 2001, from http://www.msnbc.com/news/555510.asp.

Thoits, P. A. (1983). Dimensions of life events as influences upon the genesis of psychological distress and associated conditions: An evaluation and synthesis of the literature. In H. B. Kaplan (Ed.), *Psychosocial stress: Trends in theory and research.* New York: Academic Press.

Thomas, A. M., & LoPiccolo, J. (1994). Sexual functioning in persons with diabetics: Issues in research, treatment, and education. *Clinical Psychology Review, 14,* 61–86.

Thornhill, R., & Palmer, C. T. (2000). *A natural history of rape.* Cambridge, MA: MIT Press.

Tienari, P. (1991). Interaction between genetic vulnerability and family environment: The Finnish adoptive family study of schizophrenia. *Acta Psychiatrica Scandinavica, 84,* 460–465.

Tienari, P. (1992). Implications of adoption studies on schizophrenia. *British Journal of Psychiatry, 161*(18, Suppl.), 52–58.

Tienari, P., et al. (1987). Genetic and psychosocial factors in schizophrenia: The Finnish Adoptive Family Study. *Schizophrenia Bulletin, 13,* 477–484.

Tienari, P., et al. (1990). Adopted-away offspring of schizophrenics and controls: The Finnish adoptive family study of schizophrenia. In L. Robins & M. Rutter (Eds.), *Straight and devious pathways from childhood to adulthood.* New York: Cambridge University Press.

Tiffany, S. T., Cox, L. S., & Elash, C. A. (2000). Effects of transdermal nicotine patches on abstinence-induced and cue-elicited craving in cigarette smokers. *Journal of Consulting and Clinical Psychology, 68,* 233–240.

Tiihonen, J., et al. (1992). Modified activity of the human auditory cortex during auditory hallucinations. *American Journal of Psychiatry, 149,* 255–257.

Tiihonen, J., et al. (1997). Specific major mental disorders and criminality: A 26-year prospective study of the 1996 Northern Finland Birth Cohort. *American Journal of Psychiatry, 154,* 840–845.

Tillfors, M., Furmark, T., Ekselius, L., & Fredrikson, M. (2001). Social phobia and avoidant personality disorder as related to parental history of social anxiety: A general population study. *Behaviour Research and Therapy, 39,* 289–298.

Timbrook, R. E., & Graham, J. R. (1994). Ethnic differences on the MMPI-2? *Psychological Assessment, 6,* 212–217.

Time capsule. (2000, November). *Monitor on Psychology,* p. 10.

Timpson, J., et al. (1988). Depression in a Native Canadian in Northwestern Ontario: Sadness, grief or spiritual illness? *Canada's Mental Health, 36*(2–3), 5–8.

Tobin, D. L., Johnson, C. L., & Dennis, A. B. (1992). Divergent forms of purging behavior in bulimia nervosa patients. *International Journal of Eating Disorders, 11,* 17–24.

Tohen, M., et al. (2000). Efficacy of olanzapine in acute bipolar mania: A double-blind, placebo-controlled study. *Archives of General Psychiatry, 57,* 841–849.

Tollefson, G. D., et al. (1997a). Olanzapine versus haloperidol in the treatment of schizophrenia and schizoaffective and schzophreniform disorders: Results of an international collaborative trial. *American Journal of Psychiatry, 154,* 448–456.

Tollefson, G. D., et al. (1997b). Blind, controlled, long-term study of the comparative incidence of treatment-emergent tardive dyskinesia with olanzapine or halperidol. *American Journal of Psychiatry, 154,* 1248–1254.

Tolomiczenko, G. S., Sota, T., & Goering, P. N. (2000). Personality assessment of homeless adults as a tool for service planning. *Journal of Personality Disorders, 14,* 152–161.

Torgersen, S. (1986). Genetic factors in moderately severe and mild affective disorder. *Archives of General Psychiatry, 43,* 222–226.

Torgersen, S., Kringlen, E., & Cramer, V. (2001). The prevalence of personality disorders in a community sample. *Archives of General Psychiatry, 58,* 590–596.

Toufexis, A. (1993, April 19). Seeking the roots of violence. *Time Magazine,* pp. 52–53.

Tough, P. (2001, July 29). The alchemy of OxyContin. *The New York Times Magazine,* pp. 32–37, 52, 62–63.

Tower, R. B., & Kasl, S. V. (1996). Depressive symptoms across older spouses: Longitudinal influences. *Psychology and Aging, 11,* 683–697.

Tracy, J. I., Josiassen, R. C., & Bellack, A. S. (1995). Neuropsychology of dual diagnosis: Understanding the combined effects of schizophrenia and substance use disorders. *Clinical Psychology Review, 15,* 67–98.

Tradgold, A. F. (1914). *Mental deficiency.* New York: Wainwood.

Trask, P. C., & Sigmon, S. T. (1997). Munchausen syndrome: A review and new conceptualization. *Clinical Psychology: Science and Practice, 4,* 346–358.

Traven, N. D., et al. (1995). Coronary heart disease mortality and sudden death: Trends and patterns in 35- to 44-year-old white males, 1970–1990. *American Journal of Epidemiology, 142,* 45–52.

Treatment of alcoholism—Part II. (1996, September) *The Harvard Mental Health Letter, 13,* 1–5.

Treffert, D. A. (1988). The idiot savant: A review of the syndrome. *American Journal of Psychiatry, 145,* 563–572.

Tremblay, R. E., et al. (1992). Early disruptive behavior, poor school achievement, delinquent behavior, and delinquent personality: Longitudinal analyses. *Journal of Consulting and Clinical Psychology, 60,* 64–72.

Trenton State College. (1991, Spring). *Sexual Assault Victim Education and Support Unit (SAVES-U) Newsletter.*

Trimble, J. E. (1991). The mental health service and training needs of American Indians. In H. F. Myers et al. (Eds.), *Ethnic minority perspectives on clinical training and services in psychology* (pp. 43–48). Washington, DC: American Psychological Association.

Trull, T. J. (2001). Structural relations between borderline personality disorder features and putative etiological correlates. *Journal of Abnormal Psychology, 110,* 471–481.

Tsang, H. W.-H. (2001). Applying social skills training the context of vocational rehabilitation for people with schizophrenia. *Journal of Nervous & Mental Disease, 189,* 90–98.

Tseng, W., et al. (1992). Koro epidemics in Guangdong, China: A questionnaire survey. *Journal of Nervous & Mental Disease, 180,* 117–123.

Tsuang, D., & Coryell, W. (1993). An 8-year follow-up of patients with *DSM-III-R* psychotic depression, schizoaffective disorder, and schizophrenia. *American Journal of Psychiatry, 150,* 1182–1188.

Tsuang, M. T., et al. (1998). Co-occurrence of abuse of different drugs in men: The role of drug-specific and shared vulnerabilities. *Archives of General Psychiatry, 55,* 967–972.

Tuiten, A., et al. (2000). Time course of effects of testosterone administration on sexual arousal in women. *Archives of General Psychiatry, 57,* 149–153.

Tune, L. (1998). Treatments for dementia. In P. E. Nathan & J. M. Gorman (Eds.), *A guide to treatments that work* (pp. 90–126). New York: Oxford Press.

Turner, R. M. (2000). Understanding dialectical behavior therapy. *Clinical Psychology: Science and Practice, 7,* 95–98.

Turner, S. M., & Beidel, D. C. (1989). Social phobia: Clinical syndrome, diagnosis, and comorbidity. *Clinical Psychology Review, 9,* 3–18.

Turner, S. M., Beidel, D. C., & Jacob, R. G. (1994). Social phobia: A comparison of behavior therapy and atenolol. *Journal of Consulting and Clinical Psychology, 62,* 350–358.

Turner, S. M., Beidel, D. C., & Townsley, R. M. (1992). Social phobia: A comparison of specific and generalized subtypes and avoidant personality disorder. *Journal of Abnormal Psychology, 101,* 326–331.

Turner, S. M., McCann, B. S., Beidel, D. C., & Mezzich, J. E. (1986b). *DSM-III* classification of the anxiety disorders: A psychometric study. *Journal of Abnormal Psychology, 95,* 168–172.

Turovksy, J., & Barlow, D. H. (1995, Summer). Albany Panic Control Treatment (PCT) for panic disorder and agoraphobia. *The Clinical Psychologist, 48*(3), 5–6.

Tuschen-Caffier, B., Pook, M., & Frank, M. (2001). Evaluation of manual-based cognitive-behavioral therapy for bulimia nervosa in a service setting. *Behaviour Research and Therapy, 39,* 299–308.

Tutty, L. M. (1992). The ability of elementary school children to learn child sexual abuse prevention concepts. *Child Abuse and Neglect, 16,* 369–384.

U

U.S. Bureau of Justice Statistics. (1999). *National Crime Victimization Survey.* Washington, DC: Author.

U.S. Department of Health and Human Services (USDHHS). (1986b). *NIDA capsules: Heroin.* No. 11. Rockville, MD: U.S. Department of Health and Human Services, Public Health Service, Alcohol, Drug Abuse, and Mental Health Administration, National Institute on Drug Abuse.

U.S. Department of Health and Human Services (USDHHS). (1991b). *Vital statistics of the United States 1988.* (Vol. 2. Part A. Mortality.) Washington, DC: U.S. Government Printing Office. (DHHS Pub. No. PHS 91–1101).

U.S. Department of Health and Human Services (USDHHS). (1992). *NIDA capsules: LSD (lysergic acid diethylamide)* No. 39. Rockville, MD: U.S. Department of Health and Human Services, Public Health Service, Alcohol, Drug Abuse, and Mental Health Administration, National Institute on Drug Abuse, National Institute on Drug Abuse.

U.S. Department of Health and Human Services (USDHHS). (1993). *National household survey on drug abuse: Highlights 1991.* (DHHS Publication No. (SMA) 93-1979). Washington, DC: U.S. Government Printing Office.

U.S. Department of Health and Human Services (USDHHS). (1999a). *Mental health: A report of the Surgeon General.* Rockville, MD: U.S. Department of Health and Human Services, Substance Abuse and Mental Health Services Administration, Center for Mental Health Services, National Institutes of Health, National Institute of Mental Health.

U.S. Department of Health and Human Services (USDHHS). (1999b). *Mental health: A report of the Surgeon General—Executive summary.* Rockville, MD: U.S. Department of Health and Human Services, Substance Abuse and Mental Health Services Administration, Center for Mental Health Services, National Institutes of Health, National Institute of Mental Health.

U.S. Department of Health and Human Services (USDHHS). (2001). *Mental health: Culture, race, and ethnicity: A supplement to mental health: A report of the Surgeon General—Executive summary.* Rockville, MD: U.S. Department of Health and Human Services, Substance Abuse and Mental Health Services Administration, Center for Mental Health Services, National Institutes of Health, National Institute of Mental Health.

U.S. Department of Justice. (1994). *Crime in the United States: 1993. Uniform crime reports.* Washington, DC: Author.

U.S. finds heavy toll of rapes on young. (1994, June 23). *The New York Times,* p. A12.

Ullmann, L. P., & Krasner, L. (1975). *A psychological approach to abnormal behavior* (2nd ed.). Englewood Cliffs, NJ: Prentice-Hall.

Unger, J. B., Cruz, T. B., & Rohrbach, L. A. (2000). English language use as a risk factor for smoking initiation among Hispanic and Asian American adolescents: Evidence for mediation by tobacco-related beliefs and social norms. *Health Psychology, 19,* 403–410.

Unützer, J., et al. (1997). Depressive symptoms and the cost of health services in HMO patients aged 65 years and older: A 4-year prospective study. *Journal of the American Medical Association, 277,* 1618–1623.

Update on Alzheimer's Disease. Part I. (1995, February). *Harvard Mental Health Letter, 11*(6), 1–5.

Ursano, R. J., et al. (1999). Acute and chronic posttraumatic stress disorder in motor vehicle accident victims. *American Journal of Psychiatry, 156,* 589–595.

V

Van Ameringen, M. A., et al. (2001). Sertraline treatment of generalized social phobia: A 20-week, double-blind, placebo-controlled study. *American Journal of Psychiatry, 158,* 275–281.

Van Balkom, A. J. L. M., et al. (1997). A meta-analysis of the treatment of panic disorder with or without agoraphobia: A comparison of psychopharmacological, cognitive-behavioral, and combination treatments. *Journal of Nervous & Mental Disease, 185,* 510–516.

Van Ommeren, M., et al. (2001). Psychiatric disorders among tortured Bhutanese refugees in Nepal. *Archives of General Psychiatry, 58,* 475–482.

Van Praag, H. M. (1988). Editorial: Biological psychiatry. *Journal of Nervous and Mental Disease, 176,* 195–199.

Van Son, M. J. M., Mulder, G., & Londen, A. V. (1990). The effectiveness of dry bed training for nocturnal enuresis in adults. *Behaviour Research and Therapy, 28,* 347–349.

Vega, W. A., et al. (1998). Lifetime prevalence of *DSM-III-R* psychiatric disorders among urban and rural Mexican Americans in California. *Archives of General Psychiatry, 55,* 771–778.

Viagra fails to help women. (2000, May 22). MSNBC staff and wire reports. *MSNBC Web Posting.* Retrieved July 8, 2000, from http://www.msnbc.com.

Viglione, D. J. (1999). A review of recent research addressing the utility of the Rorschach. *Psychological Assessment, 11,* 251–265.

Vincent, J. B., et al. (1999). Genetic association analysis of serotonin system genes in bipolar affective disorder. *American Journal of Psychiatry, 156,* 136–138.

Virkkunen, M., & Linnoila, M. (1993). Brain serotonin, Type II alcoholism and impulsive violence. *Journal of Studies on Alcohol* (Suppl. 11), 163–169.

Virkkunen, M., et al. (1994). CSF biochemistries, glucose metabolism, and diurnal activity rhythms in alcoholic, violent offenders, fire setters, and healthy volunteers. *Archives of General Psychiatry, 51,* 20–27.

Visser, S., & Bouman, T. K. (2001). The treatment of hypochondriasis: Exposure plus response prevention vs. cognitive therapy. *Behaviour Research and Therapy, 39,* 423–442.

Voelker, R. (2000). Recessive Alzheimer gene? *Journal of the American Medical Association, 284,* 1777.

Vogler, G. P., DeFries, J. C., & Decker, S. N. (1985). Family history as an indicator of risk for reading disability. *Journal of Learning Disabilities, 18,* 419–421.

Volkow, N. D., et al. (1997). Relationship between subjective effects of cocaine and dopamine transporter occupancy. *Nature, 386,* 827–830.

Volkow, N. D., et al. (2001). Association of dopamine transporter reduction with psychomotor impairment in methamphetamine abusers. *American Journal of Psychiatry, 158,* 377–382.

Volpicelli, J. R., et al. (1994). Naltrexone and the treatment of alcohol dependence. *Alcohol Health & Research World, 18,* 272–278.

W

Wade, C., & Tavris, C. (1994). The longest war: Gender and culture. In W. J. Lonner & R. S. Malpass (Eds.), *Psychology and culture* (pp. 121–126). Boston: Allyn & Bacon.

Wade, N. (2000, May 9). Scientists decode Down syndrome chromosome. *The New York Times,* pp. C1, C3.

Wade, N. (2001a, February 11). Genome analysis shows humans survive on low number of genes. *The New York Times,* pp. 1, 42.

Wade, N. (2001b, February 11). Long-held beliefs are challenged by new human genome analysis: Genome analysis shows humans survive on low number of genes. *The New York Times,* p. A20.

Wade, T. D., et al. (2000). Anorexia nervosa and major depression: Shared genetic and environmental risk factors. *American Journal of Psychiatry, 157,* 469–471.

Wagner, B. M. (1997). Family risk factors for child and adolescent suicidal behavior. *Psychological Bulletin, 121,* 246–298.

Wagner, R. K., & Torgesen, J. K. (1987). The nature of phonological processing and its causal role in the acquisition of reading skills. *Psychological Bulletin, 101,* 192–212.

Wahlbeck, K., et al. (1999). Evidence of clozapine's effectiveness in schizophrenia: A systematic review and meta-analysis of randomized trials. *American Journal of Psychiatry, 156,* 990–999.

Wahlbeck, K. et al. (2001). Association of schizophrenia with low maternal body mass index, small size at birth, and thinness during childhood. *Archives of General Psychiatry, 58,* 48–52.

Wahlberg, K. E., et al. (2001). Long-term stability of communication deviance. *Journal of Abnormal Psychology, 110,* 443–448.

Wakefield, H., & Underwager, R. (1996). Commentary on Kenneth Pope's review. *Clinical Psychology: Science and Practice, 3,* 366–371.

Wakefield, J. C. (1992a). The concept of mental disorder: On the boundary between biological facts and social values. *American Psychologist, 47,* 373–388.

Wakefield, J. C. (1992b). Disorder as harmful dysfunction: A conceptual critique of *DSM-III-R's* definition of mental disorder. *Psychological Review, 99,* 232–247.

Wakefield, J. C. (1997). Normal inability versus pathological disability: Why Ossorio's definition of mental disorder is not sufficient. *Clinical Psychology: Science and Practice, 4,* 249–258.

Wakefield, J. C. (2001). Evolutionary history versus current causal role in the definition of disorder: Reply to McNally. *Behaviour Research and Therapy, 39,* 347–366.

Wakeling, A. (1996). Epidemiology of anorexia nervosa. *Psychiatry Research, 62,* 3–9.

Wakschlag, L. S., et al. (1997). Maternal smoking during pregnancy and the risk of conduct disorder in boys. *Archives of General Psychiatry, 54,* 670–676.

Walker, E. F., & Diforio, D. (1997). Schizophrenia: A neural diathesis-stress model. *Psychological Review, 104,* 667–685.

Walker, L. E. (1979). *The battered woman.* New York: Harper & Row.

Walker, L. E. (1988). The battered woman syndrome. In G. T. Hotaling, D. Finkelhor, J. T. Kirkpatrick, & M. A. Straus (Eds.), *Family abuse and its consequences: New directions in research* (pp. 139–148). Newbury Park, CA: Sage.

Walkup, J. T., et al. (2001). Fluvoxamine for the treatment of anxiety disorders in children and adolescents. The Research Unit on Pediatric Psychopharmacology Anxiety Study Group. *The New England Journal of Medicine, 344,* 1279–1285.

Wall, T. L., et al. (2001). A genetic association with the development of alcohol and other substance use

behavior in Asian Americans. *Journal of Abnormal Psychology, 110,* 173–178.

Wallace, J. (1985). The alcoholism controversy. *American Psychologist, 40,* 372–373.

Waller, N. G., & Ross, C. A. (1997). The prevalence of biometric structure of pathological dissociation in the general population: Taxometric and behavior genetic findings. *Journal of Abnormal Psychology, 106,* 499–510.

Walsh, B. T., et al. (1997). Medication and psychotherapy in the treatment of bulimia nervosa. *American Journal of Psychiatry, 154,* 523–531.

Walsh, B. T., et al. (2000). Fluoxetine for bulimia nervosa following poor response to psychotherapy. *American Journal of Psychiatry, 157,* 1332–1334.

Wampold, B. E., et al. (1997a). A meta-analysis of outcome studies comparing bona fide psychotherapies: Empirically, "All must have prizes." *Psychological Bulletin, 122,* 203–215.

Wampold, B. E., et al. (1997b). The flat earth as a metaphor for the evidence for uniform efficacy of bona fide psychotherapies: Reply to Crits-Christoph (1997) and Howard et al. (1997). *Psychological Bulletin, 122,* 226–230.

Wang, X., et al. (2000). Longitudinal study of earthquake-related PTSD in a randomly selected community sample in North China. *American Journal of Psychiatry, 157,* 1260–1266.

Warheit, G. J., Vega, W. A., Auth, J., & Meinhardt, K. (1985). Psychiatric symptoms and dysfunctions among Anglos and Mexican Americans: An epidemiological study. In J. R. Greenley (Ed.), *Research in community and mental health* (pp. 3–32). London: JAI Press.

Warner, L. A., et al. (1995). Prevalence and correlates of drug use and dependence in the United States. *Archives of General Psychiatry, 52,* 219–229.

Waterman, J., et al. (1986). Challenges for the future. In K. MacFarlane, et al. (Eds.), *Sexual abuse of young children: Evaluation and treatment* (pp. 315–332). New York: Guilford Press.

Watson, C. G., et al. (1997). Lifetime prevalences of nine common psychiatric/personality disorders in female domestic abuse survivors. *Journal of Nervous & Mental Disease, 185,* 645–647.

Weaver, T. L., & Clum, G. A. (1995). Psychological distress associated with interpersonal violence: A meta-analysis. *Clinical Psychology Review, 15,* 115–140.

Weber, B. (1996, July 6). First arrests in New York under sex-offender law. *The New York Times,* p. B24.

Webster-Stratton, C., & Hammond, M. (1997). Treating children with early-onset conduct problems: A comparison of child and parent training interventions. *Journal of Consulting and Clinical Psychology, 65,* 93–109.

Wechsler, D. (1975). Intelligence defined and undefined: A relativistic appraisal. *American Psychologist, 30,* 135–139.

Weems, C. F., Berman, S. L., Silverman, W. K., & Saavedra, L. M. (2001). Cognitive errors in youth with anxiety disorders: The linkages between negative cognitive errors and anxious symptoms. *Cognitive Therapy & Research, 25,* 559–575.

Weinberg, G. (1972). *Society and the healthy homosexual.* New York: St. Martin's Press.

Weine, S. M., et al. (2000). Profiling the trauma related symptoms of Bosnian refugees who have not sought mental health services. *Journal of Nervous & Mental Disease, 188,* 416–421.

Weiner, I. B. (1994). The Rorschach inkblot method (RIM) is not a test: Implications for theory and practice. *Journal of Personality Assessment, 62,* 498–504.

Weiner, K. E., & Thompson, J. K. (1997). Overt and covert sexual abuse: Relationship to body image and eating disturbance. *International Journal of Eating Disorders, 22,* 273–284.

Weiner, M. F. (1996, July). What new treatments for Alzheimer's disease are being explored? *The Harvard Mental Health Letter, 13*(1), 8.

Weiner, R. D. (2000). Retrograde amnesia with electroconvulsive therapy characteristics and implications. *Archives of General Psychiatry, 57*, 591–592.

Weisberg, R. B., et al. (2001). Causal attributions and male sexual arousal: The impact of attributions for a bogus erectile difficulty on sexual arousal, cognitions, and affect. *Journal of Abnormal Psychology, 110*, 324–334.

Weisman, A., et al. (1993). An attributional analysis of expressed emotion in Mexican-American families with schizophrenia. *Journal of Abnormal Psychology, 102*, 601–606.

Weisman, A. G., et al. (1998). Expressed emotion, attributions, and schizophrenia symptom dimensions. *Journal of Abnormal Psychology, 107*, 355–359.

Weisman, A. G., et al. (2000). Controllability perceptions and reactions to symptoms of schizophrenia: A within-family comparison of relatives with high and low expressed emotion. *Journal of Abnormal Psychology, 109*, 167–171.

Weiss, R. D., & Mirin, S. M. (1987). *Cocaine*. Washington, DC: American Psychiatric Press.

Weissman, A. N., & Beck, A. T. (1978, November). *Development and validation of the Dysfunctional Attitudes Scale: A preliminary investigation.* Paper presented at the meeting of the American Educational Research Association, Toronto, Canada.

Weissman, M. M. (1999). Depressed adolescents grown up. *Journal of the American Medical Association, 281*, 1707–1713.

Weissman, M. M., & Markowtiz, J. C. (1994). Interpersonal psychotherapy: Current status. *Archives of General Psychiatry, 51*, 599–606.

Weissman, M. M., et al. (1989). Suicidal ideation and suicide attempts in panic disorder and attacks. *The New England Journal of Medicine, 321*, 1209–1214.

Weissman, M. M., et al. (1991). Affective disorders. In L. N. Robins & D. A. Regier (Eds.), *Psychiatric disorders in America: The Epidemiologic Catchment Area Study* (pp. 53–80). New York: Free Press.

Weisz, J. R., Pilkonis, P. A., Woody, S. R., & Follette, W. C. (2000). Stressing the (other) three Rs in the search for empirically supported treatments: Review procedures, research quality, relevance to practice and the public interest. *Clinical Psychology: Science and Practice, 7*, 243–258.

Weisz, J. R., et al. (1988). Thai and American perspectives on over-and undercontrolled child behavior problems: Exploring the threshold model among parents, teachers, and psychologists. *Journal of Consulting and Clinical Psychology, 56*, 601–609.

Wekerle, C., & Wolfe, D. A. (1993). Prevention and child physical abuse and neglect: Promising new directions. *Clinical Psychology Review, 13*, 501–540.

Welch, M. R., & Kartub, P. (1978). Socio-cultural correlates of incidence of impotence: A cross-cultural study. *Journal of Sex Research, 14*, 218–230.

Welkowitz, L. A., et al. (1999). Instructional set and physiological response to CO_2 inhalation. *American Journal of Psychiatry, 156*, 745–748.

Wells, K. B., et al. (2000). Impact of disseminating quality improvement programs for depression in managed primary care: A randomized controlled trial. *Journal of the American Medical Association, 283*, 212–220.

Weltzin, T. E., et al. (1994). Prediction of reproductive status in women with bulimia nervosa at past high weight. *American Journal of Psychiatry, 151*, 136–138.

Wender, P. H., Rosenthal, D., Kety, S. S., Schulsinger, F., & Welner, J. (1974). Cross-fostering: A research strategy for clarifying the role of genetic and experiential factors in the etiology of schizophrenia. *Archives of General Psychiatry, 30*, 121–128.

Wender, P. H., et al. (2000). ADHD in adults. *Journal of the American Academy of Child & Adolescent Psychiatry, 39*, 543.

Wenzlaff, R. M., & Grozier, S. A. (1988). Depression and the magnification of failure. *Journal of Abnormal Psychology, 97*, 90–93.

Wertlieb, D., Weigel, C., & Feldstein, M. (1987). Stress, social support, and behavior symptoms in middle childhood. *Journal of Clinical Child Psychology, 16*, 204–211.

West, M. A. (1985). Meditation and somatic arousal reduction. *American Psychologist, 40*, 717–719.

Westen, D. (1998). The scientific legacy of Sigmund Freud: Toward a psychodynamically informed psychological science. *Psychological Bulletin, 124*, 333–371.

Westen, D., & Shedler, J. (1999). Revising and assessing axis II, Part II: Toward an empirically based and clinically useful classification of personality disorders. *The American Journal of Psychiatry, 156*, 273–285.

Wetzler, S., & Marlowe, D. B. (1993). The diagnosis and assessment of depression, mania, and psychosis by self-report. *Journal of Personality Assessment, 60*, 1–31.

Wexler, B. E., et al. (2001). Functional magnetic resonance imaging of cocaine craving. *American Journal of Psychiatry, 158*, 86–95.

What is catatonia? (1995, February). *Harvard Mental Health Letter, 11*(8), p. 8.

What is PTSD? (1996). *American Journal of Psychiatry, 154*, 143–145. [Editorial]

Whiffen, V. E., & Gotlib, I. H. (1993). Comparison of postpartum and nonpostpartum depression: Clinical presentation, psychiatric history, and psychosocial functioning. *Journal of Consulting and Clinical Psychology, 61*, 485–493.

Wickelgren, I. (1997, June 27). Marijuana: Harder than thought? *Science, 276*, 1967.

Wickenhaver, J. (1992, September 8). After the "Wild Man": Can an insane system be cured? *Manhattan Spirit*, pp. 13, 28.

Wickizer, T. M., Lessler, D., & Travis, K .M. (1996). Controlling inpatient psychiatric utilization through managed care. *American Journal of Psychiatry, 153*, 339–345.

Widiger, T. A. (1991). DSM-IV reviews of the personality disorders: Introduction to special series. *Journal of Personality Disorder, 5*, 122–134.

Widiger, T. A. (1992). Generalized social phobia versus avoidant personality disorder: A commentary on three studies. *Journal of Abnormal Psychology, 101*, 340–343.

Widiger, T. A., & Clark, L. A. (2000). Toward DSM-V and the classification of psychopathology. *Psychological Bulletin, 126*, 946–963.

Widiger, T. A., & Costa, P. T., Jr. (1994). Personality and personality disorders. *Journal of Abnormal Psychology, 103*, 78–91.

Widom, C. S. (1989a). Child abuse, neglect, and adult behavior: Research design and findings on criminality, violence, and child abuse. *American Journal of Orthopsychiatry, 59*, 355–367.

Widom, C. S. (1989b). Does violence beget violence? A critical examination of the literature. *Psychological Bulletin, 106*, 3–28.

Widom, C. S. (1991). Childhood victimization: Risk factor for delinquency. In M. E. Colten & S. Gore (Eds.), *Adolescent stress: Causes and consequences* (pp. 201–221). New York: DeGruyter.

Wiersma, D., et al. (1998). Natural course of schizophrenic disorders: A 15-year follow-up of a Dutch incidence cohort. *Schizophrenia Bulletin, 24*, 75–85.

Wiersma, D., et al. (2001). Cognitive behaviour therapy with coping training for persistent auditory hallucinations in schizophrenia: A naturalistic follow-up study of the durability of effects. *Acta Psychiatrica Scandinavica, 103*, 393–399.

Wig, N. N., et al. (1987). Distribution of expressed emotion components among relatives of schizophrenic patients in Aarhus and Chandigarh. *British Journal of Psychiatry, 151*, 160–165.

Wilbur, C. B. (1986). Psychoanalysis and multiple personality disorder. In B. G. Braun (Ed.), *Treatment of multiple personality disorder*. Washington, DC: American Psychiatric Press.

Wilkie, F. L., et al. (1998). Mild cognitive impairment and risk of mortality in HIV-1 infection. *Journal of Neuropsychiatry and Clinical Neuroscience, 10*, 125–132.

Wilkinson, D. J. C., et al. (1998). Sympathetic activity in patients with panic disorder at rest, under laboratory mental stress, and during panic attacks. *Archives of General Psychiatry, 55*, 511–520.

Wilkinson-Ryan, T., & Westen, D. (2000). Identity disturbance in borderline personality disorders: An empirical investigation. *American Journal of Psychiatry, 157*, 528–541.

Williams, J. B., et al. (1992). The Structured Clinical Interview for DSM-III—(SCID). II: Multisite test-retest reliability. *Archives of General Psychiatry, 49*, 630–636.

Williams, J. E., et al. (2000). Anger proneness predicts coronary heart disease risk: Prospective analysis from the Atherosclerosis Risk in Communities (ARIC) study. *Circulation, 101*, 2034–2039.

Williams, J. M. (1984). *The psychological treatment of depression: A guide to the theory and practice of cognitive-behavior therapy.* New York: Free Press.

Williams, J. W., et al. (2000). Treatment of dysthymia and minor depression in primary care: A randomized controlled trial in older adults. *Journal of the American Medical Association, 284*, 1519–1526.

Williams, K., E., Chambless, D. L., & Ahrens, A. (1997). Are emotions frightening? An extension of the fear of fear construct. *Behaviour Research and Therapy, 35*, 239–248.

Williams, P. G., Wiebe, D. J., & Smith, T. W. (1992). Coping processes as mediators of the relationship between hardiness and health. *Journal of Behavioral Medicine, 15*, 237–255.

Williams, R. B., et al. (1997). Psychosocial correlates of job strain in a sample of working women. *Archives of General Psychiatry, 54*, 543–548.

Wills, T. A., & Cleary, S. D. (1999). Peer and adolescent substance use among 6th–9th graders: Latent growth analyses of influence versus selection mechanisms. *Health Psychology, 18*, 453–463.

Wills, T. A., & Filer Fegan, M. (2001). Social networks and social support. In A. Baum, T. A. Revenson, & J. E. Singer (Eds.), *Handbook of health psychology* (pp 3–18). Makwah, NJ: Lawrence Erlbaum Associates, Inc.

Wilson, G. T. (1987). Chemical aversion conditioning treatment for alcoholism: A re-analysis. *Behaviour Research and Therapy, 25*, 503–516.

Wilson, G. T. (1991). Chemical aversion conditioning in the treatment of alcoholism: Further comments. *Behaviour Research & Therapy, 29*, 415–419.

Wilson, G. T. (1994). Behavioral treatment of childhood obesity: Theoretical and practical implications. *Health Psychology, 13*, 371–372.

Wilson, G. T. (1997). Behavior therapy at century close. *Behavior Therapy, 28*, 449–457.

Wilson, G. T., & Fairburn, C. G. (1998). Treatment for eating disorders. In P. E. Nathan & J. M. Gorman (Eds.), *A guide to treatments that work* (pp. 501–530). New York: Oxford University Press.

Wilson, K., et al. (1992). Levels of learned helplessness in abused women. *Women and Therapy, 13*, 53–67.

Wilson, K. K. (1997, April). *The disparate classification of gender and sexual orientation in American psychiatry.* Psychiatry On-Line. Retrieved April 28, 1997, from http://www.priory.com/psych/disparat.htm.

Wilson, M. I., & Daly, M. (1996). Male sexual proprietariness and violence against wives. *Current Directions in Psychological Science, 5*, 2–7.

Wilson, S. A., Becker, L. A., & Tinker, R. H. (1997). Fifteen-month follow-up of eye movement desensitization and reprocessing (EMDR) treatment for posttraumatic stress disorder and psychological trauma. *Journal of Consulting and Clinical Psychology, 65*, 1047–1056.

Winefield, H. R., & Harvey, E. J. (1994). Needs of family caregivers in chronic schizophrenia. *Schizophrenia Bulletin, 20*, 557–566.

Winerip, M. (1991, December 18). Soldier in battle for the retarded. *The New York Times*, pp. B1, B6.

Winerip, M. (1999, May 23). Bedlam on the streets. *The New York Times*, pp. 42–49.

Wing, R. R., & Polley, B. A. (2001). Obesity. In A. Baum, T. A. Revenson, & J. E. Singer (Eds), *Handbook of health psychology* (pp. 263–279). Mahwah, NJ: Erlbaum.

Wingert, P. (2000, December 4). No more "afternoon nasties." *Newsweek*, p. 59.

Wingert, P., & Kantrowitz, B. (1997, October 27). Why Andy couldn't read. *Newsweek*, pp. 54–64.

Winkleby, M. A., Kramer, H. C., Ahn, D. K., & Varady, A. N. (1998). Ethnic and socioeconomic differences in cardiovascular disease risk factors. *Journal of the American Medical Association, 280*, 356–362.

Winston, A., et al. (1991). Brief psychotherapy of personality disorders. *Journal of Nervous & Mental Disease, 179*, 188–193.

Winston, A., et al. (1994). Short-term psychotherapy of personality disorders. *American Journal of Psychiatry, 51*, 190–194.

Winter, G. (2000, October 29). Fraudulent marketers capitalize on demand for sweat-free diets. *The New York Times*, pp. A1, A26.

Wise, T. P. (1978). Where the public peril begins: A survey of psychotherapists to determine the effects of Tarasoff. *Stanford Law Review, 135*, 165–190.

Wittchen, H., et al. (1994). *DSM-III-R* generalized anxiety disorder in the National Comorbidity Survey. *Archives of General Psychiatry, 51*, 355–363.

Wolfe, D. A., et al. (2001). Child maltreatment: Risk of adjustment problems and dating violence in adolescence. *Journal of American Academy of Child & Adolescent Psychiatry, 40*, 282–289.

Wolpe, J. (1958). *Psychotherapy by reciprocal inhibition.* Stanford, CA: Stanford University Press.

Wolpe, J., & Lazarus, A. A. (1966). *Behavior therapy techniques.* New York: Pergamon Press.

Wolpe, J., & Rachman, S. (1960). Psychoanalytic "evidence": A critique based on Freud's case of Little Hans. *Journal of Nervous and Mental Disease, 131*, 135–147.

Women under assault. (1990, July 16). *Newsweek*, p. 23.

Wonderlich, S. A., et al. (1997). Relationship of childhood sexual abuse and eating disorders. *Journal of the American Academy of Child and Adolescent Psychiatry, 36*, 1107–1115.

Wong, J. L., & Whitaker, D. J. (1993). Depressive mood states and their cognitive and personality correlates in college students: They improve over time. *Journal of Clinical Psychology, 49*, 615–621.

Wood, J. M., Nezworski, M. T., & Stejskal, W. J. (1996). The comprehensive system for the Rorschach: A critical examination. *Psychological Science, 7*, 3–10.

Wood, J. M., Nezworski, M. T., & Stejskal, W. J. (1997). The reliability of the comprehensive system for the Rorschach: A comment on Meyer. *Psychological Assessment, 9*, 490–494.

Wood, J. M., et al. (1992). Effects of 1989 San Francisco earthquake on frequency and content of nightmares. *Journal of Abnormal Psychology, 101*, 219–234.

Wood, M. D., Vinson, D. C., & Sher, K. J. (2001). Alcohol use and misuse. In A. Baum, T. A. Revenson, & J. E. Singer (Eds.), *Handbook of health psychology* (pp. 280–320). Mahwah, NJ: Erlbaum.

Woodward, A. M., Dwinell, A. D., & Arons, B. S. (1992). Barriers to mental health care for Hispanic Americans: A literature review and discussion. *Journal of Mental Health Administration, 19*, 224–236.

Wootton, J. M., et al. (1997). Ineffective parenting and childhood conduct problems: The moderating role of callous-unemotional traits. *Journal of Consulting and Clinical Psychology, 65*, 301–308.

Wren, C. S. (1997a, August 20). Saying "no" to drugs but dying in violence. *The New York Times*, p. A16.

Wren, C. S. (2001, June 26). Powell, at U.N., asks war on AIDS. *The New York Times*, pp. A1, A4.

Wright, I. C., et al. (2000). Meta-analysis of regional brain volumes in schizophrenia. *American Journal of Psychiatry, 157*, 16–25.

Wulfert, E., Greenway, D. E., & Dougher, M. J. (1996). A logical functional analysis of reinforcement-based disorders: Alcoholism and pedophilia. *Journal of Consulting and Clinical Psychology, 64*, 1140–1151.

Wyatt v. Stickney, 334 F. Supp. 1341 (1972).

Wyatt, G. E. (1990). The aftermath of child sexual abuse of African American and White American women: The victim's experience. *Journal of Family Violence, 5*, 61–81.

Y

Yairi, E., Ambrose, N., & Cox, N. (1996). Genetics of stuttering: A critical review. *Journal of Speech and Hearing Research, 39*, 771–784.

Yates, W. R. (2000). Testosterone in psychiatry: Risks and benefits. *Journal of the American Medical Association, 57*, 155–156.

Yatham, L. M., et al. (2000). Brain serotonin2 receptors in major depression: A positron emission tomography study. *Archives of General Psychiatry, 57*, 850–858.

Yeh, M., Takeuchi, D. T., & Sue, S. (1994). Asian-American children treated in the mental health system: A comparison of parallel and mainstream outpatient service centers. *Journal of Clinical Child Psychology, 23*, 5–12.

Yeung, P. P., & Greenwald, S. (1992). Jewish Americans and mental health: Results of the NIMH Epidemiologic Catchment Area Study. *Social Psychiatry and Psychiatric Epidemiology, 27*, 292–297.

Young, A. S., et al. (2001). The quality of care for depressive and anxiety disorders in the United States. *Archives of General Psychiatry, 58*, 55–61.

Young, K. S. (1999). Evaluation and treatment of Internet addiction. In L. VanderCreek & T. L. Jackson (Eds.), *Innovations in clinical practice: A source book* (Vol. 17, pp. 19–31). Sarasota, FL: Professional Resource Press/Professional Resource Exchange.

Young, M. A., et al. (1994). Interactions of risk factors in predicting suicide. *American Journal of Psychiatry, 51*, 434–435.

Young, T., et al. (1996). The gender bias in sleep apnea diagnosis. *Archives of Internal Medicine, 156*, 2445–2451.

Young, T. J., & French, L. A. (1996). Suicide and homicide rates among U.S. Indian health service areas: The income inequality hypothesis. *Social Behavior and Personality, 24*, 365–366.

Young, T. K., & Sevenhuysen, G. (1989). Obesity in northern Canadian Indians: Patterns, determinants, and consequences. *American Journal of Clinical Nutrition, 49*, 786–793.

Youngberg v. Romeo, 102 S. Ct. 2452, 2463 (1982).

Z

Zahn-Waxler, C., et al. (1996). Behavior problems in 5-year-old monozygotic and dizygotic twins: Genetic and environmental influences, patterns of regulation, and internalization of control. *Development and Psychopathology, 8*, 103–122.

Zalewski, C., & Archer, R. P. (1991). Assessment of borderline personality disorder: A review of MMPI and Rorschach findings. *Journal of Nervous & Mental Disease, 179*, 338–345.

Zamanian, K., et al. (1992). Acculturation and depression in Mexican-American elderly. *Gerontologist, 11*, 109–121.

Zanardi, R., et al. (1996). Double-blind controlled trial of sertraline versus paroxetine in the treatment of delusional depression. *American Journal of Psychiatry, 153*, 1631–1633.

Zane, N., & Sue, S. (1991). Culturally responsive mental health services for Asian Americans: Treatment and training issues. In H. F. Myers et al. (Eds.), *Ethnic minority perspectives on clinical training and services in psychology* (pp. 49–58). Washington, DC: American Psychological Association.

Zeiss, A. M., & Breckenridge, J. S. (1997). Treatment of late life depression: A response to the NIH Consensus Conference. *Behavior Therapy, 28*, 3–21.

Zhou, J-N., et al. (1995). A sex difference in the human brain and its relation to transsexuality. *Nature, 378*, 68–70.

Zickler, P. (2000). Brain imaging studies show long-term damage from methamphetamine abuse. *NIDA Notes, 15*(3), 11, 13.

Ziedonis, D. M., & Trudeau, K. (1997). Motivation to quit using substances among individuals with schizophrenia: Implications for a motivation-based treatment model. *Schizophrenia Bulletin, 23*, 229–238.

Zielbauer, P. (2000, May 22). Sex offender listings on Web set off debate. *The New York Times online.* Retrieved May 24, 2000, from http://www.nytimes.com

Zilbovicius, M., et al. (1995). Delayed maturation of the frontal cortex in childhood autism. *American Journal of Psychiatry, 152*, 248–252.

Zito, J. M., Safer, D. J., dosReis, S., Gardner, J. F., Boles, M., & Lynch, F. (2000). Trends in the prescribing of psychotropic medications to preschoolers. *Journal of the American Medical Association, 283*, 1025–1030.

Zlotnick, C., Bruce, S. E., Shea, M. T., & Keller, M. B. (2001). Delayed posttraumatic stress disorder (PTSD) and predictors of first onset of PTSD in patients with anxiety disorders. *Journal of Nervous & Mental Disease, 189*, 404–406.

Zoellner, L. A., Craske, M., G., & Rapee, R. M. (1996). Stability of catastrophic cognitions in panic disorder. *Behaviour Research and Therapy, 34*, 399–402.

Zoellner, L. A., Foa, E. B., Brigidi, B. D., & Przeworski, A. (2000). Are trauma victims susceptible to "false memories"? *Journal of Abnormal Psychology, 109*, 517–524.

Zola, S. M. (1999). Memory, amnesia, and the issue of recovered memory: Neurobiological aspects. *Clinical Psychology Review, 19*, 915–932.

Zorumski, C. F., & Isenberg, K. E. (1991). Insights into the structure and function of GABA-benzodiazepine receptors: Ion channels and psychiatry. *American Journal of Psychiatry, 148*, 162–172.

Zotter, D. L., & Crowther, J. H. (1991). The role of cognitions in bulimia nervosa. *Cognitive Therapy & Research, 15*, 413–426.

Zubenko, G. S., et al. (1997). Mortality of elderly patients with psychiatric disorders. *American Journal of Psychiatry, 154*, 1360–1368.

Zubin, J., & Spring, B. (1977). Vulnerability—New view of schizophrenia. *Journal of Abnormal Psychology, 86*, 103–126.

Zucker, K. J., & Green, R. (1992). Psychosexual disorders in children and adolescents. *Journal of Child Psychology and Psychiatry, 33*, 107–151.

Zuckerman, M. (1980). Sensation seeking. In H. London & J. Exner (Eds.), *Dimensions of personality.* New York: Wiley.

Zvolensky, M. J., & Eifert, G. H. (2001). A review of psychological factors/processes affecting anxious responding during voluntary hyperventilation and inhalations of carbon dioxide-enriched air. *Clinical Psychology Review, 21*, 375–400.

Zvolensky, M. J., et al. (2001). Assessment of anxiety sensitivity in young American Indians and Alaska Natives. *BTR, Behaviour Research and Therapy, 39*, 477–493.

Zweig-Frank, H., & Paris, J. (1991). Parents' emotional neglect and overprotection according to the recollections of patients with borderline personality disorder. *American Journal of Psychiatry, 148*, 648–651.

Zwilich, C. W. (2000). Is untreated sleep apnea a contributing factor for chronic hypertension? *Journal of the American Medical Association, 283*, 000. [Editorial]

PHOTO CREDITS

Chapter 1   Page 2 Wassily Kandinsky, (1866–1944) Russian, "Sweet Pink"/Sotheby's, London/SuperStock/© 2003 Artist Rights Society (ARS), New York/ADAGP, Paris; p. 5 (top) SuperStock, Inc.; p. 5 (left) Bob Daemmrich/Stock Boston; p. 5 (right) Steve Goldberg; p. 6 Catherine Karnow/Woodfin Camp & Associates; p. 9 Bierwert/American Museum of Natural History; p. 10 The Granger Collection; p. 11 The Granger Collection; p. 12 Courtesy of the Library of Congress; p. 13 CORBIS; p. 15 CORBIS; p. 16 (left) The Granger Collection; p. 16 (right) The Granger Collection; p. 21 Irven De Vore/Anthro-Photo File.

Chapter 2   Page 32 Alejandro Xul Solar, (1925), Latin American "Patria B"/Christie's Images/SuperStock/Museo Xul Solar Fundacion Pan Klub; p. 39 Ron Chapple/Getty Images Inc.; p. 41 (top) AP/Wide World Photos; p. 41 (bottom) Lew Merrim/Photo Researchers, Inc.; p. 42 Frank Siteman/Stock Boston; p. 44 Lucas Films/Picture Desk, Inc./Kobal Collection; p. 45 (left) Culver Pictures Inc.; p. 45 (center) Library of Congress; p. 45 (right) PhotoEdit; p. 48 (top) The Granger Collection; p. 48 (bottom) B.F. Skinner Foundation; p. 51 (left) Nancy Sheehan/Index Stock Imagery, Inc.; p. 51 (right) Laura Dwight Photography; p. 52 (left) Corbis/Rogers Ressmeyer/CORBIS; p. 52 (right) Ann Kaplan/Corbis/CORBIS; p. 52 (bottom) Tracey Saar; p. 53 Gabor Demjen/Stock Boston; p. 55 (left) Albert Ellis Institute; p. 55 (right) Aaron T. Beck, M.D.; p. 56 Hugh Rogers.

Chapter 3   Page 63 Dubuffet, Jean. "Ontogenese", (1975), © Copyright ARS, NY. Musee des Beaux-Arts Andre Malraux, Le Havre, France; p. 66 Greenlar/The Image Works; p. 68 K. Kai/The Image Works; p. 73 The Image Works; p. 74 Spencer Grant/PhotoEdit; p. 76 Pictor, New York; p. 83 Pearson Education/PH College; p. 84 Reprinted by permission of the publishers from Henry A. Murray, THEMATIC APPERCEPTION TEST, Cambridge, Mass.: Harvard University Press, © 1943 by the President and Fellows of Harvard College, © 1971 by Henry A. Murray; p. 84 (Video 3.1) Penn State; p. 90 Susan Rosenberg/Photo Researchers, Inc.; p. 92 David York/Medichrome/The Stock Shop, Inc.; p. 93 (top) Priest, Chris/Photo Researchers, Inc.; p. 93 (bottom) Brookhaven National Laboratory; p. 94 (top) Visuals Unlimited; p. 94 (left and right) Magnetic Resonance Imaging of the Brain in Schizophrenia, pg. 35–44, 1990; 47:35/Archive of General Psychiatry/American Medical Association.

Chapter 4   Page 96 Paul Klee (1979–1940), Swiss, "Variation II", Bauhaus Archive/ET Archive, London/SuperStock/© 2003 Artist Rights Society (ARS), New York/VG Bild-Kunst, Bonn; p. 100 Zigy Kaluzny/Getty Images, Inc.; p. 101 (top) Corbis/Sygma; p. 101 (bottom) Albert Rocarols/Getty Images Inc.; p. 102 Grantpix/Photo Researchers, Inc.; p. 104 Susan Rosenberg/Photo Researchers, Inc.; p. 105 (Video 4.1) Penn State; p. 111 Will Hart; p. 112 D. Young-Wolff/PhotoEdit; p. 113 Zigy Kaluzny/Getty Images Inc.; p. 115 From the *Wall Street Journal* – permission, by Cartoon Features Syndicate; p. 116 Rhoda Sydney; p. 121 James Wilson/Woodfin Camp Associates; p. 123 Bisson Bernard/Corbis/Sygma; p. 124 Michael Newman/PhotoEdit.

Chapter 5   Page 130 Diana Ong, "Medicine Man", B. (1940), SuperStock, Inc.; p. 133 Phyllis Picardi/Stock Boston; p. 134 (top) Biology Media/Science Source/Photo Researchers, Inc.; p. 134 (bottom) Marcus Townsend/CORBIS; p. 136 (left) Esbin/Anderson/Omni-Photo Communications, Inc.; p. 136 (right) Bob Daemmrich/Stock Boston; p. 138 A. Ramey/PhotoEdit; p. 139 Lawrence Migdale/Stock Boston; p. 14 Charles Gupton/Stock Boston; p. 143 Jeff Greenberg/David R. Frazier Photolibrary, Inc.; p. 146 Joel Gordon Photography; p. 148 (top) William Johnson/Stock Boston; p. 148 (bottom) Zigy Kaluzny/Getty Images Inc.; p. 153 Andy Levin/Photo Researchers, Inc.; p. 154 Alon Reininger/Woodfin Camp & Associates.

Chapter 6   Page 158 © Miriam Schapiro, "Free Fall", (1985), paper and acrylic on canvas, 90" x 64". Collection: Mr. and Mrs. Lee Sachs, Steinbaum Krauss Gallery, NYC.; p. 162 Walter Smith/CORBIS; p. 162 (Video 6.1) Pearson-Patients as Educators; p. 166 (left) Geri Engberg/Geri Engberg Photography; p. 166 (top) SuperStock, Inc.; p. 166 (bottom) David E. Dempster/Pearson Education/PH College; p. 169 Tony Stone Images; p. 170 Picture Desk, Inc./Kobal Collection; p. 170 (Video 6.2) Pearson-Patients as Educators; p. 172 (left) Allan Tannenbaum/The Image Works; p. 172 (right) Charles Piatiau/CORBIS; p. 174 Getty Images Inc./085652-001; p. 175 M.H. Sharp/Photo Researchers, Inc.; p. 185 Laima E. Druskis/Pearson Education/PH College; p. 188 Georgia Tech Communications; p. 189 Lori Grinker/Contact Press Images, Inc.

Chapter 7   Page 194 Naoki Okamoto. "Untitled". Living-Asian. B. (1990), SuperStock, Inc.; p. 195 AP/Wide World Photos; p. 197 (left) Film Still Archive/The Museum of Modern Art; p. 197 (center) Film Still Archive/The Museum of Modern Art; p. 197 (right) Film Still Archive/The Museum of Modern Art; p. 197 (Video 7.1) Penn State; p. 199 (Video 7.2) CDA; p. 204 Werner H. Muller/Peter Arnold, Inc.; p. 207 Frank Siteman/Stock Boston; p. 211 Matthew Borkoski/Stock Boston; p. 213 Karp, Ken/Omni-Photo Communications, Inc.; p. 214 Margo Granitsas/The Image Works; p. 216 Pictor, New York; p. 217 UPI/CORBIS.

Chapter 8   Page 224 Alexej von Jawlensky, "Evening", (1929), ARS/Christie's Images/CORBIS; p. 226 (Video 8.1) Pearson-Patients as Educators; p. 227 Joel Gordon Photography; p. 228 Nate Guidry/Impact Visuals Photos and Graphics, Inc.; p. 230 (top) Dan McCoy/Rainbow; p. 230 (bottom) Ted Mahieu/Corbis/Stock Market; p. 233 Jonathan Exley/Getty Images, Inc.; p. 233 (Video 8.2) Pearson-Patients as Educators; p. 237 Lisa Quinones/Black Star; p. 238 Barry Yee/Liaison Agency, Inc.; p. 239 Carroll Seghers/Photo Researchers, Inc.; p. 240 Patrick Ramsey/International Stock Photography Ltd.; p. 246 SuperStock, Inc.; p. 247 Sybil Shackman; p. 251 Michal Heron/Ms. Michal Heron; p. 263 Joel Gordon/Joel Gordon Photography.

Chapter 9   Page 266 Klee Paul, "Beware of Red", (1940), Oil on canvas. Private Collection, Milan, Italy © Photograph by Erich Lessing. © 1998 Artists Rights Society (ARS), New York/VG Bild-Kunst, Bonn./Art Resource, N.Y.; p. 269 Savino/The Image Works; p. 271 Mark Foley/AP/Wide World Photos; p. 272 Greg Smith/Corbis/SABA Press Photos, Inc.; p. 272 (Video 9.1) Pearson-Patients as Educators; p. 274 Picture Desk, Inc./Kobal Collection; p. 275 Picture Desk, Inc./Kobal Collection; p. 276 Douglas Kirkland/CORBIS; p. 277 CORBIS; p. 279 (top) Joel Gordon Photography; p. 279 (bottom) David R. Frazier Photolibrary, Inc.; p. 282 Laima E. Druskis/Pearson Education/PH College; p. 284 Bob Daemmrich/Stock Boston; p. 286 Bob Daemmrich/Stock Boston; p. 288 Richard Renaldi; p. 292 Andy Belcher/ImageState.

Chapter 10 Page 298 Christopher Richard Wynne Nevinson, "A Bursting Shell", (1915), London, Tate Gallery. B. 1889—d. 1946. 928 x 724 x 76 mm./ Art Resource, N.Y.; p. 300 (Video 10.1) CDA; p. 301 (left) Walter Bibikow/ Getty Images Inc.; p. 301 (right) Lawrence Migdale/Getty Images Inc.; p. 301 (bottom) MGM-Pathe/Kobal Collection; p. 304 Mario Beauregard/ CORBIS; p. 305 (Video 10.2) CDA; p. 308 Ken Fisher/Getty Images Inc.; p. 309 (left) D. Wells/The Image Works; p. 309 (right) Paul Chesley/Getty Images Inc.; p. 310 AP/Wide World Photos; p. 313 Don Farrall/Getty Images, Inc./PhotoDisc, Inc.; p. 315 (top) Peter Matthews/Black Star; p. 315 (bottom) Joel Gordon Photography; p. 323 Robert Essel/Corbis/Stock Market; p. 327 Richard Hutchings/PhotoEdit; p. 330 Joel Gordon Photography; p. 331 Jeff Greenberg/Lonely Planet Images/Photo 20-20.

Chapter 11 Page 340 Pablo Picasso, (1881–1973), Spanish, "Girl Before a Mirror"/Superstock/© 2003 Estate of Pablo Picasso/Artists Rights Society (ARS), New York. SuperStock, Inc.; p. 341 (Video 11.1) CDA; p. 342 Sisse Brimberg/Woodfin Camp & Associates; p. 343 Tony Freeman/PhotoEdit; p. 343 (Video 11.2) CDA; p. 344 Michael Weisbrot/The Image Works; p. 345 Jill Greenberg/Jill Greenberg Studio, Inc.; p. 345 (Video 11.3) CDA; p. 353 Tony Freeman/PhotoEdit; p. 355 Joel Gordon Photography; p. 358 Alex Wong/Getty Images, Inc.; p. 359 Russell D. Curtis/Photo Researchers, Inc.; p. 363 Pictor, New York; p. 366 Ogust/The Image Works.

Chapter 12 Page 370 Bharati Chaudhuri. "Invisible Tension", (1992), (1951)/SuperStock, Inc.; p. 372 (left) George Holton/Photo Researchers, Inc.; p. 372 (right) Lee Snyder/Photo Researchers, Inc.; p. 372 (Video 12.1) Pearson-Patients as Educators; p. 374 Corbis/Sygma; p. 377 Randy Matusow; p. 378 Fredrik D. Bodin; p. 386 Roy Morsch/Corbis/Stock Market; p. 394 Ira Wyman/Corbis/Sygma; p. 395 AP/Wide World Photos.

Chapter 13 Page 400 Gino Severini, (1883–1966), Italian, "The Head", Pushkin Museum of Fine Arts, Moscow, Russia/SuperStock/© 2003 Artist Rights Society (ARS), New York/ADAGP, Paris/SuperStock Inc.; p. 402 (left) The Granger Collection; p. 402 (right) CORBIS; p. 403 R. Flynt/The Image Works; p. 405 Pictor, New York; p. 409 (Video 13.1) Pearson-Patients as Educators; p. 412 Jonathan Nourok/PhotoEdit; p. 414 "Soulful Feelings", © Artwork by Danny Gayder, a participating artist of VSA arts, website *http://www.vsarts.org.;* p. 416 Bob Benyas Photography; p. 417 Grunnitus/Photo Researchers, Inc.; p. 418 Mitchell Funk/Getty Images Inc.; p. 419 CORBIS; p. 420 Monte S. Buchsbaum, M.D., Mount Sinai School of Medicine, New York, N.Y.; p. 423 (left) Nancy C. Andreasen, M.D./University of Iowa Hospitals & Clinics; p. 423 (right) Nancy C. Andreasen, M.D./University of Iowa Hospitals & Clinics; p. 424 Monte S. Buchsbaum, M.D./Mount Sinai School of Medicine, New York, N.Y.; p. 430 Amy Etra/PhotoEdit.

Chapter 14 Page 438 Rufino Tamayo (1899–1991), "Dos Caras," Schalkwijk/Art Resource; p. 440 Tony Freeman/PhotoEdit; p. 441 Michael Newman/PhotoEdit; p. 444 Erika Stone; p. 445 (Video 14.1) CDA; p. 446 George Goodwin; p. 449 Richard Hutchings/Photo Researchers, Inc.; p. 450 Yoav Levy/Phototake NYC; p. 451 Tony Freeman/PhotoEdit; p. 452 Paul Conklin/PhotoEdit; p. 453 Stephen Vaughan/Globe Photos, Inc.; p. 455 Will & Deni McIntyre/Photo Researchers, Inc.; p. 460 (Video 14.2) CDA; p. 461 Jose Azel/Aurora & Quanta Productions; p. 463 Pascal Quittemelle/Stock Boston; p. 466 Jeff Greenberg/PhotoEdit; p. 467 David Young-Wolff/PhotoEdit; p. 468 Jean Claude LeJeune/Stock Boston.

Chapter 15 Page 478 Paul Klee, (1879–1940), Swiss, "Allegorische Figurine", Christie's Images/SuperStock/© 2003 Artist Rights Society (ARS), New York/VG Bild-Kunst, Bonn; p. 480 Frank Siteman/Stock Boston; p. 483 Jeff Persons/Stock Boston; p. 485 Steve Weber/Getty Images Inc.; p. 486 (top) Spencer Grant/Stock Boston; p. 486 (bottom) Robert Ginn/PhotoEdit; p. 489 (top) Mark J. Terrill/AP/Wide World Photos; p. 489 (left) Robert P. Friedland, MD, Case Western University; p. 489 (right) Robert P. Friedland, MD, Case Western University; p. 490 AP/Wide World Photos; p. 490 (Video 15.1) Films for Humanities; p. 492 (top) Cecil Fox/Science Source/Photo Researchers, Inc.; p. 492 (bottom) Karen Kasmauski/Woodfin Camp & Associates; p. 494 AP/Wide World Photos; p. 496 Robin Carson/Library of Congress; p. 497 AP/Wide World Photos.

Chapter 16 Page 500 Rufino Tamayo, (1899–1991), "Title Unknown" (Abstract)/ Superstock/MUSEUM RUFINO TAMAYO; p. 503 Wally McNamee/Corbis/Sygma; p. 504 Jerry Wechter/eStock Photography LLC; p. 507 Peter Byron/Photo Researchers, Inc; p. 508 Albert Bandura; p. 509 Harvey Finkle; p. 512 Freda Leinwand Photography; p. 514 Esbin-Anderson/ The Image Works; p. 516 Les Stone/Corbis/Sygma; p. 518 Stephen Ferry/ Liaison Agency Inc.; p. 523 Steve McCurry/Magnum Photos, Inc.; p. 524 R. Sidney/The Image Works; p. 526 Anthony Bolante/Reuters/Getty Images, Inc.; p. 526 (Video 16.1) CDA; p. 528 LaPorte County Child Abuse Prevention Council; p. 529 Doug Plummer; p. 531 John Coletti/Index Stock Imagery, Inc.

Chapter 17 Page 536 P. Filonov, (1883–1944), "Man in the World", Russian State Museum, St. Petersburg, Russia/SuperStock; p. 537 AP/Wide World Photos; p. 539 AP/Wide World Photos; p. 541 Custom Medical Stock Photo, Inc.; p. 542 (left) AP/Wide World Photos; p. 542 (right) AP/Wide World Photos; p. 544 Picture Desk, Inc./Kobal Collection; p. 545 AP/Wide World Photos; p. 546 AP/Wide World Photos; p. 547 AP/Wide World Photos; p. 548 AP/Wide World Photos.

AUTHOR INDEX

Larsen, R. M., 85
Larson, C. L., 505
Larson, G., 144
Larson, R. W., 468
Latané, B., 290
Lauerman, C., 111
Laumann, E. O., 371, 385
Law, M., 503
Lawson, W. B., 121, 127
Lazarus, A. A., 110, 147
Lazarus, R. S., 136, 140
Lazovik, A. D., 90
Leary, W. E., 334, 529
Leavitt, F., 85
Leckman, A. L., 336
LeDuff, C., 299
Lee, 320
Lee, C. C., 115
Lee, D. T. S., 229
Lee, I. M., 148
Lee, T. M. C., 228
Leekam, S. R., 445
Leff, J., 425, 426
Lefley, H. P., 9, 117, 121, 427
Lehman, D. R., 148, 353
Lehrer, M., 152
Lehrer, P. M., 152
Leibel, R. L., 355
Leibenluft, E., 231
Leiblum, S. R., 388, 394, 397
Leibson, C. L., 460
Leichsenring, F., 249, 251
Leitenberg, H., 377
Lemonick, M. D., 488, 489
Lenhart, L., 465
Lentz, R. J., 433
Leocani, L., 181
Leon, G. R., 346
Lerew, D. R., 178
Lerman, C., 322
Lesch, K. P., 35, 180
Leserman, J., 155
Lesser, I., 121
Lessler, D., 115
Letourneau, E., 387, 397
Levenson, J. L., 153
Levenstein, S., 144
Levin, H., 472
Levine, A., 454, 457
Levine, J., 82
Levitan, R. D., 246, 349
Levy, S. R., 470
Lewin, T., 422
Lewinsohn, P. M., 61, 227, 237, 238, 243, 246, 250, 256, 260, 466, 468, 469, 470
Lewis, D. A., 128, 424
Lewis, D. O., 206
Lewis-Hall, F., 125
Lex, B. W., 308
Ley, R., 180
Li, Y. M., 492
Liberman, R. P., 186, 432, 433

Libet, J. M., 238
Lichstein, K. L., 366, 487
Lichtenberg, P. A., 482
Lichtenstein, E., 318
Lieber, C. S., 308
Liebowitz, M. R., 167, 458
Lightsey, O. W., Jr., 243
Lilienfeld, S. O., 64, 85, 178, 272
Lin, K., 431
Lin, T. Y., 432
Lindamer, L. A., 121
Lindsey, K. P., 127
Linehan, M. M., 260, 294
Link, B. G., 503
Linnoila, M., 505, 510, 515
Liotti, G., 275
Lipman, E. L., 520
Lipper, S., 383
Lipsey, M. W., 113
Lipton, R. B., 144, 145
Lira, L. R., 528
Lisanby, S. H., 256
Litz, B. T., 172
Livesley, W. J., 178, 283, 289
Livingstone, M., 455
Lobel, M., 142
Lochman, J. E., 288, 464, 465, 506
Lochner, B., 140
Locke, B. Z., 271
Lockwood, G., 109
Locy, T., 459
Loeber, R., 463
Loewenstein, R. J., 202, 207
Loftus, E. F., 208, 209
Lohman, J. J. H. M., 145
Lohr, B. A., 522
Londen, A. V., 473
Long, N., 464
López, B., 445
LoPiccolo, J., 388, 396, 397
Loranger, A. W., 281, 293
Lorefice, L. S., 383
Lovaas, O. I., 445, 447
Lowe, M. R., 347
Lubin, B., 85
Luborsky, I., 249
Luborsky, L., 100
Lueschen, G., 328
Luntz, B. K., 289
Luria, A. R., 87
Lurigio, A. J., 128
Lutgendorf, S. K., 155
Lyketsos, C. G., 486
Lykken, D. T., 290, 506
Lymburner, J. A., 547
Lynch, F., 461
Lynn, S. J., 207
Lyon, F. R., 456, 457
Lyons, J. S., 349, 527

Macaruso, P., 453
McAleer, J. L., 507

McBride, H., 487
McBride, P. A., 35, 447
McBurney, D. H., 504
McCabe, M. P., 345
McCabe, S. B., 243
McCann, B. S., 68
McCarty, D., 306
McCaul, M. E., 332, 333
McCauley, J., 520
McClearn, G. E., 37
McClelland, D. C., 84
McCloskey, L. A., 514, 527
Maccoby, E. E., 472
McCombs, A., 464
McCord, J., 289
McCord, W., 289
McCoy, L., 68
McCrady, B. S., 323, 329, 332
McCrae, R. R., 213–214
McCullough, L., 76
McDermott, J. F., 232
McDermut, W., 113
McDougle, C. J., 447
McEachin, J. J., 447
McElrath, J. V., 528
McElreath, L. K., 487
McElroy, S., 351
McFarland, B. H., 255
McFarlane, A. C., 515
McFarlane, M., 304
McGinn, D., 299
McGinn, L. K., 109
McGlashan, T. H., 273, 275, 418, 424
McGovern, P. G., 150
McGovern, T. F., 19
McGrath, E., 226
McGrath, P. J., 254
McGue, M., 322, 323
McGuffin, P., 180, 421, 449, 450, 456
McGuire, P. K., 413
Machan, D., 299
Machleidt, W., 432
McKay, J., 330
McKay, J. S., 523
McKenna, M. C., 153
MacKenzie, T. D., 317
Mackin, R. S., 137
McKinney, K., 531, 533
McLaughlin, C. J., 111
McLellan, A. T., 321
McMahon, P. M., 522
MacMillan, H. L., 518, 520
McMurtrie, B., 358
McNally, R., 68, 175, 180
McNeil, D. G., Jr., 497
McNeil, T. F., 424
McNiel, D. E., 540, 543
McNulty, J. L., 73
MacPhillamy, D. J., 238
McQuiston, J. T., 229
Maddi, S. R., 142

Maeder, T., 547, 548, 549
Magdol, L., 514
Maher, B. A., 9
Maher, W. B., 9
Mahler, M., 45–46, 104, 286–287
Maier, S. F., 132, 133, 244, 245
Maj, M., 408
Maki, K. M., 191
Malaspina, D., 422
Maldonado, J. R., 200, 201, 202, 203, 209
Maletsky, B. M., 383, 384
Malgady, R. G., 138
Malmo, R. B., 145
Malone, K. M., 260, 261
Maloney, K. C., 350
Mandal, M. K., 401
Mann, J. J., 35, 260, 471, 505
Mannarino, A. P., 142, 520, 527, 529
Mannuzza, S., 462
Mansell, W., 177, 347
Manzetta, B. R., 146
Marangell, L. B., 247
Marcus, D. K., 239
Marcus, E. B., 357
Marder, S.R., 430
Marengo, J., 411
Margolin, G., 514
Marino, L., 64
Mark, D. H., 144
Mark, M. M., 153
Markovitz, J. H., 150
Markowitz, J. C., 155, 249
Marks, E., 84
Marks, G., 73
Marks, I., 76, 189
Marks, J. S., 353
Marks, M., 176
Marlatt, G. A., 125, 326, 327, 334, 336
Marlowe, D. B., 82
Maroules, N., 531, 533
Marsh, D. T., 434
Marshall, D., 371
Marshall, W. L., 383, 522
Martin, D., 444, 459
Martin, D. J., 114
Martin, H., 197
Martin, J., 487
Martin, P. R., 145
Martin, S. E., 509
Martins, C., 427
Marx, E. M., 235
Maslow, A., 52
Mason, M., 144
Masters, W. H., 386, 394, 395, 397
Mastri, A. R., 494
Matarazzo, J. D., 85
Mathalno, D. H., 424
Mathes, S., 85
Mathias, R., 299, 314
Matson, J. L., 452

SUBJECT INDEX

Wechsler scales, 77, 78–79
Weight-loss programs, 358–359
Wellbutrin (buproprion), 120
Wernicke's disease, 484–485
Weyer, Johann, 12
White Americans, non-Hispanic
    alcoholism and, 309
    anxiety disorders and, 173
    child sexual abuse and, 528
    coronary heart disease and, 149
    expressed emotion and, 426–427
    homicide rates for, 509
    mental health of, 58
    schizophrenia and, 431–432

smoking and, 317
substance dependence and, 304
suicide and, 257
use of mental health services and, 126
Wish-fulfillment fantasies, 141
Witchcraft, 11–12
Withdrawal syndromes, 301–302, 303, 312, 313
Working alliance, 113
World Health Organization (WHO), 9, 293, 317, 409
Worldview, 9
Writing, therapeutic benefits of, 134
Written expression disorder, 454

Wyatt v. *Stickney*, 542–544

Xanax (alprazolam), 118, 120, 183
X-Files, 209

Youngberg v. *Romeo*, 545–546

Zar, 69, 204
Zoloft (sertraline), 119, 120, 183, 247, 254
Zolpidem (Ambien), 120, 365
Zoophilia, 382
Zyban (bupropion), 330

DSM-IV CLASSIFICATION (AMERICAN PSYCHIATRIC ASSOCIATION 2000)

AXIS I
CLINICAL SYNDROMES

DISORDERS USUALLY FIRST DIAGNOSED IN INFANCY, CHILDHOOD, OR ADOLESCENCE

- **Learning Disorders**
  Reading Disorder
  Mathematics Disorder
  Disorder of Written Expression
  Learning Disorder Not Otherwise Specified

- **Motor Skills Disorder**
  Developmental Coordination Disorder

- **Communication Disorders**
  Expressive Language Disorder
  Mixed Receptive/Expressive Language Disorder
  Phonological Disorder
  Stuttering
  Communication Disorder Not Otherwise
    Specified

- **Pervasive Developmental Disorders**
  Autistic Disorder
  Rett's Disorder
  Childhood Disintegrative Disorder
  Asperger's Disorder
  Pervasive Developmental Disorder Not
    Otherwise Specified

- **Attention-Deficit and Disruptive Behavior Disorders**
  Attention-Deficit/Hyperactivity Disorder
    Predominantly Inattentive Type
    Predominantly Hyperactive-Impulsive Type
    Combined Type
  Oppositional Defiant Disorder
  Conduct Disorder
  Attention-Deficit/Hyperactivity Disorder
    Not Otherwise Specified
  Disruptive Behavior Disorder Not Otherwise
    Specified

- **Feeding and Eating Disorders of Infancy or Early Childhood**
  Pica
  Rumination Disorder
  Feeding Disorder of Infancy or Early Childhood
    Not Otherwise Specified

- **Tic Disorders**
  Tourette's Disorder
  Chronic Motor or Vocal Tic Disorder
  Transient Tic Disorder
  Tic Disorder Not Otherwise Specified

- **Elimination Disorders**
  Encopresis
  Enuresis

- **Other Disorders of Infancy, Childhood, or Adolescence**
  Separation Anxiety Disorder
  Selective Mutism
  Reactive Attachment Disorder of Infancy
    or Early Childhood
  Stereotypic Movement Disorder
  Disorder of Infancy, Childhood, or
    Adolescence Not Otherwise Specified

DELIRIUM, DEMENTIA, AND AMNESTIC AND OTHER COGNITIVE DISORDERS

- **Delirium**
  Delirium Due to a General Medical Condition
  Substance Intoxication Delirium
  Substance Withdrawal Delirium
  Delirium Due to Multiple Etiologies
  Delirium Not Otherwise Specified

- **Dementia**
  Dementia of the Alzheimer's Type
  Vascular Dementia
  Dementias Due to Other General Medical
    Conditions
    Dementia Due to HIV Disease
    Dementia Due to Head Trauma
    Dementia Due to Parkinson's Disease
    Dementia Due to Huntington's Disease
    Dementia Due to Pick's Disease
    Dementia Due to Creutzfeldt-Jakob Disease
  Substance-Induced Persisting Dementia
  Dementia Due to Multiple Etiologies
  Dementia Not Otherwise Specified

- **Amnestic Disorders**
  Amnestic Disorder Due to a General Medical
    Condition
  Substance-Induced Persisting Amnestic
    Disorder
  Amnestic Disorder Not Otherwise Specified

SUBSTANCE-RELATED DISORDERS

- **Alcohol Use Disorders**
  Alcohol Dependence
  Alcohol Abuse

- **Alcohol-Induced Disorders**
  Alcohol Intoxication
  Alcohol Withdrawal
  Alcohol Intoxication Delirium
  Alcohol Withdrawal Delirium
  Alcohol-Induced Persisting Dementia
  Alcohol-Induced Persisting Amnestic Disorder
  Alcohol-Induced Psychotic Disorder
  Alcohol-Induced Mood Disorder
  Alcohol-Induced Anxiety Disorder
  Alcohol-Induced Sexual Dysfunction
  Alcohol-Induced Sleep Disorder
  Alcohol-Related Disorder Not Otherwise
    Specified

- **Amphetamine Use Disorders**
- **Amphetamine-Induced Disorders**
- **Caffeine-Induced Disorders**
- **Cannabis Use Disorders**
- **Cannabis-Induced Disorders**
- **Cocaine Use Disorders**
- **Cocaine-Induced Disorders**
- **Hallucinogen Use Disorders**
- **Hallucinogen-Induced Disorders**
- **Inhalant Use Disorders**
- **Inhalant-Induced Disorders**
- **Nicotine Use Disorder**
- **Nicotine-Induced Disorder**
- **Opioid Use Disorders**
- **Opioid-Induced Disorders**
- **Phencyclidine Use Disorders**
- **Phencyclidine-Induced Disorders**
- **Sedative, Hypnotic, or Anxiolytic Use Disorders**
- **Sedative, Hypnotic, or Anxiolytic-Induced Disorders**
- **Polysubstance-Related Disorder**
- **Other (or Unknown) Substance Use Disorders**
- **Other (or Unknown) Substance-Induced Disorders**

SCHIZOPHRENIA AND OTHER PSYCHOTIC DISORDERS

- **Schizophrenia**
  Paranoid Type
  Disorganized Type
  Catatonic Type
  Undifferentiated Type
  Residual Type

- **Schizophreniform Disorder**
- **Schizoaffective Disorder**
- **Delusional Disorder**
- **Brief Psychotic Disorder**
- **Shared Psychotic Disorder (Folie à Deux)**
- **Psychotic Disorder Due to a General Medical Condition**
- **Substance-Induced Psychotic Disorder**
- **Psychotic Disorder Not Otherwise Specified**

MOOD DISORDERS

- **Depressive Disorders**
  Major Depressive Disorder
  Dysthymic Disorder
  Depressive Disorder Not Otherwise
    Specified

- **Bipolar Disorders**
  Bipolar I Disorder
    Single Manic Episode
    Most Recent Episode Hypomanic
    Most Recent Episode Manic
    Most Recent Episode Mixed
    Most Recent Episode Depressed
    Most Recent Episode Unspecified
  Bipolar II Disorder
  Cyclothymic Disorder
  Bipolar Disorder Not Otherwise Specified

- **Other Mood Disorders**
  Mood Disorder Due to a General Medical
    Condition
  Substance-Induced Mood Disorder
  Mood Disorder Not Otherwise Specified